DEXA 91

D. Karagiannis (ed.)

Database and Expert Systems Applications

Proceedings of the International Conference
in Berlin, Federal Republic of Germany, 1991

Springer-Verlag Wien GmbH

Dr.-Ing. D. Karagiannis
Forschungsinstitut für anwendungsorientierte
Wissensverarbeitung (FAW)
Ulm, Federal Republic of Germany

With 351 Figures

ISBN 978-3-211-82301-9   ISBN 978-3-7091-7555-2 (eBook)
DOI 10.1007/978-3-7091-7555-2

Preface

The Database and Expert Systems Applications – DEXA – conferences are dedicated to providing an international forum for the presentation of applications in the database and expert systems field, for the exchange of ideas and experiences, and for defining requirements for the future systems in these fields.

After the very promising DEXA 90 in Vienna, Austria, we hope to have successfully established with this year's DEXA 91 a stage where scientists from diverse fields interested in application-oriented research can present and discuss their work.

This year there was a total of more than 250 submitted papers from 28 different countries, in all continents. Only 98 of the papers could be accepted.

The collection of papers in these proceedings offers a cross-section of the issues facing the area of databases and expert systems, i.e., topics of basic research interest on one hand and questions occurring when developing applications on the other.

Major credit for the success of the conference goes to all of our colleagues who submitted papers for consideration and to those who have organized and chaired the panel sessions.

Many persons contributed numerous hours to organize this conference. The names of most of them will appear on the following pages. In particular we wish to thank the Organization Committee Chairmen Johann Gordesch, A Min Tjoa, and Roland Wagner, who also helped establishing the program. Special thanks also go to Gabriella Wagner and Anke Rückert.

Dimitris Karagiannis
General Conference Chairman

Contents

SESSION 4 C   Foundation of Object Orientation

SESSION 5 A   Multimedia Databases and Hypertext

SESSION 5 B   Applications in Science, Technology, and Industry

SESSION 5 C   Heterogenous and Multidatabase Systems

SESSION 8 C   Medical Information Systems

Conference Committee

International Conference on Database and Expert Systems Applications
Freie Universität Berlin, Germany — August 21–23, 1991

General Chairman
D. Karagiannis, FAW-Ulm, Germany

Program Committee

H. Afsarmanesh	University of Amsterdam, Netherlands
H. J. Appelrath	University of Oldenburg, Germany
K. Bauknecht	University of Zürich, Switzerland
J. Bing	NRCCL Oslo, Norway
M. L. Brodie	GTE Laboratories Inc., USA
B. Croft	University of Massachusetts, USA
W. S. Cellary	Technical University of Poznan, Poland
A. L. Furtado	University of Rio de Janeiro, Brazil
G. Gardarin	INRIA, France
G. Gottlob	Technical University of Vienna, Austria
P. Henderson	University of Southampton, GB
O. Herzog	IBM Deutschland, Germany
K. Hirota	Hosei University, Japan
W. Horn	University of Vienna, Austria
D. Hsiao	Naval Postgraduate School, USA
M. Jarke	University of Passau, Germany
Y. Kambayashi	University of Kyushu, Japan
H. Krallmann	FU Berlin, Germany
J. Liebowitz	George Washington University, USA
F. Lochovsky	HKUST, Hong Kong
V. Lum	Naval Postgraduate School, USA
V. Marik	Technical University of Prague, CSFR
G. Müller	University of Freiburg, Germany
M.-A. Neimat	HP Laboratories Palo Alto, USA
E. Neuhold	GMD-IPSI, Germany
S. Nishio	University of Osaka, Japan
G. Ozsoyoglu	University Case Western Research, USA
B. Page	University of Hamburg, Germany
M. Papazoglou	Australian National University, Australia
B. Pernici	University of Udine, Italy
D. Queeney	IKOSS GmbH, Germany
G. Quirchmayr	University of Linz, Austria
I. Ramos Salavert	Technical University of Valencia, Spain
C. Rolland	University Paris I, France
C.-R. Rollinger	University of Osnabrück, Germany
N. Roussopoulos	University of Maryland, USA
D. Schütt	Siemens AG, Germany
H. Schweppe	FU Berlin, Germany
E. Simon	INRIA, France
J.C. Smith	University of British Columbia, Canada
A. Spaepen	University of Leuven, Belgium
A. Steiger-Garcao	University of Lissabon, Portugal
R. Studer	University of Karlsruhe, Germany
S.Y.W. Su	University of Florida, USA
S. Sugita	National Museum Osaka, Japan
K. Tanaka	Kobe University, Japan
C. Thanos	IEI-CNR, Italy
J. van Bemmel	Erasmus University Rotterdam, Netherlands
C. van Dorsser	ORIGIN Technology in Business, Netherlands
Y. Wand	University of British Columbia, Canada
G. Wiederhold	Stanford University, USA

Organizing Committee Chairmen

J. Gordesch	FU Berlin, Germany
R. Wagner	University of Linz, Austria
A Min Tjoa	University of Vienna, Austria

Organizing Committee Members

A. Rückert	Germany
G. Wagner	Austria

List of Referees

Each paper was carefully reviewed by three persons. Most of this work was done by the Program Committee. However, invaluable help was provided by the referees listed below.

H. Amano
P. Andlinger
F. Andres
J. Angele
S. Arikawa
H. Arimura
A. F. Batzias
C. Beierle
B. Bergsten
P. Boria
V. Botti
M. Breunig
H. Brunk
R. Bruns
F. Bry
M. A. Casanova
M. Chignell
B. Convent
J. de Jesús Pérez Alcázar
D. Densow
C. Draxler
H. Eirund
K. Faidt
P. Fankhauser
D. Fensel
G. Fleischanderl
A. Gammerman
C. Gierlinger
F. Gire
J. Gonzalez-Diaz
W. Grafik
H. Gust
A. M. Haeberer
M. Haraguchi
T. Härder
R. Haux
A. Hecht
H. Heller

A. S. Hemerly
H. Herre
G. Heyer
F. Hinz
U. Hoppe
E. Hovy
W. Huang
G. Jakobson
P. Jasiński
H. Jasper
M. Jeusfeld
A. Karduck
F. Kastner
H. Kawano
D. Keim
S. Keronen
H. Kindler
W. Klas
S. Kobayashi
U. Kohl
A. Krall
R. Krishnamurthy
K. Kuhn
E. Kühn
T. Kunishima
D. Landes
A. Lehmann
Q. Li
B. Liu
R. Marzi
G. R. Meijer
A. Miethsam
T. Morzy
B. Müller
W. Nejdl
M. L. Nelson
P. Nemeth

S. Neubert
S. Nittel
C. Peltason
A. Perkhoff
A. V. Peterson
P. Petta
U. Pletat
M. A. Rezende
B. Rieger
J. Risius
F. Röhner
G. Saake
G. Salzer
J. Sauer
P. Schäuble
S. Schebiella
S. Schmidt
M. Schrefl
S. Shimojo
Y. M. Shyu
D. Specht
M. Spies
P. Steffens
A. Stein
M. Stumptner
T. Takagi
B. Teufel
U. Thiel
H. Thoma
R. Traunmüller
V. Turau
P. Valduriez
B. Walter
K. Winkelmann
T. Wu
S. Yamaguchi
M. Yoshikawa

OO AND ACTIVE FORMAL INFORMATION SYSTEM SPECIFICATION.

Isidro Ramos, Oscar Pastor, Vicente Casado.

DSIC (DEPARTAMENTO DE SISTEMAS INFORMATICOS Y COMPUTACION) UNIVERSIDAD POLITECNICA DE VALENCIA 46071 VALENCIA (SPAIN)

ABSTRACT

Formal methods for Information System Specification is a field with a wide work background. Using an Object-Oriented model with a well-defined logical framework it is possible to execute the specifications as deductions in the formal first order theory equivalent to each specification, as was shown by Ramos [2]. The system implemented there is a powerful tool for rapid prototyping and constitutes a useful environment for open and passive IS that we call MOL (Micro-Object-Logic). Using ideas for graphical object oriented design from [4] , a wide spectrum OO specification language is presented in Bearing et al.[5] dealing with Open and Active Specification of IS (OASIS). The present paper is a first working version of this enhanced OASIS, built by adding to MOL active capabilities for expressing active relationships between objects by means of the triggering relationships. By active we mean that the objects involved are necessary for changes of state to take place, which is done by defining triggering conditions.

We then present what we mean by OO model. The third section states our class definition. The fourth presents the provided interaction mechanisms between objects and finally we present the prototype as it has been implemented, giving the syntactic language constructions and commenting on the most relevant implementation features.

I. INTRODUCTION

According to Wand and Lindgreen [1] [6], the world is made up of objects. Objects describe concrete beings, that is, specific entities rather than types or classes. We put objects together in types by means of the abstraction mechanisms. We call class the set of properties, all of which characterize certain objects. A class is a precise characterization of structural and behavioural properties that a collection (or type) of objects all share.

Objects are known to (or observable by) the world through their properties. The specific set of properties used to describe a given object depends on the point of view and the purpose of modelling. We recognize properties only through attributes

The value of an attribute at a certain time is called a state variable. The set of state variables defines the state of the object.

From a static point of view, the allowed states of an object are determined by the set of static object laws, being these laws constraints on the allowed combinations of the values of attributes (static constraints).

A transition between two states is termed an event. An event is an abstraction of a change of state in the object system. It is discrete, has no duration and occurs at a certain point in time. An event will occur (will be relevant) if a given precondition associated with it is satisfied. These preconditions constrain the occurrence of events.

From a dynamic point of view, we can also have temporal laws describing relationships between valid states (dynamic constraints)

Objects are not independent. We have the sharing of events as a first mechanism of interaction between objects. We can also have active relationships by means of a triggering mechanism. Potentially, every condition defined in terms of the relevant object events and/or attributes may serve as a trigger.

A trigger is a relationship between an event and one or more other events that at a certain level of abstraction expresses the cause for the proper agents to carry out the execution of other events. A triggering relationship is defined by giving the event to trigger, the destination and the condition that will trigger it when fulfilled.

II. CLASS DEFINITION

Following the formal logic and OO framework presented in Ramos[2], we define a class as a first order theory, composed of an alphabet, a first order language, a given set of axioms of different types and a set of rules of inference.

The alphabet of our theory is made up of the set of class events and attributes.

Between the set of events, we can distinguish between **private and shared**. Private events are those belonging to only one class. Shared events appear in more than one class.

The set of attributes is composed of **constant** attributes and **variable** attributes. Constant attributes do not change their value during the object existence. Variable attributes change on occurrence of their relevant events according to dynamic laws.

The axioms composing our theory are those presented as follows:

1.-Relevant events, those which represent successful occurrences of events, i.e., events that have been activated by a valid agent and have satisfied the constraints associated to them.

2.- Static integrity constraints: those which state static relationships between attributes that must hold in every state to be considered valid. They are built using a first order logic whose wff are:

1.- a predicate representation of an attribute is a wff
2.- if A, B are wff, then A,B A;B not(A) are wff
3.- our wff are only those obtained by 1,2.

3.- Dynamic integrity constraints: those which establish dynamic properties from the events and/or attributes, relating more than one state. They are expressed by means of a temporal extension of the first order logic used in i), adding the events to the alphabet of our wff.

4.- Variable attributes definition: those which express the axiomatic definition of the variable attributes in terms of their relevant events. The chosen expressivity (clausal, functional or both)

characterizes the specification language version. When using a clausal style for defining the variable attributes we have R-OASIS (RELATIONAL OASIS). Using a functional one we have F-OASIS (FUNCTIONAL OASIS). Blending both together we have a functional and relational expressivity.

Taking a relational logic approach, the variable attribute definition is given by clauses. The head is an attribute name and the body is the declarative attribute definition following its relevant events and/or its attributes.

attribute:-axiomatic_definition

5.- Event preconditions: these axioms relate every relevant event with the conditions that must hold for the successful event occurrence. The condition is expressed in terms of events and attributes of the theory representing the class being defined. We can represent it easily using a clausal expressivity, its head being the event and its body the corresponding condition.

event:-precondition

6.- Triggering relationships :they define active relationships between objects, expressing which conditions may potentially serve as triggers of events from other classes. We can express them in the form:

destination::event:-wff

which means that the given event will be activated and sent to the indicated destination (an object, all the objects of a class,etc.) as soon as the condition expressed by wff will hold. This condition will be given using the events and attributes belonging to the alphabet of the theory, as in the previous case. We can realize that we have a special kind of event preconditions that relate events of any other class with conditions expressed in terms of events and attributes of the class being defined.

III. INTERACTION BETWEEN OBJECTS

Objects are not independent due to the existence of special relationships between them.

Having defined our classes as first order theories, we can consider two interaction mechanisms between objects:

  1.- shared events
  2.- triggering relationships

We are going to determine both mechanisms in terms of the induced relations between the corresponding theories.

A. SHARING OF EVENTS

We have already stated that shared events are those belonging to more than one class. This implies that a relation exists between the theories sharing this kind of events, expressed in the existence of different types of axioms using the same shared event in the theories considered (those sharing the event).

The relationship between classes produced by the shared events allows us to identify the existence of an aggregated complex class that takes these events as private.

B. TRIGGERING

The triggering relationships between classes are our tool for modelling

an active pattern of communication in our object society. This is done by specifying for each class which events can be asked for and from which classes when a given condition is satisfied. We can determine if the event is to be sent to all the objects of the class, to a special subset of them or to individual instances.

The triggering axioms presented above are those theory components which take into account the expression of these active communication patterns.

IV. THE SPECIFICATION LANGUAGE

Uing from MOL works and dealing with an OO, open and passive specification of IS, we present an active enhancement by means of the introduction of triggering expressions. This leads us to our Active-MOL (OASIS) in which the introduction of an active pattern of communication allows us to specify which events will be sent to their corresponding destination classes once the defined triggering condition will hold.

The structure of the enhanced language, how the specification is executed and the most relevant features of the implemented environment are discussed subsequently.

A. STRUCTURE

A Conceptual Schema, as a definition of an object society, is built according to the following template:

Conceptual_Schema <name>
<specification body>
end_Conceptual_Schema

The body is composed of the specification of the **domains, the elementary** and **the complex** classes, the three constructions provided by OASIS.

Domains (primitive classes)

The domains denote the data subspecification that are used as object surrogates and attribute classes. Their type is an ADT. Our object society will be built taking them as the basic data level used to declare elementary classes.

The actual OASIS implementation provides as predefined the basic domains nat, bool and string with their usual operations.

We treat **time** as domain, implicitly defined and necessary for applying the Kowalski event calculus to the specification language. It appears as the last argument of the predicates representing events and attributes, fixing respectively the instant of an event occurrence or the time in which we want to make an observation (i.e. to know some attribute values). We represent time as discrete and left-bounded using the natural numbers.

Each domain declared has an associated default value, the main constant, given between parenthesis after the domain name:

nat(0), bool(true),...

It is considered the default value for non-defined attributes.

Elementary classes

Elementary classes are those built without using class operators. They define the structural and behavioural properties that a collection (or type) of objects all share.

Their syntactic representation follows the template:

```
     CLASS NAME
   ATTRIBUTES
    CONSTANT
      <ATTRIBUTE_NAME:CLASS_NAME> KEY,
      <ATTRIBUTE_NAME:CLASS_NAME>
          ...
    CONSTRAINTS
      <ADMISSIBILITY CONDITION FOR CONSTANT
ATTRIBUTES>
    VARIABLES
      ATTRIBUTE_NAME(ELEMENTARY_CLASS_NAME,
DOMAIN_NAME,TIME)
      CLAUSES <VAR.DEF>
          <CLAUSAL_DEFINITION>.
       ...
   EVENTS
    PRIVATE
      <EVENT_NAME>(<PARAMETERS>,TIME);
        ...
    SHARED
              <EVENT_NAME>(<PARAMETERS>,TIME);
       ...
   PRECONDITIONS
    <EVENT_NAME>(<PARAMETERS>,TIME) IF

      <EVENT_ADMISSIBILITY_CONDITION>
       ...
   TRIGGERING

DESTINATION_CLASS::<EVENT_NAME>(<PARAMETERS>,TIME)
IF
          <TRIGGER_CONDITION>
       ...
   END CLASS
```

First, we specify the structural properties of the class by means of the attribute declaration. We distinguish between constant attributes, those whose values do not change with time, and variable attributes, those whose values change over time depending on the relevant event occurrences. Between the constant attributes, we identify the key that is the object surrogate for class instances. For every variable attribute declared, we give its axiomatic definition in terms of their relevant events and/or attributes. The actual implementation uses a relational or clausal style for the deductive definition. So, we are dealing with an active and relational version of MOL (R-OASIS).

Using as an example the specification of an artificial lake (see fig.1), we will begin by declaring their constant and variable attributes. Constant attributes are its name (acting as key), capacity security limit and minimum reserve level. We declare the actual level as a variable attribute, giving its axiomatic definition in terms of its relevant events (those changing the level value). In the example, we do it using a relational expressivity, defining the level value in an instant t in function of its previous value (in the instant t-1) and its relevant events occured at time t.

```
ELEMENTARY CLASS ARTIFICIAL_LAKE
    ATTRIBUTES
     CONSTANT
       NAME:STRING KEY;
       CAPACITY:NAT;
         SEC_LIMIT:NAT;
         MIN_LEVEL:NAT;
     STATIC CONSTRAINTS
                        CAPACITY>SEC_LIMIT AND
SEC_LIMIT>MIN_LEVEL
     VARIABLES
       LEVEL(ARTIFICIAL_LAKE,NAT,TIME)
                              C L A U S E S
L:ARTIFICIAL_LAKE;R:RESERVOIR;Y,C:NAT;
                        T,T1:TIME;
       LEVEL(L,Y,T):-T1 IS T-1 AND LEVEL(L,Y1,T1) AND
         ((NOT(UNLOAD(L,C,T) OR LOAD(L,C,T) OR
                        PASS_AL(L,R,C,T) OR
PASS_R(L,R,C,T)) AND Y IS Y1)        OR
(UNLOAD(L,C,T) AND Y IS Y1-C) OR
         (LOAD(L,C,T) AND Y IS Y1+C) OR
         (PASS_R(L,R,C,T) AND Y IS Y1-C) OR
         (PASS_AL(L,R,C,T) AND Y IS Y1+C)).
     EVENTS
       PRIVATE
         LOAD(L,C,T)
         UNLOAD(L,C,T)
       SHARED
         PASS_R(L,R,C,T)
         PASS_AL(L,R,C,T)
     PRECONDITIONS
         UNLOAD(L,C,T) IF LEVEL(L,Y,T) AND Y-
C>MIN_LEVEL
     TRIGGERING
         SELF::DESTROY IF LEVEL(L,Y,T) AND
Y>CAPACITY
         SELF::UNLOAD(L,C,T) IF LEVEL(L,Y,T) AND
Y>SEC_LEVEL
         OBJECT:: STOP IF LEVEL(L,Y,T) AND
Y<CAPACITY
    END ELEMENTARY CLASS
```

Fig. 1: example of a class specification in OASIS.

An important feature of this enhanced OASIS is the possibility of specifying static integrity constraints between the constant attributes. Objects will be brough into existence only if this constraints on their constant attributes hold.

In our example, we can state a constraint to avoid having a security limit greater than the capacity.

Afterwards, we declare the events that are relevant to the class. We distinguish between private and shared events. Private events are those that only affect the elementary class being defined. We have two overloaded private events that are those creating and destroying class instances (**new** and **destroy**). We also have four specials private events acting over any instance of our object society and control the liveness state of the object. They can make an object active (**start**), or pause it while remaining active (**pause**), or to reactivate it again (**resume**) or, lastly, leave its active state (**stop**). These events act over any object, independently from the class to which they belong.

Shared events affects several elementary classes simultaneously. They allow us to define object interactions, and can act as private events of a complex aggregated class, relating the component classes (those sharing these events)

4

Again in our example, we have declared private events of the artificial lake class those of water **load** and **unload**. We could declare water exchange shared events between artificial lakes and water reservoirs related to them. The names assigned to these events are **pass_r** (representing the pass of a given quantity of water from an artificial lake to a reservoir) and **pass_al** (representing the movement of water in the other way).

Next we specify for every private event its admissibility condition. It states which condition must hold in order to have a valid event occurrence. We specify it in terms of events and/or attributes of the class we are defining.

For the new and destroy overloaded private events, we have resp.ectively the non existence/existence of the affected object as the default precondition.

Similarly, for the special activity events we have implicitly predefined preconditions. For **start**, the referenced object must not have received any of the other activity events. For **pause**, the object implicated must be alive in the sense that it must be in an active state (it has received a start or resume event before this one). For **resume**, the object must also obviously exists and has to be in a paused state. For **stop**, the only condition is the object existence.

In our prototype, all these events are predefined and assumed by default together with their corresponding preconditions.

In the chosen example, a precondition for the private event of releasing water would be define stating that the level of the artificial lake is greater than the minimum security level.

Last, we define the triggering relationships that will make our specification active. This activity is one of the most interesting features of OASIS, and allow us to evolve from an open and passive specification of information systems (OPSIS) given in MOL to another open and active specification of IS (OASIS).

Our system uses a similar mechanism to the used in KNOs. The difference consists of the messages sent. In KNOs the messages are objects as any other object that can also send messages, having a cyclic definition of object. OASIS uses the proper events as messages, considering them as degenerated objects whose life is the instant in which they are produced, having no attributes or events.

They are expressed by means of the syntax:
<DESTINATION>::<EVENT>
IF <EVENT_ADMISSIBILITY_CONDITION>
where destination specifies the receivers of the event, event is the triggered event and we specify the condition that will activate the trigger mechanism in the event´s admissibility condition.

We have four key words for the destinations:

1.- **self:** the triggered event destination is the object itself .

2.- **object:** the event destination is a unique object that will be asked for to trigger the event. Obviously, the object must be in conditions to receive this event, otherwise the trigger will fail.

3.- **class:** we send the triggered event to all the actual class instances (the class of the object considered).

4.- **society:** the event destination is all the instances of our object society.

When the destination is all the class instances, an event copy is triggered for every object, checking if they are valid. The trigger is considered successful if at least one of the event copies triggered is valid.

As an example of our trigger system expressivity, an artificial lake instance could send to itself a destroy event (a suicide!) if its capacity is exceeded. Or trigger a water unload event if its security level is reached.

Complex classes

Complex classes are those defined using class operators. The actual OASIS version provides at the moment only one kind called **relationships.** They represent an aggregation between classes that takes their shared events as private. When defining such a relationship we are dealing with a complex class whose instances have as surrogate space the Cartesian product of the surrogate spaces of the component classes. This new complex class will have its own set of attributes and events as emergent properties.

Their syntactic definition is given using the same constructs we use for elementary classes definition, with one difference: we have to specify explicitly what the events for creating (new) and destroying (destroy) complex class instances are.

An example including the presented language features is given in the appendix. It is about a simple river dams system involving a set of artificial lakes that are related to several water reservoirs. We can exchange water between any artificial lake and its related reservoirs in both directions. The specification declares two elementary classes (artificial_lakes and reservoir) and one complex class stating a relationship between them (the channel class).

B. IMPLEMENTATION

A specification in OASIS being equivalent to a clausal formal theory, as shown in Ramos[2], we are able to translate our specifications to a relational programming language, having the possibility of executing (or animating) them, with the added active capabilities. Every Conceptual Model specification is a first order theory, having the OO-DB extension as model (declarative semantics) and the deductive mechanism as the operational semantics. The OO-DB is implemented in R-OASIS over the standard model of the clausal theory equivalent to the IS specification.

In this way, we have built a prototyping environment composed of a graphical syntax driven editor, a translator that translates OASIS Conceptual Schemas into PROLOG logic programs and a prototyper that allows us to animate our specifications.

The translator reads a textual specification in OASIS and analyzes it syntactically. Then it generates the PROLOG logic program that represents the clausal theory to which the specification is equivalent.

The prototyper animates the specification, saving it when a prototyping session finishes, and loading the saved context to initiate another one if desired (object persistence).

The prototyper has two operating modes:

- manual: this is the mode which allows the introduction of events by external agents and the execution of queries about the society state. It provides a working environment similar to the one shown in Ramos et al.[7], although it has no active capabilities

- automatic: this mode deals with the event triggering. The implemented mechanism consider triggers to be service requests to other objects at given time instants. It allows us to deal with an active system, in which all the specified class triggering conditions are continuously checked (following a turn-around strategy).

At the beginning of a session time takes the value 0. Every valid event is included in the system with its corresponding time occurrence point. Time is then incremented in one unit. We represent time points by natural numbers. Issues dealing with more complex time representations are being developed now (as discussed in Barbic et al. [3]).

The prototyper begins the animation in an automatic mode and we have to generate an interruption (in a controlled way) for to change to manual mode operation. In our implementation we capture the signal **sigint** of UNIX generated from the keyboard by means of typing [CONTROL-C]. To do this we use an interruption management system from PROLOG that treats this sign properly. Afterwards, the system checks possible holding triggering conditions. If it finds one, the prototyper generates the trigger by itself if possible, or asks the user for the needed parameters. In both cases, the user is informed about the triggers in progress as well as if they succeed or fail (because of precondition violation)

The events that can be triggered are both those defined in the specification and those predefined. The prototyper checks the correctness of the triggered event destination.

V. CONCLUSIONS

Starting from a formal class definition and from a precise characterization of what we mean by OO, we have built a working environment that gives us a powerful set of software tools for specifying open and active Information System within an OO and logic model. We can execute our specifications generating the logic programs that represent the clausal theory equivalent to the specification.

We are already working on future extensions of the OASIS environment, according to Bear et al [5]. In short, those extensions are:

i) definition and implementation of classical abstraction mechanisms as class operators. This will give us a constructive way of defining Conceptual Schemas.

ii)implementing graphical and friendly environments, using OO design methods.

iii) developing a more flexible way of axiomatizing time.

iv)improve the system expressivity by dealing with concurrence and paralellism.

v) implement different OASIS versions in order to have a wide expressivity spectrum for the Specification Language..

Our prototype runs on SUN 3/60 and HP 9000 workstations. It includes editors, translators and prototypers. BIM-PROLOG and ZYX_PROLOG respectively are used as the implementation languages.

REFERENCES

[1] Y.Wand. "A Proposal for a Formal Model of Objects" Object-Oriented Concepts, Databases and Applications Kim,W.Lochovski,S. eds. : pp.537-559 ACM Press Addison-Wesley 1989
[2] I.Ramos "Logics and OO-Data Bases: A Declarative Approach." DEXA 90 Springer Verlag 1990.
[3] F.Barbic, R.Maiocchi, B.Pernici "Automatic Deduction of Temporal Information." Universidad Politécnica de Milano. Interim report. 1990
[4] S.Bear,P.Allen,D.Coleman,F.Hayes. "Graphical Specification of Object Oriented Systems" OOPSLA 90
[5] S.Bear,D.Coleman,P.Hayes,O.Pastor:"OASIS: An Object-Oriented Specification Language" (submitted to DOOD 91)
[6] P.Lindgreen ed. "A framework of Information Systems Concepts" FRISCO Interim Report. IFIP WG8.1 1990.
[7] I.Ramos et al. "A Conceptual Schema Specification for Rapid Prototyping" XI-IASTED Conference on Applied Informatics .-Insbruck 1990

APPENDIX

CONCEPTUAL SCHEMA RIVER_DAMS
ELEMENTARY CLASS ARTIFICIAL_LAKE
    ATTRIBUTES
      CONSTANT
        NAME:STRING KEY;
        CAPACITY:NAT;

        SEC_LIMIT:NAT;
        MIN_LEVEL:NAT;
      STATIC CONSTRAINTS CAPACITY>SEC_LIMIT AND
SEC_LIMIT>MIN_LEVEL
      VARIABLES
        LEVEL(ARTIFICIAL_LAKE,NAT,TIME)
                      C L A U S E S
L:ARTIFICIAL_LAKE;R:RESERVOIR;Y,C:NAT;
                T,T1:TIME;
      LEVEL(L,Y,T):-T1 IS T-1 AND LEVEL(L,Y1,T1) AND
      ((NOT(UNLOAD(L,C,T) OR LOAD(L,C,T) OR
                PASS_AL(L,R,C,T) OR
PASS_R(L,R,C,T)) AND Y IS Y1)   OR
(UNLOAD(L,C,T) AND Y IS Y1-C) OR
        (LOAD(L,C,T) AND Y IS Y1+C) OR
        (PASS_R(L,R,C,T) AND Y IS Y1-C) OR
        (PASS_AL(L,R,C,T) AND Y IS Y1+C)).
    EVENTS
      PRIVATE
        LOAD(L,C,T)
        UNLOAD(L,C,T)
      SHARED
        ..PASS_R(L,R,C,T)
        PASS_AL(L,R,C,T)
    PRECONDITIONS
      UNLOAD(L,C,T) IF LEVEL(L,Y,T) AND Y-
C>MIN_LEVEL
    TRIGGERING
      SELF::DESTROY IF LEVEL(L,Y,T) AND
Y>CAPACITY
      SELF::UNLOAD(L,C,T) IF LEVEL(L,Y,T) AND
Y>SEC_LEVEL
      OBJECT:: STOP IF LEVEL(L,Y,T) AND
Y<CAPACITY
END ELEMENTARY CLASS

ELEMENTARY CLASS RESERVOIR
    ATTRIBUTES
      CONSTANT
        RNAME:STRING KEY;
        RCAPACITY:NAT;
        RSEC_LIMIT:NAT;
        RMIN_LEVEL:NAT;
      STATIC CONSTRAINTS
      RCAPACITY>RSEC_LIMIT AND
RSEC_LIMIT>RMIN_LEVEL
      VARIABLES
        RLEVEL(RESERVOIR,NAT,TIME)
                    C L A U S E S
R:RESERVOIR;L:ARTIFICIAL_LAKE;Y,C:NAT;
                T,T1:TIME;
      RLEVEL(R,Y,T):-T1 IS T-1 AND RLEVEL(R,Y1,T1) AND
      ((NOT(RUNLOAD(R,C,T) OR RLOAD(R,C,T) OR
                PASS_AL(L,R,C,T) OR
PASS_R(L,R,C,T)) AND Y IS Y1) OR
(RUNLOAD(R,C,T) AND Y IS Y1-C) OR
        (RLOAD(R,C,T) AND Y IS Y1+C) OR
        (PASS_R(L,R,C,T) AND Y IS Y1-C) OR
        (PASS_AL(L,R,C,T) AND Y IS Y1+C)).

    EVENTS
      PRIVATE
        RLOAD(R,C,T)
        RUNLOAD(R,C,T)
      SHARED
        PASS_R(L,R,C,T)
        PASS_AL(L,R,C,T)
    PRECONDITIONS
      UNLOAD(L,C,T) IF LEVEL(L,Y,T) AND Y-
C>MIN_LEVEL
    TRIGGERING
      SELF::DESTROY IF RLEVEL(L,Y,T) AND
Y>RCAPACITY
      SELF::RUNLOAD(R,C,T) IF RLEVEL(R,Y,T) AND
Y>RSEC_LEVEL
      CLASS:: PAUSE IF RLEVEL(L,Y,T) AND
Y<RCAPACITY
END ELEMENTARY CLASS

COMPLEX CLASS CHANNEL(ARTIFICIAL LAKE, RESERVOIR)
    VALUE
L:ARTIFICIAL_LAKE;R:RESERVOIR,T,T1,T2:TIME;C:NAT;
      CHANNEL(L,R,T):-(PASS_R(L,R,C,T1) AND T1<=T) OR

PASS_AL(L,R,C,T2 AND T2<=T).
    EVENTS
      PRIVATE
        PASS_R(L,R,C,T)
        PASS_AL(L,R,C,T)
    PRECONDITIONS
    PASS_R(L,R,C,T) IF EXISTS(L,T) AND EXISTS(R,T).
    PASS_AL(L,R,C,T) IF EXISTS(L,T) AND EXISTS(R,T).
END COMPLEX CLASS
END CONCEPTUAL SCHEMA.

Roles: A Methodology for Representing Multifaceted Objects

M.P. Papazoglou

Australian National University,

Dept of Computer Science, Canberra ACT 2601

Australia

Abstract

Most of the efforts in the object modeling arena have concentrated on modeling object structure and behavior, with the behavior of objects being delimited by static schema definitions. Although very little has been accomplished in modeling object dynamics, it is widely accepted that the pattern of object interaction is not static, but evolves to adapt to environmental requirements and changes. In this paper we argue in favor of a model for representing object dynamics whereby objects may be represented from diverse, distinct ontological perspectives with each perspective describing different states of an object within the same application domain.

1 Introduction

Among the mandatory properties for object data models several structural properties such as the need of a rich typing system, support of inheritance, and of complex and composite objects have been already identified [1], [2]. Emphasis has also been placed on modeling object behavior where traditionally methods have been used to operate on the state of objects and, thus, represent behavior. More recently, it has been suggested to incorporate rules within the object model for expressing additional object behavior very much in the same way that active data values and daemons are used in knowledge-based systems utilizing frame concepts [2]. It is worth mentioning that all the previous activities have predominantly emphasized static properties of objects.

To reason about a particular problem domain requires not only the ability to describe both the structure and behavior of its components, it also requires representing component dynamics. Therefore, an important aspect of data intensive applications is the demand for representing changes in state and behavior: *objects of interest do not remain static with regard to the rest of the environment they must also possess the ability to evolve.* Unfortunately, dynamic aspects of object data models such the evolution of objects, the management of type changes [3], [4] as well as the notion of dynamic configuration in which the object components are not bound but specified according to user requirements [5] have received only a marginal treatment so far. Another important dynamic aspect in the object world is the ability to describe particular entities from diverse, distinct ontological perspectives, whereby each perspective describes different states of an entity within the same application domain. The ability to express multifaceted object states - referred to as *object roles* in this paper - allows for modeling versatility, richer expression of semantics and permits capturing dynamic aspects of models which are not captured by the current generation of object-oriented database systems.

The purpose of this paper is to present a methodology for representing and manipulating polymorphic object state and behavior in the process of modeling data intensive applications. In this paper we view the object-oriented paradigm under a modeling-driven perspective where the use of objects amounts to adopting data modeling constructs that are direct mappings of problem domain concepts. Evolution of objects is supported by allowing them to undertake or relinquish numerous ephemeral roles. Below, we first examine the usage of the term role in the literature and succinctly report on related activities in the areas of database modeling and knowledge-based representation. We then introduce the basic object model primitives required to support role definition and role manipulation. Finally based on the basic model, we elaborate on the details of extending it with the concepts and primitives which support role definition and role generating activities and operations.

2 Review of Related Work

The role concept has received some attention and has been studied from diverse standpoints by different communities including the AI and data management communities. In the following we will examine the definition and use of the role concept and related research activities by both these communities.

In the database literature several models have been proposed for representing roles during the data modeling process. In our view the most important contribution to the field of role modeling is exemplified by the seminal work of Bachman on the role data model [6]. The definition of the role concept in the role model is taken from the theatrical context and is used to mean a behavioral pattern which may be assumed by modeled entities in a problem domain. The purpose of the role model was to contrast this approach with conventional record-based database systems where logical records were used to represent all aspects of modeled entities and to break-out the one-to-many relationship pattern, carried over from hierarchical and network data models. The role data model introduced a static part for modeled objects called the *entity*, which was derived from its corresponding entity-type, and a dynamic type called the *role-type*. An entity established existence, while the role type established behavior for that entity. An entity could play several roles simultaneously, but only a single occurrence of each role type was permitted per entity. Moreover, a role type was permitted to be associated with several entity types.

The term role has also been used with the relational model but bears a different connotation. It describes way in which an attribute relates to a particular domain [7], [8], [9]. Research activities have concentrated on the issue of providing users with automatic navigation by means of a universal scheme which allows users to traverse through the attribute space based solely on non-qualified attribute names. To present the data as a consistent semantic whole two constraints were imposed on universal schemes: the *universal relation scheme assumption* over the universe of attributes U and the *unique role assumption* [8], [9]. The

8

universal relation scheme assumption states that any attribute in U must correspond to the same class of entities where it appears, while the unique role assumption states that the role of an attribute is unique within a single stored relation so that connections among sets of attributes are unambiguous and accesses to the database are formulated only in terms of attributes. This assumption requires not only that an attribute always represent the same class of entities, but also that it always represent that class of entities under the same role.

The work of Maier et al. [7] utilizes the notion of the object, which corresponds to a unit of retrieval having its own attributes, to develop a universal relation scheme where every attribute is unambiguously associated with the same class of entities wherever it appears. For example, consider a database schema where the attribute *name* may be used to signify the names of employees in an employee relation and same the attribute identifier *name* may be used to signify the names of managers in a manger relation. In [8] it is proposed to solve the problem of distinguishing between the overloaded attribute name in both the employee and manager contexts in terms of a universal relation scheme which uses role relationships to facilitate the expressing of attributes over the same domain to obtain distinct meaning. Some form of renaming is also suggested.

The concept of role in the AI community has been traditionally used to describe attributes by relating objects to each other through the use of binary relationships in the modeled problem domain [10], [11], [12]. In the remainder of this section, we will restrict our attention to the role concept as suggested by the knowledge representation system KL-ONE [10]. The principal elements of KL-ONE are called structured conceptual objects or Concepts and are used to group individual objects into collections indirectly by way of descriptions that collectively apply to all members of such a collection. The term concept is known in data modeling as class.

Concepts are taxonomized around an **is-a** hierarchy where inheritance is introduced along the lines of super-concepts that are used to describe more generic concepts and sub-concepts which describe the more specific concepts. The local internal structure of a concept expresses essential differences between itself and its super-concepts represented in terms of Roles and Structural Descriptions. Roles, describe the potential relationships (i.e., properties, parts, etc) between instances of a given concept and those of other closely associated concepts in the application domain. KL-ONE roles act as generalized attribute descriptors representing potential relationships between the properties of an individual object and the values that this object may assume, i.e., the objects it may reference.

In KL-ONE a *role set* is used to describe the commonalities between a set of potential functional roles that can be played by several distinct concepts at a time. Role sets carry constraints which specify the descriptions of potential role fillers and also express cardinality information. As concepts can be specified in terms of their super-concepts so can role sets. Restriction relations may be established between related role sets to indicate that subtyping inheritance exists between a specific role set and its descendants (more specific role sets).

The role concept used in this paper is builds on the role data model as defined by Bachman [6] and attempts to refine and extend it in several directions based on modeling primitives from the object-oriented paradigm. Some preliminary work on this model was reported in [13] were we indicated how the role concept can be used in conjunction with knowledge-based facilities, while in [14] we reported on how roles may improve the versatility and modeling power of spatial objects.

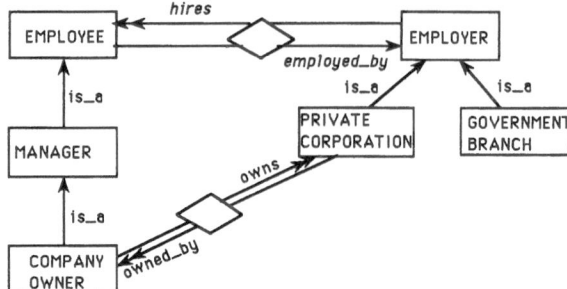

Figure 1: Rudimentary schema for an employee object-base.

3 Object Modeling

To provide a sound basis for discussion we summarize as much of a basic object model as needed to introduce the treatment of roles and delineate those features that we consider as essential. The discussion will focus on objects which have three major characteristics: they all instantiated from *type* descriptions; their instances are grouped into object collections, or *classes*, on the basis of similarity; relationships between any pair of objects may be represented by a fully-fledged object referred to as a *relationship type*.

3.1 Types and Classes

Typically, an object-base is a collection of typed objects of varying granularity where each object belongs to a single type. A type T is a description of the structural and behavioral properties of a set of objects which exhibit the same characteristics and which make up the instances of that type. An individual object reflects an abstraction which combines structure and behavior. A type defines a set of attributes $att(T)$ which encode the internal state of each of its objects.

A type also defines a set of procedural methods, which provide the external interface to its objects, i.e. methods prescribe the operations $ops(T)$ that can be performed on objects and as a result they control the behavior of their associated objects. Attributes and methods are typed in the sense that they have associated types. The type of an attribute is used to constrain the range of the attribute values, while the type of a method is used to constrain the possible return values of the method. Any operation op_i in $op(T)$ can be legally applied to the object o_T, where o_T is an instance of T. Furthermore, any attribute att_i in $att(T)$ is defined for o_T. We also may define a set of type invariants $invs(T)$ which pertain to every object o_T of type T and every invariant inv_i in the set $invs(T)$ must be satisfied by o_T.

In the object model we organize types around a *type* (or *inheritance*) lattice [4], a directed acyclic graph, which supports the notions of generalization and specialization via **is-a** relationships and is used to represent the conceptual schema for an object-base.

Figure-1 illustrates a rudimentary object-base schema in terms of types and relationships, whereby all employees and their subtypes like managers and company owners are persons. However to simplify things, and as we are interested only in the properties of persons as employees, the type **Person** has been omitted from the rudimentary schema. Note that the type **Person** is itself also a subtype of the predefined type **Object** which also does not appear in Figure-1. A typical definition of an **Employee** type for Figure-1 is given in Figure-2.

The notion of class is associated with all instances of a given type. A class is based on the same specification as a type, but it includes the run-time notions of object creation by cloning the prototype for the class, and the *extent*, which is the set of all objects that are instances of the type at any given point in time [1]. Thus objects which correspond to a single type in the inheritance lattice, are grouped together and treated as a single unit, viz. their corresponding class.

```
Person Type Employee {
rank: string;
salary, working_hrs: int;
research_projects :
[1 : Max_projects] → Project
/* invariants: */
working_hrs >= 34;

/* methods: */
do_project_work :
Employee → set − of Project
report_progress_work :
Employee → set − of Report
:
} /* Employee */
```

Figure 2: Definition of type Employee.

Whenever a new type instance is created its corresponding object identifier (OID) is automatically added to the extent of its corresponding class. Here, it is worth mentioning that if an object identifier is added to the extent of a class, then it is automatically added to the extent of all of its superclasses. Class operations include iteration over their member objects and associative retrieval of objects by specification of predicates in terms of the object properties. Classes are viewed as objects themselves and have properties of their own. Class properties are clearly not identical to the properties of their qualifying types: their purpose is to not to check program correctness, but rather to create and classify objects. In this sense we implicitly define a class-lattice which parallels the inheritance lattice and that groups objects according to their type.

3.2 Relationship Types and Objects

An attractive property of the object model is the use of inter-object relationships to facilitate the process of associating the basic units of information, viz. the typed objects. Types, and consequently objects, are related to each other through the use of binary associators which are existence dependent on the objects they associate. The arguments of an associator can, thus, be uninstantiated variables signifying types or names of actual objects. The concept (or semantic) associator is used to bind objects together semantically to form a *relationship network*.

A relationship network may be defined by appropriately interconnecting a set of triplets < t1, R, t2 > where t1 and t2 are types and R is their defining relationship; t1 is the origin of the relationship, while t2 is its destination. For example, the relationship type **hires**, expressed as < *Employer, hires, Employee* >, connects an **Employer** object with a set of **Employee** objects - the destination of the relationship.

4 The Role Concept Revisited

The term role in this paper is used to specify a scenario of behavior (undertaken by an object) which is determined on the basis of the collection of properties that are associated with the object in the center of interest and are responsible for bringing the role into existence.

To understand the implications of these issues and in particular to comprehend how roles impact the behavior of objects we must first consider how objects join their associated class extents. We illustrate this process by means of the simple schema of the employer-employee object-base schema depicted in Figure-1. Figure-1 shows the type lattice definition for the object-base schema of the sample object-base used in this text, whereas Figure 3 illustrates the class lattice associated with this particular inheritance lattice. Figure 3 also shows the particular OIDs associated with the type instances of the types depicted in Figure-1.

Consider for example, the OID *pc1* which is associated with an object of type **Private_Corporation**. When this OID is generated it is not included only in the extent of its corresponding class **Private_Corporation** but also in the extent of its superclass **Employer**. This insertion operation is based on the principle of shallow copying ala-Smalltalk where references are established to the "copied" objects. If the collection of properties is derived by instantiating the object from its type definition then we may speak of the *static*, or *predetermined*, role of an object.

The set of the diverse static roles played by an object is obviously determined by its position in the class hierarchy. The position of the object in the class hierarchy is detected by the presence of an OID for this particular object in a directed path (or paths in the case of multiple-inheritance in which case we speak about a class lattice and not of a hierarchy) reachable from some user created class at the top of the hierarchy to the lowest possible level in the hierarchy. The set of roles for a given object may then be determined by backtracking from that lowest level - which includes the OID for this particular object - in the class lattice to return to the top of the lattice. For example, in the case of the object signified by the OID *pc1* we may speak of the static role of an **Employer** object (the object at the top of the class lattice) as that of a **Private_Corporation**, see Figure 3.

As a general rule the OID for the particular object which is the current focus of attention must appear in the extent of all classes in the class lattice which generate its successive roles. The notation $< oid^{C_1}, oid^{C_2}, ..., oid^{C_n} >$ indicates changes to state for the same OID which signify the set roles undertaken by the same object. In this notation the symbol C_i with $i \geq 1$ symbolizes the name of the role defining classes with the most generalized role defining class appearing on the left. For example a valid static role defining chain for the schema of Figure-1 would be $< oid^{Employee}, oid^{Manager}, oid^{Company\_owner} >$.

We shall denote role relationships by $R_2 \rightarrow R_1$, where R_2 is a role undertaken by R_1. The symbol $\rightarrow$ is taken to mean *role_of* and the relation induced by it is obviously transitive. In the previous example, $MANAGER \rightarrow EMPLOYEE$ and $COMPANY\_OWNER \rightarrow MANAGER$, therefore $COMPANY\_OWNER \rightarrow EMPLOYEE$. The role concept is not symmetric: the fact $R_2 \rightarrow R_1$ does not imply the converse relation. Hence, an object can only exist in the role context of R_2 *iff* it already exists in the role context of R_1. In all cases it is assumed that a supertype/subtype relationship exists between objects in the role contexts R_1 and R_2, i.e., objects in R_2 are all subtypes of objects in R_1.

4.1 Transient Roles

In the dynamic case, a role specifies a defined behavioral pattern which is not prescribed by the inheritance lattice and may be assumed by the objects themselves. This type of object dynamism can be achieved by further subdividing and specializing the objects contained in the nodes and the leaves of the class lattice, and

10

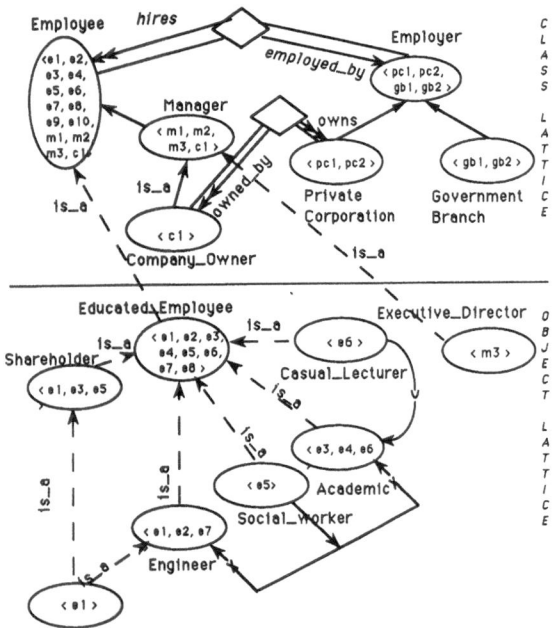

Figure 3: The class and object lattice for the object-base schema in Figure-1.

defining subclasses dynamically. Each of the new classes which are created in this manner may be though of as a *role defining class* and each of its member objects may be thought of as a role played by its counterpart superobject. We now expand on this aspect.

Figure 3 shows how the class lattice becomes an *object lattice*. Consider for example the case of an **Employee** object with OID e_1 which dynamically obtains the role of an **Educated_Employee** and an **Engineer** as indicated by the dashed lines in Figure 1. Dashed lines here indicate the existence of *transient roles*, i.e., roles which an object may choose to assume or relinquish. In the previous example, the role sequence $< e_1^{Employee}, e_1^{Educated\_Employee}, e_1^{Engineer} >$ defines one static role, namely that of $e_1^{Employee}$, and two transient roles, namely $e_1^{Educated\_Employee}, e_1^{Engineer}$ for the employee object with OID e_1. We imply that we have now introduced two classes, namely **Educated_Employee** and **Engineer**, that do not correspond directly to the schema types in Figure 1. The class **Employee** from which these two new classes have been created is referred to as their *role of origin*.

In the previous example, roles were introduced at the leaf-level of the class lattice. Although, role defining objects may also be introduced at intermediate levels of the class hierarchy, e.g, as a further specialization of the objects in class **Manager**. The invariant for role creation is that role defining classes should not intercept the **is-a** edges between any two existing classes in either the class or the object lattice. Consider for example, the two role defining sequences $< e_3^{Employee}, e_3^{Educated\_Employee}, e_3^{Academic} >$, $< e_1^{Employee}, e_1^{Educated\_Employee}, e_1^{Engineer} >$ for objects which specialize **Educated_Employee** objects into **Academic** and **Engineer** objects, respectively. Dynamic role/relationships ala KL-ONE are also possible as we shall see in a forthcoming section.

As already established from the context of Figure 3 a partic-

ular object may concurrently play more than one roles. Therefore, the existence of all the roles of interest for a given object fully characterize that object, e.g., the **Employee** object with OID e_1. Thus, a many-to-many correspondence exists between a given role and a given object: an object may play several different roles and a role may be played by different objects. For example, the employer role may be associated with the role instances private corporation and government, see Figure 1. In a counter example, the role instances social worker, shareholder, and educated employee may all characterize an employee object. Multiple roles are used to partition an object into areas of independent interest.

4.2 Classification of Transient Roles

We may identify four different semantic relationships that any two given objects may have with respect to each other (under the perspective of their roles):

1. Objects may belong to different domain classes and hence will play different roles.
2. Objects may originate from the same domain class and may play the same role.
3. Objects may originate from the same domain class and may play distinct *non-exclusive* or *mutually exclusive* roles.
4. Objects may originate from different domain classes (having some common ancestor in the lattice) and may play the same role. This category is in fact exemplified by multiple inheritance.

Objects which belong to the first category are role-defining objects which have no direct or indirect **is-a** relationship to each other. They have different OIDs and nothing in common if they originate from classes which belong to partitioned domains in the lattice, e.g., **Government_Branch** and **Educated_Employee** objects. Or they could have a few things in common such as **Executive_Director** and **Academic** objects, which have different OIDs and share only some common **Employee** properties together, see Figure 3. In a forthcoming session we will indicate how we can couple these non-related objects together and generate relationship roles.

The second category objects originate from the same domain classes and play the same dynamic role. For example, consider two different **Educated_Employee** objects signified by their respective OIDS, e_1 and e_2, which assume the additional role as **Engineer** objects.

The third category objects originate from the same domain class and play distinct dynamic roles which are referred to as non-exclusive roles as they do not affect one another. It is also possible to have mutually exclusive roles where an objects blocks another and prevents it from assuming an additional role. In this text all roles are assumed to be non-exclusive, unless otherwise stated. This aspect will be treated in section 4.3.

The fourth category concerns itself with role-defining objects which originate from different domain classes and play the same role. Obviously, these are objects which have the same OID and play a common role, which is a further specialization of two existing roles. For example, consider the **Educated_Employee** object with OID e_1, which has joined the extent of both classes **Shareholder** and **Engineer**. As these two classes may have a common subclass called **Engineer_Shareholder**, the object e_1 may then join the extent of this class in which case the role defining sequences for this particular object will be:

$$< e_1^{Employee}, e_1^{Educated\_Employee}, e_1^{Shareholder}, e_1^{Engineer\_Shareholder} >$$
$$< e_1^{Employee}, e_1^{Educated\_Employee}, e_1^{Engineer}, e_1^{Engineer\_Shareholder} >$$

This indicates that the ordering of roles is a partial order, i.e., a role may have several successors in which case we have a branching role sequence.

4.3 Role Interaction

Role interaction is taken to mean how objects in role defining class extents may relate to one another. Role interaction patterns have an effect which is similar to that of the operators for relinquishing, suspending and assuming roles. We may identify three types of role interaction: *role blocking*, *role dominance* and *role linkages*. Role interaction is closely related to role generation operations which is accounted for in some detail in a companion publication [15].

4.3.1 Role Blocking

This category of role interaction is mainly exemplified by the concept of mutual-exclusion. Two roles stemming as specializations from a single role defining class are mutually exclusive if an object in this class's extent is hindered (or blocked) from assuming both of them and is forced to select either one.

Consider for example, the **Educated_Employee** objects which may wish to assume the additional roles of **Engineer**, **Academic** and **Social_Worker** objects. In this case it would be wise to consider their respective subclasses as being mutually exclusive, i.e., objects which appear in the extents of the classes **Engineer**, or **Academic**, are not allowed to appear in the extent of class **Social_Worker** and vice-versa. In this case we may speak of mutually exclusive roles. This is indicated in Figure 3 by the presence of the arcs intercepted by the symbol X which are directed from the blocking towards the blocked roles. Obviously, all roles which are not of type mutually exclusive are called non-exclusive. It is apparent that if two or more role defining classes are mutually exclusive then all of their subclasses are also mutually exclusive, e.g., **Engineer_Shareholder** objects cannot be members of the class **Social_Worker** and vice-versa.

4.3.2 Role Dominance

In some cases it may also be necessary to consider role dominance during interaction. For example, the **Educated_Employee** role **Academic** may be dominant with respect to the **Casual_Lecturer** role. Here we assume that casual lecturers are non-academics, however, they possess the right to join the ranks of academic once they lose their role as casuals. This relationship is signified by the horizontal arcs intercepted by the symbol ⊆ and directed from the dominant role to the dominated role, see Figure 3.

Consider the case of an **Educated_Employee** object which takes on the transient role of **Casual_Lecturer** and then tries to assume the role of an **Academic**. From Figure 3, we note that the role of **Casual_Lecturer** dominates the role of **Academic**. The dominant role means that although the object's OID (say e_6) may join the extent of **Casual_Lecturer** and **Academic** the object can be seen only in its role of **Casual_Lecturer**. Its behavior as an **Academic** is suspended, and any further dynamic roles which stem from **Academic** are also barred. This object may lose its **Casual_Lecturer** role only after a role changing event takes place, e.g., after the corresponding person obtains his/her doctorate and is hired as a proper academic, in which case it assumes the behavior of an **Academic**.

The *relinquish* and *suspend* role operations (which relinquish and suspend a given role, respectively [15]) can be exemplified by dominant roles which wish to give up their status in favor of one of their dominated roles. Consider the use of a simple rule-based sublanguage with an *if-then* structure, and the following rule:

if Casual_Lecturer.Qualification = "Phd" **and**
Casual_Lecturer.Appointment = "Full-time"
then relinquish < *Casual_Lecturer* > [**assume** < *Academic* >]

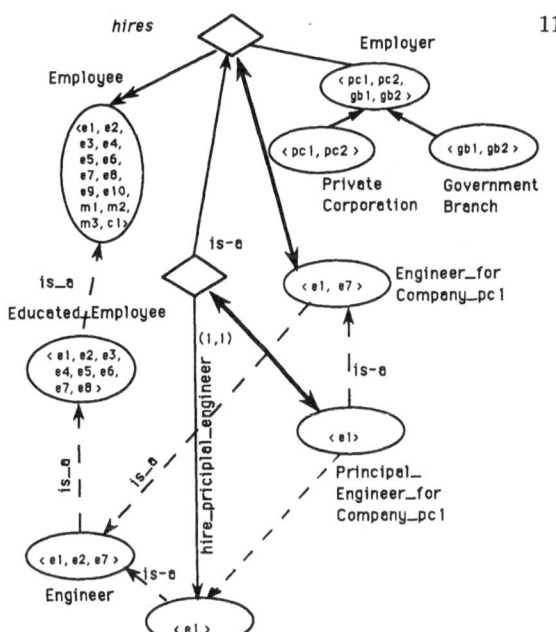

Figure 4: Defining dynamic object roles via the use of relationships.

This rule specifies that an object which plays the roles **Casual_Lecturer** and **Academic** may assume the academic status only after its attributes qualification and appointment in the casual lecturer status have obtained the appropriate values. In which case it leaves the extent of **Casual_Lecturer** and obtains a proper **Academic** status. All **Casual_Lecturer** properties and values are then lost.

A given role may dominate more than one other roles, however, a restriction which is imposed here is that a given role may not be dominated by more than one roles. If an object relinquishes its dominant role then it immediately appears in the extent of the dominated role(s) provided that this role is not suspended in the consequent of a rule, like the one specified above. If an object has more than one dominant roles and only one role is specified in the consequent of the rule then only the specified role is assumed by the relevant objects and the others are lost.

4.3.3 Role Linkages

In the role model a relationship may be used to act as a predicate and capture the commonality among a set of individual role playing objects (e.g., what kind of academic qualifications all officers of a particular company may have in common).

Here, we may speak of role defining relationships which are used to relate objects playing one role with other such objects in the class or object lattice. Such relationships relate two classes of objects and generate a new role for a subset of the objects which are included in the extent of the role defining class at the destination of the relationship type. Consider for example the relationship type **Hires** between the types **Employer** and **Employee**. This relationship type accepts the class of **Employer** objects as its origin and the class of **Employee** objects as its destination and imposes the constraint that a single **Employer** object may be related to a set of **Employee** objects. This relationship is a polymorphic relationship which can be used at the subtype level of the class *Employer* and can make references to subtypes of **Employee** objects like **Educated_Employee Engineer** and so on. The

12

statement:

create *Engineer_for_Company_pc_1* **as hires** (pc_1, **set-of** *Engineer*)

generates a new role called **Engineer_for_Company_pc_1** and populates it with the **Engineer** objects that are associated with the particular **Private_Company** identified by the OID pc_1. The new role is a subtype of the class **Engineer** which is the destination of the role defining relationship **Hires**. This situation is illustrated in Figure 4 where the presence of the double-headed thick arrow indicates the generation of a new role via the use of a role defining relationship. Other such roles may be defined once we relate **Private_Corporation** and **Government_Branch** class objects with **Academic** or **Shareholder** objects.

By the same token if we define a subtype of the relationship type **Hires**, say **Hire_Principal_Engineer**, then we may able to generate a new role called **Principal_Engineer_for_Company_pc_1** for the **Private_Company** identified by the OID pc_1. It is interesting to note that since the role **Engineer_for_Company_pc_1** was created by th relationship type **Hires** and **Hires_Principal_Engineer** is its subtype, then the class associated with that role, namely **Principal_Engineer_for_Company_pc_1**, is a subtype of **Engineer_for_Company_pc_1**. This operation parallels the *restriction* relation in KL-ONE and may be defined as follows:

If a class C_1 which is the destination of a relationship type R_1 has a subclass C_2, and if a relationship type R_2, defined as having C_2 as its destination, is a subtype of R_1, then every set of roles generated by imposing R_2 is a proper subset of the set of roles generated by imposing R_1 on C_1, provided that R_1 and R_2 designate the same class of origin, say C_3. Moreover, R_2 satisfies all the constraints imposed on both R_1 and R_2.

Observe that in Figure 4 the lower and upper bound which define the range cardinalities for the set of objects generated by the role defining relationship are both set to 1, meaning that there is only a single **Principal_Engineer** per **Private_Company**, indicated by a single-headed arrow in Figure 4. From Figure 4 we obtain, $C_1 = Engineer$, $C_2 = Principal\_Engineer$ and $C_3 = Private\_Company$, while $R_1 = Engineer\_for\_Company\_pc_1$ and $R_2 = Principal\_Engineer\_for\_Company\_pc_1$.

5 Conclusions

A role model was introduced and described in terms of a basic object model and several operations on roles were suggested and accounted for. With the role model objects are described in terms of roles for extending and influencing their life cycle behavior. Roles were seen to naturally supplement the basic object model modeling constructs with dynamic properties and features of the modeled problem domain and to be orthogonal to the notions of types and classes. The operations on roles resulted in modeling additional behavioral aspects, other than those specified in schemas. Modeling situations which involve precedence and exclusion among the behavioral aspects of objects are also possible. Another appealing property is the generation of additional object behavior in terms of relationships established between existing classes of objects. A full implementation of an initial prototype of the role model is underway. The implementation is based on a modeling substrate which relies on a tight coupling of the object-oriented database system Ontos [16] and the C Language Integrated Production System (CLIPS).

References

[1] M. Atkinson, et al. "The Object- Oriented Database System Manifesto", *Procs. 1st Deductive Object-Oriented Database Conf.*, Kyoto 1989.

[2] M. Stonebraker, et al. "Third Generation Data Base System Manifesto", *Procs. of the Object-Oriented Database Task Group Workshop*, pp. 68-83, Atlantic City, May 1990.

[3] A. Skarra, S. Zdonik "The Management of Changing Types in an Object-Oriented Database", in *Research Directions in Object-Oriented Systems*, B. Schreiver, P. Wegner eds., MIT Press, 1987.

[4] J. Banerjee *et al.*, "Data Model Issues for Object- Oriented Applications", *ACM Trans. on Office Automation Systems*, vol. 5, no. 1, pp. 3-26, 1987.

[5] J. Joseph et al. "Strawman Reference Model for Change Management of Objects", *Procs. of the Object-Oriented Database Task Group Workshop*, pp. 68-83, Atlantic City, May 1990.

[6] C.W. Bachman "The Role Concept in Data Models", *Procs. VLDB 77 Conf.*, pp. 464-476, 1977.

[7] D. Maier., D. Warren "Specifying Connections for a Universal Relation Scheme Database", *Proc. ACM SIGMOD Conf.*, pp. 1-17, 1982.

[8] D. Maier, D. Rozenshtein, J. Stein "Representing Roles in Universal Scheme Interfaces", *IEEE Trans. on Software Eng.*, vol. 11, n. 7, pp. 644-652, July 1985.

[9] D. Maier et al. "PIQUE: A Relational Query Language without Relations", *Information Systems*, vol. 12, no. 3, pp. 317-335, 1987.

[10] R. Brachman, J. Schmolze "An Overview of the KL-ONE Representation System", *Cognitive Science*, vol. 9, no. 2, pp. 171-216, Apr. 1985.

[11] A. Borgida, et al. "CLASSIC: A Structural Data Model for Objects", *SIGMOD Record*, vol. 18, no.2, pp. 58-67, June 1989.

[12] R. Brachman, et al. " The CLASSIC knowledge Representation System, or, KL-ONE: The Next Generation", *Workshop on Formal Aspects of Semantic Networks*, Feb. 1989.

[13] M. P. Papazoglou, C. Hoffmann "The Role of Knowledge in an Active Information Environment," *1st Int'l Conf. on Tools for AI*, pp. 376-385, Virginia Oct. 1989.

[14] Q. Li, M.P. Papazoglou, J.L. Smith "Dynamic Object Models with Spatial Application", *Computer Software & Applications Conference: COMPSAC-91*, Tokyo, Japan, Sept. 1991.

[15] M. P. Papazoglou "Representing and Manipulating Polymorphic Objects", *submitted for publication*, May 1991.

[16] T. Andrews, C. Harris, J. Duhl "Ontos Object Database", Ontologic Inc., Burlington, MA, 01803, March 1990.

The ALDOUS90 Project :
Merging Object-Oriented Databases and Knowledge-based Systems

F.-Y. VILLEMIN, A. PAOLI, I. TOURRILHES & M. LE

CENTRE D'ETUDE ET DE RECHERCHE EN INFORMATIQUE DU CNAM
292, rue Saint Martin 75141 PARIS CEDEX03 (France)

ABSTRACT

The ALDOUS90 project is originated in the difficulties met in realizing complex expert systems (in CAD, CASE, ...) using commercial shells such as KEE : they provide a good set of facilities for developing expert systems, but as the amount of data increases, their performance drastically decreases. Object-oriented databases, such as O2 of the GIP-ALTAIR, optimize object management which is not done in these shells. The ALDOUS90 is aimed at giving O2 functionalities similar to KEE : a first-order rule language, a context mechanism (versions), a context management system (a powerful inference engine), an extended ATMS (to maintain consistencies of versions, schemas and objects), an extended RETE algorithm (to select rules), an inferential distance algorithm (to solve conflicts in multiple inheritance) and a device to add default values to classes.

0   Introduction

Expert systems in some domains require a huge amount of data: CAD, CAM, CASE , intelligent user-interfaces as met in document retrieval, office automation, image manipulation, ...

Today, existing expert systems are programmed using shells (such as KEE™[1], ART™[2]...). Applications (expert systems) are limited due to the lack of efficiency in data management of the shells. To overcome these problems, engineers have to add, at the knowledge level, tricks to increase the performance [Benay & all 89]. But, data-level efficiency is the main concern of databases designers. It seems very tempting to merge database and expert system technologies to get better shells for data-intensive applications. Most of commercial shells (KEE™, ART™, ..) provide an object-oriented language (more or less a frame language) together with a rule-based mechanism for implementing inferential knowledge.

Recently a new database paradigm appeared relying on object-oriented programming. Many prototypes or commercial systems are now available (ORION [Banerjee & all 87], Gemstone [Maier & all 86], ONTOS [Andrews & Harris 87]...). The O2 system of GIP-ALTAIR[3] was chosen for its merges, in its principle, the relational and the object-oriented database models [Lécluse & all. 88].

The basic idea behind the ALDOUS90 project is to find what it is needed to add to object-oriented database systems such as O2 to get functionalities of expert system shells such as KEE™, and, try to appreciate what could be gained from it. This paper describes the motivations behind ALDOUS90 and its structure and behavior (which are fully explained in [Paoli 91, Lé 91, Tourrilhes 91]).

1   The O2 Model

In object-oriented database systems, data are organized into objects. Each object has its own identity : data and their behavior are encapsulated under this object identity. Manipulations on data are done via methods attached to objects.

In O2 [Lécluse & all. 88], users may access data within a programming language (CO2, an extension of C) directly on the complex values of objects. A complex object is an object with attributes having for values other objects, eventually complex ones. O2 is a strongly typed system. Classes define types (a type is the name of a class). Built-in types and type constructors in O2 are :

1) The symbol **ANY** is associated to the predefined class "object",
2) Atomic type : integer, float, boolean, char, string...,
3) If $t_1,..., t_n$ are types and $a_1,..., a_n$ are attributes, then the tuple : $[a_1:t_1,..., a_n:t_n]$ is a type,
4) If t is a type, the set $\{t\}$ is a type,
5) If t is a type, the list $<t>$ is a type.

Methods are defined using their signature : the signature of a method m belonging to a class C is an expression : "$m : C \times t_1 \times ... \times t_n \rightarrow t$" where t is the type of the result, $t_1,..., t_n$ are types of the parameters (t, $t_1,..., t_n$ are class names defined in the schema). The body of a method is a CO2 program.

In O2, objects are instances of classes. Object identity and encapsulation are adopted : each object receives an unique object identifier "OID", and, object manipulation is done via methods associated to the classes of objects.

---

[1]KEE™ is a trade mark of Intellicorp.

[2]ART™ is a trade mark of Inference Corporation.

---

[3]GIP-ALTAIR is a consortium founded by IN2 (a Siemens subsidiary), INRIA and the LRI (University of Paris XI).

In order to maintain the database consistency, in O2 it is forbidden to remove a class, if it has instances, subclasses, or if it is referenced by other classes, or, some methods, and to remove an instance, if it is referenced by other instances. But it is allowed to declare new classes, to add methods to a class, to modify the values of attributes of a class.

In O2, there is a multiple inheritance of structures and of methods : a sub-class inherits of types and methods defined in its super-classes. Conflict resolution is done statically and user-defined : by redefining types or methods in sub-classes where a conflict appears.

2   KEE™ vs O2

In O2, classes are similar to abstract data-types. They describe a set of objects having the same structure and the same behavior. In O2, Objects are seen a structural process, while in KEE™ they form a conceptual point of view : an object is a prototype of a concept. A class is a prototype of a typical (standard) object, a typical situation or a typical event. A class is described as a "frame", i.e. : a set of attributes, and, for each attributes a set of "facets". There are two sort of facets : the declarative ones, to specify properties of information stored in the attributes, and, the procedural ones, to express how to compute and to use, values associated to attribute.

In KEE™ a class describes the default information about a set of entities. KEE™ is not strongly typed : there is no constraint on the class hierarchies. As in O2, inheritance is related to inclusion of sets of instances of classes : the conflict in names have to be solved by the user, and the inheritance mode is mentioned in a facet.

Similarities and differences in the data model of O2 (V1) and of KEE™ are shown in the table below.

In KEE™, inferential knowledge is implemented as a set of productions (rules). Rules are non-monotonic. In order to maintain the overall consistency, KEE™ uses different contexts, called KEE-worlds™[4] [Filman, 1987], [Morris & Nado, 1986] (similar to ART™'s Viewpoints™[5]), and an ATMS [de Kleer, 1986]. KEE-world™ are somewhat databases versions : objects can have different values at the same time, but in different versions of the base.

3   ALDOUS90 : a KEE-like model above O2

In order to extend O2 to have the functionalities of KEE needed to write complex expert system, we suggest to add to O2 a first-order rule language, a context mechanism (versions), a context management system, an extended ATMS [de Kleer 86] (to maintain consistencies of the versions, and, of schemas and objects in each version), an extended RETE algorithm [Forgy 82] to select rules in a context, to implement the inferential distance algorithm [Touretzky 84] to solve conflicts in multiple inheritance, to add to classes, specific methods to implement default values.

---

[4]KEE-world™ is a trade mark of Intellicorp.

[5]Viewpoints™ is a trade mark of Inference Corporation.

	O2(v1)	KEE
Class	YES	YES
Prototype	NO	YES
Object	YES	YES
Type/Value	YES	NO
Method	YES	YES
Facet	NO	YES
Default Value	NO	YES
Exceptionnal Attribute/Methods	YES	YES
Structure Inheritance	YES	YES
Value " "	NO	YES
Multiple Inheritance	YES	YES
Conflict resolution	NO(1	YES(2
Recovering a schema from an object	NO	YES
Dynamic evolution of the schema	NO	YES

(1) conflict in names have to be solved by the user
(2) inheritance mode is mentioned in a facet

Table : KEE™ vs O2

Due to restriction in O2, we had to build (inside O2) an accessible meta-schema. The meta-schema is an O2-schema such that the schema of each version is an instance of this schema. The mechanisms used to maintain the consistency of the database are also used to maintain the meta-schema consistency.

4   The Rule Language

Inferential knowledge is expressed as rules :
       "IF" <condition> "THEN" <action>

Conditions (and actions) consist in conjunctions of elementary conditions (and actions) : elementary conditions and actions refer to constants, messages and pairs (<class>, <attribute>).

Elementary conditions are atomic laterals (atomic predicates or negation of atomic predicates).

Elementary actions are simple updates of the base : assignment "=" of a value to an attribute, assert "+=" or retract "-=" of a set to another set, adjunction or deletion of a value, of an instance, of an attribute (modification is the composition of a deletion of the old item followed by the adjunction of the new item).

This rule system is non-monotonic : some rules may retract items used in their conditions for selection : such rules are called "action rules", and, pure monotonic ones are called "deduction rules".

The problem of assignment of drivers and trucks described by Filman [Filman 87] is expressed by four O2 classes :
Class : Set-of-drivers (unique instance : the set of drivers)
     - name : string;
     - value : set-of Driver;
Class : Trip
     - name : string;
     - truck : Truck;

- driver : Driver;
- distance : integer;
- driver-cost : integer;
- truck-cost : integer;

Class : Truck
 - name : string;
 - location : integer;
 - unit-cost : integer;

Class : Driver
 - name : string;
 - location : integer;
 - unit-cost : integer;

The initial database (context W_0) may contain instances such as :

(trip$_1$, [name :"Indianapolis-Chicago", truck : nil, driver : nil, distance : 50, cost : nil])

(truck$_1$, [name : "Canonball", location : "Indianapolis", unit-cost : 10])

(set-of-drivers$_1$, [name : " ", value : {driver1, driver2, driver3}])

(driver$_1$, [name : "White", location : "Indianapolis", unit-cost : 7])

(driver$_2$, [name : "Green", location : "Indianapolis", unit-cost : 7])

(driver$_3$, [name : "Grey", location : "Detroit", unit-cost : 3])

Some of the rules to assign driver to trip and to compute costs of trips are :

R_1 : "**If** Trip->driver == nil **Then choice** Trip->driver in Set-of-drivers"

R_2 : "**If** Trip->truck != nil
   Then Trip->truck-cost = Trip->truck->unit-cost * Trip->distance"

R_3 : "**If** Trip->driver != nil
   Then Trip->driver-cost = Trip->driver->unit-cost * Trip->distance"

R_4 : "**If** Trip->truck->location != Trip->driver->location **Then False**"

R_5 : "**If** Trip->driver->name == "White"
   & Trip->truck->name == "Canonball"
   Then False" ("White" is disable)

5   The Context Management System (CMS) [Lé, 1991]

As in KEE™ rules are invoked in forward chaining. Hypotheses (assumption) are treated into different contexts. The contexts are organized into a hierarchy, the root of which is the database. An ATMS is used to maintain the consistency of the contexts in the tree and of data inside a context.

The use of a meta-schema aside objects in the database (due to the impossibility to recover the schema of an object) requires an a priori static and lexicographical analysis of the set of rules : every mentioned modification of the schema is reported into the meta-schema (There no dynamic modification of schema in O2).

The role of the CMS is to build a consistent tree of consistent contexts. At the present stage, the CMS implements no control on the rules : it builds a new context for each selectable rule. In a near future, it will be controlled to express expert reasoning.

The behavior of the ALDOUS90 system is sketched in figure 1.

The CMS stops when no rule is applicable in any context. Otherwise, it takes a leaf context, sends it to the filter which checks whether some rules are selectable, then analyses the resulting inferences : for deduction rules, it creates a new (son) context for each rule, and, sends the inference to the ATMS, and, for action rules, the CMS first sends to the ATMS the deleted facts, which returns all the other facts to be deleted, creates a new context, and the rest of the inference is treated as in a deduction rule.

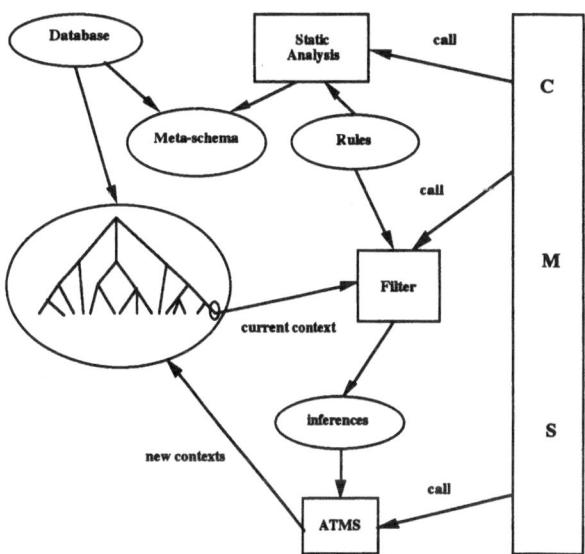

Figure 1: Structure of ALDOUS90

The meta-schema is unique and stands for the meta-schema of all versions. There is no copy of data in each version : each OID receives a list of pair for each attribute : <(Context : value)>.

In the example above, in the context W_0 the rule R_1 is firable three times, since **CHOICE** means a unique value for driver and Set-of-driver contains three drivers, three new contexts W_1, W_2 and $W3$ are thus created.

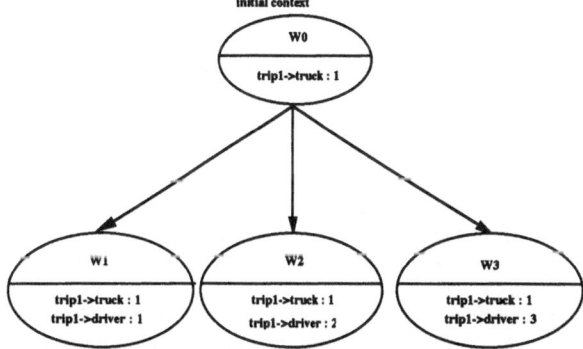

Figure 2 : Contexts created by firing the rule R1 in context W0

The schema of the base is modelized by the meta-schema (in O2 it has to be built by the user as an O2 object). It is used by rules to reason on the database schema considered as an instance of the meta-schema : every update of the schema is a new instance.

In ALDOUS90 the CMS creates the new instances of the meta-schema for every update of the schema. For a given version (or ALDOUS90 context), an object is consistent in this version if it is valid in regards with the update generating the version :

 - every instance of a class is consistent if its class is consistent,
 - every instance of a class having an attribute with value being a complex object is consistent if it is consistent,
 - the schema of the version of a class is consistent if its meta-classes and its attributes schemas and its methods are consistent.

If a schema or a method are not valid in the version, the version is inconsistent. It is therefore possible to remove a class, or an attribute in a class, or a method to a class in a new version :
- every instances, subclasses or methods of a removed class are removed,
- every instances referenced by a removed instance are removed,
- every classes having attributes defined by a removed class are removed.

(in any case, their labels are no longer included into the context label).

The meta-schema being a subset of the database, the mechanisms used to maintain the consistency of the database also maintain the consistency of the meta-schema.

As mentioned above, in O2 it is required to have a meta-schema aside objects in the database since it is impossible to recover the schema from an object. In a multiple versions database it seems useful to have an unique (non-versionized) and accessible meta-schema so that the schema of each version is an instance of this meta-schema.

6   The filtering algorithm [Tourrilhes, 1991]

A filtering algorithm determines which rules are selectable (conditions satisfied) for a given state of the fact base (database). It is a time consuming operation. Some algorithms provide a high efficiency, such as RETE [Forgy, 1982] which is based upon two main ideas :
- different rules often share common elementary conditions. Therefore we can separate the checking of elementary conditions from the instanciation of rules : a fact is unified with elementary conditions only once per cycle.
- applying a selectable rule usually modifies only a small set of facts in the base : it is only necessary to compare this set with elementary conditions of selectable rules (at the preceding cycle) and to withdraw the rules no longer selectable, and to add rules that become selectable. At each cycle, only a small set of fact is considered.

These ideas are implemented as a directed network : input nodes being elementary conditions, and, output nodes being a rule name. Facts are propagated through the network.

In ALDOUS90, facts are 4-tuples (object, attribute, value, context). The RETE algorithm has been extended to consider :
- contexts (it is necessary to determine all the facts holding in a given context).
- default values, and, inherited values and thus to solve inheritance conflicts (a non valued attribute of an instance of an object may inherit of a default value defined in the schema of the current context).

To solve the inheritance conflicts (and the default value problems), we have implemented in ALDOUS90 an inferential distance algorithm [Touretzky, 1984], which is based on an implicit ordering of defaults

In the example for the four (first) given rules a RETE network, extended to classes (no inheritance problem here) is shown figure 3.

The condition part of a rule holding in a context W_j will hold in its cach son context W_j, unless there is an update of a fact involved in this condition. This case is easily detected by the CMS (it checks if the facts returned by the filter still hold in the context W_j in which it computes the action part of the rule. This test is done in linear time while retesting in a context using RETE is much more expensive in time [Albert, 88].

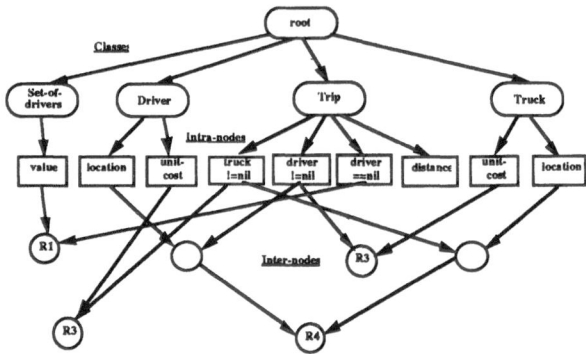

Figure 3 : The RETE network of the rules

The condition part of a rule holding in a context W_i will hold in its son contexts $W_{i+1},..., W_{i+k}$ unless there is an update of a fact involved in this condition. This case is easily detected by the CMS (it checks if the facts returned by the filter still hold in the context W_j in which it computes the action part of the rule. This test is done in a linear time while retesting in a context using RETE is much more expensive in time [Albert, 88]. An agenda with lists is implemented in the CMS (in the context W_i, when a condition part of a rule is found holding by the filter, a new line consisting of the list $\{W_i\}$ is added to the agenda, when son contexts $W_{i+1},..., W_{i+k}$ of a context W_i are created, W_i is withdrawn from the the lists and $W_{i+1},..., W_{i+k}$ are added, when an inconsistent context W_i is found W_i is deleted from all the lists and a line consisting of an empty list is removed).

7   An extended ATMS [Paoli, 1991]

A classical Assumption-based Truth Maintenance System (ATMS) [de KLEER, 1986], maintains for each fact in the base a special structure, its node, which stores all sets of assumptions (hypotheses) under which the fact holds.

The input to an ATMS is a set of propositional literals L, a set of propositional clauses C constructed from those literals, and a distinguished set of *assumptions* $A \subset L$.

An *environment* is a subset of A. An environment E is inconsistent (called *nogood*) if the union of E with C is not satisfiable. A *choose* is a clause whose literals are all assumptions and is often written *choice* $\{A_1,..., A_m\}$. A literal l is said to *hold* in environment E if l follows from the union of E and C under the rules of propositional logic. A nogood is *minimal* (with respect to subset) if it contains no other nogood as a subset.

The ATMS problem is to find all minimal nogoods and   to identify for every literal $l \in L$ - A a set of environments $\{E_1,..., E_k\}$ (called the *label*) having the four properties :
1 - Soundness : l holds in each E_i.
2 - Consistency : E_i is not nogood.
3 - Completeness : Every consistent environment E in which l holds is a superset of some E_i.
4 - Minimality : No E_i is a proper subset of any other.

For each inference performed, the CMS sends to the ATMS : the instantiated conditions of the rule, and, the instantiated actions. The ATMS computes the labels (or modifies labels) of deduced facts.

Action rules being non-monotonic, the CMS first applies the retract part. The ATMS must supply all the facts which do not hold anymore, and therefore, have to be also retracted in the new context.

Then the CMS applies the assert part and as above (deduction rules) the ATMS returns the environments.

The main improvement to the standard ATMS is the introduction of nodes related to contexts. They are represented by two entities : context environment and context assumption.

Since the ATMS deals only with propositions, for inference with values being complex objects, their references are translated into new propositions for the ATMS. The facts involving complex objects receive in their context assumptions, extra assumptions on the existence of the complex objects.

A standard relational database can be seen a first order theory, axioms of which are :

- for each relation R in the schema and each tuple $(c_1,..., c_n)$ of R, an instanciated predicate $R(c_1,..., c_n)$

- for each constraint a first order formula describing this constraint.

In a standard relational database predicates are defined extensionally (its extension is the table), while in a deductive relational database some relations are defined intentionally. In general an answer to a query $\{x \mid Q(x)\}$, with $x = (x_1,..., x_n)$, is the set of tuples $C = (c_1,..., c_n)$ such that $Q(C)$ is a theorem of the theory. To compute an answer, some axioms are needed (completion axiom, unique name axiom and domain closure axiom).

The problem of extending the deductive model to object-oriented databases is to find :

(1) a first order model of complex objects which allows decidable queries,

(2) completion, unique name and domain closure axioms for complex objects,

(3) algorithms to ensure consistency through updates of objects.

The logical model of relational database is extended to complex objects. The representation, we suggest, is based on versions of objects. An object O with attributes $a_1,..., a_n$ having value v_{ij} (if an attribute is not valued, v is nil) in a version (or context) W_j is denoted by a proposition (F):

$$(F) \quad O \mid —(((a_1, W_0) = v_{01}) \wedge ((a_2, W_0) = v_{02}) \wedge... \wedge ((a_n, W_0) = v_{0n})) \vee$$
$$((a_1, W_1) = v_{21}) \wedge ((a_2, W_1) = v_{22}) \wedge... \wedge ((a_n, W_1) = v_{2n})) \vee$$
$$..............................$$
$$((a_1, W_m) = v_{m1}) \wedge ((a_2, W_m) = v_{m2}) \wedge... \wedge ((a_n, W_m) = v_{mn})))$$

This representation has several advantages :

- these is only one OID for each complex object regardless the number of its versions : the unique name axiom is valid,

- if all v_{ij} are non-complex objects, this formula is an instance of the completion axiom for object O,

- it implies the validity of the domain closure axiom,

- the model supports the negation by failure.

In order to modelize messages, we suppose that methods do not contain references to objects other than the ones mentioned in the parameters or call to other methods and have not side effects. A message is represented by a triple :

<<receiver name> <method name> <param_1>,..., <param_n>>

The extended ATMS introduces nodes related to contexts represented by two entities :

- context assumption : conjunction of new hypotheses corresponding to the context. Since an action can assert new assumptions or retract assumptions, it is noted context assumption : $+(F_1) \wedge -(F_2) \wedge ....$ with "+" and "-" standing respectively for "assert" or "retract" an assumption F_i,

- context environment : conjunction of context assumptions of the context and of its parent contexts. It is computed by the ATMS using its father context environment.

Each context is seen by the ATMS as a context node storing the context labels. A context label is a unique environment. Facts holding in several contexts have for label the set of minimal context environments of these contexts. The ATMS maintains two sets of nodes one for the different versions and an other one for the objects. If object holds in two successive versions the label of the later one is subsumed by the label of the former one, which greatly simplifies computation and representations (pointers).

8   Example

The example is an adaptation of Filman's one [Filman, 1987] with objects and rules (R1 to R4) mentioned above.

(a) - W_0 is the initial context in which the initial instances hold. Its context environment is $\{\}$ and its ATMS node is $<W_0, \{\{\}\}>$. In W_0, the (action) rule R_1 "If Trip->driver == nil **Then choice** Trip->driver **in** Set-of-drivers" is fired, the effect of which is to create three son contexts W_1, W_2 and W_3. The context assumption for a W_i is $(+(trip_1->driver : driver_i), -(set-of-drivers->value : \{1, 2, 3\}), +(set-of-driver->value : \{1, 2, 3\}-\{i\})$, and W_1, e.g., is justified by : $[W_0, (trip_1->driver : nil), +(trip_1->driver : driver_1), -(set-of-drivers->value : \{1, 2, 3\}), +(set-of-drivers->value : \{2,3\})] \rightarrow W_1$, and the fact $(trip_1->driver : driver_1)$, by $[(trip_1->driver : nil), +(trip_1->driver : driver_1), -(set-of-drivers->value : \{1, 2, 3\}), +(set-of-drivers->value : \{2, 3\}] \rightarrow (trip_1->driver : driver_1)$ in W_1.

(b) - The (deduction) rule R_3 : "If Trip->driver != nil **Then** Trip->driver-cost = Trip->driver->unit-cost * Trip->distance" is fired in W_1, asserting the fact $(trip_1->cost : 350)$, leading to the node : $<(trip_1->cost : 350), \{[+(trip_1->driver : driver_1), -(set-of-drivers->value : \{1, 2, 3\}), +(set-of-drivers->value : \{2,3\})]\}>$. There is no context assumption in these justifications because these rules are deduction ones.

(c) - In the context W_2, the (deduction) rule R_2 "If Trip->truck != nil **Then** Trip->truck->cost = Trip->truck->unit-cost * Trip->distance" is fired, asserting in the context W_2 (no new context is created because, it does not modify the current set of assumptions) the new fact $(trip_1->truck-cost : 500)$, leading to the node : $<(trip_1->truck-cost : 500), \{[\}\}>$ Then, in the same context W_2, the (deduction) rule R_3 "If Trip->driver != nil **Then** Trip->driver-cost =Trip->driver->unit-cost * Trip->distance" is fired, asserting $(trip_1->driver-cost : 350)$. Thus the node $(trip_1->driver-cost : 350)$ has the same label as $(trip_1->truck-cost : 500)$. The fact $(trip_1->driver-cost : 350)$ holds in the two contexts W_1 and W_2, but with different justifications.

(d) - In the context W_3, the rule R_4 : "**If** Trip->truck->location != Trip->driver->location **Then** **False**" is fired, giving the justification : $[(trip_1->truck : truck_1), (trip_1->driver : driver_3), (truck_1->location :$

18

"Indianapolis"),(driver$_3$->location : "Detroit")] → **False**. The label of context W3 is a **nogood** : {⊦(trip$_1$->driver : driver$_3$), -(set-of-drivers—> value : {1, 2, 3}), +(set-of-drivers->value : {2, 3})} . W3 is inconsistent. When a context is detected inconsistent, no more fact is included in it and no more rule is fired in it.

Filman's example does not mention updates of an object :

(e) - If in the context W1, an (action) rule is : " **If** ... **Then** driver$_1$->unit-cost = 3" is fired (the condition is not explicited). The context W4 is created, justified by [W1, -(driver$_1$->unit-cost : 7)] → (driver->unit-cost : 3). Universally holding premises being removed, the result of this action is supposed to hold in the belief " +(driver$_1$-> **unit-cost : 7**) ", which it is necessary to add it to the label of W$_0$, and as well in the label of (drive r2->unit-cost : 7). Modifications of labels are propagated, yielding the new labels such that : <W0, {⊦(driver$_2$->unit-cost : 7)}}>, <W1, {⊦(trip$_1$->driver : driver$_1$), +(driver$_2$->unit-cost : 7) }}> and <W4, {⊦(trip$_1$->driver : driver$_1$), +(driver$_2$->unit-cost : 7), -(driver$_2$->unit-cost : 7) }}>(this last label is simplified in : <W4, {⊦(trip$_1$->driver : driver$_1$)}}>.Thus the fact : (trip$_1$->driver-cost : 350) does not hold any more in W$_4$. A new firing of rule R3 will compute the new value of "trip$_1$->driver-cost".

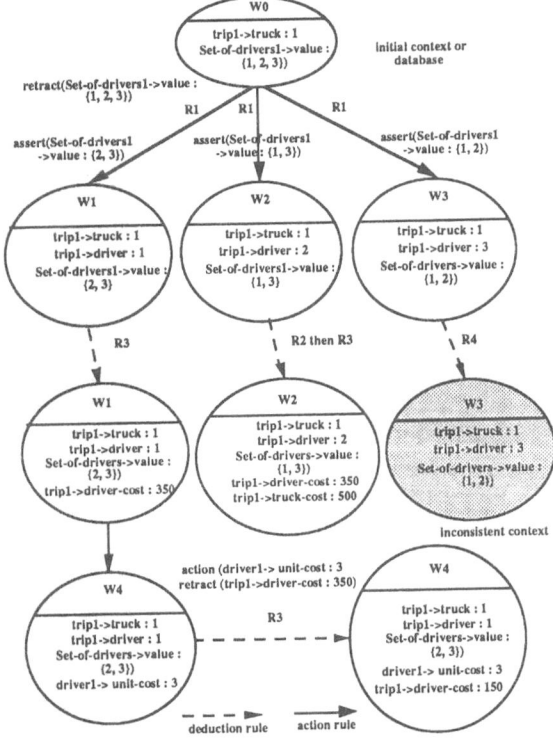

Figure 4 : Behavior of ALDOUS90

Conclusion

Some obvious modifications of O2, such that an access to the meta-schema (e.g. via a "SCHEMA-OF"), would greatly improve the performances of our system : our simulation of versions, if theoritically accurate, is not efficient.

In its current implementation, ALDOUS90 solves assignments problems with an efficiency similar to a dedicated constraint solving algorithm for it makes only 16 elementary assignments(trip $_i$, driver$_j$, truck$_i$) instead of 18 (use of unary nogoods as node constraints).

Expert reasoning is usally expressed as a meta-knowledge, such that meta-rules for reasoning about the rules

Commercial systems (KEE™, ART™) provide mechanisms to implement meta-knowledge : classes of rules (or "knowledge source"), conflict resolution mechanisms to choose which rule among the selected ones has to be applied, agenda to order rule applications, weight on rules to enforce priority... Our main concern is now to add to our system meta-rules and a blackboard mechanism.

Acknowledgements

The ALDOUS90 project is partially supported by the PRC-BD3.

REFERENCES

[Albert, 88] ALBERT L."Présentation et évaluation de la complexité en moyenne d'algorithme de filtrage dans les moteurs d'inférence", Revue d'Intelligence Artificielle, Vol 2, n°1, 1988.

[Andrews & Harris, 87] ANDREWS T. & HARRIS C., "Combining language and database advances in an object-oriented development environment", OOPSALA 87, October 1987.

[Banerjee & all. 87] BANERJEE J., CHOU H. T., GARZA J. & KIM W. "Data model issues for object-oriented applications", ACM trans. on Office Information Syst. 5, 1 1987.

[Benay & all. 89] G. BENAY, M. VAZEILLES & F.- Y. VILLEMIN, "Conception intelligemment assistée de systèmes temps-réels", Actes Congrès Systèmes Experts, Avignon 1989.

[Filman, 1987] FILMAN R.E., "Reasoning with worlds and truth maintenance in a knowledge-based programming environment", Communication of ACM, Vol 31, n°4.

[Forgy, 1982] FORGY C.L., "RETE : a fast algorithm for the many pattern/many object pattern match problem", Artificial Intelligence, n°19, 1982.

[de Kleer, 1986] de KLEER J., "An Assumption-based TMS", Artificial Intelligence, n° 28, 1986.

[Lé, 1991] LE M., "Base de données et base de connaissances : le gestionniare de monde", Mémoire d'ingénieur CNAM, 1991.

[Lécluse & all. 88] LECLUSE C., RICHARD P., and VELEZ F., "O2, an Object-Oriented Data Model", Proceeding of ACM-Sigmod, Chicago, June 1988.

[Maier & all. 86] MAIER D., STEIN J., OTTIS A. and PURDY A., "Development of an Object-Oriented DBMS", OOPSALA 86, september 1986.

[Morris & Nado, 1986] MORRIS P.H., NADO R.A., "Representing actions with an assumption-based truth maintenance system", Proc. of the 5th National Conference in Artificial Intelligence, 1986.

[Paoli, 1991] PAOLI A., "Base de données et base de connaissances : le maintien de la cohérence", Mémoire d'ingénieur CNAM, 1991.

[Touretzky, 1984] TOURETZKY D.S., "Implicit ordering of defaults in inheritance systems", Proc. of A.A.A.I., 1984.

[Tourrilhes, 1991] TOURRILHES I., "Base de données et base de connaissances : le filtrage des règles", Mémoire d'ingénieur CNAM, 1991.

Object Oriented Databases for Maintenance Expert Systems

J.C. Burneau
TéléDiffusion de France-CERLOR
1, rue Marconi-F-57070 METZ
Tel. 87 20 32 00, Fax. 87 76 33 63

O. Thiery
CRIN-URA 262
Campus Scientifique-BP 239
F-54506 VANDOEUVRE CEDEX
Tel. 83 91 20 00, Fax. 83 41 30 79

ABSTRACT

We describe in this paper a particular category of expert systems: the Maintenance Expert Systems, that are dedicated to diagnosis and reparation of electro-mechanical equipment. STEAMER is a Maintenance Expert System of broadcasting equipment, realized in the French broadcasting company "TéléDiffusion de France". We show that object oriented databases are the most convenient way for building voluminous knowledge bases. We then explain that many designers take part in the specifications of the systems, what leads us to propose a new concept, named multiple specialization. We conclude that the complete realization of STEAMER validates the proposed concepts.

1. INTRODUCTION

"TéléDiffusion de France" is the French public broadcasting company in charge of transmitting every TV or radio programme using hertzian or cable networks. In order to improve the availability of its broadcasting equipment, "TéléDiffusion de France" nowadays carries out studies about artificial intelligence based computer programmes for maintenance assistance. The STEAMER[1] project started in early '89 in FMS laboratory (Systems Reliability and Maintainability) [1]. STEAMER is a Maintenance Expert System (MES) that helps operational maintenance engineers in diagnosing failures of a TV-transmitter. Realization of STEAMER needed specific

---

[1] STEAMER stands for *Maintenance Expert System for Broadcasting Equipments* in French

concepts, methods and tools that have been analyzed before the expert programme itself.

We describe in section 2 what a MES consists in and explain the reasons for storing knowledge into a database. We then justify that the use of an object oriented database is relevant. Then we explain why the standard object oriented model is not sufficient.

In section 3 we propose a concept to be added to OO model. That concept corresponds to the *view* concept in relational model and allows many developpers to simultaneously design and implement the OO database.

2. MAINTENANCE EXPERT SYSTEMS, DATABASES AND OO MODEL

2.1. Definition of a MES

A radio or TV-transmitter is mainly made of electronics, often contains electro-mechanical modules and sometimes includes hydraulic cooling circuits: such a variety of components can fail in various and sometimes vicious ways (let us just imagine cooling-water dropping on electronics...). That is why the maintenance process, composed of diagnosis, repair and acquisition of experience, is so important. Having to deal with a great number of broadcasting stations, maintenance engineers have to learn more and more schemata, more and more techniques depending on the technologies used in these stations.

A computer-based tool, with its large storage capacity, allows operational staff people to perform practical tasks, like testing or fixing, while the computer locates and explains the failures. Hence the computer should reason the same way the expert does, that is, with an equipment-based reasoning, taking into account parameters like accessibility, safety and simple logic : one cannot test a block that still is behind a grid... The Maintenance Expert System built within TDF, STEAMER, should therefore be constructed around a modelization of the equipments it will maintain and have the same reasoning mechanism as the expert's.

2.2. Need for a database

The "expert system" expression is often associated with concepts of rule or inference engine. In fact, this is now a well-known way for formalizing knowledge. But as we mentioned above, TV-transmitters are made of a very important number of components : formalization of such an equipment would lead to a very large set of rules, very difficult to maintain. In opposition to such *first generation* expert systems, *second generation* ones are based on *deep knowledge* : the real structure of the equipment to be maintained is formalized, then a more or less precise representation of the way every component runs is added. The expert's reasoning is based on those structural and functional specifications. Therefore no specific structures like rules are needed : a *database* is the most common and convenient way for storing the large amount of knowledge that results from structural and functional modelizations.

2.3. MES and OO databases

We however have to take into account that structural and functional knowledge is static knowledge, while diagnosis reasoning mainly consists in treatments, that is, dynamic knowledge. Standard models for databases, like Relational or Entity-Relationship models, do not allow an easy formalization of both static and dynamic aspects in the particular domain we deal with (e.g. Standard Query Language would not apply to specific diagnosis reasoning) : a MES should be built using a model that mixes static and dynamic specifications. Such a model does exist, it is named *object oriented model* [2][3]. It allows real entities to be represented using objects. An object is made up of

values, this is the static representation. The behaviour of an object is represented by *operations*, this is the dynamic part of the object. Furthermore concepts of *class* and *inheritance* allow static and dynamic knowledge to be shared among many objects, the resulting OO specification being more readable and maintainable than those obtained with standard models. That is why a detailed comparative study of standard models vs OO model lead us to choose OO information structures for designing the expert system.

2.4. Multi-designer realization

As above mentioned, a 2nd generation expert system mainly consists in a large amount of knowledge. We state that designing a MES implies collecting knowledge about the structure of equipment to be maintained and about the diagnosis reasoning. A third knowledge structure is needed for building the user interface of the application. Developing a MES therefore involves at least three designers who differently observe a single real information. The resulting specifications are almost independent one of another, each consisting in a particular view on the real equipment. Object oriented model includes multiple inheritance that could be used for regrouping multiple specifications, but we show in next section that every problems are not solved using that concept. That is why we propose a new concept, named *multiple specialization*, that enlarges the inheritance definition by allowing independent specifications to be connected through a single structural representation.

3. THE MULTIPLE SPECIALIZATION CONCEPT

Let us consider an example that none of standard inheritance nor multiple inheritance can solve. We want to formalize the whole knowledge about a particular component of electro-mechanical equipments. That component is named *relay* and is used for switching high voltage outputs using a low voltage input. When considered as part of an equipment, relays can be categorized depending on the voltage of their input, either

12 or 220 volts : a class RELAY is specialized with classes LOW_POWER_RELAY (12 volts input) and HIGH_POWER_RELAY (220 volts input). But when considered by an operational engineer, a relay is said in an *up* or *down* position, depending on whether the high voltage signal is switched on or off[2] ; the corresponding definition consists in a class RELAY, specialized with classes RELAY_UP and RELAY_DOWN. Last, let us imagine how the graphist, who is building the user interface of the MES, considers the relays : the class RELAY is now specialized with classes named GREEN_RELAY and RED_RELAY.

Considering a single class RELAY, three different designers build three different specialization hierarchies. An instance of RELAY should therefore be simultaneously instance of, say, LOW_POWER_RELAY when considered by structural knowledge designers, RELAY_UP when considered by engineers and RED_RELAY when considered by graphists. Every expert domain corresponds to a particular *vision* of an object. We name *aspect* one of those particular points of view about the class RELAY. We now try to formalize aspects using inheritance and multiple inheritance, admitting the following definition for inheritance in object oriented model : *an instance of a class is also instance of every upper class in the inheritance hierarchy.*

3.1. Inheritance

Using only specialization for representing aspects of the class RELAY leads to figure 1.

However, because of the definition of inheritance we have admitted, such a definition does not allow an instance of class LOW_POWER_RELAY, for example, to be simultaneously an instance of RELAY_UP or RED_RELAY. Inheritance does not allow different aspects to be formalized.

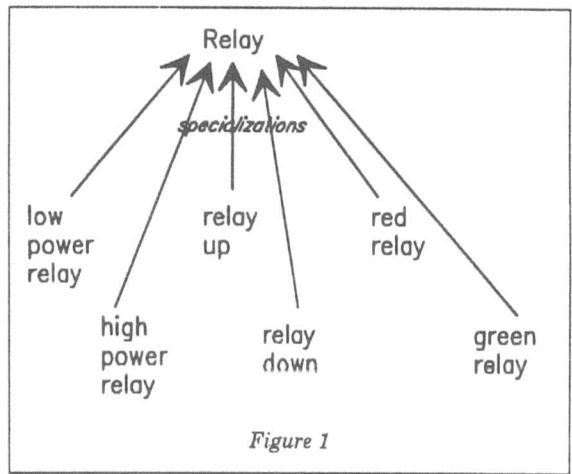

Figure 1

3.2. Multiple inheritance

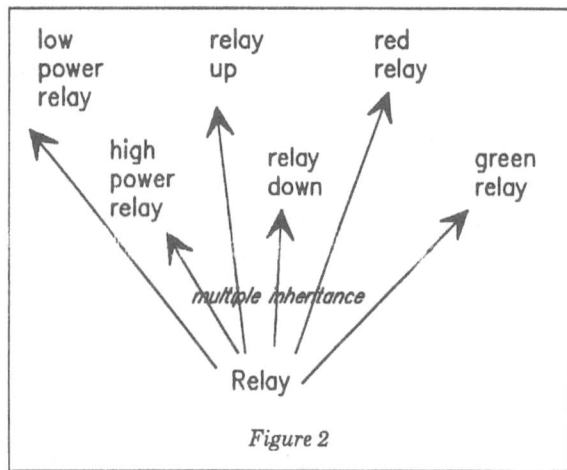

Figure 2

Figure 2 describes the class RELAY when inheriting from every specialization of every aspect. The inheritance definition now enables an instance of RELAY to be simultaneously instance of LOW_POWER_RELAY, RELAY_UP and RED_RELAY... but also of RELAY_DOWN, HIGH_POWER_RELAY and GREEN_RELAY ! Conflicts then appear if homonym properties are defined on more than one aspect, what could happen because we defined aspects as being independently designed. [4][5][6]

---

[2] We are not concerned here by an evolution from the up state to the down state or reciprocally.

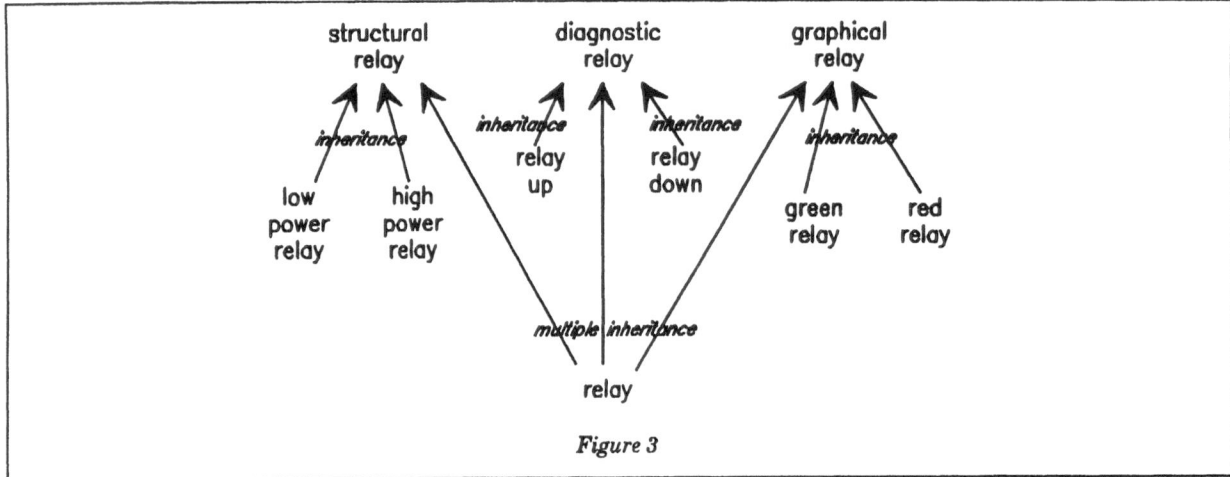

Figure 3

Another use of multiple inheritance is shown on figure 3 : RELAY inherits from classes that correspond to aspects, which classes are themselves specialized. However, in that case, the inheritance definition does not allow an instance of RELAY to be simultaneously instance of LOW_POWER_RELAY, RELAY_UP or RED_RELAY : different designers can not consider instances in the inheritance hierarchies they design. That is why we conclude that multiple inheritance does not allow the formalization of different design aspects on a class.

3.3. Creation of artificial classes

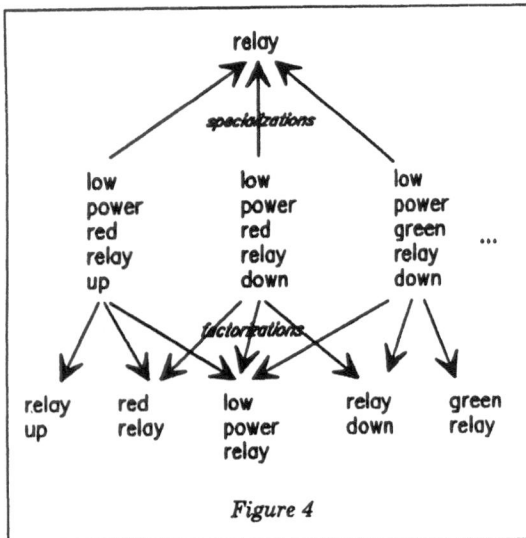

Figure 4

Figure 4 shows how the aspects of RELAY could be formalized, using artificial classes that correspond to the «cartesian product» of every specialization of aspects. Artificial classes inherit from aspect specializations in order to hold corresponding properties. The total number of classes for representing n aspects, the ith aspect being specialized by S_i classes, is

$$\prod_{i=1}^{n} S_i \quad + \quad \sum_{i=1}^{n} S_i$$

Such complex schemata are unusable for designing such important programmes as MES's.

3.4. Our proposition : multiple specialization concept

We have shown that standard inheritance does not allow multiple expert's reports about a single object to be represented. That is why we introduce a new concept, that we call *multiple specialization*. That concept allows different designers to formalize independent knowledges about a single class that describes real structural objects. Multiple specialization corresponds in OO models to the *view* concept in relational databases. We define that concept as follows :

(1) Let us consider a class C, multi-specialized in $C_1,...,C_n$. Every instance of C *is also instance* of $C_1,...,C_n$.

(2) The multiple specialization being a particular inheritance, the inheritance definition remains valid : an instance of a class C_i is also instance of C, hence (1) an instance of a class C_i is also instance of C_j, $j \neq i$.

Applying multiple specialization to the above example leads to figure 5.

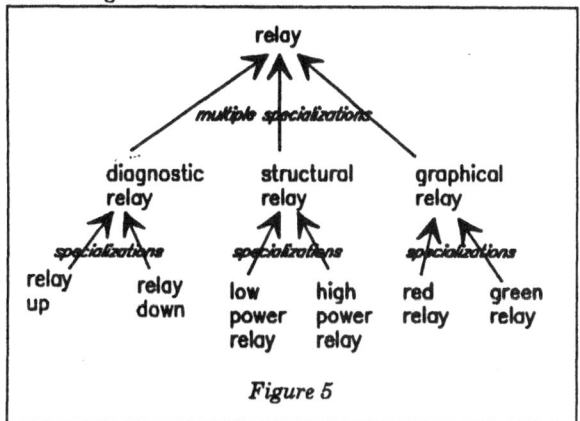

Figure 5

When an instance is created in RELAY, following definition (1) of multiple specialization, it also exists in classes RELAY_UP, LOW_POWER_RELAY and RED_RELAY (this being just an example of combination). Any designer may handle any relay-object, the properties he applies to the object depending on the aspect the designer works in : every designer has its own sub-hierarchy and defines only behaviours that are relevant for his domain without taking care of other designer's needs.

Following the definition (2), any property defined on class RELAY can be used in sub-hierarchies. But a property that is defined on an aspect cannot be accessed from another aspect. We then define the *publication* concept, that allows aspects to share properties among each other. Considering a property that is defined on an aspect class, that property can be *published* by the corresponding designer. It then exists on the structural class as a *virtual property* and, following definition (1), it is inherited by other aspect classes. A property needs to be published only if it is defined on an aspect and needed by another aspect. Therefore, every designer has to ask for particular behaviours in other aspects : the publication of properties always depends on preliminary discussions. These discussions also avoid homonym properties to be published on the structural class, what solves homonymy problems.

The *multiple specialization* concept is particularly interesting in the context of Maintenance Expert Systems,

where at least three designers, each of them handling a particular expert domain, interact for the construction of an application. That concept has been validated by the realization of a complete MES.

4. CONCLUSION

Diagnosis reasoning is a good example of an expert reasoning, that is often based on a modelization of a real universe. Data structures needed by a maintenance assistance computer-based tool have to fit to reality, what lead us to choose and to extend the object oriented model. The intervention of many experts during the design of a Maintenance Expert System explains why the multiple specialization is necessary.

STEAMER is a MES that has been fully designed using concepts described in this paper. It is composed of 760 classes and contains around 4000 objects that represent the real equipment. STEAMER results of the work of 7 men·year. We are now able to state positively that our object oriented model is relevant in the context of second generation maintenance expert systems.

REFERENCES

[1] P. Woda, J.C. Burneau, "STEAMER : SysTème Expert d'Aide à la Maintenance des Equipements de Radiodiffusion", proc. 10th international workshop "Exprert Systems and their applications", Avignon, France, 1990

[2] B.J. Cox, "Object Oriented Programming : an evolutionary approach", Addison-Wesley Pub. Comp. Ed., 1986

[3] G. Masini, A. Napoli, D. Colnet, D. Léonard and K. Tombre, "Les langages à objets : langages de classes, langages de frames, langages d'acteurs", InterEditions Ed., 1989

[4] L. Cardelli, "A semantic of multiple inheritance", Lecture Notes in Computer Science, vol 173, p 51-67, Springer Verlag Ed., 1984

[5] R. Ducournau, M. Habib, "La multiplicité de l'héritage dans les langages à objets", proc. "Mardis Objets du CRIN", Nancy, 1988

[6] P. Dugerdil, "Les mécanismes d'héritage d'OBJLOG", proc. "Mardis Objets du CRIN", Nancy, 1988

Student Admission: Expert and Database Systems

Paul O'Neill and Ala Al-Zobaidie

School of Computing and Information Technology
Thames Polytechnic,
London SE18 6PF, U.K.

Abstract

The widespread use of relational Database Management Systems (DBMS) has meant an increase in the number of application databases. Having to cope with such a large amount of data especially when used in decision making systems leads to a number of problems. The introduction of Expert Systems (ES) has enabled us to apply the domain knowledge of experts to stored data, perhaps already existing in a Database (DB). The integration of ES and DB can be seen as an attempt to combine the best facilities of both technologies. The Student Admission: Database & Expert system is an example of just one application where such problems arise. This paper looks at various integration approaches as well as the method used in this system.

1. Introduction

Each year Thames Polytechnic receives applications for its courses through the Polytechnic Central Admissions System (PCAS) and the British Technical Education Council (BTEC) examining board. Each School within the polytechnic has an admissions tutor who must select the students they believe to be most suitable for enrolment as undergraduates at Thames. Selection criteria and rules for this process are decided on by the Polytechnic and individual Schools. They are then applied by the admissions tutor.

The Student Admission system was developed to overcome problems encountered in the School of Computing and Information Technology (CIT) at Thames Polytechnic. Due to the number of applications and the variety of courses involved the admissions tutor handles a mass of information. This concerns not only each applicant but also the various examining bodies and their related qualifications.

The admissions tutor has to take into account an applicants references and relevant work experience as well as the results of the Schools applicant interviews. These interviews aid the tutor's decision whether a student can communicate effectively and if they show a keen interest in the course applied for. The interviewers are polytechnic lecturers who usually do not have the domain knowledge of the tutor. The admissions tutor must be able to supply the school with statistical data on the number of students who have applied for a particular course and their academic standards. The type and number of admission recommendations (i.e. whether conditional or unconditional) must also be made available. Any solution to the problem of the student admission system must include the ability to manage large of amounts of data.

The introduction of a DBMS would enable the admissions tutor to store large amounts of data effectively and efficiently. This solution should use the knowledge acquired by the admissions tutor in choosing the preferred applicants. The knowledge of the admissions tutor would best be implemented using an ES. An ES is defined in [1] as *"A knowledge base consisting of two components: a DB which contains simple facts and a knowledge source which holds general rules. The inference mechanism of an ES works by applying its knowledge source to its DB facts"*. An ES is made up of facts and rules and any solution must formalise the process of decision making into rules held in an ES.

Through examining the application requirements it becomes clear that a system with ES and DBMS capabilities is required. There are three methods of interfacing an ES with a DBMS. These are the Intelligent Database, Enhanced Expert System and the ES-DB communication approach [1]. The Intelligent DB approach can be described as the incorporation of Artificial Intelligence techniques into conventional DBs to form intelligent or deductive DBs [1]. This was also described in [2] as a "Homogeneous Approach". The second method of integration is the enhanced ES approach. In this approach the expert system is given the data management functions of a database. In the ES-DB communication approach the ES and DBMS are developed as separate entities and the two systems communicate through "message passing" [1].

The Deductive DB approach and Enhanced ES are examples of tight integration. When developing a link between these two systems a degree of inflexibility is created. The problem is the Deductive approach uses an ES as a slave front end to the DB. The ES is used for deductive filtering of the data to be stored in the database and for both the user and sub queries . The inflexibility arises because the ES is written to interact with the DB rather than to implement the domain knowledge of an expert.

The Enhanced ES approach uses DBMS functions to manage data. Usually this approach is implemented by the extension of an existing ES shell to include DBMS capabilities. This does not have the flexibility of using an independent DB which tends to contain more functions and facilities than those developed as an add on to an ES. Another problem is the need to load the DBMS modules into memory with the ES system which would require a considerable increase in main memory.

The ES-DB communication approach has problems with its implementation. To implement using the first two approaches described above, would require the development of two separate systems to include modules for control and message passing. Another problem to overcome is the time taken to load each module into main memory. In the independent module approach of ES-DB communication there exists the overhead of creating an extra program module for control and process management. However this method does give added benefits which outweigh this disadvantage.

Section two of this paper looks at the development of an ES and DB system. An example of a sample session will be given as well as an explanation of the hardware and software used to implement the package. This is followed by a conclusion and an outline of possible future research, problems and possible solutions.

2. The Expert System

The student admission expert system was developed at Thames Polytechnic in conjunction with the CIT admissions tutor, for the two undergraduate degree courses. Although it was envisaged that extra courses could be added to the system in the future especially the non-degree courses of the British Technical Education Council (BTEC) examining body.

The first step in developing the ES was to spend time with the admissions tutor in a process of knowledge elicitation. Knowledge elicitation enables the knowledge engineer to extract knowledge of a domain from the domain expert. Then followed the process of knowledge acquisition, which is the process of formulating elicited knowledge into rules. At all stages of the ES development the rules were checked with the admissions tutor for their accuracy.

An example of an admission rule is as follows:

```
IF
        <student failed external course>
    AND
        <student interview unacceptable>
THEN
        <student unacceptable>
ENDIF.
```

An example of the decision tree for evaluating references is shown in figure 1.

3. The Student Database

Within the polytechnic there is a large database which holds information on prospective students who are applying for undergraduate courses. This system is used by all the schools in the polytechnic. Each of which applies its own admission rules to the data held on the DB about each student. The data is supplied by the Polytechnic Central Admission System (PCAS) and includes the applicants qualifications and references. The database could be updated to include all information for courses which award BTEC qualifications.

The student database is implemented with the Ingres DBMS which is based on the relational model. SQL is a standard feature of the Ingres system as well as a Forms editor and Report writer.

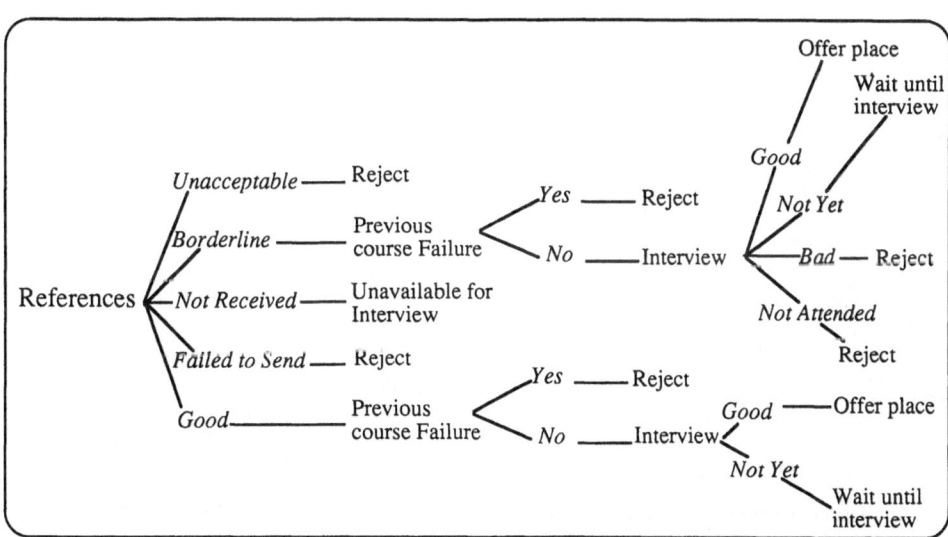

Figure 1 - The decision tree for Evaluating Student References

4. The Student Admissions: Expert & Database System.

The Student Admission system was implemented using the Inter-System communication approach with an independent communication module. A data dictionary driven approach is used by the independent module similar to the Difead system [3]. The Architecture of this system can be seen in figure 2. This approach gives both abstraction and flexibility by storing the ES rules in a data dictionary as well as metadata about the ES and DB. Metadata is knowledge stored about knowledge with which we can store data descriptions such as relationships and data format [1]. The independent module uses the metadata held in the data dictionary therefore it can communicate with the DB and ES which helps control and process management.

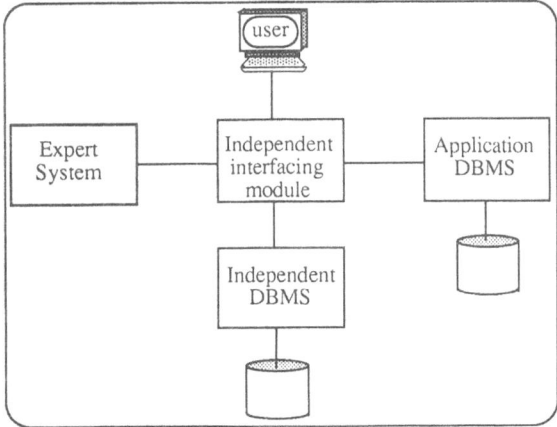

Figure 2 - The Architecture of the Student Admission System

To access the DB and data dictionaries the independent module uses embedded SQL. When a user query is first instigated an ES program will be constructed with the rules for that designated course. To achieve this the system accesses a rule set table which stores a list of rules that are specific for each course. This method allows the user to edit, update and delete the rule table rather than having to edit each ES program. The ES will then be parsed and the resultant executable file will be stored in the system directory. This file will be used every time a consultation involves that course. When the rules for a course are updated the ES programs concerned are then parsed with the new rules before use.

5. Implementation

The Student Admissions system was developed on an Opus 80286 IBM compatible Personal Computer (PC). The PC has an extended main memory of four megabytes and a forty megabyte hard disk. The operating system used was the Digital Research Dos 5.0 which loads the system files above the usual 640k Dos limit into extended memory. The use of relatively cheap PC technology would enable the various schools within the polytechnic to adopt the Student Admissions system without a huge drain on their resources.

The relational database system used was the Ingres RDBMS version 5 for the PC. Ingres contains a facility for loading its DBMS program into memory. It also has a forms editor which enabled the rapid development of screens for the independent module.

The ES was developed using the Knowledge Engineering System (KES) expert system shell. KES is a backward chaining production rule system which can be embedded in a host language (e.g. C) and this gives it the ability to use the host languages file handling and communication capabilities. The use of production rules in KES allows them to be stored in a file which can then be parsed.

The independent module was developed using the C programming language. The Microsoft C compiler version 6 was chosen because of its compatibility with the new ANSI C standard and the Ingres embedded SQL pre-processor. The C language has the ability to manage file communication that enables the passing of 'messages' between the ES and DB [3]. The C languages process management capabilities enable the loading of sub-systems into main memory. Microsoft C has a rich library of functions which allow us to construct programs rapidly.

6. A Sample Session

The user enters the independent module main menu and chooses the communication menu option. After entering this option the user chooses the applicant for qualifications, references and interview results checking. The module allows the user to choose by applicant name or PCAS number.

The system then requests the course title if this is not held in the applicants relational tuple. When a course code has been entered the rules for this course are then extracted from the DB and parsed into a KES program. These rules may have been in a previous session and so therefore are used directly by the ES.

The data from the applicant's relational tuple is passed as a communication file to the expert system. Using data in the file the ES decides whether to ask questions on the applicant's qualifications, experience etc. If further data is needed by the ES about a specific applicant then a new request is put to the user to enter the missing data directly.

The recommendation of the ES is given and then stored. At the end of a session the data entered by the user is saved along with the recommendation. The independent module updates the applicants relational tuple accordingly. The user can resume the session for a new student or Quit the system completely.

7. Conclusion

The Student Admission System when fully implemented can be used by any School within most educational establishments (in the U.K.). The rest of this section covers the advantages of using the proposed approach:

The adopted approach, stores the rules in an independent data dictionary DB where they can be edited or replaced, either by using the independent C module or the DBMS itself. Therefore there is a greater flexibility in adding new rules to the system.

The use of an independent module gives us the advantage of modularity. The separate modules (i.e. DB, ES and independent module) can be maintained and updated without the need to change other modules within the system.

The loading of a specific set(s) of rules at different stages of the ES inference avoid loading the memory with unnecessary rules that may not be applicable to the individual case. By avoiding the overhead incurred from the process, systems efficiency will be greatly enhanced.

The use of PC technology allows a department/school to use the system with existing resources. This also means that a number of popular PC DBMS and ES shells can be used.

The implementation of this work could be extended further for any type of ES shell or DB. This versatility is useful because more knowledge can be stored about both sub-systems in a data dictionary. This would enable the development of a more independent communication module. In future work the data dictionary could be extended to store more types of knowledge.

Acknowledgements

The authors would especially like to thank Mr. M. Ibrahim for his help and advice; Acknowledgement is also due to Mr. D. Parrot and Mr. M. Sutcliffe for their original research into the Student Admission expert system. The authors would also like to thank Ms. M. P. Harling for her comments during the preparation of this paper.

References

[1]   Al-Zobaidie A. and Grimson J.B., 'Expert Systems and Database systems: How can they serve each other?' Expert Syst.(The Int. J of Knowledge Eng.), Learned Information Ltd. Vol 4 No 1 (February 1987), pp 30-37.

[2]   Missikoff M. & Wiederhold G. 'Towards a unified approach for Expert and Database systems' Expert Database Systems: Proceedings from the first International Workshop, Benjamin Cummings 1986.

[3]   Al-Zobaidie A. and Grimson J.B., 'Use of Metadata to drive the interaction between Database and Expert System', Information and Software Technology, Vol 30 no. 8 1988.

[4]   Kamran Parsaye et. al., Intelligent Databases: Object Orientated, Deductive, Hypermedia Technologies, Wiley 1989.

[5]   Software Engineering System and Engineering Inc., KES Training Manual, August 1987.

Mapping Generalization and Object Sharing into Nested Relations:
An ODA Implementation

Giovanni V. Guardalben
Hi.T Srl

Via Don Carlo Steeb 7
37122 Verona, Italy

ABSTRACT

The problem of mapping object oriented database systems into a classical (or nested) relational platform has received considerable attention in recent years. In fact, relational database management systems have proven their validity in a large variety of different environments, chiefly due to their simple and provable mathematical foundations. On the other hand, object oriented database systems hold the promise of addressing the problem of complex object database applications (such as CAD, GIS, etc.). Given these facts, it seems natural to look for a link between the two different approaches to data modeling. In this paper we have tried to find ways of translating some features (i.e., inheritance, or generalization, and object sharing) of object oriented databases into (nested) relational databases. Our approach has started from the non-first normal form relational model and the translation scheme that we have devised is based on inclusion dependencies among participating nested relations. The definitions that we have obtained, have allowed us to define set operators for classes. Finally, an object oriented interpretation of the ISO-ODA standard for documents based on nested relations is described in this paper.

1 Introduction

Relational database technology has been successful at supporting standard data processing (business) applications. This success is due mostly to the simplicity of the mathematical theory (i.e., the set theory) of the relational model. However, there are now non-standard applications that need database management functions. Some of the requirements of these applications are the need for efficient support of complex objects, property inheritance and object sharing.

There are now a number of database systems that have departed completely from the relational approach and try to satisfy non-standard application requirements. However, there are situations where one would prefer to have the best from both worlds. As proposed in this paper, this can be achieved by mapping non-standard features into a relational platform. By using this approach, there are a number of benefits that can be obtained:

- Queries can be formulated in both ways: by using the traditional relational way and by using the higher level approach by means of concepts such as classes and class hierarchies.

- Questions about the non-standard approach can be reformulated in terms of the relational model, since theoretical tools are available there.

- New DataBase Management Systems (DBMS) can be generated in shorter times with the added facilities of an available relational DBMS (i.e., transaction control, multi-user support, system administration support, etc.).

Recently, there have been a few studies about non-standard data model translations into the relational data model [LY87, BO90]. In one case [LY87], the analysis focused on a semantic data model

conversion. In the other case [BO90], attribute inheritance was implemented on top of a relational system and integrity constraints, queries and locks were also mapped.

In our approach, in the mapping we have included not only class inheritance, but also the concept of object sharing. We have been able to derive the definition of class by means of inclusion dependencies with respect to other classes. Also, we have made the basic decision of mapping inheritance and object sharing into nested relations (rather than the classical flat relations). In fact, this has led to a simple, based-on-immediate-superclass attribute definition of class that has proved very useful in shedding light on class (based on nested relational) operators. This operation has proved very useful since it has allowed us to reanalyze class set operators, as defined in [RU90], by using our definition of class.

This paper consists of four sections of which the first is the introduction. In Section 2, the translation of our data model hierarchy is explained in terms of nested relations. In Section 3, we apply some of the concepts of the previous section to derive expressions for set operators and other class operators. Section 4 contains concluding remarks and the Appendix describes in details an application of our approach to model the ISO-ODA standard for documents structuring [OD88].

2 Hierarchy Translation into Nested Relations

2.1 Nested Relations

In the past years much attention has been paid to structured relations. The deficiencies of the relational model for supporting complex object applications are well documented. This has lead to the development of more general data models, in particular the nested relational data model that generalizes the flat relational model by allowing relation-valued attributes. Initially, [MA77] proposed to generalize the relational model by removing Codd's first normal form assumption [CO70]. Subsequently, a generalization of the relational algebra to relations with set-valued attributes was introduced by [SC86]. Finally, [TH86] generalized this model by allowing nested relations of arbitrary depth. [AB88] and [SC86] have independently defined an algebra for non-first normal form relations. More recently, FAD [BA87], a full data programming language including algebraic operators for complex objects, has been specified.

Recently, there have been a number of studies about powerset algebra, which is obtained by adding this operator to the nested algebra. According to [GY88], this algebra is considerably more expressive than the nested algebra and equivalent to another extension of the nested relational algebra, its least fixpoint closure.

In this paper, we follow [GY88] definition of nested relations . First, we briefly explain what are elementary and composite attributes and how relation schemes, relation instances and relations are constructed from these. Then, we summarize a nested algebra based on [GY88] and [BE90].

We assume an infinitely enumerable set U of *elementary attributes*. Attributes are either elementary or composite. The latter ones are sets of elementary or composite attributes.

Definition 2.1 *The set of all attributes $\mathcal{U}$ is the smallest set containing U such that for each finite subset Ω of $\mathcal{U}$ in which no elementary attribute appears more than once, $\Omega \in \mathcal{U}$.*

An attribute that belongs to U is called an *elementary attribute*; those of $\mathcal{U} - U$ are called *composite attributes*. A *relation scheme* Ω is a *composite attribute*, i.e., an element of $\mathcal{U} - U$. Now, we assume an infinitely enumerable set V of *elementary values* and jointly define the notions of *value*, *tuple* and *instances* as in Definition 2.1.3 in [GY88]). So, we are able to define a *(nested) relation*:

Definition 2.2 *A relation is a pair (Ω, ω), where $\Omega \in \mathcal{U} - U$ and $\omega \in I_\Omega$. Ω is called the scheme of the relation, ω is called the instance of the relation and I_Ω consists of all finite subsets of all tuples over Ω. If $\Omega \subseteq U$ then (Ω, ω) is called a flat relation.*

A nested algebra can be defined based on operators borrowed from the classical relational algebra and new operators such as nest, unnest and powerset.

Definition 2.3 (Operators) *The classical relational algebra operators of **union, difference, projection, cartesian product, rename** and **selection**. The nesting operator, ν_X, groups a subset X of the attributes Ω of a (possibly) non-first normal formal relation into a single composite attribute and groups relative tuples into a single nested tuple [GY88].*

The unnesting operator, μ_X, normalizes a subset X of the composite attributes $\Omega - U$ by turning the nested attributes in X into full-fledged elementary and composite attributes. Nested tuples are also split into separate simple and nested tuples.

2.2 Hierarchy Definition

As in [ZD90], a *class* is a template for its *instances* and every *object* is an instance of some class. An *object* contains values and some of these values may refer to *methods*, which are pieces of code to perform some actions. Classes are usually arranged in a directed graph, with the edges connecting *superclasses* to their *subclasses*. These edges are called *is-a links*. They express the inheritance relationship (or *generalization*) between the classes. Instances of a subclass are completely substitutable by instances of the superclass. One object may contain or share values that are or refer to other objects. This ability for objects to share related components is often called *aliasing* (or *object-sharing*). Objects can always be referenced through an *object identity*. This requires that there exists something about an object that remains invariant across all possible modifications of an object's value. Generalization and object-sharing can be implemented by using relations and inclusion dependencies among relations. Object identity is supported by tuple references (or *tids*) that are supported by the record managers of existing relational database systems. We assume the notion of *extended relation* as in [SI90]. Extended relations are a generalization of standard relations since they can have tuple references as attribute values, called *tid-attributes*. As in [SI90] the tid-attribute for an extended relation r is named $rTid$.

Definition 2.4 *A class, c, is a pair (Ω, ω), where $\Omega \in \mathcal{U}$ and $\Omega = \{ cTid, F_1, F_2, ..., F_n, c_{L_1}Tid, L_1, c_{L_2}Tid, L_2, ..., c_{L_m}Tid, L_m, A_1, A_2, ..., A_p \}$ and ω is the instance of the class.*

The composite attribute $F_i \in \mathcal{U} - U$, $0 \le i \le n$, i.e., the *superclass* attribute, is optional and only present if the class c is a specialization of (i.e., inherits properties from) another class Ω_{F_i}. There is a relationship between the classes' schemes and instances:

$$F_i = \{ \Omega_{F_i} - cTid \}$$

since $cTid = c_{F_i}Tid$, and

$$(\Omega_{F_i}, \omega_{F_i}) \supseteq \mu_{F_i}(\pi_{cTid, F_i}(\Omega, \omega)).$$

The last relationship is an *inclusion dependency* in the relational database making up the class hierarchy. It conveys the notion that instances of a subclass are substitutable by instances of the superclass and that *tid's* are coincident. This inclusion dependency requires the application of the unnesting operator, μ_{F_i}, on the composite attribute F_i for consistency between the superclass instances and the superclass attribute projection of the instances of the class. According to [SI90] notation, the inclusion dependency may be expressed as

$$(\Omega_{F_i}, \omega_{F_i}) \supseteq \mu_{F_i}(index_{F_i}(\Omega, \omega)).$$

The composite attribute $L_i \in \mathcal{U} - U$, $0 \le i \le n$, i.e., the *shared-object* attribute, is optional and only present if the class c shares instances of another class Ω_{L_i}. As in the case of generalization, there exists a relationship between the two classes' schemes and instances:

$$L_i = \{ \Omega_{L_i} - c_{L_i}Tid \}$$

since $cTid \ne c_{L_i}Tid$, and

$$(\Omega_{L_i}, \omega_{L_i}) \supseteq \mu_{L_i, c_{L_i}Tid}(\pi_{c_{L_i}Tid, L_i}(\Omega, \omega)).$$

Finally, the attributes $A_i \in \mathcal{U}$, i.e., the *local* attribute, may be elementary or composite. However, there is not any inter-relation dependency binding these attributes values to other relations, since they are properties only belonging to the class where they are defined. The definition of class just given, allows us to handle classes with multivalued properties, multiple inheritance and selective inheritance. Besides, a class instance may share more instances of another class (multiple object sharing). In fact, the A_i, F_i and L_i attributes are nested attributes and their instances can be relations. Multiple inheritance is achieved by allowing more than one of the superclass attributes, F_i. Each class contains a specific number of zero or more attributes F_i, each one corresponding to a class from which to inherit properties. Similarly, a class may share more objects of different classes by having more than one attributes L_i.

By selective inheritance, we intend the feature of inheriting only some of the characteristic of a superclass. With selective inheritance on a subset X of F_i, the inclusion dependency is expressed as:

$$index_X(\Omega_{F_i}, \omega_{F_i}) \supseteq \mu_X(index_X(\Omega, \omega)).$$

Similarly, only some of the attributes X of an object L_i may be shared, resulting in an inclusion dependency as follows:

$$index_X(\Omega_{L_i}, \omega_{L_i}) \supseteq \mu_{Xc_{L_i}Tid}(\pi_{c_{L_i}Tid, X}(\Omega, \omega)).$$

2.3 Derived Definitions

In the literature [RO87, OZ85 and OZ86], the benefits of properly structured nested relations have been recognized. For example, let U be a set of elementary attributed, X, Y, and Z a disjoint partition of U, and r a first normal form relation on scheme $R = \{U\}$. If the multivalued dependency $X \twoheadrightarrow Y/Z$ holds in r, then consider the relations with the Z attributes forming one nested relation and the Y attributes forming another nested relation for each X value. Some of the benefits of this approach are:

(a) X is a key for s;

(b) Y and Z are independently updatable nested relations;

(c) if we start with relation r and wish to form relation s, we need to apply the nesting operator twice once on attributed Z and once on attributed Y. if $X \twoheadrightarrow Y/Z$ holds, then the order of nesting does not modify the result.

From the concept of properly structured nested relations, [OZ85] has introduced the notion of *scheme trees*. A scheme tree is a tree whose vertices are labelled by pairwise disjoint sets of non nested attributes, where the edges of the trees represent Multi<u>V</u>alued <u>D</u>ependencies (MVD) between the attributes of the vertices of the tree. Let T be a scheme tree and let $S(T)$ denote the set of all attributes in T. Each edge of the scheme tree T represents a multivalued dependency on $S(T)$. If $P(T)$, the *path set*, is the set of all the union of all the nodes in the path from the root of T to each leaf node of T then

(a) $P(T)$ is an acyclic database scheme;

(b) the set of multivalued dependencies is equivalent to the *join dependency* $\bowtie (P(T))$.

In Fig. 1, we present the scheme tree for the class c as defined previously. The superclass attributes, F_i, and the shared object attributes, L_i, are not fully expanded down to their leaf nodes (elementary attributes) since their definition is recursive and depends on the structure of the class hierarchies. These composite attributes are the root nodes of sub-trees having a similar scheme tree to the one shown before.

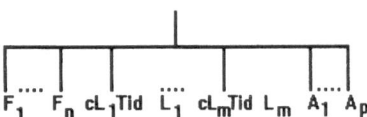

Fig.1 Scheme Tree of Class Definition

Based on the properties described previously, from the scheme tree of Figure 1, we can derive the following MVDs:

(a) $cTid \twoheadrightarrow A_1, A_2, \dots, A_p$

(b) $cTid \twoheadrightarrow F_i$

(c) $cTid \twoheadrightarrow c_{L_i}Tid, L_i$

(d) $cTid, c_{L_i}Tid, L_i \twoheadrightarrow L_i$.

Above MVDs allows us to decompose losslessly our definition of class (Definition 2.4) as follows:

Property (a): Ω decomposes losslessly into the relation schemes:

$R_1 = \{ cTid, A_1, A_2, \dots, A_p \}$

$R_2 = \{ cTid, F_1, F_2, \dots, F_n, c_{L_1}Tid, L_1, c_{L_2}Tid, L_2, \dots, c_{L_m}Tid, L_m \}$

Property (b): R_2 decomposes losslessly into the relation schemes:

$R_{3,1} = \{ cTid, F_1 \}$

$R_{3,2} = \{ cTid, F_2 \}$

$\dots$

$R_{3,n} = \{ cTid, F_n \}$

$R_4 = \{ cTid, c_{L_1}Tid, L_1, c_{L_2}Tid, L_2, \dots, c_{L_m}Tid, L_m \}$

Property (c): R_4 decomposes losslessly into the relation schemes:

$R_{5,1} = \{ cTid, c_{L_1}Tid, L_1 \}$

$R_{5,2} = \{ cTid, c_{L_2}Tid, L_2 \}$

$\dots$

$R_{5,m} = \{ cTid, c_{L_m}Tid, L_m \}$

Property (d): each $R_{5,i}$, $0 \leq i \leq m$, decomposes losslessly into the relation schemes:

$R_{6,i} = \{ cTid, c_{L_i}Tid \}$

$R_{7,i} = \{ cTid, c_{L_i}Tid, L_i \}$.

Finally, we get:

$$c = (R_1, \omega_1) \bowtie$$
$$(R_{6,1}, \omega_{6,1}) \bowtie (R_{6,2}, \omega_{6,2}) \bowtie \dots \bowtie (R_{6,m}, \omega_{6,m}) \bowtie$$
$$(R_{3,1}, \omega_{3,1}) \bowtie (R_{3,2}, \omega_{3,2}) \bowtie \dots \bowtie (R_{3,n}, \omega_{3,n}) \bowtie$$
$$(R_{7,1}, \omega_{7,1}) \bowtie (R_{7,2}, \omega_{7,2}) \bowtie \dots \bowtie (R_{7,m}, \omega_{7,m}).$$

This decomposed definition of class shows a different way of implementing a class hierarchy on a relational platform. For instance, it shows that in order to "*store*" an instance of a class only the relations based on schemes $R_1, R_{6,1}, R_{6,2}, \dots R_{6,m}$ are necessary. All inherited and shared object attribute values may be derived by cartesian join. It also shows that if Functional Dependencies (FDs) : $cTid \rightarrow A_1, A_2, \dots, A_p$ and $cTid \rightarrow c_{L_i}Tid$, $0 \leq i \leq m$, hold, then the cartesian product of

relations based on schemes $R_1, R_{6,1}, R_{6,2}, \dots R_{6,m}$ can be replaced by a single relation by the scheme of $R = \{ cTid, c_{L_1}Tid, c_{L_2}Tid, \dots, c_{L_m}Tid, A_1, A_2, \dots, A_p \}$. This is the situation when all local attributes are single valued and one object of a class cannot share more than one object of another class.

To complete our discussion of derived definitions, by applying recursively above decomposition to F_i, and L_i composite attributes, we can obtain an expression only containing A_i type attributes. This resulting expression (after the application of the unnesting operator to all composite A_i attributes) gives us a definition of class based on cartesian join of only *flat* relations.

3   Class Algebra

In Section 2.0, we have shown how to express generalization and object sharing by means of nested relations and inclusion dependencies. This approach gives us all the tools and knowledge of the relational model. More specifically, it allows us to apply (nested) relational operators to classes and to derive (class) operators that apply our definition of class (Definition 2.4)

We start by defining (class) set operators, then we analyze project, join, nest and unnest operators.

3.1 Set Operators

Recently, [RU90] has presented a framework for executing set-theoretic operations on complex objects. In his approach, set theory has been extended to the world of classes. He has borrowed the concept of object identity from data modeling research to express the effect of set operations on class members. In [RU90] model, the type of a class describes how property characteristics are to be inherited. Also, there are design rules that define how properties are inherited through set operations. The rules allow multi-valued versus single-valued and required versus optional property characteristics.

Much of [RU90] can be handled by our definition of class [see Section 2.]. In our presentation, the two classes that participate to the binary operations are called classes $c_A = (\Omega_A, \omega_A)$ and $c_B = (\Omega_B, \omega_B)$. The resulting class is called $c = (\Omega, \omega)$. The trivial case where $\Omega_A = \Omega_B$ reduces to the definition of nested algebra set operators of [GY88]. It is more interesting to derive definitions for the case where $\Omega_A \neq \Omega_B$.

Similarly to [RU90], we analyze the intersection, union, difference and symmetric difference operators (and use similar terminology).

Definition 3.1 *The intersection* $(\Omega_A, \omega_A) \cap (\Omega_B, \omega_B)$ *equals* (Ω, ω) *where*

(**collecting intersection**) $\Omega = \Omega_A \cup \Omega_B$ *and*

ω *is the relation that satisfies the set of objects*

$$O = \{\Omega', \Omega''\} \text{ [MA83]}.$$

(**extracting intersection**) $\Omega = \Omega_A \cap \Omega_B$ *and*

$$\omega = \omega' \cup \omega''.$$

Relations (Ω', ω') and (Ω'', ω'') are defined as follows

$$\Omega' = \Omega_A, \quad \Omega'' = \Omega_B,$$
$$(\Omega', \omega') = index\ (\Omega_B, \omega_B) \bowtie (\Omega_A, \omega_A) \text{ and}$$
$$(\Omega'', \omega'') = index\ (\Omega_A, \omega_A) \bowtie (\Omega_B, \omega_B).$$

In the collecting intersection case, Ω' and Ω'' are allowable schemes for subtuples of Ω and are called *objects* (as in [MA83]). Relation Ω is constrained by objects Ω' and Ω'' since for any tuple in Ω, placeholders appear on attributes $\Omega - \Omega'$ for object Ω' and $\Omega - \Omega''$ for object Ω''. In the resulting scheme placeholders play the same role as optional attribute of [RU90].

Since all inclusion dependencies (following Definition 2.4) that apply to classes (Ω_A, ω_A) and (Ω_B, ω_B) also apply to resulting class (Ω, ω), collecting intersection preserves inheritance and object sharing from classes (Ω_A, ω_A) and (Ω_B, ω_B), . We can say that resulting class (relation) is a *weak instance* of database $\{\Omega_A, \Omega_B\}$ and it satisfies the inclusion dependencies of the larger class hierarchy database. On the contrary, in general extracting intersection does not preserve inheritance and object sharing since classes (Ω_A, ω_A) and (Ω_B, ω_B) may not share all superclass or object sharing attributes.

Definition 3.2 *The union* $(\Omega_A, \omega_A) \cup (\Omega_B, \omega_B)$ *equals* (Ω, ω) *where*

(collecting union) $\qquad \Omega = \Omega_A \cup \Omega_B$ *and*

$\qquad\qquad\qquad\qquad\qquad \omega$ *is the relation that satisfies the set of objects*

$$\mathbf{O} = \{\Omega_A, \Omega_B\}.$$

(extracting union) $\qquad \Omega = \Omega_A \cap \Omega_B$ *and*

$$\omega = \omega_A \cup \omega_B.$$

Evidently, Definition 3.2 resembles Definition 3.1 with the exception of Ω' being replaced by Ω_A and Ω'' by Ω_B. In fact, with the union operator, we do not need to join instances of classes (Ω_A, ω_A) and (Ω_B, ω_B) to the index of the other class since all instances of (Ω_A, ω_A) and (Ω_B, ω_B) are included in the resulting relation.

As for the intersection operator, the collecting union operator preserves inheritance and object sharing of participating classes into the resulting class, while the same cannot be said for the extracting union.

Definition 3.3 *The difference* $(\Omega_A, \omega_A) - (\Omega_B, \omega_B)$ *equals* (Ω, ω) *where* $\Omega = \Omega_A$ *and*

$(\Omega, \omega) = (index\,(\Omega_A, \omega_A) - index\,(\Omega_B, \omega_B)) \bowtie (\Omega_A, \omega_A)$.

By result of the difference operator definition, $(\Omega, \omega) \subseteq (\Omega_A, \omega_A)$. Since $\Omega_A = \Omega$, the difference operator produces a relation that satisfies inheritance and object sharing properties of class (Ω_A, ω_A).

(collecting symm.differ.) $\Omega = \Omega_A \cup \Omega_B$ *and*

$\qquad\qquad\qquad\qquad\qquad \omega$ *is the relation that satisfies the set of objects*

$$\mathbf{O} = \{\Omega', \Omega''\}.$$

(extracting symm.differ.) $\Omega = \Omega_A \cap \Omega_B$ *and*

$$\omega = \omega' \cup \omega''.$$

Relations (Ω', ω') and (Ω'', ω'') are defined as follows

$$\Omega' = \Omega_A, \Omega'' = \Omega_B,$$

$(\Omega', \omega') = (index\,(\Omega_A, \omega_A) - index\,(\Omega_B, \omega_B)) \bowtie (\Omega_A, \omega_A)$ *and*

$(\Omega'', \omega'') = (index\,(\Omega_B, \omega_B) - index\,(\Omega_A, \omega_A)) \bowtie (\Omega_B, \omega_B)$.

Inheritance and object sharing properties are preserved as in Definition 3.1.

In [RU90] set operators are divided into *user specified* and *default* operators. User specified operators generate a selection $(\Omega_U, \omega_U) \subseteq (\Omega, \omega)$ where $\Omega_U \subseteq \Omega$ and Ω_U is defined by the user. According to the choice of attributes to include in Ω_U, inheritance and object sharing may or may not be preserved in the resulting relation. In general, only selective inheritance and selective object sharing are maintained.

3.2 Other Operators

Since they are nested algebra operators, project, join, nest and unnest operators are defined as in [GY88]. It is interesting to understand how the combination of above operators allows operations on the class hierarchy.

By projecting on $cTid$ and F_i, and unnesting on F_i, we get the set of instances of a sub-class on its superclass (superclass inclusion dependency) and similarly, by projecting on $c_{L_i}Tid$ and L_i, we get the set of instances shared from another class (object sharing dependency). And, finally by projecting on attributes $cTid$ and A_i, we get the instances of our class without inheritance and object sharing.

Since both the projection and the unnesting operators are monotone operators [BE90], we are guaranteed that by successive application of projection and unnesting the inclusion dependency constraints of Section 2 are satisfied. This is the same to say that instances of a sub-class are always contained in the superclass set of instances. On the other hand, if we apply nesting to both sides of the inclusion dependencies, the containment condition may not hold. In fact, nesting is not a monotone operator (together with scons, difference and singleton) [BE90].

By joining two classes (with the condition that the elementary attributes from which the two classes are built are disjoint), we get a class where, possibly, multiple inheritance has increased (i.e., more superclasses), more classes of objects are shared and our class specific attributes are more numerous.

The application of nesting and unnesting operators modifies the hierarchy of our class structure. By unnesting a superclass attribute, we remove a level of inheritance in our class hierarchy and the unnested attribute is split into its superclass, object sharing and class specific attributes. Similarly, by unnesting a shared object attribute, we remove an object sharing condition and basically embed the shared object attribute into our class.

The effect of nesting only some of the attributes of a class does not produce a reasonable class hierarchy. On the other hand, if we apply nesting to all attributes (except the $cTid$) we generate a subclass devoid of any specific and object sharing attribute. To be a class, this resulting class must satisfy the inclusion dependency.

4. Conclusions

In this paper, we have developed a formal framework for understanding the connection between a data model supporting inheritance and object-sharing and the nested relational model. The translation of inheritance and object-sharing to nested relational schemas is shown to be based on inclusion dependencies among nested relations at different hierarchical levels or different hierarchies. By using the nested relational model, we have been able to define a class with superclass and shared-object attributes only referring to adjacent (in hierarchical terms) classes. In this way, the resulting definition of class is simple and class operators can be derived easily. Furthermore, since the nested relational model allows attribute values which can be relations themselves, our data model supports multivalued properties, which can be inherited, shared or just local. By adding more superclass and shared-object attributes, multiple inheritance and multiple object sharing is supported.

Our model is based on the ability to make references through an object identity as defined in the concept of extended relation of [SI90]. Object identity is a simple attribute who is supported directly by the record managers of existing database systems. By means of object identity, we are able to decompose our definition of class (Def.2.4) in terms of *1)* a relation with the class id and the class local attributes, *2)* relations with the class id and participating classes object ids and *3)* relations with participating classes ids and relative nested data attribute. This alternate definition (and others equivalent) can be used to perform query efficiency optimizations.

We have employed our class definition to derive class operator expressions. Since our data model is mapped into nested relations, most class operators match nested relational model operator definitions. However, we have studied set operators with more attention, especially in situations where the participating classes do not have the same schema. Recently, this aspect of class creation by set operations has been analyzed by [RU90]. We have adopted the same terminology as in [RU90] and according to our data model, we have been able to obtain alternate definitions of set operators. This has helped us analyze how inheritance and object sharing are preserved after set operator application. Finally, we have made a few considerations on the meaning of other nested relational operators in our approach of classes.

Currently, we are applying the data model defined in this paper to the Office Document Architecture (*ODA*) hierarchical data structures. ODA [OD88] is a ISO standard model for office document structure and processing. Since this model also include support for office document *object* processing, we are trying to add features for storage of limited (in nature) processing methods. Method signatures can be included in present model, but we are seeking more sophisticated methods for storing the operations that we want to perform on an object. The underlined constraint is to build our data model on top of a commercially available (nested) relational DBMS. Details of the application of our approach to model the ODA standard are given in the appendix following these conclusions.

Appendix:

An ODA Implementation Based on Nested Relations

According to the ODA [OD88] standard, there are two primary structures of ODA documents, the logical structure and the layout structure. Logical structures describe logical characteristics of documents, such as titles, articles, etc., and layout structures describe their layout characteristics, such as size and positions. Furthermore, each structure entails a specific and a generic structures. A specific structure represents an instance of a real document, wheres a generic structure is a template of similar specific structures. In [MU89], the ODA data model has been interpreted according to principles of object-orientation. We have found that our approach based on generalization and object sharing using nested relations provides a suitable platform on which to build an object oriented ODA data management system.

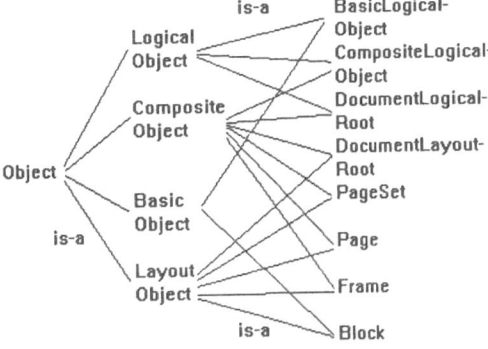

Fig.2 ODA Class Hierarchy

We start the description of our ODA implementation by showing the class hierarchy of ODA object classes (see Fig. 2). For each object type [MU89], we find an ODA object metaclass (see Fig. 3). An ODA object metaclass declares attributes and constraints of object classes of the corresponding object type. So object metaclasses are classes of object classes.

Object metaclasses are a useful tool to interpret ODA *generic classes*. In fact, generic classes are templates of specific classes and they are meant of establish *constraints* and to provide *default values* for specific objects.

Based on our definition of class, a metaclass is a class and it can be defined as follows

$m = (\Omega_m, \omega_m)$ where

$\Omega_m = \{ mTid, C, D, m_{L_c} Tid\, L_c \}$ and

C is a set of constraints on attributes,

D is a set of default attribute values and

$m_{L_c} Tid\, L_c$ is a shared object attribute (i.e., classes which are instances of this metaclass).

Since each instance of m is a class, then m is a metaclass. Based on what instances of m we decide to use, we are able to establish a relationship between a class and a set of defaults and constraints.

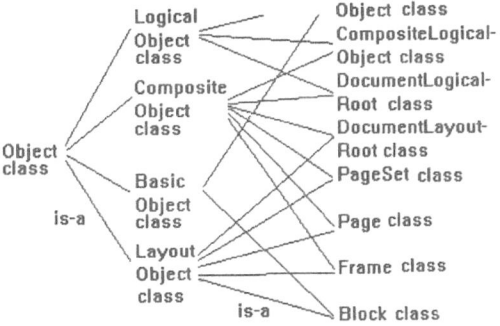

Fig.3 ODA Metaclass Hierarchy

Now, we turn our attention to the definition of ODA classes as in Fig. 2. In our definition of the ODA hierarchy, for each class we give the attributes that deal with generalization and object sharing and omit details on local attributes, since they are implementation dependent.

On top of the hierarchical structure, we find the class *Object*. Since it is located at the root of the hierarchy tree, it only contains local attributes. So the class object is defined as

Object: $Ob = (\Omega_{Ob}, \omega_{Ob})$, where

$\Omega_{Ob} = \{ ObTid, A_1, A_2, ..., A_p \}$.

There are four is-a links from the *Object* class to the *LogicalObject*, *CompositeObject*, *BasicObject* and *LayoutObject* classes. So, we can define

LogicalObject: $LoOb = (\Omega_{LoOb}, \omega_{LoOb})$, where

$\Omega_{LoOb} = \{ LoObTid, A_1, A_2, ..., A_p, F_{Ob} \}$

CompositeObject: $CoOb = (\Omega_{CoOb}, \omega_{CoOb})$, where

$\Omega_{CoOb} = \{ CoObTid, A_1, A_2, ..., A_p, F_{Ob} \}$

BasicObject: $BaOb = (\Omega_{BaOb}, \omega_{BaOb})$, where

$\Omega_{BaOb} = \{ BaObTid, A_1, A_2, ..., A_p, F_{Ob} \}$

LayoutObject: $LaOb = (\Omega_{LaOb}, \omega_{LaOb})$, where

$\Omega_{LaOb} = \{ LaObTid, A_1, A_2, ..., A_p, F_{Ob} \}$.

F_{Ob} represents the attributes inherited from the *Object* class, and A_1 to A_p are local attributes of each class.

There are now eight classes which inherit attributes from the four defined before. Most of them inherit attributes from more than one class, so we exploit our definition of generalization to handle multiple inheritance. We list now the definition of the following classes:

BasicLogicalObject: $BaLoOb = (\Omega_{BaLoOb}, \omega_{BaLoOb})$ where

$\Omega_{BaLoOb} = \{ BaLoObTid, A_1, A_2, ..., A_p, F_{LoOb}, F_{BaOb} \}$

CompositeLogicalObject: $CoLoOb = (\Omega_{CoLoOb}, \omega_{CoLoOb})$ where

$\Omega_{CoLoOb} = \{ CoLoObTid, A_1, A_2, ..., A_p, F_{LoOb}, F_{CoOb} \}$

DocumentLogicalRoot: $DoLoRo = (\Omega_{DoLoRo}, \omega_{DoLoRo})$ where

$\Omega_{DoLoRo} = \{ DoLoObTid, A_1, A_2, ..., A_p, F_{LoOb}, F_{CoOb} \}$

DocumentLayoutRoot: $DoLaRo = (\Omega_{DoLaRo}, \omega_{DoLaRo})$ where

$\Omega_{DoLaRo} = \{ DoLaObTid, A_1, A_2, ..., A_p, F_{LaOb}, F_{CoOb} \}$

PageSet: $PaSe = (\Omega_{PaSe}, \omega_{PaSe})$ where

$\Omega_{PaSe} = \{ PaSeObTid, A_1, A_2, ..., A_p, F_{LaOb}, F_{CoOb} \}$

Page: $Pa = (\Omega_{Pa}, \omega_{Pa})$ where

$\Omega_{Pa} = \{ PaTid, A_1, A_2, ..., A_p, F_{LaOb}, F_{CoOb} \}$

Frame: $\quad\quad\quad Fr = (\Omega_{Fr}, \omega_{Fr})$ where

$\Omega_{Fr} = \{ FrTid, A_1, A_2, ..., A_p, F_{LaOb}, F_{CoOb} \}$

Block: $\quad\quad\quad Bl = (\Omega_{Bl}, \omega_{Bl})$ where

$\Omega_{Bl} = \{ BlTid, A_1, A_2, ..., A_p, F_{LaOb}, F_{CoOb} \}$

The F_x composite attributes refer to inherited attributes from the previous four basic classes (on the hierarchical structure). From this point on, the hierarchy of the ODA data model may change according to user specifications. There are two possible ways of doing this: by means of the Document Application Profile (DAP) and by means of direct user specifications. In the hierarchy we have built, the user builds on top of DAPs (in fact, there can be more than one hierarchically specified DAPs) but not viceversa. There is at least one set of DAPs for every document. A DAP may contain further refinements of basic objects to define user objects such as paragraphs, footnotes, etc.

So far, we have only dealt with generalization. Our model supports also object sharing and indeed we find that our classes need this feature. Let's start from the logical structure. A logical structure contains a (logical) root and many composite and simple logical objects. So, we augment the definition of the *DocumentLogicalRoot* class to share *BasicLogicalObject* and *CompositeLogicalObject* class instances. Similarly, a *CompositeLogicalObject* is an aggregate of many *BasicLogicalObjects*, so in its definition a *CompositeLogicalObject* contains a shareable *BasicLogicalObject* attribute. We apply the same concept for the layout structure, so our class definitions become:

BasicLogicalObject: $\quad\quad$ does not change.

CompositeLogicalObject: $\quad \Omega_{CoLoOb}$ becomes

$\Omega_{CoLoOb} = \{ CoLoObTid, A_1, A_2, ..., A_p, F_{LoOb}, F_{CoOb} . BaLoObTid, L_{BaLoOb} \}$

DocumentLogicalRoot: $\quad \Omega_{DoLoRo}$ becomes

$\Omega_{DoLoRo} = \{ DoLoObTid, A_1, A_2, ..., A_p, F_{LoOb}, F_{CoOb},$
$\quad\quad\quad BaLoObTid, L_{BaLoOb}, CoLoObTid, L_{CoLoOb} \}$

DocumentLayoutRoot: $\quad \Omega_{DoLaRo}$ becomes

$\Omega_{DoLaRo} = \{ DoLaObTid, A_1, A_2, ..., A_p, F_{LaOb}, F_{CoOb},$
$\quad\quad\quad PaSeTid, L_{PaSe}, PaTid, L_{Pa}, FrTid, L_{Fr}, BlTid, L_{Bl} \}$

PageSet: $\quad\quad\quad \Omega_{PaSe}$ becomes

$\Omega_{PaSe} = \{ PaSeObTid, A_1, A_2, ..., A_p, F_{LaOb}, F_{CoOb}, PaTid, L_{Pa}, FrTid, L_{Fr},$
$BlTid, L_{Bl} \}$

Page: $\quad\quad\quad\quad \Omega_{Pa}$ becomes

$\Omega_{Pa} = \{ PaTid, A_1, A_2, ..., A_p, F_{LaOb}, F_{CoOb}, FrTid, L_{Fr}, BlTid, L_{Bl} \}$

Frame: $\quad\quad\quad\quad \Omega_{Fr}$ becomes

$\Omega_{Fr} = \{ FrTid, A_1, A_2, ..., A_p, F_{LaOb}, F_{CoOb}, BlTid, L_{Bl} \}$

Block: $\quad\quad\quad\quad$ does not change.

In Section 3.1, we have redefined set operators according to our definition of class. Set operations on instances of different classes are often used in queries on our ODA data model. For instance, the intersection operator may be employed to derive all objects that belong both to *DocumentLogicalRoot* and *BasicLogicalObject* classes. In the collecting intersection situation, the selected objects, which are single object documents (for instance, a page with just one article) have attributes from both classes. On the contrary, the extracting intersection case allows the retrieval only of properties common to *DocumentLogicalRoot* and *BasicLogicalObject* objects.

The union set operator may be usefully employed to retrieve all document layout objects within a page. To achieve this, we can apply the union operators to *Block* and *Frame* classes. The resulting collection could contain either *Block* and *Frame* attributes (collecting union) or only common attributes of *Block* and *Frame* objects (extracting union).

Finally, difference and symmetric difference operators may be used to retrieve very peculiar collections of objects. For instance, we may wish to get all composite logical objects and all simple layout objects (or viceversa) by means of the same set operation. To do this, we may use symmetric difference of *CompositeObject* and *LayoutObject* classes.

More frequently, the difference operator can be employed to extract all frames with more than one block in a page by subtracting *Block* objects from *Page* objects.

References

[AB88] S.Abiteboul and C.Beeri. *On the power of languages for the manipulation of complex objects.* Technical Report 846, INRIA, May 1988.

[BA87] F.Bancilhon, T.Briggs, S.Khoshafian and P.Valduriez. FAD powerful and simple database language. In *Intl. Conf. on VLDB*, Brighton, pages -, 1987.

[BE90] C.Beeri and Y.Kornatzky. The many faces of query monotonicity. In *Intl. Conf. on Advances in Database Technology EDBT'90*, Venice, pages 120-135, 1990.

[BO90] S.Bottcher. Attribute inheritance implemented on top of a relational database system. In *6th Intl. Conf. on Data Engineering*, Los Angeles, pages 503-509, 1990.

[CO70] E.F.Codd. A relational model of data for large shared data banks. In *Communications of ACM 13:6*, pages 377-387, 1970.

[GY87] M.Gyssens and D.Van Gucht. The powerset algebra as a result of adding programming constructs to the nested relational algebra. In *Techn.Rep. 87-26*, Univ.of Antwerp, 1987.

[GY88] M.Gyssens and D.Van Gucht. The powerset algebra as a result of adding programming constructs to the nested relational algebra. In *ACM SIGMOD Intl. Conf. on Management of Data*, pages 225-232, 1988.

[LY87] P.Lyngbaek and V.Vianu. Mapping a semantic database model to the relational model. In *ACM SIGMOD Intl. Conf. on Management of Data*, pages 132-142, 1987.

[MA83] D.Maier. *The theory of relational databases*, Computer Science Press, 1983.

[MA77] A.Makinouchi. A consideration of normal form of not-necessarily-normalized relations in the relational data model. In *Intl. Conf. on VLDB*, Tokyo, pages 447-453, 1977.

[MU89] M.Murata. An object-oriented interpretation of ODA. In *Woodman'89*, Rennes, France, pages 91-100, 1989.

[OD88] ISO/DIS 8613, *Information processing - Text and office systems* - Office Document Architecture (ODA) and interchange format.

[OZ85] G.Ozsoyoglu and L.Yuan. A normal form for nested relations. In *4th ACM SIGACT-SIGMOD Symposium on Principles of Database Systems*, pages 251-260, 1985.

[OZ86] G.Ozsoyoglu and L.Yuan. Notions of dependency preservation for nested relations. In *XP/7.52 Workshop on Database Theory*, Austin, 1986.

[RO87] M.A.Roth and H.F.Korth. The design of non-1NF relational databases into nested normal forms. In *ACM SIGMOD Intl. Conf. on Management of Data*, pages 143-159, 1987.

[RU90] E.Rundesteiner and L.Bic. Set operations in a data model supporting complex objects.In *Intl. Conf. on Advances in Database Technology EDBT'90*, Venice, pages 286-300, 1990.

[SC86] H-J.Schek and M.H.Scholl. The relational model with relation-valued attributes. In *Information Systems*, V6, N1, 1986.

[SI90] J.J.Sieg and E.Sciore. Extended relations. In *6th Intl. Conf. on Data Engineering*, Los Angeles, pages 488-494, 1990.

[TH86] S.J.Thomas and P.C.Fischer. Nested Relational Structures. In *The Theory of Databases*, P.C. Kanellakis, ed. JAI Press, pages 269-307.

[ZD90] S.B.Zdonik and D.Maier. *Readings in Object-Oriented Database Systems*, M.Kaufmann Pub.Inc., pages 1-32, 1990.

AN OBJECT MODELING METHOD FOR
OFFICE INFORMATION SYSTEMS DESIGN

I.T. Hawryszkiewycz

University of Technology, Sydney
Key Center for Advanced Computing Sciences
PO Box 123 Broadway NSW 2007, Australia

ABSTRACT

The paper describes a modeling method for information systems
with a significant group support component. The proposed
modeling method satisfies representation, state transition and
decomposition criteria. Representation is satisfied by basing the
model on semantics that consider information systems systems
as composed of activities that support teams of roles each of
which is responsible for some of the tasks that make up the
activity. Decomposition is supported by defining applications in
terms of a number of levels, and specifying standard techniques
for combining levels and supporting coordination between
objects at each level. The modeling approach places importance
on defining generalized object modules that can be adapted to
particular applications and thus encourage module reusability.

1 INTRODUCTION

One important question in the trend to more open office systems
is whether design methodologies and modeling methods for such
systems will be different to those now used in practice. Many
conventional design methodologies are oriented towards
constructing systems with a fixed structure of both data and
function and do not support semantics found in open operations.
Thus the option for supporting open system design by extending
conventional methodologies is not easy given their emphasis on
data structure and functionality but no semantics to represent user
coordination and responsibilities of roles within system
activities. What is needed for open systems are methodologies
that define activities in terms of coordination between actors and
include ways for dynamically changing the coordination. This
paper examines the possibility of providing such methodologies
by using object oriented techniques.

The proposed modeling method uses generalized objects to
model system components. These objects can be freely
interconnected and dynamically changed. Furthermore, the
methodology considers software engineering issues for building
such systems, in particular object reusability and modularity. It
classifies objects into a set of levels and develops standard ways
for integrating objects at these levels. These objects can then be
implemented using an object oriented system. Furthermore, such
modeling techniques must be amenable to a development
environment based the notion of synthesis rather than
decomposition.

2 MODELING OBJECTIVES

The goal here is to develop a modeling method that naturally
represents open systems and which at the same time is in some
ways complete. There is at this stage no widely accepted theory
for design model completeness, but a framework has been
suggested (Wand, 1990). This framework categorizes a
modeling method into three parts, namely, representation, state
transition and decomposition. Briefly, representation defines a
set of ontological constructs that are necessary for modeling
systems, state transitions define system responses to external
inputs and decomposition defines a logical way for structuring
models in well defined parts. We will indicate how our model
satisfies these criteria.

We add two other criteria, namely, the modeling method must
use a minimal but expanding set of concepts and that models can
be easily converted to an implementation.

Turning to semantic requirements we now describe the
constructs needed to model systems and then describe how they
satisfy the completeness guidelines.

3 THE PROPOSED SYSTEM SEMANTICS

Representation criteria require the model to represent all 'things'
in the system. Our model views an information system as a set of
activities. Each *activity* has a goal and accomplishes this goal by
executing a number of *tasks*. These tasks are the responsibility of
roles that are assigned to persons who are known as role *actors*.
Sometimes the role actors may depend on the task environment.
For example an approver actor would depend on the kind of
approval sought. Thus the system is made up of actor groups
that cooperate by carrying out the tasks needed to meet some
goal. A simple example of this may be arranging travel. The
tasks here are to make a travel request, get the request approved,
and then arrange for the purchase and delivery of the tickets.
This may be assigned to three roles, namely, the requestor,
approver and arranger role. It is possible for tasks to be made up
of subtasks and for tasks to create their own activities.

Another important model components is *coordination* between
roles in an activity. To encourage reusability, our models
separate coordination from task modules and provide generalized
coordination modules that can be reused in systems. Earlier
research has identified coordination methods that are used in our
models. These range from systems where each role is an
autonomous agent (Makunichi, 1990) with sufficient knowledge
to deal with any incoming messages to more specialized
coordination support as for example, *sequencing*, which
specifies relationships between team members or *client-
server,*(Winograd, 1986), which specifies one role making a
request on another as well as mediation (Kreifelts, 1989) and
conflict resolution (Martial, 1990) patterns. In our example travel
arrangement is modeled as a role sequence, starting with the

requestor and then followed by the approver and arranger. This sequence may be dynamically varied by, for example, the approver asking for more information from the requestor, the approver checking if other similar requests have been made more complex communications between requestor and arranger and so on.

Actors in our case become the external stimula that can set role states and in turn initiate activities. They can also dynamically change the system structure by creating new tasks, reallocating existing tasks to roles, delegating tasks from one role to another, subdividing tasks, creating new activities by assigning the new subtasks to new roles, or changing the coordination patterns. We now turn to decomposition.

4 OBJECT ORIENTED REPRESENTATION

Most design methodologies suggest that to manage design complexity, problems must be decomposed into levels of identical purpose and generalized semantics defined for each level. To assist design our model structures the object library in the way shown in Figure 1. There are two major dimensions in this classification. The first is a distinction between procedure and organizational objects. Here:

(a) Procedure objects define computational semantics, with object states activating methods in the procedure object. External objects cannot access the methods directly but can only initialize the procedure to some state.

(b) Organizational Objects may either be fact or rule type objects. Fact objects correspond more to data base components, such as person data, appointments and so on. They are usually designed using standard database design techniques. Organizational rules on the other hand contain knowledge about organizational policies, as for example, who approves orders when the regular approver, say the department head is away, or when budgets must be presented.

The second dimension is to define object *levels*. At the highest level there are two main object *domains*. The application domain deals with particular application semantics, such as for example, banking or insurance. This domain includes the procedure semantics as well as a domain applicable knowledge base composed of organizational objects. The other domain concerns the distribution of information and cooperation between information system workers. This, for example, may be passing on tasks between users, or in general directing information between persons concerned with a common task. This second domain is known as *group support* or CSCW (Computer Assisted Cooperative Work). The CSCW part of most information systems is continually growing due to the trend of information systems to move from personal support to group support, and the growing number of less structured applications. Furthermore, this component posseses many common characteristics across applications and thus there is the possibility of simplifying the design of the group support component through reuse of generic group support modules.

Objects in these two domains can be further classified. These more detailed domain levels are based on the natural semantics of information systems.

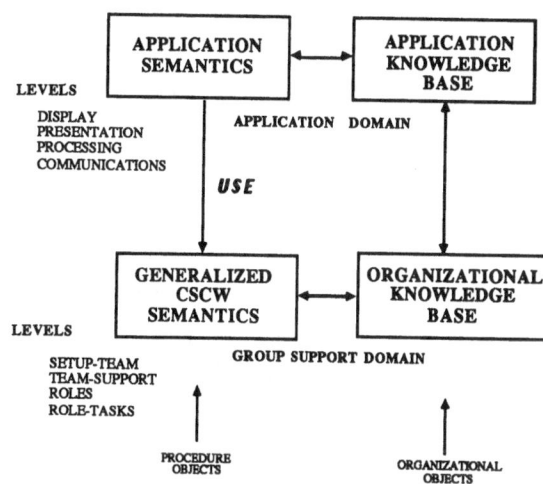

Figure 1 - Object Classification

4.1 The Application Domain Levels

The application dependent component is made up of the following levels:

Display Level - The display level interacts with system actors through display devices. General display procedure objects are made available to display information or to get responses from users. The procedure objects in the level may use the knowledge, such as where particular person can be found, display device descriptions, and how to map document structures to display devices. The display level is used by the presentation level.

Presentation Level - The presentation level knows the protocol of presenting information to users. There may be different kinds of protocols. For example there may be a protocol to carry out a single interaction with a user to get information. It presents information to an actor and asks for a reply. This knowledge includes the formulation of the question and the selection of display object. This knowledge is contained in the procedure and methods for sending a question and receiving a reply, and the context references to objects that contain presentation knowledge.

Processing Level - This level includes computational objects for application or domain dependent processing. These may include general objects for an application domain, such as banking. It may also include objects to support more generalized functions such as document processing. For document processing, for example, the generalized semantics may include semantics such as attaching a note to a document, or the insertion deletion of sections and document rearragement. Processing objects use presentation objects to obtain or display information.

Communications Level - This level concerns the distribution of information between roles. It uses knowledge used here includes determination of actors to communicate with. The communications level is made up of any number of procedure objects which may fall into one or more hierarchies. Designers may then select any one of these objects for their application.

4.2 The Group Support Levels

The group support part sets up an activity and is made up of four levels, namely, set-up-team, team support, role and task levels. In summary, the purpose of each level is:

Setup Team Level - The setup team level is used to select a particular team management strategy by nominating roles, their tasks and coordination between the roles,

Support Team Level - The team support level coordinates the roles by monitoring their states. It may do things like initiating or terminating a role or changing its direction. It also provides general activity support tasks.

Role Level - The role level describes role level semantics. It has one role object for each team role, and

Role Task Level - The role task level describes the tasks assigned to each role. It that has one object for each activity permitted for the role.

The semantic idea is that SET-UP has a broad goal and uses a TEAM-SUPPORT structure that coordinates a number of ROLES each of which can use any number of processing actions to achieve the broad goal.

You should note that an application need not contain all of the above levels, and can in fact contain more that one of any of the levels.

Objects in each level can be organized into an inheritance structure that increasingly specializes level semantics. Thus each level has a generalized object that defines the broad level semantics, and specialized objects that define detailed semantic object. Thus we may have approval as a generalized objects, with travel approval, part approval and so on as specialized objects. Detailed description of such specialization are outside the scope of this paper and can be found elsewhere (Hawryszkiewycz, 1991). We now describe how objects are combined to form systems. To do this we need to describe object structures in more detail.

4.3 Object Structure

Objects in our model are similar to those used in other work (Chrysanthis, 1990, Woo and Lochovsky, 1986). Objects in our model have five features namely:

(a) Properties that contain private attribute values of object instances as well as references to shared objects,

(b) States that define the valid states for the object. The system state is the composition of all the object states.

(c) Methods that describe the kinds of operations allowed for the object. Such operations are defined using an object oriented language.

(d) Rules and Local Constraints to the object, describing any constraints between object properties as well as the actions to be taken on an object entering a given state.

(e) Context, which defines those object properties that can be shared with other objects and in some ways corresponds to the notion of establishing an application environment. It can be implemented as database views or as messages.

States allow objects to be developed independently of other objects. External inputs are actors that change role states. These changes in turn lead to roles communicating with other roles through the team structure. These roles can then carry out their tasks. We now describe how objects are put together to model systems.

5 COMBINING LEVELS

Systems are constructed by selecting and integrating objects from a number of levels. Object integration uses the notion of objects at one level(i) *using* objects at another level(i+1). Usually, objects at level (i) are at a higher semantic level than objects at level (i+1) and consequently level(i) semantics are elaborated or customized in terms of level (i+1) objects. This customization is made in *adapting objects* each of which selects a library object and redefines its features. The adapting objects are then combined into a hierarchical structure that corresponds to domain object levels in the way shown in Figure 2. Here adapting objects are represented by rectangular boxes and library objects by circles. During execution the adapting object at level (i) creates a level(i+1) objects and initiates the object.

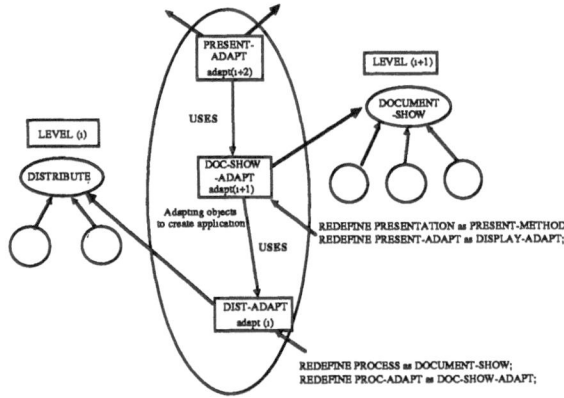

Figure 2 - Combining Levels

A special system procedure is used to specify level generation. This procedure is defined as:

```
procedure setadapt (LEVEL-TYPE, leveltyperef,
              ADAPT-TYPE, adaptyperef);
leveltyperef = make (LEVEL-TYPE);
adaptyperef = make (ADAPT-TYPE);
leveltyperef = parent (adaptyperef);
* = parent (adaptyperef);
```

Here make (x) creates an object of type X and A=parent(B) makes A a parent of B. In the example in Figure 2 the adapting object at a level (i) selects the communications level object, DISTRIBUTE, and adapts it by redefining its general features by specific objects at level (i+1), in this case, DOCUMENT-SHOW and DOC-SHOW-ADAPT as specified in the REDEFINE clause of adapt(i). These specific objects are then created by object(i). This redefinition process is here called *adaption*, to mean that we adapt the high level objects to the needs of the application. In Figure 2 object, DISTRIBUTE, includes the following method:

method SETUP-PROCESSING

(level dependent computation that may change the context)

```
for each element in circulation-list do
begin
setadapt (PROCESS, doc, PROC-ADAPT, docadapt),
state = 'setup';
end;
```

The adapting object, DIST-ADAPT, in Figure 2, customizes DISTRIBUTE by redefining PROCESS as DOCUMENT-SHOW and PROC-ADAPT as DOC-SHOW-ADAPT. The customized DISTRIBUTE object now creates one process 'DOCUMENT-SHOW' for each person on the circulation list. The next time this same object could be used to distribute another process. Of course most generalized objects would have many more functions, such as for example sending reminders or keeping backups and so on. The object at level (i+1) is then adapted to a presentation level object that presents documents in a chosen way.

5.1 Object Coordination

Objects communicate with each other by passing information between levels and coordinating object activities through object states. Information is passed by inheritance. Objects at level (i+1) inherit the features of their level(i) parent objects. Every object only has one parent and objects create their children. We restrict inheritance to the context and states. Thus, consistent to software engineering processes, the lower level objects cannot access the private data and methods of the higher level object. However, it is possible to pass data to lower levels through the inherited context, and to read and set states of the parent object.

The other aspect of communication is object coordination. Coordination uses object states to determine what methods to initiate or whether to change the state of some other object. There are alternative ways for coordinating two objects. Suppose we have two objects, namely, the owning object X and the owned object B. Object X has created object B, and object B inherits the properties of object X. Alternatives for

coordination depend on where control rests. We can have the owner in control, the child in control, child asking for orders or independence between the objects. The first alternative is used here and it can be generalized as:

$$COORD(X, out:(<o1, s1>, ... <on, sn>),$$
$$in:(r1,b1>, ... <rn,bn>)$$

This can be explained as follows. Suppose object, Y, has this coordination structure. Then whenever object Y is in one of the states o1,.. on it will set object X to the corresponding state s1,..sn. Whenever object X is in any of the states r1,..rn then object Y will be set to the corresponding state b1, .. bn. There could be specializations of this generalization, as for example, the semantics of 'doing a job', here called DOJOB. It assumes two standard states, namely (start, finish). The coordination structure is specified as:

```
Procedure DOJOB (X, state-1, state-2);
   if state-1 then initiate (X, start);
   if state(X) = finish then state = state-2;
```

This simply means that on reaching state 'state-1', the object requires JOB X to be done. When this job is finished, the object is set to state 'state-2'.

5.2 Standard Adaption Structure

A standard diagramming technique shown in Figure 3 is used to elaborate adapting objects. Here each adapting object is represented by a rectangular box made up of four parts. The first part is the adapting object name, the second part is the name of the generalized object being adapted, the third part is the redefinition structure and the fourth, the coordination structure. It is thus possible to represent the whole application by adapting objects. Each adapting object refers to a previously defined generalized object and the redefinition and coordination parts specify how these generalized objects are to be adapted and used.

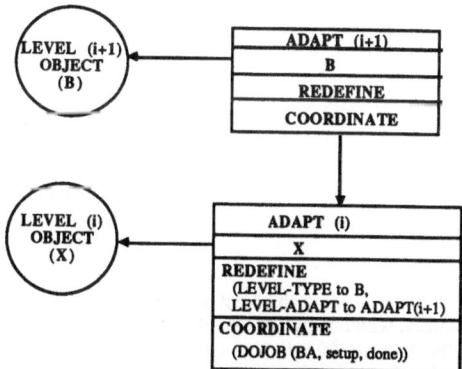

Figure 3 - Standard Adaption Structure

Furthermore, the coordination structure is such that objects can be developed independently of activities or knowledge about

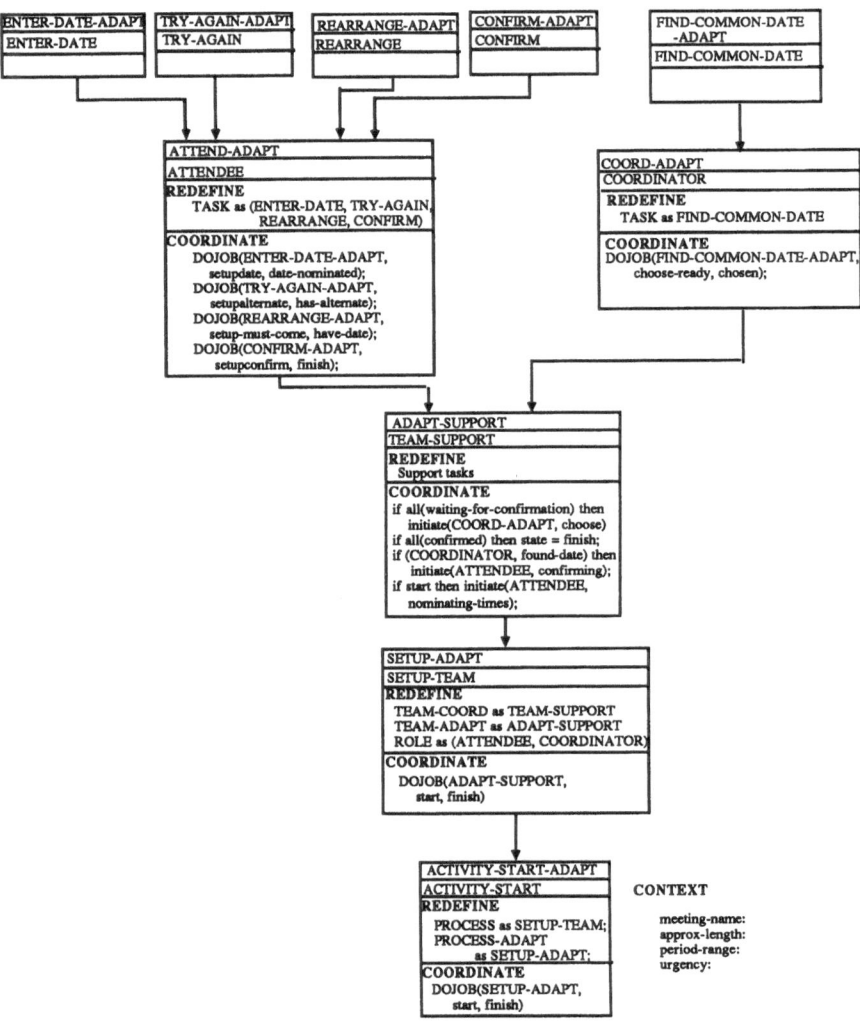

Figure 4- Date Planning system

any other objects. All each object does is set its own state. The coordination, which is part of the adapting object, decides what other objects are to be activated given the state of the adapting object.

5.3 Coordination Objects

Our methodology goal is, rather than having one coordination structure, to provide a variety of coordination structures that can be used to construct CSCW applications and which reflect the semantics of the application. DOJOB is one such coordination object. There are others, some of which such as the client server coordination as described elsewhere (Hawryszkiewycz, 1991).

6 ACTIVITY STRUCTURES

A typical activity structure is shown in Figure 4. It illustrates the DATE PLANNING SYSTEM. Such systems are designed to have a number of potential attendees agree on a suitable meeting date. Here meeting attendees are first required to nominate their available times for the meeting. Once all attendees have nominated their times, the coordinator examines these dates to see if there is a common meeting date. If so, then a confirmation is sent to the attendees by with the selected date. The ATTENDEEs then record this selected date in their calendars. If no common date is found, the coordinator can ask the attendees to nominate an alternate time, or simply say that the meeting is important by setting the state to 'must-come' and the attendees must then rearrange their calendar.

In Figure 4, the DATE PLANNING system is modeled as an activity that has two roles, the ATTENDEE and the COORDINATOR. The whole activity is initiated by the module ACTIVITY-START-ADAPT, whose context includes details of the meeting, its estimated length and a time range. This adapting object adapts the generalized object, ACTIVITY-START, to the particular task. Thus ACTIVITY-START contains the methods used to start an activity, using the generic objects, PROCESS and PROCESS-ADAPT. The adapting object redefines these generic objects as SETUP-TEAM and SETUP-ADAPT. The generalized object, SETUP-TEAM knows how to set up teams, whereas its adapting objects redefines the actual roles. This object in turn creates the team object and its adapting object which, includes the coordination structure for the roles.

The ATTENDEE is assigned a number of tasks, including, ENTER-DATE, to find a suitable date, CONFIRM, to confirm a selected date, TRY-AGAIN, to find an alternate time, and REARRANGE, to simply fit in a nominated time into their schedule. REARRANGE may itself initiate an activity that changes other meeting times. The tasks can access organizational objects to get access to retained data. These tasks are initiated by the role methods.

Coordination uses the ideas of triggers and events. The idea is that each procedure object can have any number of actions (each implemented by a pricedure object method) and the completion of an action becomes an event. This event can set states in other objects. These states then trigger actions in these other objects. The way in which this is done using the object structure is shown following.

RULES

    if state =- 'nominating-times' then NOMINATE;
    if state = 'date-nominated' then RESPOND-WAITING;

METHODS

    method NOMINATE;
    (make any changes to the context)
    setupadapt(ENTER-DATE, e, ENTER-DATE-ADAPT, ea)
    state = 'setupdate';

    method RESPOND-WAITING;
    (any intermediate computation)
    state = 'waiting-for-confirmation';

This definition shows that the ATTENDEE role state 'nominating-times' triggers method NOMINATE. Method NOMINATE creates a new ENTER-DATE procedure object. The ATTENDEE coordination structure then sets event 'setupdate', which starts the procedure object ENTER-DATE using coordination object DOJOB. When the date is entered object ENTER-DATE is finished. This, through DOJOB, sets the state of ATTENDEE-ADAPT to 'date-nominated', which triggers action RESPOND-WAITING. This action, after any intermediate computation' sets event 'waiting-for-confirmation' which may then trigger an action in object TEAM-SUPPORT ADAPT. This object in turn may trigger an action in object

COORD-ADAPT. In Figure 4 COORD-ADAPT shows only one task, namely, FIND-COMMON-DATE. This task is activated when all ATTENDEES have nominated their available times and are in state 'waiting-for-confirmation'. This sets the COORD-ADAPT state to 'choose' and subsequently triggers action CHOOSING, which in turn starts FIND-COMMON-DATE-ADAPT to find if there is a common nominated date.

RULES

    if state = 'choose' then CHOOSING;
    if state = 'chosen' then CHECK-DATE;

METHODS

    method CHOOSING
    (search to find common date);
    state = 'choose-ready';

    method CHECK-DATE
    if found then
      (set up found date in context)]
      state= found-date;
    if not(found) then state = 'not-found';

State 'found' becomes an event that triggers SETUP-ADAPT and eventually signals the end of the activity. Statre 'alternate-time' initiates a request to attendees for an alternate date.

6.1 Structure Properties

One interesting outcome of this method of hierarchical coordination is that the whole structure is correct if the individual coordination structures are themselves correct. Thus by choosing preproven coordination objects, correct system behaviour can be achieved.

7 DYNAMIC EVOLUTION

A formal semantic model provides the ability to formally define change semantics. One goal here is to provide a minimum number of change constructs, which can be specified in terms of the level at which a change is made. For example, changes can be made by roles within their levels of responsibility or within the team. Three levels of change are identified, namely:

    . change within a role responsibility,
    . change at a team level effected by one role on the team,
and

    change by a role at the activity level.

Role types may of course be different and each type may have abilities to only make changes at some of the above levels.

Changes within a roles responsibilities are the simplest. For example, a role can create a new task, add a method to a task or change a method. It can create a new activity and pass its context to this activity. In summary, the allowed changes are those that allow a role to create new child objects while preserving the semantic level structure. Such change makes it possible to realize some of the natural semantics found in task

40

organization. One such semantic is delegation which can be implemented in the way shown in Figure 5. Here the role initially had two tasks, TASK-A and TASK-B. It decides to delegate task, TASK-B. To do this it creates a new activity with one role. TASK-B is now included as part of the adaption for the new role. Roles can then make changes to any of their existing activities.

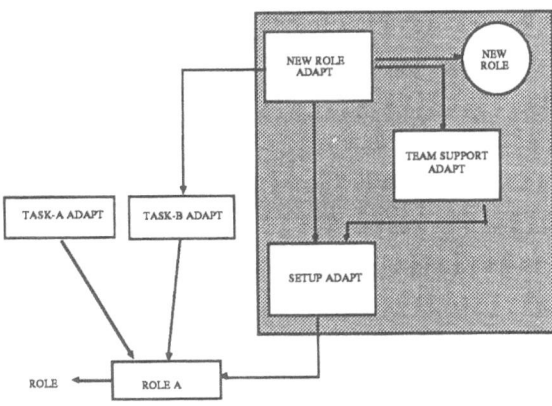

Figure 5 - Delegation

Change is implemented using generalized semantics associated with roles. These semantics are part of the generalized role object and are implemented by methods within that object. Thus a role actor would first select a change level, then select objects within this level and then change these objects or add new objects to the level.

8 IMPLEMENTATION

The models described here follow the basic ideas of object oriented systems and can be implemented using such systems. Inheritance is used to customize library objects to a particular problem. Redefinitions involve actual class names. When this is directly not implementable in an ODBMS then the same effect can be realized by regenerating the redefined method using the redefine parameters, and making this regenerated method a method in the adapting object. The context can be implemented either as database views or as messages.

9 SUMMARY

This paper described a modeling method that can be used to design open information systems. The modeling method uses object oriented techniques. It proposes an approach where an information system is specified in terms of a number of levels with generalized objects provided at each level. The generalized objects are redefined to a particular application needs and integrated to make the application.

ACKNOWLEDGEMENT

This work was carried out by the author in cooperation with GMD in Germany and the author wishes to acknowledge the many discussions with Thomas Kreifelts and Gerd Woetzel of GMD that helped formulate the ideas in this paper.

BIBLIOGRAPHY

Chrysanthis, P, et.al. (1990): "A Logically Distributed Approach for Structuring Office Systems" in Lochovsky, F.H., Allen, R.B. (eds): Proceedings of the Conference on Office Information Systems", Cambridge, Massachussetts, 1990.

Hawryszkiewycz, I.T. (1991): "The Object Oriented Approach in CSCW" Arbeitspapiere der GMD, Gesellschaft fur Mathematic und Datenverarbeitung, Schloss Birlinghoven, Germany.

Hewitt, C. (1986): "Offices are Open Systems", TOIS, Vol. 4, No. 3, July 1986, pp. 271-287.

Kim, W., Lochovsky, F. (eds). (1989): "Object Oriented Concepts, Databases, and Applications", ACM Press, Addison-Wesley.

Kreifelts, T., et.al. (1989): "A Design Tool for Autonomous Group Agents", in Proceedings of the First European Conference on Computer Supported Cooperative Work, 13-15 September 1989, Gatwick, London, UK.

Martial, F. von,. (1990a): "A Conversation Model for Resolving Conflicts among Distributed Office Activities" in Lochovsky, Allen, 1990a.

Maruichi, T., Ichikawa, M., Tokoro, M. (1990): "Modeling Autonomous Agents and their Groups" in Demazue, Y., Muller, J-P., (eds.) Decentralized AI, Elsevier Science Publishers B.V. North-Holland, 1990.

Tsichritzis, D., (ed). (1989): "Object Oriented Development", Centre Universitaire D"Informatique, Universite De Geneva.

Wand, Y., Weber, R. (1990): "Towards a Theory of Deep Structure of Information systems" Proceeding of the 11th International Conference on Information Systems, Copenhagen, 199, pp.61-72..

Weiberg, R., Guimares, T., Heath, R., (1990): "Object Oriented Systems Development" Journal of Information Systems Management, Vol.7, No. 4, Fall 1990, pp.18-26.

Winograd, T., Flores, F. (1986): Understanding Computers and Cognition: A New Foundation for Design", Ablex Publishing Corporation, Norwood, New Jersey, 1986.

Woo, C.C., Lochovsky, F.H. (1986): "Supporting Distributed Office Problem Solving in Organizations", TOIS, Vol. 4, No. 3, July 1986, pp. 185-204.

An Interface/application Builder
with Transmission Control Facility for SGML document Databases

Yoshio Nakano, Hidekazu Tanigawa and Yoshihiko Imai

MATSUSHITA ELECTRIC INDUSTRIAL CO., LTD
KANSAI INFORMATION & COMMUNICATIONS RESEARCH LABORATORY
1006 KADOMA KADOMA-SHI OSAKA JAPAN 571

Abstract

This paper presents a document-based application builder called
STUFF, using which one can create various document-based applications such as a bug report management system, a development
schedule management system, and so on.

STUFF applies SGML (Standard Generalized Markup Language)
to describe document structures, and all documents developed by
STUFF are stored in SGML-DB. In SGML-DB, not only document
contents and document structures but also their handling schema
(user interface schema and transmission control data) are stored, so
modifications of the application, such as changing document structures and altering user interfaces, become easier.

We applied SGML as the common specification language for the
three components in SGML-DB: document structures, user interface elements and transmission control data. This greatly increases
portability of the applications as well as the documents. STUFF
has facilities for constructing document-based applications to access
the components in the SGML-DB and interpret them.

Another feature of STUFF is the control of the transmission of
documents and messages in SGML-DB. Depending on a change
of document contents, STUFF, using prestored network directing
the flow of transmission, control where, what, and how documents
should be transmitted. This is an augmentation of active databases.

1 Introduction

The development of high-performance workstations, networks and
support tools has led to a great increase in their use. However, the
productivity of software development has made less progress than
that of hardware[1].

According to our survey of present software development, the
development process consists of the following tasks:

- Programming
- Developing documents
- Transmitting information between developers

Although in our investigation the working ratio of the above three
tasks is approximately 1:1:1, the support tools currently available to
develop documents and to transmit information between developers
are still at an early stage of development.

We have developed STUFF (document management System
builder passing Tagged information between User interFace block
and Function elements) to facilitate the construction of document-
based applications, such as a bug report system and a schedule
management system, required in software development.

STUFF applies SGML (Standard Generalized Markup Language)[3]
to describe document structures, and all documents developed by
STUFF are stored in an SGML-document-base(SGML-DB). Since
documents in STUFF are purely logical objects, documents can be
modified or converted in various ways.

STUFF also guarantees document portability so that any document in SGML-DB can be converted to an SGML document, which
is a text file having document contents with logical tags.

STUFF keeps a user interface schema for each document type in
the database. The user interface schema, which is also described
using SGML, are systematically built from document structure decompositions. Using the same language, SGML, to define a document structure and the corresponding user interface schema helps
systematic construction of user interfaces and easy modification of
document structures. This greatly improves the maintenance efficiency of document management systems, comparing with those of
4GL systems.

STUFF can not only manage information but can also support
information transmission between developers which is necessary to
software development. Conventionally, E-mail has been used to automate information transmissions in POSTGRES or OBE. These
systems can send mail to a certain destination address, which is
dynamically selected by queries when a specified condition is satisfied. Besides this, STUFF uses a directed network of transmission,
which enables hierarchical control of transmission and transmission
status management.

The major purpose of this paper is summarized as follows:

1. To introduce a new document database concept: SGML-DB.

2. To clarify the requirements of document-based applications in
   software development.

3. To introduced an original method to construct a user interface
   in a document development.

4. To introduced an augmented active database to handle total
   information transmission.

The remainder of the paper is organized as follows. The following section describes basic concepts and the overall configuration of
STUFF. SGML-DB and document transmission control, that are
main features of STUFF, are presented in sections 3 and 4, respectively. Another feature of STUFF, UI schema is given in section 5.
In section 6, STUFF organization is presented.

2 Basic concepts and overall configuration of STUFF

STUFF is a document-based application builder, using which one
can create various document-based applications such as a bug report
management system, a development schedule management system,
and so on.

From an abstract view of document management process in software development, we made a simple task model in which the management process consists of three basic tasks which are document
development, storage, and transmission. STUFF supports these
three basic tasks.

Apart from storing documents in a database, STUFF also manages document structures, user interface schema (UI schema), and
transmission control data in a database, called SGML-DB. That is,
SGML-DB manages not only document data and their schema but
also their handling schema (UI schema and transmission control
data).

Since UI schema, document structures, and transmission control data correspond well to the above three basic tasks: development, storage, and transmission, respectively, building a document-based application requires only the specification of these data to STUFF, and STUFF has facilities to automatically construct the application from the specified three types of data.

We applied SGML as the common specification language for the three types of data. When an application is used, STUFF accesses its specifications from the SGML-DB, and interprets them. We also use SGML to specify the protocol for transmissions between STUFF and SGML-DB. To implement the SGML-DB, we use a RDBMS, and SGML protocols are converted to RDBMS schema where tags in SGML correspond to attributes in RDB, and this is also managed in the RDB.

Figure 1 summarizes the overall configuration of SGML-DB and STUFF. SGML-DB contains documents with the following handling schema:

- document schema
- user interface schema
- transmission control data.

STUFF has facilities to construct document-based applications from the above handling schema.

Next, we briefly explain how to make the handling schema in SGML-DB, and how they are used. We first make document structures. Here, we use "document" in a logical meaning, so we define a document structure as a predefined set of logical elements and relations among them. A document is an instance having the document structure. The details of the structure will be further described in section 3. Based on the structures, an appropriate database schema will be created, shown as "document schema" in the figure.

Next, we discuss how to make documents (instances) to be handled in the management system. To begin with, we shall consider a hyper text to explain user interface definition. A hyper text may be viewed as a document in our definition. Hyper text systems also usually contain user interfaces in quite natural form. Applying this idea to our user interface schema, we recursively decompose the whole document structure into substructures which correspond to user interface elements such as menus, forms, and so on. The result of this decomposition becomes the "UI schema" in the figure. Optionally, paper layouts of documents may be defined.

As mentioned earlier, in group development of software, documents have to be transmitted among developers. In a bug report system, a bug found by a person has to be announced to the manager, and the manager then determine who should be in charge of the problem. Thus, a document needs to be transmitted according to the contents, the type, the state of development, and so on. Furthermore, the flow of the transmission needs to change dynamically. Therefore, "transmission control" has to be defined, as shown in the figure.

Since a document-based application is realized only defining the above mentioned items, the system can be modified fairly easily. Schema modification of database is left to the function of the database itself. This increases the flexibility of STUFF which is necessary in software development.

3 SGML-DB

3.1 Why use SGML?

In this section, we describe the document structure of STUFF and a new document database named "SGML-DB". We, first, briefly explain what is SGML and why we use it.

SGML stands for Standard Generalized Markup Language, established in 1986 as the international standard ISO 8879- 1986(E) for text and office systems. [3]

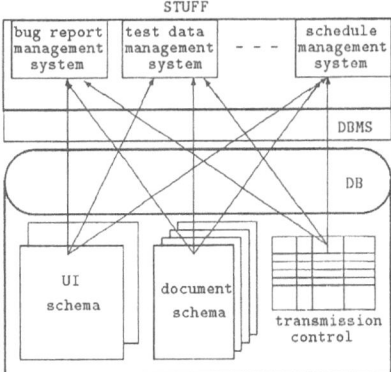

Figure 1: overall configuration of STUFF

SGML was originally designed to mark up formatting commands used in electronic publishing. However, I can be used for purposes other than just electronic publishing or making fair copies of documents. [5]

According to the range of SGML standards described in ISO 8879 -1986(E), SGML is a language to prescribe logical document structures, so a SGML document does not depend on its processing system for example the document formatter.

In SGML, a generic document structure is defined by the grammar description called "DTD" (Document Type Definition), so an SGML document means an instance of a DTD. Figure 2 and 3 show examples of a document and its DTD, respectively. Note that we do not support the full specification of the SGML, and this is limited by user interface elements which STUFF prepares.

```
<BUG_REPORT>
    <CREATE_REPORT>
        <SUMMARY> Cannot edit some characters.
        </SUMMARY>
            ...
        <TEST_REPORT>
            <DATE>1991/3/14
                ...
        </TEST_REPORT>
            ...
    </CREATE_REPORT>
    <ANALYZE_REPORT>
        ...
    </ANALYZE_REPORT>
        ...
</BUG_REPORT>
```

Figure 2: example of a document

```
<!ELEMENT BUG_REPORT ( CREATE_REPORT &
                ANALYZE_REPORT & FIX_REPORT )+ >
<!ELEMENT CREATE_REPORT ( SUMMARY & DATE & PERSON &
        SOFTWARE & VERSION & STATUS_OF_TROUBLE &
        TEST_REPORT )+ >
<!ELEMENT TEST_REPORT ( DATE & PERSON & ENVIRONMENT
        & RESULT )+ >
<!ELEMENT SUMMARY ( #text ) >
<!ELEMENT DATE ( #date ) >
```

Figure 3: document type definition

We use SGML to describe document structures in our system because it is guaranteed that any document in the system, having any structures, can be converted to plain texts with recognized markups. We use the same language, SGML, not only for describing document structures, but also for defining UI schema and transmission control data.

As is briefly mentioned in the previous section, document structures and their handling- UI schema and transmission control data- are closely related from a view point of logical documents. Using the same language makes it much easier for us to decompose a document structure into substructures which correspond to user interface elements. Also, transmission control is performed based on the contents of documents, so references from the document structures to the control becomes easier when the same language is used. These will be shown in sections 4 and 5.

3.2 documents in SGML-DB

Document contents are also managed in SGML-DB. SGML format is used for an internal document passing inside of STUFF, and when documents in SGML-DB go out of STUFF, they are converted into SGML forms. STUFF also has a facility to insert SGML form documents into SGML-DB.

We show an example of an SGML document to insert(get) into(from) SGML-DB in Figure 4. The value, distinguished in <field Value id= Tag name> of the information in the figure, is to be inserted as the attribute value in the database. Information following the <Record> expresses one record in the database.

```
<Record>
<fieldValue id=bug No>zz00-12
<fieldValue id=rank>A
<fieldValue id=summary>Mistake in Japanese
                            translation
<fieldValue id=status>When input Japanese,
            I can't translate romaji-kanji.
```

Figure 4: Example of a SGML formed document

3.3 UI schema in SGML-DB

We decompose a document structure to create a user interface definition. We use the document type definitions show in Figure 3 to show how the decomposition progresses. The decomposition starts at the root of the document structure, which is "BUG_REPORT". "BUG_REPORT" consists of the three elements: "CREATE_REPORT", "ANALYZE_REPORT", and "FIX_REPORT", as shown below.

```
<!ELEMENT BUG\_REPORT ( CREATE_REPORT &
          ANALYZE_REPORT & FIX_REPORT )+ >
```

We may assign this structure to a user interface element "menu" such as the following:

```
<mainMenu> bug report management system
    <subMenu> create  <form> CREATE_REPORT
    <subMenu> analyze <form> ANALYZE_REPORT
    <subMenu> fix     <form> FIX_REPORT.
```

This assignment of document structure to user interface elements, presently, has to be done by hand. We think semi-automated assignment may be possible.

We have currently prepared the following four types of user interface elements.

- Menu to control the system structure and form (screen)

- Form to define each user interface screen.

- Field to define each input item which composes a form

- Button to control forms and to process information interactively.

In this subsection, we will show how menus are managed in SGML-DB. Menus are managed in the menu table inside SGML-DB as shown in Table 1.

In the menu table, the "menu ID" attribute is an identifier of the menu item. The attributes "child", "brother" and "from ID" show the user interface structure.

Table 1: menu table

ATTRIBUTE	meaning
menu ID	identifier of menu item
string	display string for menu item
child	child menu ID of the menu
brother	brother menu ID of the menu
form ID	child form ID of the menu
:	:

How other user interface elements are managed in SGML-DB, will be described in detail in section 5.

3.4 Transmission control data in SGML-DB

Assuming that a software project is going on with a large number of developers, leakage, delay and loss in documents transmission clearly reduce the efficiency of the software development. Conversely, if too much information is delivered in E-mail form to the software developers, the effort to read only useful mail from many junks becomes tremendously large, and consequently this decreases the productivity. So it may be very important to appropriately control transmission of information in software development.

STUFF provides the following transmission control facilities.

- Autonomous Transmission
  As in an active database, STUFF sends documents or messages to developers in E-mail whenever contents in the document database change. To use the autonomous transmission, the following four items are managed in SGML-DB:

  - Document look up queries
  - Predefined messages to be sent
  - Directed network of transmission
  - Queries for personal assignment inside the network nodes

In short, whenever contents in the document database change, the automatic transmission facility in STUFF accesses the transmission control table as shown in Table 2, and decides the documents to be sent, predefined messages to be sent, directed network of transmission, and personal assignment inside the network nodes.

Table 2 shows a database schema to manage the four items.

Table 2: transmission control table

ID	MESSAGE	COND	TO WHOM	WHAT
1	insert		select address from bug_tab	select from bug_tab where ...
				select from test_tab where ...
:	:	:	:	:
:	:	:	:	:
3	solution	solve ='yes'	select address from user_tab where ...	select from bug_tab where ...
		solve= 'no'	select address from answer_tab where ...	select from bug_tab where ...
				select from test_tab where ...

The transmission control will be described In detail in section 4.

- Transmission status management

  The manager of the development should be able to find out the status of the transmissions easily. For instance, if a bug report transmitted to person A should have been passed to person B, but still stays at person A and has not been checked. STUFF provides the following facilities.

  - Graphical display of the transmission network indicating the current node of the document.
  - Automated reminder sent to the person where the document has been staying for longer than a specified period. This is done by sending a E-mail.

To manage the transmission status, the directed network of transmission and the conditions to decide a node where the document stays are managed in a table , called the "status table", inside SGML-DB. When a manager needs to display the transmission status of a specified document, the transmission status management facility in STUFF accesses the "status table" and the document in SGML-DB, and compares the conditions in the "status table" and the document contents, and decides the node where the document stays.

4   Document transmission control

We show transmission control in STUFF in section 3. In this section, we further describe the autonomous transmission.

When a content of a document in the database changes, the transmission control facility in STUFF retrieves information from the transmission control table (Refer to Table 2.) in the database. The table consists of node identifiers, messages, conditions to transmit the node, queries for personal assignment and document look up queries. The node identifiers and the conditions to transmit the node construct the directed network of transmission, which specifies the global control of transmission. The queries for personal assignment are used to select candidates to whom a document or a message will be sent. These mechanisms enable a hierarchical description of transmission flow.

We shall explain how this mechanism works with using Table 2 as an example. Transmission control is similar to a state transition machine. Current state of the machine is kept in the corresponding document, and modified by a user. When the state changes, corresponding ID comes to the table(Table 2). Assume now ID is '3', this selects the "solution" record in the table. Assume the "solution" attribute value in the bug report (document) is 'no', this retrieves the query sentence "select address from the answer_tab where..." from the transmission control table. Using the dynamic SQL, it is then evaluated. This evaluation results in the assignment of the person to whom the transmission occurs. Note that if "solution" was yes, the other query sentence would be selected. This corresponds to transmit to a different node in the network according to the condition.

In the next step, to determine the document to be sent, the retrieval sentences "select address from bug_tab where..." and "select from test_tab where...." in the table, are evaluated. In this case, a bug report and a test data are selected and sent to the person who has been already assigned. As shown in the example, document transmission flow can be easily specified (and modified) because it is managed in the database.

We briefly explain how our transmission control described here differs from the related works. POSTGRES [9][10][11] is a DBMS extended from RDBMS INGRES. The POSTGRES provides facilities for active databases, which are alarms and triggers. The alerter and the trigger both are a mechanism to activate a database command whenever a specified content of the database changes, or specified conditions are satisfied.

Another related work is OBE (Office-By-Example) [12] [13], which handles a wide range of office automation and was derived from Query-By-Example, released by IBM in 1978. OBE's function, similar to that of STUFF, is the trigger. In OBE, one can write expressions to specify the trigger condition. When the expression associated with a trigger is satisfied, the trigger activates an action or evaluates another trigger expressions. There are two types of triggers: modification triggers evaluating database changes and time triggers evaluating time, date and fixed time intervals.

Comparing STUFF's transmission control with OBE's trigger facilities, the reminder facility in STUFF, which sends E-mail automatically when a time period has passed, is the same as the time trigger.

On the other hand, the modification trigger in OBE, and the alerters and the triggers in POSTGRES, are similar but less powerful facilities to those in STUFF. The transmission control in STUFF manages the transmission flow using a directed network of transmission for the global controls as well as queries for personal assignment for the local controls, both implemented with a database. Since OBE supports only the local control in our meaning by using a modification trigger, STUFF might be superior to OBE on this point.

5   UI schema

As we described in section 3 we have currently prepared four types of user interface elements: menu elements, form elements, field elements and button elements.

How user interface elements are managed in SGML-DB, we will describe in detail in this section.

5.1   Menu elements

Menu elements show the user interface structure and the control of menus and forms. An example of menu elements was shown in section 3.3. <mainMenu> identifies a top menu in a system. <subMenu> identifies a sub-menu under a top menu, and it is paired with a <form> tag. This is the user interface structure. A <form> tag defines a form that is displayed when a sub-menu is selected. This is the control of the user interface.

As mentioned earlier, menus are managed in the menu table in SGML-DB as in Table 1.

5.2   Form elements

Form elements define fields and buttons in forms, also the positions of fields and buttons. An example of form elements is shown in Figure 5. Elements to distinguish the form are described after the <form> tag. Fields and comments in the form are defined by <field> and <heading> tags. A Field position in the form is specified as <v>, </v>, <h> and </h>. The position information shows positioning relations without defining coordinate values. Format can be defined without depending on display system (character terminal, X terminal and so on.).

```
<form>insertion_result_form
    <v>
        <h><heading>bug No is
            <field>project
            <field>code
            <heading>-
            <field>number
            <heading>                      </h>
        <h> <heading>output:CTRL/V
            <heading>return top menu:TAB   </h>
    </v>
```

Figure 5: Example of form element

Form elements are managed in the form table in the database as in Table 3.

In the table, the "form ID" attribute identifies a form. The "item pointer" attribute indicates the pointer of items, fields, comments and buttons, constructing a form. These items are managed in other tables.

Table 3: form table

ATTRIBUTE	meaning
form ID	identifier of form
item pointer	pointer to top item(field,comment,button)
⋮	⋮

5.3   Field elements

Field elements show field types, length and nominated data to compose forms. (Refer to Figure 6 , 7.) The field element in Figure 7 shows how to specify a field after selecting data from nominated data in the pop-up menu.

```
<field>soft_name<dataType>char<length>10
<field>date<dataType>date
<field>name<dataType>kanji<length>4
```

Figure 6: example of field elements(1)

```
<field>rank<dataType>char<length>1
    <value>A<comment>very important
    <value>B<comment>important
    <value>C<comment>not so important
```

Figure 7: example of field element(2)

Field elements are managed in the field table in the database as shown in Table 4.

The "field ID" and the "field name" attribute is the identifier and name to specify a field.

5.4   Execution button elements

The execution button elements as shown in Figure 8, perform the following facilities.

- The name to distinguish a button is described after a <button> tag.

- Button character sequence is described after a <string> tag.

- The starting function name (Command name) is described after the <execCommand> tag.

- Message character sequence during the on screen operation is described after the <message> tag.

- The data with the form specified after the <form> tag is converted into the tagged data and given to the function identified by the <execCommand> tag. This function is then executed.

- The process after executing the function part is described after the <afterService> tag.

Button elements are managed in the button table in the database as in Table 5.

5.5   Related works in user interface building

UIMS is a software architecture to try to build a user interface subsystem separately from the application's body. This separation enables rapid prototyping and easy modification of user interface specifications.[11]

The major UIMS are as follows:

- Oregon Speedcode Universe prototyping system (OSU)[12], a Macintosh high-speed development tool, studied at Oregon State University. It can add functions to the user interface.

Table 4: field table

ATTRIBUTE	meaning
field ID	identifier of field
field name	field name(= attribute name in DB)
data type	for example char, text, date and so on.
length	length of data
⋮	⋮

```
<button>insert<string>INS
 <execCommand>insert
    <message>during inserting bug report
 <form>insert_form
 <afterService>show output_form
    <resultForm>output_form
    <fieldValue id=bug_no>BUG_NO_field
```

Figure 8: example of execution button

- Serpent, developed at Software Engineering Institute

- Mode, Smalltalk general purpose UIMS, developed at University of North Carolina

STUFF's UI schema realizes the separation of user interface as well as UIMS. The main difference is that UIMS still requires programming efforts to control the user interface, while STUFF's user interface elements contain user interface controls as well as user interface definitions. So programming to build the user interface is not required in STUFF, anymore.

6   STUFF Organization

6.1   Internal structure of STUFF

STUFF consists of a "body block" and "function elements", and the "body block" consists of an "element handling block" and a "UI block", as shown in Figure 9. The "UI block" reads UI schema and controls user interface behavior. Each "function element" performs a single function such as database access, print out, and transmission control. The "element handling block" transfers user inputs to the corresponding "function element" in a SGML form, and this activates the function. Output of the function will be returned to the "element handling block", and passed to the "UI block".

Referring back to Figure ??, the document management process consists of the three basic tasks: document development, storage, and transmission. Support of each task is realized in the "body block", DB access elements in the "function elements", and transmission control in the "function elements", respectively. This shows the total support of document management performed by using STUFF.

As we show in section 3, SGML is used as the internal information passing protocol in STUFF. Using SGML for the internal information passing increases the modularity of the blocks inside STUFF. Suppose the current "UI block" built for a bitmap display window system, is to be replaced by a character terminal version. The system designer only has to consider the SGML protocols relevant to the block, and he can work on the design in his own way inside the block.

We further describes functionalities in the "function elements".

6.2   Summary of function elements

We can summarize the function elements as follows:

Table 5: button table

ATTRIBUTE	meaning
button ID	identifier of button
button name	unique name of button
exec command	execution command when button is selected.
⋮	⋮

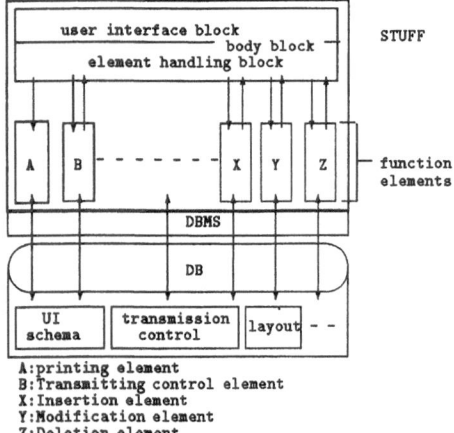

A:printing element
B:Transmitting control element
X:Insertion element
Y:Modification element
Z:Deletion element

Figure 9: STUFF structure

1. **Storage elements**

   STUFF provides the four functional elements: Data insertion, Modification, Deletion, and Selection, written in embedded SQL, independent of DBMS. These elements use a table storing correspondences of tags to the attributes, to access the database.

2. **Transmission elements**

   These have already been described in Section 3.4.

   - Transmission control element
   - Graphical display of transmission network
   - Automated reminder

3. **Document development elements**

   - Selective reporting element
     This selects substructures or elements in document, and creates a report view of them.

   - Statistics reporting element
     This computes statistics of the number of documents which satisfy given conditions.

   - Printing element
     STUFF has a formatter which lays out document contents according to their tags. How the contents are formatted is stored in a "style file", so rewriting of the style file enables formatting in different styles.

7 Conclusion

In this paper, we have described STUFF, a builder to construct document-based applications for software development support.

We mainly focused on the three STUFF features: "SGML DB", document transmission control, and UI schema. Internal structures was also described.

The SGML DB is a first trial of using SGML in a document management system. The introduction of SGML realizes the high portability of stored documents as well as easy modification of document structures. In addition to this, SGML document structures help in creating user interface definitions. We introduced a simple and efficient way of decomposing document structures and defining user interfaces from the decomposition.

The document transmission is efficiently controlled by STUFF. We introduced a network flow model in transmitting documents in E-mail, and realized a new active database superior to the similar functions in OBE and POSTGRES.

Further studies should be completed on selecting a suitable database model from among relational databases, extended relational databases, and object-oriented databases.

References

[1] Mr.Tanigawa.H., bug report management system for group development of software(in Japanese), Proc.of Joint Symposium related with electronics in Kansai Japan, S8-9, Oct.1990.

[2] Mr.Tanigawa.H., Constructing information management system which is noticed form definitions and control(in Japanese), IPSJ Special Interest Group on Database Systems,Technical Report 91-DBS-81,Jan.1991.

[3] International Standard ISO 8879-1986(E) Information processing - Text and office systems - Standard Generalized markup Language (SGML)

[4] Mr.Yamakawa.T.,DTP searching from OA industry(in Japanese), ,Proc. of Information Processing VOL.31 NO11 p1508-1517, Nov. 1990.11

[5] Mr.Shibano.K.,SGML and full text database(in Japanese), IPSJ Special Interest Group on Information Basic technology,Technical Report 89-FI-14-2,vol.89.No66,p1-8,July 1989

[6] Mr.Yamazaki.S.,Document structure specifying language (SGML) and electric publishing(in Japanese),Nikkei Computer 1989.7.28

[7] Ed Lee,User-Interface Development Tools, IEEE software May 1990

[8] T.G.Lewis and et al., Prototypes From Standard User Interface Management Systems, HICSS'89,pp.397-406(Jan.1989)

[9] M.R.Stonebraker and et.al., QUEL as a Data Type, PROC.1984 ACM-SIGMOD Conf.on the Mgt.of Data,May 1984.

[10] M.R.Stonebraker and et.al., The Design of POSTGRES, Proc.1986 ACM-SIGMOD Conf.on the Mgt.of Data,June 1986

[11]
M.R.Stonebraker and et.al., The POSTGRES Data Model, Proceedings of the 13th VLDB Conference,Brighton 1987

[12] M.M.Zloof, Office-By-Example:A business language that unifies data and word processing and electronic mail, IBM Systems Journal, VOL.21, NO.3 ,pp.272-305,1982

[13] M.M.Zloof, data processing and word processing, Office-By-Example(OBE) unifying E-mail, Nikkei Electronics, pp.195-223, 1983.3.14.

[14] Clarence A.Ellis and et. al., Office Information Systems and Computer Science, ACM Computing Surveys,Vol.12 No.1, March 1980

Rationale and Design of Serendip, a Database Programming Language

Michel Adiba   Christophe Lécluse   Philippe Richard

LGI-IMAG B.P. 53X
38041 Grenoble Cedex, France

Altaïr B.P. 105
78153 le Chesnay Cedex, France

Abstract

In this paper, we propose a database programming language. This language, named Serendip is designed in order to provide features from semantic data models and from programming languages. From the programming languages world, we took the notions of abstract data types and general computing. From the semantic data models, we took the declarative way of specifying data, the integrity constraints and the most important relationships between data (ISA, classification and membership).

1 Introduction

From the beginning of the 80's up to now, there have been a lot of proposals for extending relational database systems in order to cope with the problem of application programming. Database systems are more and more sophisticated and now range from the "rough" C+SQL systems up to fully integrated softwares, usually called *database programming languages* (DBPL). Database programming languages are gaining a great importance in database research. However, although such systems have received a lot of attention from both the theoretical and practical points of view in the last few years, there is still a debate about the goals and the definition of such systems.

Database programming languages are the leading point of two independent trends. On one hand, the programming language community has felt the need to manipulate bulk data, and to keep them on secondary storage in a comfortable way. This have led to the persistent programming languages field[6]. On the other hand, the limitations of existing database systems, and mainly the lack of computational power, have incited the database community to consider programming language design. Among the variety of proposals for database programming languages, one can distinguish between imperative proposals such as PS-Algol[7] or Pascal/R[17], functional proposals such as Adaplex[18], logic languages such as LDL[9], and object-oriented systems such as Gemstone[10], Orion[12] and O_2[14]. All these proposals are intended to allow a better programming of applications and to increase the application programmer's productivity. Indeed, the programmer needs not any more to worry about the impedance mismatch between the database and the programming language paradigms. He/she manipulates persistent data without having to be aware of the fact that they persist and do not have to translate data from one type structure to another when making them persistent (as it is necessary in the embedded approach).

The object-oriented database systems are special cases of DBPLs which are based on object-oriented languages. This approach of database programming is probably the most active one and has led to numerous system definitions and implementations. We can analyze the reasons of this success as follows. Object-oriented languages implement some of the most prominent features (for example inheritance and object identity) that can be found in most semantic data models (see [11]), and these semantic data models are a basis for the design of database system applications.

Oject-oriented languages provide a form of modularity, through the use of encapsulation. This modularity is a must for the design of large applications and for software reusability. Object-oriented languages provide a great dynamicity and extensibility as new types can be added to the system and will be used in the same way as system predefined types.

Last but not least, the object-oriented approach for database programming is one of the first proposals in the field, with the Gemstone system[10].

Two of the authors of this paper have contributed to the design and implementation of an object-oriented database system prototype[14]. One of the main lessons we have drawn from this experimentation is that the object-oriented approach is certainly a good approach for defining a DBPL but it does not solve all problems if used in a rigid way. The main problems we have encountered in the design of an object-oriented database system are the following:

- The great dynamicity and flexibility of object-oriented languages are hard to combine with the need of performance and reliability which are prominent issues for databases. In an object-oriented system, new classes can be added (and even dropped) dynamically and this is difficult to combine with optimization and safety.

- Object-identity can become cumbersome when dealing with complex structures which are classical in database applications and correctly handled by some traditional systems.

- The definition of operations as methods which are attached to classes make the definition of symmetric operations (for example the join operation) awkward. Moreover, operations without arguments (for example creation of entities) are hard to handle properly.

Another important problem to which the designer of an OODBS is faced, is to define a design methodology which would be consistent with the object-oriented approach. Up to now, there exists a lot of proposals for database design. They range from the Abrial proposal[2] to sophisticated semantic data models such as IFO[1] or INSYDE[13]. Most of them are "paper" proposals and are intended to be an intermediate level between the natural language definition of the application and its implementation using a (classical) database system. These data models generally offer a great power of expression through rich semantic concepts. They help the application designer to formulate the characteristics of his/her application and to test whether the application meets its requirements before implementing it in a relational database system. Although some models integrate dynamicity, most of them are purely static. None of these propositions are directly usable in the context of an OODBS. We thus decided to provide the semantic models features in our language rather than to try to find a new methodology for an OODBS.

Section 2 presents a proposal for the Serendip language which is intended to fulfill the requirements of Section 2. We present some concluding remarks in Section 3.

2 The Serendip language

In this section, we present the language Serendip. Our goal is to define a database language which mixes the computational power of programming languages and concepts of semantic data models. We do not define new semantics features but integrate in Serendip a set of concepts which are widely encountered in existing semantic models and widely accepted by the database community of research. The Serendip language is not supposed to be "complete" (for example, we do not consider temporal aspects here), and we shall discuss about possible extensions at the end of this paper.

2.1 Entities

Entities are "things" of the real world which are of interest for a given application, and we distinguish between two kinds of entities: *printable* and *non printable* entities. Printable entities can be thought of as concrete entities and correspond to classical structures. Printable entities include atomic entities such as 35 or "chris" but also tuples like [name: "chris", salary: 50000]. They also include collections like the set {1, 3, 6, 88} or the list <56, 77, 99, 100> or relations.

Non printable entities are abstract entities which correspond to "objects" of the real world which are not printable, for example a person.

2.2 Types

Types are used to describe entities and every entity is instance of a type. Entities are the extensional part of the database, while types are the intentional part. Types can be abstract or concrete.

Concrete types are structures which are recursively built using base types (**integer, real, string**), constant types ("male", 99, ...), range constraints and type constructors (set, tuple, list, disjunction, relation). The instances of the concrete types are the printable entities. Note that a type definition associates a name to a type expression. The names "Age" and "Number", for example, are two names designing the *same* type integer. We also allow the construction of enumerated types such as Week or Category.

Another interesting case is the type **relation** which is used to capture the relational abstraction. The "Married" relation is used to model a symmetrical relationship between objects of type Person (which is defined in figure 1). The **relation** type definition has an optional clause which allows to specify what attributes constitute the key. For example the key of the stock relation is the **prod** attribute. As it is shown in Section 2.5, data access on relation types is made in a declarative way through an SQL-like filter.

Abstract types characterize abstract (non printable) entities like persons or towns. They are defined in a way similar to [16], that is, an abstract type has a name and a list of features describing its behavior. In the classical theory of abstract data types, these features describing a type are operations. In the Serendip language, we shall consider two different features: operations and properties. This distinction comes from semantic models where we have, on one hand, some semantic links between (abstract) entities, and on the other hand, some operations describing the behavior of the entity. Figure 1 contains some abstract types definitions.

```
type Person is abstract
    property age → Age
             name → string
             address → Address

    operation
          update_add(Person, Address) → Person
end Person
```

Figure 1: Abstract Type Definitions

Properties allow for describing (directed) links between entities. A property has a name and links two types. For example, a person will have a property **age** associating an instance of type Age to him/her.

We shall see in Section 2.5 that properties can be either stored or derived, that is, computed using a general expression. However, this information is part of the implementation and does not appear in the specification of the abstract type.

Operations describe the behavior of the instances of an abstract data type. At the specification level, an operation has a name and a signature which describes its arguments and result. Operations play a role similar to methods in object-oriented systems such as O_2, although they do not have any distinguished argument like the *receiver*. Operations are attached to their defining type in the sense that they are all defined in the same logical unit which is the type. However, they are not attached to the type in the sense of object-oriented languages.

We shall see when discussing views in Section 2.4 that we can also define operations independently of any types. These operations correspond to the so-called functional abstractions of the CLU language[15].

2.3 Subtyping

The *is-a* relationship is a central primitive in most semantic data models. In the Serendip language, this relationship is expressed in terms of subtyping. The subtyping relationship mainly corresponds to the inheritance of object-oriented systems. However, as stated in [8] the term *inheritance* is somewhat misleading and we shall rather use *subtyping* or *is-a*. The subtyping relationship is explicitly stated by the user for abstract types as it corresponds to a strong modeling decision. Subtyping of concrete types, however, is inferred using similar rules to that of Galileo[4]. The semantics of subtyping in Serendip is a substitution semantics. This means that where a value of a type T is awaited, we can provide a value of a subtype of T. In the case of relations, this means for example that an Employee entity can be a value of the husband or the **wife** attribute of the relation married.

Notice that we do not put any extensional meaning to the subtyping relationship. That is, we do not interpret it in terms of inclusion of sets of instances. Most object-oriented systems, including O_2, overload the concept of inheritance with both an intentional meaning (subtyping) and an extensional meaning (classification of entities). In Serendip, the subtyping has only an intentional meaning. We shall come back to classification in Section 2.7. The following describes a set of types and subtypes.

type Customer **isa** Person
    property number → **integer**
           limit → Money
           category → Category

    operation
       change_category (Customer, Category)
             → Customer
       orders(Customer, Orc) → {Order}
end Customer

type Product **is abstract**
    property reference → **integer**
           description → **string**
           price → Money
           available → **boolean**
           substitute → Product

    operation
       validate_product(Product, {Product})
             → [prod: Product, bool: **boolean**]
end Product

type Special_offer **isa** Product
    property limit_time → Time
end Special_offer

type Orc **is**
    relation (order: Order, customer: Customer)

type Order **is abstract**
    property reference → **integer**
           date → Date
           lines → {Order_line}
           total → Money
           products → {Product}
    operation
       from (Order, Orc) → Customer
end Order

type Order_line **is abstract**
    property product → Product
           quantity → **integer**
           sub_total → Money
end Order_line

Properties and operations of an abstract type

are *inherited* by its subtypes. This means that the properties declared for the Person type can be used for the Customer type provided that Customer is declared as a subtype of Person. Note that in this example, we assume the existence of a toolbox providing general purpose types such as "Date" or "Money" together with the corresponding operations[5].

As we allow multiple supertypes for a type, there can be property names conflicts between the supertypes. A conflict arises when two non comparable parent types have a property or an operation with the same name and which is not inherited from a common parent. In this case, the user has to specify the role played by each property or operation. In order to solve these name conflicts, a type definition can contain a renaming clause

2.4 Views

At the conceptual level, a database application can be seen as a set of tasks manipulating the data. Each task can be described as a set of operations. Some of these operations are run by users through a human interface[3] and some are run by others operations. Up to now, we only have presented the definition of data types in Serendip. The notion of *view* provides the connection with the database.

A Serendip view specification is made of a name, a list of operations, a list of instance names and some integrity constraints. The instances are a way to distinguish some entities that are relevant to the application. They are also the entry points to the database. The use of instances together with operations is redundant from a programming point of view in the same way as properties and operations are in an abstract data type definition. The Serendip language provides the designer with both notions because they correspond to two different design choices. As for properties, we shall see in the following subsection that instances can be stored or computed from other elements.

We have defined abstract types as a way to structure complex applications in some independent meaningful pieces. However, we insisted on the fact that types only describe the intentional part of the application, that is the structural and behavioral aspects of the entities of an application. Views describe the extensional part of the application.

The instances of a view describe the entities that are the entry points of the application. They play a role similar to class extensions in object-oriented systems, but are more general as they are not necessarily sets of objects and are not necessarily stored.

A view corresponds to one functionality of the application. In our current example, we shall have one view for managing products, one view for managing customers and one view for managing orders. Of course these three views are not independent as they take part in the same application, but each view implements one task of the application.

This notion of view provides an alternative to the classical vision of databases. Traditionally, a relational database is defined by a conceptual schema, and by several application programs which share data through external schemas. In our proposal, schemas, application programs and data are encapsulated in views and abstract data types that allow for building complex database applications with great flexibility.

2.5 Abstract types implementation

In Serendip, specification and implementation of abstract data types are done in two distinct steps. Up to now, we have only shown how abstract types are specified by the programmer. In this section, we shall concentrate on the implementation part. An implementation of an abstract type consists of:

- Private property or operation definitions for internal use only. These properties are not visible from the other types and they are a support for the visible properties and operations implementations.

- Property implementations. The programmer can express how a given property is implemented. By default, a property will correspond to a stored reference. This is equivalent to attributes in conventional databases. In Serendip, we can also specify that a property is derived and express the computation. A typical example is the age of a person computed from the birth date. In the Order_line type above, we can express that the subtotal of an order line corresponds to the product of the price by the quantity.

- Operation implementations. As classical in object-oriented systems, we allow the user to give multiple implementations of an operation for multiple subtypes of the arguments. The

selection of the appropriate code is done at runtime following the actual parameters.

2.6 Views implementation

We have seen in the examples above that a view specification corresponds to the external specification of one functionality of an application. The implementation of a view is made of (1) some private types definitions, the view can use types that are not to be shared by other views nor reused in some other applications. Such types can be declared locally in the view implementation; (2) some private instances and operations definitions, private instances and operations can be defined as a support for implementing the public ones; (3) operation implementations, view operations are implemented in the same way as abstract types operations; (4) instance implementations, the programmer can express how a given instance is implemented. The instance can either be stored or computed using a general expression.

2.7 Specialization hierarchies

As explained in Section 2.3, subtyping is an intentional concept and does not capture the classification of entities in specialization/generalization hierarchies. The object-oriented concepts of class and inheritance mix both intentional and extensional aspects and correspond to subtyping and classification hierarchies.

In the Serendip language, we tried to clearly separate the two. In this subsection, we show how we can express specialization hierarchies using the instances and the view mechanism.

2.8 Integrity constraints

The notion of integrity constraint has received considerable attention in the relational framework but also in semantic data models. What we want to do here is to show how integrity constraints can take place in the Serendip framework based on abstract data types and views.

The first question we have to address in this context is the definition of an integrity constraint. If we take the classical definition from which integrity constraints are declarative specifications of consistent database states, then we face to a problem: Serendip types are already a specification of consistent database states. For example the date property of the type Order ranges over the Date type. This simple example shows that we have to separate typing aspects and integrity constraints. Types are used to *statically* check the consistency of the programs (using mainly structural considerations) that run over the database. Integrity constraints are additional properties that can only be checked *dynamically*.

We shall consider two kinds of integrity constraints:

2.8.1 Range constraints

Range constraints are a trivial case of integrity constraints. We have seen in Section 2.2 that (atomic) types expressions can be built using range expressions. It is clear that we cannot statically ensure that the instances of such types will stay beyond the limits of the range. The Serendip compiler will thus have to generate some code to check this property at run-time. Range constraints will be enforced permanently, that is, any violation will interrupt the program and raise an exception.

2.8.2 General constraints

Range and key constraints are generally not sufficient to express the semantics of an application. We often have to deal with more general conditions over the instances. For example, we would like to say that all bad customers have an order limit which is only 1000, or that the price of the substitute for a product is less than the price of the product. In order to express such general properties, we must give a constraint definition language which roughly correspond to first order logic. We can write, for example:

constraint
    all c **in** bad_ones : c.limit < 1000
    all p **in** stock :
        p.prod.substitute.price < p.prod.price

We can notice easily that key constraints could be expressed in such a language. However we do not know, at the moment, what is exactly the class of integrity constraints that we will be able to implement efficiently. We thus look at key constraints as the minimum we should provide and we will try to isolate a subset of the general language that can be efficiently implemented.

We have said that range constraints were permanently enforced. We clearly cannot do the same

for keys and general constraints. Indeed, if a constraint links two newly created entities, there is necessarily a period of time where the connection between the entities is not established.

In the Serendip language, the transactional unit is the view operation. Every view operation is a transaction. An important consequence of this choice is that the Serendip language will require an underlying transaction system supporting nested transactions as we allow view operations to call other view operations.

When a view operation is run, all the integrity constraints *of that view* are supposed to be satisfied and when the operation terminates, these integrity constraints are checked before committing the transaction. If one of the integrity constraint is violated by the operation, the transaction is aborted and an exception is raised.

It is important to note that views define a scope for the integrity constraints. The constraints defined within a view are tested only when committing the operations of that view.

3 Conclusion

In this paper, we have defined a semantic database language which incorporates both the advances of semantic data models and that of database programming languages. Our goal was to take the best of the two worlds while keeping the performance and feasibility of databases. The major points of our proposal are the following: (1) Serendip incorporates what we think are the most important and useful features of semantic data models: abstraction, object identity, ISA relationship, complex structures and a declarative definition of integrity constraints; (2) Serendip is based on the notions of abstract data types and views. Abstract data types provides modularity, extensibility and reusability. Views provide logical independence and allow to have different views on the same objects. Views also give an intuitive definition of applications in terms of inter-related tasks; (3) Serendip is safe. We claim that safety is necessary for database application programs. In particular, this means that compiled programs should not fail at run-time due to type errors, therefore, we designed Serendip such that it can be statically typed. This can be ensured since in Serendip, we do not allow non strict inheritance which forbids static typing[4]. For instance, a type can inherit properties but is not allowed to redefine their types. In the same way, operations can have distinct implementations depending on their actual arguments but are not allowed to redefine their signature; (4) as opposed to object-oriented systems, Serendip offers a declarative way of defining integrity constraints and maintain them automatically. Furthermore, these integrity constraints have a scope which is the view where they are defined.

References

[1] S. Abiteboul and R. Hull. IFO: A Formal Semantic Database Model. *ACM Transactions on Database Systems*, 12(4), December 1987.

[2] J. R. Abrial. Data Semantics. *Data Base Management*, 1974.

[3] S. Adiba and C. Collet. Management of Complex Objects as Dynamic Forms. In *VLDB International Conference*, 1988.

[4] A. Albano, L. Cardelli, and R. Orsini. Galileo: A Strongly Typed, Interactive Conceptual Language. *ACM Transactions on Database Systems*, 10(2), June 1985.

[5] G. Arango. *Toolboxes: a Practical Approach to Reusability in an Object-Oriented Environment*. Technical Report, GIP Altaïr, 1989.

[6] M. Atkinson and P. Buneman. Types and Persistence in Database Programming Languages. *ACM Computing Surveys*, June 1987.

[7] M. Atkinson, K. Chisholm, and W. Cockshott. PS-algol: an Algol with a Persistent Heap. *ACM SIGPLAN Notices*, 17(7), July 1981.

[8] C. Beeri. Formal Models for Object-Oriented Databases. In *DOOD 89*, December 1989.

[9] C. Beeri, S. Naqvi, R. Ramakrishan, O. Schmueli, and S. Tsur. Sets and Negation in a Logic and Database Language (LDL1). In *ACM PODS International Conference*, 1987.

[10] G. Copeland and D. Maier. Making Smalltalk a Database System. In *ACM SIGMOD International Conference*, June 1984.

[11] R. Hull and R. King. Semantic Database Modeling: Survey, Applications and Research Issues. *ACM Computing Surveys*, 19(3), September 1987.

[12] W. Kim, J. Banerjee, H. T. Chou, J. F. Garza, and D. Woelk. Composite Object Support in an Object-Oriented Database System. In *ACM SIGMOD International Conference*, May 1988.

[13] R. King and D. McLeod. A methodology and Tool for Designing Office Information Systems. *ACM Transactions on Office Information Systems*, 1985.

[14] C. Lécluse and P. Richard. The O_2 Database Programming Language. In *VLDB International Conference*, August 1989.

[15] B. Liskov and A. Snyder. Exception Handling in CLU. *IEEE Transactions on Software Engineering*, SE-5(6), November 1979.

[16] B. Liskov and S. Zilles. Programming with Abstract Data Types. *ACM SIGPLAN Notices*, 9(4), 1974.

[17] J. W. Schmidt and M. Mall. *Pascal/R Report*. Technical Report 66, Fachbereich Informatik, Université de Hambourg, July 1980.

[18] D. W. Shipman. The Functional Data Model and the Data Language DAPLEX. *ACM Transactions on Database Systems*, 6(1), March 1981.

General Transitive Closures and Aggregate Functions *

Johann Eder

Universität Wien
Institut für Statistik und Informatik
Liebiggasse 4/3-4, A-1010 Wien / AUSTRIA
eder@ifs.univie.ac.at

Abstract.

General transitive closures are a convenient operation for processing recursive structures with relational languages, because they are easy to understand, efficiently to implement and expressive enough to support a broad range of practical applications. To further extend the expressiveness of general transitive closures, we study the use of aggregate functions together with general transitive closures. While general transitive closures are restricted to express linear recursion, general transitive closures with aggregate functions can be used to express some nonlinear recursions too. We will give some conditions for general transitive closures with aggregate functions to be well formed and bottom up evalueable. We show how these constructs can be integrated in an extended SQL.

Keywords: deductive databases, recursive query processing, SQL, general transitive closure

1 Introduction

There is a common understanding in the research community that relational database systems have reached their limits in supporting the demands for new sophisticated information systems. In particular the fact that relational query languages are not computationally complete and the representation of complex objects is cumbersome has triggered a lot of research in deductive databases and object oriented databases.

For introducing deduction we present here a rather pragmatic approach. We believe that many yet unsupported applications demand comparable modest deductive capabilities. Therefore, we will present an extension of SQL for processing of a class of recursive queries rather than introducing general recursive capabilities. Since SQL is the standard query language for relational databases these extensions should be easy to use and to integrate with existing databases. A major advantage of such an approach is that with the increased capabilities of SQL investments in systems and already collected data as well as in training of programmers and end-users can be used and nevertheless new kinds of applications can be built.

Recursion is integrated into the view definition of SQL in form of generalized transitive closures ([7]). A unique aspect of our approach is that it also covers relations containing duplicates (multiset relations) to be compatible with SQL ([8]). As a positive side effect, expressiveness is increased when general transitive closures are extended to multiset relations. The semantics of this new construct is defined in a formal way to open possibilities for automatic query optimization and it is defined procedurally to be better understood by traditional programmers. Since recursively defined views can be used in queries like all other views, end users can take advantage of the increased functionality without knowing anything about recursive queries or deduction. Furthermore, tools built upon SQL like report writers or fourth generation languages can be used unchanged on top of recursively defined views.

In this paper we extend our approach by introducing aggregate functions in the definition of general transitive closures. This extension allows some non linear recursive queries to be expressed while general transitive closures are restricted to linear recursion.

This development differs from the mainstream research in deductive databases where deductive query languages are developed within the paradigm of logic programming (see [4] for an overview) as it follows a pragmatic approach introducing only small extensions and maintaining full upward compatibility with SQL.

In [12] a different approach for introducing general transitive closures as means for recursive query processing is reported. Our approach however is fully integrated into relational languages and does not require the graph metaphor for expressing recursive queries.

Previous proposals for extending SQL with a capability for processing recursive structures like [5] or the tree traversal construct of [11] differ from this approach as they work on limited sets of graphs (or relations) and their semantics is only defined procedurally.

In [1] relational algebra is extended with the operator alpha to express a certain class of recursive queries. For non-linear recursions a special relation-valued attribute delta containing the history of the traversal is introduced transforming intermediate relations to non first normal form.

The approach in [10] also extends SQL and deals with duplicates - like our approach. However, it is based on calculus in a more top down approach while we build upon an algebraic fixpoint operator with a bottom up approach and provide an easier procedural interpretation of general transitive closures.

The remainder of this paper is organized as follows: In section 2 we review previous work on general transitive closures for recursive views in SQL. In section 3 we discuss aggregate functions and define an aggregation operator. In section 4 we define aggregate closures and discuss their properties. In section 5 we extend the view definition of SQL to formulate aggregate closures, and in section 6 we draw some conclusions.

*This work was partly supported by the Austrian *Fonds zur Förderung der wissenschaftlichen Forschung* under contract P6772P.

2　General Transitive Closures

Recursion is often introduced into relational query languages by means of a fixpoint operator [2]. This means, that a query can be formulated as lfp (R = f(R)), where R is a relation, f is a relational expression, and lfp is the least fixpoint operator. The semantics of this construct is to evaluate R to the least set fulfilling the equation. This general recursive construct has the disadvantage, that a fixpoint does not always exist, and general recursion can be very inefficient to evaluate. Therefore, it seems more promising, to restrict the expression f so that a fixpoint always exists, and efficient evaluation algorithms can be developed.

For this purpose we start from the well known transitive closures and generalize transitive closures as long as the recursive expressions remain well defined and bottom up evaluable.

The transitive closure of a binary relation R is defined as least fixpoint of

$$V = R \cup comp(R, V)$$

Thereby, comp stands for a composition, which is defined as equi-join with the join attributes projected out.

To overcome some shortcomings in the expressiveness of the transitive closure, the definition can be extended in the following ways:

- The equi-join can be replaced by a theta-join or by a selection on the cartesian product.

- The projection may be extended to a projection-expression where the values of some attributes can be defined by evaluable functions like arithmetic expressions or string expressions.

The notion of a general transitive closure was introduced in [6] and [12]. In [7] it was applied to relational languages.

Definition 2.1 (General transitive closure) *We define the general transitive closure of a relation R by a composition expression compex by the least fixpoint of the following equation:*

$$V = R \cup compex(R, V)$$

Compex stands for a composition expression, which is a selection on the cartesian product of R and V together with a projection which may include functions like arithmetic and string expressions. So compex can be described as projex(select P R x GR)). In other terms, the compex expression can be described as a usual SELECT statement of SQL.

Since general transitive closure is defined by union, R and GR have to have the same schema. So the composition expression has to project the cartesian product of R and GR on this schema. The expressions in this projection allow the computation of attribute values of a tuple in the projected relation in terms of attribute values of it's corresponding tuple in the cartesian product R x GR.

The selection on the cartesian product of R and GR can be regarded as transitivity condition, as it determines, if two tuples can be connected. In the general transitive closure the transitivity condition is more general than just identity of attribute values.

Example : The relation *direct* containing inforamation about direct flights consists of the following attributes: $from - city$ and $to - city$ for the connected cities, *departure* for the time the plane departs, *arrival* for the time it arrives, and *distance* for the distance of the flight. The query, we want to formulate, shall produce a table containing all flight connections between cities together with the total distance of each flight. We define, that there is a connection between two cities, if there is a direct flight between these two cities, or there is a connection from the first city to an intermediate city and a direct flight from the intermediate city to the second city, which departs after the arrival of the connection from the first city.

The relation *connection* (short 'C') is defined as general transitive closure of the relation *direct* (short 'D'), i.e as least fixpoint of the following equation:

$$C = D \cup \pi_{C.from, D.to, C.dist+D.dist} \sigma_{D.from=C.to, D.dep<C.arr} D \times C$$

There are two reasons for extending the concept of general transitive closures to relations containing duplicates:

- Increasing expressiveness. In particular, general transitive closures of multiset-relations allow to process reconvergent structures.

- Making general transitive closure suitable for relational languages which allow duplicates in tables.

The operations of relational algebra extend very natural to multiset-relations. In [8] we formally defined these operations in accordance with the respective definitions in SQL. We will not distinguish between operations on set-relations and multiset-relations, where it is not necessary. For the multiset-union we will use the symbol $\sqcup$, e.g. $[a, a, b, b, c] \sqcup [a, a, b, d] = [a.a, a, a, b, b, b, c, d]$.

Definition 2.2 (General transitive closure of multisets) *The general transitive closure of a multiset-relation R by a (multiset-) composition expression compex is defined by the least fixpoint of the following equation:*

$$V = R \sqcup compex(R, V)$$

The expression compex consists of a multiset-selection on the multiset-cartesian product of R and T together with a multiset-projection which may contain functions like arithmetic or string expressions in terms of attributes of the cartesian product. So compex can be regarded as SELECT statement of SQL without duplicate elimination.

Example : This example deals with the well known parts hierarchy problem or bill of materials problem. A relation *comp* is given with the attributes part, subpart and quantity. A tuple $< a, b, c >$ of this relation means that part a contains c pieces of part b. In this relation a certain part can be subpart of different aggregates. (For example the same type of screw may be used in different machines or even in different subparts of a single machine). We wish to formulate the query which parts in what quantity a given aggregate consists of.

We define the relation *parts* as general transitive closure of multisets of the relation *comp*. So the relation *parts* is defined as least fixpoint of the following equation:

$$parts = comp \sqcup \pi_{comp.part, parts.subpart, comp.quantity*parts.quantity}$$

$$\sigma_{comp.subpart=parts.part} comp \times parts$$

Theorem 2.1 *A least fixpoint for the general transitive closure of multisets always exists.*

We define $\mathcal{P}^m(D)$ as the set of all multisets over the domain D. We define the partial order $\leq$ as follows: $M_1 \leq M_2$, iff all elements of M_1 appear in M_2 with at least the same cardinality. It is easy to see, that $(\mathcal{P}^m(D), \leq)$ is a complete lattice, and that $M_1 \sqcup compex(M_1, M_2)$ is continous and monotone with respect to $\leq$. Therefore, Tarski's fixpoint theorem [13] can be applied and the existence of a least fixpoint is assured.

3 Aggregate Functions

3.1 Definition of Aggregate Functions

In SQL aggregate functions are powerful constructs for formulating queries. In the syntax of SQL aggregate functions are interwoven with projection and arithmetic expressions. To be better able to reason about aggregate functions we introduce a special aggregation operator. This aggregation operator has the property that the result has the same scheme as the 'input'-relation - a property we need for recursive views.

In literature aggregate functions for relational query languages have been introduced in various ways. As we aim at extending SQL we will formalize aggregate functions as they are defined in SQL.

Definition 3.1 (aggregation) *The syntax of the aggregation operator agg applied to a relation R with schema S is defined as follows:* $agg_L R : \forall a \in S : a \in L \vee \Theta(a) \in L, \Theta \in \{min, max, sum\}$. *We call L the aggregation list,* $G = \{a \in S \mid a \in L\}$ *the grouping attribute(s) and* $A = S - G$ *the aggregated attributes.*

The semantics of the aggregation operator is defined as follows: Let $P = agg_L R$, *.* $\forall t \in agg_L R$:

1. $\exists t' \in R : t[G] = t'[G]$
2. $\forall t' \in agg_L R : t \neq t' \rightarrow t[G] \neq t'[G]$
3. $\forall a \in S, min(a) \in L : t[a] = min(\pi_a \sigma_{G=t[G]} R)$
4. $\forall b \in S, max(b) \in L : t[b] = max(\pi_b \sigma_{G=t[G]} R)$
5. $\forall c \in S, sum(c) \in L : t[c] = \sum \pi_c \sigma_{G=t[G]} R$

Example: Let R be a relation with the attributes a, b, c, and d. $agg_{a,min(b),max(c),sum(d)} R$ would read in SQL as follows:

```
Select a, min(b), max(c), sum(d)
From    R
Group by a
```

3.2 Properties of Aggregate Functions

In this section we will discuss some properties of aggregate functions. For the following propositions let D be domain, and R a set-relation and M, M', N multiset-relations over D. Further let agg_L be an aggregate function for relations over D.

Proposition 3.1 (set result) $agg_L M$ *is a set-relation, irrespective whether R is a set- or a multiset-relation, and the grouping attributes are a key (superkey) of the result relation.*

Proposition 3.2 $\forall t \in D : agg_L\{t\} = \{t\}$

It is easy to see that the application of an aggregate operation on a singleton relation results in this very relation.

Proposition 3.3 (idempotence) $agg_L(agg_L R) = agg_L R$

Each tuple of $agg_L R$ represents a different partition of R. A subsequent application of agg_L keeps the partitioning and Prop. 3.3 follows from Prop.3.2. Hence agg_L is idempotent.

Proposition 3.4 $agg_L(M \sqcup M') = agg_L(M \sqcup agg_L M')$. *and if* $agg_L M = agg_L M'$, *then* $agg_L M \sqcup N = agg_L M' \sqcup N$

It is easy to see, that in the case of multiset-relations and multiset-union the aggregation operation can be applied to a part of a relation first, without changing the result.

Note however, that this proposition does not hold for set-relations and set-union in general, because of the 'sum'-aggregation.

Proposition 3.5 *If L does not contain sum, the following proposition holds: Let $\{ M \}$ be the set of all tuples contained in the multiset-relation M:* $agg_L M = agg_L\{M\}$

This means, that if L does not contain sum, then the aggregate of a multiset- relation is the same, irrespective whether duplicates have been eliminated or not.

Proposition 3.6 $\nexists a \in S, sum(a) \in L - agg_L R \cup R' = agg_L R \cup agg_L R'$

If the aggregation contains only min und max, then the aggregation can be applied to a part of a relation first.

Proposition 3.7 *If K is a key of the relation R and $\forall a \in K : a \in L$, then* $agg_L(R) = R$.

Since K is subset of the grouping attributes, each partition imposed by those attributes consists of exactly one tuple, as the values of the key-attributes are unique.

Proposition 3.8 *The set of grouping attributes A is a superkey in* $agg_L R$.

All aggregated attributes are functional dependent from the grouping attribute, according to the definition of aggregation.

The propositions above will be needed in the sequel to discuss whether aggregate closures are well formed and bottom up evaluable.

4 Aggregate Closure

4.1 Extending general transitive closure with aggregate functions

The extension of the general transitive closure concept with aggregate operations increases expressiveness, since general transitive closures are restricted to linear recursions, while the introduction of aggregate functions will allow to express several non-linear recursions.

For aggregate closures the fixpoint with respect to the subset relation cannot be used (since $agg_L R \not\subseteq R, and R \not\subseteq agg_L R$). Therefore, we have to define an different partial order which includes the subset order.

Definition 4.1 ($\preceq_L$) *Let $r,t \in D$. $r \preceq_L t$ with respect to the aggregator agg_L with grouping attribute $A :\Leftrightarrow$*

$$\forall a \in S : \begin{array}{lll} a \in L & \rightarrow & r[a] = t[a], \\ min(a) \in L & \rightarrow & r[a] \leq t[a], \\ max(a) \in L & \rightarrow & r[a] \geq t[a], \\ sum(a) \in L & \rightarrow & r[a] \leq t[a]. \end{array}$$

Let $R, T \in \mathcal{P}(D)$. $R \preceq_L T$ with respect to the aggregator $agg_L :\Leftrightarrow$ $\forall r \in R \exists t \in T : r \preceq_L t$.

Note: Since the result of an aggregate operation is a set, we do not have to extend the lattice to multisets.

For the following let G be the grouping attribute of the aggregation L, and $\mathcal{P}(D)^G \subseteq \mathcal{P}(D)$ be the set of all relations over D which have G as superkey.

Proposition 4.1 *$\preceq_L$ is a partial order on $\mathcal{P}(D)^G$.*

It is easy to see that $\preceq_L$ is reflexive, anti-symmetric and transitive.

Note: There is another partial order with reverse inequality in the case of sum. However, for the rest of this consideration we will stay with the above definition for sake of simplicity. The results can be easily transferred to the other partial order.

Theorem 4.1 *$(\mathcal{P}(D)^G, \preceq_L)$ is a complete lattice.*

Proof: With prop. 4.1 we know, that $\preceq_L$ is a partial order on $\mathcal{P}(D)^G$. We now have to show, that for any subset of $\mathcal{P}(D)^G$ inf and sup exist. We define Lmin as an aggregation list, where sum is replaced in L by min, and Lmax as an aggregation list where we replace in L min by max, max by min and sum by max. Let $R \subseteq \mathcal{P}(D)^G . inf(R) := agg_{Lmin}((\bigcup R) \bowtie (\bigcap_{X \in R} \pi_G X), sup(R) := agg_{Lmax} \bigcup R$. It is easy to verify, that inf(R) is a greatest lower bound and sup(R) is a least upper bound.

Definition 4.2 (Aggregate closure) *The aggregate closure ac of a relation R by a composition expression compex, and an aggregate operation agg_L is defined by the least fixpoint of the following equation:*

$$V = agg_L(R \cup compex(R, V))$$

The aggregate closure ac_m of a multiset-relation M by a composition-expression compex and an aggregate operation agg_L is defined by the least fixpoint of the following equation:

$$V_m = agg_L(M \sqcup compex(M, V_m))$$

Example: This example is taken from the anti-trust control problem. A relation *owns* is given with the attributes owner, company and share. A tuple $< a, b, c >$ of this relation says that an owner a has a share of c percent of company b. Companies can themselves be owner of other companies. We want to formulate a query to determine which companies are controlled by a given

owner. A company is controlled by an owner, if this owner, together with the companies he controls, holds more than 50% of this company. We want to specify the query to derive a relation *controls*, with the attributes owner, company, and share expressing all control - relationships determined by the *owns* relation. We define a relation controls (short C) as aggregate closure of the relation has-share (short H) by

$$agg_{owner,company,sum(share)} H \sqcup \pi_{C.owner, H.company, H.share}$$
$$\sigma_{C.company=H.owner, C.share>50} H \times C$$

Like for general transitive closures, the procedural definition of the semantics of aggregate closures is given through (naive) fixpoint evaluation.

```
Vold := ∅;
Vnew := R;
while Vnew ≠ Vold do
      Vold := Vnew;
      Vnew := agg_L (R ⊔ compex(R, Vold))
endwhile;
```

This algorithm serves only for a procedural definition of the semantics, a query against an aggregate closure is evaluated with more efficient algorithms like differential fixpoint evaluation [9].

4.2 Monotonicity of Aggregate Closures

General transitive closures have the nice property that the fixpoint always exists, and that this fixpoint is bottom up evaluable. However this does not hold for aggregate closures where the fixpoint iteration may not terminate for three reasons:

1. There is an infinite number of tuples in the result. This may only happen, if attributes in the grouping list are computed by arithmetic expressions in the compex expression. This problem also occurs for general transitive closures.

2. Values of some tuples are infinite. This problem may also occur for general transitive closures, when attributes are computed and no bound is specified for the growth of values for these attributes. (For a discussion thereof see [7])

3. There does not exist a fixpoint. This problem cannot appear for general transitive closure. We will demonstrate this problem through the following example:

   Let R be a relation with the schema {a, b, c}. Let the aggregate closure V of R be defined as $V = agg_{a,b,sum(c)} R \sqcup \pi_{V.a, R.b, R.c} \sigma_{V.b=R.a, V.c>30, V.c<50} R \times V$. Let the relation R consist of the following tuples:

a	b	c
x	y	10
x	z	40
z	y	20
y	z	20

It is easy to see, that a fixpoint for this equation does not exist. Therefore, we have to derive some conditions which are sufficient that the fixpoint of an aggregate closure exists, and that it is bottom up evaluable.

Since the first two problems were already analyzed for general transitive closures, we will concentrate on the third problem. Unfortunately, it is not possible to define a partial order with respect to which the aggregate closure transformation is monotone. For checking the existence of a fixpoint we, therefore, have to check, whether the transformation is increasing. And we will give sufficient conditions for that. For the following let T denote the aggregate closure transformation, i.e. $T(V) = agg_L(R \cup compex(R, V))$, and V^i is the value of Vold in the fixpoint iteration algorithm after the ith iteration.

First we have to define a new partial order, based on the observation, that T(V) may contain more tuples than V, but 'better ones'. Therefore, the inequalities for min and max in $\preceq_L$ have to be reversed. Note, that $\preceq_L$ is the order for chosing among several fixpoints, while $\preceq_L^+$ is the order for which the sequence $(T^i(\emptyset))$ shall be monotone.

Definition 4.3 $(\preceq_L^+)$ *Let* $r, t \in D$. $r \preceq_L^+ t$ *with respect to the aggregator* agg_L *with grouping attribute* $G :\Leftrightarrow$

$$\forall a \in S: \quad \begin{aligned} a \in L & \rightarrow r[a] = t[a], \\ min(a) \in L & \rightarrow r[a] \geq t[a], \\ max(a) \in L & \rightarrow r[a] \leq t[a], \\ sum(a) \in L & \rightarrow r[a] \leq t[a]. \end{aligned}$$

Let $R, Q \in \mathcal{P}(D)$. $R \preceq_L^+ Q$ *with respect to the aggregator* $agg_L :\Leftrightarrow$ $\forall r \in R \exists t \in Q : r \preceq_L^+ t$.

Definition 4.4 (increasing) *The transformation T is increasing, iff for all* $i \geq 0$: $V^i \preceq_L^+ V^{i+1} = T(V^i)$.

If the transformation T is increasing, then the sequence $(T^i(\emptyset))$ is monotone, and the problem described above cannot appear, i.e. the fixpoint iteration cannot dangle between two different relations.

To check whether the transformation is increasing one has to analyze, which aggregate functions are used, whether there is one or more aggregated attributes, whether it is a set or multiset aggregate closure, whether aggregated attributes appear in the selection condition, and whether attributes depend on aggregated attributes.

Here we will give a sufficient condition for T being increasing which is easier to check.

Definition 4.5 (tuplewise monotone) *A composition expression compex is tuplewise monotone with respect to* $\preceq_L^+$, *iff* $\forall t, t' \in D : \{t\} \preceq_L^+ \{t'\}, \forall r \in R : compex(\{r\}, \{t\}) \preceq_L^+ compex(\{r\}, \{t'\})$.

For the definition of tuplewise increasing we take the order $\preceq_L$ (without +!), so that for example a tuple in T(t) has a higher value in a min attribute than t.

Definition 4.6 (tuplewise increasing) *A composition expression compex is tuplewise increasing with respect to* $\preceq_L$. *iff* $\forall t \in D : \forall r \in R : \pi_{S-G}\{t\} \preceq_{L-G} \pi_{S-G}compex(\{r\}, \{t\})$ *or* $compex(\{r\}, \{t\}) = \emptyset$.

Theorem 4.2 *If T is a set transformation without the sum - aggregate function, and compex (of T) is tuplewise monotone and tuplewise increasing, then T is increasing.*

Proof by induction. Obviously, $\emptyset \preceq_L^+ R$. We assume that $V^{i-1} \preceq_L^+ V^i$. We have to show that $V^i \preceq_L^+ V^{i+1}$, i.e. $\forall t \in V^i, \exists t' \in$

$agg_L(R \cup compex(R, V^i))$ with $t \preceq_L^+ t'$, which follows from the induction hypothesis, compex being monotone and increasing and the properties of aggregation.

Theorem 4.3 *If T is a multiset transformation and compex (of T) is tuplewise monotone and tuplewise increasing, and all values of attributes aggregated by sum are positive, then T is increasing.*

Proof by induction in analogy to the proof of Theorem 4.2. For the sum aggregated attributes we use the fact that since compex is a tuplewise monotone multiset operation for all sets Q, Q': $Q \preceq_L^+ Q'$ implies that $| Q | \leq | Q' |$ and $|$ compex(R. Q) $| \leq |$ compex(R. Q') $|$.

To develop an efficient algorithm for checking whether a transformation is increasing which also covers more cases than those of the previous theorems is subject of current research.

5 Extending the view definition in SQL

The formulation of recursively defined tables by means of general transitive closure or aggregate closure of set- or multiset-relations is proposed to be embedded in the view definition of SQL. The following syntax of the view definition statement is an extension of that in standard SQL.

```
CREATE VIEW <view-name> (<attributed-column-list>)
AS [DISTINCT | ALL] FIXPOINT of [<type>]
             <table-name> [(<column-list>)]
[AGGREGATE  <aggregate-list> ]
BY SELECT <list>
   FROM  <table name>, <viewname>
   WHERE <constraint-list>
```

Example: As an example of this view-definition we formulate the view needed to solve the anti-trust problem of example 4. The base table is the table owns with the attributes owner, company, and share.

```
CREATE VIEW controls (owner, company, share)
AS FIXPOINT OF owns
BY
AGGREGATE  owner, company, sum(share)
SELECT     c.owner, o.company, o.share
FROM       controls c, owns o
WHERE      c.company = o.owner
   AND     c.share > 50
```

Traversal recursions as reported in [12] are special cases of this construct. We will give an example for the formulation of graph related recursions. The relation G with the attributes a, b, w represents a graph such that a tuple $< a_1, b_1, w_1 >$ stands for a directed arc from node a_1 to node b_1 with weight w_1.

Shortest path:

```
CREATE VIEW short (a, b, w)
AS FIXPOINT of G
AGGREGATE a, b, min(w)
BY SELECT G.a, short.b, G.w + short.w
FROM      G, short
WHERE     G.b = short.a
```

In general, that an aggregate closure represents a graph traversal can be determined through an analysis of the appearance of the attributes in the view definition. Let R be the base relation and V the defined view. If the attributes of V (resp. R) can be partitioned into 3 sets A, B, W, such that A ∪ B is the grouping attribute of the aggregation, the project-expression list of compex is V.A, R.B, f(V.W, R.W) and the where-condition of compex is V.B = R.A, then the aggregate closure represents a graph traversal problem. Such views can be analyzed using the path-algebra described in [3]. However, this consideration demonstrates that aggregate closures are more expressive than graph traversals.

6 Conclusion

Aggregate closures - an extension of general transitive closures - have been introduced to meet demands for increased functionality of query languages for relational databases. The approach is rather pragmatic as it employs comparable modest extensions to SQL with the aim to support a range of practical applications while maintaining full compatibility with SQL and being secure and easy to understand. It has been shown, that the introduction of aggregate functions in the definition of recursive views increases the expressiveness of general transitive closures. However, this extension has the drawback that the existence of fixpoints is no longer guaranteed, but we gave a sufficient condition for aggregate closures to be well formed and bottom up evaluable.

Further research includes the development of an efficient algorithm for analyzing the existence of a fixpoint of an aggregate closure and for guaranteeing termination of the fixpoint iteration as well as the adoption of efficient fixpoint algorithms for aggregate closures.

References

[1] R. Agrawal. Alpha: An extension of relational algebra to express a class of recursive queries. *IEEE Trans. on Software Engineering*, 15(3):335–347, 1988.

[2] Alfred Aho and Jeffrey Ullmann. Universality of data retrieval languages. In *Proc. ACM Symp. on Principles of Programming Languages*, pages 110–120, 1979.

[3] B. Carre. *Graphs and Networks*. Claredon Press, Oxford, 1979.

[4] Stefano Ceri, Georg Gottlob, and Letizia Tanca. *Logic Programming and Databases*. Springer Verlag, 1990.

[5] E.K. Clemons. Design of an external schema facility to define and process recursive structures. *ACM Trans. on Database Systems*, 6(2):295–311, 1981.

[6] U. Dayal and J. M. Smith. Probe: A knowledge-oriented database management system. In M. Brodie and J. Mylopoulos, editors, *On Knowledge Base Management Systems*. Springer-Verlag, 1986.

[7] J. Eder. Extending SQL with general transitive closure and extreme value selections. *IEEE Transactions on Knowledge and Data Engineering*, 2(4):381–390, 1990.

[8] J. Eder. General transitive closure of relations containing duplicates. *Information Systems*, 15(3):335–347, 1990.

[9] U. Güntzer, W. Kiessling, and R. Bayer. On the evaluation of recursion in (deductive) database systems by efficient differential fixpoint iteration. In *Proc. 3rd Intern. Conf. on Data Engineering*, pages 120–129, 1987.

[10] I. S. Mumick, H. Pirahesh, and R. Ramakrishnan. The magic of duplicates and aggregates. In *Proc. of the 16th International Conference on Very Large Databases*, pages 264–277, 1990.

[11] Oracle Cooperation. *SQL*Plus Users's Guide*, 1987.

[12] A. Rosenthal, S. Heiler, U. Dayal, and F. Manola. Traversal recursion: A practical approach to supporting recursive applications. In *Proc. of the ACM SIGMOD International Conference on Management of Data*, pages 166–176, 1986.

[13] A. Tarski. A lattice theoretical fixpoint theorem and it's applications. *Pacific Journal of Mathematics*, n.5, 1955.

A DEDUCTIVE DATABASE SYSTEM
WITH APPLICATIONS TO ROUTE PLANNING

Malcolm C. Taylor
Department of Computer Science
University of Houston
Houston, TX 77204

Bogdan D. Czejdo
Department of Mathematical Sciences
Loyola University,
New Orleans, LA 70118

ABSTRACT

The issue of deductive query optimization has received widespread attention, yet the problem of dealing with functions defined on complex data structures remains unresolved. In this paper we present an approach which allows for abstract data types and arbitrary user-defined functions within the framework of an extended relational model. Functions may appear in both rules and queries, and the optimization process uses a combination of term rewriting and distribution of selections. Our approach provides a clean integration of functions into both the language and the optimization algorithm, and yields efficient strategies for a wide range of queries. The technique is demonstrated on a route planning application.

1. INTRODUCTION

In recent years there has been considerable interest in building *deductive databases,* which support intelligent inference as well as straightforward retrieval of data. These systems have almost exclusively used the relational data model as a starting point [6, 8, 14], which is natural in view of that model's theoretical foundation on first order predicate logic. Most of the research in this area has focused on the optimization of queries over recursively-defined relations [1-5, 7, 8, 12, 13, 16]. Certainly one of the most effective approaches to that problem is the magic sets method [3, 5] in which the system builds a magic set of possibly-relevant facts, and uses that set to modify the existing rules in such a way that only the possibly-relevant facts are generated.

Recognizing the success of the relational model, many researchers have sought to extend that model to include support for more complex data structures. One attraction of an extended relational model is that existing ideas on query optimization can be adapted to work on the more complex data structures [15]. Deductive rules can also be handled in this framework. The firing of a rule can be compared to executing a query which derives new facts from those stored in the database. Thus rules may be translated into an extended relational algebra. Each deduced relation can then be defined by a query. An important class of queries, involving a selection on a deduced relation, can be optimized by distributing the selection through the query so that it is executed sooner. This approach was first introduced in [2], and later refined in [1, 7, 12, 13]. We shall refer to this approach as 'distributing selections' (DS). DS can handle recursive rules, but it has not been used with abstract data types and arbitrary user-defined functions. Although DS in its basic form has been shown to be less effective than magic sets [13], it can be made equivalent by introducing a rule rewriting phase (in the style of the magic sets method) before translating into relational algebra.

An approach to optimization of general queries over complex data structures is presented in [15]. This work was developed in the context of a distributed environment, but the ideas can easily be adapted to a centralized environment also. Domains can be defined in terms of tuple and set constructors, and deductive rules are supported. But there is no support for user-defined functions, nor can recursive rules be handled.

In this paper we extend the approach of [15] to handle both recursion and abstract data types with user-defined functions. Since recursive rules are handled in other approaches, the emphasis in this paper is on abstract data types and functions. Data types are defined in the style of an algebraic specification [9, 11]. Functions may appear in both rules and queries, and query optimization uses term rewriting in the manner of OBJ [11] in addition to distributing selections. This approach leads to a clean integration of abstract data types and functions into the DS algorithm. We present an example of a route planning application, to illustrate our approach to query optimization.

The rest of the paper is structured as follows. In section 2 we show how deductive rules can be expressed in an extended relational algebra, and show how functions can be defined in an equational style. Section 3 introduces the route planning application. The main contribution of this paper is in section 4, where we discuss the optimization of queries in the presence of recursion and arbitrary user-defined functions. Four classes of transformations are identified, with different degrees of optimization being feasible for each class. Section 5 concludes the paper.

2. EXTENDED DATA MODEL

All rules are represented internally in an extended relational algebra, though a more convenient language can be provided externally for users. In [15] an extended relational algebra is formally defined. It includes an operation EXT (for 'extend') which adds a new attribute to a relation. Its syntax is

<relation> EXT (<attribute> = <definition>)

The <definition> can be a constant, or an expression involving existing attributes of the relation. Conditional definitions are also allowed.

Another operation, called REP (for 'replace'), replaces one attribute by another. In the simplest case, the new attribute takes the values of the replaced attribute, in which case the operation just renames the attribute. More generally, the new attribute is derived from existing attributes in the same way as for EXT. The general syntax is

<relation> REP (<attribute> BY <attribute> [= <definition>])

The <definition> is omitted when the intention is just to rename an attribute.

The rules are held in the form of abstract syntax trees. For each deduced relation, a tree is constructed with a UNION operation as the root, and with each branch below the root corresponding to one of the rules for deducing the relation. If there is only one rule for deducing a particular relation, the UNION vertex is omitted. After a join is performed, we use a convention that attributes taken from the left-hand operand of the join have 'LEFT.' appended to the front of their name, and attributes taken from the right-hand operand have 'RIGHT.' appended to the front of their names. This ensures uniqueness of attribute names in derived relations, and helps the query optimizer to identify correct transformations.

To support complex objects we require complex relations, in which an attribute may take values of type tuple, or type relation, or indeed of type complex relation. The operators such as select, project and join must be generalized to work on complex relations. Additionally, we need operators to transform a complex relation into an equivalent normalized form, and vice-versa. The semantics of these operators, and a set of semantics-preserving transformations for expressions involving them, have been documented in [15], so we shall not repeat them here. Instead we concentrate in this paper on ways of dealing with abstract data types and functions.

To support abstract data types, we allow the definition of arbitrarily complex structures, with associated user-defined functions. To identify semantics-preserving transformations on expressions involving arbitrary functions, is a hard task. Each function is defined by an equational specification with an initial interpretation [9]. For each abstract data type, there are certain functions whose role is to generate values of the type. Any value of the type has a canonical form which involves the generators. All other functions are defined in terms of their behaviour against these canonical forms. The syntax of function specifications is:

<function-name> (<argument-list>) == <expression>

<function-name> (<argument-list>) == <expression> IF
<condition>

The former is needed for unconditional definitions, whereas the latter allows the definition to be conditional on the values of the arguments. This is similar to the form of specification supported in OBJ [11]. The reason for defining functions in this way is that we wish to use term rewriting to simplify query expressions, replacing each occurence of a function by the expression in its definition. This will be illustrated in section 4.

As a first example of an abstract data type, we consider NELIST (non-empty list) which requires two generators:

LIST : ITEM -> NELIST

CONS : ITEM X NELIST -> NELIST

Any non-empty list can be expressed as either LIST(I) or as CONS(I,L), where I is an item and L is a list. Other functions that might be defined for type NELIST are FIRST (to get the first item on a list), LAST (to get the last item on a list), BELONGS (to check whether or not a given item is on a list) and LENGTH (to find the number of items on a list). These functions can be defined as follows:

FIRST(LIST(I)) == I
FIRST(CONS(I,L)) == I
LAST(LIST(I)) == I
LAST(CONS(I,L)) == LAST(L)
BELONGS(X,LIST(I)) == X=I
BELONGS(X,CONS(I,L)) == X=I OR BELONGS(X,L)
LENGTH(LIST(I)) == 1
LENGTH(CONS(I,L)) == 1 + LENGTH(L)

These definitions are very straightforward, since in no case is the definition dependent on the value of the arguments. Conditional definitions are needed in the next example, which is for the SET abstract data type. The generators for SET are:

EMPTY : -> SET
ADD : ITEM X SET -> SET

In this case EMPTY is a function, with no arguments, which returns the empty set. ADD is a function which adds a new element to a set.

We can specify additional functions such as MEMBER (to test whether an item belongs to a set) and INTERSECT (the usual set operation).

MEMBER(X, EMPTY) == FALSE
MEMBER(X, ADD(I,S)) == X=I OR MEMBER(X,S)
INTERSECT(EMPTY,X) == EMPTY
INTERSECT(ADD(I,S),X) == ADD(I,INTERSECT(S,X)) IF
MEMBER(I,X)
INTERSECT(ADD(I,S),X) == INTERSECT(S,X) IF NOT
MEMBER(I,X)

In the case of the SET data type, there are other properties that need to be specified. First, a set contains no duplicates. Second, the ordering of the elements is immaterial. These two properties are captured by the following:

ADD(I,ADD(I,S)) == ADD(I,S)
ADD(I,ADD(J,S)) == ADD(J,ADD(I,S)) IF J < I

Note that the latter definition needs to be conditional in order to guarantee termination of the term rewriting process.

Further, we may specify certain relationships among the defined functions:

MEMBER(A,INTERSECT(X,Y)) == MEMBER(A,X) AND
MEMBER(A,Y)

Functions may appear in both queries and rules. Our query processor uses the function definitions to optimize and simplify query expressions which involve functions.

In the remainder of the paper we shall use both the SET and NELIST data types, in designing an expert database system for a route planning application.

3. ROUTE PLANNING APPLICATION

We shall consider an example involving a number of locations linked by roads, where the expert database system is intended to assist in planning routes from one location to another. As a base relation, we assume the following:

ROAD(START,FINISH,ROADLENGTH,SUITABILITY)

Each tuple describes a road, giving its START and FINISH locations, the length of the road, and the set of vehicle types for which the road is considered suitable. From this base relation we wish to deduce the following:

ROUTE(JOURNEY,DISTANCE,VEHICLES)

Each deduced tuple describes a journey in terms of the sequence of locations passed through. The first attribute, JOURNEY, is a non-empty list, since even the null journey involves one location. The second attribute, DISTANCE, gives the total distance of the journey. The third attribute, VEHICLES, gives the set of vehicle types for which the complete journey is suitable.

First of all, corresponding to each ROAD tuple we have a two-vertex journey from the START location to the FINISH location. The distance of this journey is the road length. It is suitable for the same types of vehicles for which the road is suitable. More precisely, we use the following rule:

ROUTE(JOURNEY = CONS(S,LIST(F)), DISTANCE=R,
    VEHICLES=Y) :-
    ROAD(START=S, FINISH=F, ROADLENGTH=R,
        SUITABILITY=Y)

Next we can say that if there is a road which starts at A and finishes at B, and if there is a route L which starts at B, then there is a route which goes from A to B and then follows L. The total distance travelled on this route will be equal to the length of the road from A to B plus the distance along the route L. The route is suitable for those vehicles which can use both the road from A to B and the route L. We introduce the following rule:

ROUTE(JOURNEY=CONS(A,L), DISTANCE=D1+D2,
        VEHICLES=INTERSECT(X,Y)) :-
    ROAD(START=A, FINISH=FIRST(L), ROADLENGTH=D1,
        SUITABILITY=X) AND
    ROUTE(JOURNEY=L, DISTANCE=D2, VEHICLES=Y)

The above two rules can be translated into extended relational algebra as follows:

ROAD EXT(JOURNEY=CONS(START,LIST(FINISH)))
    REP(ROADLENGTH BY DISTANCE)
REP (SUITABILITY BY VEHICLES)
    PROJECT(JOURNEY,DISTANCE,VEHICLES)

(ROAD JOIN(LEFT.FINISH=FIRST(RIGHT.JOURNEY)) ROUTE)
    EXT(DISTANCE=LEFT.ROADLENGTH+RIGHT.DISTANCE)
EXT(VEHICLES=INTERSECT(LEFT.SUITABILITY,
        RIGHT.VEHICLES))
EXT(JOURNEY=CONS(LEFT.START,RIGHT.JOURNEY))
    PROJECT(JOURNEY,DISTANCE,VEHICLES)

As an example of a query for this application, suppose we wish to drive a truck from the Astrodome to the Galleria, via the University of Houston. We would like to find a good way of making this journey. It can be expected that there will be a large number of possible

routes, so we need to restrict the search in some way. Suppose we specify that the routes of interest are to contain no more than ten locations (i.e., at most nine roads). Then informally we have altogether five selection conditions:

FIRST(JOURNEY) = 'Astrodome'
LAST(JOURNEY) = 'Galleria'
BELONGS('UH', JOURNEY)
MEMBER('Truck', VEHICLES)
LENGTH(JOURNEY) <= 10

One way of executing this query would be to first materialize the entire ROUTE relation, then apply the selections to it. That approach would be very inefficient, however, since it involves generating a lot of irrelevant tuples. Instead we try to optimize the query execution by performing selections as early as possible. Our approach to query optimization is described in the next section.

4. QUERY OPTIMIZATION

In this paper, we shall consider only queries which are selections against deduced relations. Each query is represented as an abstract syntax tree, whose root contains the selection operation, and the rest of which represents the deduced relation. This representation gives an initial strategy for executing the query, which involves first materializing the entire deduced relation and then selecting just the required tuples. We try to improve upon this initial strategy by distributing the selection through the query graph so that selections are applied as early as possible.

When the deduced relation is defined by simple, non-recursive rules, the optimization technique is a standard one based upon the commutativity and distributivity of relational algebra operations. The optimizing transformations involving the operations of the relational algebra are well known [10]. Those involving extensions to the relational algebra are presented in [15].

Query optimization is often complicated by the presence of recursive rules and/or user-defined functions. We discuss these two cases in turn.

4.1 Optimization with recursive rules

A recursive rule is one in which the deduced relation appears as an argument in its own definition. When we try to construct the abstract syntax tree, we run into difficulties because we cannot create a vertex representing the deduced relation which we are defining. The difficulty can be resolved by introducing a pointer which loops back to the root of the tree. We shall refer to this pointer as a 'recursive edge'. Thus the "tree" becomes a cyclic graph in the presence of recursive rules.

The procedure for distributing selections through cyclic query graphs is necessarily more complex than in the non-cyclic case. This is because, in general, the selection may or may not traverse the recursive edge. If the selection does traverse the recursive edge, it is safe to distribute the selection down into the loop. If, on the other hand, it does not traverse the recursive edge, we must proceed in a different way. Below, we shall identify more precisely the degree of optimization attainable in various circumstances. We assume that the initial query graph has the form shown in figure 1, where the expressions p and q involve EXT and REP operations, and possibly selections. R1 and R2 are base relations, from which a deduced relation is defined.

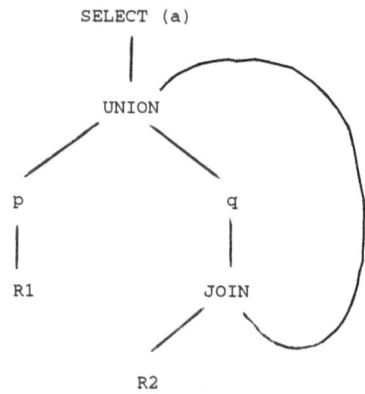

Figure 1: Initial query graph

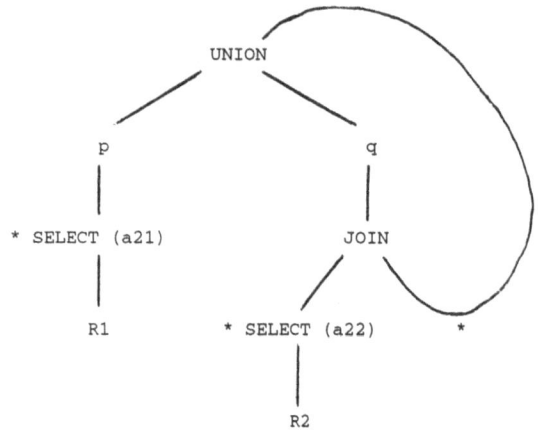

Figure 3: Optimized query graph - case (ii)

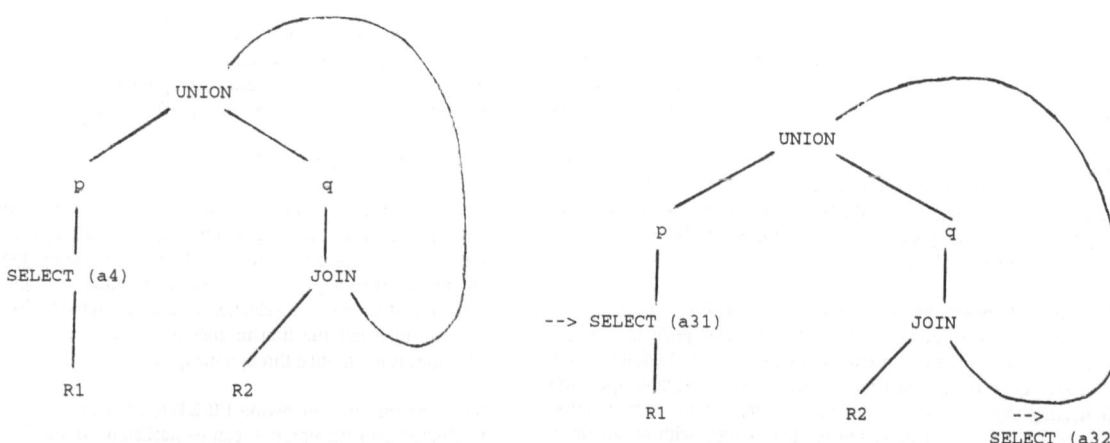

Figure 2: Optimized query graph - case (iv)

Figure 4: Optimized query graph - case (iii)

The query consists of a selection from a deduced relation, using predicate a. We first distribute the selection over the union, then push it down past p and q, and try to push it past the join. Four situations are possible at this stage:

(i)   we were unable to push the selection past the join.

(ii) the selection is pushed past the join, but it is pushed down the left branch of the join.

(iii) the selection is pushed past everything, and through the right branch of the join, and the condition that returns to the union is different from the one we started with.

(iv) the selection is pushed past everything, and through the right branch of the join, and the condition that returns to the union is the same one that we started with.

Case (iv) offers the most optimization. In this case the graph can be optimized as shown in figure 2. The point here is that the select is always being performed at the earliest possible stage of query execution. After the selection is pushed past p, the selection predicate may change (to a4).

Case (ii) offers less optimization because the selection is not pushed through the recursive edge. In this case the optimized graph is as shown in figure 3. An asterisk is placed by the recursive edge, and also by each instance of the selection which did not traverse the recursive edge. To evaluate this graph, we initially treat the marked vertices in the same way as any others. But after a marked edge is traversed, marked vertices are ignored. The result is the union of many terms, each of which involves one or more relations being joined together. In each case, the selection is applied only to the relation which is joined last. Therefore the selection is applied at a late stage of execution, after many irrelevant facts may already have been generated. This approach easily generalizes to the case of multiple recursive rules defining the same relation, and to non-linear recursive rules. In general, as a SELECT vertex is pushed down through a query graph, it may either stop at some position or be pushed through a recursive edge which returns it to the root. If there is some recursive edge through which the SELECT vertex is not pushed, that edge is marked. The positions at which the SELECT vertex stopped are also marked in this case.

Case (iii) offers substantial optimization, though the query expression becomes very complex because the selection predicate changes at each iteration. The optimized expression looks as in figure 4. The recursive edge is marked with an arrow and a selection operation, indicating that the selection predicate changes after each iteration. The original selection operation is also marked with an arrow, to indicate that the predicate for this operation needs to be re-evaluated at each iteration.

Case (i) offers little or no optimization, because the selection operation cannot be pushed down to the base relations. This situation is quite similar to case (ii), but worse in the sense that the selection can only be applied after all the relations have been joined.

4.2 Optimization with functions

Function symbols may appear in rules and also in queries. We only consider selection queries, but the selection predicate may be a complex one involving a number of user-defined functions. Optimization proceeds in similar fashion to that described above, with the aim being to push the selection operation down through the query graph in order to reduce the number of tuples generated. The presence of functions affects the optimization process in the following ways:

(i)   a function expression of form f(x) may appear in the selection predicate, where x is defined in the form of g(y) within some EXT or REP command. Pushing the selection down past the EXT or REP, we introduce a term of the form f(g(y)) in the selection predicate. When this happens, we try to simplify the term by matching it with the left-hand side of some statement of the definition of the abstract data type. If such a match can be found, we replace the term by the right-hand side of the same statement in the abstract data type definition. In other words, our query optimization uses term rewriting in the manner of (for example) OBJ [11].

(ii) The effects of the optimization technique can also be different. As a result of term rewriting we can find arbitrary expressions appearing in selection predicates. For example, if f(g(y)) == h(y) OR j(y), we find a disjunction appearing in the selection predicate. This of course would hinder the further pushing down of the selection operation. Another possibility is that the definition of f(g(y)) may be conditional on the value of y. In that case term rewriting is not appropriate, and we therefore would not push the selection down.

(iii) Even though we may be able to push the selection right through the graph, sometimes the selection predicate may change on each iteration. This situation would prevent us from finding a straightforward optimized query expression, though a (complex) optimized expression may still be obtainable.

The above discussion shows that optimization is feasible in the presence of functions, though certain cases may provide difficulties. In the next subsection we illustrate our optimization technique by considering an example from the route planning database.

4.3 Route planning example

We now consider optimization of the example query introduced in section 3. As usual, we build an initial query graph by using the rules defining the deduced relation ROUTE, and adding the selection (figure 5). In trying to push the selection down through the graph, we can treat each of the selection conditions individually. We shall examine in detail the transformations made as each of these five selections is distributed through the query graph.

When the selection involving FIRST(JOURNEY) = 'Astrodome' is distributed over the union, it can be pushed down the left branch all the way to the base relation. When it is pushed past the EXT vertex, however, the condition is modified to FIRST(CONS(START,LIST(FINISH))) = 'Astrodome', and then (using term rewriting) to START = 'Astrodome'. Similarly, on being pushed down past the EXT in the right branch, the selection condition is modified to FIRST(CONS(LEFT.START, LIST(RIGHT.FINISH))) = 'Astrodome', and then (using term rewriting) to LEFT.START = 'Astrodome'. Now when this condition is pushed past the join, it takes the left branch and the condition becomes START = 'Astrodome'. Consequently the selection does not traverse the recursive edge, which means that the selection cannot be applied on every iteration. Very limited optimization is achieved in this case.

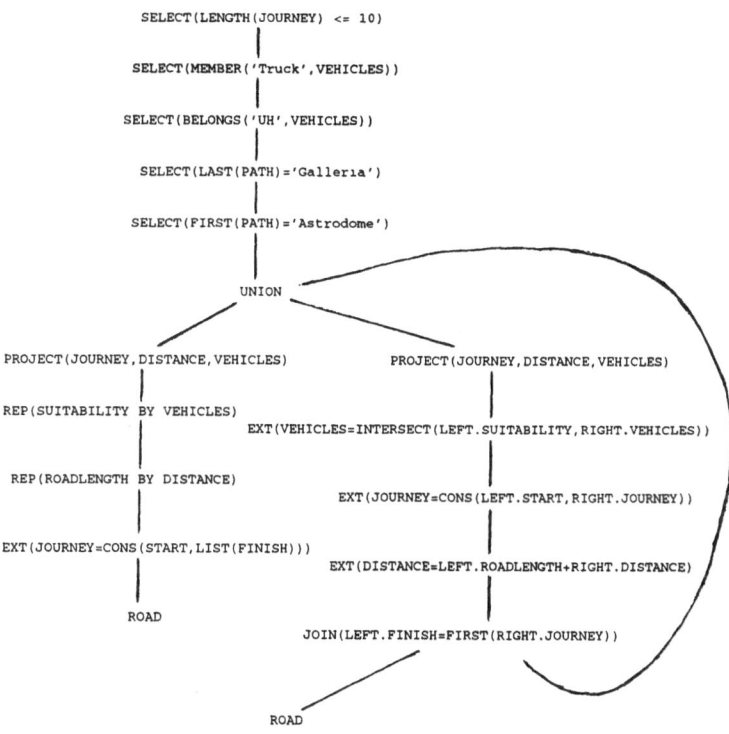

```
                        SELECT(LENGTH(JOURNEY) <= 10)
                                     |
                        SELECT(MEMBER('Truck',VEHICLES))
                                     |
                        SELECT(BELONGS('UH',VEHICLES))
                                     |
                        SELECT(LAST(PATH)='Galleria')
                                     |
                        SELECT(FIRST(PATH)='Astrodome')
                                     |
                                   UNION
```

PROJECT(JOURNEY,DISTANCE,VEHICLES)   PROJECT(JOURNEY,DISTANCE,VEHICLES)

REP(SUITABILITY BY VEHICLES)
                                    EXT(VEHICLES=INTERSECT(LEFT.SUITABILITY,RIGHT.VEHICLES))

REP(ROADLENGTH BY DISTANCE)
                                    EXT(JOURNEY=CONS(LEFT.START,RIGHT.JOURNEY))

EXT(JOURNEY=CONS(START,LIST(FINISH)))
                                    EXT(DISTANCE=LEFT.ROADLENGTH+RIGHT.DISTANCE)

ROAD
                                    JOIN(LEFT.FINISH=FIRST(RIGHT.JOURNEY))

                                    ROAD

Figure 5: Initial graph for the query to find routes from Astrodome to Galleria .

When the selection involving LAST(JOURNEY) = 'Galleria' is distributed over the union, it too can be pushed right down through the left branch. On passing the EXT vertex, the condition is modified to LAST(CONS(START,LIST(FINISH))) = 'Galleria', and then to LAST(LIST(FINISH)) = 'Galleria', and finally to FINISH = 'Galleria'. When the same condition passes through the right branch, it is modified to LAST(CONS(LEFT.START,RIGHT.JOURNEY)) = 'Galleria', and then to LAST(RIGHT.JOURNEY) = 'Galleria'. When the selection is pushed past the join, the condition LAST(JOURNEY) = 'Galleria' passes back through the recursive edge to the union. Since this is the same condition that we started with, very good optimization results from this transformation.

When the selection involving BELONGS('UH',JOURNEY) is distributed over the union, it too can be pushed right down through the left branch. On passing the EXT vertex, the condition is modified to START = 'UH' OR BELONGS('UH',LIST(FINISH)), which is then simplified to START = 'UH' OR FINISH = 'UH'. When the same condition passes through the right branch, it is modified to LEFT.START = 'UH' OR BELONGS('UH',RIGHT.JOURNEY). Since this is a disjunction of two conditions, one of which applies to the left branch and the other of which applies to the right branch, it cannot be pushed past the join. Consequently, very little optimization is achieved by this transformation.

When the selection involving MEMBER('Truck',VEHICLES) is distributed over the union, it is pushed through the left branch and modified to MEMBER('Truck',SUITABILITY). When the same condition passes through the right branch, it is modified to

MEMBER('Truck',LEFT.SUITABILITY) AND MEMBER('Truck', RIGHT.VEHICLES). Since this is a conjunction of two conditions (one involving the left branch and the other the right branch) it can be split so that one part is pushed through the left branch of the join and the other is pushed through the right branch of the join. Since the condition pushed through the recursive edge is the same one that we started with, very good optimization is achieved by this transformation.

When the selection involving LENGTH(JOURNEY) <= 10 is distributed over the union, the condition pushed through the left branch is modified to LENGTH(CONS(START,LIST(FINISH))) <= 10, and then to 1 + LENGTH(LIST(FINISH)) <= 10, and then to 1 + 1 <= 10. This final condition is easily simplified to TRUE. When the same condition is pushed through the right branch, it is modified to LENGTH(CONS(LEFT.START,RIGHT.JOURNEY)) <= 10, then to 1 + LENGTH(RIGHT.JOURNEY) <= 10, which simplifies to LENGTH(RIGHT.JOURNEY) <= 9. Consequently the condition LENGTH(JOURNEY) <= 9 traverses the recursive edge. This means that a selection can be applied at every iteration, but the selection condition changes each time. So very good optimization is achieved by this transformation, even though there is the added complication of keeping track of changes in the selection condition. In fact, the early application of this selection is essential to guarantee the termination of the execution.

66

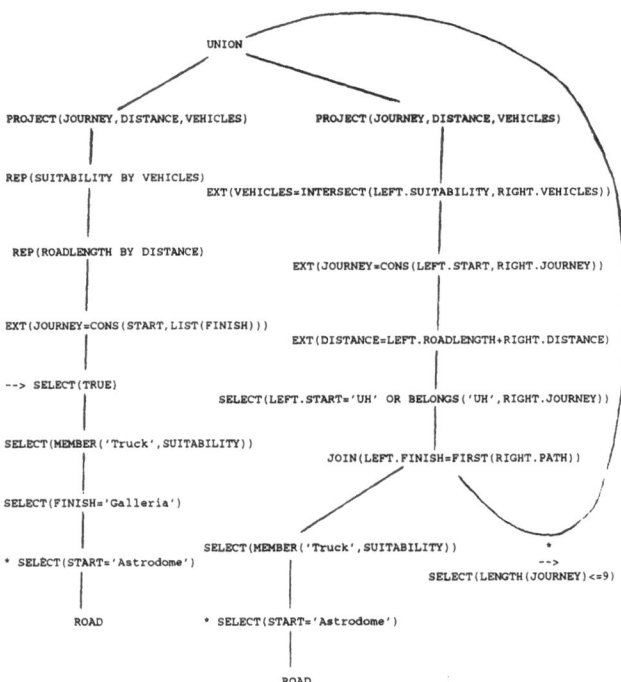

Figure 6: Optimized graph for the query of figure 5

Thus we see that very good optimization results from the two conditions LAST(JOURNEY) = 'Galleria' and MEMBER('Truck', VEHICLES). In terms of the categorization we introduced in section 4.1, case (iv) applies to each of these. Little or no optimization is possible using FIRST(JOURNEY) = 'Astrodome' and BELONGS('UH',JOURNEY), since these conditions can only be applied at a very late stage. Cases (ii) and (i), respectively, apply to these selections. On the other hand, LENGTH(JOURNEY) <= 10 plays a very important role in the optimization. Indeed, it is this condition that ensures the termination of the query. This is an example of case (iii). The final optimized query graph is shown in figure 6.

5. CONCLUSION

We presented an approach to deductive query optimization which allows for abstract data types and arbitrary user-defined functions within the framework of an extended relational model. In this way we support some of the features of object-oriented systems, in addition to deductive inferencing. Functions may appear in both rules and queries, and the query optimization process uses a combination of term rewriting and distribution of selections. This provides a clean integration of functions into both the language and the optimization algorithm. While the degree of optimization attained is dependent on the nature of the rules and the query, very efficient strategies are found for a wide range of queries. The effectiveness of the technique was demonstrated on an example from a route planning application.

REFERENCES

[1]   R. Agrawal, P. Devanbu, "Moving selections into linear least fixpoint queries", IEEE International Conference on Data Engineering, 1988.

[2]   A. Aho, J. Ullman, "Universality of data retrieval languages", conference on POPL, 1979.

[3]   F. Bancilhon et al, "Magic sets and other strange ways to implement logic programs", ACM International Symposium on PODS, 1986.

[4]   F. Bancilhon, R. Ramakrishnan, "An amateur's introduction to recursive query processing strategies", ACM SIGMOD Conference, 1986.

[5]   C. Beeri, R. Ramakrishnan, "On the power of magic", ACM international symposium on PODS, 1987.

[6]   J. Bocca, "On the evaluation strategy of EDUCE", International conference on management of data, 1986.

[7]   S. Ceri, L. Tanca, "Optimization of algebraic equations for evaluating Datalog queries", International Conference on Very Large Databases, 1987.

[8]   D. Chimenti et al, "The LDL system prototype", IEEE-TKDE 2:1, 1990.

[9]   H. Ehrig, B. Mahr, "Fundamentals of algebraic specification 1: equations and initial semantics", Springer-Verlag, 1985.

[10]   R. Elmasri, S. Navathe, "Fundamentals of database systems", Benjamin-Cummings, 1989.

[11]   J. Goguen, J. Meseguer, "Rapid protoyping in the OBJ executable specification language", Technical Report CSL-137, SRI International, 1982.

[12]   M. Kifer, E. Lozinskii, "Filtering data flow in deductive databases", ICDT, 1986.

[13]   N. Miyazaki, "Selection propagation in deductive databases: from pushing selections to magic sets", Data and Knowledge Engineering 5, 1990.

[14]   M. Stonebraker, L. Rowe, "The design of POSTGRES", International Conference on Management of Data, 1986.

[15]   M. Taylor, "Logical optimisation of distributed knowledge base queries", Computer Journal 33:1, 1990.

[16]   L. Vieille, "Recursive axioms in deductive databases: the query-subquery approach", International conference on expert database systems, 1986.

Using Relaxation Techniques
to Evaluate Queries in Deductive Databases *

Susumu Suzuki[†]   Toshihide Ibaraki[††]   Masahichi Kishi[†]

[†] Information Network Engineering, Aichi Institute of Technology
Yachigusa, Yagusa, Toyota, 470-03 Japan
[††] Applied Mathematics and Physics, Engineering, Kyoto University
Yoshida honmachi, sakyou-ku, Kyoto, 606 Japan

ABSTRACT

Relaxation method is a general framework used to improve the efficiency of answering a query $q(\mathbf{a}, \mathbf{x})$ given to a deductive database P. It first solves problem $(q'(\mathbf{a}', \mathbf{x}'), P^{RLX})$, where P^{RLX} is a relaxation of the original database P and $q'(\mathbf{a}', \mathbf{x}')$ is the modified query to P^{RLX}, to derive a set $PREL$ of predicate occurrences that is known to contain the answer set ANS in P, and construct database P^{MDF} by augmenting P with the restriction that solution space is constrained to $PREL$, and finally solves problem $(q(\mathbf{a}, \mathbf{x}), P^{MDF})$ to get the desired answer set ANS. If the relaxation P^{RLX} is properly defined, $(q'(\mathbf{a}', \mathbf{x}'), P^{RLX})$ can be efficiently solved since P^{RLX} is simpler than P, and $(q(\mathbf{a}, \mathbf{x}), P^{MDF})$ can also be efficiently solved as the solution space is restricted. Several methods are proposed to construct such relaxations. It is also argued that the original form of magic set method [2] can be described in the context of the relaxation method.

1   Introduction

Given a query $q(\mathbf{a}, \mathbf{x})$, where $\mathbf{a}$ is a vector of constants and $\mathbf{x}$ is a vector of variables, in a deductive database $P = (R, F)$, specified by a set of Horn rules R and a set of facts F, we consider to derive the set of all answers ANS to the query. It is assumed that each rule in R is range restricted (i.e. every variable in the head of a rule appears in its body) and includes no negation, and every argument of each predicate is not a function. Let $N(P)(= \{p, q, r, \ldots\})$ be the set of all predicate names in P, $C(P)(= \{a, b, c, \ldots\})$ the set of all constants in P, $PO(N(P), C(P))(= \{p(a, \ldots, a), p(a, \ldots, b), \ldots, q(a, \ldots, a), q(a, \ldots, b), \ldots\})$ the set of all forms obtained by substituting constants to the arguments of predicates. We call each element in $PO(N(P), C(P))$ a predicate occurrence (abbreviated to po). Note that a po $p(\mathbf{a})$ may not be a fact of an extensional predicate defined in F. A form $p(\mathbf{c}, \mathbf{y})$, where $\mathbf{c}$ is a constant vector and $\mathbf{y}$ is a variable vector, is also called po, and stands for all po $p(\mathbf{c}, \mathbf{a}), p(\mathbf{c}, \mathbf{b}), \ldots$ obtained by substituting constant vectors for $\mathbf{y}$.

---
*This work was supported in part by Scientific Grant in Aid by the Ministry of Education, Science and Culture of Japan. Suzuki was also supported by a grant from Nitto Foundation.

From now on, unless otherwise specified, constants are denoted by $a, b, c, \ldots$, constant vectors by $\mathbf{a}, \mathbf{b}, \mathbf{c}, \ldots$, variables by $x, y, z, \ldots$, variable vectors by $\mathbf{x}, \mathbf{y}, \mathbf{z}, \ldots$, EDB predicates(i.e. extensional database predicates used in F) by $A, B, C, \ldots$, and IDB predicates(i.e. intensional database predicates not in F) by $p, q, r, \ldots$. Let $IMP(P)(\subseteq PO(N(P), C(P)))$ denote the set of all predicate occurrences that can be deduced from P. Then the answer to a query $q(\mathbf{a}, \mathbf{x})$ is the set:

$$ANS = \{q(\mathbf{a}, \mathbf{x}) \mid q(\mathbf{a}, \mathbf{x}) \in IMP(P)\}.$$

Many methods have been proposed for efficient evaluation of queries in deductive databases [2] - [8], [10] - [14]. To reduce the number of intermediate predicate occurrences in $IMP(P)$ generated to answer a query is an important idea to improve efficiency.

Definition: If some derivation tree that derives a po $s(\mathbf{d}) \in IMP(P)$ includes a po $p(\mathbf{z})$ as one of its nodes, $p(\mathbf{z})$ is said to be relevant to $s(\mathbf{d})$ (expressed as $(p(\mathbf{z}), P) \to *s(\mathbf{d})$). If $p(\mathbf{z})$ is relevant to some answer $q(\mathbf{a}, \mathbf{b})(\in ANS)$ to a query $q(\mathbf{a}, \mathbf{x})$, $p(\mathbf{z})$ is relevant to query $q(\mathbf{a}, \mathbf{x})$. The set of relevant po's to a query $q(\mathbf{a}, \mathbf{x})$, $REL(q(\mathbf{a}, \mathbf{x}), P)(\subseteq IMP(P))$, is therefore defined by

$$REL(q(\mathbf{a}, \mathbf{x}), P) = \{p(\mathbf{z}) \mid (p(\mathbf{z}), P) \to * q(\mathbf{a}, \mathbf{x})\}.$$

Set $REL(q(\mathbf{a}, \mathbf{x}), P)$ is usually referred to as the relevant set. □

In other words, the relevant set consists of all predicate occurrences that can be used to derive answers, among those deducible from P. Therefore, if we can know set $REL(q(\mathbf{a}, \mathbf{x}), P)$ in advance, we can restrict the search of answers only within the relevant set, thereby improving the efficiency of the answering process. However, as obvious from definition, computing the relevant set is equivalent to giving the exact answer set ANS, and therefore we try to generate sets of po, $PREL$, which is a relaxation of $REL(q(\mathbf{a}, \mathbf{x}), P)$, i.e., satisfies

relaxation condition: $PREL \supseteq REL(q(\mathbf{a}, \mathbf{x}), P)$.

This set of predicate occurrences $PREL$ is called a potentially relevant set. The original database P is then solved for the query $q(\mathbf{a}, \mathbf{x})$ under the additional constraint that only those predicate occurrences contained in $PREL$ are generated during its process of searching the set of answers ANS. The notion of relevant facts was first introduced in [7] and was explained in [3]. The above definition of a potentially relevant set is more general in the sense that not only facts but also predicate occurrences are taken into account. The efficiency of our method depends on the size of its potentially relevant set $PREL$.

We propose in this paper a general frameworks of relaxation method and give several methods to derive $PREL$, as well as examples that show its effectiveness. The well known magic set method [2], which eliminates irrelevant predicate occurrences by adding a restriction derived from the constants in a query to P, can also be discussed within the framework of the relaxation method, though there are some nontrivial differences in the details of computation process. [4] showed that a number of known methods could be defined within the framework of the generalized magic set method. It is not difficult to see that most of such methods can also be viewed as special cases of the relaxation method. There are however some cases of the relaxation method that are not regarded as the generalized magic set method, and some cases of the generalized magic set method that are not regarded as the relaxation method.

2   An Example

We give an example of a deductive database and a query, and derive its relevant set. This example is used throughout this paper.

Example 1: Let a deductive database $P1 = (R1, F1)$ consist of a rule set $R1 = \{r1, r2, r3, r4, r5\}$:

$r1 : p(x_1, x_2, y_1, y_2) \quad :- \quad A(x_1, y_1), B(x_2, y_2).$

$r2 : p(x_1, x_2, z_1, z_2) \quad :- \quad p(x_1, x_2, y_1, y_2), A(y_1, z_1), B(y_2, z_2).$

$r3 : s(x_1, x_2, y_1, y_2) \quad :- \quad C(x_1, y_1), D(x_2, y_2).$

$r4 : s(x_1, x_2, z_1, z_2) \quad :- \quad s(x_1, x_2, y_1, y_2), C(y_1, z_1), D(y_2, z_2).$

$r5 : q(x_1, x_2, y_1, y_2) \quad :- \quad p(x_1, x_2, y_1, y_2), s(x_1, x_2, y_1, y_2).$

and a fact set $F1$:

$$
\begin{aligned}
F1 \;=\; & \{A(i,j) \mid j = i + 1, 51 \le i < 100, i : \text{integer}\} \\
\cup\; & \{A(i,i) \mid 51 \le i \le 100, i : \text{integer}\} \\
\cup\; & \{B(i,j) \mid j = i + 1, 1 \le i < 100, i : \text{integer}\} \\
\cup\; & \{B(i,i) \mid 1 \le i \le 100, i : \text{integer}\} \\
\cup\; & \{C(i,j) \mid j = i + 1, 1 \le i < 100, i : \text{integer}\} \\
\cup\; & \{C(i,i) \mid 1 \le i \le 100, i : \text{integer}\} \\
\cup\; & \{D(i,j) \mid j = i + 1, 51 \le i < 100, i : \text{integer}\} \\
\cup\; & \{D(i,i) \mid 51 < i \le 100, i : \text{integer}\}.
\end{aligned}
$$

A query to P1 is
$$q(x_1, x_2, 75, 75).$$

This problem can be interpreted as follows. There are two vehicles Vp and Vs on grids of dimension two with axes 1 and 2. A po $A(x_1, y_1)(C(x_1, y_1))$ means that the first coordinate

x_1 of Vp(Vs) can move directly to y_1, and $B(x_2, y_2)(D(x_2, y_2))$ means that the second coordinate x_2 of Vp(Vs) can move to y_2. Similarly, $p(x_1, x_2, y_1, y_2)$ ($s(x_1, x_2, y_1, y_2)$) means that the location (x_1, x_2) of Vp(Vs) in two-dimensional grid can reach location (y_1, y_2), and $q(x_1, x_2, y_1, y_2)$ means that both Vp and Vs, starting from (x_1, x_2), can reach (y_1, y_2). The query $q(x_1, x_2, 75, 75)$ therefore asks to compute the set of all initial locations (x_1, x_2), from which both Vp and Vs can reach $(75, 75)$:

$$ANS1 = \{q(x_1, x_2, 75, 75) \mid q(x_1, x_2, 75, 75) \in IMP(P1)\}. \square$$

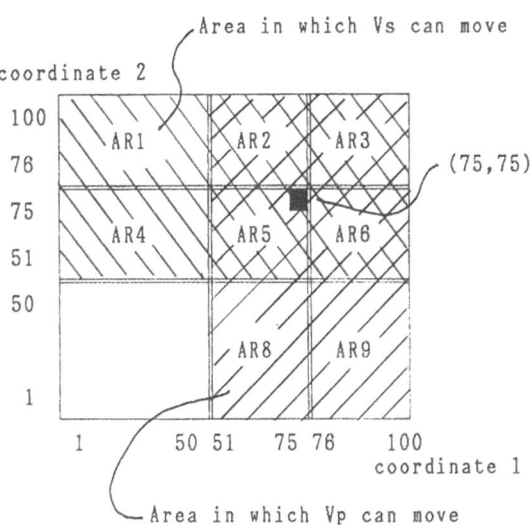

Fig.1 Two dimensional areas in which vehicles Vp and Vs can move

Fig.1 shows the areas in which Vp and Vs can move. Let $AR1, \ldots, AR9$ be the areas as shown in Fig.1, respectively. Then, Vp can move in $AR2 \cup AR3 \cup AR5 \cup AR6 \cup AR8 \cup AR9$ and Vs in $AR1 \cup AR2 \cup AR3 \cup AR4 \cup AR5 \cup AR6$. It is easy to see that the answer set for this example is

$$ANS1 = \{q(x_1, x_2, 75, 75) \mid (x_1, x_2) \in AR5\}.$$

Let $IMP_p(P1)(\subset IMP(P1))$ be the set of predicate occurrences with predicate name p, which can be deduced from $P1$, and $REL_p(q(x_1, x_2, 75, 75), P1)$ ($\subset REL(q(x_1, x_2, 75, 75), P1)$) be the set of relevant predicate occurrences with predicate name p. $IMP_p(P1)$ in the above problem example is given by

$$
\begin{aligned}
IMP_p(P1) = \\
\{p(x_1, x_2, y_1, y_2) \mid x_1 \le y_1, x_2 \le y_2, (x_1, x_2), (y_1, y_2) \\
\in AR2 \cup AR3 \cup AR5 \cup AR6 \cup AR8 \cup AR9\}.
\end{aligned}
$$

In order to derive REL_p, note that predicate occurrences of P that can be used in rule $r5$ to derive some answer $q(z_1, z_2, 75, 75)(\in ANS1)$ are $p(z_1, z_2, 75, 75)$ satisfying $(z_1, z_2) \in AR5$, and those that can be used in rule $r1$ or rule $r2$ to derive its predicate occurrences

$p(z_1, z_2, 75, 75)$ ($(z_1, z_2) \in AR5$) are $p(x_1, x_2, y_1, y_2)$ satisfying $(x_1, x_2), (y_1, y_2) \in AR5$ and $x_1 \le y_1, x_2 \le y_2$. Therefore, we have

$$REL_p(q(x_1, x_2, 75, 75), P1) = \{p(x_1, x_2, y_1, y_2) \mid$$
$$x_1 \le y_1, x_2 \le y_2, (x_1, x_2), (y_1, y_2) \in AR5\}.$$

3 Outline of Relaxation Method

Now, we will explain the idea of the relaxation method. The potentially relevant set $PREL$ becomes smallest when it is precisely equal to the relevant set REL. The relaxation method tries to compute a potentially relevant set $PREL$ that is close to REL, without spending too much computation time, by solving $(q'(\mathbf{a}', \mathbf{x}'), P^{RLX})$, where P^{RLX} is a relaxation of P and $q'(\mathbf{a}', \mathbf{x}')$ is the query $q(\mathbf{a}, \mathbf{x})$ modified to meet the relaxation of P. Here a database P^{RLX} is called a relaxation of P, if there is a mapping f from the set of po's of P to the set of po's in P^{RLX} such that the following *relevancy condition* holds:

Let $q'(\mathbf{a}', \mathbf{x}') = f(q(\mathbf{a}, \mathbf{x}))$. Then, for any $p(\mathbf{y}) \in REL(q(\mathbf{a}, \mathbf{x}), P)$, $p'(\mathbf{y}')(= f(p(\mathbf{y})))$ belongs to $REL(q'(\mathbf{a}', \mathbf{x}'), P^{RLX})$.

The relaxation method then proceeds as follow.
(1) Solve $(q'(\mathbf{a}', \mathbf{x}'), P^{RLX})$ to obtain $REL(q'(\mathbf{a}', \mathbf{x}'), P^{RLX})$. Let $PREL = f^{-1}(REL(q'(\mathbf{a}', \mathbf{x}'), P^{RLX}))$.
(2) Solve $(q(\mathbf{a}, \mathbf{x}), P)$ by restricting the domain of po's for search to set $PREL$ (i.e., ignoring all po's $\notin PREL$ generated in the computation). The database P restricted to $PREL$ is denoted by P^{MDF} and called a modified database of P. In other words, the answer set ANS of $(q(\mathbf{a}, \mathbf{x}), P)$ can be obtained by solving $(q(\mathbf{a}, \mathbf{x}), P^{MDF})$, say, by the semi-naive method [1], i.e.,

$$\begin{aligned} ANS &= \{q(\mathbf{a}, \mathbf{x}) \mid q(\mathbf{a}, \mathbf{x}) \in IMP(P)\} \\ &= \{q(\mathbf{a}, \mathbf{x}) \mid q(\mathbf{a}, \mathbf{x}) \in IMP(P) \cap PREL\} \\ &= \{q(\mathbf{a}, \mathbf{x}) \mid q(\mathbf{a}, \mathbf{x}) \in IMP(P^{MDF})\} \end{aligned}$$

The relaxation method gives the correct answer set ANS since relaxation condition

$$PREL \supseteq REL(q(\mathbf{a}, \mathbf{x}), P)$$

follows from the relevancy condition of f associated with relaxation P^{RLX}. The computation of the relaxation method is mostly spent on solving the relaxation $(q'(\mathbf{a}', \mathbf{x}'), P^{RLX})$ and the modified database $(q(\mathbf{a}, \mathbf{x}), P^{MDF})$. Therefore, it is important how to define relaxations P^{RLX} which are easy to solve and yet are close approximations of the original P. In the following, we present two examples which are both based on the so-called argument elimination strategy.

4 Relaxation Method Based on Argument Elimination Strategy

From now on, we denote relaxation j of database $P1$ of Example 1 by $P1^{RLXj}$, the mapping from the set of po's

of $P1$ to the set of po's in $P1^{RLXj}$ by fj, the po set $fj^{-1}(REL(q'(\mathbf{a}', \mathbf{x}'), P1^{RLXj}))$ by $PRELj$ and the modified database, which is database $P1$ restricted to $PRELj$, by $P1^{MDFj}$.

Example 2: A relaxation $P1^{RLX1} = (R1^{RLX1}, F1^{RLX1})$ is constructed from $P1$ of Example 1 by considering coordinate 1 only. First, the set of rules $R1^{RLX1}$ is given by

$$\begin{aligned} r6 : p_1(x_1, y_1) &:- A(x_1, y_1). \\ r7 : p_1(x_1, z_1) &:- p_1(x_1, y_1), A(y_1, z_1). \\ r8 : s_1(x_1, y_1) &:- C(x_1, y_1). \\ r9 : s_1(x_1, z_1) &:- s_1(x_1, y_1), C(y_1, z_1). \\ r10 : q_1(x_1, y_1) &:- p_1(x_1, y_1), s_1(x_1, y_1). \end{aligned}$$

The mapping $f1$ from the set of po's of $P1$ to the set of po's in $P1^{RLX1}$ is then defined by

$$\begin{aligned} f1 : \quad & p(x_1, x_2, y_1, y_2) \to p_1(x_1, y_1), \\ & s(x_1, x_2, y_1, y_2) \to s_1(x_1, y_1), \\ & q(x_1, x_2, y_1, y_2) \to q_1(x_1, y_1), \\ & A(x_1, y_1) \to A(x_1, y_1), \quad B(x_2, y_2) \to \varepsilon, \\ & C(x_1, y_1) \to C(x_1, y_1), \quad D(x_2, y_2) \to \varepsilon, \end{aligned}$$

where ε means that $P1^{RLX1}$ does not have the corresponding EDB predicate in it. The set of facts in $P1^{RLX1}$ is similarly given by

$$\begin{aligned} F1^{RLX1} &= \{A(i, j) \mid j = i + 1, 51 \le i < 100, i : \text{integer}\} \\ & \cup \{A(i, i) \mid 51 \le i \le 100, i : \text{integer}\} \\ & \cup \{C(i, j) \mid j = i + 1, 1 \le i < 100, i : \text{integer}\} \\ & \cup \{C(i, i) \mid 1 \le i \le 100, i : \text{integer}\}. \end{aligned}$$

This relaxation $P1^{RLX1}$ describes a necessary condition of $P1$ in the sense that it characterizes the conditions concerned with the first coordinates, even though the vehicles move in the two dimensional plane. For example, if a po $p(x_1, x_2, y_1, y_2)$ can be deduced from $P1$, the corresponding po $p_1(x_1, y_1)(= f1(p(x_1, x_2, y_1, y_2)))$ is also deduced from $P1^{RLX1}$ (though the converse is not always true). Extracting only the first coordinate of query $q(x_1, x_2, 75, 75)$ for $P1$ gives query $q_1(x_1, 75)(= f1(q(x_1, x_2, 75, 75)))$ for $P1^{RLX1}$. The relevant sets $REL_{p_1}(q_1(x_1, 75), P1^{RLX1})$, $REL_{s_1}(q_1(x_1, 75), P1^{RLX1})$, $REL_{q_1}(q_1(x_1, 75), P1^{RLX1})$ become

$$REL_{p_1}(q_1(x_1, 75), P1^{RLX1}) = \{p_1(x_1, y_1) \mid 51 \le x_1 \le y_1 \le 75\}$$
$$REL_{s_1}(q_1(x_1, 75), P1^{RLX1}) = \{s_1(x_1, y_1) \mid 51 \le x_1 \le y_1 \le 75\}$$
$$REL_{q_1}(q_1(x_1, 75), P1^{RLX1}) = \{q_1(x_1, 75) \mid 51 \le x_1 \le 75\}.$$

Therefore this $f1$ satisfies the relevancy condition:

$$\{f1(r(\mathbf{y})) \mid r \in \{p, s, q\}, r(\mathbf{y}) \in REL(q(x_1, x_2, 75, 75), P1)\}$$
$$\subseteq REL(q1(x_1, 75), P1^{RLX1}).$$

$(REL_p(q(x_1, x_2, 75, 75), P1)$ is given in section 2.)
Let

$$\begin{aligned} PREL1 &= f^{-1}(REL_{p_1}(q_1(x_1, 75), P1^{RLX1})) \\ & \cup f^{-1}(REL_{s_1}(q_1(x_1, 75), P1^{RLX1})) \\ & \cup f^{-1}(REL_{q_1}(q_1(x_1, 75), P1^{RLX1})), \end{aligned}$$

and the modified database, which is database $P1$ restricted to $PREL1$, be now given by $P1^{MDF1} = (R1^{MDF1}, F1^{MDF1})$, where its rule set $R1^{MDF1}$ is obtained by adding predicates representing the derived constraints to rules 1 - 5:

$$r11 : p(x_1, x_2, y_1, y_2) \quad :- \quad p_1(x_1, y_1), A(x_1, y_1), B(x_2, y_2).$$
$$r12 : p(x_1, x_2, z_1, z_2) \quad :- \quad p_1(x_1, z_1), p(x_1, x_2, y_1, y_2),$$
$$A(y_1, z_1), B(y_2, z_2).$$
$$r13 : s(x_1, x_2, y_1, y_2) \quad :- \quad s1(x_1, y_1), C(x_1, y_1), D(x_2, y_2).$$
$$r14 : s(x_1, x_2, z_1, z_2) \quad :- \quad s_1(x_1, z_1), s(x_1, x_2, y_1, y_2),$$
$$C(y_1, z_1), D(y_2, z_2).$$
$$r15 : q(x_1, x_2, y_1, y_2) \quad :- \quad q_1(x_1, y_1), p(x_1, x_2, y_1, y_2),$$
$$s(x_1, x_2, y_1, y_2).$$

and its fact set $F1^{MDF1}$ is defined by

$$F1^{MDF1} = F1 \quad \cup \quad REL_{p_1}(q_1(x_1, 75), P1^{RLX1})$$
$$\cup \quad REL_{s_1}(q_1(x_1, 75), P1^{RLX1})$$
$$\cup \quad REL_{q_1}(q_1(x_1, 75), P1^{RLX1}).$$

(Though relevant predicate occurrences $p_1(\mathbf{x}, \mathbf{y})$, $s_1(\mathbf{x}, \mathbf{y})$, $q_1(\mathbf{x}, \mathbf{y})$ of $P1^{RLX1}$ are treated as facts of $P1^{MDF1}$ in this formulation, they can also be defined by rules.) Finally, the po set $IMP(P1^{MDF1})$ is generated by solving $P1^{MDF1}$ in the bottom up manner (e.g., by the semi-naive method). Then, the following answer set $ANS1$ is derived.

$$ANS1 = \{q(x_1, x_2, 75, 75) \mid (x_1, x_2) \in AR5\}. \quad \Box$$

In general, a pair (f, P^{RLX}) constructed by the the argument elimination strategy satisfies the relevancy condition, if the following conditions hold:

1. Every rule r in P^{RLX} is range restricted.

2. Let r be any rule of P and r' the relaxed rule in P^{RLX} corresponding to r. Then, for any IDB predicate $p(\mathbf{x})$ in rule r, rule r' has the corresponding IDB predicate $p'(\mathbf{x}')(= f(p(\mathbf{x})))$.

It is easy to show that $(f1, P1^{RLX1})$ defined in the above example satisfies these conditions.

To see the efficiency of the relaxation of Example 2, note that set $IMP_p(P1^{MDF1})$, for example, is given by

$$IMP_p(P1^{MDF1}) = \{p(x_1, x_2, y_1, y_2) \mid$$
$$x_1 \le y_1, x_2 \le y_2, (x_1, x_2), (y_1, y_2) \in AR2 \cup AR5 \cup AR8\},$$

which does not contain po's corresponding to the areas $AR3, AR6$ and $AR9$, even though $IMP_p(P1)$ generated from $P1$ contains them. Since the area of search is smaller, we may say that this relaxation method solves problem $(q(x_1, x_2, 75, 75), P1)$ more efficiently.

Example 3: It is possible to define another relaxation $P1^{RLX2}$ by extracting the information of the second coordinate from $P1$. The process is similar to Example 2. Then we can combine these two restrictions together to obtain yet

another relaxation $P1^{RLX1\cdot2}$. The computation of the answer set in the modified database $P1^{MDF1\cdot2}$ from $P1^{RLX1\cdot2}$ is restricted to the following po set:

$$PREL1 \cdot 2 =$$

$$\{p(x_1, x_2, y_1, y_2) \mid x_1 \le y_1, x_2 \le y_2, (x_1, x_2), (y_1, y_2) \in AR5\}$$

$$\cup \{s(x_1, x_2, y_1, y_2) \mid x_1 \le y_1, x_2 \le y_2, (x_1, x_2), (y_1, y_2) \in AR5\}$$

$$\cup \{q(x_1, x_2, y_1, y_2) \mid x_1 \le y_1, x_2 \le y_2, (x_1, x_2), (y_1, y_2) \in AR5\}.$$

It is easy to see that $PREL1 \cdot 2$ is much smaller than $PREL1$ or $PREL2$, and the efficiency of the relaxation method using $P1^{RLX1\cdot2}$ can be higher than that using $P1^{RLX1}$ or $P1^{RLX2}$ alone. $\Box$

For a database $P = (R, F)$, denote the number of different variables in a rule r by $rule\_deg(r)$ and $\max_{r \in R}\{rule\_deg(r)\}$ by $db\_deg(P)$ and the number of different values of constants appeared in F of P by $cnum(P)$. The processing time for P by the semi-naive method can be roughly estimated as $cnum(P)^{db\_deg(P)}$. The argument elimination strategy used in Example 2 and 3 can be considered to reduce the size of a relaxation P^{RLX} to a manageable level, by decreasing $db\_deg(P)$. In Example 2, $db\_deg(P1) = 6$, $db\_deg(P1^{RLX1}) = 3$ and $cnum(P1) = cnum(P1^{RLX1}) = 100$.

5 Relaxation Methods Based on Other Strategies

There are various strategies of defining relaxations. We have investigated so far the following strategies:

1. Argument elimination(as discussed in section 4),
2. Predicate decomposition,
3. Rule decomposition,
4. Constant grouping.

Though we omit detailed explanation, the argument elimination, the predicate decomposition and the rule decomposition construct a relaxation P^{RLX} by decreasing $db\_deg(P)$, while the constant grouping decreases $cnum(P)$. We now give an example below, in which another relaxation $P1^{RLX3}$ of database $P1$ of Example 1 is constructed by following the strategies of predicate decomposition, rule decomposition and constant grouping together.

Example 4: Consider for database $P1$ of Example 1 a mapping $f3 = (f3_t, f3_c)$ that consists of a mapping of predicates $f3_t$ and a mapping of constants $f3_c$:

$$f3_t : \quad p(x_1, x_2, y_1, y_2) \rightarrow p_2(x_1, y_1, y_2) \wedge p_3(x_2, y_1, y_2),$$
$$s(x_1, x_2, y_1, y_2) \rightarrow s_2(x_1, y_1, y_2) \wedge s_3(x_2, y_1, y_2),$$
$$q(x_1, x_2, y_1, y_2) \rightarrow q(x_1, x_2, y_1, y_2),$$
$$A(x_1, y_1) \rightarrow A(x_1, y_1), \quad B(x_2, y_2) \rightarrow B(x_2, y_2),$$
$$C(x_1, y_1) \rightarrow C(x_1, y_1), \quad D(x_2, y_2) \rightarrow D(x_2, y_2),$$
$$f3_c : \quad f3_c(10(k-1) + j) = I_k,$$
$$j = 1, 2, \ldots, 10, \quad k = 1, 2, \ldots, 10.$$

For example,

$$
\begin{aligned}
f3(p(x_1, x_2, y_1, y_2)) &= p_2(f3_c(x_1), f3_c(y_1), f3_c(y_2)) \\
&\quad \wedge p_3(f3_c(x_2), f3_c(y_1), f3_c(y_2)), \\
f3(p(55, 5, 75, 65)) &= p_2(I_6, I_8, I_7) \wedge p_3(I_1, I_8, I_7).
\end{aligned}
$$

Further, consider a relaxation $P1^{RLX3} = (R1^{RLX3}, F1^{RLX3})$ that consists of the following rule set $R1^{RLX3}$:

$r16$: $\tilde{p}_2(x_1, y_1, y_2) :- A(x_1, y_1), B(x_2, y_2).$

$r17$: $p_3(x_2, y_1, y_2) :- A(x_1, y_1), B(x_2, y_2).$

$r18$: $p_2(x_1, z_1, z_2) :- p_{21}(x_1, y_2, z_1), B(y_2, z_2).$

$r19$: $p_{21}(x_1, y_2, z_1) :- p_2(x_1, y_1, y_2), A(y_1, z_1).$

$r20$: $p_3(x_2, z_1, z_2) :- p_{31}(x_2, y_2, z_1), B(y_2, z_2).$

$r21$: $p_{31}(x_2, y_2, z_1) :- p_3(x_2, y_1, y_2), A(y_1, z_1).$

$r22 \sim r27$: rules defined for s similarly to $r16, \ldots, r21$

$r28$: $q(x_1, x_2, y_1, y_2) :- p_2(x_1, y_1, y_2), p_3(x_2, y_1, y_2),$
$s_2(x_1, y_1, y_2), s_3(x_2, y_1, y_2).$

and the fact set $F1^{RLX3}$:

$$
\begin{aligned}
F1^{RLX3} &= \{E'_i(\mathbf{x}'_i) \mid E(\mathbf{x}) \in F1, \ E'_i(\mathbf{x}'_i) \in f3(E(\mathbf{x}))\} \\
&= \{A(I_i, I_j) \mid j = i + 1, 6 \le i < 10, i : \text{integer}\} \\
&\cup \{A(I_i, I_i) \mid 6 \le i \le 10, i : \text{integer}\} \\
&\cup \{B(I_i, I_j) \mid j = i + 1, 1 \le i < 10, i : \text{integer}\} \\
&\cup \{B(I_i, I_i) \mid 1 \le i \le 10, i : \text{integer}\} \\
&\cup \{C(I_i, I_j) \mid j = i + 1, 1 \le i < 10, i : \text{integer}\} \\
&\cup \{C(I_i, I_i) \mid 1 \le i \le 10, i : \text{integer}\} \\
&\cup \{D(I_i, I_j) \mid j = i + 1, 6 \le i < 10, i : \text{integer}\} \\
&\cup \{D(I_i, I_i) \mid 6 \le i \le 10, i : \text{integer}\}.
\end{aligned}
$$

Note that $P1^{RLX3}$ contains restriction on both coordinate 1 and coordinate 2 of $P1$, even though

$$
db\_deg(P1^{RLX3}) = 4 < db\_deg(P1) = 6. \qquad \square
$$

The notion of constructing a simplified database P' by the strategy of predicate decomposition is also found in [9], where it is discussed when P and P' become equivalent.

6 Comparison with the Magic Set Methods

The well known magic set methods construct the restriction to be added to the original database P by introducing the predicates that contain only the arguments carrying the binding information from the constant vector $\mathbf{a}$ in a query $q(\mathbf{a}, \mathbf{x})$ [2, 4, 10, 11, 12]. The set of such rules is called the magic rule set R^{magic}, and the resulting po. set is the magic set MS. The relaxation method using the argument elimination strategy, as exemplified in section 4, is similar to the magic set methods. In this section, the relaxation method using the argument elimination strategy is compared with the magic set methods. The original magic set method was introduced in [2]. The generalized magic set method [4] and the magic templates method [10] are generalizations of the original magic

set method that can treat a wider class of databases and can generate stronger restrictions. The Alexander method [11, 12] is also based on the same idea as the generalized magic set method.

First, we show that, for a general database $P = (R, F)$, the relaxation method can define a modified database P^{ADN_MDF} that generates the same po set $IMP(P^{ADN\_MDF})$ as $IMP(P^{magic})$ generated by the original magic set method. For a general database $P = (R, F)$, the original magic set method first constructs the adorned rule set R^{ADN} from R by replacing each predicate $p(x_1, \ldots, x_m)$ in rule $r \in R$ with predicate, e.g., $p^{bbf \cdots f}(x_1, \ldots, x_m)$, adorned with some sequence of length m of b's and f's, where b(f) means that the corresponding argument (does not) carries the binding information from the constant vector $\mathbf{a}$ in a query $q(\mathbf{a}, \mathbf{x})$. (Those rules not carrying the binding information are not included in R^{ADN}.) For example, a rule for query $q(a, x)$,

$$
r : q(x, y) :- A(x, x'), B(y, y'), q(y', x'),
$$

gives an adorned rule:

$$
r' : q^{bf}(x, y) :- A(x, x'), B(y, y'), q^{fb}(y', x').
$$

The original magic set method then constructs the rule set R' by replacing each rule r' of R^{ADN} by the rule r'' that is obtained from r' by eliminating all arguments with adornment f. For example, the above rule $r'(\in R^{ADN})$ becomes

$$
r'' : q^{bf}(x) :- A(x, x'), q^{fb}(x').
$$

of R'. (If a rule $r'(\in R^{ADN})$ has more than one intensional predicate in its body, r' is first decomposed into rules $r1', r2', \ldots$ so that each rj' may contain only one intensional predicate in its body, and then the arguments with f are eliminated from each rj'.) The magic rule set R^{magic} is then obtained from R' by interchanging the head predicate of each rule with the intensional predicate in its body. The magic set $MS(= IMP((R^{magic}, \{q^b(\mathbf{a})\} \cup F)))$ is then deduced in the bottom up manner. Finally, P^{magic} is the database $P^{ADN} = (R^{ADN}, F)$ argumented with the restriction that solution space is constrained to MS (it is achieved by adding the predicates of R^{magic} to the rules of R^{ADN} in certain manner). It is known that P^{magic} is equivalent to P with respect to query $q(\mathbf{a}, \mathbf{x})$ in the sense that both have the same answer set ANS.

Now it is not difficult to observe that the rules in the above R' can be regarded as those obtained from R^{ADN} by the argument elimination strategy of Section 4, and $P^{ADN\_RLX} = (R', F)$ is a relaxation of P^{ADN}. The relaxation method, however, does not construct R^{magic} but directly evaluate P^{ADN_RLX} in the bottom up manner. Then, to obtain the relevant set $REL(q^b(\mathbf{a}), P^{ADN\_RLX})$, it again evaluates P^{ADN_RLX} in the opposite direction (i.e., in the top down manner) from $q^b(\mathbf{a})$ under the added restriction of $IMP(P^{ADN\_RLX})$. Finally, P^{ADN_MDF} is obtained by adding restriction REL to P^{ADN} in the same way as adding MS to P^{ADN}. The following expression:

$$
IMP(P^{magic}) = IMP(P^{ADN\_MDF}),
$$

follows from the above definitions of MS and REL, even though

$$MS \supseteq REL(q^{\mathbf{b}}(\mathbf{a}), P^{ADN\_RLX}).$$

Although the complexity of computing MS and REL is generally difficult to compare, the computation time of the last phase, i.e., computation of $IMP(P^{magic})$ and $IMP(P^{ADN\_MDF})$, is much less than the computation of the original $IMP(P^{ADN})$.

To illustrate the above approach, we consider the original magic set method applied to Example 1. (In this example, adorned database $P^{ADN} = (R^{ADN}, F)$ is not introduced.) It is not difficult to show that the original magic set method generates the following set of po's:

$IMP(P1^{magic})$
$= IMP_p(P1^{magic}) \cup IMP_s(P1^{magic}) \cup IMP_q(P1^{magic})$
$= \{p(x_1, x_2, y_1, y_2) \mid$
$\quad x_1 \leq y_1, x_2 \leq y_2, (x_1, x_2), (y_1, y_2) \in AR5 + AR8\}$
$\cup \{s(x_1, x_2, y_1, y_2) \mid$
$\quad x_1 \leq y_1, x_2 \leq y_2, (x_1, x_2), (y_1, y_2) \in AR4 + AR5\}$
$\cup \{q(x_1, x_2, y_1, y_2) \mid$
$\quad x_1 \leq y_1, x_2 \leq y_2, (x_1, x_2), (y_1, y_2) \in AR5\},$

where $P1^{magic}$ is the database obtained by adding the magic set restriction $MS1$ to $P1$. If relaxation $P1^{RLX4}$ is defined by eliminating the first and second arguments from each predicate p, s, q in $P1$, the modified database $P1^{MDF4}$ from $P1^{RLX4}$ satisfies

$$IMP(P1^{MDF4}) = IMP(P1^{magic}).$$

Next, we give a case where the relaxation method is more efficient than the original magic set method. Comparing the above set $IMP(P1^{magic})$ with $IMP(P1^{MDF1\cdot2})$ of Example 3, where $IMP(P1^{MDF1\cdot2}) = PREL1 \cdot 2$, we see that $IMP(P1^{MDF1\cdot2})$ is a proper subset of $IMP(P1^{magic})$. This is because more flexible utilization of sideways information passing [4] is possible in the framework of the relaxation method. For example, relaxation $P1^{RLX1\cdot2}$ of Example 3 includes predicates $p1(x_1, y_1)$ and $p2(x_2, y_2)$ to restrict not only the third and fourth arguments of predicate $p(x1_1, x_2, y_1, y_2)$ in P but also its first and second arguments. The relaxation method can utilize sideways information passing through extensional and/or intensional predicates of P, while the original magic set method can utilize only sideways information passing through extensional predicates. Furthermore, in the body $p_1(x_1, y_1) \wedge s_1(x_1, y_1)$ of rule $r10$ in P^{RLX1}, the relaxation method makes use of sideways information passing not only in the direction from variable $x_1(y_1)$ of predicate $p(x_1, x_2, y_1, y_2)$ to variable $x_1(y_1)$ of predicate $s(x_1, x_2, y_1, y_2)$ but also in the opposite direction in rule $r5$ of $P1$. The relaxation method can utilize cyclic sideways information passing between predicate arguments, while the original magic set method can utilize only acyclic sideways information passing.

The generalization family of the original magic set method can also generate restriction sets that cannot be generated by the original magic set method. There are some such generalized restriction sets which cannot be realized by the relaxation method, and there are some restriction sets generated by the relaxation method which cannot be realized by the generalization family of the original magic set method.

7 Conclusions

The relaxation method has the following advantages:

1. It can utilize various restrictions flexibly and efficiently.

2. It is intuitively easy to understand how to define restrictions. Therefore, there is a chance to find useful relaxations that reflect the essence of a given database in natural way.

REFERENCES

[1] F.Bancilhon,: Naive Evaluation of Recursively Defined Relations, *On Knowledge Base Management Systems - Integrating Database and AI Systems, Blodie and Mylopoulous, Eds., Springer-Verlag, Berlin, pp.165-178, 1985.*

[2] F.Bancilhon, D.Maier, Y.Sagiv and J.Ullman,: Magic sets and other strange ways to implement logic programs, *Proc. 5th ACM SIGMOD-SIGACT Symp. on Principles of Database System(PODS), 1986*

[3] F.Bancilhon and R.Ramakrishnan, : An amateur's introduction to recursive query processing strategies, *Proc. ACM-SIGMOD Conf. on Management of Data(SIGMOD), Washington,D.C., 1986.*

[4] C.Beeri and R.Ramakrishnan,: On the power of magic, *Proc. 6th ACM SIGACT-SIGMOD-SIGART Symp. on Principles of Database Systems(PODS), San Diego, Calif., 1987.*

[5] A.V.Gelder,: A Message Passing Framework for Recursive Query Evaluation, *Proc. SIG-MOD. 1986*

[6] L.Henschen and S.Naqvi,: On Compiling Queries in Recursive First-Order Data Bases, *JACM 31, pp.47-85. 1984.*

[7] E.Lozinskii,: Evaluating Queries in Deductive Databases by Generating, *Proc. 11th Int. Joint Conf. on Artificial Intelligence. 1985.*

[8] D.Mckay and S.Shapiro,: Using Active Connection Graphs for Reasoning with Recursive Rules, *Proc. 7th Int. Joint Conf. on Artificial Intelligence. 1981*

[9] J.F.Naughton, R.Ramakrishnan, Y.Sagiv and J.D.Ullman,: Argument Reduction by Factoring, *Proc. VLDB. pp.173-182. 1989.*

[10] R.Ramakrishnan,: Magic templates: A spellbinding approach to logic programs, *Proc. 5th Int. Conf. and Symp. on Logic Programming(ICLP/SLP). Seattle. Wash.. 1988.*

[11] J.Rohmer, R.Lescoeur and J.M.Kerisit,: The Alexander method, a technique for the processing of recursive axioms in deductive database, *New Generation Computing 4(3), 1986.*

[12] H.Seki,: On the power of Alexander templates, *Proc. 8th ACM SIGACT-SIGMOD-SIGART Symp. on Principles of Database Systems(PODS), Philadelphia. Penn.. 1989.*

[13] J.Ullman,: Implementation of Logical Query Languages for Databases, *TOLD, 10(3), pp.289-321. 1985.*

[14] L.Vieille,: Recursive axioms in Deductive Databases. The Query/Subquery Approach, *Proc. First Int. Conf. on Expert Database Systems. Charleston. 1986*

Data-Structure Builder for VLSI/CAD Software

Doohun Eum
Artificial Intelligence Section
Electronics and Telecommunications Research Institute
Daejun, 305-606 South Korea

Toshimi Minoura
Computer Science Department
Oregon State University
Corvallis, OR 97331, USA

Abstract

Relational database systems have successfully solved many business data processing problems. The primary reason of this success is that the relational data model provides a simple, yet flexible view of data as tables. In studying VLSI/CAD data, we noticed that they are often represented in formats similar to relational tuples. Therefore, they can be stored easily in relational tables. However, it is generally agreed that conventional relational database systems are inefficient for VLSI/CAD applications, since such applications often access large amounts of data repetitively.

In order to solve this problem, we designed a data mapping subsystem that converts VLSI/CAD data stored in relational tables into internal data structures so that they can be efficiently manipulated in C. By using our data mapping language, we could reduce the amount of code required by the data-structure construction parts of some real VLSI/CAD tools to about 1/10 of that required by C implementation.

Key Words and Phrases: relational database, CAD database, mapping language, data conversion, VLSI/CAD.

1. Introduction

VLSI circuits are becoming more and more complex, and good CAD software tools are essential in their design. A database management system can play a central role in storing and integrating design data, enabling a quick development of new CAD tools.

Current VLSI/CAD systems generally use a file system provided by an operating system to store design data. Although these systems show good performance, they do not achieve a level of integration that accrues from a centralized database management system. For example, to use *rnl*, which is a timing logic simulator described in the VLSI design tools reference manual [1], one needs to create a network description *.net* file or a *.cif* file. The file is then translated by a program (*netlist* for a *.net* file or *mextra* for a *.cif* file) into an intermediate circuit description *.sim* file. Finally, the *presim* program is used to convert the *.sim* file into a binary file suitable for use by *rnl*. However, if the user finds it necessary to change, for example, the value of a capacitance while *rnl* is being executed, he must exit from *rnl*, modify the *.net* file, and repeat the entire process. As seen in this example, a VLSI/CAD system built on top of a file system does not provide a good environment for the integration of design tools.

During the past several years, many researchers observed that conventional database systems are not adequate for CAD applications [2, 3, 4, 5, 6]. Some of them investigated the data modelling issues and made various proposals [3, 4, 7, 8, 9, 10, 11]. Very few researchers [12, 13] have discussed the issues of supporting rapid development of new design tools. Despite a popular belief in *object-oriented* data models, we found that the formats of most VLSI/CAD data are relational in essence.

Relational database systems have proven very successful in business data processing applications. The primary reason of this success is that they provide a simple table-view of data and impose little preconceived structures. However, current relational database systems cannot efficiently support repetitive access of large amounts of data required by CAD application programs.

In this paper, we introduce a data mapping facility, which we call a *data-structure builder*. The data-structure builder is built on top of a relational database management system, and it converts VLSI design data stored in relational tables into data structures best suited for each VLSI/CAD program. This data conversion process follows a script written in a non-procedural mapping language. The script identifies the tuples in relational tables from which the records for such entities as transistors and nodes are constructed, and then it provides linkages among those records so that the data structure can be efficiently manipulated by a conventional programming language. Besides constructing the data structure, the script can also initialize certain fields by using declarative SQL statements. We show in this paper that the data-structure builder can significantly reduce the amount of programming required for data conversion in VLSI/CAD programs.

2. Overview

From the data stored in relations, the data-structure builder constructs the internal data structure to be used by a VLSI/CAD program. A VLSI/CAD program performs this data conversion at the beginning of its execution so that the data structure can be efficiently accessed during the rest of its execution. The data structure thus constructed consists of records and explicit pointers among them. For a circuit simulation program, we provide records for such entities as transistors and nodes, and there should be pointers from the record representing a node to the records representing the transistors connected to that node. For a layout program, records are provided for the rectangles that represent regions in various (e.g., diffusion, polysilicon, and metal) layers. Pointers link related records and provide traversal paths. We call the internal data structure thus constructed a

74

structured view.

The system architecture for the data-structure builder is shown in Fig. 2-1. The data-structure builder consists of a simple *input scanner* and a *mapping subsystem*.

The input scanner, which is based on a finite state automaton, reads the design data in such formats as the *.cif*, *.sim*, and *.ca* formats, and it then stores them in appropriate relational tables.

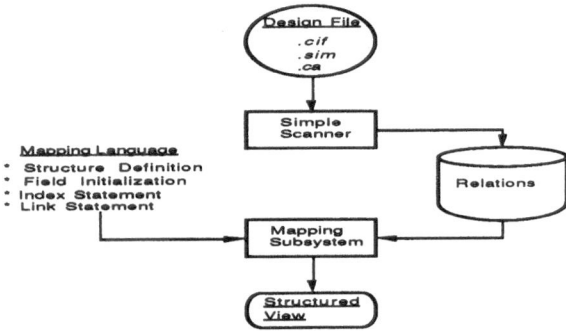

Fig. 2-1. Architecture of data-structure builder.

Under this architecture all the CAD tools share the centralized relational database. Nonetheless, each CAD tool can have a different internal data structure most suitable for its own use. The mapping subsystem performs the required data conversion between these two forms of data, following a script written in a non-procedural language.

The data conversion script consists of three parts: the record-definitions part, the index-statements part, and the link-statements part. The record-definitions part specifies the records to be constructed, and the link-statements part specifies pointers to be provided among them. The index-statements part specifies an indexing mechanism for fast access to the indexed records. Field initialization statements, which may involve SQL statements, are used within each record definition part.

Node

nname	npot
Vdd	3
Gnd	0
in	1
out	1

Cap

id	cnode	cval
c1	out	0.03

Trans

id	gate	source	drain	twidth	tlength	e
t1	in	out	Vdd	8.0	8.0	2
t2	in	out	Gnd	8.0	4.0	0

Fig. 2-3. Relational tables for CMOS inverter.

We now show this data conversion process by using a simple example involving only one CMOS inverter. Fig. 2-2(a) shows the circuit diagram of the CMOS inverter. The *.sim* file of the circuit is shown in Fig. 2-2(b). The relational tables to be constructed from the *.sim* file are shown in Fig. 2-3.

Information concerning nodes in the circuit is stored in table *Node*. Each node has a node name (*nname*) and a node potential (*npot*). The potential values of 0, 1, and 3 represent the logic values *low, intermediate or unknown*, and *high*, respectively.

Table *Cap* stores information on capacitances. Each capacitance has a capacitance number (*id*), the node name (*cnode*) of the node to which the capacitance is connected, and a capacitance value (*cval*) in pF. Only one node to which a capacitance is connected is shown because the other end of the capacitance is assumed to be grounded.

Table *Trans* stores information on transistors. Each transistor has a gate node, a source node, and a drain node representing its connection. Attributes *twidth* and *tlength* of table *Trans* represent in *lambda* the width and the length of the gate area of each transistor. Attribute *ttype* represents transistor type (2 for PMOS and 0 for NMOS). A resistor, which is a two-terminal device, is represented in table *Trans* with the value of attribute *gate* set to *Vdd* (a resistor in NMOS is sometimes formed in this way) and the resistance value stored in attribute *twidth*.

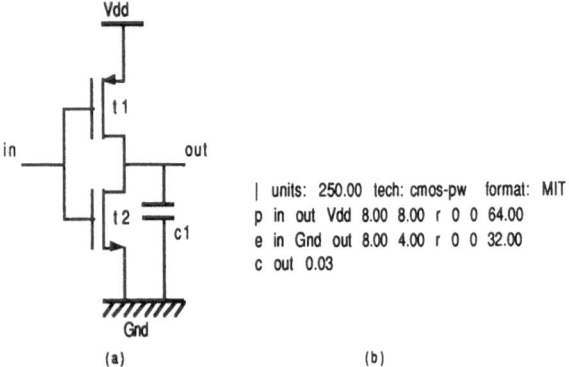

Fig. 2-2. A circuit diagram (a) and a *.sim* file (b) for a CMOS inverter.

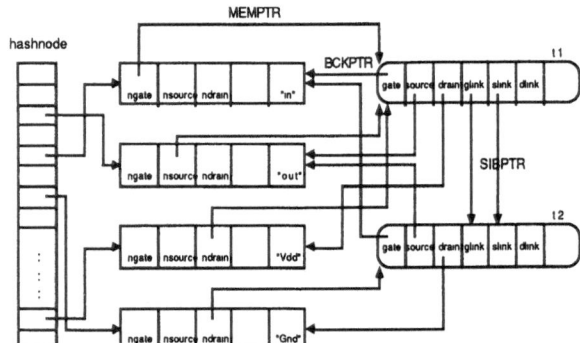

Fig. 2-4. Structured view for CMOS inverter.

Fig. 2-4 shows the data structure (structured view) used by program *presim* for the logic simulation of the circuit. The current *presim* program using a file system uses about 22 pages of programming statements to construct this structured view.

The script given in Fig. 2-5(a) creates the records for the nodes and transistors.

```
FOR EACH Node                    /* for each tuple in table Node */
PROVIDE STRUCT node {            /* node record definition */
  struct trans_*ngate;           /* list of gates connected to this node */
  struct trans *nsource;         /* list of sources connected to this node */
  struct trans *ndrain;          /* list of drains connected to this node */
  struct node *hnext;            /* link in hash bucket */
  float ncap = (CGA-CPA) * LAMBDA * LAMBDA *
          "Select SUM(twidth * tlength)
          From Trans Where Trans.gate = %Node.nname" +
          "Select SUM(cval)
          From Cap Where Cap.cnode = %Node.nname";
                                 /* capacitance of this node */
  float vlow = LOWTHRESH;        /* low logic threshold for this node */
  float vhigh = HIGHTHRESH;      /* high logic threshold for this node */
  short tplh;                    /* low to high transition time */
  short tphl;                    /* high to low transition time */
  long ndelay;                   /* delay of last transaction */
  long ctime;                    /* time of last transaction */
  short npot = Node.npot;        /* current potential of this node */
  short nflag;                   /* flag word */
  char *nname = Node.nname;      /* name of node */
  char statestatus;              /* whether node has been set to 0 or 1 */
}

FOR EACH Trans                   /* for each tuple in table Trans */
PROVIDE STRUCT trans {           /* trans record definition */
  struct node *gate;             /* node to which gate is connected */
  struct node *source;           /* node to which source is connected */
  struct node *drain;            /* node to which drain is connected */
  struct trans *glink;           /* gate link in node connection list */
  struct trans *slink;           /* source link in node connection list */
  struct trans *dlink;           /* drain link in node connection list */
  float twidth = Trans.twidth * LAMBDA;
  float tlength = Trans.tlength * LAMBDA;
  float tnumber;                 /* transistor number */
  int ttype = Trans.ttype;       /* type of transistor */
}

PROVIDE STRHASH INDEX hashnode
ON node(nname)                   /* provide string hash index on node name */
```

Fig. 2-5(a). Record definition.

The following convention is used in this paper. We use identically spelled names for a relational table and for the record type for the records created from the tuples in that table. However, the names of relational tables are started with an upper-case letter (e.g., Node and Trans) and those of the record types with a lower-case letter (e.g., node and trans). As we assume that upper-case letters and lower-case letters are different, these names are actually different. The first FOR EACH ... PROVIDE STRUCT ... statement (PROVIDE-STRUCT statement) creates a *node* record for each

tuple in table *Node*. The record definition is similar to the structure definition in C language. The body of PROVIDE-STRUCT statement is applied to each tuple in a relational table.

In the PROVIDE-STRUCT statement for the *node* records, the capacitance field *ncap* is initialized with the expression involving the SQL statements. The CMOS-PW technology is assumed, and CGA (capacitance of gate area) and CPA (capacitance of poly area) are electrical parameters. For each node, the gate areas (each of which can be computed as twidth * tlength) of the transistors to whose gates the node is connected are added and then multiplied by the capacitance per unit area (CGA - CPA). This result and other capacitances connected to the node are added to get the total capacitance for that node. The constant, LAMBDA, is the conversion factor from *lambda* to *microns*. Field *npot*, which represents the current potential of the node, is also initialized to the value of attribute *npot* in table *Node*.

The second PROVIDE-STRUCT statement creates a *trans* record for each tuple in table *Tran*. The PROVIDE ... INDEX ... statement (PROVIDE-INDEX statement) creates a hash table on the basis of string values for *nname* field of *node* records.

The scrip given in Fig. 2-5(b) creates pointers between the *node* records and the *trans* records.

```
LINK node AND trans (ONE-MANY)
WHERE Node.nname = Trans.gate
WITH    MEMPTR : ngate
        BCKPTR : gate
        SIBPTR : glink

LINK node AND trans (ONE-MANY)
WHERE Node.nname = Trans.source
WITH    MEMPTR : nsource
        BCKPTR : source
        SIBPTR : slink

LINK node AND trans (ONE-MANY)
WHERE Node.nname = Trans.drain
WITH    MEMPTR : ndrain
        BCKPTR : drain
        SIBPTR : dlink
```

Fig. 2-5(b). Link statements.

The first LINK ... AND ... statement (LINK statement) provides pointers for gate connections between the *node* records and the *trans* records. The gate connection relationship is one-many because there are usually many transistors whose gates are connected to a node. In the WHERE clause, the set of transistor records to be linked to a node record is specified as Node.nname = Trans.gate. For each node record, a pointer chain is created that begins at the field *ngate* of the *node* record as specified by MEMPTR (member pointer), and that threads through the fields *glinks* of the selected *trans* records as specified by SIBPTR (sibling pointer). Also, a back pointer (BCKPTR) is created in each *trans* record to its owner *node* record in the field *gate*.

The second and third LINK statements provide similar pointers for the source and drain connections, respectively, producing the structured view as shown in Fig. 2-4.

3. Mapping Language

In this section, we show a BNF grammar for the major constructs of the mapping language for writing data conversion scripts, and we then explain the semantics of those constructs. In describing the grammar, we use the following conventions.

1. [A] represents an optional (zero or one) occurrence of A.
2. A | B represents an occurrence of A or B.
3. Terminal symbols are represented in two ways: Reserved keywords appear as themselves in bold characters, and punctuation characters and operators are enclosed in single quotation marks.
4. Syntactic units appear in italic characters (e.g., *struct-statement*).

struct-statement

A *struct-statement*, which is used to construct records for the tuples in a relation, has the following syntax:

struct-statement ::= **FOR EACH** *table-name*
 PROVIDE STRUCT *record-type*

record-type ::= *record-type-name* '{' *field-list* '}'

field-list ::= *field-declaration* ';' [*field-list*]

field-declaration ::= *type-specifier declarator* ['=' *expression*]

The type of the records to be constructed from the tuples in a table *table-name* is specified by *record-type*. The syntax of *record-type* is similar to that of a structure type in C. Selected attributes of each tuple and additional properties are grouped into the fields specified by *field-list*, forming a record type *record-type-name*.

The declaration of a field may include an *expression* that initializes the field. An expression can be formed from the attributes of the current tuple and SQL statements enclosed in double quotation marks. A SQL statement may include parameters preceded by percent marks. This SQL statement is submitted to the database management system as a character string with the parameters replaced by the actual values for a particular record. Nested record type definitions are not allowed.

index-statement

An *index-statement*, which is used to construct an indexing mechanism for fast accesses to records, has the following syntax:

index-statement ::= **PROVIDE** *index-kind* **INDEX** *index-name*
 ON *record-type-name* '(' *field-name* ')'

index-kind ::= **STRHASH**
 | **BSTREE**
 | **NUMHASH**

The name of an index is specified by *index-name*. The field

to be indexed is specified as *record-type-name* '(' *field-name* ')', which indicates that the index should be provided for field *field-name* of record type *record-type-name*.

We support three kinds of indexes: STRHASH (string hashing), NUMHASH (number hashing), and BSTREE (binary search tree). Indexing mechanism STRHASH is based on hashing on character strings. Indexing mechanism NUMHASH is based on hashing on numbers. Indexing mechanism BSTREE uses a binary search tree on character strings.

simple-link-statement

A *simple-link-statement*, which is used to provide pointers between two record types, has the following syntax:

simple-link-statement ::= *link-clause*
 where-clause
 with-clause

link-clause ::= **LINK** *record-type-name*
 AND *record-type-name* '(' *mapping-kind* ')'

record-type-name ::= *type-name* [*alias*]

mapping-kind ::= **ONE-ONE**
 | **ONE-MANY**

where-clause ::= **WHERE** *predicate*

predicate ::= *condition* [**AND** *predicate*]

condition ::= *item-name* '=' *item-name*

item-name ::= *table-name* '.' *column-name*
 | *record-type-name* '.' *field-name*

with-clause ::= **WITH** **MEMPTR** ':' *field-name*
 [**SIBPTR** ':' *field-name*
 [**BCKPTR** ':' *field-name*]]

A *link-clause* is used to provide pointers from the records of the type *R1* indicated by the first *record-type-name* to the records of the type *R2* indicated by the second *record-type-name*. An *alias* is allowed to link records of the same record type. The kind of the relationship type between the two record types should be specified by *mapping-kind*, which may be *one-one* or *one-many*.

A *where-clause* specifies the condition for establishing the linkages. The *predicate* in *where-clause* specifies that record *r1* of type *R1* and record *r2* of type *R2* are to be linked if *predicate* is true when it is evaluated using the attribute values associated with *r1* and *r2*. An attribute used in the *predicate* may be a column name of a table (*table-name* '.' *column-name*) or a field name of a record-type (*record-type-name* '.' *field-name*).

A *with-clause* identifies the fields where pointers are stored. We use three kinds of pointers: MEMPTR (member pointer), SIBPTR (sibling pointer), and BCKPTR (back pointer). For one-many relationship, both MEMPTR and SIBPTR must be provided, and BCKPTR is optional. For one-one relationship, MEMPTR must be provided, and BCKPTR is optional.

We now describe the data structure used by the pointers for each kind of relationship.

1. (one-one) Suppose that we have one-one relationship from records of type *R1* to records of type *R2*. We provide, for each record *r1* of type *R1*, a direct pointer MEMPTR that points to the corresponding record *r2* of type *R2*. We then create a back pointer from *r2* to *r1* if the BCKPTR clause is provided. The resultant data structure is shown in Fig. 3-1(a).

2. (one-many) Suppose that we have one-many relationship from records of type *R1* to records of type *R2*. We create, beginning at the MEMPTR field of each record *r* of type *R1*, a pointer chain that threads through SIBPTR fields of all the type *R2* records *r1*, *r2*, ..., *rk* related to *r*. We then create back pointers from each of *r1*, *r2*, ..., *rk* to *r* if the BCKPTR clause is provided. The resultant data structure is shown in Fig. 3-1(b).

Although our language allows only one-one and one-many relationship types to be specified, we can create a many-many relationship type by using two one-many relationship types.

Suppose we want to establish a many-many relationship from records of type *R1* derived from relation *P1* to records of type *R2* derived from relation *P2*. As we handle this case by two one-many relationship types, we first create a view relation *P3* from which intermediate records of type *R3* can be derived. Assume that the many-many relationship must be established according to the values of fields *f1* of *P1* and *f2* of *P2*. Then the query to create *P3* is as follows:

> Select *k1*, *k2*
> From *P1*, *P2*
> Where *P1.f1* = *P2.f2*.

The *k1* and *k2* denote the keys of relations *P1* and *P2*, respectively. A new record type *R3* can now be constructed from *P3* with a *struct-statement*. We then provide two *simple-link-statement* statements to construct two one-many relationships: *R1* to *R3* and *R2* to *R3*. The resultant data structure, which is similar to the multilist representation of links in a network model [14], is shown in Fig. 3-2.

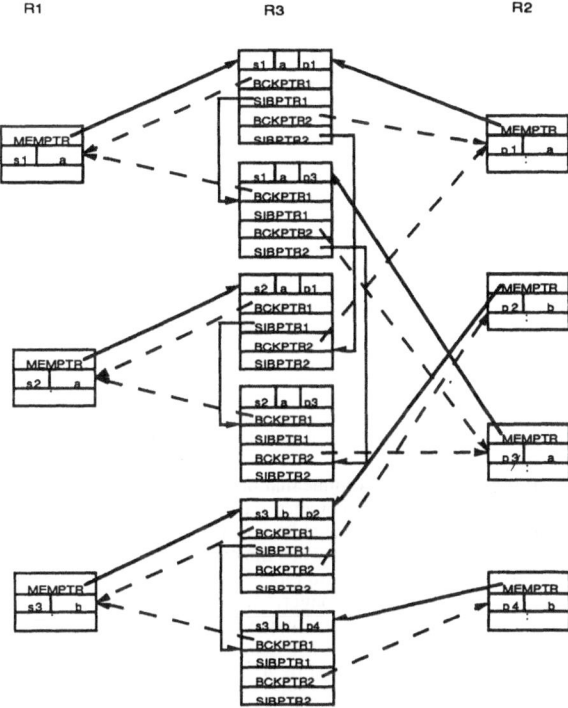

Fig. 3-2. Data structure for many-many relationship.

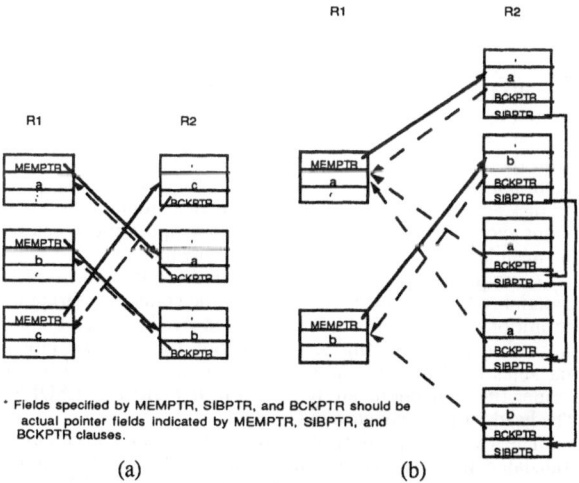

* Fields specified by MEMPTR, SIBPTR, and BCKPTR should be actual pointer fields indicated by MEMPTR, SIBPTR, and BCKPTR clauses.

(a)   (b)

Fig. 3-1. Data structure for one-one relationship (a) and one-many relationship (b).

4. Additional Examples

Three of the most widely used formats for the representation of VLSI design data are the *.sim*, *.ca*, and *.cif* formats, and many programs accept design data in these formats. The *.sim* format is used to describe MOS transistor networks and their parameters. The *.cif* format allows a hierarchical description of VLSI geometry in a concise manner. The *.ca* format allows us to describe VLSI circuit layouts at a higher level than the *.cif* format. Fig. 4-1 shows how design data in these formats are used by some VLSI design tools.

The data conversion process required by the timing and logic simulator *presim/rnl*, which uses the *.sim* format, was discussed in Section 2. In this section, we show the structured views for the interactive graphics display program *vic*, which uses the *.ca* format, and the CIF library routine *readcif*, which uses the *.cif* format. As an example, we use a layout of a 2-bit adder constructed with the layout assembly program *cfl* (Coordinate Free LAP) [1]. *Cfl* is a library of subroutines intended to facilitate the construction of VLSI circuit layouts. *Cfl* produces a set of *.ca* output files, each of which contains the layout of a cell in a hierarchical description of the circuit. *Caesar* can convert those *.ca* files into a single *.cif* file so that it can be used by programs like *readcif* that use the *.cif* format.

78

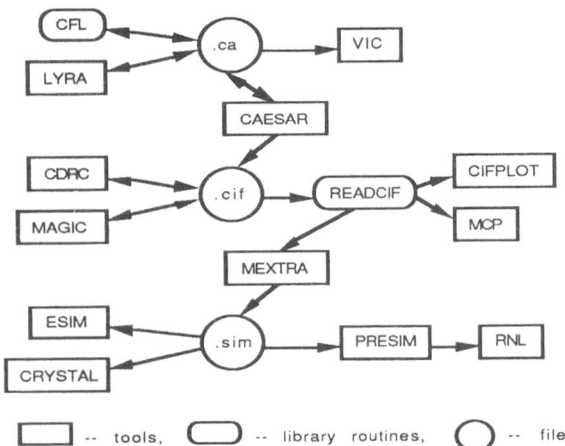

Fig. 4-1. VLSI design tools and data formats used by them.

Readcif is a library routine that builds a data structure from a *.cif* file in Manhattan geometry. Fig. 4-2 shows part of the structured view of the 2-bit adder constructed by *readcif*. There is one-many relationship between the *cell* record type and each of the *call*, *box*, and *label* record types. *Readcif* accepts Manhattan polygons and wires and converts them to boxes. The current *readcif* program uses about 21 pages of programming statements to build this structured view, which can be constructed by our mapping script in 2 pages. Fig. 4-3 shows the structured view of the 2-bit adder used by program *vic* for graphics display. The current *vic* program uses about 24 pages of programming statements to build this structured view, which can be constructed by our mapping script in 3 pages.

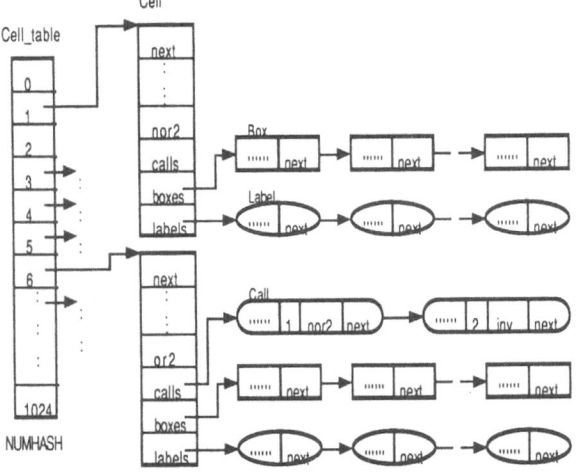

Fig. 4-2. Structured view of a 2-bit adder for *readcif*.

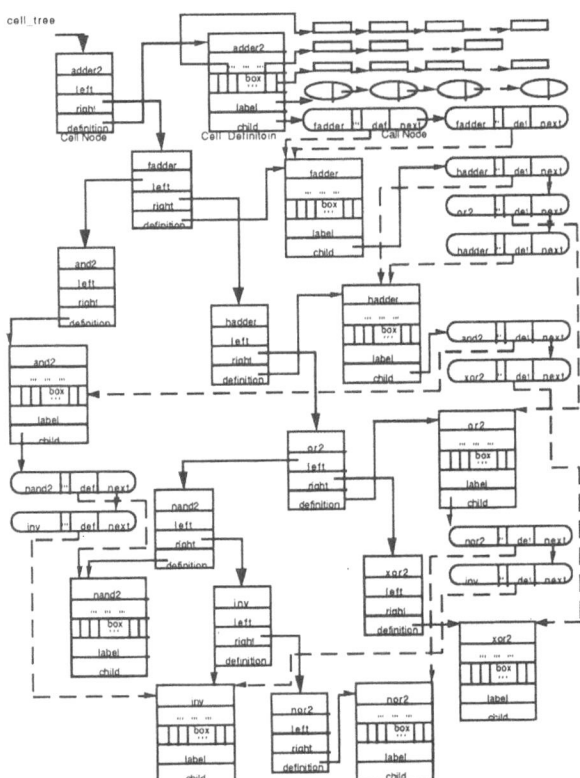

Fig. 4-3. Structured view of a 2-bit adder for *vic*.

5. Implementation Strategy

In this section, we discuss the implementation strategy of our data-structure builder. We translate the mapping script into INFORMIX_ESQL/C [15]. INFORMIX_ESQL/C is C with extentions for embedded SQL statements. At the beginning of a program execution, the generated code reads the design data from the database for initial C-structure building. Since the major portion of a typical VLSI/CAD program is CPU-intensive, the disk access overhead at the beginning of a program execution is not excessive. Fig. 5-1 shows how a script is processed by the mapping subsystem of our data-structure builder.

A script file is preprocessed into two files: the function file containing C-functions and the header file containing structure definitions. The global variables used by the functions are defined at the beginning of the function file, and the global variables used by the application program are defined in the header file. Functions are produced in INFORMIX_ESQL/C. The header file is produced in C.

The record type definition of each *struct-statement* is translated into a corresponding C-structure definition and a *record_build* function call that constructs the records of that type. The field initialization expression provided for a field definition is translated into a *field_init* function call. The *index-statement* is translated into an index structure definition and an *index* function call that constructs the indexing structure. The *link-statement* in a script is translated into a *link* function call. The *link* function links the constructed records by using the sort-join method based on the fields specified in the link statement.

The function *init()*, which calls each of the functions mentioned above, is provided at the beginning of an application program.

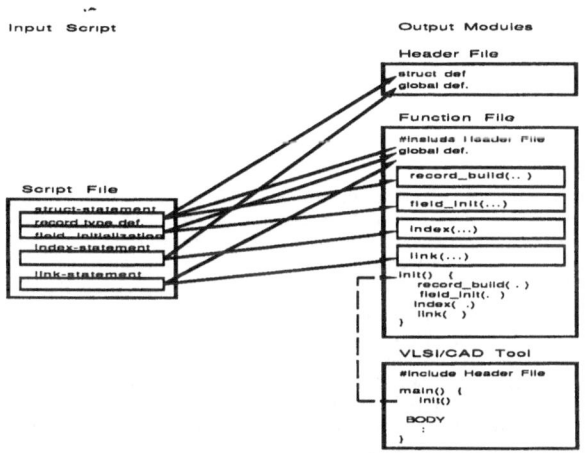

Fig. 5-1. Mapping subsystem strategy.

6. Conclusion

In integrating various VLSI/CAD tools, design data must be stored in a centralized database. We designed and implemented a data mapping subsystem that converts various VLSI/CAD design data stored in relational tables into an internal data structure that can be efficiently manipulated in C. This data conversion process follows a script written in a non-procedural mapping language. Besides constructing the data structure, the script can also initialize certain fields by using declarative SQL statements.

The results obtained from applying our technique to some real VLSI/CAD tools have shown that our approach, compared to C implementation, requires only about 1/10 of code for this data conversion in VLSI/CAD programs as shown in Fig. 6-1.

tool version	presim/rnl	vic	readcif
C implementation	22 pages	24 pages	21 pages
data-structure builder	2 pages	3 pages	2 pages

Fig. 6-1. Amount of code required for data conversion process.

References

[1]   *VLSI Design Tools Reference Manual*, TR #87-02-01, Department of Computer Science, Univ. of Washington, Seattle, Wash., 1987.

[2]   Eastman, C.M. System facilities for CAD databases. Proc. 17th ACM/IEEE Design Automation Conf., 1980, pp. 50-56.

[3]   Haskin, R.L., and Lorie, R.A. On extending the functions of a relational database system. Proc. 1982 ACM Conf. Management of Data, Jun. 1982, pp. 207-212.

[4]   Batory, D.S., and Kim, W. Modeling concepts for VLSI CAD objects. *ACM TODS 10*, 3 (Sep. 1985), 322-346.

[5]   Kim, W., Chou, H.T., and Banerjee, J. Operations and implementation of complex objects. *IEEE Trans. Software Eng., 14*, 7 (July 1988), 985-996.

[6]   Harkwick, M. Why rose is fast: Five optimizations in the design of an experimental database system for CAD/CAM applications. Proc. 1987 ACM Conf. on Management of Data, Dec. 1987, pp. 292-298.

[7]   Afsarmanesh, H., and Knapp, D. An extensible object-oriented approach to data bases for VLSI/CAD. Proc. VLDB, 1985, pp.13-24.

[8]   Ketabchi, M.A., and Berzins, V. Modeling and managing CAD databases. *IEEE Computer*, Feb. 1987, pp. 93-102.

[9]   Hollaar, L., Nelson, B., Carter, T. and Lorie, R.A. The structure and operation of a relational database system in a cell-oriented integrated circuit design system. Proc. 21st ACM/IEEE Design Automation Conference, 1984, pp. 117-125.

[10] Stonebraker M., and Rowe, L.A. The design of POSTGRES. Proc. 1986 ACM Conf. on Management of Data, May 1986, pp. 340-355.

[11] Wiederhold, G. Views, objects, and databases. *IEEE Computer,* Dec. 1986, pp. 37-44.

[12] Katz, R.H. A database approach for managing VLSI design data. Proc. 19th ACM/IEEE Design Automation Conference, 1982, pp. 274-282.

[13] Chen, G.W., and Parng, T.M. A database management system for a VLSI design system. Proc. 25th ACM/IEEE Design Automation Conference, 1988, pp. 257-262.

[14] Ullman, J.D. *Principles of Database Systems* MD: Computer Science Press, 1983.

[15] Informix, *Informix-ESQL/C*: Embedded SQL and tools for C, Programmer's Manual, Informix Software Inc., Menlo Park CA, July 1987.

KNOWLEDGE REPRESENTATION STRUCTURES FOR THE EVALUATION OF PRODUCTION PLANNING AND CONTROL SYSTEMS

I.P. Tatsiopoulos and N.D. Mekras

National Technical University of Athens, Dept. of Mechanical Engineering
Sector of Industrial Management & O.R., 28is Octovriou 42 - 106 82 Athens - Greece

Abstract

This paper describes the knowledge representation of an expert system which helps solving the problem of evaluating software packages for production planning and control (PPC). It addresses this problem on the basis of the package's functionalities and features as compared with the production management theory for the various types of production systems. A frame-based knowledge representation model is proposed whose objects and relations describe a typology of production systems and a generic PPC software package. A dual taxonomy of production systems is used based both on functional types and industrial sectors.

The above knowledge forms the knowledge base of an expert system that can help those who design Production Planning and Control (PPC) systems. This expert system gathers and processes the above knowledge and gives as inference results the functionalities and the module features of the software package that are required in the PPC system of a manufacturing firm.

1. Introduction

The large variety and complexity of the commercial software packages offered to support the production planning and control function (PPC) requires a difficult expert evaluation of these packages in order to cover the needs of a particular manufacturing firm. The selection problem derives from the lack of standardisation out of a large variety of different types of manufacturing settings and the lack of know-how on behalf of the potential buyers as to the real capabilities of PPC software packages.

It is suggested here that an industry-specific PPC software evaluation procedure should be developed, based on the knowledge domain of production management theory about the needs of the utilizing production system, according to its characteristic structures and processes (e.g. industrial sector, type of production flow, product variety, production volume, factory layout, etc). This knowledge domain should be incorporated in the form of a generic software package with specific modules and features for a series of production management methodologies (MRP II, JIT, OPT) and industrial sectors (e.g. clothing industry, foods industry, plastics industry, etc).

The reported efforts in the literature for the evaluation of PPC software packages have their origin in different science fields using different approaches. Two main research streams can be identified, the industrial engineering and the artificial intelligence approach.

An example of the industrial engineering approach is the well accepted PPC software evaluation system BAPSY of the TH Aachen [18], which uses multicriteria and value analysis methods to compare different PPC commercial software packages and select the most appropriate for a specific manufacturing firm. Another production management systems design methodology is the Burbidge connectance model [1].

Representatives of the expert systems technology are:

- The system TWAICE of Nixdorf Computer [11], which is mainly a software configuration system to support the Nixdorf COMET integrated manufacturing package and the needs of its customers for customization and consultation.
- The GRAI system [3] which is a computerisation of the GRAI method for the design of production management systems.
- The CASE-I system [19], [20], [21], for the selection and implementation of production management software and the controllability engineering method [4], which is suitable for diagnosis and design of PMS from a more business management-oriented point of view.

Section 2 of this paper addresses the problem of evaluating software packages on the basis of their pure technical characteristics, as compared with each other and with the production management theory for the various types of production systems. A knowledge-based model is proposed whose objects and relations are described through two main knowledge bases: (a) the type of production system and (b) the generic PPC software package.

Section 3 contains a description of the knowledge representation structures which are going to be used for the description of the production system and of the generic PPC software package.

All the above knowledge forms the knowledge base of an expert system that can be used as a decision support tool to help those who design Production Planning and Control systems and want to select the appropriate PPC software for their firm.

The programming language that has been used, is the Prolog language, by which the knowledge representation structures and the inferencing mechanisms have been developed [10], [22].

2. Expert evaluation problem

The proposed expert system aims at judging the degree of "suitability" of every particular software feature. There is a broad spectrum of "Suitability" of a particular software module from very good to very bad. For this reason there is often a temptation to use quantitative methods like value analysis which specify the decision on a numerical scale, say from 1 to 100. However, the factors talked about in this study are general guidelines, often not very well specified, and in a real-world situation they may not be known with great accuracy. This suggests that a 0 to 100 decision may be a meaningless break-down given the fuzziness of the factors that go into making the decision. A better choice would be to limit ourselves to a three-way decision: CRITICAL, DESIRED, NOT NECESSARY.

The requirements for all functional production types will be based on a taxonomy according to functional characteristics (e.g. product standardisation, factory layout, etc) and the knowledge domain of production management theory about the needs of a particular production type. The industry sector-specific requirements are imposed by technological processes, special problem areas, objectives, measures of performance and environmental factors, even aliases of production management terms which are characteristic of each separate industrial sector.

For the determination of PPC requirements of a specific manufacturing firm, a "normative" approach [2], using an "ideal" generic PPC software package will be followed at this stage for three main reasons:

a) It is quite common that the proposed information system embodied in the production management generic software package may be fundamentally different from existing patterns (in its content, form, complexity, etc.), so that anchoring on an existing information system or existing observations of information needs will not yield a complete and correct set of "ideal" requirements.
b) In practice there is not usually enough time at this stage to proceed to a detailed analysis of the company's current production information processing and organisational procedures.
c) A database of existing commercial packages would not be practical to maintain, given the continuous release of updated versions and new products in this field.

The systematization of expert knowledge needed at this stage includes:

- Description of the Generic PPC Software Package using hybrid techniques of Data Dictionaries [7] and object - oriented programming (OOP).
- Description of the firm's production structure and classification of the firm's production system according to a knowledge base of functional production types and industrial sectors.
- Comparison with the methods included in the generic software package, which are formulated in classes of technical features.
- Selection of technical features suitable to be included in the "ideal" software package.

There follows a more detailed discussion of the main knowledge bases.

3. Knowledge representation

The PPC software applications are well structured. Therefore, frames and semantic nets are the most appropriate representation formalisms. Nets represent objects and relations among objects, thus modelling the structure of systems in a natural way.

Relations

The relevant set of relation types for PPC applications is the following :
classification link : is_a_subclass_of
assembly link : is_part_of
instance connection : is_instance_of

Objects

Objects are the nodes of a network. Real-life objects or instances of object classes are described by their attributes (slots) and values of these attributes [6], [14]. Therefore, an object-attribute-value triplet is needed for class members.

The above data abstraction mechanisms are applied in PPC system modelling to construct the two main knowledge bases, the production systems taxonomy and the generic PPC software package.

3.1. Production systems taxonomy

Many authors have proposed classifications of production systems, e.g. Schmenner [12], Schmitt et al [13] and Kettner et al. [9]. Their common characteristic is that they adopt a narrow view of the physical production system dealing only with functional characteristics like shop layout and process flow classifications, which are not enough to determine production management requirements. Factors like management objectives and measures of performance, main problem areas, special technological processes and specific environmental constraints, which are connected to the various industrial sectors and subsectors, are equally important for the determination of PPC requirements.

The proposed taxonomy in this study is of a twofold nature, a functional taxonomy and a taxonomy based on industrial sectors. For the first one, a system of classes of parameters and values has its origin in the Schomburg [15] classification model which was built specifically for engineering firms. However, the taxonomy proposed here is extended and built in a software tool using object-oriented programming concepts. This software tool facilitates the connection of the functional taxonomy to the industrial sectors taxonomy and all relative classes, i.e. problem areas, objectives, environmental factors and aliases (terminology of production management across industrial sectors). An example of relations between objects in the knowledge base of the production system taxonomy is given in the schema of figure 1. Also in figure 2, an example is given that shows the object attributes and their values used in the same knowledge base.

As far as industrial sectors and subsectors are concerned, the formal classification of the National Greek Statistical Service has been used. For the classes of functional production characteristics, the classification model of Schomburg [15] enlarged by Tatsiopoulos [19] is used. This model uses 10 classes (attributes), each one of them having several values, as follows.

Values of Production system attributes

01 - Product Standardisation
- 01.1 - Non-catalogued customized products
- 01.2 - Catalogued products with non-standard, customized options
- 01.3 - Catalogued products with standard options

02 - Product structure
- 02.1 - single component products
- 02.2 - one-level bills of materials
- 02.3 - multi-level bills of materials
- 02.4 - scrap recycling
- 02.5 - yield variability

03 - Form of independent demand (products)
- 03.1 - Production of individual order
- 03.2 - Production of blanket order
- 03.3 - Non-seasonal production to stock
- 03.4 - Seasonal production to stock
- 03.5 - Assembly to order

04 - Form of depend demand (components, raw materials)
- 04.1 - Dependent on the customer order
- 04.2 - Mixed - mainly dependent on the customer order
- 04.3 - Mixed - mainly independent on the customer order
- 04.4 - Independent of the customer order

05 - Form of Purchasing
- 05.1 - Insignificant buy
- 05.2 - Mixed
- 05.3 - Mainly buy

06 - Process form (time dimension)
- 06.1 - One-off production with transfer
- 06.2 - One-off production without transfer
- 06.3 - Small Batch Production
- 06.4 - Serial intermittent batch production
- 06.5 - Batch flow process
- 06.6 - Lot Production (raw material dependent)

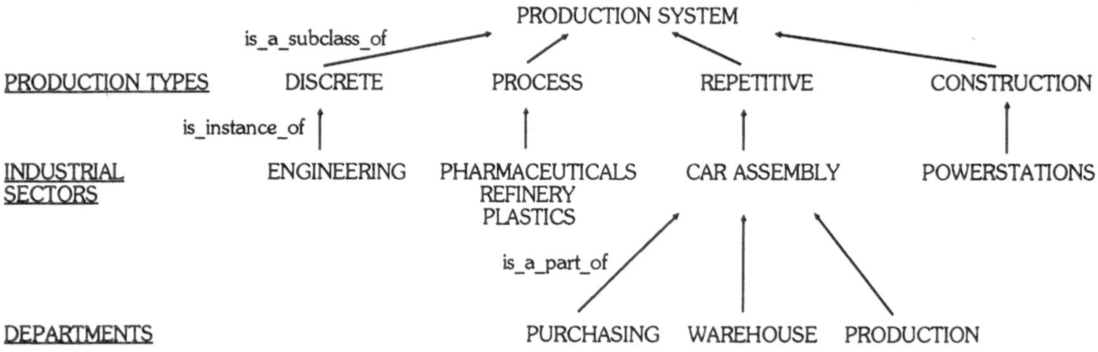

PRODUCTION SYSTEM
is_a_subclass_of
PRODUCTION TYPES
DISCRETE
PROCESS
REPETITIVE
CONSTRUCTION
is_instance_of
INDUSTRIAL SECTORS
ENGINEERING
PHARMACEUTICALS
REFINERY
PLASTICS
CAR ASSEMBLY
POWERSTATIONS
is_a_part_of
DEPARTMENTS
PURCHASING
WAREHOUSE
PRODUCTION

Figure 1. Object relations in the production systems taxonomy knowledgebase.

DISCRETE
is_a_subclass_of
PRODUCTION SYSTEM
REFINERIES
is_instance_of
PROCESS
PLASTICS
has_attribute (slot)
PRODUCT STANDARDISATION
PRODUCT STRUCTURE
has_value
ONE-LEVEL BILL OF MATERIALS

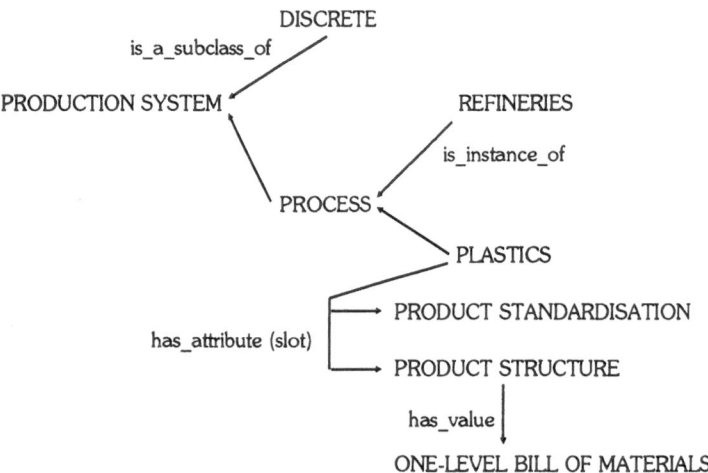

Figure 2. Objects, attributes and values in the production systems taxonomy knowledge base.

06.7 - Lot Production (process dependent)
06.8 - Production with by-products and co-products
06.9 - Worker-paced line flow
06.10- Machine-paced line flow
06.11- Continuous flow
07 - Shop-layout (space dimension)
    07.1 - Construction shop
    07.2 - Functional organization (job-shop)
    07.3 - Functional layout with sequenced operations
    07.4 - Cellular layout
    07.5 - Flexible manufacturing system
    07.6 - Product line layout
08 - Existence of Hybrid Production Structures
    08.1 - By product group (e.g. product group A in a
             job-shop, product group B in a flow shop)
    08.2 - By manufacturing function (fabrication in a
             job-shop, assembly in a flow shop)
    08.3 - By management issue (e.g. paced production of
             projects)
09 - Process complexity
    09.1 - One operation per component
    09.2 - A few operations per component
    09.3 - Many operations per component
    09.4 - Sequential routing
    09.5 - Networked form of routing
10 - Warehouse structure
    10.1 - Single warehouse
    10.2 - Multiple warehouses geographically adjacent
    10.3 - Multiple warehouses geographically distant
    10.4 - Receiving warehouse geographically distant
    10.5 - Assembly components from multiple warehouses
    10.6 - Quality status tracking important

3.2. Generic PPC software package

Most of the available commercial software modules for production management belong to large integrated packages of manufacturing management software which follow in general the MRP II design philosophy. Even though they use slightly different names for their modules, it can be said that the terminology and content of the most functions offered is fairly standard as in the following example:

PDM = Production Data Management
CRP = Capacity Requirements Planning
MPS = Master Production Scheduling
SFC = Shop Floor Control
MRP = Material Requirements Planning
PUR = Purchasing

An excellent review of most of the available packages and their characteristics both from large hardware manufacturers and independent software houses in Central Europe can be found in [5], while a review of american packages can be found in [16].

Object-oriented methodologies have been used, in order to describe and document a parameterised generic PPC software package which contains, in terms of parametric "modules" and "features", all the knowledge domain of PPC information technology and production management theory. In figure 3, an example is given which shows object relations in the generic PPC software package knowledge base. Also in figure 4, an example is given that shows object attributes and their values used in the same knowledge base.

Module attributes (features) - the example
of the MRP module

The concept of module feature is characteristic in the world of commercial software being of a rather verbal nature. Usually it represents some sort of functionality and how it is performed. Its analytical

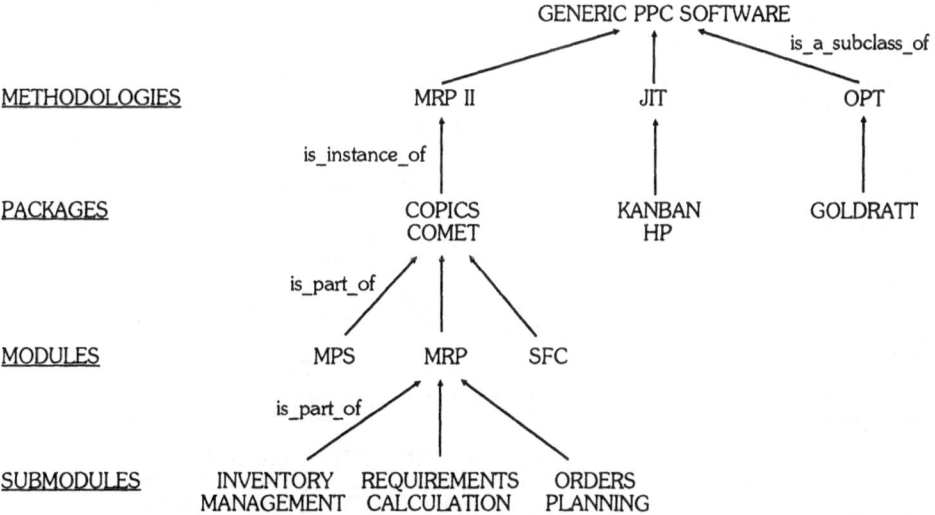

Figure 3. Object relations in the Generic PPC software package knowledge base.

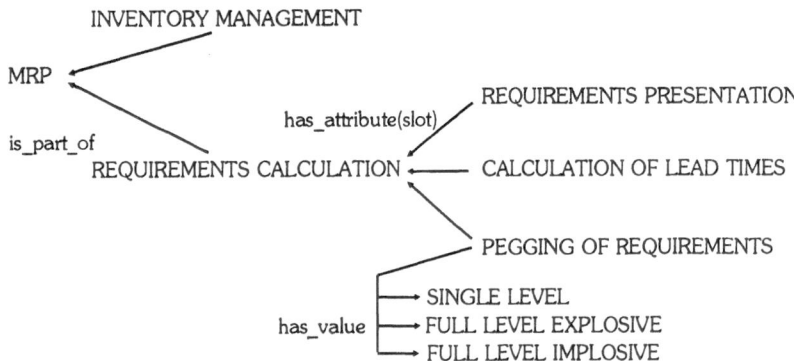

INVENTORY MANAGEMENT

MRP

is_part_of

REQUIREMENTS CALCULATION

has_attribute(slot)

REQUIREMENTS PRESENTATION

CALCULATION OF LEAD TIMES

PEGGING OF REQUIREMENTS

has_value

SINGLE LEVEL
FULL LEVEL EXPLOSIVE
FULL LEVEL IMPLOSIVE

Figure 4. Objects, attributes and values in the Generic PPC software knowledge base.

description and documentation would require extensive data flow diagrams and flowcharts which is not practical for our purposes.

Therefore, the "feature" is described by a short phrase and a set of values corresponding to alternative methods of performing its function. In this study an attempt is undertaken to codify, standardise and store in a knowledge base all known PPC software features and their alternative values. In terms of the requirements of the production management system, first we are interested in the very existence of a specific feature and then in its value, i.e. the method used. Next is given an example of codified features for the MRP module.

01. MRP operation (BATCH, INTERACTIVE, BOTH)
02. Form of MRP explosion (REGENERATIVE, NET-CHANGE, BOTH)
03. Requirements presentation (BY PERIOD, BY DATE, BY JOB)
04. Calculation of lead times (BY ITEM, BY PARENT-SON RELATION, BY BATCH PROCESS TIME) ·
05. Form of orders issued (WORK ORDER, FLOW ORDER, BOTH)
06. Pegging of Requirements (SINGLE LEVEL, FULL LEVEL EXPLOSIVE, FULL LEVEL IMPLOSIVE, MRP BY CONTRACT)
07. Selection of depth of requirements explosion (YES,NO)
08. Simulation net-change capabilities (YES,NO)
09. Lot sizing techniques (USER INPUT, PROGRAMMED RULES OF THUMB, PROGRAMMED OPTIMIZING)
10. Phantom items (YES,NO)
11. Blanket material acquisitions for large orders (YES,NO)
12. Allocations (BY PRODUCTION ORDER, BY CONTRACT, TIME-PHASED, AUTOMATIC MULTI LEVEL, ALL, NO)
13. Allocation of safety stocks (USER INPUT, PROGR.RULES OF THUMB, MATHEMATICAL)
14. Backflushing (YES,NO)
15. Government contract support, i.e. purchase and production orders by contract (YES,NO)
16. Lot tracking (YES,NO)
17. Variable Yield (YES,NO)
18. Configuration control (YES,NO)
19. Support of co-product and by-product creation (YES,NO)

After the creation of the two knowledge bases, a knowledge process mechanism, which is the inference engine of the expert system [6], [8], [22], processes the knowledge bases and gives as inference results the functionalities and the module features of PPC software that can be used by the types of the production systems.

A PPC software structure derived from a certain production system type can be covered by the existence of a particular software module and/or the value of a module feature. For example the module MRP has as a submodule, the 'know about the consequences of a late purchase order on the progress of a customer order' which is required by the production system attribute value, 'demand dependent on the customer order' and is covered by the software module feature MRP-06 (full level implosive).

4. Examples of representing knowledge using Prolog

In this section we shall give examples, that show how objects, relations and attributes that have been described in section 3, are implemented in Prolog language [10], [22], creating by this way the knowledge bases of the production systems taxonomy and of the generic PPC software.

If we consider the example of figure 1, that shows object relations in the production systems taxonomy, we can use the following Prolog code to make the representation of this knowledge.

```
is_a_subclass_of( "DISCRETE" , "PRODUCTION SYSTEM" ).
is_a_subclass_of( "PROCESS" , "PRODUCTION SYSTEM" ).
is_a_subclass_of( "REPETITIVE" , "PRODUCTION SYSTEM" ).
is_a_subclass_of( "DISCRETE" , "PRODUCTION SYSTEM" ).

is_instance_of( "ENGINEERING" , "DISCRETE" ).
is_instance_of( "PHARMACEUTICALS" , "PROCESS" ).
is_instance_of( "REFINERY" , "PROCESS" ).
is_instance_of( "PLASTICS" , "PROCESS" ).
is_instance_of( "CAR ASSEMBLY" , "REPETITIVE" ).
is_instance_of( "POWERSTATIONS" , "CONSTRUCTION" ).

is_a_part_of( "PURCHASING" , "CAR ASSEMBLY" ).
is_a_part_of( "WAREHOUSE" , "CAR ASSEMBLY" ).
is_a_part_of( "PRODUCTION" , "CAR ASSEMBLY" ).
```

Also the knowledge, that is described in figure 2 and shows attributes and values of objects, can be implemented in Prolog as follows.

```
is_a_subclass_of( "DISCRETE" , "PRODUCTION SYSTEM" ).
is_a_subclass_of( "PROCESS" , "PRODUCTION SYSTEM" ).

is_instance_of(" REFINERY" , "PROCESS" ).
is_instance_of(" PLASTICS" , "PROCESS" ).

has_attribute( "PLASTICS" , "PRODUCT STANDARDISATION" ).
has_attribute( "PLASTICS" , "PRODUCT STRUCTURE" ).

has_value( "PRODUCT STRUCTURE" , "ONE LEVEL BILL OF
                                   MATERIALS" ).
```

In case we want to represent general information describing objects, their relations and their attributes we can use rules like in the following example :

```
has_attribute( X, "PRODUCT STANDARDISATION" ) :-
                is_instance_of( X, "PROCESS" ).
```

The previous rule declares that the attribute "PRODUCT STANDARDISATION" is found in all the instances of the "PROCESS" production type.

5. Conclusions

The proposed expert system for the PPC software packages' technical evaluation, can be applied during projects in manufacturing firms seeking to buy/develop and implement integrated production management software. In all these cases the main problem is to define suitable software requirements in the form of desired module attributes (features) as compared with the characteristics of a certain type of manufacturing setting. Such evaluation and selection decisions are far too complex to be faced either by quantitative multi-criteria methods or by simple guessing. The systematic description of knowledge that AI technology requires is a valuable distillation of a vast amount of experience [17] which only can lead to a rational decision. This gave the initiative for starting an AI project in order to codify the required knowledge across the above described guidelines in an actual expert system. A prototype system is now implemented using the Prolog language. It is expected that the above expert system will be of great help to both potential buyers of production management software facing the selection and implementation problem and to software houses facing the software configuration problem for each particular customer. It also is expected to be a significant educational tool that will help those trying to implement advanced production management methods and software in uninformed production environments.

References

[1] Burbidge,J.L., A Production System Variable Connectance Model,Cranfield Institute of Technology, Cranfield, 1984.

[2] Davis, G.B. and Olson, M.H., Management Information Systems, McGraw Hill,1985.

[3] Doumeingts, G. et al, Knowledge-based System for the Design of Production Management Systems, in: J. Browne (Ed), Knowledge Based production Management Systems, Elsevier (North-Holland), IFIP, 1989.

[4] Eloranta, E et al, 'Model-based reasoning in manufacturing systems design' in Browne, J (ed), Knowledge Based Production Management Systems, Elsevier/North - Holland, Amsterdam, Netherlands, 1989.

[5] Foerster, H., Hoff, H. and Missen, E., Marktspiegel PPS-Systems auf dem Pruefstand, Verlag, Koeln, Germany, 1986.

[6] Frost, R, A, Introduction to Knowledge Base Systems,William Collins & Sons, London, UK, 1986.

[7] Gane,C. and Sarson,T., Structured Systems Analysis, Prentice-Hall, 1979.

[8] Keller, R., Expert System Technology, Prentice-Hall, Englewood Cliffs, NJ, USA, 1987.

[9] Kettner,H., J.Schmidt and H.R.Greim, Leitfaden der systematischen Fabrikplanung, Carl Hanser Verlag, Munchen, 1984.

[10] Malpas, J., Prolog: A relational language and its applications, Prentice-Hall, Englewood Cliffs, NJ, USA, 1987.

[11] Mensel,G.und J.Michel, Moeglichkeiten des Einsatzes wissenbasierter Systeme in der Fertigung, ZwF 80 11, pp. 495-500, 1985.

[12] Schmenner,R.G., Production/Operations Management, SRA Chicago, 1981.

[13] Schmitt,T.G., T.Klastorin and A.Shtub, Production classification system: concepts, models and strategies, pp.563-578, Int.J.Prod.Res., 1985.

[14] Schneider, H.-J. and Karagiannis, D., 'Intelligent Knowledge Bases of CAD Environments : The Hybrid System KANON', NATO ASI Series, Vol. F49, pp 161- 196, Springer-Verlag, Berlin, 1988.

[15] Schomburg, E., Entwicklung eines Betriebstypologischen Instrumentariums zur Systematischen Ermittlung der Anforderungen an EDV - Gestuetzte Productionsplanungs - und - Steuerungssysteme im Maschinenbau, Dissertation, TH Aachen, Germany, 1980.

[16] Sepehri, M., 'Newest manufacturing software packages offer modules which meet specialized needs', Ind. Eng. Vol 28, pp 32-43, 1985.

[17] Sheil,B., Thinking about artificial intelligence, Harvard Business Review, July-August, 1987 .

[18] Speith,G. and U.Brief, BAPSY - ein Instrumentarium zur Beurteilung und Auswahl von Produktionsplanung - und steuerungs - Systemen, FIR mitteilungen , TH Aachen, Nr. 43 (Juni), 1982.

[19] Tatsiopoulos, I., P., 'A systematization of knowledge for the selection and implementation of materials management software' in Browne, J (ed), Knowledge Based Production Management Systems, Elsevier / North - Holland, Amsterdam, Netherlands, 1989.

[20] Tatsiopoulos, I.P., 'Requirements analysis of production management software systems', in Computer Integrated Manufacturing Systems, Vol 3, pp 207-215, Butterworth - Heineman Ltd, 1990.

[21] Tatsiopoulos, I.P. and Pappas I.A., 'Design of fault-tolerant production management systems for small and medium sized firms,in Eloranta, E (ed), Advances in production management systems, Elsevier / North - Holland, Amsterdam, Netherlands, 1990.

[22] Weiskamp, K. and Hengl, T., Artificial Intelligence Programming with Turbo Prolog, John Wiley & Sons, New York, USA, 1988.

An Information System for the Mining Industry

A. Baumewerd-Ahlmann* A. B. Cremers[+] G. Krüger* J. Leonhardt[#] L. Plümer[+] R. Waschkowski*

+ Universität Bonn Institut für Informatik III Römerstr. 164; D - 4300 Bonn 1	* Universität Dortmund Lehrstuhl Informatik VI P.O.Box 500 500, D-4600 Dortmund 50	# DMT - Ges. für Forschung und Prüfung mbH Inst.f. Lagerstätte und Vermessung Westhoffstr. 17; D - 4630 Bochum 1

ABSTRACT[1]

This paper describes the conception and prototypic implementation of a comprehensive planning information system for the mining industry. Such a system has to cope with two classes of requirements resulting from the application domain characteristics: Because mine planning is a task of high responsibility - preventing all conceivable risks for miners and environmental factors -, the system must provide complete, correct, consistent and actual information. On the other hand, the spatio-temporal dimension of mining objects and their complex relations demand advanced modelling techniques and mechanisms for manipulation and integrity constraint checking.

The progress in database theory research - especially object-oriented approaches - allows for the first time to profit from database technology in such a complex domain. A first prototypic implementation including essential mining objects and several applications (topological scanning) was tested with existing productional data from one mine. It yielded promising results with respect to performance and fruitful experiences for the future overall system development.

1 Introduction

Planning of mining activities comprises comprehensive analyses of the geological situation and the characteristics of coal deposits as well as design and control of workings. Due to the particular risks of underground workings, risk assessment, and precautions make up an essential and highly responsible part of the mining engineer's and especially the markscheider's[2] profession. He has to guarantee

- the security of miners
- the safe and undisturbed operation of a mine
- the protection against negative effects on the environment.

The actual project aims at the development of a relational database supporting the complex tasks of markscheiderology and mine planning in general. These tasks are shortly described in the following chapter as an introduction to the characteristics of the application domain. Chapter 3 summarizes the previous computer support, the existing data basis, and application programs. The manifold requirements, a planning information system for the mining industry has to satisfy, are the subject of the fourth chapter, before in the next chapter the object-oriented conceptual model is presented. Finally chapters 6 and 7 outline the current state of the prototypic implementation and its utilization for applications based on geometric computations and knowledge based techniques.

2 Information management in the mining industry

The main tasks of markscheiders are to provide sufficient knowledge about the location and quality of a deposit, to determine, whether it can be exploited technically resp. economically, and finally to plan the working and provide the basis for safe and undisturbed operation of a mine (cf. [1]):

- evaluation of a deposit
- planning and designing a mine
- surveys of seams and all structures underground
- representation of all quality parameters, geological, and geometric information about the deposit and the mine in maps and manuals
- calculation of expected coal output
- recognition and prevention of risks
- assessing dislocations and damages caused by the working

In order to evaluate a deposit a lot of geometric, physical, geological and chemical information is needed. The quality of a deposit can be described by the following parameters, which are determined by samples from special drillings as well as from regular production, analyzed in laboratories:

- quantity and thickness of coal seams
- ratio of seams and barren-ground
- rate of sulphur, cinders, and volatile components of the coal

In addition to the material properties the geological constellation of the deposit has to be inspected: depth, thickness and dip of the different layers of coal and geological anomalies like tectonic faults or zones of folding. The results of surveys, geological and stratigraphic findings are described in large-scale maps.

The next step is planning the layout of a mine, designing shafts, runways and so on. Besides the coordinates and the axis of a runway resp. shaft the profile and inclination must be represented requiring not only 2-dimensional maps, but also 3-

---

1   This work was sponsored by the European Coal and Steel Community, and in parts by the North-Rhine-Westfalian Ministry for Economy, Small Industries and Technology in its program for mining-technology.

2   "Markscheiderology" (in German: "Markscheidewesen") is one of the disciplines of the mining art and comprises any work involved in prospecting, investigation, and assessment of mineral resources, deposit projection, planning surveys, and mapping of underground workings and surface installations.
   The German "Markscheider" is an engineer with full academic qualification and with special knowledge in the field of markscheiderology. His works on the subject of mining surveying are of public credibility, and the mine plans signed by him are officially recognized as if certified by a notary.

dimensional views. The drawings describe the complete geometry of the mine, shafts, runways, working fields, boreholes etc. Every artificial hollow space underground must exactly be recorded, (independent of its state: planned, in use, abandoned, refilled), since it is relevant for the stability resp. dislocations of the underground works and the ground surface. The risks of such movements demand constant monitoring and controlling of the mine geometry. Conducting surveys, preparing maps and plans for various purposes and managing maps in general is a particular subdomain of markscheiderology. All information about a deposit or a mine are subject to laws and rules, and the instructions about archiving the data in maps, plans, manuals, and other documents have to be obeyed strictly [2]. These official regulations, security of the miners, the safe and undisturbed operation of the mine and environmental protection require a very high degree of accuracy, correctness, completeness, consistency, and availability of information.

Protection against risks like rock bursts, inbursts of water, explosions, fire, and toxic gases underground plays a crucial role in the mining industry. Moreover the effects of the working itself (horizontal and vertical dislocations) on the mine and the environment have to be calculated to avoid or minimize damages. Completeness plays a crucial role in the information system, since data, which are not available (in the database), cannot be provided for risk assessment and precautions. Incomplete data might be a source of additional risks.

3   Previous support by computer aided methods

Having summarized the complex tasks of mining engineers and especially of the markscheiders let us now turn to the previous computer support for these tasks for fixing clearly the starting-point of the information system described in this article. In order to support and improve the manual processing of deposit data since the 1970's computer programs were developed for several specific mining applications [3]. (Most of numerical calculations and CAD-programs are implemented in FORTRAN. Particularly in the field of risk protection only some prototypes are existing, which are currently tested.)
- calculating the coal reserves of a mine
- interactive graphical construction of deposits based on geological findings (cf. DIGMAP, [4])
- CAD-oriented programs for drawings and graphical outputs (e.g.: TEKTODRAFT, [5], AutoCAD, [6])
- estimating the rock pressure in a planned working area using different implemented models (e.g.:GESANG [7])
- calculating horizontal and vertical dislocation, especially subsidence damage
- topological scanning and risk protection using knowledge based systems
- identification of geological strata from drilling samples (cf. chapter 6 for more details)

The programs are based on various files about deposits, mines, workings, drilling samples, geological findings, and lab data concerning quality parameters of seams having different formats and structuring concepts. The basic data, for instance, for calculation of coal reserves and for constructing the drawing of a mine are similar, but incompatible. Up to now no database management systems are used to provide a coordinated information management.

Two different types of workstations for markscheiders are in use at several sites. They have been designed for different tasks and are not fully compatible, so that only a subset of all existing programs can run on each of them.
In the information system development it is necessary to face specific requirements resulting from the characteristics of markscheiderology, which claim solutions beyond conventional relational database techniques. These requirements will be discussed in the following chapter.

4   Requirements for an information system

It was demonstrated in the previous chapter, that the actual situation in mining information management practise is characterized by a great variety of heterogeneous, special purpose application programs, each using its own data and a tailored data structuring. The resulting redundancy and semantic overlapping of data stored in various file structures not only cause problems regarding data availability and compatibility, but also the risk of undetected inconsistencies between them. In order to improve the technical support for markscheiders, it seems indispensable to develop an integrated information system coordinating all relevant data management tasks for the different planning and assessment activities (cf. [8], [9], [3]). In recent years, the need for adequate database support became more and more obvious, but the shortcomings of conventional commercially available systems and technology turned out to be a decisive impediment regarding these applications. This chapter outlines the specific requirements, which such an information system must satisfy, and describes arising problems.

Mine planning is a task of high responsibility, because it has to avoid any potential risk (of explosion, dislocation, etc.) for miners and environmental quality. Therefore it involves complex analyses and preventive measures against possible hazards for the future working. As well as the economic questions of estimating the quantity, quality and position of coal-deposits, these risk assessment tasks - as described above - have to be founded on actual, correct, reliable and complete information about the planning area.
An information system integrating all relevant data existing in the organization helps the planner to check the **completeness** of the available information with respect to a special problem and to decide, if further data collection (e.g. by drilling) will be necessary. The information from different sources - like lab-data resulting from drilling or coordinates from mine surveying - can more easily be compared and proved for **correctness**, already during the data input stage. Thus, this proceeding assures the highest possible degree of **reliability** in the basic data for the various design, prediction and analysis tasks. Let us illustrate the importance of completeness and reliability by a simple example: If a runway is planned to be advanced at point x, the miner underground has no possibility to recognize, that behind the face (very near point x) there is a water zone with a height of 200 meters. If the database would not include this information, advancing at point x would immediately cause the bursting of the water at a pressure of 20 atm. The example shows, that there are problems of risk assessment, which cannot be solved locally, but need comprehensive global information. As every database application is based on the Closed World Assumption (i.e.: everything that is not found in the database really does not exist), the claim for completeness has to be taken into account carefully.

By making available for each user / each application all the relevant data of the mine, it is guaranteed that they always access the most **actual** state. There should be no time lag between data input by one department and data access by another one. This fact improves data reliability, too.

Using current database techniques, one can avoid data redundancy, and the remaining overall **consistency** checking is automatically performed by the system, whereas the administrator only has to define the specific constraints. The formulation of semantic integrity constraints, however, in terms of relational database techniques gets rather difficult. So - in order to satisfy the completeness and correctness requirements - it should be assured for example, that there is no gap, i.e. no lacking point, in the geometric description of a line object.

In order to allow a more flexible way of interaction between the different application programs, a possibility is needed to create a **well defined standardized interface** between them, instead of individual ad hoc solutions. Here, the use of a unified database offers - based on standard data manipulation features - well founded semantics on which the applications may set up. An important requirement is, that data created or collected by geological / geometric tools like DIGMAP (c.f. [4]) should be usable by actual and future applications - regardless of the programming language used. Similarly, the results of - even complex - queries and evaluations should be usable by graphic presentation programs (e.g. TEKTODRAFT [5], AutoCAD [6]). The graphic presentation of planning conditions and results is crucial in an application domain like mine planning.

The technical barrier, which is caused by the lack of interfaces between a traditional language like FORTRAN and modern tools for knowledge based systems, may be overcome in this way, because interfaces to standard data manipulation languages (esp. SQL as quasi standard) are rather common. To give an example: the expert system for risk detection in mine planning, which is currently developed using a high level KBS tool (c.f. [10]), can access the needed DIGMAP data via the database correctly.

A planning information system for mining tasks has to be open for further modifications and additions, i.e. it has to be designed and implemented in a **modular**, adaptable and flexible way. New databases should be addable as well as new integrity constraints, new application views or higher level application programs. As the different application programs for planning and prediction are used at different sites, a **decentralized access** to the information system has to be granted. That is, in the operational state, the system must run in a heterogeneous (network) environment.

Whereas most of the above listed requirements can be satisfied using the conventional mechanisms of a relational database system, the conceptual modelling needs extended instruments because of the following characteristics of mining objects and their relationships. They have to be appropriately specified and - only in a second phase - mapped to relational concepts for implementation (cf. chapter 5).

Objects dealt with in mine planning typically are related to a **spatial location**, i.e. they can approximately be described by geometric objects - points, lines, surfaces, volumes (e.g. measuring points, boreholes, electric lines, hollow spaces, see above chapter 2). Furthermore, objects **above ground** and

objects **below ground** have to be distinguished. As the discussion concerning geographic (and CAD) databases has shown, mapping geometric information to database relations and queries is a non-trivial problem. Even for geometric search problems in mine planning, relational query facilities often are not sufficient. Consider for example topological scanning (cf. chapter 6 for details): if there were a neighborhood relation between points, the transitive closure of this relation must be constructed for getting all relevant points. Several approaches based either on extended relational models or on new, object oriented techniques are currently under development (cf. for example: [11], [12], [13], [14], [15]). They especially offer the possibility to use - or even to define one's own - geometric data types and support queries including geometric operations like "inside" or "intersects".

Some classes of mining objects (below ground) are further characterized by **temporal aspects**. The "stratigraphic height" describes the time of formation for all geological objects, denoted in meters above a basic stratum. Whereas this temporal attribute has a static character (it is used for qualitative analyses), the second and especially the third one express the dynamic character of mining objects: "creation time" and "date of measurement". The creation (or modification) time is kept for all existing objects created by mine workings, such as shafts, underground workings, boreholes.[1] The date of measurement gives exact temporal information to those points, which have been fixed or controlled by some kind of measurement. Both the information is important, because due to tectonic and underground working effects the location of mining objects is dynamically changing over time (by horizontal or vertical dislocation for example).

The dynamic changing of essential mining objects requires an appropriate support for temporal queries by the information system. Typical questions concerning this aspect are: "Give the actual position of object x" or "Show the history of object y". They are needed for the prediction of future changes and working effects and for evaluating previous calculations. In order to satisfy such requirements, it is necessary to develop a technique for representing and querying different "versions" of mining objects and for recording an object's history (cf. also [16], [17]).

Ex.: If the roof of an abandoned underground working has dislocated, the actual geometric description must be modified and the former one stored as the preceding version.

There is an additional problem caused by the temporal dimension of mining objects. Because the objects come from a variety of sources, including historical plans, the needed temporal attribute value is not always available for all objects of one class. This means, that the system must provide mechanisms for handling **incomplete information**. It should be possible to insert such an object with unknown creation or measurement time, and, nevertheless, to include it into the respective query results (e.g. looking for "actual" objects). The above statements illustrate, that the multi-dimensional character of mining objects requires complex adapted representation and management mechanisms in a supporting information system.

---

[1] Underground workings usually are advanced stepwise, therefore the creation date is significant for subobjects, too (e.g. the single points of a runway).

Markscheiders generally distinguish two different object states: **actual and future objects**. The state "actual" applies to all existing objects, i.e. those in use, abandoned or refilled (see above). The concept of "future" objects includes planned, projected as well as predicted (i.e. expected) objects, which often can be derived from existing objects. The two states have to be clearly separated because of organizational and above all security reasons, such that they form two different kinds of object classes connected by a semantic relation. This relation, which also might be interpreted as a sort of versioning, has to be recorded explicitly in the data model, otherwise a comparison of the real situation with the previous planning or prediction would not be supported.

The classification according to the state is orthogonal with respect to the other structuring types (esp. the object structuring and hierarchy) and to the distinction between above and below ground. Whereas actual objects may have several versions, the future objects are unique: there is one and only one version of planned objects (released by the markscheiders).

Several object classes are specializations of more general super classes, often building a **partition** of them. This hierarchical relationship corresponds to the usual classification in the definition of mining concepts (e.g. shaft *is-a* underground structure *is-a* hollow space). Furthermore, several object types are composed of or related to **subobjects**: a runway may have a fire-dam or an emergency door as components. Some of the subobjects depend on the super object (e.g. the support which is created together with drifting of a runway), others exist autonomously (e.g. points which may belong to several lines - crossings, branchings). This distinction implies different referential and existential integrity constraints, which have to be guaranteed. (A simple example: The runway must exist before a fire-dam belonging to it can be inserted.)

The following chapter will shortly explicate, how the database design for the mining information system can cope with these requirements.

5   A conceptual model for the mining information system

The different characteristics of mining objects imply different structuring types, which are illustrated in fig.1 (cf. [18]). Thus, complex structured objects (in different states and located in a 2 to 5 dimensional space) make up a class hierarchy, and an appropriate data modelling technique is needed, which allows to represent structural as well as semantic relations. The direct mapping to relational terms would be too far away from the user's resp. application's view. More adequate formal description methods are offered by data models currently developed in the context of object oriented database systems (c.f. [19], [20], [21], [22]).

The general definition of object oriented database systems and their characteristics (e.g. in the Object Oriented Database Manifesto of 1989, [23], [24]) shows parallels to the requirements identified for mining applications:

- structural object orientation, i.e. representation of complex objects (aggregation, sequences and sets)
- object classes and hierarchical relationships like generalization / specialization
- object versions and manipulation of dynamic objects

As a consequence of these considerations, an extended entity relationship approach was chosen for conceptual modelling (cf. [15]), which allows to represent explicitly the different aspects of mining objects and relations. The advantages of such high-

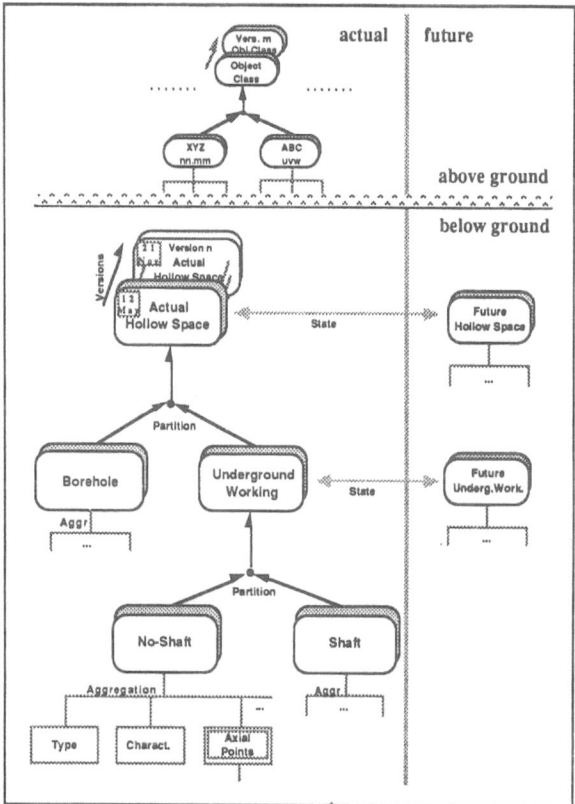

Fig. 1: Structuring Types for Mining Objects

level modelling were often stated in the database literature (cf. e.g. [25], [26]). But, as the information system is implemented with current commercial database technology, it cannot be based on a real object-oriented system. Therefore, in a second step the model must be mapped to (flat) relations.

The basic elements of the classical entity relationship model (cf. [27]) are entities, relations between entities and attributes of entities or relations. In the extended (structurally object-oriented) approach entities are viewed as objects. They can be subdivided into atomic and complex objects, allowing aggregation, list and set as constructors for complex objects. Object types may be declared as generalization or - more restrictively - as partition of subtypes.

The main elements of the mine planning database correspond to the application domain concepts, e.g. hollow space, shaft, etc. They are connected in two directions: in a partition and a structural hierarchy. In the structural relations the composition of the complex domain objects and their corresponding constructors are specified. At present database design for the actual objects below ground has been finished. Fig. 2 shows a part of the model for hollow spaces.

The spatio-temporal properties of the essential mining objects in the data model are related to the basic geometric object: the point. (The point object type includes additional optional attributes concerning the precision and method of measurement.) This definition gives a rather unconventional view of a point as a 5-dimensional object.

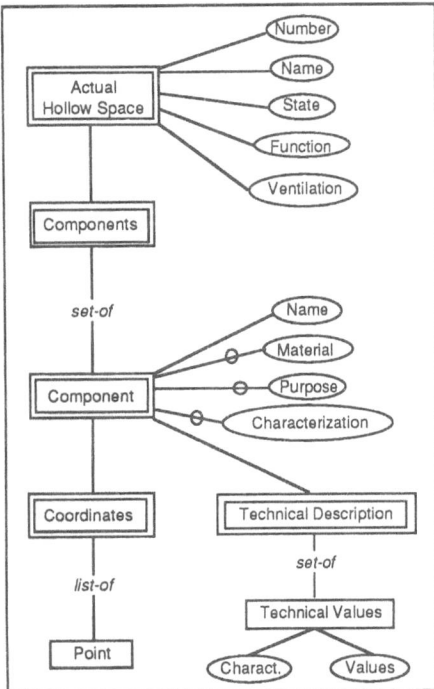

Fig.2a: (Partial) Structure of the "Actual Hollow Space" Object

The geometric description of the extended objects like runways, shafts, hollow spaces is composed of lists of points. Compared to a point set the choice of lists has the advantage, that information about the ordering of line and polygon points is kept explicitly and can directly be used for complex geometric and graph algorithms like topological scanning (see below). The importance of keeping ordering information on points implies that it is expressed explicitly in the relational implementation, too.

The conceptual model was mapped to relations by adding specific features, in order to guarantee the correct manipulation of complex objects. Structural information is flattened into attributes pointing to the sub- or superobject(s), and the inherent integrity constraints - e.g. concerning dependent subobjects as mentioned above - are checked by special supervising procedures. The problem of shared subobjects - like points belonging to several lines - is solved by locating the respective attributes in the subobject relation. The end user will only work on views and apply these special interface functions. The implementation of the version management will be realized in a similar way.

6 Implementation

The first practical phase of the described information system was the integration of existing data. It was less a problem of syntactical conversions, but of "semantic compatibility". Basic problems are null values, various values of one attribute in different files, different representation formalisms. The meaning of data cannot be derived from the format of a file alone, since meaning mostly is distributed between data files and the corresponding program. E. g.: a record of a file must not be

considered as an isolated object, if the ordering in the file is crucial for the ordering in which the records must be processed by a program. Therefore the formulation of integrity constraints and consistency checks have been an important part within the integration of several files concerning the same objects of the application domain.

The actual prototype of the information system is implemented in C and Oracle on a SUN 3/60 (Unix operating system). It is planned to run the final system with DB2 on an IBM mainframe.The most relevant objects of the application domain are implemented, namely geometric objects (the 5-dimensional points described in chapter 5 and sequences of these points) and basic parts of a mine (runways, shafts, fire-dams etc.). Interfaces are implemented to existing data files describing the structure of the mine.

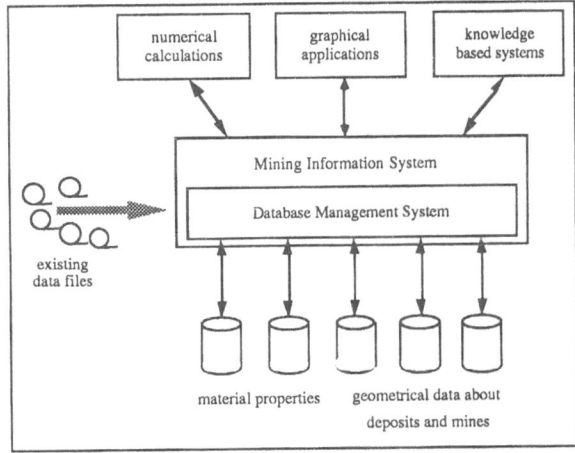

Fig. 3: Architecture of the Information System

Already in the first phase of the stepwise realization of the proposed integrated information system data for several applications are provided via the SQL interface:
- systems dealing with risk assessment and protection
- graphical systems for map construction

All geometric data exported from the database can directly be processed by graphical systems like DIGMAP and AutoCAD to produce a graphical output.

Tests of the runtime behavior of the current prototype, using data of a real mine and involving a large amount of geometric objects and joins, are promising. The tests also include interaction with application programs (for risk assessment and correlation of geological strata) producing graphical output. The results assure that the information system will be able to manage large amounts of data and to allow the interaction with additional applications.

The next phase is concerned with the implementation of the deposit data: geological informations, seams, quality parameters and so on. Integration of the CAD-system TEKTODRAFT, programs for calculating the pressure of strata, and numerical applications like calculation of coal reserves are going on. Furthermore a substantial part of the future work is devoted to integrity checks, verification and practical tests at a mine.

7 Applications

To describe the relation of the information system to various applications in greater detail, in the following paragraph some programs are presented which claim that all data are available in one integrated database. Especially knowledge based approaches for risk assessment presuppose a quick and easy access to actual and complete information about a mine and its environment.

- Topological Scanning [3], [28]

  Given the coordinates of a fire spot the program determines all runways and hollow spaces, which are menaced by fire or toxic gases. First a graph representing the topological properties of the mine is constructed using the geometric information of the database. Thereby the problem can be transformed to graph search, and an algorithm for reachability in graphs can be applied to calculate the danger zone recursively.

  A variant of this algorithm can be used to determine the danger zone, if water bursts into the hollow spaces underground. (This modification is actually implemented, cf. [29])

- Risk assessment in mine planning [10]

  A comprehensive knowledge based system for risk assessment is developed at the Technical University of Clausthal-Zellerfeld. Based on a flow-chart description of the planning process it supports a systematic construction of mine structures, avoiding faults and omissions, and identifies critical points in the design.

  The system is implemented with Nexpert Object, having a SQL interface to databases, but no interface to FORTRAN. Since most of the programs in the domain mine planning are implemented in FORTRAN 77 and the data are structured accordingly a database is necessary providing access to the existing geometric data via a SQL interface.

- SCHIKORRE - Correlation of geological strata

  Starting from drilling samples this expert system identifies geological strata, especially seams. It analyses material properties of the samples, determines similarities with respect to thickness and quality parameters resulting in a correlation between the different samples. In order to integrate these results with existing geological data access and transfer to a database system is necessary.

As shown in the article information management for the mining industry must be considered as a domain, which exceeds the current relational data base technology. Therefore extensions of commercial database systems are necessary to cope with all requirements.

8 References

[1] Leonhardt, W.J.C.: Analyse von Dateistrukturen zur Lagerstättenbearbeitung, Diplomarbeit am Fachbereich Informatik der Universität Dortmund, 1988

[2] Keune, W.: Graphische Datenverarbeitung bei der Herstellung von Normen, in: Das Markscheidewesen, 1989, Heft 1, pp. 190-197

[3] Leonhardt, J.: Anforderungen an ein modernes Informationssystem zur Verbesserung bergmännischer Planungsarbeiten, Schlußbericht über das von der EGKS geförderte Forschungsvorhaben, Essen, 1989

[4] Dann, R./ Schulte-Ontrup, R.: DIGMAP - Das Software-System im Markscheidewesen der Ruhrkohle AG, Das Markscheidewesen, 1989, Heft 1, pp. 177-182

[5] Palm / Lanser: Das Kartographiesystem TEKTODRAFT, 1989

[6] AutoCAD Release 10, Installation and Performance Guide, Autodesk AG, 1990

[7] Griesenbrock, P.: GESANG - Gebirgsdruckschätzung nach Angaben des Grubenbildes, Bergbau-Forschung Essen, 1986

[8] Cremers, A.B./ Krüger, G./ Plümer, L.: Bericht über das Entwicklungsvorhaben "Anforderungen an ein modernes Informationssystem zur Verbesserung der bergmännischen Planungsarbeiten" der Bergbau-Forschung Essen, 1988

[9] Cremers, A.B./ Krüger, G./ Plümer, L.: Bericht über das Entwicklungsvorhaben "Anforderungen an ein modernes Informationssystem zur Verbesserung der bergmännischen Planungsarbeiten" der Bergbau-Forschung Essen, 1989

[10] Pollmann, H.J./ Reitze, A.: Erkennen verschiedener Gefahren aus dem Bergmännischen Rißwerk, Text und Anlagen, 1989

[11] A. Buchmann (ed.): Design and implementation of large spatial databases. Proc., 1. Symposium SSD '89, Santa Barbara, California, July 17/18, 1989, Springer-Verlag, Berlin etc., 1990

[12] Mainguenaud, M./ Portier, M.-A.: Definition of CIGALES: A Geographical Information System Query Language, in: Tjoa, A.M./ Wagner, R. (eds.): DEXA90, Proc. of the Int. Conf. in Vienna, Austria, 1990, pp. 275-280

[13] Härder, Th. (ed.): Datenbanksysteme in Büro, Technik und Wissenschaft. GI / SI-Fachtagung, Zürich, März 1989, Springer-Verlag, Berlin etc., 1989

[14] Güting, R.-H.: Geo-Relational Algebra: A Model and Query Language for Geometric Database Systems, in: Schmidt, J.W.et al. (Eds.), Advances in Database Technology - EDBT '88, Proceedings, Springer-Verlag, Berlin etc., 1988, pp. 506-527

[15] Ramm, I./ Neumann, K./ Lipeck, U.W./ Ehrich, H.-D.: Eine Benutzerschnittstelle für geowissenschaftliche Datenbanken, Technische Universität Braunschweig, Institut für Informatik, 1985

[16] Kim, W./ Lochovsky, F.H. (Eds.): Object-Oriented Concepts, Databases, and Applications, Addison-Wesley Publ. Company, Reading (Mass.), 1989

[17] Wilkes, Wolfgang: Der Versionsbegriff und seine Modellierung in CAD, CAM-Datenbanken Hagen, Fern-Uni.-Gesamthochschule, Diss., 1987

[18] Cremers, A.B./ Krüger, G./ Plümer, L.: Bericht über das Entwicklungsvorhaben "Verbesserung der Grubenrisse" der Bergbau-Forschung Essen, 1989

[19] Dittrich, K. (Ed.): Advances in Object-Oriented Database Systems, Springer-Verlag, Berlin etc., 1988

[20] Kim, W.: Object-Oriented Databases: Definition and Research Directions, IEEE Transactions on Knowledge and Data Engineering, Vol.2, No.3, Sept. 1990, pp. 327-341

[21] Lockemann, P.C.: Object-Oriented Information Management, Decision Support Systems, Vol. 5, No. 2, 1989, pp. 79-102

[22] Zdonik, St.B./ Maier, D. (Eds.): Readings in Object-Oriented Database Systems, Morgan Kaufmann, San Mateo (CA), 1990

[23] Atkinson, M./ Bancilhon, F./ De Witt, D./ Dittrich, K./ Maier, D./ Zdonik, St.: The Object-Oriented Database Manifesto, Proc. DOOD '89, Kyoto, Dec. 1989

[24] Committee for Advanced DBMS Function: Third-Generation Data Base System Manifesto, Memorandum No. UCB/ ERL M90/28, University of California, Berkeley (CA), April 1990

[25] Dittrich, K.: Object-Oriented Database Systems: The Notion and the Issues, in: Dittrich, K./ Dayal, U. (Eds.), Int. Workshop on Object-Oriented Database Systems 1986. Proceedings, IEEE Computer Society Press, New York, 1987, pp. 2-4

[26] Adiba, M.E.: Management of Multimedia Complex Objects in the '90s, in: Blaser, A. (Ed.), Database Systems of the 90s, Proc. of the Internat. Symp., Berlin, Nov. 1990, Springer-Verlag, Berlin etc.,1990, pp. 34-54

[27] Chen, P.P. (ed.): Entity-relationship approach to information modeling and analysis, North Holland, Amsterdam, 1983

[28] Cremers, A.B./ Krüger, G./ Plümer, L.: Bericht über das Entwicklungsvorhaben "Grundlagen für ein modernes Informationssystem für die bergmännische Planung" der DMT, Bochum, 1990

[29] Baumewerd-Ahlmann, A./ Cremers, A.B./ Krüger, G./ Plümer, L./ Waschkowski, R.: Bericht über das Entwicklungsvorhaben "Informationssystem für die Verbesserung der betrieblichen und sicherheitlichen Planung - Erkennung von Gefährdungen durch Standwasser und Gebirgsschlag" der DMT, Bochum, 1990

Intelligent Network Management
A Network Management Support System using AI Techniques

JAN VAN OORSCHOT, WIL KORREMANS, and KEES VOS

Delft University of Technology
Faculty of Electrical Engineering
Mekelweg 4, P.O. Box 5031, 2600 GA Delft, The Netherlands
E-mail: JPMvOorschot@et.tudelft.nl

ABSTRACT

A prototype of a network management assistant tool has been developed, in which monitor stations continually extract information from the network. A real time dynamic Source Destination Matrix (SDM) is implemented in the monitor to retain network data on the level of connections. A central control unit, combined with an embedded expert shell, constitutes the interactive interface to the network manager. The communication module, providing remote control and interrogation facilities to the control unit, is designed to be compatible with the Simple Network Management Protocol (SNMP).

INTRODUCTION

The large scale introduction of computer networks in the last decade caused a substantial change in the way people and organisations interact, especially in business and scientific environments. Because vast interests are at stake nowadays with the use of this new and powerful medium, reliability and performance aspects became very important. Optimal performance of a computer network requires adequate network management activities. Some principal issues can be distinguished:

- Topology management.
- Capacity management.
- Security aspects.
- Trouble shooting activities.

For this kind of management real time system information about traffic, routing aspects, occurring system malfunctions etc. must be available. Several kinds of traffic analysers have been developed so far, providing large amounts of information about the network involved. However, for a proper interpretation of this information a lot of experience and expertise is required.

The Intelligent Network Management Project (INEMA) at the Delft University of Technology aims to create an efficient network management environment capable of gathering all needed network information. This paper concentrates on a way of integrating AI aspects to provide an intelligent network management assistance function.

The next section gives an overview of the requirements for a system as described above. ' Intelligent Network Management Environment' shows the way these requirements are implemented. General ideas behind the development of reasoning systems are briefly discussed in 'Building an Integrated Expert System'.

Further, 'System Parts' gives a detailed description of the system parts. Finally some conclusions are drawn about what has been accomplished until now and what has to be done further.

SYSTEM REQUIREMENTS

Several tools for network monitoring are already developed and available. In most cases statistical data is produced concerning traffic loads and the contribution of specific hardware addresses to the total load. Mayor problems are:

- The scope of these systems is usually only one isolated part of the network (edge/segment).
- A lot of system knowledge is required for the proper interpretation of the large amounts of data.

To extend a monitor system to a valuable management tool more requirements should be met:

- The scope of the system must cover all parts of the network system to be managed. This implicates, in most cases, the use of multiple monitor stations.
- The communication protocol used within the system must meet the proposed standard for network management: the Simple Network Management Protocol (SNMP). This also makes the occasional use of information from other SNMP hosts possible.
- The system should provide a Performance Database facility for the recording of long term system behaviour.
- Raw data has to be reduced to relevant information by the use of intelligent information filters and evaluators.
- The system should perform signaling and advise functions.
- The operational system must be easily adaptable to new knowledge or insight in the domain without the need to rebuild the system.

A lot of domain knowledge and experience is required to implement and maintain a system, that meets all this requirements.

INTELLIGENT NETWORK MANAGEMENT ENVIRONMENT

Expertise must be integrated in the network management environment in the design stage and continuously updated afterwards. This reason along with the scarce availability and cost of this kind of expertise makes the introduction of AI techniques very plausible. An embedded expert system rather then conventional programming techniques could cover a substantial part of the features as described in the requirements:

- Knowledge can be encoded in a very abstract and accessible manner in the production rules of the expert system. These rules are written in symbolic language and can easily be adapted. There is no recompilation of the system software necessary to change the production rules.
- A well designed expert system for the assistance to network management can perform intelligent functions like: interpretation of retrieved data, diagnosis of the current system state, advising, signaling, and detection of security violations.

An implementation of the system using these techniques has been developed in the network management project as described in the introduction. A layout of the system is given in Figure 1.

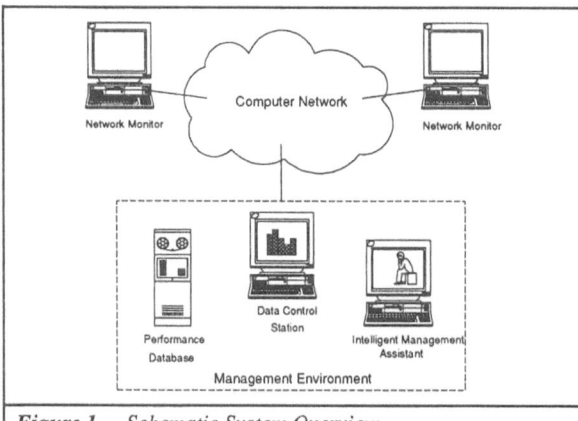

Figure 1.   *Schematic System Overview.*

Depending on the topology, network monitors can be located in several parts of the network. Each monitor collects all relevant information like traffic load, number of packets, number of collisions, protocol types used, or contents of specific packets. This information is stored in local dynamic structures. A communication module, based on the SNMP, makes the monitor accessible.

The central data control unit will interrogate the network monitors at regular intervals or on special request. The data retrieved has to be preprocessed into relevant information and stored in a local Performance Database, or has to be delivered directly to the requesting application.

The Intelligent Management Assistant part will be the main workstation of the network manager. A powerful expert shell must provide the intelligent features as described above.

The first stage implementation of the management system has some practical restrictions:

- The computer network principally may be any network. The prototype system, however, is developed for the analysis of DUneT, the Delft University Campus Ethernet.
- The control unit, database function, and embedded expert shell are integrated modules on a single PS/2 workstation.
- For the implementation of the intelligent assistant part, a public domain expert shell CLIPS (C-Language Integrated Production System: see [2]) has been embedded in the system. The developed features are discussed in 'System Parts'. CLIPS appears to be very useful, but the use of other, maybe even more powerful shells, might be considered for later versions.

BUILDING AN INTEGRATED EXPERT SYSTEM

In recent years the term 'Artificial Intelligence' has often been used as *the* magic word, promising solutions for all kinds of problems. Though this new approach to problem solving provides some interesting new prospects, the appliance must be considered very carefully.

To estimate the benefit of AI techniques, some basic understanding of the ideas behind expert systems is required. AI focuses on *problem solving techniques* rather then on the use of exact algorithms.

In AI algorithms are not used to *solve a problem*. They are used instead to *implement a problem solving process*. It is rather important to see the difference.

A problem can only be solved by conventional algorithms, if the problem has a well defined model or structure. In complex domains, like network management, it is hard if not impossible to model a significant part of the set of problems that may occur. Problems may even never have occurred before. AI aims not to model these problems, but to model the management or decision making process.

A lot of theory exist about decision making and the way human thought accomplishes to perform problem solving. An extensive discussion goes beyond the scope of this paper. We refer to the theory of H.A. Simon [8][9]. We confine ourselves to mentioning some leading ideas:

- A good deal of evidence exists that the complexity of problem solving processes is a *complexity assembled out of relatively simple interactions among a large number of simple elements*. The basic idea behind an expert system is to implement or model these simple elements and simulate the process of interaction between them.
- The simulation of a decision making process should cover only relevant issues. There is no need, for instance, for the expert system to get *nervous* when the process to be managed crashes. A proper *level of abstraction* will isolate a limited set of relatively simple processes to be simulated.
- In human thought problems are not reduced to a mathematical form. Keywords are judgment, intuition, insight, and heuristic approach. Elements of a problem are connected to each other on symbolic bases in some kind of a neurologic network. The simulation of human thinking and problem solving, in principal, need nothing more than basic *symbol manipulation features* like matching, copying, association, reading etc. PROLOG and LISP like languages are therefore more convenient for implementing a reasoning process than traditional programming languages, because of their symbolic and declarative nature.

Problems appear to a manager as a, usually incomplete, set of symptoms. A simulated problem solving process, using the ideas stated above, must manipulate these symptoms into modelled solutions. It has to recognize subproblems, estimate and retrieve missing information, find possible courses of action, and finally choose between them.

A few more indispensable definitions are given below:
- An *expert system* is a knowledge processing unit (combination of hardware and software), designed to replace or sustain an expert. It reacts to its environment in a way much alike the way a human expert reacts. Knowledge is added to the system in an symbolic encoded form. Expert systems can be designed as stand-alone units or be integrated in other systems. We refer to '*Expert System Applications to Telecommunications*' [5] for a more extensive discussion of expert systems.

- When an expert system is integrated in other systems to establish extended features, the knowledge processing part is called an *expert shell*. It is the kernel of the expert system and is the part of the system that performs the actual reasoning process.

- A *production rule* is used in a forward chaining reasoning process to represent a piece of knowledge. It associates a set of conclusions or actions to a list of connecting premises to be satisfied. A premise is satisfied when it matches with an existing fact. Production rules will be discussed further in 'Management Assistant System'. A set of production rules together with a set of initial facts is called a *program*.

- An expert system usually has some kind of *inference mechanism* that controls the evaluation of program rules.

The implementation of expert systems is very application dependent. The performance of expert systems is hard to predict. This nature makes its implementation rather complicated. A suitable and often applied method of development is 'prototyping', in which preliminary versions are build and evolved to a final form using practical experience.

A prototype of an intelligent network management assistant as implemented in the network management system is described in the next section.

SYSTEM PARTS

The Network Management Support Tool developed can roughly be split into four parts:

- One or more monitor stations.
- A communication module.
- A central control unit or management station.
- A management assistant tool.

MONITOR STATION

The main component of the monitor station consists of a small multitasking operating system, called the 'Network Packet Dispatcher' (NPD) [6], combined with a network interface card that enables the monitor to receive all network packets. The NPD provides an environment on which programmers can develop flexible and well structured monitoring programs without having to deal with complex packet handling activities. This operating system dispatches well defined events to various event driven 'Dispatcher Application Programs'.

An NPD application program is developed to build and maintain a real time dynamic 'Source Destination Matrix' (SDM). The elements of this data structure contain information about pairs of Ethernet card addresses that cause traffic over the network segment to which the monitor is connected. In the current version of the matrix module the information stored is limited to the number of packets and the number of bytes transported between two stations forming a connection. A SDM is a very useful tool in network management when considering aspects like capacity management, topology management, and trouble shooting activities because of its detailed information on the level of connections between various stations in the network.

The SDM is implemented as a half sparse matrix in which fast accessibility of the elements is realized by means of a hashing function on the addresses of a connection to obtain the row and column indexes in the matrix. Most connections cause network traffic in both ways which would have resulted in the existence of two matrix elements for each connection. By combining these two elements to one, containing send and receive fields, the SDM is

restricted to a half matrix. In order to minimize memory usage the matrix elements are allocated dynamically only for those combinations of addresses that caused traffic on the network. For this reason the elements in a row or column are connected to linked lists. In this way only a sparse number of matrix elements, compared to the number of possible connections, are used to store information. An example of the SDM layout is presented in Figure 2.

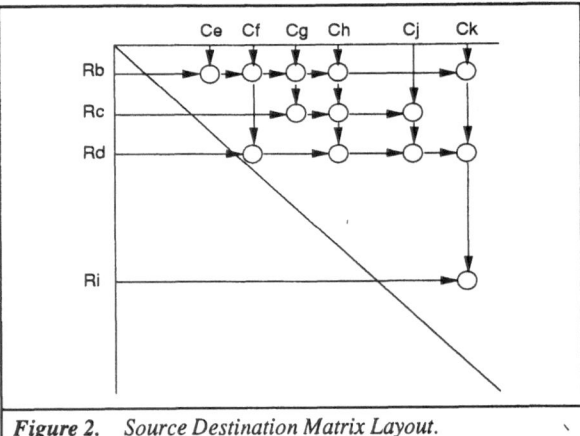

Figure 2. *Source Destination Matrix Layout.*

A matrix element is implemented as a structure containing the required number of fields for network information and matrix control.

The SDM module supports reset and garbage collection facilities to control the size of the matrix. The reset facility may be triggered by some control variables to prevent the monitor program from collapsing if, for example, the number of different addresses exceeds the capacity of the hash table. For some other reason, like the intention to impose the whole system into a zero state, a remote reset, invoked by the control unit, may be necessary.

Activating the reset facility results in deallocation of the matrix elements which leads to the loss of all information added to the matrix after the last time the elements have been interrogated by the management station.

A less rigourous way to control the size of the matrix, in case that the monitor program is expected to run out of internal memory, is called garbage collection. Using a threshold to invoke garbage collection this activity minimizes the amount of lost information by deallocating only the least recently updated elements of the matrix.

For the implementation of garbage collection several methods, like counters, time stamps, and a linked list are considered. However, the time critical environment, provided by the NPD, imposes functions to be *short* in order to reduce the number of lost packets. Counters and time stamps require a time consuming matrix traverse to find the elements concerned. For this reason a method is chosen in which all newly created elements are connected to a double linked list. Each time an element is updated it is replaced to the head of the list. When garbage collection is triggered, elements from the tail of the list are deallocated until the number of matrix elements is decreased below the threshold. Deallocation may result in unrecoverable loss of information.

Between two invocations of the SDM, by the management station, an internally triggered reset or garbage collection may take place after which the information in the elements concerned must be handled differently. A version number in the structure of a matrix element is introduced to reveal the status of the information received by the management station.

While composing and maintaining the SDM another table, called the 'Connection Top Ten' (CTT), is build in which the ten connections with the highest value in a specified field of the matrix element structure are stored. This CTT offers the manager a quick impression of which connections contributed most to the network load.

The monitor program supports the following requests for information:
• Network load as packets per second and Kbytes per second.
• A complete Source Destination Matrix.
• A list of addresses that have send packets to a specified address.
• A list of addresses that have received packets from a specified address.
• The Connection Top Ten.

COMMUNICATION MODULE

The exchange of information between the management station and several monitor stations, scattered over the network, requires both communication interfaces and a communication protocol. In a first set-up of the project the interaction of programs with the network was realized via the NetBIOS (Network Basic Input Output System) protocol. This protocol provides a reliable session service and an unreliable (broadcast) datagram service.

Communication interfaces, based on NetBIOS datagram service, are developed using the DNPAP NetBios (NB) library. This abstract function library, on top of NetBIOS, is suitable for both MS-DOS and OS/2. A simple communication protocol is designed to synchronize the datagram exchange between monitor and management station. Due to the choice of an unreliable datagram service the interface of the management station is extended with a time-out mechanism to prevent the protocol from collapsing in case of a lost datagram.

The above mentioned major design decisions to implement communication as a datagram service and to send a table of information one element at a time were made knowing that future versions of monitor and management station have to support the SNMP. This protocol is a proposed standard to pass management information between network management stations and agents responsible for performing network management functions requested by the management stations.

Supporting the SNMP instead of the NetBIOS protocol creates possibilities for the management part of the project to interrogate not only the monitor part but all devices in the network provided with a SNMP agent. Another advantage is for the monitor part to be able to operate as an agent for other network management stations which makes its application programs of more universal value.

In order to simplify the transformation to SNMP the developed interfaces are adapted to support SNMP-like requests such as 'GET-FIRST' and 'GET-NEXT' where all necessary information, for an agent to decide which element of a table has to be send, must be contained in the request. This design decision is made to keep the amount of intelligence in an SNMP agent as small as possible, offering the possibility of concurrent requests for the same table of information by several network management stations.

In case of a request for a complete table of information the management control unit asks for the first element by means of a 'GET-FIRST' request. The monitor station responds by sending the element in which the requested variable has the lowest value when considering a lexicographical order. Further the control unit repeatedly sends a 'GET-NEXT' request, containing the last received value of the specified variable, asking for its lexicographical successor. The interrogation process is terminated by a datagram from which the control unit can conclude that the table has been send completely.

CONTROL UNIT

The control unit is designed to be the workstation of the network manager providing an interactive environment in which all management activities are distributed and coordinated. A major task of this system part is the periodical interrogation of the monitor stations to collect data from all over the network. This information is stored in internal memory for short term invocation. For example one local overall SDM is build and maintained combining the matrices of the different monitor stations in the network.

Network trend analysis for capacity or topology management requires the accessibility of historical performance data. For this reason, among others, the control unit supports database functions to store network performance data after it has been processed or reduced to relevant information for long term usage.

Most of the information, collected by the monitor stations, is related to Ethernet card addresses represented as hexadecimal numbers. In the human interaction with the system it is very inconvenient to deal with a vast amount of addresses represented as numbers. A symbolic name module is implemented to rename Ethernet card addresses into symbolic names to ease human interaction.

In order to support the management activities, described in the introduction, an expert shell is embedded. It evaluates network performance data to guide or assist the network manager in his process of decision making. The shell will be discussed in detail in the next subsection.

MANAGEMENT ASSISTANT SYSTEM

Having defined and briefly explained in 'Building an Integrated Expert System' the characteristics of an expert system, we will have a closer look now at the way of utilizing this mechanism to build a network management assistant tool. The current system stage and implemented applications are discussed and an outline for developing applications using the provided features is given.

Current System Stage

The expert shell CLIPS, used in the project, is based on a forward chaining strategy. It uses production rules to manipulate available facts into relevant information. CLIPS contains three main data structures: the *Fact List*, the *Rule Base* and the *Agenda* (see Figure 3). The *Inference Machine* is a central pattern matching algorithm that controls the program flow.

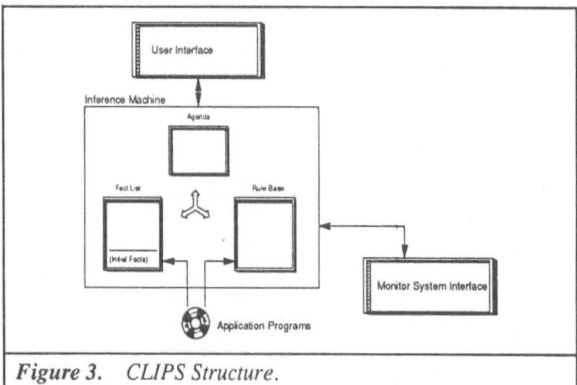

Figure 3.   CLIPS Structure.

The original version of CLIPS uses a command line prompt to interact with the user. For the purpose of this project the shell is augmented with a window oriented interface and a program development environment, providing edit and program trace facilities.

The Inference Machine matches facts in the Fact List with premises of rules on the Rule Base, using the Rete algorithm [3]. It places rules, that find a matching fact for all premises, on the Agenda. This is done for all possible sets of matching facts. Rules are 'fired' from the Agenda in order of rule defined priorities. When a rule fires, the action part of the rule is activated.

The current state of the system is defined by the contents of the Fact List. A *fact* is a set of character strings, called *atoms*, in a LISP like syntax representing any process data. A process starts with a set of initial facts, and facts are inserted and retracted during the program evaluation. Facts can be used for several purposes. Examples are:

- *Explicit program flow control*;
  example: (Estimate SystemLoad)
- *Representation of structural system information*; Several fact modules can be defined and dynamically inserted, representing for instance the system topology, user profiles, etc.
  example: (Location StationId SegmentId)
- *Representation of occasional system information*;
  example: (SecondId 243 SystemLoad 380 KbSec)
- *Representation of intermediate evaluation results*;
  example: (Traffic Stat1 Stat2 2543 Kb)

The Rule Base contains the set of *production rules* provided by the application program. CLIPS is designed by NASA Space Centre to be used as a fully integrated expert system. Interface functions are defined to declare and implement external C-language functions, which can be called by the action part of a rule for value results as well as for side effects.

IF	Fact 1
	$\vdots$
	$\vdots$
	Fact n
THEN	[Request to system for more information]
	[Request to user for more information]
	[Assert/retract facts to/from Fact List]
	[Activate system functions for return value]
	[Activate system functions for side effect]
	[Show system condition detected (trap)]
	[Display choice menu for actions to take]
	[Update statistical information]
	[Load new knowledge module]
	etc.

Figure 4. *General Form Production Rule.*

During the evaluation process new rules can be loaded from file when necessary. The action part of a rule can simply assert or retract facts to/from the Fact List, but can also activate the collection of new kinds of information, load new program modules, or ask the user for new instructions etc. (see Figure 4).

```
(defrule GetChoice                    ;rule name
    (declare (salience 100))          ;define rule priority
    ?fact <- (GetChoice)              ;match with fact 'GetChoice'
                                      ;  and bind the fact to the
                                      ;  variable '?fact' for later
                                      ;  retraction from the list
    =>                                ;'THEN'
    (retract ?fact)                   ;retract 'GetChoice'
    (bind ?answer (GetChoice))        ;call external in C-language
                                      ;  implemented interface
                                      ;  function and assign result
                                      ;  to variable ?answer
    (assert (choice ?answer))         ;assert result to fact list
)
```

Figure 5. *Example of simple production rule in CLIPS*

A rule is a representation of a small piece of knowledge provided by a domain expert and encoded by a knowledge engineer. It can incorporate for instance the recognition of a subproblem, a solution, or a trap. It can also be used in the application program to perform simple procedural tasks like interfacing to the user (see Figure 5).

A CLIPS demonstration application, 'TRACE', using some system features has been implemented. This application produces several requests to the monitor system and performs some simple interpretation of the retrieved data. Picture 6 gives a sample screen of this application. When 'TRACE' is running, about 500 rules per minute are fired. The features of 'TRACE' are:

- It provides a window interface with menu choices and dialogue boxes.
- All traffic to or from a user defined address (changeable at any moment by the user) is detected and displayed. A warning is generated when a new partner address is detected. A full trace report can be called in, showing all partners, the amount of traffic and a general conclusion about the traffic type (from traffic direction and mean packet length).
- It visualizes the current network load (percentage-bar); The user can influence some load display settings.
- It displays the current Connection Top Ten, composed by the monitor system; The addresses, amount of traffic and mean packet length is shown.

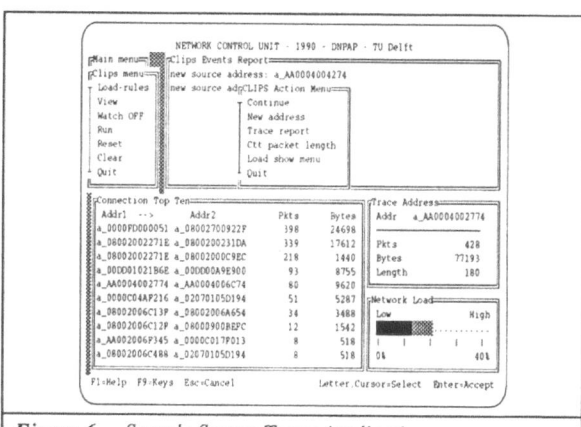

Figure 6. *Sample Screen Trace Application*

Another 'off-line' CLIPS application has been developed. It evaluates the allocation of Ethernet user stations connected to a multi-segmented Ethernet, given a certain source destination matrix. The program minimizes the system load by estimating within user defined restrictions, like irreplaceable stations or maximum segment/bridge loads, the optimal distribution of the given stations over the available segments.

Outline for Development of Applications

In the current system stage the essential ingredients to build an expert system are present. Apart from some simple evaluation features in the described applications, however, little real 'expertise' has been supplied so far. Compared to a hypothetical simulation of a human being, the system stage can be imagined as the construction of a 'robot', that can observe, think and talk, but has nothing learned yet. It can be 'told' to carry out simple actions, like in 'TRACE', but it first starts to react cognitive, when it is able to recognize a great variety of system states, and reacts to it using an heuristic approach.

Further development to a knowledge system, actually containing system *expertise*, requires a time consuming process of knowledge acquisition, knowledge engineering and in some cases software engineering to conceive new features.

In the development of new applications the use of scenario templates can be very useful. Such a template describes isolated system states to be detected (see Figure 7).

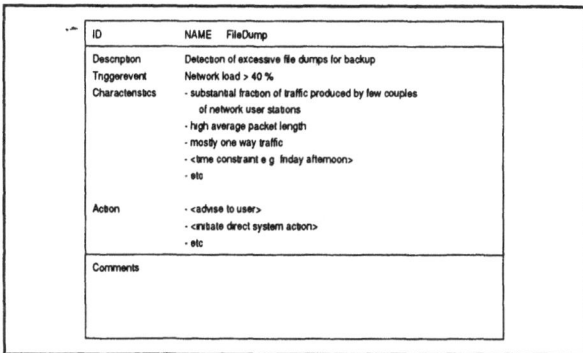

Figure 7. *Example Scenario Template*

The domain knowledge, needed to build the system as described, must be supplied by a domain expert through a process of knowledge acquisition. This includes interviews, domain studies, observations of managers activities etc. The knowledge has to be encoded in program modules by a knowledge engineer. The whole of this process may take an amount of time in the order of months or even years.

All external features manipulating the underlying soft-/hardware have to be implemented by the system's software engineer(s). An Abstract Program Interface (API) must be defined for these extended features (names of function calls; arguments; effect etc.).

The performance of the management assistance tool must continuously be reviewed by the domain expert(s). With the resulting recommendations, the system can evolve to its final form.

CONCLUSIONS

Computer Network Management is a rather new and complex/complicated domain. Flexible tools are indispensable to collect all essential system information. The nature of the problems to be solved makes it very suitable for application of Artificial Intelligence techniques.

A useful set-up for a management assistance system has been established. It consists of a monitor system with an external interface prepared for the support of the Simple Network Management Protocol, an implementation of a Source Destination Matrix, a remote control station, a database facility and an embedded expert shell for symbolic knowledge processing.

We summarize the benefit of using an expert shell, based on a production rule mechanism, in a network management environment.

* The shell provides the possibility of adding network management expertise and heuristic problem solving approaches to the system in an accessible and modular way.

* The symbolic syntax of programs improves the possibility for the expert user to review or even edit parts of the knowledge.
* The abstract symbolic interface between the shell and the underlying system enables the executed shell application to manipulate the system for retrieval of all information, that appears to be necessary for the completion of the reasoning process. Using this interface, new applications can be build easily by the knowledge engineer or the experienced user without recompiling the underlying software.
* When the development of the expert system has reached an acceptable stage, the system will exhibit such an intelligent behaviour, that the network system can be managed by operators without the direct (expensive) availability of human domain experts.

In the further development of the system the emphasis should be on the acquisition of domain knowledge. Guide-lines for the interactive evolution to a viable an efficient expert system are given in subsection 'Management Assistant System' of 'System Parts'.

ACKNOWLEDGEMENTS

This paper was written in partial fulfilment of the requirements for the Master's degree in Electrical Engineering at the Delft University of Technology. At the Laboratory of Computer Architecture and Digital Techniques, the Data Network Performance Analysis Project (DNPAP) has been initiated by J.P.M. van Oorschot, headed by Prof. G.L. Reijns. The main attention of this research group is focused on the analysis and modelling of complex network structures, in order to increase overall network performance.

We thankful made use of the existing expert shell CLIPS [2], obtained from public domain, which appeared to be very useful.

REFERENCES

[1] Comer, Douglas, *Internetworking With TCP/IP*; Prentice/Hall International, Inc. 1988.

[2] Culbert, Chris, *CLIPS Reference Manual*, Version 3.0, NASA / Johnson Space Centre, Houston, July 1986.

[3] Forgy, C.L., *Rete: A Fast Algorithm for the Many Pattern / Many Object Pattern Match Problem*, Artificial Intelligence 19, page 17-37, North-Holland, 1982.

[4] Kaarela, Kari et Al., *Building Embedded Real Time Expert Systems*, Technical Research Centre of Finland (VTT), 1989.

[5] Liebowitz, Jay (editor), *Expert System Applications to Telecommunications*, Whiley Interscience, New York, page 3-44, 191-198, 267-303, 1988. ISBN 0-471-62459-4

[6] Thio, Ling, *The Network Packet Dispatcher - an Event-driven Multi-tasking Operating System for Network Monitors*, to be published, Delft, 1990.

[7] Oorschot, J.P.M. Van, and Winter, D. de, *Intelligent Network Management. An initiating report of a joint project on Network Management*; Participants: TU-Delft / ITI-TNO. June 1989.

[8] Simon, H.A., *The New Science of Management Decision* (revised edition), Prentice Hall International Inc, 1977

[9] Simon H.A., *The Sciences of the Artificial*, MIT Press 1972.

[10] Tanenbaum, A.S., *Computer Networks*, Prentice/Hall International, Inc., 1988.

Computer-aided Production
of Multilingual Historical Reference Works

Reinhard Härtel   Peter Lauppert

Forschungsinstitut für Historische Grundwissenschaften
Körblergasse 20, A-8010 Graz

ABSTRACT

The production of indexes attached to the editions of historical texts and — based on those editions — of multilingual historical reference works is, above all, a difficult problem of structuring data. Furthermore there are very particular requests in sorting, e. g. in sorting certain ambiguous strings in a manner which is different from the normal sorting rule. It can be that many different sorting rules must cooperate in a complex system: among many others the classifying of grammatical types of word connections or the very different relations between persons or places. Concerning the output a minimum of correct usage of (natural) language must be observed, and the same holds true of the case of translations. The problem of translation presents itself in different ways, according to the respective type of information. The program-package "HISTREG" is designed for the solution of these problems and it has been completed in parts now.

Introduction

The production of multilingual historical reference works is, above all, a difficult problem of standardizing historical data. Not only technical problems have to be solved, but also fundamental problems of structuring data. The project presented is sponsored by the Austrian *Fonds zur Förderung der wissenschaftlichen Forschung* and will be finished soon. It is carried out — apart from the two authors mentioned above — by Ingeborg Baumgartner, Peter Luttenberger and Gabriela Stieber. It is concerned with fields of historical data in which a structured collection of data and facts can also be relevant for several historical disciplines, and where the data have always been similar to one another in many ways. Especially in these fields efforts in standardization will probably be successful, a lot more than within the range of fundamental discussion where the issues are too diverse.

The indexes attached to the editions of historical texts are, no doubt, parts of the former fields. On the one hand such indexes can provide you with a large number of further information, on the other hand the range of information-types normally is not too various. Solutions for which a wide acceptance can be expected are most possible here. Cumulating particular indexes according to the respective demands would create precious reference works, under condition that the singular indexes or data bases are compatible. And, of course, all this should be possible without difficulties for the user.

For this purpose, quite a lot of basic work had to be done for preparation, of course. There are certainly several rules concerning the editions of historical texts, but there are none for the setting up of indexes.

Indexes are among the earliest applications of the possibilities provided by the computer in the human sciences. But normally these indexes give information in a very limited way. On the other hand the indexes of the editions of historical texts have gained a very high or sophisticated level, but there is no uniformity between them, as old and more recent project reports show (cf., e. g., [1] and [9]). This is due to the nature of the cause itself, as has been mentioned correctly by others [13]. Even specific restrictions of the profile of index-capacities can be explained for this reason [11]. Wherever the requests have been most extreme, the usability of the system is restricted to this only one project [12]. Wherever indexes are set up automatically the matter in hand are often systems far below this level of complexity which is the standard in conventional indexes. The progress in this respect cannot be called considerable [2].

Some years ago a prototype of a computer-aided index of a certain standard of complexity was produced [3] and presented [4]. On the basis of the experiences made during the development of this index, more general solutions have been planned. Several editors respectively groups of editors of various intentions (history and linguistics, middle ages and modern times, narrative texts and other documents) have now decided to cooperate for the purpose of giving their indexes a common structure which is to be as homogeneous as possible, yet flexible enough. Their intention is further to use a common software and at the same time to regard usability as widely as possible. First ideas [5] and more concrete plans [6] were presented to and discussed by the scientific community. The first solutions within the software package

"HISTREG" now programmed by Peter Lauppert and Peter Luttenberger were just presented to and discussed by the participants of the *Montpellier Computer Conference* of the *Association of History and Computing* [7]. Further ideas on the problems of data structuring have been put up for discussion [8].

Special Requests

It seems advisable to stress here that the requests to such an index system are quite different from the requests to (e. g. prosopographical) historical data bases [10]. On the one hand, a printed index has to satisfy fewer kinds of requests than a historical database normally has to, on the other hand there are many other special requests: There are very particular demands in sorting, e. g. in sorting certain ambiguous strings in a manner which is different from the normal sorting rule applied to a special task. It can be that many different sorting rules must cooperate in a complex system: e. g. alphabetical, chronological and the classifying of grammatical types of word connections.

There is also the problem of the appropriate consideration of the different versions of one single text, respectively the problem of the names and words not contained in the published text, but only in the notes or comments which have been added to the same text. Where various indexes are to be cumulated, there will soon be the problem of translating different (natural) languages concerning various elements of the data base.

Concerning the output a minimum of correct usage of (natural) language must be observed, and the same holds true of the case of translations. There are side effects which have to be suppressed. The problem of translation presents itself in different ways, according to the respective type of information. For expressions like "number" or "see" simple lists of foreign words or symbols will be sufficient. The problems with the names are a lot more difficult. As far as persons are concerned, surnames, nicknames and family names often cannot be translated according to the same rules. Titles of nobility are generally derived from place names, but neither the possibility to translate nor the translation itself need necessarily be corresponding between title of nobility and the respective place name. On the other hand, the correlation between the two must not be neglected in the index.

In the following lines a fictitious (and at the same time very simple) example is to show this kind of problems which have to be solved. Let us assume that in the edition of a 19th century historical text on page 118 is spoken about the Austrian Prime Minister, Prince Alfred of Windischgrätz, in the following way: *der österreichische Ministerpräsident, Fürst Alfred von Windischgraetz*. Put like this the aristocratic title (*Windischgraetz*, normalized Windischgrätz) refers to the once Styrian town of Windischgraz, today situated in Yugoslavia and now called "Slovenji Gradec". Let us further assume that in this

same edited text on page 231 appears this very town of Windischgraz. In this connection it has to be stated that the place name of Windischgraz can be translated, not however, the aristocratic title Windischgrätz. In the index of a historical edition or in a historical reference work (in English) containing names the respective entries might run as follows:

Alfred (*Alfred*), see Windischgrätz

Austria (*österreichisch*), Prime minister: Windischgrätz

österreichisch, see Austria

Slovenji Gradec, town in Slovenia (Windischgraz), p. 231

Windischgrätz (*Windischgraetz*), Alfred of, Prince, p. 118, Prime minister: Austria

Windischgrätz, see Windischgraz

Windischgraetz, see Windischgrätz

Windischgraz, see Slovenji Gradec

Windischgraz, see Windischgrätz

Not even for the place names alone a simple table of translations will be sufficient: frequently the application of the official name which is valid in the respective country will be requested (e. g. Venezia instead of Venice or Venise), and generally only a certain number of place names can be translated into definite other languages. Some editors prefer the typographical distinction, i. e. names (or words) which appear in the index as you can find them in the source, or normalized names (or words). Both of them, e. g., can appear as a headword, because the one name can be identified, and the other not. For this reason there will be typographical requests with repercussions to the structuring of data. In the index the results may appear as follows:

Cosa, see *Coza*

Coza (*Cosa*), unidentified place in Northern Italy, p. 45, p. 78

Venice (*Venecia*, *Venetia*), town in Northern Italy, p. 68, p. 102

Venecia, see Venice

Venetia, see Venice

Despite of all these difficulties it will be important not to demand too much of the capacities of the editor and his collaborators and it will be necessary to find a structure of data for the input which is as simple as possible. This will, of course, be achieved by the strict separation of the input of the data themselves on the one hand and of all means for identifying, translating etc. on the other hand. It must be the choice of the editor to trust these fields of work to different collaborators.

Furthermore the categories according to which the material will be structured have to be as closely related as possible between themselves, e. g. the categories applied to persons, places and words. All the relationships of a person (e. g. profession, kinsfolk) can be understood as an "aspect" of the person concerned, according to the type of relationship with or without an "object" (e. g. the term "mother" always requires the "object", whose mother it is). There remain only three fundamental "models" for the input.

There are three basic requirements to a database so that the problems described can be handled. The first one is a flexible structure. This is needed because no or several entries must be possible in each field (e. g. a person who is related to no or to several different persons). The second one is a variable length of fields. This is absolutely necessary because a field can be empty or must hold an undefined number of characters. When working on large editions it is unreasonable to be bound to a specific fieldlength. This would waste a large quantity of data. When joining data of more editions it would be impossible to run the application on affordable machines. The third one is the different number of relations. The program has to deal with relations to one or more records of the same database (e. g. a person is the son of another person, etc.) and with relations to other databases (e. g. a person works in a certain place, etc.). Another problem is the use of different natural languages which affects all of the three requirements mentioned and makes the use of an existing database-system impossible.

Technical Solution

A further problem is the decision to use the right operating system. The application should run on small machines (like PCs) and if available on larger machines. This fact let us to opt for the programming language C which is very popular among languages on different operating systems (MS-DOS, UNIX, etc.). There is also a large number of programming-tools (e. g. for indexation, etc.)

The solution that has been adopted by Graz University is the following. For the purposes of developing software for multilingual historical reference works we can divide the data into three groups: personal, place-related and word/object-related data. The different groups of data are connected in several ways. For that reason it is necessary to build up relations between them. There can be relations between people (e. g., because of family relationship), places and people (e. g., inhabitants of a town), objects and people (e. g., due to property), or between objects and places (e. g., the site of a mill). Once the data and relations have been entered, the software almost automatically establishes the cross-references. Although the ultimate aim is to produce printed indexes, the user naturally does not have to decide on a certain output format during data entry. Formats only have to be determined before printing.

Although the software can solve most problems automatically, it still requires human interference in some situations. One of the most important problems is the unambiguous assignation of the same names to different persons. It is impossible to do this completely automatically, because the identity of a person can often only be determined on the basis of the context, in which it occurs. Hence the user has to assign the name to the person of his choice on his own. It is not the aim of this project to develop a name/person identification. This software, however, helps in providing a choice of possible answers.

Technically we have solved this problem by using a multi-lingual thesaurus, which is the core of the system. For that reason its possibilities are explained in a more detailed way here. With its aid it is possible to create hierarchic connections between single register-entries. These connections can be made both automatically or manually. The automatic linking, however, is restricted to the connecting of orthographically identical names and words. In this process a semantic coherence is, of course, not guaranteed. As the system cannot recognize such a semantic connection, it has to be checked by the user and (if necessary) to be corrected by a manual intervention. In the case of manual connection the assignments of the single names and words to the register-entries are carried out individually by the user. But here too the system offers some help. For one name or word the entire assignment possibilities are found and shown by the system in connexion with the context passage and references. If none of these possibilities shown are accepted by the user, he has the choice to search for any other available possibility of classification or, if there is no possibility at all, he can set up a new one.

The further step in this process concerns — if necessary — the input of the required translations into the languages wanted. This is considerable made easier through the already structured data-stock (besides normally only several keywords are translated, e. g. place-names, titles or brief descriptions). How many and what languages are used is up to the user and depends on the purpose of register usage and also depends on the wish of how many data-bases in how many languages are to be cumulate. For those data-bases must at least have one language in common, otherwise this one language chosen has to be completed later. If in the data-stock more than one language is taken into account, the very same index can be put out in those various languages through a simple command.

If sufficient data have been entered, the output options are manifold. The program provides adjustable alphabetical order for special, language specific characters, it enables you to print either the normalized forms of words and names or the words as they are written in the source text, and it supplies the option of additional sorting according to dates etc. The typographic module can produce hard copies for correction or files. In order to make the output as flexible as possible, the distinction of output-data has been made according to their nature (headwords, references, chronological data etc.). Each kind has an unmistakable marking which is put before and behind the respective element of the output. So the individual adaption to any typesetter is guaranteed for the user, for this marking can simply be replaced according to the respective typesetter.

Finally, we plan to develop a user interface, which will make data entry and processing a lot easier. We will also add an error handling routine to prevent errors in an early stage. A menu oriented design is to ensure easy handling of the program and allows unexperienced users to use this program.

Summing up we can say that this software package facilitates the creation of indexes for historical editions. Its real strength, however, is the ability of joining several smaller indexes to a large one and to create big historical data bases almost automatically. Technical details can be explained in a better way during a demonstration.

REFERENCES

[1] G. Battelli. *Una proposta per un indice dei registri pontifici.* In L. Fossier, A. Vauchez, editors, *Informatique et histoire médiévale. Communications et débats de la Table Ronde CNRS [...].* Rome, Ecole française de Rome, 1975.

[2] L. Fossier. *Onomastique médiévale et indexation automatique.* In *Le médiéviste et l'ordinateur* 18, 1987.

[3] R. Härtel. *Die älteren Urkunden des Klosters Moggio (bis 1250)* (Publikationen des Historischen Instituts beim Österreichischen Kulturinstitut in Rom 2/6/1). Wien, Verlag der Österr. Akademie der Wissenschaften, 1985.

[4] R. Härtel, *Prototype d'un index cumulatif pour les éditions de textes.* In *Le médiéviste et l'ordinateur* 18, 1987.

[5] R. Härtel. *Le Texte: suffit-il ?* In J.-P. Genet, editor, *Standardisation et échange des bases de données historiques. Actes de la troisième Table Ronde internationale tenue au L.I.S.H. [C.N.R.S.] Paris, 15–16 mai 1987.* Paris, Centre National de la Recherche Scientifique, 1988.

[6] R. Härtel, *Mehr als ein Anhang: Das computererstellte Register.* In: A. Schwob, K. Kranich-Hofbauer, D. Suntinger, editors, *Historische Edition und Computer. Möglichkeiten und Probleme interdisziplinärer Textverarbeitung und Textbearbeitung.* Graz, Leykam, 1989.

[7] R. Härtel and P. Lauppert. Towards Multilingual Historical Reference Works. In *Montpellier Computer Conference. Montpellier, 4–7 septembre 1990. Volume des resumés.* Montpellier, Association for History and Computing 1990.

[8] R. Härtel. *Überlegungen zur Erschließung historischer Texte.* In H. Ebner, H. Haselsteiner and I. Wiesflecker-Friedhuber, editors, *Geschichtsforschung in Graz. Festschrift zum 125-Jahr-Jubiläum des Instituts für Geschichte der Karl-Franzens-Universität.* Graz, Institut für Geschichte der Universität Graz, 1990.

[9] J. Mathieu. *Indexation automatique des suppliques d'Urbain V.* In *Le médiéviste et l'ordinateur* 18, 1987.

[10] H. Millet, editor. *Informatique et Prosopographie. Actes de la Table Ronde du CNRS, Paris, 25-26 octobre 1984.* Paris, CNRS, 1985.

[11] F. Neiske. *Die Erforschung von Personennamen und Personengruppen des Mittelalters mit Hilfe der Elektronischen Datenverarbeitung.* In K. F. Werner, editor, *L'histoire médiévale et les ordinateurs. Medieval History and Computers. Rapports d'une Table ronde internationale, Paris 1978.* München, Saur, 1981.

[12] M. Panzeri. *Automatic indexes of literary sources for Art History. The "Notizie" ... by Federico Alizeri.* In *Cologne Computer Conference. Cologne, September 7th-10th, 1988. Volume of Abstracts.* Cologne, Center for Historical Social Research, 1988.

[13] K. Schmid and J. Wollasch. *Zum Einsatz der EDV im Quellenwerk "Societas et Fraternitas".* In K. F. Werner, editor, *L'histoire médiévale et les ordinateurs. Medieval History and Computers. Rapports d'une Table ronde internationale, Paris 1978.* München, Saur, 1981.

A Friendly and Intelligent Approach
to Data Retrieval in a Multimedia DBMS

Daniel A. Keim[1], Kyung-Chang Kim, Vincent Lum

Department of Computer Science[2]
Naval Postgraduate School
Monterey, CA 93943 - 5100

Abstract

Manipulation of multimedia data is not straightforward as in conventional databases. One main problem is the retrieval of multimedia data from the database with the need to match the contents of multimedia data to a user query. In order to achieve a content based retrieval, in our approach, we use *natural language captions* which allow the user to describe the contents of multimedia data. In a similar manner, users will specify their queries on multimedia data contents in natural language form. A problem is that different or even the same user describe the same thing differently at different times which results in the descriptions of the contents of multimedia data to rarely exactly match the descriptions of the user queries. Hence, partial or approximate match between descriptions of multimedia data and user queries is generally required during multimedia data retrieval. We propose an intelligent approach to *approximate match* by integrating both object-oriented and natural language understanding techniques. In order to make the query specification process easier we also develop a graphical user interface supporting incremental query specification and a natural way of expressing joins. The Multimedia Database Management System (MDBMS) described in this paper incorporates the capabilities as mentioned above.

1. Introduction

A multimedia database management system supports the management of multimedia data, which includes image and sound among others, in addition to supporting conventional databases. Multimedia systems are currently gaining a lot of attention because technology today has made it possible to capture and store multimedia data in computers. Many applications like military, publishing or instructional routinely need multimedia data. Although the cost of the hardware required to handle multimedia data is decreasing rapidly, the software needed to manage such data is lacking or does not match the needs.

In this paper we present a Multimedia Database Management System (MDBMS). The system allows sophisticated handling of multimedia data featuring an intelligent data retrieval as well as a graphical interface for user interaction. Besides describing the overall system architecture the important parts of the system such as Parser, Matcher and Graphical User Interface will be presented in more detail.

One important achievement of the MDBMS system is the efficient method for the retrieval of multimedia data by way of inexact matching. In conventional databases, retrieval of standard numerical and alphanumeric data is handled by utilizing the *content* of the data. The fundamental problem that one must face in the context of a multimedia database is the question of how to provide content search. There is no easy solution. It is difficult to find the appropriate data conveniently and efficiently based on the contents of the multimedia data because they are intrinsically rich in semantics. In developing an efficient retrieval method for multimedia data, we concluded that it is not possible to utilize the content directly with today's technology since it is mostly unstructured complex data like an image or a sound.

In our MDBMS system we use the approach of content based search by means of verbal descriptions on the contents of multimedia data. We argue that the well known keyword approach to content description is not suitable because it has been known to be imprecise and the users often have difficulty in focusing the search to data of interest. Hence, we adopt the natural language approach to content description as a more viable option. The methodology we adopt consists of associating natural language captions to each multimedia data and using the description to retrieve the relevant data. More precisely, the description of a multimedia data is matched against the description of a user query which is also expressed using natural language captions. The major problem with this approach is that it is generally the case that the description of a multimedia data does not exactly match the description of a user query. The reason is that it is difficult for different users or even the same user at different times to describe the same thing identically because they can use synonyms, generalize/specialize categories and so on. Hence, the key to efficient retrieval is to automatically perform partial or approximate match of the description of multimedia data to the description of a user query whenever exact match is not possible. In this paper, we propose an intelligent approach to approximate matching by integrating object-oriented and natural language understanding techniques.

1. The author's permanent address is Institut für Informatik, Universität München, Theresienstr. 39, 8000 München 2.
2. This research was supported in part by NOSC, Direct Funding and the German Scholarship Foundation.

The second issue addressed in this paper regards new ways of interaction with the user. The user interface is an important part which strongly determines the effectiveness in using a system. In order to achieve a natural way of interacting with the MDBMS system we are developing a graphical user interface incorporating advanced features to make the query specification easier compared to query languages like SQL. We found that in order to formulate complex queries a user partitions it into smaller pieces and put them together at a later stage. This behavior is reflected in the principle of *incremental query specification* which is supported by our graphical user interface. In addition, we observed that, for a given database, the joins necessary to specify most of the queries directly correspond to natural language expressions. This leads to the principle of *natural expression of joins* also supported by our graphical user interface. Both principles are of general use not only for multimedia systems or graphical user interfaces but for any database query interface.

This paper makes three contributions. The first contribution is that context description of multimedia data is possible using natural language captions which can be interpreted automatically using domain dependent knowledge. The second contribution is the formulation of a general scheme to retrieve multimedia data with special emphasis on approximate match. As far as we know, very little research on partial or approximate matching has been conducted in the area of natural language processing. The third contribution is the identification and application of two principles in the construction of a graphical user interface that help to make the query specification process easier.

The paper is organized as follows: Section 2 discusses related work. Section 3 addresses fundamental problems and outlines the architecture of the Multimedia Database Management System (MDBMS). Section 4 describes the natural language interpretation capabilities of the parser, Section 5 the approximate match algorithm used for retrieval of multimedia data and Section 6 gives a short overview of the user interface. Finally, Section 7 gives the summary.

2. Related Work

Several multimedia projects have been undertaken by various researchers in both academia and industry over the past several years. The MINOS system [5] developed by a team at the University of Toronto manages highly structured multimedia objects. Sophisticated browsing and user interface features allow browsing of the schema as well as synchronized updates. The MCC database program [15] also undertook several multimedia projects and identified requirements for a data model suitable for multimedia applications. [10] has developed a framework to classify and compare the different multimedia projects.

The user interface is an important part of a database system especially when dealing with multimedia data because of their non-textual nature. Most of the research in the area of user interfaces focus on the entity-relationship [12] or the more complex sematic and object-oriented data model [1,3] allowing queries to be directly specified within the schema. In contrast, we use an extension of the relational model to handle and manipulate the media data. In order to allow an easy query specification we provide a graphical user interface which incorporates incremental query specification and a natural way of expressing joins, differing in many ways from the well know OBE interface [16].

Another important aspect of a multimedia database system is the content retrieval of media data. In [9], we introduced the approach of contents based search by means of natural language descriptions. This approach is related to research on artificial intelligence (AI) and information retrieval (IR). In the area of AI a variety of methods have been developed for the processing of natural language. [6] exemplifies the current state of the art. Most of the work done focus on complete understanding of natural language requiring extensive knowledge bases with general world knowledge. Our approach is somewhat simpler. We are only dealing with a subset of natural language being broad enough to allow a natural description of the media data but easier to understand than general language. Furthermore, we found that for most applications the knowledge base is domain specific allowing us to deal with a much smaller one for each domain. Both aspects contribute to an acceptable performance which is critical for a database system.

In the domain of IR there had been early interest in using AI techniques [14]. More representative of modern attempts are the IRUS system [2] which is designed for processing heterogeneous data bases through natural language queries and the IOTA system [4] which tries to improve the qualitative performance of IR systems in replacing keywords by noun groups. The approach we propose is somewhat different from the intelligent IR systems proposed so far. It is clear that most of the work in these systems is mainly concerned with natural language processing, particularly query processing, and deductive capabilities based on an extended semantic model of document content. Our approach also shares these characteristics. However, in most systems the concept of matching between system and user concepts is based on exact matching while our approach is based on approximate matching. Even in systems with approximate matching capabilities, the matching function used is primitive or superficial at best compared to our approach which integrates object-oriented technology and natural language understanding to improve the quality of the matching.

3. Architecture of Multimedia Database Management System (MDBMS)

In this section, we outline the architecture of the MDBMS. The architecture consists of the various components

104

of the MDBMS system. Before we continue, definitions and various issues associated with the data model used in the MDBMS system are addressed.

3.1 Definitions and Background

As mentioned before, multimedia data consists of unformatted data such as text, image, voice, signals, etc. in addition to alphanumeric data. We define a multimedia database management system (MDBMS) as a system that manages all multimedia data and provides a mechanisms to handle concurrency, consistency, and recovery in addition to providing a query language and query processing.

Despite differences in data model and implementation aspects, all research projects on MDBMS have decided to organize multimedia data using the abstract data type (ADT) concept. This is generally accepted as the adequate approach. However, none of the projects have addressed the problem of content retrieval of multimedia data.

The fundamental difficulty in handling multimedia data is intrinsically tied to its very rich semantics. To illustrate the difficulty, let us look at an image of ships. How are we to know what type of ships are in the picture? As another example, let us suppose that there is a picture of a dog and a cat. How do we know if they are chasing each other or playing? To answer queries posed on images, for example, a person must draw from a very rich experience encountered in life to derive at a good answer. One must have a sophisticated technique to analyze the contents of the images to get the semantics of the different things in the images. Technology today is not advanced enough to expect systems to have this kind of capabilities to answer multimedia queries. However, we can use both AI and IR technology to do the next best thing. We can abstract the contents of multimedia data into words or text and use the text description equivalent of the original multimedia data to match a user query. This principle we will use in designing a MDBMS to handle multimedia data for different applications.

Figure 1 shows the format of a multimedia data which consists of the registration, raw and description data. Raw data is the bit string representation of the image, sound, signal, etc. obtained from scanning or digitizing the original multimedia data. Registration data generally enhances the information about raw data and is not redundant. The con-

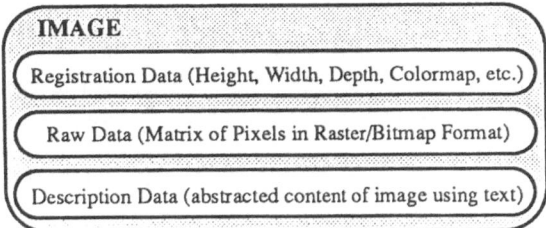

IMAGE

Registration Data (Height, Width, Depth, Colormap, etc.)

Raw Data (Matrix of Pixels in Raster/Bitmap Format)

Description Data (abstracted content of image using text)

Figure 1: Example for the Multimedia Data Format

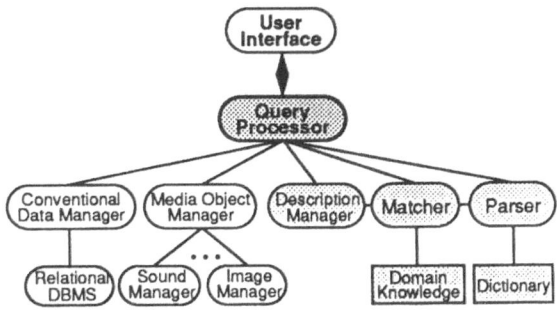

Data Access Subsystem   Intelligent Retrieval Subsystem

Figure 2: Architecture of MDBMS System

tents of a multimedia data is described by the description data. Description data cannot be automatically derived by the computer given the technology today. We assume that users will supply the description data for multimedia data in a natural language form.

3.2 Architecture

In this section, we present the various components of our MDBMS. This is a modified version of the architecture of the MDBMS discussed in [9]. Our proposed architecture enhances the performance of the matcher component and adds the capabilities of the user interface which are lacking in the architecture proposed in [9].

As shown in Figure 2, the components break down into user interface, query processor, data access and intelligent retrieval subsystem. The data access subsystem consists of conventional and media manager and controls the access to the actual data stored in relational and media DBMS. The intelligent retrieval subsystem is composed of parser, generator, matcher and description manager. The query processor accepts queries from users and executes them by calling the other components. When a new description for a multimedia data is entered, for example, the query processor calls the parser. The parser uses the dictionary to produce first-order predicates and returns them to the query processor. The query processor then hands the predicates over to the description manager which links the description to its multimedia data.

When the query processor receives a query the first task is to decompose the query into subqueries affecting only conventional or media part. The conventional subquery is passed to the conventional data manager without modifications. For the text description, the query processor calls the natural language parser to obtain the equivalent query predicates. The predicates are then handed to the matcher. The matcher tries to match the query with multimedia data by comparing the predicates of the query with that of the stored multimedia data. The matcher does this by calling the description manager and using domain knowledge. In addition, if an exact match is not possible, the matcher automatically switches to approximate match. As the solution to the natural language part of a query, the query processor receives links to the qualified multimedia data. After combing them with the results of the conventional subquery the final results are retrieved by the Data Access Subsystem.

The query processor, conventional and media object manager, description manager, parser and matcher have already been implemented as part of the MDBMS prototype system developed at the Naval Postgraduate School [7,9,11].

4. Natural Language Understanding in the Parser

In this chapter we describe the natural language understanding capabilities of the parser. We outline that in order to accomplish the goal of content retrieval of multimedia data, full understanding of natural language is not necessary. However, a restricted interpretation is necessary which is done by the parser component using the application dependent dictionary as a semantic basis.

4.1 Natural Language Descriptions

As mentioned, we propose to perform retrieval of multimedia data by matching the natural language descriptions with query specifications. We believe that unrestricted natural language processing is very difficult to achieve given the AI technology today. We found that the language needed to describe multimedia data is much more formal than everyday English. Hence, instead of natural language description, we use captions to describe multimedia data. Captions are a natural but special, stylized way of writing descriptions with a subset of natural language and not as difficult to parse and interpret as general natural language.

Additionally, for a particular multimedia application the universe of discourse is usually quite constraint. Nouns tend to be concrete and most multimedia databases emphasize still photographs and other fixed time graphics to which few verbs can be applied thereby easing a difficult aspect of natural language processing. Important is that we use natural language only to access entities in a database making complete understanding unnecessary. The details of captions and their restrictions for our objectives are beyond the scope of this paper and are given in [7,13].

4.2 Dictionary

Besides the captions themselves, our system requires auxiliary information from a dictionary. The dictionary or lexicon is necessary for parsing and gives each possible natural language word its semantic: its part of speech, its grammatical form and the form of literals needed to represent it. Many of the words - for example, conjunctions and qualifying adjectives - are consistent in meaning across a wide range of domains; thus we can borrow their interpretation from existing natural language systems and include them in our dictionary. The words that significantly change between

applications are nouns and few verbs. They need to be defined for every application domain separately, but mostly their meaning is straightforward. To simplify matching, we are trying to limit the properties and relationships to a small set of primitives, for example we will not distinguish between the relationship asserted by the terms 'within', 'inside', 'part of', 'containing' and 'comprising'. This can be done without loss because in order to achieve efficient retrieval it is not necessary to capture the full meaning of an English expression, but just the main intent.

4.3 Natural Language Interpretation

The parser translates the text description into a set of predicates called *meaning list*, thereby reducing imprecision and ambiguity of the natural language descriptions considerably. These predicates state facts about the real world entities involved with multimedia data like their properties and relationships. As in most parsing methods, we chose the use of first-order predicate calculus as a formal representation of the description data. The parser depends on the dictionary to turn the descriptions into predicates. It is the parser's task to use the dictionary to resolve synonyms and to check the syntactic context to resolve lexical ambiguities.

An example of a natural language description and its translation into an equivalent set of predicates is shown below.

Description: *"A car with red body"*

Predicates: $car(x)$, $component(x,y)$, $body(y)$, $color(y,red)$

Our parser also provides a mechanisms to automatically partition a query into subject, verb and object components. This is essential in that, during data retrieval we use the partitioned components to match against domain-dependent knowledge which also break down into subject, verb and object categories. Other important features of the parser are the use of *supercaptions*, a generalization of captions, and *frames for stereotypical actions*, allowing a set of predicates to be derived from terms in the description.

Our current implementation of the parser uses augmented-transition network parsing and interpretation routines. It is implemented in Quintus Prolog and running on a SUN SPARC workstation. The details of parser and predicates are beyond the scope of this paper and are given in [9,13].

5. Matching

In this chapter, we propose new ways of matching natural language descriptions of multimedia data with query specifications. The key to our matching process is the use of domain knowledge represented using the notion of class hierarchy borrowed from the object-oriented field.

5.1 Domain-Dependent Knowledge

To represent domain-dependent knowledge, we chose the object-oriented data model. The object-oriented model supports highly structured, complex objects and can capture

106

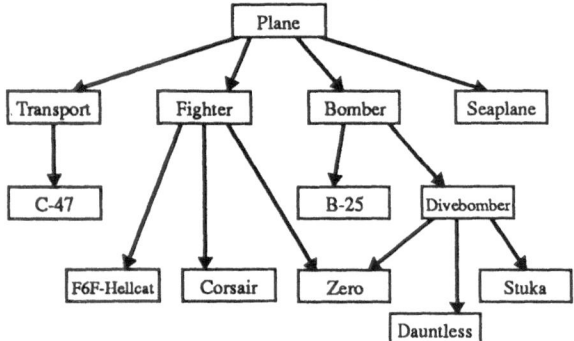

Figure 3: Generalization Hierarchy of a Plane

naturally any mini-world entity. It supports generalization and specialization abstraction which permits conceptual generalization on the contents of the captions. Researchers [7,15] have identified the use of the object-oriented model in multimedia database applications as an appropriate and viable option. Without loss of generality, in this paper we will restrict our domain of discourse to the domain of the military history of US forces in the Pacific during World War 2. The main reason is that we tested our current prototype MDBMS in a military application based on the domain of the US military history. For our purposes, we will apply the approximate matching technique to this domain; however, we claim that it can be applied to other multimedia applications as well.

Figure 3 shows an example of the generalization hierarchy of plane, a noun concept in our domain of discourse. It is the domain-dependent knowledge on planes that participated in the Pacific during World War 2. We assume that the reader is familiar with object-oriented concepts such as object, class, inheritance along class hierarchy or lattice and methods. We also assume that the direction of the arrow in Figure 3 is from a class to its subclass.

5.2 Partial Matching Algorithm

In this section, we will discuss our partial matching algorithm by following through an example. Suppose that we have images of planes stored in the multimedia database and the images are described as transport planes. Let us now assume that a user gives a query asking for all planes which are C-47s. Even though there is no exact match, we should retrieve all transport planes stored because any C-47 is a transport plane according to the domain-dependent knowledge. Now, if the user asks for all fighter planes, we cannot simply retrieve all transport planes because they may not be what the user wants. However, a user asking for planes would more likely retrieve the stored transport planes than if he was to ask for fighter planes because a transport plane is still a plane but is not a fighter plane.

The goal of our algorithm is also to minimize the influence of the definition of the hierarchy which depends on the

designer. The generalization hierarchy designer might have a view of the domain dependent knowledge which may not be consistent with the view of other people. This phenomenon might bias some specific branch of the generalization hierarchy over other branches during partial matching. Hence, our major objective is to come up with a weight ranking scheme that is both fair and accurate which can be used to determine whether stored multimedia data should be retrieved given a user description.

5.2.1 Weight Ranking within a Class Hierarchy

The weight ranking strategy used is a consequence of the semantics of the class hierarchy (lattice) or the IS-A hierarchy concept supported by the object-oriented data model. Given a class C in a generalization (class) hierarchy for a noun or a verb concept, we can introduce the following two general heuristics:

Heuristic 1: *All subclasses of C (specializations) have positive weights.*

Heuristic 2: *All superclasses of C (generalizations) have negative weights.*

Heuristic 1 says that given a class C specified in a user query, all subclasses of C in the class hierarchy to which C belongs are specializations of the class and more weights (positive) are given. Heuristics 2 says that given a class C specified in a user query, all superclasses of C in the class hierarchy to which C belongs are generalization of the class and less weights (negative) are given. This reasoning follows directly from the definition of a class (IS-A) hierarchy and relationships among classes along the class hierarchy in the context of an object-oriented data model.

The assignment of negative weights to generalization is intuitively clear. The assignment of positive weights to specialization is based on the fact that specialization inherits all properties of the parent nodes in addition to having its own additional information. Hence, we feel that positive or more weights should be assigned to the nodes in the paths towards specialization hierarchy.

In the following, we discuss the weight ranking algorithm resulting from the heuristics. There are three different situations in which weights can be assigned to classes in a class hierarchy (see Figure 4). Suppose that the class specified in a user query is class C. As before, we assume that the direction of the arrow is from a class to its subclass. The first situation, shown in Figure 4(a), is to assign weight to a class

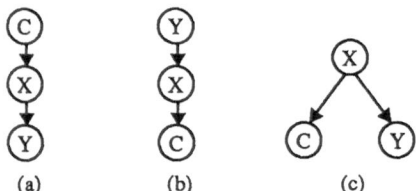

(a)   (b)   (c)

Figure 4: Three Situations in a Class Hierarchy

(X or Y) which is a subclass of class C. The second situation, shown in Figure 4(b), is to assign weight to a class (X or Y) which is a superclass of class C. The third situation, shown in Figure 4(c), is to assign weight to a class (Y) which is a subclass of a superclass (i.e. X) of class C.

The assignment of weights for the three situations is done as follows: First, we assign a weight of 0 to the class C specified in the user query. Class C is the reference point to all other classes in the class hierarchy during approximate matching. For classes which are subclasses of class C, we assign *positive weights* because they are specialized version of class C. Specialized versions of class C have more specific and definite information than C itself and hence are assigned positive weights instead of 0. For our purposes, all subclasses of C are assigned the same positive weight.

For classes which are superclasses or subclasses of superclasses of class C, we assign *negative weights* because they are generalized version of class C. Generalized versions of class C have less and more general information than C itself and hence are assigned negative weights. Different generalization versions have different negative weights. However, in assigning negative weights, we have to minimize the influence of the definition of the model. It is true that the further away a class is from class C in the class hierarchy, the more negative weight is assigned to the class.

In most systems, the assignment of weight of a class is linearly inverse proportional to the depth level of the class relative to the level of the class C specified in the user query. We believe that this is not the correct approach because the relative distance of a particular class to the class of interest, in this case class C, with respect to other classes is not the absolute but some artificial distance caused by a particular designer's view of the domain knowledge. The main problem with this approach is that some classes belonging to some lengthy branch could be unfairly disqualified because of higher negative weights. Our weight ranking system tries to minimize the bias against some lengthy branch of a class hierarchy over other shorter branches.

Given that class C is the class specified by user query as shown in Figure 4, the assignment formulas of weights for classes in a class hierarchy according to the three different situations mentioned are as follows.

(1) Class specified by user query (i.e. class C in figure 4)

$$weight = 0$$

(2) Subclass of class C (i.e. class X or Y in 4(a))

$$weight = \alpha, \text{ where } \alpha \text{ is a integer constant}$$

(3) Superclass of class C (i.e. class X or Y in 4(b))

$$weight = -\left(\alpha \times \sum_{i=1}^{n} (\frac{1}{\beta})^{i}\right),$$

where α, β are integer constants and n is level # of superclass relative to class C

(4) Subclass of a superclass of class C (i.e.class Y in 4(c))

$$weight = -\left(\alpha \times \sum_{i=1}^{h} (\frac{1}{\beta})^{i}\right) - \left(\gamma \times \sum_{j=1}^{l} (\frac{1}{\upsilon})^{(l+1-j)}\right),$$

where $\alpha, \beta, \upsilon, \gamma$ are integer constants; h is level # of superclass relative to class C and l is level # of subclass relative to superclass

In our scheme, a class which is assigned a positive weight is always selected during partial matching. A class with a negative weight can be selected provided that it does not exceed a threshold value set by the user.

To understand the weight assignments for different classes, we next give some examples using the class hierarchy of Figure 3. Given a user query, if the image corresponding to the user description is not found in the database, the system automatically proceeds with approximate matching. For a given query, the weight assignment formulas are used to calculate the weights for some of the classes in the class hierarchy. For the sake of argument, we assume that the values of α, β, γ and υ are 40, 2, 48 and 2 respectively.

(1) **"A transport plane sank in the Pacific"**
Transport = 0, C-47 = 40, Plane = -20,
Fighter = - 44, Corsair = -56

(2) **"A F6F-Hellcat sank in the Pacific"**
F6F-Hellcat = 0, Plane = -30, Seaplane = -54,
Stuka = -72, C-47 = -66

(3) **"A bomber sank in the Pacific"**
Bomber = 0, Stuka = 40, B-52 = 40, Plane = -20,
Seaplane = - 44, C-47 = -56

In the examples shown, all classes which are assigned positive weights are selected during partial matching. In example (1), the positive weight of 40. for the class C-47 means that the image whose description is *"A C-47 sank in the Pacific"* is selected during partial matching. As shown in the examples, all classes which are subclasses of the class which is specified in a user query are assigned positive weights. All classes which are superclasses or subclasses of the superclasses of the class which is specified in a user query are assigned negative weights. For these classes, the weight of a class is inversely proportional to the depth level of the class relative to the level of the class specified in the user query along the class hierarchy although they are not strictly linear. In example (2), the class Seaplane has a negative weight of -54. This means that the image whose description is *"A Seaplane sank in the Pacific"* has a weight of - 54. Class Stuka has a negative weight of -72 and class Stuka is further away from F6F-Hellcat than class Seaplane is from F6F-Hellcat.

Suppose the weight of a class is linearly but inversely proportional to the depth level of the class relative to the level of the class C specified in the user query. If we assign a negative constant weight, say -10, for each level away from class C, the class which is 5 levels away from class C will have a negative weight of -50 compared to a negative value of -20 for a class which is 2 levels away from class C. For example, if the user query is "**A Transport sank in the Pacific**", the weight of class Transport is 0, class Seaplane is -20 and class Stuka is -40. Using our formulas, the same user query will assign weights of classes Transport, Seaplane and Stuka to be 0, -44 and -62 respectively. The weight of class Stuka is more biased against relative to the weight of class Seaplane using the linear method over our method.

It is very difficult to quantify how much closer class Seaplane is to class Transport over class Stuka to class Transport as both Seaplane and Stuka are types of planes. Our formulas are designed to minimize bias as best as possible. A user is more likely to select a threshold value such that class Stuka is less likely selected during approximate matching over class Seaplane using the linear method compared to using our dynamic method. Another difficult task is to set the value of the constants to be applied in our assignment formulas as well as the threshold value. The user must choose the correct values for the constants and the threshold value depending on the number of objects that qualify during approximate matching. Hence, it is necessary for the system to interact with the user through the user interface throughout the matching process.

5.2.2 Weight Ranking for a Group of Class Hierarchies

In this section, we extend the ranking of weights for classes belonging to different generalization hierarchies. For each class hierarchy selected by the user query, the classes within the class hierarchy are assigned weights using the weight ranking system discussed in Section 5.3.1.

The global ranking of weights for different class hierarchies is a problem because the weights assigned within each class hierarchy now have to be considered with respect to weights assigned for other class hierarchies and they have to be meaningful globally. Only the user is able to determine the priority order of importance of the class hierarchies because it depends on his intent. To combine independently calculated weights of two class hierarchies (CH) the following weight formula can be used.

$$\text{Weight} = \alpha\,(\text{Weight (CH1)}) + \beta\,(\text{Weight (CH2)})$$

The constant values α and β determine the priority order of CH1 and CH2. They are to be specified by the user. However, if the weight of CH1 or CH2 is zero, the constants α and β are set to one; hence, no information from the user is needed in this case.

For a practical system, the number of class hierarchies involved in the weight assignment is obviously large since many noun and verb concepts are involved. It is not difficult to see that our weight ranking scheme can be easily extended to assign weights for classes involving many class hierarchies.

5.2.3 Application of Weight Ranking Algorithm

The application of the weighting algorithm just presented requires a parser to understand the natural language specifications in the multimedia data descriptions and the user queries. As stated earlier, the descriptions are parsed and stored in the system as predicates. The queries are processed as follows.

When a query is received from the user, the parser separates the natural language specification into smaller component groups, namely subject noun, verb and object noun phrases. Each of these will actually become predicates. When these predicates match exactly with the predicates in the descriptions of certain multimedia data, those multimedia data will be retrieved. However, there may be other descriptions of multimedia data that are actually of interest to users but those descriptions are not stated as logically implied by the query. This latter category is expected to be the usual case rather than the former for reasons stated earlier.

To find the latter, we suggest that the system searches in the noun and verb generalization hierarchies of the object classes and assigns weights to the descriptions as given in the weight assignment algorithm, using the appropriate weighting factors (ω and δ in the previous section) as received from the user. Only the multimedia data with combined weight exceeding the threshold value set by the user will then be retrieved.

The separation of the natural language query can be in smaller components than the three groups just stated. For example, a complex noun phrase may be separated into a number of small noun groups and the weighting algorithm is applied to these groups to obtain a combined weight. Naturally, the finer the granularity of the separation, the larger and the more complex the processing is needed.

6. Graphical User Interface

The goal of a graphical user interface is to support the query specification process allowing the user to efficiently use the database system. It should allow inexperienced users to retrieve data from the database without having to know a specific query language. In today's database management systems the user is forced to think in terms of data model and query language, differing a lot from his way of thinking. Often a user can express a query easily in natural language, but has difficulties to express it in some given query language.

Most queries involve both media and formatted data. For the media part of the query we use our intelligent matching algorithm which is directly processing natural language captions. For conditions on formatted data, natural language expressions are mostly too imprecise to be directly processed. We try to overcome this problem by providing a graphical user interface supporting a natural query specification.

The data model adopted in our system is an extended relational data model. Despite some drawbacks the relational model has great advantages: It is well known, widely used and has a firm theoretical basis. For our purpose, we extend the relational model to capture media data types and, as shown below, we also extend the query language to allow the manipulation of media data and facilitate the query specification process.

Before describing the user interface of the MDBMS system, we first outline ways to achieve a natural query specification process.

6.1 Towards a Natural Query Specification

Usually, every user can describe a query (or at least the desired result) easily in natural language. Unfortunately, natural language expressions representing a query are imprecise and difficult to automatically translate into a formal query language to be understood by a database management system. We argue that the gap between the user's way of expressing a query in natural language and database manipulation languages like SQL can be improved considerably.

When comparing the user's natural language (NL) expression for a query with corresponding SQL statements the first difficulty is that the table and attribute names do not exactly match. In a graphical user interface this problem is easy to overcome. All table and attribute names can be presented to the user who simply selects the desired ones using a pointing device (e.g. mouse).

Another difficulty is related to joins between tables. Mostly the join condition is hidden in the user's NL expression. In examining a large number of queries expressed in natural language as well as SQL we found that, in most cases, the join condition directly corresponds to some specific NL expressions. Additionally, the number of joins used in most of the queries was small compared to the number of possible joins. This can be explained by two facts. First, the number of semantically meaningful joins is restricted and second, some of the most frequently used joins are already intended at the design time of the database. In order to provide a natural way of expressing joins, in our system we allow database designer and user to define and name joins prior to its actual use. A predefined join can involve more than two tables (e.g. two tables are joined by means of a third table) thereby providing a simple way of expressing m:n relationships. Once defined and named, all predefined joins can be used to specify a query. Predefined joins differ from views: First, the result of a predefined join is not a table as in the case of a view but a specific connection between tables. Second, predefined joins allow connections between different levels in nested queries and even recursive joins can be expressed. An example for predefined joins is given in the next section.

Another thing we learned in examining the process of query specification is the handling of complex queries. Given a complex data retrieval task the user partitions it into smaller subtasks which are easier to handle. Starting with the clear parts of the query the user deals with all parts and combines the results into the final solution. In our system we support this way of handling complex queries by an incremental query specification to be described in the next section.

Finally, we observed that a special category of queries is easy to express in NL but rather complicated in a formal query language. Additional operators, closely related to corresponding NL expressions, allow an easier and clearer query specification. Considering for example a query like *'Select the name of planes which can carry all weapons of the category air-to-air'* we found that a special *'all'* operator greatly enhances the readability and understandability of the SQL-like query making it similar to the user's NL expression. For the example, we presume to have the tables *plane, weapon, plane_weapon* and a predefined join named *carries* expressing the m:n relationship between planes and weapons.

```
select p_name from plane
where  plane carries weapon
       and  w_nr = all ( select w_nr from weapon
                              where category = 'air-to-air')
```

SQL statements expressing the same query without the all operator are rather complicated. Two possibilities are:

```
1. select p_name from plane
   where ((select w_nr from plane_weapon A
         where plane.w_nr = A.w_nr)
               contains
         (select w_nr from weapon
           where category = 'air-to-air') )
```

```
2. select p_name from plane
   where not exists
         (select * from plane_weapon B
         where B.w_nr in (select w_nr from weapon
                              where category = 'air-to-air'))
               and not exists
               (select * from plane_weapon C
               where  C. p_nr = B.p_nr
                       and  C.w_nr = B.W_nr) )
```

6.2 Description of the Graphical User Interface

In this paper, we will give a general idea of our graphical user interface by presenting a small example of the retrieval process. Due to space limitations we will only describe a small fraction of its capabilities.

After selecting the database the user gets the system menu providing the main database manipulation functions: insert, delete, update or retrieve (see figure 5). When selecting retrieval, the user gets the query specification window and his first step is to select the tables to be used in the query. For each selected table a list with all attributes will be displayed in a separate window and all predefined connec-

110

tions involving at least one of the selected tables will appear in the *Connections* window. To specify the result list (projection) the user has to move the desired attributes to the *Result List* window. Now only the conditions need to be specified. Using connections, attributes of the selected tables and operators provided by the *Tool Box* the query can easily be built using the mouse. In the *Query Representation* window the query is displayed graphically. Each part of the query is represented by a small box, simple conditions by a single, subqueries by a double box, and the connection lines are labeled with the kind of connection used. An advantage is that every part of the query can be addressed for edit or delete at any time during the query specification process. To enhance the clarity of display parts of the query can be grouped together and displayed as one box (zoom in). If the user wants to see the query in full detail at a later stage he can use the zoom out option.

To support incremental query specification we allow the user to start with any part of the query and combine the separate parts at a later stage. Additionally, we provide an option to save and reload any part of the query for later use.

Another important part is the way of specifying the natural language description part of a query necessary when media data are involved. If the user selects a media attribute in the specification of the condition, automatically a special description editor will be displayed in a separate window where the media description can be specified. The description editor has special features including buttons to check the description, present the hierarchy for a word and enter the weight of the different parts of the description needed for the approximate matching.

To get an impression of the user interface, the specification for the query *'Select the name, air base and image of planes which can carry all weapons of category air-to-air and where the image shows "plane attacking a hostile plane"'* is displayed in figure 5.

For the representation of results we choose a combined form and list oriented approach. Generally, the results are presented as a list. Media attributes are represented as buttons allowing to access the media data. By clicking to a row of the list a single tuple can be obtained in a form. Due to space limitations we can not elaborate on these features.

In this paper, we presented only a small part of our graphical user interface. The data definition, insert, update and deletion operation, query processing and optimization issues, representation of results, predefined joins, special operators and their semantics are far beyond the scope of this paper and will be presented in a later paper [8].

7. Summary

A major problem faced in a multimedia database system is the retrieval of multimedia data such as a sound or an image. Media data is intrinsically rich in semantics and con-

ventional search methods used in databases and information retrieval systems may not work or are of little use. Most research on intelligent IR systems are concerned with natural language processing and deductive capabilities based on extended semantic models of document content. However, most of them deal with exact matching or primitive partial matching using simple linear methods.

Another problem faced in today's database systems is the lack of a natural way to specify complex queries. It is caused by the gap between the user's way of thinking and the query languages used in most systems. Although a lot of work has been done in the area of user interfaces for database systems no query language comes close to the natural query specification process used by humans.

In this paper, we discussed these fundamental problems and outlined the architecture of our MDBMS system. One contribution of our paper is the formulation of a partial matching algorithm that uses domain knowledge, represented using an object-oriented data model, and a weight ranking system to assign weights to different multimedia data stored in a database and selects those multimedia data that partially match a given user query description. Our parser, unlike others, provides an interpretation of natural language descriptions needed to achieve an intelligent retrieval of multimedia data. Further research is necessary to improve the parser to also automatically derive adjectives and other caption components for complete understanding and processing of captions in the context of partial matching.

A second contribution of this paper is our graphical user interface. It shortens the gap between the user's way of thinking and formal query languages by using graphical user interaction. In our system, we support incremental query specification, predefined joins and special operators to make the query specification process user friendly. The user is guided as much as possible allowing a quick and almost faultless query specification. Further research is necessary to come even closer to the user's way of query specification e.g. by allowing the user to directly communicate with the system in natural language.

We believe that our system provides a simple and elegant approach to both retrieval of multimedia data and query specification. The simplicity of our retrieval method lies in exploiting the semantics of generalization and specialization abstraction of the object-oriented model; the simplicity of the user interface lies in the natural way of query specification being directly obtained from queries expressed in natural language.

We also believe that our approaches are general ones that can be readily applied to other areas. Our retrieval method can be used for other applications in IR and AI and the ideas of our user interface can be easily applied to most database query interfaces.

References

[1] Agrawal, R. et al. "OdeView: The Graphical Interface to Ode", Proc. ACM-SIGMOD 1990 Int'l Conf. on Management of Data, Atlantic City, pp. 34-43, 1990.

[2] Bates, M. and B. Bobrow, "Information Retrieval using a Transportable Natural Language Interface," Proc. of the 6th. ACM SIGIR Conf. on R&D in Information Retrieval, Bethesda, MD, 1983.

[3] Bryce D. and Hull, R. "SNAP: A Graphics Based Schema Manager", Proc. IEEE Int'l Conf. on Data Engineering, Los Angeles, CA, pp. 151-164, 1986.

[4] Chiaramella, Y. and B. Defude, "A Prototype of an Intelligent System for Information Retrieval: IOTA," Information Processing and Management, vol. 23, no. 4, pp. 285-303, 1987.

[5] Christodoulakis, S. et. al., "Multimedia Document Presentation, Information Extraction, and Document Formation in MINOS: A Model and a System, " ACM TOOIS, vol. 4, no. 4, pp. 345-383, 1986.

[6] Grosz, B.J. et. al., "TEAM: An Experiment in the Design of Transportable Natural Language Interfaces," Artificial Intelligence, pp. 173-243, 1987.

[7] Holtkamp, B. et. al., "Demon- A media Object Model incorporating Natural Language Descriptions for Retrieval Support," Tech. Report NPS52-90-019, Naval Postgraduate School, Monterey, CA, 1990.

[8] Keim, D. A. and Lum, V. "A Graphical Database Interface for a Multimedia DBMS Supporting a Natural Query Specification Process", in preparation

[9] Lum, V. and K. Meyer-Wegener, "A Multimedia Database Management System Supporting Content Search in Media Data," Tech. Report NPS52-89-020, Naval Postgraduate School, Monterey, CA, 1989.

[10] Masunaga, Y. "Multimedia Databases: A Formal Framework," Proc. IEEE CS Office Automation Symp. IEEE CS Press, Washington, pp. 36-45, 1987.

[11] Meyer-Wegener, K. et. al., "Managing Multimedia Data," Tech. Report NPS52-88-010, Naval Post-graduate School, Monterey, CA, 1988.

[12] Rogers, T. R. and Cattell, R. G. G. " Entity-Rela-tionship Database User Interfaces" in Readings in Database Systems, edited by M. Stonebraker, 1988.

[13] Rowe, N. and E. Guglielmo, "Exploiting Captions for Access to Multimedia Databases," to appear in IEEE Computer, 1991.

[14] Spark, K. Jones, "Artificial Intelligence: What can it offer to Information Retrieval," Proc. of the Informatics 3, Aslib, ed., London, 1978.

[15] Woelk, D. and W. Kim, "Multimedia Information Management in an Object-Oriented Database System," Proc. of VLDB, Brighton, England, 1987.

[16] Zloof, M. M. "Query-By-Example: A Data Base Language," IBM Systems Journal, 4, pp. 324-343, 1977.

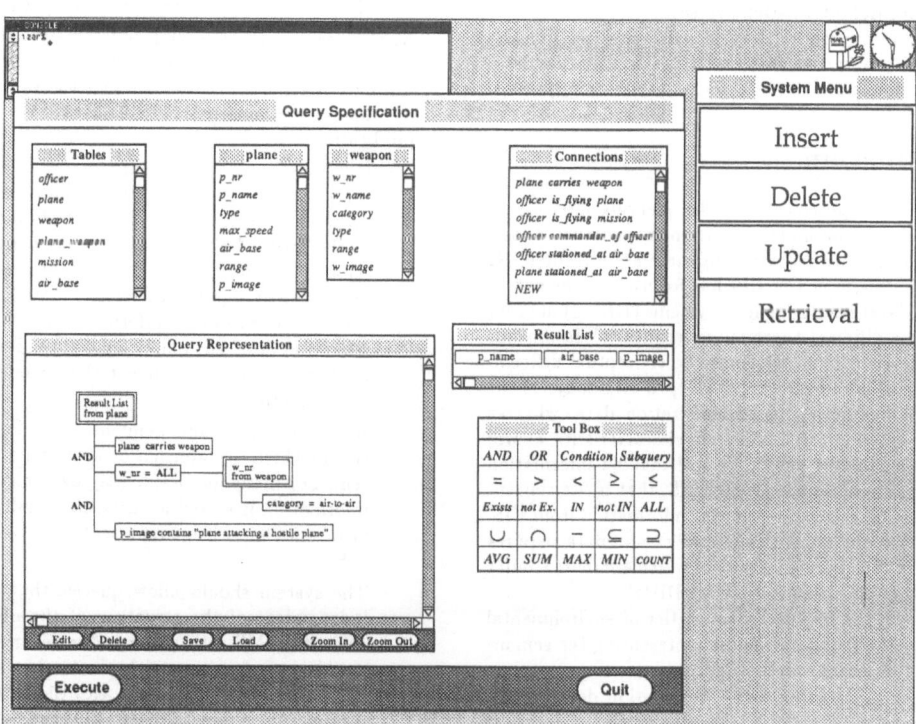

Figure 5: Screen after Specifying the Query

An Information Retrieval View of Environmental Information Systems

Norbert Fuhr

Universität Dortmund, Informatik VI, Postfach 500500
W-4600 Dortmund, Germany

Abstract

In the design of future enviromental systems, the semantics of the data as well as the kind of queries to those systems have to be considered. Enviromental data is frequently uncertain and incomplete. Heterogeneous data structures as well as multimedia data have to be managed by the system. For interactive queries, the system should allow vague queries and query formulations that are independent of the specific structure of the data and its representation. For vague queries and imprecise data, methods developed in information retrieval can be applied. Heterogeneous data structures can be handled with concepts from object-oriented database management systems. In multimedia information systems, the problem of full integration of the different media is yet unsolved, especially in case the information a user searches for is stored in different media. We claim that the retrieval interface offered by current database management systems is not sufficient for interactive use. In addition, functions like ranking, browsing, zooming, relevance feedback and cooperative support should be provided. Finally, we emphasize the need for empirical studies for the design of future environmental information systems.

Keywords: information retrieval, environmental information systems, heterogeneous data structures, multimedia data, vague queries, imprecise data, interactive information systems.

1 Introduction

In this paper, the requirements for the querying interface to future environmental information systems are discussed, and some important concepts for this component are presented. So far, much of the discussion of EIS has focused on the extension of current database managment systems (DBMS) in order to cope with the different types of environmental data. This approach, however, cannot overcome the conceptual deficiencies of today's DBMS which were developed originally for the management of bussiness and administration data, whereas environmental data has totally different characteristics, as will be shown below. In this paper, we will take an information retrieval (IR) oriented perspective on EIS, that is, we concentrate on the task of retrieving relevant information from EIS. We will show that the semantics of queries and data requires new functions in the querying interface which are more similar to those of IR systems than to those of DBMS.

First, we describe the major characteristics of environmental data, especially the requirements for representing the semantics of the data in an information system:

- Environmental data (like e.g. observation data or values of properties of pollutants) is frequently imprecise or

missing. In conventional DP MS, these cases are treated more or less as exceptions, whereas they are quite regular in EIS. In a similar way, the management of texts (or multimedia documents) can not be supported adequatly by restricting to string search methods and Boolean query languages. More advanced IR techniques assume an imprecise representation of the semantics of documents.

- Environmental data has different forms of representations, since facts as well as texts or elements of a knowledge representation formalism should be managed by an EIS. Even for the storage of facts, a large number of data types is required (For example, a series of measurement results should be represented as a pointwise specified function in order to allow the interpolation of values).

- The structure of environmental data is heterogeneous. This fact may be caused by the different origin of the data as well as by the different application contexts for which data is collected.

- Observation data mostly refers to specific geographic locations and a certain time. For this reason, EIS should offer special support for spatial and temporal data.

Now we regard the querying functions of EIS. Here we concentrate on interactive queries, since the interactive use of EIS leads to new requirements, whereas the program interface to information systems has been discussed extensively in other publications.

- Queries submitted to EIS are frequently vague. Due to the complexity of the application field, a user cannot give a precise and complete specification of his information need in the form of a single query statement. Instead, users tend to formulate queries with vague conditions, and they modify their query statement iteratively, depending on the responses from the information system (e.g. think of a request about "The pollution of ground water with nitrate in farming areas"). Current DBMS offer no support for vague queries.

- Requests may be independent of the form of representation in which the information asked for is stored in the system. For many queries, it may be irrelevant whether this information is stored as facts, in a multimedia document or in some knowledge representation language within the EIS.

- The system should allow queries that are more or less independent of the structure of the objects stored. In current DBMS, it is assumed that every query refers to a certain set of objects with identical or similar structure. This approach is in conflict with the heterogeneous structure of environmental data, thus requiring several query statements for a single request. The semantics of interactive queries can be better supported by allowing a certain kind of abstraction from the specific object structures.

In the following, we first present a conceptual model for EIS. Then we discuss several concepts that should be included in future EIS. Finally, the steps towards the development of these systems are discussed.

2 A conceptual model for EIS

We describe a conceptual model for EIS in order to clarify some essential problems in the design of these system. For the specification of our model, we start with the application requirements, from which the functions that are to be provided by the EIS are derived. This approach is different from the traditional method of developing information systems, where first a DBMS is selected (according to the major requirements of the application), and then the specific application problems have to be solved by additional application programs. As we will show, the requirements of EIS can hardly be fulfilled with current DBMS, not even when the EIS is implemented on top of such a system. Instead, the new functions required by EIS should be integrated in the basic information system.

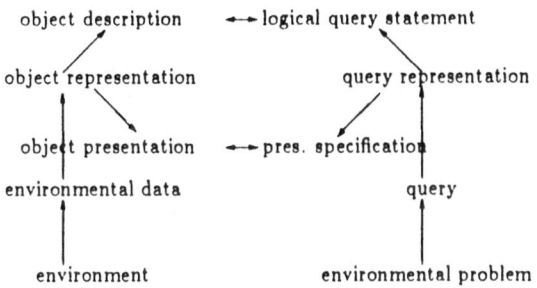

Figure 1: Conceptual model

Figure 1 shows our conceptual model for EIS. Observations of the environment produce environmental data, which can be measurement results or data derived from these values, as well as written reports or even multimedia documents with graphics, photos, voice annotations or videos. Current work on multimedia information systems focuses on the storage of multimedia objects [46] [24] and on transformations of the conceptual and the layout structure of multimedia documents. As mentioned in the beginning, we are mainly interested in the semantics of environmental data. For this reason, we introduce the object representation level in our model: Here the semantics of the objects stored in the database is represented. For example, at this level, a series of measurement results should be represented as a pointwise specified function, and the spatial and temporal distribution of these values also should be represented, e.g. for allowing the interpolation of values. For texts, the representation may range from a sequence of strings (as in most of today's commercial IR systems) up to a knowledge-based formalism like a semantic network. In the case of multimedia documents, the representation of the semantics of this kind of objects will be a major problem for future research.

Current approaches allow the assignment of keywords to an object, and semantic links may be established between different objects. An object's representation forms the basis for its description as well as for its presentation. The object description is used for answering queries by the EIS; only knowledge that is part of an object's description can be referred to in a query. So multimedia documents may allow for the storage of all kinds of knowledge, but the crucial point is, whether there are appropriate means for accessing this knowledge. If the system provides only poor descriptions of multimedia objects, then most of the information that is relevant to a request can hardly be retrieved. So the quality of the description of objects has a major impact on the overall quality of an EIS.

The presentation of objects in response to a query also depends on the representation of objects. Here different views of an object should be provided, in order to present that portion of an object that is relevant for a query. For example, in a fulltext document, only the relevant passages should be displayed. From a map stored in the system, only the geographic region that is referred to by the query should be presented.

This separation of the different levels of objects is similar to the object-oriented database management system (OODBMS) approach, where the concept of encapsulation separates between the internal data and the externally visible attributes of an object [10] [23]. We go one step further and distinguish between the raw data and its representation as parts of the internal data. The externally visible attributes are provided by certain operators that can be applied to the objects. Here we separate between operators giving the description of the object and those yielding different presentations (or views).

On the request side of our conceptual model, we also distinguish several levels corresponding to those of the data side. An environment problem leads to a query from a user. This information need is mapped onto a query representation, that is, the system's understanding of the query. The mapping can be performed automatically (e.g. if the system allows the user to enter a natural language statement), but mostly this has to be done by the user himself by formulating his query in a certain query language. From the query representation, the system derives the logical query formulation, that is, the conditions relating to the object descriptions (and their logical combination). Furthermore, the presentation specification also is derived from the query representation, that is, for the objects that are answers to the logical query statement, the specification of the view in which they are to be presented.

With the conceptual model, we can also illustrate the problem of imprecise data and vague queries. Already a single measurement result has a limited precision, therefore it should not be treated as a precise value (which is the standard case in today's DBMS). Furthermore, measurement results may be incomplete for various reasons. A second kind of imprecision is caused by the mapping from environmental data onto object representations. For text and multimedia documents, representations (as well as the descriptions) always will be uncertain and incomplete. An information system should take this imprecision into account, so query langues assuming precise descriptions (like e.g. Boolean text retrieval) are inappropriate.

With the queries, imprecision and vagueness also play an important role. The query statement formulated in order to solve an environmental problem may ask for information that does not really solve the problem. In the next step, the user's query has to be mapped onto the query representation. Since a natural language statement is more expressive than any formal representation, there is a loss of information here. For complex problem solving tasks, users often formulate vague queries (e.g. with different vaque criteria that are in conflict with each other). Current DBMS do not allow vague conditions, they require the specification of precise values instead. So a user's query for "a high proportion of nitrate" may lead to a series of query statements with varying values.

The discussion in this section has shown that major requirements for future EIS are powerful representations for environmental data, the consideration of the imprecision of these representations in query processing, and the support of vague queries.

3 Concepts for EIS

3.1 Vague queries and imprecise data

In the field of IR, vague queries and imprecise representations have been discussed in the context of text retrieval. Whereas today's commercial IR systems are still based on simple string search methods, better representations for text content have been developed and tested succesfully in IR research: Stemming algorithms [35] [27] [26] help in searching for different derivations of a word stem, machine-readable dictionaries [38] and robust parsers support the identification of noun phrases. Text indexing approaches either use a free vocabulary, that is, every term (single word or phrase) can be part of a document's description [39] [14], or they are based on a controlled vocabulary, where only index terms from a thesaurus can be assigned to a document (even if this term does not occur within the text of the document) [28] [15]. In order to cope with the imprecision of these descriptions, probabilistic IR models have been developed. In these models, it is assumed that a single query-document pair is either relevant or nonrelevant, where the relevance of different pairs is independent of each other. Now the probabilistic models aim at the estimation of the probability $P(R|q_k, d_m)$ that a query-document pair with representations q_k and d_m will be judged relevant by the user. In response to a query, documents are ranked according to decreasing values of these estimates. It can be shown theoretically that this strategy yields an optimum retrieval quality

In order to estimate the probability of relevance $P(R|q_k, d_m)$, probabilistic models are applied similar to a machine learning procedure [14]. First, relevance information for some query-document pairs must be given, from which the probabilistic parameters of the model are derived. These parameters are used for the estimation of the probability of relevance for other query-document pairs.

For vague queries and imprecise data in databases, different approaches have been developed. Fuzzy databases [36] are based on fuzzy logic [47]. The system VAGUE described in [30] applies the vector model developed for text retrieval [37] to databases. In [13], a probabilistic model for this task is presented. Here imprecise data (like null values or disjunctive information) is stored as a probability distribution over the domain of the attribute. With this approach, the limited pre-

cision of measurement results or the distribution of statistical values can be represented adequately. A vague query is a set of vague conditions, where each condition consists of an attribute name and either a unary predicate (like "low", "high", "several") or a binary predicate (like "similar to", "preferably higher then") in combination with a comparison value. The user may assign different weights to the conditions in the query (according to their importance), whereas the system computes indexing weights for attribute values with respect to query conditions. Based on these two kinds of weights, the system ranks the objects according to their probability of relevance. In this approach, attribute values can be of arbitrary complexity, e.g. a user may ask for similar chemical substances like in [31].

A different strategy for vague querys has been developed in the hypertext/hypermedia approach [8]. Here objects are regarded as nodes of a graph, and the edges represent semantic links between different objects. These links are used for browsing from a given object to similar objects. In contrast to the document clustering approach developed in text retrieval [44], most hypertext approaches support different types of links, so browsing can be more specific. The SATELLITE system ([34]) uses the browsing mechanism for navigation in an OODBMS. As described in [12], browsing and probabilistic retrieval can be regarded as two different search strategies for vague queries that complement each other.

In the field of artificial intelligence, formalisms for representing uncertainty — especially probabilistic approaches — have gained more attention during the past five years [19] [20]. The probabilistic network approach described in [33] provides a theoretical foundation for probabilistic rule-based approaches, like e.g. in expert systems for diagnosis. The paper [42] presents a probabilistic model for representing vague terminological concepts in a semantic network, where default assumptions are assigned probabilistic weights.

3.2 Heterogeneous data structures

In contrast to classical data models like the hierarchical, the network and the relational model, OODBMS are no longer based on the assumption of a uniform structure of the data to be managed by the system. Objects with identical structure form object classes, which in turn are elements of an inheritance hierarchy. Due to the inheritance mechanism, a certain class inherits the elements of the internal structure as well as the operators applicable to objects of this class from its superclass.

For the requirements of EIS, the following properties of OODBMS are important:

- A collection of data that should be treated as a unit at a certain level of the application can be declared to form a composite object, and the OODBMS provides operations for manipulating composite objects as a whole. In contrast to this approach, in relational databases the data belonging to a single object often is spread over several relations, thus requiring expensive joins for most operations on the object.

- OODBMS query models (e.g. [22], see also [17] for a survey) exploit the class hierarchy for a top-down approach, where a query may refer to the objects in a class and all its subclasses. However, only attributes occurring in all these classes may be used in the conditions forming the query.

- In [41], a bottom-up approach for queries in OODBMS is presented. Following the concept of method overloading, equivalent operators for different object classes are defined, so there is a single operator for several classes (with different implementations).

However, these approaches are not sufficient for interactive queries in EIS. A major drawback of most of the OODBMS query models is the rigid treatment of data structures. For example, if an attribute is set-valued in one class and single-valued in a second class, then it is impossible to formulate a single query that refers to this attribute in both classes. The approach from Neuhold and Schrefl helps to overcome this problem, but here the appropriate operators have to be defined explicitly. For the application discussed here, the OODBMS should allow to ignore certain aspects of the structure of objects. In [9], the concept of "connection under logical independence" is formulated for this purpose: Here a user only enters a set of attribute conditions, from which the system derives the correct query statement with respect to the data structures of the system. If more than one correct statement is possible, the user is asked to resolve the ambiguity. The "universal relation" model is a well-known example of this concept [29]. Future EIS also may require the coupling of different databases for a single application. This problem of interoperability of heterogeneous databases has become a major field of database research recently [32].

3.3 Scientific data

In contrast to relational DBMS that can handle only a few data types required for business and administration data, EIS should be able to manage a diversity of data types that occur in scientific data, e.g. spatial data, temporal data and statistical data. For these kinds of data, appropriate data types, operators and predicates have to be supported by the DBMS. For example, for spatial data union, intersection and difference operators and predicates for testing overlap, containment or proximity are required [16]. Furthermore, operators that derive new data values should also be integrated in the system, such as statistical operators, interpolation or Fourier analysis [11]. Since a large proportion of the data stored in EIS relates to a specific point of time or time period, the system should support the notion of valid time [43].

3.4 Multimedia information systems

According to the different kinds of environmental data, an EIS should be able to store knowledge in different forms of representation. Allthough there is increasing research activity concerning multimedia information systems, there is little work on the retrieval problem in these system. Moreover, the integration of the different representation forms is only discussed for the storage and the display of multimedia objects. For retrieval, only links between objects (or parts of objects) with different forms of representation have been considered so far.

The combination of knowledge representation methods and databases has been termed "knowledge base management sys-

tems" [5] [40]. Here two different strategies for this combination should be mentioned:

- Deductive databases combine relational databases with logical knowledge representation methods [7].
- Semantic data models aim at the integration of terminological knowledge and integrity constraints [18].

Some object-oriented data models try to combine these two approaches, like e.g. the model described in [21]. The CLASSIC database system described in [3] is based on the semantic network formalism KL-ONE [4].

For EIS, it would be desirable to allow query formulations that are independent of the form of representation. In our example query about the pollution with nitrate, we might search for these terms in text documents. However, if we are also interested in measurement results concerning this problem, we have to formulate a different query. In order to overcome this problem, a knowledge-based component would be required as part of the EIS, which translates representation-independent queries into representation-specific ones.

3.5 Interactive information systems

The query interface of today's information systems has been designed originally as an interface to application programs: in response to a precise query, a set of answers is returned. For interactive use, however, vague queries as well as iterative querying strategies should be supported (like e.g. in IR or in the hypertext approach). Based on the interface provided by current DBMS, three different approaches to interactive interfaces have been developed [9]:

- Query formulation aids help the user in transforming his information need into a correct query statement. The RABBIT system [45] present the concepts of the underlying database as a semantic network. Instead of formulating a query, the user navigates through this network. The "Knowledge Explorer" described in [25] helps to solve terminological problems: If a concept named by the user is not an attribute of the database, the system uses the database schema and an additional dictionary for proposing possible attribute names.

- Database browsers show a certain proportion of the database in the form of a set of tuples or objects which are located together (according to a predefined neighbourhood relation). In order to move the view shown by the browser to those elements of the database the user is interested in, he must use navigation commands. In most browsers, however, the set of possible navigation commands and the simplified presentation of the database structure pose severe restrictions on the set of queries that can be answered this way.

- The concept of generalization is in contrast to the usual top-down approach from a query formulation leading to concrete elements of the answer. Here the user first specifies a single object that is an answer to his intended query, and then the system derives the query statement by generalizing from this specific element. A well-known example of this approach is the system "Query by example" [48].

For interactive multimedia information systems, additional querying functions are needed:

- Ranking of objects instead of retrieving just a set of objects is needed due to imprecision of environmental data and the vagueness of queries. Starting with the objects with the highest probability of relevance, the user may look through the list of ranked objects as long as he wants to, without being forced to modify his query in order to achieve the desired number of objects.

- Browsing is a more associative search strategy, which may be favourable for rather vague information needs.

- Zooming allows to view a set of objects at different abstraction levels. Similar to the bird's eyes view in hypertext systems, one can also define zooming views for databases, e.g. by providing statistical information about the distribution of attribute values in a set of objects.

- Relevance feedback is a method for implicit reformulation of the query statement. Besides the binary relevance judgements used in IR, more sophisticated feedback techniques are also possible. For example, the system RABBIT mentioned above offers several options for criticizing a certain answer object, thus modifying the query.

Finally, future EIS also should provide active support in the information search process. Cooperative interfaces to information systems [2] try to correct misunderstandings, queries are over-answered and the system proposes reformulations of the query.

4 Steps towards the development of future EIS

In this paper, we have mentioned a large number of concepts that are relevant for future EIS. Currently, many EIS are implemented based on a relational DBMS, but most of these approaches show serious difficulties when attempts are made to integrate any of the concepts described before. So there are two questions that should be answered before a new EIS for a specific application is going to be developed:

- To what extend can a system based on today's DBMS architecture support the intended application?
- Which concepts should be provided by a hypothetical/future system in order to give full support to the application?

While the first question is only relevant for the users of the specific application, the second one is directed towards the development of future EIS. By collecting enough evidence for the necessity of certain concepts, the research activity in this field can be stimulated.

In a related application area, we have performed empirical studies in order to identify relevant concepts and to propose the design of future information systems: In the project "Access to materials data banks: user studies and system desighn", we have regarded materials data banks (containing values of properties of materials) [1]. This application is similar to EIS about properties of chemical substance that act as pollutants (see e.g. [31]). In this project, 15 search dialogs with existing materials data systems were observed, where 14 of the dialogs did not give satisfactory results for the user. The analysis of the dialogs showed that this result was mainly due to the fact that certain important concepts of the application were not supported by the system. So we think that similar

studies should be performed with EIS, in order to predict the success of systems currently under development as well as for guiding research work in this field.

The discussion in this paper has concentrated on the conceptual level of EIS. In order to develop future EIS, also the problems of the lower levels of the system have to be solved. For example, internal representations for the different types of data have to be developed together with implementations of the corresponding operators and predicates. Furthermore, storage and access methods and query processing strategies have to be devised. A major approach for integration these new concepts into new types of DBMS are extensible database management systems [6]. Although this approach seems to be promising for some of the concepts discussed here, we think that the IR-oriented concepts cannot be integrated in the systems proposed so far. Here the basic concepts underlying traditional DBMS (that is, Boolean logic and closed-world assumption) are in conflict with IR concepts like vague queries, imprecise data or interactive querying. For this reason, we think that future EIS require the design of a completely new type of information systems.

References

[1] K. Ammersbach, N. Fuhr, and G. Knorz. Empirically based concepts for materials data systems. In: *Proceedings of the 1988 CODATA Conference*, Karlsruhe, Germany, 1988.

[2] L. Bolc and M. Jarke, editors. *Cooperative Interfaces to Information Systems*. Springer, Berlin et al., 1986.

[3] A. Borgida, R.J. Brachman, D.L. McGuinness, and L.A. Resnick. CLASSIC: A structural data model for objects. In: *Proceedings of the ACM SIGMOD International Conference on the Management of Data*, pages 58–67, New York, 1989. ACM.

[4] R.J. Brachman and J.G. Schmolze. An overview of the klone knowledge representation system. *Cognitive Science*, 9(2):171–216, 1985.

[5] M.L. Brodie and J. Mylopoulos, editors. *On Knowledge Base Management Systems*. Topics in Information Systems. Springer-Verlag, Berlin et al., 1986.

[6] M Carey and L. Haas. Extensible database management systems. *SIGMOD RECORD*, 19(4):54–60, 1991.

[7] S Ceri, G. Gottlob, and L. Tanca. *Logic Programming and Databases*. Springer, Berlin et al., 1990.

[8] J. Conklin. Hypertext: An introduction and survey *IEEE Computer*, 20(9):17–41, 1987.

[9] A D'Atri and L. Tarantino. From browsing to querying. *IEEE Data Engineering Bulletin*, 12(2):46–53, 1989.

[10] K.R. Dittrich. Object-oriented database systems: The next miles of the marathon. *Information Systems*, 15(1):161–167, 1990.

[11] J C French, A.K. Jones, and J L. Pfaltz. Summary on the final report of the NSF workshop on scientific database management *SIGMOD RECORD*, 19(4):32–40, 1991.

[12] N. Fuhr Hypertext und information retrieval. In: P A Gloor and N.A. Streitz, editors: *Hypertext und Hypermedia*, pages 101–111, Berlin et al., 1990. Springer.

[13] N. Fuhr. A probabilistic framework for vague queries and imprecise information in databases. In: D. McLeod, R. Sacks-Davis, and H. Schek, editors: *Proceedings of the 16th International Conference on Very Large Databases*, pages 696–707, Los Altos, Cal., 1990. Morgan Kaufman.

[14] N. Fuhr and C. Buckley. A probabilistic learning approach for document indexing. To appear in: ACM Transactions on Information systems, 1991.

[15] N. Fuhr, S. Hartmann, G. Knorz, G. Lustig, M. Schwantner, and K. Tzeras. AIR/X - a rule-based multistage indexing system for large subject fields. In: *Proceedings of the RIAO'91, Barcelona, Spain, April 2-5, 1991*, 1991.

[16] O. Günther and A. Buchmann. Research issues in spatial databases. *SIGMOD RECORD*, 19(4):61–68, 1991.

[17] A. Heuer and M.H. Scholl. Principles of object-oriented query languages. In: H.-J. Appelrath, editor: *Datenbanksysteme in Büro, Technik und Wissenschaft*, pages 178–197, Berlin et al., 1991. Springer.

[18] R. Hull and R. King. Semantic database modelling: Survey, applications, and research issues. *ACM Computing Surveys*, 19(3):201–260, 1987.

[19] L.N. Kanal and J.F. Lemmer, editors. *Uncertainty in Artificial Intelligence*. North-Holland, Amsterdam et al., 1986.

[20] L.N. Kanal and J.F. Lemmer, editors. *Uncertainty in Artificial Intelligence 2*. North-Holland, Amsterdam et al., 1988.

[21] F. Kifer and G. Lausen. F-logic: A higher-order language for reasoning about objects, inheritance, and scheme. In: *Proceedings of the ACM SIGMOD International Conference on the Management of Data*, pages 134–146, New York, 1989. ACM.

[22] W. Kim. A model of queries for object-oriented databases. In: *Proceedings of the Fifteenth International Conference on Very Large Databases*, pages 423–432, Los Altos, Cal., 1989. Morgan Kaufman.

[23] W. Kim and F.H. Lochovsky, editors. *Object-Oriented Concepts, Databases. and Applications*. Addison-Wesley, Reading, Mass., 1989.

[24] W. Klas, E.J. Neuhold, and M. Schrefl. Using an object-oriented approach to model multimedia data. *Computer Communications*, 13(4):204–216, 1990.

[25] M. Kracker and E.J. Neuhold. Schema independent query formulation. In: F. Lochovsky, editor: *Proceedings of the 8th International Conference on Entity-Relationship Approach*, pages 233–247, 1989.

[26] R. Kuhlen. *Experimentelle Morphologie in der Informationswissenschaft*. Verlag Dokumentation, München, 1977.

[27] J. B. Lovins. Development of a stemming algorithm. *Mechanical Translation and Computational Linguistics*, 11:22–31, March 1968.

[28] G. Lustig, editor. *Automatische Indexierung zwischen Forschung und Anwendung*. Olms, Hildesheim, 1986.

[29] D. Maier, J.D. Ullmann, and M.Y. Vardi. On the foundations of the universal relation model. *ACM Transactions on Database Systems*, 9(2):283–308, 1984.

[30] A. Motro. Vague: A user interface to relational databases that permits vague queries. *ACM Transactions on Office Information Systems*, 6(3):187–214, 1988

[31] A.J. Musgrave, B. Page, and M. Stopp. Infuchs - ein informationssystem für umweltchemikalien, chemieanlagen und störfälle - prototyp für die entwicklung dialogorientierter datenbankanwendungen im umweltschutz. In: B. Page, editor: *Informatik im Umweltschutz. Anwendungen und Perspektiven*, pages 144–177, München, Wien, 1986. Oldenbourg.

[32] M.T. Ozsu and P. Valduriez. *Principles of Distributed Database Systems*. Prentice-Hall, Englewood Cliffs, N.J., 1991.

[33] J. Pearl. *Probabilistic Reasoning in Intelligent Systems: Networks of Plausible Inference*. Morgan Kaufman, San Mateo, Cal., 1988.

[34] X. Pintado and D. Tsichritzis. SaTellite: A navigation tool for hypermedia. In: *Proceedings of the Conference on Office Information Systems*, New York, 1990. ACM.

[35] M. F. Porter. An algorithm for suffix stripping. *Program*, 14:130–137, July 1980.

[36] H. Prade and C. Testemale. The possibilistic approach to the handling of imprecision in database systems. *IEEE Data Engineering Bulletin*, 12(2):4–10, 1989.

[37] G. Salton, editor. *The SMART Retrieval System - Experiments in Automatic Document Processing*. Prentice Hall, Englewood Cliffs, New Jersey, 1971.

[38] G. Salton. Automatic text indexing using complex identifiers. In: *Proceedings of ACM Conference on Document Processing Systems (December 5-9, 1988, Santa Fe, New Mexico)*, pages 135–144, New York, 1988. ACM.

[39] G. Salton and C. Buckley. Term weighting approaches in automatic text retrieval. *Information Processing and Management*, 24(5):513–523, 1988.

[40] J.W. Schmidt and C. Thanos, editors. *Foundations of Knowledge Base Management*. Springer, Berlin et al., 1989.

[41] M. Schrefl and E.J. Neuhold. Object class definition by generalization using upward inheritance. In: *Fourth International Conference on Data Engineering*, pages 4–13, Los Angeles, 1988. IEEE Computer Society.

[42] L. Shastri. Default reasoning in semantic networks: A formalization of recognition and inheritance. *Artificial Intelligence*, 39:283–355, 1989.

[43] R. Snodgrass. Temporal databases: Status and research directions. *SIGMOD RECORD*, 19(4):83–89, 1991.

[44] P. Willett. Recent trends in hierarchic document clustering: A critical review. *Information Processing and Management*, 24(5):577–597, 1988.

[45] M.D. Williams. What makes RABBIT run? *International Journal on Man-Machine Studies*, 21:333–352, 1984.

[46] D. Woelk and W. Kim. Multimedia information management in an object-oriented database system. In: *Proceedings of the 13th VLDB Conference*, pages 319–329, Los Altos, Cal., 1987. Morgan Kaufman.

[47] L.A. Zadeh. Fuzzy sets. *Information and Control*, 8:338–353, 1965.

[48] M.M. Zloof. Query-by-example: A data base language. *IBM Systems Journal*, 16(4):324–343, 1977.

Enhancing Text Retrieval Semantically

Edgar B. Wendlandt, Lieutenant

United States Coast Guard
Information Systems Center
Alexandria, Virginia 22310 USA

James R. Driscoll

Department of Computer Science
University of Central Florida
Orlando, Florida 32816 USA

Abstract

Current information retrieval systems focus on the use of keywords to respond to user queries. We propose the additional use of surface level knowledge in order to improve the accuracy of information retrieval. Our approach is based on the database concept of semantic modeling (particularly entities and relationships among entities). We enhance the concept of query-document similarity by recognizing basic entity properties (attributes) which appear in text. We also enhance query-document similarity using the linguistic concept of thematic roles. Thematic roles allow us to recognize relationship properties which appear in text. We include several examples to illustrate our approach.

1   Introduction

Recent information retrieval systems accept natural language queries against large collections of text [11, 14]. These systems scan the query for keywords and sort the documents retrieved from the text collection based on their similarity to the query. In addition to matching keywords, these systems improve performance by using various techniques such as stop lists (removal of useless words), stemming, co-occurrence patterns, synonyms, and query reformulation. We believe that these systems can be further improved by imposing a semantic data model upon the "surface level" knowledge found in text.

Semantic modeling was an object of considerable database research in the late 1970's and early 1980's. A brief overview can be found in [2]. Essentially, the semantic modeling approach identified concepts useful in talking informally about the real world. These concepts included the two notions of entities (objects in the real world) and relationships among entities (actions in the real world). Both entities and relationships have properties.

The properties of entities are often called attributes. There are basic or surface level attributes for entities in the real world. Examples of surface level entity attributes are SIZE, COLOR, and POSITION. These properties are prevalent in natural language. For example, consider the phrase "large, black book on the table," which indicates the SIZE, COLOR, and POSITION of a book.

In linguistic research, the basic properties of relationships are discussed and called thematic roles. Thematic roles are also referred to in the literature as participant roles, semantic roles, and case roles. Examples of thematic roles are BENEFICIARY and TIME. Thematic roles are prevalent in natural language,

they reveal how sentence phrases and clauses are semantically related to the verbs in a sentence. For example, consider the phrase "purchased for Mary on Wednesday" which indicates who benefited from a purchase (BENEFICIARY) and when a purchase occurred (TIME).

In this paper, we describe an approach to text search that includes assigning thematic roles and entity attributes as document identifiers. Our environment concerns searching documents and using their contents to perform the intelligent task of answering a question. This is explained in Section 2. In Section 3, we review conventional information retrieval methods in order to display the basic underlying concepts of determining text relevance. We detail our semantic modeling approach in Section 4, and present extended concepts for determining text relevance in Section 5. A detailed example that illustrates our method appears in Section 6. Concluding remarks appear in the discussion in Section 7.

2   Text Retrieval Environment

At the University of Central Florida (UCF), we are developing a prototype intelligent hypertext system for searching text by using "portions" of relevant text to build a response to a query [4]. Currently our work is motivated by the desire to provide convenient access to information contained in the numerous and large public information documents maintained by Public Affairs at NASA Kennedy Space Center (KSC).

The documents maintained by Public Affairs at NASA KSC consist of press releases, and other printed information created at KSC, and other NASA offices using various word processors. There are also documents from outside contractors, such as Rockwell, which produces the "NASA National Space Transportation System Reference" more often called the "shuttle manual." During a launch at KSC, about a dozen NASA employees access these printed documents to answer media questions. The amount of text is visually overwhelming. The shuttle manual alone is just over 1000 pages (it is three inches thick). The planned document storage for NASA KSC Public Affairs is around 300,000 pages (approximately seventy-five feet of stacked pages) with about 5,000 pages added or replaced annually. Electronically, the storage is manageable; approximately 900 megabytes of disk space is expected.

Our work for NASA KSC has been to research hardware and software requirements for an intelligent interactive high speed text data search system to automate the manner in which media questions are answered. Our prototype system is aimed at expository text databases. Our prototype takes advantage of IR techniques to find relevant text, and it uses general world knowledge to further pinpoint an answer to a query.

This work has been supported in part by NASA KSC Grant NAG 10-0058 Project 2A, NASA KSC Cooperative Agreement NCC 10-003 Project 2, and Florida High Technology and Industry Council Grant 4940-11-28-721.

```
┌─────────────────────────────────────────────────┐
│ NATURAL LANGUAGE QUERY ON THE SHUTTLE BASE        │
│                                                   │
│ < 1 >: What are the dimensions of the cargo area  │
│        in the shuttle?                            │
│                                                   │
│ EMPTY WORDS: What, are, the, of, the, in, the.    │
│                                                   │
│ KEYWORDS: dimensions, cargo, area, shuttle.       │
└─────────────────────────────────────────────────┘
```

Figure 1: Natural Language Query

CLASSES	NB DOCS	KEY-WORDS
1	1	dimensions,cargo,shuttle.
2	1	cargo, area, shuttle.
3	1	dimensions, area.
4	2	dimensions, shuttle.
5	4	cargo, area.
6	30	cargo, shuttle.
7	12	area, shuttle.
8	7	dimensions.
9	40	cargo.
10	147	area.
BOTTOM OF LIST		

Figure 2: Document Classes

Finding relevant text is not new and there are commercial systems which already perform this activity; we mention here an example of relevant text retrieval. For a demonstration to NASA KSC, the one thousand page shuttle manual was used by considering each paragraph of the manual as a document. This resulted in a collection of 4902 documents. A commercial hypertext system called SPIRIT [15] was used to automatically index the collection and provide natural language access. Figure 1 is a screen generated by SPIRIT for asking the natural language query

What are the dimensions of the cargo area in the shuttle?

Figure 2 is a screen generated by SPIRIT revealing a ranked list of 245 relevant documents with CLASS 1 being the most relevant. Figure 3 is a screen generated by SPIRIT revealing the first document in CLASS 6, which contains the answer to the query. This paragraph was found by reading the single paragraph in CLASS 1 first, then the single paragraph in CLASS 2, and so on until the answer was read in the tenth paragraph. We will use this example in Section 6.

```
┌─────────────────────────────────────────────────┐
│ DOC 3976 BASE : doc 3976NCP:0/CPI:1/NBI:1 +18 1K/1K│
│ IDENTIFIER. : doc 3976                            │
│ TEXT....... :                                     │
│                                                   │
│ The shuttle will transport cargo into near Earth  │
│ orbit 100 to 217 nautical miles (115 - 250 statute│
│ miles) above the Earth. This cargo (called payload)│
│ is carried in a bay 15 feet in diameter           │
│ and 60 feet long.                                 │
│ BOTTOM OF DOCUMENT                                 │
│ ─────────────────────── INFORMATIONAL PAGE 1/1    │
│ WHAT DO YOU WANT TO DISPLAY?                       │
└─────────────────────────────────────────────────┘
```

Figure 3: Document Display

3   Conventional IR Methods

The underlying principles and algorithms of automated information retrieval systems are well-known. Two functions performed by automated systems which handle natural language queries are of particular interest to our research. First, we are interested in the function that ignores useless or empty words. These words are generally prepositions, conjunctions, and articles. Second, we are interested in the function that calculates the weighting factors. We discuss the dismissal of prepositions, conjunctions, and articles in the next section. Here, we discuss concepts associated with the calculation of weighting factors.

The calculation of the weighting factor (w) for a term in a document is a combination of term frequency (tf), document frequency (df), and inverse document frequency (idf). The basic term definitions are as follows:

tf_{ij} = number of occurrences of term T_j in document D_i

df_j = number of documents in a collection which contain T_j

$idf_j = \log(\frac{N}{df_j})$, where N = total number of documents

$w_{ij} = tf_{ij} \cdot idf_{ij}$.

When an information retrieval system is used to query a collection of documents with t terms, the system computes a vector Q with terms $(q_1, q_2, \ldots, q_t)$ as the weights for each term in the query. The retrieval of a document D_i with document vector $(d_{i1}, d_{i2}, \ldots, d_{it})$ as weights of each term in the document is based on the value of a similarity measure between the query vector and a document vector. Several similarity measures are commonly used. A crude but simple measure is calculated as follows [13]:

$$sim(Q, D_i) = \sum_{j=1}^{t} w_{qj} \cdot d_{ij}$$

In current literature the degree of similarity is most often a modification of the above based not only on term frequencies, but also on co-occurrence relationships, proximal distances, and syntactic information [3, 10, 13, 14, 17].

4   Semantic Modeling Approach

Although the basic IR approach has shown some success in regard to natural language queries, it ignores some valuable information. For instance, consider the following query:

How long does the payload crew go through training before a launch?

The typical IR system dismisses the following words in the query as empty: how, does, the, through, before, a. These words contain some valuable semantic information. The following list indicates the thematic roles triggered by some of these words:

how long ⇒ DURATION, TIME
through ⇒ DURATION, MOTION, RANGE
before ⇒ LOCATION, TIME

The goal of our prototype system is to detect this thematic information along with attribute information contained in natural language queries and documents. When the information is

120

Table 1: Partial List of Thematic Roles

Thematic Role	Description
AGENT	the thing which causes an ACTION to happen
ACTION	the verb in a sentence other than the "be-verb"
OBJECT	the thing affected by an ACTION
LOCATION	where an ACTION occurs
TIME	when an ACTION occurs
PURPOSE	the reason the ACTION happens
BENEFICIARY	the thing for which an ACTION is performed
INSTRUMENT	the thing with which an ACTION is performed
MANNER	the way an ACTION is performed

present, our system uses it to help find the most relevant paragraph to a query. In order to use this additional information, the basic underlying concept of text relevance needs to be modified. The major modifications include the addition of a lexicon with thematic and attribute information, and a modified computation of the similarity measure. The details of these modifications appear in Section 5. The following is a discussion of thematic role and attribute triggers.

4.1 Thematic Roles

Thematic roles originated from work described by Fillmore who introduced six cases (thematic roles) [5]. Other alternate approaches can be found in [1] and [8]. To explain thematic roles consider the following example taken from [16]:

Mary made coffee for John with a percolator.

There are four noun phrases in this sentence, each of which fits into a particular thematic role as follows:

Noun Phrases	Thematic Role
Mary	AGENT
coffee	OBJECT
for John	BENEFICIARY
with a percolator	INSTRUMENT

Four corresponding questions can be answered now:

What was made? →OBJECT → coffee
Who made the coffee? → AGENT → Mary
For whom was coffee made? → BENEFICIARY → John
What made the coffee? → INSTRUMENT → a percolator

Thematic roles can also be used to answer many other types of questions. Several well known thematic roles are described in Table 1. There are thirty-three thematic roles discussed in [9]. Even though thematic roles have been of interest for some twenty years, most detailed information about them has appeared quite recently in linguistic literature. Still, exact definitions are hard to locate. As a point of interest, there is now a debate over thematic roles about whether they are a product of our language, whether they are independent of our language and have their ultimate origins in facts about the world, or whether they are components of our mental representation of objects and concepts.

The presence of thematic roles in text can be detected by considering the following:

A. Certain words suggest specific thematic roles. For example, all verbs other than the "be-verbs" (is, are, was,...) become candidates for an ACTION. As another example, the word "noon" implies TIME.

B. Prepositions and certain conjunctions trigger thematic role possibilities. For example, the preposition "for" can trigger the BENEFICIARY or DURATION thematic roles. The conjunction "as" can possibly trigger the MANNER or TIME thematic roles.

C. Normally, verbs cause thematic grids of the form AGENT followed by ACTION as in

John ran.

or of the form AGENT followed by ACTION followed by OBJECT as in

John chased the dog.

Grids can then be optimally followed by some of the other thematic roles as in

John chased the dog into the house.

But there are other thematic grids. For example, there is a class of verbs (represented by the verbs "load" or "spray") which can have a grid which specifies an AGENT, ACTION, LOCATION, OBJECT order, as in

John loaded the truck with furniture.

Here "the truck" is a LOCATION rather than an OBJECT.

4.2 Entity Attributes

Entity attributes are generally considered descriptors of a subject or object. Questions asking for a particular fact about an item usually make reference to an attribute. For example,

How much does the space shuttle weigh?

references the WEIGHT attribute of an object. Some of the more common attributes are COLOR, SIZE, and ORDER. The best way to describe the use of entity attributes is by example.

Refer to the query and answer paragraph of Section 2, Figure 1 and Figure 3, respectively. Note that the query and the paragraph containing the answer had several words relating to the attributes of the "cargo area". In the query, the word "dimensions" indicates that the user wants to know about the SIZE of something. Therefore, the answer must contain some information about SIZE. The paragraph with the answer also contains words indicating that the attribute of SIZE is present. The words "feet," "diameter," and "long" all indicate that the attribute SIZE may be present. It is obvious how this information could help improve the retrieval of the most relevant paragraph.

The use of attributes also requires some additional information. Like thematic roles, a precise list of entity attributes is hard to find. Our system uses a modified thesaurus as a lexicon and a source of attribute information. For example, *Roget's Thesaurus* contains a hierarchy of word classes to relate words [12]. For our research, we have selected several classes from the middle levels of this hierarchy as attributes.

5 General Approach

It was noted that current automated systems generally ignore words which can act as triggers of certain thematic roles. By incorporating a lexicon of thematic role and attribute triggers, valuable information about a document and a query can be considered. Although the use of the lexicon of triggers for these semantic concepts does not imply any type of understanding, it does improve the relevance ranking of the desired document.

5.1 Definitions

A complication arises when trying to apply this semantic knowledge to the standard similarity measure calculation. The relationship between triggers and the thematic roles or attributes is many-to-many. The following table illustrates a portion of this relationship.

Word	Possible Thematic Roles Triggered
by	CONVEYANCE, INSTRUMENT, LOCATION
carry	LOCATION, none (refer to item C in Section 4.1)
in	DESTINATION, INSTRUMENT, LOCATION, MANNER, PURPOSE
into	LOCATION, DESTINATION
on	LOCATION, TIME
to	DESTINATION, LOCATION, PURPOSE

In order to deal with this complication one must consider the probability of a particular thematic role or entity attribute being triggered. In this section, we use the term *category* as an equivalent for the concept of thematic roles or entity attributes, and we let s be the total number of *categories*. We let f_{ik} be the frequency of the kth trigger in document D_i, and we let r be the total number of triggers. We must define some additional terms to account for probabilities.

Probability (P_{jk}) : The likelihood of *category* c_j occurring due to the k_{th} trigger. For example, assuming a uniform probability distribution, the DESTINATION *category* triggered by the word "to" above has probability:

$$P_{DESTINATION,to} = 0.33$$

Expected Category Frequency (ecf_{ij}): The expected number of times a *category* c_j occurs in document D_i. This is derived from the Laws of Expectation of independent sets [7].

$$ecf_{ij} = \sum_{k=1}^{r} f_{ik} P_{jk}$$

Probability Not Present (PN_{ij}): The probability of *category* c_j not occurring in document D_i altogether.

$$PN_{ij} = \prod_{k=1}^{r} (1 - P_{jk})^{f_{ik}}$$

Probability Present (PP_{ij}): The probability of *category* c_j occurring in document D_i.

$$PP_{ij} = 1 - PN_{ij}$$

Expected Document Frequency (edf_j): Given a set of N documents, this is the expected number of documents containing *category* c_j.

$$edf_j = \sum_{i=1}^{N} PP_{ij}$$

Inverse Document Frequency (idf_j): The inverse document frequency of *category* c_j for a set of N documents.

$$idf_j = \log(\frac{N}{edf_j})$$

Weight (w_{ij}): The weight of *category* c_j in document D_i.

$$w_{ij} = ecf_{ij} \cdot idf_j$$

5.2 Procedure and Implementation

Another complication arises when using semantic knowledge. Two characteristics of *categories* cause the complication. First, the number of *categories* is rather small (approximately 60) compared to the number of indexing terms typically found in a large collection of documents. Second, *categories* occur frequently in most text collections. These two characteristics cause the weights of categories to be smaller in magnitude than the weights of keywords.

Consequently, we have found it useful to first retrieve a set of documents based on keywords only, and then consider only these documents for a combined keyword, thematic role, and attribute analysis. This is done by appending the s *category* weights calculated above to the t term weights of each document vector D_i and the query vector Q. The document vector D_i becomes $(d_{i1}, d_{i2}, \ldots, d_{it}, d_{i(t+1)}, d_{i(t+2)}, \ldots, d_{i(t+s)})$. Similarly, the query vector Q becomes $(q_1, q_2, \ldots, q_t, q_{t+1}, q_{t+2}, \ldots, q_{t+s})$. The final calculation for similarity is the same as before, except for the range of the index term j as follows:

$$sim(Q, D_i) = \sum_{j=1}^{t+s} w_{qj} \cdot d_{ij}$$

6 Detailed Example

Our example is from Section 2 and based on an arbitrary question, posed to the SPIRIT system [15] , and against the text collection known as the space shuttle manual. The query is

What are the dimensions of the cargo area in the shuttle?

The boldface words of the query were regarded as keywords. The other words were regarded as *empty* by the SPIRIT system. The SPIRIT system returned a list of ordered documents based on the similarity measures between the query and the document collection. In this case the answer was found in the tenth paragraph.

In order to illustrate our method, we select the first ten paragraphs as a document space to apply the semantic extension described in Section 5. Since we do not know the values of the query and document vectors computed by SPIRIT, we recompute the vectors based on the new document space. Applying the conventional IR calculations described in Section 3 yields the following results for analysis of the above query.

Keyword	Qf_j	df_j	idf_j
dimensions	1	4	0.4393
cargo	1	6	0.2632
area	1	5	0.3424
shuttle	1	5	0.3424

In our calculations of idf we used N = 11 instead of N = 10 to compensate for the possibility that a keyword, a thematic role, or an attribute could show up in all ten paragraphs. Also, note

Table 2: Similarity Measures Computed by Paragraph

1	2	3	4
Document Number	keywords only *	thematic role attributes only *	combined* value
D_1	0.380 (3)	0.947 (1)	1.327 (1)
D_2	0.704 (1)	0.026 (10)	0.730 (3)
D_3	0.310 (4)	0.403 (4)	0.714 (5)
D_4	0.310 (5)	0.266 (5)	0.576 (6)
D_5	0.310 (6)	0.415 (3)	0.726 (4)
D_6	0.187 (9)	0.081 (8)	0.268 (10)
D_7	0.304 (7)	0.158 (6)	0.461 (7)
D_8	0.187 (10)	0.123 (7)	0.310 (9)
D_9	0.421 (2)	0.028 (9)	0.449 (8)
D_{10}	0.256 (8)	0.535 (2)	0.791 (2)

* new paragraph rank is in parentheses

Table 3: Values by *category*

No.	*Category*	Qf	edf	idf	$Qf \cdot idf$
1	AMOUNT	1.0	8.00	0.138	0.138
2	DESTINATION	0.2	5.12	0.332	0.067
3	INSTRUMENT	0.2	3.37	0.513	0.103
4	LOCATION	1.2	9.89	0.046	0.050
5	MANNER	0.2	4.46	0.392	0.078
6	PURPOSE	0.2	5.62	0.291	0.058
7	SIZE	1.0	5.00	0.342	0.342

$$
\begin{aligned}
&= \log(\frac{11}{9.89}) \\
&= 0.0462 \\
w_{10,4} &= ecf_{10,4} \cdot idf_4 \\
&= 1.73 \cdot 0.0462 \\
&= 0.0799
\end{aligned}
$$

Since there are $s = 7$ *categories* in the query (refer to Table 3), we have the following:

$$
\begin{aligned}
sim(Q, D_{10}) &= \sum_{j=1}^{s} w_{qj} \cdot w_{10,j} \\
&= 0.138 \cdot 0.0 + 0.067 \cdot 0.244 + 0.103 \cdot 0.205 + \\
&\quad 0.050 \cdot 0.080 + 0.078 \cdot 0.157 + 0.058 \cdot 0.214 + \\
&\quad 0.342 \cdot 1.370 \\
&= 0.535
\end{aligned}
$$

If we consider only thematic roles and attributes found in D_1 through D_{10}, and use only the semantic calculations presented in Section 5, we obtain the results shown in Table 3 for an analysis of the query. Referring back to the paragraphs in Table 2, we obtain (for *sim*) the similarity measures shown in Column 3. Note that paragraph D_{10} is now ranked number two! This result is actually ignoring the original keyword ranking of the ten paragraphs; so, Column 4 reveals, perhaps, a more appropriate analysis considering both keywords and *categories*, using the keyword and semantic calculations presented in Section 5. Again, paragraph D_{10} is ranked number two!

that query frequency, Qf_j, is the number of times the jth keyword appears in the query.

Continuing the basic IR approach, we obtain the similarity measures shown in Column 2 of Table 2 for the ten retrieved documents. The new ranked positions of the ten paragraphs are shown in parenthesis. Note that paragraph D_{10} is now ranked number eight. Referring to Figure 3 in Section 2 , we see that paragraph D_{10} has two occurrences of "cargo" and one occurrence of "shuttle." A sample similarity measure calculation is as follows:

$$
\begin{aligned}
sim(Q, D_{10}) &= \sum_{j=1}^{t} w_{qj} \cdot w_{10j} \\
&= 0.2632 \cdot 0.5264 + 0.3424 \cdot 0.3424 \\
&= 0.2558
\end{aligned}
$$

Below we show a sample computation of the similarity measure based on the occurrence of *categories* in the query and paragraph D_{10}. The details are only shown for one *category*, LOCATION, for the sake of brevity. In this sample a uniform probability distribution was assumed, so the words "in," "into," "to," and "carried" trigger the *category* LOCATION with probabilities 0.2, 0.5, 0.33, and 0.5, respectively. This can be observed by reference to the trigger table in Section 5.1.

$$
\begin{aligned}
ecf_{10,4} &= \sum_{k=1}^{4} f_{10,k} P_{4,k} \\
&= 2 \cdot 0.2 + 1 \cdot 0.5 + 1 \cdot 0.33 + 1 \cdot 0.5 \\
&= 1.73 \\
PN_{10,4} &= \prod_{k=1}^{4} (1 - P_{4,k})^{f_{10,k}} \\
&= (1 - 0.2)^2 \cdot (1 - 0.5)^1 \cdot (1 - 0.33)^1 \cdot (1 - 0.5)^1 \\
&= 0.11 \\
PP_{10,4} &= 1 - PN_{10,4} \\
&= 1 - 0.11 \\
&= 0.89 \\
edf_4 &= \sum_{i=1}^{11} PP_{i,4} \\
&= 1.0 + 1.0 + 1.0 + 1.0 + 1.0 + 1.0 + \\
&\quad 1.0 + 1.0 + 1.0 + 0.89 + 0.0 \\
&= 9.89 \\
idf_4 &= \log(\frac{N}{edf_4})
\end{aligned}
$$

7 Discussion

The initial test results of our prototype system are convincing, even though the system is still in its infancy stage. The following table shows a comparison between retrieval of the most relevant document of a conventional IR system and our semantic system.

Query	Ranking (Keyword)	Ranking (Combined)
What type of liquid fuel is used on the shuttle?	3	1
What are the dimensions of the cargo area?	10	2
What is the total number of times that the shuttle has been launched?	6	1
What type of food do astronauts eat during a shuttle mission?	2	1
How many general purpose computers are on board the shuttle and what functions do they serve?	5	2

The middle column shows the ranking of the paragraph with the answer by the conventional IR method. The rightmost column shows the same paragraph's ranking after the thematic and attribute information was incorporated along with the keyword based ranking. Note that in no case did the paragraph with the answer drop further down in the rankings.

The incorporation of thematic and attribute information closely parallels the conventional IR approach with one exception. The exception is that instead of computing thematic and attribute weights during the initial indexing of a collection of documents, we only index a subset of the documents. This subset is composed of those documents returned by the conventional method. The reason for only indexing a subset of the original document collection must be considered. In current indexing schemes the *idf* plays a critical role. The property of interest is that the more often a keyword occurs, the smaller the *idf*; hence the keyword becomes less significant in the retrieval process.

This becomes very significant when considering a list of only thirty-three thematic roles and twenty-five attributes, and the fact that prepositions, which commonly occur in all text, trigger thematic roles. The likelihood of a thematic role such as LO-CATION occurring in many more documents than any of the keywords is high. This phenomenon has a tendency of skewing the combined similarity measure in favor of the keyword components.

By selecting the higher ranking documents of a retrieval based on keywords the likelihood of occurrence of the keywords is also increased. This in effect "normalizes" the weights for keywords and categories to the same order of magnitude. Other schemes may be selected to normalize the contributions of the keywords and *categories*, but this simple method has shown some success.

A factor which may be a topic for further research in the area of Computational Linguistics is the appropriate probability for the thematic roles or attributes of a given trigger. In our system we have made the simplifying assumption that multiple *categories* of a trigger each occur with equal probability. For example, if five thematic roles are triggered by "on", then 0.20 is the probability of each of those roles. Statistical research is needed to determine more precise probabilities, or an analysis of a corpus as in [6] may be used. Even with this simplifying assumption our system seems to have the ability to help retrieve the most relevant document.

Another factor to consider is the matching of the positions of keywords with thematic roles and attributes within a query or a document. This would be an extension of recognizing longer phrases of keyword combinations to improve the similarity measure calculation. An extension of our analysis needs to be made so that a query having a DURATION thematic role with filler "training period" would yield a significant contribution to the similarity measure of a document also having a DURATION thematic role with filler "training period." Roughly, this corresponds to using prepositional phrases as document identifiers.

At the present time we are preparing for an exhaustive testing of our semantic extensions to text retrieval. Our tests will be performed in the text retrieval environment discussed in Section 2. The document collection will be growing periodically. The base document will be the space shuttle manual, but other important texts such as press releases will be incrementally added. The plan is to use real media questions about the space program and monitor conventional, semantic, and combined rankings of retrieved text.

References

[1] B. Bruce, "Case System for Natural Language," *Artificial Intelligence*, Vol. 6, pp. 327-360, 1975.

[2] C. Date, *An Introduction to Database Systems, Vol I*. Addison Wesley, 1990.

[3] F. Debili, C. Fluhr, and P. Radasoa. "About Reformulation in Full-Text IRS", *Information Processing and Management*, Vol. 25, pp.647-657, 1989.

[4] J. Driscoll, "Intelligent Interactive High Speed Data Search", *NASA KSC Cooperative Agreement NCC10-003 Project 2*, June 1989.

[5] C. Fillmore, "The Case for Case", *Universal in Linguistic Theory*, New York: Holt, Rinehart and Winston, 1968.

[6] N. Fuhr, S. Hartmann, G. Lustig, M. Schwantner, and K. Tzeras. "AIR/X - a Rule-Based Multistage Indexing System for Large Subject Fields", *Proceedings of International Conference on Intelligent Text and Image Handling (RIAO-91)*, pp.606-623, 1991.

[7] J. Hodges, Jr. and E. Lehmann, *Basics Concepts of Probability and Statistics*, Holden-Day, 1964.

[8] R. Jackendoff, "Semantic Interpretation in Generative Grammar," *MIT Press*, 1972.

[9] M. Nagao, J. Tsujii, and J. Nakamura, "The Japanese Government project for Machine Translation," *Computational Linguistics*, Vol. 11, No. 2-3, April-September, 1985.

[10] L. Rau, P. Jacobs, U Zernik, "Information Extraction and Text Summarization Using Linguistic Knowledge Acquisition", *Information Processing and Management*, Vol. 25, No. 4, pp.419-428, 1989.

[11] K. Ray and J. Driscoll, "New Directions for Hypertext Systems," *DATABASE Magazine*, August 1990.

[12] *Roget's International Thesaurus*, Harper & Row, New York, Fourth Edition, 1977.

[13] G. Salton, *Automatic Text Processing*, Addison-Wesley, 1989.

[14] A. Smeaton, "Incorporating Syntactic Information into a Document Retrieval Strategy: an Investigation", *Organization of the 1986-ACM Conference on Research and Development in Information Retrieval*, pp.103-113, 1986.

[15] *SPIRIT Version 2.1 User's Manual*, SYSTEX Company, Ferme Du Moulon, 91190 Gif Sur Yvette, France (French Edition), May 1986.

[16] P. Winston, *Artificial Intelligence* (2nd Edition), Addison Wesley, 1984.

[17] U. Zernik and P. Jacobs, "Tagging for Learning: Collecting Thematic Relations from Corpus", *Proceedings of COLING-90*, Vol. 1, pp.34-39, 1990.

THE COMMONSENSE BUSINESS REASONER

Robert C. Goldstein

University of British Columbia
Vancouver, B.C. Canada

Veda C. Storey

University of Rochester
Rochester, N.Y. USA

Abstract

The *Commonsense Business Reasoner* is a knowledge-based system whose function is to provide commonsense reasoning capabilities for business expert systems. A generic business model provides the basis for the system. This model is described as is the system's ability to acquire and reason with commonsense knowledge.

Keywords:
Expert Systems, Commonsense Reasoning, Business Applications, Knowledge Modelling.

1 INTRODUCTION

One of the well-known problems associated with expert systems is that, while they possess a high degree of expertise in their specific application area, they usually know very little about anything outside that area. As a result, they often ask questions that appear unnecessary or trivial to the user. This not only increases the effort required to use these systems, but also detracts from their credibility as experts. In an effort to address some of these problems, a knowledge-based system, called the *Commonsense Business Reasoner*, has been developed. This system was built as a prototype of tools that could be incorporated into business expert systems to give them some general knowledge of the business world and the ability to both acquire more knowledge and use their knowledge to reason about business problems. This should make it possible to develop expert systems that are easier to use and display a higher degree of "intelligence".

The paper is divided into four sections. Section 2 discusses commonsense reasoning and the approach taken in this research. Section 3 introduces the Commonsense Business Reasoner and describes the structure of the system, its knowledge representation, and its reasoning capabilities. Section 4 summarizes and concludes the paper.

2 COMMONSENSE REASONING

The importance of commonsense reasoning for expert systems has been raised by many researchers [Kolata, 1982; McCarthy, 1983; Meltzer, 1985; Buchanan, 1988]. Buchanan [1988], for example, identifies three kinds of knowledge that expert systems lack: 1) successively deeper layers of knowledge in their task areas to use when their shallow, compiled knowledge fails to reach a satisfactory answer; 2) commonsense knowledge; and 3) knowledge about how to learn from experience, which is clearly related to commonsense reasoning. Dahlgren [1988] describes commonsense knowledge as "a set of naive beliefs, at times vague and inaccurate, about the way the world is structured". Alternatively, Ein-Dor [1985] defines commonsense as "what any participant in a culture expects any other participant in that culture to know when meeting for the first time and before any exchange takes place between them." He identifies four important aspects of commonsense reasoning as: 1) knowing the generally known facts about the world; 2) being able to interpret specific occurrences in terms of more general concepts; 3) being able to relate causes and effects; and 4) being able to recognize inconsistencies within or between statements. Commonsense involves both a body of widely known knowledge, which we call "general world knowledge", and a method for reasoning with this knowledge.

Commonsense reasoning, in general, is currently an active area of research. In particular, the CYC project [Lenat et al., 1990] is an ambitious attempt to automate an extremely large collection of knowledge about the world. Although this work is very interesting, it is

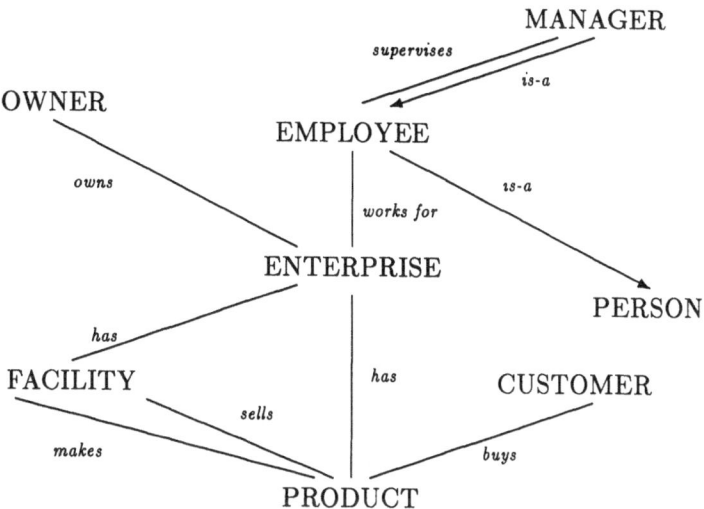

Figure 1: Generic Business Model

not closely related to ours. We are concentrating on a small subset of general knowledge; namely, that related to business applications. We also wish to explore the possibilities of a much more parsimonious approach to the problem.

2.1 Approach to Business Commonsense Reasoning

Our approach to commonsense reasoning is based on the paradigm used by Hayes [1979, 1985] in his studies of "naive physics", and in Dahlgren's "naive semantics" [1988]. This paradigm deals with representing, in machine-processable form, what people commonly believe to be true about the world. This type of knowledge is referred to as "naive" because it captures human intuition rather than scientific fact. For example, *flight* is a property commonly (naively) ascribed to birds even though there are certainly species of birds that cannot fly.

Two distinct types of knowledge are represented — classificatory and generic. The first has to do with the meanings of words, and the other, with relationships among the objects which these words name. For classificatory knowledge, Dahlgren's naive semantics employs a taxonomic hierarchy of concepts which is referred to as an ontology. Each concept inherits all of the properties of its parent and has an associated set of distinguishing characteristics. There is one such ontology for nouns and another for verbs, although it is possible to unify them into a single structure.

Generic knowledge generalizes across instances of objects and actions. Generic knowledge of objects consists of their typical properties; for example, employees receive salaries. Generic knowledge of actions consists of implications, such as when something is bought, money is given in exchange for it, and ownership is transferred from the seller to the buyer.

2.2 Naive Business Model

We have constructed a naive model of a business organization that involves concepts of people, employment, types of businesses, and exchange. The model, which is presented in Figure 1, is purposely constructed at a very high level of abstraction and is intended to capture knowledge that is generally understood about business enterprises. The main elements are: owners, managers, employees, customers, products or services, and facilities. The *buys* relationship between customer and product/service is an example of an exchange transaction, as is the *employment* relationship between employee and enterprise. Each of these represents the exchange of value; for example, money, for a good or service. The *buys* relationship also involves concepts such as ownership, desire for, and affordabillity. The person concept is relevant because employees are people, and owners and customers *may be* people. Recognizing when an owner or customer is a person as opposed to an enterprise makes it possible to attach the relevant superclass properties.

3 COMMONSENSE BUSINESS REASONER

The Commonsense Business Reasoner is a knowledge-based system for reasoning about business problems which

126

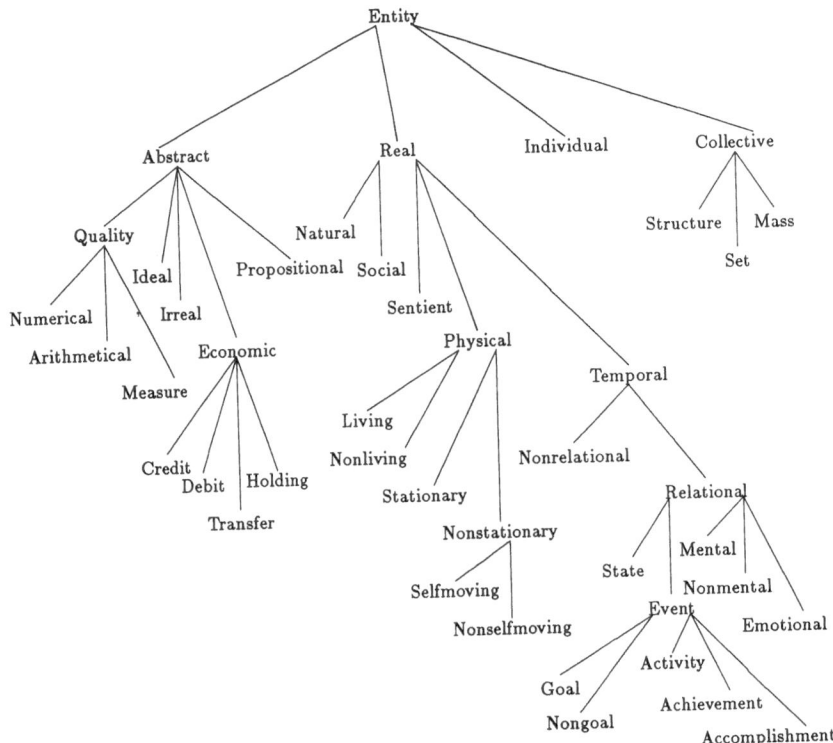

Figure 2: Ontology [Lord and Dahlgren, 1990]

is implemented in Arity Prolog. When provided with a term relevant to the business world, the system examines its knowledge base and returns all of the information it can find concerning that term. For example, given *Customer*, the Commonsense Business Reasoner lists essential and typical attributes of a customer as well as relationships between customers and other objects in its model. Some of the attribute information may well be inherited from more general concepts such as *Person*, and additional information can also be found by following the relationship linkages. Most of the information will probably not be explicitly attached to the *Customer* concept in the knowledge base, but rather, is derived from the structure of the Generic Business Model.

The Commonsense Business Reasoner has two knowledge bases. One contains knowledge about the Generic Business Model and is called the *Business Commonsense Base (BCB)*. The second, called the *Ontological Knowledge Base (OKB)*, classifies the terms in the BCB based on their ontological attributes. The ontological knowledge is used to determine the appropriate location in the BCB for newly acquired facts.

3.1 Ontological Knowledge Base

The Ontological Knowledge Base contains lexical knowledge that is used to classify the terms in the Business Commonsense Base based on a hierarchy of characteristics. A possible ontology [Lord and Dahlgren, 1990] is shown in compact form in Figure 2. The OKB consists of three types of predicates: *ontology*, *feature*, and *onto*.

Each branch of the OKB is represented by a predicate of the form:

ontology (Super_class, N, Sub_class)

where:

- Super_class and Sub_class are nodes in the ontological hierarchy and Super_class is the parent of Sub_class.

- N is an integer used to distinguish sets of mutually exclusive branches within the ontological hierarchy. For example, in Figure 2, "abstract" and "real" are mutually exclusive subsets of "entity." Their ontology predicates would have the same value of N. Similarly, "individual" and "collective" are mutually exclusive. Their predicates would also have the same value of N, but it would be a different value from that for the "abstract" and "real" predicates to indicate that one choice from the first subtree could be combined with one from the second.

To illustrate, the ontology branches whose parent is "Physical" are represented by the following set of predicates:

```
ontology(physical,1,living)
ontology(physical,1,nonliving)
ontology(physical,2,stationary)
ontology(physical,2,nonstationary)
```

The set of nodes that applies to an object defines its *ontological classification*. For example, based on Figure 2, *person* may be considered to have the ontological classification {REAL, PHYSICAL, LIVING, SOCIAL}. Each ontological class can have associated features. For example, a "physical" entity may have *components*; a "living" entity has *behaviours*; and a "social" entity can have *roles*. This information is stored in the OKB in a set of predicates of the form:

```
feature (Ontological_class, Feature_type)
```

where:

- Ontological_class identifies a node in the hierarchy.

- Feature_type is a feature type associated with that ontological class.

Some typical *feature* predicates relevant to the ontology of Figure 2 are:

```
feature(real,has_att)
feature(real,function)
feature(physical,component)
feature(living,behaviour)
feature(living,habitat)
feature(sentient,goal)
feature(social,role)
```

The feature predicates are used for two purposes. First, an object's ontological classification defines the features it can have, and therefore, the structure of its representation in the BCB. Second, it is used to relate a new object to those already known.

Both the *ontology* and *feature* predicates are static, at least in the sense that they are never modified as a result of interaction with users.

The *onto* predicate is used to map BCB terms onto the ontological hierarchy. Its general form is:

```
onto (Term, Ontological_class)
```

where:

- Term is a term in the BCB.

- Ontological_class identifies a node in the ontology hierarchy.

The *onto* predicates are used to determine the set of features potentially relevant to an object about to be added to the BCB, or to identify the set of BCB objects having a particular feature. Some of the *onto* predicates relevant to the *Person* term would be:

```
onto(person,real)
onto(person,individual)
onto(person,social)
onto(person,living)
onto(person,selfmoving)
```

3.2 Business Commonsense Base

The Business Commonsense Base contains knowledge about terms relevant to the business world. The BCB uses a frame-based knowledge representation scheme where each term is represented by a frame. The slots store individual features. The general form of a slot is:

```
slot: (Frame_Name, Slot_Type, Slot_Name, Value,
              Inheritable, Source)
```

where:

- Frame_Name — a term relevant to the Generic Business Model.

- Slot_Type — whether the slot is inherent or typical (following Dahlgren [1988]).

- Slot_Name — the name of a feature type.

- Value — the value of the feature type.

- Inheritable — whether the feature is inheritable by the frame's descendants. A value of "not-inheritable" indicates that the feature is only relevant to this frame and not to its descendants.

- Source – where the information came from. (This is used in the resolution of inconsistencies between terms in the BCB.)

BCB frames may be divided for convenience into two groups, representing nouns and verbs respectively. The difference is that certain feature types apply to nouns and others to verbs.

3.2.1 Nouns

Lord and Dahlgren [1990] identify a list of approximately fifty feature types for nouns. A subset of these, relevant to the business world, has been adopted for this system. Both the comprehensive list and the subset used for the BCB are subject to extension as the need arises. Some of the most common noun feature types are:

128

- has_att — indicates that the object has a certain attribute; e.g., *person* has the attribute "name". Any type of object may have attributes.

- behaviour — e.g., *people* "eat"; *animals* "eat grass". The behaviour feature type applies to living, physical objects [Dahlgren et al., 1989].

- function — what something does; e.g., a *customer* "buys" and an *employee* "produces." A function applies to a social thing (e.g. an employee) or a non-living physical thing (e.g. a truck).

- ako — stands for "a kind of" and represents a subset; e.g., a *manager* is a kind of "employee."

- haspart — e.g., a "department" is part of a *company*.

- synonym — e.g., *employee* means the same as "worker."

To illustrate, the *Employee* frame might initially consist of the following slots:

slot(employee,inherent,has_att,job-title,inheritable,source1)
slot(employee,inherent,function,work,inheritable,source1)
slot(employee,typical,function,product,not-inheritable,
       source1)
slot(employee,typical,function,sell,not-inheritable,source2)
slot(employee,typical,function,serve,not-inheritable,source1)
slot(employee,inherent,ako,person,inheritable,source1)
slot(employee,inherent,synonym,worker,inheritable,source2)

3.2.2 Verbs

Typical feature types for verbs are [Lord and Dahlgren, 1990]:

- subject — e.g., "customer" buys.

- object — e.g., "product" is bought.

- ako — a kind of; e.g., "produce" and "sell" are kinds of work.

- what_next — captures the notion of sequence; e.g., "owns" follows buys.

- indirect object — e.g., a salesperson sells a "customer" a computer.

- synonym — e.g., "supervise" is a synonym for manage.

- inverse_opposite — e.g., "buy" is the opposite of sell.

- inverse_synonym — e.g., "customer buys product" means the same thing as "product is-bought-by customer", but has the subject and object interchanged (similar to Dahlgren et al.'s [1989] "paraphrase" feature type.)

Other verb feature types can be goal, consequence (what happens because of something), implies, causes, what-enables, when, where, and how [Dahlgren et al. 1989].

To illustrate, the *buy* frame might initially include the following slots:

slot(buy,inherent,ako,transaction,inheritable,source1)
slot(buy,inherent,subject,buyer,inheritable,source1)
slot(buy,typical,object,product,inheritable,source1)
slot(buy,typical,indirect_object,company,inheritable,source1)
slot(buy,typical,indirect_object,employee,inheritable,source2)
slot(buy,inherent,what_next,value,pay,inheritable,source1)

3.3 Processing Capabilities

The Commonsense Business Reasoner has two predicates which allow it to carry out its main functions of retrieving and inserting knowledge.

3.3.1 Retrieval of Existing Knowledge

The predicate *tell_me* is used to retrieve all of the information that the system knows about something. This includes all of a frame's inherent and typical features and their values, and any other features that it can obtain, either through inheritance or from related frames.

For example, in retrieving information from the *Manager* frame, the Commonsense Business Reasoner would discover that:

1. *Manager* is a kind of *Employee* which, in turn, is a kind of *Person*.

2. *Manager* has the function "supervise".

3. *Manager* has a synonym, *Supervisor*.

Thus, additional facts about *Manager* will be obtained from the *Employee*, *Person* and *Supervisor* frames. From the *Supervise* frame, the system would retrieve further information about this function of a *Manager*; for example, that *Managers* supervise *Workers*.

3.3.2 Addition of New Knowledge

The *add_fact* predicate provides a mechanism for easily updating the system's knowledge. First, the system asks the user for the name of an object to be added to the BCB. If there is not already a frame for that object, the system engages the user in a dialogue to determine the object's ontological classification. If the emergent classification matches that of a known object, it is possible that the new object is related to the one already known. Either the new one is a kind of the old, or the old is a kind of the new. If a new object is a kind of the old, then it must have some additional features which the system will ask the user to specify.

4 SUMMARY & CONCLUSION

Most expert systems for business applications lack the commonsense reasoning capabilities that are inherent in human experts. This paper has reported on an approach to commonsense reasoning for business expert systems that is based on a high-level generic model of the business world. This model forms the basis of a frame-based system, called the *Commonsense Business Reasoner* that is able to retrieve knowledge about certain business concepts and modify its knowledge base to include newly acquired information.

Future research will concentrate on testing the Commonsense Business Reasoner and augmenting it with learning capabilities. The system currently relies upon a user to augment its knowledge base. Machine learning techniques need to be incorporated to allow the system to update itself based upon the knowledge that it obtains from each application to which it is applied. The main task here is to identify knowledge that is important or general enough to add to the BCB and to determine the appropriate location within the knowledge structure. In addition, mechanisms are needed to help the system determine the proper way to organize classes of things. For example, when should a class be split into two subclasses as more knowledge becomes available? To illustrate, supppose that the knowledge base contained information on stores. As more knowledge becomes available, the system needs capabilities to recognize that *Store* can be further divided into *Grocery Store*, *Department Store*, etc.

Finally, the Commonsense Business Reasoner will be integrated with an existing expert system for evaluation using real-world problems.

5 BIBLIOGRAPHY

1. Buchanan, B., "Expert Systems: Working Systems and Reseach Literature", in Savory, S.E. (Ed.), *Expert Systems in the Organization: An Introduction for Decision-Makers*, Ellis Horwood, 1988, pp.34-75.

2. Dahlgren, Kathleen, *Naive Semantics for Natural Language Understanding*, Boston MA: Kluwer Academic Publishers, 1988.

3. Dahlgren, K., MacDowell, J. and Stabler, E.P., "Knowledge Representation for Commonsense Reasoning with Text", *Computational Linguistics*, 1989, pp.149-170.

4. Ein-Dor, P., "Representing Commonsense Knowledge: A Survey", Working Paper No. 864/85, Israel Institute of Business Research, Tel Avi University, June 1985.

5. Hayes, Patrick J., "The Naive Physics Manifesto", in D. Michie (Ed.) *Expert Systems in the Micro Electronic Age*, Edinburgh: Edinburgh University Press, 1979.

6. Hayes, Patrick J., "The Second Naive Physics Manifesto", in J. R. Hobbs & R. C. Moore (eds) *Formal Theories of the Commonsense World*, Norwood, NJ: Ablex, 1985.

7. Kolata, Gina, "How Can Computers Get Common Sense?", *Science*, Vol. 217, No. 24, September 1982, pp.1237-1238.

8. Lenat, D.B., R. V. Guha, K. Pittman, D. Pratt, and M. Shepherd, "CYC: Toward Programs With Common Sense", *CACM*, Vol.33, No.8, August 1990, pp.30-49.

9. Lord, C. and Dahlgren, K., "Representation of Business and Financial Knowledge in the NewSelector System", Working Paper, IBM L.A. Scientific Center, Jan. 1990.

10. McCarthy, John, "Some Expert Systems Need Common Sense", *Annals of the New York Academy of Sciences*, Vol.426, 1983, pp.129-137.

11. Meltzer, Bernard, "Knowledge and Experience in Artificial Intelligence", *AI Magazine*, Vol. 6, No. 1, Spring 1985, pp.40-42.

6 ACKNOWLEDGEMENTS

This research was supported by the Information Systems Research Bureau, Faculty of Commerce and Business Administration, University of British Columbia, and by the William E. Simon Graduate School of Business Administration, University of Rochester. The authors wish to thank Hugo Chan, University of British Columbia, for his work on the implementation of the system.

Building Expert Databases:
L-CATA - An Intelligent Logic Based Travel Assistant.

David Cleary   John Zeleznikow

Database Research Laboratory,
Applied Computing Research Institute, La Trobe University,
Bundoora, Victoria, 3083, Australia.

ABSTRACT

The task of successfully integrating artificial intelligence into databases is a difficult one. We argue that significant research results can be achieved by building Expert Database prototypes. Our Expert Database System, L-CATA (a Logic based Computer Aided Travel Assistant), provides intelligent travel advice. L-CATA is a deductive database system written in TURBO-PROLOG. We outline L-CATA's query specification, search strategies, database and user-interface. L-CATA maintains a database of direct flights to which is applied a traveller's query specification comprising constraints, user-rules and goals. If the traveller is dissatisfied with the retrieved answer set he/she can either modify his/her query specification or specify that L-CATA is to repeat its search but with certain constraints violated in order to optimise his/her goals.

1   Introduction

Recently, there has been an increased emphasis on adding intelligence to databases [4]. We envisage two alternative methods for carrying this out.
(1)   Adding intelligence to hierarchical or network databases (or more generally object-oriented databases) by using the object-oriented paradigm.
(2)   Extending relational databases with rules. First order logic is used as the data model.
The papers of Vossos et al. [11] and Yuen et al. [15] demonstrate our approach to adding intelligence to object-oriented databases. This paper discusses the second alternative.

We believe the task of adding intelligence to databases is a difficult one. Rather than developing general techniques for constructing expert databases, we believe it will be fruitful to build specific prototypes, and then generalise the techniques developed in constructing these prototypes. For this reason we are building L-CATA an intelligent logic based travel assistant which provides intelligent travel advice.

1.1 Intelligent Travel Advice using L-CATA

The advice offered by L-CATA enhances and complements that which a travel agent can provide to a prospective traveller. Existing flight information and reservation systems can not return itineraries with the least changes of airline, cheapest fare or suggest that flying Melbourne to London and taking a ferry to Dublin is cheaper than flying directly Melbourne to Dublin. L-CATA does not attempt to model a travel agent but rather provides either a travel agent or a prospective traveller with intelligent access to a large database of flight information.

To use L-CATA the prospective traveller or travel agent composes a query and poses that query to the system. A query consists of the specification of origin and destination for the itinerary, a set of constraints and user-rules to be met by the itinerary and a set of goals specifying parameters of the itinerary to optimise. A possible query could state that the origin is Melbourne, the destination is Dublin, and the following constraints and user-rules are to be satisfied;
(1)   I will not pay more that $2500.
(2)   I will not visit Kuwait, Baghdad, Vienna or Rome.
(3)   I will only fly on Qantas, KLM or Cathay Pacific.
(4)   I will pay up to $3000 if I fly through Paris and the maximum number of legs is three.
(5)   I will visit Rome if the maximum elapsed time of the flight is twentytwo hours and I fly Cathay Pacific.
and the following goals are to be optimised;
(1)   I want the cheapest flight.
(2)   I want the flight with least elapsed travel time.
The system will attempt to retrieve itineraries that match the query specification.

The L-CATA database has two sections. The *itinerary database* contains specifications of complete flight itineraries from an origin to a destination. It includes specifications for round world tickets, package deals and established flights paths. The *direct flight database* contains specifications of direct flights between two locations. The current L-CATA prototype has concentrated on retrievals from the *direct flight database*.

Before complete itineraries can be retrieved from L-CATA's *direct flight database* that database must be searched to find all the routes between the specified origin and destination. These routes are then added to the *itinerary database* so that the user specified goals can be applied to the entire set of possible itineraries. If the prospective traveller is still dissatisfied with the itineraries retrieved from L-CATA's entire database, then he/she has no alternative but to modify his/her query.

The original CATA system was introduced by Bodi and Zeleznikow [1]. Yan and Zeleznikow [14] developed a logic framework and formal specification for L-CATA, whilst techniques for evaluating queries were discussed by Yan and Zeleznikow [13]. This paper discusses L-CATA's query specification scheme, database and user interface. A full description of the L-CATA system, together with the associated code for the current L-CATA prototype may be found in Cleary [5].

Cleary [5] documents the development and implementation of search strategies for retrieval of routes from L-CATA's *direct flight database*. L-CATA's search strategy attempts to intelligently prune the *direct flight database's* search space whilst carrying out this retrieval. As well as using system heuristics to carry out the pruning, L-CATA makes use of the constraints and user-rules supplied in a query specification. In searching the *direct flight database* L-CATA must be able to optimise different parameters of the search and handle constraints that the user has specified are violable. L-CATA could be given a query from a prospective traveller stating that he/she wishes to travel from Melbourne to Dublin at a minimal price and that his/her destination is violable. Based on this query, the closeness of Dublin to London and the availability of non-air transport between Dublin and London L-CATA's search could retrieve itineraries from Melbourne to London.

1.2 Adding Intelligence to Databases with Deductive Databases

Current DBMSs do not provide the ability to easily process information in the form of inference rules, integrity constraints, class hierarchies or inheritance. To process information of this type the concept of an expert database system (EDS) has been introduced. To build EDSs requires the integration of database and AI technologies [3]. There have been comparatively few significant results in the field of DBMS-AI integration. This is demonstrated by the fact that in the late 1980's there were no commercial EDSs in existence.

Various options have been proposed for creating EDSs. Gardarin and Valduriez [7] propose three architectures for an EDS. Existing DBMSs and AI systems can be *loosely coupled* together. Using this scheme the user still sees two distinct systems. The AI system is used for specifying rules and the DBMS is invoked for database access functions. Existing DBMSs and AI systems can be *tightly coupled* together. The AI system is built as a layer on top of the DBMS making the DBMS invisible to the user. Such a system can be extended to allow rules as well as facts to be stored and retrieved from the database. The third architecture *tightly integrates* database and AI functionality. Such a system requires rebuilding the entire DBMS from source and adding a deductive component.

Relational DBMSs can be extended with logic programming techniques from AI towards deductive databases. A deductive database consists of explicit facts and rules from which implicit facts can be inferred. Deductive databases offer an interface and evaluation process through which users can manipulate not only facts, as in relation databases, but also inference rules and integrity constraints. Retrieval from a deductive database utilizes the theorem proving techniques of first order logic. First order logic is a powerful data modelling tool, has well understood semantics and logic programming languages allow easy query specification.

Typically the knowledge base of a deductive database comprises a small number of rules and a large number of facts. Computer programs written in logic programming languages such as *PROLOG* would normally store their entire rule and fact base in the main memory of the machine carrying out the inferencing. Because of its large size, however, the knowledge base of a deductive database is usually stored in secondary memory. Although deductive database systems have been implemented through extending the PROLOG language, current research is underway to develop specific deductive database languages. Two such languages are LDL [9] and RDL1 [8].

1.3 Implementing L-CATA

L-CATA is a deductive database system. It is planned that future work on L-CATA will be carried out using a specific deductive database language. The current L-CATA prototype, however, has been implemented in the language *TURBO-PROLOG* [10]. The L-CATA system, including the database of flight information, the user's query specification, the query evaluation scheme and the database search scheme is entirely implemented using *TURBO-PROLOG's* logic based scheme. This unified implementation simplifies the process of applying the constraints and user-rules from the query specification to L-CATA's search and retrieval processes.

Given the lack of a specific deductive database language we chose to implement our prototype in TURBO-PROLOG because of its speed of execution, its provision of facilities for maintaining a dynamic database and developing a user friendly interface and because it generates easily portable executable code running on a standard IBM PC/Compatible.

Previous work on L-CATA [14] proposed three logic based architectures for knowledge base specification and query retrieval. "Proposal 1" developed an intelligent front-end interface between an existing (probably relational) commercial air-travel database and the prospective traveller. "Proposal 2" extended an existing logic based expert database core with the air-travel information. "Proposal 3" built its own logic based expert database core integrating the air travel information.

Both the existing prototype system and new work presently underway have concentrated on "Proposal 3". "Proposal 1" could have moved us away from our investigations of deductive databases introducing a series of new problems relating to interfacing different database schemes. In the future, however, we may still choose to follow "Proposal 2" if it allows us to more easily produce an integrated L-CATA system.

2 Query Specification in L-CATA

An L-CATA query specification consists of a set of user supplied constraints, user-rules and goals. Constraints are facts that must be satisfied by a retrieved result. User-rules are conditional statements specifying that a particular fact may be satisfied by a retrieved result if a series of other facts are also satisfied by that retrieved result. Goals are facts that specify what particular parameter of the query should be optimised within any retrieved results. Each item in a query is expressed as a Horn Clause .

Definition 1: A *query* to L-CATA is a typed first order formula of the form;

```
<-- C1,..,Cm,R1,..,Rn,G
```
where C_i is a constraint, R_j is a user-rule and G is a goal.

Definition 2: A *constraint* within an L-CATA query is a typed first order formula of the form;

```
<-- C
```
Examples are;
(1) Destination of the flight is London but that is violable;
```
destination(london,violable)
```
(2) I will not pay more than $2500 and that is inviolable;
```
maximum_cost(2500,inviolable)
```
(3) I will not visit Kuwait but that is violable;
```
wont_visit(kuwait,violable)
```

Definition 3: A *user-rule* within an L-CATA query is a typed first order formula of the form;

```
H <-- B1,..,Bm
```
where $1<=i<=m$.
Examples are;
(1) I will pay up to $3000 if I fly through Paris and the maximum number of legs is three;
```
maximum_cost(3000) if
    visit(paris),
    maximum_legs(3)
```
(2) I will visit Rome if the maximum elapsed time of the flight is twenty two hours and I fly Cathay Pacific;
```
visit(rome) if
    maximum_time(22),
    fly(cathay_pacific)
```

Definition 4: A *goal* within an L-CATA query is a typed first order formula of the form;

```
<-- G
```

An example is;
(1)   I want the cheapest flight;
```
minimise(cost)
```

Yan and Zeleznikow [14] allow predicates to take sets as the values of their arguments. They consider as a possible constraint; `wont_visit(middle_east_airports)` where `middle_east_airports` is the set of all the airports in the Middle East. L-CATA could be extended to handle predicates with arguments of this type by interpreting them as the set of constraints each with a single Middle Eastern airport as the value of its argument. The current L-CATA implementation, however, only allows non-complex terms as arguments for predicates.

3   L-CATA's Search Strategy

A major task for the L-CATA system is one of route finding. L-CATA's search procedure extends TURBO-PROLOG's backward chaining depth first search method for evaluating goals to produce a variation of the A* search algorithm [12].

L-CATA attempts to find optimal routes between the user specified origin and destination. L-CATA maintains an agenda of partially expanded routes sorted by the closeness of the last location in each partial route to the destination. Each item on the agenda is itself a list of the *best* partial routes to a particular location. Users specify which of the route parameters are to be optimised and the accumulated value of those parameters determines which are the *best* partial routes to a particular location. The partial routes comprising the first item on the agenda are expanded until a route to the destination is found. L-CATA wants to supply the user with not just one route to the destination but a number of the *best* routes, therefore, having successfully retrieved a route L-CATA makes use of TURBO-PROLOG's backtracking ability to continue the search to find other routes. The search procedure used by L-CATA is not an optimal search but should find routes close to the optimal route within a few iterations. On completion of this search, L-CATA returns the set of possible routes that satisfy the user's query specification.

3.1 Customising L-CATA's Search

L-CATA's search procedure enables it to find a close to optimal route between origin and destination within a small number of iterations. Nevertheless, many of the routes retrieved may be considered unsatisfactory by the user. To limit and direct its search L-CATA makes use of both system and user supplied heuristics. These heuristics are specified as constraints.

System heuristics are used to limit L-CATA's search space. For example;
(1)   Ensure that the search stays bounded by the smallest geographical region encompassing both the origin and the destination.
(2)   Ensure that with each iteration partially expanded routes end at locations nearer the destination.
(3)   Ensure that times for connecting flights are not less than minimum or greater than maximum stopover times.

User supplied heuristics produce a search that precisely matches an individual's requirements. These heuristics are specified as the constraints and user-rules in a query specification. A constraint can be viewed as a fact that limits one particular aspect of L-CATA's search. Examples are;
(1)   The destination of the flight is London.
(2)   I will not pay more than $2500.
(3)   I will not visit Kuwait.

The only compulsory user supplied constraints are the origin and destination. Users are able to specify many other constraints however. The user can specify maximum price, maximum distance, and maximum number of airline changes. The user can modify the default minimum and maximum stopover times. The user may have a number of locations that he/she is not willing to visit and a number of airlines that he/she is not willing to fly. L-CATA allows the user to specify such requests as constraints.

3.2 Violability of L-CATA Clauses

When considering their concept of *goal optimisation*, Yan and Zeleznikow [13] introduced the idea of having two classes of constraint and user-rule clauses, *violable* and *inviolable*. They noted that to optimise his/her goals a user may be prepared to accept routes that do not exactly meet his/her query specification. They cited the example of a prospective traveller wanting to fly Melbourne to Frankfurt and wishing to minimise the cost of his trip. The traveller may be willing to fly Melbourne-Frankfurt (and travel Paris-Frankfurt overland) if this change of itinerary results in a cheaper fare. Retrieval from L-CATA's database therefore consists of two phases. The first phase retrieves routes that exactly match the query constraints and user-rules. The second phase retrieves routes that match only those constraints and user-rules that are specified by the user as inviolable. In order to carry out this two phase search prospective travellers have to specify which constraints and user-rules are violable and which are not.

4   L-CATA's Database

Database systems written using traditional programming languages store their databases externally in files and manipulate those files using purposely determined procedures. A TURBO-PROLOG program is a database of facts and rules. Adding information to a TURBO-PROLOG program is equivalent to adding new facts and rules to that database. The same depth first, backward chaining search control mechanism used in implementing the program is used for manipulating the added database. L-CATA's database can be divided into three sections;
(1)   The program code that implements L-CATA.
(2)   The set of instances of constraints, user-rules and goals predicates generated from a query to L-CATA.
(3)   The set of instances of predicates used by L-CATA in carrying out its search of direct flights to determine all possible routes.

4.1 Program Code

L-CATA's program code consists of a set of Horn Clauses. The program code includes the algorithms for implementing the search of the *direct flight database* and the user interface through which the user poses queries to L-CATA. The Horn Clauses making up a logic program such as L-CATA have both a logical and a procedural interpretation. In the logical interpretation of L-CATA executing the program is seen as a process of attempting to show that the L-CATA goals are a logical consequence of the database of facts and rules. L-CATA's procedural interpretation, on the other hand, views the database of facts and rules as procedure specifications.

4.2 Query Specification Database

The database generated by a query to L-CATA consists of instances of constraint, user-rule and goal predicates. This database is maintained by asserting and retracting clauses into the L-CATA system during runtime using the TURBO-PROLOG system predicates; `assert` and `retract`.

4.3 Direct Flight Database

To carry out its search for possible routes between origin and destination L-CATA maintains a static database of direct flights, valid airports and valid airlines. Each database item is represented as a TURBO-PROLOG fact clause. The current prototype uses TURBO-PROLOG V1.1. which requires that the entire direct flight database be loaded into main memory before L-CATA can begin its search. Although this strategy makes for very quick retrieval of clauses from the database it has the major disadvantage of limiting the maximum size of the database to the size of main memory. For a large database a preferable solution to the problem of retrieval is to store the database in external files and only move clauses into main memory when required.

5   L-CATA's User Interface

L-CATA makes use of a user-friendly menu-driven user interface. The interface has been implemented to allow it to be extended for use with the full system. It allows continual modification of the current query specification before and after retrieval of flights from the database. L-CATA's user interface is written using TURBO-PROLOG augmented with routines for managing menus and generally improving the screen display from the TURBO-PROLOG TOOLBOX.

L-CATA starts up by displaying its main menu. From the main menu a user can select one of the three editors in order to manipulate his query specification; constraint editor, rule editor or goal editor. A user can select to retrieve routes from the database of direct flights matching the current query specification. He/she can also select to load a previous query specification or to save or delete the current query specification.

5.1 Query Specification Editors

Having chosen one of L-CATA's three editors, the user can either view the clauses associated with the particular editor, or delete or add new clauses. Clauses are displayed and manipulated within the editor in a logical form as opposed to the form in which they are stored within L-CATA's database. We delete clauses from an editor by selecting them from the menu of current clauses. Users add new clauses to the current query specification within an editor by typing in the entire logical form of the clause. L-CATA then parses that clause. If the user's input is a valid clause then the corresponding database form of the clause will have been generated during the parse and added to L-CATA's query specification database.

5.2 Retrieval of Flights

Having specified his query the user can then select the flight retrieval option from L-CATA's main menu. From within L-CATA's flight retrieval section the user instigates the search of L-CATA's *direct flight database* in order to retrieve routes matching the current query specification. Before this search

begins, however, the user is able to select whether the constraint violability switch will be turned on or off during the search. If the constraint violability switch is off all user supplied constraints are considered during the search whilst if it is on those constraints specified as violable may not be considered if in neglecting them the user's goals can be further optimised.

Having retrieved the set of possible routes via the direct flight database search the user is able to view each route in turn. Routes are viewed in the order specified by the current optimisation parameter. For each route information regarding all the direct flights making up that route as well as accumulated information for that complete route is displayed. In cases where the user specified destination is violable, L-CATA's *direct flight database* search suggests alternative destinations. In such cases, L-CATA also displays the suggested alternative destination and the distance of the alternative destination from the original.

6   Query Retrieval Results

The current L-CATA implementation applies its search to a database of four-hundred and fifty direct flight clauses, fifty location clauses and ten airline clauses. The direct flight tuples correspond to sections of routes from the Pacific to Europe via the Middle East or the United States.

Applying a user's query specification to L-CATA's database produces the following results for numbers of retrieved routes and retrieval times (See Table 1).

These results highlight a number of design decisions;

(1)   Changing the search goal does not alter the retrieval time. L-CATA is simply applying the same algorithm to a different parameter of the search.

(2)   Processing user-rules takes only a small percentage of L-CATA's retrieval time. Retracting the user-rules from the query specification produces no noticeable change in retrieval time.

(3)   Turning the violability switch on produced a large increase in the number of routes retrieved with only a small increase in processing time. This was a result of the destination being violable in this particular query. Processing time spent on expanding partial routes ending at locations near the specified destination was not wasted.

(4)   Retracting the constraints that limit retrieval to routes departing within a one day period produced proportional increases in both number of routes retrieved and retrieval time.

7   Conclusion

In order to solve various AI-Database integration problems we are developing L-CATA an intelligent logic based travel assistant. We have developed a logic based scheme for specifying precisely a user's query specification. Using this scheme a query is specified as a set of constraints, user-rules and goals. The current L-CATA prototype makes use of the

Table 1
Query results from L-CATA operating on an IBM PC/Compatible, 80386, 20MHz.

Routes Retrieved	Retrieval Times	Goal	User-rules	Violatability	Departure Range
6	5 seconds	closeness	yes	off	1 day
6	5 seconds	cost	yes	off	1 day
4	5 seconds	closeness	no	off	1 day
33	6 seconds	closeness	yes	on	1 day
30	24 seconds	closeness	yes	off	7 days

scheme in the search for and retrieval of routes from a *direct flight database*. This prototype also implements Yan and Zeleznikow's [14] concept of goal optimisation.

Current work on L-CATA is investigating extending the search procedure to incorporate an *itinerary database*, handling incomplete query specifications and improving the means by which violable constraints are handled during the search procedure.

REFERENCES

[1]   Bodi, A. and Zeleznikow, J. (1989), "CATA: An Expert Database for Intelligent Travel Assistance", in Pau, L.F., Motiwalla, J., Pao, Y.H. and Teh, T.T. (eds.) *Expert Systems in Economics, Banking and Management*, North Holland, pp. 177-186.

[2]   Bocca, J., Decker, H., Nicolas, J., Vieille, L. and Wallace, M. (1986), "Some Steps Towards a DBMS Based KBMS" in *Information Processing 86*, pp. 1061-1068.

[3]   Brodie, M.L. (1988), *"Future Intelligent Information Systems: AI and Database Technologies working Together"* in Brodie, M.L. and Mylopolous, J. (eds) Readings in Artificial Intelligence and Databases, pp. 623-641.

[4]   Brodie, M.L. and Mylopolous, J. (eds.) (1988), *"Readings in Artificial Intelligence"*, Morgan Kaufmann.

[5]   Cleary, D.C.G. (1990), *"L-CATA - a Logic Based Computer Aided Travel Assistant"*.   La Trobe University.

[6]   Freitag, B. and Biernath, O. (1988), "An Airtravel Expert Database", in *Proceedings of the Third International Conference on Data and Knowledge Bases"*, Morgan Kaufmann, pp. 32-46.

[7]   Gardarin, G. and Valduriez, P. (1989), *Relational Databases and Knowledge Bases*, Addison-Wesley.

[8]   Kiernan, G., de Maindreville, C. and Simon, E. (1990), "Making Deductive Databases a Practical Technology: A Step Forward", in *SIGMOD Record* 19 (2), pp. 237-246.

[9]   Naqvi, S. and Tsur, S. (1989), *A Logical Language For Data And Knowledge Bases*, Computer Science Press.

[10] Rich, K.M. and Robinson, P.R. (1988), *Using Turbo Prolog (Second Edition)*, Borland Osborne/McGraw Hill.

[11] Vossos, G., Dillon, T., Zeleznikow, J. and Taylor, G. (1991), "An Object Oriented System for Legal Reasoning - IKBALS", to appear in *Australian Computer Journal*

[12] Winston, P.H. (1984), *Artificial Intelligence Second Edition*, Addison-Wesley.

[13] Yan, S. and Zeleznikow, J. (1990), "Query Evaluation And Goal Optimisation In A Logic Based Expert Travel System" to appear in *Applied Artificial Intelligence - An International Journal*.

[14] Yan, S. and Zeleznikow, J. (1990), "L-CATA: A Logic-Based Expert Travel System" to appear in *Computer Science in Economics and Management*.

[15] Yuen, H. Zeleznikow, J. and Dillon, T. (1990), "Improving Organizational Design Methodology Using an Object-Oriented Database", in*"The Impact of Information Technology on Systems Management"*, Institute of Management Consultants, Hong Kong, pp. 254-260.

Using a Meta-Knowledge Method for Developing an Educational Knowledge-Based Application

Christoph Lell

Department of Management Information Systems, Wirtschaftsuniversität Wien
Augasse 2–6, A–1090 Wien, Austria

Abstract

We present a methodology for executable, conceptual modelling of information systems. This methodology was used to implement a knowledge-based, educational information system. In particular we focus on the possibility of using a near-English specification language as supported by the SYLLOG Expert Database System.

The conceptual modelling input to the proposed methodology consists of generic knowledge, organization-specific knowledge, and of meta-knowledge about how to merge a number of generic and specific components into a single application knowledge-base for a particular organization. The result is a tailored expert database application consisting of the components, which we call *mini knowledge-bases*. The conceptual modelling inputs (generic, specific, and meta) and the application knowledge-base output of the method are all written as near-English, nonprocedural specifications, which are directly executed by the SYLLOG expert database system. The SYLLOG system also automatically generates SQL queries as needed and is also used as the single specification language for the implementation of the educational information system.

1 Introduction

The development of future information systems will make heavy use of the group of systems known as knowledge-base management systems, expert database systems, or deductive databases. Although such systems hold out the promise of easing the "application programming bottleneck", a number of issues need to be addressed including knowledge modelling, knowledge acquisition, as well as knowledge management and maintenance.

While there are numerous, well known approaches and methodologies for traditional, relational database design and information systems modelling (e.g., the entity relationship approach [9], semantic data models such as RM/T [11] and SDM [14], dependency theory [16]) no such generally accepted methods exist for building knowledge-based information systems. While the methods mentioned above have made it easier for a user to model an information system, several concerns still remain unresolved. The problems addressed in this paper concerning current techniques for conceptual modelling of databases and knowledge-bases are the following:

1. After completion of the modelling phase, there often still exists a problematic implementation gap between the model agreed upon and the intended application. There can be several reasons for this gap including the generality of the model used, requirements that change during modelling, or the inadequacy of the system chosen for implementation to represent certain facets of the model.

2. Graphical modelling techniques, while easy to learn and use, might not capture the full application. This makes it necessary to annotate the graphical representation. This addition falls outside the methodology itself.

3. When generic knowledge about a class of applications is available we would like to use it in different contexts. The process of systematically merging and integrating this generic knowledge with specific application knowledge in the same application class can be problematic. In particular, syntactic techniques can lead to errors that can be avoided by a semantic meta-knowledge approach that we describe.

Problem (1) be avoided by implementing the conceptual model in the same form or language that the application itself uses. By defining an executable specification of the conceptual model in a near-English form this gap can be significantly reduced.

For problem (2) recent research [10] seems to indicate that graphical modelling techniques are severely restricted in their ability to represent rules and goals that are critical to an application. In cases where these restrictions play a vital role the usual procedure is to annotate the model, which ultimately leads to such problems as leaving out information, burying information, or the inability to verify these annotations.

Problem (3) concerns different types of knowledge in a large knowledge-based information system. By distinguishing between

- independent knowledge that is the same for all domains or organizations in an application class and

- organization dependent knowledge,

knowledge management and maintenance is significantly simplified [27]. We address the issue of partitioning and composing knowledge by a technique using modular knowledge-bases and a meta-level knowledge-base. This approach can be viewed as a generalization of inheritance techniques, as we no longer restrict meta-level reasoning to a predefined set of inheritance sets.

By addressing these issues, a general meta-level approach to knowledge management is developed. The input to the methodology consists of generic knowledge, organization-specific, and meta-knowledge about how to integrate a number of generic and specific components into a single application. The components are small knowledge modules or knowledge bases that we shall call mini knowledge-bases (mini-KB). The conceptual modelling inputs (generic, specific, and meta) and the application knowledge-base output of the method, are all written as near-English, nonprocedural specifications, which are directly executed by the SYLLOG expert database system.

While there is an overwhelming number of papers concerned with knowledge acquisition and several with knowledge management very few address the possibility of using small manageable modules as a means for building knowledge-bases. Moreover, most use separate knowledge acquisition and consultation tools.

A technique for modelling of deductive databases uses the concept of a conceptual schema and applies it to the area of deductive databases [12]. The method uses a diagrammatic tool consisting of a small set of primitives and a graphic interface language for the modelling of the deductive database. Additionally a query language has been developed which uses extended Prolog syntax. We believe that this approach can be used in the early stages of conceptual modelling, but will fail to represent all the semantics that an application might need. This is due to the limited set of primitives available in the proposed methodology. Furthermore, this approach attempts to model the complete application in one diagram, whereas our approach attempts to separate the application into distinct, modular parts.

A recent paper [13] describes a knowledge representation language for university requirements. Whereas the application is very similar to the one presented in this paper the solution and the modelling methodology is different. In [13] a set theoretic language (similar to Prolog) is used and it is up to the knowledge engineer to translate the degree requirements into that language. Our methodology and the application use the near-English capabilities of SYLLOG to define the degree requirements thus making it possible for a university clerk to write the requirements.

SYLLOG was developed by Adrian Walker of IBM Laboratories in Yorktown Heights and belongs to the class of declarative languages such as *Datalog* [1]. The educational application was developed on an IBM mainframe under the VM/CMS operating system.

We first describe the methodology and the basic ideas used in the modelling framework. This is followed by a description of the application and how the methodology is put to use during the implementation. We finish with a short discussion of further research.

2 Guiding Principles Used

This section gives an overview of the methodology and the principles used during the implementation of the educational knowledge-based information system described in Section 3.

The goals stated in the previous section are achieved by integrating four distinct concepts into one framework. These ideas are used in one general methodology and are the basis for the described application. The methodology makes use of the following ideas:

1. executable specifications,

2. near-English rule representation,

3. a distinction between generic application knowledge and specific application knowledge (i.e., the knowledge pertaining solely to the target organization), and

4. a meta-model in the same near-English executable form.

The methodology is supported by the SYLLOG Expert Database System. SYLLOG supports direct execution of near-English specifications. The integration of general and specific application knowledge is achieved by splitting the knowledge into distinct knowledge modules and the use of a meta-knowledge-base. By implementing the meta-model in SYLLOG we are able to avoid an additional level of complexity and offer a general framework for conceptual modelling. The following sections describe the three basic parts of the framework: SYLLOG, knowledge modules, and meta-knowledge.

2.1 SYLLOG Expert Database System

Several next-generation database systems supporting rules, integrating logic programming and relational databases, or making use of declarative programming have been proposed in the last few years. These are all in a prototype stage and are directed towards different goals [8]. These include LDL [18], NAIL! [17], ALGRES and its successor LOGRES [7], and POSTGRES [21].

The SYLLOG Expert Database System [26] is an expert and data system shell which makes use of the concept of syllogisms to build knowledge-bases without the need for programming. The system uses a near-English language with very few restrictions, executable specifications, and improved declarativeness for Prolog-like programs.

SYLLOG uses the notion of *strong declarative specification* to distinguish its power from ordinary declarative programming, as e.g. used in Prolog. In general the inference engine of a knowledge-base system imposes a certain order of execution e.g., by using certain chaining techniques. In many cases the programmer will have to take this into consideration when writing an application. Rather than having the user concern himself with procedural aspects, it is the system's responsibility to use the knowledge procedurally [15]. Issues such as the use of forward and backward chaining techniques, loop control, and negation (if the programs are stratified) are delegated to the system and can be ignored by the author of an application. This is achieved via a new theory of the strongly declarative use of knowledge consisting of formal semantics and proofs for the computation techniques used in SYLLOG[1].

The design of SYLLOG addresses the fact that we cannot know in advance, and hard code into database systems, all of the inheritance and other reasoning methods that will be needed.

For example using property inheritance in an expert database system is just one special reasoning mechanism and others are possible and might be demanded by the users in the future. By contrast, SYLLOG offers the user an easy way to specify any reasoning mechanisms or semantic, data constructs they find necessary. The result is an open system, and together with the modular technique described lets the user construct tailored information systems. The meta knowledge-base is used to describe the available reasoning techniques and semantic, data constructs and to organize the final application knowledge-base.

2.2 Knowledge Modules

The second basic part of the modelling approach is the use of

• generic knowledge about classes of organizations (such as universities), and

• specific knowledge about individual organizations (such as New York University).

This is achieved by partitioning the conceptual model into separate, modular knowledge-bases that we will call *mini knowledge-bases* (mini-KB) and that either belong to an application class group, to an organizational rule group, or to organizational facts.

A graphic representation of the proposed types of modular knowledge bases is given in Figure 1.

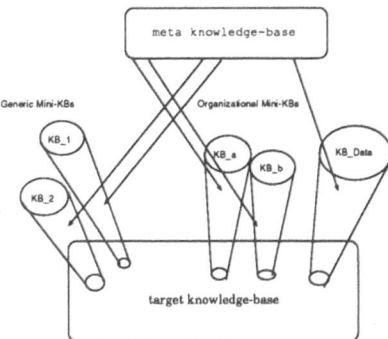

Figure 1: The Integration Process

The *target* knowledge-base is the implemented information system. The *meta* knowledge-base is the knowledge-base containing the rules and facts concerning how to combine the generic and organizational KBs to form the *target* knowledge-base. The knowledge-bases KB_1, KB_2 contain broad application knowledge and can often be seen as an independent application in their own right. The knowledge-bases KB_a, KB_b contain specific, organizational knowledge that pertain only to the enterprise being modelled. Finally, the actual facts and organizational data of the enterprise are contained in the KB_Data knowledge-base.

2.3 Integration via Meta-Knowledge

The process of identifying, choosing, and finally merging the necessary and appropriate mini-KBs for the intended use of the final knowledge-base is a problem that is itself ideally suited for a knowledge-base system.

A similar problem can also be found in the multidatabase environment, where the local databases are not aware of the existence of other database systems [6]. This results in general update and consistency problems. In our case the generic mini-KBs can be viewed as separate applications that are not aware of each other. While we do not consider the update problem, there remains the problem of integrating the various mini-KBs into one application without causing consistency problems.

The methodology chosen is a meta-level approach in which we use meta-knowledge to bootstrap an application, without the need for a separate knowledge acquisition tool. The meta knowledge-base contains facts about the available mini knowledge-bases and their functionality, and rules concerning the way these are to be integrated with each other and the factual organizational knowledge.

Generally there are two strategies that can be used for integrating the mini-KBs. One is a syntactic merging strategy, the other is a semantic, knowledge-based strategy. The syntactic method scans the target knowledge-base for all the rules stored within it and looks for the modules where the rules have been defined and in which modules the facts are stored. These mini-KBs are then plugged into one knowledge base.

While this is a very straightforward method, it has serious drawbacks:

- Modules can be incompatible with one another, so that additional rules will be needed. A purely syntactic approach will not know about these additional rules.

- Rule-Specialization is a problem.

  Example: Assume an educational knowledge-base includes the rule that all non-core courses are elective courses. If we were to add a KB that says that both non-core **and** non-major courses are elective courses, the first rule would still be part of the knowledge base. All major courses would still be identified as electives, because they are non-core courses.

- The syntactic approach will identify all knowledge modules where a certain rule is defined, regardless of that fact that the module makes no sense in the context of the target knowledge-base.

To circumvent some of these problems a meta knowledge-base approach was taken. By using a knowledge-base containing some of the semantics of the mini-KBs and appropriate merging and integrating rules an improved mechanism is available to guide the integration process. This meta knowledge-base is itself a SYLLOG knowledge-base and therefore does not add an additional level of complexity to the conceptual modelling framework.

All the necessary generic and organizational mini-KBs for the required application and the corresponding domain are identified through the meta knowledge-base. The facts and rules contained in the meta knowledge-base describe the functionality of the generic mini-KBs and how they need to be combined for the final knowledge-based application.

3 The Application

This section describes the application built with the proposed modelling methodology and gives an overview of SYLLOG and its use. We first describe the application domain and then show how SYLLOG is used in the mini and meta knowledge-base environment.

The application domain which was chosen to show the feasibility of a modular or mini knowledge-base approach is the educational environment. Several graduate programs of major universities were modelled and implemented.

The application was developed in a bottom-up manner. Initially, the generic knowledge about all the subsumed educational programs was identified. The result was the definition of a set of small, modular, generic applications. These distinct applications were then implemented as SYLLOG mini knowledge-bases. The result is a set of modular, mini knowledge-bases that together form a model of the education domain and that enables us to use meta knowledge to tailor a specialized educational knowledge-base according to our needs.

The generic knowledge-bases that were implemented included applications for the following objectives:

- a course prerequisite structure,

- a named set structure,

- degree program requirements including
  - required courses and
  - elective courses,

- tracking of student progress, and as a result thereof,

- advising based on past progress and available courses, and

- calculation of grade point averages.

Some of these generic knowledge-bases can not only be viewed in the context mentioned above, but on a more general level are implementations of generic methods. For example the knowledge-base for the prerequisite structure conceptually reasons over a directed acyclic graph (dag), while the knowledge-base concerned with elective course requirements conceptually reasons over a named set. Although a similar, conceptual structure for all modules involved in the final knowledge-base can be considered desirable, it is by no means necessary. As mentioned above an additional knowledge-base is used in cases where different and initially incompatible conceptual structures are involved.

In our case an educational program consists of elective courses and required courses, so the graph and named set structures (or their respective modules) are needed. The incompatibility is overcome by adding a knowledge-base concerned solely with bridging the gap between these two types of requirements. With the addition of this knowledge module, educational programs consisting of required and elective courses can be easily represented.

The organizational domains that were implemented together with the generic knowledge-bases included degree programs at New York University (NYU), Columbia University and City University of New York (CUNY).

3.1 Mini-KBs – The Generic Knowledge Modules

In this section we illustrate the use of SYLLOG in the generic educational mini-KBs.

Rules in a SYLLOG knowledge-base are so-called *syllogisms* or logical implications written in near-English. Given a KB, SYLLOG presents a menu from which a sentence can be selected and tailored in order to ask a question. After a question has been asked SYLLOG returns with either a yes-no answer or an answer table, depending on the type of question that was asked and automatically provides various kinds of explanation.

Rules and facts in the SYLLOG system are written in near-English with so called *example words*. These example words, which can be viewed as attribute names in the relational framework, are preceded by such words as: a_, an_, eg_, this_, that_, some_ etc.

Rules are divided by a single line in an *IF* and *THEN* part.

Examples:

(1)
a_student completed a_course with grade some_grade
that_student has taken that_course

(2)
a_student has taken a_course
not: that_student completed that_course with grade **F**
not: that_student completed that_course with grade **INC**
that_student has successfully completed that_course

(3)
the only prerequisite for some_course is an_other_course
a_student has successfully completed that_other_course
that_student is eligible to enroll in that_course

Syllogism (1) states that a student completing a course, regardless of the final grade, has taken that course.

Syllogism (2) tells us what requirements are necessary for a student to successfully complete a course, i.e., students must have enrolled in the course and have completed the course without an incomplete or failing grade.

The interpretation of syllogism (3) is: *If there is only one prerequisite for a certain course and a student has completed that prerequisite without the grade* **incomplete** *or failing the course, then that student may enroll in that course.*

The generic mini knowledge-bases contain syllogisms that are applicable to all organizations in a certain application class, even though most organizations will need only a subset of the available generic modules.

Three further example syllogisms used in the educational application illustrate the generic mini KB functionality, as well as showing some of SYLLOG's capabilities.

(4)
this_course is a prerequisite for some_intermediate_course
that_intermediate_course is a prerequisite for a_final_course
that_course is a prerequisite for that_final_course

(5)
a_student has this_type_of_specialization in some_field_of_study
a_course is in that_field_of_study
that_course is a that_type_of_specialization course for that_student

(6)
a_crse is a some_type course for some_std
sum the_p: that_std completed the_crse with grade the_p = the_pts
count the_crse: that_std completed the_crse with grade the_p = the_cs
the_pts / the_cs = the_gpa
that_std has a gpa of this_gpa in the that_type courses

Note that Syllogism (4) is recursive and by adding an integrity constraint syllogism we can check for any loops in the prerequisite structure. Essentially integrity constraints do not differ in the way they are defined from all the other syllogisms. Such a syllogism may look like this:

this_course is a prerequisite for some_intermediate_course
the_course equal that_intermediate_course
there is a loop in the prerequisite structure

The current version of SYLLOG is not normally set up to check integrity constraints automatically. Rather, a user checks a constraint by asking the question:

there is a loop in the prerequisite structure

and the user can then examine the loop by asking for an explanation.

Syllogism (5) makes special use of SYLLOG's near-English capabilities. This rule together with the appropriate facts in an organizational knowledge-base tells us what kind of courses students are taking (such as **major** or **minor**). The various types are either predefined or can also be defined through a syllogism.

Regardless of the *name* for the electives, **major**, **minor**, or **specialization** (which may vary from one organization to another), this rule will correctly identify the course using the appropriate name.

Syllogism (6) uses the aggregation operations, such as *sum*, and *count*, to compute the grade point average (gpa) for certain groups of courses. While the exact mapping from grade name to number of grade points awarded is part of the organizational mini-KB, the computation method is generally applicable.

3.2 Organization Dependent Mini-Kbs

This section describes the type of knowledge stored in the specific, organization dependent mini-KBs. For each generic knowledge module used in the final application either one or two corresponding organizational knowledge-bases will also be included. The application dependent mini-KBs consist of:

Organizational Rules: These specialized rules need to be included for an organization when we tailor the generic mini-KBs for specific needs of that organization's application. The actual tailoring is done by adding further mini-KBs. Some of these additional rules are needed to capture the semantics of an organization, while other rules in these modules might map the organizational knowledge to compatible rules available in the generic modules.

Facts: The organizational data stored in these mini-KBs is used by the generic knowledge-bases and any specialized rules included in the organizational modules.

3.2.1 Organizational Knowledge

In the examples above, syllogism (2) is an example for specific organizational knowledge. The reason for this is that not every university using the final knowledge-base will use the same notation for an incomplete grade. Instead of using **INC** to denote an incomplete grade another organization might use **IP**. In that case the *IF* part of syllogism (2) would be changed. While this is a simple example, such naming conventions are in fact crucial in some areas, such as medicine.

Another example illustrating the use of organizational knowledge is the definition of various named sets of courses. Educational institutions may have different ways of defining what an *elective* course is (Syllogism (7) below), or a program may include requirements for seminars in a certain field, e.g., students need to complete a seminar in their field of specialization.

Example: We can say generically, that an **elective** course is any course that is not a course in the field of specialization or part of the core requirements. A **major_seminar** course is a course that is a seminar and held in the field of a student's specialization.

(7)
not: a_course is a specialization course for some_student
not: a_course is a core course for that_student
that_course is a elective course for some_student

(8)
a_student has specialization some_field
a_course is in seminar
that_course is in that_field
that_course is a specialization_seminar course for that_student

Example: The doctoral program in business administration at NYU requires a student to choose a major and a minor field. The generic mini-KBs needed include the *prerequisite, set, specialization, electives,* and *gpa* mini-KBs. The specific rules for NYU can be found in the NYU organizational mini-KBs **NYU_prerequisite**, **NYU_set**, **NYU_elective**, and **NYU_gpa**[1]. In addition to the specific rules, the organizational data concerning NYU needs to be added to these mini-KBs.

- The named sets **major**, **minor**, **major_seminar**, and **minor_seminar** are missing in the respective generic *named set* mini-KB. The rules for these named sets can be found in the **NYU_set** KB and can be then accessed in the final knowledge-base. The definition for the **major** and **minor_seminar** sets are the following syllogisms:

(9)
a_student has major some_field
a_course is in that_field
that_course is a major course for that_student

(10)
a_student has specialization some_field
a_course is in seminar
that_course is in that_field
that_course is a specialization_seminar course for the_student

- Certain grades have no numerical value and will therefore not be included in the grade point average. However, the exact value or abbreviation for these grades may differ. These names must be defined in the NYU_gpa module to insure compatibility with the generic *set* knowledge-base, which has the general knowledge of incomplete or audited courses. At NYU audited classes receive the grade R and incomplete classes receive the grade IP. In this case the following two rules are added to the mini-KB NYU_gpa:

(11[1]) | *a_student completed a_course with grade* IP |
|---|
| *that_student completed that_course with an incomplete grade* |

(12) | *a_student completed a_course with grade* R |
|---|
| *that_student audited that_course* |

3.2.2 Organizational Facts

Up to this point only rules have been discussed and there has been no mention of the way the actual data is stored in SYLLOG.

From the user point of view facts in SYLLOG are stored in tables, with a header sentence divided from the actual data by two lines. All the organizational data is stored in these SYLLOG tables. (In the underlying system, these may actually be SQL tables).

The organizational facts in a knowledge-base storing prerequisite course information include the following tables:

(1)

the only prerequisite for	*this_course is*	*this_other_course*
	statistics_201	statistics_101
	research_seminar	research_methods

(2)

this_student	*has enrolled in*	*this_course*
Allen		economics_101
Allen		statistics_101
Fred		economics_101
Fred		statistics_101

(3)

this_student	*completed*	*this_course*	*with grade*	*this_grade*
Allen		economics_101		A+
Allen		statistics_101		B
Fred		economics_101		INC
Fred		statistics_101		3.0

As table (2) illustrates, numerical values may be used together with alphanumerical values.

The rules together with the data can now be used by the inference engine to generate the appropriate answers and explanations. Questions in SYLLOG can be asked by choosing the appropriate query or statement from the system's knowledge via a menu and drop-down windows. In cases where all the *example words* are fixed, SYLLOG returns with a yes–no answer. When *example words* are left empty the result of a question will be an answer table for all those *example words*.

The query: Fred *is eligible to enroll in* statistics_201 results in the following answer and the explanation:

> *Yes, that's true*
> *Because....*

the only prerequisite for statistics_201 *is* statistics_101
Fred *has successfully completed* statistics_101
Fred *may take* statistics_201

Fred *has taken* statistics_101
not: Fred *completed* statistics_101 *with grade* F
not: Fred *completed* statistics_101 *with grade* INC
Fred *is eligible to enroll in* statistics_101

Fred *completed* statistics_101 *with grade* 3.0
Fred *has taken* statistics_101

The query: *this_student is eligible to enroll in* statistics_201 results in the following answer table:

this_student is eligible to enroll in statistics_201
Allen
Fred

4 Integration of Mini Knowledge-Bases

The previous section contained the description of an application that was modelled using the meta knowledge approach. In this section the meta KB itself is described.

The meta knowledge-base controls the merging of the generic mini-KBs with the organizational mini-KBs, in this case the specific university rules and data.

The facts and rules stored in the meta-KB contain the names of all the generic, organizational, and data mini-KBs available in the educational application class. Furthermore the meta-KB contains the facts and rules for merging and integrating the generic and specific knowledge-bases.

The target knowledge-base can be viewed as composed of various input objects, the objects being the mini-KBs. The input mini-KBs can be grouped by the way they are actually used in the target application.

- Knowledge-bases that are totally independent and thus do not make use of any rules defined in other knowledge modules in the application class.

- Knowledge-bases that need to be accessed together with other knowledge modules to function correctly.

- Knowledge-bases that are necessary for compatibility reasons, e.g. when two knowledge-bases interact, additional rules may be needed in order to integrate these KBs correctly.

The following example meta knowledge-base shows a segment of the facts and rules concerned with constructing the target knowledge base [2].

this_kb contains generic information about	*this_property*
prerequisite	prerequisite_structure
set	named_sets
specialization	specialization
specialization	major
advise	advising
gpa	grade_point_average
help1	combines_K1_K2

this_kb contains specific information about	*this_property*	*for*	*this_uni*
NYU_prerequisite	prerequisite_structure		NYU
NYU_gpa	grade_point_average		NYU

qtu: I would like to build a KB for some_organization

qtu: I would like to build a KB with this_property

if you use	*this_kb*	*you will also need*	*this_additional_kb*
	advise		prerequisite
	advise		set
	specialization		set

I would like to build a KB with some_type_of_property
this_kb contains generic information about that_type_of_property
to build a KB for your organization you need that_kb

to build a KB for this organization with this property you need some_kb
if you use that_kb you will also need this_second_kb
to build a KB for your organization you need that_second_kb

I would like to build a KB with this_property
I would like to build a KB for this_organization
a_kb contains specific information about that_property for that_organization
to build a KB for your organization you need that_kb

The tag "qtu" (query-the-user) signals the dialogue component of SYLLOG to prompt the user for certain values. The following example, based on the meta-knowledge above, shows how the query-the-user facility is used [3].

Example: If we are not sure ahead of time for which organization and what type of KB we would like to build the qtu capability comes in handy.

After we ask SYLLOG the question:

to build a KB for your organization you need this_mini_kb

SYLLOG asks for the name of the university and the properties or functionality of the target knowledge-base. SYLLOG needs to know the name of the organization and the objectives in order to tell us what mini-kbs we actually need for our application.

The following two tables show the selections (table entries) that were made by a user for *functionality* and for *organization*.

I would like to build a knowledge base with	*this_functionality*
	prerequisite_structure
	major
	advising

I would like to build a knowledge base for	*this_organization*
	NYU

Based on these selections SYLLOG returns with an answer table containing the necessary mini-kbs for our target application.

The result is given in the following answer table:

to build a knowledge base for your organization you need this_mini_kb
prerequisite
specialization
set
advising
NYU_prerequisite
NYU_specialization
NYU_set
NYU_data

The module NYU_data contains the actual facts for the NYU application. After the appropriate knowledge modules have been identified, they are loaded into the SYLLOG workspace as one knowledge-base.

5   Directions for Further Work

A rigorous formalization of the proposed, modular approach is needed. This includes the need to capture the semantics of the modules. A knowledge acquisition tool written as a SYLLOG knowledge-base, which is able to help in distinguishing generic from organizational knowledge would be an additional aid.

Other areas for further work concern the applicability of the proposed approach to other research areas in knowledge-base systems.

- Can the modular approach be used for modelling applications in a distributed knowledge-base environment?

- Does the proposed approach allow simple versioning? Can the meta knowledge-base itself be used for version control? These questions are especially interesting in complex systems using large-scale knowledge-bases [2].

A further point for investigation is the applicability of the proposed methodology regarding the size of the information system. Is this modular approach cost-effective only for very large applications or is it also cost-effective to develop small and middle sized applications with this technique?

6   Conclusion

We have presented a method for conceptual modelling in a knowledge-based environment. The approach makes use of the ability of the SYLLOG Expert Database System to execute near-English specifications directly over SQL databases. This capability can help in bridging the gap between a conventional conceptual semantic data model and the intended application. A second aspect of the method is the way the knowledge-base is managed and maintained by making use of a meta-knowledge technique.

The meta-knowledge technique is itself a SYLLOG knowledge-base, and we therefore avoid an additional level of complexity, by capturing the complete technique in one framework. The input knowledge modules that are used to form the target information system are grouped as

- generic knowledge modules, that are usable in the application class being modelled and

- specific, organizational knowledge modules that pertain to a certain organization in the application class.

The approach is demonstrated in an educational environment and the modelling of various degree programs of academic institutions.

By adding capabilities for knowledge acquisition, knowledge management, or versioning we suggest that this is an approach to be considered for the modelling and implementation of large knowledge based information systems.

Acknowledgements

The author wishes to thank Adrian Walker, Peter Sheridan, and Daphne Tzoar of the IBM T. J. Watson Research Center, Hawthorne, N. Y. for their encouraging discussions and comments.

This work was sponsored in part by the Austrian Chamber of Commerce.

References

[1] Apt, K. R., Blair, H., Walker A., Towards a Theory of Declarative Knowledge in *Foundations of Deductive Databases and Logic Programming* J. Minker (Ed.), Morgan Kaufman, 89–148, 1988.

[2] Bobrow D.G., Katz R.H., Context Structures/Versioning: A Survey, in [3].

[3] Brodie M., Mylopoulos J., *On Knowledge Base Management Systems*, Springer-Verlag, 1986.

[4] Borgida A., Survey of Conceptual Modeling of Information Systems, in [3]

[5] Bancilhon F., Ramakrishnan R., An Amateur's Introduction to Recursive Query Processing Strategies, *Proceedings ACM SIGMOD Conference on Management of Data*, 16–52, 1986.

[6] Breitbart Y., Silberschatz A., Multidatabase Update Issues, in *Proceedings SIGMOD 1988*, ACM Press, pp. 135–142, 1988.

[7] Ceri S., Crespi Reghezzi S., Lamperti F., Lavazza, Zicari R., ALGRES: An Advanced Database System for Complex Applications, *IEEE Software*, 1988.

[8] Ceri S., Gottlob G., Tanca L., *Logic Programming and Databases*, Springer-Verlag Berlin Heidelberg, 1990.

[9] Chen P., The Entity-Relationship Model - Toward a Unified View of Data, *ACM Transactions on Database Systems*, Vol. 1, No. 1, pp. 9–36, March, 1976.

---

[3] See [20] for a detailed description of this type of user-interface.

[10] Carasik R., Johnson S., Patterson D., Von Glahn G., Towards a Domain Description Grammar: An Application of Linguistic Semantics, *Software Engineering Notes*, Vol. 15, No. 5, Oct. 1990, pp. 28–43.

[11] Codd E.F., Extending the Database Relational Model to Capture More Meaning, *ACM Transactions on Database Systems*, Vol. 4, No. 4, pp. 397–434, December 1979.

[12] Dart P., Zobel J., Conceptual Schemas Applied to Deductive Databases, *Information Systems*, Vol. 13, No. 3, pp. 273–287, 1988.

[13] Golumbic M.C., Markovich M., Tiomkin M., A Knowledge Representation Language for University Requirements, *Decision Support Systems*, Vol. 7, No. 1, pp. 33–45, 1991.

[14] Hammer M., McLeod D., Database Desrition with SDM: A Semantic Database Model, *ACM Transactions on Database Systems*, Vol. 6, No. 3, September 1981.

[15] Kowalski B., Lenat D., Soloway E., Stonebraker M., Walker A., Knowledge Management, in *Proceedings of the Second International Conference on Expert Database Systems*, Kerschberg L. (ed.), Benjamin Cummings, pp. 63–69, 1988.

[16] Maier D., *Theory of Relational Databases*, Computer Science Press, Rockville, MD., 1983.

[17] Morris K., Ullman J.D., Van Gelder A., Design Overview of the NAIL! System, *Proceedings International Conference on Logic Programming*, London, 1986.

[18] Naqvi S., Tsur S., *A Logical Langauge for Data and Knowledge Bases*, Computer Science Press, New York, 1989.

[19] New York University, *New York University Bulletin, Leonard Stern School of Business*, New York University, New York, 1990.

[20] Sergot M., The Query-The-User Facility for Logic Programming in: p. Degano, E. Sandewall: *Integrated Interactive Computing Systems*, North-Holland, Amsterdam, pp. 27–41, 1983.

[21] Stonebraker M., Hanson E., Hong C., *The Design of the POSTGRES Rules System*, Proc. 1987 IEEE Data Engineering Conference, Los Angeles, CA., Feb. 1987.

[22] Schmidt J., Thanos C., *Foundations of Knowledge Base Management*, Springer-Verlag, 1989.

[23] Teorey T., Yang D., Fry J.P., A Logical Design Methodology for Relational Databases Using the Extended Entity -Relationship Model, *ACM Computing Surveys*, 1986.

[24] Tzoar D., Walker A., *The Syllog Expert System Version 0.8 Notes for Users*, I.B.M. T.J. Watson Research Center Yorktown Heights, N.Y., 1990. Informal notes, available from ADRIAN@IBM.COM.

[25] Ullman J.D. *Principles of Database and Knowledge-Base Systems, Volumes 1 and 2*, Computer Science Press, 1988.

[26] Walker A., McCord M., Sowa J., Wilson W., *Knowledge Systems and Prolog*, Addison Wesely, 1990.

[27] Wiederhold G., Rathman P., Barsalou T., Lee B. S., Partitioning and Composing Knowledge, *Information Systems* Vol. 15, No. 1, pp. 61 –72, 1990.

TARPS: A Prototype Expert Database System For
Training and Administration of Reserves Officer Placement

Magdi N. Kamel   George A. Zolla

Department of Administrative Sciences
Naval Postgraduate School
Monterey, CA 93943

Abstract

The billet assignment duration for Training and Administration of Reserves (TAR) officers is normally two to three years. A placement officer determines where the TAR officer's subsequent assignment will be based on the officer's qualifications and billet requirements. This assignment is vitally important because it significantly affects the officer's career opportunities for promotion and command. This paper describes the design and implementation of a prototype expert database system that will enhance the placement officer's ability to efficiently select the optimum billet for each officer. The prototype integrates a rule based expert system with officer and billet databases to produce a list of billets that match an officer's qualifications and desires.

1. INTRODUCTION

The placement officer's primary responsibility is to select the best possible assignment for officers who are transferring out of their current assignments. The four placement officers who serve at the Training and Administration of Reserves (TAR) branch of the Naval Military Personnel Command (NMPC-4417) are responsible for approximately 2200 officers and 2200 billets. The present method of billet selection is done manually. First the placement officer goes through the list of officers due for new assignments and takes the officers input for where they want to go. Second he methodically goes through a list of billets to see which ones will be open at the right time and have requirements that match the officer qualifications. Complicating the task further is that the officer and billet information are in separate databases. These databases, Officer Assignment and Information System (OAIS) and Officer Billet Description Information System (ODIS) are not linked and have only rudimentary query capabilities. They do, however, contain an enormous quantity of information on both the officers and the billets. The OAIS database contains officer information. This information includes: Name, Rank, Social Security Number (SSN), Designator, Homeport, Billet Title, Planned Rotation Date (PRD), Subspecialty, and Additional Qualification Designator (AQD).

The ODIS database contains billet information. This information includes: Unit Identification Code (UIC), Billet Sequence Code (BSC), Billet Title, Activity, Homeport, Rank, Designator, PRD, Subspecialty and Additional Qualification Designator (AQD). UIC specifies the Naval activity and the BSC identifies the specific billet in that command. Rank and Designator are specific qualifications. PRD determines if a timely match can be made. Homeport is the number one priority for most officers when requesting a billet. AQD defines the type of equipment the officer is qualified in.

There are many rules that experts use to match officers with billets. For example, a billet may be specified for a particular rank but may accept a higher or lower rank. These rules are normally assimilated by experience since they are not specified in a single structured instruction. Training and transition for a new placement officer requires a minimum of two to three months of overlap with an experienced placement officer before he is ready to make placement decisions. Subsequently, the officer in training, accesses the databases for information on officers and billets and applies his expert knowledge to make a selection.

At the Naval Military Personnel Command there are several branches that have similar responsibilities covering all the officers in the U.S. Navy. A study of all these branches show that the billet selection process is nearly the same everywhere but no advanced computer system is being designed to help the placement officers.

There have been attempts to produce computer based systems to enhance the decision process. Rapp [11] used a model based on the classical transportation model of linear programming to design a system for assignment of officers during a massive mobilization to the U.S. Marines. Strouzas [14] designed a database application to integrate billets and officers for the Greek Navy. Alston [1] designed an expert system based on PROLOG to assign enlisted personnel to maintenance billets in aviation squadrons. Although interesting, none of the above approaches seem to be well suited to the placement officer's decision process. Rapp's linear programming model produces only one billet for each officer. It does not allow placement officer interaction to share expertise and additional knowledge that may be important, nor does it consider the wishes of the transferring officer on where or what type of billet he wants. Strouzas' database application automates query selection of billets and personnel but does not build any decision model for officer placement. Alston's model deals only with squadron level enlisted personnel assignments.

Because the process of officer placement uses expert knowledge, an expert system is a good choice for implementation [2]. The placement officer could use the expert system as an assistant to filter the available choices to a reasonable number, then personally make the final decision [6]. Additionally, the process of officer placement meets the general requirements for an expert system as specified by Turban and Waterman [15]:

1. The task requires only cognitive skills.
2. At least one genuine expert, who is willing to cooperate, exists.
3. The experts involved can articulate their methods of problem solving.
4. The task is not too difficult.
5. The task is well understood, and is defined clearly.
6. The solution to the problem has a high payoff. (The task is important).
7. The Expert System can preserve scarce human expertise.
8. The expertise will improve performance and/or quality.
9. The system can be used for training.

Because the databases provide information for the knowledge base, the placement process is ideal for a computer based system that combines an expert system (ES) with the available database management system (DBMS) [3]. This combination is known as an expert database system (EDS) [12]. The coupling of the expert system and database could be either tight or loose. In a tightly coupled architecture, the expert system controls the DBMS with the ES functioning as a front end data entry system for the database or, alternatively, the database management system controls the ES [9]. In a loosely coupled architecture, both subsystems retain their original structure and appearance. A loosely coupled architecture is best suited for the officer placement application. The expert systems component uses it's rule base, placement officer input, and access to the two databases to propose a selection while the databases could be manipulated independently.

This paper presents the design and implementation of a prototype expert database system for placing TAR officers in their upcoming duty assignments. The organization of the paper is as follows. Section 2 explains the domain of expertise needed for the expert system. Section 3 develops a rule base. Section 4 details the design of the expert system and its interface with both databases and the expert user. Finally, Section 5 draws some conclusions and states objectives for future research.

2. DOMAIN OF EXPERTISE

Gathering the expertise needed to build an expert system is often the most difficult part of the development of the system [8]. Since one of the authors of this paper, George Zolla, has served as a TAR placement officer, he is the domain expert. Having an expert readily available greatly enhanced the process of building and testing this system.

Placing an officer into an available billet can be perceived in two different ways. If the priority is placed on assigning the best qualified officer to a billet, then the problem can be viewed as starting from the billet and working backward to find the best qualified officer to fill that billet. However, this method does not consider the officer's wishes or career requirements. If, on the other hand, we view the problem from the officers perspective, the solution would be to find the exact billet that fills his needs and desires. In most branches of NMPC there are two officers working on officer placement, one who works with the officer being reassigned and one who works with the commands that are trying to fill their billets. Each of these officers is an expert, one queries the officer database to find the best qualified officer for the billets and the other queries the billet database to find the best possible billet for the officer.

In NMPC-4417, the placement officer manages both the billets and the officers. He can choose to prioritize either one. This paper will choose the approach that prioritizes the officer's wishes. It will attempt to find the best billet available for his career needs. This approach increases retention and morale but must be realistically balanced against command requirements. No officer can be placed in a requested billet just because he wants it, there must be a need and he must be qualified to fill that need.

The first step used by the placement officer is to retrieve the transferring officer's record from the NMPC database and review his qualifications. The following officer information will be required for this simple prototype: Name, Rank, Social Security Number (SSN), Designator, Present Homeport, Planned Rotation Date (PRD), and Requested Homeport. This data gives a good sketch of the officer's qualifications and what the billet requirements need to be. For example, it would be beneficial to put a pilot in a billet that has a pilot designator code and it would be beneficial to place a commander in a billet that is rank coded for commander. In addition, the officer's requested homeport will show his requested geographic location.

The next step is to retrieve the billet attributes needed for billet identification and officer matching. The minimum billet attributes needed are as follows: Unit Identification Code (UIC), Billet Sequence Code (BSC), Rank, Designator, PRD of the incumbent officer, and Homeport. These attributes are just a small portion of billet requirements but they represent the most important aspects for a first examination.

Armed with officer qualifications and billet requirements, the next step would normally be querying the billet database with the officer qualifications and requested homeport to find what matches could be made. Since the databases are not linked, the placement officer is forced to do a very long and complicated query to produce a list of billets in the requested geographic area that match the officer's qualifications. However, the placement officer still wouldn't have any information on the personnel that are in the selected billets nor the incumbent's PRDs.

In practice, the placement officer keeps a paper

list (slate) of each of his commands and their billets. The slate displays each billet plus its required rank and designator codes. Directly below the billet information is a strip of paper showing the officer assigned with his name, rank, SSN, designator and PRD.

The process of billet selection is not simply based on exact matches for rank, designator and PRD. There are rules that allow the billet to be filled by an officer of a different rank than specified. Normally an officer of the next higher or next lower rank can fill the billet. Billet designators do not exactly match officer designators, they define what officer designators may be assigned to these billets. There are billet designators that allow any officer to be assigned. Some pilot billets may be filled by Naval Flight Officers and some Naval Flight Officer billets may be filled by pilots. There are also billets that require an officer with any warfare specialty.

PRDs do not have to be an exact match either. There may be an overlap of officers and at times there may be a gap. Normally a plus or minus 2 month window is acceptable. Similarly, other rules are used by the expert to determine the allowable Additional Qualification Code (AQD) and Subspecialty Codes.

The following simplistic cases with fictitious names are provided to clarify the assignment process:

CASE 1. Lt Nickerson makes a morning telephone call and schedules a meeting with the placement officer at NMPC-4417 in Washington, D.C. for the afternoon to discuss his next duty assignment. Before he arrives, the placement officer checks the officer database and finds that Lt Nickerson is a 1317 (TAR pilot) stationed at Norfolk, VA flying the F-14 Tomcat. His PRD is June of 1991 and his duty preference shows that he is requesting Fighter Squadron Three Zero One, an F-14 squadron at Naval Air Station Miramar, California as his next duty assignment. The placement officer mentally goes through his knowledge base and deduces that this officer could be assigned to a LT, LTJG or LCDR billet. As a pilot he is eligible to fill a pilot or Naval Flight Officer billet (1317 or 1327). His PRD of 9106 probably could be adjusted by plus or minus 2 months. The placement officer then determines what commands are located at Miramar, California. He manually checks each command's billets (slates) to determine what billets match Lt Nickerson qualifications and which billets have incumbents with PRDs aligned with June of 1991. A review of these billets suggest there are no matches in Fighter Squadron Three Zero One but Fighter Squadron Three Zero Two, also an F-14 squadron at Miramar, California has a billet with a PRD of August, 1991. Lt Nickerson arrives for the meeting and is very happy to accept the billet at Fighter Squadron Three Zero Two because he has received his geographic preference and will continue to fly the F-14.

CASE 2. Lt Wood calls NMPC-4417 to request orders to his next duty assignment. While he is on the telephone, the placement officer retrieves his record from the OAIS. Lt Wood is a 1307 (Non-flying aviation officer) stationed at Naval Air Station Glenview, Illinois with a PRD of September 1991. He has no homeport preference in the database. He states that he would like to be transferred to Atlanta, Georgia. With a designator of 1307 he qualifies for 1300 (non-flying aviation) and 1000 (any officer) billets. A check of the Atlanta area shows that the only Atlanta commands, Naval Air Station Atlanta and Naval Reserve Center Atlanta have no billet openings that match his qualifications. The placement officer conveys this information and Lt Wood states that Boston would be his second choice for duty. A review of the commands at Boston reveals no billets available for him. Dallas, Texas is Lt Wood's third choice. Reviewing the commands located at Dallas reveals a 1300 Lt billet open in July 1991. Lt Wood accepts the billet.

To summarize the current process: First the officer's qualifications and desires are retrieved from OAIS. Next, the placement officer applies a set of rules to the officer's qualifications to determine what billets he is qualified to fill. Finally, the placement officer manually queries all the billets at the requested homeport to find any billets that are expected to be open and match the officer's qualifications. If no matches are found, the search must be expanded to include other geographic locations. This manual process is exceedingly tedious and time consuming. Automating the process would provide the placement officer with more time to communicate with transferring officers and to consider placement options resulting in improved decision making.

3. RULE BASE

To transform the processes that are currently in use to an expert system, a collection of IF THEN rules [7] needs to be developed. These rules will be applied to the information retrieved from the officer database just as the placement officer applies his knowledge of the rules to the information he retrieves from the officer database. There are three main areas that use rules: Officer Rank, Officer Designator and Officer PRD. For this simple prototype, the placement officer will manually enter the officer's request for homeport. Manual insertion of the requested homeport was chosen because in most cases the officers do not make their final decision for homeport preference until the last possible moment making the homeport preference in the database outdated.

The first set of rules will determine billet ranks available to the officer. If the officer's rank is LCDR, he would be qualified to fill a billet for a CDR, LCDR or LT. This is illustrated in the following example:

```
IF      OFFICER_RANK = LCDR
THEN    BILLET_RANK = CDR
        BILLET_RANK = LCDR
        BILLET_RANK = LT
```

The second area that requires a rule base is billet designator. For example, if the officer's designator is 1327, he is qualified for assignment to billets with designators of 1000, 1050, 1300, 1301, 1320, 1321, and 1322. The rule for this example is written as:

```
IF      OFFICER_DESIGNATOR = 1327
THEN    BILLET_DESIGNATOR = 1000
        BILLET_DESIGNATOR = 1050
        BILLET_DESIGNATOR = 1300
        BILLET_DESIGNATOR = 1301
        BILLET_DESIGNATOR = 1302
        BILLET_DESIGNATOR = 1320
        BILLET_DESIGNATOR = 1321
        BILLET_DESIGNATOR = 1322
```

The third area that needs a rule base is officer Planned Rotation Date (PRD). The system should be able to pick billets that have a PRD window close to the officer's PRD, but not necessarily an exact match. An exact match would be too restrictive and too narrowly limit the billet choices. In practice, the placement officer often looks at an entire calendar year when beginning his search for billet matches. Looking at an officer with a PRD of 9107, the placement officer would initially look at all billets with incumbent PRDs of 9101 through 9112. This rule would look like this:

```
IF      OFFICER_PRD >= 9101 AND
        OFFICER_PRD <= 9112
THEN    BILLET_PRD = 91**
```

** = any integer between 1 and 12

The final rule base is for homeport preference. There are several locations that have many homeports in close proximity. For example, an officer requesting Washington, D.C. normally means he would like to be stationed in the Washington, D.C. metropolitan area. This area includes several cities in Virginia and Maryland. The homeport rule for Washington, D.C. is written as:

```
IF      OFFICER_HOMEPORT=WASHDC
THEN    BILLET_HOMEPORT=WASHDC
        BILLET_HOMEPORT=ARLINGTON
        BILLET_HOMEPORT=ADELPHI
        BILLET_HOMEPORT=ALEXANDRIA
        BILLET_HOMEPORT=ANDAFB
        BILLET_HOMEPORT=BETHES
        BILLET_HOMEPORT=SUITLN
```

The billet rank, designator, PRD and homeport generated by the rule base would then be used to query the billet database for matches. Figure 1 illustrates the architecture of the rule base [10].

4. SYSTEM DESIGN

As indicated earlier, the TAR officer Placement System (TARPS) is designed as an expert database system that couples the officer and billet databases to an expert system [4]. The placement officer interacts with the system by providing officer information. The required officer attributes are then retrieved from the officer database, and passed to the rule base where it is processed by an inference engine to produce a list of query criteria. These query criteria plus officer input is passed to the billet database to produce a list of billets that match officer qualifications, billet requirements and the officer request. Figure 2 is a diagram showing the system architecture [5].

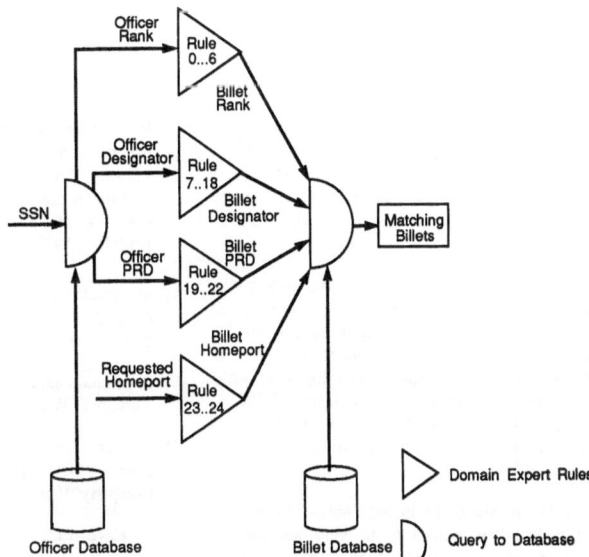

Figure 1. TARPS rule base architecture.

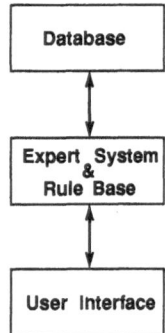

Figure 2. TARPS system architecture.

Since OAIS is composed of information on tens of thousands of officers and ODIS has information on ten of thousands of billets it is expected that performance will be negatively affected. To improve the efficiency of the expert system without affecting it's functionality, the OAIS and ODIS databases were filtered into smaller databases that included only TAR officers and TAR billets. These smaller databases are then downloaded to and accessed by the expert system.

An expert system shell was selected to couple the knowledge base and the databases because it has the ability to interface with the user and has an inference engine built in to process the rule base. The VP expert system shell was selected because of it's additional capability to query databases and ability to be implemented on microcomputers. The rule base for the prototype is expected to be about 150 rules.

5. CONCLUSIONS AND FUTURE RESEARCH

This paper addressed the feasibility of developing an expert system for placing TAR officers in their upcoming duty assignments. It also addressed the capability of capturing the required domain expertise into a rule base. The prototype demonstrates that it is possible to develop an expert system for officer placement and that it is feasible to capture a major portion of the expertise required to do so in a rule base.

The implementation of the rule base was exceptionally beneficial. The rules that govern officer assignments have previously been assimilated primarily by experience. They became so intertwined that decisions were difficult to explain. Development of the rule base produced clarification of many of the building blocks that are used to make decisions. These rules will be extremely beneficial for training new placement officers.

Trimming the databases to include only TAR officers and their billets proved to be very advantageous. It made the performance of the system very acceptable.

Filtering the billets by only four criteria: rank, designator, PRD and homeport quickly trimmed the quantity of acceptable billets down to a reasonable number. These billets consistently proved to be a very good starting point for the placement officer. In addition, the ability to rerun the system with different homeports was an effective way of quickly looking for available billets at several geographic locations.

Use of an expert system shell proved to be extremely efficient. Very little coding was required beyond incorporating the IF THEN rules. Development of an expert system interface with a programming language like PROLOG or LISP appeared to be a much more difficult undertaking.

A comprehensive system is currently being developed that will provide additional officer qualification information in the database and allow more domain expertise information to be incorporated in the knowledge base. This effort includes the addition of the promotion status attribute in the officer database to provide information that is helpful in determining the optimum billet rank. It also includes the addition of the Additional Qualification Designator (AQD). This code specifically defines the ship or aircraft where the officer qualification has been attained. Billets also have AQDs that define the type of equipment that the qualification must be in. This precludes a helicopter pilot from being considered for an F-14 squadron. Finally, the addition of a subspecialty code attribute for officers and billets will enable the new system to match officer educational background with billet educational requirements.

REFERENCES

[1] P. Alston, "A prototype expert system for assigning aviation maintenance personnel to squadron billets," Master's Thesis, Naval Postgraduate School, Monterey, CA, 1987.

[2] J. Boose, *Expertise Transfer for Expert System Design*. New York, NY: Elsevier Science Publishing Co., 1986.

[3] R.J. Brachman and H.J. Levesque, "Tales from the far side of Krypton," in *Expert Database Systems: Proceedings from the first International Conference*, L. Kerschberg, Ed., Menlo Park, CA: The Benjamin/Cummings Publishing Company Inc., 1987.

[4] M. Brodie and J. Mylopoulos, *On Knowledge Base Management Systems*. New York, New York: Springer-Verlag, 1986.

[5] P. Harmon and D. King, *Expert Systems*. New York, NY: Wiley Press, 1985.

[6] A. Hart, *Knowledge Acquisition for Expert Systems*. New York, NY: McGraw-Hill Book Company, 1986.

[7] F. Hayes-Roth, "Rule based systems," *Communications of the ACM*, vol. 28, No. 9, pp. 921-941, September 1985.

[8] F. Hayes-Roth, D. Waterman, and D. Lenat, *Building Expert Systems*. Reading, MA: Addison-Wesley Publishing Company, Inc., 1983.

[9] M. Missikoff and G. Wiederhold, "Towards a unified approach for expert and database systems," in *Expert Database Systems: Proceedings from the first International Workshop*, L. Kerschberg, Ed., Menlo Park, CA: The Benjamin/Cummings Publishing Company Inc., 1986.

[10] R.J. Mockler, *Knowledge-based Systems for Management Decisions*. Englewood Cliffs, NJ: Prentice-Hall, 1989.

[11] S.H. Rapp, "Design and implementation of a network optimizer for officer assignment during mobilization," Master's Thesis, Naval Postgraduate School, Monterey, CA, 1987.

[12] J.M. Smith, "Expert database systems: A database perspective," in *Expert Database Systems: Proceedings from the first International Workshop*, L. Kerschberg, Ed., Menlo Park, CA: The Benjamin/Cummings Publishing Company Inc., 1986.

[13] R. Sprague Jr. and E. Carlson, *Building Effective Decision Support Systems*. Englewood Cliffs, NJ: Prentice- Hall Inc., 1982.

[14] I. G. Strouzas, "Implementation of a personnel database system performing the annual reassignment of the officers of a branch directorate of the Hellenic Army General Staff," Master's Thesis, Naval Postgraduate School, Monterey, CA, 1986.

[15] E. Turban, *Decision Support and Expert Systems*. New York, NY: Macmillan Publishing Company, 1990.

Constructing Minimal Knowledge Bases by Machine Learning

O. Najmann   K. Eckstein

Universität Duisburg, FB 11, Praktische Informatik
Postfach 10 15 03, 4100 Duisburg 1, Germany

Abstract. Like databases, knowledge bases should not contain redundant information. Therefore, if knowledge is acquired, the size of the corresponding knowledge base should be kept to a minimum without loss of information. We analyze the problem of constructing minimal, i.e., non-redundant, knowledge bases using machine learning methods. Here, knowledge is represented as a decision tree. There exist a number of heuristics that control the process of learning such trees from examples. We introduce four new heuristics and analyze these and two existing ones regarding the size of the trees they produce. For this purpose, we made computer-simulated experiments to obtain average-case results. The results show that there are remarkable differences in the average performance ratio: the values range from 1.01 to 1.41; "random learning" produces overly large decision trees (65%–125% larger than necessary).

1. Introduction

During the past decades, database design theory was motivated by an economical principle—keeping the required amount of storage to a minimum. Following this principle guarantees that no redundancy in the database can occur [24]. Similarly, in an *expert system* [3, 12] it is desirable to minimize the amount of coded knowledge without loss of information. Although minimum size does not necessarily guarantee maximum computation speed for knowledge processing, this principle obviously guarantees that (1) the knowledge is more understandable, (2) it is easier to maintain. "Size" is closely related to "notational convenience," an important criterion for assessing a knowledge representation [12].

For example, if the size of a *rule-based knowledge base* is measured by the sum of the "lengths" of all rules, then among all semantically equal knowledge bases the smallest one is preferable, i.e., that one for which the sum of the rule lengths is minimal. The choice of the size function obviously depends on the *representation language* [12], and several size functions are possible for one and the same representation language. For example, another size function for a rule base is the *maximum* rule length.

Although it is perhaps possible to reduce the size of a *given* knowledge base, it is more practical to control the knowledge base's size during the *knowledge acquisition phase* [3, 8, 12].

Since sophisticated expert systems usually contain very large knowledge bases, the acquisition process is of great importance, and the problem of acquiring knowledge quickly and efficiently has led to the term "knowledge acquisition bottleneck" [5, 6].

Two approaches to overcome this "bottleneck" problem have been suggested in the past:

(1) If knowledge is acquired by humans (knowledge engineers), then intelligent systems should support these people in order to efficiently develop a knowledge base of smallest possible size. (2) Alternatively, if *machine learning methods* [4] are used for automatically acquiring (parts) of a knowledge base, then the control of the knowledge base's size is a part of these methods.

In what follows, we will concentrate on the problem of constructing knowledge bases of minimum size using machine learning methods, in particular decision tree induction algorithms [20, 21]. These methods belong to a wider class of learning methods called *concept learning methods* [4] where a (hypothetical) concept is inferred from a set of examples. We analyze these methods regarding the size of "knowledge" they produce and compare them on the basis of computer-simulated experiments. To be concrete, we analyze the ratio

$$\frac{\text{Size of heuristically computed "knowledge"}}{\text{Size of perfectly small "knowledge"}}$$

in different settings.

This optimality analysis is new; purely comparative analyses have been made by Mingers [16], Norton [17], Pagallo [18], and Pagallo & Haussler [19], limited to few heuristics and restrictive settings. For an overview of concept learning for knowledge acquisition see [25]. The principle of constructing *simple* hypotheses is known as *Occam's Razor* [1].

2. Knowledge bases and decision trees

A knowledge base is a set of expressions using a certain representation language (formalism); popular representation languages are, for instance, (see [12]): (1) production rules, (2) propositional or predicate logic, (3) associative nets and frame systems, (4) object oriented representation, (5) variable-valued logic (VL) [14], and (6) decision trees. Each of these representation languages has its own advantages and disadvantages and, under certain restrictions, transformation from one language L to a another language L' is possible.

Henceforth, we will assume that knowledge is represented as a decision tree which is a labeled directed tree. Each inner node is labeled by an *attribute name*, each leaf is labeled by a class name, and each edge is labeled by a *value* taken from the domain of that attribute which is the label of the start node of that edge. Such a decision tree is useful for representing knowledge about class membership of objects described by a set of attribute values. For better understanding, each leaf is additionally labeled by a set of numbers denoting the objects which are classified at this leaf.

Example: Let us assume that dogs are described on the basis of the attributes SIZE with domain {big, small}, COLOR with domain {black, brown, red}, and SPOTS with domain {yes, no}. A dog belongs either to the class "dangerous" (+) or "not dangerous" (−). A fictitious object collection is:

Object	SIZE	COLOR	SPOTS	Class
1	big	red	yes	+
2	small	red	yes	−
3	small	black	yes	+
4	big	black	no	+
5	big	brown	yes	−
6	small	brown	no	−

A possible decision tree which correctly classifies each of these objects is given below.

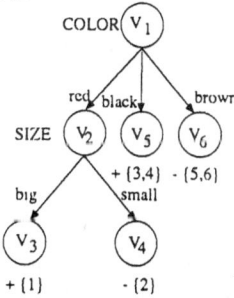

Figure 1: A decision tree for the dogs examples

"Correct classification" means that there is a unique path from the root to a leaf for each object with the property that the labels of the edges along that path are a subset of the object's attribute values and that the label of the leaf is the class to which the object belongs. A decision tree is a *hypothesis* about the object universe since it may not necessarily correctly classify unseen objects.

Initial work on decision tree induction was done by Hunt *et al.* [10] which formed the basis for research done by Quinlan [20, 21] who developed and successfully applied the ID3 algorithm. Breiman *et al.* [2] used decision tree induction methods for data analysis.

Three important criteria for the construction of decision trees are [21, 16]:

1. Accuracy
2. Size
3. Understandability

Size and understandability are often reciprocally related to each other. The construction of a decision tree with respect to to one of these criteria is usually done by a heuristic algorithm which constructs the decision tree in a recursive top-down manner [21]. This is achieved by splitting the object collection using a heuristically selected attribute into subsets according to the values of the selected attribute and applying this method recursively on these subsets until all objects in such a subset be long to one class.

Computing the "best" decision tree can, in practice, not be done in reasonable time for large object collections for that the number of possible trees explodes. Accordingly, heuristic algorithms are used to construct near-optimal decision trees.

Typical size measures [13] are:

1. the number of leaves of a tree, μ_N,
2. the height of a tree, μ_H, and
3. the weighted external path length of a tree, μ_W.

In the latter, the "weight" of a leaf is the number of objects that are classified by the path from the root to that leaf.

Example: The values of the size functions for the tree in Fig. 1 are $\mu_N = 4$, $\mu_H = 2$, and $\mu_W = 8$.

Definition: Problem "Minimum Decision Tree" (MDT) is the problem to construct a decision tree for a given object collection M such that it is minimal with respect to μ_N (μ_H, μ_W).

Remarks: 1. It must be guaranteed that M does not contain *incompatible* objects, i.e., objects with equal attribute values but different class membership. 2. We rule out *trivial* object collections, i.e., object collections which contain objects from only one class. 3. Other possible size functions, which have not been analyzed here, are "external path length" and "number of edges."

A decision tree can easily be transformed to a set of production rules or VL-rules [14] of the form "$A_1 = a_1$ and $A_2 = a_2$ and ... and $A_k = a_k \rightarrow c$" where the A_i's are attribute names, the a_i's are values from A_i, and where c is a class name. The set is constructed by computing one rule for each path from the root to a leaf [22].

There is a close relation between the size of a decision tree and the size of a rule set, namely: 1. The number of rules is μ_N. 2. The length of the longest rule measured by the number of tests is μ_H. 3. The average number of comparisons needed to classify an object is

$$\frac{1}{|M|}\mu_W,$$

where $|M|$ is the size of the object collection M; this result is valid under the assumption that the probability distribution is induced by the weights of the leaves [13].

The construction of a minimal decision tree is a combinatorial optimization problem. A related problem, namely the construction of a binary decision tree with all weights having a value of 1 and minimum (weighted) external path length was shown to be NP-complete [11]. Whether problem MDT is NP-complete is not known.

We will now review two important heuristics, introduce some new ones, and analyze all of them with respect to their performance ratio [7]. It is easy to see that all heuristics mentioned in the next section have polynomial time complexity.

3. Decision tree induction heuristics and optimal tree construction

Heuristics

Each of the following heuristics h determines the split attribute at each node on the basis of the matrix

$$\mathbf{X} = \begin{pmatrix} x_{11} & \cdots & x_{1r} \\ \vdots & \ddots & \vdots \\ x_{k1} & \cdots & x_{kr} \end{pmatrix}$$

which can be derived from an object collection M as follows: Let k be the number of classes to which objects in M belong, let r be the number of attribute values objects in M can take, then x_{ij} is the number of objects with attribute value j that fall into class i. Note that r depends on the attribute. The split attribute is that attribute which minimizes (or maximizes) the value of h.

Heuristic *ID3*: Quinlan's [20, 21] entropy heuristic, as used in ID3, chooses that attribute which maximizes its information content. With a little algebra, the original heuristic can be simplified to

$$h = \sum_{j=1}^{r} \left(\frac{X_j}{X} \left(-\sum_{i=1}^{k} g\left(\frac{x_{ij}}{X_j} \right) \right) \right) \to \min$$

where $X_j = \sum_{i=1}^{k} x_{ij}$, $X = \sum_{j=1}^{r} X_j$, and

$$g(u) = \begin{cases} u \log u, & \text{if } u > 0; \\ 0, & \text{otherwise.} \end{cases}$$

Heuristic *Chi2*: Mingers' [16] χ^2 heuristic is based on a statistical test and is defined as

$$h = \chi^2 = \sum_{i=1}^{k} \sum_{j=1}^{r} \frac{(x_{ij} - E_{ij})^2}{E_{ij}} \to \max$$

where $E_{ij} = \frac{X_j C_i}{X}$, and $C_i = \sum_{j=1}^{r} x_{ij}$.

We now introduce the following heuristics.

Heuristic *Var*: It chooses that attribute which maximizes the sum of the variances among the class frequencies:

$$h = \sum_{j=1}^{r} \text{var}(x_{1j}, \ldots, x_{kj}) \to \max.$$

Heuristic *MH*: The following heuristic chooses that attribute which minimizes the maximally possible height of any subtree assuming that there were infinitely many attributes remaining:

$$h = \max_{j \in \{1,\ldots r\}} \{\sigma(V_j)\} \to \min$$

with $V_j =$ the multiset of all numbers $x_{ij} > 0$, and

$$\sigma(V) = \begin{cases} \sum_{v \in V} v, & \text{if } |V| > 1; \\ 1, & \text{otherwise.} \end{cases}$$

Heuristic *MHR*: Like *MH* but with a restriction on the number of attributes. The only difference is to replace $\sigma(V)$ in the formula for h of *MH* with $\sigma'(V) = \min\{n, \sigma(V)\}$, where n is the number of attributes.

Heuristic *MEPL*: The following heuristic is similar to *MH* but the goal is to minimize the maximally possible external path length of the current (sub-)tree.

$$h = \sum_{j=1}^{r} \sigma''(V_j) \to \min$$

with

$$\sigma''(V) = \begin{cases} \frac{1}{2} \left(3 \sum_{v \in V} v + \left(\sum_{v \in V} v \right)^2 \right) - 1, & \text{if } |V| > 1; \\ 1, & \text{otherwise.} \end{cases}$$

Heuristic *Random*: For the purpose of comparing the heuristically constructed tree with a randomly constructed tree, a simple "random learning" heuristic was developed which chooses each attribute with equal probability.

Optimal tree construction

We now briefly describe an algorithm that solves problem MDT for a given object collection M (with n attributes) and a size function μ.

As a first attempt, one could compute all possible decision trees and then choose the smallest one. However, as the following considerations will show, only a subset need to be examined.

Our consideration starts with the observation that each of the n attributes can be chosen as the root node. In our example, this leads to three initial decision trees.

If a node v_i at some level l is the root of some subtree S, then the minimal decision tree for this "tree state" has the property that it is minimal if S is minimal (*). This can be seen from Figure 2. If all subtrees in a tree T fulfill the property (*), then T is minimal.

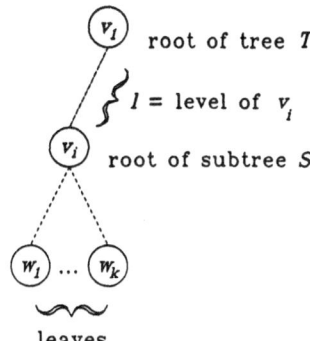

Figure 2: Pruned decision tree

Let $\mu(T_{|S})$ denote the size of the tree that is obtained by pruning all other subtrees away except that one that leads to S, then

(1) $\mu_N(T_{|S}) = k$

$= \mu_N(S)$, this fulfills $(*)$

(2) $\mu_H(T_{|S}) = \max\{\mathrm{level}(w_1)+l,\ldots,\mathrm{level}(w_k)+l\}$

$= l + \max\{\mathrm{level}(w_1),\ldots,\mathrm{level}(w_k)\}$

$= l + \mu_H(S)$

Since l is constant, the property $(*)$ is fulfilled.

(3) $\mu_W(T_{|S}) = \sum_{i=1}^{k} \mathrm{weight}(w_i)\,[\mathrm{level}(w_i)+l]$

$= \mu_W(S) + l\sum_{i=1}^{k}\mathrm{weight}(w_i)$

Since l and $\sum_{i=1}^{k}\mathrm{weight}(w_i)$ are constant, $(*)$ is fullfilled.

Remark: If the size function "external path length" were chosen, property $(*)$ would not hold but a similar condition could be formulated.

This leads to the following recursive algorithm: At each inner node select each of the remaining attributes and compute the locally best subtree $T_{|S}$ for the given "tree state". If we consider the attribute A_i, we must construct edges for all possible attribute values of A_i and compute the locally best subtrees for the end nodes of these edges. The recursion terminates if the remaining objects belong to one class.

Example: Let us construct a decision tree for the dogs examples with minimum number of leaves. We consider the attribute SIZE as a split attribute for the root node and firstly select the value 'big' (because of object 1). At this situation we must classify the objects 1, 4, and 5 with the attributes COLOR and SPOTS (Fig. 3). The tree with attribute COLOR at node v_2 has minimum number of leaves (3) and is therefore the minimal subtree at this position. After the complete generation, we have constructed the three decision trees T_1, T_2, and T_3 (Fig. 4) with different

roots. The number of leaves of these trees are: $\mu_N(T_1) = 6$, $\mu_N(T_2) = 4$, and $\mu_N(T_3) = 6$. Therefore, the tree T_2 is a tree with minimum number of leaves. A minimal tree for other size functions (μ_H, μ_W) can be constructed similarly.

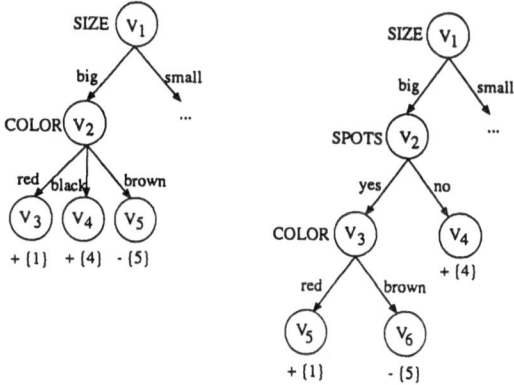

Figure 3: Alternative subtrees for root node v_2

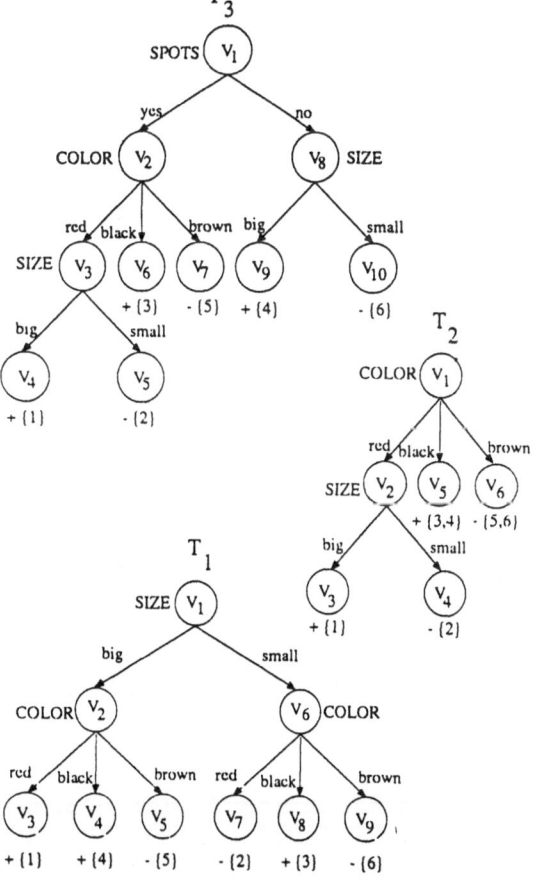

Figure 4: Three μ_N-minimal trees for *fixed* root node

4. Analysis Methodology

Since theoretical average-case analysis of the heuristics seems to be extremely difficult (to us), we have developed a methodology for obtaining the *experimental mean of the performance ratio*

$$R = \frac{\mu(T_H)}{\mu(T^*)},$$

where T_H is the heuristically constructed tree, and T^* is the optimal tree, by computer simulation.

1. Each object collection was created by randomization assuming equal probability of each attribute value and each class name.

2. The simulation was repeated until the 95% confidence interval of the mean of R had a relative size of at most ±0.01 (for the random heuristic: 0.05) (see [23] for details on sampling theory).

5. Results

The analysis was made for a random sample of ten objects, eight attributes, and two classes; two populations were considered:

Case 1: Eight binary attributes. (Size of object universe $= 2^8 = 256$.)

Case 2: Five binary attributes and three five-valued attributes. (Size of object universe $= 2^5 5^3 = 4000$.)

Although object collections of this type seem to be very small, the following results are valuable since they give an indication regarding the choice of the best heuristic in dependence of the chosen size function and population.

The results for each size function are shown in the following plots of the minimum, average, and maximum performance ratio R (Fig. 5). A value of 1.0 indicates perfect performance. In practice, values ≤ 1.10 are good, and values ≤ 1.50 are sometimes acceptable.

The ranges of the average performance ratio are summarized in the following table:

Heuristic	Range	Best Heuristic for
ID3	1.01 – 1.37	Case 1: μ_N; Case 2: μ_W
Chi2	1.02 – 1.35	Case 1: μ_N
Var	1.13 – 1.41	Case 2: μ_N
MH	1.02 – 1.41	Case 1: μ_H; Case 2: μ_H
MHR	1.02 – 1.41	Case 1: μ_H; Case 2: μ_H
MEPL	1.01 – 1.34	Case 1: μ_W; Case 2: μ_W
Random	1.66 – 2.25	*never*

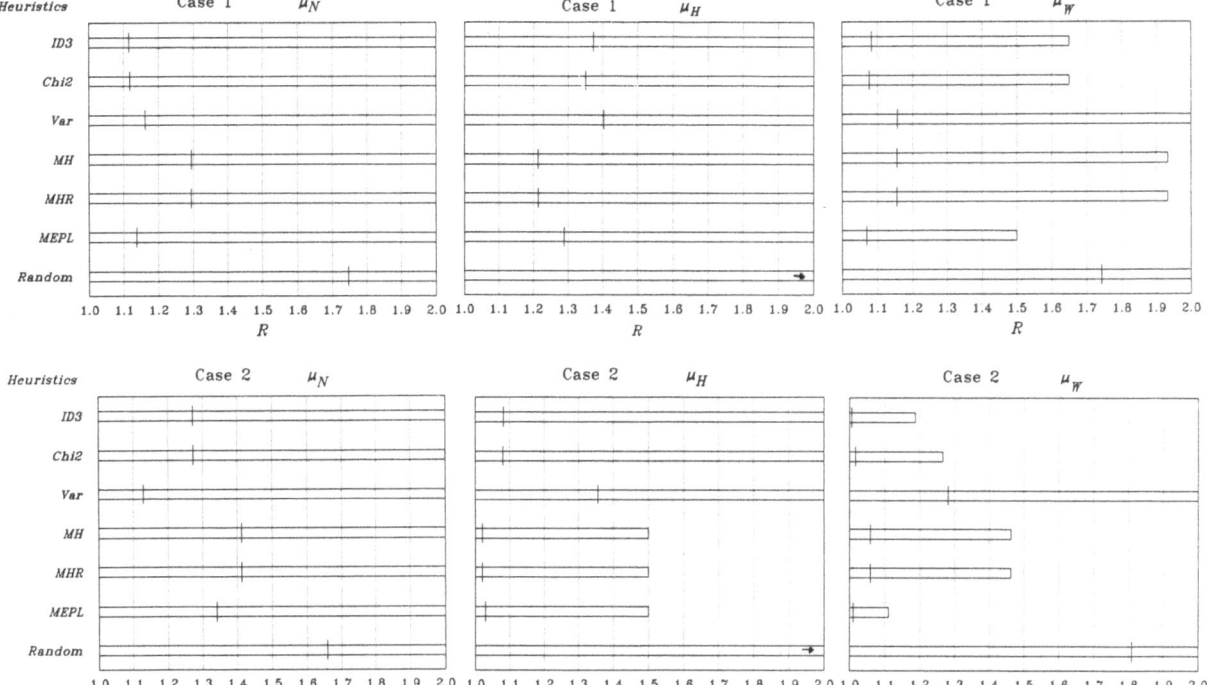

Figure 5: Each horizontal bar indicates minimum/maximum performance ratio. The vertical bar indicates the average value (if ≤ 2.0).

6. Summary

We have analyzed decision tree induction heuristics regarding the size of "knowledge" they produce. The analyses were made using randomly generated examples from two different populations. The result have shown that the choice of the best heuristic depends on the characteristics of the object collection and on the chosen size function. The values of the average performance ratio for *true*, i.e., nonrandom, heuristics range between 1.01 and 1.41. Random learning is useless: The size of the produced "knowledge" is 65%–125% greater than necessary.

We are currently analyzing the heuristics in many more settings and for other size functions.

Acknowledgements

We are grateful to Prof. Dr. Kleine Büning for his support of this research project and helpful discussions.

References

[1] Blumer A., Ehrenfeucht, A., Haussler, D., Warmuth, M. K. [1987], "Occam's razor," *Information Processing Letters*, 24, pp. 377–380

[2] Breiman, L., Friedman, J. H., Olshen, R. A., Stone, C. J. [1984], *Classification and Regression Trees*, Belmont: Wadsworth International Group

[3] Buchanan, B. G., Shortliffe, E. H. (Eds.) [1985], *Rule-Based Expert Systems*, Reading: Addison Wesley

[4] Carbonell, J. G., Michalski, R. S., Mitchell, T. M. [1983], "An overview of machine learning," *Machine Learning, An Artificial Intelligence Approach, Vol. I*, Carbonell, J. G., Michalski, R. S., Mitchell, T. M. (Eds.), Palo Alto: Tioga

[5] Feigenbaum, E. A. [1977], "The art of artificial intelligence: themes and case studies of knowledge engineering," *Proceedings of the 5th International Joint Conference on Artificial Intelligence, Cambridge*, pp. 1014–1029, Palo Alto: Morgan Kaufmann

[6] Feigenbaum, E. A. [1981], "Expert systems in the 1980s.," *State of the art report on machine intelligence*, Bond, A. (Ed.), Maidenhead: Pergamon-Infotech

[7] Garey, M. R., Johnson, D. S. [1979], *Computers and Intractability*, New York: Freeman

[8] Hart, A. [1986], *Knowledge Acquisition for Expert Systems*, London: Kogan Page

[9] Hayes-Roth, F., Waterman, D. A., Lenat D. (Eds.) [1983], *Building Expert Systems*, London: Addison Wesley

[10] Hunt, E. B., Marin, J., Stone, P. J. [1966], *Experiments in Induction*, New York: Academic Press

[11] Hyafil, L., Rivest R. L. [1976], "Constructing optimal binary decision trees is NP-complete," *Information Processing Letters*, Vol. 5, No. 1, pp. 15–17

[12] Jackson, P. [1990], *Introduction to Expert Systems*, Wokingham: Addison Wesley

[13] Knuth, D. E. [1973], *The Art of Computer Programming. Vol. 1: Fundamental Algorithms*, Reading: Addison Wesley

[14] Michalski, R. S. [1975], "Variable-valued logic and its applications to pattern recognition and machine learning," *Computer Science and Multiple-Valued Logic Theory and Applications*, Rine, D. C. (Ed.), Amsterdam: North-Holland

[15] Michalski, R. S. [1987], "Learning strategies and automated knowledge acquisition: an overview," *Computational Models of Learning*, Bolc, L. (Ed.), Berlin: Springer-Verlag

[16] Mingers, J. [1989], "An empirical comparison of selection measures for decision-tree induction," *Machine Learning*, 3, pp. 319-342

[17] Norton, S. W. [1989], "Generating better decision trees," *Proceedings of the 11th International Joint Conference on Artificial Intelligence, Detroit*, pp. 800–805, Palo Alto: Morgan Kaufmann

[18] Pagallo, G. [1989], "Learning DNF by decision trees," *Proceedings of the 11th International Joint Conference on Artificial Intelligence, Detroit*, pp. 639–644, Palo Alto: Morgan Kaufmann

[19] Pagallo, G., Haussler D. [1990], "Boolean feature discovery in empirical learning," *Machine Learning*, 5, pp. 71–99

[20] Quinlan, J. R. [1983], "Learning efficient classification procedures and their application to chess end game," *Machine Learning: An Artificial Intelligence Approach, Vol. I*, Carbonell, J. G., Michalski, R. S., Mitchell, T. M. (Eds.), Palo Alto: Tioga

[21] Quinlan, J. R. [1986], "Induction of decision trees," *Machine Learning*, 1, pp. 81–106

[22] Quinlan, J. R. [1987], "Generating production rules from decision trees," *Proceedings of the 10th International Joint Conference on Artificial Intelligence, Milan*, pp. 304–307, Palo Alto: Morgan Kaufmann

[23] Snedecor, G. W., Cochran, W. G. [1967], *Statistical Methods*, Ames: The Iowa State University Press

[24] Ullman, J. D. [1988], *Principles of Database and Knowledge-base Systems, Vol. I*, Computer Science Press

[25] Witten, I. A., MacDonald, B. A. [1990], "Using concept learning for knowledge acquisition," *Knowledge-Based Systems, Vol. 3: Machine Learning and Uncertain Reasoning*, Gaines, B., Boose, J. (Eds.), London: Academic Press

Efficient Access To Large Prolog Knowledge Bases*

Christos Garidis[†]
Institute for Parallel and Distributed
High Performance Systems
Stuttgart University
Azenbergstr. 12
7000 Stuttgart 1
Germany

Stefan Böttcher[‡]
IBM Germany Scientific Center
Institute for Knowledge Based Systems
Schloßstr. 70
7000 Stuttgart 1
Germany

Abstract

One requirement for language systems for knowledge based applications is to handle large knowledge bases efficiently. Large knowledge bases written in Prolog have a large load time from secondary storage. We describe how a Prolog system can be supported with a clustering concept for minimizing both the load time and the loaded code of large Prolog knowledge bases, which additionally enables an efficient cluster buffer managment, if knowledge base size exceeds the available main memory. Clusters are knowledge base partitions of equal size which are generated at compile time and contain semantically related clauses. The paper focusses on a comparative performance evaluation of a Prolog system supported with various cluster replacement strategies and compares "intelligent" cluster replacement strategies with conventional replacement strategies known from operating systems. The result of the performance evaluation is that the load time for Prolog knowledge bases can be reduced by using "intelligent" instead of conventional cluster replacement strategies.

1. Introduction

Prolog systems commonly store their knowledge bases via a file management system in secondary storage and load them into the main memory before execution. Developing large knowledge bases that exceed available main memories, implies the need to support Prolog systems by specific techniques for an efficient run time management of large knowledge bases.

One of the serious problems by retrieving code of Prolog knowledge bases from secondary storage is the large load time, which is quite prohibitive for a run time retrieval of large knowlegde bases. The load time of knowledge bases comprises the transfer time and the translation time; the latter incures 90% of the total load time [Boc90]. The following diagrams show an exponential load time by an increasing knowledge base size; the load times are measured by interpreting (consult) and compiling (compile) source code by QUINTUS Prolog 2.4 under AIX on a IBM RT computer:

---

*The work reported here has been carried out at IBM Stuttgart as part of the EUREKA project PROTOS (EU56): Prolog Tools for building Expert Systems. Project partners are BIM, IBM Germany, Hoechst AG, Sandoz AG, University of Dortmund and University of Oldenburg. The work of the first author was funded by IBM Germany.

[†]Current address: Berata GmbH, P.O.Box 2209, D-7030 Böblingen, Germany.

[‡]Current address: Daimler Benz, Forschung und Technik Ulm, FA/IW, Eberhard-Finckh-Straße 11, D-7900 Ulm, Germany.

w Knowledge base size
t Load time

$$t(w) = t_0 * 3^{\left(\frac{w}{w_0}\right)}$$

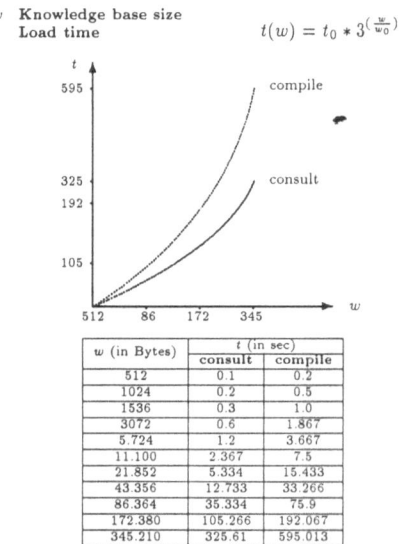

w (in Bytes)	t (in sec)	
	consult	compile
512	0.1	0.2
1024	0.2	0.5
1536	0.3	1.0
3072	0.6	1.867
5.724	1.2	3.667
11.100	2.367	7.5
21.852	5.334	15.433
43.356	12.733	33.266
86.364	35.334	75.9
172.380	105.266	192.067
345.210	325.61	595.013

The presented clustering concept was developed in order to achieve the following aims:

1. Both the real load time and the loaded code of large Prolog knowledge bases from secondary storage can be minimized, since code clusters are small load granules and clustering allows to load knowlege bases incrementally on demand.

   Code clusters have to be of an optimal physical size, which can be tested experimentally (c.f. section 4). Additionally, shallow derivations, which are a common phenomenon, need small knowledge partitions to be loaded, something that advocates for clusters.

2. Clustering facilitates intelligent buffer management. This is advantageous if the available main memory is small.

   Intelligent cluster replacement policies can reduce the I/O rate of the underlying operating system and the cluster access rate of the Prolog system.

3. Clustering facilitates code prefetching.

   Prefetching of code clusters which are needed in the near future of program execution [Gar90] can eliminate the synchronous waiting of the Prolog system for responses of the data storage system.

We specify and investigate the clustering concept for compiling Prolog systems for the following reasons:

1. Elimination of the translation time during loading by storing of compiled code in secondary storage.

2. Realization of a virtual cluster memory. Compiling Prolog systems that don't allow knowledge base modification at run time permit a relative addressing of the code contained in a cluster w.r.t to cluster address.

3. Easy integration of the clustering concept in the compile process.

At run-time, the code of the Prolog programs is loaded into main memory by a one-cluster-at-a-time access and is executed by a Warren Abstract Machine (WAM) [War83]. In order to reduce the number of load operations and the amount of code to be loaded, the goal of clustering is to combine those pieces of code on a code cluster which are executed in sequence.

Clustering concerns the procedure structure of Prolog programs, i.e. the code for all rules of a procedure is stored on the same cluster (as long as the procedure code size is less than the cluster size). Additionally, the implemented clustering algorithm supports a depth-first left-to-right proof strategy by preferably putting the left-most successor procedure on the same cluster as a given procedure. [Gar90] and [Zin89] describe the implemented clustering algorithm in detail and compared it with other clustering algorithms.

All code clusters have the same physical size in order to reduce the cluster buffer management overhead and in order to have a low and constant I/O time for the access of clusters in secondary storage.

In order to meet the goals specified above, the Prolog system has to provide system components for clustering and for cluster management. The architecture of a such Prolog system is sketched in Figure 1.

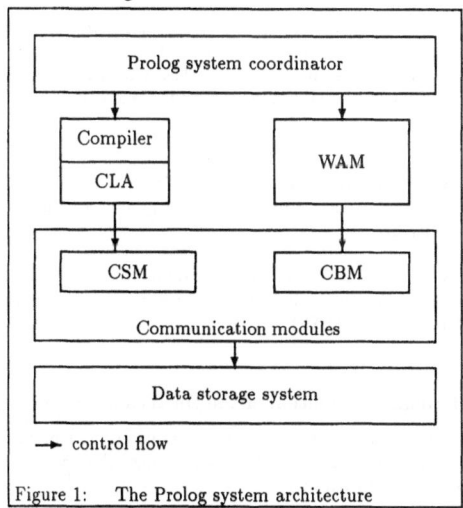

Figure 1: The Prolog system architecture

The Prolog system consists of the following subsystems: a compiler to compile arbitrary Prolog programs into code clusters containing Warren Abstract Machine code, a Warren Abstract Machine (WAM) and an external data storage system (DSS), e.g. a file system, database system, etc. to store und retrieve code clusters. In order to keep the WAM and compiler independent of specific DSS details, a cluster storage module (CSM) and a cluster buffer manager (CBM) have been designed as interfaces between the Prolog system and the data storage system. WAM and compiler are implemented as two independent processes and interact with the DSS only via the interface modules CSM and CBM. A Prolog system coordinator coordinates all system activities and performs dialog with the user.

The clustering algorithms (CLA) in the back-end of the compiler divides the Prolog program into code clusters of equal size. Whenever the WAM tries to access code which is not contained in a main memory resident cluster, we have a so called *cluster fault*. In this case, the CBM retrieves the requested cluster from the secondary storage and supersedes another cluster if the cluster buffer is full.

2. Cluster buffer management

The aim of cluster buffer management is to reduce the number of times a code cluster has to be loaded. This can be reached by applying specific cluster replacement algorithms. Their specification depends on the notion of the dynamic state of clusters. To define this notion an analysis of the cluster reference behaviour of a Prolog system is needed.

2.1. Cluster reference behaviour of a Prolog system

The cluster reference behaviour of a Prolog system is mainly influenced by the proof strategy used, which determines the control flow on the program procedures and subsequentlly on their containing clusters. In order to describe this behaviour formally, some properties of the internal state and the abstract jump instructions of the WAM should be considered.

Part of the internal state of the WAM is its *local stack* which contains two types of objects: choice points and environments.

A *choice point* is pushed on to the local stack when the first clause of a set of alternative clauses is entered and points to the next clause. On failure, backtracking is accomplished by simply finding the last choice point in the local stack and jumping to the clause it points to.

An *environment* is pushed onto the local stack every time a clause is entered if the clause has more than one subgoal with "permanent variables". It points to the subgoal, which has to be executed.

If the procedure p_s contains the jump instructions *call* p_t or *execute* p_t , control is always transferred to the procedure p_t by executing one of these instructions. The jump instruction *proceed* ends the code of an alternative in a procedure p_s und causes a control transfer to the calling procedure p_t, if the alternative succeeds. By *fail* inside of an alternative of p_s control is transfered to that procedure p_t which has pushed the last choice point on the local stack. For more details about the control structures and the jump instructions of the WAM see [War83].

Let C_i, C_j $(i \neq j)$ be clusters. A cluster reference is always issued, if a control transfer from the procedure $p_s \in C_i$ to the procedure $p_t \in C_j$ occurs.

Depending on the state of the WAM, that can be characterized either by forward proceeding or backtracking, the following kinds of cluster references are possible:

forward cluster reference: It can only be issued if a *call* p_s or *execute* p_t instruction is executed.

backward cluster reference: It can only be issued during backtracking by success, if the *proceed* instruction is executed, or during backtracking by *fail* by executing implicit jumps.

Forward cluster referencing is non-deterministic. That means, it is not decidable whether control being in a cluster C_i reaches its successor cluster C_j. This non-deterministic cluster reference behaviour is caused by the undecidability of the horn logic. In contrast to this, backward cluster referencing is deterministic. This is ensured by the stored choice point and environment information on the local stack, which during backtracking determines exactly the next procedure and subsequently the next cluster reached by the control. To formalize the possibility of reaching clusters by the control during backtracking, the cluster state is introduced. Its specification relies on the number of the choice points and environments generated during the code execution of the cluster. There are three possible cluster states:

- **passive clusters:** They possess no choice points and no environments at the time control left them. Such clusters can be considered as cluster garbage, that is not needed any more.

- **semi-active clusters:** They possess only environments at the time being leaved by the control. Such clusters can be reached by the control only during backtracking by success.

- **active clusters:** They possess choice points and possibly environments. Such clusters are reached by the control in both of the backtracking modes.

In order to manage the cluster state on the communication modules level precisely, WAM always passes appropriate information to the cluster buffer manager when choice points / environments are generated or discarded on the local stack. This information is managed by the cluster buffer manager for each cluster explicitly.

Information about the kind of a cluster reference is really needed to handle correctly the conversion from the semi-active to passive state. If a cluster, that precedes a number of semi-active clusters on the local stack, becomes passive by fail, the control will reach the last choice point on the local stack and subsequently the last active cluster, which has generated this choice point. All intermediate semi-active clusters are skipped and have to be changed to passive. Because backtracking by fail can cause skipping of semi-active clusters, backward cluster references by fail give the cluster buffer manager this information in order to handle this situation correctly.

2.2. Cluster replacement algorithms

In the operating and database system area considerable work on page replacement algorithms has been done in order to achieve an efficient buffer management for these systems. Well known page replacement algorithms like FIFO, LFU, LRU, CLOCK, LRD, etc. have been already studied extensively and experimental results of their behaviour in real system environments demonstrated in [Bel66, Den68, Ston81, EfHä84, SaSc86]. The aim of each replacement algorithm is the minimization of the buffer fault rate, and subsequently the physical I/O time, for a given buffer size and allocation. Their general assumption is that there is locality of reference; locality means that the probability of a reference to recently referenced pages is higher than the average reference probability [EfHä84].

Because Prolog programs do exhibit locality of reference [RoMa84, RoRa86], replacement algorithms based on the locality principle can be employed for the cluster buffer management too. These algorithms can be made more powerful if they exploit the already mentioned cluster type and cluster state information.

The cluster type information, that is generated at compile-time, divides the clusters of a program into two groups: the group of the normal clusters and the group of the cluster, which contain common procedure sub-trees (cps-clusters). The cluster state information provided to the cluster buffer manager by the WAM at run-time, devides clusters into the groups of the passive, the semi-active and the active clusters. Because passive clusters are not needed any more, the cluster replacement algorithms have to replace passive clusters as soon as possible (high replacement priority) and to hold active clusters as long as possible (low replacement priority) in the buffer. Additionally, they have to hold active cps-clusters longer than normal active clusters in the buffer. Taking into account both cluster type and cluster state information, the replacement priorities for the cluster groups showed in the following table are obtained:

cluster group		replacement priority
cluster type	cluster state	
normal	passive	4
cps	passive	3
normal	active or semi-active	2
cps	active or semi-active	1

Under the foregoing considerations four cluster replacement algorithms have been designed and implemented.

The algorithms named 4xFIFO and 4xLRU exploit the sequential (4xFIFO) and the local (4xLRU) cluster reference behaviour of the Prolog system and use the cluster type and cluster state information. They are obtained by applying both FIFO and LRU to each of the four cluster groups in the specified priority order.

If the duration of the active cluster state is long, it can happen that the buffer is occupied by active clusters, because they are of the lowest replacement priority. The algorithms named 4xFIFO/CWS und 4xLRU/CWS attempt to overcome this problem as follows:

1. They compute the working sets (CWS) and the current number of clusters (C) for each cluster group by each cluster reference.

2. They replace clusters fifo-wise (4xFIFO/CWS) or lru-wise (4xLRU/CWS) from that group, which has the maximum difference   (C - CWS).

3. Performance evaluation of the clustering concept

This section describes the evaluation parameters and performance evaluation criteria of both clustering algorithms and cluster replacement algorithms.

3.1. Evaluation parameters

The performance evaluation of both clustering algorithms and cluster replacement algorithms relies on the following parameters:

PCS	physical cluster size
CBS	physical buffer size
CR	total cluster references
CFR	cluster fault rate
CFR_{fr}	cluster fault rate by forward referencing
CFR_{br}	cluster fault rate by backward referencing It holds: $CFR = CFR_{fr} + CFR_{br}$
CFR_{cps}	cluster fault rate of cps-clusters
CFR_{cps-fr}	cluster fault rate of cps-clusters by forward referencing
CFR_{cps-br}	cluster fault rate of cps-clusters by backward referencing
L_a	duration of the active cluster state (aver.)

3.2. Evaluation criterium for the clustering algorithm

The optimality measure definition for the specified clustering algorithms relies on the assumption of an infinite physical buffer size, because the whole code activated by the query has to be loaded into the main memory. In this case, clusters are accessed only once (single cluster faults) because there is no need for cluster replacement. In order to define the optimality measure of a clustering algorithm, the following notions are introduced:

The **dynamic procedure tree** (*dpt*) is a trace of the procedures which are called in order to compute the an answer to a given query. It is generated by the inference process.

Similarly, the **dynamic cluster tree** (*dct*) is a trace of the code clusters which are executed in order to to compute the answer to a given query.

The optimality of a clustering algorithm is obtained by "clustering" the *dpt* with the same physical cluster size. To "cluster" the *dpt*, the physical size of the *dpt* is simply divided by the given physical cluster size. To express the optimality measure formally the following two variables are introduced, which indicate the number of cluster faults issued by loading of both trees:

C_{dpt}:number of the obtained clusters by the "clustering" of the *dpt*

C_{dct}:number of the accessed clusters, which belong to the *dct*

The cluster discrepancy

$$D_A = C_{dct} - C_{dpt}$$

can be considered as an absolute optimality measure for the clustering algorithm A. The parameter R_A, defined as

$$R_A = C_{dct}/C_{dpt} - 1$$

indicates how much more code than the code needed by the query has been loaded into the main memory. A clustering algorithm A_1 is considered to be better than A_2 according to a given query, if $R_{A_1} < R_{A_2}$.

3.3. Evaluation criteria for cluster replacement algorithms

The optimality measure definition for the cluster replacement algorithms relies on the assumption that the knowledge base size exceeds the physical buffer size. In this case, clusters can be loaded more than once (multiple cluster faults) because cluster replacement is performed. For this reason the optimality measure definition has to take into account the applied cluster replacement algorithm.

In order to get an optimality measure for a specific cluster replacement algorithm, it is compared with the well-known Belady's OPT-algorithm [Bel66], which always replaces the cluster with the longest forward reference distance on the cluster reference string. This algorithm represents an absolute lower bound for the cluster fault rate of a given cluster reference string. Its evaluation is carried out on the already derived cluster reference string.

An "upper bound" describing the "worst case" for the cluster fault rate is in our case approximated by the RANDOM algorithm, i.e. for practical purposes OPT and RANDOM are assumed to limit the realm of reasonable replacement algorithms and thereby give a optimality measure for them [EfHä84].

The optimality measure for a cluster replacement algorithm is defined formally by introducing the following parameters:

CFR_{rep}:cluster fault rate observed by applying the given cluster replacement algorithm.

CFR_{opt}:cluster fault rate observed by applying the OPT-algorithm.

The discrepancy

$$D_{CFR} = CFR_{rep} - CFR_{opt}$$

can be accepted as an absolute optimality measure for a cluster replacement algorithm w.r.t. a given clustering algorithm.

3.4. Evaluation method

For technical reasons simulation was chosen as the evaluation method. The evaluation results reported in the next section are based on two cluster reference strings derived from two large VM-Prolog [VMP] applications: the LILOG system [Herz86] and the SYLLOG system [WaTz88]. LILOG is a natural language processing system for German text understanding and consists of 3.5 MB VM-Prolog code. SYLLOG is a multipurpose expert system shell of 2 MB VM-Prolog code.

The cluster reference strings were derived from queries, which activated about 40% of the procedures of the code. These cluster reference strings were used as input for the cluster buffer manager, which was driven as simulator, providing various cluster replacement algorithms and physical buffer sizes.

The following method was applied in order to obtain the appropriate cluster reference strings: First, rules and facts of both systems were clustered (using the algorithm CLUSTER1 described in [Gar00]). The facts were clustered only if their physical size did not exceed the used physical cluster size. Because LILOG and SYLLOG contained large amounts of facts, the actually clustered code was 1126 KB (LILOG) and 542 KB (SYLLOG) respectively. Second, both systems were traced and the obtained procedure traces were further interpreted in order to get the appropriate cluster reference information. The derived cluster reference strings contain two kinds of references: the *cluster reference* concerns the control transfer from one cluster to another; the *state reference* encodes the changes of the local stack and thereby simultaneously the state changes of a given cluster, e.g. from semi-active to passive.

The value set [0.5, 1, 1.5, 2, 3, 4] (in KB) was used for the physical cluster size in order to get evidence about the cluster fault change by doubling the cluster size. The value set [10, 20, 30, 50], measured in clusters, was applied for the cluster buffer size.

4. Performance evaluation results and interpretation

The following charts and table statistics illustrate the performance evaluation results of the clustering concept. Both chart 1 and table 1 state the optimality of the investigated clustering algorithm and thereby show how much load time can be saved by clustering.

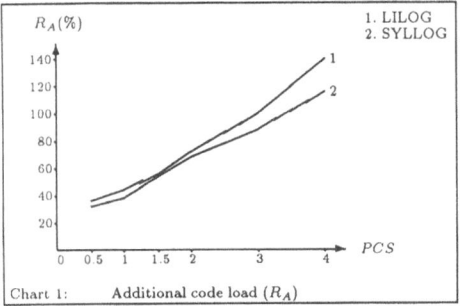

Chart 1:   Additional code load (R_A)

	LILOG				SYLLOG			
	total clustered code.		1126 KB		total clustered code		542 KB	
	activated code		462 KB		activated code:		195 KB	
PCS	Clusters			R_A(%)	Clusters			R_A(%)
	System	C_{act}	C_{dpt}		System	C_{act}	C_{dpt}	
0.5	2603	1284	924	39	1120	530	390	36
1	1398	656	462	42	600	273	195	40
1.5	1110	480	308	56	410	200	130	54
2	795	395	231	71	305	168	98	70
3	487	320	154	108	234	127	65	95
4	356	280	116	141	168	106	49	116

Table 1:   Optimality measurement for the clustering algorithm

Both Chart 1 and table 1 show that significant reduction by loading code of clustered Prolog knowledge bases can be expected, if small physical cluster sizes are used. For the physical cluster sizes 0.5 KB and 1 KB, queries that activate 40% of the total application code have loaded only 39% and 46% more clustered code than really needed. The contribution of clustering to reduce the loaded code can also be seen by comparing the number of the loaded clusters (C_{act}) with the total number of the application clusters ($System$). The achieved results show that the loaded clustered code is less than 55% of the total application code. This can be considered as another advantage of clustering.

The following charts and tables concern the performance of the cluster replacement algorithms, obtained by evaluating the physical cluster and buffer size.

The cluster replacement algorithms caused generally decreasing cluster fault rates by an increasing physical cluster and buffer size. In order to explain the behaviour of the extended cluster replacement algorithms the duration of the active cluster state (L_a) has to be taken into account. Tables 2 and 3 state that the duration of the active state of LILOG clusters is three times longer than the duration of active state of SYLLOG clusters. The influence of the duration of the active cluster state is illustrated by the charts 2 and 3. Chart 2 shows that the discrepancy between the cluster fault rates of 4xFIFO, 4xLRU and OPT in the case of LILOG is four times greater than the discrepancy between the FIFO, LRU and OPT algorithms in the case of SYLLOG. The undesired result in the case of LILOG was caused by the applied replacement priority schema for the four cluster groups. The effect of such a cluster replacement was the buffer occupation by active clusters, which have the lowest replacement priority and the longest duration. In contrast

to this, chart 3 shows that 4xFIFO and 4xLRU have a better behaviour than FIFO and LRU in the case of the SYLLOG system.

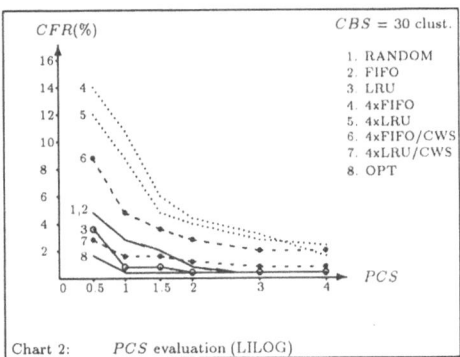

Chart 2: PCS evaluation (LILOG)

PCS	0.5		1		1.5		2		3		4	
CR	193069		174773		134806		123551		118182		121342	
L_a (in refs)	81		65		52		43		30		26	
CFR(fr, br)	fr	br	fr	br	fr	br	fr	br	fr	br	fr	br
RANDOM	91	9	91	9	90	10	90	10	90	10	91	9
FIFO	94	6	95	5	94	6	93	7	94	6	96	4
4xFIFO	83	17	83	17	84	16	96	4	97	3	81	19
4xFIFO/CWS	84	16	81	19	77	23	74	26	73	27	68	32
LRU	96	4	97	3	97	3	97	3	96	4	96	4
4xLRU	84	16	83	17	85	15	96	4	96	4	81	19
4xLRU/CWS	88	12	85	15	87	13	89	11	86	14	87	13
OPT	97	3	98	2	96	4	96	4	96	4	94	4

Table 2:   Cluster references and cluster fault rates during forward and backward referencing (LILOG)

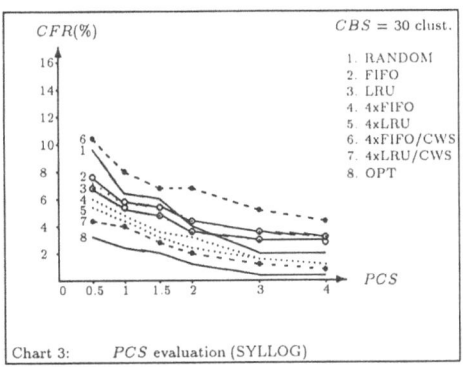

Chart 3: PCS evaluation (SYLLOG)

PCS	0.5		1		1.5		2		3		4	
CR	3533		3179		3012		2039		2901		1876	
L_a (in refs)	29		24		15		13		10		9	
CFR(fr, br)	fr	br	fr	br	fr	br	fr	br	fr	br	fr	br
RANDOM	92	8	91	8	90	10	93	7	98	2	95	5
FIFO	96	4	95	5	94	6	91	9	95	5	96	4
4xFIFO	99	1	100	0	100	0	100	0	100	0	100	0
4xFIFO/CWS	89	11	94	6	92	8	90	10	81	19	100	0
LRU	97	3	96	4	96	4	94	6	98	2	100	0
4xLRU	99	1	100	0	100	0	100	0	100	0	100	0
4xLRU/CWS	91	9	94	6	92	8	92	8	97	3	98	2
OPT	98	2	98	2	99	1	95	5	100	0	100	0

Table 3:   Cluster references and cluster fault rates during forward and backward referencing (SYLLOG)

The cluster fault rates CFR_{cps-fr} and CFR_{cps-br} of table 4 state that the algorithm 4xLRU/CWS shows a better behaviour than 4xFIFO/CWS. The reason for this is the high reference locality caused mainly by referencing the cps-clusters; table 4 shows that cps-clusters (CR_{cps}) incurred more than 70% of the total cluster references (CR). Additionally, the small CFR_{br} rates show that all extended replacement algorithms have managed backward referencing efficiently.

PCS	0.5		1		1.5		2		3		4	
LILOG												
CR	193069		174773		134806		123551		118182		121342	
CR_{cps}	134623		153445		117979		112922		106851		110775	
CFR_{cps} (%)	fr	br	fr	br	fr	br	fr	br	fr	br	fr	br
4xFIFO	0.6	0.1	0.3	0.1	0.3	0	0.3	0	0.2	0	0.2	0
4xFIFO/CWS	3	9	26	10	28	16	40	21	25	10	14	8
4xLRU	0.4	0	0.2	0	0.2	0	0.2	0	0.2	0	0.1	0
4xLRU/CWS	4	1	6	1	7	3	9	4	11	3	8	6
SYLLOG												
CR	3533		3179		3012		2039		2901		1876	
CR_{cps}	2598		2659		2675		1755		2628		1687	
CFR_{cps} (%)	fr	br	fr	br	fr	br	fr	br	fr	br	fr	br
4xFIFO	4	0	3	0	3	0	4	0	2	0	3	0
4xFIFO/CWS	16	3	15	5	11	1	4	0	2	0	3	0
4xLRU	3	0	3	0	3	0	4	0	2	0	3	0
4xLRU/CWS	8	2	7	1	9	0	4	0	2	0	3	0

Table 4: **Statistics on management of cps-clusters**

Charts 4 and 5 display decreasing cluster fault rates by an increasing cluster buffer size. The influence of the active cluster state on the fault rates of the extended algorithms retains also in the case of physical buffer size evaluation. This becomes obvious from the better behaviour of the 4xFIFO and 4xLRU algorithms, showed by the chart 5.

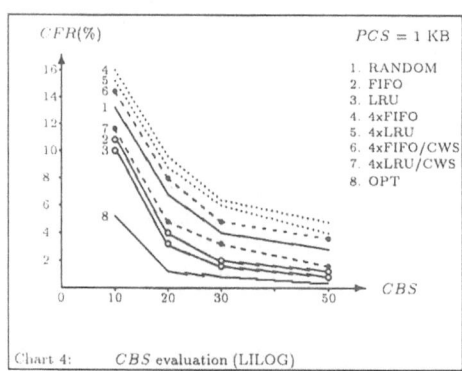

Chart 4: CBS evaluation (LILOG)

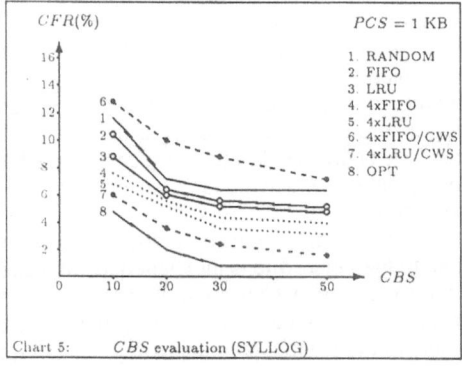

Chart 5: CBS evaluation (SYLLOG)

5. Conclusions

In the case of an infinite buffer size, the foregoing analysis showed a substantial code reduction by loading clustered code, if small cluster sizes are used. The obtained load time reduction result is a product of the number of the unloaded application clusters multiplied by the constant cluster load time. Therefore, clustering strongly reduces the load time for large knowledge bases.

The general conclusion about the cluster replacement algorithms in the case of a finite buffer size is that the extended algorithms show a better behaviour than the non-extended algorithms, if the duration of the active cluster state tends to be short.

Finally, the use of the clustering concept is not restricted to code retrieval from secondary storage into main memory, but the same underlying ideas may be used for loading pieces of code into cache memory or any other fast memory.

Acknowledgement

We would like to express our thanks to Jürgen Zink who did the performance evaluation for us.

References

Bel66   Belady, L.A.: *A study of replacement algorithms for virtual storage computers.* IBM Syst. J. 5, 2 (1966).

Boc90   Bocca, J.: *Compilation of Logic Programs to Implement Very Large Knowledge Base Systems - A Case Study: Educe*. Proc. of the 6th Int. Conf. on Data Engineering, Los Angeles, USA, Feb. 90.

BöBe89   Böttcher, S. Beierle, C.: *Database Support for the PROTOS-L System.* Microprocessing and Microprogramming, Vol. 27, 1989.

Den68   Denning, P.G.: *The working set model for program behavior.* Commun. ACM 11, 5 (1968), 323-333.

EfHä84   Effelsberg, W. Härder, T.: *Principles of Database Buffer Managment.* ACM TODS, Vol. 9, No. 4, Dec. 84.

Gar90   Garidis, C.: *Clustering-Konzepte für optimalen Zugriff auf große und datenbankresidente Wissensbasen.* PhD Thesis, Uni. Stuttgart, Dezember 90.

Herz86   Herzog O. et. al: *LILOG - Linguistic and Logic Methods for the Computational Understanding of German.* TR 1b, IBM Germany, 1986.

RoMa84   Ross M.L. McMahon A.G.: *Memory Managment of a Sequential Prolog Interpreter.* Technical Report 84/6, RMIT, 1984.

RoRa86   Ross M.L. Ramamohanarao K.: *Paging Strategy for Prolog based dynamic virtual Memory.* Symp. on Logic Programming, Salt Lake City, Utah, Sep. 86.

SaSc86   Sacco, G.M. Schkolnick, M.: *Buffer Management in Relational Database Systems.* ACM TODS, Vol. 11, No. 4, Dec. 86.

Ston81   Stonebraker, M.: *Operating system support for database managment systems.* Commun. ACM 24, 7 (1981), 412-418.

VMP   VM/Programming in Logic, *Program Description and Operations Manual.* Program Number 5785-ABH, SB11-63740, IBM, 1985.

WaTz88   Walker, A. Tzoar, D.: *The SYLLOG Expert Database System.* Notes for Users, Version 0.7, IBM T.J. Watson Research Center, 1988.

War83   Warren, H.D.: *An Abstract Prolog Instruction Set.* SRI Tchnical Note 309, 1983.

Zin89   Zink, J.: *Entwurf und Implementierung eines Meßssystems zur Evaluierung des Clustering-Konzeptes des PROTOS-L-Systems.* Diplomarbeit 607, Universität Stuttgart, Dec. 1989.

The ARPO-2: an expert system for building contracts[1]

Pilar Lasala

Statistical Methods Department. Zaragoza University
50009 Zaragoza (Spain)

ABSTRACT

The theme of expert legal systems is considered in a general form and a general model for such systems is suggested. A description is given of the ARPO-2 prototype which has been developed to deal with problems relating to building contracts. The system acts as an aid to the jurist in discovering whether it is possible to make a legal claim relative to a building contract as well as documenting the posture to be taken with respect to the case. Some results of the use of IDEAL methodology for expert system development are shown, as obtained for ARPO-2. Future lines of work are discussed, with the aim of improving this prototype.

1 A DESCRIPTION OF THE PROBLEM

All jurists, whether they be judges, magistrates, teachers within Faculties of Law or lawyers, confront, on a daily basis, the necessity of managing large volumes of legal documentation which make up the sources of law, namely legislation, judicial precedents and bibliography. This applies to both practising jurists, because all the cases they handle (be they lawyers or judges) have to be documented and to theoretical jurists, because their work consists of constructing theories by way of and by reference to the said documentation.

This volume of documentation is being constantly increased by virtue of the new laws which are being passed (laws which may, in turn, annul or repeal earlier laws), by new judgements pronounced by a variety of Courts of Justice and by other publications on legal themes. Thus, a jurist who wishes to carry out his work in the best possible way must keep himself constantly up-to-date, in order to maintain at the necessary level the legal knowledge he earlier acquired.

It is obvious that no single person can dominate all the legal documentation which exists on any matter. Nevertheless, there are individuals whose experience, developed in the course of their professional lives, has resulted in them having an almost exhaustive knowledge of the legal documentation covering certain specific matters. These individuals are experts in going to legal texts and in finding the best documentation upon which a case can be based.

In order to focus on the theme of this study, let us first consider certain observations which have been made on the nature of legal reasoning. As indicated by Susskind [8], there are three functions which can be emphasized with respect to legal reasoning, namely:

JUSTIFICATION: in general terms, it is expected of judges that they offer clear reasons for their decisions.

PREDICTION: the reasoning carried out by lawyers tries to predict judicial behaviour, whilst judges' reasoning is of a predictive nature of an instrumental type, being concerned with whether or not the law will function for society.

PERSUASION: the task of the lawyer is understood to be that of convincing the Court of the merit of the argument he presents.

It is possible therefore to consider that, in order to design an expert system which reproduces legal reasoning, one of these three functions should be chosen to be used as a model in the system. Nevertheless, these three functions take place by way of a common rational process, such that a body of legal knowledge can be applied to the facts of the case in order to reach a legal conclusion. Once this legal conclusion has been reached, some jurists can choose to justify it, others can use it as an element in their predictive calculations, whilst others can use it in their rhetorical opinions. In any of these three cases, the jurist needs to draw on the sources of law namely, the law, judicial precedent and bibliography, which support the legal conclusion.

The theme of this study is the modelling of judicial reasoning in order to reach the legal conclusions to a case, citing the sources of law upon which they are based. The subsequent use which the jurist will make of this data is not considered.

The problem which is posed is the need to make accessible to the jurist -who is inexperienced in a specific matter- the experience which is required in the search for the best legal documentation concerning that matter.

The object of the system is to improve juridical practice by permitting jurists to improve the quality of the

[1] For this research funds have been received from the General Offices of Scientific and Technical Research (DGICYT), Project PB87-0632

TABLE I: PLAUSIBILITY DIMENSION (The possibility of developing the expert system)

CHARACTE-RISTIC	CATE-GORY	TYPE	DENOMINATION OF THE CHARACTERISTIC	THRESHOLD T_{1j}	WEIGHT W_{1j}	VALUE V_{1j}
P1	E	EX	Experts exist	7	10	9
P2	E	EX	The assigned expert is genuine	8	10	9
P3	D	EX	The expert is cooperative		8	9
P4	D	EX	The expert is capable of explaining his methods but not of categorising them		7	8
P5	E	TA	Sufficient cases of proof exist: normal, typical, exemplary, tough, etc.	7	10	9
P6	D	TA	The task is well structured and understood		10	8
P7	D	TA	Only the skill of knowledge is required		10	7
P8	D	TA	Optimum results are not required, only satisfactory results		9	7
P9	D	TA	The task does not require much common sense		9	7
P10	D	DU	Management is fully committed to the project		7	10

$$\text{Valuation: } VD_1 = \prod_{k \text{ essentials}} (V_{1K} // T_{1K}) \frac{\sum_{j=1}^{10} W_{1j}}{\sum_{j=1}^{10} \frac{W_{1j}}{V_{1j}}} = 8.15$$

TABLE II: JUSTIFICATION DIMENSION (Justification for the development of the expert system)

CHARACTE-RISTIC	CATE-GORY	TYPE	DENOMINATION OF THE CHARACTERISTIC	THRESHOLD T_{2j}	WEIGHT W_{2j}	VALUE V_{2j}
J1	E	EX	The expert will not be available	7	10	8
J2	D	EX	There is scarce human experience		10	5
J3	D	TA	The need for experience exists simultaneously in many places		8	9
J4	E	TA	There is a need for experience in hostile, difficult and/or unrewarding environments	6	10	7
J5	E	TA	Alternative admissible solutions do not exist	6	8	6
J6	D	DU	A high rate of return on the investment is expected		7	8
J7	E	DU	It fulfils a useful and necessary task	7	8	8

$$\text{Valuation: } VD_2 = \prod_{k \text{ essentials}} (V_{2K} // T_{2K}) \frac{\sum_{j=1}^{7} W_{2j}}{\sum_{j=1}^{7} \frac{W_{2j}}{V_{2j}}} = 6.95$$

TABLE III: SUITABILITY DIMENSION (Suitability of the problem to the technology of expert systems)

CHARACTE-RISTIC	CATE-GORY	TYPE	DENOMINATION OF THE CHARACTERISTIC	THRESHOLD T_{3j}	WEIGHT W_{3j}	VALUE V_{3j}
A1	D	EX	The experience used by the expert is not badly organised		5	8
A2	D	TA	It has a practical value		6	9
A3	D	TA	It is more practical than strategic		7	7
A4	E	TA	It will serve needs in the long term	7	6	7
A5	D	TA	The task, which is not particulary easy, requires intensive knowledge both with respect to personal knowledge and to the manipulation of information		5	6
A6	D	TA	It is of manageable size and/or a gradual approach is possible and/or a breakdown into independent sub-tasks is possible		6	8
A7	E	EX	The transfer of experience between individuals is possible	7	7	8
A8	D	TA	It was identified as a problem within the area and the effects of the introduction of an expert system can be planned for		6	7
A9	E	TA	It does not require answers in immediate real time	7	9	7
A10	E	TA	The task does not require basic investigation and it involves little, if any, generation and understanding of natural language	7	9	7
A11	D	TA	The expert basically uses symbolic reasoning which implies subjective factors		5	4
A12	D	TA	It is basically of an heuristic type		5	7

$$\text{Valuation: } VD_3 = \prod_{k \text{ essentials}} (V_{3K} // TK) \frac{\sum_{j=1}^{12} W_{3j}}{\sum_{j=1}^{12} \frac{W_{3j}}{V_{3j}}} = 6.91$$

TABLE IV: SUCCESS DIMENSION (Possibility of success of the expert system)

CHARACTE-RISTIC	CATE-GORY	TYPE	DENOMINATION OF THE CHARACTERISTIC	THRESHOLD T_4	WEIGHT W_4	VALUE V_4
E1	D	EX	They do not feel threatened by the project; they are capable of feeling intellectually united with respect to it		8	9
E2	D	EX	They have a brilliant history in carrying out this task		6	8
E3	D	EX	There is agreement as to what constitutes a good solution to the task		5	8
E4	D	EX	The only justification to take a step towards the solution is the quality of the final solution		5	8
E5	D	TA	There is no fixed period for completion and nor is there another project dependent upon this task		6	7
E6	E	TA	It is not influenced by political changes	8	7	8
E7	D	TA	Expert systems already exist which solve this or similar tasks		8	7
E8	D	TA	There are minimal changes in habitual procedures		8	7
E9	D	TA	The solutions are explicable or interactive		5	8
E10	E	TA	The task is of an R+D or of a practical character, but not the two simultaneously	6	7	6
E11	D	DU	They are mentally adjusted to the problem and have realistic expectations with respect to both scope and limitations		6	8
E12	E	DU	They do not totally reject this technology	7	7	8
E13	D	DU	The system interacts in an intelligent and friendly way with the user		6	9
E14	D	DU	The system is capable of explaining its reasoning to the user		9	9
E15	D	DU	The insertion of the system is carried out without problems, that is to say, without it interfering with the daily routine		8	7
E16	D	DU	They are committed during the total duration of the project, including after its introduction		6	8
E17	E	DU	An adequate transfer of technology takes place	6	8	7

Valuation:
$$VD_4 = \prod_{k \text{ essentials}} (V_{4K} \; // \; T_{4K}) \; \frac{\sum_{j=1}^{17} W_{4j}}{\sum_{j=1}^{17} \frac{W_{4j}}{V_{4j}}} = 7.65$$

Valuation of the problem:
$$V = \frac{\sum_{i=1}^{4} VD_i}{4} = 7.42$$

documentation upon which they base their legal conclusions.

The aim of the system is that the inexperienced jurist, aided by the system, be capable of finding legal solutions and documentation at the same speed and with the same skill as that shown by an expert. At the same time the system will suggest procedures relevant to the case as given.

2 SUITABILITY OF ARTIFICIAL INTELLIGENCE TECHNOLOGY

The ARPO-2 prototype, described in section 5, has been developed using the IDEAL methodology [5]. This methodology propose four phases to develop an expert system:

Phase I: Identification of the problem and conception of the solution

Phase II: Development of the prototype(s)

Phase III: Construction and execution of the full system

Phase IV: Achieve the technology transfer and the system maintenance

In order to measure the suitability of artificial intelligence technology to the given problem, the task evaluation test which suggests the Phase I of IDEAL methodology has been carried out.

This knowledge engineering methodology classifies the characteristics of a problem into four dimensions: plausibility, justification, suitability and success. The category of a characteristic may be essential (E) or desirable (D); the type of a characteristic may be expert (E), task (TA) or management and user (DU).

The knowledge engineer must fix the threshold values of the essential characteristics and next evaluate the characteristics corresponding to the plausibility, justification, suitability and success dimensions. If an essential characteristic does not reach its threshold value, the given problem is rejected as being inappropriate to be solved by mean of artificial intelligence technology.

Each dimension is evaluated as shown in formulas VD_1, VD_2, VD_3 and VD_4, and the problem is finally evaluated as shown in formula V.

The results obtained for this problem are set out in Tables I, II, III and IV.

As can be seen, every essential characteristic surpasses

its threshold value and the final valuation of the problem is 7.42, by virtue of which it was considered to have passed the evaluation stage and thus it moved on to the development of a prototype which deals with a specific aspect of the problem.

3 EXPERIENCE AND LEGAL EXPERTS

In order to study the development of legal expert systems, it is necessary to give some considerations to the nature of what we understand legal experience to be. Susskind [8] distinguishes between two types of legal knowledge: academic and experiential.

Academic legal knowledge can be acquired by any one who is trained in the techniques of legal research. The raw material for this type of legal knowledge is made up of the formulation of the laws and legal commentaries upon them. Academic legal knowledge allows us to carry out the appraisal, interpretation and comprehension of the repositories of law. This knowledge also includes a level of heuristic knowledge and it is this which any student of the law tries to acquire and any teacher of law possesses to a certain degree.

Good practical jurists possess this academic knowledge, but they have, in addition, acquired an experiential legal knowledge represented by the day-to-day knowledge gained in the practical administration of the law. This knowledge cannot be acquired from legal repositories, but rather it is achieved by the personal experience of working with legal processes. Experiential knowledge is itself made up of two types: heuristic knowledge and non-heuristic procedural knowledge.

Heuristic knowledge can, in turn, be divided into four types:

Prediction on the way a Court will react to the facts of a case; that is to say, the advice of the legal expert must go beyond a pure description of the law.

Law-derivations, which are reached by the application of the techniques of legal science, in such a way that they can be associated, by way of derivation, with any formal legal source; these derivations do not have the same level of generality or the same terminology as the formulation of the law.

Meta-knowledge, which is the knowledge of how to use all legal knowledge (academic, heuristic and procedural) to solve problems. This meta-knowledge can be of two types: domain-independent or domain-specific.

Procedural heuristic knowledge, formed by the totality of the rules which indicate efficient forms of proceeding with the possibility of success, and which are legally acceptable for the resolution of legal problems; these forms of proceeding are achieved following long experience with the legal knowledge specific to the application of these forms.

Finally procedural, non-heuristic, knowledge is that knowledge which relates to how the administration of the law functions. It is the conjunction of algorithmic instructions which describe essential legal procedures.

The different types of legal knowledge, as described above, can be set out in Figure 1.

4 A MODEL OF A LEGAL EXPERT SYSTEM

The expert system which is described here must be one giving access to legal documentation, which makes it much easier to gain access to legal documents stored in databases that are accessible by means of computer.

The idea of legal expert systems which give access to databases in order to extract documentation is one that has been the subject of recent development by different research groups throughout the world, [7], [4], [1], this idea being converted, in certain cases, into intelligent systems giving access to databases.

In an ideal system, the jurist would set out in writing his version of a specific problem and, by virtue of the interactions between the program and the user, the problem being dealt with would be defined little by little and, consequently, so would the information needs that he has, such that, by way of this definition, the appropriate documentation would be recovered from the group of databases.

For the exposition of the theme, a free drafting of the problem should be carried out by jurists and not by individuals who do not possess a knowledge of the law.

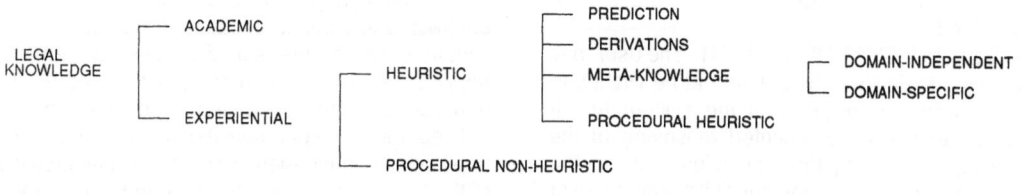

Figure 1

The jurist would express the problem to the system in his language, which is a language having certain formalities.

With respect to the legal knowledge to be included in the system, we should first remember the diagram which appears in Section 3; according to this diagram, the system will include in the knowledge base both academic legal knowledge and practical heuristic legal knowledge whilst, for the construction of the inference engine, heuristic experiential legal meta-knowledge must be used.

The user of a legal expert system must be a jurist or a student of law. A system of this type should never be used by anyone who does not possess the necessary knowledge in order to understand the terminology and the legal concepts relative to the theme being dealt with by the system.

With respect to the legal problems contemplated by the expert system, these must be very specific, as has been the case with those systems which have been developed up to now: [6], [3], [8], [9], [2], [4].

Nevertheless, the setting-up of a system of this type is too ambitious, including as it does many aspects of basic research, such as the understanding of natural language and the integration of separate database systems with expert systems. Therefore, as a first step, a prototype has been developed which adopts a partial approach to the global problem.

The system must be capable of guiding the user in his search for documentation with respect to the case as given.

To establish a model for the system, we examine the work made by a lawyer to solve a legal problem. In this process, the lawyer carry out certain activities:

- Formulation of the problem and determination of the main facts.
- Search of the legal norms that can be applied to the facts
- Application of such legal norms in order to reach a legal conclusion
- Argumentation of the legal conclusion based on law, judicial precedents and bibliography.

The system must do a similar work. To that end, it passes through four stages:

DETERMINATION OF THE ENVIRONMENT. In this stage, the system determines which subjects intervene, in what posture and what is the relationship which unites them. The individual who is consulting must be one the subjects of this relationship.

In any event, it is in this phase that the type of contract, the clauses or agreements that it includes and the relevant duration and dates are determined.

SELECTION OF THE TYPE OF ANSWER. The user may have already decided the action that he wishes to institute and only requires of the system that it indicates to him a documented reasoning of the possibility of carrying that action out; but, at the same time, there is also the possibility that the user asks the system to show him all the actions that he can institute with respect to the facts as given.

RESOLUTION OF THE CASE. In order for there to be a legal problem, there must have been a breach of contract by one of the parties; in this phase, the party who is in breach as well as the type of breach are determined.

The system guides the user by way of questions until the conclusion of reached, including the actions that can be brought and the procedural mechanisms that are available to that end.

The possible actions that are available are as follows:

An action claiming that the work be carried out
An action claiming that the work be handed over
An action claiming the payment of the work
An action claiming receipt of the work
A decennial action
An action for the rectification of defects
An action for payment of interest
An action for equivalent performance
An action for compensation
An action for specific performance
An action for the repetition of work done
Resolution

REPRODUCTION OF THE REASONING. The system concludes by showing the user the path which has been followed to reach the conclusion, the reasoning being based on the required sources of law. As an option, the user can have access to the complete text of the sources to which reference has been made.

5 DESCRIPTION OF THE ARPO-2 PROTOTYPE

The prototype, as developed, is a system by way of which access is given to legal documentation on the theme of building contracts; users must be jurists; the system asks the jurist questions and, by way of this conversation, a route is opened which leads to the legislation, the judicial precedents and the bibliography applicable to the case.

The system acts as an aid to the jurist in discovering whether it is possible to make a legal claim relative to a building contract as well as documenting the posture to be taken with respect to the case. The system must fulfil the following aims: to indicate a route to the individual who knows nothing of the theme, to complete the knowledge of the individual who knows something of the theme and to confirm the reasoning of the individual who knows more than the system.

From the legal point of view, the problem of the building contract is interesting because, in contrast to the normal situation, where the specific rules for a problem are applied first and when such specific rules exist then the general rules are not applied, in this case necessity has obliged us to forget specific rules and to turn to the application of the general rules; this is because the articles of the law are very rigid, as illustrated, for example, by the development of the concept of ruin. Therefore, use has had to be made of the more generic normative, first that which relates to buying and selling and, when even that fell short of the requirements of the normative for construction, then that governing obligations in general has been employed. Due to the lack of specific rules, the judge has had to take a step backwards and applies the basic subject matter which is available to him on contracts.

The prototype follows the squeme proposed in section 4. The relationship which unites the subjects must be a building contract, which is the theme chosen for the development of the prototype.

The system has been developed to work on IBM PS/2 computers or compatible, using the GURU tool, an environment for the development of expert systems which includes, amongst other features, the possibility of access to various databases and the use of various knowledge bases.

The role of expert has been assumed by a teacher of the Law Faculty at Zaragoza University and a Judge of the Superior Court of Aragón (Spain).

In order to formalise the knowledge representation, a model which contains two parts has been adopted, these parts being: RULE and REFERENCES.

The first has the form of rule in the habitual form:

IF condition THEN consequence

The second contains three elements:

LAW
JUDICIAL PRECEDENTS
BIBLIOGRAPHY

The rule contains the result that the expert obtains from the processing of the legal normative. The references contain the bases in the sources of law that the expert has available to him in order to obtain the corresponding rule.

6 FUTURE LINES OF WORK

The ARPO-2 prototype can be improved in three directions: by increasing the types of problem that it can handle, by permitting access to external databases and by admitting the drafting of the problem in legal language.

As was stated in Section 4, the ARPO-2 prototype, as a model of a legal expert system, deals with a very specific legal problem: the building contract. Nevertheless, it is possible to think in terms of developing a bigger system which covers the problems relating to breach of contract in general.

The difficulty which arises when dealing with bigger problems is that the knowledge base has to be so large that the search for information within it, in order to produce a reasoning, can be very slow and complicated. In order to increase the ARPO-2 prototype, we propose the construction of various knowledge bases, by means of classifying the legal normative which is common to all types of contract and that which is specific to each type. Thus, when passing through the determination of the scene phase, the type of contract which relates the parties is determined and, therefore, the group of knowledge bases which have to be referred to is restricted.

The ARPO-2 prototype is only capable of giving access to the legal documentation which is stored on the hard disk of the computer being used. An improvement in this respect would be to enable access to documentation kept on external databases, to which access can be gained by any communication medium.

The form of working on the ARPO-2 is by asking the user the necessary questions in order to carry out a reasoning. A further stage would be to develop a module which understands the legal language which relates to the theme of contracts and which would thus permit the jurist to introduce the case by way of free wording, without being limited to replying to the questions asked by the system.

It should be noted that the suggested module is not a module which understands natural language, and not even one which understands legal language in general. By restricting the need to understand language to that which relates to the theme of contracts, its development has been made easier, albeit within the level of complication that it carries with it.

REFERENCES

[1]   A. Basu, L. Ramkumar, F.D. Abramson. "An expert system for legal case research support." Proceedings DEXA 90 - Database and Expert Systems Applications, Vienna, Austria, August 1990.

[2]   G. D'Aietti. "Un Expert System in tema di locazioni commerciali." In Sistemi esperti nel diritto, A. A. Martino, ed. CEDAM, Padua, Italy, 1989.

[3]   A. Gardner. "An artificial intelligence approach to legal reasoning." MIT Press, 1987.

[4]   R.M. Di Giorgi, E. Fameli, R. Nannucci. "Expert system and database interactions in the legal domain." Proceedings DEXA 90 - Database and Expert Systems Applications, Vienna, Austria, August 1990.

[5]   J.L. Mató, J. Pazos. "Ingeniería del conocimiento. Diseño y construcción de sistemas expertos." Ed. SEPA, S.A., 1988.

[6]   L.T. McCarthy. "Reflections on TAXMAN: an experiment in artificial intelligence and legal reasoning." *Harvard Law Review* 90, 837, 1977.

[7]   L.T. McCarthy. "AI and law: How to get there from here." AAAI-90, Workshop on Artificial Intelligence and Legal Reasoning, Boston, EEUU, July 1990.

[8]   R. Susskind. "Expert systems in law." Clarendon Press, Oxford, 1987.

[9]   A. Valente. "Artificial intelligence applications in the juridical field: the SEFIT project - An expert system for accessing the special rollover fund for technological innovation." Proceedings 4º Congresso Internazionale sul tema Informatica e Regolamentazioni giuridiche, Rome, Italy, 1988.

A GRAPHICAL INTERACTIVE TOOL FOR KBS MAINTENANCE.

Frans Coenen   Trevor Bench-Capon

**Department of Computer Science, University of Liverpool,
Chadwick Building, PO BOX 147
Liverpool, L69 3BX, United Kingdom.**

ABSTRACT.

Although KBSs are now well established, very little work has
been carried out concerning the maintenance of these systems. In
this paper a KBS maintenance tool is described designed to assist
maintenance engineers in the task of maintaining the Rule Bases
(RBs) of KBSs. The tool is directed at KBSs built using an intermediate representation, between the source and the final Rule
base, which is isomorphic with the source i.e. that reflects the
structure of the source data. Essentially, the Datamap tool
described allows the maintenance engineer to navigate round the
intermediate representation to identify suspect Rules. This is
achieved using two directed biparteid graphs which graphically
display the connections between elements within individual Rules
and the connections between the Rules themselves. In addition a
number of facilities are provided to allow the user to interact with
the graphical displays and obtain answers to questions concerning
KB maintenance. These facilities support maintenance activities
where judgements are required on behalf of the maintenance
engineer.

1. INTRODUCTION.

Knowledge Based Systems (KBSs) have been in existence for
several decades now, but their general acceptance is still limited.
It is suggested that one principal reason for this is the difficulty in
maintaining such systems due to the nature of the expert
knowledge used [1]. This tends to be dynamic, in that the
knowledge will change as new discoveries are made and expert
opinions alter over a period of time. This means that KBSs, if
they are not maintained, quickly become obsolete or inaccurate.
This is especially the case in legal domains where the knowledge
may change overnight if legislation is altered.

The maintenance of KBSs tends to be adaptive maintenance
rather than the corrective or perfective maintenance as associated
with conventional systems, a categorisation first proposed in [2].
The approach to maintenance is therefore not the same since the
emphasis is on responding to external changes. Further the
structure of KBSs is such that traditional maintenance techniques
are not applicable. Given the above a surprisingly small amount
of research work has been carried out to investigate the maintenance of KBSs. What work has been carried out has largely been
concerned with formal consistency checking of Rule Bases (RBs)
such as in the COVADIS system [3], the debugging of rule bases
such as provided by the TEIRESIAS system [4], or the syntactical
editing of RBs within KBS development toolkits.

In this paper, a proposed support tool to assist the KBS maintenance engineer in the maintenance of Rule Bases (RBs) is
described. The tool is part of a suite of tools under development
as part of the Maintenance Assistance for Knowledge Engineers
(MAKE) Project, further details of which can be found in 1. The
MAKE project itself is a two year collaborative project between
Liverpool University, ICL and British Coal. The tools are essentially designed to be used in conjunction with KBSs built using
MADE (Make Authoring and Development Environment). This
is a development technique aimed at producing an isomorphic
intermediate representation [5], a brief overview of which is given
in Section 2. Currently this intermediate representation is
translated into an RB represented in Clausal Form. However the
target representation could just as easily be the Horn Clause Subset used by Prolog or straight Production Rules popular in many
expert system shells. The Datamap tool described here thus has
potential for implementation on any Rule based representation.

An overview of the Datamap is given in Section 3 and some possible uses with respect to maintenance are suggested. To
increase the usefulness of the Datamap the user will need to
access the underlying information. To this end a number of additional facilities and an alternative view option are proposed. This
interaction is described in detail in Section 4 and the proposed
additional facilities in the following Sub-sections. The discussion
includes suggestions concerning the usefulness of each facility.
Essentially the Datamap tool gives a graphical view of the RB
and allows the maintenance engineer to pose certain questions to
it. We may distinguish two categories of problem that may arise
with respect to RB maintenance, problems of structure and problems of content. Structural problems relate to the logical structure of the KB and are concerned with missing and redundant
Rules, Clauses, circular Rule paths, etc. Problems of content are
associated with the actual contents of the Rules. Essentially
there are two possibilities with regard to mistakes of content:
either the KB licences an inference which is not in fact legitimate
or the KB fails to licence a desired inference. The proposed facilities provided with the Datamap are designed to address both
questions of structure and content. The interactive facilities in
particular support content maintenance where judgements are
required on behalf of the maintenance engineer.

In the Final Section of this paper some conclusions are drawn
including the results of the demonstration of a proto-type
Datamap that has been developed.

2. THE MADE ISOMORPHIC DEVELOPMENT METHODOLOGY.

MADE is a KBS development environment based on KANT (Knowledge engineers assistANT). This is a hypertext like knowledge analysis tool originally built to assist in the development of a KBS to provide decision support for Department of Social Security (DSS) Adjudication Officers in the assessment of clams for benefits in local DSS offices [6]. The system was called the Local Office Demonstrator (LOD) System and was one of three applications built as part of the Alvey DHSS Large Demonstrator Project aimed at demonstrating the viability of KBS decision support in large, legislation based organisations [7]. It is ideally suited to the construction of KBSs in domains, such as legal domains, where the source knowledge is comprised of a significant amount of textual material, by assisting the knowledge engineer in the analysis of these source documents. The philosophy behind MADE is that knowledge can be viewed at different levels and that this ability will greatly enhance system maintenance. An advantage that is utilised by the Datamap.

The first level at which knowledge can be viewed is at the source level. KANT allows the knowledge engineer to browse one or more source documents in individual windows so that relevant Sections can be identified. These can then be analysed. The Result of the analysis is a set of Rules and a hierarchical Data Base, called the Class Hierarchy. The Rules in the Rule Base typically all branch out from a single top level node. This represents the Root Proposition which the KBS is intended to establish. The Class Hierarchy represents the vocabulary of the domain and consists of a top level Class with Sub-Classes branching from it describing different Object types. Each Object has a unique Class name and a number of slots describing Attributes of that Object and the possible Values that these Attributes may have for that Object. A feature of the Class Hierarchy is that Sub-Classes inherit Attributes of Super-Classes so as to ensure that a Sub-Class is a strict specialisation of its Super-Class. In KANT, inherited Attributes cannot be cancelled as is the case with some other development environments such as KEE. The Datamap described here is designed to assist in the maintenance of RBs and is not primarily concerned with the nature of the Class Hierarchy.

After analysis the Rule Base and Class Hierarchy are both represented using an intermediate representation. called MIR (Make Intermediate Representation). This is the second level view of the knowledge. The nature of this intermediate representation and the advantages to be gained from this type of representation have been discussed elsewhere ([8], [5] and [9]). It is thus not the intention of this paper to continue the discussion. Suffice to say that the more flexible syntax of the intermediate representation assists the knowledge engineer by allowing him to express the knowledge in the most natural way, and by maintaining a clear correspondence with the source.

The MIR Rule Base and Class Hierarchy are compiled into a target representation, the third level view of the knowledge. Currently this consists of a Clausal form referred to as CMIR (Compiled MIR). The Datamap allows the maintenance engineer to intercat and explore these second and third levels of knowledge representation in association with the RB.

The design of MADE revolves around three base windows, the KANT, MADE and MAPPE (Make APPlication Environment) Windows. From the KANT base window structures and sources can be selected and analysed. This is where the Knowledge Analysis for the Application is carried out. The MADE base window incorporates a results area in which sequences of messages produced during compilation of the MIR into CMIR are displayed. The MADE window is also the user interface through which the MAKE maintenance tools are invoked, including the Datamap described here. A full discussion of the tools available under the MAKE project is given in 1. The MAPPE Base Window provides the end user view of the application. It is divided into a hierarchy of TOPIC windows. These consist of forms to filled in by the user and can be viewed as Finite State Machines (FSM) in that Forms pass from one state to another depending on the operations performed on them. The states change according to either the user supplying an answer or by Rule initiated answers. The user can choose the order in which to address the various Sub-tasks and links to the written sources mean that the appropriate sections of legislation and guidance can be consulted at any time. This aspect is discussed in ([9]).

Finally, with respect to the RB and the intermediate representation, the following definitions, used in Sections 3 and 4 below, should be noted:-

(a) Rule.

This is an expression comprising Propositions, typically EAVs, and logical connectives. It consists of a head and a tail separated by an if or iff (read as if and only if). The head contains a single Proposition the truth or falsity of which is determined according to the truth or falsity of the Propositions contained in the body and their connectives.

(b) Clause.

This is an expression in standard Clausal Form, with a Proposition as head and a set of conjoined Propositions as tail (body). The Head Proposition is true if all the Propositions in the body are true. A single Rule will typically be equivalent to several Clauses.

(c) Proposition.

A Proposition is a triple comprising an Entity, an Attribute and a Value. The Entity may be a constant (the name of an instance) or a variable (typed to some Class in the Class Hierarchy). The Attribute will be a slot associated with the Class of which the Entity is a member. The Value will be a sub-range of the possible Values for the slot as defined in the Class of which the Entity is a member. Note that the Class Hierarchy constrains what Propositions are possible.

(d) Root Propositions and Attributes.

A Root Proposition is a Proposition which appears in the head of some Clause, and does not appear in the tail of any Clause. A Root Attribute is an Attribute associated with one or more Root Propositions. Thus a Root Proposition represents the task which the RB is designed to establish.

(e) Leaf Propositions and Attributes.

A Leaf Proposition is a Proposition which appears in the body of one or more Clauses, and in the head of no Clauses. A Leaf Attribute is an Attribute associated with one or more Leaf Propositions. The significance of leaves is that Values associated with them must be supplied to the system, not deduced. Values may be supplied either by explicit user input, or by the association of an instance with a Class the definition of which makes the Proposition true.

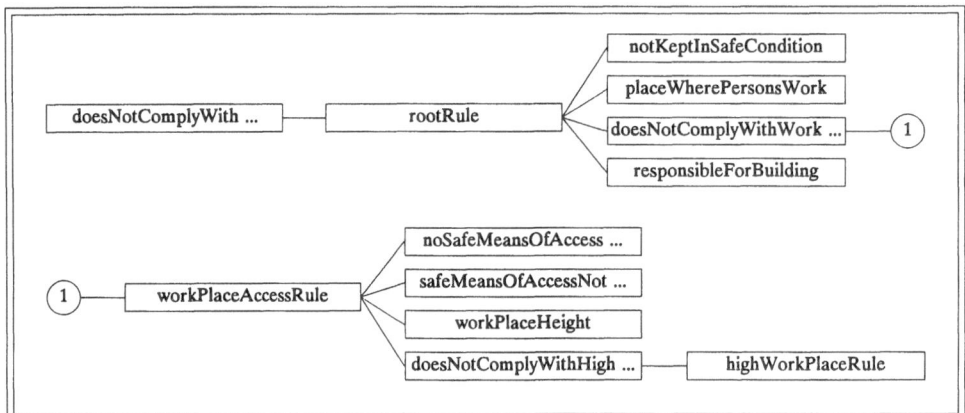

FIG 1: DATA MAP EXAMPLE 1

An example of MIR given in the Appendix. This fragment of RB has been taken from a genuine KBS designed to provide British Coal's accident claims officers and investigators with decision support. This was also developed as part of the MAKE project because it was felt that a real application was required on which proposed maintenance tools could be tested.

3. OVERVIEW OF THE DATAMAP.

The Datamap is a directed (from left to right) biparteid graph which links Attributes and Rules. On the left hand side we will find the start Attribute(s), with arcs to the Rules in which the start Attribute(s) act as the head. Arcs from these Rules will connect to Attributes in the body of these Rules. Further arcs will link to Rules in which these Attributes appear as the head (i.e. the Attribute concerning which the Rule permits inference), and so on until the Leaf Attributes are reached. It is proposed that the Datamap be invoked by a top level command selected from a KBS maintenance tool menu and that it be drawn, by default, starting with the Root Attributes. An option will be provided however to allow the maintenance engineer to select an alternative start Attribute, should he wish to investigate a sub-tree. Figure 1 shows a Datamap drawn in default mode representing the example Rule Base given in the Appendix. Note that only three levels of Attribute-Rule pairs are drawn. This is because of the limited amount of screen space that it is envisaged will be available. The information displayed in these three levels, although limited, is enough to allow the user to navigate through the RB. Using the Unfold/walk Down and the Fold/Walk Up Options described below further levels may be accessed.

The thing shown most clearly by the Datamap in Figure 1 is the relationship between Attributes and Rules. It shows in which Rules Attributes appear (through the arcs), and the role that they play in those Rules (through the direction of the arcs). By following a path through the Datamap it is possible to determine the Leaf Attributes into which a Root Attribute ultimately unfolds using the Unfold/Walk Down Option (see Sub-section 4.1). This ᵗ⁻ᵃⁿ makes it relatively easy to find a Rule which may be prob-
⁻ ⁻ᵗ⁻ᵉ behaviour of an Attribute is not as expected.

ERACTION.

described in the previous Section,
nount of user interaction by "click-

ing" on any Attribute or Rule Identifier of interest. The result will be "pop up" menus of the form shown in Figure 2 giving the user the choice of a number of options. Each of the options available is described in further detail in the following Sub-Sections.

4.1 THE UNFOLD/WALK DOWN AND FOLD WALK UP OPTIONS.

The Datamap as described above is only drawn to three levels. If the user wishes to display further levels he/she can click on an Attribute and select the "Unfold/Walk Down" Option (Figure 2). For example if, in Figure 1, the user selects the Attribute "doesNotComplyWithHigh ... " and the "Unfold/Walk Down" Option then the result will be as depicted in Figure 3. Alternatively if the user wishes to walk back up the Datamap to find defined Attributes the the "Fold/Walk Up" Option can be selected.

These Options allow the user to navigate through the Datamap. Firstly to explore how Attributes and Rules are connected to each other and secondly to trace a Root Attribute through to the Leaf Attributes associated with it and vice versa.

4.2 ALTERNATIVE VIEW OPTION.

There is a need for the maintenance engineer to also be able to inspect the relationships between Clauses and Propositions. This is the lowest level at which the knowledge displayed can be viewed and governs the "fine grain" behaviour of the system. An Alternative Datamap is therefore required and is produced in a separate window by selecting the Alternative View Option. This Datamap is drawn starting with the Head Proposition(s) con-

Alternative View	Unfold/Walk Down
Display Rule	Fold/Walk Up
Display Clauses	Head Proposition(s)
	Body Proposition(s)
	Root Proposition(s)
	Leaf Proposition(s)
	Values
	Entities

(a) Rule Menu   (b) Attribute Menu

FIG 2: DATA MAP MENUS

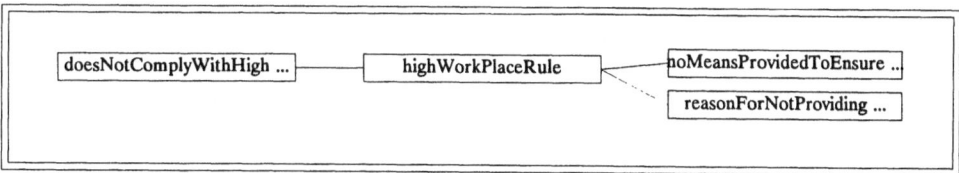

FIG 3: DATA MAP EXAMPLE 2

tained in the Rule Identifier selected. The Clause Identifiers in which this Proposition appears are then produced and displayed. This is then followed by the tail Propositions associated with these Clauses, followed by the Clauses in which these tail Propositions appear as the head. Again because of the limited amount of space available this process only continues until three levels of Proposition-Clause pairs have been displayed or until a Leaf Proposition is reached. Thus if for example the "rootRule" Identifier is selected in Figure 1 and the Alternative View Option selected from the resulting menu, an Alternative Datamap of the form given in Figure 4 will be produced.

As discussed previously the initial Datamap can be used to identify suspect Rules. These represent the second level view of the knowledge below the source documents. When identified these Rules can be examined to determine why their behaviour is unexpected. At this stage, viewing the Rule as its set of consequent Clauses is probably to be desired; typically the aberrent behaviour will be as a result of either some unwanted, malformed or missing Clause, a situation which may be difficult to identify by inspection of the Rule alone. However the provision of an Alternative Datamap Option will alleviate this situation by allowing the user to switch to the detailed Clausal Representation. In contrast if we consider Horn Clause or Prolog representations where

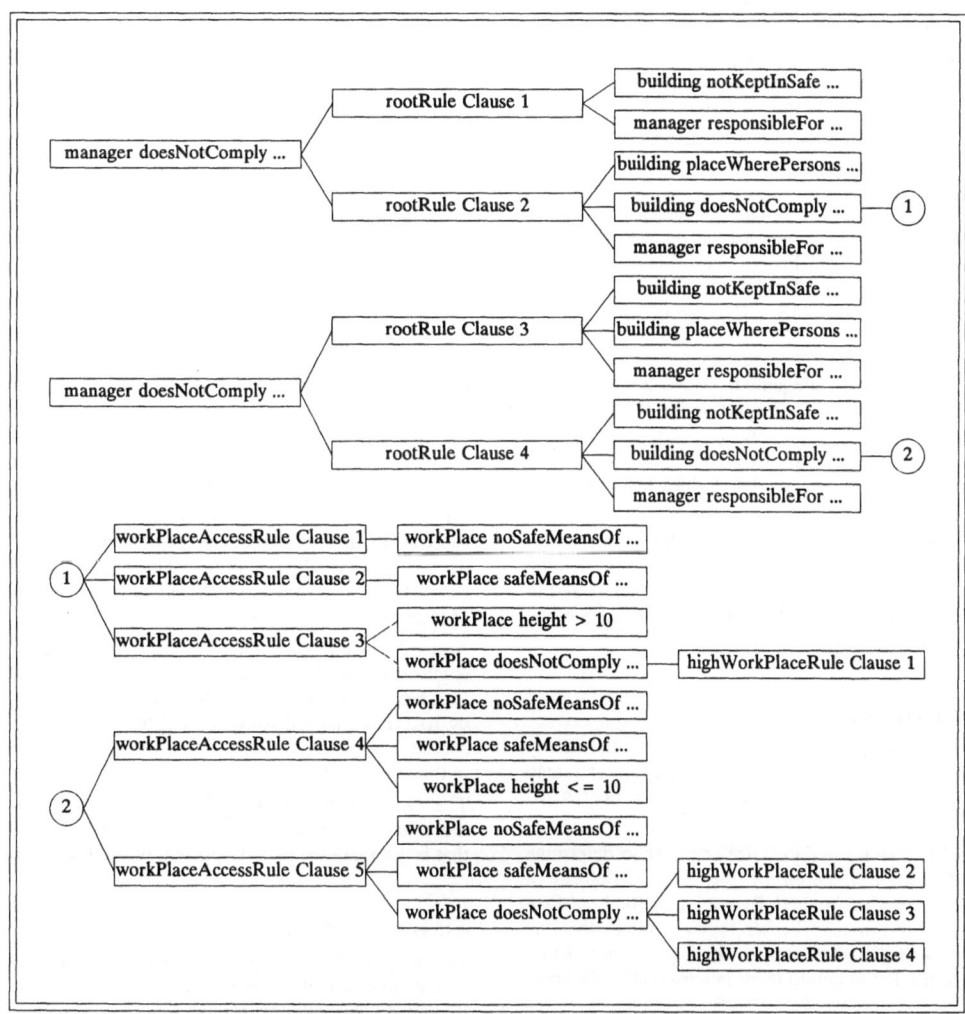

FIG 4: ALTERNATIVE DATA MAP EXAMPLE

170

Rules or Clauses are syntactically the same, then appreciation of the RB is at a single level: knowledge of the source structure provides no guidance. In the Datamap we can navigate at a more abstract level, calling up the detail when it is needed.

As with the initial Datamap each Proposition Identifier has a pop up menu associated with it as illustrated in Figure 5. By selecting the "Unfold/Walk Down" Option we can unfold the data map in the same way as described for the initial Datamap. Similarly we can walk back up the Datamap using the "Fold/Walk Up" Option.

4.3 HEAD PROPOSITION(S).

The selection of the Head Propositions Option produces a list of Head Propositions and their associated Clause Identifiers in a separate window. The Option may be used to allow the maintenance engineer to inspect the Head Propositions associated with Attributes and identify the Clauses in which they are contained without referring to the Alternative Datamap.

4.4 BODY PROPOSITION(S).

The Body Propositions Option displays the Body Propositions in which a selected Attribute appears and the Clause Identifiers associated with these Propositions. The Option will allow the user to inspect the Propositions contained in the body of a selected Rule, without referring to the Alternative Datamap.

4.5 ROOT PROPOSITION(S).

The Root Propositions Option is similar to the Head Propositions Option except that it returns "NONE" if the selected Attribute can not be linked to a Root Proposition. This Option could be used to determine whether an Attribute, and hence the associated Proposition, is a Root Attribute or Root Proposition.

The Option would also assist the maintenance engineer when determining whether the RB is adequate to establish the information that the application requires by inspecting the Root Propositions. The Root Propositions of the RB must be exhaustive with respect to the possible Values of the Root Attributes required by the task, and must partition the possible Values in the desired way.

Lastly the Root Proposition(s) Option would allow the maintenance engineer to determine whether the RB establishes anything not required. It may be that an Attribute we are not interested in appears as a Root with respect to the RB, in which case we will waste inference in establishing it.

4.6 LEAF PROPOSITION(S).

The Leaf Proposition(s) Option is similar to the Body Proposition(s) Option described above except that the Datamap will return "NONE" if the selected Attribute is not a Leaf Attribute.

This Option would allow the maintenance engineer to determine whether the information required by the RB to establish a desired Propositions can be obtained. By examining the Leaf Propositions the engineer can see whether they are things that the system user can be expected to supply. If they are not, Rules must be added to the RB to unfold them into ascertainable information.

The Option will also be of use in determining whether all Leaf

Unfold/Walk Down
Fold/Walk Up

FIG 5: ALTERNATIVE DATA MAP MENU

Propositions in the KB are required to establish a desired conclusion i.e. some Leaf Proposition may be redundant. This will involve finding all Leaf Propositions who appear only on paths leading to non-desired Root Attributes.

Finally this Option can be used to check for missing branches. The structure of the RB and Class Hierarchy must be such that all Values for Leaf Propositions can be obtained either by direct reference to the the Class Hierarchy or by explicit input by the user i.e. the completion of appropriate forms. If not further Rules may have to be added or maintenance carried out on the Class Hierarchy and/or forms available. In the MAKE application user input is defined through a task description. Linking this to the Datamap automates the finding of missing branches.

4.7 VALUES.

When selected the Values Option is used to display the Values that an Attribute may have by referring to the Propositions in which the Attribute of interest is contained. This Option would also assist in checking that there are no missing branches in the RB as described in the previous Section by allowing the engineer to match possible Attribute Values with the contents of the Class Hierarchy. There may be a possibility of introducing some automation here.

4.8 ENTITIES.

The Entities Option is similar to the Values Option described in the previous Section except that it returns the Entities associated with an individual Attribute, again by reference to the Propositions in which the Attribute is contained.

4.9 DISPLAY RULE.

When carrying out RB maintenance it will eventually be necessary for the engineer to inspect individual Rules as they are represented in the intermediate representation. This is facilitated by the "Display Rule" Option. The Option simply displays an entire Rule, in a separate window, by selecting a Rule Identifier of interest.

A possible use of this Option would be to allow the maintenance engineer to check that individual Rules represent the source data. Using an isomorphic approach to KBS development, as espoused by KANT, individual Rules should represent individual blocks of source, which can be inspected at this point by links established in the analysis phase.

This Option will also allow the maintenance engineer to inspect the "and" and "or" connections in the body of a Rule. Something that is not identifiable by inspection of the Datamap itself.

4.10 DISPLAY CLAUSE.

The Display Clause Option is similar to the previous Option except that all the Clauses that a Rule compiles into are displayed. This may be required during a maintenance session again to allow the maintenance engineer to inspect the affect of the "and" and "or" connections in Rules or simply to examine specific RB Clauses.

5. CONCLUSIONS.

A proto-type Datamap has been in operation on a pilot version of the British Coal KBS which has been developed as part of the MAKE project. This proto-type was of the form of the basic Datamap described in Section 3 and did not display all of the additional facilities described in Section 4. However in this basic form the proto-type Datamap has been demonstrated to all project members and has been very well received. It was generally considered to be a essential maintenance tool and that the additional facilities described here would make it into a very effective tool. We therefore feel that the Datamap would be a useful addition to any KBS toolkit or development methodology.

It should however be noted that redundant Rules or Clauses will not appear in the Datamap and that subsumed Clauses will not be identifiable. Additional tools have been specified as part of the MAKE project to be appended to the Datamapand to allow the maintenance engineer to identify such Rules and Clauses [10]. Finally it should also be noted that the Datamap would also allow for easy identification of cyclic paths, both at the Rule and Clause level, although this is not really an issue in systems built using the MADE methodology.

ACKNOWLEDGEMENTS.

The work described here is being carried out as part of the MAKE Project, supported by the Information Engineering Directorate of the UK Department of Trade and Industry and the UK Science and Engineering Research Council. The project collaborators are ICL, the University of Liverpool and British Coal. In addition, the authors would like to express special thanks to Chris Burton for development and demonstration of the original proto-type Datamap.

APPENDIX (MAKE RB FRAGMENT).

"rootRule"
(manager doesNotComplyWithRegulations is true
iff
(((building notKeptInSafeCondition is true)
or
((building placeWherePersonsWork is true)
and
(building doesNotComplyWithWorkPlaceAccessRule is true)))
when
(manager responsibleForBuilding includes building)))

"workPlaceAccessRule"
(workPlace doesNotComplyWithWorkPlaceAccessRule is true
iff
((workPlace noSafeMeansOfAccessProvided is true)
or
(workPlace safeMeansOfAccessNotMaintained is true)
or
((workPlace height > 10)
and
(workPlace doesNotComplyWithHighWorkPlaceRule is true))))

"highWorkPlaceRule"
(highWorkPlace doesNotComplyWithHighWorkPlaceRule is true
iff
((highWorkPlace noMeansProvidedToEnsureSafety is true)
and
(highWorkPlace reasonForNotProvidingMeansToEnsureSafety
is other)))

REFERENCES.

[1] Bench-Capon, T.J.M. & Coenen.Practical Application of KBS To Law: The Crucial Role of Maintenance in van Noortwijk, C., Schmidt, A.H.J. & Winkels, R.G.F. (Eds) Legal Knowledge Based Systems: Aims for Research and Development, Koninklijke Vermande BV, pp 5-17,1991.

[2] Swanson, E.B. The Dimensions of Maintenance. Proceedings, 2nd International Conference on Software Engineering, IEEE, Oct. 1976.

[3] Rousett, M. On The Consistency of Knowledge Bases: The COVADIS System. Proceedings of ECAI 1988.

[4] Davis, R. Interactive Transfer of Expertise. In Buchannan, B.G. & Shortliffe, E.H. Rule-Based Expert Systems: The MYCIN Experiments of The Stanford Heuristic Programming Project, 1984. Addison-Wesley, 1984.

[5] Routen, T.W. & Bench-Capon, T.J.M. Hierarchical Formalisations. Forthcoming in International Journal of Man-Machine Studies, 1991.

[6] Storrs, G.E. & Burton, C.P. KANT, A Knowledge Analysis Tool. ICL Technical Journal, Vol 6, No 3, May 1989.

[7] Forder, J.M. & Taylor, A.D. The Local Office System. Forthcoming in Bench-Capon, T.J.M. (Ed), Knowledge based Systems for Legal Applications. Academic Press, pp 139-164, 1991.

[8] Bench-Capon, T.J.M. Deep Models, Normative Reasoning and Legal Expert Systems Proceedings of the Second International Conference on AI and Law, Vancouver. ACM Press, 1989.

[9] Bench-Capon, T.J.M. & Forder, J.M. Knowledge Representation for Legal Applications. Forthcoming in Bench-Capon, T.J.M. (Ed), Knowledge based Systems for Legal Applications. Academic Press, pp 245-264, 1991.

[10] Coenen, F. and Bench-Capon, T.J.M. Specification For Redundancy and Subsumption ID Tool. Make Report 3/91, Deliverable D5a[1]. Department of Computer Science, Liverpool University, 1991.

EXPERIENCES WITH SUPER, A DATABASE VISUAL ENVIRONMENT[1]

Annamaria AUDDINO(*), Eric AMIEL(**) and Bharat BHARGAVA(***)

(*) Ecole Polytechnique Fédérale, DI, Laboratoire de Bases de Données - Lausanne, Switzerland
(**) INRIA Rocquencourt - B.P. 105 Le Chesnay Cedex, France
(***) Department of Computer Science - Purdue University - West Lafayette, USA

ABSTRACT

We present our experiences with building SUPER, a database environment based on a structurally object-oriented entity-relationship data model, called ERC+. SUPER is designed to be a semantically rich user-friendly front-end to existing relational or object-oriented database systems. We focus on the functionalities of visual direct manipulation interfaces of SUPER, in particular the schema and the query editors. We motivate and advocate the use of object-oriented toolboxes both to support the multi-threaded event-based dialogue of direct manipulation graphical interfaces and the implementation of data models.

1. INTRODUCTION

User interfaces have evolved from command languages, where the user had a textual, sequential interaction with the computer, to graphical, direct manipulation interfaces, based on the WIMP metaphor (Windows, Icons, Menus, Pointing devices). Human-computer interaction has evolved to a multithreaded dialogue, where multiple, independent tasks are carried out simultaneously by the user. The user can switch among several tasks.

In database management systems (DBMS) the users are still bound to classical textual languages as SQL. However, visual interfaces aim at relieving the user from the syntax of a command language. This implies that some graphical denotations must be adopted to display both the objects being manipulated and the functions that are used to manipulate them on the screen. Graphical data definition interfaces have achieved a large consensus. A number of commercial tools exist, which offer graphical facilities for the definition of a database schema, according to concepts of the entity-relationship (ER) approach [9].

Many prototypes that provide graphical DBMS interfaces have been developed. Some of these support graphical data definition, as [8], Sidereus [1]. DDEW [24] extends the definition process to all phases of database design, providing an integrated environment from user requirements to physical design. Several tools provide both schema definition and visual query facilities: ISIS [14], SNAP [5], [24], Pasta-3 [16, 17]. Tools have been developed as query editors, using the the visual representation of a database for formulating queries: GUIDE [30], [13], QBD [7], [11].

Many DBMS interaction tools have a restricted view of the direct manipulation paradigm [27]. Some DBMS visual interfaces only provide the user with a language that is a visual translation of textual languages [14]. Some interfaces constrain the user's behavior, preventing him/her to store incomplete definitions of database schema or queries [8]. SNAP and Pasta-3 provide the user with flexibility both in schema definition and manipulation.
Second, since many research prototypes are based on either entity-relationship, or semantic, or object-oriented data models, they should base the data manipulation on the same schema representation as the one used at schema definition time, as suggested in [5, 13]. However, only some prototypes provide data manipulation facilities close to those defined for relational databases. Others present the results of user queries as relational tuples rather than as objects of the data model [7, 13]. As the user is not provided with the same level of abstraction of database schema representation, there is a lack of consistency. Multiple representations of the data, that is being manipulated, are often neither equivalent nor simultaneously displayed [14]. The global view of manipulated data is partitioned into complementary representations [17].

The user has to enter a specific mode to display and manipulate them [1, 24]. Finally, several existing prototypes do not provide an environment for supporting both database design and manipulation. Several visual query editors manipulate a database schema defined through textual languages. Some do not let the user update the database. Moreover, database design is often limited to a schema editor.

Some of these limitations and concerns are being dealt with in the system we are currently developing, called SUPER[2]. It is a comprehensive user environment for database interactions based on the ERC+ model [21, 22], an extended entity-relationship (ER) model for the support of complex objects. This environment [3] is based on direct manipulation, providing users with maximal flexibility during schema definition as well as query formulation. We have taken simplicity and minimality as guidelines. The environment consists of a graphical schema definition and manipulation interface, a view definition tool and a view integration tool.
To implement our visual environment and the ERC+ data model, we chose to use toolboxes [2, 18]. The toolbox approach is not only a good software engineering approach, but also particularly well-suited for implementing visual direct manipulation interfaces as well as the data models. The toolbox approach has been shown to provide both low-level extensibility of database systems and support for user-friendly database environment.

In section 2, we present a brief overview of the SUPER environment model and its main features. In section 3, we present the visual interfaces currently specified and developed, the schema editor and the query editor. Section 4 shows why and how we used toolboxes to implement the ERC+ data model and to support the direct manipulation paradigm of the interfaces. Finally, we present the future and ongoing extensions.

2. THE SUPER ENVIRONMENT

2.1 An Overview of the ERC+ Model

ERC+ is an extended entity-relationship model [21, 22], specifically designed to support complex objects and object identity. Object types may bear any number of attributes, which may in turn, recursively, be composed of other attributes. The structure of an object type may thus be regarded as a multiple attribute tree. Attributes, entities and relationships may be valued in a multiset (i.e. not excluding duplicates). An object identity is associated to entities and relationships, i.e. different instances may have exactly the same values for all their attributes. Two generalization relationships are supported on entities: the classical "is-a" and an additional "may-be-a" relationships [28]. The former corresponds to the well-known generalization concept; the latter has the same semantics, except it does not require an inclusion dependency between the subtype and the type extensions.
Moreover, formal manipulation languages (an algebra [21] and an equivalent calculus [23]) have been defined. The ERC+ algebra is a set of 10 primitive operators. Each operator manipulates one (or more) entity type(s) and returns as result an entity type.

Figure 1 shows a sample ERC+ schema. Rectangles represent entity types. Diamond boxes represent relationship types. Attributes are represented as names attached to the parent object by a line. Links are represented as lines connecting an entity type and a relationship type. A single continuous line is used to represent a 1:1 cardinality, a single dotted line represents a 0:1

---

[1] This work was performed while prof. Bhargava was visiting EPFL

[2] this research is supported by the Fonds National de la Recherche Scientifique Suisse

cardinality, a double dotted line represents a 0:n cardinality, a double line (once dotted, once continuous) represents a 1:n cardinality. Arrows represent generalizations.

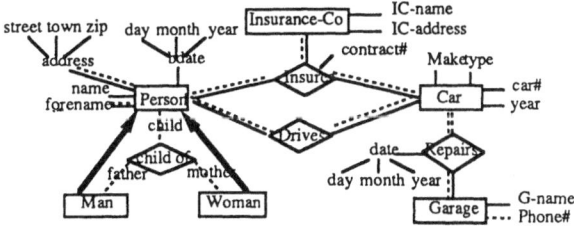

Figure 1: a sample ERC+ schema

We now highlight the characteristics of the ERC+ model that facilitate the modelling of database objects. Atomic objects are directly represented in an ERC+ database as entities, irrespective of the attribute structure. Attribute complexity and multivaluation express the usual product and set constructs of the object-oriented approach, with the advantage that they may simultaneously apply at the same node. Composite complex objects can be represented by a "main" entity type linked to its components (represented as other entity types) by relationships types bearing the semantic interpretation of "is composed of", "is component of", and so on. ERC+ does not associate specific methods to specific objects. According to [12], ERC+ might be defined as a structurally object-oriented model.

2.2 SUPER's Main Features

The SUPER environment takes advantage of ERC+ powerful semantic modelling capacities and stresses comprehensiveness and intuitiveness above all. SUPER is thus targetted to be a front-end to a relational or an object-oriented database.

One of its main features is to present a global view of user/database interaction. The same interaction paradigms are used for all user's dialogs with the different components of the database management system during both design and operation on the database. Interaction styles are consistent over the various functions and editors.
Beside schema editing and querying facilities, SUPER provides advanced features to assist users during all phases of database design and operation. For example, the interfaces are responsible for checking user actions and ensuring the desired level of consistency.

Other important features are *flexibility*, *reusability* and *backtracking*. Flexibility allows each user to follow his/her own strategy: users are not forced to follow a predefined sequence of actions. Whenever actions are not atomic, users are allowed to start some action and move to another one without being required to complete the first one. For example, during schema design process, users are allowed to leave object definitions incomplete. During query formulation process the user is allowed to independently specify the different components of a query and modify them at any time. As far as reusability is concerned, users are allowed to reuse definitions of objects already known to the system. This is useful both in schema design and manipulation. Users may need to reuse existing definitions either in the current schema or in another one. An already evaluated query may be reused to build a very similar one. Finally, the user may at any time undo erroneous actions and restore the previous state.

Our environment is also appropriate for several categories of users. The direct manipulation of ERC+ diagrams (cf. section 2.3), both in the design and operation phase, is attractive for novice or occasional users. Such users need basic functionalities reachable through easy-to-understand graphical displays. Expert users can define schemas and query them via menus and dialog boxes. Our interfaces provide several, equivalent ways to perform the same action depending on the users' level of expertise.

2.3 SUPER's Direct Manipulation Visual Interfaces

We have chosen the direct manipulation paradigm, where the user shows what to do by "grabbing" and manipulating visual representations of objects. Direct manipulation is nowadays a de facto standard for graphical, bit-mapped workstations with a multiwindowing system and a mouse. The

advantages of this approach are: first, users permanently see the information they work on (for instance, the schema diagram). Secondly, users immediately see the impact of their actions through the visual representation. Finally, users can perform intuitive physical actions (like selecting and dragging an object) to modify the graphical representation, or activate dedicated functions (through menus, labelled buttons, dialog boxes, etc.) to manipulate application objects.

Our interfaces avoid using different modes of operation, or different dialog styles, when going from one function to the other. For instance, data manipulation is based on the same schema representation as the one used at schema definition time [5, 7, 11, 13, 14, 30].

The SUPER environment consists of the following four visual tools:
- The **schema editor** is a visual data definition interface allowing designers to build an ERC+ schema and supporting two modes of interaction.
- The **query editor** is an editor that provides the user with direct and visual manipulation facilities for the specification of queries and updates.
- The **view definition tool** provides the user with an interface allowing to build views over an existing database schema. This tool gives the user the possibility to define his/her view by reusing existing definitions.
- The **view integration tool** provides an interface allowing the user to build an integrated schema from a set of user views without modifying them. This tool, which is yet to be implemented, will use the correspondences existing among the views for solving in an automatic way the conflicts arising from different representations of the same informations.

Each of these tools presents two layers: an **external** layer, dealing with user interaction, and an **internal** layer, manipulating the logical, in-memory representation of the objects visible at the interface level.

SUPER ENVIRONMENT

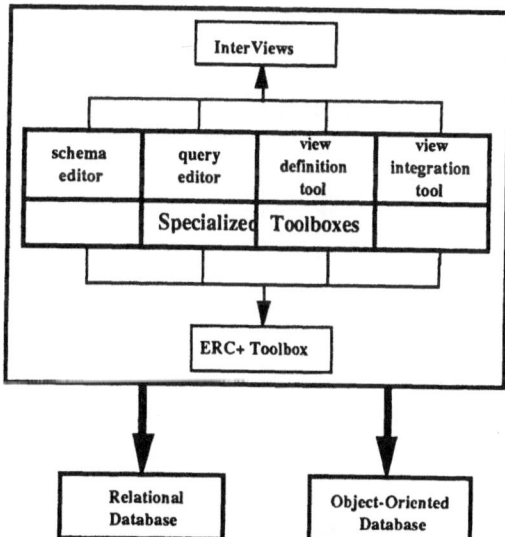

Figure 2: The SUPER Environment

Figure 2 shows the architecture of the final environment. The ERC+ toolbox [2] is independent from any particular application. It is the kernel of the internal layer of each tool. The ERC+ toolbox is specialized into a set of toolboxes, each one associated to a particular tool. Classes in these toolboxes add the properties and the behavior specific to the tool. For instance, classes in the Schema Editor toolbox will bear all the informations concerning the edition status of an object (e.g. *selected, modifying, valid,* etc.) and will have methods that make specific checks.
InterViews [18] is the graphic toolbox used for building the objects that compose the external layer of a tool, i.e. the general graphic tools (windows, menus, palettes, etc.) and visual representations of logical object.

174

3. VISUAL INTERFACES

3.1 The Schema Editor Interface

The schema editor provides two modes of operations for the schema definition. Each mode has a separate window. The **graphical** mode allows direct building of ERC+ diagrams by picking graphical symbols from a palette (corresponding to ERC+ constructs) and positioning them into the workspace provided in the associated window. With the **alphanumeric** mode, users may define schema objects by entering textual definitions through forms (called **object boxes**). Different object boxes correspond to the different ERC+ constructs (four object boxes may be seen in figure 3).

There is no notion of "mode switch", as users may freely go from one mode to the other, any time during the interaction. Users may also decide to work in only one mode (with the other window closed). The two modes are equivalent and the schema editor keeps them synchronized: all visible representations of the same object are automatically updated when users modify the object's definition. For instance, when the name of an object gets modified in an alphanumeric object box, the new name immediately replaces the old one in the diagram.

The creation of an object activates the display of the corresponding object box. An object box contains text entry areas (for entering object's name and comment), radio buttons for predefined choices (cardinality specification, for instance) and list-bars referring to objects directly attached to the current object.
The entity box (InsuranceCo) in figure 3 shows list-bars for attributes, links and generalizations defined on an entity type. A list-bar for components of a complex attribute is included in the attribute box (address). List-bars have been chosen as a standard technique to link objects. Clicking on a list-bar displays the corresponding scrollable list of linked objects. The lists group objects of the same type, linked to the same parent element (which is the schema for dictionary lists). Clicking on an object in a list displays its object box. Clicking on the New button in the list box displays an empty object box for adding a new object to the list. Using object boxes, list-bars and the attached lists, users may navigate through the schema and add or modify objects as they want. Top-down definition strategies are easily performed.

Incomplete definitions of objects are allowed for flexibility. Users may, for instance, define entity types and relationship types, and attach attributes or add generalizations later. Each user may follow his/her own strategy.

Incomplete schema definitions may be saved and reused in another session. At any time, a validation function may be activated to check whether the actual schema definition is consistent with the rules of their model. If inconsistencies or incompleteness are detected, they are reported to the user. As the editor keeps track of what has been validated (and is still valid), users may easily identify which definitions have to be refined to correct their schema.
Some model rules have to be permanently enforced (uniqueness of entity names, for instance) in order to avoid ambiguities. These rules are enforced at the ERC+ kernel level, as discussed in section 4. The default names that are provided by the system are always unique.

Reusability implies whether the object definition is to be reused in the current schema or in another schema. *Cut, copy* and *paste* operations may be used to move an object (i.e. disconnect and connect elsewhere), delete, or create a similar object elsewhere (if needed, because of uniqueness rule, the name of the object is automatically updated). The object may be a single object (an entity type, an attribute, etc.), or a collection of objects (e.g., a set of attributes may be copied from various existing objects and attached to an entity type). An object can be a subschema (a set of entities, relationships, links and generalizations where the latter two must include the objects they link). A *duplicate* operation creates an object which is identical to the original one, with the same links but with a different name.

The schema editor supports backtracking using *undo* and *redo* operations. Typically, if a user clicks on a Cancel button instead of the nearby OK button, all actions performed on the object would be lost. By undoing the erroneous click, he/she will get a second chance.

The alphanumeric mode allows schema browsing by navigation from one object to another through existing links. This navigation may use object boxes (as shown in figure 3) to allow users to see all informations about the objects on the path. A similar navigation may also be performed using a simultaneous display of the various dictionary lists. The only information provided to users in such a navigation are the names of the objects. To know more about a specific object, users have to click on its entry in the appropriate list to activate its object box. The information contained in the object box is then only available for inspection, to prevent conflicts between different actions on the same object.

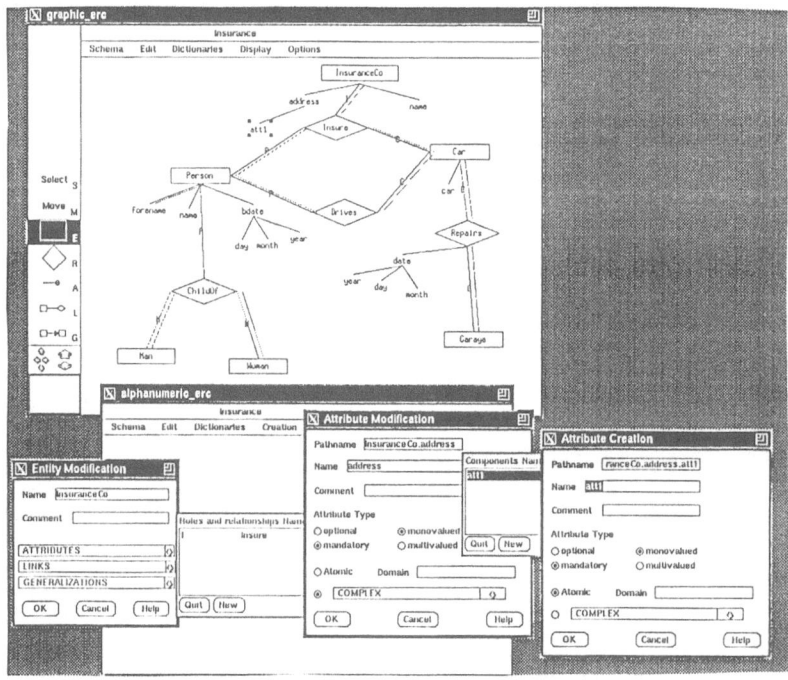

Figure 3: a screen display showing schema editor windows
(after creation of a new attribute, whose default name is att1)

Comparison with existing schema editors

The schema editor is based on simple graphic representations. We believe that basic ER symbols are easy to understand by the users. The use of "nicer" symbols as icons [15] or patterns [14] is not always effective for immediate understanding. Databases with a large number of object types require the users to memorize a large number of different symbols. Some schema editors use other representations, as in Pasta-3 [17], which characterizes the type of nodes by using a different character style instead of different graphic symbols.

The alphanumeric and graphical representations of our editor are different ways to display the overall schema. Both can be used to display all available informations about the schema. Some schema editors (as SNAP [5] and Pasta-3) do not introduce a notion of mode switch for manipulating the schema objects through different levels of detail (e.g. an entity and its attributes). Some prototypes use different representations for objects and their properties. These representations are neither equivalent nor simultaneously displayed. For instance, in Sidereus [1], a user has to enter a graphical environment to specify classes and relationships and a textual environment to specify their properties. The ER graph and the inheritance lattice used in Pasta-3 are complementary but not equivalent representations of the global schema.

3.2 The Query Editor

Our system includes an editor for graphical specification of queries and updates. We have chosen a multistep structure, as clear separation between the steps alleviates users' mental load and improves the chances of correct formulation. Users can any time modify any stated part of the query to correct or refine the current formulation. This allows users to follow their own strategy. The steps which compose the process of query formulation are:

- **Selecting the query subschema**: the portion relevant to the query is extracted from the database schema.
- **Restructuring the query subschema**: the subschema is transformed into a different structure (hierarchical in our case).
- **Specifying predicates**: predicates are stated to select only relevant data.
- **Formatting the output**: the editor is provided with data items that are to be included into the structure of the result.
- **Displaying resulting data.**

Selecting the query subschema

This step configures the schema to contain only those objects which are involved in the query. The diagram corresponding to a schema is displayed in a read-only window, called the **database schema** (DBS) window. The query subschema is extracted through a sequence of "point and click" selections on objects in the diagram. Clicks copy the designated objects into a second window, called the **working schema** (WS) window. Some automatic selection is embedded in our system. A click on a relationship type will copy the participating entity types and roles. Objects are copied with their attributes. If necessary, the users may later pick additional objects from the DBS window. Figure 4 shows the WS window for expressing the simple query "select name and address of people who insure a 1984 Ford" on the schema of figure 1.

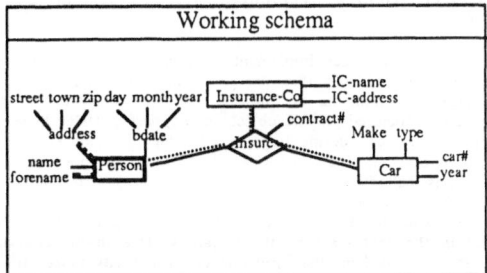

Figure 4: Working schema window after objects selection

Restructuring query subschema

Many interfaces require the subschema to be transformed into a specific structure. For instance, in [13] the query subschema is transformed into a

hierarchical structure. In our editor, the user identifies the root of the query hierarchy. The user explicitly disconnects a link to break a possible cycle. The designated link is detached from the linked entity type and attached to a copy of that entity type. The user can use pruning to remove unnecessary objects, i.e. objects which appear neither in the format of the result nor in a predicate. The resulting hierarchy is transformed into a single entity type with all other informations as attributes. This structure is displayed in a third window, called the **selection window** (SW). The user may go back to the working schema window to modify the query subschema if it is necessary.

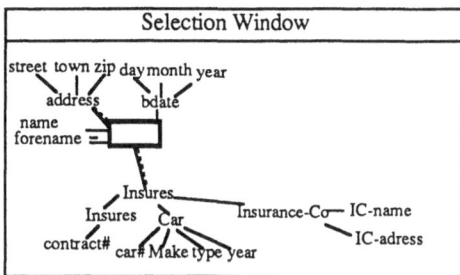

Figure 5: Transformed hierarchical structure (root is an empty box) before pruning unnecessary objects in the working schema window

Specifying predicates

Once the user has built the desired final entity type in the selection window, he/she proceeds with the specification of predicates. Predicates are expressed on the hierarchical structure resulting from restructuring. A predicate is any logical expression involving attributes of the final entity type. Predicates are expressed by using a **predicate box** associated to the root of the hierarchy. Sub-predicates are automatically generated when the user designates the attributes involved in the predicate. By default, the equality operator is used for clauses and the existential quantifier is assumed for multivalued attributes. The use of several variables associated to the same attribute is graphically achieved by the duplication of the attribute. Evaluation of the predicates can be done in any order. Each intermediate step builds a potential query that can be interpreted and executed in the fourth window.

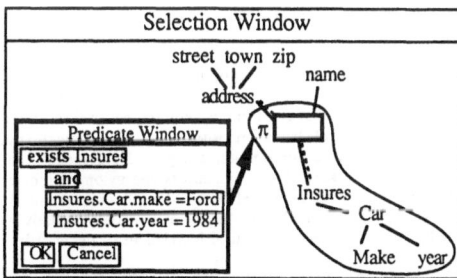

Figure 6: final state of the selection window after the specification of the predicates

Formatting the output and displaying resulting data

Some attributes of the resulting entity type in the selection window may have been kept because of some predicates defined on them. The selection window provides a *hide* (or, conversely, *show*) operator to define which attributes are to be discarded (or kept in). The last phase displays the instances, result from the query. Resulting entities are displayed according to their hierarchical structure in the **result window** (RW).

Comparison with existing query editors

We believe that visual interfaces should be based on an assertional approach rather than a procedural one that is typical of textual languages. In some query editors [11] queries are specified as a sequence of operators that transform the query subschema into a new one at each step. The multistep structure of our editor provides the user with flexibility. The different components of a query can be independently specified. They can be modified at any time for either error correction or refinements.

We provide the user with simple and powerful techniques, that avoid ambiguities. The point and click technique used for extracting the query subschema is a natural way to specify pertinent objects. Sophisticated techniques as in QBD [7] may confuse the user. Our hierarchical restructuring of a query is consistent with the ERC+ algebra, where the result of a query is an entity. The explicit disconnection of a link leads to an unambiguous interpretation of the hierarchical structure.

Several existing query editors do not allow the use of a graphical formalism for expressing predicates. Some interfaces use fill-in forms as gql/ER [31] or are based on menus for syntactic editing [13]. We tried to use a graphical formalism and an automatic generation of the predicate based on user's graphical manipulations.

Many interfaces lack the consistency in the representation of the query results. These results are often represented in a tabular form [25]. The user thus looses the level of abstraction provided by the data model, as he/she does not see the results as instances of items belonging to this model.

4. TOOLBOX FOR OBJECT CREATION AND MANIPULATION

4.1 Using Object-Oriented Toolboxes

The internal layer of our environment has to create and manipulate the logical, in-memory representation of the objects visible at the interface level. These objects include ERC+ objects such as entities, relationships, attributes, as well as interface objects such as object boxes and diagrams. In the development of the SUPER environment, we have used a toolbox approach to manipulate these in-memory representations. To implement the ERC+ objects we developed a toolbox [2], whereas an existing toolbox, InterViews [18] from Stanford University, was used to implement interface objects. We chose a toolbox approach (TA) for four reasons.

· TA helps reducing the impedance mismatch between the user interface paradigm and the programming language
Given a proper interface, toolboxes can support the direct manipulation paradigm of user interfaces, reducing the impedance mismatch between this paradigm and the programming language. The toolbox gives the system implementor total freedom to do things in any order he/she prefers. In section 4.3, we will show that, using the toolbox, a programmer can build a schema exactly as he/she would do using the direct manipulation graphical interface.

· TA is well suited for data model implementation
The toolbox approach is based on the analysis of the domain to implement for extracting the objects that constitute it, with respect to their structure and behavior. The theoretical basis on which any data model should lie encompasses such a need for domain analysis. Data models constitute domains that are built "after" their components and axioms are determined. This is not the case with empirical domains such as user interfaces or programming languages. Domain analysis for data models is nearly trivial as it can usually draw upon the mathematical foundations of the models.

· TA provides for extensibility
Extensibility is natural to the toolbox approach that might be limited to providing new tools. Object-oriented programming languages (OOPL) are best suited to implement toolboxes as they concentrate on finding and analyzing objects of a given domain and providing them with suitable methods as their interface to the outside world. OOPLs provide support for the consistency preservation requirement through the encapsulation paradigm. Inheritance and dynamic binding allow toolboxes to be easily customized and reused. This is also a natural way to address DBMS extensibility that is needed to cope with the diversity of emerging database application domains and to minimize the cost of DBMS customization. Many object-oriented database systems (like EXODUS [6], Starburst [26], GENESIS [4]) address the problem of functionalities (modular and layered architecture) which offers high-level support for extensibility; software development techniques and programming languages that provide low-level support for extensibility are needed.

· TA helps Software Engineering
Besides extensibility and reusability that are well-known properties of object-orientation, another advantage we observed is, as mentioned by [20]: "(object-oriented development) allows for bottom-up and to some extent non-hierarchic development". Indeed, the development of the interface,

which heavily uses the toolbox, took place even while the toolbox was being implemented.

Although supporting the direct manipulation paradigm enhances the intuitiveness of the use of the toolbox by upper layers implementors, it challenges the toolbox consistency requirement, as freedom without control is anarchy. To design the toolbox, we identified four requirements that can serve as guidelines or metrics in designing or evaluating a toolbox :

- **Completeness:** a toolbox should provide all the tools that will ever be needed by its clients.
- **Orthogonality:** a toolbox should avoid functional overlapping of its tools and even more, code redundancy.
- **Consistency preservation:** a toolbox should not provide ill-mannered tools that could violate the consistency of the domain.
- **Intuitiveness:** a toolbox should provide tools whose function corresponds to the usual perception of the domain and how it is manipulated.

These requirements are independent of the needs of a particular application that would use the toolbox. The intuitiveness requirement is "users' perception"-dependent and may be considered as a meta-knowledge on the domain. The first three requirements constitute the intra-domain specification of the toolbox, while intuitiveness is a meta-domain specification. Some of these requirements may be contradictory to some extent, particularly orthogonality and consistency preservation on one side and intuitiveness on the other. The common manipulation of a domain may include non-orthogonal (e.g. square and multiplication) or unsafe (division without zero check) tools.

A priori domain analysis encountered when dealing with data models ensures intuitiveness, as the perception of the data model, its components, axioms and operations are pre-defined explicitly. Proper naming, for instance, is trivially achievable by following the data model's nomenclature. The completeness of the querying operators is ensured if the algebra is complete. The fact that consistency, completeness and intuitiveness are well defined by the ERC+ model, allowed the toolbox interface to remain unchanged and made the concurrent development possible.

Another guideline for building a toolbox has been presented in [19]. Each kind of tools is responsible for a different kind of tasks:

- **constructors:** for creating new objects of the domain;
- **observers:** for giving information about objects of the domain;
- **modifiers:** for modifying objects of the domain;
- **iterators:** for yielding, one at a time, components of objects of the domain.

This division of responsibilities ensures a minimum of orthogonality, and isolates the potential trouble-makers, modifiers, that are the only tools allowed to have side-effects. This facilitates the debugging process. Moreover, it offers the client a consistent and intuitive interface to the domain, and decreases the misunderstandings over specifications that have always been a source of errors in structured development.

4.2 Object-Oriented Toolboxes for Implementing Visual Interfaces

ERC+ interface has been implemented through the use of InterViews, a library of C++ classes that provides basic interactive objects and composition mechanisms to build a complex interface. In addition, manipulable structured graphic objects are supported. Using these classes, the implementor can define large manipulable diagrams such as ERC+ schemas. A diagram object in ERC+ schema is the composition of several basic objects (called *pictures*). For instance, an entity is the composition of a rectangle and a label. These composed objects maintain a state. All functions needed for dragging, zooming, rotating, etc. a graphic object are defined in the root class of the hierarchy. Due to object-orientation inheritance mechanism, the implementor only needs to redefine these functions only if a particular behavior is needed.

As all interface objects are instances of C++ classes, the interface programmer does not have to call directly the underlying window manager. The modification of the behavior of one object does not affect the rest of the interface. On one side, we are not constrained to follow a predefined "look and feel" for the interface. On the other, all basic objects that usually compose an interface are provided by the toolkit.

We have extensively used the mechanism of *subjects* and *views* provided by InterViews. Subjects are the objects manipulated at the internal level (for instance, the logical representation of an entity type provided by the ERC+ toolbox). Views are their visual representations. In our environment, we need to simultaneously display several visual representations of the same logical object. InterViews allows to associate a list of visual representations for each subject. When the user modifies an object through one of its visual representations, the corresponding update function on the subject is triggered. The subject notifies all its views that a modification has taken place, so that they can update their state and appearance according to the subject's new state. This allowed us to implement the synchronization between all the visual representations of ERC+ objects.

Finally, the object-orientation of InterViews provides the support for representing the event-driven dialogue of direct manipulation interfaces. Each component of an interface is an object that can be viewed as an agent that can receive events and send messages to other components of the interface. That allowed us to implement the **multiagent** model, an architectural abstraction of human-computer interaction [10]. The facility for implementing event-driven dialogue allowed the implementation of an interface allowing unconstrained user's behavior. As each component of the interface is an independent agent, the sequencing of events is reduced to a minimal. An user's action is seen as an interaction with one agent. The user is not compelled to complete an action as other actions (other agents) are active.

4.3 The ERC+ Toolbox

This section gives an overview of the ERC+ toolbox design and interface to upper layers. Like InterViews, the ERC+ toolbox is a C++ class library providing the four abstractions of the ERC+ model: entity, relationship, attribute types and schemas with operations on them. The operations include creation, attaching attributes to entities, linking entities to relationships, etc.. The interface of class relationship_type is presented below as an example of what is provided to the upper layers implementors :

```
class relationship_type: public ....
{
public:
// constructors
    relationship_type(char* a_name, char* a_comment = NULL);
// modifiers
    bool      attach(entity_type&, cardinality, char* a_role);
    bool      detach(entity_type&, char* a_role);
    bool      attach(attribute_type&);
    bool      detach(attribute_type&);
// observers
    attribute_type*  get_attribute(pathname);
    shared_set       get_attributes();
    shared_set       get_links();
    shared_set       get_entities();
    entity_type*     get_entity(char* a_role);
    virtual bool operator==(element&);
    // definition needed to implement denomination axioms
// iterators
    attribute_type*  init_attribute();
    attribute_type*  next_attribute();
    entity_type*     init_entity();
    entity_type*     next_entity();
    link_type*       init_link();
    link_type*       next_link();
};
```

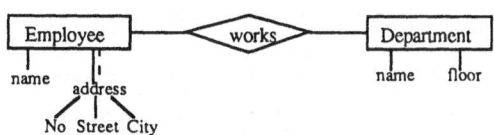

Figure 7: example of an ERC+ schema

Below is an example of how to build the schema shown in figure 7 using the ERC+ toolbox :

```
ERC_schema mall ("Mall");
entity_type employee ("Employee");
simple_attribute_type nameE ("Name", string_dom, cardinality()).
```

```
complex_attribute_type address ("Address", no_dom, cardinality(1)).
simple_attribute_type no ("No", int_dom, cardinality());
simple_attribute_type street ("Street", string_dom, cardinality());
simple_attribute_type city ("City", string_dom, cardinality());
address.attach (no);
address.attach (street);
address.attach (city);                  // homogeneous handling
employee.attach (nameE);                // of attributes
employee.attach (address);
entity_type department ("Department");
simple_attribute_type nameD ("Name", string_dom, cardinality());
department.attach (nameD);
relationship_type works ("Works");
mall.insert (employee);                 // attributes
mall.insert (department);               // are inserted
mall.insert (works);                    // automatically
works.link(employee, cardinality());
// default role: Employee
works.link(department, cardinality(1));
// default role: Department
```

We note that building a schema using the toolbox matches the direct manipulation paradigm required by our environment.

Enforcing Consistency through Encapsulation

In the ERC+ data model, the consistency preservation means enforcing denomination axioms and the structural invariants between objects. For example, adding an attribute to an entity also registers the attribute as belonging to the entity's schema. The consistency is enforced using the C++ constructor mechanism which allows for the control and enforcement of the initialization. For example:

```
entity_type a_relation("Name of the entity");
```

is the good way to create an entity. Denomination axioms are further preserved by making the objects structure protected. Thus, consistency can be checked inside the modifiers which all return a boolean indicating whether they succeeded or failed due to the consistency violation. For example:

```
an_entity.attach(an_attribute);
```

is the good way to add an attribute to an entity and fails if an_entity already has an attribute with the same name as an_attribute.

But modifiers are not the only way to access the internals of an object. The observers must also be careful not to yield the real structure of the objects. For example, our observers return shared sets, sets that only share their members with the real sets. Thus the user has access to the actual members, but not to the actual sets and thus will not be able to directly insert a member, as in:

```
an_entity.get_attributes().insert(an_attribute);
```

The other aspect of validity, connectivity, does not apply at every step of schema building and thus is not invariant across schema definition operations as consistency is. The toolbox may only provide a boolean observer valid for class ERC_schema.

Achieving Intuitiveness While Preserving Consistency

In order to reduce the impedance mismatch between the direct manipulation paradigm of the user interface and the programming language, the user should be able to create a schema as he/she would draw it. Moreover, intuitiveness means that the user is provided with expressive power and flexibility. Insertion into a schema illustrates these points. Intuitively, only entities and relationships need to be explicitly inserted into a schema: their attributes and links should be inserted transparently at the same time. Explicit insertion of attributes could lead to orphan attributes that are yet in a schema. For example, a schema named Company containing an entity Employee with an attribute Name should be definable in any of the following ways (assuming variables for employee, name and company have already been defined):

```
employee.attach(name);
company.insert(employee);
```
or:
```
company.insert(employee);
employee.attach(name);
```

The final state should be the same with both employee and name having company as their schema and company containing employee and name in its entity and attribute types sets. This kind of flexibility is paid by greater complexity, as consistency must still be preserved without any assumptions on the order things will get done. But it is worth the effort as the toolbox users have less preconditions and special cases to watch for. They are less likely to do things the wrong way because any way is good. Nevertheless, linking an entity to a relationship requires both objects to belong to the same schema, thus they must be inserted before they are linked.

5. CONCLUSIONS AND FUTURE WORKS

In this paper we have presented experiences with building SUPER, a comprehensive database user environment using the ERC+ data model. SUPER is intended to be a semantical front-end environment to existing relational or object-oriented database systems. It is based on the direct manipulation of objects and functions. Users are provided with the maximal flexibility to follow their own strategy for schema definition as well as for query formulation. The graphical interactions are simple but powerful. The visual interfaces support multiple interaction styles, well-suited for various categories of users. Data manipulation is assertional and object-based. The interaction styles are consistent over the various functions and editors.

We have focused mostly on the external layers, the visual direct manipulation interfaces and their support by the innermost layers and the toolboxes. The schema and query editor have been analyzed, with a focus on functionalities and the underlying design choices. Finally, we have shown the suitability of toolboxes to implement the data models and to support the direct manipulation paradigm.

The schema editor has been implemented in C++, in a UNIX environment complemented with the user interface toolbox InterViews. The schema editor code is about 13,000 lines of code. The ERC+ toolbox code is about 6,000 lines of code. It runs on Sun (3 and 4) workstations. The development took 24 man/months, in a team of six persons. The query editor is currently being implemented.

The next step concerns the specification of a view definition graphical facility. Its first goal will be to allow users to define views over an existing schema. We intend to develop a similar interface for definition of views in the initial phase of database design, as a formal way to express user requirements. These views will be used as input to an integration tool, which will automatically perform their integration according to explicitly defined interview correspondences [29]. Finally, we intend to define tools to cover the other phases of the database design process.

ACKNOWLEDGEMENTS

The authors wish to thank prof. S. Spaccapietra and all the people that worked and are working at the Database Laboratory of the EPFL for the specification and implementation of the SUPER project, A. Aimar, Y. Dennebouy, Y. Dupont, E. Fontana, M. Gentile, Z. Tari and L. Tieche.

REFERENCES

[1] A. Albano, L. Alfò, S. Coluccini, R. Orsini: "An Overview of Sidereus, a Graphical Database Schema Editor for Galileo", in *Advances in Database Technology - EDBT '88*, J. W. Schmidt, S. Ceri, M. Missikof eds., pp. 567-571, Springer-Verlag, 1988

[2] E. Amiel: "Object-Oriented Programming for Data Model Implementation", in *Data Management - Current Trends*, N. Prakash ed., pp. 223-243, Tata McGraw-Hill, 1990

[3] A. Auddino, Y. Dennebouy, Y. Dupont, E. Fontana, S. Spaccapietra, Z. Tari: "SUPER: A Comprehensive Approach to DBMS Visual User Interfaces", to appear in *Proc. of the 2nd Working Conference on Visual Database Systems*, Budapest, 1991

[4] D. S. Batory et al.: "GENESIS: An Extensible Database Management System", *IEEE Transactions on Software Engineering*, vol. 14, no. 11, pp. 1711-1730, November 1988

[5] D. Bryce, R. Hull: "SNAP, a Graphics-Based Schema Manager", in *Proc. of the 2nd IEEE Int'l Conf. on Data Engineering*, pp. 151-164, Los Angeles, 1986

[6] M. Carey et al.: "The Architecture of the EXODUS Extensible DBMS", in *Proc. Int'l Workshop on Object-Oriented Database Systems*, pp. 52-65, 1986

[7] T. Catarci, G. Santucci: "Query by Diagram: A Graphic Query System", in *Proceedings of the 7th Int'l Conf. on Entity-Relationship Approach*, pp. 157-174, Rome, 1988

[8] E. Chan, F. Lochovsky: "A Graphical Database Design Aid Using the Entity-Relationship Model", in *Entity-Relationship Approach to Systems Analysis and Design*, pp. 259-310, North-Holland, 1980

[9] P. P. Chen: "The Entity-Relationship Model - Towards a Unified View of Data", *ACM Transactions on Database Systems*, vol. 1, no. 1, pp. 9-36, March 1976

[10] J. Coutaz: "Architecture Models for Interactive Software: Failures and Trends", in *Proc. of the IFIP WG 2.7 Conference Engineering for Human-Computer Interaction*, Napa Valley, 1989

[11] B. Czejdo, R. Elmasri, D. W. Embley, M. Rusinkiewicz: "A Graphical Data Manipulation Language for an Extended Entity-Relationship Model", *IEEE Computer*, vol. 23, no. 3, pp. 26-36, March 1990

[12] K. R. Dittrich: "Object-Oriented Database Systems", in *Entity-Relationship Approach - Ten Years of Experience in Information Modeling*, S. Spaccapietra ed., pp. 51-66, North-Holland, 1987

[13] R. A. Elmasri, J. A. Larson: "A Graphical Query Facility for ER Databases", in *Entity-Relationship Approach - The Use of ER Concept in Knowledge Representation*, P. P. Chen ed., pp. 236-245, North-Holland, 1985

[14] K. J. Goldman, S. A. Goldman, P. C. Kanellakis, S. B. Zdonik: "ISIS, Interface for a Semantic Information System", in *Proc. of ACM SIGMOD '85, Int'l Conf. on Management of Data*, pp. 328-342, Austin, 1985

[15] I. P. Groette, E. G. Nilsson: "SICON, an Iconic Presentation Module for an E-R Database", in *Proc. of the 7th Int'l Conf. on Entity-Relationship Approach*, pp. 137-155, Rome, 1988

[16] M. Kuntz, R. Melchert: "Pasta-3's Graphical Query Language: Direct Manipulation, Cooperative Queries, Full Expressive Power", in *Proc. of the 15th Int'l Conf. on Very Large Data Bases*, pp. 97-105, Amsterdam, 1989

[17] M. Kuntz, R. Melchert: "Ergonomic Schema Design and Browsing with More Semantics in the Pasta-3 Interface for E-R DBMSs", in *Entity-Relationship Approach to Database Design and Querying*, F. Lochovsky ed., North-Holland, 1990

[18] M. A. Linton, J. M. Vlissides, P. R. Calder: "Composing User Interfaces with InterViews", *IEEE Computer*, vol. 22, no. 2, pp. 8-22, February 1989

[19] B. Liskov, J. Guttag: *Abstraction and Specification in Program Development*, MIT Press/Mc Graw Hill, 1986

[20] P. H. Loy: "A Comparison of Object-Oriented and Structured Development Methods", *ACM SIGSOFT*, January 1990

[21] C. Parent, S. Spaccapietra: "An Algebra for a General Entity-Relationship Model", *IEEE Transactions on Software Engineering*, vol. 11, no. 7, pp. 634-643, July 1985

[22] C. Parent, S. Spaccapietra: "About Complex Entities, Complex Objects and Object-Oriented Data Models", in *Information Systems Concepts - An In-depth Analysis*, E. D. Falkenberg, P. Lindgreen eds., pp. 347-360, North-Holland, 1989

[23] C. Parent, H. Rolin, K. Yétongnon, S. Spaccapietra: "An ER Calculus for the Entity-Relationship Complex Model", in *Entity-Relationship Approach to Database Design and Querying*, F. Lochovsky ed., North-Holland, 1990

[24] D. Reiner et al.: "A Database Designer's Workbench", in *Entity-Relationship Approach - Ten Years of Experience in Information Modeling*, S. Spaccapietra ed., pp. 347-360, North-Holland, 1987

[25] T. R. Rogers, R. G. G. Cattell: "Entity-Relationship Database User Interfaces", in *Proc. of the 6th Int'l Conf. on Entity-Relationship Approach*, pp. 323-335, New York, 1987

[26] P. Schwarz et al.: "Extensibility in the Starburst Database System", in *Proc. Int'l Workshop on Object-Oriented Database Systems*, pp. 85-93, 1986

[27] B. Shneiderman: "Direct Manipulation: A Step Beyond Programming Languages", *IEEE Computer*, vol. 16, no. 8, pp. 57-69, August 1983

[28] S. Spaccapietra, C. Parent, K. Yétongnon, M. S. Abaidi: "Generalizations: A Formal and Flexible Approach", in *Management of Data*, N. Prakash ed., pp. 100-117, Tata McGraw-Hill, 1989

[29] S. Spaccapietra, C. Parent: "View Integration: A Step Forward in Solving Structural Conflicts", to appear in *IEEE Transactions on Knowledge and Data Engineering*, 1991

[30] H. K. T. Wong, I. Kuo: "GUIDE: Graphic User Interface for Database Exploration", in *Proc. of the 8th Int'l Conf. on Very Large Databases*, pp. 22-32, Mexico City, 1982

[31] Z. Q. Zhang, A. O. Mendelzon: "A Graphical Query Language for Entity-Relationship Databases", in *Entity-Relationship Approach to Software Engineering*, Davis et al. eds., pp. 441-448, North-Holland, 1983

A Flexible and Extensible Index Manager
for Spatial Database Systems*

Hans-Peter Kriegel[1], Peter Heep[2], Stephan Heep[3], Michael Schiwietz[1], Ralf Schneider[1]

1 Institut für Informatik, Universität München, Leopoldstraße 11, D-8000 München 40

2 NANU NANA GmbH, Lange Straße 48, D-2900 Oldenburg

3 Praktische Informatik, Universität Bremen, Bibliothekstraße, D-2800 Bremen 33

Abstract

The management of spatial data in applications such as graphics and image processing, geography as well as computer aided design (CAD) imposes stringent new requirements on socalled spatial database systems. In this paper we propose a flexible and extensible index manager for efficient query processing in spatial database systems by integrating spatial access methods. An essential ingredient for efficient query processing is spatial clustering of objects. In our approach an extensible set of alternative access paths is provided, in order to accelerate queries on properties which are not supported by clustering. Clustering and alternative access paths are organized in such a way that redundant storage of objects as well as time consuming reorganizations are avoided. This guarantees flexibility with respect to storage and access of the objects as well as efficient query processing. To support the index manager, we propose a storage method for handling arbitrary long objects, which is suitable in an environment that demands for clustering and multiple indexing.

1 Introduction

The demand for using database systems in application areas such as graphics and image processing, computer aided design (CAD) as well as geography and cartography is considerably increasing. The important characteristic of these applications is the occurance of spatial objects. The management of spatial objects imposes stringent new requirements on socalled spatial database systems.

One characteristic of spatial databases is that the description of spatial objects is a combination of nonspatial, atomic attributes and additional spatial attributes. Spatial attributes may contain an arbitrary long description as well as a spatial location and spatial relations to other spatial objects which have to be supported for query processing. Efficient query processing can only be achieved by integrating spatial access methods and index methods into spatial database systems.

For example, in a geographical database system a spatial object could be a lot. The description of the spatial object lot consists of the nonspatial attribute 'owner' as well as the spatial attributes 'boundary polygon' and 'MBB' the minimum bounding box of the lot. The boundary polygon is an example of a spatial attribute of arbitrary length. Additionally, the boundary polygon gives an exact specification of the spatial location and it implies the neighbour relationship as a spatial relation. Because no available query processing concept is able to support polygons directly, minimum bounding boxes are used as a spatial attribute approximating size, location and spatial relationship of polygons. For efficient query processing, the lots should be clustered according to their spatial location using available spatial access methods (SAMs) for multidimensional rectilinear boxes (see [KSSS 89], [KS 88]). Assume, in our example we want to retrieve lots according to their owner. Obviously, we need an alternative access path which organizes lots according to the nonspatial attribute owner. In order to handle the combination of clustering by spatial access methods and additional alternative access paths, an index manager is needed. In particular the index manager should avoid redundant storage of objects as well as time consuming reorganizations.

In the next chapter we specify some modeling concepts which are essential to spatial database systems. Such concepts impose requirements for our underlying flexible and extensible index manager and are therefore described here. Next we present the conceptual features of our proposal. In this context we derive what kind of metadata has to be provided for the index manager. In chapter 4 we describe the realization of this index manager. In chapter 5 we propose a storage method for handling arbitrary long objects supporting the index manager. The paper concluds with a summary that points out the main contributions of our proposal.

2 Conceptual requirements in spatial databases

The support of applications which use spatial data, such as CAD or geographic applications, asks for modeling capabilities that exceed those of relational database systems. There exist a lot of proposals for data models and data modeling capabilities for this reason. Some of them are concerned with general capabilities, e.g. the functional data model [Ship 81], POSTGRES [SR 86] or the EXODUS proposal [CDRS 86] and others are directly concerned with the modeling of spatial data like [Guet 89]. In the following we do not propose a new data model but we would like to describe those modeling capabilities which every spatial database system should support in our oppinion in any case. Furthermore, we will emphasize that our index manager may be integrated in a straightforward way into systems which provide those modeling capabilities.

On the conceptual level we consider a (structured) object as a record consisting of a set of attributes that are referenced by their names. In the following we describe the set of available attribute types, the internal structure of a record and of a database.

2.1 The attribute types

This section deals with the description of the *six* attribute classes which should be included in a spatial database system.

First of all such a spatial database system should include the attribute types of the traditional relational model with relations of normalized form. Attribute types are only system given *atomic* types of fixed length, e.g. INTEGER, REAL, CARDINAL and STRINGS. These types, called atomic attribute types, are system supported by a set of type dependent operations such as comparison operations, identity checking and others.

For spatial databases, the available attribute types should be augmented by types for simple spatial objects as proposed in [Guet 89]. In order to support geometric database systems, we introduce a class of *atomic geoattribute* types for point objects as well as 2 and 3-dimensional rectangular objects. This class consists of the types Point_2D, Point_3D, INTERVALL, RECTANGLE and RECTANGULAR SOLID. These types are considered as atomic types even though they are composed. As a consequence type dependent operations on these objects are supported. An example for such an operation is the predicate Intersects (R,S) which is defined on two rectangles R and S.

* This work was supported by grant no. Kr 670/4-3 from the Deutsche Forschungsgemeinschaft (German Research Society)

An essential feature of new data models is the representation of arbitrary and variable length objects or attributes as described for example in [CDRS 86]. This feature is used to accommodate objects which are difficult to decompose in atomic types, e.g. unstructured objects such as text. Our approach provides an attribute type called *complex*. Due to the hidden structure of an attribute of type complex only special read and write operations, but no additional operations such as comparison operations, are assigned to this type.

An additional feature which we require are *user-defined* types in order to support extensibility of the database system. Their internal representation may be based on the type complex. For an efficient handling the user may define special operations to gain more type specific accuracy, e.g. more sophisticated read and write operations. These operations are strictly bound to their special types. Their description is given in a procedural manner and is declared to the system at the time of type definition. As an example we consider the type polygon. An instance of this type can on the logical level be described by the number of points and an ordered point list. User defined type definitions may contain procedures for reading and writing an arbitrary point of a point list.

The values of all attributes described until now are explicitly given. An attribute of type *derived* is handled differently. A special derivation procedure defines the type of such an attribute. An example is given by a procedure computing the minimum bounding box (MBB), which is of type rectangle, from a user-defined attribute of the type polygon. The existence of a derivation procedure automatically extends the record by the derived attribute. For simplicity we assume that the type of a derived attribute is atomic, such that its value can be stored in the attribute directly. If the procedure evaluates to more complex types, a procedural (uninterpreted) or object identifier based representation is necessary. A detailed discussion of such representations for complex objects can be found in [JS 90] and [KC 86].

User-defined and *derived* attributes are supported by user-defined operations. We distinguish between operations which provide a change of data, e.g. write operations, and those that generally leave data unchanged, e.g. comparison operations. Because 'changing' operations need additional activities, they must be separately handled.

A helpful feature which should be included is object identity which allows identification of a record by its own system given unique identifier (surrogate). This surrogate is represented by an additional atomic data type called *object identifier* (OID) which remains hidden to the user, however it has a central significance for indexing purposes (see chapter 3).

2.2 The record structure

For the index manager to be proposed some kind of metadata which describes the structure of records has to be included. This metadata can be provided by specifying a record descriptor shown in example 1 (see fig. 1).

AttrNo	AttrName	Type	Update Mode
1	boundary	polygon	pointer
2	name	STRING	-
3	population	INTEGER	-
4	MBB	RECTANGLE	*

Fig. 1: Example 1: Description of a record

Thus a fixed structure defined by the record descriptor is attached to each record. For each single attribute this record descriptor contains the name and the type of the attribute and the update mode which propagates object changes. Derived attributes are locked for direct manipulation which is denoted by a '*' within the update mode field (see attribute 'MBB' in example 1). A trigger is attached to each attribute which contains related derived attributes. This trigger is defined by an update mode pointer representing derivation procedures which are called in the case of changes of the attribute. In example 1 the entry within the update mode of the

attribute 'boundary' refers to a procedure computing the minimum bounding box of the polygon and adding the value to the attribute 'MBB'. For the rest of the attributes no special update mode information is necessary. For simplification and internal purposes every single attribute obtains a system given attribute number.

2.3 Relations and cluster

All data models provide the possibility to aggregate collections of records of the same type which are known as sets or relations. The concept of combining sets of those relations to one cluster seems to be suitable for spatial databases. A cluster defines an area within secondary storage where all data belonging to the corresponding relations is accumulated. Then, a database consists of a set of such clusters. The idea of combining different relations and thus differently typed objects to the same cluster is based on a possible common connection between objects belonging to different structures. For example, in a geographic database, objects describing cities and agricultural areas are to be stored, where the attribute 'population' which is relevant for cities is meaningless for agricultural areas. City and agricultural objects are therefore differently structured and thus assigned to different relations. Yet, a common reference is given by the spatial location. This relationship should be used within geographical queries, such as, 'what agricultural areas and what cities are included in a given region?'. An efficient query support by access paths is only possible by introducing a component which we call an index manager.

3 The concepts of the index manager

As outlined before, any single object is assigned to an unique relation within a cluster. With respect to application demands atomic attributes as well as combinations of atomic attributes are candidates for indexing. The index manager facilitates the support of any number and combination of attributes. In the following we assume m attributes should be supported as indexes.

As a first attempt a single m-dimensional ($m \geq 1$) (super-)index may be formed over all the m attributes. Such an index defines object organization and localization on secondary storage. Additional to managing problems in the case of a high number of attributes the main problem due to this approach is the performance of any m-dimensional access method degenerates in the case of partial match queries specifying $n \ll m$ attributes. Thus, the number of attributes managed by one index has to be limited for the sake of efficiency. Because every query relevant attribute should be supported by indexing, more than one index turns out to be necessary. In our approach, arbitrary one- or multidimensional access methods may be assigned in arbitrary combination on the attributes of any object type. This index manager, introducing the concept of cluster and inverted indexes, is described in the following sections. A lot of index structures have been proposed in literature for different purposes([BM 72], [NHS 84], [SK 90]). Some of them excellently manage point data but are not suitable for spatial data, whereas others are exclusively proposed for spatial data management ([Gutt 84], [RL 85], [GB 88], [BKSS 90], see also [Same 90]). Thus an additional advantage arises when using more than one single index. Contrary to using one single index, any attribute as well as any combination of attributes may be organized using a tailorcut access method. Spatial data should be supported by spatial access methods whereas point data should be organized by efficient point access methods. Special superimposed coding structures, e.g. known for text representation, may be included as well (see [Ston 83]). This kind of open architecture is most adequate to face the requirements mentioned above.

3.1 The different types of indexes and their interaction

In this section, we describe the meaning and the interaction of the concepts *cluster index*, *inverted index* and *relation index.*

The clustering of records and relations is a central design goal of our approach. Objects belonging to different relations and therefore consisting of different internal structures may be grouped to a cluster with respect to a common relationship, e.g. their spatial location. Because different relations may be accommodated in one cluster, such a cluster is called heterogenous. A heterogenous cluster generally makes sense in an environment of many different object classes consisting of only a few objects, which are similar to each other with respect to some essential semantic property.

The cluster property is defined by those attributes contributing to that common relationship. The position of a record on secondary storage is (uniquely) defined by the *cluster index* which also provides an access path to the objects. Choosing the cluster index on attributes of high selectivity and considering an application dependent semantic suitability of the attributes will lead to good query performance. High selectivity is characterized by a low number of duplicates. Another criterion is the number of attributes handled by the cluster index. For the sake of efficiency too many cluster attributes should be avoided to prevent deterioration of partial match query performance.

Because a set of records cannot be physically clustered by different cluster indexes without object redundancy and on the other hand one index may not support an arbitrary number of key attributes for performance issues, we use a second type of indexes. Due to the indexing based on a given clustering of the objects, those indexes are called *inverted indexes*. These indexes perform no clustering on the objects themselves but on pointers to the objects. They describe alternative access paths to the object instances organized under the given clustering by the cluster index. For the cluster index any arbitrary but suited one- or multidimensional access method may be applied. For inverted indexes a variety of different index structures can be applied for different indexes. Therefore any particular query can be supported by an index meeting application specific requirements. As different applications may use the same attributes for selections, the attribute sets of different indexes are not restricted to be disjoint.

The notion of a relation corresponds to a semantic clustering of equally typed objects. The explicit clustering is performed by a cluster index which may be unified for several different relations. To support an efficient access to a single relation within a cluster, a special inverted index, called *relation index*, may be defined over the primary key or the surrogate of that relation. That relation index provides a partial indexing on those records of the cluster index belonging to the relation.

3.2 Architecture of the index manager

Our objective is a superimposed system optimizing the access to a set of objects by adapting to the requirements of a flexible internal management. The global architecture of our proposal of an index manger is shown in fig. 2. A central aspect is the interaction of one cluster index and a set of inverted indexes.

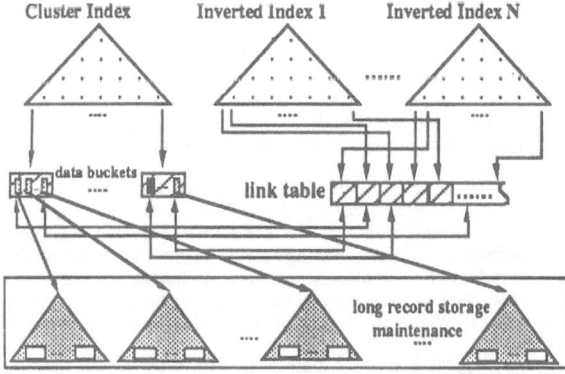

Fig. 2: Architecture of the index manager

As described before, objects of the same type and structure may be combined to relations and sets of relations to a cluster. The cluster index provides the location of the data objects on secondary storage data pages. However, inverted indexes organize only references to such clustered objects. Special access paths can be modeled using suitable inverted indexes on single relations or multirelational

indexes over different clusters. As mentioned before, an inverted index is called a relation index if it is defined over the primary key or surrogate of a single relation. In addition, an arbitrary number of different set oriented access paths may be modeled within one or many clusters. As the data objects and their clustering is dynamic an additional structure, called link table (see chapter 4), that enables a dynamic referencing to the clustered objects is necessary.

3.3 Metadata for the index manager

The following three structures are used as metadata for the index manager: the index list, the record descriptor and the index descriptor.

The necessary information on the set of indexes used within one database is managed in the form of an index list. The index list consists of the following entries:

- index Id
- access method description
- pointer to that access method
- type of the index: (cluster index, inverted index or relation index)
- key dimension (number of key attributes)
- key types of every dimension
- relation counter: number of relations managed by the index
- key attributes: key names within each relation

As mentioned before three types of indexes may be assigned to each single relation. The association between the relation attributes and the attributes used for indexing is given by assignments within a relation descriptor. The relation descriptor consists of:

- name of the relation
- pointer to the corresponding record descriptor
- one cluster index
- one or none relation index
- set of inverted indexes

Every single index is represented by an index description, that consists of:

- the number of the index within the actual list of indexes (see Chapter 4)
- the array of key attributes used for indexing

A compatibility checking of the relation descriptor attribute types and the indexed attributes, described by the corresponding entry within the index list, is performed by the system.

3.4 Creation and deletion of indexes

In spatial databases an index management has to adapt dynamically. Therefore creating new and deleting old indexes has to be supported. This dynamic is different for cluster and inverted indexes.

A cluster index is created when the objects are inserted and physically clustered on secondary storage. Defining the internal secondary storage location of the objects, a deletion of the cluster index involves a global reorganization of all data. Although not explicitly excluded, this possibility will lead to a complete reorganization of both the cluster index and the link table. An adaption of the inverted indexes however is not necessary. Creation of an additional cluster index is not provided, because of redundant object storage. Inverted indexes may be created in parallel to the cluster index at object insertion time or at any time later on. Creating a new inverted index, all relations or, more exactly, all clusters affected by the new index require an explicit examination. The index is build on the surrogates of the objects. Thus the location of any object within a datapage does not change. As the deletion of an inverted index neither affects the cluster index nor the objects themselves it can be performed in constant time.

4 Realisation of a dynamic index manager

In the last section the static architecture of a global index management system is described on conceptual level. The aspect of dynamic behaviour was considered only for creating and deleting a whole (inverted) index and therefore on the level of query support, but not for the dynamic behaviour of the objects itself. In spatial database applications objects are not static. New objects appear whereas old ones should be deleted or updated. Thus an object management must be provided in a dynamic way just as for the index management. The used index structures themselves are dynamic by definition, i.e. efficiently support insertions, deletions and updates. The global index management, however, has to be made dynamic explicitly.

As the references to the objects used for inverted indexing depend on the explicit clustering of those objects, any object change affecting the clustering location must be taken into account within the inverted indexes in form of new reference assignments. Therefore, in order to avoid a global scan of all inverted indexes, the objects themselves are referenced by a dynamic assignment structure called linktable. This linktable provides the correspondance between the datapage addresses in inverted index and cluster index. References managed by inverted indexes represent no explicit pointers to cluster index data page locations but to locations within the linktable, where the actual object position is stored.

The linktable concept

The function of the linktable is to link the object surrogates or references organized by the inverted indexes to the object instances positioned within the datapages of the cluster index. The linktable organizes a direct reference between the object surrogates and the cluster index datapages. Every object of all object clusters in the database is represented by exactly one specific entry within that linktable, whereas any of the inverted indexes generally is a partial index, i.e. not every object of the linktable and therefore of the database is organized.

Maintainance of the linktable: The dynamic behaviour of the cluster index in case of insertions and deletions is propagated to the location of the records which are never fixed to a specific datapage. In case of a datapage split the locations of all records transmitted to the new datapage are changed. Therefore all pointers to those objects within the inverted indexes have to be adapted to the new position in order to maintain a valid reference. As the reference between the object surrogates and the datapages containing the records is provided by the global linktable only the corresponding object entries within the linktable have to be adjusted. Most important, a particular treatment of every single inverted index, which would highly decrease in performance with an increasing number of such indexes, is avoided by introducing the global architecture of a linktable. Therefore the update performance does not depend on the number of inverted indexes.

As a datapage split will typically affect more than one object, an immediate adjustment of all entries affected by that update seems to be inefficient. Notice, that there is no demand for an actual linktable entry of an object in the time between two inverted index accesses to that object. Just in the case of an access to an object the corresponding linktable entry has to be actual. For supporting a delayed adjustment we use a reorganization protocol. If an object is not placed at the location given by its linktable entry, there exists a unique protocol entry containing the actual position of that record. By copying the object address to the corresponding linktable entry, the object reference is actualized and the protocol entry removed. Though, in the case of a not actual link table entry, the search for an object leads to at least one additional page access. For that reason, the linktable adjustment in the case of an access should be the exception. Using a background process the linktable is adjusted in parallel while queries and other database operations are performed.

The protocol file is organized as a search structure using the object surrogates as primary keys. We employ an AVL tree, a well known type of balanced primary key search structure storing the triples (surrogate, datapage, offset) using the surrogate as search key. Multiple updates of one and the same object are protocolled only once. Only the last object position is stored, whereas all previous positions are neglected by deleting the old entry in the case of an entry inserted, bound to the same unique surrogate. Therefore any object may only be represented once within the protocol file.

Implementation aspects: As every object is uniquely represented within the linktable and the set of objects is not static, the linktable provides a dynamic organization. The management of one-dimensional pairwise disjoint and static entries is the objective of the linktable. A one-dimensional hashing scheme seems to be best suitable guaranteeing a one-access exact match query, randomly distributed key values provided. Because an exact match query is the only relevant type of query in the linktable we suggest the use of the following hashing scheme: Let the surrogates be instanciated by cardinal values assigned randomly to the objects. Taking their bitstrings, interpreting them as a binary number between zero and one, and inverting that bitstring, we receive uniformly distributed values within the range (0,1]. An efficient management of such values is provided by the one dimensional orderpreserving linear hashing scheme (see [Lars 80], [KS 86]).

A linktable entry consists of a key part and an info part. The key part contains the surrogate as search key for accessing purposes, whereas the info part contains a pointer to the object position in terms of an address within the cluster index data file consisting of a page address and an offset value. Changing the location of an object causes an actualization of the corresponding linktable. Notice the important property that the key part, and therefore the access to that entry remains unchanged for the time of existence of that object.

Query management: The access to objects using an inverted index consists of a three level query. The first is a query to the index returning a set of object surrogates fullfilling the application query condition, followed by an access to the linktable for every single object surrogate, and finally reading the objects from their locations within the datapages of the cluster index. Accessing an object using the linktable requires the evaluation of a hash function and generally exactly one additional page access. To avoid multiple access to the same datapage, range queries to inverted indexes are treated in a breadth first manner. The set of object pointers is collected before running a set oriented access to the objects themselves.

An additional feature of the linktable and the multiple index scheme is the possibility of surrogate based query processing on different inverted indexes in parallel, minimizing the set of accesses to the objects. In other words, one query with different selection conditions may be distributed to different inverted indexes. This provides an important extension of join and selection indexes as proposed by Valduriez [Vald 87]. Valduriez neither includes the concept of multidimensional application oriented indexes nor a global, delayed updated, link structure. His notion of a join index corresponds to our concept of a multi-cluster or multi-relation inverted index.

5 A storage method supporting the index manager

In chapter 2 we described which objects have to be supported in spatial database systems and in chapter 3 and 4 we introduced a flexible index manager for those objects. Some types of indexes and global object clustering are basic to support an efficient access to objects.

Permitting an arbitrary object length we cannot assume that each object fits in a single datapage of the cluster index. In such cases the storage of objects is twofold: some more essential attributes, e.g. attributes used for indexing, reside in the datapages of the cluster index whereas others, e.g. variable length attributes, are evacuated. Just as an access to attributes not being evacuated is efficient an access to evacuated ones should never increase excessivly.

At the logical level each object occurance (a record) may be stored within a datapage of a cluster index introduced in chapter 4. However due to efficiency limitations for index structures the number of entries within such a datapage may not be arbitrary small and thus there is a restriction to the length of records at this level. A solution for such is to evacuate records or portions of them by adding an external storage layer which handles long objects (long fields). In this context we have to take into account an efficient access to all types of fixed length attributes as well as to any portions of variable length attributes. How can this be done?

The first idea is using one of the well known storage systems which support long objects. We describe some of them in the next section including their problems with respect to the requirements of storing and accessing records. Then we introduce a new storage method derived from the EXODUS storage manager [CDRS 86] combined with storage management at the level of a cluster index. This storage method utilizes efficient access and update to indexed and atomic attributes as well as to variable length attributes, portions of those and also to sequences of attributes.

5.1 Previous work in storage management

Well known storage systems which support the storage of objects of (virtually) any length are the Wisconsin Storage System (WiSS) [CDKK 85], the Starburst Long Field Manager [LL 89] and the EXODUS Storage Manager [CDRS 86].

In WiSS socalled "long data items" are proposed. A long data item consists of two parts, a number of data segments and a directory to those segments where a segment is considered to be at most one page long. Therefore WiSS supports pageoriented access within long objects. However, there is no semantic access at page level, i.e. interpreting data is up to the user.

The Starburst Long Field Manager stores long objects by a long field descriptor which is a tuple in a relation with maximum size of 255 Bytes. The descriptor consists of pointers to "buddy segments" which are portions of storage in a socalled Buddy-System. In Starburst long fields are handled, in the case of reading and writing, as entities and therefore no partial updates are allowed.

In EXODUS the basic unit of data is a storage object which is virtually unlimited in size. A storage object is internally represented by a B$^+$-tree indexed on byte positions within the object, with the B$^+$-tree leaves as data blocks (this is derived from the storage management in INGRES [Ston 83]). Small storage objects may span a maximum of one page (a degenerated B$^+$-tree). For storage objects any amount of data may be read or written.

Taking one of these storage managers the global problem of storing and accessing long objects or attributes can be solved. However for objects in our sense none of the above storage mangers is adequate. Using WiSS allows no semantic access to long attributes at page level which is basicly the same in Starburst. Storing objects in our sense in Starburst leads to another problem: at the level of the cluster index a record may completely fill a datapage or exceed the page capacity if there are some long attributes with descriptors of maximum length in additon to the other attributes. EXODUS seems to be suitable for the requirement of individual access to any portion of data. However EXODUS is guided by the idea that a long object covers a relation structure (or something similar), which is similarly handled in WiSS.

5.2 A storage method depending on object structure

Storing records we distinguish between short and long ones at the level of the cluster index where short ones are completely stored in the datapages. A record is called short, if a given maximum record length defined for the datapage entries of the cluster index is not exceeded. Long records are split in such a way that some attributes are stored in the datapages of the cluster index and the remaining ones are stored as an interpretable byte string in a B$^+$-tree which is derived from the B$^+$-tree introduced for use in EXODUS [CDRS 86]. Remaining of attributes at the level of the cluster index is handled by the following three rules:

1. An attribute for which a cluster index is defined has to reside there.
2. Attributes supported by an inverted index should reside there, because high access frequency is assumed.
3. Access to atomic attributes (typically a few bytes) should be considerably faster than access to long attributes.

Setting these concepts into action, some additional information is needed: Each object in our system is therefore preceeded by a predefined structured header, see fig.3. The first entry in the header is the object identifier which is inter alia needed for clustering

purposes. The next entry points to the record description where information about attribute types and indexing is stored. These are the basic facts which influence the evacuation decision. For evacuation purposes we store entry pairs (evacuation flag, attribute length) for each attribute containing the information whether an attribute is evacuated or not and its actual length. The entry pairs are stored in the sequence given by the record descriptor.

RECORD WITHIN THE CLUSTERINDEX

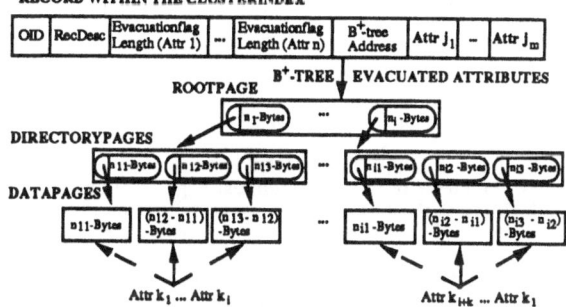

Fig. 3: The record storage structure

Generally, the attributes which are not evacuated can be named Attr j_1,...,Attr j_m, $j_i \in \{1..n\}$, $i \in \{1..m\}$. Those attributes are stored directly in the datapages of the cluster index. The remaining attributes Attr k_1,...,Attr k_l, $k_i \in \{1..n\}$; $k_i \neq j_i$, $i \in \{1..m\}$, are stored in a B$^+$-tree, which can be accessed by a pointer. There are many strategies for evacuation, each having application specific advantages. A simple strategy is given when the complete record with all attributes is stored in a B$^+$-tree. In this case an access to an atomic attribute leads always to multiple page accesses. Another strategy is to place a maximum number of attributes in the datapages of the cluster index with no regard to the structure of the attributes, e.g. take the first n attributes. If queries rarely refer to these attributes, query performance will degenerate. Our approach is to apply a heuristic strategy which first tries to store all indexed attributes and then all atomic attributes in the datapages of the cluster index. With this strategy the access to indexed or atomic attributes is sped up to the greatest possible extent. On the other hand for some kind of attributes it is sensible or necessary to evacuate them, e.g. because of their length or low query frequency. In particular attributes of type complex are candidates for evacuation.

The strategies mentioned above do not guarantee for indexed or atomic attributes not to be evacuated, except for attributes defining clustering. Furthermore, no statement with respect to the number of accesses to evacuated attributes is possible. Due to these facts we introduce a specific storage strategy for evacuated attributes by taking the record structure and the length information into account in the operations of the B$^+$-tree. The B$^+$-tree introduced in EXODUS [CDRS 86] manipulates an arbitrary number of bytes not considering the structure which is inherent to the byte string, i.e. the interpretation of the byte string is left to a higher level in the system. Our variant of this B$^+$-tree is able to store attributes in such a way that no attribute covers multiple datapages of the B$^+$-tree if it spans less than the page capacity. Attributes that span multiple pages are stored in the smallest possible number of datapages, as defined later. This can be done by using the header information, more precisely by using the length information of the attributes.

The following fundamental properties of the B$^+$-tree are retained:

- Datapages are allowed to vary from being half full to completely full (50% full convention)
- An entry of a directory page consists of a byte counter and a pointer to a page on the next level
- The root page has a minimum of two entries and the other directory pages have a minimum of n and a maximum of 2n + 1 (for a short time overfilled) entries.

In general we have an ordered subset of attributes $Attr_i$, $i \in \{1..k\}$, $k \in \{2..n\}$, of the record $R=Attr_1,...,Attr_n$. A subsequence $Attr_i,...,Attr_j$, $j \geq i$, will be inserted into a datapage, if this page is, as a consequence, minimally filled and the next attribute $Attr_{j+1}$ would overfill this page. For $i = 1$ the attribute $Attr_i$ is stored in the first datapage, and the attributes $Attr_{j+1},...,Attr_k$ are distributed to the following datapages in the same way. If for a sequence $Attr_i,...,Attr_j$ the 50 % full convention is not fullfilled, the attribute $Attr_{j+1}$ is split. By this strategy one page is filled completely and the next right page can be handled in the usual way. In the worst case only the first attribute is covered by a single page and all other attributes are covered by at least two pages even if most of the attributes could be covered by a single page. To avoid a disadvantageous storage in such a case, a datapage is allowed to be underfilled if it fullfills the 50 % full convention together with its right neighbour page. The rightmost page is allowed to be underfilled if the left neighbour page fulfills the 50 % full convention and the last attributes cannot be stored there. Thus the 50 % full convention can be guaranteed in the whole B+-tree. For attributes that span multiple pages, a number of pages is filled completely, lets say p. The remaining bytes, which span less than a page, will be stored on the current page (the first bytes of the attribute) or on the page that follows the p pages (the last bytes of the attribute).

The algorithms introduced in EXODUS can be used in our approach with little modifications. These are the operations to search for, to insert, to update and to delete arbitrary sequences of bytes. As an additional feature each attribute of a record can be handled as a null value, which is modeled by the length information in the record header. Therefore a null value is known at the level of datapages in the cluster index.

6 Conclusions

The index manager we proposed is suitable for efficient query processing in spatial database systems. As pointed out in the paper efficient query processing is achieved by supporting an extensible set of access paths. The index manager organizes cluster and inverted indexes facilitating these access paths and fullfilling two essential demands: non-redundant storage as well as avoidance of time consuming reorganizations within a dynamic environment. For additionally supporting the index manager, we proposed a specific storage method for handling arbitrary long objects.

Starting point for our concept was the problem to design and implement a Bioindication database system [KS 90] in an interdisciplinary project in which lichen were used as a biological indicator for environmental pollution. This project lead to the design of a multi-level query processor for structured spatial objects [Krie 91]. Another application area for our concept is the storage management in object oriented database systems. This concept can be used to instantiate a class hierarchy index, see [KKD 89].

The goal for our future work is to implement the extensible index management presented in this paper as well as the above mentioned query processor in an object oriented geographical database system in order to verify efficiency and flexibility with respect to query processing of structured spatial objects. The efficiency will be particularly determined by the physical implementation of the presented logical concept.

References

[BM 72] Bayer, R. & E. McCreight, 'Organization and Maintenance of Large Ordered Indexes', Acta Informatica, Vol.1, No.3, 173-189, 1972.

[BKSS 90] Beckmann, N., H.P. Kriegel, R. Schneider & B. Seeger, 'The R*-tree: An efficient and robust access method for points and rectangles', in Proc. 1990 ACM SIGMOD International Conference on Management of Data , 322-331, Atlantic City, USA, May 1990.

[CDKK 85] Chou, H.-T., D.J. DeWitt, R.H. Katz & A.C. Klug, 'Design and Implementation of the Wisconsin Storage System', Software Practice and Experience, Vol. 15(10), 943-962, October 1985.

[CDRS 86] Carey, M. J., D.J. DeWitt, J.E. Richardson & E.J. Shekita, 'Object and File Management in the EXODUS Extensible Database System', Proc. 12th Int. Conf. on Very Large Data Bases, Kyoto, Japan, August 1986.

[GB 88] Günther, O. & J. Bilmes, 'The Implementation of the Cell-tree: Design alternatives and performance evaluation', Technical Report TRCS88-23, University of California, Santa Barbara, October 1988.

[Guet 89] Güting, R.H., 'Gral: an extensible relational database system for geografic applications', Proc. 15th Int. Conf. on Very Large Data Bases, 33-44, Amsterdam, The Netherlands, August 1989.

[Gutt 84] Guttman A.: 'R-trees: a dynamic index structure for spatial searching', Proc. ACM SIGMOD Int. Conf. on Management of Data, 47-57, June 1984.

[JS 90] Jhingran, A. & M. Stonebraker, 'Alternatives in Complex Object Representation: A Performance Perspective', Proc. 6th Int. Conf. on Data Engineering, 94-102, Los Angeles, February 1990.

[KC 86] Khoshafian, S.N. & G.P. Copeland, 'Object Identity', Proc. of OOPSLA, 1986.

[KKD 89] Kim, W., K.-C. Kim & A. Dale, 'Indexing Techniques for Object-Oriented Databases', in Kim W. & F. Lochovsky, (Eds.), 'Object-Oriented Concepts, Databases, and Applications', Addison-Wesley Publishing Company, Inc., 371-394, 1989.

[Krie 91] Kriegel, H.P., P. Heep, S. Heep, M. Schiwietz & R. Schneider, 'An Access Method Based Query Processor for Spatial Database Systems', Proc. Int. Workshop on DBMS's for geographical applications, Capri, May 16-17, 1991.

[KS 86] Kriegel, H.P. & B. Seeger, 'Multidimensional order preserving linear hashing with partial expansions', Proc. Int. Conf. on Database Theory, Lecture Notes in Computer Science 243, 203-220, 1986.

[KS 88] Kriegel, H.P. & B. Seeger, 'PLOP-Hashing: a grid file without directory', Proc. 4th Int. Conf. on Data Engineering, 369-376, Los Angeles, February 1988.

[KS 90] Kriegel, H.P. & R. Schneider, 'Entwurf eines Bioindikations-Datenbanksystems', in Proc. 5.Symposium 'Informatik für den Umweltschutz', Wien, September 1990.

[KSSS 89] Kriegel, H.P., M. Schiwietz, R. Schneider & B.Seeger, 'Performance Comparison of Point and Spatial Access Methods', in Proceedings "Symposium on the Design and Implementation of Large Spatial Databases", 89-114, Santa Barbara, USA, July 1989.

[Lars 80] Larson, P.-A., 'Linear Hashing with partial expansions', Proc. 6th Int. Conf. on Very Large Data Bases, 212-223, 1980.

[LL 89] Lehman, T.J. & B.G. Lindsay,'The Starburst Long Field Manager', Proc. 15th Int. Conf. on Very Large Data Bases, Amsterdam, The Netherlands, August 1989.

[NHS 84] Nievergelt J., H. Hinterberger & K.C. Sevcik: 'The grid file: an adaptable, symmetric multikey file structure', ACM Trans. on Database Systems, Vol. 9, 1, 38-71, 1984.

[RL 85] Roussopoulos N. & D. Leifker: 'Direct spatial search on pictorial databases using packed R-trees', Proc. ACM SIGMOD Int. Conf. on Managment of Data, 17-31, May 1985.

[Same 90] Samet, H., 'The Design and Analysis of Spatial Structures', Addison-Wesley Publishing Company Inc., 1990.

[Ship 81] Shipman, D., 'The functional data model and the data language DAPLEX', ACM Transactions on Database Systems, Vol. 6, No. 1, March 1981.

[Ston 83] Stonebraker, M., H. Stettner, N. Lynn, J. Kalash & A. Guttman, 'Document Processing in a Relational Database System', ACM Transactions on Office Information Systems, Vol. 1, No. 2, April 1983.

[SK 90] Seeger, B. & H.P. Kriegel, 'The Buddy Tree: An Efficient and Robust Access Method for Spatial Databases', Proc. 16th Int. Conf. on Very Large Data Bases, Brisbane, Australia, August 1990.

[SR 86] Stonebraker, M. & L. Rowe, 'The Design of POSTGRES', Proc. 1986 ACM SIGMOD Conf. on Management of Data, Washington DC, May 1986.

[Vald 87] Valduriez, P., 'Join Indices, ACM Transactions on Database Systems', Vol. 12, No. 2, June 1987.

KRISHNA - Concurrency Control Algorithms based on Dynamic Attributes

Vijay Kumar and James Mumper

Computer Science Telecommunications
University of Missouri-Kansas City
5100 Rockhill
Kansas City, MO 64110, U.S.A.
kumar@vax2.cstp.umkc.edu

Abstract: Three new concurrency control mechanisms that utilizes the dynamic attribute of concurrent transactions for resolving conflicts are presented. Our study shows that their performance is superior to all well-known two-phase concurrency control mechanisms. There are a large number of such algorithms but we report our findings since our approach has some unique features worth exploring.

1 Introduction

Concurrent execution of transactions is managed by Concurrency Control Mechanisms (CCMs) to preserve database consistency. A large number of CCMs have been developed in the past and can be classified into *two-phase* and non two-phase categories. Algorithms belonging to the two-phase category use lock and unlock operations on database *entities* dynamically and algorithms belonging to the non two-phase category follow a pre-assigned order of execution which eliminates the need for locking. The interleaving of the operations of concurrent transactions may create *conflicts* which must be resolved. A common way of resolving conflicts is by rolling-back and/or blocking one of the conflicting transactions. All two-phase CCMs apply these operations dynamically in the sense that the execution order of transactions are not pre-determined and is decided when a conflict arise between transactions. It is at this time the algorithm decides whether to use roll-back or blocking to resolve conflict. There are a number of ways these operations can be applied and each way defines a CCM. In non two-phase algorithms, on the other hand, usually roll-back is used to resolve conflicts.

Although this area seems to overworked, still there is plenty of scope to find innovative ways of serializing concurrent execution. This is especially true in the area of object-oriented database management systems. The proliferation of CCMs motivated much performance work to identify an optimal mechanism. These works (there are a large number of papers in this area but we list only a few here) [1, 5, 6] show that no one CCM is the best for all types of workloads and CCMs based on two-phase policy outperform other commonly known non-two-phase CCMs in most cases.

We categorize well-known two-phase CCMs on the basis of their conflict resolution policy as follows:

Category A: Algorithms of this category use execution status (running or blocked) of conflicting transactions to resolve conflicts. Algorithms Running Priority (RP) [3], and Cautious Waiting (CW) [4] belong to this category.

Category B: Algorithms that use the age (timestamp) of conflicting transactions to resolve conflicts. Wound-Wait (WW) and Wait-Die (WD) belong to this category [7].

Category C: Algorithms that take action only on the transaction requesting an item (requestor) to resolve conflicts. General Waiting (GW) and Immediate Restart (IR) [9] belong to this category.

The conflict resolution policy of all these algorithms may be called ad hoc since the roll-back or blocking is not guaranteed to be applied on the "right" transaction. For example, in WD and WW mechanisms transactions which may not create a deadlock are rolled-back to resolve conflicts. In CW, RP, GW or IR, a large requestor (transaction making a request for a data item) may be rolled-back or blocked leaving a smaller transaction to proceed. Such redundant or expensive roll-backs or blocking have significant effect on the performance of these algorithms [5]. If the "right" transaction is selected and subjected to roll-back and blocking then the cost of conflict resolution can be minimized. We propose that a right transaction can be selected for resolving conflict if the *execution status* of every transaction is continuously maintained and used to resolve conflicts. We have used this approach to develop algorithms which resolve conflicts on the basis of information available when it arises and not on the basis of a predefined policy. Such decision we believe would be the best for a particular conflict at that particular time.

A transaction during its execution life under these CCMs acquires several "attributes". The value of these attributes can be used to defines completely the execution status of a transaction. Some of the examples of such attributes are: number of conflicts, number of entities locked by the transaction, the time duration the transaction waited for the desired data items, number of times the transaction was blocked, number of times the transaction was rolled-back etc. We call these attributes *dynamic attributes* of transactions, and the values of a subset of these attributes give a transaction a unique status. The values of these attributes can be used as a measure of the progress of a transaction, and can be used to resolve conflicts "intelligently" and efficiently. By intelligently we mean selecting the best possible operation (blocking or roll-back) and by efficiently we mean the conflict resolution is free from outside influence or from some predefined policy.

So far as we know, no CCM except Optimized Cautious Waiting [6] has used one of these attributes to resolve conflicts between concurrent transactions. In [6] the amount of CPU utilization of a transaction was included in resolving conflicts and the performance study of that algorithm showed some improvement. In this paper we report three new CCMs that use a subset of dynamic attributes of transactions for resolving conflicts and compare their performance with commonly know two-phase CCMs in a varieties of environments. Two of the three CCMs presented here are not as intelligent as the third one in the sense that some redundant roll-backs are possible. A higher priority requestor may be rolled-back or blocked allowing a lower priority transaction to proceed. In spite of this, however, we show that these three algorithms performs better than some of the other CCMs studied here.

2   Dynamic Attributes of Transactions

We define a finite Dynamic Attribute Set (DAS) as:

DAS = {a_1, a_2, ..., a_n}; where a_is are dynamic attributes.

Theoretically, n can be as large as possible. Intuitively, however, a small value of n may give us the optimal cardinality of DAS. By optimal cardinality we mean the cardinality of DAS which is sufficient to make the best conflict resolution decision. On the basis of our experience and since some of these attributes are more informative than others, we have selected the following dynamic attributes to create a Conflict Resolution Set (CRS) Õ DAS. We believe that a CRS precisely define the status of a transaction at the time of conflict under two-phase CCMs:
Conflict Resolution Set (CRS) = {number of locks acquired,number of conflicts accumulated so far, number of roll-backs suffered so far, number of blockings accumulated so far}

A CRS is an ordered set and the position of a member in the set defines its weight, i.e., the number of locks acquired has a higher weight than the number of conflicts accumulated, and so on. This order, however, may depend upon the processing environment and the workload type, and can be modified if necessary. Reordering of CRS could be done either for every transaction or for a set of transactions. In this report, we have not investigated its effect but we have reorganized CRS statically. We selected number of locks acquired by a transaction since

under the two-phase policy the progress of a transaction depends on its successfully acquiring the desired locks. So the number of locks gives a measure of transaction maturity (i.e., how far it has progressed in its execution) in terms of its resource utilization. We selected number of conflicts since this parameter is inherent to concurrent execution of transactions and may change more frequently than other dynamic attributes. The number of roll-backs suffered by a transaction gives information about transaction's CPU usage and its stay in the system indirectly. The number of blockings also provide similar information but the degree of transaction's stay in the system and its CPU usage may differ significantly. It depends on the conflict resolution policy to a large extent, in some cases the number of blockings may carry more weight than the number of roll-backs and vice-versa. For example, in Immediate Restart (IR) a transaction may have roll-backs but no blockings. Similarly, in General Waiting (GW), a transaction may have a number of blockings but no roll-backs.

The order of CRS can be redefined to identify the best combination for resolving conflicts. One of the aims of our experiment is to discover whether or not there exist an optimal order or the set does not have to be an ordered set. We would also like to find if the cardinality of the CRS has any relationship with the performance of the algorithm.

3   An Intelligent Conflict Resolution Scheme

The algorithms proposed in this paper resolve conflicts by rolling-back and/or blocking one of the conflicting transactions. Unlike other CCMs, to resolve a conflict an operation (roll-back or blocking) is decided instantaneously at the time of conflict. We define an additional term before we explain our scheme.
Priority: Every transaction is associated with a priority that is computed on the basis of the values of the members of CRS (Conflict Resolution Set). This priority is time variant. It has a unique value at an instant of time, and it may either remain the same or increases with time but never decreases. We define two types of priority and either can be used in the algorithm. In this report we present our experiments related to absolute priority only.
Absolute priority: individual attribute value is used to compute absolute priority.
Average priority: the entire conflict resolution set is used to compute the average priority.

We assume the following:
T_j and T_k = two conflicting transactions.
DAS_j and DAS_k = DASs of T_i and T_j's respectively.
P_j and P_k = Priorities of T_i and T_j on a conflict.
DAS_j = {a_1, a_2, ..., a_n} DAS_k = {b_1, b_2, ..., b_n}

Algorithm for assigning absolute priority to conflicting transactions:

if $(a_1 > b_1)$ then $P_j > P_k$
else if $(a_1 = b_1)$ then
    if $(a_2 > b_2)$ then $P_j > P_k$
    else if $(a_2 > b_2)$ then
      ----
      if $(a_n > b_n)$ then $P_j > P_k$
      else if $(a_n = b_n)$ then $P_j = P_k$

Algorithm for assigning average priority to conflicting transactions:

$$\text{Compute}\quad a = \frac{\sum\limits_{i=1}^{n} a_i}{n} \quad\text{and}\quad b = \frac{\sum\limits_{i=1}^{n} b_i}{n}$$

if $(a>b)$ then $P_j>P_k$ else if $(a = b)$ then $P_j = P_k$ else $P_j<P_k$

We define CRS (Conflict Resolution Set) of cardinality four for our algorithms with the following attributes at the time of the current conflict:
E_j and E_k = No. of locks T_j and T_k had at a conflict.
C_j and C_k = No. of conflicts T_j and T_k had at a conflict.
R_j and R_k =No. of roll-backs T_j and T_k had at a conflict.
B_j and B_k = No. of blocking T_j and T_k had at a conflict.
P_j and P_k = priorities of T_j and T_k respectively.

Computation of absolute priority

if $(E_j > E_k)$ then $P_j > P_k$
else if $E_j < E_k)$ then $P_j < P_k$
   else if $(E_j = E_k)$ then
     if $(C_j > C_k)$ then $P_j > P_k$
     else if $(C_j = C_k)$ then
       if $(R_j < R_k)$ then $P_j > P_k$
       else if $(R_j = R_k)$ then
         if $(B_j > B_k)$ then $P_j>P_k$ else $P_j = P_k$

As mentioned before the order of these element could be changed dynamically in computing absolute priority. We, however, have not studied its effect in this work. There may be an optimal order of these elements giving the best value of absolute priority. We aim to discover if there exists an optimal order. The average priority can be computed as follows:

$$a = \frac{E_j + C_j + R_j + B_j}{4} \quad\text{and}\quad b = \frac{E_k + C_k + R_k + B_k}{4}$$

if $(a>b)$ then $P_j > P_k$ else if $(a=b)$ then $P_j = P_k$ else $P_j<P_k$

If the holder (transaction holding the data item) is subjected to blocking then this may create a deadlock and if it is rolled-back then the algorithm will become preemptive (aborting the active holder). We introduce three CCMs called KRISHNA1, KRISHNA2 and KRISHNA3.

KRISHNA 1: If the priority of the requestor (T_r) > the priority of the holder (T_h) then block the requestor (T_r) else if the priority of the requestor (T_r) = the priority of the holder (T_h) then select one of the transaction randomly for roll-back else roll-back the requester (T_r).
KRISHN 2: If the priority of T_r > the priority of T_h then if T_r is blocked, roll-back T_R else block T_r else if the priority of T_r = the priority of T_h then select one of the transaction randomly for roll-back else roll-back T_r.
KRISHN 3: If the priority of T_r > the priority of T_h then if T_h is blocked then roll-back T_h else block T_r else if the priority of T_r <= the priority of T_h then if T_h is blocked then roll-back T_r else block T_r.

Figure 1 traces the working of KRISHNA1,2 and 3.

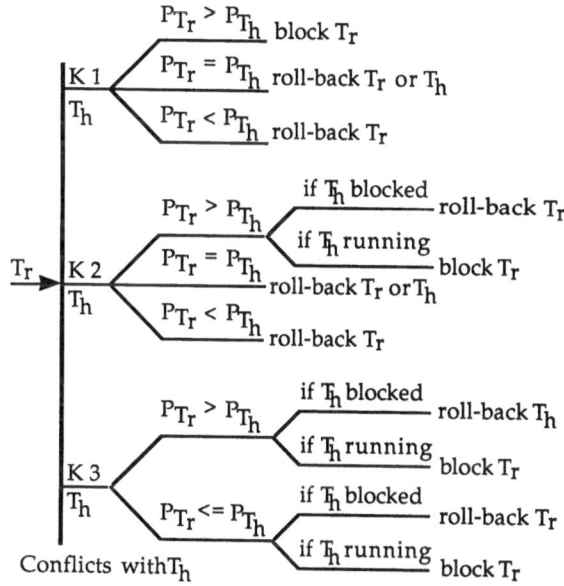

Figure 1: Working of KRISHNA 1, 2 and 3

4 Performance Measurement

We compare the performance of KRISHNA1, 2 and 3 with CW, GW, IR, RP, WW and WD. In particular we want to study: CPU utilization, Roll-back and Blocking rates, Resiliency towards stress situations, The optimal order of CRS and Throughput.
We give a brief description of CW, GW, IR, RP, WW and WD. A conflict between T_r and T_h is resolved under these algorithms as follows:
WW [7]: If T_r started up earlier than T_h then wound (roll-back) T_h otherwise block T_r.
WD [7]: If the T_r started up earlier than T_h then block T_r (T_r waits for T_h to release the desired data item) otherwise T_r dies (rolls-back).
CW [4]: If T_h is in a blocked state (waiting for a data item) then roll-back T_r but if T_h is active (in a ready state may be under suspension) then block T_r.
IR [9]: Simply restart T_r.
RP [3]: If T_h is in a blocked state (waiting for a data item) then roll-back T_h and grant the lock to T_r but if T_h is running then block T_r.

188

6 Analysis

We discuss the expected behavior of KRISHNA1, 2 and 3. As explained earlier every conflict resolution policy's aim is to find the minimum cost activity. We say an activity is a minimum cost activity if it uses minimum amount of resources and its effect is minimum on the multiprogramming level. The conflict resolution policies of all algorithms except KRISHNA1, 2 and 3 are based on some approximation of this requirement. This is the reason that some resolution policies are expensive in most of the transaction processing environments. The policies of KRISHNA1, 2 and 3 on the other hand, incorporates the cost analysis aspect in their resolution policies. In other words, it includes those aspects of transactions (dynamic attributes) that have significant effect on the processing cost. We, therefore, believe that the inclusion of cost analysis aspect is likely to improve the performance of KRISHNA1, 2 and 3.

We identify the effect of approaches taken by these algorithms with the help of some examples. Consider two transactions, T_r (requestor) and T_h (holder). T_r is older than T_h but has processed much less number of entities than T_h which is running. The roll-back and blocking cost of T_h are much higher than T_r. Under WW, however, in a conflict T_r will wound T_h indicating a poor decision. This is because WW assumes that the roll-back and blocking costs of an older requestor are always higher than the younger holder. This assumption may not always be true.

In GW, RP and WD, T_r will be blocked, but in our algorithm T_r will be rolled-back since its priority (average and absolute) will be smaller than T_h. Rolling-back T_r seems to be a better choice since it has lower roll-back and blocking costs. Some counter arguments of this choice, however, can be given and only a detailed simulation study can establish the correctness of such choice. In IR also, T_r will be rolled-back, but the difference lies in the conflict resolution policy of these two algorithms.

Now consider the situation where T_r has more number of entities (more matured) than T_h, and T_h is blocked and older than T_r. In this situation under CW, IR and WD, T_r will be rolled-back which is not the best decision since T_r would have an expensive roll-back. The best decision would be to roll-back T_h which happens in RP and in our algorithm. In WW, T_r will be blocked. In RP a blocked transaction can be rolled-back thus the transaction expense (running + blocked + roll-back) is the highest. In CW a blocked transaction is never rolled-back so transaction's maximum expense = execution + blocking. In IR transaction expense is execution + roll-back.

We argue that our algorithms provide an optimal conflict resolution policy. We also identify that our algorithms can be tuned statically or dynamically by reordering the CRS to improve its performance. This

may be necessary to establish the compatibility between our algorithms and the environment they are implemented.

7 Simulation model of CCMs

A general simulation model for measuring the performance of these CCMs' is given in Figure 2. The model is based on a closed queuing model. There are a fixed number of terminals from where transactions originate under Poisson distribution. A transaction is regarded active if it has at least gone through CCM once and has not completed execution. The number of active transaction defines multiprogramming level (MPL). We included two I/O servers and I/O requests are served under FCFS. A transaction selects a server randomly where all I/O servers are equally likely to be selected.

If the lock request is denied then depending upon the CCM under investigation, the transaction is either blocked or rolled-back. We perform continuous deadlock detection.

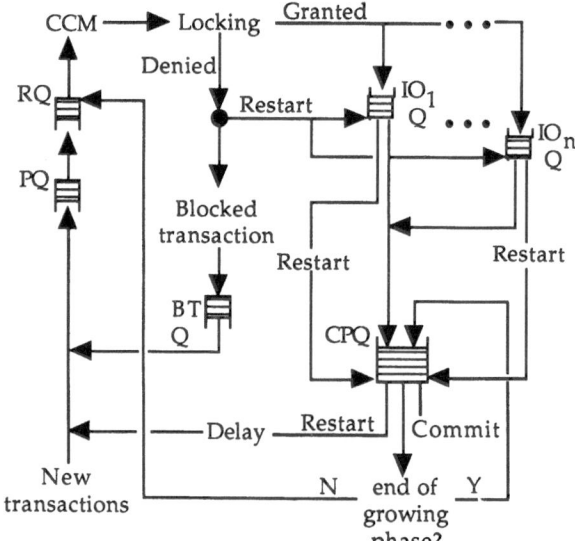

Figure 2: Simulation model

The transaction to be rolled-back is given the highest priority and is done by putting the transaction at the top of IOQ, then to the top of CPQ and is subjected to some delay before it joins the end of PQ. We employ a delay of one transaction, which has been found to be a better choice [1], before it is rescheduled for execution. A restarted transaction retains its history and requests the same set of data items.

The choice of transaction size and the type is motivated by other works in this area, notably [4,9]. The transaction size is uniformly distributed between a minimum and a maximum size. We selected this range to simulate an even workload. In [5,6,9] it is suggested that read-write ratios can be reflected by varying database size, and do not appear to change the picture of the relative performance. IN this work we have used only write-only transactions, however, in our future work we do investigation the effect of read-write ratios. Also, this size range was selected for ease of comparison with the existing results [9,1].

8   Results and Discussions

We ran a large number of simulation experiments to examine the effect of conflict resolution policy of KRISHNA 1, 2 and 3. Table 1 lists the simulation parameters and their values used in our experiments. Since our aim has been to highlight the significance of dynamic attributes, we compare the performance of KRISHNA3 with other CCMs only and do not investigate the relative performance of CW, GW, IR, RP, WD and WW. Results of other experiments will be reported in our future work.

Table 1

Parameter Description	Values
Database size (number of entities)	10,000
Largest transaction size	12
Smallest transaction size	4
Average transaction size	8
Multiprogramming level	5 - 200
I/O time for accessing a data item	35 ms
CPU time for locking/releasing an entity	1.0 ms
Number of terminals	200
Number of I/O servers	2
Av. time between two queries (exp).	10 sec.
CPU time to prepare for an I/O	10 ms
Number of CPU servers	1

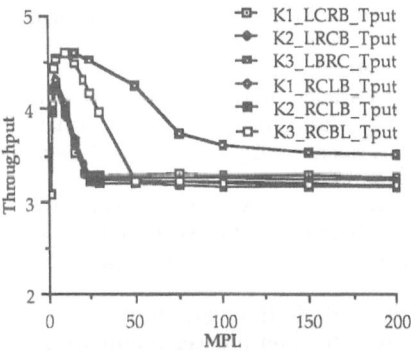

Graph 1: MPL vs. Throughput

Graph 1 shows the relationship between the throughput of KRISHNA1 (K1), KRISHNA2 (K2) and KRISHNA3 (K3) under several MPL values. The order of a CRS set used is identified by the four letters string in the name of a CCM. So LCRB indicates Number of locks, Number of conflicts, Number of roll-backs and Number of Blockings. We selected only those orders of CRS which produced the highest and the lowest throughputs. Graph 1 identifies K3_LBRC is the best performer so we selected KRISHNA3 with LBRC order of CRS for comparing performance of our scheme with

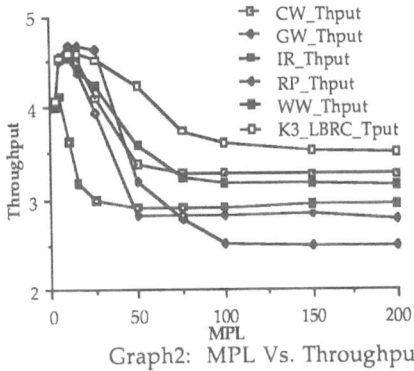

Graph2: MPL Vs. Throughput other CCMs.

Graph 2 shows the relationship between MPL and the throughput. It shows that KRISHNA 3 outperforms all two-phase CCMs we tested. The initial performance of General Waiting (GW) is the best but it declines rapidly with MPL mainly due to a higher number blockings, and deadlock treatment. We can also see from graph 2 that the throughput of KRISHNA3 declines much more slowly compared to other CCMs. This indicates that KRISHNA3 shows more resilience towards MPL increase than other CCMS.

As indicated before, an efficient CCM must guarantee forward processing of a majority of transactions most of the time and a transaction should not suffer repeated restarts. These properties of a CCM would produce a very low number of roll-backs, conflicts and blockings. Graph 3 shows the relationship between MPL and blocking rate. The blocking rate of KRISHNA3 with LBRC order is lower than all other CCMs except CW. Graph 5 shows that the roll-back rate of KRISHNA3 is the lowest of all CCMs except RP. Intuitively, in an efficient CCM, apart from other attributes, if the blocking rate is low then the roll-back rate tends to be high. This effect is shown in graph 5. Other algorithms (CW, WW and GW) do not exhibit this property.

The conflict rate of KRISHNA3 is also lower than all the CCMs except CW. These results indicate that KRISHNA3 possesses all the desirable properties of an efficient and robust algorithm. It maintains a minimum blocking rate while keeping the roll-back rate comparatively very low. This suggests that in an overloaded system KRISHNA3 is not likely to thrash so early. Graph 4 shows that the conflict rate of KRISHNA3 is the lowest of all CCMs except CW. This behavior suggests another desirable property for a CCM. An efficient CCM must synchronize the lock requests of concurrent transactions in such a way that it should improve the probability of grant.

Our results lead us to conclude that KRISHNA 3 possesses all these desirable properties thus offering the highest performance. We are in the process of studying the effect of hot spots on the behavior of KRISHNA1, 2 and 3.

Graph 6 shows that   KRISHNA3 utilizes CPU

resource much more efficiently than other CCMS (except WW). It seems to suggests that the amount of CPU utilization may add the conflict resolution capability of our algorithms. We plan to investigate the effect of this parameter in our future work.

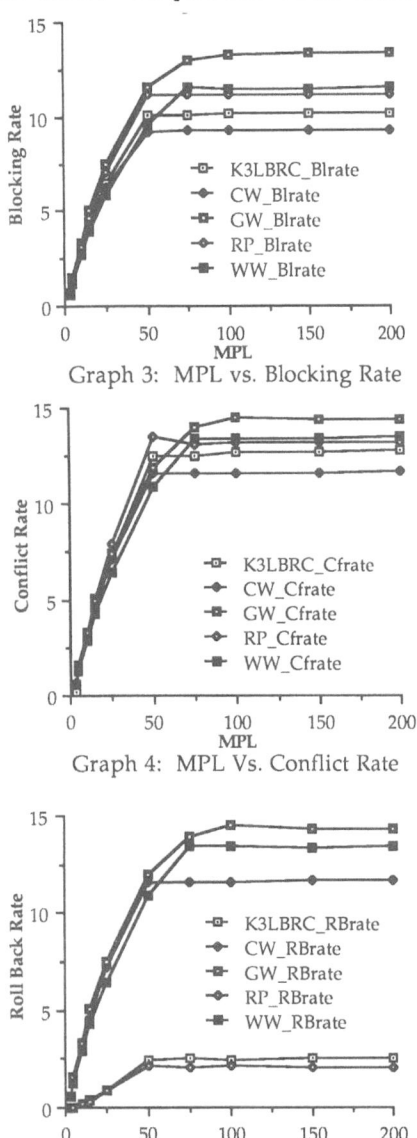

Graph 3: MPL vs. Blocking Rate

Graph 4: MPL Vs. Conflict Rate

Graph 5: MPL vs. Roll Back Rate

9   Summary

The performance study of KRISHNA1, KRISHNA2 and KRISHNA3 suggests that the dynamic attributes of concurrent transactions are very effective parameters for designing efficient concurrency control mechanisms. These algorithms may be suitable for all types of transactions, especially for real-time transactions where the values of dynamic attributes are likely to change more frequently. We are in the

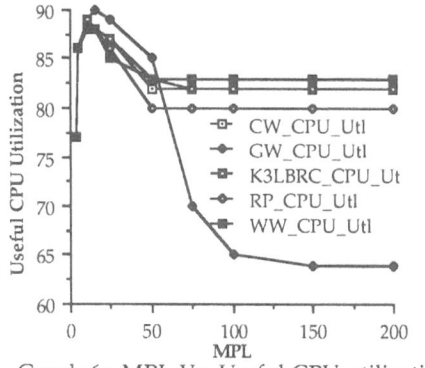

Graph 6: MPL Vs. Useful CPU utilization

process of investigating all other aspect of our algorithms and looking into ways of developing object-oriented CCMs.

References

[1] R. Agrawal, at. al., "The Performance of Alternative Strategies for dealing with Deadlocks in Database Management Systems", *IEEE Trans on SE,*, Vol. SE-13, No. 12, Dec. 1987.

[2] K.P. Eswaran, at. al., "The Notions of Consistency and Predicate Locks in database Systems", *Comm. ACM* Vol. 19, No. 11, Nov. 1976.

[3] P. Franaszek and J. T. Robinson, "Limitations of concurrency in transaction procesing", ACM TODS., 10 (1), pp. 1-28, Mar. 1985.

[4] M. Hsu and B. Zhang, "The Mean Value Approach to Performance Evaluation of Cautious Waiting", Submitted for Publication, 1987.

[5] V.Kumar, "Performance Comparison of Database Concurrency Control Mechanisms based on Two-Phase Locking, Timestamping and Mixed Approach", *Information Sciences: An International Journal*, Vol. 51, No. 3, 1990.

[6] V. Kumar and Meichun Hsu, "A Superior Two-Phase Locking Algorithm and Its Performance", *Information Sciences: An International Journal*, (Accepted for publication).

[7] D.J. Rosenkrantz at. al, "System level concurrency control for distributed database systems," ACM Trans. Database Syst., Vol. 3, No. 2, pp. 178-198, June 1978.

[8] Shemer, J.E. and Collmeyer, A.J., "Database sharing-A study of interference, roadblocks, and deadlocks", Proc. 1972 ACM SIGFIDET Workshop, pp. 147-163.

[9] Y.C. Tay at. al., "Locking performance in centralized databases," ACM TODS, 10 (4), pp. 415-462, Dec. 85.

The Design of an Efficient Data Structure for Manipulating Data in an Image DataBase System

A. Touir

Ecole Nationale Supérieure des Télécommunications 46, rue Barrault - 75013 Paris - FRANCE
e-mail: {touir}@@inf.enst.fr

Abstract: This paper reports the design of the Inverted Quadtree, a dynamic index structure for image database. The set of the inserted images are stored in a way that permits to perform content-oriented retrieval. The content search manipulates directly the bitmap representation of the image, so this structure support the pattern searching. Thus, we consider the problem to resolve as a fuzzy search of pattern in an image database. We specially describe the behavior of the proposed structure for this kind of manipulation. We analyze the distribution of the data in the base, and some operations of manipulation. We suggest a parallel processing to execute a fuzzy search.

1   Introduction

Image DataBase Management Systems (IDBMS) [9, 13] become more and more capable of efficiently manipulating unformatted data. Most approaches integrate descriptors [2, 19, 23] to access and manipulate images. Queries are then composed with criteria that are in these descriptors. The main problem of the IDBMS is the limitation of the searching capabilities to a set of previously defined criteria. However, many applications handling pictures, need to manipulate this kind of data directly. Spatial operations, editing facilities, content-oriented retrievals demand to handle the bitmap representation.

A convenient data structure has to be as compact as possible, and to support access paths corresponding to different types of manipulation. A bitmap-compatible structure seems to be an attractive solution. Quadtree [16,17] is such a structure, which provides an interesting technique to code images in a compact way [4].

The principle of the quadtree consists in proceeding with a recursive subdivision of the image into four equal-sized quadrants. Nonterminal nodes of the quadtree correspond to gray quadrants of the image and have four child. If a given children is a leaf, it corresponds to a black/white quadrant. The Morton's code [Morton66] is generally used to label the quadtree's nodes. It consists in bit-interleaving the (x,y) coordinates of the upper left corner of the quadrant corresponding to the node. This label, which we call *prefix*, may have several representations. In this paper, we suppose that a prefix is defined either by its binary label, or by its bit-length (number of bits that compose it) and its decimal value.

Some varieties of quadtrees have been proposed. Each one is more or less adapted to manipulate specific data. Linear quadtrees [7] are used to code image, where each node corresponds to a black quadrant. Nodes of the PM Quadtree [15] represent line segments data. The PR Quadtree [1] is used to code points and regions, where nodes of the MX-CIF Quadtree [10] represent rectangle data. These latter two types of quadtrees accept more than one data in a node. Moreover, using the MX-CIF Quadtree, data can be in any node (root, terminal or nonterminal nodes), whereas the use of the other kind of quadtrees allows data stored only in leaves (terminal nodes). The essential characteristics of all these types of quadtrees is to associate a quadtree to each complex object.

In this paper, we focus on query like: *"for whatever pattern, select the image that contains it"*. We propose an original method that copes with this kind of query. The problem is to execute a fuzzy search and to select an image that contains the searched pattern. Of course this kind of query could be considered as a search constraint in an advanced query specification, which combine DBMS search techniques and information retrieval capabilities.

Nowadays, existing systems [3, 8, 14] support complex domains such as images and are able to perform efficiently spatial search. However, pattern recognition operations are relatively limited to search simple shapes such as edge detection. Our aim is to allow the pattern recognition operations to be more

192

general, and the search of any pattern in all the inserted images to be possible. In this paper, we propose a new type of quadtree, called the Inverted Quadtree (IQ). In this structure the set of the inserted images is encoded into a single quadtree.

This paper is organized as follow: in Section 2, we expose the problem that we want to solve, so we define the chosen data structure, we precise its characteristics, and we describe the data file organization. The fuzzy search operation is analyzed in Section 3. In Section 4, we suggest a parallel processing to manipulate data, then we conclude in Section 5.

2 Data Definition Level

The purpose of the query processing is to select the identifiers of valid images. Thus, the search processing consists in scanning each image, in order to detect a pattern matching between the image and the searched pattern. A large part of the complexity of the operation is due to the sequential characteristic of the adopted strategy. Indeed, the use of any data structure that process grid representation of spatial data, generates an image space where each inserted image is coded and linked to a specific structure. Inserting 2 images using quadtree structure, generates 2 quadtrees. So, each image has its own set of prefixes, and the searched pattern also has its proper set. In addition, many of these prefixes are redundant. The greater the number of images is, the larger the redundancy is. Because, we are in presence of a very large database, this kind of data distribution and use of the quadtree generates an important run time and processing complexity. The main task of this level consists in :

(1) distributing data so that data storage is performed without any redundance.

(2) insuring an efficient data access.

2.1 Principle of Data Distribution

The principle of storing and distributing data consists in inverting the search. This inversion is interpreted as the linking of each prefix to the set of images where it occurs. So, the search processing uses directly the data structure to determine the identifiers of the image, where a particular prefix occurs. The search of a pattern including a set of prefixes leads us to intersect several lists of identifiers to obtain the convenient identifiers.

The image space is coded only with a single IQ. A field node of an IQ is composed with a list of Image Identifiers (ImIds). Each quadrant is linked to a node. A quadrant is black for each ImId

in the list. This space can be viewed as the superposition of all the inserted images (Figure 1) and is called the meta-image. This is the base of the proposed data structure. The access to any node is performed using a dynamic index structure. Data is distributed using a combination of this index and the B-tree [6]. The index function has (1) to order prefixes so that the disk accesses are minimize and (2) to allow the search on visiting a node once.

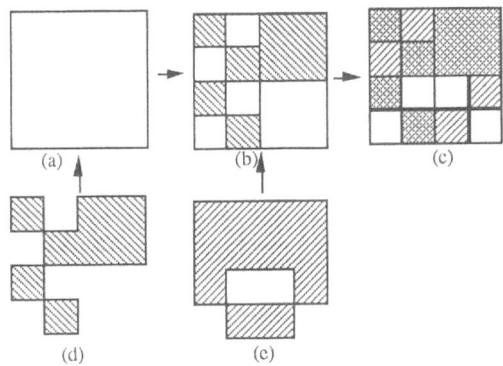

Figure 1 : building a Meta-Image

2.2. Characteristics of The IQ

In this section, we give some characteristics of the IQ and we show how to express and use it. We suppose that all the inserted images have a size of $2^N x 2^N$ pixels.

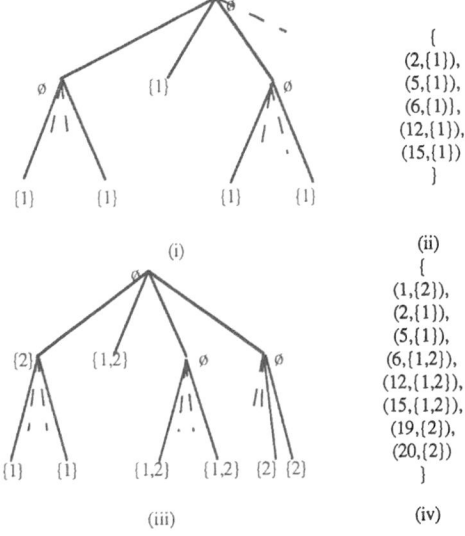

Figure 2 : evolution of the IQ corresponding to the sequence of insertions of Figure 1

The insertion of a given image consists of computing the prefixes of all the quadrants, and the insertion of the identifier of this image in all the IQ nodes that correspond to these prefixes. Figure 2.i represents the IQ, after the insertion of a first image represented in Figure1.d. Whereas Figure 2.iii represents the state of the IQ after the insertion of a second image represented in Figure1.e, while the evolution of the meta-image is represented respectively in Figures 1.a, 1.b and 1.c. Dotted lines in Figures 2.i, 2.iii represent empty nodes.

2.3. Index Structure

The pattern to be searched is coded with a linear quadtree; its prefixes have a binary representation and they are sorted with an increasing order (the quadtree order). Therefore, efficiency of the matching operation implies that the quadtree of the searched pattern and the set of the addresses of IQ nodes (on disk) have the same order. The quadtree order is the same one than the z-order [12], which can be summarized as:

For any prefix $P = p_1p_2p_3 \cdots p_{Lp} = (Lp, Vp)$, where $p_i \in \{0,1\}$, $Vp = \sum_{i=1}^{Lp} p_i*2^{(Lp-i)}$, and for any couple of prefixes $P = (Lp, Vp)$, $Q = (Lq, Vq)$: $P < Q \Leftrightarrow Vp*2^{Lq-Lp} < Vq$, is not sufficient to order all the prefixes of the IQ; for example, quadrants having prefixes P=000000 and Q=00000000 cannot be ordered. In the next, we propose a function that order any couple of prefixes. This order represents a particular labelling of the quadrants of the meta-image. Figure 3 shows (a) the labelling of the quadrants and (b) the labelling of the IQ nodes with N=3. The function used to index the set of the IQ prefixes, is defined as :

$$\mathcal{H}(P) = \frac{Lp}{2} + \sum_{i=1}^{Lp} p_i*\Omega_i$$

$$\text{where} \begin{cases} \Omega_i = \dfrac{4^{(N+1)-i/2}-1}{3} \text{ if } i \text{ is even} \\ \Omega_i = 2*\Omega_{i+1} \text{ if } i \text{ is odd} \end{cases}$$

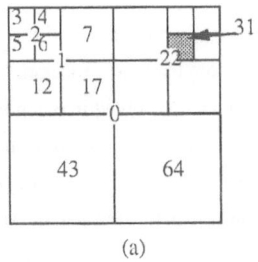

(a)

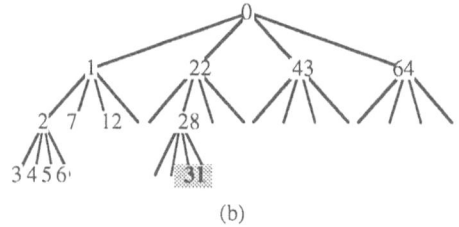

(b)

<u>Figure 3</u> : *the labelling of the quadrants and the IQ nodes (decimal values)*

The principle of the labelling consists :

(1) in associating to each quadrant, the number of the subquadrants that it contains. We consider that the meta-image as a special quadrant, so it contains $(4^{(N+1)}-1) / 3$ subquadrants; we note Ω or Ω_0 this number. The quarter of the meta-image contains $(4^{(N+1)-1}-1) / 3$ subquadrants and is related to a prefix of two-bit length; we note this latter number by Ω_2. The half of the meta-image is (theoretically) associated to a prefix of one-bit length, therefore the number of subquadrants that it contains, is $\Omega_1=2*\Omega_2$. So any quadrant related to a prefix of Lp-bits length, contains $\Omega_{Lp}=(4^{(N+1)-LP/2}-1) / 3$ subquadrants.

(2) for any prefix $P = (Lp, Vp) = p_1p_2p_3 \cdots p_{Lp}$, p_i is associated to Ω_i, $i \le Lp$.

Figures 2.ii and 2.iv show the evolution of sets of couples (node index, list of *ImIds*) that define the IQ. In Figure 3.a where N=3, the prefix P=010110= (Lp=6,Vp=22) is associated to the quadrant number 31. This number is obtained by associating Ω_1 to the first bit (from the left), Ω_2 to the second one, Ω_3 to the third one, and so forth. Thus, in the example, the address of P is $\mathcal{H}(P)=\Omega_2+\Omega_4+\Omega_5+Lp/2= 31$.

2.4. IQ File Organization

As it is described above, data has to be organized so that several kind of manipulations can be performed efficiently. Even though, the manipulated data is 2-dimentional, the Morton's code and the used index function permit to manipulate it as a 1-dimentional data. Thus point access method is required in our case. The IQ can be viewed as an efficient way to code all the inserted images, but it is not sufficient to be used as an access method. Indeed, its use to access to any node generates a page fault. A combination of the index function described above and the B-tree seem an attractive way of distributing data. This kind of storage is efficient in that the set of indexes is bounded by Ω, so the depth of the B-tree is bounded too. Because the hashing

194

function is bijective, the use of prefixes allows to determine the addresses of their correspondents nodes and vis versa. In an ImIds field, a single bit is associated to each ImId. So the use of 8-bits byte to code the fields nodes, allows us to insert eight images. Thus, if the fields have α 8-bits bytes size, the IQ file could range from 1 to an upper bound $8*\alpha$ images.

3 Data Manipulation and Fuzzy Search Analysis

In this section, we give an idea about the complexity of the displacement of the pattern through the IQ, then we expose and analyze the principle of the fuzzy search. We consider a pattern composed of M_pref prefixes. These prefixes address a set of quadrants having a total of M_pix pixels. This pattern is contained in a minimal rectangle having (L*l) pixels.

3.1 Moving in the IQ

A filtering can be executed in a possible position, if the minimal rectangle that contains the pattern is inside the meta-image. Assuming that the minimal rectangle that contains the meta-image has a size of (2^N*2^N) pixels and the pattern is included in a (L*l) minimal rectangle, the total number of possible positions is $(2^N-L+1)*(2^N-l+1)+1$. Therefore, the larger this rectangle is, the less the number of translations is. This operation is costly [22, 20]. However, the translation can be done simultaneously with the filtering [21]. Such a processing allows the filtering to be stopped in a given position, if it is shown that the pattern cannot exist in that position; so, no image contains the pattern in such a position. The translation is then broken and it is executed again in another position. To reduce the number of translations, the user can indicate a particular region that could contain the pattern. If this region is (R * r) pixels size, the number of translations is then reduced to (R-L+1)*(r-l+1)+1.

3.2 Filtering Criteria

We present now, the principle of the filtering; first we give the definition of a naive global matching between a pattern and an image, then we introduce a new definition which is more precise.

We say that a prefix P matches with a prefix Q, if its correspondent quadrant is included in the one of Q. Thus, an image I contains a pattern M, if all the prefixes of M match with some prefixes of I. This definition is not sufficient and not precise. Indeed, let us suppose that we find a pattern represented by

{0000001010, 0000011000, 0000100, 0000111}, and it exists an image having a prefix P=0000, we note that all the prefixes of M match with P, and consequently I contains M. It is obvious that this kind of matching is not precise. To improve the filtering, we introduce two matching criterias corresponding to two filtering levels. The first is a microscopic level (or prefix level) represented by Definition1, and the second is a macroscopic level (or pattern level) represented by Definition2.

__Definition 1__ : Let $Q = q_1q_2q_3...q_{Lq} = (Lq,Vq)$ and $P=p_1p_2p_3...p_{Lp}=(Lp,Vp)$ be two prefixes of M and I respectively; we say that Q matches with P to within a factor δ,

$$\text{match}_\delta(Q,P) = \begin{cases} Lq = Lp + \delta, \delta \geq 0 \\ \text{and} \\ p_i = q_i, \ i = 1, ..., Lp \end{cases}$$

We note that : if $\delta = 0$, Q and P represent the same quadrant ; if $\delta = 2$, the quadrant associated to Q is included into the one of P and it has a quarter size of the one of P.

__Definition 2__ : We note N_pref the number of prefixes of an image that match the pattern, and N_pix the number of pixels addressed by the set of N_pref prefixes. We define the filtering ratio (or the filtering distance) between M and I by:

$$d(M,I) = \frac{1}{2} * \left(\frac{N\_pref}{M\_pref} + \frac{N\_pix}{M\_pix} \right).$$

Note that if $d(M,I) = 1$, the search is an exact one. Furthermore, because for any image I, $M\_pref \geq N\_pref$ and $M\_pix \geq N\_pix$, $d(M,I) \leq 1$. Thus, the precision of the search could be defined by the user. This means that the user gives a precision coefficient K $(0 \leq K \leq 1)$, and the system searches any image I that verifies $d(M,I) \geq K$.

According to these definitions, we can compare the filtering distance of two images I1, I2 to a given pattern M. We note d(M,I1) > d(M,I2) if

$$\left(\frac{N\_pref_1}{M\_pref} + \frac{N\_pix_1}{M\_pix} \right) > \left(\frac{N\_pref_2}{M\_pref} + \frac{N\_pix_2}{M\_pix} \right)$$

4. Parallel Processing

In this section, we suggest a method that permits to perform the fuzzy search using more than one processor. Actually, the operations described above run only with one processor; the use of the parallel processing is not yet implemented in our system. First, we give the usual algorithm for parallel image processing, then we introduce how to execute a parallel fuzzy search.

4.1 Parallel Image Processing

The principle of the quadtree parallel coding of an image, consists of (1) subdividing this image into some sub-images and (2) assigning to each processor a sub-image that has to be coded. According to the quadtree subdivision, the generated sub-images are about 4^i, if the subdivision is stopped at a given level i. The level where the subdivision would be stopped varies with the number of the available processors. Thus, if there are more than 4^i, (and less than $4^{(i+1)}$) processors, the number of these ones in addition will be idle. This kind of use of the parallel processing is not well optimized. Indeed, the informations contained in one image, are generally unevenly distributed. One image could have data concentrate in one or two sub-images, so just two processors process the coding, whereas the others are idle. To remedy this problem and to improve the parallel processing, [5] proposed a method that permits to distribute the sub-images so as to obtain an uniform charge on processors. The principle of distributing sub-images uniformly on processors, consists of assigning to each processor a set of sub-images. All these sets have more or less the same quantity of data but not the same number of sub-images. So data is almost well balanced in all the active processors.

In our case, we do not need to find a strategy of distributing data uniformly. In fact, the use of the B-tree and the IQ, allows to distribute data uniformly. That is why, we do not need to balance the processing, since it is naturally distributed uniformly. Thus, all the processors would almost have the same charge. Thus, the updating operations are processed using the classical algorithm described above. We discuss in the following section which tasks will be assigned to the processors to process a parallel searching.

4.2 Parallel Searching

In this section, we introduce the principle of the parallel fuzzy search that we adopt. Assuming that the searched pattern is contained in a minimal rectangle having (L*l) pixels size, the number of processors that we possess is NP, the total number of possible positions is $(2^N-L+1)*(2^N-l+1)+1$. So the parallel searching consists of assigning to each processor, a set of positions where the pattern has to be searched in. In the contrarily of the updating operation, where the number of processors NP has to be a power of 4, otherwise the processors in addition will be idle, this operation allows the use of all the available processors. We give, first, an example of executing a parallel search (fig4), then we introduce the general case of executing this operation.

In the example of Figure 4, we suppose that the number of processors is 4, the meta-image has a size of (16*16) pixels, and the minimal rectangle that contains the searched pattern has a size of (11*8) pixels. The content pattern can be any thing. So the total number of possible positions where the pattern has to be searched in, is 55. This set of positions is distributed uniformly into these processors. The minimal rectangle that contains all the possible positions is represented in a bold line, the boundaries searching of a given set of positions, for each processor is represented with a bold dotted line. We note that the first, the second and the third processor have to search the pattern in 13 positions, whereas the fourth one has to search it in 15 positions. We consider the last processor as the gathering one. In fact, Its task is to execute the search in all the positions that are not executed by any processor.

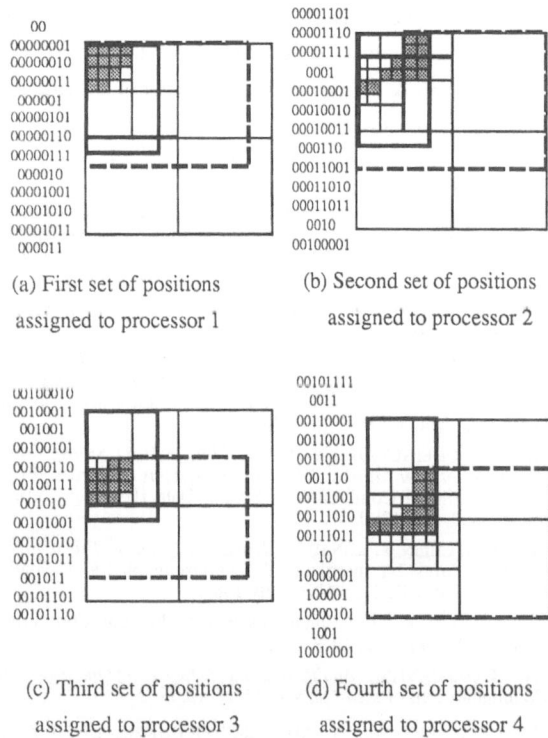

(a) First set of positions
assigned to processor 1

(b) Second set of positions
assigned to processor 2

(c) Third set of positions
assigned to processor 3

(d) Fourth set of positions
assigned to processor 4

<u>Figure 4</u>: *distribution of the set of positions*

So, the general algorithm of executing a parallel fuzzy search can be considered as :

1)- Computing the $[(2^n-L+1) \times (2^n-l+1)+1]$ positions, and the minimal rectangle that contains them.

2)- Distributing this set of positions as follows :

  a)- for i=1 to (NP-1) do

  associate to the processor i the positions that are between

$((i-1)*([(2^n-L+1) \times (2^n-l+1)+1]/NP)+1)$ and

       $(i*([(2^n-L+1) \times (2^n-l+1)+1]/NP))$

       b)- associate to the NP^{th} processor the positions that are between $((NP-1)*([(2^n-L+1) \times (2^n-l+1)+1]/NP)+1)$ and

      $((2^n-L+1) \times (2^n-l+1)+1)$

3)- Each processor executes partial fuzzy search in its associated set of positions

5. Conclusion

The main contribution of this paper can be described as the proposition of a new Quadtree-based data structure allowing a fuzzy search of pattern in an image database. We have investigated different types of manipulations with this structure, and we have shown that it is well adapted for content-oriented retrieval and fuzzy search. We have suggested a parallel processing for the fuzzy search using this data structure. In a forthcoming work, we will study the behavior of this structure using parallel processing.

6. References

[1] C.H. ANG, H. SAMET, "Node Distribution in a PR Quadtree", In Proceedings 1st International Symposium on Large Spatial Databases, Santa Barbara, USA, July 1989.

[2] S.K. CHANG, C.W. YAN, T. AMDT, D. DIMITROFF, "An Intelligent Image Database System", IEEE Transactions on Software Engineering, Vol.14, N°5, 1988.

[3] S.K. CHANG, E. JUNGERT, Y. LI, " The Design of Pictorial Database Based Upon the Theory of Symbolic Projections", In Proceedings 1st International Symposium on Large Spatial Databases, Santa Barbara, USA, July 1989.

[4] J.P. CHEINEY, B. KERHERVÉ: "Image Data Storage and Manipulations for Multimedia Database Systems", In Proceedings 4th International Conference on Spatial Data Handling, Zurich, Switzerland, July 1990.

[5] C.H. CHIEN, T. KANADE : "Distributed Quadtree Processing", In Proceedings 1st International Symposium on Large Spatial Databases, Santa Barbara, USA, July 1989.

[6] D. COMER, "The Ubiquitous B-tree", In ACM Computing Surveys , Vol.11, N°2, 1979.

[7] I. GARGANTINI: "An Efficient Way to Represent Quadtrees", In Communications of the ACM, Vol .25, N° 12, 1982.

[8] T. JOSEPH, A. F. CARDENAS, " PICQUERY: A High Level Query Language for Pictorial Database Management", IEEE Transactions on Software Engineering, Vol.14, N°5, 1988.

[9] K. MEYER, V.Y. LUM, C.T. WU :"Image Management in Multimedia Database System", In Proceedings IFIP TC 2/WG 2.6 Working Conference on Visual Database Systems, Tokyo, Japan, April 1989.

[10] G. KEDEM, "The Quadtree-CIF tree: a Data Structure for Hierarchical on-line algorithms", In Proceedings 19th Design Automation Conference, Las Vegas, USA, June 1983.

[11] G.M. MORTON, " A Computer Oriented Geodetic Database and a New Technique in File Sequencing" IBM Ltd., Ottawa, Canada, 1966.

[12] J. A. ORENSTEIN, T.H. MERRETT, "A Class of Data Structure for Associative Searching", ,In Proceedings 3rd ACM SIGACT-SIGMOD Symposium of Principles of DataBase Systems, 1984

[13] J. A. ORENSTEIN, F. A. MANOLA, "PROBE Spatial Data Modeling and Query Processing in an Image DataBase Application", IEEE Transactions on Software Engineering, Vol.14, N°5, 1988.

[14] N. ROUSSOPOULOS, C. FALOUTSOS, T.SELLIS, "An Efficient Pictorial DataBase System for PSQL", IEEE Transactions on Software Engineering, Vol.14, N°5, 1988.

[15] H.SAMET, "The Quadtree and Related Hierarchical Data Structures", In ACM Computing Surveys , Vol.16, N°2, 1984.

[16] H. SAMET: "Applications of Spatial Data Structures", Addison-Wesley, 1990.

[17] H. SAMET: "The Design and Analysis of Spatial Data Structures", Addison-Wesley, 1990.

[18] C.A. SHAFFER, H. SAMET, "Optimal Quadtree Construction Algorithms", In Computer Vision, Graphics and Image Processing, Vol 37,N°3, 1987.

[19] H.TAMOURA, N.YOKOYA: "Image Database System: A Survey", In Pattern Recognition, Vol.17, N°1, 1984.

[20] A. TOUIR,- B. KERHERVÉ: "Shape Translation in Images Encoded by Linear Quadtree", In Proceedings IFIP TC 5.10 Working Conference on Modeling in Computer Graphics, Tokyo, Japan April 1991.

[21] A. TOUIR: "Search Algorithms in Image Databases", Internal Report ENST/INF/BD/90_10

[22] T.R. WALSH: "Efficient Axis-Translation of Binary Digital Pictures by Blocks by Linear Quadtree Representation" Computer Vision, Graphics and Images Processing Vol .41, N°3, 1988.

[23] D. WOELK, W. KIM, W. LUTHER, "An Oriented Approach to Multimedia Databases",In Proceedings ACM SIGMOD'86 International Conference on Management of Data, Washington, USA, May 1986.

High Performance Data Parallel Recursion

Norbert Duppel

University of Stuttgart, IPVR
Breitwiesenstr. 22
D-7000 Stuttgart
duppel@ipvr.informatik.uni-stuttgart.dbp.de

ABSTRACT

The purpose of this paper is twofold. First we give results of a high performance implementation of data parallel recursion. Two algorithms demonstrate a linear growth in the range from 1 to 15 CPUs, and there is reason to believe that this will continue up to 45 resp. 25 CPUs.

The first algorithm is usable for arbitrarily large amounts of data, for the faster second one the result has to fit in the main memory available on all CPUs together. These algorithms can be perfectly used for transitive closure processing, and also for generalized transitive closures as e.g. bill-of-materials.

Second we give an algorithm for the integration of this data parallel algorithms in a general Deductive Database. We demonstrate the compilation of arbitrary recursive Horn logic rules into our data parallel algorithm. In fact we have just finished the integration in the Parallel Deductive Database developed at Stuttgart university.

1. Introduction

In the mass of papers which appeared in the last years on the topic of deductive processing, the need for parallel algorithms is generally acknowledged, as response times are often unacceptable. A lot of energy was put in the area of parallel deductive languages, but the parallel access of data in a deductive database is only rarely considered.

Parallel deduction can be achieved on the rule level and on the data level. Rule level parallelism appears in three important kinds: AND- parallelism on the rule level, OR-parallelism on the rule level and pipelining.

On this level parallelism results from the many data streams, which are defined by the rule system. These streams are - apart from the availability of their input - independent of each other and can so be under work independently or in a pipeline. There are several implementations of non-parallel deductive databases [1,2,3,...], but to our knowledge there is almost none including real concurrency [4,5].

The main drawback of rule level parallelism is the **restriction of the degree of parallelism** by the structure of the rule system. Most of the time only one processor can be used for the computation of a simple transitive closure, which is defined by a single recursive rule with two different predicates. So not much performance gains can be expected by the introduction of these kinds of parallelism for queries, which involve only a few recursive rules. On the other hand

transitive closures and other linear problems are most important in the area of recursion.

The only alternative is the introduction of **parallelism on the level of tuples resp. data**. The much greater number of tuples offers a much greater potential of parallelism, but of course also the danger of too much overhead in the processing of too small units of parallel execution.

In this paper we introduce a **high performance data parallel implementation** for the semi-naive computation of function free Horn logic recursive predicates [6]. Semi-naive computation is the method of choice, if there are·no instantiations. Additionally a lot of rule transformations have been investigated [7,8,9,10,...] that allow the efficient use of instantiations in a slightly modified semi-naive computation. Our algorithm is general, i.e. there are no restrictions on the type of recursion and it can be combined with several rule transformations, e.g. magic sets. For linear rules we demonstrate a nearly linear speed up in the range of 1 to 15 processors and there is reason to believe, that this remains true at least until about 45 resp. 25 processors. So performance is excellent and we believe that this data parallel algorithm can be used widely. The implementation was done on a Tandem multi processor system (TXPs) on top of the relational database NonStop SQL.

2. Definitions

We define a Deductive Database like in [11]. It describes a database which contains explicitly stored **basc predicates** (base relations) and rule-defined (function free Horn clauses) **virtual predicates** (virtual relations). In the Horn clause

$$P(X,Y) <\text{-} Q_1 (X,Z) ,..., Q_n (Z,Y)$$

we call P(X) the **head** of the rule and the conjunction of $Q_1(...), ..., Q_n(...)$ the rule **body**. Predicates Q_i may be base predicates, virtual predicates or selection predicates. **Selection predicates** are used to select only tuples with certain attribute properties. Examples are:

$$X = "John"$$

$$salary \ BETWEEN \ 0 \ AND \ 50$$

For safety of computation we consider so-called range restricted rules [7]. A **query** is syntactically a rule body, i. e. a conjunction of predicates (and at least one of them is no selection predicate). On the set of virtual predicates occurring in a rule system we define two relations as follows:

(1) P => Q,   if ∃ rule: Q <- ..., P, ...

(2) P =>> Q, if (P => Q) OR   ($\exists$ predicates P_1, P_2, ..., P_n:
P => P_1 AND P_1 => P_2 AND ... AND P_n => Q)

A predicate P is called **recursive**, if P =>> P. Predicates P and Q are called **mutual recursive**, if P =>> Q AND Q =>> P. Mutual recursion is an equivalence relation on the set of recursive predicates in a rule system. It partitions these predicates in disjunct subsets, called **recursive cliques**.

We often use the term "clique" not only for the set of predicates, but also for those rules, whose head is a clique predicate. Those rules are either **exit rules** or **recursive rules**: there is no recursive predicate in the body of an exit rule, but there is at least one in the body of a recursive rule.

3.   The SCHEDULER

In the project PROSPECT at Stuttgart university the so-called SCHEDULER was developed, which is an utility for the control of parallel execution schemes. Basic objects are tasks, events and server classes. A **task** is the unit of execution. In our context it means the execution of a database operation corresponding to a rule. Tasks are executed by **servers**. A server class consists of several servers each executing the same sequential program. For execution tasks are sent to the SCHEDULER, which propagates them to an available server. So if N tasks are sent to the SCHEDULER and N servers are available on different processors, they are all computed in parallel.

An **event** is basically a counter, which fires when the counter reaches zero. For each task a start event and a termination event can be defined. A task is not executed before its start event has fired. The termination of the task decreases the counter of its termination event by 1. The counter of an event can also be explicitly changed.

Class events support the termination detection of massive parallel computations. After their definition for a certain server class they fire if no more task exists for this server class, i.e. a (typically recursive) computation in this server class has finished. More details can be found in [12,13].

From the mass of features of the SCHEDULER two are essential for our purposes: low overhead on messages by message bundling and sophisticated dynamic load balancing among all servers in a class. Fig. 1 shows a typical process configuration consisting of a main program, the SCHEDULER process and two server classes.

4.   An illustrative example

The SCHEDULER is an excellent basis for the implementation of data parallel deduction. We now illustrate the basic ideas by a description of the computation of the transitive closure of a graph G. The following two rules define our problem:

TC(X,Y)   <-   G(X,Y);

TC(X,Y)   <-   TC(X,Z), G(Z,Y);

We assume, that the graph G is stored in a database relation G(G1,G2), and we want to compute its transitive closure and insert in into relation TC. Note that Horn logic "predicates" and database "relations" are synonyms in our context.

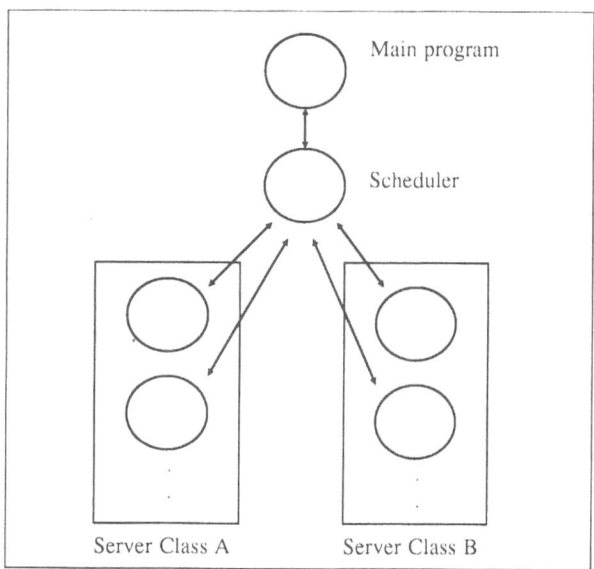

Fig. 1: Process configuration with two server classes

In rules data flows from the rule body (right side) to the rule head (left side). Given tuples for all predicates in the rule body, we can derive tuples of the head predicate. So the first rule leads to an insertion of all tuples of G into TC.

The second rule says: Find a tuple (v1,v2) of TC and a tuple (g1,g2) of G which hold v2=g1. Then you can derive a tuple TC(v1,g2). For our algorithm we change this interpretation a little bit:

Given a tuple (v1,v2) of TC, we have to look for a tuple (v2,g2) of G and can then derive (v1,g2) of TC.

Remember that the first rule produces many tuples for TC. For each of them we have to look in the graph for appropriate tuples. On the other hand again tuples for TC are now produced. They in turn must be used for further derivations, and so we have a recursive computation.

We now give a more formal description of the algorithm. Assume there is a tuple (v1, v2) of TC. For further derivations we have to insert this tuple in the body of the second rule. The inserted constants can be propagated in the rule, as the replaced variables occur elsewhere:

TC(v1, Y) <-   TC(v1, v2), G(v2, Y)

Predicate TC is satisfied by the inserted tuple by definition. Thus it can be deleted and we obtain:

TC(v1, Y) <-   G(v2, Y)

This reduced rule exactly follows our interpretation given before: we only have to look for appropriate tuples in G. So the following SELECT statement suffices for the computation of other new tuples (v1,Y) from the assumed tuple (v1,v2) of TC:

```
SELECT v1, G.G2
FROM G
WHERE G.G1 = v2
```

Several notes have to be made:

- The derived tuples of TC can be fed in again in the algorithm. We then get a recursive computation.

- A cycle in the data leads to an infinite computation. This can be avoided, if only **new** tuples are recursively fed in again. Then the computation will stop when TC is computed.

- If we start with all nodes/arcs existing in the graph (according the first rule), the transitive closure of the graph is computed.

- All these "tasks" are totally independent of each other and can be **executed concurrently**.

This independent execution of a "task" is a prerequisite for the usage of the SCHEDULER for the control of the computation. We can define the above described algorithm applied to an input tuple as a SCHEDULER task. Its code is given in Fig. 2.

```
INPUT:    tuple (v1,v2)

open cursor C for
    SELECT G.<Attribute2>
    FROM G
    WHERE <Attribute1> = v2;
fetch C into x;
while NOT end-of-cursor do begin
    INSERT INTO TC VALUES(v1, x);
    if NOT duplicate-error then {new tuple}
        Define_Task(v1,x); {define follower task}
    fetch C into x;
end
```

Fig. 2: Task to compute a transitive closure

Note, that relation TC must be created with key on both attributes to recognize duplicate tuples. Note that the database operations only differ in their input parameters. Only for a new tuple (i.e. no duplicate error results from the INSERT) another task is defined. This implements a semi-naive computation.

The computation is initiated by the main program as shown in Fig. 3. The first rule produces some tuples for TC, which build the starting point for the parallel computation. Remember that these initial tasks define new tasks themselves. After initiation the main program only has to wait until no more tasks are active or ready for execution. The SCHEDULER offers a mechanism for this: the class events (s. chapter 3).

```
The main program initiates the computation as follows:

1.)   Fetch all tuples of the graph;
      For each tuple (v1,v2) do
          Define_Task(v1,v2);
2.)   Wait for the termination
```

Fig. 3: Main program for the transitive closure

It is important to state, that the database operations in the code of the task are the result of a rule compilation as illustrated before. So we can generalize this algorithm for general recursive processing. These ideas, as well as the performance aspects, are discussed in the next chapters.

5. The algorithm

We now describe the algorithm for a data parallel computation of the predicates of a recursive clique. In a first phase the rule system is analyzed in the main program and the database operations of the tasks are determined according to the recursive rules. Input are the rules of the recursive clique and the query predicate with its instantiations. We first have to broadcast the database operations to the servers, then the second phase begins: the database access. The initial tasks are determined according to the (non-recursive) exit rules and sent to the SCHEDULER for execution. The main program now awaits the end of the recursive computation.

Phase 1: Rule compilation (main program)

For the moment we assume that the rule system is linear, i.e. in the body of each recursive rule there is exactly one predicate of the recursive clique. For each recursive rule we construct the according database operations as follows:

Assume we have the following rule and a tuple $(q_1, q_2, ...)$ for the recursive predicate Q in the rule body:

$$P(P_1, P_2, ...) <- ..., Q(Q_1, Q_2, ...), ...$$

Insert this tuple in the rule body and propagate the constants to the other predicates: if a replaced variable Q_j also occurs in another predicate, it can be replaced everywhere by constant q_j. After predicate Q is deleted from the rule body, the rule is transformed into an equivalent SQL statement. If two variables Q_i and Q_j are equal, the condition $q_i=q_j$ must be added to the SQL statement (or be checked elsewhere in the task). In the sequel we call this database operation "Select-from-body". A second database operation called "Insert-into-head" is simply constructed as "INSERT INTO <P> VALUES (...)".

For each recursive rule we now have the following information: name and structure of the input predicate Q, name and structure of the output predicate P and the database operations SELECT-from-body and INSERT-into-head.

This information about all rules is broadcast to each server at the end of the first phase.

Example (P, Q are recursive):

$$P(X, Z) \quad <- \quad B1(W, X), Q(X, Y), B2(Y, Z)$$

Insert tuple $Q(q_1,q_2)$ and propagate constants:

$$=> \quad P(q_1, Z) \quad <- \quad B1(W, q_1), Q(q_1, q_2), B2(q_2, Z)$$

Delete predicate Q which is fulfilled:

$$=> \quad P(q_1, Z) \quad <- \quad B1(W, q_1), B2(q_2, Z)$$

Transform into SQL ("SELECT-from-body"):

```
=>    SELECT q1, B2.<attribute2>
      FROM B1, B2
      WHERE B1.<attribute2> = q1
      AND B2.<attribute1> = q2
```

Remember, that q_1 and q_2 are parameters for the dynamic SQL operation, which are replaced during task execution by the actual task input tuple values. As both joins defined by the original rule involved predicate Q, which is now substituted by a fixed tuple, the transformed rule contains no join at all and is therefore very cheap.

Phase 2: The data parallel computation

The input information of a task consists of a tuple t and the name of the predicate P, to which it belongs. The initial tasks for the computation are defined by the main program according the exit rules. An exit rule

P(P1, P2, ...) <- ...

is transformed in a database operation, and the tuples for P are fetched. For each tuple t a task is defined:

Define_Task(P, t);

The code of the task is mainly the same as in Fig. 2. The only generalization is, that all database operations are performed with input tuple t, that were determined from a rule with head predicate P. The server is given in Fig. 4.

```
while TRUE do begin
   read message;
   if "broadcast message" then{ it contains all database
                           statements and predicate names }
      repare all database operations
   else              { message: ( predicate: Q, tuple: t) }
      for each rule with pred. Q in the rule body do begin
         open cursor C for according SELECT using t;
         fetch C;
         build new tuple t^new;
         determine head predicate P;
         while NOT end-of-cursor do begin
         INSERT INTO P VALUES ( t^new);
            if NOT duplicate-error then
               Define_Task ( P, t^new );
            fetch C;
            build new tuple t^new;
         end
      end {for/else}
end; {while}
```

Fig. 4: Server for the data parallel computation

From a non-linear rule we generate N database operations if there are N clique predicates in the rule body. Due to lack of space we do not consider them further on.

6. Performance validation by measurements

Performance is the only reason for the development of our tuple-oriented strategy. In the following we will argue in three steps: First we give results from the transitive closure computation described in the beginning. Second we conclude on the performance of linear rule processing, and finally we deal with non-linear rules.

Note that the dominant performance factor is the database access in the task, as it is done for each tuple!

6.1. The transitive closure (TC)

Our transitive closure processing was intensively studied during the development of the SCHEDULER (see chapter

3). Environment for the implementation was a Tandem multi processor system with the relational database NonStop SQL. The system follows the shared-nothing approach, i.e. neither memory nor discs are shared by the processors. Data access is therefore RPC-based.

For the measurements data about roads around Stuttgart is used: the graph contains 304 edges connecting 101 nodes, the transitive closure consists of 13736 edges and 16968 duplicates are produced. For a computation with N processors the graph relation and the result relation are both partitioned over N discs.

Several conclusions could be drawn [12]:

- A linear speed-up and scale-up with increasing number of processors was reached with a factor of 0.9. Measurements were made in the range of 1 to 15 processors. There is no bottleneck in the computation, not even in the SCHEDULER, which distributes the tasks. All major components except the SCHEDULER and the interprocessor bus are evenly distributed over the system. As the SCHEDULER consumes only about 20% of its CPU and the load of the interprocessor bus is almost as low, there is reason to believe that throughput growth remains linear until about 45 processors.

- The single processor performance is equal to a standard semi-naive evaluation, which is a good strategy given only one processor.

- The result of our compilation of the rules defining TC differs only in the usage of dynamic SQL instead of static SQL, as the SQL statements are dynamically derived from the rules. Fig. 5 gives the result of our measurements in the range from 1 to 15 processors. The lower curve was measured with only one server on each CPU, the upper one with two servers. Then the CPUs are fully utilized and more servers do not change the results significantly. Note that we give the throughput to demonstrate its linearity.

There are three important conditions for this excellent behaviour:

- The data must be partitioned across the discs, so that costs for the data access (I/O and CPU path length) are distributed over all processors.

- There is indexed access on the graph relation, i.e. the tuples are stored in a partitioned B-tree, which allows to directly access them.

- The messages between the SCHEDULER and the servers must be bundled to reduce message overhead. The SCHEDULER does not send single tasks to a server, but a bundle of tasks. The servers as well send the tasks they define not one by one but in bundles. This bundling of messages is invisible to the SCHEDULER application programmer. The bundling factor is dynamically determined according to the number of tasks which are ready for execution.

6.2. Linear rule performance

A linear rule contains exactly one recursive predicate Q in its body:

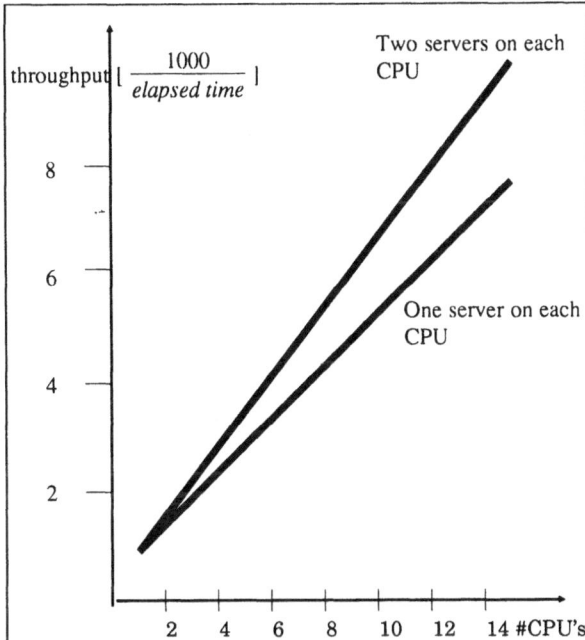

Fig. 5: Measurement of transitive closure performance

P(...) <- ..., Q(...), ...

This predicate is removed after the tuple was inserted and the constants were propagated. All other predicates are stored in the database, either as base relations or as intermediate results. Let us now look at the resulting database access in certain situations:

If **no other predicate** remains, then operation "Select-from-body" is empty, which results in excellent performance! Note that the whole rule could have been eliminated by optimization techniques described in [5,14].

If a **single predicate** remains, then each task only has to SELECT from a single predicate. This is a cheap operation, especially if there is an indexed access. This is the case in the transitive closure computation.

If there are **two or more predicates** left, the database access seems to be more costly. Consider two examples, where small characters indicate constants, R and S are base relations, and the rules are already transformed:

(1)   P(...) <-   S(Z,v), R(v,X)

(2)   P(...) <-   S(v,Z), R(Z,X)

In the first example no join condition is left, as the join variable was obviously replaced by constant v. Again the database access is cheap. In the second example in each task a join of S and R has to be computed. But this join can be **avoided in the task**, as we can precompute a new virtual predicate SR defined by the rule

SR(A,Z,X) <- S(A,Z), R(Z,X)

We then replace it in rule (2), which is now reduced to

(2)   P(...) <-   SR(v,Z,X)

Thus the problem is reduced to the single predicate case described above.

Note that this precomputation can be determined at rule compilation time and thus be integrated in other precomputations, e.g. the computation of Q and/or R, if they themselves are virtual predicates defined by other rules. In general we can avoid any join in the task by a precomputation. This is analogous to the precomputation of a loop-invariant during code optimization of compilers.

7. Improved duplicate elimination

In this chapter we give a variant of the algorithm that differs in the method of duplicate elimination. Consider once again Figures 2 and 4. In each task the definition of further tasks depends on the success of the insertion of the produced tuple. If the tuple was already inserted before, the task also was defined before and is therefore now ignored.

In essence the primary key of a database table is used for duplicate elimination. Of course there are cheaper techniques of duplicate elimination, e.g. hashing techniques:

> Instead of a try to insert the tuple, it is sent to a special server, which eliminates duplicates among the incoming tuples by inserting them in a hash table (extendible hashing). If a tuple is new, it is inserted in the result table and a follower task is defined. So the original task is divided into two: a fetch and an insert task.

This technique can be realized using the SCHEDULER by the introduction of another server class, which contains only a single elimination server.

The new processing structure shows a different behaviour:

- The number of tasks as a whole is greater, as each fetched tuple is sent to the elimination server via an additional task.

- Duplicate elimination is much cheaper as long as the hash table fits in main memory: the number of INSERT operations is strongly reduced, all remaining operations are successful.

- The insertion of tuples is cheaper, as no key is needed on the relation. It also should not be partitioned.

Fig. 6 shows the results of measurements, where one CPU was reserved for the elimination server. It is the curve labelled "One elimination server". Until 6 processors we get a linear curve, which shows an improvement of almost 50% to the previous algorithm. Then the elimination server gets the bottleneck of the computation.

Unfortunately the 15 processor system was not available for these measurements, so that we can only present results in the range from 1 to 8 processors.

8. Multiple elimination servers

The bottleneck produced by the single elimination server can be avoided by the addition of further elimination servers. But for correct duplicate elimination we have to ensure that a tuple t, which is produced several times in different fetch servers is always sent to exactly the same elimination server. Only then we can be sure, that the duplicates will be recognized.

202

Our approach to ensure this with minimal overhead is the usage of another hash function in the fetch servers:

> With N elimination servers we use a hash function with N hash classes. A fetch server hashes each produced tuple, and according to the hash value the tuple is sent to the appropriate elimination server. If tuple t is produced several times, it results always in the same hash value and is surely sent to exactly the same elimination server.

Fig. 6 also shows the curve for two elimination servers. Until 6 processors it is identical to the single server curve. But then no bottleneck keeps from a further linear growth.

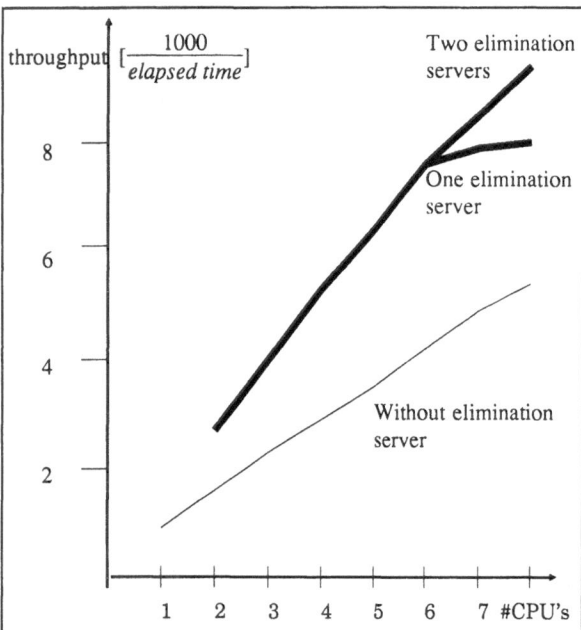

Fig. 6: Performance with duplicate elimination by hashing

There are several advantages in the use of multiple elimination servers:

- The number of servers can be adjusted to avoid bottlenecks.

- An elimination server on each CPU ensures a well-balanced load, which has a strong impact on linear growth.

- The amount of main memory available for the hash table used for duplicate elimination is the sum of the memory available on all CPUs.

Note that the SCHEDULER in this case produced not more than about 30 % of CPU load. This limits the linear growth to about 25 CPUs, which is a great number today. A direct communication path from the fetch servers to the elimination servers could defer this limit.

9. Conclusion

In this paper we give results of a high performance implementation of data parallel recursion. Two algorithms demonstrate a linear growth in the range from 1 to 15 resp.

8 CPUs, and there is reason to believe that this will continue up to 45 resp. 25 CPUs.

The first algorithm is usable for arbitrarily large amounts of data, for the faster second one the result has to fit in the main memory available on all CPUs together. These algorithms can be perfectly used for transitive closure processing, and also for generalized transitive closures as e.g. bill-of-materials [15].

Second we give an algorithm for the integration of this data parallel algorithms into a general Deductive Database. We demonstrate the compilation of arbitrary recursive Horn logic rules into our data parallel algorithm. In fact we have just finished the integration into the Parallel Deductive Database developed at Stuttgart university.

References

[1] Dayal, U., Smith, J.; PROBE: A Knowledge-Oriented DBMS, Proc. Islamorada Workshop On Large Scale Knowledgebase And Reasoning Systems, 1985

[2] Ullman, J. D.; Implementation of Logical Query Languages for Databases, ACM Transactions on Database Systems, Vol. 10, No. 3, pp 298-321, 1985

[3] Lefebvre, A., Vieille, L.; On Deductive Query Evaluation in the DedGin System, Proc. 1st Int. Conf. on Deductive and O-O Databases, 1989

[4] Boral, H.; Parallelism in BUBBA, Proc. Int. Symposium on Databases in Parallel and Distributed Systems, Austin, Tx, 1988

[5] Duppel, N., Gugel, D., Maier, J., Reuter, A., Schiele, G.; Proc. Workshop on PROSPECT, University of Stuttgart, 1990

[6] Bayer, R.; Query Evaluation and Recursion in Deductive Database Systems, Technical University of Munich, internal review, 1985

[7] Bancilhon, F. and Ramakrishnan, R.; An Amateur's Introduction to Recursive Query Processing Strategies, ACM SIGMOD, Vol. 15, No. 2, p. 16, 1986

[8] Bancilhon, F., Maier, D., Sagiv, Y., Ullman, J.; Magic sets and other strange ways to implement logic programs, Proc. 5th ACM SIGMOD-SIGACT PODS, 1986

[9] Beeri, C., Ramakrishnan, R.; On the power of Magic, MCC Technical Report DB-061-86, 1986

[10] Sacca, D., Zaniolo, C.; Magic Counting Methods, Proc. ACM SIGMOD, 1987

[11] Gallaire, H., Minker, M.; Logic and Databases: A Deductive Approach, ACM Computing Surveys, Vol. 16, No. 2, 1984

[12] Schiele, G.; Eine Testumgebung zur Untersuchung paralleler Verarbeitungsstrategien in komplexen Transaktionen, Informatik Fachberichte, No. 204, Springer Verlag, 1989

[13] Gugel, Dieter; Verteilte parallele Verarbeitung komplexer Transaktionen - Entwurf geeigneter Basismechanismen, Diplomarbeit am Institut für Informatik, Universität Stuttgart, 1989

[14] Duppel, N.; Implementation of a Parallel Deductive Database, Proc. GFKl 1991, Salzburg, 1991

[15] Staiger, R.; Massively parallel bill-of-material processing (in German), Studienarbeit No. 844, IPVR, university of Stuttgart, 1990

A Form System
for an Object-Oriented Database System [1]

Christine Collet Eric Brunel

Laboratoire de Genie Informatique, IMAG
BP 53X, 38041 Grenoble, France

ABSTRACT

This paper describes the interactive system FO2 implemented on top of an object-oriented database system. FO2 uses the form model described in [3] and [8]. The form notion offers a formal and homogeneous approach for describing and manipulating structural, semantic, and interface aspects of new database applications. Data are represented by Abstract Forms. An Abstract Form (called FA) may be viewed as a nonfirst normal form relation to which a set of rules describing the behavior of the FA occurrences is associated. For every FA, FO2 builds Presentations allowing an end-user to get on the screen the forms for querying and updating the occurrences of the FA. FO2 has been implemented with a bootstrap approach and we have forms to define forms. Here we give a general presentation of the FO2 system and a description of the FO2 kernel implemented using O_2, an object-oriented database system[6].

1 Introduction

The well known form notion is traditionally used to build screens and to describe some database user dialog in order to access and update data [27], [30], [23]. Most of 4th Generation Languages offer a form concept [11] but the approach is rather artificial because of the use of SQL as a programming language. Further, in office automation, the form notion has been used to increase the database system capabilities with some specific tools such as word processing, editors , electronic mail, and office procedure automatization [31], [32], [14], [29], [7], [13], [20]. In order to design a system integrating, in a homogeneous way, the features of a DBMS and those of an application generator we propose to extend the form notion [3], [8]. This approach breaks the separation between application programs and the DBMS, and gives the possibility to manage at the same time structural and semantic aspects of data. The form notion allows designing such a system with a top-down approach by taking the form notion at the interface level and extending this notion in several ways. First, we allow multimedia data in the form fields. Second, we consider a form as a complex object inside the database [5], [2], [16], [21]. Third, because of the interactive nature of a form displayed on the screen, actions can be performed upon the form, letting the system react accordingly. The "dynamic" nature of the objects is achieved through an "event-action" mechanism. Therefore, an application is defined by forms that capture the complex objects of the application, their behavior, and their presentations on the screen.

[1]This work was supported in part by the Gip Altair, IN2-INRIA-LRI, Le Chesnay, France.

```
Customer: [Name: string, Orders: {Order: [Year: integer,
              Design: CLU: □ | Name: string, Amount: integer] },
          TotalAmount: integer   ]
                              Schema
(10, Customer: [Name: John,
     Orders: {Order: [Year: 1989, Design: CLU:□, Amount: 100],
              Order: [Year: 1989, Design: Name: DB4, Amount: 300]},
              TotalAmount: 400     ] )
                              Occurrence
```

Figure 1: Schema and Occurrence of the FA Customer

This paper is organized as follows. Section 2 briefly describes the main concepts of the form model and lists the key choices taken to develop the FO2 system implementing this model. FO2 runs on SUN workstations and has been implemented on top of O_2, an object-oriented database system [6]. Section 3 presents an overview of the FO2 system. Section 4 describes the two components of the system. Finally, section 5 summarizes our results.

2 Form Model

2.1 Abstract Form

The Abstract Form(FA) is the main concept of the form model. A FA is the representation of a class of complex objects. To define the FA concept, we took an approach similar to the one developed for nonfirst normal form relations [4], [12], [18], [1], [26], [24], [28], or complex objects [5], [2], [16], [21]. The extension of a FA is a set of occurrences (or complex objects). The intention of a FA is twofold: first, a **schema** describes the common structure of the objects; second, **rules** express the behavior of the objects.

2.1.1 Schema

A FA schema is defined by using a combination of the tuple([...]), set({...}), list(≺...≻), and alternative (|) constructors and atomic domain names. The schema Customer in Figure 1 describes the structure of a class of customers of a warehouse of products. The product named 'CLU' is the most ordered and appears as a constant schema (CLU: □) specifying one of the possible choices for naming the ordered products. Each customer occurrence has a unique identifier in the FA Customer, a name, the set of product orders that were placed, and the amount to pay for the orders. In the occurrence of Figure 1, identified by *10*, the set Orders is a heterogeneous set of Order due to the alternative constructor used to define the Design attribute.

2.1.2 FA_Expressions

FA_expressions have to be considered as a formalism (i.e., part of the form model) and not as a user language. They are built using operations for querying, updating FAs, and doing specific calculations as those in a programming language. FA_expressions to query FAs use quantifiers and operations such as select, prune, nest, or unnest. These operations are defined recursively because in the context of an occurrence, an attribute and its value may define a FA. For example, to find the name of the customers who never placed an order of the "CLU" product, the following FA_expression can be written:

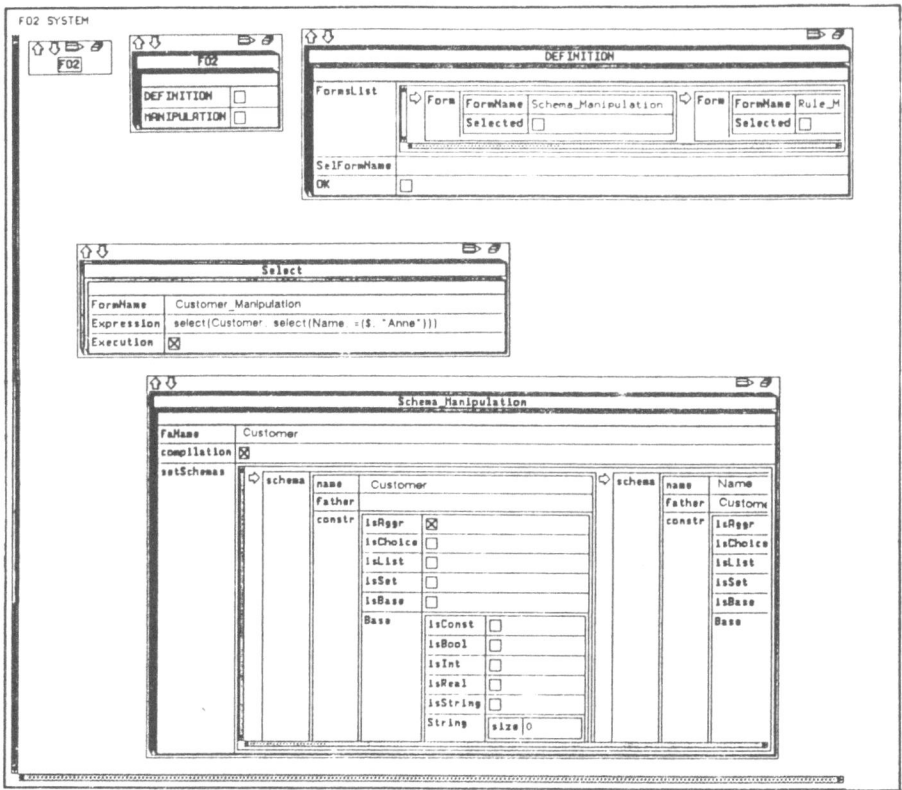

Figure 3: Screen of the FO2 system

prune(select(Customer, select(Orders, ∀select(Order, select(Design, not(CLU)))), Orders, TotalAmount)

The first part of the prune operation (i.e., the select operation) retrieves the set of customers who never placed an order of the "CLU" product. The second part of the prune operation ("Orders, TotalAmount") defines the attributes of the retrieved occurrences that have to be pruned. Operations to update FAs concern a set of occurrences (i.e., create, delete, modify) or only one occurrence (i.e., assign, remove).

2.1.3 Rule

Complex object behavior is treated here in the precise framework of the interaction between a user and a form. A rule can express integrity constraints, object status (e.g., mandatory, modifiable), calculations, exceptions, and so on. The CalcTotal rule in Figure 2 is attached to the schema Customer of Figure 1 and to every Customer occurrence. This rule is intended to control the assignment of a value to the attribute Amount of a product order, and to calculate the TotalAmount due by the customer. The rule becomes active when values are assigned to the variables: ?c(an identifier of occurrence of Customer), ?i(an internal index to denote an order in the set Orders), and ?p(an amount of order). Then the BEFORE clause is executed: if Amount is positive, then the modification operation is accepted and the AFTER clause is executed, otherwise the operation "cancel_evt" is performed and the modification operation is rejected. The execution of the CalcTotal rule results in assigning to the form the current value of the TotalAmount component: the last value, if the event is rejected, or the result of the calculation, if the event is accepted.

A WHEN clause can have more then one event; the activation of the rule is done when an event of the clause occurs and the other events have been accepted. A manipulation context is maintained for each occurrence O of a FA. This context lists the update operations that have been performed against O and that are significant for the activation of the rules attached to O.

```
WHEN     assign(?c.Orders{?i}.Order.Amount, ?p);
BEFORE if ( ≺(?p, 0), cancel_evt;);
AFTER    assign(?c.TotalAmount, 0);
         FA(AMOUNT, ?c.Orders.Order);
         For(AMOUNT, ?A) assign(?c.TotalAmount,
                          +(?c.TotalAmount, ?A.Amount));
```

Figure 2: Rule CalcTotal in the FA Customer

2.2 Presentation

A Presentation gets a form (an object on the screen) from FA occurrences. A Presentation is twofold: a format that express how an occurrence has to be displayed and some specific operations that are allowed on the form. To describe a format we do not propose new presentation technics but we rather use the notion of box and the dialog between a user and a form is based on the event notion [15]. The specific operations are not tied to a format; this approach allows to get forms on the screen having different behaviors for a given FA and a given format. The invocation of a specific operation might be seen as the opening of a context (i.e., a transaction) for executing elementary operations/events on the form.

3 General presentation of FO2

3.1 User aspects

Figure 3 shows a screen produced by FO2. The FO2 form is used to choose one of the two FO2 environments, both represented by a form. The DEFINITION form shows a list of system forms (names) that can be used to define, modify or delete forms. The MANIPULATION form shows a list of user forms that have been defined using FO2. A form is chosen by clicking the "Selected" box or directly by typing the form name in the "SelFormName" field. When the user validates his or her choice by clicking the "OK" box, the DEFINITION form or the MANIPULATION form displays the selected form.

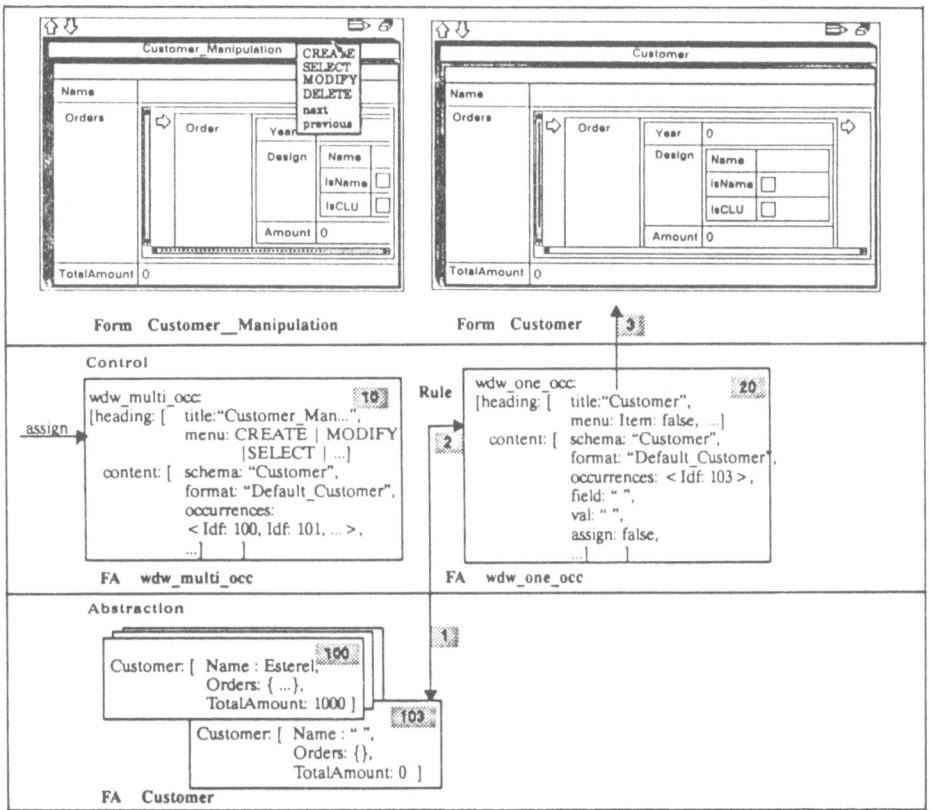

Figure 4: Behavior of the FO2 system

Generally speaking, when a user wants to define a form she or he has to define a FA (i.e., a schema and rules) through forms. Figure 3 shows the aspect of the Schema form during the specification of the Customer schema. Let us assume that the compilation of the Customer schema has been performed. The FO2 system provides the user with two new (user) forms called Customer_Manipulation and Customer showed in figure 4.

The form Customer_Manipulation can be viewed as a factory with a stock (the set of customers of the warehouse). It can only be manipulated through a menu which has items that allow creating a new customer, modifying or deleting an existing customer. A customer is extracted from the stock (i.e., the database) using the SELECT operation. The next and previous operations allow displaying of the "next" or "previous" customer among the selected customers, respectively. The definition of form is comprised of its name, the name of the FA schema it uses, the name of a format, and the name of a window FA (the *Window* component) specifying the frame used to display the form. The *Window* component for Customer_Manipulation is *wdw_multi_occ*, the name of the window FA that describes the specific operations giving a factory behavior to that form.

The form Customer is displayed when a user clicks CREATE or MODIFY from the menu of Customer_Manipulation. The Customer form can be edited in a flexible manner using the *cut, copy,* and *paste* operations and the *new* operation to insert a new element in a set or a list. Let us assume the user types a positive value in the field Amount of an order line and a Carriage Return to validate her or his entry. The CalcTotal rule will become active and a new value is displayed for the field TotalAmount. The form Customer may be compared to the manufacturing process of a customer during which controls are executed. The *Window* component of Customer is *wdw_one_occ* describing a window for editing.

3.2 Run-time Aspects

Figure 4 gives a static view of the FO2 System and shows that we use the PAC model[10] to structure FO2. This model provides modularity and independence between the semantics and the interface aspects of an interactive system which is structured in three parts: the Abstraction part, the Presentation part, and the Control part.

The Abstraction part defines the concepts and the functions of the system. This part is represented in Figure 4 by the FA Customer. The context used for rules activation(see section 2.1.3) is not illustrated in Figure 4. The Presentation part defines the input and output behavior of the system as perceived by the user. It is composed in Figure 4 of: (i) for output, the form Customer_Manipulation, (ii) for input, mouse actions that the user can perform to select an item from the menu. The Control part maintains the consistency between the two previous parts by storing an extensive knowledge about the two worlds served : the FA world and the Presentations world. In Figure 4, the Control is comprised of an occurrence of the *wdw_multi_occ* FA with an identifier, say *10*. This occurrence is comprised of: (i) a heading that gives the title and the menu of the form, (ii) a contents giving the components used to build the form (i.e., the schema and the occurrences of a FA, and a Presentation).

Let us assume the user has clicked CREATE from the menu of the Customer_Manipulation form. The Presentation manages the form and "notifies" the control part of the user action by asking for the execution of "*assign(wdw_multi_occ{10}. heading.menu,* CREATE". The Control part "interprets" the selection of the CREATE item from the menu as: (1) the creation of a new occurrence for the FA Customer with an identifier, say *103*; (2) the creation of a new occurrence of the *wdw_one_occ* FA with an identifier, say *20*, and some "*assign*" operations that set values to attributes of that occurrence.

The above actions are achieved through a rule of the FA wdw_multi_occ. If the "assign(...)" operation is validated then the Control asked the Presentation to display the Customer form. Notice that the creation of occurrences belonging to FAs of the Control Part is the means for the Abstraction to ask the Presentation for displaying forms.

4 FO2 Implementation

4.1 The O_2 platform

The FO2 system has been implemented on top of the object-oriented system O_2. This section presents only the basic elements of the O_2 system (prototype of September 1989) useful to understand how the FO2 system has been implemented. For a more complete description of the O_2 system, the reader is referred to [6], [21].

The O_2 data definition language [22], is used to describe a schema. A schema consists of classes related by an inheritance relationship. A class describes the internal structure(type) of objects and their behavior(methods). An object is a pair(identity value). A type is constructed recursively using O_2 atomic types, class names, and set, list or tuple constructors. Methods implementation is the writing of CO_2 code or $BasicO_2$ code [22]. Persistency in O_2 is provided by naming objects and values. For example, the expression "*add object Extend_Customer: FA_Custo mer*" declares the name "Extend_Customer" for a FA_Customer object. The O_2 system also provides the notion of an application as a set programs manipulating classes of the database. Programs represent tasks of the application and are coded using one of the O_2 programming languages. One particular application of the O_2 system is the Object-Oriented Programming Environment(OOPE) having classes such as the class OOPE_class which describes the structure of classes and their behavior.

LOOKS is a user interface generation tool [25] that provides primitives to create, remove, edit, save, and maintain consistency of the presentations of objects or values. These primitives may be used in a method implementation or a program of an application. Figures in Section 3 give examples of O_2 presentations. A presentation has a menu whose items show the names of methods that can be activated on the object. This menu can be changed by overriding the method "activable_methods" of the object. Classic editing operations such as cut, copy, paste, create are performed on a presentation using the mouse and the keyboard.

4.2 Implementation Choices

Among the operations to manipulate the FAs, we implemented: the *select* operation which retrieves occurrences of a FA, the update operations *create*, *modify*, *delete* and *assign*, the "*FA*" operation which defines a temporary FA, an iteration function *for* which can be applied on a set or list of occurrences, and a set of basic functions ($+$, $=$, $\succ$, string concatenation, and so on). The rule definition limits the WHEN clause to have only one event. FO2 generates a default Presentation for every FA. The format is defined using the FA schema [9] and specific operations are provided for a standard manipulation of forms. This functionality is an aid for the designer during form specification and also increases productivity. Further, this allows form applications to be developed with homogeneous interface aspects.

An initial implementation of the form model [9] showed that a form can be built only from occurrences and schemas, i.e., FA. The implementation also showed the advantage of using bootstrapping techniques: rapid implementation and evaluation of the model and the language itself by developing the forms definition environment. FO2 has been developed using a bootstrap approach too and we have defined a FA for every key concept of our model. The Schema and Rule FAs are only used for the implementation of FO2 and an application programmer cannot use them to write FA_expressions. This is justified by the requirement for safe manipulation of the data. The FA Evt for the description of events and the FA Algebra for the description of query FA_expressions are used only during the execution of an application.

By considering FA_expressions and rules as FA occurrences we get a system that makes no distinction between data and programs. However, to adopt the philosophy "everything is an object," we should define a FA for each major syntactic operations of the language. The syntactical checks would be incorporated in the schema of these FAs and the semantics ones would be defined in the rules attached to these FAs. With that kind of representation, we can provide a friendlier way of expressing queries, and facilities such as programming-by-examples or by menus to define rules.

Concurrency is not considered in FO2. Transactions are managed using the mechanism proposed by the O_2 system and nested transactions necessary for rules execution are not provided. Therefore, every valid update operation (not cancelled by the execution of a BEFORE clause of a rule) is committed to the database.

4.3 The FO2 Kernel

4.3.1 Abstraction part

The Abstraction part is implemented by a set of O_2 classes providing functions to manipulate objects as FA occurrences, to manage events, to trigger and execute rules. Figure 5 shows the main classes of the Abstraction part. The name of a class is given in an oval and the type declaration of the class is given below the oval. The names of the main methods of a class are also given beside the oval.

The FA class

The FA class describes the common structural and semantic properties of FA occurrences. Methods of the FA class codes query and update operations, and the execution mechanism of these operations including the activation and execution of rules.

A FA S is implemented by an O_2 class, say FA_S which is a subclass of the FA class. The FA_S class is the result of the compilation of the schema S (see below). Methods of the FA_S class describe the query and update operations for S. Every occurrence of S is represented by an object of FA_S having the attributes: (i) *FAname* whose value is the string denoting the FA to which the occurrence belongs ("S"), (ii) *idf* whose value is the occurrence identifier, (iii) *ctxt* whose value is a set of objects describing the update operations that have been performed on the occurrence, (iv) *rules* whose value is a set objects representing the rules attached to S and we say that the attribute rules refers the rules of S, and (iv) *schema* whose value represents the occurrence.

The subclasses FA_Schema, FA_Rule, FA_Evt and FA_Algebra in Figure 5 can be viewed as the result of the compilation of the FA schemas Schema, Rule, Evt and Algebra, respectively. An instance of one these subclasses is manipulated using the methods resulting of the compilation of the corresponding FA. However, the subclasses also code internal functions of the FO2 system through additional methods such as Compile, sendEvt, execSelect that have been explicitly defined. Notice that an instance of the FA_Schema(FA_Rule) class has an attribute *rules* whose value refers the rules of Schema(Rule) coding the semantics of schemas(rules) update.

The FA_Schema class

The class FA_Schema in Figure 5 implements the FA Schema. An instance of the FA_Schema class, say O_S, represents the definition of a schema S. The method Compile is the main function of the FA_Schema class. When this method is applied to an object O_S, the following actions are executed:

• the definition of the subclass FA_S representing the schema S. The type the FA_S class is on the form `tuple(schema:M(S))` where M (Figure 6) is the mapping function between the constructors of the FA model and those of the O_2 model. A list or a set in FO2 has a name for its elements and is represented by a list of O_2 tuples. The O_2 model has no alternative constructor and we use the tuple constructor to represent an FO2 alternative. Assume the schema C: A1:*d1* | A2:*d2* | ... | An:*dn*. Each subschema Ai:*di* of C is mapped into an O_2 tuple having two attribute descriptions "isAi:boolean" and "Ai: M(di)". The semantics of the alternative constructor is managed through the methods generated for the update of the O_2 list.

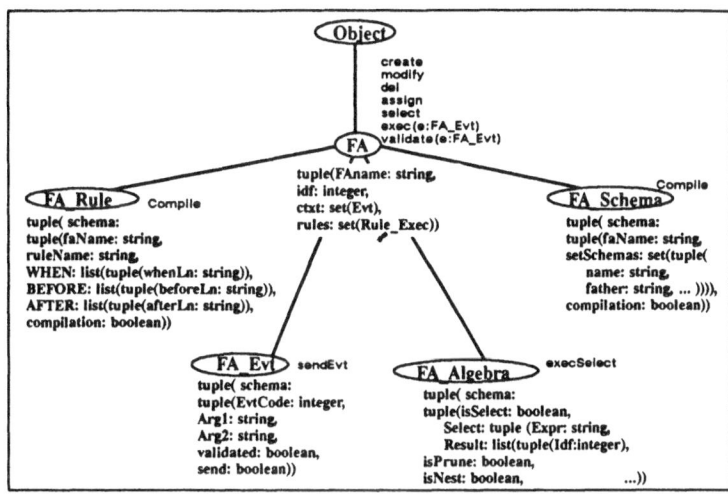

Figure 5: Main classes of the Abstraction

The function M is defined recursively by:

$$M([A1:d1, ..., An:dn]) = tuple(A1:M(d1), ..., An:M(dn))$$
$$M(\prec A:d \succ) = list(tuple(A:M(d)))$$
$$M(\{A:d\}) = set(tuple(A:M(d)))$$
$$M(A1:d1 \mid ... \mid An:dn]) = list(tuple(isA1: boolean, A1:M(d1)),$$
$$...$$
$$tuple(isAn: boolean, An:M(dn)),$$
$$M(D) = D$$
$$M(A:) = nothing$$

Figure 6: Mapping function M

The FA_S class description is an object of the OOPE_Class class of the programming environment of O_2. The compilation of this object updates the hierarchy in Figure 5 by creating a subclass FA_S of the FA class. Methods of the class FA_S are taken from the definition of the FA class. The methods *create* and *del* are overloaded because the CO_2 language does not provide genericity. New methods are defined to execute a Select operation, to read attributes values of an FA_S object, to set values to attributes of an object of FA_S. The definition of these methods is done using the OOPE_method class and the OOPE_class class of OOPE.

• the definition of the prototype object of the class FA_S "Extend_S:FA_S". The creation of a new occurrence of the FA S is done by applying the method create to Extend_S. The value of the idf attribute of this object is the value of the next occurrence identifier for the FA_S and the attribute rules refers the rules of the FA_S.

• the definition of a named value "FA_S: set(FA_S)". Every new occurrence of S belongs to the set FA_S.

• the definition and compilation of a class Default_S, representing the default format for the FA S. The type of the class default_S is M(S). In case of a window FA wdw_S, the Default_wdw_S created is a subclass of the Default_wdw class coding the commun features of the window FAs(see section 4.4). If attributes close, next and previous are present in the schema of wdw_S, the class Default_wdw_S inherits the methods close, next, and previous from Default_wdw. For every alternative $Item_1$ of the menu attribute, a method $Item_1$ is defined.

The FA_Rule class

The class FA_Rule implements the FA Rule. An object of that class represents a rule. The compilation of a rule builds an internal representation of that rule that allows its activation and the execution of its BEFORE and AFTER clauses. This rep-

resentation is an object of the Rule_exec class. For example, for the rule CalcTotal in Figure 2, the method compile creates the $R_{CalcTotal}$ object illustrated in Figure 7. The attributes bodybefore and bodyafter have as value identifiers of objects of the OOPE_class_method class that belongs to OOPE. These identifiers refer the definitions of the methods before_CalcTotal and after_CalcTotal of the FA_Customer class. The bodies of these methods are pieces of CO_2 code generated from the BEFORE and AFTER clauses of the CalcTotal rule. The code generation is based on the transformation of an update operation into an event creation.

The FA_Evt class

When a update operation is invoked through a form or a rule, we say that an event occurs and an occurrence of the FA Evt representing this event is created. Then this occurrence is used to process the corresponding operation. This approach introduces a form of genericity in our language. For example, it is possible to write the operation "create(?F, ?v)" where ?F is a variable for the name of a FA.

The main function of the class FA_Evt is to control the execution of an event. Figure 7 illustrates the O_{assign} object that represents an event occurring when the operation "assign(Customer{100}.Orders{1}.Order.Amount, 50)" is invoked. The execution of that event is done by applying the method SendEvt to O_{assign}. The following actions are executed:

• find the class corresponding to the FA Customer and the object corresponding to the FA Customer occurrence with the identifier 100. The FA_Customer class and the $O_{Customer}$ object shown in Figure 7 are found. Note that when an event corresponds to an occurrence creation, it is not possible to find the corresponding object that does not exist yet. In that case, the object found is the prototype object of the class.

• apply the exec method to $O_{Customer}$. The exec method executes the code of the "assign" operation taking into account the rules attached to the Customer schema. This method search for rules that can be activated, executes the BEFORE clauses, validates the event (the value "50" is assigned to the Amount attribute of the first tuple of the Orders list), executes the AFTER clauses. When the method exec terminates, it returns a boolean value used by the Abstraction to notify the Control of the result of the event execution.

During the BEFORE clauses execution, the event can be rejected (cancel_evt) and the operation "assign(Customer...)" is not accepted. If this operation is invoked from a form, the rejection of the operation is notified to that form that comes back to the state it had before the operation invocation: the form is refreshed using the $O_{Customer}$ object that has not been changed by the operation.

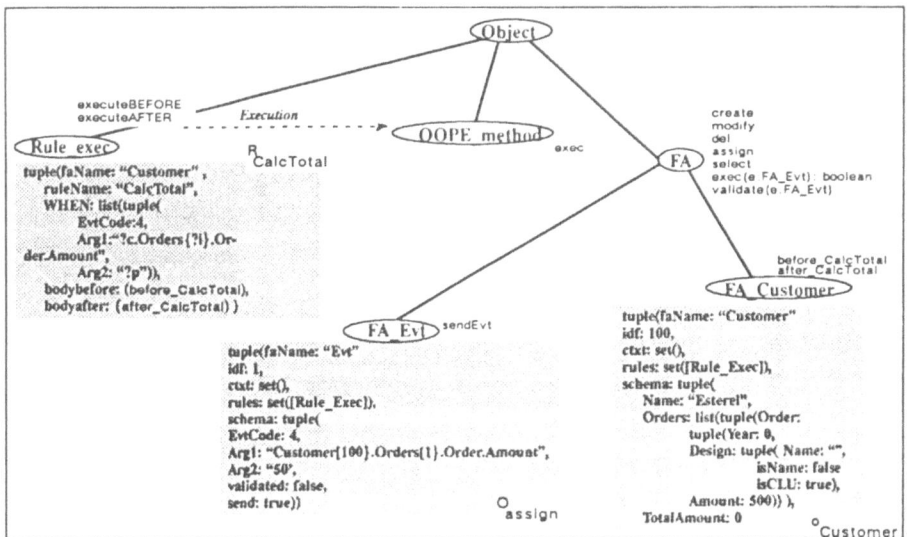

Figure 7: Execution of an update operation

Also during the AFTER clauses execution, other rules may be activated. Assume the execution of one of these rules fails. Then, the operation ""*assign(Customer...)*' stops and operations executed since the beginning of the execution of the rule CalcTotal have to be undone. One solution to cancel these operations is to attach a transaction to each invoked operation. The transaction is committed if the operation is accepted, otherwise the transaction is aborted. The transactions commands have to be put in methods of classes of the Presentation part. O_2 manages transactions through programs and not through methods. Unfortunately, if an operation, say O is not validated because of the non validation of an operation of one of the AFTER clauses of the rules activated by O, inconsistency is produced between the Abstraction and the Presentation.

4.3.2 Presentation part

The Presentation part manages the Input and Output image of the system. The input behavior captures an external event such as a mouse click and sends its representation to the Control part. The output behavior displays, erases, and refreshes forms. To manage events the Presentation translates an event on an O_2 presentation into an update operation request and send it to the Control part. Assume the Presentation part has to display the Customer_Manipulation form in Figure 4. This is done by:

• creating an object, say DC that belongs to the Default_Customer class. Its value is the one of the attribute schema of a FA_Customer object. The DC object contains exactly the information we want to display.

• creating an object, say DW, of the class Default_wdw_multi_occ.

• "encapsulating" DC in DW(DC is becoming the value of DW), creates an O_2 presentation for DW and displays it. The user can only activate one of the methods of DW by selecting an item from the menu associated to the presentation.

To get the a Customer form in Figure 4, the Presentation part will use an object DW of the class Default_wdw_one_occ that has a method through which the Control is notified of an editing event.

4.3.3 Control part

The Control part maintains consistency and realizes the communication between the two previous parts. The abstraction level of the communication protocol from the Control part to the other parts depends on the two worlds served :

• The communication between the Control part and the Presentation part is done by excuting methods of the O_2 Interface object. This object maintains a link for every form on the screen. A link provides the identifiers of the different components of a form (objects belonging to a FA_... class, a Default_... class, a wdw_... class, and an O_2 presentation). The main function of the Interface object is to update the screen after the process of a user action, i.e. to refresh every form and to create new forms for every new occurrences of window FAs.

• The communication between the Control part and the Abstraction part is done by updating the FA Evt through the window FAs wdw_multi_occ and wdd_one_occ.

4.4 The FO_2 Application

The application FO2 is an O_2 application that uses the classes of the kernel to create and initialize objects defining the schema and rules of the FAs that build FO2. Objects created are those defining the system FAs(Schema, Rule, Evt, Algebra), the window FAs (wdw_multi_occ, wdw_one_occ), and also others FAs used to manage forms definitions, forms display, queries (i.e., to express a select operation) and user functions (i.e., to add new functions to the FA_expressions language). Here we only detail the window FAs.

A **window FA** is used to handle the acquisition and the management of external events provided by a Presentation. FO2 provides two window FAs: (i) wdw_one_occ that allows the description of a manufacturing form, i.e., a form interested in editing events, and (ii) wdw_multi_occ allows the description of factory forms, i.e, forms interested in high level events (selection of an item from a menu).

Every form F on a screen has an underlying FA, say F_a, and an underlying occurrence of window FA, say WF_a. The occurrence WF_a processes an event by asking the Abstraction to execute operations (against F_a) corresponding to the event. The process of an event is realized by a rule of the window FA. Such an approach has the following advantages:

• the management of an event provided by FO2 through the wdw_multi_occ and wdw_one_occ can be redefined by changing the rules of these FAs.

• a new way of interacting with a form can be defined simply by creating a new window FA. Further, some parts of the semantics of a form can be moved from its abstraction part to its control part.

Due to its communication role, a window FA has a standard schema (see figure 4). A new window schema, say wdw_S, may have less attributes than the standard schema. It may have a **Menu** attribute describing the specific operations available for a form built with wdw_S. The fixed attributes **Field**, **Value**, **Assign**, **Create**, and **Delete** of wdw_S will be used when there is a need to represent a request for an update operation that has to be performed by the Abstraction.

5 Conclusion

The FO2 system shows that an "event-action" mechanism provides a framework for describing the semantics of an application. It also shows that object-oriented technology and complex object technology can be integrated: from a FA schema it is possible to generate a class having methods used to: (i) get a minimal manipulation of objects (i.e., methods to read and write an attribute value) and, (ii) get a manipulation of a set of objects (the extension of the class) as it is done for N1NF relations. However, for performance consideration there is a need to reduce exchanges between the Abstraction part and the Presentation part. This could be done by coding one part of a form semantics at the Presentation level. This approach confronts the designer with the problem of how to divide the semantics of an application in its abstracts objects (FAs) and its interface objects (Forms).

Complex forms and application generators

The FO2 system may be viewed as an application generator. FO2 addresses identifiable and simple interactive applications. From schemas and rules definitions, FO2 produces a complete application that can be executed without adding functions to the generated code. The only notions needed to "program" a form are the FA_expression language, the event execution principle, and the interactive manipulation of a form. However, a programming-by-example or by menu tool may be considered to facilitate the writing of FA_expressions and the definition of rules. Further, the form model does not support shared objects and specialization, and it is difficult to have a modular development of applications. An example form model having these characteristics is presented in [17]. Another approach for an application generator is to "wrap" database objects in some graphic objects to which are associated actions. However, with this approach a designer has to learn the language of the underlying DBMS and the primitives of generator to know how to express the semantics of an application. An example of such a generator is given in [19].

Forms and database interfaces

The form model offers a structure to build an environment interacting with a DBMS and having the following characteristics:

• Extensibility and integration. The FA concept can be used to integrate the data manipulated by different tools and the FA_expression language can be extended with the specific functions of the tools.

• Homogeneity and portability. The applications are developed using the same formalism and have the same look and feel. The portability can be insured by providing an interface between the environment and the underlying DBMS.

• Distribution. Bookkeeping information can be maintained for every FA occurrence[17], and forms can migrate from one workstation to another over the network connected to the DBMS.

References

[1] S. Abiteboul, N.Bidoit, "Non First Normal Form Relations: an algebra allowing data restructuring". *Proceedings of ACM SIGACT-SIGMOD Symposium on Principles of Database System*, 1984.

[2] S. Abiteboul, S. Grumbach, "Bases de données et objets structurés," *TSI, Vol 6, No 5*, December 1987.

[3] M. Adiba, C. Collet, "Management of complex objects as dynamic form," *14th VLDB conference*, Los Angeles, August 1986.

[4] F. Bancilhon, P. Richard, M. Scholl, "Verso: A Relational Backend Database Machine," *Proceedings of International Workshop on Database Machines*, San Diego, 1982.

[5] F. Bancilhon, S. Koshafian, "A Calculus for Complex Objects," *Proceedings of ACM Symposium on PODS*, Boston, March 1986.

[6] F. Bancilhon, C. Delobel, P. Kannelakis, "The O_2 Book," *Preliminary Version*, October 1989.

[7] F. Barbic, M. Carli, B. Pernici, G. Bracchi, "A tool for form definition in office information systems specification," *New applications on Databases edited by G. Gardarin. On proceedings of ICOD-2 Conference Workshop*, Cambrigde University, September 1983.

[8] C. Collet, "Les Formulaires complexes dans les bases de données multimédia," *Thèse de Docteur de l'USTMG*, Grenoble, November 1987.

[9] C. Collet, "FAKIR, un système pour la définition et la manipulation interactive d'objets complexes," *Colloque sur l'ingénierie des interfaces Homme-Machine*, Sophia-Antiapolis, May 1989.

[10] J. Coutaz, "Interface Homme-Ordinateur," *Thèse de doctorat d'état de l'Université Joseph Fourier*, Grenoble, December 1988.

[11] A. doucet, C. Lepenant, "Language de quatrième génération et générateurs d'interfaces," *Rapport technique, GIP Altaïr No 3-87*, March 1987.

[12] P. Fisher, S.T. Thomas, "Operators on Non-First-Normal-Form Relations," *Proceedings of the 7th International Software Application Conference*, Chicago 1983.

[13] N.H Gehani, "High level form definition in office information systems," *The Computer Journal, Vol 26, No 1*, 1983.

[14] S. Gibbs, "An Object-Oriented Office Data Model," *Technic al Report CSRG-154*, January 1984.

[15] M. Green, "A Survey of Three Dialog Models," *ACM Trans. Graphics*, July 1986.

[16] R.H. Gutting, R. Zicari, D.M. Choy, "An Algebra for structured office documents," *IBM Research Report RJ5559*, San Jose, March 1987.

[17] H. Hämmäimen, E. Eloranta, J. Alasuvanto, "Distributed Form Management," *ACM Trans. on Information Systems, Vol 8, No 1*, January 1990.

[18] B. Jaeschke, "Recursive algebra for relations with relation valued attributes," *Lecture notes IBM Europe Institute*, Davos, 1984.

[19] R. King, M. Novak, "FaceKit: A Database Interface Design Toolkit," *Proc of 15th VLDB Conf.*, Amsterdam, September 1989.

[20] H. Kitagawa, M. Gotoh, S. Misaki, M. Azuma, "Form Document Management System SPECDOC - its Architecture and Implementation," *ACM SIGQA on Office Information System*, Toronto, June 84.

[21] C. Lécluse, P. Richard, F. Velez, "O_2, An Object-Oriented Data Model," *Proceedings of the ACM-SIGMOD Conference*, Chicago, 1988.

[22] C. Lécluse, P. Richard, "The O_2 Database Programming Language," *Proceedings of the 15th VLDB Conference*, Amsterdam, August 1989.

[23] Oracle, "Users manual for SQLForms," *Oracle Corporation*, Menlo Park, California, Original issue: October 1987.

[24] P. Pistor. F. Andersen "Designing a generalized NF2 model with an SQL-type language interface," *Proceedings of the 12th VLDB Conference*, Kyoto, August 1986.

[25] D. Plateau, R. Cazalens, B. Poyer, "A customizable abstract I/O server for complex object edition," *Rapport technique GIP Altaïr No 28-89*, March 1989.

[26] M.A. Roth, H.F. Korth, A. Silberschatz, "Extended Algebra and Calculus for -1NF Relational Databases," *Technical report - Computer Science Dept - University of Texas*, Texas, 1985.

[27] L.A. Rowe, ""Fill-in-the-form" programming," *Proceedings of the 11th VLDB Conference*, Stockholm, August 1985.

[28] H.J. Schek, M.H. Scholl, "The relational model with relation-valued attributes," *Informations Systems Vol 11, No 2*, 1986.

[29] N.C. Shu, "FORMAL: A Forms-Oriented, Visual-Directed application development System," *IEE Transactions on Software Engineering*, 1985.

[30] M. Stonebraker, "The Ingres Paper, anatomy of a relational Database system," *IEE Addison-Wesley Publishing Company*, 1986.

[31] D. Tsichritzis, "Form Management," *Communications ACM, Vol 25, No 7*, July 1982.

[32] M. Zloof, "Office-By-Example: a business language that unifies data and word processing and electronic mail," *IBM Research Journal, Vol 21, No 3*, 1982.

Supporting User Interactions with OODB's: A Declarative Approach.[*]

F. Staes
Origin/Technology Support
HCM-524

NL - 5611 CA Eindhoven
The Netherlands

L. Tarantino
University of L'Aquila
Dipt. di Ing. Elettrica
Poggio di Roio
I - 6704 L'Aquila
Italy

B. Verdonk
Research Center Alcatel - Bell
Francis Welleplein 1

B - 2018 Antwerpen
Belgium

D. Vermeir
University of Antwerp
Dept of Math. and Comp. Sc.
Universiteitsplein 1
B - 2610 Wilrijk
Belgium

Abstract

In this paper we discuss the graphical interaction environment to the object-oriented knowledge base system KIWIS. This environment provides both customizable views on the data and several interaction paradigms with different complexity. This is achieved by exploiting some characteristics of LOCO, the knowledge representation language of KIWIS. LOCO is based on a tight integration between the logic and the object-oriented paradigm, offering powerful modeling capabilities as well as declarative query capabilities. We discuss here the characteristics of LOCO which allow to effectively construct and maintain individual user's views, and to achieve the property of closure under query: a query is an object which can be saved and used as an operand to another query, hence allowing incremental queries.

Introduction.

As the utilization of information systems grew, the need arose for adapting them on one side to the new kinds of applications, and on the other side to the ever growing user population. These new necessities made the information systems evolve in several interrelated directions: *from the representation power standpoint*, new data models are being defined to extend the universe of real world objects that can be handled by the information system, *from the usability standpoint*, a growing interest is given to the problems related to the human-computer interaction.

The object-oriented approach has recently received a great deal of attention from the area of database management systems (DBMS's) for new applications such as CAD-CAM, AI, etc.. The well established technology of relational DBMS's is not able to provide effective and efficient solutions to the problems which these applications raise, on one hand because of the lack of high level data abstraction primitives, and on the other hand because of the strong separation between data and operations on them. The attempts of coupling the relational approach with other paradigms have proven to be rather restrictive, also because the different natures of the paradigms give rise to the impedance mismatch problem.

Nevertheless, relational systems still represent a landmark as regards the management and the manipulation of persistent data. Furthermore, with respect to the interaction point of view relational systems show superior features profitable for the end users: query languages are based upon declarative paradigms, and query models satisfy the property of *closure under query* (the result of querying a relation is still a relation). This lets end users easily extract information from the database, possibly through an incremental process in case of complex queries.

It is argued, e.g. in [1,2], that in order to meet the expectations of end-users the advantageous interaction characteristics of relational systems must be included in the object oriented paradigm. In this paper we discuss how this is achieved in the KIWIS[3] system through the use of the LOCO language, the native knowledge representation formalism of KIWIS.

LOCO is an object-oriented database programming language which models the salient features of the object-oriented approach [2,4,5]: complex objects, object identity, inheritance and defaults; and integrates them with the logic programming paradigm . This greatly enhances the capabilities of the language: on one hand, including the object-oriented concepts yields superior modeling capabilities, while, on the other hand, the deductive approach allows for clear formal semantics as well as declarative query capabilities, as enjoyed by relational systems.

Moreover, in order to address needs and requirements of both naive and expert users, the KIWIS system provides a friendly, flexible and customizable interaction environment. This environment assists the user in all the phases of the interaction (learning and training, goal definition, query construction and interpretation, and answer presentation) by providing several interaction paradigms with different usage complexity, fully integrated in a graphical dialogue environment based on the direct manipulation of the visible objects. This is achieved through an advanced graphical User Interface Development System (UIDS) which is fully integrated in LOCO.

The remainder of the paper is organized as follows. In section 2 we recall the basic concepts of the LOCO language while in section 3 we discuss the main issues that have to be addressed in the interaction environment to an object oriented database system. Section 4 will be devoted to introducing the novel features of the LOCO language, namely object-terms and virtual objects. These features enhance LOCO in that they provide tools for incremental queries and for the construction and maintenance of different views of the knowledge base. Finally, in section 5 the implementation of the user interface is sketched.

LOCO core.

LOCO (LOgic for Complex Objects) [6] is a database programming language which aims at integrating the logic and object-oriented programming paradigm.

In LOCO the properties of objects are described using an extended logic program, i.e. a logic program where negation may also occur in the rule heads. Hence to LOCO an object is just a logical theory. (Multiple) inheritance and defaults are modeled by introducing a partial order on the objects. The partial order (also called instance-of relation) allows information to flow from an object to its instances. The instance-of relation is sufficiently general and powerful to be useful to model e.g. delegation, classification and/or generalization hierarchies, while it also provides facilities for non-monotonic reasoning.

Objects as theories

In object-oriented languages, an object has, besides an identity that remains fixed throughout its lifetime, properties that may be either passive (such properties are often called "instance variables") or active ("methods").

In LOCO, we use logic to describe the properties of an object, i.e. we identify an object with a logical theory. In particular, an object is represented by a set of rules of the form

$$H :- B_1, B_2, ..., B_n. \qquad (n \geq 0)$$

where the head H of the rule is a literal, i.e. a positive or negative atom, and each B_i, $0 \leq i \leq n$, in the body of the rule is either a literal or an extended literal, i.e. an expression of the form $X.p$ where X is the name of an object (or a variable) and p is a literal. Intuitively, an extended literal $X.p$ should be read as "p is true at object X" or "X has

[*] This work has been supported in part by the EEC under the Esprit programme (contract EP2424)

property p", while a literal p refers to the truth of p at the "current" object (see below), in other words p and $Self.p$ are equivalent. The only differences between a rule and a clause as used in a "traditional" logic program are that the head H of a rule can be a negative atom and the object reference in an extended literal.

As an example consider the following LOCO knowledge base:

```
/* Example 1 */
sheratonBrussels = {
    rate(3500).
    conferenceRoom(atlanta).
    conferenceRoom(memphis).
    image(sheratonImage).
    bigConferenceFacility:-
        conferenceRoom(X),
        X.info(name=_, size=N),
        N >= 50. };
atlanta = {
    info(name="Atlanta",size=50).
    facility("overhead").
    facility("video").
    facility("slides"). };
```

The first 4 rules in *sheratonBrussels* are facts, i.e. rules with an empty body. The second rule is a fact whose argument refers to another object *atlanta*. Informally, facts in objects may be regarded as the equivalent of "instance variables" in traditional object-oriented languages. The last rule defines the property *bigConferenceFacility* of *sheratonBrussels*. It illustrates the possibility for a literal in the rule body to refer to a property of another object: *sheratonBrussels* has facilities to organize big conferences if it has conference rooms which offer space for at least 50 persons. Informally, rules can be interpreted as the equivalent of "methods" in object-oriented languages.

Note that integers and strings are predefined objects in LOCO. Like in Prolog, variable names begin with a capital letter while dummy variables are denoted by '_'.

Multiple inheritance

An important feature of the object-oriented programming paradigm is the ability to structure objects in hierarchies such that properties of lower level objects ("instances" or "subclasses") may be derived using rules at the higher level objects (usually called "classes"). In LOCO, such inheritance will be obtained by allowing the objects that constitute a program to be structured in a "specificity" partial order, denoted "≤". For example, an extended version of Example 1 could be:

```
/* Example 2 */
hotel = {
    bigConferenceFacility:- ...
    threestars:- michelin.mention(Self). };
(hotel) sheratonBrussels = {
    rate(3500).
    conferenceRoom(atlanta).
    conferenceRoom(memphis).
    image(sheratonImage). };
michelin = {
    mention(parkhotel).
    mention(sheratonBrussels).
    ... };
```

The construction $(o_1... o_n)$ o indicates that the object o is more specific than each of the objects o_i, $1 \le i \le n$, i.e. $o \le o_i$. We say that an object a is an instance of an object b if $a \le b$.

Informally, the rules defined at an object do not constitute the entire knowledge about that object; objects can also use the rules defined at more general (less specific) objects. E.g., *sheratonBrussels*, being an instance of *hotel*, will have the property *threestars*, by using the rule

threestars:- michelin.mention(Self).

and by substituting *sheratonBrussels* for *Self*. (In analogy with many other object-oriented languages, the keyword *Self* in LOCO always re-

fers to the object where the rule is "used", in this case *sheratonBrussels*).

It should be stressed that objects "inherit" rules, not conclusions, from higher objects. This corresponds to dynamic binding in traditional object-oriented languages. The specificity order can be used to define default properties, as is illustrated in the following example:

```
/* Example 3 */
confRoom = { facility("overhead"). };
(confRoom) atlanta = {
    info(name = "Atlanta", size = 50).
    facility("slides").
    facility("video"). };
(confRoom) memphis = {
    info(name = "Memphis", size = 15).
    ¬ facility("overhead"). };
```

Since *atlanta* is an instance of *confRoom*, it inherits the *facility("overhead")* property of the latter.

If several rules conflict, the rule which is defined at the more specific object "wins". Thus, *memphis.¬facility("overhead")* will hold. We say that, for *memphis*, the *facility("overhead")* rule at *confRoom* is overruled by the *¬facility("overhead")* rule at the more specific object *memphis*. If conflicting rules are defined at incomparable objects, the sceptical approach is taken and both rules are said to be **defeated**. This is illustrated below using a familiar example from non-monotonic logic.

```
/* Example 4 */
quaker = { pacifist. };
republican = { ¬pacifist. };
(quaker republican) nixon;
```

Here neither *nixon.pacifist* nor *nixon.¬pacifist* will be true.

Theoretical background.

In essence, a LOCO program associates with each object o, an extended logic program P_o. The entire knowledge of the object o does, however, not only consist of P_o, but also of the logic programs associated with objects o', where $o \le o'$, in this way modeling (multiple) inheritance. The extended (ordered) logic program representing the entire knowledge of the object o is therefore given by:

$$P_o^* = \{ r \mid r \in P_{o'}, o \le o' \}$$

The semantics of ordered logic [7] allow us to associate with each extended (ordered) logic program P_o^* a unique well-founded model, taking into account the overruling and defeating mechanisms of LOCO and providing a sound way to determine, for each object o in the LOCO knowledge base, what is true about it.

An overview of the KIWIS User Interface.

In this section we give an overview of the graphical interaction environment of the KIWIS system, focusing on those user-oriented characteristics that were some of the motivations that made LOCO evolve (and enhance) from its core. More detailed discussions on the various aspects of the user interface can be found in [8-11].

Display Model.

Different users may have different perceptions of the reality modeled in the knowledge base, and of the way in which such reality is represented by means of the knowledge representation model. Classifications of end users may be done according to several parameters . As extremes of a multi-dimensional parameter space we find the very naive user and the knowledge engineer.

- Naive users do not know the knowledge representation model. Furthermore, they are not able to formulate requests by using a formal query language. Hence, they need an interface that presents the information according to their real-world vision, and that allows to access and manipulate data by means of easy-to-use commands.
- On the other extreme, the knowledge engineer has a deep knowledge of the data model, the database context and of the data manip-

212

ulation language. He needs presentation and interaction techniques powerful enough to fully exploit the capabilities of the system.

To meet the above multi-user requirements, the KIWIS User Interface supports multiple interaction paradigms, and at the same time the possibility to customize the graphical representation of objects. The approach we take in KIWIS is to associate with each object a unique graphical representation (customized or default) which is to be used by each of the interaction paradigms. The Display Model takes care of the mapping from objects to their graphical representation, thus hiding the customizations from the interaction paradigms.

Default Display Model: the Default Display Model (DDM) associates a standard visualization with each object in the knowledge base. Such a visualization reflects the internal representation of objects in that an object is displayed by means of all its properties (inherited or locally defined). We illustrate the DDM by means of the object *sheratonBrussels* defined in example 1 and whose visualization is given in figure 1. As we can see from the figure, a graphical window is associated with an object and contains the representation of the object's properties. Since a property is defined by a pair <property_name, property_values>, each property representation consists of a string corresponding to the name of the property followed by the graphical representation of its values.

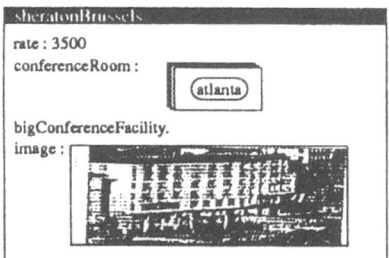

Figure 1: The Default Display Model.

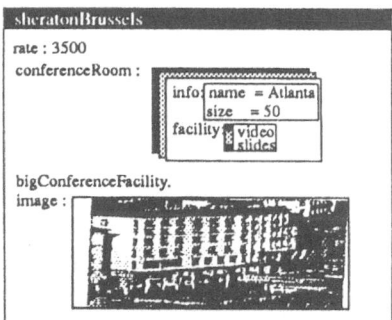

Figure 2: A Tailored Representation

The way in which the property values are displayed depends fully on the nature of these values (objects). The default representation of a predefined object (like strings and integers) is its value (e.g. "*3500*") while a user-defined object yields a button representation (e.g. *atlanta*).

If a property has several values, the values are represented using a layered layout. In this layout one of the values is shown while the others are hidden behind it. The next value can be selected by clicking in the shaded area behind the currently displayed value. It is also possible to get a menu of all possible values. Note that buttons are used to cut short an object representation. If the user wants to see the definitions of the underlying objects, he can open a new window or zoom by clicking the corresponding buttons. One can observe that the DDM is a very simple direct mapping from the internal structure of an object to

its graphical representation; however this is not a limitation, because it is exactly this conceptual simplicity that allows us to define a number of tailoring capabilities that make it very flexible.

Tailoring the default display model: When displaying a hotel to a user, it is clearly more informative to have a more complete presentation of its properties, rather than some reference (e.g. a button) to their values. For instance, according to the representation as given in figure 1, the user has to click on the button labeled *atlanta* to access the features of this conference room; furthermore, because of the layered layout used for properties with more than one value, only one value is visible. Let us consider instead the representation given in figure 2: here the object *atlanta* is expanded, and, in it, the values of the property *facility* are listed in a scrollable window.

These and other adjustments of the visualization characteristics can easily be specified both in an interactive graphical way (by the end user and the knowledge engineer) and in a textual way, by using LOCO (by the knowledge engineer). Some of the tailoring possibilities offered are: hiding of properties, ordering of the properties, setting the level of depth, i.e. the level on which buttons are used to represent user defined objects instead of showing their contents. For example, in figure 2 the level of depth is set to 2 in order to expand the user defined object *atlanta*. Another tailoring option is the choice between a layered layout (as used for the *conferenceRoom* property in the object *sheratonBrussels*) and a table layout (as used in the *facility* property of the object *atlanta* in figure 2) if a property has more than one value.

It is worth noting that the adjustments specified at an object *o* will be inherited by all the subobjects of *o*, that is, they become defaults in the sub-hierarchy rooted at *o*.

Customized Display Model: Clearly, the object representations as provided by the DDM are not always the best possible, even when extensively tailored. Furthermore, the tailoring capabilities are not sufficiently rich to allow for the definitions of *views*, as provided in the relational model, i.e. "imaginary" objects defined in a precise way from real (stored) objects. In real multi-user applications the possibilities of defining and maintaining views is however crucial, e.g., for preventing unauthorized access or for providing predefined abstraction of the knowledge base suitable for particular tasks. For example, an operator of a service agency organizing conferences may prefer to see the conference rooms of any hotel grouped and displayed by size. To this user, the representation depicted in figure 3 is certainly more intuitive than the one in figure 2 and allows a simpler interaction.

We will see in the following section that LOCO provides for view definitions that become objects in the database, and as such, could be represented according to the DDM. In order to help the knowledge engineer in the task of constructing customized displays that stray from the DDM, KIWIS supports a collection of built-in (graphical) objects. These User Interface Description Objects (UIDO's) are fully integrated in LOCO, so that the knowledge engineer can define and maintain an application environment - from KR over integration of external sources [3] to UI definition - using a single language.

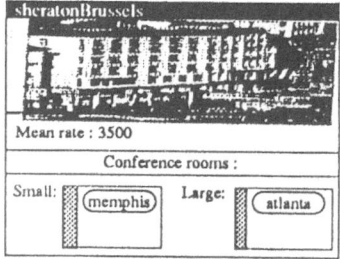

Figure 3: A Customized view of sheratonBrussels

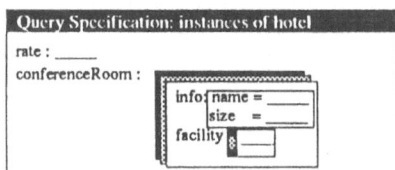

Figure 4: A Query Specification Window.

Interaction Paradigms.

KIWIS offers a number of interaction paradigms varying from browsing to querying, thus covering in a continuum the gap from very naive users to sophisticated ones. The interaction is carried out in a uniform framework, based on the direct manipulation of the graphical representations as defined in the Display Model. In the following subsections we shortly describe the browsing and querying paradigms, while we refer to [9] for a more detailed discussion of the other paradigms.

Browsing: Naive users can "get acquainted" with a KIWIS application by using its friendly navigational capabilities. The simplest navigation process is based on the elementary browsing paradigm: the user examines a concept and its neighborhood, a new element is selected in such a neighborhood to become the current one, and so on iteratively. In terms of the Display Model, the user starts from the visualization of an object, and, by clicking on the buttons used to cut short the object's representations, he visits new objects, thus disclosing new portions of the knowledge base.

Querying: More expert users may want to express their goals in a more direct way, even if they are not able to formulate standard queries in LOCO. To support these users, KIWIS offers an Object-Oriented Query By Example interface that allows to formulate queries by providing examples of the desired answer, thus extending the QBE[13] query language.

A definition environment is provided for building examples and for handling previously generated queries (if the retrieved answer is not satisfactory) under the system's assistance. Queries are formulated either by filling in object representations visualized on the screen according to the display model, or, starting from objects previously retrieved while browsing, asking the system to generalize the retrieved example by substituting some constants with variables. It is worth noting that the query can be saved and reused later in an incremental query process. We will discuss in the next section how LOCO handles queries in order to provide the closure under query property.

As an example, let us consider the query specification window depicted in figure 4. It allows to formulate a query whose target is restricted to the single (class) object hotel. The hotel is visualized according to the representation defined in the Display Model, but the fields representing property values are now editable (for instance, the user may specify '< 4000' at the rate property). The user can also indicate which of the properties he wants to be presented in the answer by using the tailoring capabilities of the Default Display Model.

A pop-up menu is associated with each of the editable fields. Options within these menus include, among others, the possibility to define a link condition between properties of two (or more) query specification windows[11]. Using this facility, one can define explicit join conditions as discussed in [12].

As we will see in the following section, queries are new objects stored in the database. Therefore, they can be represented using the Display Model and manipulated using the traditional interaction paradigms. For a more detailed discussion on the OOQBE interface we refer to [11].

LOCO extensions.

In this section we discuss new features of LOCO which have been added to the language, as it was presented in [6], to be able to support

the requirements of the user interface, among other reasons. In particular we will show 1) how the introduction of so-called object constructors (that allow for general object terms) greatly improve the construction and the management of individual user's views, 2) how the introduction of so-called virtual objects (that allow to impose existence conditions on object terms) can be put to good use to model incremental queries.

Object terms

As pointed out above, one of the strong points of the UIDS is that it allows the graphical customization of object representations. Especially in the CDM this customization can be far reaching and is essentially based on the capability to define and maintain different views of the knowledge base. This capability can not be offered by LOCO in a consistent way with just the basic features we have described so far. Reconsider for example the customization of the sheratonBrussels object. The idea is that a particular user wants the conferencerooms of sheratonBrussels, and more generally of any hotel, grouped and displayed by size. One way to satisfy the user's request could be to associate with each hotel object in the knowledge base, an object describing the user's view of that hotel and to display this object. For sheratonBrussels this associated view object could be defined as:

```
/* Example 6 */
johnSheratonBrussels = {
    rate(3500).
    image(sheratonImage).
    smallConfRoom(memphis).
    largeConfRoom(atlanta). };
```

The problem with this approach is that it becomes necessary to synchronize updates and additions to the sheratonBrussels and johnSheratonBrussels object (and similarly for every hotel object in the knowledge base). Besides being time consuming and error-prone, this will also increase memory usage, without adding any information. A better approach is the introduction of a so-called object constructor johnHotelView:

```
/* Example 7 */
johnHotelView(Hotel) = {
    rate(R) :- Hotel.rate(R).
    smallConfRoom(X) :- Hotel.conferenceRoom(X),
        X.info(name=_, size=N), N < 50.
    largeConfRoom(X) :- Hotel.conferenceRoom(X),
        X.info(name=_, size=N), N >= 50.
    image(B) :- Hotel.image(B). };
```

The above LOCO program defines an object constructor johnHotelView. The object constructor allows to construct objects johnHotelView(h) for each hotel object h. The fact that h should be a hotel is not explicitly specified in the above LOCO program. In the next section we shall indicate how this restriction can be imposed. The logic program defining the properties of the object johnHotelView(h) is the logic program associated with the object constructor johnHotelView, where Hotel is instantiated with h. Note that in this example all properties of johnHotelView(h) can be computed from the properties at the object h. The object identifier of johnHotelView(h) is the concatenation of the object identifier of johnHotelView and the object identifier of h.

The introduction of object constructors allows us to define and maintain different views of the same knowledge base while overcoming the problems mentioned above. Introducing object constructors also implies that we have extended the set of objects in LOCO from simple constants to general (object) terms $f(o_1,..., o_n)$. A LOCO program can then be considered as a mapping from object terms $f(o_1, o_2,..., o_n)$ to logical theories (sets of clauses).

Just like with constants, the inheritance can be generalized to arbitrary object terms. Assume for instance that a new user, fred, wants to refine the view john has of hotels. This can be achieved by the following LOCO program

```
/* Example 8 */
johnHotelView(Hotel) = { ... };
(johnHotelView(Hotel)) fredHotelView(Hotel) =
    { threestars:- Hotel.threestars. };
```

The above program states that for any hotel object *h*, *fredHotelView(h)* will inherit the different properties *rate,...* from *johnHotelView(h)*. Fred refines the view of john in that he adds the additional *threestars* property to his view. Note that the above LOCO program does not declare *fredHotelView* to be an instance of *johnHotelView*, rather it declares, for any hotel *h*, *fredHotelView(h)* to be an instance of *johnHotelView(h)*. In other words, declarations involving variables are to be read as shorthands for the set of their ground instances.

Virtual objects

The introduction of object constructors and object terms, allows us to at least customize a user's view on objects in the knowledge base. However, it does not allow us to restrict the view to certain objects. In Example 7, for instance, there was no way to specify that *johnHotelView(o)* should only exist if *o* is a hotel object. Therefore, we introduce existence conditions on object terms.

```
/* Example 9 */
johnHotelView(Hotel) = {
    rate(R) :- Hotel.rate(R).
    smallConfRoom(X) :- Hotel.conferenceRoom(X),
                X.info(name=_, size=N), N < 50.
    ...
    } :- hotel.instance(Hotel).
```

Here, the *virtual object johnHotelView(h)* exists only if *h* is an instance of the object *hotel*. Thus the condition *hotel.instance(Hotel)* can be considered as a restriction on the 'domain' of the object constructor *johnHotelView*.

Obviously, existence conditions may be much more complex than in Example 9. A user may want to define a view on hotels with facilities for big conferences. If the knowledge base is as in Example 2, the view could be defined as.

```
/* Example 10 */
view(X) = {
    rate(R) :- X.rate(R).
    image(B) :- X.image(B).
    } :- hotel.instance(X), X.bigConferenceFacility.
```

Object terms with existence conditions, or virtual objects, are the analogue of the entity-creating rules in [14,15]. However, unlike in [14] and [15], LOCO associates object identifiers with the object constructors themselves. As such, these constructors are part of the LOCO knowledge base, although they are not included in the object hierarchy. As will become clear in a moment, associating object identifiers with object constructors can be put to good use to model incremental queries.

Incremental queries

Given a LOCO knowledge base consisting of a set of object terms as described above, we obviously would want to retrieve information from it with minimal human effort. Unlike data objects which are stored in the permanent database, queries are processed interactively during a work session. As such, it is difficult to build a system that supports a generalized query reuse scheme, nor is it easy to define a query procedure in one session and use it in another, or to combine queries.

LOCO tackles this problem by allowing query entities to be stored in the permanent database as well. Consider the simple example where we want to query the knowledge base of Example 2 for all hotels with big conference facilities which are affordable (rate < 4000). This query can be expressed in LOCO as

```
/* Example 11a */
?hotel.instance(X), X.bigConferenceFacility, X.rate(R), R<4000.
```

LOCO will return a set of *(X,R)* tuples, one for each hotel *X* which has big conference facilities and whose rate *R* is lower than 4000. However, using the *view* object of Example 10, there is another way to specify the query:

```
/* Example 11b */
?view(X).rate(R), R<4000.
```

LOCO will return the same set of *(X,R)* tuples as in the first query. Remember that *view(x)* (example 10) is only defined if *x* is an instance of hotel and has big conference facilities. Therefore, the above query causes the system to find *x* such that *hotel.instance(X), X.bigConferenceFacility* is satisfied, and then to construct the oid of the object *view(x)* (through concatenation of the oid of *view* and the oid of *x*). If *view(x)* has a *rate(r)* such that *r* does not exceed 4000, both *x* and *r* are returned. In other words, the query *hotel.instance(X),X.bigConferenceFacility*, is retrieved from the KB through the object constructor *view*, and used to construct a new query. Note that in Example 11, the semantic equivalence of the two queries is based on the fact that in *view(h)* the rate property is defined in terms of the rate property at *h*.

Let us consider another query which seems similar to the one of Example 11. Given the knowledge base of Example 2, we are now interested in all 'three-star' hotels which offer big conference facilities. I.e.

```
/* Example 12a */
?hotel.instance(X), X.bigConferenceFacility, X.threestars.
```

Following Example 11, we could reformulate this query as.

```
/* Example 12b */
?view(X).threestars.
```

In this case however, the first query will return, among others, sheratonBrussels, while the second query will not return any solutions. The reason for the problem should be clear: the *threestars* property is not defined in the *view(h)* object; hence querying *h* and *view(h)* for the property *threestars* is no longer semantically equivalent. The most obvious way around this problem is to include the rule

```
    threestars:- X.threestars.
```

in the definition of the *view* object in Example 10. However, this is contrary to the idea of customization and views. A very simple solution consists in adding a (built-in) dummy property to the definition of *view*:

```
/* Example 13 */
view(X) = {
    dummy.
    rate(R) :- X.rate(R).
    image(B) :- X.image(B).
    } :- hotel.instance(X), X.bigConferenceFacility.
```

For any object *x* satisfying the initial query (the one associated with the *view* object), the object *view(x)* exists and satisfies the property *view(x).dummy*. Therefore, the queries *hotel.instance(X), X.bigConferenceFacility* and *view(X).dummy* will return the same objects *x*. Clearly then we can reformulate the query in Example 12a correctly as follows

```
/* Example 12c */
?view(X).dummy, X.threestars.
```

The few examples given above illustrate how incremental queries can be modeled in LOCO, through a combination of object constructors and existence conditions on object terms. In this respect object constructors and virtual objects together offer a functionality similar to that of abstract objects in [16]. It is important to note that, although the above examples all are typical selection queries where the selection is done on instances of the class object hotel, more complex queries involving a combination of selection, projection, implicit and explicit joins [12] can also be modeled. For more details we refer to [10].

User Interface Implementation.

In this section we briefly outline how the Display Model can be described in the LOCO language.

Remember that the purpose of the Display Model was to associate a unique (default or customized) representation with each of the objects in the knowledge base. In order to implement this idea, the UI first defines a number of primitive UI Description Objects, such as verticalList, horizontalList,... in LOCO [17].

The Display Model considers the graphical representation of an object as a view on that object. This view describes how the object is to be displayed on the screen. According to the DDM, properties of an object are to be displayed in a vertical list. Therefore, the DDM view of an object is an instance of the *verticalList* object and has a property *element(x)* for each property defined within the original object.

$(verticalList)\ ddmView(Object) =$
$\{\ element(ddmPropertyView(Y)) :- Object.\_prop(Y). \};$

Given an object *o*, the built-in *_prop(Y)* binds *Y* to each of the property names defined within *o*. The elements of the vertical list are not the property names themselves, but the graphical representations of the actual properties. Therefore *ddmView(Object)* is a vertical list whose elements are themselves graphical representations defined by the object constructor *ddmPropertyView*.

The DDM stipulates that a property *p* is represented by means of its name followed by a colon and the graphical representation of all argument tuples $x_1,...,x_n$ such that $p(x_1,...,x_n)$ holds. Hence *ddmPropertyView(Property)* is an instance of *horizontalList*:

$(horizontalList)\ ddmPropertyView(P) = \{$
$element(name(P)).$
$element(" : ").$
$element(ddmValueView(X)) :- ... \};$

The third element in the horizontal list is the representation of the collection of argument tuples $x_1,...,x_n$. There are two ways to represent this collection of tuples: a stack layout and a table layout (cfr figures 1 and 2). If we choose for a stack layout, *ddmValueView(X)* is an instance of the UIDO *stack*:

$stack = \{\ display :- ... \};$
$(stack)\ ddmValueView(X) = \{\ element(Y) :- ... \};$

Being an instance of *stack*, *ddmValueView(X)* will inherit the display method from *stack* which in turn will use the property *element(Y)* to know which argument tuples to display.

Obviously this is only a sketch of the DDM. A complete implementation of the DDM in LOCO has been developed in the framework of the KIWIS project as part of the UIDS. Current work on the UIDS focuses on the implementation of the OOQBE where graphical queries are mapped to virtual objects in LOCO and are as such stored in the knowledge base. Future work on the UIDS will involve support for updating the knowledge base, as well as an enhancement of the tailoring and customization facilities of the Display Model.

Conclusions.

In this paper we have discussed the graphical interaction environment to the object-oriented knowledge base system KIWIS. We have first introduced the Display Model which, independent of the interaction paradigms, provides a uniform graphical representation of the objects in the knowledge base. The LOCO implementation of the Display Model is based on the idea that the graphical representation of an object is nothing but a special view of that object which can therefore easily be implemented using the concept of object term in LOCO.

Further, we have illustrated with a number of simple examples the browsing and querying interaction paradigms of the KIWIS system. We have indicated how queries can be constructed incrementally in LOCO by mapping them to to object constructors with existence conditions. In [12], another query model to OODB's is proposed which also supports the closure under query property. Unlike in our model however, [12] creates new object identifiers to store the results of a query (instead of the query itself). When updates occur, this may cause problems since the newly created objects may no longer be consistent

with the objects they are derived from. The problem of where in the hierarchy to place the query (results) is an open problem both in [12] and in our model, and is subject to further investigation.

Acknowledgments.

The authors are indebted to Els Laenens for introducing the idea of virtual objects in LOCO and for many insightful discussions.

References

1   J. D. Ullman, *Principles of database and knowledge-base systems*, Pergamon Press, Rockville, Maryland, 1988.

2   F. Bancilhon, "Object Oriented Database Systems" in *Proceedings of ACM-SIGMOD*, Austin, TX, March 1988.

3   The KIWIS team, "The KIWIS Knowledge Base Management System" in *Proceedings of the Conference on Advanced Information Systems Engineering*, Trondheim, Norway, May 1991.

4   P. Wegner, "The Object-Oriented Classification Paradigm" in *Research Directions in Object-Oriented Programming*, The MIT Press, Cambridge, Massachusetts, 1987.

5   W. Kim, "Object-Oriented Databases: Definition and Research Directions" *IEEE Transactions on Knowledge and Data Engineering*, vol. 2 (3), pp. 327-342, September 1990.

6   E. Laenens, B. Verdonk, D. Vermeir, and D. Sacca, "The LOCO language: Towards an integration of Logic and Object-Oriented Programming", Workshop on Non-Monotonic Reasoning and Logic Programming, Austin (TX), 1990.

7   E. Laenens, "Ordered Logic", Ph.D. Thesis, University of Antwerp, Antwerp, Belgium, December 1990.

8   F. Staes, E. Laenens, and L. Tarantino, "Towards a flexible User Interface for Knowledge Bases" in *Proceedings of the 1990 IEEE Workshop on Visual Languages*, pp. 143-148, Skokie, Illinois, 1990.

9   A. D'Atri and L. Tarantino, "From browsing to querying" *IEEE Data Engineering*, June 1989.

10   F. Staes, L. Tarantino and B. Verdonk, "*A Logic Based Approach for supporting queries in object oriented databases*", To appear in the Proc. of the IFIP Conference on the Object Oriented Approach in Information Systems, Quebec City, 1991, Elsevier.

11   F. Staes, L. Tarantino, and B. Tiems," *OOQBE: Object Oriented Query By Example*", 1991, submitted for publication.

12   W. Kim, "A Model of Queries for Object-Oriented Databases" in *Proceedings of the 15th Intl. Conf. on Very Large Databases*, pp. 423-432, Amsterdam, NL, August 22-25, 1990.

13   M. M. Zloof, "Query by Example", *IBM Systems Journal*, vol. 16, no. 4, pp. 324-343, 1977.

14   W. Chen and D. S. Warren, "C-Logic of Complex Objects" in *Proc. of the Eight Symposium on Principles of Data-base Systems*, pp. 369-378, 1989.

15   M. Kifer and G. Lausen, "F-Logic: A Higher-Order Language for Reasoning About Objects, Inheritance and Scheme" in *Proceedings of ACM-SIGMOD*, pp. 134-146, 1989.

16   J. Zhu and D. Maier, "Abstract Objects in an Object Oriented Data Model" in *Proceedings of the second Intl. Conf. on Expert Database Systems*, 1988.

17   F. Staes, E. Laenens, D. Vermeir, and L. Tarantino," *A seamless integration of graphics and dialogues within a logic based object-oriented language*", Journal of Visual Languages and Computing, vol. 1, pp. 313--332, 1990.

A Query Interface for an Object Management System

Xuequn Wu

Department of Computer Science
University of Dortmund
P.O.Box 500 500, D-4600 Dortmund 50, Germany

Abstract

This paper presents the query interface EQL of the object management system $InORM$, which is based on a relation-object model. We describe the requirements and design objectives of an interface of an object management system in an integrated software factory and then review the facilities and main features of the interface EQL. The EQL supports object-oriented database capabilities such as encapsulation, method invocation, inheritance, and navigational queries while maintaining the relational capabilities. Moreover, the closure property is provided in a simple way and content-based queries for documents and programs are supported. The EQL has demonstrated that a useful, general purpose interface could be built for an object management system, on which a high-level integration of tools can be reached.

1 Introduction

The object management system (OMS) is the data repository in a software factory or a software development environment, which is responsible for retaining, accessing and modifying the vast amount of objects and associated information which are generated all along the software life cycle.

In the last years several research efforts in the area of software factory have focused on the developing uniform OMSs as a framework for tool integration and communication. For instance, the PCTE OMS [2] and the DAMOKLES OMS [3] are the results of the efforts, and they are the OMSs of the state-of-the-art. However, all such OMSs have a data model based only on object structures (structured object-oriented data model [7]) and provide only limited query facilities.

In comparison with these OMSs we proposed and developed $InORM$ database system [14] as an OMS which is based on an relation-object model (or an integrated relational and object-oriented data model). It is fully object-oriented according to the "manifesto"[4]. The interface to

$InORM$ is EQL that is an object-oriented extension to the SQL query language [1]. With the EQL the essential object-oriented concepts and relational concepts are integrated in a uniform framework, so that the EQL supports relational and object-oriented database capabilities. While the EQL can be used to introduce new abstract data types for objects, handle inheritance, query and manipulate complex objects, and invoke methods of objects, the basis of the EQL is relational in nature. Objects and values are organized into relations. Moreover EQL provides closure property [6] and natural language processing capability that supports content-based queries for large objects such as documents and programs.

The next section summarizes those aspects of the OMS $InORM$ that are necessary to follow the paper. Section 3 gives requirements for the interface of an OMS which are not or are only partially supported by existing OMSs, and which are design objectives for EQL. Then the main features of EQL is given in section 4. Section 5 presents some conclusions.

2 An Overview of the $InORM$ Object Management System

This section describes those features of the $InORM$ that are necessary to follow the remainder of the paper.

The $InORM$ is based on an integrated relation-object model. An object has a system-created surrogate that is systemwide unique. Objects in the OMS are typed. There are three sorts of types:

- the predefined types
- the user-defined abstract data types (UADTs)
- the complex types

The predefined types include primitive types and parameterized types which are Tuple, Set and List [13]. The primitive types are NUMBER, CHAR and LONG_FIELD, with having predefined methods. The type LONG_FIELD is offered to handle large data objects as well as unformatted data such as software documents. The parameterized types have fixed structures and methods.

The UADT is similar to the abstract data types defined in POSTGRES[11], which can be introduced to the OMS by the user. In comparison with predefined ones there must be mechanisms to program new methods outside the OMS and to register them into the OMS.

With parameterized types users can define new types and in this case the interface of the parameterized type may be augmented through several user-defined methods. A so defined type is called a complex type. The complex types can be used to define types for complex objects.

Types are organized in a type hierarchy that supports generalization and specialization. A type may be declared to be a subtype of another type. In that case, all instances of the subtype are also instances of the supertype, i.e. there is a containment relationship between the supertype and the subtype. It follows that attributes and methods defined on the supertype are inherited by the subtype. And as objects of a subtype can be used in the place where a supertype of that subtype is expected.

Relationships can be established between objects with reference specifications and relations. There are three types of reference specifications: REFERENCE, PART and RELATE.

With REFERENCE such a relationship between two objects is established that the referenced object is indpendent of the referencing object. It means that if the referencing object is deleted, the referenced object still remains in the object base.

PART describes that the referenced object is a part object of the referencing object and therefore is dependent of the referencing object. Moreover, with PART reference, not only a type but also an instance object can be shared as a part of more than one object. With the sharability of part objects, the propagational deletion of part objects are now so executed, that the referenced object remains in the object base until the last object that references it is deleted.

Similar to relational database systems, relations are used to make associations between the different objects in the object base. However, a value of an attribute could be a complex object or an object of a UADT type. RELATE is introduced To enforce some integrity constraints to the objects in such relationships.

The relations are the first class constructs of the $\mathcal{InORM}$ system. Objects are organisded into relations. A relation is then a collection of objects or a collection of instances of a relationship as mentioned above.

The schema of the object base consists now of two parts: 1) The type system that include all defined types and the hierarchy of the types according to inheritance. 2) The schemas for relations, each of which groups some types defined in the type system.

3 Requirements for an OMS Interface

We identify here some requirements for an OMS Interface, which were not or were only partially fulfilled by existing OMSs. They include:

1. To provide powerful and general purpose query facilities. The tools of a software factory could then be integrated at a high-level;

2. To access and manipulate sets of objects. Neither PCTE nor DAMOKLES provide such operations. Because of the relational nature of EQL, that is well supported by EQL;

3. To be extensible. The interface could then be extended to include some facilities which will be used by several different tools. That avoids the repeated implmentations of the facilities in different tools and reduces the works of the tool writers. It is supported by EQL through the user-defined methods which are provided neither by PCTE nor by DAMOKLES;

4. To support reusability of the developed facilities. That could be supplied by EQL through method inheritance while by PCTE and DAMOKLES there is no such inheritance;

5. To support content-based object retrieval. There are many large objects in the object base such as documents and programs. In existing OMSs such objects are only retrieved through alphanumeric attributes and their contents are treated as a non-interpreted whole. However, the alphanumeric attributes could catch only very little semantics of the contents;

6. To ensure that the results of queries are available in a form that allow them to be used as operands of other queries so that the exchange of query results between tools and composition of queries could be possible;

7. To make it easier to store the query results in the object base. Although there are many cases where the results of a query need only be trnsient, e.g. for display purpose, there are also occasions where we wish to make the results of a query persistent.

The last two items (6. and 7.) require the OMS interface provide the closure property. The most object-oriented database systems either do not provide the property, or provide a costly implementation of the property.

218

There are other important requirements which will not be addressed in this paper, some of them are

- version and configuration management,

- view concept that could provide, for an object, different representations for different tools,

- integrated development of consistent documents in the software engineering process.

The first two points are partly treated in [15, 12], and the third point is described in [10]. '

4 The EQL Query Interface

This section describes the EQL query interface of the $\mathcal{InORM}$ OMS. The main features of the EQL is illustrated with examples.

We now give the running example. Figure 1 shows a simple schema for a relation Projects which contains one or more Project objects.

A Project object has a name, and may be related to a manager (an Emloyee object) and to a set of subtasks.

One subtask may contain a list of Doc_Info. Each Doc_Info has a name and is related to a document (a Document object) and to a set of workers (Employee objects) who establish the document.

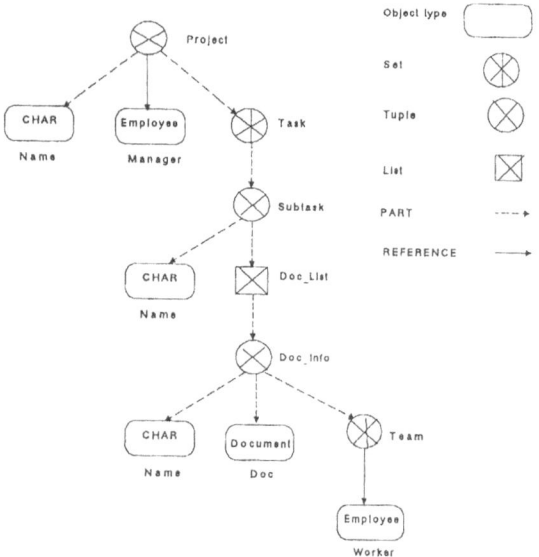

Figure 1: A simple schema

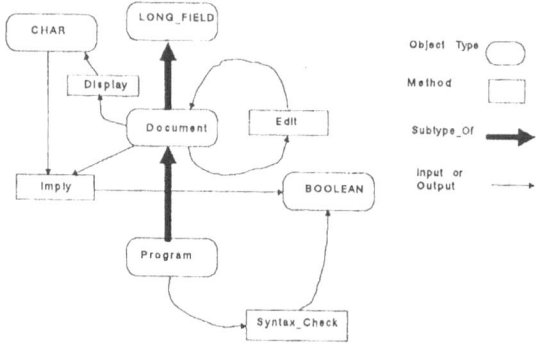

Figure 2: A type hierarchy

The type Employee may be a subtype of a type Person. It could have attributes such as name, address, rank etc., references to other types, and some methods defined on it.

The figure 2 shows a type hierarchy related to type Document with some methods defined on it. Document is a subtype of the type LONG_FIELD. The methods Edit, Display and Imply are defined for Document. Imply could test if the semantics described by a character string match the semantics contained in a Document object. Therefore it could be used to support content-based retrieval. Program is in turn a subtype of Document. It inherits all methods connected to document, while having its own specific method Syntax_Check that checks the syntax of a Program object.

4.1 Path Expression

A Path from an object to another object (objects) is specified by a dot notation. This is consistent with the view given in SQL that a dot followed by an attribute name represents attribute selection. A sequence of object and/or attribute names seperated by dots is called a path expression. An example for path expression is shown as follows:

```
SELECT d.Doc, d.Team.Worker
FROM p IN Projects,
     d IN p.Task.Subtask.Doc_List
WHERE p.Name = "InORM";
```

The example selects all documents of project $\mathcal{InORM}$ and their corresponding workers. Here p is connected to the Project object having name $\mathcal{InORM}$. Along the path expression p.Task.Subtask.Doc_list d is connected to a Doc_Info object. Starting from d along d.Doc and d.Team.Worker, the corresponding Document objects and Employee objects can be accessed respectively. The dot notation is uniformly used for the objects which are either values of the primitive types or referenced with REFERENCE or PART or RELATE.

4.2 Object Method Invocation

It is possible to invoke methods of objects in a select statement. While the path to the component objects of a complex object is specified with the path expression, the syntax for invoking methods is the same as that of invoking aggregate functions in SQL (e.g. COUNT,AVG). That is, method names are followed by arguments which are enclosed in brackets.

The following example shows the functional semantics of the methods that enables nested invocation of methods. The example displays the first document of the subtask Parser for project $\mathcal{InORM}$.

```
SELECT Display(NTH(1, s.Doc_List).Doc)
FROM p IN Projects, s IN p.Task
WHERE p.Name = "InORM"
  AND s.Name="Parser";
```

The method NTH is defined for the list type and in the example it returns the first document of the list s.Doc_List.

4.3 Closure Property and Navigational Query

Most existing database systems, which are intended to be "pure" object-oriented, have problem with providing closure property. Sometimes it is difficult to determine types for query results. That is not serious when the results are only for display purpose. However, that is particularly a problem when the results of queries are further operated on by other query operations or when one wants to store the results in the database.

One approach for providing the closure property for object-oriented databases is to dynamically modify the type hierarchy. That is, when a query creates a result, the type hierarchy will be searched to see if there is a type that can describe the result. If such a type does not exist, a new type has to be created and put into a appropriate place within the type hierarchy. This approach is discussed in [9]. The problems here are twofold: on the one hand, searching the type hierarchy and modifying the type hierarchy (when a new created type is put into the type hierarchy) could be very costly; On the other hand, with creating new types for results of queries the type hierarchy may expand very quickly and could be hardly to be managed.

In comparison with the "pure" object-oriented databse systems, the $\mathcal{InORM}$ benefits by its relational nature and supports the closure property in a very easy way. All the objects and the values in $\mathcal{InORM}$ are organized into relations. The queries are carried out on relations and the query results are again relations, where the schemas about relations will be updated, but the type hierarchy will remain unchanged because no new object type is created. So EQL

supports the closure property of query operations as found in SQL.

Although most object-oriented programming languages proceed in a navigational style, most SQL-like database language do not support navigational queries. It is well-known that such queries are needed in many new database applications, for instance, in a software development environment.

The closure property mentioned avove is a prerequisite for navigational queries. In EQL the assign statement, which is originally introduced in [5], is used to store query results. An example is given as below:

```
ASSIGN TO Project_Manager:
    SELECT Name, Manager
    FROM Projects;
```

With this assign statement a new relation Project_Manager will be created that has two attributes of type CHAR and (referenced) Employee. One could give new attribute names for the new relation. With syntax "ASSIGN TRANSIENT TO ..." one could also create a transient relation that exists merely as the OMS is switched on.

While EQL supplies relations, one can create a variable connected to an object. It is then possible to ignore the relational concept, and to query with the variable directly. The following statement creates a variable of type Document.

```
DECLARE VARIABLE doc FOR Document;
```

The variable can then be connected to an Document object with an assign statement.

The navigational queries can be performed in EQL by iteratively assigning the result of a query to a relation or variable, and then performing a query on the result to get a new result. For the sake of the limited space no examples for that will be given.

4.4 Content-Based Retrieval

As already outlined in the preceding sections the large objects such as documents or programs are usually retrieved through alphanumeric attributes attached to them. The drawback of this approach is that the alphanumeric attributes can only catch very little semantics of the contents of the large objects. As an alternative, we introduce natural language processing capability into EQL to support content-based retrieval. This is ilustrated by the following example:

```
SELECT p.Name, d.Doc, d.Team
FROM   p IN Projects,
       d IN p.Task.Subtask.Doc_List
WHERE  Imply(d.Doc, "a parser for a query
              language of an object-oriented
              database system");
```

To be able to understand natural language different items are needed. Firstly, we need a grammar for a subset of the English language that defines the syntactic scope of our natural language processing component. Then we need a parser for the Document object content data or for the queries. The parser uses a dictionary to perform parsing. The dictionary holds a vocabulary along with the parts of speech information, defining the scope of contents, in particular, the application domain. Synonymous information is also defined there. We regard the dictionary to be the place where all knowledge is deposited for the system. Finally, we need a component for the evaluation of descriptions in queries and their matching with object contents. All these items together constitute the natural language processing component. As a detailed discussion of this component is beyond the scope of this paper, and it can be found in [8].

5 Conclusions

The EQL Interface for the object management system $\mathcal{InORM}$ is unique in that it is based on a relation-object model. It provides object-oriented capabilities while maintaining relational capabilities and closure property. Consenquently, it is much more powerful than those interfaces of most existing OMSs and provides a high-level basis for integrating tools. The EQL has demonstrated that a useful, general purpose interface can be built for an OMS.

References

[1] *ISO/TC 97: "Information Processing Systems - Data Language SQL"*. International Standards Organisation, 1986. Draft International Standard ISO/DIS 9075.

[2] PCTE - A Basis for a Portable Common Tool Environment: Functional Specification. Technical report, CEC, 1988. Version 1.5.

[3] K. Abramowicz et al. Datenbankunterstützung für Software-Produktionsumgebung. In *Proc. of the BTW Conf.*, Darmstadt, 1987.

[4] M. Atkinson, F. Bancilhon, D. DeWitt, K. Dittrich, D. Maier, and S. Zdonik. The Object-Oriented Database System Manifesto. In W. Kim, J.-M. Nicolas, and S. Nishio, editors, *Proc. of the First Intl. Conf. on Deductive and Object-Oriented Databases*, Kyoto, Japan, Dec. 1989. North-Holland.

[5] D. Chamberlin, M. Astrahan, et al. SEQUEL 2: A Unified Approach to Data Definition, Manipulation, and Control. IBM Research Report RJ 1798, IBM Research Laboratory, San Jose, 1976.

[6] C. J. Date. *An Introduction to Database Systems*, volume I. Addison-Wesley Publishing Company, fourth edition, 1986.

[7] K. Dittrich. Object-Oriented Database Systems: The Notion and the Issues. In K. Dittrich and U. Dayal, editors, *Proc. Intl. Workshop on Object-Oriented Database Systems*, 1986.

[8] B. Holtkamp and V. Y. Lum. Integration of Alphanumeric and Media Data. Technical Report 48, University of Dortmund, Department of Computer Science, Software Technology, 1990.

[9] W. Kim. A Model of Queries for Object-Oriented Databases. In *Proc. of 15th VLDB conf.*, 1989.

[10] J. Neuhaus. Document Representation and Data Integration with an Object-Oriented Database in a Software Factory (in german). Master's thesis, University of Dortmund, Department of Computer Science, 1991. in preparation.

[11] L. A. Rowe and M. R. Stonebracker. The POSTGRES Data Model. In *Proc. of 13th VLDB Conf.*, 1987.

[12] X. Wu. *Relationale Benutzerschnittstelle für eine Objektbank in einer Software-Entwicklungsumgebung zur Entwicklung modularer Systeme*. PhD thesis, University of Dortmund, February 1989. Research report 306/89.

[13] X. Wu. An Object-Oriented Data Model with a SQL-Style Query Language. In *Proc. of the Eighth IASTED Intl. Symposium, Innsbruck*, 1990.

[14] X. Wu. InORM: A System to Integrate Relational and Object-Oriented Approaches. In *Proc. of the 9th IASTED Intl. Symposium, Innsbruck*, 1991.

[15] X. Wu and K.-D. Kreplin. Ein Versionskonzept und ein zugehöriges Transaktionskonzept für eine modulare Softwareentwicklung. In *Proc. of GI-Conf. "Databases for Software Engineering"*, Dortmund, 1987.

An Indexing Model for Complex Object Hierarchies in Object-Oriented Databases

Farshad Fotouhi   T.G. Lee   William I. Grosky

Computer Science Department, Wayne State University
Detroit, Michigan 48202   United States of America

ABSTRACT

Recently, many specialized indexing schemes have been proposed for object-oriented database systems. These indexing techniques can be classified as indexing schemes for class hierarchies, for nested object hierarchies, and for complex object hierarchies. There are indexing schemes for complex object hierarchies such as the single class index and the class hierarchy index, but with these indexing schemes, we need traversal to get the result of a query. In this paper, we propose a hybrid indexing technique called a *generalized index* which can support complex object hierarchies as well as other hierarchical structures without traversal.

1. Introduction

Object-oriented database systems (OODBS) have recently become a very active research area for several reasons. One reason is that these systems, such as VBase [1], IRIS [9], POSTGRES [22], Gemstone [19], Exodus [7,12], and Orion [4], overcome the rather limited modeling capabilities of traditional database systems. Traditional systems are not adept at handling advanced applications such as CAD/CAM [2], OIS [3], and AI [21]. Another reason is that OODBS provide powerful concepts for application development and programming: modularity, encapsulation, inheritance, overriding, protocols, and polymorphism.

In this paper, we have chosen the object-oriented data model given in [4] since it not only has the properties of an OODBS (versions [13], composite objects [4], dynamic schema evolution [5], and multimedia data management [25]), but also supports a formal query model. Figure 1 shows the schema for a computer database. In this figure, circles represent classes, thin edges denote the *is-a* relationship, while thick edges represent the *is-part-of* relationship. A label associated with an edge represents a complex attribute, while a label associated with a node represents a primitive attribute. The root of the class hierarchy is the system-defined class **object**. That is, the class **object** is a superclass of any class in the class hierarchy.

We can classify different possible hierarchical structures in an object-oriented schema into three domains. These are the class hierarchy, the nested object hierarchy, and the complex object hierarchy. The class hierarchy is a hierarchy of classes in which an edge between a pair of nodes represents an *is-a* (generalization) relationship; that is, the subclass is a specialization of the superclass and the superclass is a generalization of the subclass. This hierarchy is usually represented as a rooted directed acyclic graph. The nested object hierarchy is a hierarchy of classes in which an edge between a pair of nodes represents either an *is-part-of* (aggregation) or an association relationship. Finally, the complex object hierarchy is the union of the nested object and class hierarchies. Each complex attribute is represented by a node in the complex object hierarchy. An edge between a pair of nodes represents an *is-a*, *is-part-of*, or an association relationship. The class hierarchy and the nested object hierarchy are viewed as special cases of the complex object hierarchy.

There are four different types of query graphs which can be constructed against an object-oriented schema. These are as follows:

1. A single class query graph is a graph in which the scope of the access of the query includes only a specific class, as in the query, **Find all microcomputers running under DOS**. See Figure 2a.

2. A class hierarchy query graph is a graph in which all the edges represent the *is-a* relationship, as in the query, **Find all computers running under DOS**. See Figure 2b.

3. A nested object query graph is a graph in which all the edges represent the *is-part-of* relationship, as in the query, **Find all computers running under DOS and manufactured by IBM**. See Figure 2c.

4. A hybrid query graph is a graph with mixed type of edges; that is each edge either represents the *is-a* or the *is-part-of* relationship, as in the query, **Find all computers running under DOS and manufactured by IBM**. See Figure 2d.

Many authors [6,8,18,20] have proposed specialized indexing models to speed-up query processing for queries whose graphs are of the forms 1-3 above. For example, [14] has proposed the class-hierarchy index for type 2 queries, while [6] has proposed a multilevel index scheme for type 3 queries. Note that any relational database indexing scheme can be used for type 1 queries. Both a single class index and a class hierarchy index can be used for queries of type 4, but the retrieval performance of these indices are not good for this type of query. This is due to the fact that one may have to execute a reverse traversal from the indexed class hierarchy to the query's target class hierarchy, which is quite expensive.

The organization of this paper is as follows. Section 2 presents a generalized indexing model for efficient support of a variety of structures in OODBS. In Section 3, we discuss our assumptions and we derive the cost expressions for queries using a single class index, a class hierarchy index, and a generalized index, respectively. In Section 4, performance of these three indices are analyzed in terms of retrieval cost. Finally, our conclusions are given in Section 5.

2. The Generalized Index

In the previous section, we mentioned some of the existing indexing methods for both class hierarchies and nested object hierarchies. However, up to the present time, no one has proposed any indexing methods for complex object hierarchies. Our approach is a hybrid of the approaches discussed previously.

We now describe the structure of the generalized index. This structure maintains given attribute values, path names which end at this attribute, classes which contain objects having the given attribute values, and the UID's of these objects. This information is stored in a tree structure referred to as an index tree.

Conceptually, this tree has a constant height of 5 and each level of the tree contains the following information (see Figure 3):

- Level 1 *(Domain level):* The nodes on this level represent the various domains of specific attributes. This level separates non-compatible domains into separate subtrees.

- Level 2 *(Value level):* Each node on this level represents a primitive value from the corresponding domain of its parent node.

- Level 3 *(Path level):* The nodes on this level represent path names as well as attribute names. For example, the value **IBM** on level 2 may point to two nodes at level 3 labeled **Company.Name** and **Company.Manufacturer.Name**, respectively.

- Level 4 *(Class level):* Each node on this level represents a class containing at least one object whose complex attribute represented by its parent node takes on the value represented by its grandparent node.

- Level 5 *(Identity level):* Each node on this level represents a UID of an object contained in the class represented by its parent node whose complex attribute represented by its grandparent node takes on the value represented by its great grandparent node.

Thus, in an index tree, each path from the root to a leaf consists of a 5-tuple (D,V,P,C,I). Operations on index trees and properties of our generalized indexing scheme can be found in [10,11,16,17].

3. Cost Expressions for Queries

In this section, we make certain assumptions underlying our development of cost formulas for the so-called type-hos query graph with respect to the single class index, the class hierarchy index, and our generalized index. A type-hos query is a hybrid query of type 4 consisting of a single predicate against a nested attribute. An example type-hos query is **Find all computers manufactured by IBM**. This query uses the path **Computer.Manufacturer.Name**. Cost analyses for other types of queries as well as for insertions, deletions and modifications are derived in [17].

Our assumptions are as follows:

a. *File Structures:* The data structure of each index is based

on a B-tree [6,14,15,17]. The reference [17] describes the file structures of each index in detail.

b. *Parameters:* The parameters we have considered in the cost expressions are classified as logical parameters and index-related parameters. The logical parameters describe the characteristics of the class hierarchy, the paths, and the objects. The index parameters describe the characteristics of the index file.

c. *Types of Costs:* Category 1 cost (N_a) is the cost of accessing all index pages of the target class hierarchy in order to find the list of UID's associated with a given key value. This corresponds to accessing the leaf and non-leaf nodes of the index tree for a given value. Category 2 cost (N_b) is the cost of accessing all pages of a class hierarchy which contain instances of an indexed attribute. Finally, category 3 cost (N_c) is the cost of accessing all pages in order to support either forward traversal, from C(m) to C(m+i), or reverse traversal, from C(m) to C(m-i), for m > i.

d. *Types of Predicates:* The predicate '=' is called a type 1 operator, while predicates such as '<', '≤', '>', '≥', '≠' are called type 2 operators.

e. *Other assumptions:* We assume that the length of all key values are the same. This implies that the length of all non-leaf nodes is the same for all indices. We also assume that there are no multivalued attributes, no partial instantiations exist along the path, all lengths and sizes are in bytes, the leaf nodes of the indices are linked, and that the costs of unions and intersections are 0.

The attribute of our query may be a nested attribute of the complex object hierarchy. The operator is either a type 1 or a type 2 predicate. Thus, a single key query is of the form <attribute (type 1 operator) value> and a range query is of the form <attribute (type 2 operator) value>.

Given the type-hos query graph of Figure 4a, Figure 4b-4d illustrates the three indexing techniques we are comparing: a single class index, a class hierarchy index, and a generalized index.

3.1 Cost Formula for Single Class Index

In this indexing scheme, there are *b* index trees for an ending class hierarchy CH_n. To obtain the set of UID's satisfying the value *val*, we have to access all the indices which contain this value. Then, reverse traversal is needed to get the UID's of the target class hierarchy CH_1. An algorithm to do this can be written as follows:

SingleClassIndexRetrieve(P,Pred);
{*Input:*   P : path; Pred : (attribute operator *val*);}
{*Output:*   TOIDS : set of UID's in the target class hierarchy;}

begin

     T = set of index trees associated with value *val* in predicate Pred for class hierarchy CH_n;

     IOIDS = ∅;

     for each index tree t ∈ T do

         IOIDS = IOIDS ∪ RetrieveOid(*val*,t);

$$\text{TOIDS} = \text{ReverseTraversal}(P, \text{IOIDS}, CH_n, CH_1);$$
end.

Based on this algorithm, the total number of accesses (N_{sc}) needed is

$$N_{SingleClass} = \sum_{j=1}^{b} N_a(j, val, Pred) + \sum_{j=1}^{n-1} N_c(j), \text{ where,}$$

(i) $N_a(j, val, Pred)$ is the cost of accessing the jth index tree associated with a subclass $C_{j,n}$ in a class hierarchy CH_n for value val of the predicate Pred.

(ii) $N_c(j)$ is the cost of accessing the file associated with a class hierarchy CH_{j+1} in order to get 'back-pointer' UID's of class hierarchy CH_j.

(iii) b is the number of subclasses in a class hierarchy having the same value.

(iv) n is the length of path P.

Case 1: Type-1 Predicate

$$N_a(j, val, Pred) = \begin{cases} N_{sc}(j, val, Pred) + 1 \text{ if } LS(j, val, Pred) \le L_p \\ \\ N_{sc}(j, val, Pred) + \left\lceil \dfrac{LS(j, val, Pred)}{L_p} \right\rceil \\ \\ \text{if } LS(j, val, Pred) > L_p \end{cases}$$

where,

(i) $N_{sc}(j, val, Pred)$ is the number of non-leaf nodes of the jth index tree associated with subclass $C_{i,n}$ in class hierarchy CH_n for value val of the predicate Pred.

(ii) $LS(j, val, Pred)$ is the size of a leaf node of the jth index tree associated with subclass $C_{j,n}$ in class hierarchy CH_n for value val of the predicate Pred.

(iii) L_p is the page size.

and

$$N_c(j) = \begin{cases} R\left(A(j+1), N_{Pages}(j+1), N_{Records}(j+1)\right) \\ \quad \text{if } S_{Records}(j+1) \le L_p \\ \\ A(j+1)\left\lceil \dfrac{S_{Records}(j+1)}{L_p} \right\rceil \text{ if } S_{Records}(j+1) > L_p \end{cases}$$

where,

(a) $R(r,p,q)$ is the formula developed by Yao [24] to estimate the approximate number of block accesses in the case where the size of a record is less than that of a block, where r is the cardinality of a set of records which takes p pages to store and out of which one is to choose q records at random.

(b) $N_{Records}(j)$ is the number of records in the files associated with class hierarchy CH_j.

(c) $N_{Pages}(j)$ is the number of pages needed for the files associated with class hierarchy CH_j.

(d) $A(j)$ is the cardinality of the set of records to be chosen from the class hierarchy CH_j. We have that $A(j) = k(j) \times \ldots \times k(n)$, where $k(i)$ is the number of records from the class hierarchy CH_i which have the same A_i value. In turn, $k(i)$ is the quotient of the number of distinct objects in CH_i by the total number of distinct values of A_i.

Case 2: Type-2 Predicate

In this case, there is more than one key value in a range specified for the query. Hence, the cost is as follows:

$$N_a(j, val, Pred) = \begin{cases} N_{sc}(j, val, Pred) + \left\lceil \dfrac{N_{Keys}}{NL_{Records}} \right\rceil \\ \\ \quad \text{if } LS(j, val, Pred) \le L_p \\ \\ N_{sc}(j, val, Pred) + N_{Keys}\left\lceil \dfrac{LS(j, val, Pred)}{L_p} \right\rceil \\ \\ \quad \text{if } LS(j, val, Pred) > L_p \end{cases}$$

where,

(i) $NL_{Records}$ is the number of records per leaf node.

(ii) N_{Keys} is the number of key values in the range specified by the predicate Pred.

(iii) $N_c(j)$ is defined as in (iv) above, with $A(j) = N_{Keys} \times k(j) \times \ldots \times k(n)$.

3.2 Cost Formula for Class Hierarchy Index

In this indexing model, one index file exists for the class hierarchy CH_n, since it is maintained on an attribute for a class hierarchy consisting of m classes. To retrieve the set of UID's satisfying the value val, we need access only a single index tree. It is then necessary to execute a reverse traversal to get the result. An algorithm to do this can be written as follows:

ClassHierarchyIndexRetrieve(P,Pred);
{*Input:*   P : path; Pred : (attribute operator val);}
{*Output:*   TOIDS : set of UID's in the target class hierarchy;}

begin
    T = class hierarchy index tree associated with CH_n;
    IOIDS = RetrieveOidFromIndexTree(val,T);
    TOIDS = ReverseTraversal(P,IOIDS,CH_n,CH_1);
end.

The formulas for $N_{ClassHierarchy}$ are similar to that of the previous case for $N_{SingleClass}$, except that both $N_{sc}(j,val,Pred)$ is replaced by $N_h(val,Pred)$, and $LS(j,val,Pred)$ is now independent of j and is written as $LS(val,Pred)$. Their new semantics are as follows.

(i) $N_h(val,Pred)$ is the number of non-leaf nodes of the index tree associated with class hierarchy CH_n for value val of the predicate Pred.

(ii) $LS(val,Pred)$ is the size of a leaf node of the index tree associated with class hierarchy CH_n for value val of the predicate Pred.

3.3 Cost Formula for Generalized Index

This index model provides a direct association between an ending object and the corresponding starting object along the path. To retrieve a list of UID's, we need to access only a single index tree. Therefore, the total number of accesses needed is $N_g = N_a(val,Pred)$, where the latter expression is the cost of accessing the index tree associated with the target class hierarchy CH_1.

Case 1: Type-1 Predicate

$$N_{GIndex} = \begin{cases} N_G(val,Pred) + 1 \\ \quad \text{if } LS(val,Pred) \leq L_p \\ N_G(val,Pred) + \left\lceil \dfrac{LS(val,Pred)}{L_p} \right\rceil \\ \quad \text{if } LS(val,Pred) > L_p \end{cases}$$

where,

(i) $N_G(val,Pred)$ is the number of nodes of the index tree associated with the target class hierarchy CH_1 which must be accessed for value val of the predicate Pred.

(ii) $LS(val,Pred)$ is the size of a leaf node of the index tree associated with the target class hierarchy CH_1 for value val of the predicate Pred.

Case 2: Type-2 Predicate

$$N_{GIndex} = \begin{cases} N_G(val,Pred) + \left\lceil \dfrac{N_{Keys}}{NL_{Records}} \right\rceil \\ \quad \text{if } LS(val,Pred) \leq L_p \\ N_G(val,Pred) + N_{Keys} \left\lceil \dfrac{LS(val,Pred)}{L_p} \right\rceil \\ \quad \text{if } LS(val,Pred) > L_p \end{cases}$$

4. Analysis

We select the length of the path P, namely n, as the parameter of analysis for the retrieval cost. We do this for the following reasons. The reverse traversal cost depends on the length of the path P, and thus this influences the cost of using the single class index and the class hierarchy index, since both of them have a term for the reverse traversal cost. Also, the number of objects in class hierarchy CH_i, $1 \leq i \leq n$, which have the same value for attribute A_i, depends on the length of the path P.

As seen in the formulas above, the cost of processing a single predicate query using either the single class index or the class hierarchy index has a term for the reverse traversal cost from class hierarchy CH_n to class hierarchy CH_1. On the other hand, the cost of processing the query using our generalized index depends only on the height of the index tree, which is fixed. In general, the value of,

$$(*) \qquad \sum_{j=2}^{n} \left(\prod_{i=j}^{n} k(i) \right)$$

is the most significant factor in the retrieval cost expressions due to the fact that the accessing cost of the index is small compared with the reverse traversal cost. We analyze the following cases:

1. *Case 1:* For this case, we have that $k(1) = ... = k(n-1) = 1$, while $k(n)$ is arbitrary. That is, the cardinality of the set of objects retrieved from the target class hierarchy is constant, regardless of the length of path P. However, the reverse traversal cost still increases as the length of the path P increases. Thus, the retrieval cost using the generalized index is constant, while the retrieval cost using either the single class index or the class hierarchy index increases as the length of P increases. See the graph displayed in Figure 5a.

(2) *Case 2:* We assume that the cardinality of the set of objects retrieved from the target class hierarchy increases as the length of the path P increases. That is, $k(1), ..., k(n) > 1$. Since we are using a B-tree to simulate the generalized index tree, which always has a fixed height of 5, the height of our generalized index tree will increase depending on the value of expression (*) above. However, the change of this height is so small as to be negligible. On the other hand, the retrieval cost of both the single class index and the class hierarchy index increases rapidly with a small variation in the path length, since the reverse traversal cost increases with the product shown in (*) above. See the graph displayed in Figure 5b.

5. Conclusions

Unlike a relational database whose schema can be viewed as a set of independent relations, the schema of an object-oriented database consists of different types of hierarchical structures. Therefore, given a query against such a database, we may encounter many different types of query graphs, such as a single class query graph, a class hierarchy query graph, a nested object query graph, and a hybrid query graph. Thus, an indexing scheme for object-oriented databases must be able to provide efficient support for a variety of query types.

In this paper, we have proposed an indexing scheme for complex object hierarchies in order to speed-up query processing for object-oriented databases. We have shown the improved performance of query retrieval when such indexing is used for a particular type of query. This improved performance generalizes to other types of queries as well as to insertions, deletions, and modifications [17]. Also, this indexing method allows us to share the value of indexed attributes among the classes whose domains are identical and thus facilitates processing the query in a parallel framework. This is currently under investigation.

REFERENCES

[1]   T. Andrews and C. Harris, 'Combining Language and Database Advances in an Object-Oriented Development Environment,' *Proceedings of the Conference on Object-Oriented Systems, Languages, and Applications*, Orlando, Florida, September 1987, pp. 430-440

[2]   H. Afsarmanesh, D. Knapp, D. McLeod, and A. Parker, 'An Extendible Object-Oriented Approach to VLSI/CAD,' *Proceedings of the Eleventh International Conference on Very Large Databases*, Stockholm, Sweden, August 1985, pp. 13-24

[3]   M. Ahlsen, A. Bjornerstedt, S. Britts, C. Hulten, and L. Soderlund, 'An Architecture for Object Management in OIS,' *ACM Transactions on Office Information Systems*, Volume 2 (1984), pp. 173-196

[4]   H. Banerjee, H.T. Chou, J. Garza, W. Kim, D. Woelk, and N. Ballou, 'Data Model Issues for Object-Oriented Applications,' *ACM Transactions on Office Information Systems*, Volume 5 (1987), pp. 3-26

[5]   J. Banerjee, W. Kim, H.J. Kim, and H.F. Korth, 'Semantics and Information of Schema Evolution in Object-Oriented Databases,' *Proceedings of the ACM Conference on Management of Data*, San Francisco, California, May 1987, pp. 311-322

[6]   E. Bertino and W. Kim, 'Indexing Techniques for Queries on Nested Objects,' *IEEE Transactions on Knowledge and Data Engineering*, Volume 1 (1989), pp. 196-214

[7]   M.H. Carey, D.J. DeWitt, D. Frank, G. Graefe, M. Muralikrishna, J.E. Richardson, and E.J. Shekita 'The Architecture of the EXODUS Extensible DBMS: A Preliminary Report,' *Proceedings of the International Workshop on Object-Oriented Databases Systems*, Pacific Grove, California, September 1986, pp. 52-65

[8]   A. Deshpande and D. Gucht, 'An Implementation or Nested Relational Databases,' *Proceedings of the Fourteenth International Conference on Very Large Databases*, Los Angeles, California, August 1988, pp. 76-87

[9]   D.H. Fishman et. al., 'IRIS: An Object-Oriented Database Management System,' *ACM Transactions on Office Information Systems*, Volume 5 (1987), pp. 48-69

[10]   F. Fotouhi and T.G. Lee, *Cost Analysis of the Generalized Index Model*, Technical Report CSC-90-011, Computer Science Department, Wayne State University, Detroit, Michigan, 1990

[11]   F. Fotouhi, T.G. Lee, and W.I. Grosky, 'The Generalized Index Model for Object-Oriented Database Systems,' *Proceedings of the Tenth Annual International IEEE International Phoenix Conference on Computers and Communications*, Phoenix, Arizona, March 1991, pp. 302-308

[12]   G. Graefe and D.J. DeWitt, 'The EXODUS Optimizer Generator,' *Proceedings of the ACM International Conference on Management of Data*, San Francisco, California, May 1987, pp. 160-172

[13]   W. Kim and H.T. Chou, 'Versions of Schema for Object-Oriented Databases,' *Proceedings of the Fourteenth International Conference on Very Large Databases*, Los Angeles, California, August 1988, pp. 148-159

[14]   W. Kim, K.C. Kim, and A. Dale, 'Indexing Techniques for Object-Oriented Databases,' In *Object-Oriented Concepts, Applications, and Databases*, edited by W. Kim and F. Lochovsky, Addison-Wesley Publishing Company, Reading, Massachusetts, 1989

[15]   D. Knuth, *The Art of Computer Programming*, Volume 3, Addison-Wesley Publishing Company, Reading, Massachusetts, 1979

[16]   T.G. Lee and F. Fotouhi, 'Indexing Methods for Object-Oriented Database Systems,' *KESA Newsletter*, Volume 19 (1990), pp. 43-46

[17]   T.G. Lee, *The Generalized Index for Query Optimization in Object-Oriented Database Systems*, Ph.D. Thesis, Wayne State University, 1991

[18]   D. Maier and J. Stein, *Indexing in an Object-Oriented Data Model*, Technical Report CS/E-86-006, Computer Science Department, Oregon Graduate Center, Portland, Oregon, May 1986

[19]   D. Maier, J. Stein, A. Otis, and A. Purdy, *Development of an Object-Oriented DBMS*, Technical Report CS/E-86-005, Computer Science Department, Oregon Graduate Center, Portland, Oregon, 1986

[20]   M. Missikoff, 'A Domain Based Internal Schema for Relational Database Machines,' *Proceedings of the ACM Conference on the Management of Data*, June 1982

[21]   M. Stefik and D. Bobrow, 'Object-Oriented Programming: Themes and Variations,' *AI Magazine*, Volume 6 (1986), pp. 40-62

[22]   M. Stonebraker and L.A. Rowe, 'The Design of Postgres,' *Proceedings of the ACM Conference on the Management of Data*, Washington, D.C., June 1986, pp. 340-355

[23]   D. Woelk, W. Kim, and W. Luther, 'Multimedia Information Management in an Object-Oriented Database System,' *Proceedings of the Thirteenth International Conference on Very Large Databases*, Brighton, England, September 1987, pp. 319-330

[24]   S.B. Yao, 'Approximating Block Accesses in Database Organizations,' *Communications of the ACM*, Volume 20 (1977), p. 260

226

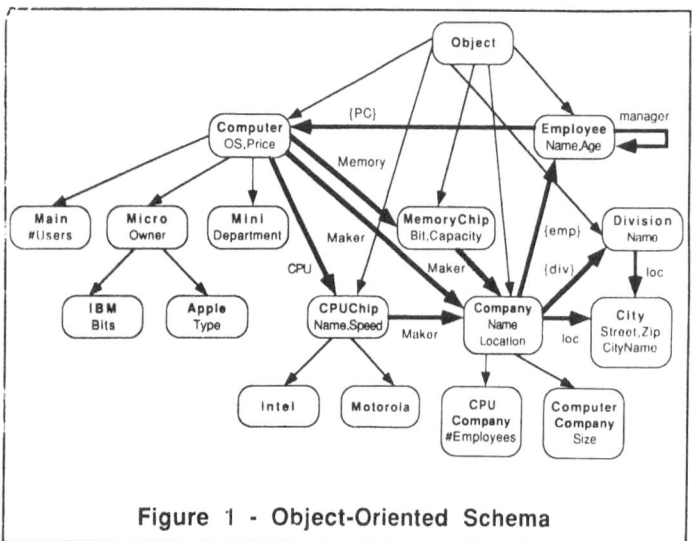

Figure 1 - Object-Oriented Schema

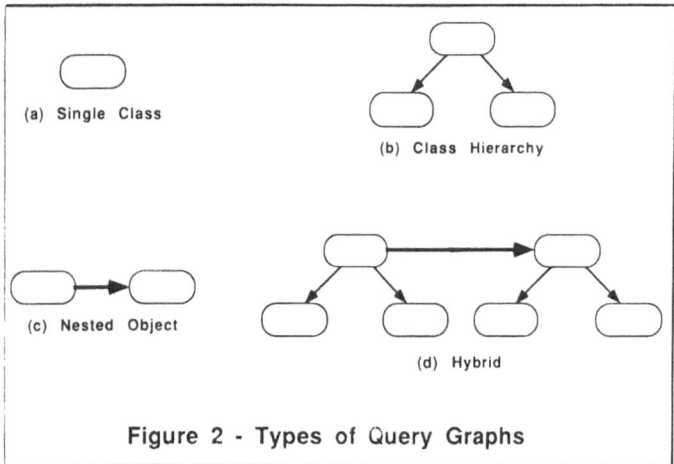

Figure 2 - Types of Query Graphs

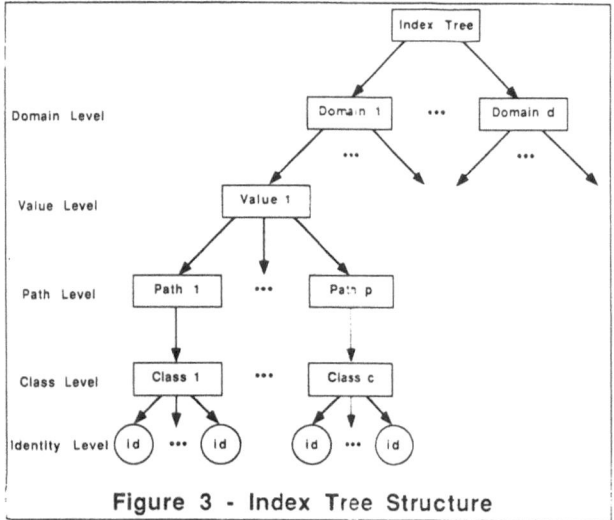

Figure 3 - Index Tree Structure

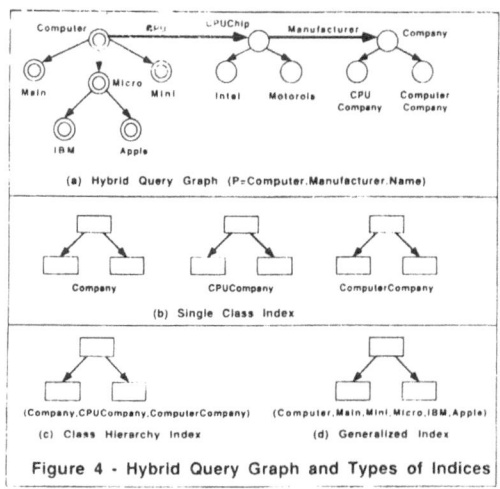

Figure 4 - Hybrid Query Graph and Types of Indices

Figure 5a - Performance of Retrieval
[k(1) = k(2) = ... = k(n-1) = 1, k(n) = 10]

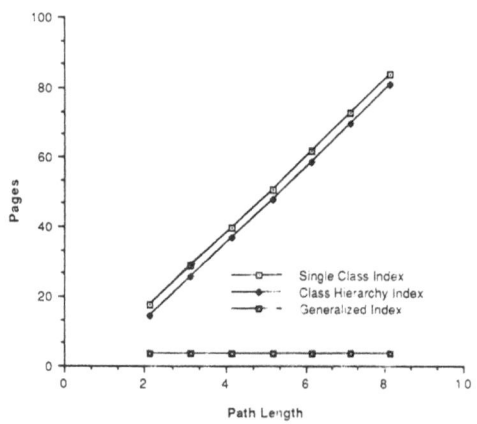

Figure 5b - Performance of Retrieval
[k(1) = k(2) = ... = k(n-1) = 2, k(n) = 10]

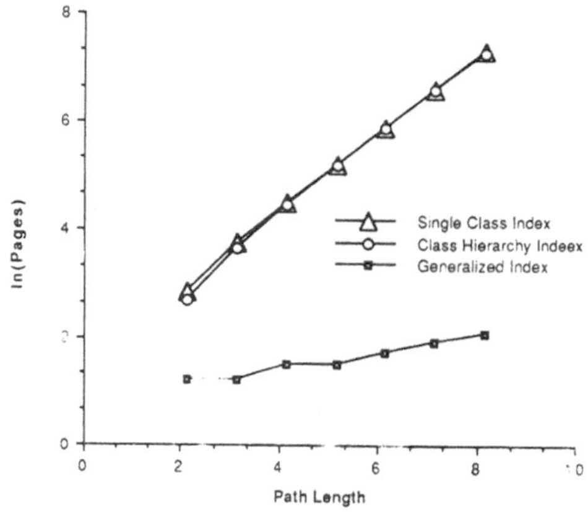

An Object-Oriented Executable Requirements Specification Language*

Oscar Barros   Germán Pavez

Industrial Engineering Department - University of Chile
P.O.Box 2777
Santiago/Chile

ABSTRACT

An end user-, object-oriented requirements specification language, suitable for transaction-processing data base applications, is presented. Such language is formal and hence computer processable, allowing for specification execution and simulation, thus facilitating a prototype development approach.

1. INTRODUCTION

In the process of developing data base applications, a requirements determination and specification front-end step is generally recognized. Methods for requirements specifications have been developed that range from informal narrative approaches using plain natural language, to very formal specification techniques that are computer processable [6,10,12].

Currently, academic and practical work is being done in the direction of formalizing the statement of requirement specifications and providing computer support for them. Representative approaches of this work are :

i) CASE products [5] that partially formalize specifications by some sort of computer-supported diagramming -DFD, ER, state transition, etc.- and dictionary or repository documentation, and which attempt to interface with 3rd generation languages, data base products or 4th generation languages for code generation.

ii) Languages like SREM [1], Taxis [8], Paisley [13] and others that formalize specifications in a way which is close to the computer implementation and thus are able to execute specifications.

iii) Object-oriented programming and design, which provide formal languages like OPAL [9], IRIS [7] and others [11] that are suitable for analysts.

iv) Formal languages like CML [4] and others that formalize specifications in a way which is close to users views of the system but that have not yet been successful in either providing specifications that are processable themselves or generate code in a suitable language that implements the specification.

Our work make progress along the lines of the fourth type of approach above in that:

i) We provide a formal language and interface which is problem and thus user oriented.

ii) We give computer support that allows to directly execute specifications, thus facilitating rapid prototyping and simulation.

iii) We attempt to generate code in a language suitable to implement specifications above.

Main difficulties in accomplishing tasks above are in that formality is not usually friendly to users and structural and behavioral characteristics of systems do not mix well, thus generating the so called impedance mismatch. We have attempted to solve these problems by using the ideas of object-oriented development and databases [3,7] as a framework, which, we have found, provide a nice match between problem-oriented or real-life entities and computer implementation of such entities.

In what follows we give a summary of the language and describe the computer support we provide for it.

2. DESCRIPTION OF THE LANGUAGE

2.1. General Ideas

They key idea for specification that we apply is to convert problem entities into persistent computer objects that simulate the former. Thus we want to keep a close match between problem structure and computer implementation structure, in order to facilitate specification understanding by end users.

In specifying computer objects, we adopt the common concepts proposed for this in the literature [7,9]. Thus we define classes of objects, which in our case will be classes of problem entities. Other entities are introduced as "attributes" (in a very general sense) needed to describe classes. For example, an invoice is an entity needed to describe the obligation of a client (problem entity) to pay for a product or service, and addresses is an entity used to describe an attribute of invoice. Since these "attributes" may be complex data types, we will use two well known type constructors to specify them: the "setof" and "recordof" constructors [9]. However there are no limitations to define other data types needed for object specification.

As usual, we distinguish between object structure and object behavior, the latter being specified by means of methods [9]. Thus the general pattern of object specification is:

```
class   class_name
        structure
                oid object_id
                attributes
                        attribute_list
        methods
                method_list
end
```

---
* Finantial suppport for this work from FONDECYT is appreciated

2.2. Structure Specification

For each of the objects identified as in Section 2.1, a structure specification is written according to the following scheme:

class   class_name
    structure
        oid
        object_id : T [constraint];
        attributes
            C_1 ` : [qualifier] T1 [constraint];
            .
            .
            Cn   : [qualifier] Tn [constraint];
end;

Contraints can also be used within recordof data-types as shown below :

T = **recordof** (C_1 : [qualifier] T1 [constraint] ;
           .
           .
      Cn : [qualifier] Tn [constraint] ;);

The recordof and setof type constructors work according to the following main rules :

a) **Recordof**

- Defines and n-tuple, where each component has a unique **name** and a type.
- Record types can be **setof** of another previously defined type
- The i'th component of record T is denoted $T.c_i$
- Recursive structures are allowed, i.e. a component of T can be of the type **setof**(T).

b) **Setof**

- Allows to represent sets, arrays and lists.
- If T = **setof**(T_o), To is the base type of the set, and should be previously defined.
- Repeated elements are allowed; the specification T = **setof**(To:unique) is used when no repetition is required.

In Figure 1, an example of structure specification of the entity CLIENT, identified in a credit management application, is presented. Attributes in Figure 1 are the ones necessary to characterize a client in terms of credit risk and to know his state of orders and debt at any given moment, where the specification of data-types ORDERS and INVOICES are :

ORDER_DETAIL= **recordof**(product_code : **oid** PRODUCTS;
                 quantity   : **integer** <= 999););
ORDERS   = **recordof** (order_number : **integer** <= 9999;
               order_date : **DATE**;
               detail   : **setof**(ORDER_DETAIL););
INSTALLMENTS= **recordof**(installment_no: **integer** <= 99;
               amount   : **integer** <= 9999;
               due_date   : **DATE**;
               installment_status: **integer in** [1,3];);
INVOICES   = **recordof**(invoice_number: **integer** <= 9999;
               invoice_date : **DATE**;
               inv_detail : **setof** (INSTALL-
               MENTS););

Notice that invoices are paid in installments, each with a given due date, and that ORDERS make reference to PRODUCTS, which is another class with the obvious attributes of product_code, description and price.

2.3. Behavior Specification

As stated before, we attempt a behavior specification which is as non-procedural as possible. In doing this we use logical-based **preconditions**, whenever is possible, to indicate processing rules that should be satisfied previous to the execution of **actions** associated to a method. Hence the general structure of a method is the one shown in Figure 2, where "->" indicates that the method is applied to a given object of a class; and, alternatively, "=>" that the method is applied over a set of objects in a class; parameters of the method can be **recordof**, **setof** or objects; there is an optional data-type returned by the method;under **local** there are variables that participate in the method and their corresponding types; and **preconditions** are to be satisfied by parameters.

We define logical quantifiers on sets, which will serve for specifying **preconditions** in a declarative way and also to be included in expressions of the type "where", "when" and others to be explained later. The "some" quantifier is as follows :

some element **in** set_class_name(condition)

```
class  CLIENT
  structure
    oid
      client_number  : integer;
    attributes
      client_name   : unchange string[20] not null;
      address     : string[30];
      financial_state: integer <=99999;
      account_balance: integer <=credit_limit;
      active_or_dismissed: boolean;
      credit_limit    : integer <=0.1*finantial_state;
      orders     : setof(ORDERS:unique);
      invoices     : setof(INVOICES:unique);
end
```

Figure 1. Example of structure specification

wich checks the existance of an element in a class or set that satisfies a given condition; it returns true when there is at least one such an element. In a similar way "none" and "all" quantifiers are defined.

As an example of the use of **preconditions** with the logical quantifiers above, we show, in Figure 3, the processing of a payment transaction for the class defined in Figure 1, with parameters inv_number, install_no and amo_paid which, given that an invoice and corresponding installment with such attribute values exist, changes the attribute installment_status of CLIENT to "3", which means paid, and updates account_balance with amo_paid.

We provide a set of instructions to perform the usual operations of querying, updating, deleting and inserting objects in a class, common to relational languages, such as SQL, and also object-oriented languages, such as OPAL, as shown bellow :

Select

This statement finds the elements from a list of sets and/ or classes that satisfy a given optional condition, as follows:

```
select expression_list
    from  var_name1 in set_class_name1
        [,var_name2 in set_class_name2
                    .
                    .
            ,var_nameN in set_class_nameN]
        [where select_condition]
```

This sentence always generates a **setof**, which can be used in another set expression; e.g.:

```
set_name:=select_statement;
return select_statement;
```

This plays the rol a cursor performs in other languages and allows to link **select** to other statements in transaction processing, as we will see later.

```
method class_name      ->   method_name ([parameter_list])
                            [:data_type];
[local
        var_name1  :  data_type1;
        [var_name2  :  data_type2;
            .            .
            .            .
        var_nameN  :  data_typeN;]]
[preconditions
        var_name1 ===> precondition_list1
        [var_name2 ===> precondition_list2
            .                .
            .                .
        var_nameN ===> precondition_listN]]
actions
        statement_list
end ;
```

Figure 2. Method specification schema

An example or **select**, which uses the class specified in Figure 1, is given in Figure 4, where we use the type:

```
DEL_INV = recordof(
                    invoice_number:integer,
                    installment_no:integer);
```

Other similar sentences for **update, delete, insert, min, max, count, sum, average,** and **sort** in sets are provided.

Besides common instruction above, we provide others that allow to specify full transaction processing, including transaction input, complex logic calculation and output production, as follows:

Input

This instruction allows to enter a variable -simple, **recordof, setof** or complex object- from any of several input devices:

```
input var_name [from input_device]
            [where condition]
```

The example in Figure 7 shows the way transactions can be entered with **input** and left ready for processing within a method.

```
method   CLIENT->Process_payment(
                            inv_number : integer
                            install_no : integer
                            amo_paid  : integer);
local
    inv : INVOICES;
    inst: INSTALLMENTS;
preconditions
    inv_number ==>rule some inv in client.invoices(
                inv.invoice_number = inv_number):
                error "Invoice", inv_number, "does
                            not exist";

    install_no ==>   rule some inst in invoices.installments(
                inst.installment_number=install_no):
                error "Installment",install_no, "does
                            not_exist";
end;
actions
    inst.installment_status=3 /*paid*/;
    account_balance = account_balance-
                            amo_paid/*update balance*/;
end;
```

Figure 3. Example of **method** and **preconditions**

Output

This statement puts data on a given device:

output expression_list
[**to** output_device]
[**from** var_name1 **in** set_class_name1
[,var_name2 **in** set_class_name2
:
,var_nameN **in** set_class_nameN]]
[**where** condition]

The example in Figure 5 shows the use of **output** together with the link to the method used in Figure 4.

For each

for each   var_name1 **in** set_class_name1
[,var_name2 **in** set_class_name2
:
,var_nameN **in** set_class_nameN]
[**where** condition]
do
 statement_block

For each can be used within a method with **preconditions**, in which case, if there is also a **where** statement, **preconditions** have priority.

In Figure 6, we give an example of transaction processing using **for each**, where :

PAYMENT_TRANSACTION = **recordof**(
client_no: **integer**,
invoi_no : **integer**,
insta_no : **integer**,

```
method CLIENT->Delinquent_payments( ): setof(DEL_INV);
local
  inv  : INVOICES ;
  inst : INSTALLMENTS ;
actions
  return select inv.invoice_number,inst.installment_no
      from  inv in invoices,
            inst in inv.installments
      where  inst.installment_status=1/*not_paid*/
      and inst.due_date < date( ) /*current_date*/;
end;
```

Figure 4. Example of **select**

When

This expression allows the conditional execution of a group of actions, based on case logic :
when case condition1 **then**
statement_list1
[**case** condition2 **then**
statement_list2

case conditionN **then**
statement_listN]
[**otherwise**
statement_list]
end

In Figure 7, an example of use of **when** is shown, integrating, at the same time, several of the previous features we have presented and some new ones. In particular, in entering several orders for products, calculating invoices amount and updating class CLIENT with new orders, invoices and installments, we illustrate the use of input from screen and the passing of transactions to a method; the statement **sum**, which is similar to **select**; and the creation/updating of sets by means of the statement **union**. In the example, the following data type has been used:

ORDER_IN = **recordof**(
client_no : **oid** CLIENT;
order : ORDERS;
number_of_installments: **integer** >= 1);

```
method  CLIENT->Print_delinquent_payments( );
actions
  output  client_number, client->Delinquent_payments( )
  to printer;
end;
```

Figure 5. Example of **output**

```
method CLIENT=>Process_payment_transactions(
                 pay_trans: setof (PAYMENT_
                            TRANSACTION));
local
  c : oid CLIENT ;
  pt: PAYMENT_TRANSACTION ;
actions
  for each pt in pay_trans
    where some c in class CLIENT(c->OID( )=pt.client_no)
  do
  c->Process_payment(
                pt.invoi_no,
                pt.insta_no,
                pt.amo_paid);
```

Figure 6. Example of transaction processing

```
method CLIENT=>Invoicing and_updating( );
local
   c      : oid CLIENT;
   order_in: ORDEN_IN;
actions
   for each order_in from screen
   where some c in class CLIENT(c->OID( )=order_in.client_no)
do
      c-> Invoicing_and_updating(order_in);
end;
methodCLIENT->Invoicing_and_updating
                           (order_in:ORDER_IN);
local
   invoice_amount: integer;
   order_detail  : ORDER_DETAIL;
   i             : integer;
   date          : DATE;
   inst          : INSTALLMENTS;
   prod          : oid PRODUCTS;
   inv           : INVOICES;
actions
   invoice_amount:= sum prod->price( )*order_detail.quantity
                      from order_detail in order_in.order
                      where some prod in class PRODUCTS(
                      prod->OID( )=order_detail.product_code);
   account_balance:=account_balance+invoice_amount;
   orders := orders union {order};
when
case order_in.number_of_installments = 1 then
   invoices:=invoices union{((client->Assign_invoice_no(),{ ));
otherwise
   inv.invoice_number:=client->Assign_invoice_no( );
   inv.invoice_detail:={ };
   date :=date( ) + @00/01/00;
   for i :=1 to order_in.number_of_installments do begin
   inst.installment.no:=i;
   inst.amount:=invoice_amount/order_in.number_
                                  of_installments;
   inst.status:=1/* not due */;
   inst.due_date:=date;
   inv.inv_detail=inv.inv_detail union {inst};
   date:=date+@00/01/00;
end;
   invoices:=invoices union {inv};
end;
```

Figure 7. Example of **when** and other features

3.   COMPUTER SUPPORT

In this section we give a brief account of the software that supports the language outlined in Section 2.

3.1.   User Interface

User interface is alternatively a graphic editor that allows to draw an entity-relationship diagram or a specification editor that interprets instructions explained above. In the case the graphic editor is used, the software will automatically produce an outline of the specification, defining classes and data types. Then, the analyst or user will complete the specification with attributes, integrity constraints and methods. The software provides interactive syntaxis checking, so that errors are corrected on the spot.

3.2.   Specification Validation and Simulation

In order to allow the user to conceptualy validate a specification, the software provides a graphical representation of the behavioral components of the system. Such representation is of the object data flow type [2]. The software will actually execute the specification allowing to perform all the methods over the classes. Thus processing of inputs, updating, calculations, output production and so on will be simulated and the user will be able to see the full functionality of the system.

3.3.   Code Generation

Once a specification is refined through simulated prototyping, actual code will be produced in standar SQL plus a host language. The code will be generated by first converting objects into normalized tables. Then methods written in our specification language will be translated into standard SQL, when feasible. Other methods, not directly mapped into SQL, will be translated into SQL and C.

4.   SUMMARY AND CONCLUSION

We have shown an object-oriented language suitable for the specification of transaction-oriented data base applications directly by end users of such applications. Such language is formal and hence computer processable, allowing for specification execution, thus facilitating a prototype development approach.

Main conclusion is that it is feasible to mix formality and friendliness in a specification language, using a mostly declarative approach, and, at the same time, to integrate structural and behavioral aspects of database applications.

232

REFERENCES

[1] Alford, M. "SREM at the Age Eight; The Distributed Computing Design System." *IEEE Computer*, vol.18, p.36, april 1985.

[2] Bailin, S.D. "An Object-Oriented Requirements Specification Method." *Comm ACM*, vol. 32, p. 608, 1989.

[3] Booch, G. "Object-Oriented Development." *IEEE Trans. Software Eng.*, vol. SE 12, p. 211, 1986.

[4] Borgida, A. "Features of Languages for the Development of Information Systems at the Conceptual Level." *IEEE Software*, p. 63, july 1985.

[5] Chikofsky, E.J. and B.L.Rubenstein "CASE: Reliability Engineering for Information Systems." *IEEE Software*, p.11, march 1988.

[6] Davis, A.M. "A Comparison of Techniques for the Specification of External System Behavior." *Comm ACM*, vol. 31, p.1098, 1988.

[7] Kim, W. and F.H.Lochovsky (eds.) "Object-Oriented Concepts, Databases, and Applications." *ACM Press Frontier Series*, Addison-Wesley, Reading, Mass, 1989.

[8] Mylopoulos, J. Ph.A.Bernstein and H.K.Wong "A Language Facility for Designing Database Intensive Applications." *ACM Trans. Database Syst.*, vol. 5, p. 1985, 1980.

[9] Ullman, J.D. "Principles of Database and Knowledge-Base Systems, Volume I." *Computer Science Press, Rockville*, Maryland, 1988.

[10] Webster, D.E. "Mapping the Design Information Representation Terrain." *Computer*, p. 8, december 1988.

[11] Wirfs-Brock, J. and R.E. Johnson "Surveying Current Research in "Object-Oriented Design." *Comm. ACM*, vol. 33, p. 105, 1990.

[12] Yadav, S.B., R.R. Brovoco, A.T.Chatfield and T.M.Rajkumar "Comparison of Techniques for Information Requirement Determination." *Comm. ACM*, Vol. 31, p. 1090, 1988.

[13] Zave, P. "An Operational Approach to Requirements Specification for Embedded Systems." *IEEE Trans. Software Eng.*, vol. SE-8, p.250. 1982.

Functional and Object-Oriented Specification of Information Systems

José. H. Canós and Oscar Pastor

Departament de Sistemes Informàtics i Computació

Universitat Politècnica de València. Camí de Vera, s/n   46020 València (Spain)

Phone + 34 6 3877350   Fax + 34 6 3877359

e-mail joseh@garbi.aii.upv.es (J.H. Canós) plo@garbi.aii.upv.es (O. Pastor)

Abstract

One of the main trends in software development in the last years is to use prototypes for validating requirements specifications at early phases of the software lifecycle. Moreover, the *Automation-BasedParadigm* provides an alternative to software construction, using formal methods as a basis for introducing automation in the development process. Among these methods, formal specification languages appear as the necessary tool for generating prototypes in an automatic process. **FMOL** is a formal Functional and Object-Oriented specification language, developed for specifying OO-Databases Conceptual Schemata. This paper describes the language and presents an enhancement of the prototyping environment introduced in [1]: the addition of logic variables that provides a powerful query language through the execution of specifications via conditional narrowing.

1   Introduction.

Prototyping allows to transform the classical *waterfall* software lifecycle in order to validate software requirements specifications at early stages of software development. Following this technique, developers and final users can test together a first version of the final product, reducing the high application's maintenance costs. There are basically two approaches for prototyping. One of them deals with the introduction of an intermediate phase in the classical lifecycle in which the prototype is developed and tested, generating feedbacks to previous stages if necessary. The other approach is more radical, attempting to define a new software lifecycle without the classical lifecycle errors.

In the early 80's Balzer proposes the *Automation-Based Paradigm* [2], which main goal is the automation of the software development process. This automation is reached through the use of *formal methods*. Among these methods, formal specification languages appear as a necessary tool for prototype generation in an automatic process, in which the operational semantics of the formal language provides the specification executability. In this way, the Analyst must only write the problem's formal specification, and this is the prototype itself. The new lifecycle is concluded with an automatic formal transformation of the formal specification into an efficient implementation that will be the final product.

FMOL is a functional and Object-Oriented Language that blends an objectual and functional logic at the semantic level to specify open and passive Information Systems. Specifications written in FMOL can be animated in a proto-typing environment presented in [1] and now enhanced substantially.In this paper we describe the language and the environment enhancements. Section 2 presents the Object-Oriented Model that FMOL implements. Next, we make a description of the Language (section 4). In section 5 we show how FMOL specifications can be transformed into equivalent logic programs, and in section 6 the prototyping environment is presented.

2   The OO-Model.

Being our main objective to produce a logic program from an OO Specification Language and using a functional expressiveness, we have to precise what do we mean by Object-Oriented. There is not still a wide accepted formalization of what an object is. We propose here a blend between ontological concepts as presented in [3] and the most recent definitions from IFIP WG 8.1 [4] in order to provide a formal model to specify Information Systems from an OO approach.

One of the tasks of the IS Analyst is to specify a *system view* of the *Object System* in order to produce the *Conceptual Model specification*. An OO view is useful because of the closeness of OO concepts to real world phenomena. In this way, the semantic gap (the difference between what the system is and how it is to be represented) is narrower, because we can argue that the world is made of objects. Objects describe concrete beings, that is, specific entities rather that types or classes. By means of the abstraction mechanisms we put together objects in types. We call *class* a set of properties all of which characterize certain objects. A class is a precise characterization of structural and behavioural properties that a collection (or *type*) of objects all share.

Objects are known (or observable) to the world through their properties. We recognize properties only through attributes.The value of an attribute at a certain time is called a *state variable*. The set of state variables define the *state of the object*.

When an object is created, it is brought into existence and when it is destroyed, it finishes its existence (life). Each object has a name that identifies it during its existence.

An object has *dynamic* and *static* aspects in the sense that they do or do not change over time. From a static point of view, the allowed states of an object are determined by the set of static object laws, being these laws constraints on the allowed combinations of the attribute values (*static constraints*).From a dynamic point of view, we can also have temporal laws stating relationships between valid states (*dynamic constraints*).

We call *process* the cause of a change of state of an object. It is limited in time. It has elementary parts responsible for a single unified change of state that we call *Events*. An event is an abstraction of a change of state in the object system. It is discrete, has no duration and occurs at a certain point in time. The event concept is relative to the abstraction level. Objects are not independent. We have the *event sharing* as a mechanism of interaction between objects.

In the following section we show how our environment fits this OO model.

3 Object-Oriented Representation of Information Systems.

Considering a Conceptual Schema as a society of interacting objects [5], we can distinguish two kind of aspects:

- structural (anatomical), refering to the structural object composition. For simple classes, these aspects would be given by the corresponding typed attributes. Their type must be one of the predefined ADT (domains, or data subspecification). In classes built over other classes we have a richer situation because of the use of class definition operators as aggregation, specialization ,etc.

- behavioural (physiological), alluding to the object lives represented by the set of events and admisible traces.

And we have an observation function that relates both aspects, allowing us to know the structure as a function of the behaviour.

Class definition. Following these ideas, an object class may be formalized as a 4-tuple $(\mathcal{X}, \mathcal{A}, \mathcal{T}, \mathcal{O})$, where:

- $\mathcal{X}$ is the event set, including private and shared events. *Private events* belong to only one class. *Shared events* belong to more than one class. We have two special members of $\mathcal{X}$: those representing the creation and destruction of objects (resp. the **new** and **destroy** events).

- $\mathcal{A}$ is the typed attributes set, including *constant attributes* (those whose values do not change during the object live) and *variable attributes* (those changing depending on event occurrence)

Among the constant attributes we have to choose the key ones. They will be used for representing the object class surrogate space. Every object instance has to have its own and unique surrogate identifying it during its life. They are typed: every attribute takes its actual value from its type.

- $\mathcal{T} \subset \mathcal{X}^*$ is the lifecycle set, equivalent to the admisible event sequences. They will represent the possible objects' lives.

Every object life (or *trace*) will be made up of events of the event set $\mathcal{X}$ of its corresponding class. The precise specification of the correct traces for the class being defined will characterize the object behaviour.

Each trace representing an object instance will be composed by an initial creation event **new**, assigning to the object its surrogate and constant attributes, an adequate (correct) sequence of object class event occurrences and finally, a (optional) deletion event **destroy** finishing its existence.

- $\mathcal{O} : \mathcal{T} \to \mathcal{O}(\mathcal{A})$ is the observation function. Using it we will obtain for a given trace representing an object its corresponding set of pairs attribute-value giving us the object attribute values as a function of the event sequences.

Classes are built over *domains*. Domains contain a set of values and a set of operations on these values. They contain neither events nor variable attributes. Its type is the carrier set of the corresponding Abstract Data Type. They denote the data subspecification, and are used as object surrogates and attribute types. Their instances always exist, they are neither created nor destroyed and they do not have a changing state (i.e. class **Nat**, **Bool**, with obvious types $\{0,1,2\ldots\}$, $\{$**true**,**false**$\}$).

If a class has events and attributes, and it's not built using class operators, it is an *Elementary class*. We call *Complex classes* those defined using class operatorssuch as aggregation, specialization, ...

With respect to the $\mathcal{O}$ implementation, we have built in FMOL an event-oriented system, using a functional expressiveness for defining the observation function.In an event-oriented system, event occurrences are stored and we only evaluate the observation function when user wants to know something about one/many object lives. So, we have a backward inference, and the possibility of using an axiomatic implementation of the observation function for deducing the attribute values, connecting with all the logic programming theory results.

The variable attribute definition is done in terms of the relevant events of the attribute. And we will determine our set of correct traces by specifying preconditions that must be satisfied for an event occurrence.

4 The FMOL Specification Language

FMOL is a Specification Language that blends the functional and the OO programming paradigms at a semantic level. Its functional view is present in the observation function representation through the axiomatic and equational definition of variable attributes. Its objectual approach is given by its support to the class definition presented above.

First we are going to present the language structure.

A Conceptual Schema specification in FMOL is done according to the template:

Conceptual Schema *name*
specification_body
end Conceptual Schema

where the body contains the specification of the three FMOL units: domains, elementary classes and complex classes.The specification of a simple library conceptual schema including a book class is presented as an example in the Appendix A.

The specification body includes the definition of all entities composing the Conceptual Schema. These entities are domains, classes and relationships.

- domains denote the data subspecification. They are used as object surrogates and attribute types. Its type is an ADT and usually they are predefined.

- A class is declared by giving first its set of attributes (constant and variables). The variable attribute definition is done axiomatically using a functional style as shown below. Second we determine its set of events, distinguishing between private and shared. Finally, we precise what do we mean by correct traces fixing the preconditions related with each event. An event will be relevant (i.e. will happen) if it is activated by the system and its associated precondition holds. The following is the class specification of the books in a library

```
class book;

    constant attributes
    code:string key
    title:string


    variable attributes
    available(b:book):bool;
      equations r:reader
        available(b)=true if T=T1'newbook(b);
          available(b)=false if T=T1'loan(b,r);
          available(b)=true if T=T1'return(b);
              else available(b) at T1
          end_equations

    is_of_library(b:book):bool
        equations
    is_of_library(b)=true if T=T1'newbook(b)
                else is_of_library(b) at T1
        end_equations;
```

```
    private_events
        newbook(x:book)


    shared_events (reader)
        loan(x:book s:reader);
        return(x:book s:reader)


    preconditions T,T1:traces  x:book
        T=T1'newbook(x) if not is_of_library(x)

    end_class;
```

- We call *complex classes* those defined by using class operators. FMOL in its actual state allows to define complex class by aggregation. These complex classes are the relationships. When dealing with such a relationship, we have a complex class with some restrictions with respect to its components:

  1. its surrogate space is the cartesian product of the component class surrogate spaces

  2. the events shared between the component classes are private events of the relationship.

For example, the shared events loan and return between reader and book elementary classes are private events of the has_book relationship.

At this moment, other class operators are being implemented, in particular those corresponding to the classical abstraction mechanisms used in Semantic Modeling: generalization/specialization and grouping/ownership.

5 The Equational-Logic Program equivalent to a FMOL Specification.

A specification in FMOL is equivalent to a first order equational theory [6]. Logic Programming provides us with software tools to manipulate these resulting theories (e.g., Axis [7] or RAP [8] presentations). We can execute a given specification by generating its equivalent logic-functional program.

In this version of FMOL, we have chosen RAP, a functional language with conditional narrowing as operational semantics and a declarative semantics based on initial-algebras. Among its main features, RAP includes the executability of specifications; by executability we mean not only functions evaluation for given arguments, but also solving simultaneous equations based on a specification. This fact will allow to have available a powerful query language associated with FMOL. Let us describe how a FMOL specification can be transformed into a equivalent object program.

A RAP specification is composed by a signature plus a set of axioms (i.e., a *Presentation*). This presentation can be built incrementally, so that in fact it will be composed by a type —formally, Abstract Data Types— hierarchy. A FMOL specification must be therefore transformed into a RAP specification, i.e., we must to specify the Abstract Data Type representing our conceptual schema. Let's see how translating is accomplished.

We make an incremental translating, specifying first the conceptual schema components, i.e., classes and relationships:

Classes. Classes are specified as types, in which the class identifier is declared as the main **sort**. A **constructor** is introduced in order to be able to generate class instances uniquely identified (this is the object surrogate). Class attributes and events are not declared at this point, because they must be evaluated in the conceptual schema context. So, they will be introduced as operators of the type representing the conceptual schema (see below).

Relationships. Relationships are transformed into boolean-valued operators.

Once we have described the conceptual schema components, we build the whole system specification from them. We include here class attributes and events, and also the relationships. As before, a sort representing the conceptual schema is introduced. This sort will be added as the last argument of any operator's domain, because objects attributes, relationships and event preconditions must be evaluated with respect to the conceptual schema state, represented by a term of the sort.

Events are introduced as **constructors** of the sort, while attributes are now **function** symbols having as codomain the sort corresponding to the attribute's type. Similarly, relationships are introduced as boolean operators (note that any FMOL relationship specification contains always a variable attribute with the same name of the relationship and of type **bool**).

6 Specifications Animation and Queries.

The main interest of the formal specification languages is the ability to generate automatically a prototype from the source specification. This prototype can be executed, having so an animated specification of the conceptual schema.

We saw in section 2 that objects *evolve* through events occurrence. Their state can be observed by evaluating the attributes over the objects' lifecycle. So, a conceptual schema animation will be carried out as an *admissible* event sequence. By admissible we mean that events will be added to the sequence only if their corresponding preconditions hold.

But another important feature of a prototyping environment must be the existence of a *User Language* that allows users to query the first order theory equivalent to the specification of the conceptual schema. Through the queries we can know, for example, the value of an object's attribute, the extension of a relationship, etc.

FMOL specifications animation. We will see now the way FMOL specifications are animated. As a part of the FMOL environment, a prototyper manages event occurrences. For each specification being animated, a menu including all possible events is generated. Users (acting as *agents*) can at any moment select one of them; once an event has been selected, user is prompted for event arguments (if any). Next, a sequence of tests are started by the animator:

- *Do exist all the objects supplied as event arguments?*. We distinguish two cases:

    1. If the selected event is **new**, the object to be created must not exist.
    2. Otherwise, all objects must exist.

  If the answer is *no*, event is rejected.

- *Does hold the event precondition?*. If it does, event is accepted and added to the system *trace*. Otherwise, event is not accepted.

The system trace is a term of the sort corresponding to the conceptual schema (see section 5) that represents the conceptual schema *animation history*, that is, the admissible event sequence up to now. It will be the state with respect to which queries will be solved.

The FMOL User Language. An User Language associated to FMOL has to be defined in the prototyping environment. This language will allow us to query the system state. We define now the syntax and semantics of the user language.

- Syntax.

  Terms. Terms relative to the presentation equivalent to a FMOL conceptual shema specification are defined inductively as follows:

    1. Given the set of sorts $\{S_1, \ldots, S_n\}$, for each S_i there is a unique set of names $\{X_{i1}, \ldots, X_{im}\}$ that will be named variables of the sort S_i. These variables are terms of type S_i.
    2. Any constant of a domain's sort is a term of this sort.
    3. Let S_C be a sort coming from a class C, and S_A be the sort of the key attribute of C. There exists a mapping $I_C : S_A \longrightarrow S_C$ that gives a class instance from a element of S_A.

Let be $s \in S_A$; then $I_C(s)$ is a term of sort S_C. For example, book('El Quijote')

4. For each class, given the n-ary operator set (the events) $o_i : S_{i1} \times S_{in} \longrightarrow S_j$, and given n terms $t_1, \ldots, t_n$ of type $S_{i1}, \ldots, S_{in}$ respectively, $o_i(t_1, \ldots, t_n)$ is a term of sort S_j for all i. For example, newbook(book('El Quijote'))

5. Let f be a n-ary operator corresponding to a class' attribute, and let $t_1, \ldots, t_n$ terms of its arguments' types. Then $f(t_1, \ldots, t_n)$ is a term.

6. The only terms are those defined by 1, ..., 5.

Well-Formed Formulas Its definition is the following:

1. If t_1 and t_2 are terms, then $t_1 = t_2$ is a well-formed formula.

2. Only are well-formed formulas those generated by 1.

- **Semantics.**

We take the terms of the sort representing the Conceptual Schema (the interest sort) as the domain of the interpretation. Its type is T, the set of traces. Attributes, events, event preconditions and relationships are represented as operators. The wff will be set of equations with logic variables evaluated over terms of the interest sort.

Queries. One of the main features of the FMOL environment is the powerful query language provided by the operational semantics of the object language employed. The Conditional Narrowing algorithm used by RAP allows users to solve equations representing database queries with respect to the presentation equivalent to the conceptual schema specification. These equations are, of course, well-formed formulas of the User Language.

Examples.

1. *What books are available in a library state in which only the books* **Hamlet** *and* **El Quijote** *have been inserted?*.

This query can be written as follows:

```
available(B,new_book(book('El Quijote'),
    newbook(book('Hamlet),nil))) = true.
```

The answer from the system will be:

```
B = book('El Quijote').

More Solutions?
```

If we ask for more solutions, B = book('Hamlet) will be the next answer. If we ask again for more solutions, we will get No more solutions.

2. *Is* **Hamlet** *available in a state in which the book* **Hamlet** *has been loaned to the reader* **34526** *after created?*. The query will look as:

```
available(book('Hamlet),loan(book('Hamlet),
    reader(34526),newbook(book('Hamlet'),
    nil))) = X.
```

The system answer will be now:

```
X = false

More Solutions?
```

Being this one the only answer found.

7   Conclusions

We have built an environment composed of a set of Software tools with the common objective of using formal specification techniques based on functional and objectual logics, their fusions and extensions, providing a higher expressivity without loosing a well defined declarative and efficient operational semantics. With these techniques, the software validation by automatic prototyping is guaranteed, and furthermore, they allow to approach topics such as soundness, completeness, etc. in a formalized framework. They allow also to deal with dynamic aspects animating the equational theory equivalent to the specification.

Working with RAP as object language, we can use logic variables when querying the prototype (i.e. the presentation in RAP equivalent to the FMOL specification). We have a logic programming environemnt dealing with the three emergent logic programming paradigms: functional, objectual and relational.

A graphical environment has been implemented allowing to build FMOL specifications in a user-friendly environment.

An intensive work is now in progress for incorporating in the FMOL expressiveness class operators corresponding with the classical abstraction mechanisms. Having already including aggregation by means of the relationships, we are working in the inclusion of specialization/generalization and grouping/ownership class operators.

We are also adding active capabilities to FMOL by defining triggered relations between events of different classes. When a condition holds, an event can be sent to any other system object.

238

We provide with all these capabilities a working implementation of an automated life cycle for Software Production. This environment is intended to improve the final Software product quality and to reduce the classical problems related with the so-called 'Crisis of Software'.

References

[1] Ramos, I., Canós, J.H., Forradellas, R. and Oliver, J., *A Conceptual Schema Specification System for Rapid Prototyping*, Proc. of the XI IASTED , Feb. 1990.

[2] Balzer, R., Cheatman, T.E. and Green, C., *Software Technology in the 1990's: Using a New Paradigm*, IEEE Computer, Nov. 1983..

[3] Wand, Y., *A Proposal for a Formal Model of Objects*, Object-Oriented Concepts, Databases and Applications, Ed. by W. Kim, ACM Press, 1989.

[4] Lindgreen, P. ed., *A Framework of Information Systems Concepts*, Interim Report from IFIP WG 8.1 Task Group FRISCO, 1990.

[5] Sernadas, A. , Sernadas, C. and Ehrich, H.-D, *Object-Oriented Language Features for Information Systems Specification*, INESC 89.

[6] Ramos, I., *Logics and OO-Databases: A Declarative Approach*, Proc. of the DEXA-90, Springer-Verlag, 1990.

[7] Coleman, D., Dollin, C., Gallimore, R., Arnold, P. and Rush, T., *An Introduction to the Axis Specification Language*, Technical Report, Hewlett-Packard Labs., Bristol, UK, 1988.

[8] Hussmann, H., *Rapid Prototyping for Algebraic Specifications. RAP System Users's Manual*, Version 2.0, Report Universität Passau, Fakultät für Mathematik und Informatik, July 1989.

[9] *BIM Prolog Reference Manual*, ISS, Belgium, 1989.

Formal Model of an Object-Oriented Database
with Versioned Objects and Schema

Wojciech Cellary

Institute of Computing Science
Technical University of Poznań
60-965 Poznań, Poland

Geneviève Jomier

Université Paris-Dauphine and
GIP Altaïr, BP 105
78153 Le Chesnay Cedex, France

Tomasz Koszlajda

Institute of Computing Science
Technical University of Poznań
60-965 Poznań, Poland

Abstract

A formal model of an object-oriented database is presented, where both objects and database schema may be multiversion. A concept of *database version* is introduced. A database version comprises one version of each multiversion object and class that are bound together to represent a global state of the real world modeled. In this way, a multiversion database reflects a number of different consecutive real world states and state variants that are clearly distinguished and identified. Since both objects and schema are multiversion, real world states modeled may differ from one another by values, structure and behaviour.

Key words and phrases: object-oriented databases, multiversion databases, formal database model, object versioning, class versioning, schema versioning, apparent versions

1 Introduction

Conventional object-oriented databases are monoversion. Each object contained in such a database has exactly one value associated with it. A database as a whole reflects one state of the real world it models. Such a "real world" may be, for example, an enterprise; the structure of the enterprise is reflected by the database schema composed of classes that describe objects contained in the database, where objects correspond to real world entities. The state of the enterprise is represented by the state of all the objects contained in the database. In many applications, such as Computer Aided Design *(CAD)* or Computer Aided Software Engineering *(CASE)*, a user needs to view and to manipulate different versions of the same object. The versions of an object correspond either to consecutive states of the entity it models, following its evolution, or to its different variants. For example, in a *CASE* application, an object which contains the source of a program may exist in many versions corresponding to successive releases of this program. It may also exist in many versions because of different program variants corresponding to different operating systems.

Versioning facilities for object oriented databases have been proposed in [3,4,6,9]. A survey of them concerning engineering databases is presented in [7]. In these approaches, a real world entity is represented by a multiversion object that is a set of object versions representing consecutive entity states or state variants. In the approach proposed in [10] types of an entity

may also be versioned. These are represented by multiversion classes that are sets of class versions. However, the problem that remains unsolved in these approaches is how to represent relationships between object and class versions that appear in the real world. This problem was pointed out in [1,11,12]. Consider a "real world" *Garden* composed of two entities *Flower* and *Tree*. The consecutive states and variants of these entities are presented in Figure 1. They are represented in the database as shown in Figures 2 and 3. In such a database it is difficult to ask a question about the global state of the garden. Even if particular versions of different objects and classes are related with one

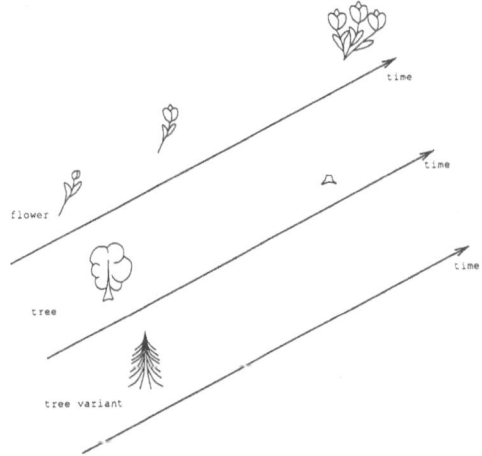

Figure 1: Consecutive entity states and state variants in the "real world" *Garden*

another by static or dynamic references, either these references are not sufficient to bind together the object and class versions that represent one real world state, or they are very hard to manage.

In [8] an improvement has been proposed concerning classes. In this approach, particular class versions are collected together in a consistent schema version. The unit of versioning is the entire database schema instead of a class. Each version of the database schema represents a variant of the structure of the real world modeled. However, each schema version is related with a collection of multiversion objects. The problem remains of relations between schema versions and object versions, and relations among versions of different objects.

A database model where consecutive real world states and state variants are represented instead of consecutive states and state variants of particular entities has been proposed for the first time in [2]. A situation presented in Figure 1 is perceived as shown in Figure 4. In this model, the unit of versioning is the entire database instead of separate objects. A multiversion database is considered to be a set of logically independent database versions as shown in Figure 5. Each database version is composed of a version of each object stored in the database; however, identical object versions are shared by several database versions. Database versions represent consecutive states or state variants of the real world modeled as shown in Figure 6. In this figure solid line circles represent object versions that exist physically, while dashed line circles represent object versions that exist only logically, because of object version sharing by database versions.

In this paper an extension of the model proposed in [2] is presented. In [2] only objects were multiversion, not classes. In the model proposed in this paper a database version comprises both object and class versions. All the class versions contained in

Figure 4: Consecutive real world states and state variants

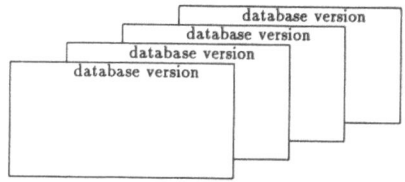

Figure 5: Multiversion database as a set of database versions

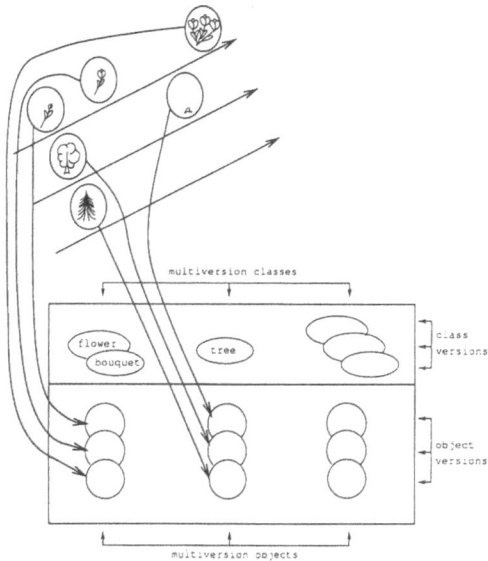

Figure 2: Representation of consecutive entity states and state variants in a database

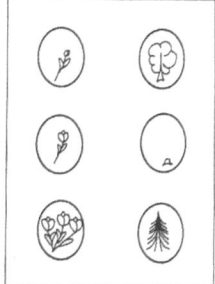

Figure 3: Object versions in a database

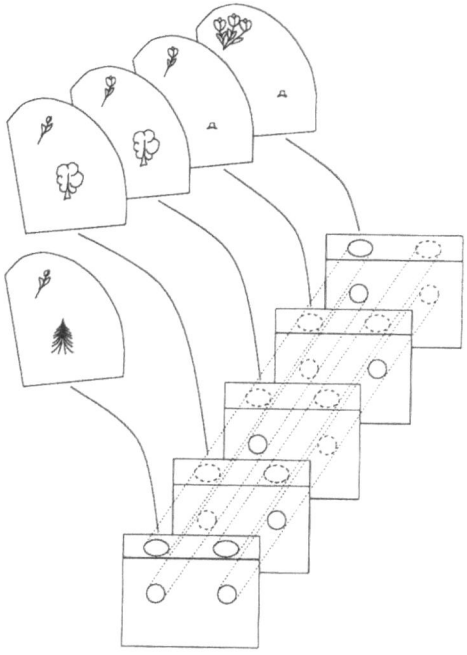

Figure 6: Representation of consecutive real world states and state variants by database versions

one database version compose a database schema version. This schema version is the description of the structure and behaviour of the object versions contained in the database version. Thus, class and object versions of one database version are bound together to represent one state of the real world that may differ from another one by values, structure and behaviour of its entities. The aim of this paper is to formalize this model. To this end, in Section 2 a formal model of a monoversion object-oriented database is presented, as the basis for the multiversion database model. Section 3 is devoted to the multiversion database model. Section 4 concludes the paper.

2   Model of a Monoversion O-O Database

To define a monoversion o-o database classical notions of *class* and *object* are assumed [5]. A class is a collection of attributes and methods. Domains of attributes may be simple, such as numbers, strings etc., or complex, which are classes. An object is a collection of attribute values. An attribute value of a complex domain is itself an object. A class is also an object of a particular kind. A class is denoted c, an object is denoted o. The set of all the classes is denoted C; the set of all the objects is denoted O. Objects and classes are related by the instantiation relation $R_{inst} : O \to C$ which means that each object is an instance of a class.

A *database schema* is a triple:

$$s = (C, \prec_{inh}, R_{dom}),$$

where:

- C is the set of classes, each class identified by a unique *class identifier*;
- $\prec_{inh}: C \to C$ is the *inheritance relation* partially ordering set C ($\prec_{inh}$ is a *DAG*);
- $R_{dom} : C \to C$ is the *domain relation*. Two classes are related by this relation if the first one is the domain of an attribute of the second one. R_{dom} is cyclic.

A *monoversion o-o database* is a quadruple:

$$db = (s, O, R_{inst}, R_{ref}),$$

where:

- s is the database schema;
- O is the set of objects, each object identified by a unique *object identifier*;
- $R_{inst} : O \to C$ is the *instantiation relation* (an object is an *instance of* a class); and
- $R_{ref} : O \to O$ is the *reference relation*. R_{ref} is cyclic.

The reference relation reflects relationships between entities of the real world. Two objects are related by this relation if the first one is an attribute value of the second one. An object o_i may be related to an object o_j by the reference relation R_{ref} only if the class of o_i is related to the class of o_j by the domain relation R_{dom}, i.e.

$$\forall(o_i, o_j \in O) : o_i = R_{ref}(o_j) \Rightarrow R_{inst}(o_i) = R_{dom}(R_{inst}(o_j)).$$

An example of a monoversion o-o database is presented in Figure 7. The schema of this database is composed of six classes: *object*; *engine*, *car* and *assembly_line* inherited from *object*; *ex-1500* inherited from *engine*; and *Golf* inherited from *car*. The in-

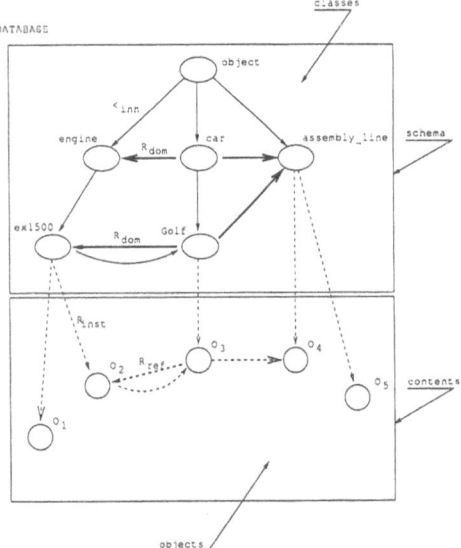

Figure 7: Monoversion o-o database

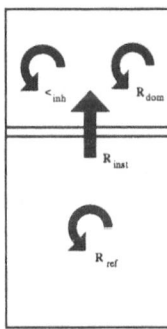

Figure 8: Monoversion o-o database

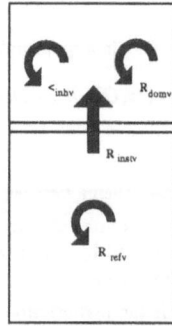

Figure 9: An o-o database version

242

heritance relation is presented by the thin solid line arrows. The domain relation between classes is presented by the thick solid line arrows. The database contains five objects; two of them are instances of the *ex1500* class, one is an instance of the *Golf* class, and the remaining two are instances of the *assembly_line* class. The instantiation relation is presented by the thin dashed arrows. The reference relation between objects is presented by the thick dashed arrows. A monoversion o-o database will be symbolized as presented in Figure 8.

3 Model of a Multiversion O-O Database

The model of a multiversion o-o database is an extension of that of a monoversion o-o database. In a monoversion database, one state of the real world is represented; a multiversion database is required to represent several consecutive real world states and state variants. To this end, the concept of *database version* is proposed. A database version corresponds exactly to a monoversion database; however, it is composed of class versions instead of classes, and of object versions instead of objects (Figure 9). A multiversion database may be viewed, on one hand, as a set of database versions, and on the other hand, as a set of multiversion classes and objects, as presented in Figure 10.

The formal model of a multiversion o-o database is the following. A *class version* is denoted cv, an *object version* is denoted ov. The set of all the class versions is denoted CV_Σ; the set of all the object versions is denoted OV_Σ. Object versions and class versions are related by the instantiation relation $R_{inst\Sigma} : OV_\Sigma \to CV_\Sigma$ which means that each object version is an instance of a class version.

A *database schema version* is a triple:

$$sv = (CV, \prec_{inhv}, R_{domv}),$$

where:

> $CV \subseteq CV_\Sigma$ is a set of class versions. Class versions are identified by *class identifiers* unique in a schema version;
>
> $\prec_{inhv} : CV \to CV$ is the *inheritance relation* partially ordering set CV ($\prec_{inhv}$ is a DAG);
>
> $R_{domv} : CV \to CV$ is the *domain relation*. Two class versions are related by this relation if the first one is the domain of an attribute of the second one.

An *o-o database version* is a quadruple:

$$dbv = (sv, OV, R_{instv}, R_{refv}),$$

where:

> sv is the database schema version;
>
> $OV \subseteq OV_\Sigma$ is a set of object versions. Object versions are identified by *object identifiers* unique in a database version;
>
> $R_{instv} \subseteq R_{inst\Sigma}$ is the *instantiation relation*; and
>
> $R_{refv} : OV \to OV$ is the *reference relation*.

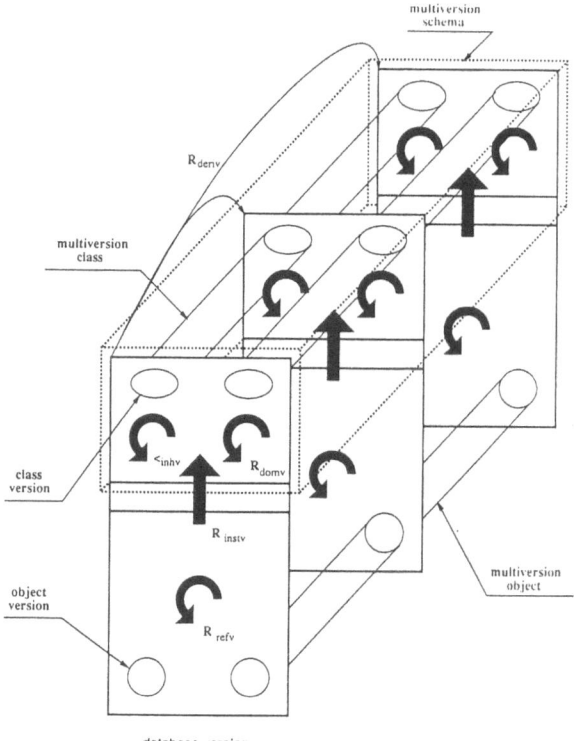

Figure 10: Multiversion o-o database

An object version ov_i may be related to an object version ov_j by the reference relation R_{refv} only if the class of ov_i is related to the class of ov_j by the domain relation R_{domv}, i.e.

$$\forall(ov_i, ov_j \in OV) : ov_i = R_{refv}(ov_j) \Rightarrow$$
$$R_{instv}(ov_i) = R_{domv}(R_{instv}(ov_j)).$$

O-O database versions reflect consecutive states and state variants of the real world modeled.

A *multiversion o-o database* is a pair:

$$mdb = (DBV, \prec_{deriv}),$$

where:

> DBV is the set of all the database versions, each one of them identified by a unique *database version identifier*; and
>
> $\prec_{deriv} : DBV \to DBV$ is the derivation relation. It reflects a history of operations that derive a new database version. The notation: $dbv_i = \prec_{deriv}(dbv_j)$ means that database version dbv_i was derived from database version dbv_j.

Notions of multiversion class and multiversion object are now introduced that are not equivalent to any notions in monoversion databases.

A *multiversion class*, denoted mc, is the set of all the class versions that reflect the same kind of entities of the real world. Each class version of a multiversion class belongs to a separate database version:

$$mc = \{cv_i \mid \forall(cv_i \in dbv_k, cv_j \in dbv_l) : cv_i \neq cv_j \Rightarrow dbv_k \neq dbv_l\}.$$

All the versions of a multiversion class bear the same class identifier. A class version is identified by the pair: class identifier and database version identifier. This pair is unique in the whole multiversion database. However, several pairs may identify the same class version, i.e. a class version may be shared by several database versions.

A *multiversion object*, denoted mo, is the set of all the object versions that reflect the same real world entity. Each object version of a multiversion object belongs to another database version:

$$mo = \{ov_i \mid \forall(ov_i \in dbv_k, ov_j \in dbv_l) : ov_i \neq ov_j \Rightarrow dbv_k \neq dbv_l\}.$$

All the versions of a multiversion object bear the same object identifier. An object version is identified by the pair: object identifier and database version identifier. This pair is unique in the whole multiversion database. However, several pairs may identify the same object version, i.e. an object version may be shared by several database versions.

The set of all the multiversion objects is denoted $MO = \{mo_1, \ldots, mo_n\}$.

A *multiversion database schema* is defined as the set of all the schema versions:

$$ms = \{sv_1, \ldots, sv_N\}.$$

Now, a multiversion o-o database may be alternatively defined as a quadruple:

$$mdb = (ms, MO, R_{inst\Sigma}, R_{ref\Sigma}),$$

where:

ms is the multiversion database schema;

MO is the set of all the multiversion objects;

$R_{inst\Sigma} = \bigcup_{DBV} R_{instv} \mid \forall(mo_i \in MO), \forall(ov_j, ov_k \in mo_i) :$ class versions $R_{inst\Sigma}(ov_i), R_{inst\Sigma}(ov_j)$ belong to the same multiversion class;

$R_{ref\Sigma} = \bigcup_{DBV} R_{refv}$.

Two object versions, which belong to the same multiversion object, may be instances of different class versions that, however, must belong to the same multiversion class.

4 Conclusions

The main advantage of the multiversion o-o database model presented in this paper is the notion of *database version* as a unit of consistency. By this notion, appropriate object and class versions are bound together to represent consecutive states and state variants of the entire real world modeled that may vary by their values, structure and behaviour. It is important to notice that up to date there was not a clear proposition in the literature how to identify an appropriate class version from an object version. More precisely, when switching from a version of a multiversion object to another, how to identify a class version corresponding to it ? In the model proposed in this paper it is identified immediately, because switching concerns the entire database version comprising all the required object and class versions, instead of a version of an object.

The notion of database version concerns not only object and class versions, but also relationships among them. In the multiversion database models developed up to date, the instantiation, domain, inheritance and reference relationships were defined on the global sets of all the class and object versions. In our model, each such relationship is split into a set of relationships $(\{R_{instv}\}, \{R_{domv}\}, \{\prec_{inhv}\}, \{R_{refv}\})$ whose scope is limited to a database version, i.e. which are defined on the sets of class and object versions contained in a database version. In this way also these relationships are versioned.

A version manager according to the model described in this paper has been implemented in the Institute of Computing Science of the Technical University of Poznań in collaboration with the GIP Altaïr in France, where object-oriented database O_2 is developed. At this moment, the prototype of the version manager concerns only object versions. It is under development to concern both objects and schema.

References

[1] Agrawal, R., and H. V. Jagadish
On Correctly Configuring Versioned Objects.
Proc. 15th VLDB Conf., Amsterdam, August 1989, pp. 367-374.

[2] Cellary, W., and G. Jomier
Consistency of Versions in Object-Oriented Databases.
Proc. 16th. VLDB Conf., Brisbane, Australia, August 1990, pp. 432-441.

[3] Chou, Hong-Tai, and Won Kim
A Unifying Framework for Version Control in a CAD Environment.
Proc. 12th VLDB Conf., Kyoto, August 1986, pp. 336-344.

[4] Chou, Hong-Tai, and Won Kim
Version and Change Notification in an Object-Oriented Database System.
Proc. 25th ACM/IEEE Design Automation Conf., Anaheim, June 1988, pp. 275-281.

[5] Goldberg, A., and D. Robson
Smalltalk-80: The Language and its Implementation.
Addison-Wesley, Reading, MA 1983.

[6] Katz, R. H., E. Chang and R. Bhateja
Version Modeling Concepts for Computer-Aided Design Databases.
ACM SIGMOD Int. Conf. on Data Management, 1986, pp. 379-386.

244

[7]   Katz, R. H.
      Toward a Unified Framework for Version Modeling in En-
      gineering Databases.
      ACM Computing Surveys, Vol. 22, No 4, December 1990,
      pp. 375-408.

[8]   Kim, Won and Hong-Tai Chou
      Versions of Schemas for Object-Oriented Databases.
      Proc. 14th VLDB Conf., Los Angeles, Calif., 1988, pp. 148-
      159.

[9]   Klahold, P., G. Schlageter, R. Unland and W. Wilkes
      A transaction model supporting complex applications in in-
      tegrated information systems.
      Proc. ACM SIGMOD Int. Conf. on Management of Data,
      Austin, Texas,
      in SIGMOD RECORD, Vol. 14, No. 4, December 1985, pp.
      388-400.

[10] Skarra, A.H., and S. Zdonik
      The Management of Changing Types in an Object-Oriented
      Database.
      Proc. OOPSLA, Portland, Oregon, October 1986.

[11] Vidyasankar, K., and C. N. G. Dampney
      Version   Consistency   and   Serializability   in   Design
      Databases.
      ICDT'88, 2nd Int. Conf. on Database Theory, Bruges, Bel-
      gium, August 1988,
      in Lecture Notes in Computer Science No. 326, pp. 368-382.

[12] Zdonik, S. B.
      Version Management in an Object-Oriented Database.
      Int. Workshop on Advanced Programming Environments,
      Trondheim, Norway, June 1986.

Meta Variables and Inheritance in an Object-Oriented Data Model

Yanjun Lou and Z. Meral Ozsoyoglu

Department of Computer Engineering and Science
Case Western Reserve University
Cleveland, OH 44106, USA

Abstract

In this paper, we discuss the properties of an object-oriented data model that combines the simplicity of relational data model and features of object-oriented data models. Meta variables are introduced for information hiding, data abstraction, and type inheritance. Type inheritance hierarchies are built up by instantiating meta variables in types. Partial order is defined on classes as well as on types to describe inheritance relationship. The concept of named values bridges the concepts of values in logical models and objects in object-oriented models. With union values, values can be formed from its subset values. Semantics of the model is analyzed and key features are also discussed.

1 Introduction

Recently, object-oriented databases have been the focus of a lot of experimental work and research, e.g., [F+ 87, Ban+ 88, ZdMa 90, Kim 90]. Considerable amount of research has been conducted on integrating object-oriented database features such as complex objects, object identity, inheritance and encapsulation into logic programming [BaKh 86, AbKa 89, KiLa 89]. However, as it has been pointed out in [Banc 88, AbKa 89], very little progress has been made on understanding the principles of object-oriented databases. And, this is partly because much of the terminology in object-oriented databases is overloaded and not commonly agreed upon by the experts in this field. More recent works [AbKa 89, LeRi 89b] are important steps toward clarifying the concepts and defining a formal model for object-oriented databases. In this paper, we also discuss several concepts in object-oriented databases, and propose an object-oriented data model which, we hope, will serve as basis for an object-oriented database system incorporating deductive capabilities.

One of the most important features of an object oriented system is inheritance, which, in turn, is composed of two parts: data inheritance and method inheritance. Data inheritance is about object classification. An object in a subclass is also an object in the corresponding superclass. For example, a student is also a person, and a graduate student is also a student etc. On the other hand, a subclass object may have more attributes. A student must take courses, while a person does not necessarily do so. A graduate student has a thesis advisor and a student may not. One of the commonly accepted semantics of multiple inheritance is described by Cardelli [Card 88]. That is, a subtype (subclass) has more attributes (methods) than its supertype (superclass). LOGIN [AiNa 86], IQL [AbKa 89] and F-Logic [KiLa 89] are using this semantics. However, under this interpretation, the structural differences among objects in a class due to data inheritance may create problems when methods are defined on classes. It is very hard to take care of all those structural differences, especially in a deductive framework. In other words, how to apply a method defined on superclasses to subclasses? This problem must be solved before an object-oriented deductive query model can be developed.

Cardelli once pointed out that when a subclass object is used as an object in its superclass, its structural details that are not in the superclass will be lost [CaWe 85]. There are also cases that can not be handled by the semantics given in [Card 88], such as parametric polymorphism. Cardelli and Wegner [CaWe 85] introduced quantifiers $\exists$ and $\forall$ to solve those problems. Even though IQL adopted the semantics of Cardelli [Card 88], it seems only data inheritance is achieved. It is not clear from [AbKa 89] what is the method and how methods are being inherited among classes and their subclasses. In this paper, we take a different approach to attack this problem. We introduce *Meta variables*, which, we believe, will overcome some of those difficulties. A meta variable is a type variable, i.e., it takes types as its values. Thus a type with a meta variable as its attribute actually represents a set of types. Utilizing meta variables, type hierarchies can be built, and inheritance relationship can be established. Meta variables also play the role of information hiding and data abstraction, since a meta variable hides part of the details of the subtypes from supertype. All information will be kept when a value or object is used as an object of its supertype. In other words, type and its subtype have the same structure at a higher level. This feature makes it possible for a rule based language to have *method inheritance* since the structural barrier between instances of a type and that of its subtypes is removed. Meta variable virtually plays the role of *parameter* (or meta parameter) in a type.

Values in O_2 [Ban+ 88, LeRi 89b] do not have identifiers. The role played by values is really limited. They can only appear in objects and are not addressible directly. In IQL [AbKa 89], in addition to the concept of values, relations are part of the data model. A relation is actually a set value with an identifier, which makes it accessible, and relational operations are easily applicable. Following this direction, we introduce the concept of *named values*. A named value is a value with an identifier. A set value with an identifier is a relation. Thus the concept of named values is more general than relations introduced in IQL. Not only can we define operations directly on relations, we can also define operations on other types of values.

We introduce the concept of *union value* which allows a value to be formed from its subvalues. The value-subvalue relationship makes it possible to establish a value hierarchy. That is, a value inherits data from its subvalues. For example, all the students in a university is a value, and is the union of students from each college. We can operate, access the students in the university by an identifier, and we also can operate and access the students in each college. There is a *data inheritance* relationship between the students in a university and the students in one of its colleges. Union values facilitate binding several values together and organizing smaller values into bigger ones.

In integrating object-oriented features with deductive language, method definition and method inheritance are the key issues. The introduction of meta variables makes objects in a class having the uniform structures. This is the most important support for a query model with methods and method inheritance. However, in this paper, we will focus on the data representation and structural inheritance. The query model is discussed in [LoOz 90b].

The rest of the paper is organized as follows. Next section presents the syntax of the model. In section 3, we discuss the semantic issues. Section 4 addresses the inheritance problem specifically and a partial order similar to that in O_2 [LeRi 89b] is presented. We highlight the major features of the model in section 5 and discuss related work. Finally, we discuss future research directions and conclude this paper.

2 Meta Variables in Data Model

In this section, we introduce meta variables into our data model. The presentation follows the notation in O_2 [Ban+ 88, LeRi 89b] and IQL [AbKa 89]. The reader may find it useful to refer to those papers when necessary.

We assume the existence of the following countably infinite and pairwise disjoint sets of atomic symbols:
   1) basic type symbols $\mathcal{B}$ $\{B_1, B_2, \ldots\}$, specifically $\perp$ is a basic type symbol;
   2) meta variables $\mathcal{M}$ $\{m_1, m_2, \ldots\}$;
   3) types $\mathcal{T}$ $\{\tau_1, \tau_2, \ldots\}$;
   4) type IDs $\mathcal{T}_{ID}$ $\{T_1, T_2, \ldots\}$;
   5) class names $\mathcal{C}$ $\{C_1, C_2, \ldots, \}$;
   6) identifiers $\mathcal{N}_{id}$ $\{p_1, p_2, \ldots\}$.

2.1 Types

Types are defined the usual way as in [Ban+ 88, LeRi 89b, AbKa 89]. Basic symbol $B \in \mathcal{B}$ is a type. A class name $C \in \mathcal{C}$ is a type. A type name is a type. And we have tuple types and set types. Especially, a meta variable $m \in \mathcal{M}$ is a type.

In our presentation, type ID's and class names start with capital letters and basic types are denoted by bold face symbols. The following are examples of types:

   - $[Name, age, m_1]$ is a tuple type, where *Name* is a type, **age** is a basic type, and m_1 is a meta variable.

   - $[deptname, \{Personnel\}, \{Faculty\}, \{Student\}, \{TA\}]$ is a tuple type, where **deptname** is a basic type, *Personnel*, *Faculty*, *Students* and *TAs* are class names, $\{Personnel\}$ etc. are set types.

If there exist meta variables in a type, we call this type *meta type*. The set of types defined is denoted by $\mathcal{T}$.

Meta type is a type in which meta variables hide part of the structural information from the current type. So if we specialize the part hidden by the meta variable, we will get another type, that is , a subtype. Thus, the instantiation of the meta variables is the key point in type inheritance.

In this paper, we restrict the number of meta variables in a type to at most one. It is easy to show that multiple meta variables in a type can be represented by types that have only one meta variable. In particular, a conventional type can be seen as a meta type without meta variable.

Definition 2.1 *Meta variable instantiation* η is a function from $\mathcal{M}$ to $2^{\mathcal{T}}$ such that every meta variable is mapped to a set of types. For a meta variable m, we call its image under η, $\eta(m)$, the *domain* of m. □

Each type in $\eta(m)$ represents the structure that is hidden by m. There is also a case that a meta variable does not hide any thing in the subtype (i.e., the subtype does not have any attributes corresponding to the meta variable). So, there is at least one element in $\eta(m)$ to represent this situation. The basic type symbol $\perp$ is used for this purpose and is omited if there is no confusion.

Definition 2.1 can be extended to types in a natural way[*]:

   1. Basic types: For every basic type τ, $\eta(\tau) = \{\tau\}$.

   2. Type IDs: For every type ID, T, $\eta(T) = \eta(\tau)$, where τ is the type T denotes.

   3. Tuple types: For every tuple type $\tau = [\tau_1, \ldots, \tau_n]$, $\eta(\tau) = \{[\tau_1', \ldots, \tau_n'] | \tau_1' \in \eta(\tau_1) \; or \ldots or \; \tau_n' \in \eta(\tau_n)\}$.

   4. Set types: For each set type $\tau = \{\tau_1\}$, $\eta(\tau) = \{\{\tau_1'\} | \tau_1' \in \eta(\tau_1)\}$.

The transitive domain of m is denoted by $\eta^\star$:
$$\eta^1(m) = \eta(m).$$
$$\eta^k(m) = \cup_{\tau \in \eta^{k-1}(m)} \eta(\tau) \cup \eta^{k-1}(m).$$
$$\eta^\star(m) = \cup_{k=1}^\infty \eta^k(m)$$

Let τ_1 and τ_2 be two types from $\mathcal{T}$, m be a meta variable in τ_1. If τ_2 can be obtained by substituting m in τ_1 by an element from $\eta(m)$, i.e., $\tau_2 \in \eta(\tau_1)$, then we call τ_2 *subtype* of τ_1, and τ_1 is called *super-type* of τ_2. τ_2 is also called *instance type* of meta type τ_1. This concept is similar to the partial order defined in [Card 88]. The importance of meta variable will be further addressed in Section 4.

The function η is very important in discussing type inheritance. For a finite set of types $\mathbf{T}$, the interrelationship between types can be visualized through a DAG. A DAG for a set of types $\mathbf{T}$ is a graph $< \mathbf{T}, E >$, where each type $\tau \in \mathbf{T}$ is a node, and there is an edge $e \in E$ from τ_1 to τ_2 if $\tau_2 \in \eta(\tau_1)$. We call DAG's introduced by η, *type inheritance hierarchies*.

The following is an example showing the role played by η. Multiple inheritance [Card 88] is now represented by meta variables. The problem addressed in [AbKa 89], i.e., legal instances with attributes that do not appear in the schema, is virtually eliminated.

Example 2.2 (Type hierarchy) Suppose we have the following types:

   - $[Name, \mathbf{age}, m]$,
   - $[Name, \mathbf{age}, [GPA, m_1]]$,
   - $[Name, \mathbf{age} , [m_2, \mathbf{sal}]]$,
   - $[Name, \mathbf{age}, [GPA, \mathbf{sal}]]$,

where m, m_1 and m_2 are meta variables.
$$\eta(m) = \{[GPA, m_1], [m_2, \mathbf{sal}]\},$$
$$\eta(m_1) = \{\mathbf{sal}\}, \text{ and}$$
$$\eta(m_2) = \{GPA\}.$$

Function η can be extended to types, as shown below:
$$\eta([Name, \mathbf{age}, m]) = \{[Name, \mathbf{age}, [GPA, m_1]],$$
$$[Name, \mathbf{age}, [m_2, \mathbf{sal}]]\},$$
$\eta([Name, \mathbf{age}, [GPA, m_1]]) = \{[Name, \mathbf{age}, [GPA, \mathbf{sal}]]\}$ and $\eta([Name, \mathbf{age}, [m_2, \mathbf{sal}]]) = \{[Name, \mathbf{age}, [GPA, \mathbf{sal}]]\}$.

We use *Persontype* as a shorthand for $[Name, \mathbf{age}, m]$, *Studenttype* for $[Name, \mathbf{age}, [GPA, m_1]]$, *Stafftype* for $[Name, \mathbf{age} , [m_2, \mathbf{sal}]]$ and *Tatype* for $[Name, \mathbf{age}, [GPA, \mathbf{sal}]]$. Then we have the following type inheritance hierarchy.

---
[*]The extension of η is made similar to the extension of σ, the mapping from class names to types in [LeRi 89b]

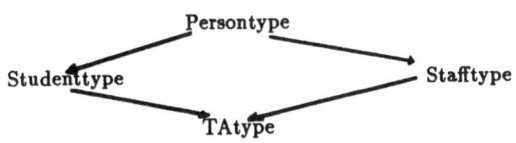

Fig. 1: Type Hierarchy

It should be pointed out that general type hierarchies can be modeled by meta variables. New elements can be put into or deleted from the domain of a meta variable. New subtypes can be introduced or removed and type hierarchy will change accordingly.

The concept of type in our model is used to model the structure part of data. Every class name is associated with a type . This type is called the *schema* of the class. Every identifier also has a type. This type restricts the values that the identifier takes.

Let C be a finite set of class names and N be a finite set of identifiers. A *schema* σ is a function from $C \cup N$ to T.

As in [LeRi 89b], this definition can be extended to types in a natural way.

- Basic types: for every basic type τ, $\sigma(\tau) = \tau$.
- Type IDs: For every type ID T, $\sigma(T) = \sigma(\tau)$, where τ is the type T denotes.
- Tuple types: $\sigma([\tau_1, \ldots, \tau_n]) = [\sigma(\tau_1), \ldots, \sigma(\tau_n)]$.
- Set types: $\sigma\{\tau\} = \{\sigma(\tau)\}$.

Schema σ functions as structure abstraction. Applying σ to a type actually brings out the parts in a type hidden by class names and type ID's. Those structures associated with class names represent the structures of objects which the classes can take.

- For class name *Dept*, $\sigma(Dept)$=[deptname, { *Personnel*}, {*Faculty*}, {*Student*}, {*TA*}].

- For class name *Student*, $\sigma(Student)$= [*Name*, age,[GPA, m_1]].

- Recursive structures can also be specified. For a class name P, $\sigma(P)$ = [a, $\{P\}$] (see [AbKa 89]).

- Let o_1 be an identifier, then its type is given by: $\sigma(o_1)$=[*Name*, age, [GPA, m_1]].

2.2 Values

In addition to the values defined in [LeRi 89b], we introduce the *union values* into our model. There are many situations in which one value is the union of several values. Sometimes we need to address the union of the values as a whole (union value) and sometimes we need to use one of them. This concept together with the concept of named values discussed in the next subsection will make it possible to collect a set value from several subset values.

Suppose every basic type B_i has a set of symbols $\mathcal{D}_i$ associated with it, and *null* is the only symbol associated with type $\perp$. $\mathcal{D}$ is defined as $\mathcal{D} = \cup_i \mathcal{D}_i$.

Definition 2.3 (values)
1. Every element $d \in \mathcal{D}$ is a value, called *basic value*; specifically, *null* is a basic value.
2. Every object identifiers $p \in \mathcal{N}_{id}$ is a value.
3. If $v_1, v_2, \ldots, v_k$ are values, then $\{v_1, v_2, \ldots, v_k\}$ is a *set value*, v_i is called *element value* of $\{v_1, v_2, \ldots, v_k\}$. { } denotes the empty set value.
4. If v_1 is a value, $\ldots$, v_n is a value , then $[v_1, \ldots, v_n]$ is a *tuple value*. v_i is called *attribute value* of $[v_1, \ldots, v_n]$.
5. If $v_1, \ldots, v_n$ are values, then $v_1 \mid \ldots \mid v_n$ is a *union value*. v_i is called *subvalue*. □

We denote the set of values thus defined as $\mathcal{V}$.

Here the union values are introduced to model the *value hierarchy* for set values, i.e., a value is composed of its subvalues. If an identifier denotes, directly or indirectly, a set value, it can also be used as a subvalue(see section 2.3 and 3).

Example 2.4 (cf. Example 2.2).

- { [['john', 'smith'], 23, [3.65, 15000]], [['bill', 'rich'], 25, [2.90,12000]]} is a set value of type $\{Tatype\}$.

- Let p_1 be a set value of type $\{Tatype\}$, { [['don', 'gorden'] 19, [3.82]], [['mary', 'king'], 20, [3.25]]} be a set value of { *Studenttype*}, then $p_1 \mid$ {[[['don', 'gorden'] 19, [3.82]],[['mary', 'king'], 20, [3.25]]} is a union value of $\{Studenttype\}$.

- Similarly, let p_1 be a set value of type $\{Tatype\}$. Then $p_1 \mid$ {[['harry', 'bull'], 32, [23,000]} is a union value assigned to p_3 and finally,

- Let p_2 be a set value of type $\{Studenttype\}$, and p_3 be a set value of type $\{Stafftype\}$. Then $p_2 \mid p_3$ is a union value assigned to p_4. □

2.3 Named Values, Objects and Classes

A *named value* is a value with an identifier. When a named value is put into a class, it is called an *object*, and its identifier is the object identifier. *A Named value specifies the structural part of the object.*

A relation in relational model is a named value which is composed of a relation name (identifier) and a set of tuples (tuple values). Instead of modeling relation directly, as has been done in [AbKa 89], we model named values, which may be tuples, sets or even atomic values. Named values are different from objects in that they can be manipulated directly by operations. This approach combines the advantage of value oriented systems and that of object oriented systems.

Let N be a finite set of identifiers. A *mapping* δ for N is a partial function from N to $\mathcal{V}$ such that every identifier $p \in N$ is assigned a value $v \in \mathcal{V}$.

Each application of δ opens one level of encapsulation of values or named values.
- Basic values: For every basic value v, $\delta(v) = \dot{v}$.
- Set values: $\delta(\{v_1, \ldots, v_n\}) = \{\delta(v_1), \ldots, \delta(v_n)\}$ and $\delta(\{\}) = \{\}$.
- Tuple values: $\delta([v_1, \ldots, v_n]) = [\delta(v_1), \ldots, \delta(v_n)]$.
- Union values: $\delta(v_1 \mid \ldots \mid v_n) = \delta(v_1) \mid \ldots \mid \delta(v_n)$ if there exists v_i, $\delta(v_i)$ is not a set value; otherwise, $\delta(v_1 \mid \ldots \mid v_n) = \delta(v_1) \cup \ldots \cup \delta(v_n)$.

The mapping of union values deserves more discussion here. Union value is defined for set values. On the other hand, one or more of the subvalues may be identifiers which are mapped by δ, directly or indirectly, to set values.

Example 2.5 (Named value) We continue with Example 2.4, where only values are given. Here δ associates a value with each identifier. It can be easily seen that p_1 denotes a set of *Tatype* values, p_2 denotes a set of *Studenttype* values, p_3 denotes a set of *Stafftype* values and p_4 denotes a set of *Persontype* values. If δ is applied more than one time, the named values will be opened gradually.

- $\delta(p_1)$={ [['john', 'smith'], 23, [3.65, 15000]], [['bill', 'rich'], 25, [2.90, 12000]]}

- $\delta(p_2)$= $p_1 \mid$ {[[['don', 'gorden'], 19, [3.82]], [['mary', 'king'], 20, [3.25]]]}

- $\delta(p_3)$= $p_1 \mid$ {[['harry', 'bull'], 32, [23000]} and finally,

- $\delta(p_4)$=$p_2 \mid p_3$.

Through δ and the union value, we can build named value hierarchies.

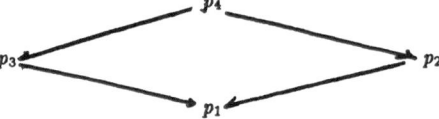

Fig. 2: Named Value Hierarchy

Note: There is no clear agreement on whether a set is an object [Kim 90, ZdMa 90]. In our model, set of objects is not an object[†]. But a set is a value, which can be assigned to an object. Note that an object must have an oid and a value. First of all, $\{m\}$ is a type (*parameterized type*), where m is a meta variable. The domain of m includes all the relevant types. All set properties such as membership, subset relationship are defined on $\{m\}$. By the type-subtype relationship defined above, every relevant set type is a subtype of $\{m\}$ and share its methods. Second, set at a time operation is a well known advantage of Datalog over Prolog. By allowing set as value of an object, the set value will be encapsulated. A computation can be applied to each and every element in the set. Also a class is an object with a set value which is the set of objects assigned to it. We can apply a method of the class to all the objects in the class at the same time. In general, the type of a set is related to the type of the objects that it is allowed to contain [ZdMa 90]. If T_2 is a subtype of type T_1, then every instance of $\{T_2\}$ (a set of value of type T_2) is also an instance of type $\{T_1\}$. For example, a *set of graduate students* is also a *set of students*. Both *set of students* and *set of graduate students* inherit methods from $\{m\}$ if they are in the domain of m. In addition, *set of graduate students* can inherit methods defined on *set of students*. Instead of defining type-subtype relationship by attribute set [Card 88], in our model the type-subtype relationship between set types is determined by meta variables. This is an alternative solution to the controversy on this topic.

2.4 Databases

A *database schema* S is a tuple $< N, C, \sigma, \prec >$, where N is a set of identifiers, C is a set of class names, σ is a map from $N \cup C$ to types, and $\prec$ is a partial order on class names.

Note: If an identifer is assigned to a class, it takes the type of the class as its type. In this case, it is not necessary to assign a type to the oid. But a named value, if not assigned to a class, needs to be typed in order to type-check its value. In the definition given above, if an identifier belongs to a class, the type of the identifier should be consistent with the type of the class.

Example 2.6 Let *Personnel* be a class name of type *Persontype*, *Student* be a class name of type *Studenttype*, *Staff* be a class name of type *Stafftype*, and *TA* be a class name of *Tatype*. Further, we have *Student* $\prec$ *Personnel*, *Staff* $\prec$ *Personnel*, *TA* $\prec$ *Student*, and *TA* $\prec$ *Staff*. Then we have a class inheritance hierarchy as shown below.

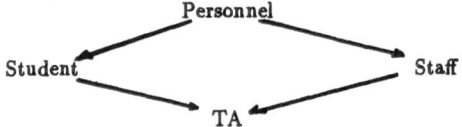

Fig. 3: Class Inheritance Hierachy

[†]This is consistent with Kim [Kim 90].

Let C be a finite set of class names. An *identifier assignment* π for C is a function which assigns a finite set of identifiers to each class name in C such that if $C_1 \prec C_2$, then $\pi(C_1) \subseteq \pi(C_2)$.

As discussed before, each class is also an object. For each class name C, there is an oid o_C, $\delta(o_C) = \pi(C)$, such that the corresponding object is an instance of a class of type $\{C\}$. If there is no confusion, we also use C as the object identifier for the object corresponding to the class C instead of o_C.

A named value whose identifier is assigned to a class is called the object of that class. For example, a relation in relational model is a named value (set of tuples). A relation name is an identifier which can be assigned to a class. In this case, the relation becomes an object.

A *database instance* I_S is a tuple $< \pi, \delta >$ of schema $< N, C, \sigma, \prec >$, where π is an oid assignment for C, and δ is a partial function from N to values.

3 Semantics

If there is no identifier in a value, then we call it *pure value*. The interpretation of types associates a set of pure values to each type.

The *closure of* δ, $\delta \times \delta \times \ldots$, i.e., repetitive application of δ, is denoted as $\delta^\star$. For any value or identifier o, $\delta^\star(o)$ is a pure value.

As pointed out in [AbKa 89], there are some problems using Cardelli's multiple inheritance semantics. The advantage of meta variables, especially in a deductive framework, is that a type and its subtype have the same structure. Part of the subtype structure is hidden, or more accurately, is abstracted through meta variable.

The interpretation of types is similar to that in [LeRi 89b], and is focused on types with meta variables.

Let σ be a schema and a δ be a mapping. An interpretation under σ and δ is a function that associates a set of pure values $I(\tau)$ to each type, satisfying the following properties:

1. For each basic type B_i, $I(B_i) = \mathcal{D}_i$;

2. For each type ID T, $I(T) = I(\tau)$, where τ is the type that T denotes.

3. For each class name C, $I(C) = \pi(C)$.

4. For each tuple type $\tau = [\tau_1, \tau_2, \ldots, \tau_n]$, where $\tau_1, \tau_2, \ldots, \tau_n$ are not meta variables,
$$I(\tau) = \{[v_1, v_2, \ldots, v_n] \mid \forall i \in \{1, 2, \ldots, n\}, v_i \in I(\tau_i)\};$$

5. For each set type $\tau = \{\tau'\}$, where τ' is not a meta variable,
$$I(\tau) = \{\{v_1, v_2, \ldots, v_n\} \mid n \geq 0, 0 \leq i \leq n, v_i \in I(\tau')\},$$
in particular, $I(\{\}) = \{\}$.

6. For each meta type τ, $I(\tau) = \cup_{\tau' \in \eta(\tau)} I(\tau')$ (1).

Equation 1 specifies type inheritance. The union applies to all instance types. This is possible because at the level of τ, there is no structural difference among all instance types since meta variables hide the difference.

There are semantical requirement for the values assigned to an object in a class. That is, for a class C, the value of every object in C must be an instance of type $\sigma(C)$. More formally, we have the following equation:

$$\delta^\star(\pi(C)) \subseteq I(\sigma(C)).$$

3.1 The Implicit Class Associated with a Type

In [Card 88], type inheritance is implicit, i.e., if the set of attributes in type τ_1 includes that of type τ_2, then τ_1 is a *subtype* of τ_2. In [AbKa 89], in addition to type inheritance, *isa* hierarchies on classes are introduced to establish inheritance relationship among classes. In this subsection, we want to make a connection between class inheritance and type inheritance, and if possible, set up a uniform characterization. Intuitively, all the named values with the same type should share a common set of methods. For example, if john is a named value of type *Studenttype* (here *Studenttype* is a type ID, or a shorthand for a structure), then whatever class it is assigned, it is a student and there are common properties that hold for all students. In the following, we are trying to define a class for each type so that all classes with this type are subclasses of this class. Methods can be defined on this class and shared (inherited) by all classes with this type.

Definition 3.1 (Implicit Class of a Type) For every type $\tau \in \mathcal{T}$, there is a class name C_τ, such that $\sigma(C_\tau) = \tau$, and
$$I(C_\tau) = \{o | o \in \mathcal{N}_{id}, \delta^*(o) \in I(\tau)\}.$$
□

Now, when we are talking about methods defined on types τ, we mean the methods defined on the class C_τ. Thus in the schema $< N, C, \sigma, \prec >$, the partial order $\prec$ is extended by the following rules:

1. For each class name C with $\sigma(C) = \tau$: $C \prec C_\tau$.

2. Any identifier p with $\sigma(p) = \tau$ will automatically be an object identifier in class C_τ.

4 Inheritance by Partial Order
4.1 Semantics of Inheritance

Corresponding to the two interpretations given in the last section, we define the partial order on types. The term *refinement* used in [LeRi 89b] is used here to name the partial order.

Definition 4.1 (Partial order on types under I) Type τ_1 is a *refinement* of type τ_2 under interpretation I, denoted as $\tau_1 \leq_I \tau_2$, if and only if $I(\tau_1) \subseteq I(\tau_2)$. □

Definition 4.2 (Partial order on types) Type τ_1 is a *refinement* of type τ_2 $(\tau_1 \leq \tau_2)$ if and only if for every interpretation I, $\tau_1 \leq_I \tau_2$. □

The word *refinement* reminds us its meaning in software engineering. Here it carries the same connotation as information hiding. Since the type hierarchies defined are built up through the domains of meta variables, we achieved data abstraction and information hiding.

Example 4.3 In Example 2.2, *Tatype* is a refinement of *Studenttype*. Similarly, Class name *TA* is a refinement of class name *Student* in Example 2.6. □

4.2 Syntactical Descriptions of Inheritance

In section 2, we defined one level type inheritance. The partial order $\prec$ on classes is given by the users. Following the discussion of inference rules and type checking algorithms in [Card 88, CaWe 85], we have a *patial order* $(\leq)$ on types in general, as shown in the following theorem:

Theorem 1 *(syntactical inference rules for types)*

1. *For any type τ, $\tau \leq \tau$;*

2. *For any class names C_1 and C_2, $C_1 \leq C_2$ if $C_1 \prec C_2$ or $C_1 = C_2$;*

3. *For meta variable m and any type $\tau \in \eta(m)$, $\tau \leq m$;*

4. *If $\forall i \in \{1, \ldots, n\}, \tau_i \leq s_i, [\tau_1, \tau_2, \ldots, \tau_k] \leq [s_1, s_2, \ldots, s_k]$;*

5. *If $\tau_1 \leq \tau_2$, $\{\tau_1\} \leq \{\tau_2\}$.*

If we let the domain of m be the set of all types for every meta variable m, i.e., $\eta(m) = \mathcal{T}$, and every tuple type have one meta variable as its attribute, then we get the type inheritance given in [Card 88].

Theorem 2 *The multiple inheritance semantics given by Cardelli in [Card 88] is a special case of the multiple inheritance discussed in this paper.*

5 Features of the Data Model
5.1 Named Values: Bridge between the Value-Oriented Model and Object-Oriented Model

In the relational model, relation schemas and relations are the principle concepts, and the model is closed under relational algebra. The results of an operation is also a relation, which can be used as an operand immediately. But in Object-Oriented Database Systems [Banc 88], where methods are applied to objects in classes, it is not clear which class the resulting object belongs to, and how encapsulation works.

In O_2, values as well as objects can be used to construct more complex objects. IQL [AbKa 89] introduces relations into its data model, so that relational data model is properly included. Extending this idea, we introduce *named values* to further address the importance of values in object-oriented data model. Both values and named values are used in constructing other values and named values. Furthermore, named values are directly accessible.

- Relations are special cases of named values, i.e., a named set value whose elements are tuple values. Thus relations in IQL are properly included in our model.

- Named values are more general since an identifier can be mapped to a basic value, a tuple value, a set value or a union value.

- Identifiers are allowed in named values. Recursive named values, data abstraction and information hiding are achieved. Duplicate data can be represented through named values, that is, the same value could be assigned to different identifiers.

- Named values are objects if their identifiers are assigned to classes.

- Named values can be operated directly. For example, named set values can be handled as nested relations and relational algebra is applicable.

5.2 Meta variables: Information Hiding and Data Abstraction

In [Card 88], inheritance is implicit, i.e., if type τ_1 has more attributes than type τ_2, then τ_1 is a subtype of type τ_2. There are advantages and disadvantages of this approach. Some inheritance implied by the system may not be desirable and the user may not be aware of its existence. On the other hand, some inheritance can not be modeled, such as parameterized types and parameter polymorphism. Another example is that the inheritance between two types with exactly the same structure can not be handled properly, as there is no corresponding mechanism in [CaWe 85, Card 88] to handle this situation. On the other hand, as has been pointed out in [AbKa 89], this approach will lead to legal instances with attributes that do not appear in the schema.

In F-Logic [KiLa 89] a lattice structure is used to cope with inconsistency solving. This is a nice feature, but inheritance is not only a way of inconsistency solving. Furthermore, some inconsistency should be reported instead of being hidden.

Another problem that raises a lot of interest recently is data abstraction. Cardelli and Wegner [CaWe 85] used universal and existential quantifiers to represent abstract data structures and hide details from users. Inspired by this approach, the meta variables are introduced in our model to achieve the goal of information hiding, data abstraction, and inheritance. A meta variable in a type hides part of structural detail in the subtype. Through the instantiation of meta variable, a type hierarchy is built up, with its root being the most abstract data type, and all the leaf types being detailed structures. The types between the root node and leaf nodes expose the hidden structure to a certain degree.

Through meta variables, polymorphism of types is achieved explicitly. Instances in a type and instances in its subtypes have the same structure if looked from the supertype point of view. We believe this uniform structure shared by a type and all its subtypes will play an important role for an object-oriented database system in a logical framework, as the barrier applying a method defined on a type to it subtype is removed.

5.3 New Features of Inheritance

In PROLOG, predicates with more arguments are transformed into predicates with fewer arguments by rules (projection in relational algebra). In LOGIN [AiNa 86], a special rule is introduced to define partial order. The resolution steps to achieve inheritance in PROLOG are replaced by partial order checking. Actually the partial order forms a semilattice on data. If two terms are not directly unifiable, their *glb* is calculated . The unification algorithm is modified accordingly.

Sciore [Scio 89] addressed the problem of polymorphism of classes and objects. As pointed out there, specialization hierarchies are typically treated as type-level constructs and are used to define various inheritance mechanisms. Specialization at object level creates a more flexible and powerful notion of inheritance by allowing objects to define their own inheritance path. Object inheritance is also a mean of data abstraction, as subobjects and components of an object are, in some sense, encapsulated.

In our model, features of inheritance described in IQL [AbKa 89] and O_2 [Ban+ 88, LeRi 89b] are maintained, such as the *isa* hierarchy on classes and type inheritance. In addition, we have extended inheritance mechanisms, and added new features.

- Since meta variables hide structural difference of objects of a class and its subclasses, methods defined on a superclass can be applied to its subclasses.

- Meta variables play the role of parameters in a type. The instance types of a meta type are derived by exposing the structures hidden by the meta variable. This is exactly the meaning of *parametric inheritance* as discussed in [CaWe 85]. The multiple inheritance semantics of our model is more general than that given in [Card 88].

Method inheritance in a deductive framework is one of our ongoing research topics. Detailed discussion can be found in [LoOz 90b].

6 Conclusion

We have presented a data model that takes advantage of the simplicity of the relational model and has most of the features of the object-oriented data models. We developed the named value concept which is more general than the concept of nested relation in IQL [AbKa 89] and value O_2[LeRi 89b]. Meta variables are introduced to implement information hiding, data abstraction and inheritance. The concept of *isa hierarchies* in [AbKa 89] is kept. The type inheritance is based on the class inheritance and meta variables. Different from the multiple inheritace semantics discussed in [Card 88], type-subtype relationship is determined through meta variable domains. Meta variables, functioning as parameters in types, also model parametric inheritance. For each type τ we defined a special class C_τ that takes all named values with type τ as its objects. All classes with type τ now is subclasses of C_τ. Through this simple treatment, the concepts of class inheritance and type inheritance are unified naturally. We also presented a nice feature of values. The concept of union value, together with other constructs of values, make it possible to define a value by its subvalues. *Value hierarchy* or *value inheritance* is an extension and complements to other inheritance mechanisms.

One of our goal is to have a data model that can be used to support a rule based language with object-oriented flavors. Meta variables hide the structural difference between type and its subtypes, thus clear the way for the unification algorithm, which, at current form, can not handle predicates with different numbers of arguments. Through meta variables, a type and its subtypes have the same structure at a higher level, which makes inheritance staightforward. A rule based language based on this model is described in [LoOz 90b].

References

[AbHu 87] Abiteboul S., and R. Hull, *IFO: A Formal Semantic Data Model*, ACM Transaction on Database systems, Vol.12, No.4, pp.525-565(1987).

[AbKa 89] Abiteboul S., and P. Kanellakis, *Object Identity as a Query Language Primitive*. In Proc. ACM SIGMOD, pp. 159-173(1989).

[AiNa 86] Ait-Kaci, H. and R. Nasr, *LOGIN: A Logic Programming Language With Built-in Inheritance*, J. Logic Programming, 3:185-215, 1986.

[Banc 88] Bancilhon, F., *Object Oriented Database Systems*. In Proc. ACM PODS, pp.240-250(1988).

[Ban+ 88] Bancilhon, F., et al., *The Design and Implementation of O_2, an Object-Oriented Database System*. In Proc. OODBS2 Workshop, Badmunster RFA, 1988

[BaKh 86] Bancilhon, F.and S. Khoshafian, *A Calculus for Complex Objects*, ACM PODS , pp.53-59(1986).

[Card 88] Cardelli, L., *A Semantics of Multiple Inheritance*. Information and Computation, 76:138-164,1988.

[CaWe 85] Cardelli, L., and P. Wegner, *On Understanding Types, Data Abstraction and Polymorphism*. In Computing Surveys, Vol.17, No.4, Dec. 1985.

[F+ 87] Fishman, D. et al. *Iris: an Object-Oriented Database Management System*. ACM TOIS Vol.5, No. 1, pp. 46-69, 1987.

[KiLa 89] Kifer, M., and G. Lausen, *F-Logic: A Higher-Order Language for Reasoning about Objects*, Inheritance and Scheme. In Proc. ACM PODS, pp. 134-146(1989).

[Kim 90] Kim, W., *Object-Oriented Databases: Definition an Research Directions* , IEEE Trans. on Knowledge and Data Engineering, Vol. 2, No. 3, 1990

[LeRi 89b] Lecluse, C., P. Richard, Modeling Complex Structures in Object-Oriented Databases. ACM PODS, pp. 360-368. (1989)

[LoOz 90b] Lou, Y. , and M. Ozsoyoglu. *LLO: A Deductive Language with Methods and Method Inheritance*, ACM SIGMOD'91, Denver, May 1991.

[Scio 89] Sciore, E., *Object Specialization*, ACM Trans. Information Systems, Vol. 7, No.2, pp. 103-122, 1989.

[ZdMa 90] Zdonik, S. B. and D. Maier, *Fundamentals of Object-Oriented Databases*, in Readings in Object-Oriented Database Systems, S. B. Zdonik and D. Maier (eds), pp. 1-32, 1990

Uncertainty Management in Object-Oriented Database Systems*

Katsumi Tanaka, Susumu Kobayashi and Tomomi Sakanoue[†]

Dept. of Instrumentation Engineering
Kobe University
Rokkodai, Nada, Kobe 657, Japan

Abstract

In this paper, we propose an approach and basic constructs to realize a fuzzy database processing capability on an Object-Oriented Database (OODB) system. The proposed approach can manage several types of uncertainties: (1) uncertain objects, (2) uncertain relationships between instance objects, (3) uncertain *instance-of* relationships, and (4) uncertain *is-a (subclass/superclass)* relationships. A notable feature is the usage of extensibility offered by OODB systems. That is, it is possible to add these several uncertainties without restructuring a database schema. We will describe our prototype fuzzy OODB system and briefly show the functionalities of the system by using an example movie database.

1 Introduction

Recently, the importance of accommodating *imprecision* in database systems is paid much attention (for example, see Motro[1]), and several efforts have been done to store and/or query an imprecise data in databases. Indeed, for example, very-large knowledge bases (VLKB), CAD databases including a lot of design knowledge, OIS(office information systems) applications and databases for groupwares should include human knowledges, and so, should contain a lot of vague data, which are difficult, impossible or needless to be defined precisely. To handle such a vague data in the usual database framework, it requires to add/rewrite many complicated application programs and/or to do a radical change against the conventional database schemas which handled only precise data. Moreover, the ability to pose imprecise queries is strongly desired, but conventional RDB query language (e.g., SQL) does not provide this facility.

For these reasons some database systems, which have the functions to handle vague data and vague queries, have been reported so far (for example, see Buckles and Petry[2], Motro[3], Raju and Majumdar[4], Morrissey[5], Umano[6]) and all of these except Morrissey[5] are based on extensions of the relational database model to the fuzzy relational database model, since the relational database model has an established logical foundation.

The fuzzy relational database systems, however, have some following drawbacks:

*This research was supported in part by the Scientific Research Grant-in-Aid from the Ministry of Education, Science and Culture of Japan.

[†]Currently with Fujitsu Ltd.

Semantic Ambiguity

In the fuzzy relational data model, a fuzzy relation is defined as a fuzzy subset of Cartesian product of n domains (each domain may be a fuzzy set). That is, each tuple in a fuzzy relation is associated with the tuple's membership-function value, which is represented as a value of attribute μ (membership function). For example, suppose that we have the following tuple t in a fuzzy relation Employee(Name, Job, Salary, μ):

$$t = (\text{John, Engineer, 60000, 0.67})$$

According to the mathematical definition of the fuzzy relation, the value 0.67 means only the degree to what extent this tuple t is possible to belong to the relation. This interpretation is easily misunderstood, and users may understand the meaning of this tuple in either of the following ways:

- The degree that 'John' is an employee is 0.67.
- The degree that John's job is 'Engineer' is 0.67.
- The degree that John's salary is 60000 is 0.67.

Lack of Complex-object Management

In the above example, suppose that the degree that John is an employee is 0.9, the degree that John's job is 'Engineer' is 0.8, and the degree that John's salary is 60000 is 0.6. If we introduce fuzzy domains, then this information can be represented as:

$$((\text{John}, 0.9), \text{Engineer}, 0.8) \text{ and}$$
$$((\text{John}, 0.9), 60000, 0.6)$$

Conventional relational database systems are not sufficient to handle these complex objects, and we may need NF^2 extensions.

Lack of Extensibility

After creating a database schema, if users wish to extend a domain into a fuzzy domain, then we will need a drastic schema change. That is, if we wish to change the domain of attribute Salary into the fuzzy domain, say FuzzySalary, which may includes the values 'high', 'low', and salary-values with membership grades. First of all, we should add attributes denoting the membership functions, and sometimes, we may have to decompose the original relation schema.

Lack of Imprecise Schema Definition

In conventional fuzzy relational database systems,

data and queries can be imprecise, but, the database schema itself cannot be imprecise. This situation is also the same in conventional OODB systems. But, in some applications, it is very difficult to define a precise database schema (table skeletons in the case of RDB, and class hierarchies in the case of OODBs).

Object-oriented DBMSs (OODBMSs)[7] provide a richer modelling capability, strong complex-object management capability and a higher extensibility compared with relational databases. Therefore, in order to compensate the above drawbacks, we propose an approach to realize the fuzzy database functionalities based on the OODB model.

We introduce basic constructs to realize the fuzzy processing capability on OODBs. In our approach, several kinds of uncertainties are realized: (1) uncertain objects, (2) uncertain relationships among instance objects, (3) uncertain *instance-of* relationships between instance objects and class objects, and (4) uncertain *is-a (subclass/superclass)* relationships among classes. A notable feature of our approach is the usage of extensibility offered by OODBMSs. That is, our approach in this paper makes it possible to add these several uncertainties without restructuring a database schema.

Also, we will describe our prototype fuzzy OODB system, which was implemented on the commercial OODBMS Versant[8] and is currently running. An example database is a collection of textual data and PostScript image data concerned with movie information. By using this example database, we will briefly show the functionalities of our prototype system.

In section 2 we describe several types of uncertainties that appear in OODBs. In section 3 we propose a way to build a fuzzy database based on the OODB model, and introduce basic constructs that support to manage uncertain information. Section 4 describes our prototype fuzzy database and implementation issues by an example movie information database. Section 5 concludes the paper with some comments on future research direction.

2 Uncertainties in OODB

Fuzzy relational database systems have been intensively investigated, and have already several advantages: for example, the applicability of the relational algebra, and its strong mathematical foundations. As described in Section 1, they, however, have several disadvantages, most of which come from the record-based and value-based features of the relational model.

In the OODB model, each *instance* (object) has its own identity, and is associated with a *type* (or *class*), which is intuitively a description of its data structure and its operational interface. The structural part of a type (class) can be recursively constructed by several type constructors such as *tuple*, *set*, and *list*. The operational part of a type (class) consists of method name, argument types, type of returned object, and the implementation (code) of the method. The operation for an object is executed by sending a message to it. When the object receives a message, the method corresponding to the message is invoked and the object behaves like the modeled entity. A class is like a template such that similar objects can share method implementation codes and data structure. Classes are organized into a hierarchy, called a *class hierarchy*. Between an instance object and its associated class, we say, there is an *instance-of* relationship. In a class hierarchy, two classes are connected by an *is-a* (or *subclass/superclass*)

relationship. If class C2 is a subclass of class C1, then the data structure and method implementation codes are *inherited* to each instance object belonging to C2.

Several types of uncertainties appear in OODB model, and these are classified into the following types;

- Uncertain objects

- Uncertain relationships among instance objects

- Uncertain *instance-of* relationships between instance objects and class objects

- Uncertain *is-a (subclass/superclass)* relationships among class objects

The details for these types are described in the following.

2.1 Uncertain Objects

This type of uncertainty appears when it is difficult to represent the object itself precisely. For example,

1. Michael's birthplace is 'New York' or 'Washington D.C'.

2. Linda's age is *young*.

In this example, Michael's **birthplace** is a single object, which itself is not represented precisely. This is a kind of *disjunctive* information. In the latter example, the **age**-value of the object *Linda* is not an integer, but a fuzzy predicate *young*. These uncertain objects are able to be represented by a fuzzy set and a membership function[9] as follows:

$$NewYork\_or\_WashingtonDC = \{ 0.9/NewYork,$$
$$0.8/WashingtonDC \} \ (\text{fuzzy set})$$

Here, 0.9 and 0.8 denote the grade values (of membership functions) of the fuzzy set. *NewYork* and *WashingtonDC* are regarded as object names. The following is a definition of *young*, where μ_{young} is a membership function which maps each **age**-value to its grade.

$$\mu_{young}(20) = 1, \ \mu_{young}(21) = 0.9, \ ...$$

Note that in both of the above examples, the attributes **birthplace** and **age** are *not* set-valued. We need to distinguish fuzzy sets strictly from ordinary set-valued attributes. Of course, it is desired that these objects represented above are handled in the same way with the regular precise data.

According to Morrissey[5], this type of uncertainty is classified into (1) *p-domain* which is represented by enumerating each component distributively, (2) *p-range* which is represented with lower and upper limit, and (3) *null value* which are the objects that are unable to be represented by concrete objects. (*unknown*, *not applicable*, and so on.)

However, in this paper, we will concentrate ourselves into only uncertain objects that are represented as *fuzzy-objects* as shown above.

2.2 Uncertain Relationships Between Instance Objects

In OODB model, the relationships between instance objects are represented as attributes. Although the objects themselves are precise, their relationship may become imprecise. This type of uncertainty arises when assigning a value to an attribute, and it is independent of the uncertainty of the value. For example,

John might be perhaps a friend of Susan.

In this statement, *John* and *Susan* are supposed to be the regular precise objects. The uncertainty arises, however, when assigning *John* to the attribute friend of *Susan* object.

2.3 Uncertain IS-A Relationships

In OODB model, the class hierarchy is constructed to inherit and share the methods and data structures that are defined in the superclass and, at the same time, it corresponds to a classification of conceptual groups of real world entities. Then an uncertainty of is-a relationship arises when regarding a class hierarchy as a classification hierarchy.

For example, suppose to build a database concerned with sports players. It is natural to define the classes according to the categories of sports players; ball game players, swimming players, athletic players and so on.

When defining a class WaterPoloPlayer as a subclass of both of BallGamePlayer and SwimmingPlayer, users may wish to represent some uncertainties of the is-a relationships between class WaterPoloPlayer and BallGamePlayer and SwimmingPlayer with some grades.

The grade that represents the uncertainty of is-a relationships may not have a significant meanings when a class hierarchy is used to inherit and share methods and data structures, but we emphasize the importance of the ability to represent the uncertainty when a class hierarchy is used to represent a categorical hierarchy for grouping instance objects.

2.4 Uncertain Instance-of Relationships

This type of uncertainty corresponds to the uncertainty of *categorization of instances*. In usual OODB model, each object is enforced to belong to exactly one class with no impreciseness. But, it is desirable to introduce some impreciseness to the *instance-of* relationships between instance objects and classes.

In the preceding example, suppose a certain player who surely plays baseball and also is believed to play american football in the non-baseball season. In this case, users may wish to represent the player as a single object and let it belong to both of the class BaseballPlayer and AmericanFootBallPlayer with some uncertainty.

3 Fuzzy Database Constructs for OODB

The uncertainties described in Section 2 are independent each other and so, it is important to make a clear distinction on representing these types of uncertainties. Note that it is difficult to handle all of these uncertainties concurrently with a clear distinction in the relational model because of its flat and record-based structure. In this section we propose basic constructs that manage several types of uncertainties for OODBs. As will be described below, the proposed basic constructs can be implemented so that the added facilities may be *transparent* to users as much as possible.

3.1 Fuzzy-Object Classes

These classes are defined by users as subclasses of ordinary built-in classes (for example, integer, string etc.) or ordinary user-defined classes in order to make those conventional classes be able to handle fuzzy-objects (uncertain objects). Suppose that we have a built-in class Integer. If a user wishes to store a fuzzy integer (for example, *young*), then he can add FuzzyInteger class as a subclass of Integer class (see Fig.1). This FuzzyInteger class is a fuzzy-object class, and each of its instance object can represent a fuzzy-object.

Each fuzzy-object class has mainly two attributes objectName and contents. The objectName value stands for a fuzzy predicate such as *young*, which can be used as a value of some attribute of other objects. The contents-value is a list of tuples with the following format:

(grade, a pointer to its component object)

That is, a contents-value represents a single fuzzy set. For example, as shown in Fig.1, the *young* fuzzy-object has the following:

objectName: young

contents: {(0.7, a pointer to 30), (0.9, a pointer to 25), ⋯}

This data structure enables to handle the fuzzy object as a single object. Moreover, to define the FuzzyInteger class as a subclass of the precise atomic type class Integer makes it possible to handle a fuzzy integer as a special type of integer. For example, a fuzzy integer *young* can be assigned to the attribute Age whose domain is defined as integer. Therefore, no change on the database schema is needed.

When a fuzzy-object receives a message, the object passes the message to each of the component objects and gets the return values and the grades if the message is applicable. Then, overloading (redefining) of the methods defined in the original class makes it possible to handle the fuzzy-object in the same way as the precise objects. In the similar manner as described above, users can define fuzzy-object classes for user-defined classes.

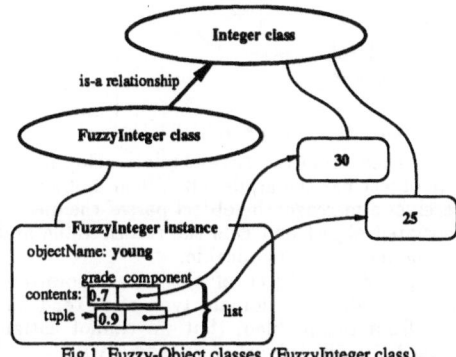

Fig.1 Fuzzy-Object classes (FuzzyInteger class)

3.2 FUZZY-INSTANCE-OF Class

This class is introduced to realize the fuzzy instance-of relationships between classes and instance objects. For users, the existence of this FUZZY-INSTANCE-OF class and its instances are invisible. Each instance object of this class represents a fuzzy instance-of relationship between a class and its instance object.

Suppose that a user wishes to make a Movie object belong to both of Action class and Dramatic class with some uncertainties. Our system will make two objects (whose contents are the same), where one belongs to Action and the other belongs to Dramatic class. Next, an instance object of the FUZZY-INSTANCE-OF class is produced, and this object contains the grade information of the instance-of relationships (see Fig.2).

The data structure of this class is similar to that of a fuzzy-object classes except that contents attribute contains the corresponding class name and the grade of the instance-of relationship. For users, this FUZZY-INSTANCE-OF object and two objects (for Action and Dramatic) are invisible, and a single Movie object belongs to these classes with some certainties for users.

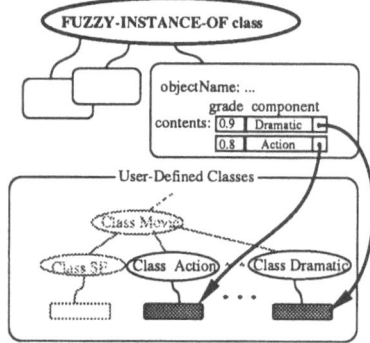

Fig.2 FUZZY-INSTANCE-OF class

3.3 FUZZY-RELATIONSHIP Class

This class manages the uncertain relationships among instance objects. Each instance object of this class has a tuple that consists of the grade of the relationship and a pointer that points to the associated object (see Fig.3).

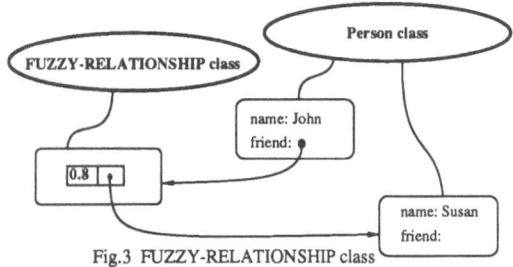

Fig.3 FUZZY-RELATIONSHIP class

This figure shows that the friend relationship from *John* to *Susan* object has the grade 0.8. When a object of this class receives a message, the object passes the message to the associated object and gets the return value and the grade if the message is applicable.

The type of the object of this class, however, has nothing to do with the domain type of friend and so, it suffers from the problem that we cannot assign the FUZZY-RELATIONSHIP object to friend attribute without changing its domain definition. In order to do it, we need

to define a subclass that is derived from the attribute domain's class (say, Person) and the FUZZY-RELATIONSHIP class by multiple inheritance.

3.4 FUZZY-CLASS-HIERARCHY Class

This class manages the uncertainty of the class hierarchy. Each instance object of this class corresponds to each of the user-defined classes and consists of a string that represents the corresponding class name and two lists that represent fuzzy is-a relationships to its superclasses and subclasses (see Fig.4).

Each list consists of some tuples, each of which holds a pointer pointing to other object of this class and the grade represents the uncertainty of the is-a relationship between the corresponding class and the pointed class. The two lists convey the fuzzy information of superclasses and subclasses, respectively.

In this method, the representation and the storage of the grade of the uncertainties of is-a relationships is independent from the inner structure of the user classes.

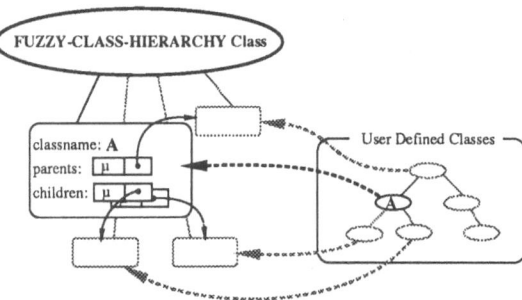

Fig.4 FUZZY-CLASS-HIERARCHY Class

4 Prototype Fuzzy OODB System and Example

We implemented a fuzzy OODB system on Versant OODBMS, which uses the proposed basic constructs and an example movie information that consists of textual data and PostScript image data. The movie information may cause several uncertainties. First, it is difficult to make a clear classification of the movie categories, so that is-a relationships will become imprecise. Next, it is difficult to assign a movie to a certain category since a movie may have various factors. Then, it will be needed to represent the uncertainty of instance-of relationships. Also, the values contained in a movie information may be imprecise. For example, the year of movie's story will be not determined precisely.

4.1 System Overview

The system overview that we build is shown in Fig.5. This system is a prototype of a fuzzy database system[1]. In this system, we defined the following additional classes for convenience.

Base class

This class is the root class of this system. To derive the user-defined classes from this class enables to append the uncertainty to the object. The object of this class has a tag that distinguishes whether the object is precise or not. This tag is used in order to manage the imprecise retrieval for convenience, and users need no awareness of its value.

---

[1] The function that manages the uncertainty of relationship between instance objects has not yet been implemented.

GRADE class

When the query is executed, a fuzzy object returns a value and some grades must be represented in order to show how much the fuzzy object satisfies the query. So, we use a variable that holds these grades. The object of this class has a pointer that points the return value for the query and three floating point numbers that represent the grades of is-a relationship, instance-of relationship and satisfaction to the condition of the query.

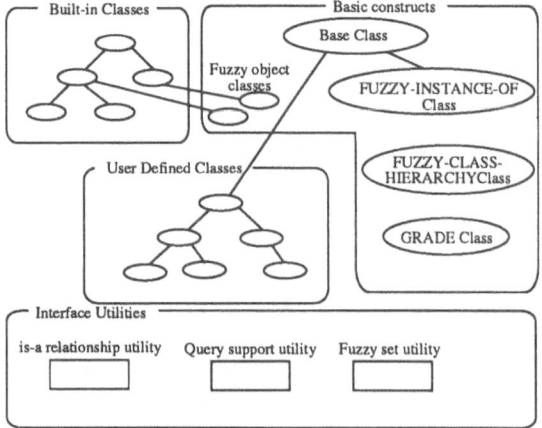

Fig.5 System overview

Also, we implemented the following interface utilities.

IS-A relationship utility

The objects of FUZZY-CLASS-HIERARCHY class can be handled by this utility. In a window shown in Fig.6, the grades of is-a relationships can be browsed and tuned up by user interactions. Also, it is possible to generate the objects of FUZZY-CLASS-HIERARCHY class automatically by specifying the name of the root class of the user classes.

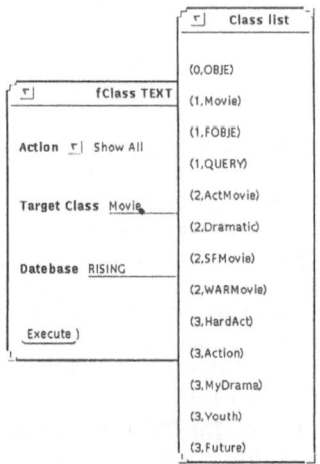

Fig.6 is-a relationship utility

Fuzzy set utility

The objects of fuzzy-object classes can be handled by this utility. In a window shown in Fig.7, the grade associated with a component object can be browsed and tuned up by user interactions. Also, it is possible to generate a fuzzy object on this window.

Fuzzy Set Window	recent
	(0.083333,1981)
Task Complete	(0.166667,1982)
	(0.250000,1983)
Predicate recent	(0.333333,1984)
	(0.416667,1985)
Task	(0.500000,1986)
Show	(0.600000,1987)
Function	(0.700000,1988)
Sygmoid1	(0.800000,1989)
	(0.900000,1990)
	(1.000000,1991)

Fig.7 Fuzzy set utility

Query support utility

Fig.8 shows a window of this utility. In this window, it is possible to pose basic queries by specifying target class name and plural conditions that consist of fuzzy objects.

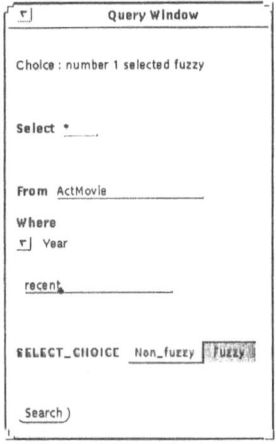

Fig.8 Query support utility

4.2 Example

We first defined some classes according to movie categories like **Action**, **SF**, **Dramatic**, and further defined their subclasses by the detailed categories of movies. Since the class hierarchy may not be precise from the standpoint of movie categorization, we add some grades to is-a relationships among these classes. Also, since a movie may have more than one categories, such as the action and dramatic, we made some movie objects belong to more than one class with some uncertainties. As for fuzzy-objects, each movie object has two attributes **Year** and **Movie_Year**, which are allowed to take fuzzy-objects (e.g., *recent*, *about1989*, *Now*) as their values. Here, **Year** represents the time when the movie was produced. The attribute **Movie_Year** represents the time which the movie's story assumes. The following shows the examples of the retrieval and its results.

256

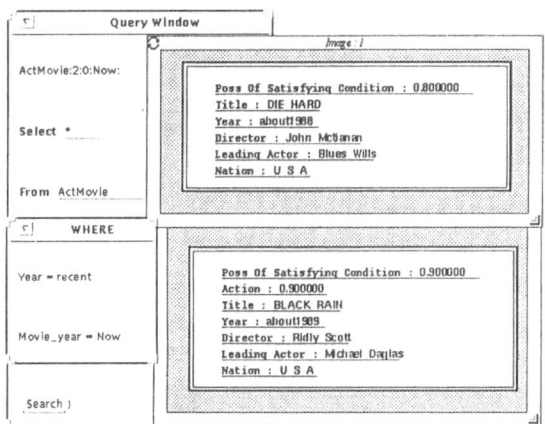

Fig.9 Retrieval by uncertain conditions

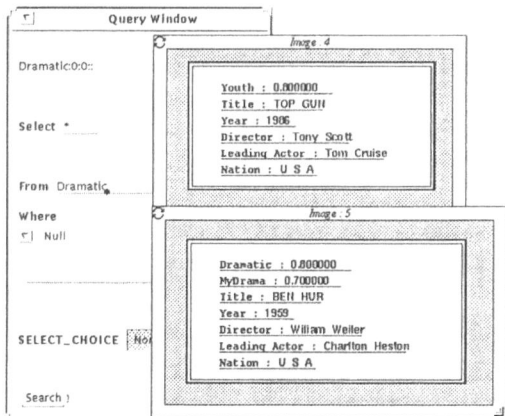

Fig.10 Retrieval in the fuzzy class hierarchy

Fig.9 shows a query containing fuzzy qualifications, which is to retrieve all the movie objects, such that (1) its category is an action movie, (2) it was produced *recently*, and (3) its story assumes the *present* day.

```
select *
from ActMovie
where Year = recent and Movie_year = Now
```

The value of **Poss Of Satisfying Condition** in each *Image* window indicates the grade of a resulting object. That is, it shows how much each resulting object satisfies the conditions specified in **where** clause. In order to calculate the grade values, we used the following ordinary computation method:

For each comparison operator (e.g., **Year = recent**), we use the *min-max* method to compare a (possibly fuzzy) object with another (possibly fuzzy) object. This method first takes the minimum grade for each corresponding component object, and then, takes the maximum value among them. In the example of *Image 2*, a fuzzy-object *about1989* (the value of **Year**) is compared with *recent*. These two fuzzy-objects are currently defined as follows:

$$about1989 = \{ ..., 0.9/1988, 1.0/1989, 0.9/1990, ... \}$$
$$recent = \{ ..., 0.8/1988, 0.9/1989, 1.0/1990, ... \}$$

The minimum values in comparison of these component values are *0.8* on *1988*, *0.9* on *1989* , and so on. Then the result of the evaluation is the maximum value *0.9*. In the similar manner, the second condition **Movie_Year = Now** is evaluated, and the evaluation result is 0.8. Since these two conditions are connected by **and**, we take the minimum value from {0.9, 0.8}, that is, 0.8 as the final value.

Also, **Action: 0.9** in this window indicates that the retrieved object has a grade *0.9* as an **Action** movie. (The grade of instance-of relationship between the object and class **Action** is *0.9*.)

Fig.10 shows a query concerned with fuzzy is-a relationships, which retrieves all the **Dramatic** objects. The query is: **select * from Dramatic**. In Fig.10, **Dramatic: 0.8** and **MyDrama: 0.7** in the *Image:5* window indicate that class **MyDrama** is a subclass of class **Dramatic** with a grade **0.8**, and this movie has a grade **0.7** as **MyDrama**.

5 Conclusions

In this paper, we introduced basic constructs to realize the fuzzy processing capability on conventional OODBs. These basic constructs are implemented so that users can easily extend their OODBs to fuzzy OODBs without restructuring their database schemas.

In this paper, we did not describe (1)*fuzzy integrity constraints*, (2)a general computation algorithm to compute final grades from several types of uncertain information, and (3)inheritance and overloding of fuzzy membership functions. These kinds of more general uncertainty management facilities are the subject of a future research.

References

[1] Motro,A., *Accommodating Imprecision in Database Systems: Issues and Solution*, ACM SIGMOD RECORD, Vol.19, No.4, pp.69-74, December 1990.

[2] Buckles,B.P. and Petry,F.E., *A Fuzzy Representation of Data for Relational Databases*, Fuzzy Sets and Systems, Vol.7, No.3, pp.213-226, May 1982.

[3] Motro,A., *VAGUE: A User Interface to Relational Databases That Permits Vague Queries*, ACM Trans. on Office Information Systems, Vol.6, no.3, pp.187-214, July 1988.

[4] Raju,K.V.S.V.N. and Majumdar,A., *Fuzzy Functional Dependencies and Lossless Join Decomposition of Fuzzy Database Systems*, ACM Trans. on Database Systems, Vol.13, No.2, pp.129-166, June 1988.

[5] Morrissey,J.M., *Imprecise Information and Uncertainty in Information Systems*, ACM Trans. on Information Systems, Vol.8, No.2, pp.159-180, April 1990.

[6] Umano,M., *Perspective and Trends of Fuzzy Databases*, proc. of Advanced Database System Symposium'89, pp. 207-214, December 1989.

[7] Atkinson,M. et al., *The Object-Oriented Database System Manifesto*, in *Deductive and Object-Oriented Databases*, pp.223-240, North-Holland, 1990.

[8] VERSANT Object Technology, *VERSANT System Manual*, Sept. 1990.

[9] Zadeh,L.A., *Fuzzy Sets as a Basic for Theory of Possibility*, Fuzzy Sets and Systems, Vol.1, pp. 3-28, 1978.

A Framework for Strong Typing and Type Inference in (Persistent) Object Models

Alfons Kemper
Lehrstuhl für Informatik III
RWTH Aachen
W-5100 Aachen
kemper@informatik.rwth-aachen.de

Guido Moerkotte
Fakultät für Informatik
Universität Karlsruhe
W-7500 Kalrsruhe
moer@ira.uka.de

Abstract

In this paper a coherent framework of *subtyping* is developed that achieves *strong typing* in (persistent) object models without compromising flexibility and expressiveness. The typing framework is based on the concept of *substitutability*—meaning that from the type consistency perspective objects exhibiting a particular functional characteristic are substitutable for objects of another kind without compromising type safety. We deduce substitutability from the functional specification of object types, called the *type signature*. Utilizing our framework we show that inheritance-based subtyping on tuple-structured types cannot generally be extended to set-structured or any other collection types, e.g., lists, without sacrificing static verifiability of type consistency.

1 Introduction

Until recently, typing was not a "hot" topic in database research as opposed to the programming language area, e.g., [3, 6]. All conventional data models (relational, CODA-SYL network, and hierarchical model) and their associated database programming languages uniformly provide static type specificity. The recent emergence of object oriented data models as the (presumably) next-generation DBMS has led to a relaxation of static typing in favor of increased flexibility and expressiveness. Unfortunately, in most newly developed object models the increase in flexibility had to be paid for dearly: database operations could no longer be guaranteed type safe. In order to achieve a high degree of reusability of built-in database operators and user-defined operations type constraints were either completely or partially abolished for the sake of flexibility.

*This work was partly supported by a grant from the Deutsche Forschungsgemeinschaft (DFG; German Research Council) within the interdisciplinary cooperation project SFB 346, sub-project A1 "Cooperation in Distributed Object Bases".

In some data models no type information is kept. Objects can be freely created using the built-in type constructors. This approach is typically termed *loose* typing. This typing strategy has its roots in the programming language LISP; one representative data model adhering to this is FAD [2].

The *dynamically* typed models let the database designer specify the outer level of the objects; but the components (attributes, set elements, etc.) are untyped, i.e., they may refer to any object. The precursor of this approach in the programming language area is Smalltalk-80 [8], which gave rise to some developments in the database area, e.g., GemStone [4] and—to some extent—Orion [11].

The two above mentioned classes of object oriented data models cannot guarantee type safety of database operations at compile time. We argue that the lack of type safety in object bases constitutes a much more severe problem than in object oriented programming languages: an object base is a highly shared, persistent resource which is modified by a variety of more or less knowledgeable users. Furthermore, many database facilities, e.g., access support, concurrency control, recovery, etc., are inherently more difficult and less efficient and robust under dynamic typing.

Therefore, a third class of object models was designed along the lines of Simula 67 [5] in order to try to reconcile type safety and object oriented features, such as inheritance, subtyping, operator overriding (refinement), and late binding [1]. This approach is typically called *strong* typing: all expressions in the language can be verified type consistent at compile time even though the exact type cannot always be determined. However, in all models that we know of there are either some loopholes where dynamic type checking is still required or, the constraints imposed by strong typing severely reduce flexibility. An example of the former is O_2 [12], in which the designers consciously incorporated some features that prevent static type verification for the sake of expressiveness. These features include (cf. Section 6): *retyping of attributes* in a subtype (this, in general, violates strong typing even if the new type is a subtype of the original one), *exceptional attributes* (attributes that are only present in some instances of the type, but not in all) and *subtyping on set- and list-structured object types*.

Our main contribution in this paper is the development of a unifying framework within which static verification of type consistency can be studied. The framework is based on the notion of object substitutability, meaning that objects exhibiting a particular functional behavior can be substituted for objects having a corresponding functional specification. The concept of object substitutability is studied in the context of a typed object model by analyzing the *type signatures* which constitutes the set of abstract operation signatures that are applicable on the respective instances of this type. In a step-wise fashion we extend a basic (miniaturized) object model by further object-oriented concepts and analyze the requirements upon these features to retain strong typing.

The remainder of this paper is organized as follows. In section 2 we describe the essentials of an object oriented data model, GOM (Generic Object Model), which—as the name implies—generalizes the most salient constructs of recently proposed [1, 15] models in one coherent research vehicle. In subsequent sections the base model is extended: in Section 4 subtyping and subtype substitutability is included. In Section 5 operator refinement (overriding) is being integrated in the base model. In Section 6 we analyze the potential "loopholes" of various concepts which potentially prevents static type consistency verification. Section 7 concludes the paper.

2 The Basics of GOM

In this section the most basic features of the object model GOM are presented—for the sake of simplicity the actually implemented model has been severely "miniaturized" (a more thorough presentation of the "real" object model GOM can be found in [10]). GOM includes a set of base types represented by the base type symbols *int*, *bool*, *char*, *float*, and *string*. For base types we have values (e.g., 1, 2, ..., "henry", ...). In addition there exists the built-in type *ANY* that forms the root of the type hierarchy. Besides basic values we can have objects which are instantiations of complex (e.g., user defined) types. Let $\mathcal{T}$ denote the set of defined types. Then a new object of type $t \in \mathcal{T}$ is created (instantiated) by the following expression: $t\$create$. We use the following two built-in type and object constructors: *tuple* and *set* denoted by [] and {}, respectively[1].

A unique identifier (e.g., $id_0, id_1, \ldots$) is associated with every GOM object. The incorporation of subtyping, i.e., the substitutability of an instance of a subtype for an instance of a supertype (cf. Section 4), requires that each database object "knows" to what *direct* type it belongs. Therefore, a (complex) object is represented as a triple (OID, v, t) consisting of the *object identifier OID*, the *(complex) value v*, and the *type t* of which the object was instantiated.

---

[1]GOM also provides *lists* which are—from the perspective of typing—treated analogously to sets.

2.1 Type Definitions

In the type definition we allow for single inheritance only. But as long as no type conflicts occur our results are adaptable for multiple inheritance. But, if type conflicts occur—due to name clashes in a system supporting multiple inheritance—these cannot be resolved in the context of strong typing.

Let $s, t, t_i^j \in \mathcal{T}$ $(1 \le j \le m, 1 \le i \le n_j + 1)$ be type symbols, and x_v^w $(1 \le w \le m, 1 \le v \le n_w)$ be pairwise distinct identifiers (for formal parameters). Then a type definition is:

type t **supertype** s **is**
  body *Structural-Representation*
  operations
    declare $op_1 : t \| x_1^1 : t_1^1, \ldots, x_{n_1}^1 : t_{n_1}^1 \to t_{n_1+1}^1$ **is** $impl_1$;
    ...
    declare $op_m : t \| x_1^m : t_1^m, \ldots, x_{n_m}^m : t_{n_m}^m \to t_{n_m+1}^m$ **is** $impl_m$;
end type t;

In this case s is called the *supertype* of t, and t is called a (direct) *subtype* of s. If the **supertype** clause is missing **supertype** ANY is implicitly assumed. We denote by $\le_T$ the reflexive, transitive closure of the subtype relation which is demanded to be cycle free. If $t \le_T s$ and $s \ne t$ then t is called a *proper subtype* of s.

The operator declarations constitute formal signatures of the respective operators which determine the validity of invocations. The type t is called the receiver type of operation op_i. Such an operation is invoked as $e_0.op_i(e_1, \ldots, e_{n_i})$ where the e_j are expressions of appropriate type. The actual argument types and the expected result type of an invocation is matched against the signature—at compile time. The implementation of the operators—denoted here as *impl*—has to be verified type consistent with respect to their formal signature (cf. Section 3).

2.2 Tuple- and Set-Structured Types

We distinguish between tuple-structured types and set-structured types. Let $a_1, \ldots, a_n$ be pairwise distinct attribute names Then a tuple-structured type has the following *Structural-Representation*: $[a_1 : t_1; \ldots; a_n : t_n]$

For a tuple-structured type the following operations are implicitly declared (and defined) in the **operations** clause of the type. For every attribute a_i $(1 \le i \le n)$ the system provides an operation *read_a_i* to read the attribute value and *set_a_i* to associate a new object with the attribute[2]. The signatures of these implicitly generated operations are as follows:

declare $read\_a_i : t \| \to t_i$;
declare $set\_a_i : t \| t_i \to$ **void**;

---

[2]Assigning an object to a variable (or attribute) means to establish a reference from the attribute to the object, i.e., the object identifier of the assigned object is stored. Referencing and dereferencing is implicit in GOM.

Set-structured types are structurally represented as: $\{t_1\}$. The difference to a tuple-structured type is that a different set of pre-defined operations is supplied. For a set-structured type these are the primitive operations to *insert* a new element—more precisely: to insert a reference to the particular object—and to remove one element (*removeOne*) as well as the test *isNotEmpty* whether the set is not empty. The signatures of these operations are:

declare *insert* : $t\|t_1 \to$ **void**;
declare *removeOne* : $t\| \to t_1$;
declare *isNotEmpty* : $t\| \to$ *bool*;

The semantics of these operations should be obvious.

For these pre-defined operations no implementation has to be provided—their implementation is implicit and, by default, correct and type consistent with respect to the formal signature.

2.3   Restrictions on Type Definitions

At this point we enforce very stringent restrictions on the type definitions, which are—somewhat informally—stated below:

1. the transitive closure of the subtype hierarchy, modelled by the relation $\le_T$, has to be cycle-free.

2. if an operation name *op* has been introduced in a type *s* it must not be reused in any subtype *t* of *s*.

3. if an attribute *a* has been introduced in a type *s* it must not be reused as an attribute name in any subtype *t* of *s*. This is actually a consequence of requirement 2 when considering the predefined operations on tuple types. However, it is possible to add new attributes (of distinct name) within the subtypes of *s*.

4. if a type *s* has the clause **body** $\{t_1\}$ then subtypes *t* of *s* must not have a **body** clause—that is, the supertype specifies the structural representation once and for all. It is merely possible to add further application-specific operations that are different from the implicit set operations.

These restrictions rule out any name clashes that may otherwise occur. Later on—in Section 5—we will relax the restriction on operator name uniqueness and show how refinement of operators will fit in with our typing framework.

2.4   The Language

The implementation of an operation must obey the syntax of the following (mini-GOM) language:

```
Stmt ::= Stmt; Stmt|          Exp ::= self |
         begin Stmt end |             Variable |
         while (Exp) Stmt |           Exp.OpName(Exp,...,Exp) |
         return Exp |                 TypeName$create
         Exp |
         Variable := Exp
```

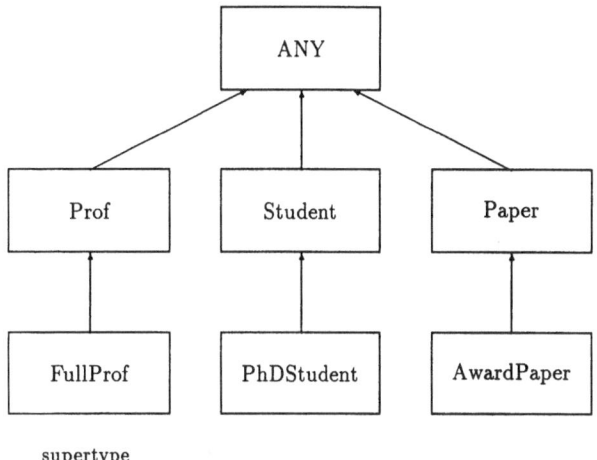

Figure 1: University Type Hierarchy

The subsequent discussions will be illustrated by an example type hierarchy modeling (part of) a university. The type hierarchy is sketched in Figure 1. Some of the types are defined in Figure 2.

```
type Prof supertype ANY is
  body [Name: string;
        Sal: float;
        Boss: Prof]
  operations
  declare incSal: Prof‖x: float→void is
    self.set_Sal(self.read_Sal * (1 + x));
  declare writePaper: Prof‖p: PhDStudent→Paper is
    return (Paper$create);
    ...         !! predefined operations to read and set attributes

end type Prof;

type FullProf supertype Prof is
  body [Asst: Prof]
  operations
  declare read_Asst: FullProf‖→Prof;
  declare set_Asst: FullProf‖Prof→void;
end type FullProf;
```

Figure 2: Sample Type Definitions

2.5   Type Signatures

Our framework of type consistency verification will be entirely based on the analysis of the functional specification of the type definitions. The basis forms the following definition of type signature:

Definition 2.1 (Type Signature)
For the above type definition of t we define the signature Σ_t as follows: $\Sigma_t := \{(op_1 : t_1^1, \ldots, t_{n_1}^1 \rightarrow t_{n_1+1}^1), \ldots, (op_m : t_1^m, \ldots, t_{n_m}^m \rightarrow t_{n_m+1}^m)\} \cup \Sigma_s$

Thus the signature of a type constitutes the set of all operation signatures—including the (inherited) ones, that were specified in any supertype of t. Note that this recursive definition is bounded by the signature Σ_{ANY} which merely includes the built-in operation ($EQ : ANY \rightarrow bool$), i.e., the test for equality of two objects.

Our example types have the following type signatures:

Σ_{Prof}={ (incSal: *float* → **void**),
  (read_Name: → *string*), (set_Name: *string* → **void**),
  (read_Sal: → *float*), (set_Sal: *float* → **void**),
  (read_Boss: → Prof), (set_Boss: Prof → **void**) } $\cup \Sigma_{ANY}$
$\Sigma_{FullProf}$={ (read_Asst: → Prof), (set_Asst: Prof → **void**) }
  $\cup \Sigma_{Prof}$

3   Static Type Checking

We now define the concept of *substitutability* which specifies conditions under which we can safely substitute objects of one "kind" for objects of another "kind".

Definition 3.1 (Substitutability)
An object o' is substitutable for an object o iff for every operation op and all objects $o_1, \ldots, o_n$ the following holds: if $o.op(o_1, \ldots, o_n)$ is a valid invocation of op—that is, o "understands" the operation invocation—then $o'.op(o_1, \ldots, o_n)$ is also a valid invocation of op and $o'.op(o_1, \ldots, o_n)$ is substitutable for $o.op(o_1, \ldots, o_n)$.

This definition does not account for any semantics—it merely specifies syntactical requirements. Thus an object is substitutable for another object when it is—from a typing perspective—as "knowledgeable" with respect to the operations it "understands". Moreover, the return objects of its operations have to be at least as "good" as the return values of the object being substituted.

Proposition 3.1 (Substitutability in all Places)
Let o_j for $(0 \leq j \leq n)$ and o_i' be objects. If o_i' is substitutable for o_i then if the invocation $o_0.op(o_1, \ldots, o_i, \ldots, o_n)$ is valid then also $o_0.op(o_1, \ldots, o_i', \ldots, o_n)$ is a valid invocation and the result $o_0.op(o_1, \ldots, o_i', \ldots, o_n)$ is substitutable for $o_0.op(o_1, \ldots, o_i, \ldots, o_n)$.

The proof of this proposition is rather easy: as long as o_i is not used as a receiver for any operation invocation no information can be deduced from o_i. Information can only be derived from o_i or o_i', respectively, if they are used as the receiver of some operation during the execution of op. But then o_i' is as "good" as o_i (since the prerequisite of the proposition states that o_i' is substitutable for o_i).

In the remainder of this paper we will study substitutability only in the context of type extensions and not on the basis of individual objects. The following proposition forms the basis for this:

Proposition 3.2 (Substitutability of Type Instances)

For any type t and any two instances (objects) o_1 and o_2 of type t o_1 is substitutable for o_2 and o_2 is substitutable for o_1.

The validity of this proposition is just a consequence of the typing philosophy obeyed in GOM: all objects of one type have the same functional interface. We do not allow the addition of further operations (or attributes) at the instance level.

Definition 3.2 (Type Schema and Variables)
When we define a new type r with type signatures Σ_r and direct supertype s, we have to include the following information in the schema $\mathcal{S}$:

$$\mathcal{S} := \mathcal{S} \ \cup \ \{(r \leq_T s)\}$$
$$\cup \ \left(\bigcup_{(op:t_1,\ldots,t_n \rightarrow t_{n+1}) \in \Sigma_r} \{(op : r \| t_1, \ldots, t_n \rightarrow t_{n+1})\} \right)$$

The set $\mathcal{X}$ encompasses all global variables defined in the object base. For a variable declaration $\textbf{var } x : t$ we update this set as follows:

$$\mathcal{X} := \mathcal{X} \cup \{(x : t)\}$$

For simplicity we restrict the use of variables in this discussion to global variables and formal parameters. But only the former are being added to $\mathcal{X}$.

Before we can start verifying the type safety of individual operations we have to compile this schema information for the entire object base schema, i.e., for all (newly defined) types. The completeness of the schema information is necessary because of possible recursive interdependencies of operation invocations.

Then we have to verify for each individual operation—except for the implicit ones to read and modify attributes and to handle sets —the type consistency of the implementation. The following definition forms the basis for the verification process:

Definition 3.3 (Static Type Consistency)
The operation ($\textbf{declare } op : r \| x_1 : t_1, \ldots, x_n : t_n \rightarrow t_{n+1}$ is $impl;$) is verified type consistent if

$$(\mathcal{S}, (\mathcal{X} \cup \{(\textbf{self}:t_0), (x_1:t_1), \ldots, (x_n:t_n)\}) \vdash impl : t_{n+1})$$

can be deduced by using the type inference rules in Figure 3.

4   Substitutability of Subtype Instances

The typing rules presented so far do not provide for substitutability of subtype instances for supertype instances. Thus, our type hierarchy—so far—merely constitutes a simple inheritance mechanism. The following program fragment highlights this:

$$S, (\mathcal{X} \cup \{x : t\}) \;\vdash\; x : t \qquad [\text{I}1]$$

$$S, (\mathcal{X} \cup \{\mathbf{self} : t\}) \;\vdash\; \mathbf{self} : t \qquad [\text{I}2]$$

$$S \cup \{(t \leq_T s)\}, \mathcal{X} \;\vdash\; t\$\mathbf{create} : t \qquad [\text{I}3]$$

$$S \cup \{(op : t_0 \| t_1, \ldots, t_n \to r)\}, \mathcal{X} \;\vdash\; (op : t_0 \| t_1, \ldots, t_n \to r)[\text{I}4]$$

$$\frac{S, \mathcal{X} \vdash e_0 : t_0, \ldots, e_n : t_n, (op : t_0 \| t_1, \ldots, t_n \to t_{n+1})}{S, \mathcal{X} \vdash e_0.op(e_1, \ldots, e_n) : t_{n+1}} \qquad [\text{I}5]$$

$$\frac{S, \mathcal{X} \vdash e : t \text{ for } t \in \mathcal{T}}{S, \mathcal{X} \vdash e : \mathbf{void}} \qquad [\text{I}6]$$

$$\frac{S, \mathcal{X} \vdash e : t}{S, (\mathcal{X} \cup \{x : t\}) \vdash (x := e) : \mathbf{void}} \qquad [\text{I}7]$$

$$\frac{S, \mathcal{X} \vdash e_1 : \mathbf{void}, e_2 : t_2}{S, \mathcal{X} \vdash (e_1; e_2) : t_2} \qquad [\text{I}8]$$

$$\frac{S, \mathcal{X} \vdash e : t}{S, \mathcal{X} \vdash \mathbf{return}\ e : t} \qquad [\text{I}9]$$

$$\frac{S, \mathcal{X} \vdash \alpha : bool, e_1 : \mathbf{void}, e_2 : \mathbf{void}}{S, \mathcal{X} \vdash \mathbf{if}(\alpha) e_1\ \mathbf{else}\ e_2 : \mathbf{void}} \qquad [\text{I}10]$$

$$\frac{S, \mathcal{X} \vdash \alpha : bool, e : \mathbf{void}}{S, \mathcal{X} \vdash \mathbf{while}(\alpha) e : \mathbf{void}} \qquad [\text{I}11]$$

Figure 3: Type Inference Rules for Static Typing

var Fritz: Prof; Einstein: FullProf; Newcomer: Prof;

...

(1) Fritz.set_Boss(Newcomer);   !! **ok**
(2) Fritz.set_Boss(Einstein);   !! **illegal** (so far)

The variable *Einstein* is constrained to objects of type *Full-Prof*, which is a subtype of *Prof*. Unfortunately our preliminary type inference system presented so far does not yet account for subtype substitutability.

The subsequent proposition is the key to provide the additional flexibility of subtype substitutability for our strongly typed object model:

Proposition 4.1 (Substitutability of Subtypes)
For any two types $t, s \in \mathcal{T}$ such that $t \leq_T s$ and any two objects o_t of type t and o_s of type s o_t is substitutable for o_s.

The proof of this proposition is based on the fact that—so far—we do not allow name clashes in our type hierarchy and that a subtype inherits *all* operations of its supertype. Therefore, a subtype instance "knows" more than a supertype instance and, therefore, can safely be substituted wherever a supertype instance is required. Sometimes, the "*inherit all*" paradigm causes problems concerning the "natural" modeling of some applications. These problems are investigated in [9] where a solution based on a constraint approach is proposed.

In order to exploit Proposition 4.1 we have to "relax" our type inference system of Figure 3 by three further rules:

$$S \cup \{(t \leq_T s)\}, \mathcal{X} \;\vdash\; t \leq_T s \qquad [\text{I}12]$$

$$\frac{S, \mathcal{X} \vdash t \leq_T r, r \leq_T s}{S, \mathcal{X} \vdash t \leq_T s} \qquad [\text{I}13]$$

$$\frac{S, \mathcal{X} \vdash e : t, t \leq_T s}{S, \mathcal{X} \vdash e : s} \qquad [\text{I}14]$$

Using these additional type inference rules the statement (2) above becomes valid.

5 Refinement of Operations

So far our object model lacks the flexibility to adapt operations that were inherited from a supertype to the particular characteristics of the subtype instances. A very typical example is the revision of an inherited *volume* operation in a geometric object type hierarchy. In a strongly typed object model this adaptation of inherited operations is possible; but it has to be constrained with respect to the signature of the inherited operation. The following is the key definition that constrains adaptation to (valid) *refinement*:

Definition 5.1 (Operation Refinement)
*For $(1 \leq i \leq n + 1)$ let t_i and t_i' be types and (**declare** op : $t_0 \| x_1 : t_1, \ldots, x_n : t_n \to t_{n+1}$ **is** impl;) an operator declaration with t_0 being the receiver type of op. Then (**declare** op : $t_0' \| y_1 : t_1', \ldots, y_n : t_n' \to t_{n+1}'$ **is** impl';) is called a (valid) refinement of op iff the following conditions hold:*

*1. $t_i \leq_T t_i'$ for $(1 \leq i \leq n)$—the (new) argument types have to be **super-types***

*2. $t_{n+1}' \leq_T t_{n+1}$—the (new) result has to be a **sub-type***

We can extend this definition to valid refinements of types:

Definition 5.2 (Type Refinement)
A type t is a (valid) type refinement of another type s iff for every operation signature $(op : t_1, \ldots, t_n \to t_{n+1}) \in \Sigma_s$ there exists an $(op : t_1', \ldots, t_n' \to t_{n+1}') \in \Sigma_t$ such that the latter is a (valid) operation refinement of the former.

Proposition 5.1 (Substitutability of Refined Types)
Let t and s be types such that t is a valid refinement of s. Then any object o_t of type t is substitutable for any object o_s of type s.

The proof is based on the observation that the refined operations are "better" in the typing sense than the original versions: they yield "better" output with less specific input (parameters).

In GOM we ensure that every (new) type t is a valid refinement of its supertype. This is achieved by enforcing the requirements of Definition 5.1 on all inherited operations that are re-declared and re-implemented within the new (sub-)type t.

If a type t being a subtype of type s refines an inherited operation op we have to revise the definition of the type signature in the way that the inherited (original) signature of op which is included in Σ_s is replaced by the refined signature. Thus, we get:

$$\Sigma_t := \{\ldots, (op : t'_1, \ldots, t'_n \to t'_{n+1}), \ldots\}$$
$$\cup \left(\Sigma_s \setminus \{(op : t_1, \ldots, t_n \to t_{n+1})\}\right)$$

It is straightforward to extend this to more than one refined operation in a subtype.

We want to highlight (valid) operation refinement on an example. In our University there exists an operation *writePaper* in which it takes a *Prof* and a *PhDStudent* to write a *Paper*. However, if a *FullProf* is going to write down his/her thoughts only a "general" *Student* is necessary to create one that is even awarded (*AwardPaper*). Therefore, the inherited *writePaper* operation is being refined within type *FullProf* as follows:

declare writePaper: FullProf∥s: Student → AwardPaper **is**
    return (AwardPaper$create); !! if it only were that easy

As can be seen *FullProfs* are "better" than "normal" *Profs* since they are able to produce "better" output, i.e., *Award-Papers*, with "less qualified" input, i.e., "general" *Students*. Thus, whenever a "normal" *Prof* shall write a *Paper* one can substitute him/her by a *FullProf* without any loss of type safety.

In our type inference system it is only possible to substitute instances of subtypes where supertype instances are required. This is more stringent than Proposition 5.1 states—from the type safety point of view it is sufficient to require that the type of the substituted object is a refinement of the constrained type. However, this—in general—leads to the problem of unintended substitutability [10, 7], e.g., substituting a *Person* object by a *Wine* object because they just happen to have the same functional specification consisting of *Name* and *Age* attributes. Our view is that the user should indicate the desire for substitutability explicitly by relating the types accordingly in the subtype hierarchy. Therefore we only allow substitutability of (explicit) subtype instances where supertype instances are required.

6 Truths that Hurt

In this section we analyze a few commonly encountered "loopholes" that conflict with strong typing.

6.1 Retyping of Attributes is Illegal

It is not possible to redefine inherited attribute types without violating subtype substitutability. This will be shown by way of an example. Reconsider the type hierarchy of Figure 1 and let us sketch the two type definitions of *Paper* and *AwardPaper*:

type Paper **supertype** ANY **is**
  body [Author: Prof]
  operations
    declare set_Author: Prof→**void**;

    declare read_Author:→Prof;
  end type Paper;

type AwardPaper **supertype** Paper **is**
  body [**refine** Author: FullProf] !! **ILLEGAL**
  operations
    declare set_Author: FullProf→**void**;
    declare read_Author:→FullProf;
  end type AwardPaper;

Unfortunately, the type *AwardPaper* is not a valid refinement of *Paper*. This can be concluded from the type signatures:

$$\Sigma_{Paper} = \{ (\text{read\_Author}: \to \text{Prof}),$$
$$(\text{set\_Author}: \text{Prof} \to \textbf{void}), \ldots \}$$
$$\Sigma_{AwardPaper} = \{ (\text{read\_Author}: \to \text{FullProf}),$$
$$(\text{set\_Author}: \text{FullProf} \to \textbf{void}), \ldots \}$$

The attribute assignment operation *set_Author* of *Award-Paper* is not a legal refinement of the respective operation of *Paper*. Furthermore, the type signatures show that attributes must not be retyped by supertypes of the original attribute types either, e.g., typing the attribute *Author* of *AwardPaper* with *Person* which is a supertype of *Prof* would lead to a type conflict, as well—this time the *read_Author* operation would cause the conflict.

Consider the following program fragment to illustrate the potentially occurring type conflict:

var p: Paper; Newcomer: Prof; ap: AwardPaper
. . .
(1) p.set_Author(Newcomer); !! okay
(2) p := ap;   !! okay, subtype substitutability
(3) p.set_Author(Newcomer); !! potential type violation

The principle of subtype substitutability demands that the statement (2) is valid since the variable *p* can legally be associated with an *AwardPaper* instance. After executing (2) *p* and *ap* refer to the same object of (actual) type *AwardPaper*. However, then the statement (3) may lead to a type violation since the variable *Newcomer* could refer to an "ordinary" *Prof* which is then assigned as the *Author* of the *AwardPaper* instance—a clear type violation.

6.2 Subtyping of Collection Types

Many people are tempted to view a collection type with element type t_1 as a subtype of a collection type with elements of type t_2 if $t_1 \leq t_2$ holds. For instance, one is tempted to treat the type *FullProfSet* as a subtype of *ProfSet* where *ProfSet* and *FullProfSet* have the structural representation {*Prof*} and {*FullProf*}, respectively.

We will now prove that the intuitive—and tempting—attempt of treating *FullProfSet* as a (substitutable) subtype of *ProfSet* is wrong. Suppose we have the following (persistent) variable declarations:

```
var ManyFullProfs: FullProfSet;
var ManyProfs: ProfSet;
```

If *FullProfSet* were a *legal* subtype of *ProfSet* the assignment

```
ManyProfs := ManyFullProfs;
```

would be valid and result-in the sharing of the set object referred to by *ManyFullProfs*.

The dilemma is, that over the variable *ManyProfs*, one could insert *Prof* instances into the set object of type *FullProfSet*, e.g.:

```
ManyProfs.insert(SomeProf);
```

This has the catastrophic side effect that the object to which *ManyFullProfs* and *ManyProfs* refer is no longer properly typed.

Again, we will consider the type signatures to give a more formalized proof:

$$\Sigma_{ProfSet} \supseteq \{(\text{insert} : \text{Prof} \rightarrow \textbf{void})\}$$
$$\Sigma_{FullProfSet} \supseteq \{(\text{insert} : \text{FullProf} \rightarrow \textbf{void})\}$$

The signature of *insert* in $\Sigma_{FullProf}$ is not a valid refinement of *insert* in Σ_{Prof} because the *insert* operation of *FullProfSet* requires an instance $\leq_T$ *FullProf* whereas *ProfSet* is "happy" dealing with instances $\leq_T$ *Prof*. Thus, *FullProfSet* instances cannot safely be substituted for *ProfSet* instances.

The consequence of this discussion is that two set-structured types with *different* element types cannot possibly be related as sub- and super-type. However, subtyping of collection types need not be forbidden generally; but, only collections with *identical* element types can possibly be valid subtypes of each other.

7 Conclusion

In this paper we presented a formal framework within which strong typing of object models can be studied. For this purpose the concept of substitutability was developed on the basis of analyzing operation signatures. We presented a complete type inference system for our object model, called mini-GOM. Utilizing the framework we could analyze a few frequently encountered loop-holes that jeopardize static verifiability of type safety. It was illustrated that inheritance and subtype substitutability alone, under the constraint of strong typing, restricts the expressiveness of the model in particular for operators based on collection types. Therefore, in our (full-fledged) object model GOM we developed a framework that unifies inheritance, subtyping and polymorphism [10]. The type checker has been built along the lines of the ones developed in ML [13] and Machiavelli [14].

Acknowledgments

The GOM language—including most of the type verification—was implemented by A. Zachmann. The type inference system for polymorphic operators was realized by W. Häfelinger. Furthermore, we had valuable discussions with our colleagues H.-D. Walter and C. Kilger.

References

[1] M. Atkinson, F. Bancilhon, D. J. DeWitt, K. R. Dittrich, D. Maier, and S. Zdonik. The object-oriented database system manifesto. In *Proc. of the DOOD Conference*, pages 40–57, Kyoto, Japan, Dec 1989.

[2] F. Bancilhon, T. Briggs, S. Khoshafian, and P. Valduriez. FAD, a powerful and simple database language. In *Proc. of The Conf. on Very Large Data Bases (VLDB)*, pages 97–105, Brighton, U.K., Sep 1987.

[3] L. Cardelli and P. Wegner. On understanding types, data abstraction, and polymorphism. *ACM Computing Surveys*, 17(4):471–522, Dec 1985.

[4] G. Copeland and D. Maier. Making Smalltalk a database system. In *Proc. of the ACM SIGMOD Conf. on Management of Data*, pages 316–325, 1984.

[5] O. Dahl and K. Nygaard. Simula, an Algol-based simulation language. *CACM*, 9:671–678, 1966.

[6] S. Danforth and C. Tomlinson. Type theories and object oriented programming. *ACM Computing Surveys*, 20(1):29–72, Mar 1988.

[7] J. A. Goguen and D. Wolfram. On types and FOOPS. In *Proc. IFIP TC 2 Working Conference on Database Semantics: Object Oriented Databases—Analysis, Design, and Construction*, Windermere, UK, Jun 90.

[8] A. Goldberg and D. Robson. *Smalltalk-80: The Language and its Implementation*. Addison-Wesley, 1983.

[9] A. Kemper and G. Moerkotte. Correcting anomalies of standard inheritance—a constraint based approach. In *Proc. Intl. Conf. on Database and Expert Systems Applications*, pages 49–55, Wien, Austria, Aug 90.

[10] A. Kemper, G. Moerkotte, H.-D. Walter, and A. Zachmann. GOM: a strongly typed, persistent object model with polymorphism. In *Proc. of the BTW Conf.*, pages 198–217, Mar 1991. Springer-Verlag, Informatik-Fachberichte Nr. 270.

[11] W. Kim, H. T. Chou, and J. Banerjee. Operations and implementation of complex objects. *IEEE Trans. Software Eng.*, 14(7):985–996, Jul 1988.

[12] C. Lécluse and P. Richard. The O_2 database programming language. In *Proc. of The Conf. on Very Large Data Bases (VLDB)*, pages 411–422, Amsterdam, NL, Sep 1989.

[13] R. Milner. A theory of type polymorphism. *Journal of Computer and System Sciences*, 17:378–375, 1978.

[14] A. Ohori, P. Buneman, and V. Breazu-Tannen. Database programming in Machiavelli: A polymorphic language with static type inference. In *Proc. of the ACM SIGMOD Conf. on Management of Data*, Portland, OR, 1989.

[15] S. Zdonik and D. Maier. Fundamentals of object-oriented databases. In S. Zdonik and D. Maier, editors, *Readings in Object-Oriented Databases*, pages 1–32. Morgan-Kaufman Publ. Co., 89.

PRINCIPLES OF KNOWLEDGE AUGMENTED VISUAL DATABASES

Matthias Rhiner

Multimedia Laboratory
Department of Computer Science
University of Zurich
Winterthurerstr. 190
CH-8057 Zurich

Advanced Software Systems
IBM Switzerland
Gartenstr. 19
Postbox
CH-8022 Zurich

ABSTRACT

Visual media such as graphics and images are of increasing importance for various application types. These media often contain a considerable amount of *implicit* information that is fast and easily perceptible for human cognition. But this implicit information may be very difficult to be accessed by methods of electronic data processing. In order to reduce this *semantic gap* special techniques must be provided to establish *logical* and *physical links* between implicit information and *explicit representation* forms of it. This paper presents a method of augmenting visual objects with additional visual and textual descriptive knowledge in a logical and user interface independent way. The so called *virtual visual objects* resulting from this process are organized in a *knowledge augmented visual database* system. In this way visual data can consistently be accessed and used by different applications, without primary impact of physical constraints given by a specific application environment.

KEYWORDS

Visual databases, visual object description, visual object representation, visual knowledge representation

1. INTRODUCTION

Manifold progress in the domains of knowledge engineering, of hardware and software techniques is a challenging basis for the development of increasingly complex application systems. Modern development methods (4th generation languages, knowledge based system techniques), advanced subsystems (databases, communication) and sophisticated, visually supported user interfaces (windowing, graphics, images) make part of an integrated complex application environment.

Application support by *visual means* is one of the most impressive features in this kind of advanced software systems. *Visual representation* of crucial facts can considerably enhance the interaction with users in complex application domains. Important keywords in this context are: Ease and speed of *cognition*, clarity and associative impacts resulting from *visual apprehension*. These advantages are highly favored in interactive visual user interfaces (VUI).

It is a major requirement to support complex application types (e.g. knowledge based systems) by the integration of visual information components. But many of the advantages related with the usage of visual information are balanced by its rather difficult handling. Images, for example, may contain a very high, fast conceivable, implicit information content with regard to human viewers. But they contain none or almost none directly usable information content (explicit information representation) with regard to the requirements of electronic data processing. There has been a long tradition to automate the process of pattern and feature recognition and there are continuing tendencies with the target of automation in image understanding. But these techniques are still not applicable in a general way, except for acceptable results in very restricted and dedicated areas [1,2]. Therefore it is still a main task in the development of visually supported applications to find general methods for an *explicit knowledge representation* and integration of visual objects.

The following sections will explain concepts and techniques applicable to the domain of explicit visual object representation. Section 2 will motivate the use of databases for a common management of visual objects. Section 3 shows general requirements and consequences for the integration of visual data objects in different application environments. As a result of these requirements section 4 will introduce the concepts of *virtual visual objects* and their management in *knowledge augmented visual databases*. Section 5 finally outlines a system architecture that allows the communication and information exchange between knowledge augmented visual databases and different target applications or visual user interfaces by the means of virtual visual objects.

2. CONCEPTS OF VISUAL DATABASES

Modern application types are increasingly supported by visual techniques. Mainly graphics and images have become substantial components in a variety of application domains. But in many cases their usage is directly and uniquely related with a specific application. That means that a specifically prepared and dedicated visual object is presented within a predefined application step. This action is completely driven by the content of a controlling application. Usually there is nor object related *structural data* nor any *contextual knowledge* contained within the visual object itself.

In many application scenarios it would be interesting to profit from reusable, structured visual objects that can be embedded in different, independent processing and end-user interaction environments. Such visual objects should be organized in a globally accessible way and descriptive attributes must be assigned for this purpose. These attributes define physical and logical properties that are relevant for a general and flexible usage of the visual objects. Logical relations and methods for the physical object composition and decomposition must be exactly defined in the case of complex objects. Visual objects containing such descriptive and structural attributes will be called *knowledge augmented virtual visual objects* (KaVVO) or just virtual visual objects (VVO) within this paper. For the purpose of general accessibility and reusability knowledge augmented visual objects will be organized within existing database schemes which satisfy traditional database requirements such as consistency, multiuser access etc. Databases supporting the concepts of KaVVO will be called *knowledge augmented visual databases* (KaVDB).

Summarizing the main facts proprietary to visual objects, it can be stated that in many cases there is primarily only an implicit mental, association between visual objects and other objects (e.g. text, data tables, further visual objects etc.) related to them. In order to make these associations more explicit, two major activities have to be performed: Explicit logical correlations must be defined, and physical properties (e.g. positional and spatial correlations) of visual objects must be exposed and formalized. These tasks must be performed with regard to object integration in a generally accessible database and can be considered as a process of explicit *knowledge representation* or even *knowledge augmentation* for visual objects.

3. VISUAL DATABASE and VISUAL USER INTERFACE

In the preceding section it has been stated that usually there is a need for explicit definitions in order to integrate and link visual objects with an existing application frame consisting of conventional data types, such as text and data tables. In most cases this process must be done in a completely 'manual' way. This means that there are only few special cases where support of automatic methods can be used (e.g. mass processing of similar objects using a dedicated feature extraction and description algorithm). As a consequence the description and integration of visual objects is a very time consuming and expensive task. Therefore methods must be found in order to make 'manually' acquired and structured knowledge available to a broad range of target applications.

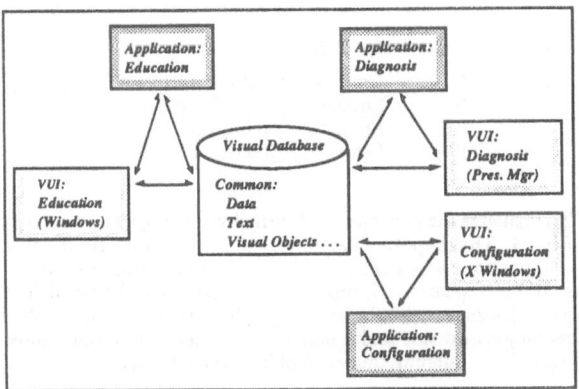

Fig.1   Database - Application - VUI Structure

As a practical example, the description of a complex engine shall be cited. This description may consist of text, data tables, images and graphical schemata. This information should be organized so that all the logical and physical relations are visualized in a problem adequate way. Knowledge structured to suffice these principles, will allow that the same set of textual and related visual information can be made accessible to different target applications. As a consequence it will be possible to implement different applications such as a configuration system (assembling the engine), a diagnosis system (finding defective parts) or an educational system (teaching the internals of the engine) using the same visual database as a kernel component for the various applications.

The aspect of reusing visual objects for different target applications and probably different VUIs brings up the topic of *object representation*. In the case of visual objects there are not only logical properties such as descriptors and references but also *physical attributes* such as dimensions (image x-size, y-size), positions (textual annotation at <xt, yt>), or pure format data (image I is of type RGB, TIFF). These physical properties must be considered for the final object instantiation in a specific target VUI, but for all the intermediate steps of object and database definitions, the logical characteristics are the decisive ones.

Referring to the example of a visual database, containing data, images, and graphics for an engine description, the following scenario can be assumed: As shown in Fig.1, different applications and VUIs (e.g. Windows™, Presentation Manager™, X-Windows) are accessing the visual database. Several of these applications may have a certain program step where a basic image, showing a specific part of the engine, is presented to the user. This image may be overlaid by a graphical schema, emphasizing the contours of some specific parts, and annotation texts describing important features.

In this scenario visual data objects and positionally dependent textual objects are mapped from a visual database to a specific VUI. The process of mapping visual objects involves different conceptual steps: In a first step it is a pure logical operation to retrieve the relevant basic image, the related graphics and annotation texts from the database. In a second step, logical and physical aspects must be considered. All spatial and positional correlations that exist between visual objects in a common context have to be adjusted (specially if overlay techniques are used). In a third and final step, the actual mapping to the destination VUI, that means rendering the physical object components within a specific presentation environment, must be performed.

The different steps, objects and methods necessary to fulfil this process of object mapping (dependent on object descriptions and object related operations) must be defined in a KaVDB. There are various approaches that can be applied to organize objects, descriptive and operational data within a database (see Fig. 2).

a) Program-Oriented

All steps necessary to retrieve visual data and construct the target object are explicitly embedded in a dedicated application program which manages database accesses, object retrieving and object handling. There is no or only very few descriptive information, concerning object characteristics, stored in the database. Most of the structural knowledge is bound to dedicated program code and has primarily no external appearance. The database mainly contains the visual objects and some, related secondary data. The target application retrieves data objects from the database (e.g. O1)

b) Encapsulated Object-Oriented

In this case the database contains objects and methods operating on them. For an application program or a VUI this means that not all the process steps for object handling must be performed at a basic level. Rather, objects and methods can be accessed and used at a conceptually higher level. For example, there might be a method defining how to retrieve and compose all components of a more complex structure, and there might be a method for representing this object in a specific VUI. This approach is based on the advanced concept that general methods (e.g. for logical object reconstruction) must be defined only once and that they must be closely related to respective object classes. A target application retrieves both, objects and methods for the usage in its environment (e.g. O1 and M11).

In this approach most of the knowledge concerning object structure and behavior is stored in the database. The information is encapsulated in the sense of pure object-oriented concepts. For the problem of representing the same object in different target VUIs it means that dedicated methods are necessary for all different environments.

c) Declarative Object-Oriented

In this approach objects and methods are represented in an open and declarative way. This means that there are object- and method-declarations, entirely defined within open database elements (e.g table rows in relational databases). These declarations, defined in a homogeneous and consistent way, represent a kind of *metalanguage* that can be interpreted in any application or VUI. The target application now retrieves object, object declarations and method declarations from the database (e.g. O1, DO1, DM11).

Compared to the previous approaches this is the most open one. The crucial idea of objects and related methods has been preserved, but the concept of hidden encapsulation has given up for the enhancement of full reusability of objects and methods within completely heterogeneous environments.

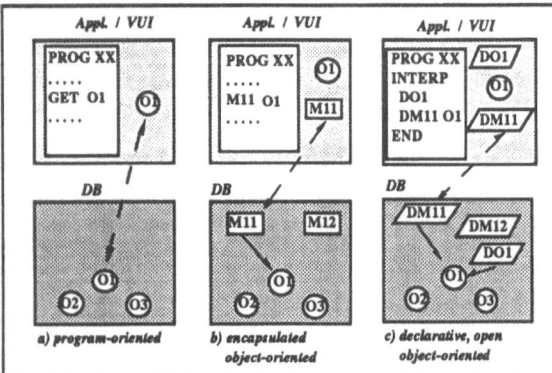

Fig. 2 Conceptual Approaches

All the approaches shown in Fig. 2 have special advantages and disadvantages. Various factors such as openness, reusability,

overhead for object reconstruction and representation, consistency control and performance are decisive factors for the implementation of real systems. Principally there are no theoretical limitations that prevent from combining concepts of the different approaches. There are even reasons that might justify the parallel usage of various concepts. For example, a combined program-oriented and declarative description might considerably increase application flexibility and performance, but may contemporarily have a negative impact on data consistency and redundancy.

The contemplations in the following sections will be dominated by the requirements of open object and method declarations with main regard to reusing of structural knowledge and special consideration of logical and physical object representation.

4. VIRTUAL VISUAL OBJECTS

This section concentrates on a structure and representation description for complex visual objects. For the beginning two formal definitions are given:

Visual Atoms: A = {A$_l$ | A$_l$ is a basic visual object}

> visual atoms are basic, physical, representable objects (e.g. single pixel, image, graphical primitiva, graphical object, metafile)

> they may be structured (e.g. graphical rectangle consisting of four lines defined in a metafile (GKS), but none of these lines is stored or accessible as an individual database element)

> they have no externally visible or referable sub-parts

> they are always declared and referenced as *one logical database entity* (e.g. lines in rectangle above can be interpreted only within the context of the whole GKS file)

Virtual Visual Objects: V = {V$_l$ | V$_l$ is a composite of V$_j$ ε V and A$_j$ ε A}

Virtual visual objects are composites of other virtual visual objects and/or atoms.

By extending the view of virtual objects beyond the range of object components alone, a VVO can be defined by the following tupel:

$$V_l = <C_{vl}, S_{vl}, M_{vl}, D_{vl}>$$

where	C_{vi} :	$\underline{C}$omponents (atoms, virtual objects) of V_i
	S_{vi} :	$\underline{S}$tructural Declaration of V_i
	M_{vi} :	$\underline{M}$ethods operating on V_i
	D_{vi} :	Secondary $\underline{D}$escription of V_i

To visualize the conception of virtual visual objects we refer to Fig. 3. The hypothetical object shown in this figure is a composite VVO with a symbolic identification V0. In its intuitive appearance it represents an image consisting of four parts that are overlaid by several graphical structures (the dashed rectangles do not make part of the object; they only show logical, surrounding frames of object components).

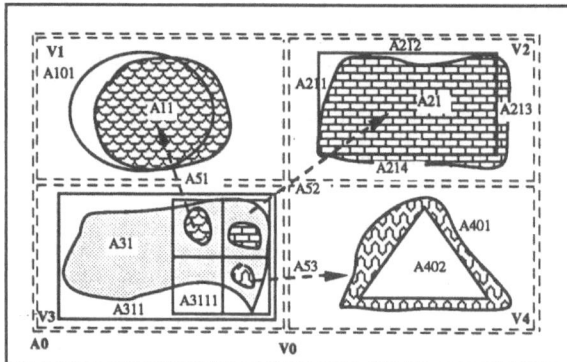

Fig. 3 Virtual Visual Object Example

In a more structural view the object V0, shown in Fig. 3, is composed by the following components:

A0 : Empty, abstract frame defining the dimensions of the whole object (outer dashed rectangle).
It will be referenced by all sub-objects for spatial and positional relations.

V1 - V4 : Four composite VVOs of different structure and level depth, making up disjoint, independent parts of the final composite object

V5 : An overlaid virtual object consisting of 3 graphical arrows, establishing a visual and mental correlation between V3 and V1, V2, V4

Mapped to a symbolic tree structure the virtual visual object V0 has the appearance shown in Fig. 4. This tree structure reflects the object composition by other virtual objects and atoms. It also shows that atoms may appear at different levels in similar structures.

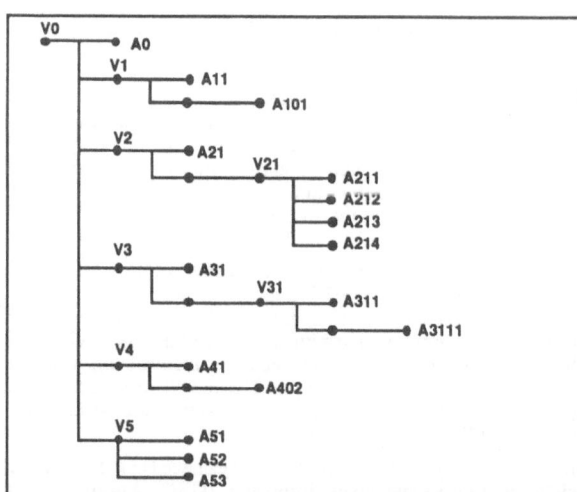

Fig. 4 Virtual Visual Object Structure

The object structure can also be declared in a more formal way. In this representation form there is a local physical view of object V0. Therefore, the parameters $<P_{xA0}, P_{yA0}>$ for effective object positioning and $<S_{xA0}, S_{yA0}>$ for object dimensions can be considered as undefined $<*,*>$ until the object is set in an inherited spatial context. All positions related with components of V0 are based on these reference coordinates. The frame size $<S_{xA0}, S_{yA0}>$ determines logical dimensions which are used as a reference coordinate system for all internal structures and for all sub-components. Again, these dimensions and all depending ones are actually assigned and adjusted only at the time when the virtual object is transformed into a real instantiation.

OId	CId	Lev	RefPosition	FrameSize	
V0	A0	0	$<P_{xA0}, P_{yA0}>$	$<S_{xA0}, S_{yA0}>$	
	V1	1	$<P_{xA0}, P_{yA0}+S_{yA0}/2>$	$<S_{xA0}/2, S_{yA0}/2>$	
	V2	1	$<P_{xA0}+S_{xA0}/2, P_{yA0}+S_{yA0}/2>$	$<S_{xA0}/2, S_{yA0}/2>$	
	V3	1	$<P_{xA0}, P_{yA0}>$	$<S_{xA0}/2, S_{yA0}/2>$	
	V4	1	$<P_{xA0}, P_{yA0}+S_{yA0}//2>$	$<S_{xA0}/2, S_{yA0}/2>$	
	V5	1	$<P_{xA0}+O_{xV5}, P_{yA0}+O_{ýV5}>$	$<S_{xA0}*Q_{xV5}, S_{yV5}*Q_{yA0}>$	

Table 1   Virtual Visual Object Representation

The description scheme for a subordinated VVO is done exactly in the same way. Again, any sub-objects must primarily be considered independent objects. All internal relations are coded in a relative way referring to position and dimension parameters that are dynamically determined by values inherited from a dominating VVO instantiation.

This method of object structuring can be evaluated from a logical and a physical point of view.

In a mainly physical sense:

Without adding much more information, this formal object declaration can be used as input code for an interpreter in a VUI which translates logical object declarations into a physical object representation (object rendering). It is the main advantage of this kind of object declaration that it does not refer to any absolute physical properties but only contains a relative and logical representation form of them. The interpreter in the respective VUI is responsible for the correct mapping of logical correlations to their physical appearance.

In a combined physical and logical sense:

The definition of virtual objects, as shown in table 1, is very flexible with respect to changes or extensions. For example, a different logical emphasis can be put on virtual object V0 by replacing the physical structure V5 (arrows indicating logical relations) or by adding an additional graphical overlay V6 that aims to visualize other object relations.

The spatial aspects and relations expressed in the formal object representation may be relevant information for different purposes. Depending from a specific application context it may

268

be interesting to know which objects VL are situated to the left of an object Vx, and which objects VO are overlapping Vx.

In a mainly logical sense:

The selected form of object representation corresponds to a open and declarative approach, as mentioned before. Therefore it is not only useable for the rendering process of objects in a visual representation form but for any purpose that needs insight into the logical object structure (e.g. dependency of object components for a configuration application). For this reason, the declarative object definition may also be considered and used as a form of *logical* and *structural knowledge representation* for the description of complex, static visual scenarios. This aspect is even reinforced if we additionally use the classical, contextual object attributes (descriptors, references, links) that can be assigned to both, atomic and virtual objects.

The definition of virtual visual objects, as presented in this section, reflects many of the problems related with visual object representation that are known in the respective literature. Primarily there is the discrepancy between logical and physical objects [3], secondarily there are the requirements resulting from complex, composite structures, and finally there is the challenge of different, heterogeneous environments [4] that can at least partially be explained and solved by the means of a consistent model for visual object description and representation.

5. SYSTEM ARCHITECTURE

An open and declarative definition of virtual visual objects is very essential for application dependent processing of VVOs and their final representation in the environment of a dedicated VUI. A knowledge augmented visual database is the repository where all the physical and logical objects and their correlations can be stored, accessed and retrieved.

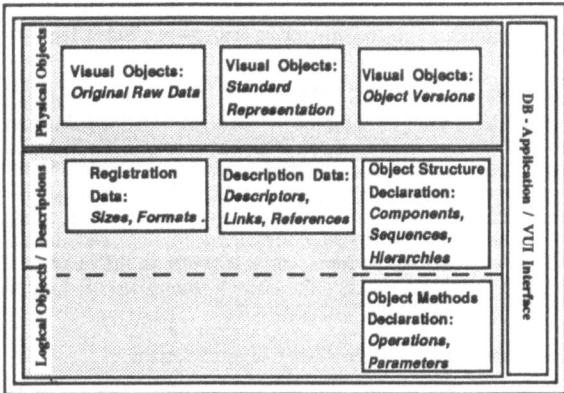

Fig. 5 Visual Database Internals

Physical components cover atomic objects such as images, for example in a pure canonical form (RGB bytemaps) or in a formatted metafile form (e.g. TIFF files). There may be several versions of the same object (e.g original raw data, and transformed versions to a format most commonly used).

Registration data (basic attributes of objects), descriptive data (object descriptors, references), structural information (structure of virtual objects), and operational descriptions (object method declarations) are organized in the logical part of the visual database .

An interpreter and transformation process, proprietary to a specific VUI, is required for the integration and "materialization" of a logical object in its final representation environment. In a first step the virtual visual object declaration must be interpreted, dissolved into sub-components and mapped into VUI internal, proprietary data and process structures. In a second step the respective physical objects must be retrieved from the database and (possibly) be transformed to the final form necessary (e.g. image format conversions such as TIFF -> TARGA™, scaling operations) for specific requirements within a VUI. Such transformations may be performed on the side of the DB-server, in an intermediate step between DB and VUI, or within the VUI itself, depending on the specificity or generality of the transformation purposes.

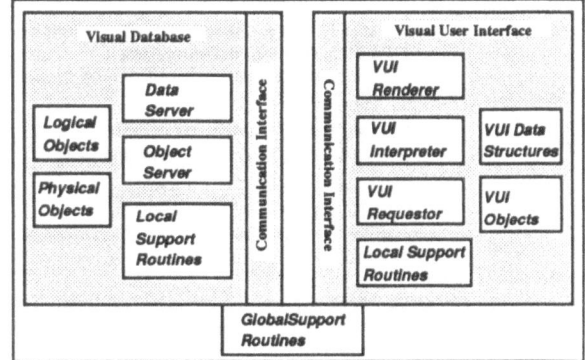

Fig. 6 System Architecture

6. IMPLEMENTATIONAL APPROACHES

The presented concepts of visual virtual objects, their impact on knowledge augmented visual databases and on interpretative visual user interfaces are not bound to a specific implementation environment. The necessary data structures can be mapped to relational or object oriented database systems without violating any fundamental concepts. In any of the two database models there are special features that can be exploited to optimize certain application components.

Several feasibility tests have been made within a relational database environment (OS/2 Database Manager™). Availability and broad, on-going experiences [e.g.5, 6] made with relational models are an important argument for the choice of a relational basis because there has never been the intent of this work to define a new extended relational DB model or object server concept. But future tests within object oriented environments (e.g. ONTOS™) shall not be excluded.

In a similar way certain feasibility studies have been done on the side of the visual user interface (OS/2 Audio Visual Connection™, a very fast programmable, interpretative, visual prototyping environment). Again, other visual user interfaces must be considered to test the concept of a general reusability of virtual visual objects in heterogeneous environments. More information concerning the experimental environment can be found in [7].

7. CRITICISM AND OUTLOOK

A concept of virtual visual elements that build the kernel for knowledge augmented visual databases has been presented in this paper. A special focus was set on the basic definition and structure of these objects that help to overcome the semantic gap between the implicit content of visual information and an external, explicit representation form of it. At this point of the on-going work a *static* solution has been developed which allows to describe the dualism of logical and physical object representation with respect to object storage, object processing and object rendering.

For the future, the additional knowledge correlated with visual objects can be exploited in a much more extensive way. As mentioned before, the structural and logical object knowledge can be accessed whenever there is a need to retrieve details concerning object structures and object correlations.

For other purposes, explicitly represented object knowledge and correlated methods should also serve in a more active way. Therefore this purpose *active methods* operating on the virtual objects must be defined in an open and declarative way for a generally applicable usage in various, heterogeneous environments. These methods will allow to extend currently static, virtual visual objects with *active, dynamic* and *temporal* features.

REFERENCES

[1] T. Kato et al. : *"Visual Interaction with Electronic Art Gallery"*; Proceedings of the International Conference on Databases and Expert Systems Applications, DEXA 1990, in Vienna; Springer Verlag Wien New York, 1990; pp. 234-240.

[2] T. Kato et al. : *"A Cognitive Approach to Visual Interaction"*; Proceedings of the International Conference on Multimedia Information Systems '91, Singapore; McGraw-Hill Publishing Company, 1991; pp. 109-120.

[3] S.-K.Chang: *"Principles of Pictorial Information Systems Design"*, Prentice Hall International Editions, Englewood Cliffs, 1989.

[4] W. Klas et al. : *"Visual Databases need Data Models for Multimedia Data"*; in: [8]; pp. 433-462.

[5] K. Meyer-Wegener: *"Image Management in a Multimedia Database System"*, in: [8]; pp. 497-523.

[6] H. Schütt et N. Streitz: *"HyperBase: A hypermedia engine based on a relational data-base management system"*, Proceedings of the first European Conference on Hypertext, ed. A. Rizk et al., INRIA, France, November 1990; Cambridge University Press, Cambridge 1990; pp. 95-108.

[7] M. Rhiner: *"Concepts of Integrating Visual Databases and Expert Systems"*, in: A.M. Tjoa and R. Wagner eds., Proceedings of the International Conference on Database and Expert Systems Applications, DEXA 1990 in Vienna; Springer Verlag Wien NewYork, 1990; pp. 474-478.

[8] Kunii T.L. ed.: *"Visual Database Systems"*, Proceedings of the IFIP TC 2/WG 2.6 Working Conference on Visual Database Systems, Tokyo, Japan, 3-7 April 1989; NORTH-HOLLAND, 1989.

Relationship Abstractions for an Effective Hypertext Design: Augmentation and Globalization

Yoshinori Hara [*]

Arthur M. Keller [†]

Gio Wiederhold [‡]

NEC Corporation
and
Stanford University [§]

Advanced Decision Systems
and
Stanford University [§]

Stanford University [§]

Abstract

Data abstractions, i.e., aggregation and generalization, are useful for representing complex objects effectively. They provide high level semantic constraints as well as extend the capabilities of entity description in the E-R model. However, corresponding concepts of relationship abstraction are not directly available, particularly in hypertext systems.

We propose two types of relationship abstractions, *augmentation* and *globalization*, aiming at the improvement of relationship design phases. The former is an abstraction which turns information held in relationships into that of attributes for existing entities. The latter is an abstraction which generates global-to-local relationship hierarchies. We show the advantages of these abstractions.

1 Introduction

Hypertext and hypermedia [YHMD88, Hala88, HaKa88, etc.] are based on a network or a graph data structure, as are semantic networks [Quil68, LeMy79] and some aspects of the structural model [Wied83]. Two advantages of graph models are navigational access and their associative connection strategy. Navigation has the potential to support users to get target information from ill-structured information spaces. Navigation is one of the most useful retrieval clues for hypermedia, since multimedia objects are essentially composed of non-specific attributes. The connection strategy is also useful for an individual user, because he or she can easily relate objects together without the requirement of specifying a database schema. This rough but simple strategy enables users to handle heterogeneous objects homogeneously in such fields as personal, office, and educational information systems.

However, recent contributions to hypertext systems depend highly on hardware/software progress and the extension of hypertext functionalities. There are very few design strategies for hypertext systems, i.e., how to organize hypertext structures effectively [JoMa90]. Consequently, whether the hypertext structures are well organized or not depends highly on the individual designer's skill [Niel90].

As for conceptual database design, several well-formulated models have been proposed in order to provide the effective mapping into the target structures. The concept of database abstractions [SmSm77] is one of the most useful ways of thinking to capture the high level semantics Two abstraction concepts, i.e., *aggregation* and *generalization*, are widely used in the object-oriented databases [ABDD89], the semantic databases[HuKi87], etc. However, they are not concerned about relationship abstraction as much, which is more essential in hypertext or other network-based knowledge representation models.

This paper proposes the relationship abstractions to support hypertext design phases. They are *augmentation* and *globalization*, which are the extension of aggregation and generalization, respectively. We show the advantages of these abstractions by using an example of a movie database.

Section 2 describes the concept of database abstractions and its problems. In Section 3, we propose a model of relationship abstractions by extending the database abstractions. Section 4 presents a hypertext design strategy using our model. In Section 5, we discuss other possible application fields such as schema integrations and visual interfaces.

2 Database Abstractions

The concept of database abstractions is a fundamental model to incorporate real world semantics into computational forms. Similar concepts are also widely used in AI and software engineering fields as well. We describe a summary of database abstractions.

2.1 Aggregation

Aggregation refers to an abstraction in which related attributes in an object are regarded as a higher level attribute. In the relational model, it is an abstraction which integrates vertical elements in a relation, i.e., attributes. In other words, the type of an attribute is extended to a more complex structure and users can capture these attributes in any levels of abstraction.

Attributes can be organized as an aggregation hierarchy using "is-part-of" relation. In the case that an aggregated attribute is for the composition of objects, we obtain a *composite object* [WoKi87]. In the structural model [Wied83], *ownership relation* can be treated as aggregation.

Usually, an aggregation hierarchy is defined such that there is no inheritance mechanism between lower level and upper level of abstractions. However, *property inheritance*, i.e., a bottom-up inheritance, can be executed in some systems in order to provide information of a higher level based on that of lower levels.

---

[*]e-mail address: hara@eclipse.stanford.edu

[†]e-mail address: ark@eclipse.stanford.edu

[‡]e-mail address: gio@cs.stanford.edu

[§]Authors' address: Department of Computer Science, Stanford University, Stanford, CA 94305-2140, U.S.A.

Aggregation is useful because it has the capability for different users to access objects at different levels of abstractions. It contributes to raising the flexibility in a utilization phase as well as to providing the extensibility in a design phase. However, this contribution is mainly to the extension of entity description in the E-R model.

2.2 Generalization

Generalization refers to an abstraction in which objects having common attributes are regarded as a generic object. In the relational model, it is an abstraction which integrates the common attributes in horizontal elements in a relation, i.e., tuples. In the object-oriented model, this abstraction is represented as a superclass-subclass relation.

A set of tuples can be organized as a generalization hierarchy using "is-a" relation. The inverse operation of generalization is called *specialization*. In the structural model, *subset relation* can be treated as generalization.

Compared with aggregation, there is a (top-down) inheritance mechanism in the generalization hierarchy. That is, the attributes in an upper level are common, so that they inherit to its lower levels. If the attribute name is the same in both levels, the value of the attribute in the lowest level is used.

Generalization is useful because it provides a high level semantic structure and its compact representation. It also contributes to the information usability both in a utilization phase and in a design phase. However, it is mainly focused on the complex structures of entities in the E-R model.

2.3 An example

Let us consider the design of a database of information about movies in order to illustrate the example of aggregation and generalization. Figure 1 shows an example of abstractions on the relational model. We can recognize how these abstractions are organized.

Note that we are not concerned with the abstraction for relationships. If we concerned about the relationship abstraction as shown in Fig. 2, they are aggregated as one aggregated object or decomposed into two many-to-one relationships. A more precise semantic structure for relationships is not yet available.

2.4 Other types of abstractions

There are some other types of abstractions besides aggregation and generalization. They are versions, time abstractions, etc. They are useful particularly for such specific applications as CASE and CAD. However, since they depend on specific semantics, these issues are beyond the scope of this paper.

3 Relationship Abstractions

In this section, we extend the concept of abstraction for relationships in the E-R model. It is similarly applicable for *associative links* in the hypertext, i.e., self relationships in the E-R model.

An objective of relationship abstraction is to prevent excess relationships. The excess causes not only a decrease in the efficiency of navigation, but also a deterioration of the semantics of relationships. As a result, the usability of hypertext information may be decreased.

Another objective of relationship abstraction is to capture high level semantic structures in a relationship. It contributes to providing fruitful queries.

3.1 The properties of a relationship

Let us consider the properties of a relationship first. Its properties are different from those of an entity, although both of them can be represented as an equivalent form in the relational model. As shown in Fig. 3, the different properties are as follows:

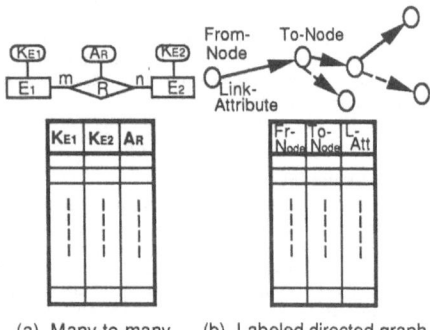

(a) Many-to-many relationship (b) Labeled directed graph

Fig. 3 The properties of a relationship

(1) The key of relationship relation R_R is the combination of two foreign keys.

The relation of relationship R_R consists of three attributes. Two of them are foreign keys of corresponding entity relations R_{E_1}, R_{E_2}. The other is an attribute of the relationship or an aggregation attribute of the relationship. Due to having foreign keys, the existence of relationships is affected by the updating of corresponding entity relations.

A labeled directed graph can be equally represented except that the relevant element sets are disjoint or not. The first two attributes are input and output node IDs. They are considered to be foreign keys. The remaining is the attribute of link types.

(2) The number of attributes in a relationship relation is few.

The number of attributes in a relationship relation is relatively fewer than that in an entity relation. There are less semantic structures in the relationship relation. Therefore, it is difficult to specify useful semantic constraints such as functional dependencies.

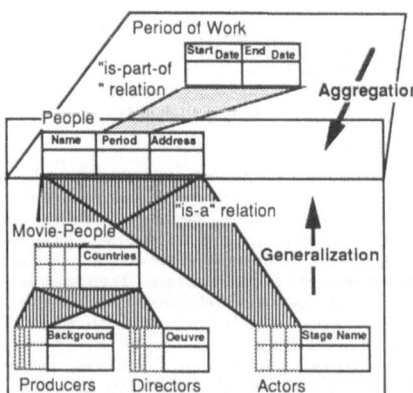

Fig. 1 Aggregation and Generalization

Fig. 2 A Many-to-Many Relationship

(3) The number of tuples in a relationship relation is relatively large.

The number of tuples in a relationship relation is on the order of the product of the number of tuples in the corresponding entity relations. In other words, the number of tuples in a relationship relation turns out to be much larger than that in an ordinary entity relation, particularly when the relationship becomes complex.

3.2 Problems of previous works

Two problems arise when we apply database abstractions to relationship relations. One is that aggregation has little meaning for relationship abstraction. This is because the number of attributes in a relationship is so few that there is little need for aggregation.

The other problem is that generalization cannot be directly applied to relationship abstraction. Except in some trivial cases, generalization is mainly focused on a class of entity objects into a generic object. Even when it is applied to a relationship, this operation is only the separation of tuples in the relationship relation.

3.3 Requirements for relationship abstraction

In order to improve relationship design and maintenance phases, we set out the following three requirements for relationship abstraction. We must extend database abstractions in order to satisfy the requirements.

Firstly, one of the essential potentials of abstraction is to translate information into a more compact representation. This involves more than the separation of information. Secondly, regardless of which operations we apply, the decomposed structures have the same information as its original information. On the other hand, the reorganized structure has no redundancy nor inconsistency compared with its original information. Thirdly, each portion of an abstracted structure can be named. That is, the abstracted relationship structure can be connected to the real world semantics.

3.4 Augmentation

There are some *visible* and *hidden* meanings in relationship attributes or link types. Let us consider a simple example of a relationship between actors/actresses and the movies they cast. This relationship is a many-to-many connection, and its relationship name is simply "casts in." However, there are several meanings behind it. The reason why an actor or an actress casts in a movie may be caused by his or her affiliation, the conductor's character of the movie, etc. These attributes often make a relationship between entities.

Augmentation proposed here is a relationship abstraction which turns information held in relationships into attributes in the corresponding entities, as illustrated in Fig. 4. It is a decomposition or an aggregation of attributes, i.e., a vertical operation which is similar to aggregation described in Section 2. However, since such a primitive attribute is related to a possible entity attribute, we can substitute the relationship information for the entity attributes and the relationship among them. This substitution often produces a more compact representation of relationship, since a real world relationship is correlated.

Several methods for augmentation can be applicable. *ACE clustering* [HaKW91] is one of them. It is a clustering method considering exceptions. A relationship relation can be turned into new attributes of entities given by the clustering. The number of the attribute values is smaller than that of original relationships.

Once we get the attributes, the original relationships can be calculated by join operation or the function between the attributes. Therefore, we recognize the reason caused by the entity attributes that makes the relationships between the entities.

Following is a summary of possible patterns for augmentation.

(1) Translated attribute types

One possible translation is that the information of relationships can be turned to some existing entity attributes, called *visible attributes*. When there is a strong correlation between relationships and some of the existing attributes, we can set them out as visible attributes.

Otherwise, we have to consider another reason that makes relationships be organized. Namely, the information of relationships can be turned to some non-existing entity attributes, called *hidden attributes*. They can be extracted by clustering the elements of entities.

(2) Mapping patterns

There are three types of mapping patterns between relationships and entity attributes. One is *overlapping mapping*, which is a many-to-many mapping between relationship elements and target attribute values. Another is *non-overlapping mapping with exceptions*, which is a many-to-one mapping from a relationship element to a target attribute value, e.g., clustering number, allowing some exceptions. The other is *recursive non-overlapping mapping*, which is plural many-to-many mappings between relationships and entity attributes. It is organized as the same attribute hierarchy as aggregation.

The most practical mapping is the second case, i.e., the non-overlapping mapping with exceptions. ACE clustering is an efficient method to organize this mapping.

(3) The relationship among attribute values

Two possible relationships among attribute values can be set out as an alternative representation for the original relationship information. The same attribute value means the simplest representation of relationship. The second simplest one is that there can be set out a relationship between two attribute values. In other cases, such translations are useless, because they turn out to be a more complex representation of relationships.

3.5 Globalization

The second relationship abstraction is defined by the degree of globality in a relationship relation. Some relationships are treated as global structures, and some are only effective within local structures. A local structure is, in other words, represented as the compensated information of its global structure. Therefore, we can organize a global-to-local relationship hierarchy, which is similar to the generalization-specialization hierarchy described in Section 2.

Globalization is a relationship abstraction which generates the global-to-local relationship hierarchy, as shown in Fig. 5. It is a grouping operation for tuples in a relationship relation, i.e., a horizontal operation similar to generalization. Since relationships in an upper level can inherit to its lower levels, relationships in the lower levels obey those in the upper level unless there is a concrete description of relationships in the lower levels.

Globalization is different from generalization by following two points. One is that the attribute in globalization is invariant and only its attribute values may

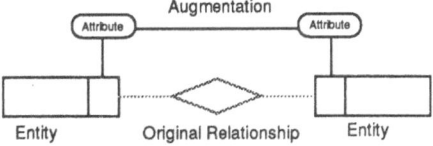

Fig. 4 Augmentation

change. In this meaning, the global-to-local relationship hierarchy is similar to the exception relationship hierarchy. The other point is that the instance of globalization can appear in any levels. On the other hand, the instance of generalization appears only in the lowest level.

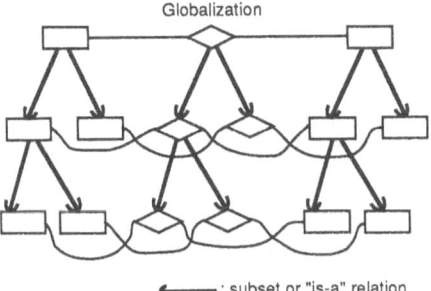

Fig. 5 Globalization

3.6 An example: A movie database

Let us consider the design of a movie database in order to illustrate the example of augmentation and globalization. Figure 6 shows an example of abstractions on the relational model. The original relationships can be translated into the attributes of each entity, and its subclasses.

We are evaluating such clusterings for a movie database with 6250 movies, 5300 actors/actresses, 22000 cast entries, and 1450 directors. Some of the "casts in" relationships can be substituted by the directors and the movie categories such as horror, drama, etc.

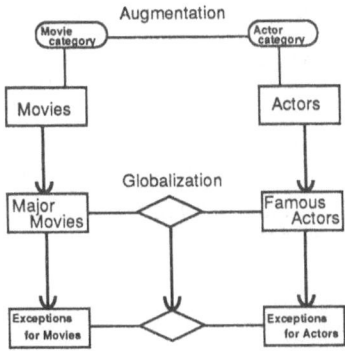

Fig. 6 An Example of Relationship Abstractions

4 A Strategy for Making Effective Hypertext Structures

In this section, we discuss a hypertext design strategy using the relationship abstractions. Hypertext systems are categorized by several viewpoints, such as scope of the user target (single or collaborative), browsing versus authoring, and task specificity [Hala88]. Here we discuss the improvement of design phases for single hypertext systems, which may be the basic component for other systems.

4.1 A hypertext design process

We have been developed several hypertext/hypermedia prototypes, such as an electronic filing system [KaHa86], an electronic encyclopedia for fine arts [HaKa88], and the PENGUIN system [BaCW89], which aims to combine database facilities with a hypertext interface. From the experiences gained with these systems, a design process for making effective hypertext structures can be set out as following five steps.

(1) Macro framework design and the focus of materials

Initially, a hypertext designer specifies a macro framework of the target system. It consists of global node structures, the relationships among them, and the focus of materials. The framework is, as it were, an implicit semantic constraint imposed on individual nodes and links.

It is important to specify the focus in the structure such as key nodes and key path sequences. They represent the author's intention, and readers are guided to read the materials according to the guidance. Otherwise, a hypertext structure is only like a complicated web.

(2) Node design

Secondly, individual nodes are specified. In this phase, the concept of database abstraction is helpful to organize nodes, as described in Section 2. A hierarchy of "is-a" relationship is also useful when combining the internal data structure with the objects seen at the human interface. When dealing with hypermedia, we also have to consider the medium to represent nodes for target objects and their access clues.

(3) Link design : a bottom-up organization

Then, relationships among the nodes are specified. There are several link types, such as *static link, dynamic link,* and *virtual link* [HaKa90]. Almost all of them are based on a bottom-up organization. That is, links are locally organized and the whole hypertext structure is formulated as a result. This linking strategy is an essential point to create a hypertext system and to maintain it.

(4) Evaluation of global consistency

An important point for good design is a feedback evaluation in any phases. In particular, the comparison between the macro framework and the link design is the most important to improve the usability of hypertext structures. However, it depends highly on the designer's skill, since there is no effective method to specify the consistency.

Of course, there are some practical rules to prevent excess links and to exclude useless links. One is to eliminate the indirect relationships from the structure, which are calculated as a transitive closure. Another method is to set out an attribute of link priority according to the user's interest. However, there is not an effective method to analyze the link design.

(5) Restructuring

The last one is a restructuring phase in order to incorporate the node/link design with the macro framework. By restructuring, a hidden but important structure may be clear, as well as the author's intention is more emphasized. When a hypertext system is larger, the evaluation and the restructuring phases are much necessary.

4.2 A design strategy using relationship abstractions

Relationship abstractions are helpful for the evaluation phase. They show an easier way to compare the link design with the macro framework. In some cases, they can automatically detect the differences between them and provide an alternative design.

Relationship abstractions are useful when the designer cannot specify the constraints in a relationship at the designing phase. The designer can recognize the constraints and improve the structure by analyzing the data. This bottom-up organization will contribute to providing an effective hypertext structure.

5 Other Applications for Relationship Abstractions

In this section, we briefly discuss other applications for relationship abstractions.

Firstly, since relationships can be organized as a higher level structure, it is possible to apply for schema integration in a collaborative environment. Usually, an individual user has his or her own view and it is difficult to integrate the whole structure. However, some common attributes are extracted by the abstractions, so that these attributes may be teated as a basis for schema integration.

Secondly, relationship abstractions can apply to improve the visual interface for recognizing large information spaces. That is, the potential exists for creating overview diagrams based on the abstractions, which are graphical browsers using aggregation. They are very important when the information space is too large for every node and link to be shown on a single map [Niel90].

6 Conclusion

We have presented the two types of relationship abstractions to improve relationship design phases. Augmentation is an abstraction which turns information held in relationship into that of attributes for existing entities. Intuitively, it is a translation of individual relationships into more stable states, since entities are likely to exist longer than relationships. Globalization is an abstraction which generates global-to-local relationship hierarchies. Local relationships provide compensated information of their global relationships. The experimental results show the effectiveness of these abstractions. They are helpful for the evaluation phase of hypertext design processes.

Acknowledgements

We would like to thank Dimitris Karagiannis, Jack Milton, Jim Diederich, Donovan Hsieh, Peter Rathmann, and Shaibal Roy for their helpful comments.

References

[ABDD89] Atkinson, M., Bancilhon, F., et al. "The Object-Oriented Database System Manifesto," *DOOD'89*, 1989, pp. 40-57.

[BaCW89] Barsalou, T., Chavez, R. M., and Wiederhold, G. "Hypertext Interfaces for Decision-support Systems: A Case Study," *MEDINFO'89*, 1989, pp. 126-130.

[Conk87] Conklin, J. "Hypertext: An Introduction and Survey," *IEEE Computer*, Vol. 20, No. 9, 1987, pp. 17-41.

[Hala88] Halasz, F. G. "Reflections on Notecards: Seven Issues for the Next Generation of Hypermedia Systems," *Communications of the ACM*, Vol. 31, No. 7, 1988, pp. 836-852.

[HaKa88] Hara, Y., and Kaneko, A. "A New Multimedia Electronic Book and Its Functional Capabilities," *User-oriented, Content-based, Text and Image Handling (RIAO)*, 1988, pp. 114-123.

[HaKa90] Hara, Y., and Kasahara Y. "A Set-to-Set Linking Strategy for Hypertext Systems," *ACM Conference on Office Information Systems*, 1990, pp. 131-135.

[HaKW91] Hara, Y., Keller, A. M., and Wiederhold, G. "Implementing Hypertext Database Relationships through Aggregations and Exceptions," *Stanford Technical Report (to appear)*, 1991.

[HuKi87] Hull, R., and King, R. "Semantic Database Modeling: Survey, Applications, and Research Issues," *ACM Computing Surveys*, Vol. 19, No. 3, 1987, pp. 201-260.

[JoMa90] Jonassen, D., and Mandl, H. (eds.) "Designing Hypermedia for Learning," *Springer-Verlag (Proc. of the NATO Advanced Research Workshop 1989)*, 1990.

[KiBG89] Kim, W., Bertino E., and Garza, J.F. "Composite Objects Revisited," *ACM SIGMOD'89*, 1989, pp. 337-347.

[LeMy79] Levesque, H., and Mylopoulos, J. "A Procedural Semantics for Semantic Networks, Associative Networks," *Academic Press*, 1979.

[Niel90] Nielsen, J. "Hypertext and Hypermedia," *Academic Press*, 1990.

[Quil68] Quillian, M. R. "Semantic Memory,". *Semantic Information Processing, MIT Press*, 1968.

[SmSm77] Smith, J. M., and Smith, D. C. P. "Database abstractions: Aggregation and Generalization," *ACM Trans. on Database Systems*, Vol. 2, No. 2, 1977, pp. 105-133.

[TWBK89] Teorey, T. J., Wei, G., et al. "ER Model Clustering as an Aid for User Communication and Documentation in Database Design," *Communications of the ACM*, Vol. 32, No. 8, 1989, pp. 975-987.

[Wied83] Wiederhold, G. "Database Design," *McGraw-Hill*, 1983.

[Wied87] Wiederhold, G. "File Organization for Database Design," *McGraw-Hill*, 1987.

[WoKi87] Woelk, D., and Kim, W. "Multimedia Information Management in an Object-Oriented Database System," *Proc. of the 13th VLDB Conference*, 1987, pp. 319-329.

[YHMD88] Yankelovich, N., Haan, B. J., Meyrowitz, N. K., et al. "Intermedia: The concept and the construction of a seamless information environment," *IEEE Computer*, Vol. 20, No. 1, 1988, pp. 81-96.

TOROS-HYPER: A Tool for the Integration of Hyper Documents into Knowledge-Based Systems

Hans Delfs

Klaus Winkelmann

Siemens AG, ZFE IS SOF 14
Postfach 3240, D-8520 Erlangen

Siemens AG, ZFE IS INF31
Otto-Hahn-Ring 6, D-8000 München 83

Abstract

We discuss the relations of knowledge representation and hyper documents and argue that expert systems can greatly benefit from the integration with a hypertext system. We present TOROS-Hyper as our approach to such an integration, based on the object-oriented programming environment TOROS. The first stage of TOROS-Hyper provides loose coupling between objects and hyper documents, i.e. certain document objects are used to access the hypertext system. The second stage is a close coupling: now the system guarantees the consistency of the link structures of the hyper document and the corresponding objects.

1 Hypertext and Knowledge Representation

We discuss, at a general level, the relationship between hypertext and knowledge representation; we then express this in more specific terms with reference to the requirements of diagnostic expert systems and derive the objectives of our current TOROS-Hyper development project.

1.1 Semantic Networks as a Common Root

The classical and oldest method of "representing knowledge" is the informal method, namely in texts and images. An infinitely small proportion of our knowledge is formal or formalized permits the algorithmic derivation of further knowledge. This includes not only expert systems, but also all types of databases. Without outlining the interesting history of the formal representation of knowledge, influenced by, among others, Leibniz, we are able to discern the notion of *semantic networks* as an important milestone in this area of research. It is essentially the idea that the meaning of a concept is contained (also) in its relations with other concepts and, indeed, can even be defined by such relations.

As early as the forties, attempts were made to develop a comprehensive knowledge-processing system based on the concept of semantic networks (Bush 1945). Interestingly, the idea then evolved in different directions, and, today, we find hypertext systems and expert systems at opposite ends of the semantic-networks spectrum:

Expert systems place the emphasis on the *complete operationalization* of knowledge: an interpreter works on formal knowledge structures, infers new knowledge and solves problems. The semantics of the knowledge structures is thus precisely defined. The term "semantic network" is, in fact, not very often used in this context. In rule-based systems, the network of concepts frequently exists only in very indirect form, whereas object-oriented knowledge bases can usually be viewed as semantic networks without any major difficulty. The original concept of semantic networks is most clearly characterized in those systems that attempt to create a basis for the representation of a very large portion of reality, i.e. tools such as KRYPTON (Brachman 1983) and KLONE (Brachman 1979), many systems for the processing of natural language, or the CYC common-sense project (Guha 1990).

Conversely, *hypertext systems* are free from the need for operationalization. Navigation within the semantic network is left up to the human user. Consequently, *semantics* recedes in importance behind the *network*. It is sufficient to guess the meaning of links on the basis of mnemonic names or from the context. The obvious advantage of such a *semiformal* method of representation is its high *flexibility* and generality.

Now, it would be naive simply to demand systems with the operationality of expert systems and the flexibility of hypertext systems. There necessarily exists a tension between both goals. However, what appears important to us is to find adequate hybrid forms that unite the useful elements of the two techniques. Even at this general level, the task is a worthwhile one - it is conceivable, for example, in the course of a knowledge acquisition, to make a gradual and systematic transition from informal representations (text, graphics) through semiformal ones (hypertext) to formal representations (executable knowledge base).

Before defining our objectives for the present project, we illustrate our motives at a practical level.

1.2 Diagnostic Expert Systems Need Hypertext

We observed the need for an integrated environment with expert system and hypertext tools during the development of various diagnosis expert systems based on the diagnosis expert system shell MAX (Delfs 89). MAX was developed in order to support the field service for complex electrical systems. It is now being successfully employed for various applications, such as the locating of faults in the power sections of thyristor-fed drives, the investigation of bearing damage in electrical machines or the putting-into-operation of feedback-control systems on drives.

We give a short review of some of our experiences during the development of MAX-applications, since the basic requirements for TOROS-Hyper are derived from there. As in other associative-heuristic diagnosis systems (Schmiedel 1991), the basic structure of a MAX application is a *diagnosis hierarchy* which represents problems and their breaking-down into subproblems. Symptoms and rules are associated with each problem. Symptoms describe the information necessary for the investigation of a problem, such as measurements, and rules indicate how it is possible, on the basis of the symptoms, to narrow down problems, to exclude causes of faults or to carry out repair measures.

MAX covers a wide range of diagnosis models, including, in particular, fault trees, such as in KLUE (Karel 1989). Nevertheless, the formal structures in the knowledge base of MAX are far from being adequate to express all the knowledge required in order to perform a diagnosis in a complex electrical system. The same is probably true of all currently known techniques of formal knowledge representation.

Examples of knowledge which may not be adequately represented by formal and operational mechanisms, such as frames or rules include knowledge about the physical-technical background, complex measuring setups, the rectification of faults, the administrative environment and the limits of the system.

It was an obvious step to capture such knowledge in nonformal documents. Normally, expert-system shells offer help texts, help files or individual graphics for such purposes. Our experience, however, showed that such documents, at least in complex domains, have a pronounced nonlinear structure: there are logical correlations and cross-references between documents.

It became necessary to provide MAX with a hypertext component in addition to the existing means of representation and processing (for more details see Delfs 90). There are more reports on expert system applications where the integration of hypertext was necessary in order to obtain a sufficient functionality (cf. e.g. Alderman 1989, Fischer 1989, Scott 1989, Timpka 1987).

1.3 Project Objectives of TOROS-Hyper

The major objective of our project is the integration of hypertext functionality into Siemens' own development environment TOROS (Toolkit for Object and Rule oriented system construction) (Delfs 1991a,b, Suda 1991). TOROS is a powerful hybrid development tool for object and rule oriented systems. It is particularly well suited for the development of knowledge based applications and was successfully used in a large number of complex engineering applications. It was also used for the implementation of the product version of the afore-mentioned MAX diagnosis shell.

TOROS is an object and rule oriented extension of the C language. It includes the usual mechanisms for the definition of classes, attributes and methods and for instantiating classes. The concept of *relations* between objects allows the modelling of semantic networks. An

efficient and flexible, fully compiled rule language is included as well as an advanced graphics library. TOROS knows persistent objects and provides operations for storing and loading object data. TOROS can run under Unix, and a DOS version is under development.

Integration of hypertext functionality into TOROS means that facilities for the definition of and navigation in hyperdocuments are added to the existing means for the formal representation of knowledge. For this purpose we will not implement a hypertext system, but instead we focus on the neat integration of an existing hypertext system into TOROS. The essential parts of TOROS-Hyper will not depend on the features of any particular hypertext system.

We can now define our objectives more precisely:

We develop a TOROS-class library for hypertext. Using this class library a TOROS-application is able to implement an interface to a hypertext documentation system. The library provides classes to represent documents (of various types) and hyperlinks between documents.
Methods of these classes (for instance, *display, follow-links, show-links*) enable the TOROS-application to access the functionality of the hypertext system.

The class-library approach means, in particular, that it is possible to define simple mechanisms that can be successively specialized for different classes of applications and that can be enriched with additional semantics. Such additional semantics will relate, for example, to the differentiation of link types and object types, which are of particular relevance for diagnosis systems.

The following requirements define the envisaged potential of TOROS-Hyper.

- Within a knowledge-based application implemented by use of TOROS the user can access background information in the form of hyper documents, and navigate within these documents.

- From within hyperdocuments it should be possible to activate inference procedures in the expert system part of the TOROS application.

- The network of TOROS objects needs to be consistent with the network of hyper documents.

- The process of integrating existing documents in a newly built knowledge-based system should be supported.

2 Architecture of TOROS-Hyper

Although it has not yet been completed, we can already outline the essential features of TOROS-Hyper here.

First of all, there is a somewhat more detailed description of the basic TOROS system.

We are implementing TOROS-Hyper in two stages of development, called loose and close coupling. To complete the picture, we include two more stages (0 and 3) here for reference:

Stage 0: Use is made not of a hypertext system, but of a linear documentation system.
Documents are represented by instances of the class 'Document', links between documents by instances of class 'Link' (as in

MAX). The method 'Display' of 'Document' tells the user where he can find the real document in the documentation system (there he may open it) and shows a menue with the links starting at this document. Technically the diagnosis system and the documentation system are separate systems.

Stage 1: Loose coupling between objects and hyperdocuments.

Stage 2: Close coupling with guaranteed consistency between TOROS objects and hyperdocuments.

Stage 3: Fully object-oriented open hypertext system as the theoretical ideal.

The concepts behind stages 1 - 3 are presented in the following.

2.1 Loose Coupling

Now a real hypertext system is used. The links between individual documents, of the kind resulting, for example, from keywords and explanations, have now been shifted to the hypertext system (see figure 1).

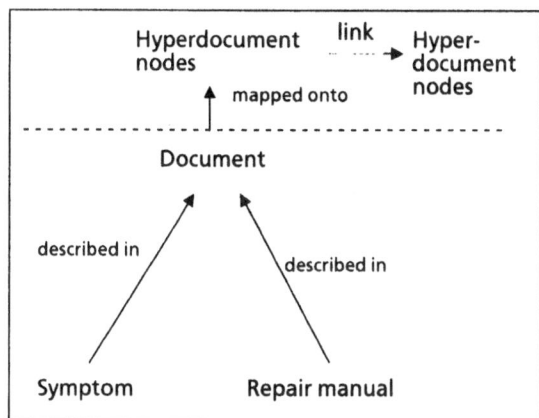

Figure 1 - Mapping objects to hyper documents.

TOROS-Hyper provides a class "document", which basically looks like this:

Class: Document

    Attributes:

        Hyper-node   / * contains the information on access to the associated node */

    Methods:

        display   /* displays the document and hands over control to the hypertext system*/

Here, we are discussing merely the execution system and not the creation system with additional methods for the creation and editing of documents.

With regard to the hypertext, the following are planned:

- Return of control to the expert system - this can be done either by termination/closing of the hyperdocument or by selection of a special "button" named "continue" or "resume".

- Activating a TOROS application from within the hypertext system. An example would be a plant documentation manual that, in the document describing a specific component, contains an expert system for the diagnosis of that component - the diagnosis is started with a "Start Diagnosis" button. The name and design of such a button are specific to the application: TOROS-Hyper simply provides the basic mechanism.

For an "active link" it is possible to specify:

- an object and
- a method.

When the button is selected, the respective method of the object is executed.

As compared with stage 0, loose coupling made it possible to use the comfort and convenience of a hypertext system for navigation in documents. Conversely, as far as the TOROS object structure is concerned, the link structure of the hyperdocument is completely hidden. Therefore, insofar as document structures reflect object structures - for example, diagnosis hierarchies or component hierarchies - it is left up to the user to keep the two consistent. This means that, if a new component is added, it must be inserted into the object hierarchy, its relations with other components (*part-of, replaceable-by* ...) must be defined, and, in addition, the corresponding document with the logically identical cross-references must be created.

Stage 2 - Close Coupling - will help to eliminate the need for precisely these additional operations.

2.2 Close Coupling

A class "link" is added to TOROS-Hyper. Links between hypernodes are represented in the TOROS application by instances of this class. The creation system guarantees that the definition of a link in the hyperdocument is also entered in the associated object and vice versa.

The basic problem in closely coupling hypertext with an object-oriented system is the semantics which has to be associated to the hypertext links. In TOROS-Hyper, the general classes "Knowledge object" and "link" can be specialized to capture this semantics.

As an illustration we look at how a diagnosis application can be implemented with TOROS-Hyper.

Figure 2 shows typical objects like Problem, Symptom, Diagnosis-rule and Repair for the formal knowledge representation in a diagnosis application (they are taken from the MAX system) and how they are now mapped to corrresponding documents via the new ".doc" objects.

There is a "hypertext class library for diagnosis" and, in addition to the general "display" method, there are methods such as

        investigate hypothesis,

        explain symptom or

        describe component.

278

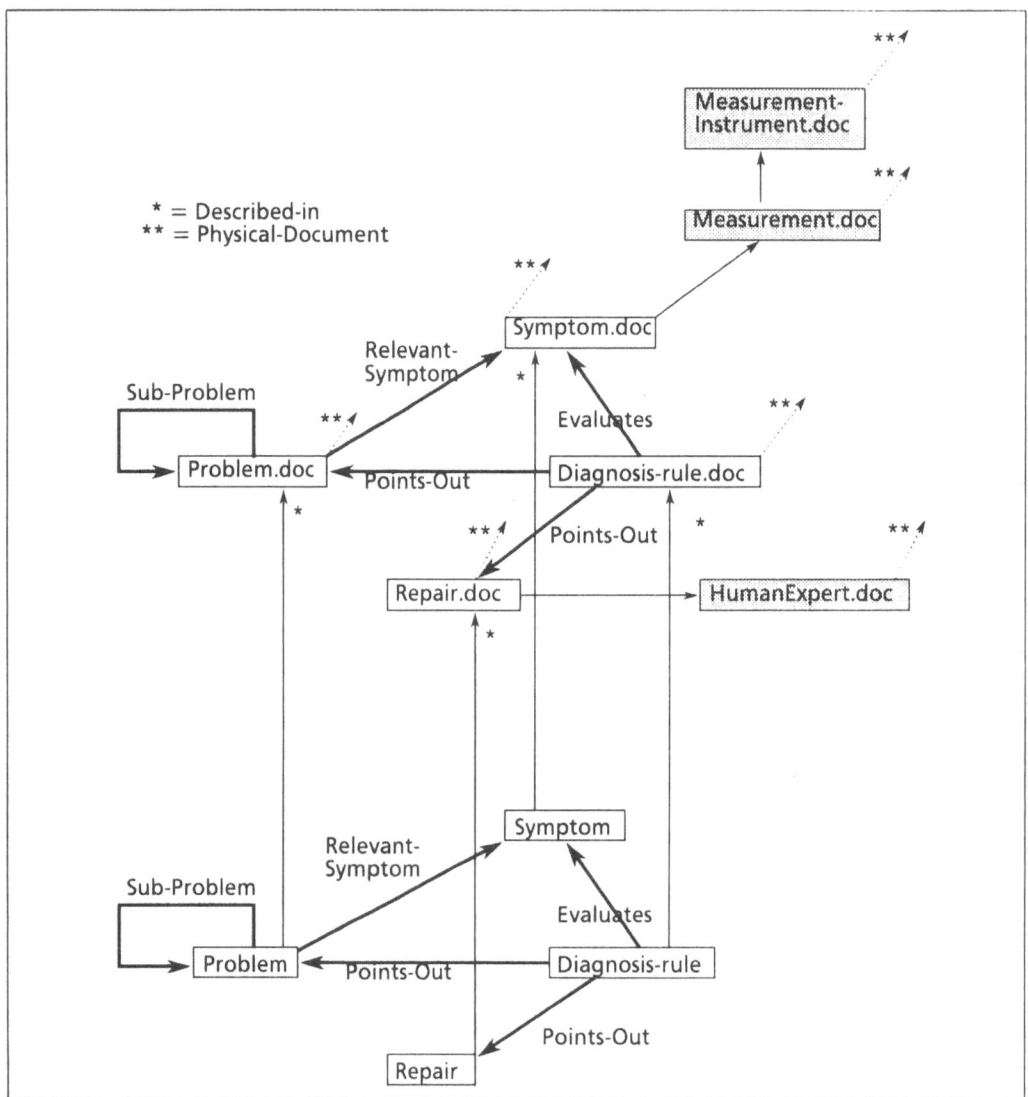

Figure 2 - Example of objects and related documents

Above all, however, it is also possible to specialize "display" in order, for example, to represent also the subcomponent (part of) structure for objects of the "Component" type.

Figure 3 shows a refined class hierarchy for diagnosis applications: there is a difference in specificity between types of links: links of the type "A is possible cause of B" ("causes") are more specific than "A may contribute to explanation of B" ("explains"), which, in turn, is more specific than the all-embracing "A has something to do with B" ("link").

Even though the precise characteristics of this application-specific level will depend greatly on the domain and on the method of knowledge modeling used, TOROS-Hyper will create the basis for the specializations outlined here.

2.3 Fully Object-Oriented, Open Hypertext System

With regard to content, stage 2 can already be viewed as the ultimate objective, namely as a "hypertext class library". Although objects and hypertext nodes are still implemented separately, they are treated conceptually as one.

Stage 3 would go beyond this to the extent that the separation between objects and documents is removed also as regards implementation.

One of the motives behind this is that some advanced hypertext systems (e.g. Intermedia) are object-oriented and, consequently, in stage 2, we still have two parallel sets of objects to handle. Normally, therefore, not all the possibilities of hypertext - such as complex objects or animations - will have their equivalent in the TOROS object model.

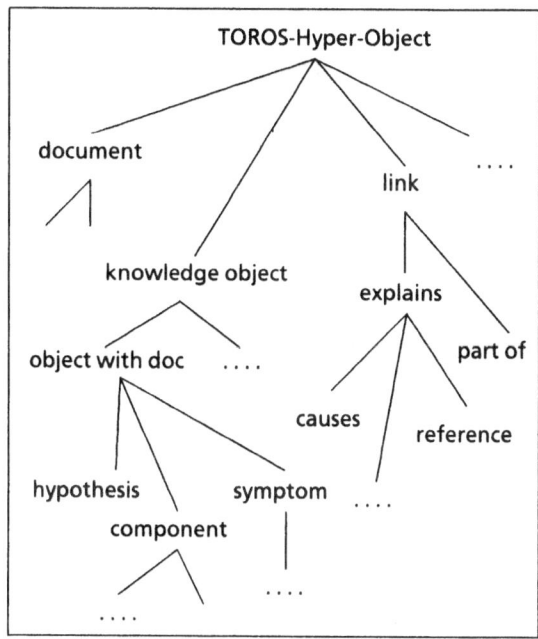

Figure 3 - refined class hierarchy for diagnosis

We call a hypertext system "fully object oriented and open" if the class hierarchy of the hypertext system can be extended and if its script language can be used as a universal programming language for the implementation of methods.

For practical reasons, we do currently not intend to implement this stage 3. Within the TOROS project this would mean the implementation of a new hypertext system with TOROS. Rather, we use the concept of stage 3 as an point of reference for design of stages 1 and 2: the consistency problems discussed above would vanish in stage 3.

3   Research Topics

In this section, we shall briefly discuss some topics that require further work.

3.1 Knowledge Acquisition and Author System

The acquisition of knowledge for an expert system can be divided into a formal part and a nonformal part, namely

- the definition of the formal knowledge structure (diagnosis hierarchy, symptoms...) for inference,

- the development of the documentation with its hypertext structure.

Frequently, one starts with nonformal knowledge and attempts to derive the formal structures from it. Since, with TOROS-Hyper, we are creating a common framework for both, a basis is also being generated for the automatic derivation of formal structures. This can be done interactively, for example, with the user being requested to specialize general links in accordance with a predetermined selection.

Above the usual level of the hypertext author system, there is now - as a result of the enhanced expressive power - a need for a meta-level, namely a system for the definition of classes and link types. It is still necessary to investigate what such a system will look like and how it will interact with other knowledge-acquisition tools.

3.2 Hypertext as User Interface

Present-day hypertext systems are based on a fixed network of documents. If hypertext is used as an output medium (instead of a print command), one quickly arrives at the need to overlay variable texts (e.g. program variables) and thus, ultimately, to compose texts and images dynamically.

As far as the input side is concerned, it is also possible today for the selecting of buttons to initiate actions by means of procedures hidden behind the buttons. Alphanumeric inputs are not normally allowed.

We are in no way advocating that hypertext should be "dressed up" with all conceivable features, but it would be worth investigating to what extent simple extensions for input and output might make hypertext a good tool for a user interface of knowledge-processing systems. For example, networks of graphically represented components play a central role in configuration systems. Hypertext can help to visualize such a network, but this would require a dynamic definition of hypertext.

3.3 Further Applications

The developments presented here are based for the most part on diagnosis systems. In essence, though, they will be generally applicable. Future fields of application will show in what ways hypertext can be profitably combined with knowledge processing. Other typical application areas of TOROS-Hyper are

- knowledge based retrieval of information in the documentation of products or complex systems,
- intelligent help facilities in configuration expert systems.

TOROS-Hyper will also be used as a means of experimentation for testing such new possibilities.

References:

Alderman 1989
    E.L. Alderman, A. Rappaport, An expert system for thrombolysis in acute myocardial infarction (ADMIT). Proceedings "Computers in Cardiology 1988", Washington, DC, 1989, p. 197 - 200.

Brachman 1979
    R.J. Brachman, On the Epistemological Status of Semantic Networks, in: R.J. Brachman, H.J. Levesque (eds.), Readings in Knowledge Representation, Morgan Kaufman 1985

Brachman 1983
    R.J. Brachman, R.E. Fikes, H.J. Levesque, KRYPTON: A Functional Approach to Knowledge Representation, in: R.J. Brachman, H.J. Levesque (eds.), Readings in Knowledge Representation, Morgan Kaufman 1985

Bush 1945
    V. Bush, As we may think, Atlantic Monthly, 176, 101-108.

Delfs 1990
H. Delfs, Diagnose-Expertensysteme brauchen Hypertext - Das Beispiel MAX. In P. Gloor, N. Streitz (Hrsg.), Hypertext und Hypermedia: Von theoretischen Konzepten zur praktischen Anwendung. Informatik Fachbericht 249, Springer Heidelberg 1990.

Delfs 1991a
H. Delfs, P. Suda, S. Verplaetse, Objekt- und regelorientierte Programmierung in C mit TOROS, unix mail 2 / 91.

Delfs 1991b
H. Delfs, U. Welz, P. Suda, S. Verplaetse, TOROS, ein C-basiertes Werkzeug zur Entwicklung von KI-Anwendungen, in K. Winkelmann (Hrsg.), Wissensbasierte System in der Praxis, Siemens Verlag, to appear 1991

Fischer 1989
G. Fischer, R. McCall, A. Morch, Design environments for constructive and argumentive design. Conference on Human Factors in Computing. Systems (CHI 89), SIGCHI Bull., special issue May 1989, p. 269 - 275.

Guha 1990
R.V. Guha, D.B. Lenat, Cyc: A Mid-Term Report. AI Magazine 11/3, 1990

Karel 1989
G. Karel, M. Kenner, KLUE: a Diagnostic Expert System Tool for Manufacturing, Intellinews, vol. 5, No. 1, Mountain View, CA, IntelliCorp 1989.

Schmiedel 1991
G. Schmiedel, Neuartige Entwicklung wissensbasierter Systeme mit DIWA, in: G. Hommel (Hrsg.), Prozeßrechensysteme '91, Informatik Fachbericht 269, Springer 1991.

Scott 1989:
C.K. Scott, B.G. Nickerson, K. Ward, ARIES: an expert system for regulatory information and compliance requirements. In: Proceedings, Canadian Nuclear Society, 10th Annual Conference 1989. Ottawa 1989.

Suda 1991:
P. Suda, H. Delfs, TOROS: A system integrating object and rule-oriented programming in a C/UNIX-environment, to appear in Structured Programming.

Timpka 1987
T. Timpka, Knowledge-based decision support for general practitioners: an integrated design. Comput. Methods Programs Biomed., vol. 25, no. 1 (1987), 49 - 60.

A Transaction Model for Hypertext

P.L. van der Spiegel   J.Th.W. Driessen   P.D. Bruza   Th.P. van der Weide *

Dept. of Information Systems, University of Nijmegen,
Toernooiveld 1, 6525 ED Nijmegen, The Netherlands, e-mail: pvds@cs.kun.nl

Abstract

This paper presents a specification of $\mathcal{H}$ypertext systems on several levels of abstraction, and describes translations between these different levels. The $\mathcal{H}$ypertext system will be organised according to a stratified architecture, which is a generalisation of the so-called Two Level Architecture.

We describe a user interface for the $\mathcal{H}$ypertext system, examine the user's elementary operations (transactions) and present the corresponding user view on the system.

Next a conceptual schema is presented, that describes $\mathcal{H}$ypertext from the perspective of the *author* (editor) of the information. We describe the user transactions in terms of operations on the conceptual schema.

An object oriented implementation of this $\mathcal{H}$ypertext system is presented. We show how the object hierarchy is derived from the conceptual schema.

1 Introduction

Current research on $\mathcal{H}$ypertext systems appears to focus around two aspects. Firstly, research is focussed on the design of powerful user interfaces. This topic received the most attention so far. Secondly, research is directed at basic concepts that constitute $\mathcal{H}$ypertext (see for example [2] and [16]).

In this paper we deal with both aspects, and relate them to each other. For this purpose we use a general architecture for $\mathcal{H}$ypertext systems. We follow the approach for Information System Architecture as sketched in [3], and consider a $\mathcal{H}$ypertext system as consisting of the following components (see figure 1):

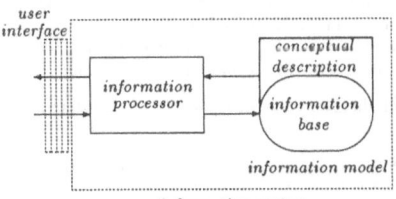

information system

Figure 1: The Information System Paradigm

1. the information model. This is also denoted as application model or as title ([2]). It consists of:

   (a) a conceptual description (specification), describing the structure of the stored information, and the rules that govern modifications of the stored information (such as constraints):

   (b) an information base, containing the stored information according to the conceptual description. This is usually referred to as an instantiation (population) of the conceptual description.

2. an information processor, that processes user requests. The information processor accepts commands from the user via a user interface, interprets them in terms of the conceptual description, and responds in accordance with the information model (both the information base and the conceptual description).

An important difference between $\mathcal{H}$ypertext systems and (conventional) information systems is the concept of *associative link*, that enables the user to jump unconstrained through the information base. In terms of the relational model the associative link may be understood as a cross-reference from any tupel of any table into any tuple of another table.

In traditional $\mathcal{H}$ypertext systems, in contrast with conventional information systems, there is almost no conceptual description of the stored data. The weaknesses of such an approach have been discussed by several authors ([7][15]). There seems to be a growing need to be able to support a conceptual description in relation with $\mathcal{H}$ypertext or documents, especially the combination of structured documents with $\mathcal{H}$ypertext applications looks promising. Our setup combines $\mathcal{H}$ypertext and document description languages, such as ODA ([4]), SGML ([10]) and TEX ([11]).

The outline of the paper is as follows. In section 2 we introduce a multi-level organisation of $\mathcal{H}$ypertext. Three levels are emphasised in this regard.

One level is concerned with the actual information, the second level with the disclosure of the information. The third level is intended to administrate the users' own routes of preference through the $\mathcal{H}$ypertext to their favourite areas of exploration. Such user behaviour, sometimes also referred to as user profile, forms a dynamic aspect, even in an otherwise read-only $\mathcal{H}$ypertext such as CD-Rom applications.

Next we describe the different components of the system, on the basis of the general architecture as presented in figure 1.

As mentioned earlier, navigation is the primary activity of the user of a $\mathcal{H}$ypertext system. For this reason the commands, given to the information processor via the user interface, consist of operations to support navigation. The user interface is a presentation of the system to the user, hiding (as good as possible) internal aspects. It reflects the internal state of the information system, and gives the user the opportunity to change this internal state (for example by clicking a button). These transactions with the system are modelled in section 3, and result in what is called the transaction model.

In section 4 the underlying conceptual schema is discussed in detail. This conceptual schema supports the multi-level organisation of the information as introduced above. We describe how user transactions are translated to operations on the conceptual schema in section 5. Finally we indicate how a transaction model can be implemented in the Object Oriented Paradigm.

* This work has been supported by the ESPRIT project APPED (2499).

2 Multi-level organisation of the information model

In [2] a new mechanism was presented to structure $\mathcal{H}$ypertext into two levels. Similar approaches are discussed in [1] and [12]. The intention of this structure was to provide a means of facilitating user orientation in Hypermedia in response to the well documented "lost in hyperspace" problem [13][14]. The bottom level of this mechanism is called the *hyperbase* and the upper level the *hyperindex*. We denote the hyperbase by $\mathcal{H}$ and the hyperindex by $\hbar$.

The hyperbase corresponds to $\mathcal{H}$ypertext as is typical in current systems (with the extension that both the conceptual description and the actual information are contained).

The hyperindex is an index, organised in the form of a $\mathcal{H}$ypertext, and is used to index the information in the underlying hyperbase. Its underlying principle is that any index term can be *refined* or *enlarged*. When the user arrives at some potentially interesting index information item, the information in the hyperbase, relevant to this particular index item, can be retrieved. In this way the user moves from the hyperindex level to the hyperbase level. This type of browsing, by navigating through the hyperindex, is termed *query by navigation* (QBN). Querying is thus reduced to a form of browsing which is an easily understood form of searching behaviour.

Users of a $\mathcal{H}$ypertext application can be compared with explorers. Slowly but surely they build up knowledge about relevant parts of the hyperbase. They need the possibility to connect relevant information (in their own subjective way). This need is administrated in our architecture by an additional level: the *hypermap*, denoted by $\bar{m}$. This hypermap can be compared with a made-to-measure road-map (one for each user), which serves as a private guide for the user on how to reach specific information. This feature supports the user, who travels around in the lonelyness of the vast information-desert, by recording a kind of historical document of what was achieved.

In this paper we restrict ourselves to the three levels we just described. However, useful extensions are possible, for example a level that indexes the hyperindex, or a hypermap for the hyperindex. Also we do not consider interlayer connections between the hypermap and the hyperindex.

The resulting structure of the information model is shown in figure 2. Details of this figure will be explained in the next section.

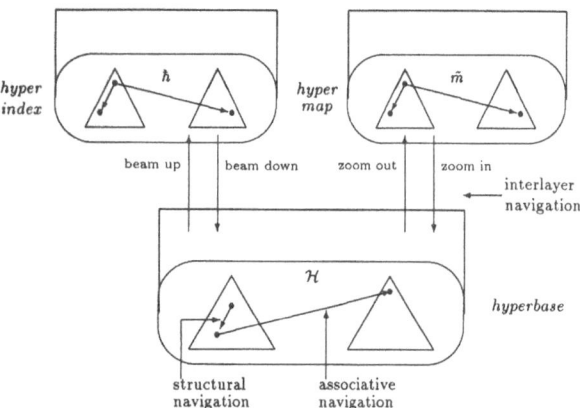

Figure 2: Multi-level organisation of $\mathcal{H}$ypertext

Each of the $\mathcal{H}$ypertext (sub)structures has its own conceptual description, information base, and set of associative links. Between the levels are connections.

3 The user interface

Now that the multi-level architecture has been introduced, we describe the behaviour of a system based on this architecture. This behaviour will then serve as a base to build the associated transaction model.

To describe the interaction of the system with a user we use the *conceptual dialogue specification technique DST* (see [5] and [6]). First the DST-technique will be introduced briefly. We use the style that was presented in [9].

The intention of a *DST-diagram* is to describe a dialogue, usually between man and machine. A DST-diagram maps out the different stable states of an information system, and the dialogue by which the user can bring about state transitions. A brief description of the intention of the symbols is as follows:

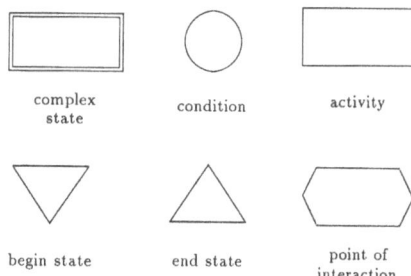

Figure 3: DST-diagram symbols

- The **begin state** and **end state** denote the states in which a dialogue begins or ends respectively.

- A **point of interaction** is a state in which the system waits for user input.

- An **activity** denotes an autarkic action of the system, i.e., an action requiring no (or only trivial) interaction with the user.

- A **complex state** denotes a subdialogue which is refined in an other DST-diagram. By means of complex states the possibility of *hierarchical decomposition* is provided.

- In a **condition** (transition guard) the system evaluates the associated condition. According to its outcome, one of the transitions is selected. Note that conditions are *not* restricted to boolean conditions.

The above symbols can be connected by so-called transition arrows, which may have an associated label.

A well formed DST-diagram is a DST-diagram that conforms to a number of rules. Some important ones of these are:

- A DST-diagram must have a unique begin state and a unique end state.

- The begin state must lead to every other state.

- The end state must be reachable from every other state.

At this point we assume that the DST-diagrams have been sufficiently well introduced to be able to understand the specifications which will follow. For more details about DST-diagrams the reader is referred to [6].

3.1 The Interaction with $\mathcal{H}$ypertext

Imagine we are sitting behind a terminal, navigating our way through the $\mathcal{H}$ypertext system, looking for information. A typical stable state will be that the system has presented some information on the screen, that we are reading and using for deciding what we want next. A collection of information that is offered as a whole to the searcher is denoted as a *presentation*. It is the central point of interaction in figure 4. We make a distinction between the presentation and the underlying object that is manifested by this presentation. We will use the term *context* to denote this underlying object.

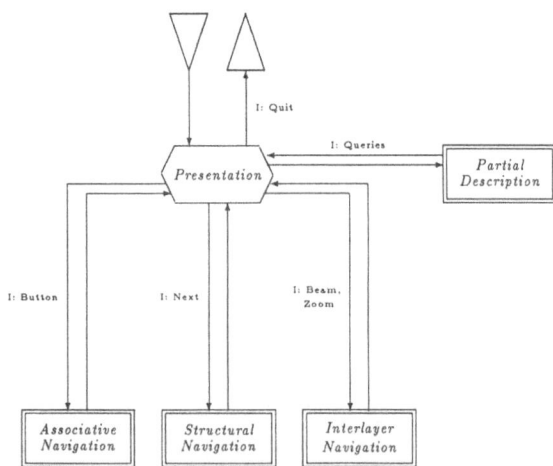

Figure 4: Top Layer DST-diagram Interaction with User

From a particular context there are several possibilities to go to an other stable point (piece of information):

1. Typical for $\mathcal{H}$ypertext systems is to offer the opportunity to have follow up on some issue that is presented on the presentation screen. For example, pieces of the text on this screen are highlighted in order to indicate that they can be selected for further reading. These pieces of text then form the *buttons* that can be pushed in order to communicate to the system what next action is required. These connections are termed *associative links*. We use the term **Associative Navigation** for this kind of traversal through the information.

2. Associative links are very flexible as they impose no restrictions on making connections between pieces of information. However, just as goto statements in programming languages, they tend to deform rapidly into a muddle. A way to overcome this would be to assign labels to associative links. A better approach, however, is to organise the information according to some structure. An example is the organisation of the information as a book, consisting of chapters, chapters consisting of sections, etcetera.

   Imposing a structure can be compared to the usage of typed variables in conventional programming languages. In this case, the $\mathcal{H}$ypertext system will enforce the compliance with the imposed structure.

   As a result, navigation over the structure is of an other nature than Associative Navigation. It is denoted as **Structural Navigation** in figure 4. Structural Navigation is characterised by the fact that it extends (enlarges) or contracts (refines) the current context. Going from a chapter of a book to one of its sections is an example of context refinement.

3. The next option is navigation between two layers: **Interlayer Navigation**. This kind of navigation is displayed in figure 2 as *beam up* and *beam down* (or *zoom out* and *zoom in*). The underlying idea is traversal from the current context into the best

suitable context within the other layer. For example, beam down from the hyperindex into the hyperbase leads to a context in which all relevant contexts are listed in order of relevance.

4. A fourth option is to give a partial description of subject of interest and to go to that subject in the hyperbase. This is often called a **query**. We will not deal with query handling in this paper but refer to [8] for this.

5. Of course there is also the possibility of leaving the $\mathcal{H}$ypertext system.

The various options are depicted in a DST-diagram in figure 4.

3.2 The user's concepts/elementary transactions

In the previous section the behaviour of the system towards the user was introduced. We will now examine the concepts related to this behaviour somewhat further.

The user is always in a certain *context*, represented by a *presentation*. That context stands for a certain *structure* that again is in a *layer*. Every navigation step leads to a change of context. The active context is left, and a new one is entered.

- During associative navigation, little can be said about the new context. We direct ourselves to information, probably in quite another context. It might even be the case that we can reach the requested information in more than one context. For example if we follow a link to the map of a city, then this map may be part of a tourist guide, but may also occur in the context of a detective book, that contains the map for reader convenience. In case of such *context ambiguity* the system has to resolve this confusion, by letting the reader select one context. When the new context is clear, the system will shift to this new context. A *context shift* takes place. The decomposition of Associative Navigation is presented in figure 5.

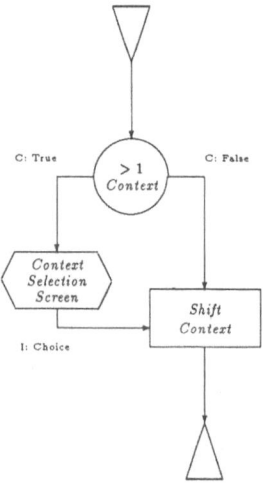

Figure 5: Refinement of Associative Navigation

- When navigating following the structure only a minor change of context takes place. We call this: *context adjustment*. The effect of structural navigation is enlargement or refinement of the current context. The decomposition of structural navigation is shown in figure 6.

- The navigation between two distinct layers (Interlayer Navigation) can be initiated by selecting in the presentation screen the

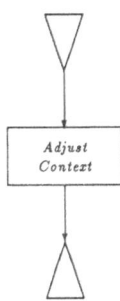

Figure 6: Refinement of Structural Navigation

desired kind of interlayer navigation (*beam up*, *beam down*, *zoom out* or *zoom in*). When the user selects a beam or zoom, the system determines the new context. This new context is in the newly selected layer. Here also a *context shift* takes place.

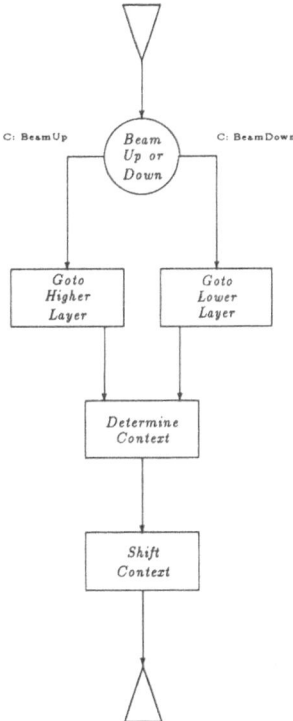

Figure 7: Refinement of Interlayer Navigation

The various possible context changes and the other concepts of the navigation process are described schematically, using an E.R. like notation, in figure 8.

4 The conceptual description

In the previous section we presented the information structure from the perspective of a person who is only consulting the information. More sophisticated views on the information exist however. In this section we present the overall underlying information structure, the conceptual description (see figure 9). This will for example be used by the author

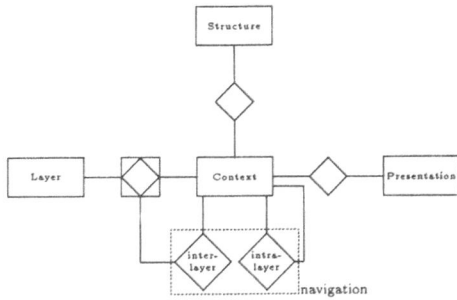

Figure 8: Schematically description of the user's concepts

of the application. We consider 𝓗ypertext as consisting of: *structure*, *presentation* and *contents*. We will discuss the information structure from figure 9 in detail in this section.

The basis of the conceptual model is a set of so called *fragments*. Fragments are elementary pieces of information, which are not decomposed structurally into smaller components. The criterion for judging whether a fragment is atomic or not is not necessarily a property of the fragment itself, but rather is dependent on the lowest level of granularity at which the information is to be considered. For example, animation can be considered as a single fragment, or as a sequence of fragments. Each fragment has associated *data* of a particular *medium* (text, video, audio, etc).

Usually information is structured in some well defined form. For example, if the information has the form of a book, it is grouped into chapters, where a chapter consists of sections, etc. There are several approaches for specifying the structure of the information. For example, context free rules are used to describe the structure of a document in SGML [10], which seems to be the emerging defacto standard for this purpose. Other possibilities in this regard are ODA [4] and TEX [11]. We basically adopt the grammar based approach of SGML. As a consequence, an information structure is described by the following components:

- A set of symbols denoting structural elements

- A set of context free rules

- A start symbol

A *rule* comprises a left hand side (relation *lhs*), which consists of a single *structural element* and a right hand side (*rhs*), which is a series of one or more structural elements (see figure 9). Each structural element in the right hand side may be qualified by one of the following occurrence indicators (*occ*):

* the so-called Kleene star, the qualified structural element may occur zero or more times.

+ the so-called Kleene plus, the qualified structural element should occur at least once.

? the qualified structural element may occur at most once.

The structure definition specifies a framework for the document structure. An *actual structure* is a hierarchy of instances of structural elements conforming to the structure definition. We call such an instance a *molecule*. The hierarchy is modelled by the relation *parent child*.

Links model cross references in the information. In our model, two types of links are distinguished: *context bound* links and *context free* links. A context free link is an association between two fragments that holds independent of any context and is in this sense absolute. A context

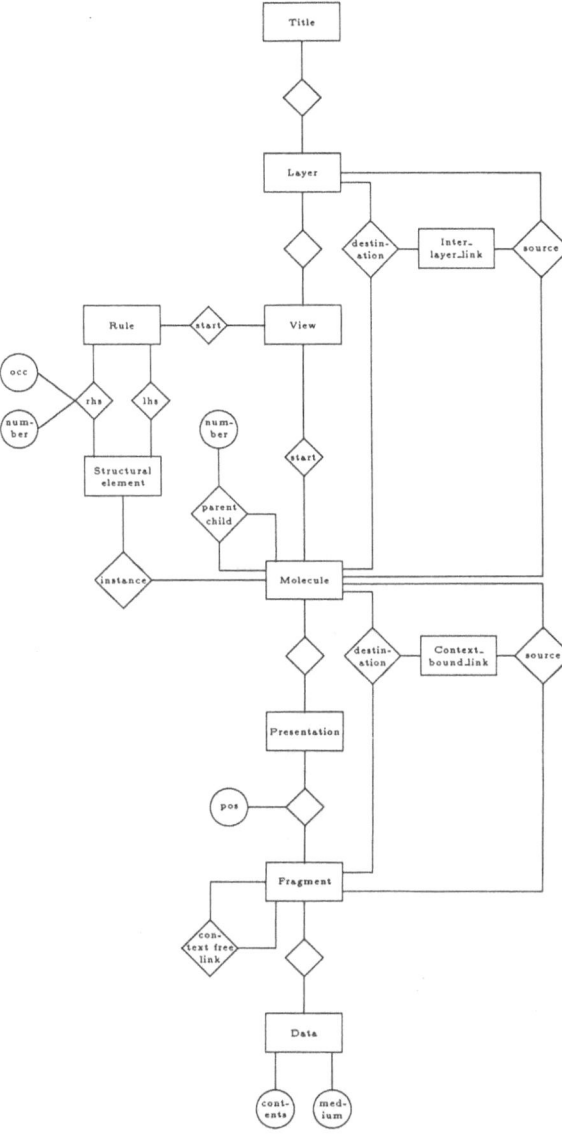

Figure 9: Conceptual Schema of the Information Model

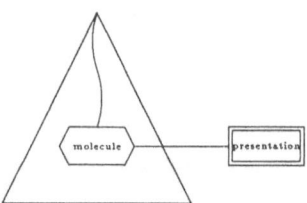

Figure 10: A context

bound link is also an association between two fragments, but its *source* and *destination* both have associated a certain context. This context is established by the associated molecule-fragment pair.

One of the most powerful aspects of Ｈypertext is the ability to define different views on the same underlying information. A *view* consists of a structural definition and an associated actual structure. Finally a view contains a set of associated links.

A set of related views together forms a *layer*. Every view has an associated unique layer. Note that in this paper we only consider the layers hyperindex, hypermap and hyperbase.

5 Translation

Up to this point we have described two ways of looking at a Ｈypertext system. The first is the view from the perspective of a user, the second is the underlying structure of the information. The relation between the two will be described in this section, on the basis of the user interface from section 3 and the internal structure of section 4.

First we consider the stable state in figure 4 which is a *presentation*. As mentioned before this presentation represents a certain abstract object, called context (see figure 8). A context corresponds to a certain molecule (see figure 9), and the path to the root of the corresponding actual structure (figure 10). This structure is related to a view.

The *layer* and the *presentation* entities from figure 8 can be mapped to the same entities from figure 9. The contents of the presentation are modelled as a partially ordered set of fragments, each on a certain position (relation *pos*) in the presentation.

Operations on the user level can now easily be translated to operations on the conceptual schema. On the elements of the conceptual schema we only need some primitive building and retrieval operations.

- Associative Navigation is achieved by following either context bound or context free links. If the destination of a context bound link consist of more than one context, one of them has to be selected.

- For Structural Navigation the *parent-child* relation over *Molecule* is used. For example, context enlargement implies taking the father of a certain molecule.

- Interlayer Navigation uses the *interlayer link* in an obvious way.

Now the operations on contexts are automatically clear. Context adjustment is a (little) modification of the path which defines the context. A context shift implies building a completely new path in a certain structure.

5.1 An object oriented prototype

In this section we give a short description of a prototype implementation in the Object Oriented Paradigm. Our approach was to implement each entity type of the conceptual schema from figure 9 as a so called class, where a class consists of a data structure and the methods for accessing the data.

The methods within a class and the inheritance structure of the classes are derived from:

1. the relation types of the conceptual schema

2. the usage as described in the transaction model.

This derivation is quite straight forward, and therefore not described in detail. For example, the procedure to present a molecule makes use of the routines that are provided by the class Presentation, that handles the construction in terms of fragments. The resulting class hierarchy is depicted in figure 11.

286

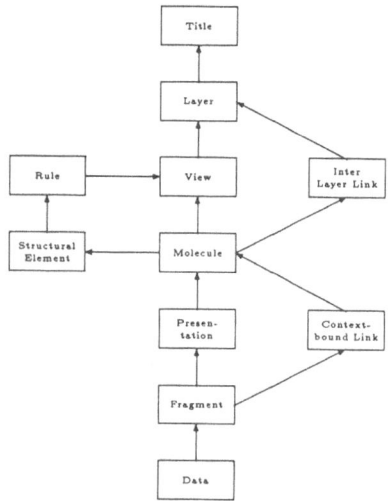

Figure 11: Class hierarchy of the prototype

6 Conclusions

In this paper we have tried to bridge the gap between conventional information systems and document oriented systems (especially *H*ypertext systems). The resulting system can benefit from the concepts of both worlds. We see that *H*ypertext manipulation can be interpreted in terms of conventional conceptual schema manipulation. The inverse however does not seem to hold. For example, there is no counterpart for query by navigation in a conventional SQL database. Further research therefore might concentrate on the meaning of such operations in the world of databases.

References

[1] M. Agosti, A. Archi, R. Colotti, R.M. Di Giorgi, G. Gradenigo, B. Inghirami, P. Matiello, R. Nannuci, and M. Ragona. New prospectives in information retrieval techniques: a hypertext prototype in environmental law. In *Online Management 89, Proceedings 13th International Online Information Meeting, London, England*, pages 483–494, 1989.

[2] P.D. Bruza and T.P. van der Weide. Two Level Hypermedia - An Improved Architecture for Hypertext. In *Proceedings of the Data Base and Expert System Applications (DEXA 90)*. Springer Verlag, 1990.

[3] J.A. Bubenko. Information system methodologies - a research view. In T.W. Olle, H.G. Sol, and A.A. Verrijn Stuart, editors, *Information System Design Methodologies: Improving the Practice*, pages 289–318. North-Holland, 1986.

[4] I.R Campbell-Grant and P.J. Robinson. An Introduction to ISO DIS 8613 - Office Document Architecture - and its Application to Computer Graphics. *Computer and Graphics*, 11(4):325–341, 1987.

[5] E. Denert. Specification and design of dialogue systems with state diagrams. In E. Morlet and D. Ribbens, editors, *Proceeding International Computing Symposium*, pages 417–424. North-Holland, 1977.

[6] E.J.T van Dinter, M.P.W. Martens, A.H.M. ter Hofstede, and S. Brinkkemper. Specification and Implementation of the Conceptual Dialogue Specification Technique DST. Technical Report 90-17, Department of Information Systems, University of Nijmegen, The Netherlands, November 1990.

[7] P. Garg. Abstraction mechanisms in hypertext. *Communications ACM*, 31(7):863–870, July 1988.

[8] F. Halasz. Reflections on notecards: Seven issues for the next generation of hypertext systems. *Communications ACM*, 31(7):836–852, July 1988.

[9] A.H.M. ter Hofstede and Th.P. van der Weide. Formalisation of techniques: Chopping down the methodology jungle. Technical report, Department of Information Systems, University of Nijmegen, The Netherlands, dec 1990. Submitted to Information and Software Technology.

[10] ISO8879. Information Processing - Text and Office Systems - Standard General Markup Language (SGML), 1986-10-15.

[11] D.E. Knuth. *The T$_E$Xbook*. Addison Wesly, reading, Massachusetts, 1984.

[12] D. Lucarella. A Model for Hypertext-Based Information Retrieval. In *Proceedings of the European Conference on Hypertext - ECHT 90*, pages 81–94. Cambridge University Press, 1990.

[13] J. Nielsen. The art of navigating though Hypertext. *Communications ACM*, 33(3):296–310, March 1990.

[14] B. Schneiderman and G. Kearsley. *Hypertext Hands-On!* Addison-Wesley Publishing Company, 1989.

[15] P. Stotts and R. Furuta. Petri-Net-Based Hypertext: Document Structure with Browsing Semantics. *ACM Transactions on Information Systems*, 7(1):3–29, 1989.

[16] F. Tompa. A Data Model for Flexible Hypertext Database Systems. *ACM Transactions on Information Systems*, 7(1):85–100, January 1989.

A Knowledge-Based System for Fault Diagnosis in Real-Time Engineering Applications

T. Patrick Martin, Janice I. Glasgow, Michel P. Féret and Todd Kelley

Department of Computing and Information Science, Queen's University
Kingston, Ontario, CANADA K7L 3N6.

Abstract

We describe the development of a knowledge-based system for fault diagnosis in complex real-time engineering devices. The characteristics of this type of application require that the system combine reasoning, database, and real-time data acquisition capabilities. We concentrate on an explanation of the knowledge and database components of this system.

1 Introduction

The monitoring and diagnosis of failures in complex real-time engineering devices, such as robots or process control systems, is an important application area for knowledge-based (KB) systems. These devices typically require constant supervision and are often situated in remote or hazardous locations. A device is usually monitored by a set of sensors which continually produce streams of data indicating the states of the various components of that device.

A device of this kind is expected to be extremely reliable so when a fault occurs it is crucial to diagnose and repair the problem as soon as possible. However, they are often so complex that the experts performing the diagnosis have a difficult time dealing with the large amount of information required to make that diagnosis. The obvious solution is to develop a KB system to aid with the diagnosis. The properties of these devices, and of the diagnosis process, introduce difficult requirements for this KB system.

Diagnosis of a fault requires data about one or more components of the device and a general knowledge of the structure and the expected behaviour of the device. Two types of data are used in the diagnosis: *sensor* data, which describes the state of the device, and *engineering* data, which describes properties of the components such as maintenance schedules and reliability projections. The sensor data used in the diagnosis may be both current and historical. Thus, the KB system is required to store and manage potentially large amounts of sensor data. It is also required to accept this data in real-time. The engineering data may already exist in a database so the design of the KB system should be flexible enough to allow the integration of that database.

Our approach to building a fault diagnosis KB system is based on the observation that there are similarities among devices which allow us to consider a "family" of devices and not just a single device. The devices within a particular family have common global characteristics: they often have the same components; they are built along the same construction patterns, and they have parts which are bound by the same dependency relations. For example, all robots have electrical motors which activate joints that carry operating components, or all car engines have cylinders, pistons, valves, etc. The regularities among members of the family also mean that diagnosis is very similar from one member to another. Thus we are able to develop a "generic" KB system for a family of devices and then customize it for particular instances of that family.

This paper describes a generic fault diagnosis system for one family of real-time engineering devices. This family of devices is characterized by a hierarchical structure, that is, a device can be viewed as a hierarchy of components or group of components. A device is composed of a set of modules. Modules are in turn made up of streams which are series of device components. Sensors are positioned throughout the device to report upon the state of various device components

The system, called the *Automated Data Management System* or ADMS, was developed under a contract with Spectrum Engineering Corporation Ltd. and sponsored by the Strategic Technology for Automation and Robotics (STEAR) program in collaboration with the National Research Council of Canada. We have applied the ADMS to a robotic device called the Fairing Servicing Subsystem (FSS)[1]. It is a suitable demonstration application since it has a moderate level of sensor density and it is made up of a complex arrangement of interactive modules. The examples provided in this paper come from this system [spec90]. Ultimately, the ADMS is to be incorporated into the Mobile Servicing System,

Canada's contribution to the International Space Station.

In Section 2 we present an overview of the system structure and describe the purpose of each of the major system modules. We then concentrate on the knowledge base and database components of the system. Section 3 discusses the knowledge base component of the ADMS. It explains how knowledge is stored and outlines the diagnosis algorithm. Section 4 describes the database component of the ADMS and how it interacts with the knowledge base component during the diagnosis of a failure. Section 5 summarizes the paper.

2 Structure of the ADMS

The system architecture used in the design of the ADMS is described in detail in Féret *et. al.* [FGLJ90]. This architecture is intended to provide developers of specific applications with an effective design foundation and organizational policy. It supports a clear delineation of the components of the generic system, of the roles of these components and of their interactions. The architecture is also flexible enough to allow the developer to incorporate existing software into one or more of the components. The structure of the ADMS is shown in Figure 1.

The Data Analysis Module (DAM)is the interface between the ADMS and the device. It receives the real-time sensor data from the device, samples the data according to rates set by the system operator and passes the data on to the Data Management Module for insertion into the database. The Data Analysis Module triggers the diagnosis process whenever it detects a fault in the incoming data. It detects a fault by comparing a reading to expected ranges of values and then categorizes that fault as being of a particular fault type (e.g. out-of-range, inappropriate or irrational). The type of fault is determined by the reading and by the current state of the device.

The Data Management Module (DMM) maintains the database and provides access to that database to the other modules in the system. The Database (DB) stores static information about the device and its components, a history of the faults that have occurred, and the sensor data passed from the Data Analysis Module. A complete description of the Data Management Module is given in Section 4.

---

1. The FSS is a robot placed at the rear of a boat to replace damaged fairings on a cable which drags an underwater detection system. The fairings are essential to prevent the detection system from drifting away from the axis of the boat.

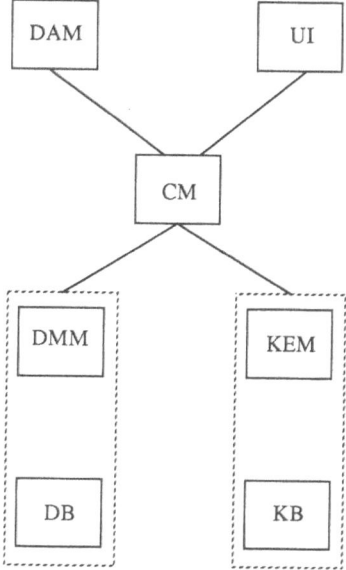

Figure 1 System Architecture

The main task of the Knowledge Engineering Module (KEM) is to perform diagnosis as accurately as possible. The first step of the diagnosis is to provide a list of potential diagnoses, possibly representing multiple faults. This list is then ranked according to various criteria such as mean time between failures, frequency of failures, or age. The ranked list is finally presented to the operator. The secondary task of the KEM is to maintain the Knowledge Base (KB). A more detailed description of the diagnosis algorithm and of the knowledge base are given in Section 3.

The User Interface (UI) provides the operator with access to the database and to the knowledge base. It also presents the diagnosis process and provides for explanations of the decision-making process. A comprehensive and consistent explanation facility is essential since it is important that the operator understands how the diagnosis process works and why specific choices are made by the program at different points during the diagnosis.

The Control Module (CM) is in charge of all the communications between the modules. It uses a simple blackboard paradigm where each task is given a priority value. A module picks up, and executes, the tasks ready for it in order of priority. A module will pass any return values from the execution of a task back to the Control Module for forwarding to the module that originated the task.

The current version of the ADMS runs on a SUN SPARC 1 workstation with the UNIX operating system. The ADMS is written mostly in C with the code for the diagnosis component written in Nial [nial85], a functional programming language developed at Queen's University. The database is implemented using the Oracle relational DBMS [oracle] and the knowledge base is implemented using the Nial Frame Language [nial87]. The user interface is implemented using X-windows [X]. Each module is implemented as a separate UNIX process and communication between the processes is via message-passing.

3 Knowledge Component

The primary purpose of the knowledge component of the system is to determine the exact location a fault occurred once it has been detected. The diagnosis process takes as input a fault, the location at which the fault was detected (by a sensor), and a fault type (determined by the Data Analysis Module). Based on this input, the current state of the device which is determined by the sensor data, and knowledge of the structure of the device, the diagnosis process must determine which component, or components, could have failed.

3.1 Knowledge Base

The knowledge base, which is maintained by the KEM, contains knowledge of the structure of the device. We view a device as a hierarchy of components or groups of components. Figure 2 shows a portion of this kind of decomposition hierarchy for the FSS. The device, in our example the FSS, is represented by the top node of the hierarchy. The device is composed of modules, for example the Nose Operator or Tail Operator. Modules are made up of streams, for example the TO_Arm, which are series of components. Streams are comprised of the individual device components, for example the Motor Starter, Fuse, Cable, etc., which can be diagnosed as sources of failure.

This structural knowledge is used to guide the diagnosis algorithm. Each node in the hierarchy can be considered as a potential pruning step, that is, the components in the subtree under that node can be eliminated from the set of possible sources of the failure. This decision is made by consulting one or more pruning rules attached to the node. A pruning rule is simply a description of a normal (or abnormal) behaviour or context for each represented entity in the device.

The association of nodes representing structural or functional entities in the device with the description of properties defining expected (or unexpected) behaviours or contexts can be considered as a tree-shaped *semantic network* [rich83]. We represent this semantic network with frames [nial87]. Each level in the hierarchy is defined by a single generic frame holding all information common to the nodes at that level. The instances of a generic frame contain the information specific to a particular node in the tree. The relation *IsPartOf* is used in the instance frames to represent the hierarchy of parts in the device.

Figure 2 contains an example of a stream substructure in the FSS. It is a series of components made up of a Motor Starter, a Fuse, a Cable, a Motor, a Joint, and a Gripper. The frame definition, in the Nial Frame Language, for this particular instance of a stream is given in Figure 3. The AKO slot gives the name of the generic frame of which the TO_Arm is an instance, namely a Stream. The CLASSIFICATION slot indicates whether the frame is GENERIC or INDIVIDUAL (i.e. an instance). The Components slot lists the components making up the stream, and the IsPartOf slot indicates the parent node in the Tail Operator structure.

The pruning rules are considered properties of individual nodes. The rules can be either general or specific. General rules apply to a type of component and are

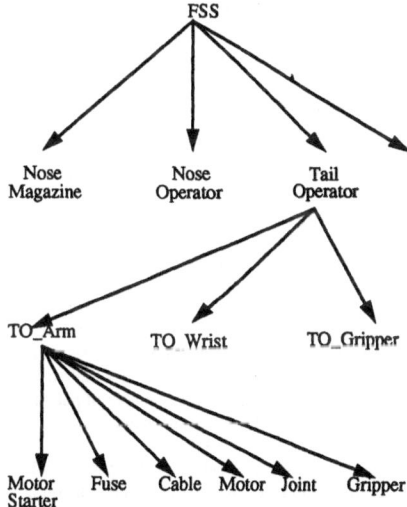

Figure 2 FSS Decomposition Hierarchy

```
fdefine TO_Arm
["AKO "VALUE ["Stream],
 "CLASSIFICATION "VALUE
     ["INDIVIDUAL],
 "Components "VALUE
     ("Motor_Starter "Fuse "Cable
      "Motor "Joint "Gripper),
 "IsPartOf "VALUE ["Tail_Operator]
]
```

Figure 3 Example Frame Definition

stored in the corresponding generic frame. Specific rules apply to a particular component and are stored in the corresponding instance frame. An example of a pruning rule is shown in Figure 4.

This rule states that if a part is missing and if the sensor which had an incorrect reading is not a Proximity Detector (i.e. the name of that sensor not one of the names of the Proximity Detectors), then all modules which are "upstream" in the part flow in the model of the device must be included in the list of possible faulty modules. All modules "downstream" in the part flow can be eliminated from further consideration.

3.2 Diagnosis Algorithm

The diagnosis algorithm is a top-down search of our semantic network. The paths followed in this search are selected according to a context which is partially defined by the sensor data contained in the database. The decomposition of the device into levels of complexity allows us to partition the diagnosis process into successive steps corresponding to the structure of the device. The diagnosis algorithm is defined by extracting pruning rules from the semantic network and building a series of pruning steps which correspond to levels and nodes in the hierarchical decomposition of the device. This extraction is done automatically.

The key problem in the algorithm is to optimize the search by eliminating branches as soon as possible in the process while preserving the validity of the final result. The efficiency of a search depends upon the effectiveness of the pruning rules. An effective set of rules will prune away all subtrees which can not contain faulty components, and leave a minimal number of potentially faulty components in the remaining subtrees.

Once the list of potential diagnoses has been produced, the diagnosis process ranks them by order of likelihood according to criteria such as age, time remaining in life expectancy, or mean time between failures. This last part of the diagnosis process is important because it determines how the list of potential diagnoses

```
conditions:
 (and (FaultType = 'PART MISSING)
      (not (Sensor in "FSS-NM-PD1
           "FSS-TM-PD1)))

effects:
 PossibleModules := cull link (module
    EACHRIGHT upstream
    "ReplacementNose "DamagedNose)
```

Figure 4 Example Pruning Rule

will be presented to the operator.

The current diagnostic process algorithm allows for multiple fault detection since it considers "all" possible components that may have a fault. Faults are diagnosed sequentially as they are detected so conflicting fault messages do not affect each other. Intermittent or recurring faults can be detected since a history is kept in the database which can be queried by the diagnostic process. In theory, multiple diagnosis processes could be spawned if multiple faults are detected but this is a topic for future research.

4 Database Component

The database stores the more structured information required by the system. We chose to take maximum advantage of the database software and to place any information easily representable as a relation in the database. The schema for our particular generic system contains seventeen relations which can be grouped into the following categories:

1. *Sensor Data*: operational data from the sensors;

2. *Fault Diagnosis*: data concerning previous diagnoses, such as the operational data triggering a particular diagnosis, the list of possible diagnoses, with reasons, for a particular fault, and the diagnosis confirmed by the operator for a particular fault;

3. *Engineering Data*: data describing all components and sensors, such as maintenance schedules, maintenance histories, predicted reliabilities and performance specifications;

4. *Failure Mechanisms*: data concerning known failures which is used by the diagnosis process in producing explanations of possible failures and possible remedial actions.

The two main tasks performed by the DMM are the insertion of the sensor data into the database, which must be performed in real-time, and the handling of queries from the KEM during the diagnosis of a fault. Our

```
sf161 is operation Comp {
    MS := getcomp "Motor_Starter Comp;
    (query_db 2 (string MS)'1'"") = 1
}
```

Figure 5 Example Pruning Rule with Query

design separates these tasks into different submodules so that, if necessary, they can be implemented as separate concurrent processes accessing the relational DBMS. It is important to minimize the delay a sensor data update may incur because of an concurrently executing diagnosis.

Queries from the diagnosis process are generated during the execution of some of the pruning rules. An example of such a rule is given in Figure 5. This rule is an example of a *sensor function* which is a boolean test on the state of a component. The failure state of a component can be described by some boolean combination of these sensor functions. The example rule "sf161" tests if the last reading for the motor starter in the stream before the occurrence of the fault was either ON (1) or OFF (0).

Queries, such as the one in Figure 5, are expressed as procedure calls of the form

query_db query_type string1 string2 string3

where "query_db" is the name of the Nial operation which sends out the query; "query_type" is an integer from 1 to 7 indicating the kind of query, and "string1", "string2", and "string3" are parameters (possibly empty) for the query. Queries are packaged in this form by the KEM and passed to the DMM where they are translated into a corresponding SQL query and then forwarded to the DBMS for execution. The results of the query follow the reverse path from the DBMS to the KEM.

The seven types of queries issued by the KEM are the following:

1. *library information*: The query returns the attribute value for the attribute name and component specified as arguments.

2. *data before fault*: The query returns a list of N readings corresponding to the last N values for the specified sensor before the fault occurred. The query issued by sf161 in Figure 4 is of this type; it requests the last reading for the sensor associated with the Motor Starter.

3. *data while motor on*: The query is similar to type two but the data starts when the motor was activated before the last fault.

4. *data for period*: The query returns all the readings for the specified sensor for the specified period of time before the fault occurred.

5. *data list while motor on*: The query returns N series of readings for the specified sensor corresponding to the last N periods of time before the fault during which the specified motor was on.

6. *fault information*: The query returns the name of the sensor which detected the most recent fault, the type of the fault and the time of the fault.

7. *mtbf information*: The query returns the predicted mean time between failures for the specified component.

There is typically a significant amount of redundancy to the queries being issued by the KEM. A very simple caching strategy is currently employed by the KEM to take advantage of this redundancy and consequently reduce the number of requests to the DMM. The KEM maintains a local cache of the last N queries and their responses. Whenever a query is encountered by the KEM it first checks this cache to see if the result is already available and only issues the query to the DMM if the result is not in the cache.

5 Summary

In this paper we discussed the use of a knowledge-based system for fault diagnosis in complex real-time engineering devices. The characteristics of these devices require that the system combine reasoning, database, and real-time data acquisition capabilities. Our approach to building such a system was to design a generic system applicable to a family of devices which could then be customized for use with particular members of this family. A prototype generic system has been built and adapted to one device.

The main topics of the paper were the diagnosis algorithm used and the representations for the knowledge and the data required by the algorithm. The structured data, such as the readings from the sensors and the characteristics of the components of the device, are kept in a relational DBMS. The structural knowledge of the device is represented in a tree-shaped semantic network and is used to guide diagnosis process. The key feature of the diagnosis process is the use of pruning rules associated with nodes in the tree to limit the search performed during a diagnosis. The interaction between the knowledge and database components during the diagnosis process was also described.

Work is continuing towards the development of a production level version of this system. This work will

292

include testing the system with larger and more complex devices and the construction of an application development package. This package will help users with the customization of the generic system for a particular device.

References

[FGLJ90] M. Féret, J. Glasgow, D. Lawson and M. Jenkins, An Architecture for Real-Time Diagnosis Systems, *Proceedings of the 3rd International Conference on Industrial and Engineering Applications of Artificial Intelligence and Expert Systems*, Charleston SC, pp. 9 – 15, July 1990.

[nial85] M.A. Jenkins and W.H. Jenkins, *The Q'Nial Reference Manual*, Nial Systems Ltd., Kingston, 1985.

[nial87] M.A. Jenkins and W.H. Jenkins, *Artificial Intelligence Toolkit for Q'Nial*, Nial Systems Ltd., Kingston, 1987.

[oracle] *Oracle Installation and User's Guide, Version 6*, Oracle Corp., 1989.

[X] C.D. Peterson, *Athena Widget Set — C Language Interface, X Window System, X Version 11, Release 4*, MIT, Cambridge MA, 1989.

[rich83] E. Rich, *Artificial Intelligence*, McGraw-Hill Publishing Co., 1983.

[spec90] *Automation of Operations Relating to an Automated Data Management System, Phase II, Milestone I Report*, Spectrum Engineering Corp. Ltd., Peterborough, October 1990.

An Expert System
to Support Mine Planning Operations

Martin Breunig*, Gernot Heyer*, Axel Perkhoff

Freie Universität Berlin,
Dept. of Computer Science,
Nestorstr. 8-9, D-1000 Berlin 31,
(breunig, heyer, perkhoff) @inf.fu-berlin.·

Michael Seewald

Technische Universität Berlin,
Dept. of Mining Engineering,
Straße des 17. Juni 135, D-1000 Berlin 12

Abstract:

Practice-oriented support of complex mine planning operations is a very ambitious domain for expert systems. The necessary prerequisites for this task are relating to the access to external databases, to the handling of uncertain knowledge and to spatial reasoning. They can be considered as fundamental requirements to recent expert systems.

The paper presented reports about an ongoing research project which concentrates on the above mentioned topics. First solutions are discussed, especially the coupling of expert systems and autonomous databases based on a logical integration of the heterogeneous data, the combination of probabilistic networks and production rules to handle uncertain knowledge and spatial reasoning, using abstract expressions with spatial context deriving from spatial data and operations. These solutions are implemented in an expert system prototype, using a typical mine planning task as background for the research work.

Keywords:
Expert System-Database-Coupling, Logical Data Integration, Uncertain Knowledge, Spatial Abstraction, Mine Planning

1 Introduction

Mine planning operations are usually very complex and ill-structured, they are fraught with uncertain and vague knowledge, and moreover, the solution process requires the handling of a large amount of technical, economical, geological and spatial data.

The Department of Mining Engineering at Technische Universität Berlin is developing in cooperation with the Department of Computer Science at Freie Universität Berlin an expert system prototype to assist the layout planning of face operations for an underground coal mine. This research work aims at investigating and at developing the scientific requirements for the usage of knowledge-based techniques in the field of mine planning.

In the following a typical mine planning task, which serves as background for the research work, is briefly outlined.

* supported by Deutsche Forschungsgesellschaft
(German Research Society) by grant no Schw 415/1-1

Thereafter some essential requirements to the expert system are discussed and a first approach to integrate external databases, to reason with uncertain knowledge and to spatial reasoning is presented. As these topics are not exclusively related to mining, the research work done is fundamental for recent expert systems.

2 The Layout Planning of Face Operations in Underground Coal Mines

In German underground hardcoal mines, the longwall mining method is generally applied (fig. 1).

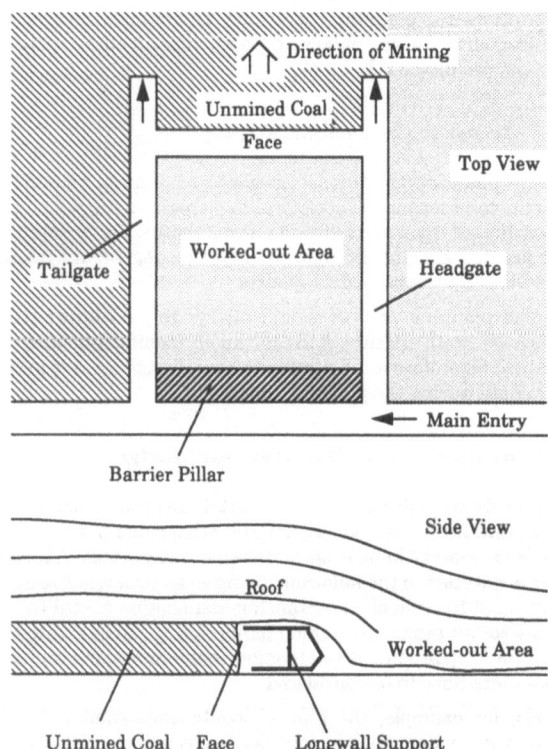

Fig. 1 : Schematic Representation of a Working Panel

About ten different layout variants of longwall mining are common. The layout planning of face operations results in selecting the most favourable variant for a given planning situation.

To select the optimal layout variant, a number of practical requirements with sometimes contradicting targets has to be taken into account. These targets are reached to a strongly diverging degree by the different layout alternatives. Whenever difficult operational conditions prevail, selection of a suitable layout ends up in finding a solution, which contains many compromises. Among the practical demands, which have to be fulfilled by the layout, e. g. the following have to be considered: All potential measures to control methane emission, mine climate, dust and spontaneous combustion, to optimize roadway-driving operations, etc.

The expert system aims at supporting the planning engineer throughout the whole planning procedure, starting with the evaluation of actual, practical requirements to the layout solution, and ending with the integration of flanking technical measures to compensate the drawbacks of the variant selected, in order to design a satisfactory and practicable layout solution [1].

3 Requirements of the Expert System

An expert system, designed for a practice-oriented support of complex mine planning operations, has to meet diverse requirements. In the following three fundamental requirements are discussed.

3.1 Access to External Databases

Mine planning operations are based on a large amount of technical, economical, geological and spatial data, which are distributed to several autonomous databases. These databases are managed by different database management systems and based on various data models.

The planning process should always rely on latest data, however, data are subject to continuous modification and updating. Therefore it is desirable to have direct access to external data during the planning process.

3.2 Reasoning with Uncertain Knowledge

In the field of mine planning, uncertainties arise from uncertain and incomplete geological and economical data as well as from expert's knowledge handling vague contexts. The latter is outlined in the following, using as an example the evaluation of the risk of a spontaneous combustion of coal in the worked-out area of a working panel (fig. 1). To evaluate the risk of a spontaneous combustion, numerous facts and parameters have to be considered.

So, for example, the risk of spontaneous combustion is partly dependent on the quantity of oxygen in the worked-out area and on the duration of its influence to the coal. However, this context cannot be formulated adequately by a production rule like "If the quantity of oxygen and its duration of influence to the coal are sufficient, a spontaneous combustion will

occur" but rather by a rule like "The more likely the quantity of oxygen and its duration of influence to the coal are to be adequate, the more likely a spontaneous combustion will occur". For reasoning with this type of uncertain contexts, a special representation formalism for uncertain knowledge has to be applied.

3.3 Operations for Spatial Reasoning

Reasoning with spatial data is an essential for mine planning operations. To give an example, "precalculation of methane emission" is presented, which uses spatial reasoning very intensively whenever certain planning situations prevail.

Methane is a volatile component of coal deposits, which is set free during the coal winning process. As it causes explosions under certain circumstances, the content of methane in the mine air is normally limited to 1%.

To evaluate the expected methane emission for a planned panel, normally a special precalculation is carried out. The results of the precalculation are depending on technical as well as on geological parameters and of course on the amount of methane, which is contained within a defined region right near the planned panel. Therefore, old workings in this region require a special treatment, as they cause a reduction of content of methane. To integrate regions with a reduced content of methane into the precalculation of methane emission in an appropriate way, the exact spatial position of the old workings as well as their spatial relation to the planned panel have to be considered. Within this context those regions of the planned panel are of special interest, which are overlapped by old workings.

Generally spatial reasoning is not based on elementary data representations. It is evident that reasoning based on abstract expressions relating to a spatial context like "overlying old working" has to be executed in the expert system. Consequently, the spatial information usually is processed on a very abstract and symbolic level. Therefore the definition of context specific spatial expressions to support spatial reasoning [2] has to be provided.

4 Realization - a First Prototype System

This chapter outlines the approaches which have been undertaken to meet the requirements to the expert system described above.

4.1 Coupling an Expert System Shell with External Database Systems

To provide direct access to distributed heterogeneous data for the mine planning procedure, the different databases have to be integrated logically and the view of the data obtained this way has to be coupled to the expert system.

In a first prototype, the hybrid expert shell BABYLON [3], which is the platform for the mine planning expert system, was coupled with the relational data base management system INGRES [4] (fig. 2).

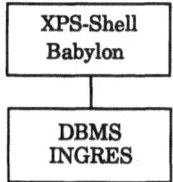

Fig. 2: System Architecture of the First Prototype

The database contains economical and technical data of working panels and old workings. These data originate from the database ZPD[1] of the German mining company Ruhrkohle AG, which is supporting the ongoing research work. The access to the database is realized as a tight coupling [5, 6] that allows loading data into the expert system at any time during the inference process. At present state only reading access to the database is realized.

To extend functionality of expert systems with regard to access to different autonomously managed data an interface for logical data integration is developed (fig. 3). The definition of application dependent schemes and user defined operations abstracts from original data representation. Goal is the transparent use of data and operations from e.g. expert systems with schemes that hide from location, representation and management.

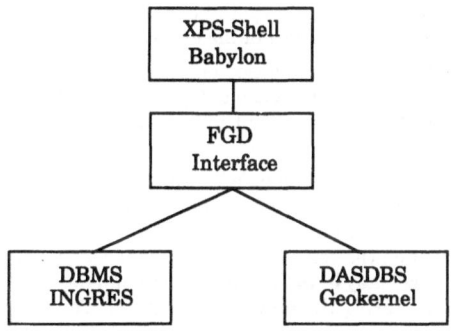

Fig. 3: Extended System Architecture

The data model FGD (Functional Global Data model) [7] represents a functional interface, which supports abstraction mechanisms of recent programming languages and semantic data models. The data manipulation language of FGD is based on functional languages like Galileo [8, 9, 10] and is extended for the integration of especially pre-existing heterogeneous databases and for accessing the data in a transparent way as described above.

The coupling of Babylon and the FGD-Interface (fig. 3) is now being developed. On the database side another data source managed by the DASDBS Geokernel [11, 12] is under realisation. The data are extracted from the graphic information system DIGMAP[2][13]. This system provides 3D-graphic support for planning purposes based on geological and spatial data about deposits.

1. Abbr. for "Zechen-Projekt-Datei" (Mine Project Database)

2. Abbr. for "Digitales Interaktives Geologisch-Markscheiderisches Analyse- und Planungssystem" (digital interactive geological and mine surveying analyse and planning system)

4.2 Using Probabilistic Networks to Reason with Uncertain Knowledge

In probability theory [14] the truth value of each fact A is represented by its probability p(A) of being true. A dependency between two facts A and B is described by the conditional probabilities p(B|A) and p(B|¬A). By this conditional probabilities it is possible to evaluate p(B), providing that p(A) is given, and vice versa. The dependencies between uncertain facts can be represented by directed, acyclic graphs, representing facts as nodes and dependencies between them as edges. Such graphs are called "probabilistic networks". A detailed description of the propagation of the probabilities in probabilistic networks is given in [15].

Probability theory can also be applied to probabilities being numerical measures of subjective belief [16]. With regard to the risk of a spontaneous combustion, for example, the evaluated quantity of oxygen in the worked-out area can be represented also by its likelihood for being sufficient to cause a spontaneous combustion, since this is the relevant aspect in this context. This likelihood results from subjective estimation of the expert.

The research work in this field aims at integrating probabilistic networks in rule-based expert systems, in order to use probabilistic networks instead of production rules, whenever uncertainty has to be represented explicitly. Production rules are leading from certain premises to certain conclusions as well as to uncertain ones. Probabilistic networks, however, usually are leading from uncertain premises to uncertain conclusions. Therefore reasoning based on certain base parameters is done by production rules. Whenever the inference process is leading to uncertain conclusions, these conclusions are representing the basic nodes of the probabilistic network. The combination of these two representation formalisms is demonstrated in figure 4, where solid arrows represent probabilistic dependencies and dashed arrows stand for discrete production rules.

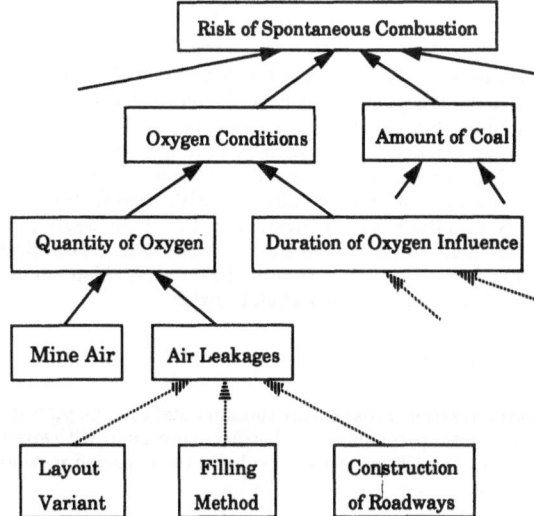

Fig. 4: Combining a Probabilistic Network (Solid Arrows) with Rule-based Reasoning (Dashed Arrows)

There are two possibilities to provide probabilities for basic nodes of a probabilistic network. The first one is to apply production rules which yield probabilities as conclusion. For example, the amount of air leakages in the worked-out area is depending on layout variant, filling method and construction of roadways chosen for the planned panel. The amount of air leakages can be investigated by a production rule like "If gastight roadside packs are constructed on both sides of the worked-out area, then the likelihood of the air leakages to be sufficient to cause a spontaneous combustion is 0.1".

The second way to obtain probabilities is based on mapping given numerical values of parameters to a scale from 0 to 1, according to their likelihood to cause a spontaneous combustion. This mapping occurs by an arithmetic function. To give an example, the duration of oxygen influence (D) in days, which is inferred by production rules, is mapped by the following function to its likelihood p(D) for causing a spontaneous combustion:

$$p(D) = \begin{cases} 0, & \text{if } D \leq 2 \\ (D-2)/40, & \text{if } 2 < D < 42 \\ 1, & \text{if } D \geq 42 \end{cases}$$

According to this function, a duration of oxygen influence to the coal of less than two days is definitely too short to cause a spontaneous combustion while a duration of more than six weeks is sufficient anyway for doing so.

Reasoning in probabilistic networks is carried out by calculating probabilities in an appropriate way. For example, the probability of sufficient oxygen conditions (C) is calculated using the probabilities for sufficient quantity of oxygen (Q) and for sufficient duration of oxygen influence (D) (see fig. 4) and also the conditional probabilities by

$$\begin{aligned} p(C) = \;& p(Q \wedge D) &*& \; p(C \mid Q \wedge D) + \\ & p(Q \wedge \neg D) &*& \; p(C \mid Q \wedge \neg D) + \\ & p(\neg Q \wedge D) &*& \; p(C \mid \neg Q \wedge D) + \\ & p(\neg Q \wedge \neg D) &*& \; p(C \mid \neg Q \wedge \neg D) \end{aligned}$$

To evaluate the risk of a spontaneous combustion the probabilities of all dependent nodes of the network are calculated bottom-up this way. Dependencies in probabilistic networks, however, can also be applied for reasoning in the other direction. For example, if the quantity of oxygen is given, the maximal duration of oxygen influence with regard to optimal safety conditions can be evaluated. For implementing the probabilistic network, the Bayesian Reasoning Tool BaRT [17] is applied, which is running in the same Lisp environment as the expert system shell Babylon.

4.3 Spatial Abstraction

Spatial relationships [18] are fundamental to mine planning. This chapter presents some abstract expressions with spatial reference, which are used to evaluate the expected methane emission.

In the context of methane emission the planning engineer is interested in all overlying panels, which are the old work-

ings situated within a certain distance above the planned panel (fig. 5). In other contexts the overlying panels can be defined differently. For example, in the context of the risk of a spontaneous combustion the definition of the overlying panels is relating only to the nearest panel above the planned panel. Therefore such spatial relationships have to be defined as context-dependent spatial operations.

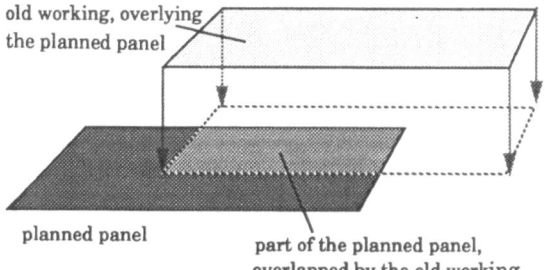

old working, overlying the planned panel

planned panel

part of the planned panel, overlapped by the old working

Fig. 5: Overlying Panels

There is an "abstraction gap" between the spatial expressions used in the expert system and the hard data and operations in the underlying systems for data handling and computational geometry. Therefore an abstraction of spatial data representations and operations [19] is required for the definition of context specific spatial expressions. These expressions may be part of rules in the expert system.

Spatial abstraction is based on transformation from Euclidian coordinate information to topological relations. This is a direct way from basic point information to spatial reasoning.

The data structure of a panel in the ZPD database consists of non-spatial attributes like number, name, etc. and of spatial attributes containing the point coordinates of the panel. Dependent on the context, the relevant aspect of the geometry of a panel may be defined by the first and the last position of the face during the mining of the panel. The positions of the face are geometric data of the working panel, which are acquired monthly. Non-spatial attributes are not to be changed by the abstraction process. For spatial analysis the planning engineer is interested in the abstract geometry rather than point coordinates of the panel. Therefore the following mapping has to be executed:

spatial-mapping:
    set of point-coordinates -> geometry of the panel

The abstraction of spatial data representations is only a first step of spatial abstraction in the expert system. The second step is an abstraction of spatial operations.

For example, the overlying panels relevant to the context of methane emission are obtained by the following operations:

overlying-panels   : panel -> panel*
degree-of-overlapping : panel -> (panel, real)*

These operations are mapping the abstract data representation panel to a set of panels, respectively (panel, real)-set.

The overlying-panels operation determines the set of all panels situated above a given panel. The data used as input and output are the panels introduced above. An advanced operation is degree-of-overlapping which delivers the set of all relevant panels situated above a planned panel, each with its percentage of overlying in proportion to the area of the planned panel.

These complex operations can be defined by a set of basic geometric operations. The degree-of-overlapping operation is defined by the abstract operation overlying-panels and the basic geometric operation area. The overlying-panels operation is defined by the basic geometric operations intersection and above (fig. 6).

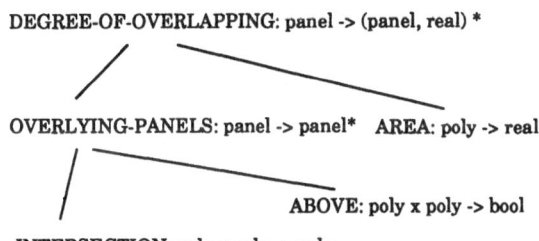

DEGREE-OF-OVERLAPPING: panel -> (panel, real) *

OVERLYING-PANELS: panel -> panel*   AREA: poly -> real

ABOVE: poly x poly -> bool

INTERSECTION: poly x poly -> poly

Fig. 6: Abstraction of Basic Spatial Operations

The first basic operation intersects two polygons yielding a polygon. If the intersection is not empty, the polygons are tested whether lying within a certain interval above each other by the second basic operation above. The third basic operation area computes the areas of the polygons in order to calculate the respective degree of the overlyings in proportion to the total area of the planned panel.

The definition of abstract spatial expressions may replace many single rules at an "atomic information level" in expert systems. For example, the degree-of-overlapping operation replaces rules like "if any z-coordinate of any panel > any z-coordinate of a panel within a window on the x-y-plane then the panels are overlying by the given percentage".

5 Conclusions and Outlook

Essential requirements of expert systems designed to support mine planning operations have been discussed. Possible solutions and the realization in a first prototype system have been presented. Mechanisms for the abstraction and condensation of basic data and operations have been considered very useful.

In future the query processing in the integrated schemes will be inquired to optimize the query evaluation. It will be examined how the uncertainties of the basic data can be investigated and considered in reasoning. Context-specific spatial abstraction on top of representation-independent basic geometric operations will be examined. Further problems to be considered are, for example, efficient data buffering in the expert system, communication and database update operations.

Acknowledgements:

We would like to thank our student collaborators Michael Walter for implementing the coup- ling of Babylon to Ingres, and Stefan Schuster, Barbara Winkler and Bernd Machenschalk for supporting the implementation of the expert system prototype. Furthermore Mr. R. Beez, Ibbenbüren Collery, for his expertise of methane emission and for providing the program for precalculation, Mr. H. Auberg, DeutscheMontanTechnologie, for his expertise in the field of spontaneous combustion and the Ruhrkohle AG for providing ZPD and DIGMAP data. Last, but not least, Prof. Dr.-Ing. H. Schweppe and Prof. Dr.-Ing. F. L. Wilke for supporting our research.

References:

[1] Wilke, F.L., Seewald, M.: The Fundamentals for an Expert System, Designed to Assist the Lay-out Planning of Face Operations for an Unterground Coal Mine, in: Proc. of the 21st APCOM-Symposium, Las Vegas, Nevada, 1989

[2] Buisson L.: Reasoning on Space with Object-Centered Knowledge Representations, in: Design and Implementation of Large Spatial Databases. Proceedings 1st Int. Symposium SSD. Lecture Notes in Computer Science 409, 1989

[3] Christaller, T., di Primio, F., Voss, A.: The AI-Workbench Babylon (in German), Addison-Wesley, Bonn, 1986

[4] Relational Technology Inc.: INGRES / SQL Reference Manual, Release 6, Alameda, Califonia, 1989

[5] Härder, T., Mattos, N., Puppe, F.: About Coupling of Database Systems and Expert Systems (in German), in: State of the Art 3, Oldenbourg Verlag, Munich, 1987

[6] Mattos, N.: An Approach to Knowledge Base Management, Doctoral Thesis, Universität Kaiserslautern, Kaiserslautern, Germany, 1989

[7] Perkhoff A.: A functional transformation language for the logical integration of heterogeneous data (in German), in: Proc. Datenbanken in Büro, Technik und Wissenschaft BTW'91, Kaiserslautern, Germany, 1991.

[8] Albano A., Cardelli L., Orsini R.: Galileo A strongly typed interactive conceptual language, ACM Trans. Database Systems, Vol. 10, No. 2, 1985.

[9] Albano A., Giamotti F., Orsini R., Pedreschi D.: The Type System of GALILEO, in: M.P. Atkinson, P. Buneman, R. Morrison (eds.). Topics in Inf. Systems, Data Types and Persistence; Springer Verlag, 1988.

[10] R. Bird, P. Wadler: Introduction to Functional Programming; Prentice Hall Int. Series in Computer Science, 1988

[11] Schek H.-J. and Waterfeld W.: A Database Kernel System for Geoscientific Applications, in: Proceedings 2nd Int. Symposium on Spatial Data Handling, Seattle, Washington, 1986.

[12] Waterfeld W., Schek H.-J.: The DASDBS Geokernel - an Extensible Database System for GIS, in: K. Turner (ed.). Three-Dimensional Modelling with Geoscientific Information Systems, Proceedings NATO Advanced Research Workshop, Santa Barbara, California, 1990

[13] Dann R., Schulte-Ontropp R.: DIGMAP - The Software System in the Surveying Department of the Ruhrkohle A.G. (in German), in: Das Markscheidewesen 96, No.1, 1989

[14] de Finetti, B.: Theory of Probability, John Wiley & Sons, New York, 1974

[15] Pearl, J.: Probabilistic Reasoning in Intelligent Systems, Morgan Kaufmann Publishers Inc., San Mateo, California, 1986

[16] Cheeseman, P.: Probabilistic versus Fuzzy Reasoning, in: Kanal, L., Lemmer, F (eds.): Uncertainty in AI, Elsevier Science Publishers, New York, 1986

[17] Booker, L., Hota, N., Hemphill, G.: Implementing a Bayesian Scheme for Revising Belief Commitments, Proc. of the 3rd AAAI Workshop on Uncertainty in AI, Seattle, Washington, 1987

[18] Freeman J.: The modelling of spatial relations. Computer Graphics and Image Processing 4, 1975

[19] Guenther O., Buchmann A.: Research Issues in Spatial Databases. SIGMOD RECORD, Vol. 19, No.4, Dec. 1990

Knowledge Base Management Systems in the Field of High Energy Physics

Renate Meyer   Gunter Schlageter

FernUniversität Hagen
Feithstraße 140
D-5800 Hagen (Germany)

Abstract

The huge amount and the complexity of data that occur in high energy physics experiments require the use of knowledge based techniques. Conventional coupling of expert systems and data base systems leads to complex application programs on top of the data base systems which makes explicit access to the knowledge about the stored data difficult or impossible. Therefore, knowledge base management systems are considered which are based on a deductive database system with external rule management. In this paper we introduce two application fields in the area of High Energy Physics, motivate the use of Knowledge Base Management Systems in this field, and present a prototype system.

1. Introduction

The amount and complexity of the data that occur in high energy physics experiments urgently require the use of 'intelligent' systems for automatic deduction and classification of events. One of the projects that approaches this problem is 'Expert Systems Applications in the field of natural science'[*]. The aim of the project is to support various aspects of the experiments by knowledge based techniques.

This paper deals with two parts of the joint project: 'An Expert System Shell for Error Diagnosis in Detectors' (short: Delphi project) and 'Error Diagnosis in the FASTBUS System' (short: FASTBUS project). We put the main emphasis on the necessary co-operation between expert system and database technology.

The first 'ad-hoc' approach was to use a system which coupled an expert system (XPS) and a database system (DBS). The coupling was realized as an application program of the DBS.

---

[*] This project is supported by the 'KI-Verbund North Rhine-Westphalia', founded by the Minister for Science and Research of North Rhine-Westphalia within the framework of the co-operation 'Applications of AI'.

This program became rather complex, because it contained a lot of coded knowledge about the structure of and the access on stored data. Since the FASTBUS project would possibly be an application of co-operating XPS, this sort of knowledge must be available to other XPS [8]. To enable access to knowledge, it is necessary that the knowledge is explicitly stored and that retrieval operators for the stored knowledge are available. To preserve the functionality of the coupled system, the stored knowledge must be used to derive new data from the stored data (intensional query mechanism). These requirements lead to the idea of a Knowledge Base Management System (KBMS) which provide an intensional query mechanism and an external rule management. The development of the KBMS, especially the rule management, is at present still in the initial state.

This paper is organized as follows. Section 2 introduces the two application areas in the field of High Energy Physics. Section 3 covers coupling between the XPS and the DBS, which represents the project work on the part of the University of Hagen up to now. Section 4 deals with our present work, i.e. with the development of a KBMS. We introduce a rough concept of a KBMS, discuss the advantages of such systems in the two presented application areas, and present a prototype system.

2. Application field

A new electron positron collider at the European High Energy Physics Research Center CERN near Geneva has started operating in July '89. In the collider ring electrons and their anti-particles, the positrons, are accelerated in opposite directions. Each time an electron collides with a positron in a so called event, many new and partially short-lived particles arise. Some particles can be identified with the help of large detector systems.

At the locations, where the particles collide, experiments were installed, and one of these is the Delphi experiment [3],[2]. There are Microstrip Detectors, Time projection chambers, Ring imagine Cherenkov-counter, as well as large Drift chambers, Scintillation hodoscopes and several electromagnetic and hadronic calorimeters. Altogether, there are 150 000 electronic channels or 500 000 components, which have to be supervised permanently during the data acquisition.

Within the Delphi experiment data is read out by the FASTBUS system ([3], [5], [4]). FASTBUS is a standardized modular databus system for data-acquisition, data processing, and control.
FASTBUS make it possible to extend a bus or split a bus into several autonomous bus segments by Segment Interconnect modules. Masters can get mastership of a bus segment and initiate data transfers to or from slaves. Several masters can access the same bus segment, however not at the same time. This architecture enables the construction of highly complicated multiprocessor/multibus systems.

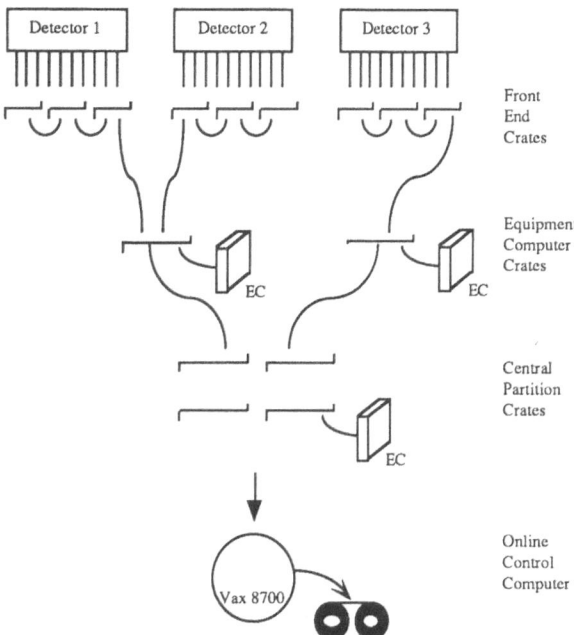

Fig.1: Layout of the Delphi Acquisition System.

In the case of the Delphi experiment, for instance, there are 172 FASTBUS crates, a large number of FASTBUS segments, around 1000 processors, and a total of at least 1000 FASTBUS modules. All these electronic modules are spread over several counting rooms. The layout of the acquisition system is tree-like (see Fig.1): On the top there are several DELPHI detectors. They feed their data into so called Front

End Electronics located in the Front End FB-Crates, whose main task is to digitize the incoming data. From there data is sent 'downwards' to the respective Equipment Computer Crates where the data is collected for each detector partition. Each partition has an Equipment Computer used for event monitoring and for initialisation of that partition. In the next step data will be sent from the Equipment Computer Crates to the Central Partition Crates. Finally, to accomplish the data taking process, the event data is read by the main online control computer which then writes it onto tape.
Each part of the system can be accessed from the VAXes via FASTBUS standard software. These routines are used to perform FASTBUS actions such as reading from or writing to certain registers in FASTBUS modules. A lot of information about the status of execution is obtained by analyzing the return code of the routines.

The specialists in detectors and FASTBUS are available only for a certain length of time. For that reason knowledge based systems which detect errors in detectors and in the acquisition system should be developed and used in the Delphi experiment.

3. A Coupled XP-DB System

During a pilot project* an XPS (Delphi Expert) detecting errors in one particular detector was developed by the universitiy of Wuppertal in co-operation with the university of Dortmund [1]. The aim of the Delphi project is to develope an XPS shell based on Delphi Expert, making it possible to build XPS used for the other detectors in Delphi experiment.

Delphi Expert was implemented by means of OPS5. To realize complex processing and graphic illustrations OPS5 was not sufficient. Therefore, Pascal procedures called from OPS5 were often used by the developers. Furthermore, external storing of data was realized by means of Pascal. Instead of Pascal files a DBS should be used turning from the XPS to the XPS shell. This step requires communication between OPS5, Pascal, and the DBS. A program environment was realized to enable communication that is independent of a special application. The program environment essentially consists of transfer and converting routines between OPS5, Pascal, and the DBS.
The project task of the Hagener group was the connection between programming environment and DBS. The central issue of this task was how to represent the complex structures and access mechanism of the programming environment within the DB. For time reasons a commercial DBS was used.

_____

* supported by the Minister for Science and Research of North Rhine Westphalia

Coupling the relational DBS Oracle with the programming environment [10] one gains from advantages of DBS like integrity and security of data, concurrent access, and efficiency by set oriented working method and optimized access.

The structure used by the programming environment is a complex object; and to access it requires a fixpoint operator. Relational DBS provide neither fixpoint operators nor to store complex objects. Only an extensive application program of the DBS makes both possible.

Such an application program was implemented in Hagen and runs together with Delphi XPS just being installed in CERN. The relational DBS Oracle was used for this implementation. The application program of the DBS was written by means of Pascal and the Precompiler of Oracle. The implementation took place on Vax workstations using the VAX VMS operating system.

4. Knowledge Base Management Systems

In the coupled system of Delphi Expert and Oracle, knowledge about the structure as well as knowledge about an access to this structure is hidden in the application program. An investigation of exemplary queries with POSTGRES and the concept of deductive DBS [7] demonstrated that systems which are able to use knowledge for the deduction of data considerably reduce the volume of the application program (see below).

The development of XPS within the FASTBUS project is still in the initial state. There exists a prototype used in the initial phase of the bus system [5]. For the overall problem a distributed solution with co-operating XPS is taking shape [4]. In such an application the knowledge of one of the cooperating XPS must be available to the others.

If a cooperating XPS is coupled with a DBS and not only data but also a part of the knowledge is transferred from the XPS to the DBS then this knowledge must also be available to the other XPS. For this, the knowledge must be stored and accessable in a suitable fashion.

The solution realized in the Delphi project does not provide these features, because a part of the transferred knowledge is hidden in the application program.

A system, that could be useful in both application fields, should manage knowledge in an explicit manner (rules, horn clauses) and make it available to other application. Furthermore, it must use the stored knowledge in the derivation process. Such system, that consists of an intensional query mechanism and an external knowledge or rule management is called **knowledge base management system** (KBMS).

Let us assume that Delphi Expert is coupled with a KBMS instead of a DBS. Then up to now the knowledge hidden in the application program will be stored explicitly in rules. In order

to derive data by means of this knowledge the intensional query mechanism is necessary.

Research in the area of deductive database systems led to wide basic knowledge with regard to the processing and optimization of the intensional mechanism [6], [14]. Besides theoretical foundations there exists practical knowledge from projects like NAIL!, LDL and POSTGRES (see [14]).

With regard to the intensional query mechanism of KBMS we have to answer the question, which of the known methods is the best one for the application [11] and the co-operation with the knowledge management. For example, it is quite possible, that the same functions or structures are used during both the access of knowledge and the derivation of data.

Deductive DBS store knowledge only in unstructured bitstrings and processed it in an internal form of rules by the query mechanism to derive new data from stored ones. An external rule management that stores knowledge in single parts and makes it available to users does not take place.

However, such kind of knowledge management would be beneficial for a coupling with an XPS: Besides the simplification of the application program this results in a higher flexibility, because knowlegde managed by a DBS may be changed, enlarged or deleted without change of source code. Furthermore, it is available to other application programs, e.g. for derivation of meta knowledge in a coupling of co-operating XPS. Operating the KBMS stand-alone this knowledge is beneficial for the user, too, e.g. if the user gets unexpected answers or the resulting data indicate some regularity the user wants to know whether it is coincidental. In such cases, it would be necessary to query the knowledge base and to get knowledge rather than data as result.

In order to meet these requirements the rule management must be able to store syntactically correct rules in a rule base. However, it is not yet clear how rules must be divided, which information about rules must be stored and which relationships between rules must be regarded to support the intensional query mechanism as well as to enable the access to knowledge. This will be clarified when the query operators for the rule base are fixed, i.e. the query language is defined. In this context some query operators proposed by [9] are of some interest: e.g. which knowledge is stored, whether the stored knowledge contradicts hypothetical knowledge or whether there exits stored knowledge meets the condition of a hypothetical knowledge.

In order to achieve the required flexibility insert, delete and update operators on the rule base are necessary.

Moreover the support of the intensional query mechanism by the rule management must be clarified. Among others the rule management must enable the access to rules.

4.1. KBMS in the Delphi Project

In the Delphi project a programming environment (PE) was developed which makes it possible to transfer elements of OPS5 to Pascal and Oracle and vice versa. In the PE these elements are called *instances* of *classes* and *PE-relation instances* of *PE-relations*. Therefore, there is an instance level and a description level. The basic structure of the PE is called the *net*. This is obtained by connecting two elements with an existing relationship at the instance level.

Parts of the net are transferred between Pascal, Oracle and OPS5 portions. These parts are query results. The queries are defined at the description level and evaluated at the instance level. The algorithm below processes the result of a query:

Algorithm Query Evaluation.

Input: query = (root-class, PE-relations, restrictions)

1. The root-class instances which satisfy the restrictions in the query are part of the result;

2. **while** new instances are found

   if ik, an instance of class k, is part of the result,

     /* Case 1: outward edges */

     for all PE-Relations (k,j) of the query

       if an instance (ik,ij) of the PE-Relation (k,j) exsists in the net

         and if ik satisfies the restrictions,

         then ij, an Instance of class j and the edge (ik,ij) are part of the result.

     /* Case 2: inward edges */

     for all PE-Relations (j,k) of the query

       if an instance (ij,ik) of the PE-Relation (j,k) exsists in the net

         and if ij satisfies the restrictions,

         then ij, an Instance of class j and the edge (ij,ik) are part of the result.

Output: result (a part of the net of instances).

When mapping the PE portions to the relational DBS only the nodes of the net are stored physically. With any query the edges are passed as parameters of the form $R(class_1,class_2,attr_1)$ and $E(X_1, ... , X_n)$ by the OPS5 or Pascal portion. The application program interprets these parameters as a relationship between instances of the *class1* and *class2*, where the instances (each an n-tuple $<X_1, ... , X_n>$) of the class *class1* are connected with the instances of the class *class2*, (via its first attribute and *attr1*.).and the instances of class *class1* meet the restrictions $E(X_1, ... , X_n)$.

The required net which consists of instances of various classes is computed by the application program. This is done by recursively searching all instances which are described by the query and connected with the root. So the application program contains complete knowledge of the description level: the net is described by relationships, instances of two classes are connected by relationships, all instances of a net are connected with each other. Additionally it contains the algorithmic knowledge how the instances of this relationship can be accessed in the DB and how to get all instances connected with the root.

In contrast to a relational DBS in a KBMS which processes explicit knowledge a rule base would exist consisting of a dynamic part which changes with every query and a static part which is valid for the whole application. The static part is stored externally. Both form a query, that can be processed by the intesional query mechanism.

dynamic:

$R_i(C_{i1},C_{i2},attr_{i1}).$ $\forall$ i ε {1,...,k};

$E_j(X_1, ... , X_{nj})$ $\forall$ j ε {1,...,k};

?- $node(class_1, X_1, ... , X_{n1}), ... , node(class_k, X_1, ... , X_{n1}).$

static:

$node(Class_j, X_1, ... , X_{nj}) :- R(C_i,Class_j,attr_i),$ *root*

     $C_i(X_1,...,X_{nj}),$

     $E_i(X_1,...,X_{nj}).$

$node(Class_j, X_1, ... , X_{nj}) :- R(C_i,Class_j,attr_i),$ *outward*

     $node(C_i,Y_1,..,attr_i,.,Y_{ni}),$

     $E_i(Y_1,...,Y_{ni}),$

     $Class_j (attr_i, ... ,X_{nj}).$

$node(Class_j, X_1, ... , X_{nj}) :- R(Class_j,C_i,attr_j),$ *inward*

     $node(C_i,attr_j,...,Y_{ni}),$

     $Class_j (X_1,...,attr_i, ... ,X_{nj}),$

     $E_j(X_1,...,X_{nj}).$

The above rules are managed by the KBMS and are processed by means of the intensional query mechanism when putting a query=(root, PE-relations, restrictions). In this case the application program only would consist of conversion routines.

The knowledge about the structures is stored in form of rules. The algorithmic knowledge is covered by the intensional query mechanism and therefore is application independent. Such a KBMS could be able to couple XPS without using the PE of the Delphi project.

4.2. KBMS in the FASTBUS Project

The FASTBUS-DBS contains structured objects (e.g. HWConf, Environment, Scopes), which are administered by the FASTBUS-System-management [12], a complex application-program for Oracle. An XPS or a set of cooperating XPSs in the FASTBUS environment has to access the FASTBUS-DBS in order to represent its specific knowledge, e.g. to describe the hardware.

The hardware is organised hierarchically and consists of nested components. Access to one of the FASTBUS components require knowledge and evaluation of the relationships between the components and subcomponents: e.g. the roots in the data acquisition tree (segment tree). Such routes are mainly described by their beginning and end segments. To access all segments of one route would require an algorithm similar to that in the Delphi environment, which successively determines and retrieves all segments connected to the beginning and end segments. The knowledge about the structure of the data acquisition tree and the routes as well as their evaluation is algorithmically incorporated in the access routines of the FASTBUS system management.

By coupling XPS and KBMS such knowledge would be stored externally as rules, and together with the intensional query mechanism would thus simplify the FASTBUS system management.

In case of cooperating XPS a part of the domain specific knowlegde would be transferred to the FASTBUS DB. The cooperating XPS must provide metaknowledge about their own knowledge base to other XPS, especially about that part that is managed externally. But this is not possible, if the knowledge is decoded within the application program. A rule management which stores knowledge in an explicit manner could provide meta knowledge by quering the rule base.

4.3. A KBMS Prototype for the DELPHI and FASTBUS Applications

Presently a KBMS prototype is being developed to demonstrate the possible applications of knowledge based DBS in the DELPHI and FASTBUS project. In addition to the intensional query mechanism the prototype contains a rudimentary rule management system and serves as a base for further developments. Consequently the main emphasis in the conception of the prototype was put on the aspect of modular structure rather than the performance aspect, so that for example an enhanced version of the rule management system could easily be incorporated. Fig. 2 illustrates the architecture of the prototype.

Since the intensional queries are defined by a set of datalog rules (= a datalog program), a *rule editor* is the user interface. The rule editor facilitates the creation of datalog rules and programs including syntax checking, and allows the user to invoke rule management functions from within the rule editor, for example in order to store rules which have been syntax-checked or to read externally stored rules. Furthermore it is possible to run a syntactically correct datalog program, i.e. to put an intensional query to the database. The intensional query mechanism is based on the semi-naive bottom-up method. After ensuring that a given datalog program is syntactically correct, the rules are transformed in such a way, that they comply with the requirements of the general semi-naive method (algebraic expressions). Then the method is applied to them in order to retrieve data from the database. The intensional query mechanism has been implemented without any additional optimization methods.

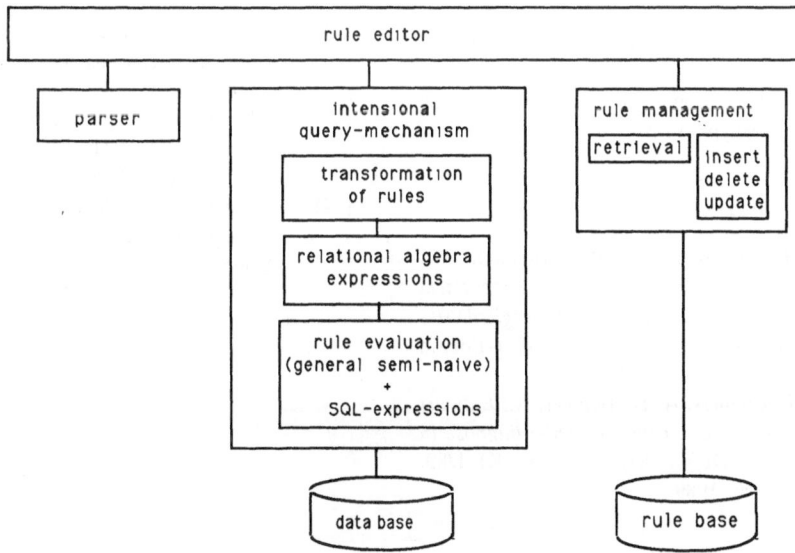

Fig. 2: Architecture of a KBMS-Prototype.

The rule management system in the prototype version is as yet very rudimentary. It does not cooperate with the intensional query mechanism. It allows the insertion, deletion and modification of individual rules, as well as the storing syntactically correct datalog programs. Reading a set of rules is possible by using the intensional query mechanism.

The prototype is presently in the implementation phase. The implementation is taking place on VAX-workstations using the VAX VMS, VAX Pascal, the' DBS Oracle and the Oracle Pascal-precompiler. To a large extent the parser and the intensional query mechanism have been completed.

5. Conclusion

The requirements to process knowledge which is available in an explicit manner, to access such knowledge and to use it in the derivation process led to the concept of KBMS. We have motivated the use of such system in the area of High Energy Physic and presented a prototype implementation.

The development of a KBMS qualitatively continues our work done in the Delphi project up to now and forms the foundation of the FASTBUS project, from the DB point of view.

The development of a query language for the rule base, the co-operation between intensional mechanism and rule management, and the completion of the prototype are considered to be the next important steps of our future work.

Acknowledgement

We are very grateful to the colleagues of A.B.Cremers' group of the Computer Science Department of Bonn and to the colleagues of K.-H. Becks' group of the Physics Science Department of the University of Wuppertal for their help and steady interest.

We also would like to thank Monir Taha and Heng Li for the implementation of the prototype system.

References

[1]   Becks, K.-H.; Cremers, A. B.; Forsbach, H.; Hemker, A.: DELPHI-Expert - *Ein Expertensystem für die Fehlerdiagnose in einem Hochenergiephysik-Experiment.*. Proceedings Anwender-Forum Expertensysteme, Wuppertal, 1987.

[2]   Becks, K.-H.; Cremers, A. B.; Hemker, A.: *Entwurf einer Expertensystemshell für die Fehlerdiagnose in Detektoren des Delphi-Experimentes.* KI 1/89, Oldenbourg-Verlag, 1989.

[3]   Becks, K.-H.: *Artificial Intelligence and Expert Systems-Applications in Data Acquisition.* Proceedings of the 1989 CERN School of Computing, CERN,1989.

[4]   Block, F.; Becks, K.-H, Hemker, A.: FB_EXPERT: *An Expert System for the Management and Error Diagnosis of FASTBUS Networks.* Proceedings of the International Workshop on New Computing Techniques in Physik Research, Lyon, Apr. 1990.

[5]   Block, F.: *FBExpert- Ein Expertensystem zur Fehlerdiagnose in FASTBUS-Systemen.* Diplomarbeit WU D 90-24, University of Wuppertal, Aug. 1990.

[6]   Ceri, S.; Gottlob, G; Tanca, L. (editors): *Logic Programming and Databases.* Springer-Verlag Berlin Heidelberg,1990.

[7]   Frach, R.; Neumann, H.: *Knowledge-Storing - Strukturwissen in Datenbanken. Effiziente Datenbankunterstützung für die Verwaltung von Expertensystem-Objekten.* Diplomarbeit, University of Hagen, 1990.

[8]   Kirn, St.; Schlageter, G; Wu, X.: *Meta-Wissen über die Kompetenz Föderativer Expertensysteme.* Research Report, No. 89, University of Hagen, Jan. 1990.

[9]   Motro, A.; Yuan, Q: *Querying Database Knowledge.* Proceeding of the ACM SIGMOD International Conference on Management of Data, Atlantic City, NJ, May 1990.

[10] Meyer, R.; Schlageter, G.: *Ankopplung der Delphi-Expert-Shell an eine relationale Datenbank.* Internal Report, FU Hagen, Mar 1990.

[11] Peter, J.: *Definite deduktive Datenbanken: Vergleich verschiedener Strategien zur Beantwortung rekursiver Anfragen.* Diplomarbeit, University of Hagen, Mar 1988.

[12] Rimmer, E.M.: *FASTBUS System Management. User Guide and Reference Manual.* Internal Report, CERN 1988.

[13] Ullman, J. D.: *Database and Knowledge-base Systems.* Vol. I: The New Technologies. Computer Science Press, 1988.

[14] Ullman, J. D.: *Database and Knowledge-base Systems. Vol. II: The New Technologies.* Computer Science Press, 1989.

A Meteorological Database for Numerical and Non-numerical Processing*

Michel Desmarais   Alain Leblanc

Centre de recherche informatique de Montréal

3744, rue Jean-Brillant, suite 500

Montréal, Canada H3T 1P1

Abstract

This paper describes the architecture and the functionality of the database software developed in Project Stratus, a project aimed at the development of a knowledge based system for low clouds forecasting. This read-only software is composed of a controlling module, DB, and three slave modules. Each of the slave modules handles a different type of meteorological data. DB integrates the three modules and offers a uniform view of the different data sources. This in turn allows highly flexible data access. DB can be accessed either interactively by the user, or within an application written in "C" or FOR-TRAN. High flexibility and efficiency is realized through the use of an object-oriented paradigm, cache-like mechanisms, and data compression algorithms. DB has been proved efficient not only in the Stratus knowledge based system, but also in more traditional data processing applications, such as a tephigram display program, a contouring display program, and a numerical analysis program to compute vertical motion.

1 Introduction

Stratus is a project aimed at the development of a knowledge based system for forecasting the low cloud portion of a terminal weather forecast (see Desmarais et al.–[3]). Although it is a knowledge based system, the role of heuristic or empirical rules is minimal. The priority in the design is given to numerical physics modelling. When no such model seems appropriate to solve a specific problem, the use of qualitative physics is considered. Only if this option also fails will heuristic rules be introduced.

Numerical modelling of atmospheric physics involves a lot of computation. For a typical day Stratus must process about 2.5Mb of data. Other applications within the project use the database, and their nature requires that each piece of data be accessible in random time. This stresses the importance of a database interface which is both efficient and flexible.

The efficiency we look for is the ability to rapidly access any record in a uniform amount of time, without having to tailor the specific application in any particular way. The flexibility factor is equally important. The database contains files coming from various sources and sometimes stored under different representations. These exact specifications are subject to numerous changes during the development phase. But it is important to allow the developers to work without the burden of updating their application at each minor modification of the database.

When the work started on the project, there was no available database tailored for meteorological data that met our requirements. Frame-like representations, relational languages, etc., traditionally used in knowledge based systems, have plenty of flexibility but are slow and memory consuming. Commercial databases also provide some degree of flexibility but require a significant programming effort in order to tailor them to the levels of functionality and performance required by the project. Their cost is also non-negligable. We thus decided to develop the database facility internally.

The software that we developed addresses the efficiency issue with an architecture containing a master module, which create subprocesses that will read the data and send it to the master through interprocesses communication channels. Each subprocess (three of them presently exist) is designed to optimize the access time to the particular data it must handle. The flexibility problem was resolved by defining a *conceptual view* of the data, where each record is described in a similar way, independent of its actual representation in the database.

The next section describes this conceptual view of the data. We then outline the architecture of the database interface and its actual implementation. Some performance results are provided and we also give an overview of the current and future developments.

2 The Conceptual Data Structure

In order to offer a flexible access to the data, it is necessary to provide a *normalized form* (not to be confused with the normal forms–see Date [2] or Codd [1]). The normalized form

*Funded by the Artificial Intelligence and Development Fund of the Ministry of Industry, Science and Technology Canada, Transport Canada, Atmospheric Environment Services of Environment Canada, and the Department of National Defence. The author wishes to thank Frances de Verteuil, Daniel Caya, and Peter Zwack for their suggestions and comments on previous drafts.

Table 1: Content of a DB record

	Index	Value
1	<value>	the value of the parameter (symbolic or numerical)
2	<var>	name of physical parameter (temperature, cloud cover, etc.)
3	<for>	forecast time or program initialisation time
4	<src>	source of physical parameter (RFE, SA, sounding, objective-analysis, etc.)
5	<time>	time tag (relative or absolute)
6	<alt>	altitude (pressure or height)
7	<lat>	latitude (a degree or station name)
8	<lon>	longitude (a degree or station name)

enables the user[1] of the database to refer to any record using a uniform syntax, independently of its actual data structure in the program. It is a conceptual view of the data that follows the *object oriented* data abstraction paradigm. It hides the internal representation of its data structures from the users of this data.

The conceptual view of the meteorological data in Stratus consists of records that contain eight fields (tuples). Table 1 enumerates these fields. The first two represent the value and the name of the parameter. The third field represents the time of forecast. It defaults to 0 in the case of observed data. The fourth field indicates the source of the data. For example, the temperature can be reported in an SA[2], a sounding, or it can come from an objective analysis, a forecast by a numerical model or some other forecasting model. The next set of fields represents a four dimensional index in time and space.

2.1 Automatic Operations on Variables

In order to provide this normalized form, DB must be capable of converting the format given by a user in his request into the actual format of the record in the file. One example is that DB may receive a request where a station name occupies the <lat><lon> fields, but the source stores the data on grid points. DB will automatically make the necessary conversion. It can also interpolate if there is no data at that particular point in time and space, giving the impression that the data is continuous.

Another feature of the conceptual view is the notion of a *virtual variable*. This allows variables, not directly in the data, to be computed on the fly. A simple use of this feature is to obtain conversion between units by specifying the unit name with the variable. It is currently used to support automatic computation of derivatives.

---

[1]Throughout this document, the "user", here can refer either to an application that makes use of the database or to a person that queries interactively the database

[2]An SA consists of an hourly report that contains meteorological observations of temperature, clouds, etc., sent from a large number of stations.

2.2 Virtual Sources

The notion of a *virtual source* is also a key feature of the normalized view of meteorological data. The basic idea behind virtual sources is to automatically integrate different sources into just one. The user specifies how the variables in a virtual sources are to be defined. This definition can be a simple binding with a variable from another source, or a complex computation involving mathematical and logical operations with several variables from different sources. Thus the exact definition of a variable could vary with the time or the exact location. The user defines the variables through a set of commands to DB, which incorporate a small high level language having the capability to manipulate the meteorological data by identifying only the conceptual data structures.

The use of a virtual source is well illustrated by the way that Stratus produces a forecast. The method is to take a prediction of the values of different meteorological variables for the time of the forecast (e.g. the temperature TT), and then produce a diagnostic of the atmosphere based on the expected values of these variable. A numerical model is available to estimate these predictions. However this model is very unreliable in the first few hours after its initialization, and then performs relatively well. So Stratus could define a virtual source for the forecast in which the variable TT is estimated from the last reported temperature for short term forecasts, and then increases the weight of the numerical model for longer term forecasts. But what is most important is that the queries for the variables of this source keep the same syntax as for the variables of a real source.

3   General Architecture

Although DB offers a unified view of meteorological data, it comprises different modules, each having their own data representation scheme. The current implementation of the database is composed of four modules. There is one module for each type of data (soundings, surface based observations, and gridded data) and one controlling module which interfaces with the client (see figure 1).

The three slave modules (GRI-DB, SON-DB, and OBS-DB) are separate processes that are spawned by the controlling module (DB) as needed. Each one of them communicates with DB by means of interprocess communication (UNIX pipes). The three slave modules receive "messages" from the DB module and reply to it through the standard input-output channel.

3.1   Cache mechanism

The slave modules serve the purpose of a first level cache (other caches are found in the slave modules themselves). When a request is made to DB, it first checks that there does not already exist a process that contains the requested record, otherwise, it will spawn that process. Each process is spawned over a data block, a file that usually contains a

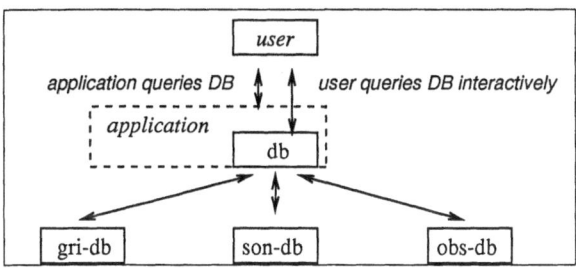

Figure 1: The architecture of DB

day of data. Spawning that process in effect loads the data from disk to the computer's main memory. Further requests within that block of data will not require a file system access and thus constitute a "cached" data block. It is possible to tailor the cache by redefining what is in a block. Data can thus be broken down into hour blocks, station blocks, etc. Note that the keyword "all" will fetch all the records within a block. If the block contains a month's worth of hourly data for a single station, the keyword "all" on the hour field will fetch all hours for that month. If the block contains a day's data for all stations, it will fetch 24 hours only. This permits some flexibility to optimize the database for a specific usage.

3.2 Implementation

All modules have been written in the "C" language, and can presently run on different architectures using the UNIX operating system. Speed was the principal factor in the choice of this language.

All the slave modules are stand-alone programs. They can be started interactively by a user directly from the terminal. Their instructions are read from the standard input, and their results are written on the standard output. Only one option during the call indicates to a slave that it is dealing with the database interface, and the only additional action from the slave will be to add a special character to the output when all the data from one request has been transmitted. This character signifies the end of the transmission to the master module . Upon call, the slave module will load one file of data into real memory. Thus any program using the standard input/output could be used as a slave, with only minor modifications to the source code.

The master module is built with a simple command language, developed using the UNIX tools "yacc" and "lex". It will spawn a new process when a new file is requested, and create and set the pipes that permit the interprocess communications.

The master module handles requests in the normalized form using the command "get", which has the following syntax

```
get <yy>/<mm>/<dd> <for> <src> <var> <hour>
<lat> <lon> <alt>
```

DB will use the parameters to locate the necessary file, initiate the required subprocess and send it the requests through the pipe. The slave returns the data through another pipe under the form of a character string. DB gives the final result to the user as a series of records contained in a unique character string, where each record has the form:

```
<value> <var> <time> <alt> <lat> <lon>
```

For instance, the call

```
get 91/05/01 0 efr  tt 12 wmw wmw all
```
normalizes:
```
1.19389 TT 301200 649 42.7507N 73.7997W
5.01014 TT 301200 709 42.7507N 73.7997W
⋮
12.3918 TT 301200 980 46.3807N 75.9598W
```

Notice the use of the keyword "all" to indicate all the levels available, and the use of the station name "wmw" (which is Maniwaki, Québec) instead of the actual latitude or longitude of the station. Doing the same call with the corresponding latitude and longitude or the x-y coordinate of the grid defined for the source would have yielded the same result.

3.3 Data Compression

Each slave module uses compressed data. Data files must be preprocessed by data compression programs. The programs load the compressed data in memory and decompress individual records on demand only. Since the compression factor is approximately 66% the saving constitutes an important gain of memory for the cache.

4 Performance

The database performance is critical for the Stratus project. It is extensively used both by the Stratus knowledge base and the applications (the tephigram and contouring display modules, and the vertical motion module). Inefficient performance could result in rejection on the part of the users.

The global performance of the database is broken down in table 2. The times are for a single day of data on an HP 9000/380 workstation. They are based on the average time to fetch the temperature over 1000 trials. The *fetch through* DB corresponds to interactive queries made to DB, whereas the *direct fetch* corresponds to queries made directly to the slave module without going through DB. Queries can fall into an internal cache[3] within the module (cache hit), in which case no data decompression is required. Otherwise, the data must first be decompressed before being processed (cache miss). Note that GRI-DB does not have a cache and thus performance breakdown is for cache miss only.

The data loading time of each module varies between 0.12 and 0.56s. Total loading time for a single day of data is

---

[3]Note that the internal modules' caches are different from the caches referred to in section 3.1, where a cache hit represents a query that falls into an already loaded sub-module containing the data.

Table 2: Database performance breakdown (times are in ms for an HP 9000/380-7 mips workstation)

	Modules		
	OBS-DB	SON-DB	GRI-DB
Loading time	311	121	560
Memory requirements	1080Kb	460Kb	800Kb
Compressed data size	422Kb	51Kb	637Kb
Fetch through DB			
cache hit	9.3	9.3	n/a
cache miss	11.7	20.4	20.5
Direct fetch			
cache hit	0.5	1.4	n/a
cache miss	0.6	13.0	15

approximately 1s. This includes all SA's, wind and temperature soundings, and 6 variables at 9 levels over a grid of 25×25 from the RFE numerical model. This constitutes approximately 250 000 individual records. Once loaded, fetching of a record from DB takes between 9ms and 21ms since all data is kept in memory. Fetching directly from the slave modules is between 5ms to 11ms faster. This is the time required by DB to parse the message and dispatch it to the correct slave program. Direct fetches vary between .5ms and 15ms, depending on the module and whether the request falls into the internal modules' caches or not. A request will generally fall within an internal module's cache if it applies to the same station and the same time.

5 Future Developments and Conclusion

The database interface developed during the Stratus project is successful in two aspects. It offers the flexibility to integrate different representations of data under a uniform syntax, and it provides the efficiency required for many different applications related to this project, in addition to the knowledge based system itself. It has been operational for more than a year, and its design allows for numerous additions to its functionality within the existing architecture. The development efforts on this project are presently oriented toward the integration of sources, and also on a training process where DB compares the forecast data coming from various sources with the observed data, so that it will learn to choose the best value to use when more than one alternative is available.

References

[1] E. F. Codd. A relational model of data for large shared data banks. *Communications of the ACM*, 13(6), June 1970.

[2] C. J. Date. *An introduction to database systems*, volume I,II. Adison-Wesley, Reading, MA, fourth edition, 1986.

[3] Michel C. Desmarais, Frances de Verteuil, Denis Jacob, and Peter Zwack. Stratus: combining a knowledge-based approach with numerical modeling in weather forecasting. In *Avignon 91, Eleventh international workshop*. AFIA, ARC, ECCAI et JSAI, 27–31 mai, Avignon, France 1991.

An Implementation Model for Multidatabase Queries

Marek Rusinkiewicz[*]   Bogdan Czejdo   David W. Embley
University of Houston   Loyola University   Brigham Young University

Abstract

In this paper we discuss an approach to formulation and processing of multidatabase queries. The proposed approach allows incremental growth of a federated database system and provides mechanisms for resolving schema incompatibilities. The implementation model assumes that global queries are evaluated by performing synthesis of (rather than decomposition into) individual site queries. The approach is based on a single language that can be used for both schema integration and query formulation. Once a multidatabase query is formulated, a query evaluation plan can be generated and translated into site queries by an incremental compiler.

1   Introduction

The early work on heterogeneous databases was based on *schema integration* with the objective of providing full *distribution transparency* of access [NSE84]. In turned out that, except for some special cases, such approach is not feasible in practice; this led to the emergence of the concept of interoperable multidatabase systems [LA86]. This concept is based on the recognition of the fact that multiple autonomous databases will continue to co-exist because of historical, political and technological reasons. Several prototype implementations, (e.g., [LR82, FS82]) were undertaken to evaluate the applicability of the new solutions.

In the discussion below, we assume an environment consisting of autonomous *local database systems (LDBSs)* which may have their own local users and applications. We assume further, that each LDBS decides to contribute a part of its informational content to the multidatabase system by presenting an *export schema*. The export schemas include information about attribute domains, which can be used to resolve attribute incompatibilities such as differences in units of measurement, representation and precision. In

[ECR87] we discussed the use of *Abstract Data Types (ADTs)* to resolve simple incompatibilities between attributes in different relations. We also discussed data manipulation operations that tolerate and help resolve relation-definition incompatibilities.

In the discussion below, we assume that the export schemas are relational. Hierarchical, network, and other data models used by the LDBMSs can be accommodated by including necessary data model translations. The problem of data model translation has been discussed in [FS82] and practical solutions are available in the form of relational query interfaces to major commercial non-relational DBMSs (e.g., IDMS/R and DATACOM/DB).

A global query, formulated in a multidatabase language such as MSQL [Lit90] must be replaced by a collection of *site subqueries*. The standard approach to this problem is to perform query decomposition [ECR87] and translation in the languages of the LDMSs (if neccesary). An alternative approach, which will be introduced in this paper is to "synthesize" site queries directly in local languages.

The remainder of this paper is organized as follows. In Section 2, we review the extended relational data model and an algebra over the model. The operators of the algebra permit to combine data from partially compatible relations and are thus useful in resolving relation-definition incompatibilities. We also discuss briefly an interactive, graphical query language based on the introduced model. Generation of query evaluation plans and construction of site queries is explained in Section 3. Section 4 summarizes our results.

2   Query Formulation in Multidatabase Systems

The idea of extending the relational data model with connectors has been proposed in [ECR86]. The application ot this concept to the formulation of multidatabase queries has been discussed in [ECR87]. Below we will review the basic operators of the extended relational algebra that have been defined in [ECR87].

Let $\mathcal{U}$ be a set of attribute names. Let $\mathcal{D}$ be a set of domains and let *dom* be a func-

---
[*]Address for correspondence: Computer Science Department. University of Houston. Houston. TX 77204-3475. email: marek@cs.uh.edu. tel: (713) 749-1471, fax: (713) 749-2378

tion from $\mathcal{U}$ to $\mathcal{D}$. Let $\mathcal{V}$ be a set of relation names. A *relation descriptor* is a triple $(N, \mathcal{A}, \mathcal{X})$ where N is an element of $\mathcal{V}$, $\mathcal{A}$ is a nonempty subset of $\mathcal{U}$, and X is a query expression that, when executed on the stored database, yields a set of tuples of the relation named N.

Let $\mathcal{R}$ be a nonempty set of relation descriptors. A *connection descriptor* over R is a 5-tuple (Ra, Aa, Rb, Ab, θ) where Ra and Rb are distinct relation descriptors in $\mathcal{R}$, Aa and Ab are each an attribute of the $Ra.A$ and $Rb.A$, respectively, $dom(Aa) = dom(Ab) = d$, and θ is a binary predicate defined over d. The definition of a connection descriptor can be generalized to relate a set of attributes, possibly defined over different domains. Let $\mathcal{C}$ be a (possibly empty) set of connection descriptors over $\mathcal{R}$. We define a *relational database schema with connectors* RC to be the pair $(\mathcal{R}, \mathcal{C})$. We also define $RC - set$ to be the set of all RCs. The $RC - set$ together with a set of operators defined over it constitute a RC-algebra.

All operators of the RC-algebra map the $RC - set$ into itself. An operator can be formally defined by giving its name, modifier list, and semantics. The operators listed below will be used in our examples.

- **Delete-Connector(C1):** deletes connection descriptor C1 from the set $\mathcal{C}$

- **Add-Connector(R1, A1, R2, A2, θ):** creates a θ-comparison connection descriptor between attribute A1 of relation descriptor R1 and attribute A2 of relation descriptor R2 and adds it to the set $\mathcal{C}$ of the current RC. A1 and A2 must be θ-comparable attributes.

- **Delete-Relation(R1):** removes relation descriptor R1 from the set $\mathcal{R}$ of the current RC and also removes from the set $\mathcal{C}$ of the current RC any connection descriptors associated with the removed relation descriptor.

- **Add-Relation(N1, A1, T):** creates a single-attribute constant relation named N1 with an attribute A1 whose tuples are given in the set T, adds the relation to the stored database, and adds its relation descriptor to the current RC.

- **Delete-Attributes(R1, Z):** removes the attributes specified in set Z from the descriptor of relation R1. The removal of all attributes is prohibited. The X component of the relation descriptor is updated by adding a projection on the set of remaining attributes. Any connection descriptor that references a deleted attribute is also deleted.

- **Join-Combine(R1, R2):** combines relation descriptors R1 and R2 into a new one. The name of the new relation is a concatenation of the names of R1 and R2. The new A component consists of all the attributes (possibly renamed) of R1 and R2. The new X component is the θ-join of

the X components of R1 and R2. If there are connectors between R1 and R2, the θ-join observes constraints imposed by the connectors. If there are no connectors, the θ-join has no constraints and becomes a Cartesian product.

- **Rename-Relation(R1, N1):** changes the name of relation descriptor R1 to be N1 and also changes the name in all connection descriptors that contain R1. Control over relation names can be useful, for example, to replace long system-generated names by shorter ones.

- **Duplicate:** creates two copies of the current RC and changes relation names to avoid name duplication. The two copies are then merged into a single RC. One of the many uses of this operator is to allow a join of a relation with itself and thus to allow for self-referencing queries.

- **Union-Combine(R1, R2):** combines relation descriptors R1 and R2 into a new one. If the connectors between R1 and R2 establish a bijective mapping between the sets of attributes of R1 and R2, then the new relation is essentially the set union of the relations for R1 and R2. The difference is that conflicting attribute names are allowed because automatic renaming is done on the basis of the connectors. When connectors between R1 and R2 exist but do not establish a bijective mapping, the new relation is essentially an outer join of the relations for R1 and R2. The difference again is that necessary renaming is performed automatically. When there are no connectors between R1 and R2, the new relation is essentially the set of tuples of both relations for R1 and R2, where the tuples are padded with *nulls* to make them compatible. The difference again is the automatic adjustment of names. The main difference between the union-combine and the outer join is the way they operate in the absence of connected attributes: for outer join we have a Cartesian product, for union-combine we have the set of appropriately padded tuples from both argument relations.

- **Difference-Combine(R1, R2):** combines relation descriptors R1 and R2 into a new one. If the connectors between R1 and R2 establish a bijective mapping between the sets of attributes of R1 and R2, then the new relation is essentially the set difference of the relations for R1 and R2. The difference is that conflicting attribute names are allowed because automatic renaming is performed on the basis of the connectors. When connectors between R1 and R2 exist but do not establish a bijective mapping, the new relation is essentially the relation R1 minus the tuples joinable (as determined by connectors) with the relation R2. The difference again is that necessary renaming is performed automatically. When there are no connectors between R1 and R2, the new relation is the relation R1.

In [ECR86] we have shown that a subset of RC-operators is relationally complete. Additional operators for performing computations and updates can be defined but these extensions will not be discussed here.

We will illustrate the basic components of the RC model using as an example a multidatabase system containing information about subscribers to journals published by computer societies. We assume that relations

```
ieee_subs(SS#, Name, Address, IEEE#)
subscription(SS#, J_Name, Exp_Date)
```

are stored at one site and that relations

```
acm_subscriber(Id#, Name, Address,
                ACM#)
journal(Id#, Journ, Expiration)
```

are stored at another site. We also assume that the connectors are declared initially that semantically link acm_subscriber relation with journal relation and ieee_subs relation with subscription relation. This multidatabase schema is represented in our model as follows: $\mathcal{R} = \{R1, R2, R3, R4\}$, $\mathcal{C} = \{C1, C2\}$, where

```
R1=(IEEE_SUBS,
    {SS#, Name, Address, IEEE#},
    ieee_subs)
R2=(SUBSCRIPTIONS,
    {SS#, J_Name, Exp_Date},
    subscriptions)
R3=(ACM_SUBSCRIBER,
    {Id#, Name, Address, ACM#},
    acm_subscriber)
R4=(JOURNAL,
    {Id#, Journ, Expiration},
    journal)

C1=(R1, SS#, R2, SS#, "=")
C2=(R3, Id#, R4, Id#, "=")
```

The application of RC operators causes the modification of the state of the model, without affecting the stored database. As an example, let us assume that the following operations have been invoked in the process of formulating a query:

```
delete_relation(IEEE_SUBS)
delete_relation(SUBSCRIPTION).
```

The state of the model then becomes: $\mathcal{R} = \{R3, R4\}$, $\mathcal{C} = \{C2\}$, where $R3, R4$ anc $C3$ are defined as above. If the operation

```
delete-attributes(ACM_SUBSCRIBER,
                  {Address})
```

is invoked later, the relation descriptor $R3$ is modified as follows:

$$R3 = (ACM\_SUBSCRIBER,$$
$$\{Id\#, Name, ACM\#\},$$
$$\Pi_{Id\#, Name, ACM\#} acm\_subscriber).$$

The algebraic operators described here can be conveniently invoked using a graphical user interface. An implementation of a graphical query language based on the above approach is described in [ECR86]. We assume that the export schemas including relation names, attribute names, and connectors are displayed as a diagram on the terminal screen together with the list of operators. A user of our graphical query language manipulates diagrams by pointing. The basic action is to select an operator and then specify the operator's modifier list either by pointing at relations, attributes, and connectors or by entering information. Application of a graphically invoked RC-operator transforms the diagram and the underlying RC model, but does not affect the stored databases. When RC operators are applied, relational algebra expressions are generated and stored as X components of relation descriptors. Then when the display operator is invoked, a final relational algebra expression is formed by specifying that a join of all X-components followed by a projection onto the marked attributes be performed.

3   Implementation Model

Various methods for processing global queries in heterogeneous distributed database systems have been discussed, among others, in [Lit83]. In general, a multidatabase query can be processed by specifying a collection of subqueries and a global query evaluation plan. A subquery specifies the data to be obtained from an individual database, and a global query evaluation plan specifies how to process the data obtained from the queries. Before a subquery is sent to its target LDBMS for evaluation, it may need to be translated into the target DBMS language.

The first phase in processing of a global query involves its decomposition into site subqueries. In the case of a homogeneous relational environment, the goal of query decomposition is to convert the global query into a coherent collection of elementary relational operations on underlying local relations or fragments. For example, [CP84] discuss equivalence transformations between expressions of extended relational algebra, correctness of distributed query processing strategies, and heuristics that lead to efficient evaluation of distributed queries. Most query decomposition algorithms proposed in the literature for homogeneous DDBMS, decompose a query into a sequence of basic relational operations, such as semi-joins, and data moves.

In our further discussion, we assume that a remote site may only support remote query access and that its local DBMS does not need to be modified in order to contribute its data to the multidatabase database system.

The applicability of different query decomposition strategies depends on the level of schema integration. A traditional approach to query decomposition and optimization, based on estimation of volume of data transfer and communication costs, is suitable for systems in which queries are formulated assuming a global integrated schema. Depending on the scope of functions provided by the site DBMSs, different plans for evaluating a compound query may become feasible. Query-decomposition algorithms based on this approach, which are suitable for heterogeneous databases are described in [RC87]. The implementation of this approach requires a separate decomposition module, which is activated after the query is formulated, to derive the "optimal" evaluation plan.

An alternative and novel approach, which is particularly suitable when the query is formulated by directly manipulating the export schemas in the manner described above, can be implemented. In this approach, instead of decomposing a global query, the system synthesizes it. Synthesis facilitates incremental construction of individual site queries and the global query evaluation plan. With our method every step in query formulation results in a complete, valid query. Thus, the incremental compilation is facilitated since each change made to a query diagram corresponds to a modification of a complete and legal query evaluation program.

We assume that as the schema diagrams are manipulated by the user, the graphical query interface generates a sequence of RC-operators as described in the previous section. Such a sequence constitutes an RC-program which is then processed by an incremental compiler to produce site queries.

To allow incremental processing of queries we will modify the definition a relation descriptor to include a list of site queries together with the query evaluation plan. Thus, a relation descriptor R is now a four-tuple (N, A, X, XL) where N and A are as defined above and X is a global query evaluation plan expressed in terms of results of site queries listed in XL. Generally, when a unary operation is specified on a particular relation Q, the descriptor for Q can be modified to reflect the effect of that operation. These modifications are achieved by appropriate manipulation of the N, A, X, and XL components of Q. A descriptor Q' of the resulting relation is produced with corresponding N, A, X, and XL components. Binary operations on relations are treated in a similar way. This model allows us to associate with each (virtual or base) relation r an expression that derives r. The restriction that each expression in XL refers only to objects in a single export schema simplifies the creation of site queries.

In evaluating a global query in a heterogeneous database, the site subqueries may need to be translated into site languages of their respective target sites. Once the local query languages of the sites involved in the query processing are known, translation of site subqueries can be performed as a separate step in processing the query [RC85]. On the other hand, query translation can be combined with

the synthesis of site queries and be performed in an incremental fashion by the RC-algebra incremental compiler. When this approach is used, the site subqueries in XL are maintained and incrementally modified in their respective site languages.

As an example, illustrating the outlined approach let us assume that Site 1 containing relations IEEE_SUBS and SUBSCRIPTION uses QUEL as its external interface and that Site 2 containing relations ACM_SUBSCRIBER and JOURNAL uses SQL as its external interface. We assume the following query is issued from Site 1: "List the IEEE#'s of IEEE subscribers who also subscribe to the ACM publication TODS."

Initially, the XL1 components in relation descriptors of each relation in Site 1 are the expressions that return the relations themselves. All other XL components are empty for these relation descriptors. Similarly, the XL2 components in relation descriptors of each relation in Site 2 are the expressions that return these relations. All other X components are empty for these relation descriptors.

The query can be formulated in several phases. In the first phase the following operators can be invoked graphically:

```
delete(SUBSCRIPTION)
add_connector(ACM_SUBSCRIBER, Id#,
              IEEE_SUBS, SS#, '=')
```

As a result, the relation descriptor SUBSCRIPTION is deleted and an additional connector is created. None of the X components has been affected.

In the second phase the following operators can be invoked:

```
add_relation(TODS, TDS, <TDS:'TODS'>)
add_connector(TODS, TDS,
              JOURNAL, Journ, '=')
join_combine(TODS, JOURNAL)
```

In this phase the new relation descriptor named TODS is created and then combined with relation descriptor for JOURNAL yielding a relation descriptor named TODS-JOURNAL. The XL2 component of this relation descriptor contains the expression:

```
SELECT *
FROM JOURNAL
WHERE Journ='TODS'
```

Next, the join-combine(TODS-JOURNAL, ACM_SUBSCRIBER) operator is invoked. The relation descriptors named TODS-JOURNAL and ACM_SUBSCRIBER are combined yielding a new relation descriptor TODS-JOURNAL-ACM_SUBSCRIBER. The XL2 component of this relation descriptor contains the following expression:

```
SELECT *
FROM ACM_SUBSCRIBER, JOURNAL
WHERE ACM_SUBSCRIBER.Id# = JOURNAL.Id#
AND JOURNAL.Journ = 'TODS'
```

Next, the join-combine (IEEE_SUBS, TODS-JOURNAL-ACM_SUBSCRIBER) operator is invoked yielding a new relation descriptor. The XL2 component of the new relation descriptor contains the above expression, and XL1 component contains the following expression:

```
RANGE OF t IS IEEE_SUBS
RETRIEVE (t.all)
```

The query evaluation module assumes that the results of subqueries are returned as temporary relations T1 and T2 and thus the X component of the new relation descriptor is the following expression:

```
RANGE OF t1 is T1
RANGE OF t2 is T2
RETRIEVE (t1.all, t2.all)
WHERE t1.SS# = t2.Id#
```

The attribute to be displayed, IEEE_SUBS.IEEE#, can now be marked resulting in the final projection being added to the X component of the only remaining relation descriptor. The projections can be pushed down the query-evaluation tree and the XL and X components will be modified as follows:

```
XL2:
    SELECT ACM_SUBSCRIBER.Id#
    FROM ACM_SUBSCRIBER, JOURNAL
    WHERE ACM_SUBSCRIBER.Id#=JOURNAL.Id#
        AND JOURNAL.Journ='TODS'

XL1:
    RANGE OF t IS IEEE_SUBS
    RETRIEVE (t.SS#, t.IEEE#)

X:
    RANGE OF t1 is T1
    RANGE OF t2 is T2
    RETRIEVE (t1.IEEE#)
    WHERE t1.SS# = t2.Id#
```

In this example a single relation descriptor was obtained by explicitly combining the relation descriptors. The XL components of this relation descriptor contain site queries and its X component describes how the results of evaluation of subqueries can be combined to yield the answer to the query.

4 SUMMARY

In this paper we have discussed processing of global queries in a multidatabase environment. We proposed a query-synthesis approach to the processing of such queries. As relation descriptors are manipulated, site subqueries can be generated and processed using incremental compilation. The site subqueries can be maintained and manipulated directly in the languages of their corresponding target sites.

Many ideas presented in this paper were used in the design of a graphical query interface to OMNIBASE – an experimental multidatabase system developed at the University of Houston [R+88].

References

[CP84] S. Ceri and G. Pelagatti. *Distributed Databases Principles and Systems*. McGraw-Hill, 1984.

[ECR86] D. Embley, B. Czejdo, and M. Rusinkiewicz. Graphical query formulation by manipulating relational schema diagrams. *Systems Science*, 12(3), 1986.

[ECR87] D. Embley, B. Czejdo, and M. Rusinkiewicz. An approach to schema integration and query formulation in federated database systems. In *Proceedings of the Third International Conference on Data Engineering*, February 1987.

[FS82] A. Ferrier and C. Strangret. Heterogeneity in the distributed database management systems Sirius-Delta. In *Proceeding of the 8th VLDB International Conference*, September 1982.

[LA86] W. Litwin and A. Abdellatif. Multidatabase interoperability. *Computer*, 19(12), December 1986.

[Lit83] W. Litwin. MALPHA: a relational multidatabase manipulation language. In *EUTECO Proceedings*. North-Holland, 1983.

[Lit90] W. Litwin. MSQL: A Multidatabase Language. *Information Sciences*, 1990.

[LR82] T. Landers and R. Rosenberg. An Overview of Multibase. In *Proceedings of the International Symposium on Distributed Databases*, 1982. Berlin.

[NSE84] S. Navathe, T. Sashidhar, and R. Elmasri. Relationship merging in schema integration. In *Proceedings of the 10th International Conference on Very Large Databases*, August 1984.

[R+88] M. Rusinkiewicz et al. OMNIBASE: Design and Implementa-

314

tion of a Multidatabase System. *IEEE CS Distributed Processing Technical Committee Newsletter*, 10(2), November 88.

[RC85]   M. Rusinkiewicz and B. Czejdo. Query transformation in heterogeneous distributed database systems. In *Proceedings of the 7-th International Conference on Distributed Computing*, 1985.

[RC87]   M. Rusinkiewicz and B. Czejdo. An approach to query processing in federated database systems. In *Proceedings of the Twentieth Hawaii International Conference on System Sciences*, 1987.

[WQ87]   G. Wiederhold and X. Qian. Modeling Asynchrony in Distributed Databases. In *Intl. Conf on Data Engineering*, February 1987.

Knowledge-Based Schema Analysis in a Multi-Database Framework

Jian Yang* Mike P. Papazoglou* Louis Marinos†

*Australian National University
Dept of Computer Science
Canberra, ACT 2601 Australia

†Erasmus University Rotterdam
Laboratory For Artificial Intelligence
3000 DR Rotterdam, Holland

Abstract

Schema analysis is a very important issue in the integration of a corporate information system. The basic problems to be dealt with during integration come from structural and semantical diversities in schemas to be merged. Before we integrate local schemas, we must ascertain how conflicts and correspondences between types in different schemas can be identified. In this paper, we present a strategy for schema analysis based on a knowledge-based version of the object-oriented paradigm and describe a methodology for discovering structural and semantic relatedness of components within disparate information sources.

1 Introduction

The main characteristics of a corporate information system, i.e. multi-database system, is that the individual information sources which comprise it are independently created and administered. They may use different data formats and diverse data models. Also they may model different aspects of the same concepts. Thus integration of data has become an area of growing interest in recent years. During this process two problems arise: first, how can we reconcile the differences between diverse local, and possibly conflicting schema definitions (for example, name differences, domain and type differences); second, how can we establish relationships between two or more diverse entities in different information sources, that are semantically related when such kinds of relationships are not expressed in their schema specifications.

The methodologies mentioned in previous research work [1], [2], [3], [4], [5] mainly cope with finding equivalent, subset, overlapping and disjoint relationships between entities (or types in the object-oriented terminology) on the basis of attribute equivalence. The conflicts that these methodologies broadly distinguish are of two kinds: naming conflicts and structural conflicts [1]. However, one may identify several limitations in current research activities conducted in the realm of schema integration:

1. The problems which they consider represent only a small fraction of the problems that one should be confronted with during the design of a multi-database system. For example, the major inter-schema property they consider is the subset relationship, while such relationships as 'role of', 'a part of', 'existence dependent on' and so on - which exist between types in different schemas - are not taken into account.

2. Attribute equivalence is the only methodology to determine type similarity, however, this concept has not been exploited to its full extent to detect rich inter-schema semantics. For instance, by employing attribute equivalence one can only determine that the type Lecturer in schema 1 and Instructor in schema 2 are overlapping. But one cannot tell in detail how and if they are semantically related to one another.

3. No specific strategy is presented for collecting the candidate entities, i.e., similar or near similar entities that need to be further analyzed and subsequently merged.

In this paper we present a strategy for schema analysis by elaborating on several techniques for collecting those types which need to be analyzed and related, and by detecting different sorts of structural and/or semantic relationships between diverse schema components (such as role relationships, category relationships, etc) - which are not currently treated by the relevant literature. Schema analysis may be thought of as the process of analyzing and comparing different schemas in order to determine the degree of correspondence among inter-schema types and detect possible conflicts between them. It is argued that without the ability to discover and represent inter-schema semantics during the schema analysis stage, there is little hope for developing general methods for integration of schemas from multiple related, partially overlapping information sources.

The methodology proposed for dealing with the ramifications of schema analysis is a knowledge-based semi-automatic process guided by heuristics as well as system-designer interaction. Information regarding inter-schema conflicts and semantics is found and stored as meta-knowledge in a knowledge base associated with each host schema. After this process, all semantically related components will implicitly be merged or connected yielding thus a universal view of the schemas in the disparate information sources. In this paper we will assume that the data model underlying the individual information sources to be merged is a variant of the object-oriented model which treats all parts of the design as objects thereby reducing the complexity of the analysis [6], [7]. This methodology can also be applied to distributed heterogeneous information-bases if some kind of object-oriented data model is chosen as the canonical data model and schema homogenization has been attained [8].

The remainder of this paper is organized as follows: section 2 covers the essential features of the proposed framework for schema analysis. In section 3 the methodology for schema comparison is presented. Finally, section 4 presents our concluding remarks and further research directions.

2 Outline of the Schema Analysis

In the distributed environment, partially overlapping information sources are very common. For example, if one information source deals with company information, it is quite unlikely to include the totality of information regarding a lecturer who is employed as a company consultant. On the other hand, a university information-base may also not have information concerning a lecturer working as a project consultant in a company. Furthermore, different applications may have different information or viewpoints on the same or similar concepts. Only by combining information about their views will the information sources be able to form an overall picture about employees [8]. Therefore, in order to resolve conflicts and give a complete account of the type of knowledge that needs to be deployed for the integration

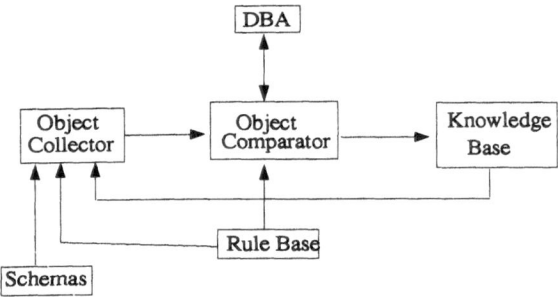

Figure 1: The framework for Schema Analysis

Type $t_{i,k}$ S_1	Related Type $t_{j,n}$
	Semantic Relationship
	Constraint
	Assertion
	Resolution

Figure 2: Frame-The Structure of The Knowledge Base

of multiple information sources, we propose a revised expert system like approach - conceptually viewed as illustrated in Figure-1. This integration framework assumes that underlying information sources are described in some variant of the object-oriented data model and extends the object management facilities at each host information source by offering orthogonal functionality. It comprises the following components:

1. Rule Base: This includes the definitions of different kinds of structural and semantic relationships between types encountered in each host schema (for further details see section 3), and the rules for guiding the Type Collector component of the integration framework to select the types to be compared. The rule base is used to identify the semantic relationships between types.

2. Knowledge Base: Each host schema has an associated knowledge base. The knowledge stored in the knowledge base is the result of the schema analysis. This component accomplishes two functions: it accumulates knowledge regarding host schemas, e.g. the type Student in schema 1 is the supertype of type Graduate-student in schema 2 and Pupil in schema 3 and so on. This knowledge will be progressively refined during the process of type comparison and confirmed by the DBA. The other function that this component accomplishes, in conjunction with the rule base, is to direct and aid the Type Collector module to collect the right schema types which need to be compared.

3. Type Collector: This module selects those types from the disparate schemas which are candidates for analysis and forwards them to Type Comparator module. This process is guided by the rule base and knowledge base.

4. Type Comparator: This is a rule-based module which checks type conflicts and determines equivalences and the degree of inter-type correspondence by establishing semantic relationships between types in the disparate information sources. Results are represented as knowledge portions regarding a particular schema type and are stored in the knowledge base. This is an interactive process, under the control of the DBA, to make sure that knowledge which is accumulated during the process of schema analysis is correct and complete.

For reasons of simplicity and brevity (as we will use several examples), we will frequently concern ourselves only with the analysis and collection of meta-knowledge regarding two schemas referred to as S_i and S_j. This process can be easily generalized and applied to n schemas. We now expand on this aspect.

We use the concept of a *frame* as the packaged structure which is used to organize and retrieve knowledge in the knowledge-base and assist the reasoning process. The concept of frame used in the knowledge base is equivalent to that of object in the object

model which underlies the disparate information sources in the distributed environment. We introduce this sharp distinction for reasons of clarity as frames are used to capture and convey meta-knowledge deployed for the purpose of schema analysis and integration, whereas objects stored in the object-base are used to reflect data and knowledge regarding modeled domain entities, see Figure 2.

The frame structure in the knowledge base is seen to comprise a name tag for the particular object type analyzed and any additional properties used to accumulate and manipulate meta-knowledge regarding this object type's links with the rest of the environment. The construct $t_{i,k}$ denotes a particular object type k in the schema S_1. *Related Type* $t_{j,n}$ represents the object type n in the schema S_j which is semantically or structurally related to $t_{i,k}$ in S_1. *Semantic Relation* signifies what kind of semantic relationships that exist between these two object types. *Constraint* indicates the conditions under which these two types are related. *Assertion* asserts information regarding the domains of different object types which may need to be associated during the process of integration. For example, knowledge that signifies that a student can work as part time employee in a company when there is no such knowledge in the host schemas. *Resolution* specifies the integration policy, e.g. the way in which the semantic relationships between object types are established and the conflicts are resolved. Each object type has a set of frames depending on the number of (semantic) relationships the type establishes with types in other schemas.

During the process of schema analysis, when a new structural or semantic relationship regarding types is established, it will be recorded in its corresponding frame structure. This cycle is repeated until no more relationships can be found. This makes it possible to relate the various types in diverse schemas to each other so that operations applicable to one type may be applied to a related type as well. Definition of the appropriate general rules for structural and semantic equivalence is the responsibility of the DBA. The DBA defines the general rules and guidelines which determine the structural and semantic similarities and equivalences among object types belonging to disparate information sources and subsequently stores them in a rule-base. The rule-base is used as an automated means for analyzing diverse host schemas and determining type and attribute similarities and interconnections. After such similarities or equivalences have been identified they need to be verified by the DBA.

The schema analysis processor described in Figure-1 is a semi-automated environment which needs constant guidance from the DBA to store the verified results of the schema analysis into the knowledge-base as a series of frames for subsequent use during the process of schema integration. After analysis is performed, unambiguous and complete meta-knowledge regarding the relationships of types in different host schemas is stored in the knowledge base which is an integrated part of each host information source. Therefore, this approach offers global visibility from the level of each host schema, and entails multiple facets (windows) which enable users to access information scattered across the entire information source network. The following section is the description of the schema analysis process.

3 The Process of Schema Analysis

Past research conducted on schema integration mainly emphasized the issues of addressing and solving structural problems, such as incompatibilities regarding identical (or similar) concepts, and the policy for global schema structuring. And has given considerable attention to a very focussed area of semantic problems, such as naming conflicts and constraint conflicts. In contrast, in this paper, we will mainly concentrate on semantic problems and relationships. In this section, we will concentrate on a series typical structural and semantic problems associated with the degree of similarity of types in disparate information sources. Resolution of inter-schema type conflicts and deviations can be achieved by means of a semi-automated tool, see Figure-1.

Even when applications and user groups are structurally disconnected, as in most governmental and large administrative setups, there is something to be gained by having an enterprise-wide view of the information resources. This potentially allows individual applications to 'bridge' themselves and understand how their respective information sources are related to one another. Regarding the entities in host schemas that are not the same but are related, we need to discover all the structural and semantic inter-schema properties that relate them. The semantic relationships considered in current research which are based on the attribute equivalence are too weak to be used as a basis to unravel and resolve problems relating to the previous cases [9], [10]. Only when we understand the semantic relationships among the entities involved in the integration process in their entirety, can we resolve any potential integration problems. The main structural conflicts we consider in a corporate information system are: *name differences, domain or type differences, ontological differences* [9], [10], [8]. Below we give brief definitions of the taxonomic scheme used to determine the degree of semantic confluence between any two individual types in the disparate information sources.

1. **Equivalence Relationship**

   There are two sub-categories here:

   - **Identical Relationship**

     For concept of identity holds between two types $t_{i,1}$ and $t_{j,2}$ in different schemas S_i and S_j, we may say that $t_{i,1}$ and $t_{j,2}$ are identical, if the same modeling constructs are used, the same perceptions are applied, and no incoherence enters into the specification even if their respective names are different.

   - **Isomorphic Relationship**

     The isomorphic relationship holds between two types $t_{i,1}$ and $t_{j,2}$ (for example the types Employee1 and Employee2 in schemas 1 and 2) iff their instances correspond to one another in a one-to-one basis but there might be some additional properties which need to be added.

2. **Generalization/Specialization Relationship**

   There are two sub-categories here which are established for non-identical and non-isomorphic types:

   - **Is-A Relationship**

     $t_{i,1}$ **is-a** $t_{j,2}$ iff the regular expression that specifies the domain for $t_{i,1}$ is a subexpression of a commuted regular expression that defines the domain for $t_{j,2}$.

   - **Conceptual Is-A Relationship**

     The relationship $t_{i,1}$ **conceptual is-a** $t_{j,2}$ holds whenever these two types have an **is-a** relationship which is not depicted by the schemas. For example, the type Person may be defined as '< name, address, birthdate, sex, address >' in schema 1, while Worker type may

be declared with a domain definition whose regular expression is < name, address, social-security-nr, birthdate, sex, ethnic-origin > in schema 2. Since the type Worker does not possess the attribute 'address', we cannot say that Worker **is-a** Person according to the true spirit of inheritance, but in the real world entity Worker is (conceptually) a specialization of Person.

3. **Category Relationship**

   Two partially equivalent object types are category-related iff they share some common properties and represent different mutually exclusive versions of a common entity. For example, the types Lecturer and Manager both belong to the Employee category and the assumption is that an object can either be a Lecturer or a Manager but not both.

4. **Role Relationship**

   The term role in this paper is used to specify a scenario of behavior (undertaken by an object) which is determined on the basis of the collection of properties that are associated with the object in the center of interest and are responsible for bringing the role into existence. The Role Relationship holds between object types iff an instance of one type has equivalent counterparts in other information sources where emphasis is placed on a different perspective. This means that different roles are played by the same conceptual object in different information sources.

5. **Is-Part-Of Relationship**

   $t_{i,1}$ **is-part-of** $t_{j,2}$ iff in the real world $t_{j,2}$ is composed of $t_{i,1}$ and cannot exist without it (e.g. Door is part of Car).

6. **Additional Association Relationship**

   The additional association relationship is a relationship which holds between object types that may be related during the process of schema integration when their respective type instances are taken into account. Such kinds of relationships are not expressed in the host schemas. For example, Lecturer in schema 1 can work as a part time consultant in Company in schema 2, but there is no such relationship in either schemas.

In our view a schema contains the knowledge regarding the structure and semantics of its underlying object-base which not only describes the actual data structure and organization within the system but also the semantics of the problem domain. Unfortunately, this type of knowledge is buried deeply in the schemas, and one needs to rely on an interactive environment to analyze schemas, extract and structure this body of knowledge. There are two sorts of comparisons considered here: one is based on the structure, while the other is based on the semantics of the schemas. Both of these comparisons take into account the types of structural conflicts and semantic confluence relationships described in the previous.

3.1 Structure-Based Comparison

In order to perform schema integration it is important to single out the set of components in the disparate information sources that present some degree of structural connectivity. Apart from the structural differences and deviations identified in the previous section a structure-based comparison is used to determine the structural relatedness between individual types belonging to diverse schemas on the basis of a set of rules (in the rule-base) which determine this kind of connectivity. The basic structural relationships between individual types in different schemas are determined on the basis of a comparison to identify common and non-common structural characteristics and correspondences.

318

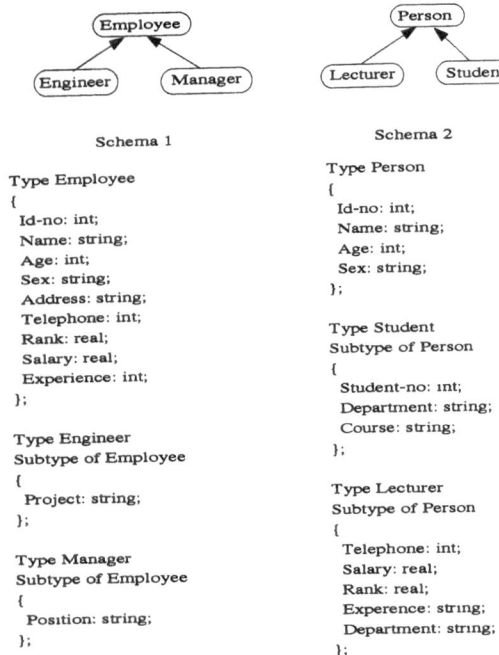

Schema 1   Schema 2

Type Employee
{
    Id-no: int;
    Name: string;
    Age: int;
    Sex: string;
    Address: string;
    Telephone: int;
    Rank: real;
    Salary: real;
    Experience: int;
};

Type Engineer
Subtype of Employee
{
    Project: string;
};

Type Manager
Subtype of Employee
{
    Position: string;
};

Type Person
{
    Id-no: int;
    Name: string;
    Age: int;
    Sex: string;
};

Type Student
Subtype of Person
{
    Student-no: int;
    Department: string;
    Course: string;
};

Type Lecturer
Subtype of Person
{
    Telephone: int;
    Salary: real;
    Rank: real;
    Experence: string;
    Department: string;
};

Figure 3: Structure-Based Comparison

A result of the structural comparison under the guidance of the rule collections (put by the DBA) in the rule-base will reveal several sorts of inter-type structural correspondences. Types may be *equivalent* (see definitions in previous section) in which they have identical domains e.g., the types Faculty in two different schemas which are identified as drawing their properties from identical domains. Types can be contained into one another, e.g., a type Faculty in one schema and Department in another. Types can be identified to be (partially or totally) overlapping with not containment relationship between them. For example, the domain of some properties of one schema type like Lecturer may totally overlap with those of the type Head in another schema, or may partially overlap with those of the type Lecturer in another schema. Finally, types may be disjoint in which case their properties originate from different domains.

The process of structure-based comparison may be fully understood in the context of a simple example. Consider two atomic object types which are of the same kind, such as Employee and Lecturer which are both of type Person and originate from two different information sources. Then identical, containment, overlapping and disjoint relationships must be established between them based on the idea of property (attribute) equivalences. In this situation, object types can be compared along their respective inheritance hierarchies. For example in Figure 3, we assume that two different information sources exist whose respective schemas need to be merged, and we attempt to compare their respective object types. We start by comparing the construct Employee in the inheritance hierarchy for schema 1 with the construct Person in the inheritance hierarchy for schema 2. Here based on the rule sets contained in the rule-base we may conclude that Employee and Person are overlapping and in fact that Person subsumes Employee. In this case we may conclude that Employee is a subtype of Person based on the attributes they possess. Subsequently, we keep on comparing along the Person hierarchy in schema 1. We then compare the attributes of Employee that do not belong to Person with those of Lec-

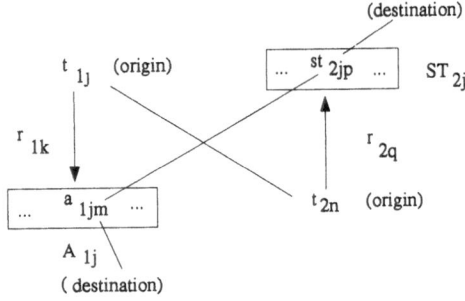

Solid and dashed lines show inter-type comparison

Figure 4: Semantic-based Comparison

turer or/and Student, and can ascertain that Employee is the supertype of Lecturer and that Employee and Student are really disjoint types (assuming that a student cannot work as a part-time employee).

Any knowledge and conclusions pertaining to the inter-type relationships in the diverse schema-types is accumulated, validated and then stored in the knowledge-base as a series of frames for subsequent use and exploitation during the process of semantic analysis which succeeds.

3.2 Semantic-Based Comparison

Owing to the diversity of concepts and perspectives modeled by the multiple information sources, it may well happen that concepts which appear to be structurally disjoint may still be semantically related. In order to find additional semantics between types which are hidden in the schema structures, such as role relationship, category relationship etc., that are defined in our rule base and can not be ascertained by the structure-based comparison, we should check the object-type relationships which associate object types in different schemas. For example, we may wish to isolate two relationships like works_for in schema 1 which associates objects of type employee (its origin) with objects of the type Private_Company (its destination) and the relationship employed_by is schema 2 which associates objects of the type Worker with those of type Factory. It is assumed that these relationships are represented as full-fledged typed objects in the underlying model. The result of this comparison will determine whether objects like Factory and Private_Company, and Worker and Employee are pairwisely related, if there are any additional types of association that can be established between them which are not expressed in the schemas 1 and 2 and so on. Such kinds of associations may not be fully captured by the structural analysis and this is where semantic analysis may prove to be extremely useful. The results of the semantic analysis are seen as a further refinement of the results yielded during the structural analysis, in which case portions of schema information stored in the knowledge-base will have to be refined to reflect the true relatedness between inter-schema types.

Inter-type relationships indicate: (1) possible semantic connections between object types outside the schema hierarchy; (2) further hidden behavior of the object types; and (3) hidden dependencies between object types. Based on this viewpoint, we briefly outline an interactive methodology for semantic inter-type comparison.

To give some rigor to this process we first define some concepts relating to two different schema types and relationships which we compare to ascertain any existing semantic links.

We define:
Schema as $S_i = \{T_i, R_i, 2 \leq i \leq n\}$,

$T_i = \{t_{i,j} \mid t_{i,j}$ an object type in schema S_i with $j > 1\}$,
$R_i = \{r_{i,k} \mid r_{i,k}$ a relationship type in S_i with $k > 1\}$.
$A_{i,j} = \{a_{i,j,m} \mid a_{i,j,m} \in T_i$, denotes the destination types in S_i
    that have direct association links with $t_{i,j}\}$.
$ST_{i+1,j} = \{st_{i+1,j,p} \mid st_{i+1,j,p} \in T_{i+1}$, the set of types in S_{i+1}
     that have structural relationships
     with types in the set $A_{i,j}$ of $S_i\}$.

The structural relationships like equivalence, containment, overlapping and so on used in the previous definitions were described in section 3.1. A concise representation of how the previous constructs are related is depicted in Figure 4.

For this semantic-based comparison we can define three types of assertions established between any two relationship types of the form $r(t_1, t_2)$, where t_1 and t_2 are types in the same information source, in different schemas. Again knowledge regarding the inter-relationship types will require guidelines and support from the rules in the rule-base. The inter-relationship type assertions are as follows:

1. **Identical** means that two relationships have exactly the same semantics in the real world although they may have different names.

2. **Compatible** means that two relationships are not identical but have similar functions.

3. **Incompatible** means that two relationships have no common properties.

Below we give a general explanation regarding semantic-based comparisons. For reasons of simplicity, we assume that we compare and analyze two schemas only, namely schema S_1 and S_2. We will use simple examples to explain the process of semantic analysis wherever intuition is deemed necessary.

For every type $t_{1,j}$ in schema 1 we find a set of types $A_{1,j}$ which have direct associations with this particular type. We then find a set of types in schema 2 which have structural relationships with types in set $A_{1,j}$ and name it $ST_{2,j}$. Now we pick a type $a_{1,j,m}$ in $A_{1,j}$ which has an association type $r_{1,k}$ with $t_{1,j}$, and the type $st_{2,j,p}$ in $ST_{2,j}$ which has a specific structural relationship with $a_{1,j,m}$. We then find a type $t_{2,n}$ in schema 2 which has an association relationship r_{2q} with $st_{2,j,p}$. This process is also described to some extent in Figure 4.

To establish semantic similarities we must then compare all four types $t_{1,j}$, $t_{2,n}$, $a_{1,j,m}$, $st_{2,j,p}$ and the two relationship types $r_{1,k}$, r_{2q}. This process will be performed in three steps and has as follows:

1. The purpose of this step is to further refine the structural relationship between the two types $a_{1,j,m}$ and $st_{2,j,p}$ which initially may have identical, contained or overlapping relationships stored in the knowledge base. If these two types are identical we then goto step-2. Otherwise use we the two types substitute for each other in the association relationships in which they participate. In which case the relationship type $r_{1,k}(t_{1,j}, a_{1,j,m})$ becomes $r_{1,k}(t_{1,j}, st_{2,j,p})$, and the relationship type $r_{2q}(t_{2,n}, st_{2,j,p})$ becomes $r_{2q}(t_{2,n}, a_{1,j,m})$. The purpose of this substitution is to establish whether the relationship types are still valid after the substitution. The relationship is valid if we can intermix types as explained and its constraints are not violated. This must be confirmed by the DBA.

Here we may distinguish between two broad cases: (i) types $st_{2,j,p}$ and $a_{1,j,m}$ may have *weak connectivity* when the relationships $r_{1,k}$ and r_{2q} are no longer valid, in which case we are satisfied with the results of the structural comparison; and (ii) the two types may have *strong connectivity*

in which case we must further refine knowledge concerning their structural association found in the knowledge-base.

Strong connectivity may differentiate between the following three cases:

(a) The two types are equivalent.
(b) The two types have a conceptual **is-a** relationship if all $st_{2,j,p}$ and $a_{1,j,m}$ type instances can substitute one another.
(c) The two types have a role relationship if some $st_{2,j,p}$ and $a_{1,j,m}$ type instances can substitute one another.

Consider for example, the case of the two relationships works_for(Employee, Company) in schema 1 and employed_by(Worker, Factory) in schema 2. All we have to do is to compare the types Company vs. Factory. If the substitution of Company by Factory in works_for and of Factory by Company in employed_by is valid, then we conclude that these objects are somehow semantically related. If not we assume that they are only structurally related as indicated in the previous section. If now the objects are semantically such related we may find that Company and Factory are identical or a Company **is-a** conceptual Factory (or vice versa) or a Company plays the role of a Factory (or vice-versa). Such knowledge refines any knowledge initially obtained from the process of structural comparison.

2. Here we check whether we can express any additional associations between the types $t_{1,j}$, and $st_{2,j,p}$, and the types $t_{2,n}$, and $a_{1,j,m}$. If we find an additional association we express it and then proceed with step-2.

Consider for example the case of the two relationships works_for(Student, Company) and studies_at(University, Student) we we have established that $t_{1,j} = st_{2,j,p} = $ Student but the fact that a student may also be employed is missing from schema 2. In this case we must introduce an additional relationship type during integration to express this fact.

3. This step involves comparison of the types $t_{1,j}$ and $t_{2,n}$ based on previous results regarding their associated counterparts $a_{1,j,m}$ and $st_{2,j,p}$. It also involves comparison of their associated relationship types $r_{1,k}$ and r_{2q}. Here we may differentiate between three cases regarding the relationship types $r_{1,k}$ and r_{2q}:

(a) $r_{1,k}$ and r_{2q} are identical: If the two $a_{1,j,m}$ and $st_{2,j,p}$ have been found to be identical or somewhat **is-a** related then $t_{1,j}$ and $t_{2,n}$ may be conceptually **is-a** or category related.
Consider the case of the relationships travels_by(Customer, Plane) and flies(Passenger, Plane). If the DBA has ascertained that these two relationships are identical and have already established that Passenger and Customer are identical or **is-a** related then it follows that Train and Plain belong to the same general category, say Means_of_Transport.

(b) $r_{1,k}$ and r_{2q} are compatible: The previous assumptions hold also here, the only additional element introduced is that the types instances of $t_{1,j}$ and $t_{2,n}$ may be role related.

(c) $r_{1,k}$ and r_{2q} are incompatible: Here no further assumptions can be made regarding the types $a_{1,j,m}$ and $st_{2,j,p}$, they are weakly connected.

The outcome of the process of semantic analysis results in a wealth of knowledge which supplements and refines that found during the process of structural analysis. This process can be enormously facilitated if a similarity-based classification scheme is employed by the schema analysis framework. In this way, one can address the problem of fitting an individual case, i.e., an individual schema type, within already existing cases by using such techniques as case-based reasoning and induction learning [11]. Learning procedures can then be used to create generalized situations represented by frames that record the similarities between a group of cases [12].

4 Concluding Remarks

Knowledge of the internal structures and semantics of conceptual schemas and their relatedness is critical to our ability to understand how their underlying information repositories are organized. Current trends in the fields of database technology and knowledge engineering dictate the need for advanced knowledge-based interactive tools for schema context diagnosis and integration. Unless one understands what the individual objects mean, how they are organized, and how they are semantically related to one another, one cannot integrate them effectively in a distributed environment. This paper presented a brief account of past research activities in schema integration, their current limitations and the unsolved problems. For such problems we proposed the use of a new framework integrating AI techniques and the object-oriented paradigm, which is more suitable not only for structural problem solving but also for dealing with semantic problems during the schema integration phase.

Out of the many research issues directly associated with the multiple information sources and the methodology for schema analysis great potential lies in formulating the the rules and criteria for schema diagnosis and integration. After consulting the host database designers, enough empirical knowledge and rules can be accumulatively derived and subsequently encoded providing, thus, online help on a whenever required basis.

References

[1] C. Batini, M. Lenzerini, S. B. Navathe,'A Comparative Analysis of Methodologies for Database Schema Integration', Computing Surveys, vol. 18, no. 4, December 1986.

[2] S. Navathe et al.,'Integration User Views in Database Design', IEEE Computer, vol. 19, no. 1, January 1986.

[3] M. V. Mannino et al, 'A Rule-Based Approach For Merging Generalization Hierarchies', Information Systems vol.13, no.3, pp. 257-272, 1988.

[4] A. P. Sheth, J. A. Larson, 'A Tool For Integration Conceptual Schema And User Views', IEEE Conf. on Data & Knowledge Eng., pp. 176-183, Los Angles, Feb. 1988.

[5] S. Hayne, S. Ram, 'Muti-User View Integration System(MUVIS): An Expert System for View Integration', IEEE Conf. on Data & Knowledge Eng., pp. 402-409, Feb. 1990.

[6] J. Banerjee et al, 'Data Model Issues for Object-Oriented Applications', ACM trans. on Office Information Systems, vol.5, no.1, pp. 3-26, Jan. 1987.

[7] S. Zdonik and D. Maier, 'Readings in Object-Oriented Database System', Morgan Koffman Publishers, San Mateo, CA, 1990.

[8] M. P. Papazoglou, 'Knowledge-Driven Distributed Information System', 14th Int'l Computer Software & Application Conference, COMPSAC-90, pp. 671-679, Chicago, Oct. 1990.

[9] W. Effelsberg, M. Mannino 'Attribute Equivalence in Global Schema Design for Heterogeneous Distributed Databases', Information Systems, vol.9, no.3, 1984.

[10] J. Larson et al., 'A Theory of Attribute Equivalence in Databases with Application to Schema Integration', IEEE trans. on Software Engineering, vol. 15, no. 4, pp. 449-463, April 1989.

[11] S. Slade, 'Case-Based Reasoning: A Research Paradigm', AI-Magazine, pp. 42-55, Spring 1991.

[12] M. Vilain et al, 'On Analytical and Similarity-Based Classification', AAAI-90 Conference, pp. 867-874, Boston, 1990.

Atomicity of Global Transactions in Distributed Heterogeneous Database Systems*

K. Vidyasankar
Department of Computer Science
Memorial University of Newfoundland
St. John's, Newfoundland
Canada A1C 5S7

Abstract. Compensating transactions are required to achieve the atomicity of global transactions in distributed heterogeneous database systems. Compensation imposes several constraints on the definition of the global transactions. In this paper we illustrate some of these constraints, and suggest ways of accommodating them.

1. Introduction

A distributed heterogeneous database system is a system which interconnects already existing autonomous database systems to support global applications that access data items in more than one database [3, 10]. Other names proposed for such a network are: federated database system [12], multidatabase system [7], decentralized system [11], etc. These systems are characterized by the autonomy of the individual sites as well as the cooperation among them.

Three different aspects of autonomy have been discussed in [3, 4, 10]:

1. *Design autonomy.* The individual sites may differ with respect to data models, physical design, data definition and manipulation languages, query processing strategies, concurrency control and recovery mechanisms, etc. One reason for the heterogeneity is that when the individual systems were designed they were probably unaware of the intended interconnection with other sites.

2. *Execution autonomy.* Each site executes its own local transactions and also subtransactions of global transactions. All these transactions are treated in the same way. That is, the site is entitled to decide when and how to execute a subtransaction, and commits it as soon as its execution is complete, without waiting for the commitment of the entire global transaction.

3. *Communication autonomy.* The sites may be willing to share with other sites only some, not all, data and transaction processing information at that site. Also, each site communicates with other sites only when it finds it convenient. Consequently each site might be inaccessible to the other sites for long periods of time.

*This research is supported in part by the Natural Sciences and Engineering Research Council of Canada Individual Operating Grant A-3182.

The cooperation of the sites is in the execution of global transactions. Each site is capable of initiating a global transaction [4, 12]. Each global transaction is decomposed into subtransactions, which may be decomposed further into smaller subtransactions, and so on. A general architecture of a heterogeneous system is given in Figure 1. Here GTM stands for Global Transaction Manager, and LTM for Local Transaction Manager. The GTM decomposes the global transactions initiated at that site and the subtransactions received from other sites into smaller subtransactions, and sends some of them to the GTMs of the other sites and the remaining to the LTM at that site; the latter are called *g-local* transactions in this paper. The LTM is responsible for executing g-local transactions and the local transactions initiated at that site.

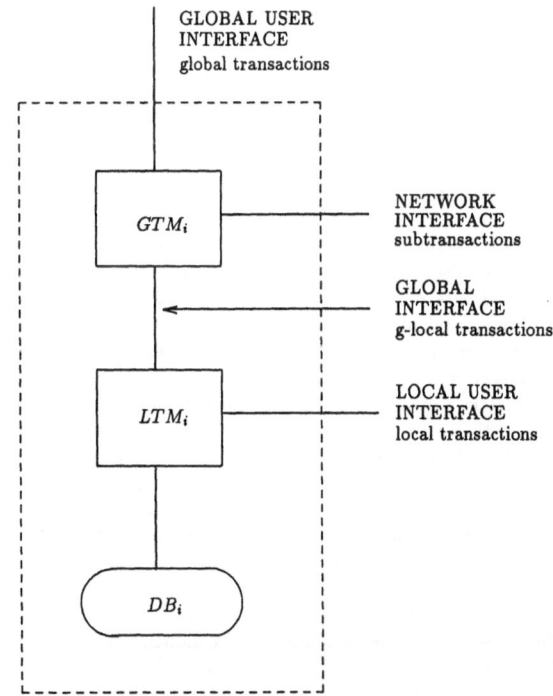

Figure 1. General architecture of site *i*.

322

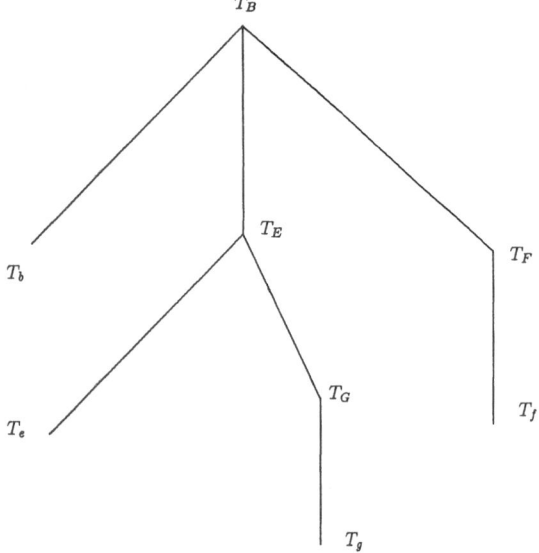

Figure 2. Global transaction T.

Figure 2 gives an example of a global transaction T that is executed at sites b, e, f and g. It is initiated at site b, and hence is denoted also as (sub)transaction T_B. The GTM at site b decomposes it into a g-local transaction T_b for its LTM, and subtransactions T_E and T_F for the sites e and f respectively. The GTM at site e decomposes T_E into T_e and T_G. Finally T_F and T_G consist simply of g-local transactions T_f and T_g at sites f and g respectively.

In heterogeneous systems, the final composition of a global transaction in terms of subtransactions and g-local transactions depends on many factors. First, there is no global or centralized knowledge of (the data contained in or the g-local transactions that can be executed by) the various sites of the entire system [11]. Each site may have only limited information about the other sites. Second, for executing a subtransaction, a site may select any one of the available sites capable of executing that subtransaction. Thus the same logical task may be composed into different global transactions at different times.

As with transactions in traditional database systems, concurrency control and guaranteeing atomicity of transactions are two major issues in heterogeneous database systems. Both these issues are more difficult than in traditional systems due to the autonomy of the local sites. The study of the concurrency control issues indicates that the global transactions need to be defined in a special way [10]. This is elaborated in section 2. In this paper, we show that the atomicity considerations also impose some constraints on the definition of the global transactions in heterogeneous systems.

Since a global transaction is composed eventually of several g-local transactions, atomicity implies that either all or none of the g-local transactions of the global transaction are executed. But each site commits the g-local transactions as soon as their execu-

tion is completed successfully, without waiting for the global commitment (execution autonomy). Hence, if all the g-local transactions of a global transaction cannot be executed successfully, then those which have been executed successfully must be rolled back *logically*, by executing *compensating transactions* [1, 4]. It is the compensating transactions that impose further constraints.

We illustrate two kinds of constraints in this paper. One concerns with the composition of compensating transactions as subtransactions of global transactions. This is dealt with in section 2. The other constraint is due to the fact that not all (sub)transactions are compensatable. Hence the set of g-local transactions constituting a global transaction cannot be arbitrary. We show in section 3 some special properties that need to be satisfied.

In this paper we are not concerned with how a subtransaction can be compensated. The design of compensating transactions is a difficult and important topic. Several papers discuss this issue [8, 13, 15]. For the purposes of this paper, we need only to distinguish which transactions can be compensated.

2. Atomicity versus Serializability

In heterogeneous database systems, a global transaction facilitates access and updates of the constituent databases. Each global transaction is eventually composed of several g-local transactions. However, the composition is influenced by the concurrency control and the atomicity issues, which are affected considerably by the autonomy of the local sites. First we consider concurrency control. To ensure that the interleaved execution of the transactions is correct, some sort of concurrency control is required. An accepted criterion of correctness is the *serializability* of the execution, that is, the effect of the execution should be equivalent to that of some serial execution of the transactions. In heterogeneous systems, each site already has a concurrency control mechanism that ensures serializability among the local transactions (including the g-local transactions of the global ones) executed at that site. Then a global concurrency control mechanism needs to be designed such that it, along with the existing local concurrency control machanisms, will ensure serializability of the global transactions (together with the local transactions). One of the earliest papers analyzing this problem is [10]. That paper gives a set of conditions under which such a global concurrency control mechanism can be designed without violating the autonomy of the local sites. One of the conditions is that:

C1. Each global transaction can have at most one g-local transaction at each site.

All the concurrency control mechanisms proposed in the literature [1, 2, 5, 14, 16] require that this condition be satisfied. This condition implies that *from concurrency control point of view* the composition of a global transaction can be considered to be a *2-level nested transaction*, a transaction consisting of some g-local transactions. A concurrent execution of 2-level nested transactions is serializable (as shown in [17]) if it is equivalent to a serial execution of its 1-level transactions in which, for each 2-level transaction, all its 1-level transactions occur consecutively. We call this the *consecutive serializability* requirement of the g-local transactions.

323

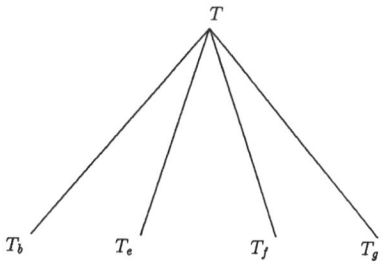

Figure 3. Two level structure of T.

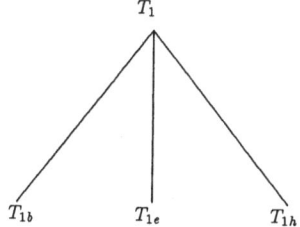

Figure 4. Global transaction T_1.

A two level structure of transaction T in Figure 2 is given in Figure 3. Figure 4 describes another global transaction T_1, with g-local transactions in sites b, e and h, in this form. The execution in the order $(T_b, T_e, T_{1b}, T_{1h}, T_f, T_{1e}, T_g)$ is serializable since it is equivalent to $(T_b, T_e, T_f, T_g, T_{1b}, T_{1h}, T_{1e})$, that is, (T, T_1).

The consecutive serializability requirement of the g-local transactions can be achieved by another condition stated in [10], namely:

C2. The global concurrency control mechanism determines a total order of execution of the global transactions, and the corresponding g-local transactions must be executed by the LTMs in each relevant site *effectively* in the same order.

By "effective order" is meant the order in which the transactions occur in any equivalent serial order of execution. (This is referred to as *serialization order* in [3].) Suppose that the order (T_{1a}, T_{2a}) is required in site a. Then the steps of T_{1a} and T_{2a} can be executed concurrently, or serially in *any* order, even in the order T_{2a} followed by T_{1a}, as long as T_{1a} occurs before T_{2a} in any equivalent serial order of the execution [3, 10].

For a concurrent execution involving T and T_1 to be serializable in the order (T, T_1), the order (T_b, T_{1b}) must be followed at the site b, and the order (T_e, T_{1e}) at the site e.

Now let us consider the atomicity issue. Consider again the transaction T in Figure 2. Suppose the execution of T_f fails and, at that time, the executions of T_b and T_e have been successfully completed and that of T_g has not started. Then the intended execution of T_g can be cancelled, and T_b and T_e must be rolled back logically by executing, for instance, compensating transactions T_b' and T_e', at sites b and e, respectively. In such cases, it seems natural to group the compensating transactions along with the transactions which are being compensated, and consider these as constituting a single global transaction. In the above example,

the g-local transactions T_b, T_e, T_b' and T_e' will form a single transaction, say T_ϕ. This approach is satisfactory from atomicity point of view, but creates problems for concurrency control, since *this has more than one g-local transaction per site* and hence violates the condition C1.

We note that sometimes, depending on the semantics of the transaction, it may be sufficient to maintain serializability only with respect to the g-local transactions of T and not T itself, that is, the consecutive serializability requirement of the g-local transactions may be relaxed to the simple serializability requirement. (The "unit of consistency" is not T, but a g-local transaction of T.) A 2-level transaction with this kind of consistency constraint has been called *saga* in [9]. If T and T_1 are considered as sagas, then the g-local transactions at the two sites b and e need not be executed in the same order. For instance, $(T_b, T_{1e}, T_{1b}, T_e, T_{1h}, T_g, T_f)$ is an acceptable order of execution. We will refer to a transaction which is not a saga as a *strict* transaction.

We propose that the transaction T_ϕ stated earlier, consisting of T_b, T_e, T_b' and T_e', be considered as a saga. Then each of the subtransactions becomes a separate global transaction from concurrency control point of view and hence the condition C1 is not violated. In addition to satisfying the concurrency control aspect, this proposal has additional merits. Note that the original intention was to execute T. But once it is realized that T cannot be executed successfully, the transaction T_ϕ has been executed. From the atomicity point of view, either a complete successful execution or nonexecution of T is required. The execution of T_ϕ is *not* equivalent to the nonexecution of T if other, local or g-local, transactions happen to be executed in the local sites in between the first g-local transaction and the corresponding compensating one. But this is the best that could be done in heterogeneous systems, respecting the autonomy of the local sites. Now by treating T_ϕ as a saga instead of a strict transaction, we are allowing more freedom in compensation. To illustrate this, consider the execution of (saga) T_ϕ and (strict) T_1 in the order $(T_b, T_e, T_{1e}, T_e', T_b', T_{1b}, T_{1h})$. This is serializable since it is equivalent to the serial execution $(T_b, T_b', T_e, (T_{1e}, T_{1b}, T_{1h}), T_e')$, that is, $(T_b, T_b', T_e, T_1, T_e')$. At the site b, the transaction T_b' is intended to compensate the effects of T_b. The compensation may depend on the other local transactions executed after T_b. Thus T_b' may not be unique with respect to T_b. At the site e, T_{1e} and possibly some local transactions have been executed after T_e. Now T_e' can be designed so as to compensate the effects of T_e knowing that these other transactions have been executed at that site. It is not affected by the design of T_b' or when T_b' is executed. Thus there is no necessity of combining T_e' with T_b' and coordinating their execution, which would be the case if we consider T_ϕ as a strict transaction.

Now let us consider another example. Suppose that an execution of a global transaction T_P consists of the execution of the following g-local transactions: $T_{a1}, T_{a1}', T_{a2}, T_{b1}, T_{b1}'$ and T_{c1}. Here the primed transactions are compensating the unprimed ones. In this execution, partial roll back has been done twice and after each time the main execution has continued. Logically, the executed transaction T_P consists finally of the g-local transactions T_{a2} and T_{c1}. We propose that these two constitute the strict component, and the remaining form a saga.

The general proposal is the following:

Proposal:

The g-local transactions of a global transaction T can be partitioned into three disjoint sets: RT, the set of transactions that were rolled back; CT, the compensating transactions that rolled back the first set; and FT, the other g-local transactions which finally logically constitute T. We propose that FT constitute the strict part, and RT and CT constitute the saga part. That is, from concurrency control point of view, we decompose T into a set of transactions: a strict 2-level transaction consisting of g-local transactions in FT, and several 1-level transactions, namely, the g-local transactions of RT and CT.□

As a consequence of this proposal, the two conditions stated earlier can be modified as follows.

C1'. Each global transaction can have at most one g-local transaction belonging to its strict part at each site. It can have any number of g-local transactions of its saga part.

C2'. The global concurrency control mechanism determines a total order of execution of the global transactions, and the g-local transactions of the strict part of the corresponding transactions must be executed by the LTMs in each relevant site *effectively* in the same order. The g-local transactions of the saga part may be executed in any order.

3. Compensatability Considerations

Suppose a g-local transaction T_b is executed at site b, and at a later stage a compensating transaction T_b' is to be executed. The effects of T_b have been visible to other local or g-local transactions executed after T_b but before T_b'. Hence any compensation of T_b would, in a strict sense, also require the logical roll back of those local or g-local transactions T_I which "saw" the effects of T_b, and, in turn, the roll back of those local or g-local transactions which saw the effects of T_I, and so on, causing a cascade roll back. But the autonomy of the sites implies that no global authority can dictate the roll back of local transactions. This means that T_b must be such that no local transactions that saw the effects of T_b need to be rolled back, when T_b is rolled back. Furthermore T_b must be compensatable despite the fact that the transactions which saw the effects of T_b are not rolled back.

In this section we give a definition of global transactions that takes into account that not all transactions are compensatable. We start with a few definitions.

Definition 3.1. A g-local transaction T_a is *compensatable* if there exists another g-local transaction T_a' (called *compensating transaction of T_a*) executable at the same site such that (i) T_a' semantically removes the effects of T_a from the database at that site, even though some other transactions T_I may have been executed at that site after T_a, and (ii) no such T_I needs to be compensated when T_a is compensated; it is *noncompensatable* otherwise.□

We note that the compensating transaction T_a' in the above definition need not be unique. There may be different choices depending upon the other transactions that are executed between T_a and T_a'.

Definition 3.2. A g-local transaction is *assured* if
(i) its successful execution is guaranteed, and
(ii) its (logical) roll back will not be required (by the global mechanism) later;

it is *unassured* otherwise.□

A compensatable transaction may or may not be an assured transaction. Similarly, an assured transaction may or may not be compensatable. It is generally assumed however, for example in [4, 8], that each compensating g-local transaction is an assured one.

Definition 3.3. A g-local transaction is *critical* if it is non-compensatable and unassured; it is *noncritical* otherwise.□

Observation 3.1. Each global transaction T may consist of a prolog P of several compensatable g-local transactions, followed by at most one critical g-local transaction t^*, and then an epilog E of some assured g-local transactions.□

The rationale is that the execution of t^* will be considered only if all the transactions in P have been executed successfully. Then if t^* is executed successfully, then all the transactions in E will be executed; otherwise, some transactions which compensate those in P will be executed. It is clear that if there are two or more critical g-local transactions and one of them is executed successfully but another one fails, then, since the first one cannot be compensated, the atomicity cannot be preserved.

As mentioned earlier, in this paper we are not concerned about how a transaction may be compensated. As long as it can be compensated somehow, it is compensatable. The following examples illustrate the various types of transactions.

Example 3.1. (Cash withdrawal from an automatic teller machine (ATM)). We assume that each ATM has a (perhaps not up-to-date) copy X_i of the current balance in the customer's account. If the amount X_i is greater than the requested withdrawal amount Y, then Y is subtracted from X_i (a g-local transaction T_i) and the withdrawal allowed (an external nondatabase operation). Actual subtraction from the "master copy" X (another g-local transaction T_j) is done afterwards, perhaps the next working day. Here T_i is the critical transaction, and, in practice, T_j is made an assured transaction possibly because of the following. (i) If during the update of the master copy X it is found that the account has been overdrawn, some penalty is levied, for instance, by way of some overdraft charges. (ii) There is a limit on the maximum amount that can be withdrawn from an ATM at any one time, and a possible loss due to such withdrawal is considered minor.□

Example 3.2. (A purchase using a credit card). Let C be a customer purchasing an article from a shop S, using a credit card issued by bank B. Then the following steps occur:
(i) C buys article from S (with the arrangement that B will pay S);
(ii) S (requests payment and) gets paid by B; and
(iii) B (charges and) gets paid by C.
Here (i) is an external operation, and (ii) and (iii) are database operations. It is a normal practice that if the purchase is for a small amount, for example, less than \$50, then the above steps occur in the given order, and both (ii) and (iii) are assumed to be assured transactions. If the purchase amount exceeds \$50, then (ii) may not be guaranteed automatically by the bank, and hence is critical. Then S phones B to get authorization for the payment, and only if the authorization is given, (i), and then (iii), which has become an assured transaction, are done. Thus (ii) being critical is determined by the purchase amount.□

Example 3.3. (Read-only transactions). We can consider

all read-only g-local transactions as compensatable since, from the database point of view, they can be rolled back simply by ignoring them. Note that the values read by a g-local transaction might be instrumental to some external "critical" operation like launching a missile. But it is reasonable to assume that such external operations will be triggered only on commitment of the global transaction, whereas the compensation issue comes up before such commitment.□

Example 3.4. An optimistic approach of concurrency control for global transactions is discussed in [5]. There the read steps of the global transaction are executed first, and the validity of their results checked. If invalid, the read steps are performed repeatedly until valid values are read. Then the write steps are executed. Only those transactions for which the sites performing the read steps and those performing the write steps are either disjoint or have only one site in common are allowed. The success of the execution of the global transaction is guaranteed in the former case. (The individual write steps are executed by the local sites repeatedly until they succeed.) In the latter case, if the first time execution of the write step at the common site is successful (with the effect that the write step is performed immediately after the read step so that both these steps together form a g-local transaction), then the write steps at the other sites are carried out, otherwise the global transaction is aborted. Aborting a global transaction is trivial in this scheme since all its subtransactions that have been executed when the decision to abort is made are read-only.

Here the critical g-local transaction is the one with a read step and a write step at the same site. All other read steps correspond individually to compensatable transactions, all other write steps are assured transactions.□

We now extend the Definitions 3.1, 3.2 and 3.3 to arbitrary subtransactions.

Definition 3.4. A subtransaction T_A is *compensatable* if there exists another subtransaction T_A' (called *compensating transaction* of T_A) whose execution will semantically remove the effects of T_A from the (global) database, even though some other transactions T_I may have been executed in the system after T_A, and no such T_I needs to be compensated when T_A is compensated; it is *noncompensatable* otherwise.□

We note that we do not make any reference to the compositions of T_A and T_A', or to the sites in which their g-local transactions are executed.

Definition 3.5. A subtransaction is *assured* if
(i) its successful execution is guaranteed, and
(ii) its (logical) roll back will not be required later;
it is *unassured* otherwise.□

Definition 3.6. A subtransaction is *1-critical* if
(i) it is a critical g-local transaction, or
(ii) it can be decomposed into a sequence consisting of a prolog P of several compensatable subtransactions, followed by exactly one 1-critical proper subtransaction t^*, and then an epilog E of some assured subtransactions.□

Now Observation 3.1 can be generalized as follows.

Proposition 3.2. Each global transaction T may consist of a prolog P of several compensatable subtransactions, followed by at most one 1-critical subtransaction, and then an epilog E of some assured subtransactions.□

By Proposition 3.2, the execution of a global transaction consists of three phases: *compensatable*, *critical* and *assured* phases. In the compensatable phase, compensatable transactions are executed. If a partial roll back decision is made at some stage, then some (assured) transactions compensating some of the already executed transactions will be executed, and then the execution of the other compensatable transactions will be continued. Thus not all g-local transactions executed in the compensatable phase need to be compensatable ones. Similarly, some transactions executed in the assured phase may be of unassured type. We illustrate these situations with an example.

Example 3.5. Figure 5 gives an execution sequence of sub-transactions for reserving flights and hotels, confirming flights and reserving cars, in that order. The critical transaction is CONFIRM-FLIGHTS, with the transactions preceding it constituting the compensatable phase and the ones following it the assured phase. The underlying assumptions are: a ticket purchase is associated with the flights confirmation, and once the ticket is purchased it cannot be returned; flights and hotel reservations are uncertain, whereas renting a car (from one agency or another) is assured; the trip (with a single air ticket) involves visiting two different places, and hence two different hotels and car rentals; and the car rentals in both places must be from the same rental agency.□

RESERVE-FLIGHTS-A	(c)	
RESERVE-HOTEL-1A	(c)	
RESERVE-HOTEL-2A	fail	
CANCEL-HOTEL-2A	(a)	
CANCEL-FLIGHTS-A	(a)	(C)
RESERVE-FLIGHTS-B	(c)	
RESERVE-HOTEL-1B	(c)	
RESERVE-HOTEL-2B	(c)	
CONFIRM-FLIGHTS-B	(*)	(**)
RESERVE-CAR-1A	(c)	
RESERVE CAR-2A	fail	
CANCEL-CAR-1A	(a)	(A)
RESERVE-CAR-1B	(c)	
RESERVE-CAR-2B	(c)	

(C) - COMPENSATABLE PHASE

(**) - CRITICAL PHASE

(A) - ASSURED PHASE

(c) - compensatable transactions

(*) - critical transaction

(a) - assured transaction

Figure 5. Transaction for Example 3.5

4. Discussion

In heterogeneous database systems compensating activity is essential to preserve the atomicity of the global transactions. Compensation imposes several constraints on the definition of the global transactions. In this paper we have illustrated some of these constraints, and have suggested ways of accommodating the constraints.

First, in section 2, we have proposed a way of splitting a global transaction defined from atomicity point of view into several transactions such that each has at most one g-local transaction per site, which is a basic requirement for achieving serializability of global transactions. Here each g-local transaction T_a which is compensated, and a g-local transaction T_a' which compensates T_a become separate global transactions. This approach appears natural since the compensating activity T_a' needs to be designed individually, at the site where T_a was executed, depending upon the other transactions executed in that site after T_a. Furthermore, there does not seem to be any need for coordinating the execution of T_a' at that site with another transaction, say T_b', at another site even though both are executed towards preserving the atomicity of the same original global transaction.

In section 3 we have shown that the transactions that need to be executed as global transactions in heterogeneous environment need to be composed so as to have at most one critical g-local transaction. The execution or nonexecution of the critical g-local transaction determines respectively the successful completion or the logical roll back of the global transaction. If such a composition is not possible, then they can be executed only by sacrificing the autonomy of the sites. That is, a few sites must be "locked" simultaneously for the execution.

We note that the concept of a single critical step has been used in other atomicity considerations. With respect to the atomicity of a transaction in a centralized database system, the execution or nonexecution of the commit step of the transaction determines its successful completion or physical roll back. And, in distributed (homogeneous) database systems where failures are considered, the global *certification* of a transaction (that is, the guarantee that the effects of the transaction will remain in the system in spite of subsequent subsystem failures) is determined by the certification in the primary site, in one method, and in a majority of the sites, in another method. In all these cases there is just one critical step. We have extended the same concept to the heterogeneous environment.

Global transactions having compensatable and noncompensatable parts have been considered in [7] also, where a new transaction model for heterogeneous database systems has been proposed. Such transactions are called *mixed* transactions in that paper.

Acknowledgement. The problem addressed in section 2 came up during discussions with N. Natarajan. J. Veijalainen contributed to the development of the global transaction concept in section 3.

References

[1] R. Alonso, H. Garcia-Molina and K. Salem, "Concurrency control and recovery for global procedures in federated database systems," *IEEE Data Engineering*, Vol. 10, No. 3, pp. 5-11, September 1987.

[2] Y. Breitbart and A. Silberschatz, "Multidatabase update issues," *Proc. ACM SIGMOD'88*, pp. 135-142.

[3] W. Du, A.K. Elmagarmid, Y. Leu and S.D. Ostermann, "Effects of autonomy on maintaining global serializability in heterogeneous database systems," *Proc. 2nd International Conference on Data and Knowledge Systems for Manufacturing and Engineering*, Gaithersburg, MD, October 1989.

[4] F. Eliassen and J. Veijalainen, "Language support for multidatabase transactions in a cooperative, autonomous environment," *Proc. TENCON'87, IEEE Regional Conference*, Seoul, 1987.

[5] A.K. Elmagarmid and A.A. Helal, "Supporting updates in heterogeneous distributed database systems," *Proc. Fourth International Conference on Data Engineering*, pp. 564-569, 1988.

[6] A.K. Elmagarmid and Y. Leu, "A hierarchical approach to concurrency control for multidatabases," *Proc. 2nd International Symp. on Databases in Parallel and Distributed Systems*, Dublin, 1990.

[7] A.K. Elmagarmid, Y. Leu, W. Litwin and M. Rusinkiewicz, "A multidatabase transaction model for InterBase," *Proc. VLDB'90*.

[8] H. Garcia-Molina, "Using semantic knowledge for transaction processing in a distributed database," *ACM TODS*, Vol. 8, No. 2, pp. 186-213, June 1983.

[9] H. Garcia-Molina and K. Salem, "Sagas," *Proc. ACM SIGMOD'87*, pp. 249-259.

[10] V. Gligor and R. Popescu-Zeletin, "Transaction management in distributed heterogeneous database management systems," *Information Systems*, Vol. 11, No. 4, pp. 287-297, 1986.

[11] J. Gray, "An approach to decentralized computer systems," *IEEE Trans. on Software Engineering*, Vol. 12, No. 6, pp. 684-692, June 1986.

[12] D. Heimbignor and D. McLeod, "A federated architecture for information management," *ACM Trans. on Office Information Systems*, Vol. 3, No. 3, pp. 253-278, July 1985.

[13] H.F. Korth, E. Levy and A. Silberschatz, "A formal approach to recovery by compensating transactions," *Proc. VLDB'90*.

[14] C. Pu, "Superdatabases for composition of heterogeneous databases," *Proc. Fourth International Conference on Data Engineering*, pp. 548-555, 1988.

[15] H. Tokuda, "Compensatable atomic objects in object-oriented operating systems," *Proc. Pacific Computer Communication Symp.*, Seoul, 1985.

[16] K. Vidyasankar, "A non-two-phase locking protocol for global concurrency control in distributed heterogeneous database systems," *IEEE Trans. on Knowledge and Data Engineering*, to appear.

[17] K. Vidyasankar, "Unified theory of database serializability," *Fundamenta Informatica*, to appear.

Application-oriented Integration of
Distributed Heterogeneous Knowledge Sources

Alexander Endrikat   Ralf Michalski

Forschungsinstitut für anwendungsorientierte Wissensverarbeitung
P.O.Box 2060, D-7900 Ulm, Germany

Abstract

Management of distributed information is one of the major challenges in today's world of interconnected open systems. Thereby, the information is stored as data in heterogeneous autonomous knowledge sources. Benefits for the management can be gained from a sensible connection and integration of data offered by adequate access capabilities. Conceptual work and implementation experiences in the FAW-WINHEDA project, which aims at better support of users in accessing and managing databases as one kind of knowledge sources, are reported in this paper. Operations making implicit knowledge and meta-knowledge explicit will come into focus. An incremental approach is used for the user-initiated, application related knowledge integration. This leads to a significant increase of accessible knowledge by means of a semantically rich representation based on an extended Entity-/Relationship-Model (ExER), which is represented in the KEE™ frame system.

1   Introduction

The realization of knowledge-based access to distributed heterogeneous knowledge sources is a great challenge today and deals with one of the central problems in the "information society": to care for connectivity and availability of distributed facts stored as data for the reason of knowledge extraction by relating data to a given context. One of the major problems in broader data usage and availability is missing knowledge about the data stored (nature, storing process etc.). Storing processes are deeply interrelated with the designers subjective perspective to the represented world and his view on the data storage system (see figure 1). In the best case, the mapping process is based on a conceptual scheme and an adequate database system is used. The result of this mapping process is a stock of data, stored in the specific syntax of the database system, with little openly represented semantics. Parts of that data, and therefore parts of the knowledge about the universe of discourse will be translated into user information via application programs and/or database query languages and lead to an increase of the users specific knowledge. The semantics of the data is regained, at

least partially, by the user interpretation and/or high level application programs.

Summarizing the present state of the situation, with the current techniques stored knowledge will usually represent the universe of discourse in an adequate way only for the designer. For the general user only parts of the semantics are available. Therefore, without participation from the designers of the knowledge sources when developping a distributed application, in our opinion, there is neither a complete integration, nor the construction of a global conceptual scheme possible. Generally, we can assume that the system designers are not available. Therefore ways and means should be identified to achieve also later at least a partial, partly automated and application specific integration of various data sources with the participation of the involved database administrators and users.

With regard to databases as data storage systems, contributions in the field of semantic integration and translation of database schemes is one of the topics in research activities on Federative Database Systems (FDBS), as it is called. A FDBS consists of distributed, possibly heterogeneous and autonomous component databases, that are part of a federation by allowing partial and controlled sharing of their data.

According to the definition in [1] the architecture concerning the data access attempted in the FAW-WINHEDA project is seen first of all as a loosely coupled federation of distributed and heterogeneous database systems. This definition is very similar to the definition for FDBS given in [2]. The autonomy of the participating components is maintained, the partial integration on a global level does not restrict local operations and application programs. Instead of specifying a global conceptual scheme which integrates all the component schemes, an incremental approach is used for the stepwise integration of partial knowledge. The user is supported by facilities to express identified relations between data elements, particularly those between data elements of different databases. Formulating those relations as extensions of the semantic level leads to a partial global conceptual scheme that is relevant to the specific application domain, subsequently called "Semantic Background Model". This approach includes flexibility on the user level. The user can execute database operations on the local DBMS as usual, or she/he can make use of the integration level.

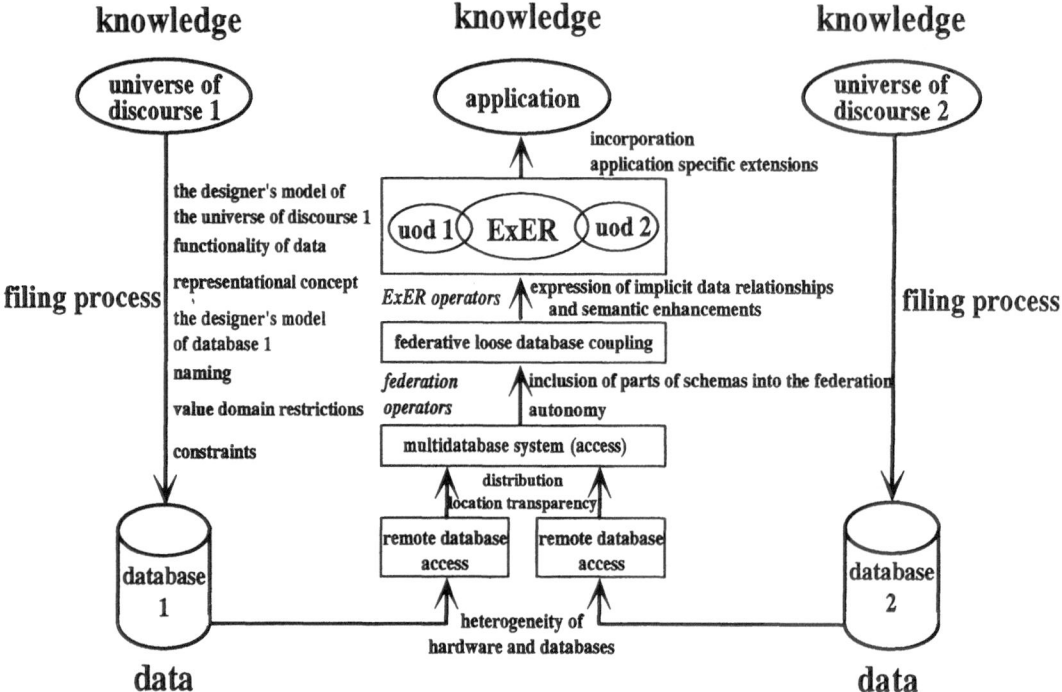

figure 1: application domain and WINHEDA bottom up approach

Subsequently the developed *three phases approach* is discussed in more detail. Chapter 2 describes the user-initiated knowledge integration approach as a first step to a gradual knowledge integration and the realization of concepts in a prototype system. Phases two and three of the approach are described briefly. Chapter 3 gives an overview on the system architecture and reports on the software and hardware configuration of the prototype system. The paper concludes with an outline of project activities ahead.

2   The Integration Approach

The approach described here consists of three subsequent phases for making distributed knowledge available and usable. These phases are considered as the base for an efficient usage of available information sources in the WINHEDA concept. They are characterized as

- bottom up and manual
- top down and manual
- top down and partly automated.

In this approach, we start from the databases as the basis (bottom) to make available higher functionalities towards the user level (top).

2.1   Bottom up and manual

One of the aims of this phase is to make technical prerequisits for parallel access to the involved multiple knowledge sources available. The second aim is the preparation of a high semantical level of representation in order to store explicit database contents and to express implicit data relationships. Particularly, this concerns relationships between overlapping databases, which are autonomous and not coupled so far.

In respect to the technical part, for all the involved knowledge sources the system must take care of uniform access capabilities out of the representation scheme. Doing this, a client/server architecture is aimed at which takes the standardization proposal for the Remote Database Access (RDA) (see [2]) into account. Up to the RDA level, problems concerning the heterogeneity of hardware and database systems have to be addressed in a standardized way (see figure 1) and to the extend possible. As a next step, building on the established level of parallel access, one then has to provide **one** logical view on the distributed data. For example this level supplies the transparent join over different databases (multidatabase level, figure 1).

One important topic in the project phases already completed has been the development of a central representation scheme. This scheme serves as a basis for the implementation of the "Semantic Background Model" of the current application domain. An extended Entity/Relationship model (ExER) was chosen which covers the classical E/R model of

Chen ([3]) and extends it by some relation concepts. ExER allows implementation of a background model on a reasonably high and transparent semantical level. This leads, at the end of the "bottom up and manual" phase, to a binding of information from the involved database systems to the corresponding concepts within the Semantic Background Model.

In doing so the modeling follows the general paradigm of "object orientation". While this could in principle also be done within the E/R model, extension concepts, such as

- object identity,

- generalization / specialization,

- aggregation on object level,

- multivalued attributes,

- grouping,

- primary key constraint,

- referential integrity constraint,

allow a much closer orientation at a structurally object-oriented representation of an application domain. The selection of ExER also in principal, allows the later integration of databases founded on other data models ([4, 5]). On the implementation side, the hybrid KEE system's frame concept supports object-oriented programming, while it's rule based component allows navigation across explicitly represented relationships between objects. Concluding: in this phase an application domain expert builts up a structurally object-oriented model of the application domain, starting from the basis of database information given. The formal frame for this building up process is given in the notation of Predicate/Transition Nets (Pr/T nets) ([6, 7]). Pr/T nets are Petri nets with individual, typed tokens. They may be used to model any kind of structured objects and the rules by which these objects are changed. A place in a Pr/T net represents a variable predicate; an assignment of objects to that place determines an actual extension of the according predicate. Transitions model static predicates, determining the relations between consumed and produced objects during the firing of the transition ([6]).

Our Pr/T net consists of a conventional uninscribed net and inscriptions of the places (also called system state) by sets of objects (i.e., ground terms), inscriptions of the arcs by sets of partially specified objects (i.e., terms) and textual inscriptions of the transitions referring to the complex ExER operators. A transition can be fired if it belongs to the operator set of the current user's usertype (see section 3.1), and if in its preset (i.e., the set of places from which an arc leads to the transition) there are objects such that all partial specifications of the corresponding arcs as well as the firing conditions (included in the transition) are met. In this context the objects are elements of the ExER models implementation system, which of course should be a frame

system. These elements (i.e., classes and instances) could, but do not have to refer to database tables and rows; at the beginning of the building up process they refer to those elements. Initially all places are empty, only the transition *prepare global data dictionary* can be fired.

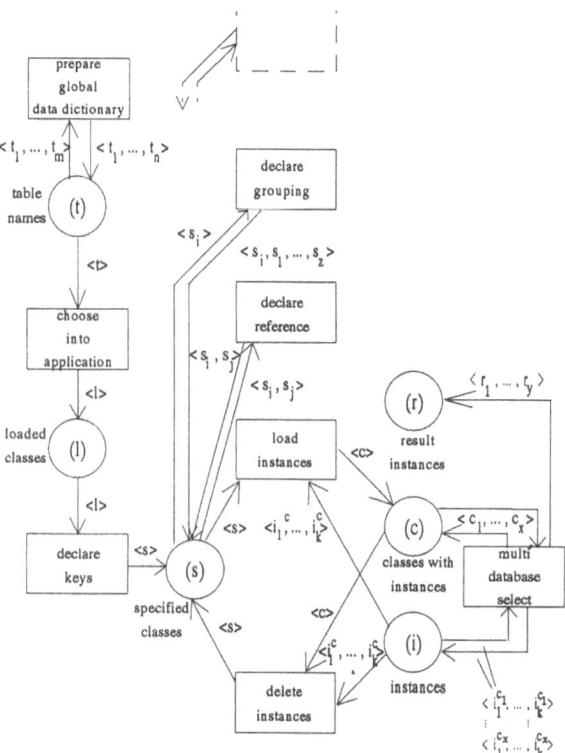

figure 2: Semi-specified Predicate/Transition Net of the building up process

The essential operators (transitions) of the building up process are *declare keys* and *declare reference*. While *declare keys* enables object identity of table rows by enforcing the primary key constraint, then classes representing tables can be used as type constraints for attribute values of other classes during execution of the *declare reference* operator. In doing so, the application domain expert can express implicit relationships between attribute values (foreign keys), especially relationships overlapping databases, and enforce referential integrity.

On the implementation side, the database tables and rows are mapped onto classes and instances of the KEE system's frame concept by the KEElink communication software. As the Pr/T net can also be represented in these frames, there is only one formalism for the representation of the concepts. The generic E/R model of the Pr/T net and its mapping onto the KEE frame system is given in [8].

2.2 Top down and manual

The development of the central representation scheme based on the ExER model offers the possibility to express explicitly, information about data and relationships included in data – even across different databases – on a semantically high level. Otherwise, this knowledge is in many cases directly coded in applications. New applications on distributed heterogeneous knowledge sources can be realized within the chosen approach, preserving the logical independence from data in a better way. Moreover, the ExER-scheme of the federative scheme provides a more powerful data basis for the application, than the mere combination of the single systems would. In this case, top down and manual means the **manual construction** of the application-oriented ExER scheme and **the manual build up** of the corresponding relationships between ExER and application objects **from above** as well as the mapping of database contents onto these relationships, based on information within the federative level.

2.3 Top down and partly automated

A long-term goal in the use of distributed heterogeneous knowledge sources must be an increase of productivity and performance by automating some of the earlier mentioned processes.

In particular, the emphasis on a manual creation of the application specific ExER scheme is motivated by two aspects. Today's database implementations do not hold the whole conceptual scheme (e.g., as formulated in an E/R-model), but only the result of mapping the conceptual scheme onto the syntax of the database system, the logical scheme. Information which is not included in the logical scheme is often lost. This causes severe restrictions in reusing database contents. Approaches related to relational database systems to store information from the conceptual level can be seen in the revised SQL standard ([9]) and the proposals for the possible standards SQL2 and SQL3. In this framework, one particularly important demand is the storage of **meta-information** about the filing process itself into the database. Such meta-information should deal at least with information about key constraints, meaningful relations, domains and cardinalities. This information would be helpful to automize parts of step 1 in the presented concept (section 2.1).

The second aspect is the missing database storage of context information which provides the meaning to data values. This leads to the challenging demand for storing **meta-knowledge** about the application domain represented by the conceptual scheme. In the future, the modeling of the basic concepts and notions of an application domain will be very important. What we need are models of new application areas, on the basis of broad and accepted ontologies, as well as models of currently used applications. Moreover, there must exist a modeling framework that allows the representation and storage of application models in a database system. Only the cooperation of those models seems to present a meaningful approach for realizing a **partial automation of the building of relations from the top**. Realizing this aim would finally lead to a partly automated assignment of ExER objects to application objects.

The content of the last section is focussed on the future research topics and on the gap between data manipulation and data storage. In our opinion, this gap is rather a breakage, and it is responsible for the difficulties in interoperability (on discussion and facets of this term see [10] and [11]) of information systems. In parallel, analysis of this gap leads to the challenge to care for reusability and further usability of future advanced information systems by enforcing their communication and cooperation features.

3 Realization Aspects

3.1 The System Architecture

The system architecture (figure 3) reflects the division of the access procedure as shown in figure 1. First, at the access level, problems of heterogeneity of hardware and database systems, as well as problems of data distribution and location transparency have to be solved. Up to the level of the *communication knowledgebases* the access process is supported by the KEElink software.

After providing such global access capabilities on the *multidatabase knowledgebase*, operations for the incremental building up and enhancement of the *application knowledgebase* can be executed. Installation of all needed operators as well as of users and usertypes (three usertypes are distinguished at the moment, see figure 3) is done interactively by a user of type *federation administrator*. According to the currently active user, the relating set of operators is offered by the *control knowledgebase*. Some user-rights (operators) can be related to different usertypes. The execution of an operator then for example, effects the connection to a database or leads to an extension of the *application knowledgebase* associated to the current user. All users working on the same

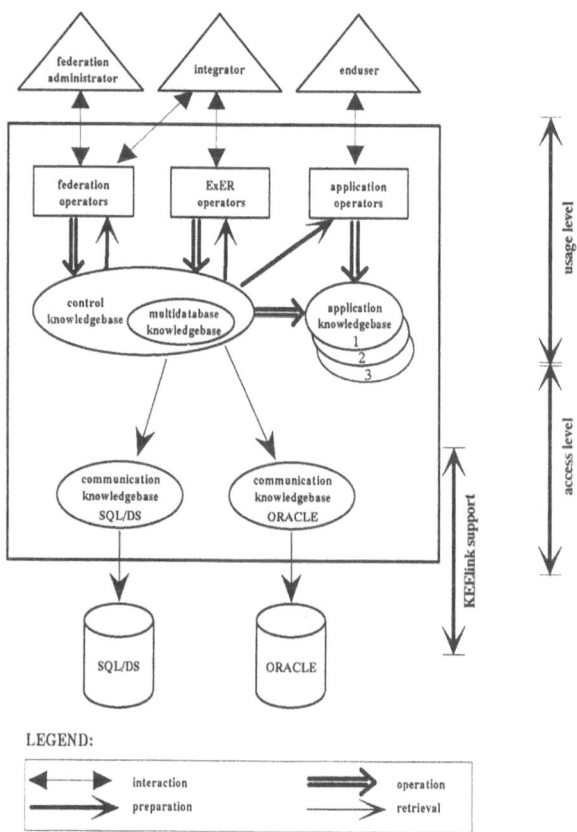

figure 3: WINHEDA system architecture

Realization of access and representation in the prototype is done by federation operators, ExER operators and application operators. The first task of the federation operators is to care for access to areas of component databases by interacting with the federation administrator. These component databases must have agreed on the federation before that. Also, the operators have to care for needed preparations of these access areas on the federation level and to allow for multidatabase select statements. The implemented (and naturally named) operators in our prototype, supporting the mentioned functionalities, are: *connect to sqlds; connect to oracle; download sqlds scheme; download oracle scheme; prepare global data dictionary; multidatabase select.*

The ExER operators realize the ExER model concepts, while application operators serve for the enduser system interaction. In addition, the following ExER operators have also been implemented respectively are in the implementation process: *show data; choose into application; declare keys; declare reference; declare generalization; declare grouping; declare aggregation; declare multivalued; load instances;*

delete instances. The current state of the application operators is: *declare synonym; reload instances; show application data; water quality comparison; department water quality comparison.* A detailed description of the concepts and operators mentioned above would exceed the limitations of this paper, but are given in [12].

3.2 The Prototype

Within the WINHEDA prototype system (figure 4), we have realized the workstation and database modules to access two different database management systems (SQL/DS, ORACLE) on two different hardware platforms (IBM mainframe, SUN workstation). The communication between the workstations (KEE-ORACLE) was based on the given standards of the TCP/IP software and the KEElink services.

The developement of the database module on the mainframe caused a variety of changes and reimplementations on the source code level of the KEElink software, by using elementary TCP/IP software services (sockets and ports).

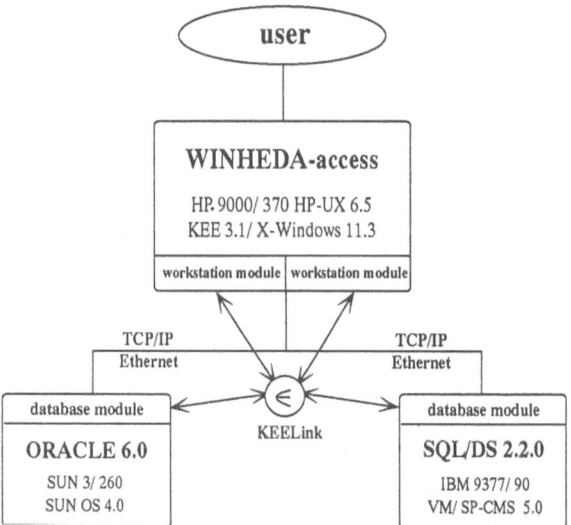

figure 4: hardware and software configuration of the prototype

4   Conclusion and outline

The goal of the WINHEDA project is the application oriented realization of concepts supporting users handling distributed heterogeneous knowledge sources. Therefore we have - in this first step - solved problems that arise out of the heterogeneity of hardware and databases, as well as the distribution and location transparency of data. Parallel to this, we evaluated the central representation scheme ExER using the procedures associated with the above mentioned phase

332

1, within an application in the field of water conservation for the State of Baden-Württemberg. The features of the prototype system have been used to build up an object-oriented Semantic Background Model for that application domain, based on database information. The WINHEDA activities in the application area are strongly related to current work at the FAW in the area of environmental information systems, in particular within the NAUDA project (Natural Language Access to Environmental Databases), which is presented in [13].

The current project work deals with the realization of the concepts reported upon as phases 2 and 3. The evaluation of these features is done as before within a specific application framework. In this respect the WINHEDA project is closely related to the TEAM activities (Telecommunication Enhanced Application Methodologies) at the FAW. The goal of these activities is to make distributed models and taxonomies of the organisation of enterprises within central services available, and to support an integrated use of hardware, software and all kinds of telecommunication services.

References

[1] A.P. Sheth and J.A. Larson. Federated database systems for managing distributed, heterogeneous and autonomous databases. *ACM Computing Surveys*, September 1990.

[2] W. Lamersdorf. Data-intensive applications in open networks: Extending the modelling, programming and communication support. In A.M. Tjoa and R. Wagner, editors, *International Conference on Database and Expert Systems Applications*, Vienna, 1990. Springer-Verlag.

[3] P. Chen. The entity-relationship model - toward a unified view of data. *ACM TODS*, 1(1), 1976.

[4] J. Winans and Hogshead Davis, K. Software reverse engineering from a currently existing IMS database to an entity-relationship model. In Hannu Kangassalo, editor, *9th International Conference on Entity-Relationship Approach*, Lausanne, CH, 1990.

[5] S.B. Navathe, S. Geum, D.K. Desai, and H. Lam. Conceptual design for non-database experts with an interactive schema tailoring tool. In Hannu Kangassalo, editor, *9th International Conference on Entity-Relationship Approach*, Lausanne, CH, 1990.

[6] H. Fleischhack and A. Weber. Rule based programming, predicate transition nets and the modelling of office procedures and flexible manufacturing systems. In G. De Michelis, editor, *Application and Theory of Petri Nets, Proceedings of the 10th International Conference*, Bonn, FRG, 1989.

[7] W. Reisig. Petri nets in software engineering. In W. Brauer, W. Reisig, and G. Rozenberg, editors, *Petri Nets: Applications and Relationships to Other Models of Concurrency, Advances in Petri Nets 1986, Proceedings of an Advanced Course*, Bad Honnef, FRG, 1986. Springer-Verlag.

[8] A. Endrikat. Die frühen Phasen des Software Engineering: Ein Prototyping-Ansatz auf der Basis höherer Petrinetze. Masterthesis, University of Ulm, FRG, 1990.

[9] International Organization for Standardization. *Database Language SQL with Integrity Enhancements, International Standard 9075*, 1989.

[10] Y. Kambayashi, M. Rusinkiewicz, and A. Sheth, editors. *First International Workshop on Interoperability in Multidatabase Systems*, Kyoto, Japan, 1991. IEEE Computer Society Press.

[11] A. Blaser, editor. *Database Systems of the 90s, International Symposium*, Berlin, FRG, 1990. LNCS No 466, Springer-Verlag.

[12] A. Endrikat, M. Luther, R. Michalski, and R. Schmitt. WINHEDA: Wissensbasierter Zugriff auf verteilte heterogene Wissensquellen. Technical report, FAW-Ulm, Germany, 1991.

[13] R. Becker, W. Gotterbarm, A. Karduck, D. Küpper, F. Liske, and D. Rösner. Natürlichsprachliches Zugangssystem zu Umweltdatenbanken. In W. Pillmann and A. Jaeschke, editors, *Informatik für den Umweltschutz, Proc. 5. Symposium*, Vienna, 1990. IF No 256, Springer-Verlag.

Semantic Interpretation of Natural Language in PROLOG: Logical Forms

Manuel Palomar, Lidia Moreno, Amparo Pascual

Departamento de Sistemas Informáticos y Computación.
Universidad Politécnica de Valencia (Spain)

ABSTRACT

In this paper we discuss a semantic interpretation, that we will use as a meaning representation language for natural language (NL): Spanish Language. The meaning of the sentences are represented as Logical Forms (LF). This LF is an extension of the First-Order Predicate Calculus (FOPC). The implementation has been made in PROLOG.

Keywords: Natural Language, Logical Form.

1. INTRODUCTION.

In NL processing must perform an study of all components, lexical, morphologic, syntactic, semantic and pragmatic.

This paper is a continuation of Moreno and Palomar work about syntactic and morphologic analysis of the spanish language [7]; we study the semantic representation of sentences that are sintactically correct.

The purpose of this study is to analyze sentences semantically.

2. THE LOGICAL FORM LANGUAGE.

In this section we discuss a LF Language, we will use a meaning representation language for NL.

We do an extension of the FOPC. When in a sentence appears determiners such as: numbers (uno, dos, ...), undefine (varios, varias,..) or comparative adjetives (mayor que, menor que,....). Then the following predicates are introduced:
   - card(P,N), the cardinal number of P is N, we could define card by the rule,
   card(P,N)<-set_of(P,P,S)&length(S,N).
The predicate set_of(X,P,S) means that the set of all X such as P holds is S.

   - mayor(N1,N2), where N1 y N2 are two numbers, they are derived from two predicates "card", which appear in the formula of the sentences; according to that the number N1 is greater that number N2.

   - menor(N1, N2), idem, but N1 < N2.

   - igual(N1, N2), idem, but N1 = N2.

   - mayor_igual(N1,N2), idem, but N1>= N2.

When indefinite determiners appear we introduce the predicate "mayor(N,1)", where N is a variable that represents a number unknown, but greater that number 1.

We also introduce the following predicates for the different types of sentences:

- imp(X, F), to represent the imperative sentences, where X is a free-variable, and F is an open well formed formula (wff).

- si-no(F), to indicate the type of sentence it is an interrogative sentence, waiting a "yes" or a "no" answer, F is a closed wff.

   - que(X, F), to indicate that is an interrogative sentence, which is introduced by the pronoun "que", where X is a free-variable, it is the object or a list of objects that holds F(open wff).

   - quien(X,F), interrogative sentence introduced by "quien" or "quienes" where X is a free-variable or list of objects that verifies F(open wff).

   - en-que(X, F), where X is a free-variable of the place or places of the question in the sentence that are represented in the open wff F.

   - cuantos(X, F), to represent the interrogative sentences, which are introduced by the pronouns "cuantos" or "cuantas". X is a free-variable which indicates the quantity of objects which hold F, and F is a open wff.

Furthermore, the rules for the quantifier scope are the following:

   1.- The quantification introduced by the determiner of the subject dominates the quantification introduced by the verb complement.

   2.- When a common noun appears and a complement of that noun, the quantification introduced by the determiner dominates the quantification introduced by the determiner of the noun.

   3.- When a verb, adjective or common noun have two or more complements, the quantification is the other way round of their aparition.

3. LINGUISTIC COVER.

While looking at the different word classes, we will say something about Spanish syntax, because the syntax has a close connection to logical form. We will constraint this study in a subset of Spanish language that is the following:

3.1. DETERMINERS.

They are main types of premodifiers of nouns. Determiners form a closed class of word. In this subset, we will consider the articles, numbers and indefinite determiners.

(i)**Articles:** The article defines the quantification of the formula associated to the sentence. Each article has to be an existencial or universal quantifier , so:

* Singular and Plural Indefinite Articles and Singular Definite Articles:
```
existe(X, P&Q)          Existencial quantifier
```

* Plural Definite Articles:
```
para_todo(X, P->Q)     Universal quantifier
```

=> Todos los rios tienen un afluente.
   (All the rivers have a flowing)
   para_todo(X,rio(X)->existe(Y,afluente(Y, X))

(ii)**Numbers:** It is a determine number. The numbers introduce the binary predicate "card(P, N)".

=> El rio tiene 2 afluentes.
   (The river has 2 flowings)
   existe(X,rio(X)&existe(Y,card(afluente(Y,X), 2))

(iii)**Indefinite:** These determiners limit the general meaning of the noun to specify its quantity but without determining it with precision. We consider the following indefinite determiners:

* Algún, alguna, alguno, algunas, algunos, algunos de los, algunas de las (something, somebody); they have the following semantic: "existe(X, P&Q)".
* Ningún, ninguna, ninguno, ningunos, ningunas, ninguno de los, ninguna de las (nothing); they have the following semantic: "no(existe(X, P&Q)".
* Cada, todo, toda, todos, todas, todos los, todas las, todo el (all, each); which semantic is: "para_todo(X, P->Q)".
* Varios, varias, varios de los, varias de las; semanticaly, we represent them by the predicate "mayor(N,1)", where N is a number that we derive it by the predicate "card(P,N)".

3.2. PRONOUNS.

The pronouns form a closed class that has features in common with both nouns and determiners. We have considered the interrogative pronouns: "que", "quien" and "quienes", because the definite pronouns have something in common with the definite articles and the indefinite pronouns essentially consist of indefinite determiner:

que(Free_variable, Open_wff)

quien(Free_variable, Open_wff)

3.3. ADJECTIVES.

The adjectives are open-class words that can modify nouns. They introduce a predicate with one or two arguments. They have one argument in the majority of cases. They will only have two arguments when there is a preposition "de", or the contract article "del" after adjective; which means a relation between thenselves: adjective(X) or adjective(X, Y).

=> El agua es cristalina. (The water is crystalline)
   existe(X, agua(X) & cristalina(X))

Another class of adjectives are the comparatives. they are the following: mayor que, mayores que, menor que, menores que, igual que, iguales que. They introduce the "es_mayor", "es_menor", "es_igual" predicates, which have two arguments that are free-variables N1 and N2. The two arguments are derived from the two predicates "card": card(P1, N1) and card(P2, N2).

=> El rio Ebro es mayor que el Turia en caudal.
(The Ebro river flow is bigger than the Turia's one)
   existe(X,rio(ebro)&card(caudal(X,ebro),N1)&
   existe(Z,card(caudal(Z,turia),N2)))&mayor(N1,N2)

3.4. COMMON NOUN.

The Common Nouns semantically introduce a predicate whose number of arguments depend on the number of noun phrases.
(1) If a preposition "de" or "del" appears after of a common noun, then we introduce a predicate with two arguments.

=> La provincia de Valencia tiene mar.
   (The province of Valencia has sea)
   existe(X,povincia(X, Valencia) & existe(Y,mar(Y,X))

(2) If this prepositions does not appear, the predicate has only single argument.

=>La provincia tiene mar. (The province has sea)
   existe(X, provincia(X) & existe(Y, mar(Y,X)))

3.5. PREPOSITIONS.

Prepositions are closed class words introducing prepositional phrases, that consist of a preposition followed by a noun phrase.

In this subset, we have only considered the prepositon "con" (with). This preposition introduce a binary predicate: "con(X, Y)"; the first argument corresponds to the noun phrase associated with the preposition, and the second corresponds to its companion in the sentence.

The preposition "de" (of) has been considered together with the nouns and adjectives: "common_noun(X, Y)" and "adjective(X,Y)".

3.6. ADVERBS.

We have considered this subset of adverbs: place, time, mode and the negation.

(i) Negation Adverbs: the adverbs which include no, ni, nunca, tampoco, jamás. They semantically introduce a predicate, with a single argument: "no(X)", where X is the structure of the verbs in the sentence. For example,

> => El rio Ebro no pasa por Valencia.
> (The Ebro river does not cross Valencia)
> no(rio(ebro)&pasar(ebro,valencia)).

(ii) Place, Time and Mode Adverbs: They introduce a predicate whose name is this adverb, and whose only argument is LF that is obtained from the adverb sentence.

> => El rio que hoy pasa por la provincia de Valencia esta contaminado.
> (The river that today crosses through the province of Valencia is polluted)
> existe(X,(rio(X)&hoy(existe(Y,provincia(Y,valencia)&pasa(X, Y))))& contaminado(X)).

> => Hoy el rio que pasa por la provincia de Valencia esta contaminado.
> (Today the river that crosses the province of Valencia is polluted)
> hoy(existe(X,(rio(X)&existe(Y,provincia(Y,valencia)& pasa(X, Y)))& contaminado(X))).

3.7 VERBS.

In Spanish language exists a great variety of verb forms, but we will consider a subset of them; Indicative mode, third person of singular or plural, in present tense or indicative mode (For the imperative sentences).

We distinguish in this paper two verb groups: If the infinitive is coupled with an auxiliary verb, or with a verb which may be considered as an auxiliary, like "ser"(to be) , "estar" (to be), "tener" (to have) and the lexical verbs.

Lexical verbs: We considere lexical verbs, with semantic information, which has not an empty of meaning. These can be classified into:

Verbs of type 0: They are the intransitive verbs. These verbs do not accept direct object or complement. They introduce an unary predicate "nom_verbo(X)", the functor is the general term of verb and the argument is the subject.

Verbs of type 1: These verbs admit indirect object or complement. They introduce a binary predicate "nom_verbo(X, Y)", the functor is the verb general term, when X is the object reference in the subject and Y is the object reference in the direct complement.

Verbs of type 2: These verbs admit direct and indirect complements. They introduce a ternary predicate "nom_verb(X, Y, Z)", where X is the object reference in the subject, Y is the object reference in the direct complement and Z is the indirect complement.

In case in which there were more complements these will be introduced as arguments of the verb. If some the complements of the verb are missing then that will be indicated by nill arguments.

Auxiliary verbs: We consider auxiliary verbs, all verbs submits to grammatical process and to combine with a normal form loosing their meaning. Only the "ser" (to be) verb is empty of meaning. The "estar"(to be) and "haber"(to have) verbs generally have not any meaning, but when they are accompanied by place complements then they mean: "estar".

> => El Ebro esta contaminado.
> (The Ebro river is polluted)
> contaminado(ebro)

> => El Veleta esta en la sierra.
> (The Veleta is in the sierra)
> existe(X, sierra(X) & esta(veleta, X))

> => Hay un pico. (There is one peak)
> existe(X, card(pico(X),1))

> => Hay un pico en la sierra.
> (There is one peak in the sierra)
> existe(X,sierra(X)&existe(Y,card(picos(Y)&esta(Y, X),1)))

We consider the verb "tener" (to have) as an auxiliary verb because it does not adduce semantic information; We comprehend "X tiene Y" (X has Y) as "X es de Y" (X is of Y),

> => Valencia tiene mar. (Valencia has got sea)
> existe(X, mar(X, valencia))

"It must exist an object X in the database, which has to be a sea and this sea has to be of Valencia".

The auxiliary verbs are verbs of type 3. For the verbs "haber" and "tener" have been implemented special complements that are "comph_" and "compt_".

3.8 SENTENCES CONSIDERED.

Sentences of communication necessary to express a database queries are:

- Enunciative sentences:
They are sentences to express, that something happens, something has happened and something will happen, both afirmative and negative mode.

> => Los rios desembocan en el mar.
> (The rivers flow into the sea)
> para_todo(X,rio(X)->existe(Y,mar(Y)&desemboca(X,Y))

-Imperative sentences:
They are sentences to express a order . The LF will be the predicate "imp": imp(X, F).

> => Obtener los rios que pasan por la provincia de Valencia.
> (Obtain the rivers which cross the province of Valencia.)
> imp(X,rio(X)&existe(Y,provincia(Y,valencia)& pasa_por(X,Y))).

-Interrogative sentences:
The interrogative sentences are the most important group of sentences for a communication with a database because they are indispensable by the queries.

The following pronouns : "que", "en que", "quien", "cuantos",... can be sentences of enunciative class with the symbols of question '?'. We have distinguished the following interrogative sentences:

* Interrogative sentences of type "si_no" (yes_no):

They are enunciative sentences with the symbol of question "?", and the only possible answer is yes or no; They are introduced by predicate "si_no": si_no(F).

=>¿El Guadalquivir desemboca en el oceano Atlántico?
(Does the Guadalquivir river flow into the Atlantic Ocean?)
    si_no(desemboca(guadalquivir, oceano(atlantico))).

* Interrogative sentences of type "quien":

They are interrogative sentences that are introduced by interrogative pronouns "quien/quienes". In the semantic the principal connector is the predicate "quien" (Who): quien(X,F).

    =>¿Quien tiene varios campos?
    (Who has more than one field?)
    quien(X,existe(Y,card(campo(Y,X),N1))&mayor(N1,1)

*Interrogative sentences of type "que":

They are interrogative sentences that are introduced by the interrogative pronoun "que" (that). The LF consists of the binary predicate "que(X,F).

    => ¿Que rios tienen tres afluentes?
    (Which rivers has three flowings?)
    que(X,rio(X)&existe(Y,card(afluente(Y,X),3)))

*Interrogative sentences of type "en_que":

They asked for the place where is found something or somebody. They are introduced by the predicate "en_que(X,F)".

    =>¿En que provincia nace el rio Turia?
    (In which province does the Turia river rise?)
     en_que(X,provincia(X)&rio(turia)&nace(X,turia))

*Interrogative sentences of type "cuantos":

They are interrogative sentences that are introduced by interrogative pronouns like :cuantos","cuantas". They are introduced by the predicate "cuantos(X,F). Thus X will be a free-variable and the second argument is the predicate "card(P,N), where N is the set of objects of database as that satisfies the open-WFF.

    =>¿Cuantos rios desembocan en el mar Mediterraneo?
    (How many rivers flow into the Mediterranean sea?)
    cuantos(X,card(rio(X)&mar(mediterraneo)&
    desemboca(X,mediterraneo,N1))

COMPOUND SENTENCES

In all compound sentences, the propositions must be composed by their subject and their predicate.We do not handle the phenomena of the ellipsis (or reduction). We have implemented the following:

a) Coordination

The compound sentence is formed by propositions between which there is not relation of dependence. Grammatical construction with the conjunctions "y" (and), "o" (or).

    \=>El rio Ebro pasa por Zaragoza y el rio Turia pasa por Valencia.
(The Ebro river cross Zaragoza and the Turia river cross Valencia.)
rio(ebro)&pasa(ebro,zaragoza)&rio(turia)&
pasa(turia,valencia))

b)Subordination:

Subordination is produced when a proposition (the subordinate) has a grammatical function in relation to the other one.

Relative subordination: The relative sentences are introduced by a relative pronoun.

    =>los rios que pasan por la provincia de Valencia no son caudalosos.
    (The rivers which cross through the Valencia province are not very flow.)
    para_todo(X,rio(X)&existe(Y,provincia(y,valencia)
    &pasa(X,Y)=>no(caudalosos(X))

These class of sentences treat the left extraposition, one of the main features of Natural Language Syntax were described by F.Pereira and implemented by L.Moreno and M.J. Palomar[7].

c) Yuxtaposition.

The yuxtaposition proposition is connected by symbols "," and ";".

    =>El Mulhacen esta en sierra nevada, cabeza de manzaneda esta en la provincia de orense.
    (The Mulhacen is in Nevada sierra. Cabeza de Manzaneda is in Orense province.
sierra(nevada)&esta(mulhacen,nevada)&
    existe(X,provincia(X,orense)&
    esta(cabeza_de_manzaneda,X)).

4.THE SEMANTIC ANALYZER.

The system have the following phases:
    1.Introduction of the sentence.
    2.Call to the syntactic analysis.
    3.If the syntactic analysis is not correct go to 6.
    4.Call to the semantic analysis.
    5.Obtain logic form.
    6.System.

To analyze semantically a sentence it is necesary a question of following type:

    oracion([sentence_to_be_analyzed],[],semantic)

Where "semantic" will be the logic form interpreted by semantic analyzer. The main features to construct the LF are the following:

i) The general structure of the noun phrase is the following:

s_nominal

det   nombre   rel

Where "det" will be the list of determiners, "rel" will be a posible relative sentence, which is contained into the noun phrase; and "nombre" will be an additional structure of the noun phrase.

ii) The structure of the verb phrase is the following:

s_verbal

verbo   s_nominal

s_verbal

adv_neg   verbo   s_nominal

Noun Phrase: The noun phrases which have been taken into account in the parser are the following:

    s_nominal <- []   (Absense of noun phrase)
    s_nominal <- nomp
    s_nominal <- nomp,com

Where "com" will be an special structure for the treating of verb complements, which are not introduced by prepositions "de" (of) or "con" (with), for this cases, we have defined two complements, their structure is:
    comcon <- nexo_con,s_nominal
    comde <- nexo_de,s_nominal
    com   <- nexo,s_nominal

Further:
    s_nominal <- nomc,rel

where "rel" will be a possible relative sentence, that can be empty (absence of relative sentence iv1), or can be a subject complement relative sentence iv2, or can be a direct complement relative sentence iv3. The rules are:

    iv1) rel <- []
    iv2) rel <- pronrel,s_verbal
    iv3) rel <- pronrel,oracion_rel

where:
    oracion_rel <- s_nominal,s_verbal_rel
    s_verbal_rel <- verbo,s_nominal
    s_verbal_rel <- adv_neg,verbo,s_nominal

Further:
    s_nominal <- nomc,nomp
    s_nominal <- det,nomc,nomp,rel
    s_nominal <- det,nomp,rel
    s_nominal <- nomp,rel
    s_nominal <- nomp,s_nominal
    s_nominal <- adj

    s_nominal <- adj,adv
    s_nominal <- adj,comd
    s_nominal <- adv
    s_nominal <- adv,s_nominal
    s_nominal <- det,nombre,rel
    s_nominal <- nombre

where "nombre" must be any rule of:
    nombre <- nomc
    nombre <- nomc,adj
    nombre <- nomc,adj,comde
    nombre <- nomc,adj,com
    nombre <- nomc,adv
    nombre <- nomc,comde
    nombre <- nomc,comcon
    nombre <- nomc,com
    nombre <- nomc,s_nominal
    nombre <- adj,com
    nombre <- adj,comde
    nombre <- adv,comde
    nombre <- adv,com
    nombre <- adv_cant,nomc
    nombre <- adv_cant,nomc,rel
    nombre <- adv_cant,comc,comde
    nombre <- adv_cant,nomc,s_nominal
    nombre <- comde
    nombre <- comcon
    nombre <- com

Verb Phrase: We have a set of special rules to recognize verb phrases introduce by auxiliary verbs ("haber" and "tener"), and another rules to recognize verb phrases introduce by the rest of verbs (type 0, 1 and 2), including "ser" and "estar" verbs.

The verb phrase rules to "haber" verb are:
    h1)s_verbal<-verbo_haber, comph1, crear_sem_vh1

where: comph1<-adv_cant,nomc,com and crear_sem_vh1, as crear_sem_vt1 are rules to use when "haber" and "tener" verb go close to the verb complement introducing the "esta(X, Y)" form.
    h2)s_verbal<-verbo_haber, comph2, crear_sem_vh1
        comph2 <- adv_cant, nomc, adj, com
    h3) s_verbal <- verbo_haber, comph11
        comph11 <- adv_cant, nomc
    h4) s_verbal <- verbo_haber, comph22
        comph22 <- adv_, nomc, adj
    h5) s_verbal <- verbo_haber, comph33
        comph33 <- det, nomc
    h6) s_verbal <- verbo_haber, comph3
        comph3 <- det, nomc, comde
    h7) s_verbal <- verbo_haber, comph44
        comph44 <- nomc
    h8) s_verbal <- verbo_haber, comph46
        comph46 <- nomc, adj
    h9) s_verbal <- verbo_haber, comph45
        comph45 <- nomc, comde
    h10)s_verbal<-verbo_haber,comph4, crear_sem_vt1
        comph4 <- nomc, com

The verb phrase rules to "tener" verb are:
    t1) s_verbal <- verbo_tener, adv_cant, nomc
    t2) s_verbal <- verbo_tener, nomc
    t3) s_verbal <- verbo_tener, nomp
    t4) s_verbal <- verbo_tener, adj_var, nomc
    t5) s_verbal<-verbo_tener,adj_al_men,adv_cant,nomc
    t6)s_verbal<-verbo_tener,det,nomp, rel,crear_sem_rel

338

```
t7) s_verbal<-verbo_tener,det,nomc,nomp,rel,
          crear_sem_rel
t8) s_verbal<-verbo_tener,compt2,crear_sem_vtl
    compt2<- nomc, com
t9) s_verbal<-verbo_tener,comptl,crear_sem_vhl
    comptl <- adv_cant, nomc, com
t10) s_verbal<-verbo_tener,compt22
    compt22<- det, nomc
t11) s_verbal<-verbo_tener,compt23, crear_sem_vtl
    compt23<- det, nomc, com
```

To the rest of the verbs we will have the following
rules:
```
s_verbal<-verbo,s_nominal, crear_sem_v
s_verbal<-adv_neg,verbo,s_nominal,
        crear_sem_v,crear_neg
```

where "crear_neg" rule is used to negation of
semantic which is introduced by the verb in negative
sentences. And the crear_sem_v rule is used to make
the semantic which is introduced by the verb.

5. CONCLUSIONS.

The LF is the intermediate representation between the
syntactic form of sentence and a pragmatic
representation of the sentence. An intermediate
semantic representation is desirable because it
provides a natural division between two separate
problems: one concerns word sense and sentence
ambiguity, and the other involves to use the
knowledge of the world and the present context to
identify the particular consequences of a certain
sentence.

The actual system provides to interpret a vaste
diversity of sentences. But, yet the language is
constrained with respect to verb forms and coordinate
sentences treating. Now we are working about the
ellipsis phenomena in the coordinate sentences, which
will improve the present system.

6. REFERENCES.

[1]   Allen, J.
"Natural Language Understanding"
The Benjamin/Cummings Publishing Company, Inc., 1987

[2]   Clocksin, W.F. / Mellish, C.S.
"Programming in Prolog" Springer-Verlag, 1981

[3]   García, A.
"Gramáticas Lógicas: Resolución de problemas en
Lenguaje Natural"Tesis Doctoral, Universidad
Politécnica de Madrid, 1987

[4]   Lázaro, F.
"Curso de Lengua Española"Anaya, 1982

[5]   Lloyd, J.M.
"Logic Programming" Springer-Verlag, 1984

[6]   Moreno, A. / Olmeda, C.
"Análisis e interpretación de los verbos del español
en un sistema NLQ" VI Congreso Anual de la SEPLN,
1990.

[7]   Moreno, L. / Palomar, M.
"Syntactic and Morphologic analysis of Natural
Language" In Proc. IASTED International Conference on
Artificial Intelligence and Neural Networks.
Zurich (Suiza), 1990

[8]   Pereira, F. /Shieber S.
"Prolog and Natural-Language Analysis" CSLI, 1987

[9]   Pereira, F. /Warren, D.
"Definite Clause Grammars for Language Analysis- A
Survey of the Formalism and a Comparison with
Augmented Transition Networks". Artificial
Intelligence, vol. 13, 1980

[10]   Saint-Dizier, P.
"An Approach to Natural Language Semantic in Logic
Programming".IRISA, Rennes, 1985

[11]   Sterling, L. / Shapiro, E.
"The Art of Prolog" MIT Press, 1986

[12]   Warren, D / Pereira, F.
"An Efficient Easily Adaptable System for Interpreting
Natural Language Queries" American Journal of
Computational Linguitics, vol. 8, n. 3-4, 1982

Map Summarization using Analogical Matching of Schema

Shigeru Shimada, Hitoshi Matsushima

Central Research Laboratory. Hitachi Ltd.
1-280 Higashi-Koigakubo Kokubunji-city Tokyo 185, Japan

Abstract

Recently in public enterprise companies, the demand for utilizing the multimedia database (MMDB) is rising. Such MMDB is used in the strategy information system (SIS) not only for special purposes such as facility management but also for the more general office sections. But there exists structural mismatch between user specified schema and a priori memolized schema of MMDB. Therefore, we express multimedia as object oriented structures and investigate analogical matching method of extracting the part of the structure that resembles the user specified scheme structure from this multimedia database. This new method is applied to an example that automatically summalize map for guidance from the residential map. As a result, we can get a prospect that an effective automatic summarization of map.

1. Introduction

1.1 Background

Strategy information systems (SIS) in public utility companies, such as electric power, gas supplies and water-sewage are being developed, by utilizing the multimedia management ability of the workstation. SISs include a system for mapping various attribute information, in order to manage facilities and serve customers, ("mapping system" is short for these as follows), using the background of digital maps and drawings. In this paper, we discuss various retrieving information from the multimedia database (MMDB), changing the retrieved results into multimedia such as figures or images, displaying the results onto overlaid map, and hyper-like retrieval.

Many practical mapping systems with these faculties have already been developed[1][2]. Especially in the fields of managing underground facilities in overcrowded metropolis centers, the preceding investigations being conducted in public utility companies, and then maps and drawings are fully digitalized into databases[3]. Additionally, the mapping system is being used for business development. Here, the contents of the database, which is utilized in various kinds of business works, change into multimedia such as figures and pictures, and show the overlay display on the residential maps[4].

1.2 Necessity of summarize function

These maps and drawings can be applied to databases, in specialized departments, such as facility management. So, if they can be applied to common databases, it is desirable to utilize for more general purposes such as planning and scheming. In order to realize these demands, it is necessary to summarize the essence of the maps and drawings for each object and omit the detailed information.

A preceding study focused on making a guide map which was mainly composed of road components[5][6]. In this study, the method of inducing a course from a starting point to an arrival point was studied, examining each road crossing point of the chosen course. From the more macro viewpoint, the method for summarizing map was proposed[7][8]. In this case, this method automatically changed the detail rate of the map, by dealing with the reduced scale of the requested summarization.

Thus, these methods could not implement the summarization mechanism to pick out only the necessary information from the detailed maps and drawings, and emphasize and express them according to importance.

1.3 Grasp of semantic meaning of summarization

The above methods lacked the technical means to select the main points of the maps and drawings. They did not have the ability to grasp the logical semantic structure of the summarized map. On the other hand, in the composing method that focuses on the logical media structure, the media is understood from the concept of a user to the display object by the top-down approach. Therefore, this method does not greatly influence the characteristics of the media, enabling a more universal algorithm. However, it was difficult to grasp the media with a complex logical semantic structure such as maps and drawings, so it couldn't be practically used. Then, we propose the next following two steps. (1) Express the multimedia construction, as objects directly, when making map and drawings. (2) Infer the user-defined summarize schema structure analogically from the scheme structure of the multimedia database.

The significance of an analogical matching among the schema structure and the processing flow of inference is explained as follows. MMDB is needed that can correspond to various retrieval requirements, for example document processing and CAD, in the distributed environment. However, in this MMDB, there is mismatch between a priori memorized schema structure of MMDB system and user demanded schema structure, so it is necessary to automatically acquire the schema structure that best suits this user requirement. Therefore, this analogical matching is equivalent to a user interface for purposed media access.

A flow of analogical matching is outlined in Fig.1. The schema structure of the desired retrieval is converted into object structure (user model). In MMDB, the schema structure

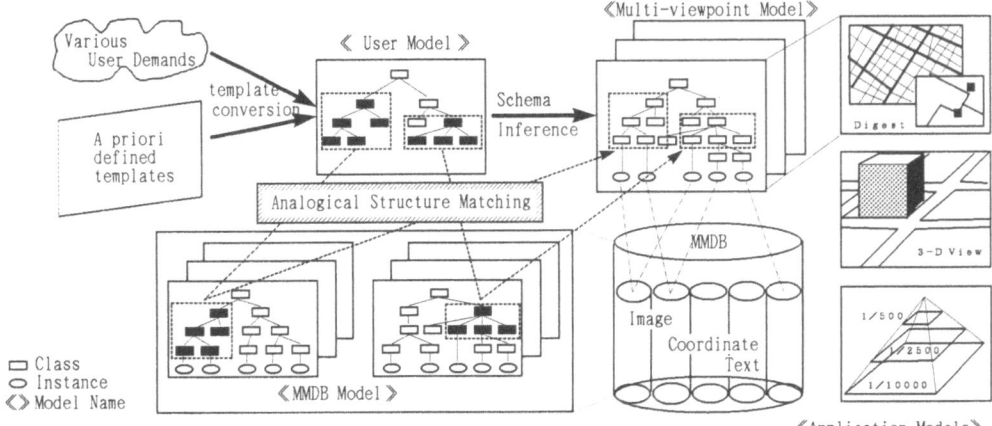

Figure 1. Flow of the analogical matching of schema

of the multimedia is assumed to be memorized a priori in an expression of an object type (multimedia model). In this state, partial correspondence between the user model and multimedia model is sought by analogical structure matching processing among models, and the contents of the user model are supplemented in the multimedia model that partially correspond and are stored as a multi-viewpoint model in compound objects. Thus, the inside method of the compound object acquired in this way is executed. Finally, multimedia accessing is performed, and a concrete media retrieval result is gained.

2. Multimedia modeling

First, we explain the terms and definitions used in this paper, and then explain the object-oriented expression of multimedia.

2.1 Merits of object-oriented expression[9]

In a system that handles various media, it is necessary to judge the media types and the processing procedures to be applied, because the procedures are different for each media, even if they have the same processing purpose. Thus, multimedia information is formed into one unit having a series of labels, such as data and procedures, and is stored and managed as a single object. This object capsulation property enables the responsibility for selecting the procedure that fits the media type of the object to be transported from the application side of media service to the supply side. This considerably reduces the development load of an application program.

This object is composed of the class that hierarchically express a common concept, and the instance which takes on a particular value for each class to define that class. Depending on necessity, each class can hierarchically produce particular instances, and the instance group produced from this class can share and inherit class variables and procedures. Therefore, the description of the multimedia structure is simplified by using object expression. Object expression also enables simple and clear program development.

2.2 Persistent Object Management

In this paper, "object" is used as a general name for class objects and instance objects, which are stored and managed in the Object Managing System(OMS). The function of the OMS is memorizing objects into files. As already proposed in OODB research, this problem is solved by realizing persistent object file management where the object appears to exist after the system has finished its work. This persistent object is useful to solve impedance mismatches which reduce uniformity of OODB usage which is accessed from object-oriented language. Already this file management mechanism of the persistent object has been put to practical use. For example, there are fundamental file I/O functions "StoreOn" or "ReadFrom" in the object-oriented language Objective-C[10], and "TypedStream" or "read/write" in the NeXT computer[11]. Additionally, there are many techniques such as peculiar file management or a high-speed retrieval mechanism in various commercialized OODBs. In this OMS fundamental mechanism, there is a special speed-up mechanism for retrieving a partial hierarchical structure, by treating the objects' tree structure as the first order structural cache and applying the B-tree index mechanism to them[12].

2.3 Object Structure
2.3.1 Structure Classification and Expression Form

Object structure describes the relationship between objects. This relationship is classified into (1) Media structure, and (2) Semantic structure based on the meaning of the object expression. The media structure is composed of entity objects, and the class object of hierarchical management. On the other hand, the semantic structure is composed of the relation object, describing the relationship between media.

And these two relationship is realized by more fundamental relationships. They are classified into following.
[ako relationship] This is class structural relationships between super-class and sub-class. And this is a simple parent-child relationship among classes.
[is_a relationship] This is almost identical to ako relationship, but the above-mentioned child class is changed into instance.
[part_of relationships] This is the dependency relationships

between instances, which manage pointers from one instance to another instance by instance variables.

[func relationships] This relationship is composed of an object expressed as the functional call for data processing (func object as short) and an object equivalent to the actual processed data, it is necessary to register the func object to the ordered collection, which is managed by instance variable.

2.3.2 List expression of object relationships

Next, let's consider the expressive form, as described above. In order to realize the analogical matching mechanism in the world of predicate logic programming, it is necessary to change the object expression into list form, such as a "prolog" complex term. This list form is mainly the expression form which can be treated as a view object on the main memory by a predicate logic programming language (such as prolog). As shown next, this list form is composed of a complex term, constant-text located on the head of the complex term, and corresponds to the predicate of first order predicate calculus.

    complex term:constant-text(term1,term2, ..,termN).

        where term: constant,variable,complex term
            constant: constant-text,integer,real

Used to express the object by this list form are the values of instance variables or information of class name etc. that are contained in instance objects, and various relationships between each objects. The list form of instance objects as following

    instance(InstanceName,POID,ClassName,

                Value#1of IinstanceVariable,...).

    InstanceName: Character string which given instance name
    POID: List of class ID and object ID
    ClassName: Character string which given class name
    InstanceVariable:List of each instance variable type

which is expressed in the retrieval items following the predicate instance. In the body of this list expression, much information such as the initial instance name, persistent object identifier, class name and instance variables are described in order. Especially, the persistent object identifier is the unique object identifier of each instance object, and is composed of the class identifier (classID, 4 bytes) and the object number (objNo, 4 bytes). Each object has a persistent identifier, called "POID". In the first list of "instance name" is the character line that responds after access has been requested to the instance method of each object, and each class has a different value. For example, the character line is "building name" in the building class, and "target part" in the target class. The instance name is the representative name of the object which is represented clearly at the time of displaying structure or editing.

3. Automatic summarization of map

The automatic creation method for a summarized map and drawing based on the semantic model of multimedia is described here. The proposed automatic summarization method is different from the road guide map generated by conventional media-oriented processing or the macro-map produced by the thinning out procedure. The creation method has a feature for acquiring the method of processing data which is necessary for completing the media structure from the user defined semantic structure.

3.1 Formulation of analogical matching

Generally, analogical matching is the inference mechanism of the following process[14]. At first, some similarity is found among a given object. Then a clue of a problem solution is gained by applying the fact already formed in the object of one side and the rule to the other object based on the similarity. The internally hidden unknown facts or rules in objects are presumed and predicted. The principle of analogical inference is following that Ai (1<i<n) is the fact formed in the domain D1, and [A1,A2,...,An->B] is a rule formed in the domain D1 regarding Ai. The following processing is performed by analogical inference. The unknown domain D2 that tries to acquire a rule from D1 is determined. When Ai'(1<i'<m) is composed in the domain D2, analogy ϕ of Ai and Ai' is calculated. B' is acquired by using ϕ^{-1} from B.

This analogical matching mechanism is formulated from the point of view of summarization. Here, the list form to be processed is used by analogical matching mechanism with the object structure. In this analogical matching processing, the ideal processing flow is when the semantic structure and media structure that are a priori defined template map in domain D1 and the semantic structure of the summarized map that is defined in domain D2 are given, then the media structure of the summarized map is inferred. However, it is difficult to formulate a method of automatically completing media structure from the semantic structure. Then the semantic structure that used processing data in the form of the func relationship between the above-mentioned semantic structure and the media structure is formed, and an analogical matching is formulated again, as shown in Fig.2. The func relationship in this figure describes a method of media processing. That is, the function call that processes the media is managed as an object, and it is added to the object that becomes the target to be processed. The semantic structure of a summarization with this func relationship is converted into media structure. The func relationship in the list form is expressed by using a predicate func and discriminates it from a predicate showing other relationships.

If the mechanism of analogical matching is described as mentioned above in the list form. The upper part is the object structure of the template, and the lower part is the object structure of the summarized map to be created. The calculation of analogy only has to evaluate the identity among the part_of structure linearly. This has been defined here as the ratio of the number of nodes that exists in the structure range of correspondence and the number of nodes that actually

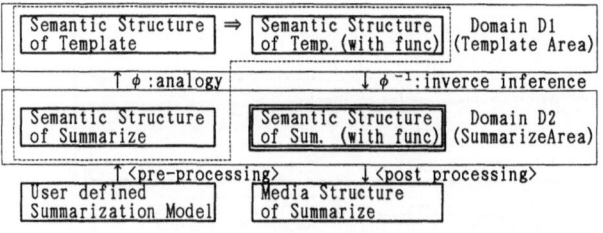

:This part of information is settled a priori

Figure 2. Formulation of analogical inference for summarization

342

correspond to the relationship. When an analogy φ is calculated by this method, and a corresponding list is added, the func relation that holds true in domain D1 is shifted and is added to domain D2 by φ⁻¹. The inference process are executed according to prolog like three steps reasoning. Thus, the assumption part corresponds to the pair among the structure where analogy φ is largest, and the conclusion part is the object structure including the func relationship drawn from the pair.

3.2 Application of the analogical matching to map summarization '

Formulation of the above-mentioned analogical matching is applied to the problem of concrete summarization of map. First, the flow of processing of the entire summarization is explained in Fig.3. The entire processing branches into four stages.

Now we explain the actual process flow of analogical schema-object inference of a summarized map, focusing on the change of the instance object structure. First, a precondition for analogical inference processing is cleared. The style of summarized map that becomes the goal of analogical matching is supposed to the simple one composed of a arrival part and a

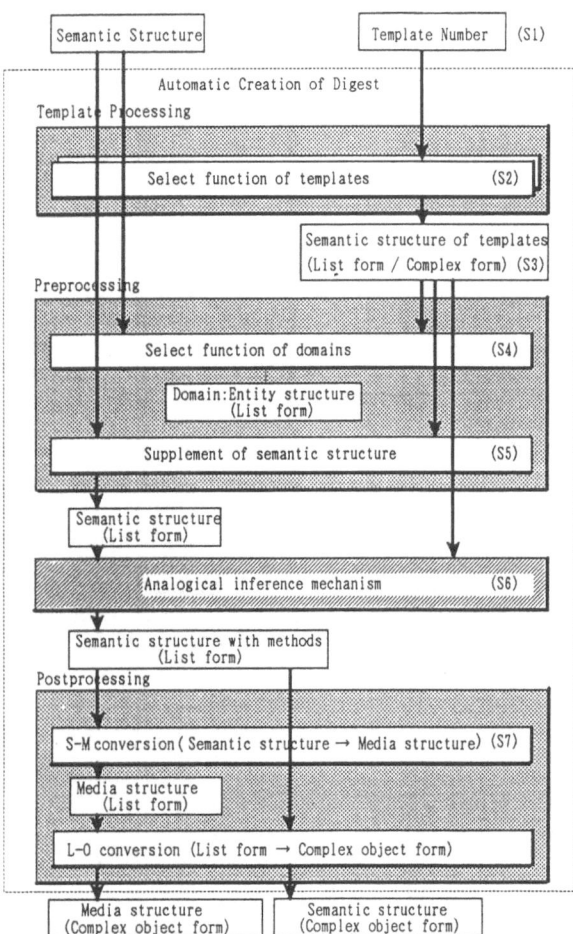

Figure 3. Whole processing flow of map summarization

```
(digest_02)┬(sdigest_02)┬(PurposePart_02)─(Purpose_02)─(To-ei)
           │             └(AroundPart_02)
           │
           └(mdigest_02)
```
(a) part-of Diagram

```
instance(InstanceName,POID,ClassName,InstanceValue,...).
instance(digest_02, (-1,299376), CutTemplate, v1, ...).
instance(sdigest_02, (-1,-1), SDigest, v1, ...).
instance(mdigest_02, (-1,-1), MDigest, v1, ...).
instance(PurposePart_02, (-1,-1), PurposePart, v1, ...).
instance(AroundPart_02, (-1,-1), AroundPart, v1,...).
instance(Purpose_02, (-1,-1), Purpose, v1, ...).
instance(To-ei, (-1,-1), Building, v1, ...).
In case the object entity does not exist, poid=(-1,-1)
```
(b) Instance Definition

```
ako(ParentClassName,ChildClassName).
ako(Object, (PObject)).
ako(Template, (CutTemplate, NaviTemplate, GuidTemplate)).
ako(DigestElement, (MDigest, SDigest, PurposePart, AroundPart,
                    PassPart, TrafficElement, FuncIcon)).
ako(FuncIcon, (Ref, Extend, Area, N_lin)).
```
(c) ako Structure

```
part_of(Parent-POID, (Child-POID...Child-POID)).
part_of(digest_02, (sdigest_02, mdigest_02)).
part_of(sdigest_02, (PurposePart_02, AroundPart_02)).
part_of(PurposePart_02, (Purpose_02)).
part_of(Purpose_02, (To-ei)).
```
(d) part_of Strucure

Figure 4. Semantic structure of user defined map summarization

circumference part (this corresponds to summarization template type 1). As a layout of a summarized map display, the arrival part should be arranged on the center of the screen surrounded by the circumference part. Then, the arrival part is expanded 2.0 times greater, and the circumference part receives an orthogonal magnification conversion reduced about 1.0--0.5 times from an inverse. The method of this orthogonal magnification conversion becomes the target of analogical inference as a func relationship. Additionally, the layout style of this summarization display, the guidance type equipped with a start part and an departure part is prepared. Also the navigation type equipped with a passage part is prepared. As follows, the details of analogical inference are explained by each processing step. While analogical inference is processed mainly in the list form, for simplification, a diagram illustrating the semantic structure of the object is used here.

(S1) Specification of template number and summarization semantic structure

The template number that gives the creating style of a summarization and the semantic structure are given by the user. As for the semantic structure of a summarized map that corresponds to the user specified template number. Especially in the arrival part, the place name that shows a concrete arrival place is given. This is named domain D1. On the other hand, the semantic structure of the user defined summarized map is only a framework that gives the composition of a arrival part and a circumference part, as shown in Fig.4(a), a arrival part (PurposePart_02) and a circumference part (AroundPart_02) exist in the lower part structure of digest_02.

(S2) Expansion into the main memory of template semantic structure

The semantic structure of the template map that corresponds to the template number selected is expanded into the main memory. The semantic structure of the summarized map that corresponds to the template number. A arrival part (PurposePart_01) and a circumference part (AroundPart_01) exist here in the lower part structure of digest_01. Especially in the arrival part, the place name that shows a concrete arrival place is given. Then, we select the most similar partial structure with the user defined semantic structure of the summarized map specified in the front step, and calculate those analogies and attach similar partial correspondence among structures.

(S3) Generation of instance object

The instance object is generated from the expression of a list type of the instance definition of each above-mentioned semantic structure. The examples of these expression of list type of the instance definition are shown in Fig.4(b)(c)(d). However, when class which is specified in each instance definition sentence is not defined, the existing instance object is retrieved from OMS, or generation of a new instance is conducted.

(S4) Selection of domain D2

The map data that corresponds to each part of the semantic structure is retrieved from the OMS and is translated into an expression of a list type, and the analogical inference domain D2 is determined. The details of the concrete processing contents are as follows. First, map data that becomes the target of map summarization is retrieved from the OMS by using a procedure (select_domain and so on) registered in the template class, then formalized into lists, and the base of the analogical inference domain D2 is obtained. In addition, this select_domain method translates map data into the coordinates of which a arrival place becomes an origin. This method can both reduce and adjust the scale. Additionally, it corrects and adds the contents of a list form already stored into the domain D2. The media structure changed in this step, and the relationship between instance definitions, ako, is_a and part_of and so on, is the conversion of data registered to OMS into a list form. The func relationship is composed of ref function to give it an offset that is applicable to each data.

(S5) Supplement of semantic structure

By using procedures (SelectData etc.) or parameters which are registered into the template class, necessary objects for composing the summarized map are retrieved and generated, and the semantic structure object of the summarization in domain D2 is supplemented. The main processing in this SelectData method is extracting elements of a map in the domain and adding these to the list form of the semantic structure as a part_of relationship defined sentence. However if the value of a parameter and an instance variable needed for processing in the above-mentioned method is undefined, the contents of a similar object are applied.

(S6) Analogical inference processing

An analogy among each semantic structure is taken in domains D1 and D2, and correspondence among the object structure that partially resembled is taken. Then, the func relationship that holds true in domain D1 is inferred to the corresponding position in domain D2 by using the analogical inference mechanism. The result is added to the semantic structure of D2. The object diagram of the semantic structure is added by analogical inference processing However, as the media structure does not change, it is omitted.

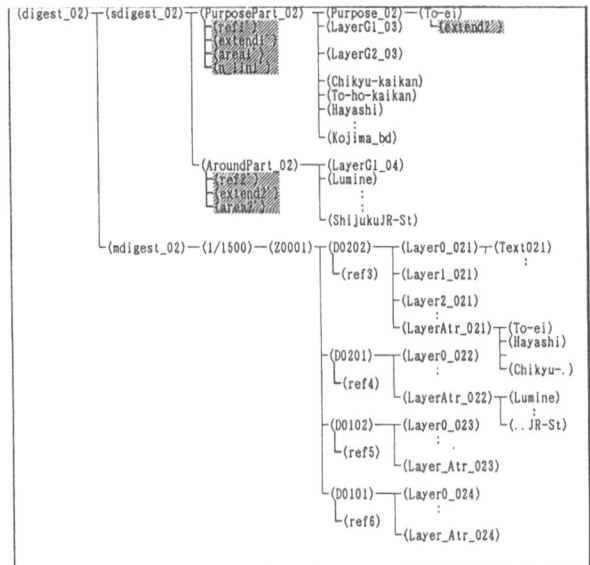

Figure 5. State of func relationship inferenced by analogical matching (method list is added)

(S7) S-M conversion processing

The semantic structure of the summarized map processed by the above supplement and analogical matching is converted into media structure. The expansion mechanism of the part_of relationship is used here, and the media structure with the func is completed. It has the following processing contents with the part_of expansion mechanism. In the list form, part_of hierarchy is resolved and described by two steps. Therefore expansion processing traces the part_of structure sequentially from the upper part to the lower part. Then, expansion processing is completed where the object that becomes the leaf of the object structure is reached. The media structure diagram of the summarized map finally completed in this S-M conversion is shown in Fig.5. The structures "digest_02" and "sdigest_02" without a change constructed by the former step is omitted.

4. Implemental situation and evaluation

The developed method of map summarization by analogical matching is applied to the creation example of a summarized map by using an actual residential map database. The display example of the residential map to be processed in Fig.6. And the result of this application is shown in Fig.7. The form of template number#2 is applied to the standard of analogical matching in the composition that sets a detailed departure part ("Restaurant Lion") and arrival part ("Kogakuin university") in both sides, and displays only a macro element of which the reduced scale degree is higher than departure or arrival parts on the circumference part (near "Shinjuku"). Especially in the departure or arrival part, in order to clearly express the actual reduced scale degree, a procedure where an orthogonal magnification process of locally multiplying the shape and the size of a character by 2.0 is added, and this processing is included into the part of the func relationship that is the target of analogical matching.

Next, predicting the performance evaluation and

344

Figure 6. Display example of original residential map near "Shinjyuku" district in Tokyo.   published from "Zenrin" Co. Ltd. by CD

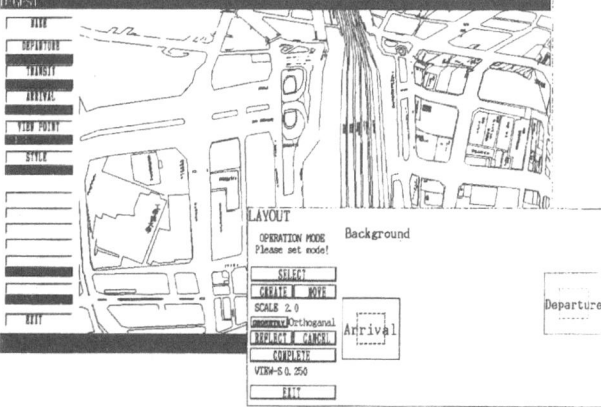

Figure 7. Example of automatic summarization of map from "Restaurant Lion" to "Kogakuin University" in "Shinjyuku district in Tokyo"

characteristics is described briefly. The summarized map created by the analogical matching method proposed in this paper aims to put it into practical use in the guidance map near the arrival position in business documents ,etc. Therefore the ratio between the data capacity of the summarized map and data capacity of the entire map which is the target of processing is the main performance evaluation item. This is evaluated as the rate of omitting an unnecessary element from the original residential map, while maintaining a clear guide map. This can be thought as a quality evaluation of the summarized map obtained by analogical matching. The entire capacity of the residential map processed in Fig.6, is 12.3 Mbytes.The capacity of the created summarized map in Fig.7 is 0.8 Mbytes, which is equivalent to a compression capacity of 6.5%. As a result, we can expect a result that prevents a communication bottle neck in the distributed processing system via LAN communication, and prevents the increase of data capacity in document processing ,etc.

5. Conclusions

The requirement for various multimedia processing is growing due to the use of workstations in the field of the strategy information processing systems of public enterprise companies. As such, it is necessary to use these map databases in general office work such as planning, documentation, etc., while conventional map databases were used in the special purpose section such as facility management, etc. In this paper, we clarify the necessity of the summarization function that makes necessary only detailed parts and conceals unnecessary information. In order to realize such demand, consider the semantic understanding the summarization that was not pursued sufficiently in the past. We proposed a new automatic method of summarization, and this method infers the retrieval method for multimedia files and the processing method for multimedia, by utilizing the analogy of a semantic structure which is given as template and user selected semantic structure of summarization. In addition, it was confirmed that data capacity will be decreased less than 1/10 compared with the former database, by applying this method to an example of map summarization from a practical residential map database.

References

[1] Matsuka,H. and Uno,S.: Canonical Geometric Modeling for Computer Aided Design, Data Base Techniques for Pictorial Applications Proc. 81, Springer-Verlag, pp233-252 (1978)

[2] Tsurutani,T.,Kasahata,Y. and Miyashita, T.: A geographic information overlay method for regional analysis, Systems and Computers in Japan, 17 no.8, pp41-48 (1986)

[3] Shimada,S.,Miyatake,T.,Mastsushima,H. and Ejiri,M.: "Knowledge-based Multimedia Database Management System and its Application to Map Information Systems", Proc. of the International Workshop on Artificial Intelligence for Industrial Applications. (1988)

[4] Shimada,S. and Chikada,N.: "Object-oriented Multimadeia Annotaion for Large-scale Mapping system", Proc. of DASFAA'91, Tokyo. Japan,(1991)

[5] Sugie,M., O.Menzilcioglu, and H.T.Kung: "CARGuide-on-board computer for automobile route guidance", Proc. of National Computer Conference, pp697-706,(1984)

[6] Kasturi,R.: Image-Analysis Techniques for Geographic Information Systems, Image Analysis Applications Kasturi,R. and Trivedi,M. (Editor), pp127-163, Marcel Dekker, Inc., New York, (1990)

[7] Aonuma,H., Imai,H. and Kambayashi,H.: A visual system of placing characters appropriately in multimedia map databases, Visual Database Systems, T.L.Kunii(Editor), Elsevier Science Publishers B.V. (North-Holland), IFIP, pp525-546, (1989)

[8] Shi-kuo Chang: Principles of Pictorial Information Systems Design, pp212-233, Prentice Hall, (1989)

[9] B.J.Cox: Object Oriented Programming An Evolutionary Approach, Addison Wesley Publishing Corp.,(1988)

[10] Objective-C Reference Manual, Release4.0, Step Stone Corp., (1990)

[11] NeXT System Reference Manual, Chapter 10, "Support Objects and Functions', and "Chapter 23,"C functions", NeXT Inc., (1989)

[12] Elisa Bertino: "Issues in Indexing Techniques for Object-oriented Databases", Proc. Advanced Database System Symposium '89, pp151-160, Kyoto Japan, (1989)

[13] Shimada,S. and Kurata,A.:"A multiple prospector and automatic message propagation mechanism for multi-media type map-based systems", Proc. Advanced Database System Symposium '89, pp279-284, Kyoto Japan, (1989)

[14] Haraguchi, M.:"Analogical Reasoning Using transformation of rules", Bull. Inform. Cybernetics, 22, pp.1-8 (1986)

[15] Misue,K. and Sugiyama,K.: A method to display the whole and details simultaneously, and the application to compound graphs, Technical Reports on Human Interface 29-5, IPS, Japan,(1990)

Goblin: a DBPL designed for Advanced Database Applications

M.L. Kersten

CWI, Kruislaan 413
1098 SJ, Amsterdam

Abstract

Goblin is a database programming language for application development and ad-hoc querying advanced databases. Its salient features include: a strong and extensible type system; classification based on type, behavior, and constraints; a core of common programming language concepts; and a trigger mechanism. Moreover, the query language framework is largely borrowed from SQL, such that manipulation of a Goblin database with flat objects appears as dealing with a traditional relational database.

The language design is strongly influenced by several envisioned application domains, such as an office automation, robotic applications, cartographic applications, and astronomy. These application domains are surveyed and their requirements on a database programming language identified.
keywords: database programming languages, application domain requirements, triggers, classes, ADTs.

1 Introduction

The main thrust of research vested in post-relational systems aims at supporting novel application domains, such as office automation, geographics, CIM/robotics, VLSI design, and astronomy. These environments require database modelling and processing facilities not being offered by commercial DBMSs. In particular, the mismatch of application programming language and database language have revived interest in the design of database programming languages (DBPL), that extend the early work in the late seventies on Pascal/R [20], PLAIN [18], and PS-Algol [2].

Although many recent DBPL papers [17, 1, 7, 16, 3] aim at these potential markets, few have taken the requirements imposed by them as a driving force for language design. To partially alleviate this situation, we believe that the application domain characteristics sketched in this paper have a significant impact on the syntax and semantics of a general purpose DBPL, such as:

- *union types and type discrimination*, to deal effectively with heterogeneous data structures,

- *classification*, to (automatically) organize objects by structure, behavior, and constraints,

- *triggers*, to model semi-autonomous processes or active objects,

- *Abstract Data Types*, to extend the type system and compiler optimizer.

We have taken the route to develop a database programming language, called Goblin, as an intermediate step towards a domain specific DBMS, i.e. with a domain specific data model, query language, and user interface. Its design has produced a balanced solution between common practice (and expertise) to write applications in a mixture of C and SQL and the need for a new full-fledged high-level programming language to obtain a seamless interface to the database management system. The rationale is that a database programming language should not force users to convert existing

software. Instead, it should attract users by providing a more convenient programming platform with an open interface to reuse existing software. A design track also followed in the O_2 project [7].

In the design process of Goblin, we have used the application characteristics as a yardstick to identify the essential language features, to exercise language expressiveness, and to select convenient syntax shortcuts. To summarize, the predominant language design issues produced by this course of action are:

- *Extensible Type System*
  Goblin supports an Abstract Data Type facility, that specify the signatures and the equations of new (external) basic types. The rationale is that a DBPL should provide a well-defined interface with an existing, possibly unsafe programming environment.

- *Type Checking*
  Goblin is a strongly typed language. The rationale is that compile time warnings pay off in development costs, but can not ensure correctness of all expressions that involve types over finite domains, such as array bounds and subranges. In those cases where information at compile time is not available it resorts to run time checks.

- *Classification System*
  Goblin supports (composite) values and objects with a clear separation of their role. A class provides an (automatic) classification scheme for objects based on their representation, their behavior, and their constraints. Variables hold unclassified data values or references to classified objects. The rationale is that a flexible classification scheme leads to a concise and modular description of the database content and its behavior.

- *Triggers*
  Goblin supports triggers to model semi-autonomous actions and it provides mechanisms to synchronize and manage trigger teams. The rationale is that triggers (like active objects, agents) are a convenient concept for capturing guarded processes in control applications.

- *SQL Compliance*
  Goblin is upward compatible with a significant subset of SQL. In particular, the semantics for querying collections of tuples using a SELECT-FROM-WHERE construct is indistinguishable from its counterpart on a traditional SQL database server. The rationale is to re-cap learning SQL and to provide an evolutionary route towards using a new programming language.

- *Parallelism*
  Goblin stimulates a programming style that supports implicit coarse-grain parallel processing. The rationale is that the effectiveness of database technology comes from optimizing independent actions over collections. It is this order independence that permits parallel processing without explicit action on the programmer's part.

The remainder of this paper illustrates the requirements imposed by the application domains that led to these choices. For each application domain, we give a necessarily short description of the problems dealt with and we indicate the requirements imposed upon a DBPL. Small examples exemplify the Goblin syntax, where we assume a general background on the semantics of most constructs used. An in-depth description of the language and the envisioned system architecture are given elsewhere[14] [15].

2   Office Automation

Database management in office automation concerns the capturing, archiving, and dissemination of documents for decision making purposes [9], [21]. These document databases are large collections of semi-structured objects, that range from simple bit maps, ascii strings, and letters, to highly regular data entry forms and EDI messages. Furthermore, collections of documents are structured in two (independent) ways: a hypertext structure and folders. The hypertext structure is caused by the (unpredictable) way office documents refer to one another, while folders emerge from (unpredictable) aggregation of heterogeneous document structures.

From a DBPL point of view, this application domain requires a rich type system to support document structuring, a flexible reference mechanism to manage hypertext structures, and variables that can hold values of different types. We will elaborate a little on these characteristics.

The first issue deals with the role of typing schemes in such office applications. In principle, a typing scheme can be used to described the classification hierarchy of office documents [4]. For, each document can be seen as a hierarchical aggregation of components, which can be described with tuple types. However, since document structures differ widely, this leads to large type descriptions.

For example, a common business letter may contain a 'your ref' and 'our ref' section, the secretary's name, the topic, a telephone extension, a logo, a bank account footnote, etc.. These properties differ per letter, per business market, and per country. Catching these differences with a single hierarchical tuple type that includes all properties yields an unwieldy structure, because many of the attributes will be set to NULL and inappropriate attributes can not easily be distinguished from missing values.

Furthermore, the structure of a document need not be complete described [6]. An office worker tends to classify a document by the major structuring criteria, leaving the detailed classification for the future, as need arises. This means that at any level in the document type hierarchy we have to permit for a non-interpreted portion. This calls for a union type constructor where one alternative permits typing a document portion as a reference to another representation, such as its bit-map or ascii string.

The second issue stems from the liberal use of references inside office documents. They appear both in specific document areas, e.g. an 'our ref' section, as well as in their content part, e.g. 'in answer to your letter dd. 12-4'. Furthermore, the format ranges from document identifiers, 'contract nr 97-33-77' to hints 'our meeting last week'. This broad spectrum of formats and their embedding in documents requires both union types and an extensible coercion mechanism. For example, a contract number can be coerced to a document id regardless its format.

The third issue stems from office practice to physically group documents into folders to simplify reference, querying, and message handling. The content of these folders is based on a simple predicate, such as a client name, and it contains different document styles, i.e. memos, EDI messages, letters, and forms. Thus, an office folder assembles items from anywhere in the database, which severally complicates type checking and storage optimization. At the language level this leads to classes over union types and a materialized view concept, which allow a programmer to (declaratively) describe object grouping.

Although querying a document base may start with a folder, subsequent selection is often based on presenting a set of <property, value-constraints> pairs. For example, find all the documents in the folder named Competition that refer to the product MilkSoap. Such queries stress the functionality of a query processor, because it should first locate all objects in the folder that have a product attribute and, thereafter, select those that satisfy the restriction.

The requirements posed by this area on a DBPL can be summarized as follows:

- It should support heterogeneous data structures,
- it should support a general general reference mechanism,
- it should support (declarative) aggregation of objects, and
- it should support querying the database both by physical aggregation and by predicates over individual document properties.

2.1   Type expressions and discriminators

Among the language facilities offered by Goblin for this domain are *tuple type expressions*, which simplify the definition of hierarchical structures, *union types* and *optional attributes*, to catch alternate structures, and *type discriminators*, to select variants from a large union type.

The union type and tuple type expressions are illustrated in the program fragment below, which describes various kinds of letters. The common part of a letter is a sender and a body. The love letter has a single receiver and no archive number; the love letter is addressed to someone; junk mail is a letter without body. Mail is a union type, which also introduces the local type Memo and ValentineCard.

```
TYPE Letter= TUPLE( sender:Person, body:string)
TYPE JunkMail = Letter - (body)
TYPE LoveMail = Letter + TUPLE(receiver:Person)
TYPE Mail =UNION(
          Memo = TUPLE( department:string, when:date),
          ValentineCard : string,
          Letter, JunkMail, LoveMail)
```

Although a union type can be used to model optional attributes, such a track would lead to a rather unwieldy type definition. For example, the type persons can be described concisely in Goblin by the following tuple type:

```
TYPE Person = TUPLE( name:string, [tel:int], [home:string], [ss:char(8)])
```

which is equivalent to the more verbose unlabeled union type that enumerates all combinations:

```
TYPE  Person = UNION(
      TUPLE ( name:string),
      TUPLE ( name:string, tel:int),
      TUPLE ( name:string, tel:int, home:string),
      TUPLE ( name:string, tel:int, ss:char(8)),
      TUPLE ( name:string, home:string),
            ... )
```

Absence of type tags to identify alternatives is resolved with *type discriminators*, i.e. an expression over the known attribute labels. For example, tramps can be characterized as Person WITH name AND NOT (tel OR home). Likewise, the telephone owners can be referred to as Person WITH tel. Such type discriminators can also be used to analyse the type property of a variable, like tmpVar ISA Mail WITH Valentine OR LoveMail.

Observe that this language feature is primarily syntax that simplifies life of the programmer. It does not pose severe problems for the language semantics. Moreover, a type discriminator embodies the 'minimal' tuple structure required in a given context. As such, it provides a handle on the validity of a piece of code after an update of the type definition.

3 Spatial Databases

Spatial database applications, such as geographics and mechanical CAD, illustrate another dimension in advanced database applications. They deal with the representation of n-dimensional data with explicit knowledge about objects, their extent, and their position in space. The basic data structures and algorithms required in this area do not neatly match the relational model. Instead, it requires handling of multiple spatial representations and data models, access methods and optimizations [11].

The primitive types dealt with include points, polygons, edges, etc.. The variety in semantics and the availability of many graphic packages hinder inclusion of such types within a DBPL implementation. Instead, one should include an Abstract Data Type facility, which permits the functions and behavior of these types to be described in an abstract and manageable way. Their actual implementation can be borrowed from the environment.

Such ADTs extend the vocabulary of the query languages. The behavior of geometric types, described by equations, aids query optimization. Provided the compiler includes a rule driven optimizer as researched in [12]

The last issues stems form the experience that no single spatial representation suites all purposes in a given application. Instead, objects are often represented in different ways, for example a constructive solid geometry representation (CSG) versus a boundary representation (BR). Such applications would benefit from a language mechanism, such as triggers and constraints, that permits concise description of propagation of updates on either representation.

Therefore, the additional requirements posed upon a DBPL are:

- it should support ADTs for interfacing and query optimization;
- it should support management of replicated data structures with different representations.

3.1 Geometric Abstract Data Types

The Abstract Data Type facility of Goblin forms the interface with (separately compiled) external libraries. Their specification tells the programmer the signature of the functions and its equations describe the (relevant) semantics. The specification is used by the Goblin compiler to type check expressions, but it can also be used optimize the code.

For example, consider a geographic application domain that requires the type point. Its partial behavior is specified below. The equality axioms illustrate that the compiler can assume that equality of point identity implies value equality and it can optimize code for expressions such as `equal(point.new(1,1),Z)` without going through the mechanism to create a point representation first.

```
CREATE ADT point
        FUNCTION new (x,y:int) :point
        FUNCTION put_x(src:point, x:int):point
        FUNCTION put_y(src:point, y:int):point
        FUNCTION get_x(src:point):int
        FUNCTION get_y(src:point):int
        FUNCTION equal(p1,p2:point):boolean
        FUNCTION copy(dst,src:point):point
        ...
        RULE get_y(new(X,Y))=>Y
        RULE equal(X,Y)=> (X=Y)
        RULE equal(new(X,Y),Z)=> (get_x(Z)=Y AND get_y(Z)=Y)
        RULE copy(X,Y)=>X
        ...

END ADT
```

An abstract data type can be implemented by a separate Goblin or C program. Conformance of their implementation with the ADT specification is left to the discretion of the programmer (or librarian).

4 Computer Integrated Manufacturing

In Computer Integrated Manufacturing (CIM) a distinction is made between the design of a production environment, i.e. the off-line environment, and the completed, running system, i.e. the on-line environment [5, 8]. The off-line environment is a highly interactive process, where a designer is focussed on finding an optimal solution for product assemblages. This involves choosing robots and sensor systems, defining the cell layout, and producing a task description for the robot systems. Once an initial design is made, the designer experiments to find defects and to improve the design.

The online environment can be characterized as a semi-autonomous system, where robot tasks have been fixed up front and the interaction with the image recognition system is well-defined and stable. That is, the focus in the on-line case shifts towards scheduling processing tasks under hard deadlines.

At the language level it implies, amongst others, support for the definitions of semi-autonomous tasks, support for hypothetical queries and a flexible simulation environment, and a (distributed) processing platform. We will illustrate these issues briefly.

Due to the nature of CIM systems, their designs are extensively tested before being taken into production. This involves both the physical design of the production cell and the programming of the robot tasks. The former requires facilities for geometric modelling, as described above. The robot tasks can be seen as threads of primitive actions, such as picking a component and moving it into place, which are triggered by scene analysis, such as the recognition of a new frame arrival. This calls for active database support, such as provided by *triggers* (active objects, actors, etc.). They allow a robot task designer to express the partial order among the tasks in terms of observed database states and events.

Once the robot tasks have been prototyped, the production cell will be simulated against a mock up state. In essence, this amounts to producing derivable database states that reflects the reachable cell states. The simulation analysis involves statistical aggregation of measurement data, such as the average production time of a piece, and the recognition of critical intermediate states, such as two robot arms in deadly embrace awaiting the other to leave a 3-D subspace. The latter area also includes hypothetical queries or 'what if' queries, such as testing the robot recovery procedures by presenting a dangerous situation.

The on-line CIM situation, i.e. the production cell is characterized as a distributed processing environment with autonomous sensory nodes, robot control, and component transport. A database system managing this environment is faced with hard deadlines, such as handling an event within 30 ms. Yet, the fixed set of actions provide ample opportunities for extensive compiler-based optimizations.

Therefore, the development aspects of the CIM design phase imposes the following requirements on a DBPL:

- it should support a trigger concept to model semi-autonomous actions,
- it should support an incremental programming style,
- it should support flexible transaction semantics and synchronization primitives for specifying cooperative behavior.

4.1 Materialized views by triggers

A place where triggers come in handy is the maintenance of materialized views. For, in an online CIM environment the scenery is viewed from different perspectives. The vision subsystem deals with bitmaps, the robot arm with trajectories, and the belt with motion, etc.. Since view materalization is in general too costly, such as rebuilding the CSG from a bitmap, we should include a mechanism to propagate updates.

This is conveniently handled by a trigger, that describes an action to be taken BEFORE or AFTER a method on an object has been applied. Alternatively, it is activated when a particular database state has occurred or a combination of event and state change.

For example, consider a sensory device that accepts new images from its vision system. This information analysis may lead to updates of edge boundary representation of the scene. The object recognizer should react on such an event, because it may affect its belief on the objects in the vision field. Such actions can be described independent of the vision and recognizer class.

```
TRIGGER updateBR AFTER vision.update {...}
```

```
CREATE CLASS recognizer TYPE objectRep
    TRIGGER validateNew AFTER new {...}
    TRIGGER notifyUser
    SELECT *
    FROM  o IN recognizer
    WHERE NOT o.locate IN robotArm.space {...}
END CLASS
```

The triggers are also used to refine actions within a single class. For example, above we have included the trigger validateNew, which could involve actions to be taken whenever an object is (implicitly) inserted into the class. The body of this trigger runs within the same transaction as the corresponding recognize.new with the same target object.

Moreover, each object comes with a backup copy, that represents its state at the previous commit. For example, let locate be an attribute of an var x:objectRep then x.locate'-x.locate denotes the distance moved (under proper assumptions about the updates).

The last trigger in the class above describes an exceptional situation based on an undesirable database state.

5 VLSI Design

VLSI design has been an early focus of advanced database applications. It deals with a precisely defined and structured domain of chip components and their layout on the wavers. Furthermore, the algorithms that exercise a chip design are highly computation intensive. The data structures managed are spatial in nature. However, as pointed out in [13], the view on the geometry differs with each query problem being addressed.

For example, a chip design consists of several information layers; the wiring structure, the cell structure, and the functional structure. The wiring level can be viewed as being composed of faces build out of edges and edges build out of points. However, this hierarchical view may not be adequate for an analysis of electrical interference, which would require the chip to structured as junctions (points) connecting wires (edges).

In both situations we have a single geometric structure, but the ways in which this structure is being navigated differs. In terms of database concepts it means that alternative (navigational) views can be defined and at the implementation level that references between structures can always be reversed. The additional requirements posed on a DBPL become:

- it supports redefinition of navigational paths;
- it supports bi-directional access over object references;
- it should support efficient manipulation of large graph-like data structures.

5.1 Object structure inversions

A recurring data structure in advanced applications is a graph, where attributes are attached to the nodes and the edges. For example, an electronic CAD contains nodes that describe components, resistors, transistores, etc., and the edges represent wires on the print. Edge attributes could be thickness, length constraints, and magnetic flux. Depending on the application this graph is either viewed as nodes with component edges or, conversely, edges with components nodes. Such data structures are describe in a OODBMS through object references with an *inversion* constraint.

In Goblin we have made path inversion part of the system nucleus. That is, with every path expression major.minor there exists a path expression of the form minor:major. The difference is the type of the expression as a whole. For let major (minor) be a component of type majorPart (minorPart) then minor:major is a bag of MajorPart. The advantage of this mechanism is that the programmer need not a priory define inversions. Moreover, the underlying object implementation is likely to keep backward references for persistency and garbage collection. Thus, it comes at no addition cost. Furthermore, the path denotation operator (dot) also applies to sets, producing sets as well.

For example, below we have defined nodes and edges. Let n denote a node variable and e an edge. Then n.links.length is a bag of integers, e:links a bag of nodes sharing e, and e:links.kind a bag of componentKind.

```
TYPE node= TUPLE ( kind:componentKind,
                   links:SET OF edge,
                   location:point)
TYPE edge= TUPLE ( bp,ep:point,
                   length:int,
                   thickness:float)
```

6 Astronomy

Astronomy illustrates an extreme case of scientific databases. It deals with capturing, archiving, and analysis of information gathered from extra-terrestrial objects and space missions. Its databases are often huge (100-6000 GigaByte) [10] and they contain a variety of data items, ranging from radio-, and telescope images, textual descriptions of observations, to highly condensed structural information, such as space catalogues.

From a DBPL viewpoint, its requirements extends those above by support for information retrieval, approximate query facilities, and statistical summaries.

A significant difference with previous domains is that the databases in astronomy have a tendency to accumulate information. Raw data obtained from observations is calibrated, summarized, and interpreted in scientific reports. Integration of all this information within the database is necessary to supports the researcher. For example, having access to the raw observatory data about an object is as important as the related scientific reports. Thus, a DBPL for this environment should be prepared to accumulate a large type catalogue and be an open language to access remote resources.

Another complicating aspect is the querying mode encountered in scientific databases. A researcher often can not identify the data of interest with a single request. Instead, he will browse the database by posing approximate or classification queries until the portion of interest is located; the working more is *browsing* and *data dredging* within the context of a general classification framework. The isolated portion is often used for a lengthly period, which calls for a materialized view, and statistical summaries are constantly being added.

To summarize, the additional requirements posed on the design of a general purpose DBPL are as follows:

- it should support an evolutionary type and classification scheme,
- it should support information retrieval over multi-media types,
- it should support approximate querying and statistical grouping,
- it should support huge (readonly) databases.

6.1 Classification of observations

A predominant action of user on scientific databases is to find a classification scheme for its observations that prove a hypothesis. The class concept as interpreted in Goblin aims at precisely this aspect, taking the common software encapsulation principle as a secondary issue. That is, a class groups objects by similar structure, behavior, and constraints. A class is either populated explicitly by creation of new objects that satisfy the class's properties or implicitly by the set-inclusion rules over classes.

For example, consider the (oversimplified) `stars` class below with `nearbyStar` and `otherStar` as subclasses based on by the Cardelli tuple type inheritance scheme. The constraints further limit their extent. Nearby stars are recognized by the low doplershift, i.e. a predicate over its instance attributes, while the remainder is collected in `otherStar` using a class predicate. Stars can be added to both subclasses, provided the constraints hold, and triggering their inclusion in the super class.

```
TYPE starRecord= (name:string, doplershift:float)
CLASS star TYPE starRecord
        METHOD calibrate(n:float) {...}
        METHOD display {...}
              ...
END CLASS

VAR cutoff float;

CLASS nearbyStar TYPE (name:string, doplershift:float)
              WHERE doplershift <cutoff
        METHOD analyse {...}
              ...
END CLASS
CLASS otherStar TYPE starRecord
              WHERE doplershift >=cutoff
              ...
END CLASS
```

The variable `cutoff` determines the class extent and browsing the database involves changing its value. Note that such changes can be used by the query optimizer to generate incremental queries, rather than re-partitioning the class `star`. For, if `cutoff'` > `cutoff` then stars in the range `cutoff'`-`cutoff` migrate from `otherStar` to `nearbyStar`.

7 Summary

Designing a database programming language involves identifying a mixture of (old and new) concepts with a sound theoretical basis that lead to a concise description of domain specific algorithms and a pleasing working environment for its users. Goblin is a step towards this ideal situation, yet much research remains to be done. A few pointers in the directions pursued are given below.

Inclusion of the type discriminator to distinguish the cases in a union type affects the type checking algorithm, because now each language expression over tuples is characterised by a type expression. Then type correctness boils down to proving subsumption among type expressions, which requires an efficient inference engine. Furthermore, the signature of ADTs enables both type checking and the equations can, in principle, be used for compiler optimization.

Although triggers conveniently describe semi-autonomous actions and can be used to refine methods, their efficient implementation is far from trivial [22]. Furthermore, research is required on design tools for trigger teams that can predict their cooperative behavior or inconsistency.

The class concept offered in Goblin uses Cardelli-like type inheritance scheme for classification by structure. Similar concise and formal semantics for classification by constraint and (more difficult) behavior are needed.

Last, but not least, the operational aspects, such as transaction management, and storage aspects, such as class implementations, require reassesment of traditional database technology.

References

[1] R. Agrawal and N.H. Gehani, *Rationale for the Design of Persistence and Query Processing Facilities in the Database Programming Language O++* Proceedings 2-nd Int. Workshop on Database Programming Languages, June 1989, pp. 25-40.

[2] M.P. Atkinson et.al. PS-Algol: An Algol with a Persistent Heap ACM SIGPLAN Notices, 17(7):24-31, 1981

[3] M. Atkinson, *Questioning Persistent Types* Proceedings 2-nd Int. Workshop on Database Programming Languages, June 1989, pp.

[4] F. Barbic and F. Rabitti, *The Type Concept In Document Retrieval* Proceedings of the 11th International Conference on Very Large Database, Stockholm, pp.34-48, 1985.

[5] L. Camarinha and A. Steiger, *An Information System Architecture fro Robot Cell Programming*, ESPRIT Project No. 623, 1987,

[6] P. Constantopoulos et. al., *Office Document Retrieval in MULTOS*, in: ESPRIT '86: Results and Achievements North-Holland , pp. 563-574, 1987.

[7] O. Deux, et. al. *The Story of O − 2* IEEE Trans. on Knowledge and Data Engineering, Vol 2. No.1, March 1990, pp. 91-108.

[8] P. Freedman and C. Michaud and G. Carayannis and A. Malloway, *A Database Design for the Runtime Environment of a Robotic Workcell*, Robitics & Computer-Integrated Manufacturing, 1989, Vol. 5, pp. 21-31.

[9] S.J. Gibbs, *Conceptual Modelling and Office Information Systems*, in Office Automation, D. Tsichritzis (ed.), Springer-Verlag, 1985, ISBN, 3-540-15129-X, pp.193-226

[10] J.L. Green, *The New Space and Earth Science Information Systems at NASA's Archive*, Government Information Quaterly, 1990, Vol 7, No 2, pp. 141-147, ISSN: 0740-624X.

[11] O. Guenther and A. Buchmann, *Research Issues in Spatial Databases* ACM SIGMOD Records, 19(4), Dec 1990, pp 61-68.

[12] R. Güting, *Gral: an extensible relational database system for geometric applications*, Proc. 15-th VLDB, Amsterdam, 1989, pp 33-44.

[13] T. Härder, Meyer-Wegener K., Mitschang B. & Sikeler A., *PRIMA - a DBMS Prototype Supporting Engineering Applications*, Proceedings 13th International Conference on Very Large Databases, Brighton 1987.

[14] M.L. Kersten, *Large Scale Handling of Complex Objects*, AI International AI Symposium 90,Nov 1990, Nagoya, Japan, pp. 151-158

[15] M.L. Kersten, M.H. vd Voort, C. vd Berg, and A.P.J.M. Siebes, *The Goblin Database Programming Language* CWI Report CS-91xx, May 1991.

[16] F. Matthes and J.W. Schmidt, *The Type System of DBPL* Proceedings 2-nd Int. Workshop on Database Programming Languages, June 1989, pp. 219-225.

[17] A. Dearle, R. Connor, F. Brown, R. Morrison, *Napier88- A Database Programming Language* Proceedings 2-nd Int. Workshop on Database Programming Languages, June 1989, pp. 179-195.

[18] R.P. van der Riet, A.I. Wasserman, M.L. Kersten and W. de Jonge. *High-level Programming Features for Improving the Efficiency of a Relational Database System* ACM Trans. on Database Systems, Vol 6, No. 3., Sep 1981, 464-487.

[19] F. Rabitti, *A Model for Multimedia Documents* in Office Automation, D. Tsichritzis (ed.), Springer-Verlag, 1985, ISBN, 3-540-15129-X, pp.227-250

[20] J.W. Schmidt, *Some high level language constructs for data of type relation*, ACM Trans. on Database Systems, Vol. 2, no. 3. (Sept 1977), 247-261.

[21] D. Tsichritzis (ed.), *Office Automation*, Springer-Verlag, 1985, ISBN, 3-540-15129-X.

[22] M.H. vd Voort and M.L. Kersten *The Facets of Database Triggers* Submitted for publication. CWI Report CS-91xx, April 1991.

[23] A.I. Wasserman et.al., *Revised Report on the programming language PLAIN* SIGPLAN Notices (ACM), Vol. 16, no. 5 (May 1981), 59-80.

A metamodel approach for the management of multiple models in CASE tools

Paolo Atzeni
Dip. di Informatica e Sistemistica
Università di Roma "La Sapienza"
Via Salaria, 113
00198 Roma, Italy

Riccardo Torlone
IASI-CNR
Viale Manzoni, 30
00185 Roma, Italy

Abstract

Many different data models are currently used in conceptual design Especially within CASE environments, it may therefore be useful to have the possibility of defining different models and managing translations of schemes from one model to another.

The constructs in the various models can be reconducted to a rather limited number of categories. Therefore, we introduce a metamodel that allows the definition models within a rather general family, which includes the models that involve constructs of these categories.

The translation of schemes can be specified rather efficiently, by means of a rule based language and a number of predefined modules that express the translations of the basic constructs.

1 Introduction

Many different data models have been proposed to be used in conceptual design (see Hull and King [13], Peckham and Maryanski [15], and Tsichritzis and Lochovski [16] for extensive surveys and tutorials), and are widely adopted in practical applications. This has negative consequences on the possibility of fruitful information exchange among different developers, especially in large projects, carried out over long periods, as standards are seldom fixed, and, when fixed, change with time. Also, analysts often change job and company, and have to adapt to new models or versions thereof. The problem is even more complex when CASE tools and environments are used, as the features and details of the models are crucial. Therefore, we believe that it is important to study the management of different models for the conceptual design of data, and the possible automation of the corresponding translation.

This work has been supported by *Ministero della Pubblica Istruzione*, within the project. "Metodi formali e strumenti per basi di dati evolute" and by *CNR, PF Sistemi Informatici e Calcolo Parallelo*, within "Sottoprogetto 6, LRC INFOKIT" and "Sottoprogetto 5, LRC LOGI-DATA+".

This may be useful in various ways: (a) different levels of expertise may correspond to different complexity of the models (for example in terms of some sophisticated details that are not of interest for a less experienced designer); (b) the work of different designers using their respective favourite models can be exchanged and integrated; (c) translations towards the implementation phases can be produced, for each conceptual model.

Ideally, the environment we envisage should allow the definition of any possible model by means of a suitable formalism that we could call a *metamodel*. Then, given two models M_1 and M_2 defined by means of the metamodel, and a scheme S_1 (the *source scheme*) according to M_1 (the *source model*), it should be able to generate a scheme S_2 (the *target scheme*) that be the "translation" of S_1 into M_2 (the *target model*). There are two crucial points in this plan:

1. It is not clear what does "any possible model" mean. The notion of model, although intuitively clear, is not formal nor precise, and it is therefore impossible to introduce a "universal" metamodel that allows the description of every possible model.

2. The translation of a scheme from a model to another model is a very difficult task, especially if considered at a general level. In fact a lot of work has been conducted on this problem, but essentially on a model by model basis: it is known how to translate from the Entity-Relationship (E-R in the following) model to the relational model [11], or from the network to the relational one [14,17], and so on, but there are no general techniques. Also, a notion of "equivalence" of database schemes, in different models, is required, and there exist many, incomparable definitions, referring to more or less general frameworks [5,8,12,14].

We propose a solution of this problem based on a language that allows (to a specialist called the *model engineer*) the definition of a wide variety of models, on the basis of a limited set of constructs that cover almost all known models.

The translation process has also to be specified by the model engineer, with reference to individual constructs (so there is no need to refer to all other models, but just to the basic constructs); also, a set of predefined, basic translations is provided, and the model engineer will often have only to combine some of them. Translations are specified by means of LOGIDATA+ [6], a rule based language for complex objects with identity. In this way, there is no complete automation of the translation, but the activity of the model engineers is greatly simplified, and most of their work is based on predefined rules. They have to put their effort in combining existing rules and rewriting those that are not considered to be suitable to the specifc model under consideration.

The rest of the paper is organized as follows. In Section 2 we present the framework for the description of models, by first describing the basic constructs used in the models and then giving the language for the definition of models, and the consequent language for describing schemes within each model. In Section 3 we show how the translation process can be specified: we first motivate the problem and illustrate the main difficulties, and then, after a brief presentation of the LOGIDATA+ model and language, we show some examples of translations.

2 The metamodel

As we said in the Introduction, it is clearly impossible to describe all the features of every possible model. However, it can be argued that the existing models use a rather limited number of constructs. Adopting a terminology that follows essentially that of Hull and King [13], it can be said that the constructs used in the known conceptual models can be reconducted to few categories: lexical types, abstract types, aggregations, grouping constructs, functions, keys, generalizations.

This approach leads to a metamodel allowing the definition of all the models whose constructs correspond to the types above. It can be argued that this approach is not "complete", as it does not cover all possible models. However, as we argued above, it is sufficient for essentially all widely used conceptual models. Also, the approach is "extensible": should a model with a completely new construct be proposed, the corresponding type could be introduced in the metamodel. In the rest of this section we discuss the set of basic constructs we have considered and the *model definition language (MDL)*, to be used by a *model engineer* to define models. It is important to note that, in a first effort, we have not considered all known constructs: for example, generalizations (or is-a) have been omitted. At this moment, we do not want to solve the whole problem, but just to show the feasibility of the approach. Because of the extensibility of our approach, it will not be very difficult to add further constructs later.

Let us fix the terminology. A *metamodel* is a formalism for the definition of models. In turn, a *model* is a formalism for the description of *schemes*, which describe the structure of *instances*, which finally contain the actual data. We use the term *concept* to refer to an element of a scheme, the term *construct* to refer to components of models, and the term *metaconstruct* for components of the metamodel. As an example, given an E-R description of persons, there may be an entity *person* with an attribute *age*; then, *age* is a concept, *attribute* is the corresponding construct, and *function* the corresponding metaconstruct, since each attribute describes a function from an entity set to a domain. To refer to the construct to which a concept correspond we will use the phrase *type of the concept*; similarly, we will use *type of the construct* to indicate the metaconstruct corresponding to a construct. In the example, the type of the concept *age* is the construct *attribute*, whose type is in turn the metaconstruct *function*.

The metamodel we consider in this paper includes the following metaconstructs:

1. *Lexical*: it allows the definition of constructs whose concepts have instances that are sets of printable values.

2. *Abstract*: it allows the definition of constructs whose concepts have instances that are sets of non-printable values; for example, *entity* is the (only) abstract construct of the E-R model. Associated with each abstract concept there can be a *key*, a constraint on a collection of functions (the notion of function in this framework is introduced below, but it follows the usual notion) defined over the abstract concept, requiring that a tuple of values of the functions (one for each involved function) uniquely identifies an element of the domain.

3. *Aggregation*: it allows the definition of constructs whose concepts have instances that are sets of (labelled or unlabelled) tuples of (simpler) concepts, called the *components* of the aggregation. There are a number of variations of aggregations constructs, on the basis of the types of the components (lexical, abstract, or aggregation concepts) and on whether only binary aggregations are allowed or n-ary ones, for every $n \geq 2$. Associated with each aggregation there is a *key*, a constraint that specifies that some components allows unique identification of the tuples. For example, the *relationship* of the classical E-R model is an n-ary aggregation construct, whose components are entities, that is concepts of an abstract construct; *maximum cardinalities* allow to determine keys. The *relation* construct of the *Semantic Binary Data Model* [3,9] is a binary aggregation construct, defined over components that can be abstract concepts and/or lexical concepts.

4. *Function*: it allows the definition of constructs whose concepts have instances that are functions from one or more concepts to another concept. Here we also have a number of possible variations: for each function construct, the metamodel allows to specify: (1) the allowed types of the argument(s) of the function, and (2) for its range; (3) whether it may have more than one argument (that is, whether it has to be monadic or it may, in general, be polyadic) (4) whether its concepts are monovalued functions, or multivalued functions, or both. As an example, the *attribute* of the E-R model is a monadic monovalued function construct whose concepts have an entity (abstract concept) or a relationship (aggregation of abstracts) as argument, and a domain as range.

Clearly, not all possible combinations of constructs form a model. We are rather liberal in this respect, but we feel that some *minimal* and *maximal hypotheses* have to be enforced. The former are needed to guarantee a basic expressive power, and the latter to avoid excessive redundancies. Let us just mention two examples, one per category: (a) each model must have at least an aggregation construct or a function construct; (b) each model must have at most one abstract construct.

Our proposed systems puts a *model definition language* at the disposal of the model engineer, whose syntax is shown in Figure 1. Figure 2 shows how it can be used to define the E-R model.

3 Scheme translation

The final goal of our research is a system that, given two models defined by means of the metamodel, is able of translating schemes from a model to the other, preserving equivalence. As we said, a first problem here is that there is no agreed definition of equivalence. Also, there are problems that arise whichever notion of equivalence we assume. Let us say that the source and target scheme are *equivalent* if there is a one to one correspondence between their respective sets of instances.

Then, there are pairs of models for which it is possible to find an equivalent target scheme for each source scheme: for example, this holds if a binary E-R model and a functional model, with suitable technical details, are considered. However, this is not true in general: it is clear that equivalence cannot be guaranteed when the source model allows finer representation of features than the target model. For example, if the source model is a variant of the E-R model that allows the distinction between $1:1$, $1:n$, $m:n$ relationships, and the target is another variant that does not (and at the same time does not provide any construct for the representation of this aspect), then for some source schemes there cannot be an equivalent target scheme. In these cases we say that there is a *loss* of information in the

```
<model-declaration> =
    MODEL <identifier> ;
    CONSTRUCTS {<construct-declaration>;}
<construct-declaration> =
    <lexical-declaration> | < abstract-declaration> |
    <aggregation-declaration> |
    < function-declaration>
<lexical-declaration> = LEXICAL <identifier>
<abstract-declaration> = ABSTRACT <identifier>
    [(KEY<identifier>)]
<aggregation-declaration> =
    <rank> AGGREGATION <identifier>
    ON <component-id> { , <component-id>}
    ; KEY <identifier>
<function-declaration> =
    <arity> <valued> FUNCTION <identifier>
    FROM <argument-id> { , <argument-id> }
    TO <range-id> { , <range-id> }
<rank> = BINARY | N-ARY
<arity> = UNARY | N-ARY
<valued> = MONOVALUED | MULTIVALUED |
    MONOVALUED OR MULTIVALUED
```

Figure 1:

```
MODEL entity-relationship;
CONSTRUCTS
    LEXICAL domain;
    ABSTRACT entity (KEY identifier);
    N-ARY AGGREGATION relationship ON entity
                        (KEY key-entities);
    UNARY MONOVALUED FUNCTION attribute
                        FROM entity, relationship
                        TO domain;
```

Figure 2:

translation process

There are also cases where it is possible to find an equivalent target scheme for each source scheme, but the intuitive information represented by the target scheme is less rich than that of the source scheme. This is especially apparent when there is an "implementation" process: it is known that, given a source scheme in the E-R model, with rather general features, it is possible to find a relational scheme that is equivalent to the source scheme, but does not represent the same semantics (in terms of understandability for humans) as the source scheme. In these cases, it is usually impossible to invert the translation: the problem of building E-R schemes from relational ones is a known difficult reverse engineering task. Here we say that the information, though preserved, is *degraded*. Making a parallel with termodynamics, we can say that in this case "energy" is preserved whereas "entropy" increases, without any chance of being decreased anymore.

Both in the case of loss of information and in the case of degradation, there are various possible translations of schemes, with incomparable properties (that is, each translation is better on some grounds and worse on others). Even when equivalent translations exist, if the models are *redundant* (that is, allow different constructs to represent individual features — for example, both aggregations and functions involving abstract concepts), there are different, reasonable translations.

Summarizing, we can say that it would be very difficult (if at all possible) to find general, automatic translations that work in every case and satisfy the preferences of each analyst. As a consequence, we believe that at least part of the translation process has to be specified by the model engineer. However, we believe that a lot of support can be provided for this specification. In our proposal this is done in two ways:

1. The translation is based on the translation of basic constructs. More precisely, for each metaconstruct (or variation of a metaconstruct) that is not present in the model, the model engineer has to specify how it is represented. In this way, it is not needed to specify the translation from each model to each other model, but we may assume that there is a *supermodel*, that involves every construct, and the translation is specified from the supermodel to every other model. In this way, the number of required translations is linear in terms of the number of models, instead of quadratic, as it would be if the process had to be specified for each pair of models.

2. As the number of construct is limited, it is possible to predefine a number of basic translations, which are put at the disposal of the model engineer. who can use them to build more complex translations.

The translations are specified by means of the declarative language (called LOGIDATA+ [6]) of a system (cur-

```
TYPE funtype = (monovalued,multivalued);
CLASS concept :   TUPLE name:string END;
CLASS refble-concept ISA concept;
CLASS lexical-concept ISA refble-concept;
CLASS abstract-concept ISA refble-concept;
CLASS abstract-concept-with-key ISA
   abstract-concept:   TUPLE key:SET OF string
                       END;
CLASS aggregation-concept ISA refble-concept:
  TUPLE components:
        SET OF TUPLE attribute:string;
                     comp:refble-concept;
             END;
        key:SET OF string;
  END;
CLASS function-concept ISA concept :
  TUPLE arguments:
        SET OF TUPLE name:string;
                     argument:refble-concept;
             END;
        range:  refble-concept;
        val:  funtype
  END;
CLASS scheme:   TUPLE name:string;
                      concepts:SET OF concept
                END;
```

Figure 3:

rently being defined) for the management of complex objects databases by means of a rule based (declarative) language.

The LOGIDATA+ model allows three main structuring constructs, *class*. *relation* and *function*. A LOGIDATA+ class is a set of *objects*, entities for. which value equality does not imply identity; *is-a* relationships between classes can be defined. A LOGIDATA+ relation is a relation as in the nested relational model, with the further possibility of including references to classes (which are implemented by means of oid's). A LOGIDATA+ function is a (partial) function in the usual sense; its domain and range may have nested structures. Figure 3 shows the declaration of a LOGIDATA+ scheme that can handle the data about models and schemes relevant in our framework.

The language used in LOGIDATA+ is rule-based, a typed extension of a pure logic programming language, with *(i)* oid-invention, as proposed by Abiteboul and Kanellakis [2] to generate new objects, and *(ii)* stratification to deal with negation (Apt et al.[4]), sets (Beeri et al. [7]), and functions (Abiteboul and Grumbach [1]). Being the language typed and recursive, type declarations should be provided for atoms that appear both in the right and in the left hand side of a rule. For the sake of space, we will omit most of them, as they will understood from the context.

As we said at the beginning of this section, the basic notion underlying our translations is that of "supermodel", a model that involves a construct for each metaconstruct in the metamodel, in its full generality. The translation process can be seen as composed of two steps: *(i)* from the source model to the supermodel; *(ii)* from the supermodel to the target model. Step *(i)* is trivial, as every scheme in any model is a scheme in the supermodel (up to renaming of constructs: that is, each entity is a *supermodel abstract concept*, and so on). Step *(ii)* can be performed by means of suitable translations of the concepts whose metatype has no counterpart in the target model into concepts of allowed types. All the model engineer has to do at the definition of the model is to specify a translation for (each aspect of) each metaconstruct for which the model has no construct. The "maximal hypotheses" mentioned in Section 2 guarantee the feasibility of the final step of this translation towards the constructs of the specific target model.

The specification of the translation of the metaconstructs has to be specified by means of the LOGIDATA+ rule based language. This task may be rather difficult in general; however, its responsibility is given to the model engineer, who is supposed to be a skilled individual (of group of individuals). Also, it can be easily seen that many translations share some specific steps, which correspond to the elimination of constructs with given types (that is, the representation of their concepts by means of concepts with other types and metatypes); an example is the elimination of aggregation concepts and their representation by means of function concepts. There are three points to note.

(a) Some of the basic translations may introduce auxiliary concepts, which have to be taken under control, possibly by ordering the various translations. For example, the elimination of n-ary aggregations may lead to the introduction of auxiliary abstract concepts, and therefore, if the target model does not contain an abstract construct, this step has to be followed by a step that eliminates abstract concepts, without introducing n-ary aggregations back. Therefore, the postconditions of each elementary step have to be specified (that is, known to the model engineer).

(b) Each translation involves the concepts corresponding to types that have to be eliminated and concepts with other types that may involve or make reference to those concepts, and that have therefore to be modified as a side effect. For this reason we assume that each translation is applied to all the concepts of a scheme.

(c) For some of the translations it may be useful to have the possibility of applying them in a selective manner. For example, to generate Entity-Relationship schemes, it is needed to replace all n-ary functions, and all unary functions from abstract concepts to abstract concepts, and from lexical to lexical, but not the functions from abstract to lexical concepts.

Without introducing details that cannot be accomodated here, we can say that for each of the elementary steps there are one or two LOGIDATA+ functions that transform a scheme into another scheme that does not contain concepts

```
FUNCTION replace-abstracts:
    TUPLE source.scheme END TO scheme;
FUNCTION replace-aggregations:
    TUPLE source:scheme; over:metaconstruct
    END TO scheme;
FUNCTION replace-functions-wrt-range:
    TUPLE source:scheme;
        with-range:metaconstruct
    END TO scheme;
FUNCTION replace-functions-wrt-arguments:
    TUPLE source:scheme;
        with-argument:metaconstruct
    END TO scheme;
FUNCTION replace-n-ary-aggregations:
    TUPLE source:scheme END TO scheme;
FUNCTION replace-n-ary-functions:
    TUPLE source:scheme END TO scheme;
```

Figure 4:

of some specific types. Specifically, we have defined the six functions in Figure 4.

It is worth noting that the two functions for replacing functions and that for replacing aggregations have a second argument, which is in fact the parameter that allows to express selectivity. We have also defined two "derived" functions, for the elimination of all functions and all aggregations, respectively:

```
FUNCTION replace-all-aggregations:
    TUPLE source:scheme END TO scheme
FUNCTION replace-all-functions:
    TUPLE source:scheme END TO scheme
```

Now, most of the useful translations can be specified by means of combinations of applications of these functions. The two rules in Figure 5 describe the translation of every scheme into the relational model (elimination of abstract concepts, elimination of functions, elimination of nested ag-

```
S = relational-scheme(source:S1),
scheme(S;name:append(Relational-for-',S1.name),
    concepts:S4.concepts)
 <- S2 = replace-abstracts(source:S1),
    S3 = replace-all-functions(source:S2),
    S4 = replace-aggregations
        (source:S3;over:aggregation).
S = E-R-scheme(source:S1),
scheme(S;name:append('E-R-for-',S1.name),
    concepts:S7.concepts)
 <- S2 = replace-polyadic-functions(source:S1),
    S3 = replace-functions-wrt-range
        (source:S2,with-range:abstract),
    S4 = replace-functions-wrt-range
        (source:S3,with-range:aggregation),
    S5 = replace-functions-wrt-arguments
        (source:S4,with-argument:lexical),
    S6 = replace-aggregations
        (source:S5,over:aggregation),
    S7 = replace-aggregations
        (source:S6;over:lexical).
```

Figure 5:

gregations) and into the Entity-Relationship model, respectively.

The predefined functions listed above are also specified by means of LOGIDATA+ rules. We cannot accomodate their specifications in this draft. We just say that the translations are based on the repeated application of functions that takes as input a concept C and generates a new concept (sometimes a set of concepts) depending on the metatype of C. For instance the function `replace-abstracts` is based on the function `r-abs-concept` that generates from lexical concepts, aggregation concepts and function concepts a new concept of the same metaconstruct, whereas from an abstract concept it generates an aggregation concept.

References

[1] S. Abiteboul and S. Grumbach. Col: A logic-based language for complex objects. In *EDBT'88 (Int. Conf. on Extending Database Technology), Venezia, Lecture Notes in Computer Science 303*, pages 271–293. Springer-Verlag, 1988.

[2] S. Abiteboul and P. Kanellakis. Object identity as a query language primitive. In *ACM SIGMOD International Conf. on Management of Data*, pages 159–173, 1989.

[3] J.R. Abrial. Data semantics. In *Data Base Management*, pages 1–59. North-Holland Publishing Company, Amsterdam, 1974.

[4] K. Apt, H. Blair, and A. Walker. Toward a theory of declarative knowledge. In J. Minker, editor, *Foundations of Deductive Databases and Logic Programming*, pages 89–148. Morgan Kauffman, Los Altos, 1988.

[5] P. Atzeni, G. Ausiello, C. Batini, and M. Moscarini. Inclusion and equivalence between relational database schemata. *Theoretical Computer Science*, 19(2):267–285, 1982.

[6] P. Atzeni and L. Tanca. The logidata+ model and language. In *East-West Workshop on Database Technology, Kiev, Lecture Notes in Computer Science*. Springer-Verlag, 1991.

[7] C. Beeri, S. Naqvi, R. Ramakrishnan, O. Shmueli, and S. Tsur. Sets and negation in a logic database language (LDL). In *Sixth ACM SIGACT SIGMOD SIGART Symp. on Principles of Database Systems*, pages 21–37, 1987.

[8] S.A. Borkin. Data model equivalence. In *Fourth International Conf. on Very Large Data Bases, Berlin*, pages 526–534, 1978.

[9] G. Bracchi, P. Paolini, and G. Pelagatti. Binary logical associations in data modelling. In *Modelling in Data Base Management*, pages 125–148. North-Holland Publishing Company, Amsterdam, 1976.

[10] M.L. Brodie. On the devlopment of data models. In M.L. Brodie, J. Mylopoulos, and J.W. Schmidt, editors, *On Conceptual Modelling*, pages 19–48. Springer-Verlag, 1984.

[11] P.P. Chen. The entity-relationship model: Toward a unified view of data. *ACM Trans. on Database Syst.*, 1(1):9–36, March 1976.

[12] R.B. Hull. Relative information capacity of simple relational schemata. *SIAM Journal on Computing*, 15(3):856–886, 1986.

[13] R.B. Hull and R. King. Semantic database modelling: Survey, applications and research issues. *ACM Computing Surveys*, 19(3):201–260, September 1987.

[14] Y.E. Lien. On the equivalence of database models. *Journal of the ACM*, 29(2):333–362, 1982.

[15] J Peckham and F. Maryanski. Semantic data models. *ACM Computing Surveys*, 20(3):153–190, 1988.

[16] D. Tsichritzis and F.H. Lochovski. *Data Models*. Prentice-Hall, Englewood Cliffs, New Jersey, 1982.

[17] C. Zaniolo. Relational views in a database system; support for queries. In *IEEE International Conference on Computer Software and Applications, Chicago*, pages 267–275, 1977.

The Development of a Knowledge-Based Database Transaction Design Assistant

X.Y. Wang   N.J. Fiddian   W.A. Gray

Department of Computing Mathematics
University of Wales College of Cardiff
Cardiff CF2 4YN, U.K.

Abstract

In this paper, we describe the development of KBTDA, a knowledge-based database transaction design assistant, with the emphasis on the types of knowledge it contains, i.e. its functionality. When applied to a database application, KBTDA first derives, with the involvement of the database designer, specific knowledge about the application. It then accepts a user-designed transaction, converts it into internal form (an And/Or tree) and performs the following processing on the transaction in that form: optimisation, safety verification, amendment and analysis. All this processing, as well as the process of deriving specific knowledge, is done interactively with end-users, and this interaction is assisted by a limited explanation/advice facility. The resulting transaction is safe, and may have been improved with respect to efficiency and reliability.

1.   Introduction

A database contains data that, together with its associated applications, model a real world enterprise. A database state is said to be consistent if it obeys the integrity constraints of the database. When users write database transactions (database update programs), they are required to ensure that the transactions are safe. A transaction is said to be safe if it always brings the database from one consistent state to another.

Designing efficient, safe and reliable transactions is a difficult task, as it requires both general knowledge concerning database systems and transaction design, and specific knowledge concerning the database on which the transaction is defined. On the one hand, various faults may exist in transactions designed by designers who lack either or both types of knowledge. The common faults include cases where the transactions are not efficient, they are unsafe, or their effects are not what the designers have in mind, i.e. they are unreliable. On the other hand, verifying transaction safety and amending unsafe transactions is a difficult, tedious and error-prone task even for designers who possess both types of knowledge. Therefore, there is a need for automatic design tools to assist transaction designers.

Several existing techniques can be used either to overcome the various types of faults mentioned above or to help to verify and amend transactions. For instance, transaction optimisation techniques based on high level syntactic or semantic information [1, 6, 14, 22, 24] can be used to enhance the efficiency of transactions; logic-based techniques for improving integrity checking [11, 13, 16, 17, 18, 22] can be used to reduce both the cost of integrity checking and the complexity of transaction

safety verification; Constraint compilers [11, 12] or techniques for synthesising transactions [19] can be used to build safe transactions from their specification; techniques regarding mechanical proofs of transaction safety [4, 10, 21] can be used to verify transaction safety automatically; and feedback generated in [22] concerning unsafe transactions and changes in cardinality of the updated relations can be used to help transaction designers to diagnose or to detect unintended results.

However, these techniques have been independently developed and no previous attempt has been made to integrate them into a comprehensive system capable of supporting the difficult and error-prone process of transaction design. The advent of knowledge-based systems has made this integration feasible. In this paper, we describe the development KBTDA, a Knowledge-Based database Transaction Design Assistant, which integrates in the framework of logic a comprehensive collection of useful techniques to form a system capable of supporting the process of transaction design.

Several existing techniques identified by other authors have been modified so that they will fit into the underlying framework of KBTDA, i.e. first-order logic. For instance, the syntactic optimisation technique proposed in [1] has been reimplemented using a set of "rewriting rules" which capture the interactions and relationships between different pairs of update operations.

These identified techniques have also been augmented with new techniques we have developed which are concerned with amending unsafe transactions and analysing transactions deemed "safe". Both issues have attracted limited attention in the literature. We believe that a deeper study of these issues is necessary and important. This is because an unsafe transaction can be amended in many ways, each semantically appropriate in a specific situation, and a transaction deemed "safe" may still contain potential semantic errors which may lead to unintended results. Our amendment method is similar to but more general and user-friendly than that described in [22] which attempts to amend an unsafe transaction by adding either integrity checks or compensating operations, and our rules for analysing transactions deemed "safe" are, to the best of our knowledge, novel.

The rest of the paper is organised as follows. In section 2, we give an overview of KBTDA. In section 3, we describe the knowledge base of KBTDA. In section 4, we discuss the implementation and identify the potential applications of KBTDA. In section 5, we draw conclusions and discuss future improvements. The example integrity constraints and transactions employed to support our illustrations are given in Appendix A, which are taken from [21, 22]. The examples illustrating our discussion are given in Appendix B to this paper.

2.   An overview of KBTDA : a Knowledge-Based Database Transaction Design Assistant

2.1.   Preliminaries

KBTDA has been developed in the context of relational

databases. A relational database is viewed as a first-order theory [9, 16]. Database integrity constraints are expressed as function-free and range-restricted horn-clauses in the language of the database theory [16, 17]. Both the integrity constraints and the database state before a transaction is applied are assumed to be consistent.

The three classes of database update operations (insert/delete/modify) are assumed to be different in their complexity (and thus in their execution costs). Here, the increasing order of complexity defined in [1], i.e. insert, delete and modify, is assumed to apply.

Update operations in a transaction are classified into two types, namely **primary operations** and **secondary operations.** A *secondary operation* in a transaction is one which is required either by a primary operation or by another secondary operation for the purpose of preserving the consistency of the database, while a *primary operation* is one which is not a secondary operation.

Database transactions are assumed to be composed of three sections, namely the **parameter section**, which contains all the parameters used by preconditions and operations; the **precondition section**, which contains conditions for ensuring the successful execution of primary operations; and the **transaction body**, which contains one or more update operations possibly connected using if-then-else control constructs.

2.2. An architectural overview of KBTDA

KBTDA has been designed as an integrated and comprehensive design tool for assisting transaction designers in the difficult, tedious and error-prone process of transaction design. It resembles an expert system with a limited explanation facility. It provides a menu interface to its end-users, who are either database or transaction designers. Figure 1 shows an overview of the architecture of KBTDA, and identifies its major components, whose names reflect their functions.

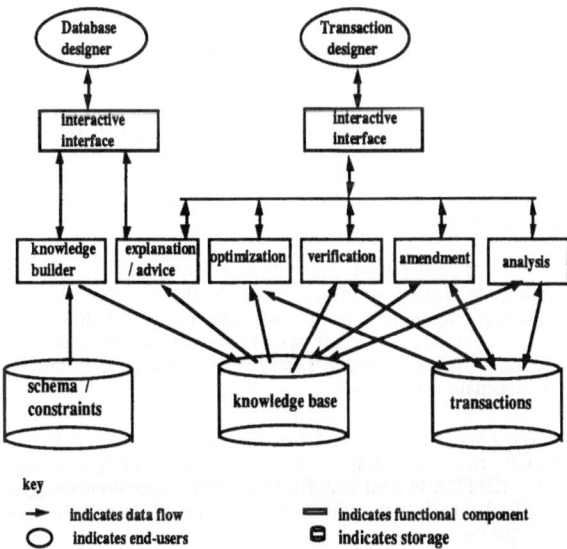

key

→ indicates data flow   ▬ indicates functional component
◯ indicates end-users   ⬭ indicates storage

Figure 1 : Architectural organisation of KBTDA

2.3. A functional overview of KBTDA

When KBTDA is applied to a specific database application, it first derives, with the involvement of the database designer, specific knowledge about that application (using the **knowledge builder**), and stores this specific knowledge in its knowledge base. It then accepts a transaction (which is either predefined or specified on-line), converts it into its internal form (an And/Or tree) and performs the following processing on the And/Or tree :

(a). optimisation, which attempts to improve the efficiency of the transaction;

(b). safety verification , which checks whether the transaction preserves the consistency of the database;

(c). amendment, which corrects any errors detected during safety verification;

(d). optimisation, as step (c) may introduce new redundancies;

(e). analysis, which attempts to detect potential semantic errors that may exist in the transaction.

All this processing is done interactively with the transaction designers, and this interaction is assisted by a limited explanation/advice facility which has been built into each end-user menu. This explanation /advice facility either explains a situation the user is facing or generates tailored advice regarding a specific situation. The message it displays is either explicitly stored in the knowledge base of KBTDA or is a combination of explicitly stored text and text generated with respect to a specific situation.

The resulting transaction is safe and may have been improved with respect to efficiency and reliability by the above processing.

3. The knowledge base of KBTDA

The knowledge base of KBTDA is composed of two constituent knowledge bases, namely the specific knowledge base and the general knowledge base.

3.1. The specific knowledge base

The specific knowledge base will be built and incorporated into KBTDA when KBTDA is applied to a specific database application. It is composed of both the structural and behavioral knowledge about this application. The former is concerned with the entities in the database and their relationships (i.e. the database schema), as well as the integrity constraints, while the latter is concerned with the operations acting on the relations in the database and their relationships.

Both types of specific knowledge are represented using facts. They are listed below.

(a). Structural knowledge : schema and integrity constraint facts

- the entities in the database
- the attributes of these entities and their features, e.g. keys or derived attributes
- the relationships between these entities
- the integrity constraints as specified in high-level specification languages
- the clausal forms of the integrity constraints.

358

(b). Behavioral knowledge : database consistency maintaining rules (DCM-rules)

Although any database update operations are physically executable on the database, not all of them are meaningful in the real world enterprise of which the database is a model, and those which are meaningful are often constrained in certain ways to preserve the consistency of the database.

The allowable update operations on the database, the properties of the database (the integrity constraints) that must be preserved by these operations, and the actions to be taken when certain properties are violated are all captured in the database consistency maintaining rules,(DCM-rules) which are in effect the physical and operational interpretations of the semantics of the application.

3.2. The general knowledge base

The general knowledge base is composed of a set of rules that correspond to a comprehensive set of techniques concerning specific knowledge building, transaction optimisation, safety verification, amendment of unsafe transactions and analysis of transactions deemed "safe". It also consists of some useful general knowledge concerning database systems and transaction design, which is used by the explanation/advice facility. These techniques and the useful knowledge are described below.

3.2.1. Technique for improving the efficiency of integrity checking KBTDA contains an integrity checking technique which is capable of either proving that a class of update operations U cannot violate an integrity constraint I, or producing a formula S whose truth guarantees that I will not be violated by U. S is frequently much easier to evaluate than I.

This technique is used to build the database consistency maintaining rules. It is based on a procedure proposed in [16] (called procedure B). However, it produces simplified integrity constraints to be tested after an update operation is applied rather than before, as with those produced by procedure B. It is more efficient than procedure B, as it is based upon syntactic criteria (which are supported by several theorems we have proved) while procedure B is based upon the resolution principle [16].

3.2.2. Transaction optimisation techniques Two types of transaction optimisation technique have been incorporated into KBTDA, namely the syntactic optimisation technique and the semantic optimisation technique. The former utilises syntactic information in the form of equivalence-preserving transformation rules, e.g. $p \wedge p \Leftrightarrow p$, or $p \wedge q \Leftrightarrow p$ if $p \rightarrow q$, while the latter utilises semantic information in the form of database integrity constraints.

Both types of optimisation technique attempt to detect transaction constructs (preconditions or operations) which either become redundant as a result of their interactions with other constructs, or can be replaced using cheaper but semantically equivalent ones. See **B.1-B.3** for examples of several types of redundancies.

3.2.3. Transaction safety verification technique Since we view a relational database as a first-order theory, the integrity constraints of the database become theorems to be proved in that theory [9, 16]. Let **DBT** be the database theory before a transaction **T** has been applied and **T(DBT)** the database theory after; Let I_{old} be the integrity constraints that are assumed to have been proved in **DBT** and I_{new} be the integrity constraints that are to be proved in **T(DBT)**. Then transaction **T** is safe if

and only if I_{new} are theorems of the conjunction of **T(DBT)** and I_{old}. Formally, this is represented as follows :

$$\mathbf{T(DBT)} \wedge I_{old} \vdash I_{new}$$

An intuitive sound and complete verification algorithm will be a theorem prover based on the resolution principle. However, such a verification algorithm is likely to be inefficient (see examples in [16]). In addition, such an algorithm cannot detect semantically unsafe situations which may result in semantically unsafe transactions (a semantically unsafe transaction is safe, but may behave in such a way that its effect is not what the designer has in mind. See **3.2.4** below).

We have designed a simple and efficient transaction safety verification algorithm. It is coupled with heuristics cutting down both the number of theorems (integrity constraints) to be proved in the new database theory and the complexity of the theorems. The former is achieved by ignoring those integrity constraints which will be violated by a certain transaction, and the latter by proving simplified forms of the theorems (integrity constraints).

This safety verification algorithm consists of two steps. In the first step, each update operation in a transaction is regarded as the last and only operation in the transaction. By matching this operation with the DCM-rules, we can obtain the set of integrity constraints that this operation may violate, together with their simplified instances and the compensating actions to be taken when these simplified instances are verified to be false. Then for each constraint in this set, an attempt is made to prove that its simplified instance is a theorem of the "current" database theory (which is represented using **DBT** and the rest of the operations in the transaction). This is done by proving the existence in the transaction body of the compensating action of the simplified instance whose effect on the database state cannot be destroyed by its subsequent operations (this guarantees the soundness of our verification algorithm). If this attempt succeeds, this constraint is said to have been enforced. Otherwise, the amendment function is called. If any operations have been inserted into the transaction as a result of the amendment, they will be treated in the same way as those in the original transaction. After all the operations in a transaction have been processed in this way, including those newly inserted ones, the resulting transaction is safe.

The first step also separates the operations in the transaction into two groups, i.e. the primary operation group and the secondary operation group. This by-product of the first step is the basis of the second step of our verification algorithm, which checks whether the preconditions of all the primary operations are in the precondition section. If there is any one missing, the amendment function is called.

3.2.4. Transaction amendment rules The transaction amendment function attempts, with the involvement of transaction designers, to identify the reasons behind any anomalous situations (unsafe or semantically unsafe situations) detected during transaction safety verification, and to amend these anomalous situations.

We have designed and incorporated into KBTDA four heuristic rules regarding transaction amendment. These rules enable KBTDA to deal with four anomalous situations we have identified which may exist in transactions. These anomalous situations are:

(d.1). where an integrity constraint which may be violated by a transaction has not been enforced in that transaction;

(d.2). where the transaction designer has chosen a different compensating action from the one chosen by the database designer to enforce an integrity constraint;

(d.3). where a precondition is found which subsumes another precondition required by a primary operation;

(d.4). where the precondition of a primary operation has not been found in the precondition section.

(d.1) above is an unsafe situation, while the rest are semantically unsafe situations.

Each of the amendment rules contains the possible causes of the situation it deals with, their respective amending actions, as well as the semantics these amending actions intend to enforce. It is activated when its corresponding situation is detected. It informs the designer about this situation, displays the possible causes of this situation and asks the designer to identify a suitable cause. It then carries out the action corresponding to the cause chosen by the designer.

These amendment rules have been designed to assist transaction designers in identifying the causes of these unsafe situations and in amending these situations, rather than to make decisions on the designers' behalf.

3.2.5. Transaction analysis rules
By designing our own transactions and analysing example transactions from previous work [3, 4, 8, 20, 21, 22], we have identified several situations that may exist in transactions verified as safe. These situations may lead to the detection of several semantic errors, e.g. an update operation has been omitted from a transaction. We have also gained some knowledge concerning the causes of these situations and developed some heuristics for helping transaction designers in identifying them. These situations, their causes, the heuristics for identifying the causes and the actions to be taken when the causes have been identified have all been encapsulated using the three analysis rules contained in KBTDA.

The first rule targets the parameters of a transaction, attempting to detect parameters which are either (a). not used in preconditions or operations, or (b). only used in preconditions. The existence of these parameters may indicate that certain update operations which use them may have been omitted. See B.5 for an application of this rule.

The second rule acts on the preconditions of a transaction, attempting to detect preconditions which are not required by any primary operations. The existence of these preconditions may cause semantic errors, e.g. that a safe transaction is wrongly aborted or that a safe transaction can never be executed.

The third rule acts on the transaction body, attempting to establish that the operations in the transaction can be divided into a number of logically disjoint subgroups (two update operations are said to be logically connected if one is a secondary operation of the other). The existence of such subgroups may indicate semantic errors, e.g. that the transaction is, in fact, a combination of several independent transactions, which should be separated. See B.6 for an illustration of this rule.

Each of the three analysis rules works as follows: when it detects its target, it either informs the designer about this situation and explains the implication of this situation, or carries out further processing, attempting to derive more information to help the designer in identifying the cause (see B.5). After the designer has chosen a cause, it executes the action that corresponds to the identified cause.

These rules have not, to the best of our knowledge, been identified before. Neither has any criterion been proposed regarding how to analyse transactions deemed "safe". The only work known to us which has a similar intention to that of our analysing rules is [22], in which attempts are made to generate some of the effects of a transaction, e.g. the changes in

cardinality of the updated relations, so that transaction designers can be alerted if some unexpected result appears.

3.2.6. General knowledge concerning relational databases and transactions
This type of general knowledge is mainly used in the explanations and advice generated by KBTDA as required by its users. It may be extended as and when necessary. The current prototype KBTDA contains background knowledge concerning relations, integrity constraints, transactions, and how integrity constraints may be violated by update operations.

3.2.7. Other heuristic knowledge
This type of knowledge is also mainly used in the explanations and advice generated by KBTDA. It includes various types of information that may be helpful to users in dealing with a situation at hand.

For instance, a user may ask for advice concerning what action to take when an entity is removed while it still has occurrences in certain relationships. Among the feedback KBTDA generates are the possible actions, and examples of real world situations where one of the possible actions is more appropriate than the others. This may help the user in making his/her decision.

4. Implementation and potential application

4.1. Implementation

KBTDA is coded entirely in PROLOG and was developed on a Sun workstation (using POPLOG-PROLOG). PROLOG was chosen for two main reasons. The first is that it has been demonstrated to be an appropriate language for defining and implementing knowledge-based systems and expert systems in general. The second is that it is an ideal language for implementing KBTDA, in which a relational database is viewed as a first-order theory and the integrity constraints and operations are viewed as first-order formulas. Most of the algorithms contained in KBTDA are based on the resolution principle, which is well represented in PROLOG. Altogether, the system code amounts to some 6,000 source lines.

4.2. Potential applications of KBTDA

The wide background and range of techniques on which KBTDA is based enable it to be applied in several areas, with or without modifications.

Firstly, KBTDA can be adapted for use as a transaction design teaching system. For this purpose, its explanation/advice facility needs to be expanded to generate more detailed explanations concerning each step it takes and advice regarding how to tackle problems.

Secondly, KBTDA can be used as a run-time integrity constraint enforcer which monitors on-line streams of update operations so that they preserve database consistency. Its transaction safety verification algorithm can be used for this purpose, as it builds safe And/Or trees from the streams of update operations submitted by users.

Thirdly, KBTDA can be used as a constraint precompiler which automatically incorporates suitable integrity checks into transactions to make them safe. Indeed, a safe And/Or tree built by its transaction safety verification algorithm represents a safe transaction in which suitable integrity checks have been included.

5. Conclusions

5.1. Summary

KBTDA, a knowledge-based database transaction design assistant has been described in this paper. It has been designed as an integrated and comprehensive design tool whose objective is to assist transaction designers in designing efficient, safe and reliable transactions. The various techniques incorporated in its general knowledge base have been presented, some are illustrated using examples.

A prototype KBTDA has been implemented using PROLOG (POPLOG-PROLOG) on a Sun workstation. Its efficacy has been demonstrated by us using a set of test transactions which successfully employ all the techniques described in this paper.

The base of the successful integration we have achieved is first-order logic coupled with logic programming technology. Apart from this, the major contribution of this research lies in the procedures and heuristic rules that comprise KBTDA's general knowledge base. In particular, the heuristics for analysing safe transactions have not, to our knowledge, been identified before.

5.2. Future improvements

KBTDA can be improved along two main lines. First, it could be expanded to accommodate more elaborate integrity constraints and update operations. The current prototype system can deal with only a limited set of integrity constraints, and with update operations which contain no functions. The solution would seem to lie in using more powerful logic.

Second, its general knowledge base could be enriched. The incorporation of additional knowledge into KBTDA could enhance its power and applicability.

Appendix A : Integrity constraints and transactions

A.1. Integrity constraints

IC_1: contains (person.pid, placement.pid);
IC_2: contains (job.jid, placement.jid);
IC_3: contains (job.jid, offering.jid);
IC_4: contains (job.jid, application.jid);
IC_5: for all x in person : x.placed is-redundant-with x.pid in placement.pid;
IC_6: null_intersection(application.pid,placement.pid);
IC_7: all c in company: is_redundant_with (c.total, sum((all p in placement where p.cid=c.cid), sal)).

A.2. Transactions

A.2.1. Fire transaction (defined in [22])

```
Transaction Fire (firee, comp,jb)
Precondition
     firee in person.pid;
     [firee, comp, jb] in placement;
Begin
     modify p in person where p.pid=firee
          by [placed=false];
     delete x from placement where x.pid=firee;
     if    [comp, jb] in offering.[cid, jid]
     then
        modify o in offering where o.cid=comp and
        o.jib=jb by [no_of_places=no_of_places+1];
     else
        insert [comp, jb, 1] into offering;
End
```

A.2.2. Fire transaction (defined in [21])

```
Transaction Fire (firee, comp,jb, sal)
Precondition
     [firee, comp, jb, sal] in placement;
Begin
     modify p in person where p.pid=firee
          by [placed=false];
     delete x from placement where x.pid=firee;
     modify c in company where c.cid=comp
          by [totsal = totsal - sal];
End
```

Appendix B. Examples

B.1. Semantically redundant precondition

Consider the two preconditions in the Fire transaction given in A.2.1. From IC_1 in A.1, we know that if the second is true, so is the first. Therefore, the first is redundant.

B.2. Semantically redundant update operations

Consider the delete operation :

delete p from placement where p.pid in application.pid

From IC_6 in A.1, we know that no tuple in relation placement satisfies the qualification predicate of this delete operation. Therefore, it is redundant.

B.3. Syntactically redundant update operations

Suppose relation placement is updated by the following two operations :

Op_1: insert [pid,cid,jid,sal] into placement
Op_2: delete p from placement where p.cid=cid

According to one of our rewriting rules :

insert R(a);delete R(b) ⇔ delete R(b) if a ∈ STS(b)

we know that the Op_1 is redundant (STS(x) represents the set of tuples satisfying predicate x).

B.4.

Consider the two Fire transactions given in A.2.1 and A.2.2. The former will be referred to as Fire(A.2.1) and the latter as Fire(A.2.2). Although they are both verified as safe in [22] and [21] respectively, Fire(A.2.1) is unsafe because it will violate IC_7 in A.1, and Fire(A.2.2) is semantically unsafe because it lacks the construct given in bold in Fire(A.2.1). Our conjecture is that this bold construct in Fire(A.2.1) is required by the operation: delete x from placement where x.pid=firee to preserve an implicit integrity constraint. This constraint states: *when a person is fired from a job, that job should be made available to others*.

B.5 below shows that the parameter analysis rule (see 3.2.5) may help to detect the omission from Fire(A.2.2) of the construct given in bold in Fire(A.2.1), while B.6 shows that the transaction body analysis rule (see 3.2.5) may help to detect the omission of the above implicit integrity constraint.

B.5. /* read **B.4** before reading what follows */
Consider transaction **Fire(A.2.2)**. The parameter **jb** is found to be used only in the precondition, and from this precondition, we know that **jb** and the third attribute of relation **placement (jid)** are defined on the same domain. Reference to the integrity constraints tells us that relations **job** (using **IC_2** in **A.1**) and **offering** (using **IC_3** in **A.1**) also contain attributes defined on that domain. Therefore the candidate relations are **placement**, **job** and **offering**. Assisted by this information, the transaction designer may be able to detect the omission of the construct (which actually acts on relation **offering**) marked in **bold** in **Fire(A.2.1)**.

B.6. /* read **B.4** before reading what follows */
The third analysis rule (see **3.2.5**) can establish that the construct given in **bold** in **Fire(A.2.1)** is not logically related to the rest of the transaction. If the designer confirms that this situation is caused by the omission of the implicit semantic rule given in **B.4**, this missing semantic rule will be captured using a DCM-rule and inserted into the knowledge base. If **Fire(A.2.2)** is submitted later, it will be verified as unsafe, as it has not enforced this newly acquired semantic rule.

References

[1] S.Abiteboul and V. Vianu. Transactions in Relational Databases (Preliminary Report). Proceedings of the 10th VLDB Conference, 1984, pp.46-56.

[2] M.Bouzeghoub, G. Gardarin and E. Metais. Database Design Tools : An Expert System Approach. Proceedings of the 11th VLDB Conference, 1985, pp. 82-95.

[3] M. L. Brodie and D. Ridjanovic. On the Design and Specification of Database Transactions. *in* On Conceptual modelling. Edited by M.L.Brodie, J.Mylopoulos and T.W.Schmidt, Springer-Verlag,1984, pp. 277-306.

[4] M. A. Casanova and P. A. Bernstein. A Formal System for Reasoning about Programs Accessing a Relational Database. ACM Transactions on Programming, 1980, Vol. 2, pp. 386-414.

[5] M.A.Casanova, L.Tucherman and A.L.Furtado. Enforcing Inclusion Dependencies and Referential Integrity. Proceedings of the 14th VLDB Conference, 1988, pp.38-49.

[6] S.Chakravarthy, J. Grant and J.Minker. Logic-based Approach to Semantic Query Optimization. ACM TODS, 1990, Vol. 15, No. 2, pp. 162-207.

[7] C.J.Date. An Introduction to Database Systems. Vol. I, Fourth Edition, Addison-Wesley Publishing Company, 1986.

[8] R. Elmasri, J. Weeldreyer and A. Hevner. The category concept: An extension to the entity relationship model. Data & Knowledge Engineering, 1985, Vol.1, pp. 75-116.

[9] H. Gaillaire, J. Minker and J-M. Nicolas. Logic and Databases: A Deductive Approach . ACM Computing Surveys, 1984, Vol.16, No.2, pp.153-185.

[10] G. Gardarin and M. Melkanoff: Proving Consistency of Database Transactions. Proceedings of the 5th VLDB Conference, 1979, pp.291-298.

[11] L. J. Henschen, W. W. McCune and S. A. Naqvi. Compiling Constraint Checking Programs from First-Order Formulas. *in* Advances in Database Theory, Vol 2. Edited by Gallaire,Minker and Nicolas, Plenum Press, N.Y., 1984, pp.145-169.

[12] M.M.Hammer and S.K. Sarin. Efficient Monitoring of Database Assertions. Proceedings of ACM SIGMOD Conference, 1978.

[13] T.Hsu and T.Imielinski. Integrity Checking for Multiple Updates. Proceedings of ACM SIGMOD Conference, 1985, pp. 152-168.

[14] J.J. King. QUIST : A System for Semantic Query Optimization in Relational Databases. Proceedings of the 7th VLDB Conference, 1981, pp. 510-517.

[15] Z. Manna. Mathematical Theory of Computation. McGraw-Hill Book Co., 1974.

[16] W.W.McCune and L.J.Henschen. Maintaining State Constraints in Relational Databases : A Proof Theoretic Basis. JACM, 1989, Vol.36, No.1, pp. 46-68.

[17] J-M. Nicolas. Logic for Improving Integrity Checking in Relational Databases. Acta Informatica, 1982, Vol. 18, No. 3, pp. 227-253.

[18] X.Qian. An Effective Method for Integrity Constraint Simplification. IEEE DE 4, 1988, pp. 338-345.

[19] X.Qian. Synthesizing Database Transactions. Proceedings of the 16th VLDB Conference, 1990.

[20] T.Sheard and D.Stemple. Coping with Complexity in Automated Reasoning about Database Systems Proceedings of ACM SIGMOD Conference, 1985, pp. 426-435.

[21] T.Sheard and D.Stemple. Automatic Verification of Database Transaction Safety. ACM TODS, 1989, Vol. 14, No. 3, pp. 322-369.

[22] D. Stemple, S. Mazumdar and T. Sheard. On the Modes and Meaning of Feedback to Transaction Designers. Proceedings of ACM SIGMOD Conference, 1987, pp. 374-386.

[23] V.C.Storey and R.C.Goldstein. A Methodology for Creating User Views in Database Design. ACM TODS, 1988, Vol. 13, No. 3, pp. 305-338.

[24] X. Wang, W.Gray and N.Fiddian. Semantic Transaction Optimization in Relational Databases. Proceedings of the 8th British National Conference On Databases, York, England, July 1990, pp. 108-123.

Integrity Constraint Enforcement through Transaction Modification

Paul W.P.J. Grefen   Peter M.G. Apers
grefen@cs.utwente.nl   apers@cs.utwente.nl
University of Twente

Abstract

The complexity of modern database applications requires powerful integrity maintenance facilities in the context of transaction processing. This paper proposes a mechanism for integrity constraint handling based on *transaction modification*. This mechanism conforms to the complete transaction model, complying with transaction atomicity and serializability. Further, the technique can be integrated into the normal query processing strategy of a relational DBMS, and can thus easily be applied in a real world system; this is shown for the PRISMA parallel database system. Transaction modification is fit for handling a large class of constraints and provides a high degree of flexibility and extensibility.

1 Introduction

In database systems the notion of transactions is used to model actions executed by applications against the database. Transactions should provide atomicity of the actions, serializability with respect to concurrent actions, and correctness with respect to integrity rules. The concepts of atomicity and serializability have been generally incorporated into the transaction concept, both in theory and in practice. Although the growing complexity of modern applications requires powerful integrity maintenance facilities, there is little agreement on full-fledged techniques in this area. Many proposals have never left the theoretical status, others have been implemented, but offer only a partial solution to the problem. Interesting proposals in the context of this paper are the following. The *query modification* technique [St75] has been implemented in the INGRES system, but deals with a limited set of constraint types, and does not comply with transaction atomicity. The work done in the context of the SABRE project [Si84, Si87] has some similarities with the ideas presented in this paper; constraint enforcement is, however, not made an integral part of a transaction specification; constraints are specified in an operational form (triggers are user defined). The work presented in [Ce90] describes only part of constraint handling, since actual enforcement is not dealt with; constraint definitions are stated in an SQL-based language; implementation of the ideas is not described.

A number of general problem areas for design and implementation of a constraint handling technique can be identified. The technique should have a high level of generality with respect to various types of integrity constraints, and to various implementation platforms (DBMSs). Further, the technique should support full transaction semantics. Finally, the high processing costs associated with constraint enforcement should be handled in an adequate way.

The transaction modification approach. This paper proposes a technique for integrity constraint handling that deals with the problems mentioned above; the technique is called *transaction modification*, and is designed to meet full transaction semantics. In this approach, transactions are modified such, that they can be executed in the regular way, but cannot violate the integrity of the database. For this purpose, constraint definitions are translated into an extension to the relational algebra. Transaction modification makes constraint enforcement an integral part of normal transaction execution, and thus fits orthogonally into the query processing strategy of a DBMS; this addresses the problem of generality with respect to implementation platforms. The problem of the high processing cost for constraint enforcement is attacked in two ways. Firstly, the technique allows for a number of optimizations that greatly reduce the amount of work. Secondly, the generality with respect to implementation platforms allows the use of a high performance relational engine that can effectively cope with high processing demands; the PRISMA database system is used as an example. The generality of the approach with respect to constraint types is guaranteed by the expressiveness of the relational algebra. Transaction modification is applicable in a distributed environment; the problems caused by relation fragmentation and the possibilities for parallelism in constraint enforcement are discussed in [Gr90a].

Organization of this paper. Section 2 discusses the basic concepts of this paper, extending the standard transaction model with transaction modification. Section 3 describes the DBMS architecture for transaction modification; it is applied in the PRISMA database system. Section 4 shows how constraints are expressed in relational algebra. The generation of constraint triggers is discussed in Section 5. An adapted version of the XRA language is used to describe relational operations. XRA is an extension to the standard relational algebra, including relational variables and assignments, standard and non-standard relational operators, and transaction brackets. Throughout this paper the same example university database is used; the scheme is given below:

```
student (studnr,name,address,dept,year_start,year_end)
exam (coursenr,studnr,date,grade)
staff (empnr,name,superior,dept)
dept (name,address,head)
```

2 Transaction model

This section first discusses the basic transaction model. Next, two new operators are defined that are necessary functional extensions to this model. The combination of these concepts allows the definition of the transaction modification principle.

2.1 Basic transaction model

A transaction T can be seen as an operator that transforms a database state D into another state $T(D)$. To transform the database state, T consists of a sequence of elementary operations o_i, so $T = (o_1; o_2; \cdots; o_n)$. In this paper, each operation o_i is a single XRA statement, such as a query, an assignment, or an update statement. The parentheses denote the transaction brackets. During the execution of the operations o_i, the database can be in a number of intermediate states; these states have no external semantics. The execution of a transaction T must satisfy three important properties. The execution of T must always be *atomic*. This means, that the effect of any execution of T on database state D must be such, that either the effects of T are completed fully, or D remains unchanged:

$$D \overset{T}{\to} T(D) \quad or \quad D \overset{T}{\to} D$$

The execution of a transaction T_1 must always be *serializable* with the execution of another concurrent transaction T_2. The effect of concurrently running transactions must be the same as the effect of some serial execution of these transactions:

$$D \overset{(T_1, T_2)}{\to} T_1(T_2(D)) \quad or \quad D \overset{(T_1, T_2)}{\to} T_2(T_1(D))$$

A database state D must satisfy a set of integrity rules $\mathcal{I}_s$ (state constraints), and a database transition must satisfy a set of integrity rules $\mathcal{I}_t$ (transition constraints). The execution of a transaction T must always be *correct* with respect to all integrity rules:

$$\mathcal{I}_s(D) \Rightarrow \mathcal{I}_s(T(D)) \quad and \quad \mathcal{I}_s(D) \Rightarrow \mathcal{I}_t(D, T(D))$$

Note, that we are interested only in the correctness of the database state before and after the transaction execution.

2.2 New operators

The transaction modification technique uses XRA as the primary constraint enforcement vehicle. Constraints are translated into XRA constructs and added to a transaction. This requires a simple extension to XRA and an operator to manipulate transactions.

The *concatenation* of two transactions T_1 and T_2 is defined as the transaction consisting of the operations of T_1 and T_2 in their respective order:

$$T_1 = (o_1; o_2; \cdots; o_m) \qquad T_2 = (o_{m+1}; o_{m+2}; \cdots; o_n)$$
$$T_1 \oplus T_2 = (o_1; o_2; \cdots; o_m; o_{m+1}; \cdots; o_n)$$

In database systems, an abort operator is used to undo all effects of a transaction in case of an error, like concurrency control deadlock, or an application generated abort. In our approach to integrity maintenance, the abort operator is used explicitly to undo incorrect transactions. This requires an operator that raises an abort state if some condition on the database state holds. The operator, *alarm*, accepts an arbitrary relational expression as its operand, and generates an abort situation if this operand is nonempty.

2.3 Transaction modification

For a set of integrity constraints $\mathcal{I}$ a transaction T_c, called *transaction modifier*, can be constructed that has one of the following two properties:

- if not $\mathcal{I}(D)$, the execution of T_c on D will be aborted; T_c is called an *aborting modifier*;
- if not $\mathcal{I}(D)$, the execution of T_c performs updates on D such that $\mathcal{I}(T_c(D))$; T_c is called a *compensating modifier*.

Now, the basic idea of transaction modification can be described as follows. Every user transaction T_u that performs updates on a correct database state D, may bring D into an incorrect state $T_u(D)$. Therefore, every such T_u is concatenated with a transaction modifier T_c as described above, resulting in a *modified transaction* T_m that cannot violate the integrity of D:

$$T_m = T_u \oplus T_c \quad such\ that \quad \mathcal{I}(D) \Rightarrow \mathcal{I}(T_m(D))$$

Given a constraint set $\mathcal{I}$, it is possible to construct one single transaction modifier T_c that can be used for all possible transactions T_u. This is very inefficient, however; in practice, T_c is generated depending on the operations in T_u using constraint filtering.

Example. If we are concerned about a correct registration of exams, we can have the constraint set $\mathcal{I} = \{I_1, I_2\}$, with:

$$I_1 \ : \ (\forall x \in exam.grade)(x \leq 10)$$
$$I_2 \ : \ (\forall x \in student)(x.year\_start \leq x.year\_end)$$

In this case we can construct the aborting $T_c = (o_1; o_2)$ with:

$$o_1 \ : \ alarm(select(grade > 10, exam))$$
$$o_2 \ : \ alarm(select(year\_start > year\_end, student))$$

The compensating form is $T_c = (o_1; o_2)$ with:

$$o_1 \ : \ delete(exam, select(grade > 10, exam))$$
$$o_2 \ : \ delete(student, select(year\_start > year\_end, student))$$

Both forms of T_c can be used to modify an arbitrary T_u. $\qquad\square$

Note, that a transaction modifier containing updates, may require the concatenation of a new modifier. This process may have to be repeated several times, and even lead to an infinite process. This problem is discussed in [Ce90].

The transaction modification technique has two important characteristics. Firstly, constraint enforcement actions are expressed in relational algebra, and can thus be handled by the normal query execution machinery of the DBMS; special purpose enforcement algorithms are not necessary. Secondly, constraint enforcement is made part of a transaction and is therefore executed fully within the semantics of a transaction, satisfying the requirements of serializability and atomicity. An approach that may seem comparable to transaction modification is *query modification* [St75]. Apart from the lower expressiveness of this approach [Si84], it also does not conform to transaction atomicity: query modification merely places a filter on the database extension to suppress individual illegal values.

364

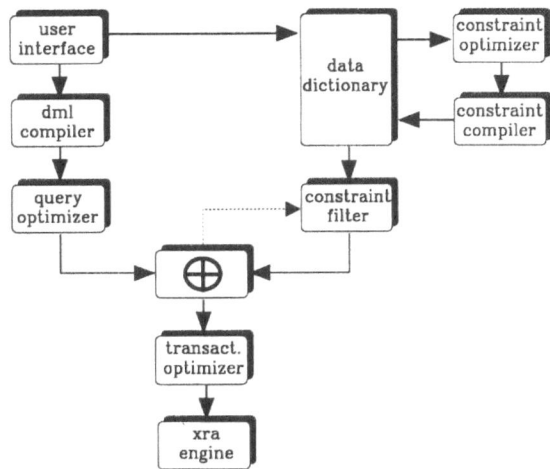

Figure 1: Abstract system architecture

3 System architecture

The first part of this section presents an abstract system architecture for integrity constraint handling through transaction modification. The abstract architecture can be mapped to a physical architecture for the development of a DBMS using transaction modification or for the integration of this technique into an existing DBMS. The latter case is shown for the PRISMA DBMS in the second part of this section.

3.1 Abstract architecture

The abstract system architecture for transaction modification is shown in Figure 1. The transaction modificator, indicated with the ⊕ operator, forms the heart of the architecture.

Architecture overview. The *User Interface* forms the interface to the system; it provides the possibility to issue both DML and DDL commands; DDL commands include constraint definitions. The *DML Compiler* and *Query Optimizer* perform the normal pre-processing of user transactions. The DML Compiler translates the user transactions from an external language into the internal relational language of the system (XRA). The transactions are optimized by the Query Optimizer. Constraint definitions issued by the user are stored in source format in the *Data Dictionary*. The *Constraint Optimizer* performs optimizations on the constraint definitions as discussed below. The *Constraint Compiler* translates the optimized constraints into XRA constructs, ready for direct enforcement. The resulting constraints are stored in the Data Dictionary. The actual transaction modification is performed by the *Transaction Modificator* and *Constraint Filter*. The Transaction Modificator concatenates a user transaction with a transaction modifier obtained from the Data Dictionary and reduced by the Constraint Filter. The *Transaction Optimizer* performs some dynamic optimizations on the execution of the modified transaction. The *Relational Algebra Engine* is the actual execution layer of the system. It provides all the usual facilities for the execution

of transactions stated in relational algebra, including locking and commit protocols.

Constraint optimization. Constraints can be optimized in a way comparable to regular query optimization. Algorithms are discussed in [Gr90a]; here only a short description of the possibilities is given. Constraints can be enforced by only examining data that has actually been changed by a transaction; this technique requires the manipulation of *differential sets* [Si87]. Integrity constraints can be rewritten such, that they can be evaluated more efficiently. In the case of distributed database systems, the integrity constraint rules can be distributed over the fragments of relations, thereby avoiding the overhead of reconstructing global relations. The usage of fragmentation knowledge in distributed systems can lead to more efficient integrity constraint rule evaluation by leaving out parts that can never be violated due to relation fragmentation. Constraint optimization can be performed before or after compilation. Post-optimization enables the use of standard query optimization techniques. Pre-optimization gives better possibilities to use the semantics of the constraints. In [Gr90a] pre-optimization of constraints in first-order logic is shown.

Constraint filtering. The most simple approach to transaction modification is to concatenate every user transaction with a transaction modifier that enforces all defined constraints. It is more efficient, however, to modify a transaction with a modifier containing only those constraints that may be violated by the transaction [Si84, Ce90]. This technique is called *constraint filtering* here. A transaction can be analyzed syntactically to identify the relations updated by the transaction. Only constraints that pertain to these relations have to be included in the transaction modifier. More efficiency can be obtained by distinguishing between insert and delete type updates. The dotted arrow in Figure 1 indicates the information flow for static constraint filtering.

Transaction optimization. The execution of the actions in a (modified) transaction in the specified order may not be the most efficient. It may be worthwile to deviate from this order to make better use of parallel processing capabilities, availability of resources and early abort situations. For this purpose, the architecture includes a *transaction optimizer*, that reschedules the execution of the actions in a transaction based on an analysis of the dependencies between the various actions.

Example. Suppose we have the following $T_m = (o_1, \cdots, o_4)$:

o_1 : $insert(student, y)$
o_2 : $insert(exam, x)$
o_3 : $alarm(select(\neg(grade \leq 10), exam))$
o_4 : $alarm(select(\neg(studnr = null), student))$

In this case the transaction optimizer schedules the execution of action o_4 before the execution of action o_2, thereby enabling early transaction abort in case of constraint violation. □

Necessary algorithms. The abstract system architecture discussed above requires a number of algorithms. *Constraint optimization* and a first step towards *constraint compilation* are described in [Gr90a]. *Constraint filtering* is a straightforward algorithm if constraints are labeled with trigger sets; generation of

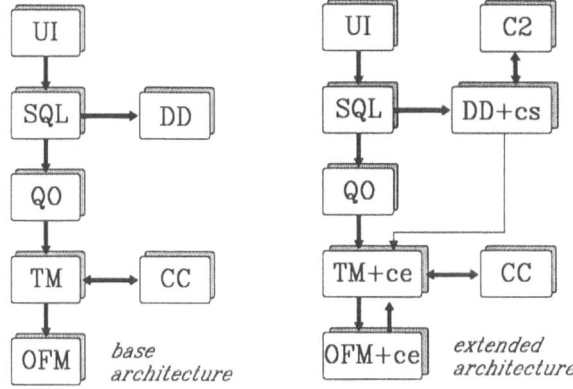

Figure 2: PRISMA/DB architecture

trigger sets is treated in Section 5. *Transaction modification* itself is fairly straightforward; it consists of two simple tasks: syntactical analysis of update statements to control the constraint filtering, and concatenation of the user transaction and the transaction modifier produced by the filtering process. *Transaction optimization* is a current topic of research.

3.2 PRISMA/DB architecture

In this section the approach to constraint handling taken in the PRISMA DBMS is discussed. First, the context of the PRISMA system is described. Next, we show how the mechanism of transaction modification is added to the system to obtain a full-fledged constraint handling subsystem.

The PRISMA/DB context. PRISMA/DB is a parallel main memory DBMS, running on shared-nothing multi-processor hardware. The system makes extensive use of parallelism in query processing; relation fragmentation is used to support the use of parallelism. The system uses XRA as its internal language. Figure 2 shows the simplified base architecture of PRISMA/DB.

The *Data Dictionary (DD)* stores all meta-data of the system, such as information on relations and their fragments. The *Concurrency Controller (CC)* controls the serializability of concurrent transactions using a two-phase locking protocol. The *User Interface (UI)* is the interface for interactive communication with one of the user language parsers of the system (only the SQL parser is shown). The *SQL Parser (SQL)* translates SQL queries into XRA; further, it informs the DD about data definition commands. The *Query Optimizer (QO)* resolves fragmentation transparency in queries, removes views, translates recursive XRA expressions, and optimizes queries. The *Transaction Manager (TM)* manages the execution of schedules produced by the QO; for this purpose, it builds execution infrastructures of temporary OFMs and tuple transport channels. The TM supports transaction serializability through locking in cooperation with the CC; transaction atomicity is achieved by means of a two phase commit protocol in cooperation with the OFMs involved in the transaction. The *One-Fragment Manager (OFM)* manages a single relation fragment or intermediate result in the database; one OFM exists for every frag-

ment or intermediate result. The OFM also executes all relational operators present in XRA.

Transaction modification in PRISMA/DB. To obtain constraint handling facilities, the abstract system architecture as depicted in Figure 1 is integrated into the PRISMA/DB architecture. The extended architecture of PRISMA/DB is shown in Figure 2. The *Data Dictionary* is extended to handle constraints. It stores constraints both in source format as specified by the user and in XRA format. The source format is necessary for automatic recompilation; the XRA format is needed for constraint enforcement. The Data Dictionary automatically activates the Constraint Compiler when necessary. The *Constraint Compiler (C2)* optimizes constraint definitions and translates these from external format into XRA constructs that are directly executable by the Transaction Manager. The C2 also resolves fragmentation transparancy for constraint definitions. Finally, it generates trigger sets that are added to the translated constraints for constraint filtering. In the current prototype implementation of the C2, only a limited set of constraint types in ad hoc format is accepted; future implementations will accept more general constraints. The *Transaction Manager* is extended to handle constraint filtering and transaction modification. During transaction execution, the TM analyzes the incoming XRA actions to record possible constraint violations. When the TM reaches end of transaction, it retrieves the constraint definitions for the possibly inconsistent fragments from the DD, and performs further filtering using the constraint triggers. Finally, the TM performs the actual transaction modification by concatenating the constraints to the transaction. The modified transaction is executed in exactly the same way as an unmodified transaction, using transaction optimization algorithms. Parallelism between transaction management and transaction execution is possible [Gr90b]. Two extensions to the *One-Fragment Manager* are necessary for constraint enforcement. The OFM must support the alarm operator, and maintain the differential sets by keeping an administration of inserted and deleted tuple values. Note, that the execution layer of the system (the OFMs) can be fully unaware of the existence of constraints.

4 Expressing constraints in XRA

Transaction modification can be applied to a large class of constraint types. This is demonstrated here by showing how various types of constraints can be expressed in XRA. A few constraint types were already discussed in [Gr90a]; the types presented below extend these ideas to a more complete spectrum. Each constraint type is described in first-order logic, and then expressed in XRA. The actual translation process is not an issue here.

4.1 State constraints

Expressing attribute and tuple state constraints in XRA is straightforward (see [Gr90a, Gr90c]). Below, further constraint types are discussed.

Relation state constraints. An *uniqueness constraint* defines that a combination of values of some attributes $i, j, \cdots, k$ in a tuple must be unique throughout an entire relation R:

$$(\forall x, y \in R \mid x \neq y)(not((x.i = y.i) \land \cdots \land (x.k = y.k)))$$

Having a *unique* operator in XRA that only takes specified attributes into account, the translation is rather simple:

$$alarm(diff(R, unique((i, j, \cdots), R)))$$

Aggregate constraints define a condition on aggregate functions over groups of tuples in a relation (or over the entire relation). In the constraint definition, a relation R is grouped based on the values of an attribute j; a condition c is specified over the results of some **aggregate function** $aggr$ that is computed over the values of attribute i of the tuples per group:

$$(\forall y \in R.j)(c(aggr(\{x.i \mid x \in R \land x.j = y\})))$$

This constraint can be expressed conveniently in XRA using the *groupby* operator. This operator takes as its arguments a list of attributes that define the grouping, a list of aggregate functions, and a relational expression. It results a virtual relation having as attributes both the grouping attributes and aggregated attributes, and consisting of one tuple per group in the operand. So, the constraint above corresponds with the following XRA construct [1]:

$$alarm(select(\neg c(\%2), groupby((j), (aggr(i)), R)))$$

Database state constraints. An important type of database state constraint is the *referential integrity constraint*:

$$(\forall x \in R.i \mid x \neq null)(\exists y \in S.j)(x = y)$$

For this type of constraints, generally two types of violation response actions are considered: the effects of the transaction are simply undone by means of a transaction abort, or "illegal" updates are made "legal" by performing additional compensating updates. The aborting case is discussed in [Gr90a], so we concentrate on the compensating case here. We have to distinguish between the types of updates that violated the constraint: the deletion of key values in the referenced relation, or the insertion of foreign key values in the referencing relation; the transaction modifier for the first case is:

$$temp1 = unique((\%1), select(\%1 \neq null, proj((i), R)))$$
$$temp2 = diff(temp1, proj((j), S))$$
$$delete(R, proj((\%2, \cdots, \%n), join(temp2, \%1 = i, R)))$$

Interrelation aggregate constraints define relations between aggregate functions computed on two relations. The general form is:

$$c(aggr_1(\{x \mid x \in R.i\}), aggr_2(\{x \mid x \in S.j\}))$$

To be able to compare the two aggregate values, they are combined into a virtual relation using a cartesian product.

$$temp1 = groupby((), (aggr_1(i)), R)$$
$$temp2 = groupby((), (aggr_2(j)), S)$$
$$alarm(select(\neg c(\%1, \%2), product(temp1, temp2)))$$

Example. If we require that there are at least as many exams as there are students, we have: $count(exam) \geq count(student)$. This constraint can be enforced using the following XRA construct:

$$temp1 = groupby((), (count()), exam)$$
$$temp2 = groupby((), (count()), student)$$
$$alarm(select(\neg(\%1 \geq \%2), product(temp1, temp2)))$$

---

[1] Anonymous attributes of an intermediate result of operations are identified by their number, e.g. %3.

4.2 Transition constraints

Transition constraints can be handled through transaction modification if some requirements are met. For all types of transition constraints, the pre-transaction state of a relation R should be explicitly available during transaction execution (denoted here as R_{old}). Further, for attribute and tuple transition constraints, the tuples in a relation on which a constraint is defined must be uniquely addressable, i.e. the relation must have a key.

Attribute and tuple transition constraints. For attribute and tuple transition constraints, it is necessary to evaluate a predicate over the old and the new value of one and the same tuple. This is possible by joining the old and the new state of the relation on a (candidate) key of the relation and evaluating the predicate over the result of the join. Note, that this solution to handle transition constraints is not very efficient (though the use of differential sets will keep the join normally small).

Example. Suppose that the grade for an exam may never be increased by more than one:

$$(\forall x \in exam)(x.grade \leq (x_{old}.grade + 1))$$

This constraint can be enforced by the following XRA construct:

$$t = join(exam, exam.studnr = exam_{old}.studnr \land \cdots, exam_{old})$$
$$alarm(select(\%1 > 1, proj((\%8 - \%4), t)))$$

Relation and database transition constraints. Relation and database transition constraints are usually **aggregate constraints**. Provided that the old and new states of the involved relations are available, they can be handled in a manner similar to the way interrelation state constraints are handled.

4.3 Complex constraints

The growing complexity of modern applications can require the handling of complex constraints. Below, one important type of complex constraint is described, the *recursive constraint*. Further, *general user defined constraints* are of great importance; examples can be found in [Gr90c].

Recursive constraints. Untill now, all constraints were specified in (an extension to) first-order logic. It is possible, however, to formulate constraints that go beyond the expressiveness of this formalism. An important example is the recursive constraint. According to the knowledge of the authors, the field of recursive constraints is still unexplored in database research. Therefore, we limit ourselves here to an illustrative example, showing how recursive constraints can be handled, provided that the underlying relational engine provides a recursion operator.

Example. In relation *staff* each employee is recorded; one of the attributes of an employee is his (or her) superior. If we want to express the constraint "nobody can be his own direct or indirect superior", we have a recursive constraint. Using the transitive closure operation of XRA, this constraint can be expressed as follows:

$$temp = closure((\%1, \%2, \%7, \%4), \%1 = \%7, staff)$$
$$alarm(select(empnr = superior, temp))$$

5 Deriving trigger sets

Constraint definitions need to be labeled with triggers to be able to perform constraint filtering at constraint enforcement time. This section describes the generation of trigger sets for constraints specified in first-order logic. In [Ni82] the use of triggers for improving constraint enforcement is discussed. Generation of triggers for constraints specified in a SQL-like syntax is described in [Ce90]. In some approaches, triggers are supplied by the user when defining integrity constraints (e.g. the QBE system [Zl78]). In the technique as proposed in this paper, triggers are generated automically by the system from the constraint definitions.

5.1 Constraint descriptors

Given a constraint definition, a *constraint descriptor* is constructed. This is a pair $I = [t, r]$ in which r is the constraint definition, now called the *rule* of the descriptor, and in which t is the *trigger set*, containing all update types that may violate the constraint.

Example. Given a constraint definition

$$(\forall x \in student.dept)(\exists y \in dept.name)(x = y)$$

we can construct the constraint descriptor $I = [t, r]$ with:

$$t = \{INS(student), DEL(dept)\}$$
$$r = (\forall x \in student.dept)(\exists y \in dept.name)(x = y)$$

The trigger set t indicates, that I has to be enforced whenever an insert (or update) is made to the *student* relation or a delete (or update) is made to the *dept* relation. □

5.2 Generation of triggers

Triggers can be generated in the constraint compilation process as described in the abstract system architecture. For each constraint, a trigger set can be constructed by inspection of the constraint definition, using the following algorithm:

- the process starts with an empty trigger set t;
- every existential quantor over a relation R or over an attribute $R.i$ adds a delete trigger on R to t;
- every universal quantor over a relation R or over an attribute $R.i$ adds an insert trigger on R to t;
- every aggregate function over an attribute $R.i$ adds both a delete and an insert trigger over relation R to t;
- the process ends with the elimination of all duplicates in t.

With respect to triggers generated from aggregate functions, some optimizations are possible by detailed inspection of the aggregate function and the predicate it is used in [Ce90].

6 Conclusions

The transaction modification technique for constraint enforcement satisfies the complete transaction model: it fully complies with transaction atomicity and serializability. Other approaches, like query modification, operate on an operation basis instead of on a transaction basis, and therefore violate transaction atomicity.

Transaction modification can easily be integrated into the normal query processing machinery of a DBMS. This has two important advantages: first, implementation of constraint handling in a DBMS is easy; secondly, all mechanisms for regular query processing apply to constraint handling too, thereby ensuring efficiency and opening ways to parallelism. The proposed technique has a strong expressiveness; new types of constraints, like recursive constraints, can be supported easily. Further, transaction modification allows for a flexible and modular system architecture, leaving room for several optimization techniques.

The transaction modification technique has been implemented in the PRISMA parallel main memory DBMS. The relatively small implementation effort clearly showed the feasability of the approach. PRISMA provides a good platform for the evaluation of the technique, addressing two issues: the usability of the technique for a broad range of constraint types and the performance of the constraint handling subsystem. This evaluation is currently being performed; the first results show that the approach performs well, both in qualitative and quantitative aspects.

References

[Ce90] S. Ceri, J. Widom; *Deriving Production Rules for Constraint Maintenance*; Proc. 16th VLDB Conference; Brisbane, Australia, 1990.

[Gr90a] P.W.P.J. Grefen, P.M.G. Apers; *Parallel Handling of Integrity Constraints on Fragmented Relations*; Proc. International Symposium on Databases in Parallel and Distributed Systems; Dublin, Ireland, 1990.

[Gr90b] P.W.P.J. Grefen, J. Flokstra, P.M.G. Apers; *Parallel Handling of Integrity Constraints*; Proc. Workshop on Parallel Database Systems; Noordwijk, The Netherlands, 1990.

[Gr90c] P.W.P.J. Grefen; *Integrity Constraint Enforcement through Transaction Modification*; Memorandum INF90-60; University of Twente, 1990.

[Ni82] J.M. Nicolas; *Logic for Improving Integrity Checking in Relational Data Bases*; Acta Informatica Vol. 18, 1982.

[Si84] E. Simon, P. Valduriez; *Design and Implementation of an Extendible Integrity Subsystem*; Proc. 1984 SIGMOD Conference; Boston, USA, 1984.

[Si87] E. Simon, P. Valduriez; *Design and Analysis of a Relational Integrity Subsystem*; MCC Technical Report Number DB-015-87; MCC, Austin, USA, 1987.

[St75] M. Stonebraker; *Implementation of Integrity Constraints and Views by Query Modification*; Proc. 1975 SIGMOD Conference; San Jose, USA, 1975.

[Wi89] A.N. Wilschut, P.W.P.J. Grefen, P.M.G. Apers, M.L. Kersten; *Implementing PRISMA/DB in an OOPL*; Proc. 6th International Workshop on Database Machines; Deauville, France, 1989.

[Zl78] M.M. Zloof; *Security and Integrity within the Query-by-Example Database Management Language*; IBM RC 6982; Yorktown Hts., USA, 1978.

Environmental Information Organization

Alan B. Carlson

Dept. of Computer Sciences
Chalmers Univ. of Tech. & Univ. of Göteborg
S-412 96 Göteborg, Sweden

Bengt G. Lundberg

Dept. of Computer and System Sciences
Univ. of Stockholm
Electrum 230 S-164 40 Kista, Sweden

ABSTRACT

The concept of information organization is introduced and discussed from the standpoint of strategic decision-making. Some information organization systems are described and an experimental system intended for organizing text-based informational items obtained from an environmental scanning process is presented and discussed. This system is based on the idea that information items are represented as natural language texts and that these informational items are organized and indexed via assigned associations based on mutual relevance. This system comprises, in part, an automatic indexing method in which informational items are used as indexes to other items allowing the result of retrieval operations to include contextual information. Further, a preliminary explanation model of the system is presented and some topics for research are pointed out.

1. INTRODUCTION

Individuals are often confronted with situations in which they have to construct a mental model from an "amorphous" mass of documents in order to find what may be relevant information. The mass of documents may be considered amorphous even though the documents have been categorized according to some scheme. There may be any number of reasons for this: the categories are of too low resolution to be of any value; they are inapplicable for the information's present use; or the categorization scheme is not at all evident. Decision-makers, especially in strategic decision-making situations, have a limited amount of time in which to construct this model. Executives must be able to quickly evaluate what the information pertains to; otherwise, there is the risk that they may ignore the information and thereby miss valuable insights.

It is important to note that while the contents of each document is important, there exists also a structure among documents [20]. In other words, there is information to be obtained from the particular way in which documents are organized in relation to one another. A structure which exists among or between documents can be exploited in order to organize them into a more structured and thereby more accessible mass.

In this paper we propose and discuss the concept of information organization in the strategic decision-making process in the form of information nets. The proposed information organization form exploits the structure which exists among documents in order to make them more accessible. The paper is organized in the following manner: in section 2 we discuss the use of information in strategic decision-making situations. In section 3, we discuss concepts of information organization. In section 4, we present and discuss an environmental scanning tool. Finally, in section 5, we present some conclusions and point out further research directions.

2. STRATEGIC INFORMATION USE

2.1 Conceptions of Information

There are a number of definitions of the term information (see e.g. [11] for several examples). However, the concept of information which we want to convey here has the following general properties:

— it is the interpretation of data,

— it is meaningful in the sense that it has real or perceived value in current or prospective action or decision [4].

According to this way of seeing information, information is the result of data having been interpreted based on current background knowledge (see figure 1 which is discussed more thoroughly in [12]).

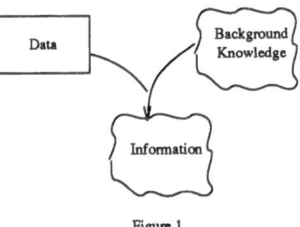

Figure 1

We are assuming that the representation of an information item is some sort of symbol, possibly complex. The symbol, due to insufficient representational facilities can be assigned several possible interpretations depending upon the structural and semantic context in which it is used. In addition, the interpretation assigned to a symbol may be influenced by other information such as explicit and implicit circumstantial information.

Another approach to the concept of information, as signifier and signified is introduced in the field of semiotics (see e.g. [5]). In this conception of information, a sign-vehicle (or roughly data) carries meaning in so far as there is exists a code in which to decipher the meaning and a human being who can apply the code. Information, then, is seen as something inherent in the process of communication.

In database systems, the data provided is assumed to be relatively univocal in that there is a relatively well agreed upon schema by which this data is interpreted into information. The more one progresses towards document systems (i.e. systems which provide data access in the form of free-text) the more ambiguous and equivocal the data becomes.

2.2 Strategic Information

By "strategic" it is usually meant anything which has a potentially large and long-term impact upon an organization [18]. This is usually contrasted with "operational" which has to do with the everyday running of the organization. The term "strategic information", then, refers to information which forms the basis for strategic or long-range decisions in organizations. Strategic information has a number of characteristics which differentiate it from information required for operational decisions Among these characteristics are that strategic information:

— tends to come more from sources outside the organization

— is often in an unstructured or semi-structured form (e.g. free-text format)

— is qualitative

— is judgemental about future events

As a result of these characteristics the information which is gathered, for example in the environmental scanning process, is highly equivocal.

Executives spend much of their time scanning the environment of information pertinent to their organization [6]. This information is used as an early warning system in order for organizations to identify and take action upon possible strategic threats and opportunities. The scanning process encompasses both oral and written material. The written material which is gathered is primarily in free-text form [6]. Much written material can be found in electronic media, e.g. in the form of memos and letters. In addition, so-called information brokers provide large amounts of free-text materials in computer friendly form [6, 9].

An information need in a strategic decision making situation can be related to the concepts of Problem-Oriented Information Need (POIN) and Concrete Information Need (CIN) [7]. A CIN has a well-defined boundary in the sense that it should be quite clear to most people what the question is about and what would constitute an acceptable answer: e.g. "How may items have been sold?" A POIN, has an ill-defined boundary, it will not be clear to all people what the question is about, nor what constitutes an acceptable answer: e.g. "How is the market responding?" A CIN may be satisfied with one document and the information need disappears when the relevant document(s) is/are retrieved. With a POIN, however, all available and relevant documents are probably not sufficient to satisfy the information need and the documents which are retrieved will probably serve to expand the boundary of the information need, possibly triggering a reformulation of the POIN. In a strategic decision making situation, there are both CINs and POINs which have to be met but the strategic scanning process is most like a POIN.

El Sawi [18] has identified two types of strategic scanning information: accommodation information and assimilation information. Accommodation information is information which is not necessarily coupled with a specific threat or opportunity but provides the background for asking relevant questions. One might call it "wisdom-increasing" information in that it alters the "filter" (world view) which executives use to sift out relevant information from irrelevant information. Assimilation information is more specific and relates to identifying specific strategic threats and opportunities. The scanning process, then, is characterized by "second-order learning" whereby accommodation information may change the frame of reference through which an executive interprets information.

3. CONCEPTS OF INFORMATION ORGANIZATION

3.1 Introduction to Information Organization

Figure 2 illustrates the most simple case of what we refer to as an information organization process. A stream of information items, or chunks of information, flows in to an individual. The individual then organizes these information items into a mental structure (an information organization) via some sort of categorization scheme. The resulting structure, including possible abstractions, forms a part of the individual's mental model of the phenomena covered in the stream of information items.

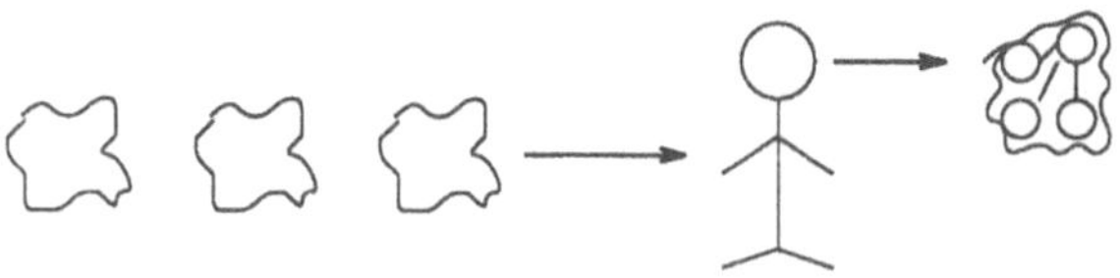

Figure 2

Information organization entails relating informational items, e.g. documents or pictures, with one another in order to generate a "context" out of these items. This context may be some sort of structure like a semantic net. One consequence of generating the context may be that two documents which previously were considered irrelevant are considered relevant when observed together. Another possible consequence is that new information may be generated (i.e. new associations come to light). Finally, because it is viewed in a context, information may be more readily located due to being anchored to other information items on the same theme.

In a sense, information organization is a generalization (albeit of only certain aspects) of database, information retrieval and hypertext techniques. These techniques deal with the classification, indexing, storage, retrieval, and presentation of informational items. The different functions may be evident to a greater or lesser degree in these systems and the functions may be automated to a greater or lesser degree in different systems.

In the next section, we intend to discuss the above mentioned techniques with respect to information organization. We do this with the hope of clarifying the concept of information organization not to generate any new insights into these techniques.

3.2 Examples of Information Organization Systems

In a traditional database system, such as a relational database system, an informational item is often called an entity or relationship and represents an abstract or concrete entity in the real world [8]. An entity is composed of an aggregate of properties, and these entities may be associated with one another via a relationship. An informational item is classified via a system of strong typing in that the conceptual schema of a database insures that an information item unequivocally belongs to a class of entities, or in the case of a relationship, a class of relationships. Thus, there is, via the conceptual schema, a relatively unambiguous interpretation of every symbol in the information organization structure. The indexing of an information item is achieved in its most simple form by relating it to a particular set of items (i.e. an entity belongs to an entity type). Entities may also be indexed by

370

properties. Sets of objects are indexed to one another via relationships. Thus, the retrieval of information items is achieved via finding a set of items which meet very precise retrieval requirements.

In an information retrieval system, the basic informational item is a document or perhaps an abstract of a document. The document may vary in size, being anywhere from a few words to several million. An informational item is usually classified by subject, i.e. by a number of keywords designating what the document is about. These keywords are often picked by the author(s) of the document. The indexing of an informational item may be achieved in basically two ways. In the first case, the subject keywords serve, as a primitive indexing mechanism. The second way an informational item may be indexed is via certain words from the document or abstract. This latter means of indexing may also be the basis for storing certain documents closer to one another, i.e. document clustering [16]. The presentation of an informational item is similar to that of database systems. The result of a query is usually a set of documents which more or less meet the information need specified in the query.

In hypertext systems the basic informational item is a chunk of free-text. This informational item differs from information retrieval items in the sense that the former constitutes a formal document with an author, title, publication date, etc. while the latter is often a piece of informal text. There are a wide variety of classification schemes, from simple visual means, i.e. the items may have several different type of icons which represent different types of text documents, to system-supported node types (e.g. gIBIS has three types Issue, Position and Argument [3]). There exist a plethora of indexing schemes based on the concept of association links. In hypercard systems, links between informational items are differentiated by the shape of the buttons. In a system like gIBIS, there are nine different link types, such as Responds-to, Refers-to and Objects-to. Retrieval in hypertext systems vary (some systems are hybrids of relational databases and hypertext systems), but it is in principle characterized by being more oriented towards content rather than form, to selection by natural language as opposed to set-level manipulation, and biased towards exploration/browsing rather than the precise satisfaction of information wants [21].

In summary, information organization involves the building of a semantic structure, i.e. organizing informational items into a structure which is meaningful for an individual. We have discussed various techniques for organizing informational items, hypertext, information retrieval and database techniques, all of which should be seen as restricted cases of information organization.

4. INFORMATION SUPPORT

4.1 Overview of an Information Organization System for Environmental Scanning

Based on the idea of semantic networks [15] and associative networks [1], an experimental tool has been developed in order to study potential principles for the organization of strategic decision information. The system is assumed to receive short news items which are automatically organized in a network in which the arcs denote that two items represent information about the same topic, at least approximately (see figure 3). Further, as shown in figure 3, a filter function has been implemented which selects news items based on a user-profile. When a set of items have been organized into a network, an information net, the user can edit the network by introducing new informational items and arcs, or deleting existing arcs. In addition, a user can search the network for items being similar to an expression representing an

information need.

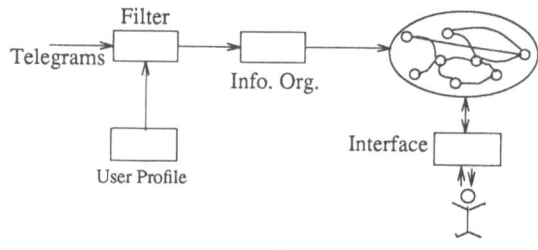

Figure 3

The news items represent some information in the form of an ordinary text and thus the similarity between two items is calculated as their textual similarity and is considered to represent the degree of mutual relevance of the two items. Other functions that have been implemented in the tool are functions for navigation in the network and zooming. The synthesized network is displayed on the screen of a personal computer with a user-defined focal item in the middle, surrounded by its neighbors (i.e. the most similar items) and further away along the radius the neighbor's neighbors, thus making the indirect association visible between items even though they may not be textually similar.

The aim assigned to the use of the tool is to simulate the information acquisition and information organization process that takes place when performing environmental scanning and a huge set of items are received which are believed to be more or less relevant to the task at hand. The system thus produces an organization of informational items which can be considered as a preparatory clustering of items to be presented to a decision maker. The set of informational items that are assumed to be relevant to a task is considered to be (at least in practice) infinite, which is the basic assumption made in the system.

The set of information items (roughly, pieces of information) that can be considered relevant to a task is assumed to be infinite. The property of being infinite derives from the assumption that a real world phenomenon can be described from an infinite set of aspects and thus, in principle, will be represented by an infinite set of informational items. Thus, it follows that a constructed information net will also be infinite (at least practically) which has to be considered when processing the net, such as when searching the net for specified items.

The assumption that the net is infinite implies in particular that not every relevant item can be assumed to be found, i.e. on has to use some sort of heuristics giving sub-optimal satisficing results when searching the net. The same applies when a new item is received and the similar items should be found and linked to the new item. In that case one has to assume that some of the similar items are not found and thus some of the relevant associations cannot be established. These properties of the search and insertion processes corresponds to the human search processes that are performed when searching for some information manually. The search process is assumed to be performed opportunistically in the sense that the search focuses in the most promising direction. In the system this corresponds to an heuristic search process which uses an opportunistic heuristic rule with a net-pruning criterion.

An important facility of the environmental scanning tool is the set of functions for manual navigating in the information net and the related redisplay of parts of the net. Assuming that a part of the net is displayed the user can click with the mouse at an item on the screen thus making the item the focal point of the redisplayed net. The focal item is then displayed together with its neighbors and the neighbor's neighbors, etc. The navigation in a net can be interpreted as a redefinition of an information need as the informational items are browsed and thus the neighboring items of the focal item can be considered to correspond to the retrieved items in a retrieval process.

The simultaneous display of related informational items supplies the user with potentially indirectly relevant information (or, circumstantial information). Assume the items A, B, and C, and that A is considered (syntactically) similar to B and that B is considered similar to C. Then, C is potentially relevant to A though not necessarily having a textual similarity with A, i.e. B constitutes a connecting item. A basic property of the environmental scanning tool is the similarity calculation that is performed in order to decide whether two items are relevant to each other. That two items are mutually relevant when they are syntactically similar is based on the cluster hypothesis in information retrieval. The cluster hypothesis states that associations between items, such as similarity measures, convey information about the joint relevance of items to information wants [17]. In our system that assumption is effectuated by the linking of found similar items and which are simultaneously shown to a user. This is described in the next section.

4.2 Information Net Generation

When a human-being receives informational items the corresponding information items are incorporated into an existing knowledge structure. It is assumed here that the knowledge structure can be simulated by a network in which informational items are the nodes and the links represent associations of mutual relevance. In what follows we will describe the information net generation procedure of the information organization tool in the case that the informational items are natural language representations of information. The objective of the net generation procedure is thus to organize informational items into a network such that the assumed corresponding mental process of a human being is simulated. When an informational item is received an existing net is searched in order to find items which are relevant to the received item (i.e. they concern the same topic). This search process is assumed to be restricted according to the principle of bounded rationality [13, 19] and to be directed in the search space (i.e. the information net) according to the heuristics "most promising direction".

The net generation procedure that is informally presented above is based on the concept of mutual relevance between informational items. In our context we consider informational items to be mutually relevant if they represent information on the same topic. Further, two items are considered to represent information on the same topic if they are similar, i.e. they include approximately the same set of words. This corresponds to the cluster hypothesis in information retrieval which states that similar documents (items) are jointly relevant to a query [17].

In the information organization tool the terms characterizing an informational item are derived as follows:

— common words are ignored, such as "the", "and", "to"

— the first five characters of a word are used as a characterizing term

Given the sets of terms of two items X and Y the similarity of the items is computed as follows:

$$\mathrm{SIM}(X,Y) = \frac{|X \cap Y|}{|X| + |Y| - |X \cap Y|}$$

i.e. the Jaccard coefficient [17].

Two items are considered mutually relevant when their similarity value exceeds an experimentally determined value (in our experiments about 10%, depending on the used texts).

When informational items are received by the system an information net is assumed to exist. Initially the net is constituted by a single node ROOT. When the system tries to incorporate a new item it searches the net for relevant items and if such items cannot be found the new item is by default linked to the ROOT node and thus a new branch of the net is constructed.

The search procedure that looks for relevant items in a net is based on a standard graph-search procedure as presented in [14]. The graph-search procedure uses two values, namely a pruning value and a link value (or, relevance threshold value). The pruning value is used to restrict the exploration of a net in the directions that do not seem promising and the link value is used as a threshold for linking a new item to the found items (normally the link value used will be greater than the prune value).

The graph-search procedure that is used is as follows:

1. Create two empty lists OPEN and CLOSED

2. Denote the new item A and select a start item R (normally the ROOT node). Insert R in OPEN.

3. If OPEN is empty then goto 6.

4. Select from OPEN the item that is most similar to the item A, denote it S. Move S from OPEN to CLOSED. Find the items that are relevant to S and insert them into OPEN if:

   — they do not exist in OPEN or in CLOSED

   — their similarity value is greater than the prune value

5. Goto 3.

6. Link item A to those items in CLOSED that are more similar than the link value.

7. Stop.

In the procedure above the similarity value between the item A and the new item constitute the heuristic function in the algorithm. With that heuristic function we cannot assume that the algorithm will stop in an infinite net (or, in a very large net it will not stop in reasonable time), i.e. the algorithm is practically unbound. In order to get a bounded algorithm one has to include a criterion of resource restriction, such as:

3. If the resources are exhausted then goto 6.

The resource restriction may concern elapsed time or number of found relevant items.

4.3 Information Net Restructuring

The information net generated can be improved from a number of standpoints. One of the preliminary findings of interaction with the experimental system is that clusters (highly dense portions of the network) are seen to grow during the interaction sessions. These clusters seem to roughly

372

correspond to "concepts" in the real world, i.e.. to abstract notions. However, since the network is composed of instances of informational items, the system is uninformed as to the existence of these "concept clusters": these are first discovered and interpreted by an information organizer during the browsing process. In addition, because the network grows in size at an alarming rate and there is a general lack of abstraction mechanisms (many items which are very similar to one another are presented together instead of, for example, displaying one "typical informational item"). Because of this, the system may be construed as increasing rather than reducing information overload in certain cases.

Similar problems have been encountered in hypertext and hypermedia systems as well as in traditional information retrieval systems [2, 16]. The usual solution is to further organize the network by implementing an hierarchical structure upon the network. We believe there are two reasons for not choosing this solution. Firstly, the organization mechanism employed in the system uses an "heuristic, opportunistic similarity algorithm" (similar to a heuristic clustering process) [16] in which an new informational item is inserted into the network as soon as a "satisfactory position" is found in the net as opposed to comparing an incoming item with all other items in the network and finding an optimal position. This heuristic algorithm imitates the way in which a human organizes information. Hierarchic clustering methods, in contrast, work best when the organizing method is optimal. A second reason for not implementing a hierarchy is that a hierarchic "information model" is not often the most natural way of organizing information and should not be forced upon an information organizer [10].

The direction which we are taking is to find and characterize portions of the network which are highly dense regions and represent these by abstract informational items (this can be performed mechanically or manually, or perhaps by a combination of these approaches although the method which we are exploring is totally automatic). A second network structure is being implemented above the instance level structure of the base system. This second level network will be used to categorize and represent particularly dense regions of the instance level (clusters) in order to deal with the problem of information overload which occurs when the instance level becomes too voluminous. A node in the second level network will, then, represent a cluster of document instances on the base level (see figure 4).

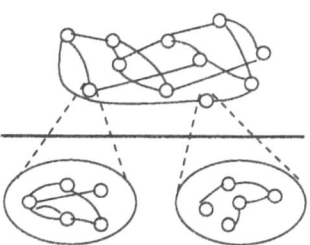

Figure 4

Another extension which is being explored is the use of labeled links. The system provides a means of manually labeling arcs between nodes. These labeled nodes help the user to augment the information net, providing a means of improving the cognitive effectiveness of the representation. However, the system itself is totally uninformed about the existence of labeled arcs and has no method of exploiting this

semantic information either in the search process or when a new informational item is to be inserted into the net.

One possible direction is the implementation of argument-based links, e.g. of the type "supports" and "contradicts". The establishment of these types of links, which the system would be informed of, would serve as a means of discriminating background information to the focal item. This will serve primarily to assist the manual browsing process by giving the user richer criteria in which to judge the most promising direction in which to continue browsing, e.g. by making use of a list of antonyms.

5. CONCLUSIONS

From the starting point of a discussion on the use of information in strategic decision-making, the concept of information organization has been introduced. Some common information organization systems have been described and an experimental system intended for environmental scanning has been discussed and presented from the standpoint of information organization. This system is based on the idea that information items are represented as natural language texts and that these informational items are organized and indexed via assigned associations based on mutual relevance which is determined form the textual similarity of informational items. This system thus comprises, in part, an automatic indexing method in which informational items are used as indexes to other items allowing the result of retrieval operations to include contextual information. Further, some possible and promising extensions to the system have been proposed and discussed.

References

[1]   Vannevar Bush, "As We May Think", *Atlantic Monthly*, July 1945.

[2]   Jeff Conklin, "Hypertext: An Introduction and Survey", *Computer*, September 1987.

[3]   Jeff Conklin and M. Begeman, "gIBIS: A Hypertext Tool for Exploratory Policy Discussion", *ACM Transactions on Office Information Systems*, Vol. 6 no. 4 (October 1988).

[4]   Gordon B. Davis and Margrethe H. Olson, *Management Information Systems*, MacGraw-Hill (1984).

[5]   Umberto Eco, *A Theory of Semiotics*, Indiana University Press (1976).

[6]   Martha S. Feldman and James G. March, "Information in Organizations as Signal and Symbol", *Administrative Science Quarterly*, Vol. 26 (1981).

[7]   Valery I. Frants and Craig B. Brush, "The Need for Information and Some Aspects of Information Retrieval System Construction", *Journal of the American Society for Information Science*, Vol. 39 no. 2 (1988).

[8]   J. Griethuysen (ed.), *Concepts and Terminology for the Conceptual Schema and the Information Base*, ISO (1982).

[9]   P. G. Huber, "The Nature and Design of Post-Industrial Organizations", *Management Science*, Vol. 30 no. 8 (1984).

[10]   William Kent, *Data and Reality*, Elsevier Science Publishers B.V. (1978).

[11]   Jonathan Liebenau and James Backhouse, *Understanding Information*, MacMillan (1990).

[12]   Bengt G. Lundberg, "An Environmental Scanning and Information Organization System", Department of Computer and Computer Sciences, University of Stockholm, 1990, Internal Report.

[13]   James G. March, "Bounded Rationality, Ambiguity, and the Engineering of Choice", *Bell Journal of Economics*, Vol. 9 (1978).

[14]   Nils J. Nilsson, *Principles of Artificial Intelligence*, Springer-Verlag (1982).

[15]   M. Ross Quillian, "Semantic Memory" in *Semantic Information Processing*, ed. Marvin Minsky, The MIT Press (1968).

[16]   G. Salton and M. McGill, *Introduction to Modern Information Retrieval*, McGraw-Hill (1983).

[17]   G. Salton, *Automatic Text Processing*, Addison-Wesley (1989).

[18]   Omar A. El Sawi, "Personal Information Systems for Strategic Scanning in Turbulent Environments: Can the CEO Go On-Line?", *MIS Quarterly*, March 1985.

[19]   H. A. Simon, *The Sciences of the Artificial*, The MIT Press (1984).

[20]   Don R. Swanson, "Historical Note: Information Retrieval and the Future of an Illusion", *Journal of the American Society for Information Science*, Vol. 39 no. 2 (1988).

[21]   Nigel Woodhead, *Hypertext & Hypermedia*, Addison-Wesley (1991).

Making C++ Object Persistent
by Using a Standard Relational Database System

Paul Andlinger *)   Christian Gierlinger **)   Gerald Quirchmayr *)

*) Johannes Kepler University Linz, Institut für Informatik, Altenbergerstr. 69, A-4040 Linz Austria
**) Johannes Kepler University Linz, FAW Forschungsinstitut für Anwendungsorientierte Wissens-
verarbeitung Institut für Informatik, Altenbergerstr. 69, A-4040 Linz Austria

Abstract

This paper describes an approach for making objects created in C++ persistent by linking C++ to a relational database system. In a first step the necessary concepts and the underlying data model are introduced. In a second step we give an overview of the API and its use in C++. To support the decomposition of complex data types into flat relations we introduce a precompiler. For the implementation of the prototype we choose the relational DBMS Oracle. In order to make the system portable to other relational DBMS we have made it as transparent as possible. Finally we give an example to demonstrate the prototypes functionality and compare the results of our approach with the demands stated in the OODB manifesto [2].

1. Introduction

One major project of our institute currently is the implementation of the "Behavior-Entity-Relationship-Model" (so called BIER-Model) which is described in [3], [4], [6], [7]. The implemented system will be a CASE-Tool for information systems design. It is characterized by the following concepts:

- the underlying data model is the E-R model which is extended by the concepts of surrogates and time dimension;
- the dynamic feature of the universe of discourse can be decomposed into elementary and complex processes;
- the dynamic component of the model is described by a Petri net based graphical representation [9]

We have implemented our model in C++ and we have come across the problem of making the instances persistent in the application programs.

The solution of this problem is in the following chapters. We introduce a general framework for making objects created with an object-oriented programming language persistent in a database. From the database point of view, persistency never was a problem, but from the programming language point of view it is a novelty [1], [2]. The object-oriented programming language we used is C++ [10], [11] and the relational database system is ORACLE.

The C++ application programmer is provided with four basic methods. The name and the function correspond to the respective statement for embedded SQL, namely INSERT, FETCH, DELETE and SELECT. With these methods the programmer is enabled to insert, delete and select objects from the database. Furthermore it is possible to fetch the selected objects, to manipulate and to restore them.

2. The Application Program Interface (API)

The user who wants to store the contents of his C++ objects in the relational database is provided with four basic methods whose denomination and functionality correspond to the respective statements of embedded SQL: INSERT, FETCH, DELETE, SELECT.

For the reason of portability to another RDBMS all access functions to the database are contained in a single class, called OBJORACLE. In the existing system these functions are realized via the Oracle Call Interface [8]. Moreover this class contains the structures and variables which are required for establishing and maintaining the connection to the DBMS (Logon Data Area, Communication Data Area).

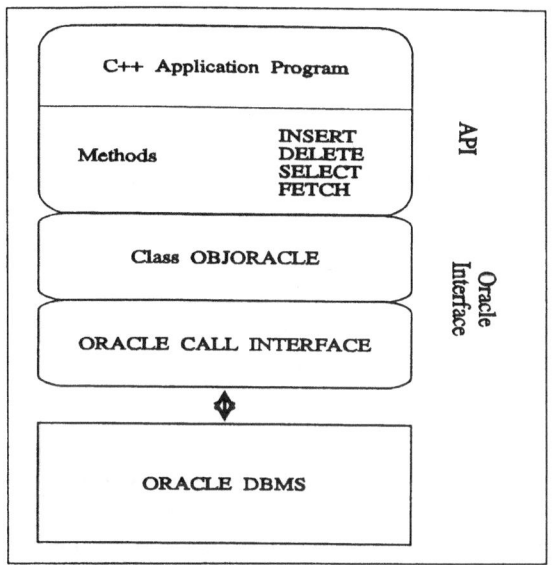

FIGURE 1: Scheme of our system

The interface functions INSERT, FETCH and DELETE must be present in each class-declaration as public methods, whereas SELECT is a method of the general class OBJORACLE. This is due to the fact that for an operation like FETCH, INSERT or DELETE there has to exist the corresponding instance of the class, but on the contrary it must be allowed to perform a SELECT on a set of stored instances of a class with the intention to create the retrieved objects afterwards. The first three functions manage the saving, loading and deleting of the proper object instances, a feature which becomes most important in the case of object inheritance.

For each access to stored objects (SELECT, FETCH, DELETE), respectively for inserting an object into the database (INSERT) at least one instance of the general class OBJORACLE must exist.

The arguments of the SELECT function are the name of the interesting class and the where-clause which specifies the condition for the objects being selected. This clause is equivalent to the where-clause of SQL and therefore it supports all the constructs allowed by the SQL implementation of the underlying RDBMS. The return value is an integer which holds the number of found objects in the database.

The definition of these methods is structurally equivalent for all classes. Each method only has to know whether the class it belongs to is a basic class (not inherited from another class) or a derived one. In case of the latter, the call of the same method of the corresponding 'upper' class has to be included in the method's definition.

Return-value	Functionname	Parameters	Lines of code
void	INSERT	pointer to class OBJORACLE	6
void	DELETE	pointer to class OBJORACLE	4
void	FETCH	pointer to class OBJORACLE	4
No. of Selected Objects	SELECT	Classname, WhereClause	

FIGURE 2: The functions of the API

The transfer of values of the instance variables from and to the database is done via their addresses. Therefore a method, which is called 'setaddresses' must be provided for storing the addresses of all instance variables in the so called datapointer-array. Additionally, the datapointer-array holds the name and the datatype of the instance variable. The last method required in each class definition is the initialization function, which is used for storing the number of instance variables and the name of the corresponding relation in special instance variables. Additionally this method handles the logon to the DBMS. Therefore it makes sense to add a call of this method to each constructor of the class. It is quite obvious that the methods 'initialization' and 'setaddresses' should be declared as private member functions.

376

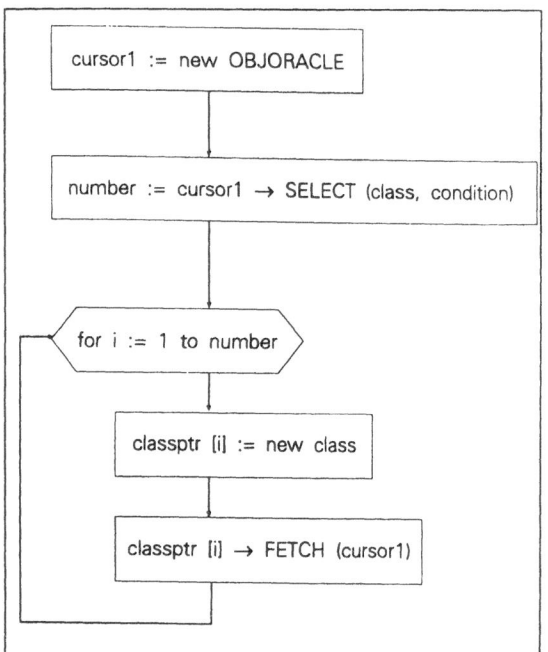

FIGURE 3: shows the typical flow of control for selecting and fetching objects.

A useful feature is that it is possible to handle more than one 'object set' (created by Select) at a time, which opens the way towards parallelism. The only thing to do is to create an own instance of OBJORACLE for each SELECT and to refer to it with the parameters of the method FETCH.

3. The Underlying Relational Data Model

As mentioned in one of the earlier chapters, we have used a standard RDBMS to store the objects of C++ classes into the database. Therefore we have had to take care of transforming the class definitions into a data model consisting of flat relations only. This is trivial for simple classes containing only attributes with standard basic datatypes. It is more interesting if there are some more complex, usually user-defined datatypes which are composed of basic ones. The definition of such a variable has to be analyzed and decomposed to atomic attributes of the relation. But how can hierarchies of objects caused by inheritance be transformed to relations? It is quite obvious that it is no acceptable solution to create a relation for each class in which each attribute corresponds to one variable (including the inherited variables) of the class. With such a design the generalization (an important feature of object-oriented modelling) cannot be correctly expressed in the database, because information of the general class would have to be stored several times in each of its subclasses which entails the problems of inconsistency an redundancy of data.

The approach chosen in this paper also requires a relation for each class declaration. But the difference to the proceeding above described is manifested in the attributes the classes consist of. Now the relations are built only with the attributes of the corresponding class definition and the inherited attributes are not in this class definition, however. This means, that if the class, is an inherited class the matching relation contains only the instance variables (of course transformed to atomic attributes) which are newly introduced in the definition of this class. Therefore it is necessary, to establish a reference to the relation of the basic class. This can easily be done by inserting a surrogate (an additional key attribute) into every relation which can then be referenced in the subclass' relations by an attribute called 'foreign key'. The addition of these two attributes enables the representation of inheritance hierarchies in the data model.

3.1. About Object Identity

It has to be considered that many objects of the same class and with the same values of their instance variables do often exist simultaneously. We could for example take a traffic simulation problem in which many motor-cars (the objects) - which need not be further distinguished - drive from the same source to the same destination at the same time. Then it makes no sense to store them one by one in the relations of the database, since they anyway can be distinguished by their surrogate key attribute alone.

That is why we have added an additional attribute to each relation, the so called count-attribute. This integer holds the number of identical objects.

3.2. Generalization, Inheritance and Weak Entities

Another aspect the data model has to cope with, lies in the semantics which is implied by generalization respectively by inheritance. So we must distinguish between basic classes holding instances of real entities and basic classes which are modelled as a generalization of several subclasses and therefore represent only weak entities, which cannot exist without entities of the corresponding subclasses. This matter of fact can be illustrated best by two small examples.

a) Let's assume that an enterprise company is interested in holding informations about its business partners. Having object-oriented design in mind, we define the following class
partners (with attributes like name, address, phone number, ...)
with two subclasses
suppliers (terms of payment, outstanding debts, ...)
customers (ordered articles, customer number, ...).
In this restricted commercially-oriented view, a partner entity lacking the information of being a supplier or a customer does not have any meaning at all and therefore it should not be allowed to exist stand alone.

b) Assume a data model for an extremely simple CAD system in which only two different symbols are allowed: a rectangle and a rectangle with crosshairs inside. Two classes are defined:
rectangle (location, dimension, color, ...) and the subclass
rectangle-with-cross (colour of cross, thickness of cross, ...)
In this example a rectangle can be seen in two ways, as a concrete entity (drawn on the screen) and as a generalization of a rectangle-with-cross.

Having in mind the last example, let us now try to store only one object (a rectangle-with-cross) in the two relations which would have been created by our data model. There would be one record in the relation *rectangle* and one in the relation *rectangle-with-cross* of which the attribute *foreign key* refers to the *surrogate key attribute* of the first relation. Then it cannot be decided whether there exist two objects (i.e. a rectangle and a rectangle with crosshairs having the same locations and dimensions) or if there exists only a rectangle with crosshairs, as intended.

So it becomes evident, that our data model has to store additional information about an entity to distinguish whether it is a weak entity only (and therefore requires at least one corresponding entity of a subclass) or a concrete instance of the class.

The count-attribute, introduced for storing multiple identical objects, offers the straight forward way to handle this information. It only has to be set to zero for weak entities and to one for concrete objects. If an identical object does already exist the count-attribute must be increased by one.

3.3. Inserting and Selecting Instances

To insert an object into the database, the instance variables of the class declarations have to be stored in the corresponding relations, beginning with the basic class up to the different subclasses (in the case of inheritance). Thereby the key of the nth subclass becomes the foreign key of the $(n+1)^{th}$ subclass.
For selecting objects from the database we have to perform a join over all concerned relations, where again the foreign key of each relation must be equal to the key of the relation next in rank. For avoiding the selection of weak entities the count-attribute of the 'lowest' relation must be zero. It is convenient to create a view for each relation corresponding to a class in which the join and the comparison of the count-attribute are performed implicitly.

4. The Precompiler

Due to the structural equivalence of the methods FETCH, INSERT, DELETE in all classes we decided to develop a precompiler for doing the 'dirty work' of inserting those member functions. The input to the precompiler is the original C++ program, but of course the header file containing the declarations of the classes is enough (and the preferred method). This file is parsed for the class informations and the precompiler builds an internal tree of classes. The precompiler output consists of the C++ input file completed with the definition of the five specific member functions. The only problem of this operation lies in the method 'setaddresses' which has to transform not only simple data types (integer, character ...) but also user defined data types (e.g. structures) into atomic attributes of a flat relation. (This problem would not occur if we had used a structured object-oriented data model but this would contradict a aim goal of the project general usability.) A similar difficulty can be seen in the extensive use of pointers and cascades of pointers by some programmers. It

378

obviously makes no sense to store pointers in the database, so in fact you have to know the 'hidden semantics' behind a pointer. Therefore the current implementation of our precompiler supports only the standard datatypes, as there are: integer, double, character, string (array of characters) and simple arrays. The decomposition of other abstract datatypes has to be done by the programmer after the precompile step.

The second task the precompiler can fulfill is the creation of the relations and views corresponding to the class declarations. In this connection the precompiler must only distinguish between basic classes and classes which inherit other classes, because the former have no foreign key attribute.

With the support of the precompiler it is possible to compose an environment, so that the objects of every class (provided the programmer did not create 'complex' user defined data types) can be made persistent without doing something else than starting the precompiler.

5. Example of a Class Declaration

The following example will try to illustrate the described model. In the first part you can see a section of a C++ class declaration and in the second passage we give the corresponding data model.

```
class BASIS {
    private:
        int a1;
        char a2[30];
}
class SUB1: public BASIS {
    private:
        int a1[3];
        int a3;
}
class SUB2: public BASIS {
    private:
        char a4[15];
}
class SUB11: public SUB1 {
    private:
        double a5;
}
```

FIGURE 4: C++ class declaration

The corresponding relational schema which has to be built by the precompiler is as follows:

BASIS	a1	a2	key	count
	num(5)	char(30)	num(5)	num(5)

SUB1	a1$0	a1$1	a1$2	a3	key	fkey	count
	num(5)	num(5)	num(5)	num(5)	num(5)	num(5)	num(5)

SUB2	a4	key	fkey	count
	char(15)	num(5)	num(5)	num(5)

SUB11	a5	key	fkey	count
	num(10)	num(5)	num(5)	num(5)

FIGURE 5: The relational scheme of the C++ class declaration of figure 4

The "select" statement, which retrieves the objects of a class by a specified condition, works upon the views created by the precompiler. For the above example the following views would have been created:

```
create view BASIS_VIEW (basis_a1,
    basis_a2, count) as
    select a1, a2, count
    from basis
    where count > 0;
create view SUB1_VIEW (basis_a1, basis_a2,
    sub1_a1$0, sub1_a1$1, sub1_a1$2,
    sub1_a3, count) as
    select basis.a1, basis.a2, sub1.a1$0,
    sub1.a1$1, sub1.a1$2, sub1.a3,
    sub1.count
    from basis, sub1
    where sub1.fkey = basis.key and
    sub1.count > 0;
create view SUB2_VIEW (basis_a1, basis_a2,
    sub2_a4, count) as
    select basis.a1, basis.a2, sub2.a4,
    sub2.count
    from basis, sub2
    where sub2.fkey = basis.key and
    sub2.count > 0;
create view SUB11_VIEW (basis_a1,
    basis_a2, sub1_a1$0, sub1_a1$1,
    sub1_a1$2, sub1_a3, sub11_a5, count) as
    select basis.a1, basis.a2, sub1.a1$0,
    sub1.a1$1, sub1.a1$2, sub1.a3, sub11.a5,
    sub11.count
    from basis, sub1, sub11
    where sub11.fkey = sub1.key and
    sub1.fkey = basis.key and sub11.count >
    0;
```

6. Comparison With the Object-Oriented Manifesto [2]

An object-oriented database always consists of a database and an object-oriented data model [5]. In our case the database is ORACLE and the data model we implemented in C++.

Let us discuss now whether our approach can be qualified as an object-oriented data model or not. We compare our model with the main features and characteristics that a system must have to be classified as an object-oriented database according to [2]. Our system partially satisfies rule 1 (complex objects), rule 2 (object identity), rule 3 (encapsulation), rule 4 (type and classes), rule 5 (class or type hierarchies), rule 6 (overriding, overloading and late binding), rule 7 (computational completeness) and rule 9 (persistence). It has to be noted that our first prototype does not get satisfy rule 8 (extensibility), rule 10 (secondary storage management), rule 11 (concurrency) and rule 12 (recovery). Therefore DBMS has to take care of the last three rules. That is why our system cannot be qualified as a full object-oriented database system. So we have avoided the denomination "object-oriented database" in the title of our paper for reasons of honesty.

7. Conclusion

We have been trying to introduce a general method for making C++ objects persistent by using a standard relational database system. We have shown the user interface, the ORACLE interface and the developed precompiler. We have sketched the problem whether our system is full object-oriented. Until now we have not solved the problem of concurrency. It also will be necessary to integrate a recovery mechanism into our prototype. In contrast to C++ multiple inheritance is not yet supported. These issues are the scope of current research work and will be discussed in forthcoming papers.

References

[1] M. Atkinson, P. J. Bayley, K. Chilsom, W. Cockshott, R. Morrison, An approach to persistent programming, Computer Journal 26(4), pp 360-265, 1983.

[2] M. Atkinson, F. Bancilhon, D. DeWitt, K. Dittrich, D. Maier, S. Zdonik, The object-oriented database system manifesto (a political pamphlet), Proc. DOOD 89, Kyoto, Japan, December 1989.

[3] J. Eder, G. Kappel, A Min Tjoa, R.R. Wagner, BIER - The Behavior Integrated Entity Relationship Approach, Proc. 5th, Int. Conference on ER-Approach, Dijon, 1986.

[4] J. Eder, G. Kappel, A Min Tjoa, R.R. Wagner, A Behavior Design Methodology for Information Systems, Proc. IEEE 6th, Int. Conference on Computers and Communications, Phoenix, 1987.

[5] K. R. Dittrich, Object-oriented database systems: the next miles of the marathon, Information Systems, Vol. 15, No. 1, pp. 161-167, 1990.

[6] Ch. Gierlinger, K. Reisinger, A M. Toja, R. R. Wagner: Update-Dependencies in Dynamic Data Models for Office Information Systems, International Conference on Organizations and Information Systems, Yugoslavia, Bled, Conf. Proc., 1989.

[7] Ch. Gierlinger, F. Kastner, R. R. Wagner, BIER '90, The Behavior Integrated Entity Relationship Model '90, in print in Bibliotheka Informatyki Szkol Wyzszych, Pub. M. Bazewicza, Wroclaw, Polen, 1990.

[8] Oracle Corporation, Pro*C User's Guide, Belmont CA, 1987.

[9] J. L. Peterson: Petri Net Theory and the Modelling of Systems, Prentice Hall, 1981.

[10] B. Stroustrup, The C++ Programming Language, Addison-Wesley 1986.

[11] R. S. Wiener, L. J. Pinson, An Introduction to Object-Oriented Programming and C++, Addison-Wesley, 1988.

Relational Database Organization Based on Views and Fragments

Günther Pernul*   Kamalakar Karlapalem   Shamkant B. Navathe

College Of Computing
Georgia Institute Of Technology
Atlanta GA30332
e-mail: kamal@cc.gatech.edu

Abstract

Traditionally data is organized at the logical level in relational databases on the basis of its semantics. But there are more abstractions of the real world to be represented. A part of this missing semantics is that of views. We include views as an integral part of the data model. After defining views on a relational scheme, we present a methodology to decompose the relations of this scheme into a set of disjoint fragments. One or more fragments represent a view. Then these fragments and *not the relations* of the relational scheme are materialized. We further develop a scheme for maintaining the consistency of a database made up of fragments (which include attributes of the left or right side of a split functional dependencies) of a non-3NF relation by introducing the concept of update clusters and virtual attributes. The methodology results in a database design where the database operations access less amount of irrelevant data in comparison to the design where the base relations are materialized. We briefly discuss the applicability of this methodology in designing databases based on centralized, distributed, parallel database environments and for secure database systems.

1 Introduction

The goal of this paper is to develop a new way of organizing a database by using the access patterns of users defined by the views on the database. We regard a relational global database scheme as consisting of a set of relational schemes, a set of interrelational dependencies and a set of views. Interrelational dependencies are used to express referential integrity and are described by inclusion dependencies. A view defines the part of the database that is being accessed by one or more users. It is possible that different views may overlap, that is, they access the same part of the database. This gives rise to a relationship between the views. The data of the database is organized as a set of disjoint fragments (relations) based on the

---
*The work of Gunther Pernul is supported by the Austrian Science Foundation under the contract J0461-PHY

views defined on the database. There are *no physically materialized base relations*. The design methodology derives this set of fragments by extracting the relationships between the views. Therefore, a view is represented by one or more fragments. The relationships between views and fragments are stored in *catalog relations*.

A view is a more general concept than a transaction, because a view can encompass a set of transactions accessing a part of the database. Moreover, at the initial stages of the design, the user and the designer may not know enough (about the applications accessing the database) to list *a priori* all the transactions. Note that a view can be easily described by the users of the database to the designer than a specific set of future transactions during the initial database design stage.

We shall define some concepts and give an overview of our design process in the next section. Section 3 describes a mixed decomposition methodology for decomposing the global scheme according to the predefined views into a set of disjoint fragments. In order to avoid known processing anomalies we normalize these fragments after mixed decomposition (Section 4.). We describe the catalog relations to support the mixed decomposition in Section 5. Section 6 presents some application areas where this methodology for designing databases can be applied. Finally we present some conclusions in Section 7.

2 Overview of the Design Process

The universe of discourse is represented by an initial global scheme R which consists of the relational schemes (representations of object types of real world), a set of global dependencies to express referential integrity constraints, and a set of user views representing the requirements of a set of users in the multiuser database environment. Thus R is defined by the triple:

$(\mathbf{RS}, \mathbf{GD}, \mathbf{V})$ where

$RS = \{RS_1(ATTR_1, LD_1), \ldots, RS_n(ATTR_n, LD_n)\}$ RS_i is the ith relational scheme consisting of a set of attributes $ATTR_i$ and a set of local dependencies LD_i (we consider functional dependencies (FDs) only). RS_i is not necessarily in third normal form(3NF).

GD as the set of global dependencies expressing referential integrity constraints.

V the set of user views described on subsets of RS.

A view in this data model can only be specified by a DBA. It is a very weak constraint on the global schema, because it encompasses all the transactions accessing a specific part of a database. A view is defined by using the following syntax (note that it is possible to define a view having access to attributes from several relations):

VIEW view-name

[AS SELECT $\left\{ \begin{array}{l} attr - name \\ rel - name.attr - name \end{array} \right\}$ [$\left\{ \begin{array}{l} attr - name \\ rel - name.attr - name \end{array} \right\}$]]

[FROM rel-name [,rel-name] ...]

[WHERE condition];

/* The syntax for the term condition is as follows */

condition $\begin{array}{l} sel - condition \\ sel - condition \end{array}$ [$\left\{ \begin{array}{l} and\ (condition) \\ or\ (condition) \end{array} \right\}$]

/* The syntax for the term sel-condition is as follows */

sel-condition [(sel-attr $< op >$ $\left\{ \begin{array}{l} constant \\ attr - name \end{array} \right\}$)]

$< op > = \{<, >, =, \leq, \geq, \neq\}$

Figure 1: View Creation Statement

Consider a global scheme R representing the universe of discourse of a company database. The company consists of a set of departments and a set of employees. The Department relation consists of attributes: {D#, D_Name, ZIP, State, Budget}. The Employee relation consists of attributes: { SSN, Name, Salary, D#}. Each employee belongs to one department. The mini world of the company database is represented by two relational schemes and four views accessing the database described by the global scheme. In this example, view V_1 has access to the whole database, while view V_2 has access only to the tuples of the department relation projected on the attributes D#, D_Name and ZIP. View V_3 has access to all employees with $Salary > 32K$, and to the Budget and State columns of the department these employees are working for. Users with view V_4 have access to all tuples of Employee.

The views are defined by using the SQL-like syntax given in Figure 1. The definition of the views are:

VIEW V_1;

VIEW V_2

AS SELECT Department.D#, D_Name, ZIP,

FROM Department;   1

VIEW V_3

AS SELECT SSN, Name, Salary, Employee.D#, Budget, State

FROM Employee, Department

WHERE $Salary > 32K$ and Employee.D# = Department.D#;

VIEW V_4

FROM Employee;

In [Pern 90] , the authors extended the RM/T model by incorporating additional catalog relations to express abstractions on views. In this paper we describe the decomposition procedure, the handling of split dependencies, normalization of fragments and the applicability of this methodology to specialized environments.

The design methodology based on the views on a global relational database scheme is as follows:

1. The global relational database scheme defined above is the input to the design process.

2. The global scheme is then decomposed into disjoint fragments based on the views defined by using the horizontal, vertical and derived horizontal fragmentation operators.

3. Further normalization of the fragments is performed (if necessary) to avoid known processing anomalies.

4. Based on the above decomposition and normalization, relationships between the fragments and views are derived and stored in the catalog relations.

3 Mixed Decomposition

In a multiuser environment different sets of users will have different views of the database defined by the database designer. These views may or may not overlap. The grouping of these views defined on the global scheme R can be represented by an undirected graph $G(V, E)$ consisting of two sets: a finite set of views V and a set of edges E. An edge exists between two views if they are overlapping.

Let R[A] represent a projection on attribute set A in relation or view R. Dom[A] denotes the domain of the set of selection attributes[1] A. $SD(V[A])$ denotes the subdomain of the selection attribute set A valid in view V.

Definition: User views V_i and V_j are said to be overlapping iff:

$$\exists A \mid (A \in ATTR(V_i) \wedge A \in ATTR(V_j))\ \text{and}\ SD(V_i[A]) \bigcap SD(V_j[A]) \neq \emptyset.$$

with A as selection attribute in V_i and V_j, and $SD(V_i[A]) \subseteq Dom[A], SD(V_j[A]) \subseteq Dom[A]$ with $SD(V_i[A])$ as the subdomain of selection attribute A valid in view V_i and $SD(V_j[A])$ as the subdomain of A in V_j respectively.

Otherwise V_i and V_j are called isolated.

We decompose the global scheme based on overlapping views into a set of disjoint fragments. In order to reflect the local dependencies within these disjoint fragments, normalization is done after the decomposition. The standard relational operators are not sufficient to decompose the conceptual global scheme R according to view definitions. For this purpose we adopt the theory of distributed database design [Chan80, Ceri84] by using the operators vertical, horizontal and derived horizontal fragmentation for generating fragments. We shall now describe the vertical,

---

[1]Selection attribute is the set of attributes in the WHERE-clause of the definition of a view used to derive a horizontal fragment

horizontal and derived horizontal fragmentation operators denoted respectively by (*), (//) and (d//).

Vertical fragmentation (*)

(*) is defined by projecting a relation R over subsets of its attributes. To make the projection lossless, a key or a surrogate as a unique identifier is included within each fragment. Note that this surrogate identifier requires additional space proportional to $(number of vertical fragments) \times (max - integer\{log_2(cardinality(relation)))\}$. Vertical fragmentation is non-overlapping, i.e. every non-key attribute belongs to one and only one fragment. A vertical fragment is specified by using the SELECT- and FROM-clause of the view definition statement shown in Figure 1. It is obvious that if every relation of the global scheme contains a surrogate or a key as a unique identifier and all relations composing the global scheme are in 3NF, then the resulting fragments are also in 3NF. If the relations are only in 2NF or less normalized, problems will arise. In Section 4, we will discuss these problems.

Horizontal fragmentation (//)

(//) is the concept of partitioning a relation R into disjoint fragments based on predicates defined on R. The predicates are defined in the WHERE-clause of the view creation statement (see Figure 1). A (//) is correct, if each tuple of R is mapped exactly in one horizontal fragment. In the case of overlapping fragments, it is always possible to generate a finer fragmentation in which all fragments are disjoint. Horizontal fragmentation is specified in the WHERE-clause during the definition of a view by using the syntax presented in Figure 1.

Derived horizontal fragmentation (d//)

(d//) is the concept of partitioning a relation RS_i by applying to it the same partitioning criterion as applied to RS_j ($i \neq j$). RS_j is called the owner-relation and RS_i the member relation. Owner and member relations are connected via a link. With a given partitioning of an owner relation and a 1 : n association between owner and member object, it is always possible to define a corresponding derived horizontal fragmentation. To express the link between an owner and member relation we use key-based inclusion dependencies. As the link is a 1 : n association the key of the owner relation is always present in the member relation as a foreign key. We recollect that inclusion dependencies are specified in GD, the set of global dependencies of R. Note that in this approach derived horizontal fragmentation is used to horizontally fragment more than one relation.

However our goal is the decomposition of the global scheme by performing a mixed decomposition in a way that the resulting disjoint fragments are representing the view structure defined on the global scheme. A fragment is also described (like a view) by the set of attributes spanned by it and by a set of conditions on the attributes. The descriptors of the fragments are generated during the mixed decompo-

sition process. The decomposition is done by using the following procedure:

Procedure Mixed Decomposition

1. Find all views which are overlapping
2. For each pair of overlapping views, perform a structured decomposition on them by applying (*), (//) and (d//) (in this order) into the smallest non overlapping grid cells.
3. Perform (*), (//) and (d//) (in this order) for each isolated view.

The number of fragments after decomposition depends on the number of horizontal and vertical decompositions. Sometimes we have to do more joins in our approach compared to the *traditional approach* of storing the base relations, but the number of tuples involved in the join is always less than or almost equal to the traditional approach. In most cases we have to join fewer tuples than in the traditional approach as we cluster the data according to the accessing behavior of the users thus reducing the number of irrelevant tuples. Relational operations will therefore operate not on the whole data, but will operate on the relevant part of data (parts of relations), the materialized fragments.

Before we will go into further details of this procedure, an example can now be given. Consider the global scheme below. For simplicity we do not use local dependencies at this step but we will extend this example in Section 4. by incorporating functional dependencies (FD's). As the selection predicates are very simple and easy to understand we do not use the syntax given in Figure 1 for the definition of the views in this example.

Suppose attribute D# is a key of relation Department and a foreign key in relation Employee. Assume furthermore Salary is a selection attribute for a derived horizontal fragmentation.

Example 1: Given $R(RS, GD, V)$ with

RS = { Department(D#, D_Name, ZIP, State, Budget);

       Employee(SSN, Name, Salary, D#) }

GD = { Employee[D#] $\subseteq$ Department[D#]}

V = {V_1: No constraints;

     V_2: attributes D#, D_Name, ZIP from Department;

     V_3: SSN, Name, Salary of Employees with $Salary > 32K$ and D#, Budget and

       State of corresponding Departments

     V_4: SSN, Name, Salary, D# from Employee
}

By applying the procedure given above to this global scheme it would lead to the following decomposition:

The global scheme is first vertically fragmented (*) into two different relations Department and Employee. Department is in a second step vertically fragmented into candidate fragments CF_1 and intermediate fragment IF_1 which is then derived-horizontally-fragmented (d//) into CF_2 and CF_3 according to the horizontal fragmentation of Employee into CF_4 and

CF_5. By using the inverse operations of the decomposition operators it is possible to construct relations Employee, Department and the global scheme R. We shall detail these inverse operators in Section 5.

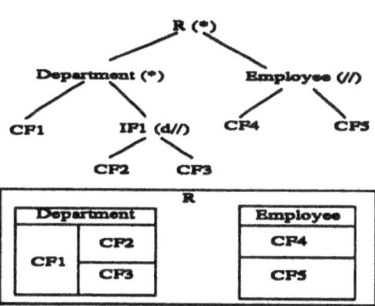

Figure 2: Decomposition Structure

We use the word candidate to indicate that this is possibly not the final fragmentation. Figure 2 shows the decomposition tree, the resulting fragmentation and the decomposition expression for this example.

This decomposition reflects the view structure in a much better way than it could be done with traditional design methodologies. For example, user V_1, by having access to the whole scheme has now access to $\{CF_1, \ldots, CF_5\}$. User V_2 has access to CF_1; user V_3 has access to CF_2 and CF_4, while user V_4 has access to CF_4 and CF_5. The structure of the decomposition is stored in catalog relations. The algorithm has been implemented for vertical and horizontal decomposition and produces disjoint fragments [Eich88].

4 Further Decomposition with Normalization

What is the effect of mixed decomposition on local dependencies? In the case of horizontal fragmentation, in the resulting horizontal fragments, some new dependencies may become valid which were not valid in the global scheme before the decomposition. This fact could be used to improve the performance of queries on the fragments [DeBr86]. But what about vertical fragmentation? As indicated in Section 3. if all relations of the global scheme are in 3NF and the key is redundantly stored in each vertical fragment, then vertical fragmentation has also no effect on functional dependencies. But consider the case where a relation which is not in 3NF is considered for a vertical fragmentation. The motivation for this case arises from the fact that for large business applications to be processed efficiently, the number of joins to be executed are reduced by storing some of the relations in non third normal form. We now consider an example taken from Section 2 by introducing some functional dependencies. For example let us see what happens if we have the following dependency structure valid in relation Department: D# $\longrightarrow$ D_Name, ZIP, Budget; ZIP $\longrightarrow$ State.

As we apply a vertical fragmentation on Department into two vertical fragments according to the

DEPARTMENT						
CF1				CF2		
D#	D_Name	ZIP		D#	State	Budget
1	EPCOT	1		1	FL	123k
2	DISNEY	3		3	FL	100k
3	Sea W.	1		2	CA	213k
4	Silicon	3		4	CA	200k

Figure 3: Decomposition of relation Department

view structure the functional dependency ZIP $\longrightarrow$ State will be split. The resulting fragmentation looks like the table in Figure 3. As we show only the impact of vertical fragmentation on a local dependency structure we do not decompose IF_1 into two horizontal fragments as done in figure 3. Henceforth in this section we shall refer to IF_1 as CF_2. Assume CF_1 and CF_2 are stored in different nodes in a distributed environment and $t_1, \ldots, t_4$ are tuples of Department. Let the dependency structure mentioned above be valid in Department. Now consider the following update operations on the relation Department:

$< op1 >$: UPDATE State = 'GA' in CF_2 where Budget = 100K;

$< op2 >$: UPDATE ZIP = '1' in CF_1 where D_Name = 'Silicon';

Both update operations, $< op1 >$ by updating the right hand side of a FD and $< op2 >$ by updating the left hand side of a FD would lead to an inconsistent database. The FD ZIP $\longrightarrow$ State will be violated by these update operations. If CF_1 and CF_2 are stored in different nodes in a distributed environment, it is only possible to preserve the consistency of the database by incurring high communication costs. In order to check the violation of integrity constraints in the local side (node holding the vertical fragment) and to avoid communication costs we introduce the concept of update clusters and virtual attributes.

An update cluster is defined as a set of attributes formed as a union of the left hand side attributes and right hand side attributes of a functional dependency which is split. In order to consistently update the relation, the database management system has to check that the functional dependency inherent in the update cluster is not violated. For each local dependency split by a vertical fragmentation, we copy the left hand side of this dependency to the candidate fragment containing the attributes present in the right hand side of the dependency and vice versa (called as *virtual attributes* thus forming an update cluster). Virtual attributes and update clusters are not seen by any user, they are only necessary for preserving the database consistency and to save communication costs in a distributed environment. The construction of the update cluster is done by the following algorithm:

```
Algorithm MAKE-UPDATE-CLUSTER:
    FOR each RS_i ∈ RS do
        FOR each FD X ⟶ Y ∈ FD(RS_i) do
            FOR each proper subset Z of XY do
                FOR each vertical fragment CF_j ∈ RS_i do
                    IF Z ∈ ATTR(CF_j)
                        THEN add XY \ Z to ATTR(CF_j) as a virtual attribute and define
                             XY as an update cluster
```

The last step in this proposed database design methodology is the normalization of fragments. This is necessary to avoid the known anomalies by performing insert, delete and update operations against fragments. In this paper we give no explicit algorithm. There are many algorithms available to produce a database free from processing anomalies. After applying any normalization algorithm to the example, it will lead to the fragmentation given below. It is assumed that the relation Employee is in 3NF. To indicate that this is the final fragmentation we do not use a suffix as a fragment any longer. Each F_i' represents an *update cluster*, * is used to indicate a virtual attribute.

CF_1: F_1 ({D#, D_Name, ZIP}{D# ⟶ D_Name, ZIP})

F_1' ({ZIP, $State^*$}{ZIP ⟶ $State^*$ })

CF_2: F_2 ({D#, State, Budget}{D# ⟶ State, Budget})

F_2' ({ZIP^*, State}{ZIP^* ⟶ State})

CF_2 holds only departments which have at least one employee with salary > 32K.

CF_3: F_3 ({D#, State, Budget}{D# ⟶ State, Budget})

F_3' ({ZIP^*, State}{ZIP^* ⟶ State})

CF_3 holds only departments which have no employee with salary > 32K.

CF_4: F_4 ({SSN, Name, Salary, D#}{SSN ⟶ Name, Salary, D#}) and $F_4[D\#] = F_2[D\#]$.

CF_4 holds only tuples with salary > 32K.

CF_5: F_5 ({SSN, Name, Salary, D#}{SSN ⟶ Name, Salary, D#}) and $F_5[D\#] = F_3[D\#]$.

CF_5 holds only tuples with salary ≤ 32K.

These fragments represent a database scheme free from processing anomalies. The allocation of fragments to the users represents the views in the multiuser environment. In the case of an underlying distributed database management system, the fragments can be allocated to nodes so as to help in reducing communication costs.

5 Catalog Relations

The catalog relations (CR) are used to store meta information about the database. In our approach they have an important role, because they store information about fragments, the relational schemes and decomposition operators, intermediate fragments, the domain of the attributes valid in fragments and the access rights of the users.

The CR consist of relational schemes: the application scheme and the data scheme. The *application scheme* is used to store the structure of the decomposition (the decomposition tree) while the *data scheme* contains information about the valid domain of the attributes in fragments and allocation of the fragments to the users.

The CR act as an interface between the database and the users. An access to fragments from a user is only possible if the user has the corresponding access right to the desired fragments indicated in the CR. Further, the CR are used to check for the integrity of the database because they have the information about the valid subdomain (condition specified) of a selection attribute in a horizontal fragment. An update of a selection attribute in a horizontal fragment may lead to the transfer of tuples to another horizontal fragment. With the information of the data scheme, the system can route the tuples to the corresponding new fragment. To reconstruct the tuples we introduce additional operations.

For example, to realize the view of user V_4 which has access to Employee which is horizontally partitioned into CF_4 and CF_5. We have to apply the inverse operation of (//), an *append* of CF_4 and CF_5. Similarly V_1 having access to the whole R is constructed by applying $V_1 \longleftarrow CF_1$ *concat* ((CF_2 *append* CF_3) || (CF_4 *append* CF_5))[2]. (||) is used to indicate the coupling of disjoint relational schemes RS_i, RS_j ($i \neq j$) belonging to R. According to our example the left hand side of (||) forms relation Department while the right hand side forms relation Employee. The *append* operation is inverse of the horizontal partitioning operation, where we append a horizontal fragment to another horizontal fragment, to generate a larger horizontal fragment. In our example CF_3 is appended to CF_2 to generate the fragment which is the projection on attributes State, Budget and $D\#$ from relation Department.

6 Applications of the Design Methodology

In this section we briefly describe three areas presented in SIGMOD Record December 90 (Lunt and Fernandez on Database Security, DeWitt and Gray on Parallel Database Systems, and Garcia-Molina and Lindsay on Distributed Databases)[3], wherein this methodology could be applied for designing spe-

---

[2] As the tuples in vertical fragments are stored in order of their key values, the inverse operation of a vertical fragmentation is a concatenation of tuples in different fragments.

[3] Proposed future research directions in certain areas of database systems

cialized databases. Details of applying this methodology are left for future research.

6.1 Secure Databases

Two different concepts of security modeling of database information are discussed in the literature:

(1). Discretionary access control is controlling the access from users to data by granting access privileges. The granting of privileges is under the discretion of the users themselves.

(2). Mandatory access control is based on the following principle: Database components (databases, files, relations, views, tuples, attributes, domains) are classified by specific security labels, called classification. Users and applications that have access to database components have a security label called clearance. For a successful data access, the security policy of an organization requires that the clearance of a user must be at least as high as the classification of the database component he/she wants to access.

In a multilevel secure database (MLS) environment security labels such as "top-secret" or "secret", consist of linearly ordered sensitivity levels and these labels are assigned to database components and users by a database or security administrator. Providing security labels for each attribute of a relational scheme or even for subset of domains of attributes leads to enormous processing overheads while simply protecting files is not sufficient in most environments. Choosing views as the granularity of protected data for the support of mandatory access controls was first proposed by [Clay83] and today several research projects (for e.g., [GaWu88],[LuDe90],[StTh90]) are investigating the use of views for both discretionary and mandatory access controls.

We believe that the proposed database organization has built-in multilevel secure capabilities. Physical fragments can be classified according to the sensitivity of the contained data by different labels of classification. By obtaining the fragment accessed by less users, the most sensitive area of the database can be determined. Fragments accessed by few users contain more sensitive data than fragments accessed by many users. This can be reflected by linearly ordered sensitivity levels and modeled by different classification labels. According to the number of fragments a particular view accesses, the level of clearance of that view is determined. The clearance label of that view must at least be as high as the highest label of classification of the data accessed by the fragments of this view. By assigning classification labels to fragments and clearance labels to users the security policy of an organization can be implemented with the proposed design methodology.

6.2 Distributed Databases

There has been a lot of work in distribution design i.e. design of distributed databases [e.g., Ceri 83, Nava 84, Nava 90]. This work assumes that the most important transactions are known a priori. There is no work in distribution design that assumes the relations

to be denormalized in lower normal forms which occurs frequently. A distribution design consists of a fragmentation scheme, i.e., the set of fragments a relation is partitioned to, and an allocation scheme, i.e., the mapping between the fragments and sites. When designing a new database the users rarely have a detailed specification of the transactions that will be run on the populated database, or the frequency with which they are executed.

User views may be constructed however, in advance without knowing specific transactions. Hence this methodology can be used to come up with the initial fragmentation scheme. For less normalized relations than 3NF, our work described in the Section 4 can be used as a scheme for maintaining database consistency. Otherwise, applications have to enforce consistency by incurring heavy communication costs.

6.3 Parallel Databases

Current parallel database systems are based on highly parallel architectures, which consist of multiprocessors based on fast microprocessors. This is because the mainframes have not been able to provide the processing capabilities required to support large relational databases. There are two types of architectures: Shared-Nothing and Shared-Memory. In case of shared-memory architectures, the secondary storage is shared among all the processors; this has a disadvantage if one needs to add more processors, as this results in increased interference for accessing the data. Thus the efficiency of such a system depends upon the concurrency mechanism provided, and the partitioning of resources. This is true for both shared-nothing and shared-memory systems. In order to optimize the execution of the database operations, data partitioning plays an important role.

One area in which no work has been done to the best of our knowledge is that of designing parallel databases so as to efficiently process the applications. We believe that our methodology to design databases can be used to decluster the relations among the different hard disks. In the current literature there are following methods of declustering besides hashing and random allocation:

rango partitioning: In this case the range of possible values taken by the key attribute are split into a set of contiguous sub ranges, and each sub-range is allocated to a hard disk.

round-robin: Each successive tuple is allocated to a hard disk in a round-robin fashion.

The above methods of declustering are heuristics and do not take into consideration optimal execution of the database operations. The time spent in executing database operations is well spent if minimal number of irrelevant tuples are processed and to the best of our knowledge none of the above methods have taken this criterion into consideration on which our methodology is based. The catalog relations can be used by the query processor to route the database operations to only those processors which have the data relevant for that operation. Moreover, the concurrency of the whole system can be increased as the processors which are not processing a database operation (because they do not have data relevant for that operation) can process another database operation.

7 Conclusions

In this paper we proposed an organization of a relational database on the basis of views. The design is based on the mixed decomposition procedure which uses the vertical, horizontal and derived horizontal decomposition operators to produce a set of disjoint candidate fragments. The final fragments are generated after a normalization step which is necessary to avoid known processing anomalies. The fragments are materialized and not the base relations. A set of fragments represents a view; hence a view can be constructed by combining fragments.

Database design based on views is not limited to the relational data model; it can be suitably applied to any data model which supports the concept of a view. This methodology can be uniformly applied for designing centralized databases and fragmentation scheme for distributed databases. This model has builtin authorization mechanism as the user accessing the database is limited to the part of the database spanned by the views he/she accesses. As the fragments are materialized, the data relevant for a specific view is *physically separated* from the *data not spanned* by this view.

The model has its limitation if there is a large number of overlapping views. In this case the decomposition leads to a high number of fragments. It should be noted that the views are defined by the database administrator and not by the users themselves, thus the number of views defined can be constrained. In general views are dynamic, hence if a newly defined view cannot be constructed by combining the existing set of fragments, a redesign (splitting) of a part of the database has to be done.

Note that along with the view definations which are given as input to the mixed decomposition procedure, the access frequencies as to how many times the views are accessed can be collected, and in case of distributed system, the information about sites from which the views are accessed. This can be used in ranking the views according to their access frequencies, and then allocating them to various disk packs in centralized system, or sites in distributed systems. A techinique similar to that given in [COPE 88] for placing relations in parallel machine Bubba so as to balance the load can be used. Moreover, if two views have very low access frequecies and are compatible vertical or horizontal fragments (i.e. either vertical fragments of a relation, or horizontal fragments of a relation), then they can be merged so as to balance the load.

The future work involves applying this methodology to organize databases for specialized environments like secure database systems, distributed database systems and parallel database systems. Current research involves efficiently processing database operations on parallel databases organized by means of this methodology, and maintaining the database consistency.

Acknowledgements: The authors would like to thank Seong Geum and Minyoung Ra, for their helpful comments. G. Pernul thanks A Min Tjoa for helpful suggestions in earlier related work.

References

[Ceri83] Ceri S, Navathe S. B, Wiederhold G,: Distribution Design of Logical Database Schemas, IEEE ToSE, SE-9, July 1983.

[Chan80] Chang, Cheng: A methodology for structured database decomposition, IEEE ToSE, vol. SE-6,2,1980.

[Clay83] B. G. Claybrook. Using Views in a Multilevel Secure Database Management System. Proc. IEEE Symposium on Research in Security and Privacy, 1983.

[Cope88] Copeland, G., Alexander, W., Boughter, E., and Keller, T. Data Placemnt in Bubba, Proc. of ACM SIGMOD, pages 99-108, May 1988.

[DeBr86] De Bra, P: Horizontal Decompositions based on Functional Dependency Set Implications, Lecture Notes in Computer Science, ICDT86, Springer-Verlag, 1986.

[Eich88] Eichler B.: Implementation of a prototype for database design according to user views, Master thesis, University of Vienna, 1988.

[GaWu88] C. Garvey, A. Wu. ASD_Views. Proc. IEEE Symposium on Research in Security and Privacy, 1988.

[LuDe90] T. F. Lunt, D. E. Denning, R. R. Schell, M. Heckman, W. R. Shockley. The SeaView Security Model, IEEE Trans. on Software Engineering, vol. 16, no. 6, June 1990.

[Nava84] Navathe, S. B., Ceri, S., Wiederhold G., Dou, J.:Vertical Partitioning Algorithms for Database Design, ACM TODS, Vol. 9, No 4, Dec. 1984.

[Nava90] Navathe, S. B., Ra, M., Varadarajan, R., Karlapalem, K., Sreewastav, K.: A Mixed Partitioning Methodology for Distributed Database Design, Technical Report UF-CIS TR-90-17, University of Florida, Feb. 1990.

[Pern90] Pernul, G., Moser P., Luef, G.: Database Design according to user views, Parbase-90, Int. Conf. on databases and parallel architectures and their applications, IEEE Computer Science Press, 1990.

[StTh90] P. D. Stachour, B. Thuraisingham. Design of LDV: A multilevel secure relational database management system. IEEE Trans. on Knowledge and Data Engineering, vol. 2, no. 2, June 1990.

A Dynamic Overwrite Protocol for Multiversion Concurrency Control Algorithms

Tadeusz Morzy

Technical University of Poznań
Institute of Computing Science
60-965 Poznań, POLAND

Abstract

The main difficulty with multiversion database systems is that of storage space, i.e. in a multiversion database we would need to keep a potentially unlimited number of versions of data items. As storage space is always limited, the number data item versions maintained in the database is also limited. This means that some write operations must overwrite old versions of data items in order to create new ones. This paper presents the novel dynamic overwrite protocol which compared to conventional natural overwrite protocol used in practice minimize the number of transactions abortions caused by the limited storage space. The main idea of this new overwrite protocol lies on finding data item versions which can be safely overwritten because no active transaction accesses them in the future.

1 Introduction

Recently, several authors in the area of database concurrency control have pointed out that, by maintaining multiple versions of data items, we can achieve concurrency control algorithms of enhanced performance [1,2,7,9,10,11,13,14,15,16,17]. Multiple versions of data items increase the degree of concurrency because they significantly reduce the contention of transactions during their concurrent access to the database. The higher degree of concurrency results since out-of-order read-only transactions can be serviced by reading appropriate older versions of data items. This approach is attractive also because of its close connection to recovery [3,5,10,12,13,14,17].

In a multiversion database system, read-only transactions are never rejected if all versions of data items are retained. However, all versions cannot be retained forever in any multiversion database systems due to the limited storage space and processing overhead. Since storage space is always limited, the total number of versions of data items stored in the database is also limited. Therefore, some write operations must overwrite old versions of data items in order to create new ones. However, if some versions are discarded (overwritten), transactions that need to read them must be aborted.

The decisions which of the existing versions to overwrite to create new versions of data items depend on the *overwrite protocol* used by a concurrency control algorithms. Most of concurrency control algorithms designed (or proposed) for MVDBSs apply the overwrite protocol which we called the *natural overwrite protocol* (*nop*). According to the *nop*, if some write operation must overwrite a version of a data item, it always overwrites the oldest version stored in the database [3,5,7]. The primary weakness of the *nop* is that it may lead to unnecessary transaction abortions because of the overwriting versions that may be needed by active read-only transactions. This results from the fact that the *nop* does not make use of the information about active transactions. Recently, Son and Haghighi [15] proposed a new protocol the main idea of which is to discard versions that will no longer be needed by any active transaction, so as to reduce the probability of abort of active transactions. In their solution, by using special timestamp assignment method for read-only transactions, each read-only transaction informs all data items which versions it needs to access. This process has an associated cost — a read–only transaction cannot begin execution until it has chosen a timestamp, a process that requires communicating with all data items it needs to access. The proposed solution has several shortcomings: it may be only used with the multiversion timestamp ordering algorithm, it allows creation of only one temporary version for each data item and does not allow inserting a new version in the middle of existing valid versions.

The contribution of this paper is twofold. First, we formulate a sufficient condition for overwriting (discarding) a version of data item under which no active transaction must be aborted due to the unavailability of this version. Then, we extend this condition to the case of multiple active transactions. Second, we propose a novel, *dynamic overwrite protocol* which, in comparison to the *nop*, reduces the probability of transaction abortions caused by limited storage space. Unlike the solution of Son and Haghighi, our protocol allows creation of an unlimited number of temporary versions and allows inserting new versions between existing valid versions.

The paper is organized as follows. In Section 2 we give an overview of the database system model used in the paper. In Section 3 we briefly present the theory of multiversion serializability. Section 4 contains the formulation of the problem. In Section 5 we state sufficient conditions under which a version can be discarded without affecting an execution of a single active transaction and a set of active transactions. In Section 6 the proposed dynamic overwrite protocol is presented. Section 7 contains the final conclusions.

2 Database system model

A multiversion database system ($MVDBS$) is a triple $KVDBS = (DB, \tau, C(\tau))$, where DB is a database, $\tau = (T_0, T_1, \ldots, T_m)$ is a set of transactions, and $C(\tau)$ is a set of all correct executions of τ called the *correctness criterion*.

A database DB is a finite collection of data items denoted $x, y, z, \ldots$. Each data item $x \in DB$ is a sequence of versions storing its consecutive values denoted $x_{p_1}^1, x_{p_2}^2, \ldots, x_{p_g}^g$, where the superscript is the index of the version and the subscript is the index of the transaction that created it. We assume that the total number of versions of data items is limited to K.

Set τ consists of transactions $T_1, T_2, \ldots, T_m$ and a fictitious transaction T_0 called the *initial transaction*. This transaction is a write-only transaction which writes the initial values of all data items of the DB. Each transaction $T_i \in \tau$, $i \in (1, m)$, is a poset $T_i = (\overline{T}_i, <_i)$, where $\overline{T}_i$ is a set of database operations issued by T_i and $<_i$ is a partial order relation which specifies the execution order of operations in $\overline{T}_i$. We assume four types of database operations: a read operation $r(x)$, a write operation $w(x)$, a commit operation c, and an abort operation a. A read operation $r(x)$ returns the value of a version of a data item x. A write operation $w(x)$ creates a new version of a data item x. This version is either added to the DB, when the current number of versions of data items is less than K, or it replaces a version of a data item stored in the database, when the current number of versions of data items is equal to K. A transaction terminates with either a commit, c, or an abort, a, operation. We assume a transaction model, in which all write operations of a transaction are executed as a single indivisible step together with a commit operation. This assumption is well fulfilled by most modern transaction oriented database systems.

In order to indicate that a given database operation belongs to a transaction T_i we use the following notation: $T_i : r(x)$ for a read operation, $T_i : w(x)$ for a write operation, $T_i : c$ for a commit operation, and $T_i : a$ for an abort operation. A set of T's read operations executed without interleaving with any other database operations is called its *read step* denoted $T_i : r(x, y, \ldots)$. In a similar way a *write step* of a transaction is defined, denoted $T_i : w(x, y, \ldots)$.

3 Multiversion serializability

A concurrent execution of a set of transactions in MVDBS is modeled by a multiversion schedule.

A *complete multiversion (MV) schedule* over a set τ of transactions is a triple

$$mvs_p(\tau) = (\overline{T}_p(\tau), <_{mvs_p}, Rd_{mvs_p})$$

where: $\overline{T}_p(\tau) = \bigcup_{i=0}^{i=m} \overline{T}_i$ is a set of all database operations involved in the transactions of the set τ; $<_{mvs_p} \supseteq \bigcup_{i=0}^{i=m} <_i$ is a partial order on $\overline{T}_p(\tau)$ compatible with the partial orders of database operations specified by the transactions; $Rd_{mvs_p} : \overline{T}_p(\tau) \to \overline{T}_p(\tau)$ is a reads-from relation over $\overline{T}_p(\tau)$, which determines the versions of data items read by transactions of τ. $Rd_{mvs_p}(T_i : r(x)) = T_j : w(x)$ if a read operation of transaction T_i reads the version of data item x created by a write operation of transaction T_j. Clearly, $Rd_{mvs_p}(T_i : r(x)) = T_j : w(x)$ only if $T_j : w(x) <_{mvs_p} T_i : r(x)$.

A MV schedule $mvs(\tau) = (\overline{T}(\tau), <_{mvs}, Rd_{mvs})$ is a prefix of a complete MV schedule $mvs_p(\tau) = (\overline{T}_p(\tau), <_{mvs_p}, Rd_{mvs_p})$, where: $\overline{T}(\tau) \subseteq \overline{T}_p(\tau)$, $<_{mvs} \subseteq <_{mvs_p}$, for each pair of operations $O_i, O_j \in \overline{T}(\tau)$, if $O_i <_{mvs} O_j$ then $O_i <_{mvs_p} O_j$. $Rd_{mvs} \subseteq Rd_{mvs_p}$, for each pair of operations $O_i, O_j \in \overline{T}(\tau)$, if $Rd_{mvs}(O_j) = O_i$ then $Rd_{mvs_p}(O_j) = O_i$.

To present a MV schedule graphically, in what follows we simply write down the database operations of $\overline{T}(\tau)$ from left to right in the order $<_{mvs}$ and additionaly we give the relation Rd_{mvs}.

A transaction T_i is *committed* in a MV schedule $mvs(\tau) = (\overline{T}(\tau), <_{mvs}, Rd_{mvs})$ if $T_i : c \in \overline{T}(\tau)$. If $T_i : c \notin \overline{T}(\tau)$, then we say that T_i is an active transaction in $mvs(\tau)$. For any $\tau' \subseteq \tau$, the *projection* of $mvs(\tau)$ onto τ' is obtained by removing from $\overline{T}(\tau)$ the database operations of transactions not in τ'. The projection of a MV schedule $mvs(\tau)$ onto the set of committed transactions in $mvs(\tau)$ is called a *committed projection of $mvs(\tau)$* and denoted $CP(mvs(\tau))$. A *continuation* of an active transaction T_k of a MV schedule $mvs(\tau)$ is a sequence of database operations (or steps) of T_k not contained in $\overline{T}(\tau)$ of $mvs(\tau)$. A *safe continuation* of an active transaction T_k of a MV schedule $mvs(\tau)$ is a such continuation of T_k, that read operations of T_k are never rejected due to unavailability of data item versions. A *continuation* of a MV schedule $mvs(\tau)$ is a sequence of database operations of active transactions of $mvs(\tau)$ and possibly some new transactions. A continuation of a MV schedule $mvs(\tau)$ contains all continuations of its active transactions. A concatenation of a MV schedule $mvs(\tau)$ and a continuation r, denoted $mvs(\tau) + r$, is a MV schedule.

Two MV schedules $mvs(\tau) = (\overline{T}(\tau), <_{mvs}, Rd_{mvs})$ and $mvs'(\tau) = (\overline{T}'(\tau), <_{mvs'}, Rd_{mvs'})$ over τ are equivalent, $mvs \equiv mvs'$, iff (1) $\overline{T}(\tau) = \overline{T}'(\tau)$, and $Rd_{mvs} = Rd_{mvs'}$. A MV schedule $mvs(\tau)$ is *serial* iff for each pair of transactions $T_i, T_j \in \tau$, either all database operations of T_i precede in $mvs(\tau)$ all those of T_j, or vice versa. This means that no interleaving of transactions occurs. A serial MV schedule $mvs(\tau)$ is *standard* if for all i,j and x, if $(T_j : w(x), T_i : r(x)) \in Rd_{mvs}$ then $T_j : w(x)$ is the last write operation preceding $T_i : r(x)$ in $mvs(\tau)$ that creates a new version of x. Since mvs is a serial MV schedule, the "last write operation preceding a read operation" is well defined.

A standard serial MV schedule in MVDBS corresponds to a serial monoversion schedule in monoversion DBS. This follows from the definition of a transaction and the definition of a standard serial MV schedule. On the basis of the notion of equivalence and a standard serial MV schedule, we can formulate the following correctness criterion called *multiversion serializability* [3].

> A multiversion schedule $mvs(\tau)$ is multiversion serializable if its committed projection $CP(mvs(\tau))$ is equivalent to any standard serial multiversion schedule of the same set of transactions.

We can determine whether a MV schedule is multiversion serializable by analyzing a graph called a *multiversion serialization graph* $(MVSRG(mvs(\tau)))$. A MV schedule $mvs(\tau)$ is multiversion serializable iff an acyclic $MVSRG(mvs(\tau))$ can be constructed [3,4]. Deciding whether an MV schedule is multiversion serializable is *NP*-complete problem [3,4,12], so practical multiversion concurrency control algorithms enforce the stronger correctness criterion called *DMV-serializability*.

In order to present a formal definition of the *DMV*-serializability we introduce the notion of the transaction precedence relation in a multiversion schedule $mvs(\tau)$, denoted by $\to\to$. For a multiversion schedule $mvs(\tau)$ and a data item x the precedence relation $\rightarrow\rightarrow$ over a set of transactions τ is defined as follows:

1. For every two operations $T_i : w(x)$ and $T_j : r(x)$, $i \neq j$, if $Rd_{mvs}(T_j : r(x)) = T_i : w(x)$, then $T_i \rightarrow\rightarrow T_j$;

2. For every two operations $T_i : w(x)$ and $T_j : w(x)$, $i \neq j$, if $T_i : w(x)) \prec_{mvs} T_j : w(x)$, then $T_i \rightarrow\rightarrow T_j$;

3. For every three operations $T_i : w(x), T_j : r(x)$ and $T_k : w(x)$, $i \neq j \neq k$, such that $Rd_{mvs}(T_j : r(x)) = T_i : w(x)$, if $T_i : w(x) \prec_{mvs} T_k : w(x)$ then $T_j \rightarrow\rightarrow T_k$, else $T_k \rightarrow\rightarrow T_i$

Using the precedence relation $\rightarrow\rightarrow$ we can formulate the DMV-serializability criterion.

A multiversion schedule $mvs(\tau)$ is DMV-serializable iff the graph of its precedence relation $\rightarrow\rightarrow$ is acyclic.

Using the DMV-serializability criterion, testing the correctness of a multiversion schedule $mvs(\tau)$ is now reduced to testing the acyclicity of the graph of the precedence relation $\rightarrow\rightarrow$. It is called the DMV-serializability graph of a schedule $mvs(\tau)$ and denoted $DMVSRG(mvs(\tau))$.

4 Problem formulation

Any multiversion concurrency control algorithm, besides deciding at each moment whether to grant, delay, or abort an arriving read or write operation of a transaction, and which of the existing versions of a data item accessed should be presented to a read operation, must also decide which of the existing versions of a data item, if any, to overwrite. This latter decision is made by a *version control manager*, which realizes a given *overwrite protocol*. Most of version control managers designed so far or proposed for use in MVDBSs apply the same overwrite protocol which we called *natural overwrite protocol* [2,3,5,7,13].

The *natural overwrite protocol (nop)* may be defined as follows. When a write operation create a new version do:

1. If the total number of versions of all data items is less than K, then add this version to the database; otherwise,

2. If the total number of versions of all data items is K, then overwrite the "oldest" version stored in the database.

The principal weakness of the natural overwrite protocol is that it may lead to unnecessary transaction abortions and, thus, to MVDBS performance degradation. To illustrate this fact, consider the processing of database operations by the well-known multiversion timestamp ordering algorithm due to Reed [13] combined with the natural overwrite protocol [3].

Example 1

Given transactions T_0, T_1, T_2, T_3, with $TS(T_i) = i$ for $i \in (0,3)$ presented in Figure 1. Assume that the above transactions are processed according to the $MVTO$ algorithm complemented by the natural overwrite protocol in MVDBS with the system-imposed upper bound on the number of versions $K = 4$.

Assume that transactions issue their operations in the following order (read from left to right)

$T_0 : w(x,y)$ $T_0 : c$ $T_1 : r(x)$ $T_2 : r(x,y)$ $T_2 : w(x,y)$
$T_2 : c$ $T_3 : r(x,y)$ $T_3 : w(x,y)$ $T_3 : c$ $T_1 : r(y)$

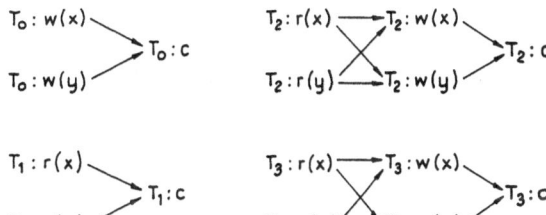

Fig. 1: A set of transactions from Example 1

The MVTO algorithm schedules this sequence of database operations as follows. Transaction T_1 reads a version x_0^1 created by T_0. Similarly, transaction T_2 reads versions x_0^1 and y_0^1 created by T_0. Transaction T_2 creates new versions x_2^2 and y_2^2 of x and y. According to the *nop*, versions created by the transaction T_3 overwrites versions x_0^1 and y_0^1 created by T_0. The DB state at T_3's commitment is: $DB = \{(x_2^1, x_3^2), (y_2^1, y_3^2)\}$. Therefore, a read operation $T_1 : r(y)$ has to be rejected because there is no version $y_{p_i}^i$ of y whose timestamp $W\_ts(y_{p_i}^i) < TS(T_1)$. This means that transaction T_1 must be aborted.

However, transaction T_1 is aborted unnecessarily. If versions created by T_3 overwrite versions x_0^1 and y_2^2, then a read operation $T_1 : r(y)$ may access the version y_0^1 retained in the DB. It is easy to prove that the MV schedule $mvs(\tau)$ with the reads-from relation Rd_{mvs} in which $T_1 : r(y)$ reads the version y_0^1 is multiversion serializable.

$\square$

As follows from the above example, the *nop* may lead to unnecessary transaction abortions. Therefore, by replacing the *nop* protocol by a protocol which will make use of the information about active transactions, the number of transaction abortions can be reduced.

5 Safe continuation of transactions

Now, we examine in a formal manner the problem of ensuring a safe continuation of an active transaction when the upper bound of the number of valid versions is attained and the necessity of overwriting one of them appears. We state a sufficient condition under which a version may be overwritten without affecting an execution of an active read-only transaction.

To formulate this condition, let us analyse a modified DMV-serialization graph called MV *schedule state* graph and denoted $MVSSG(mvs(\tau))$. At any time, $MVSSG(mvs(\tau))$ represents a current state of the MV schedule $mvs(\tau)$ produced by a scheduler of a concurrency control algorithm Alg used in MVDBS. $MVSSG(mvs(\tau))$ is $DMVSRG(mvs(\tau))$ with additional type of nodes called version nodes and some arcs (T_i, T_j) replaced by pairs of arcs $(T_i, x), (x, T_j)$, where x is a version node. If $mvs(\tau)$ is multiversion serializable, more precisely, if it is DMV-serializable, then $DMVSRG(mvs(\tau))$ is acyclic. $DMVSRG(mvs(\tau))$ acyclic implies $MVSSG(mvs(\tau))$ acyclic. Since each schedule $mvs(\tau)$ produced by a correct concurrency control algorithm must be DMV-serializable, so $MVSSG(mvs(\tau))$ is always acyclic. In the following, for ease of presentation, we will say that $MVSSG(mvs(\tau))$ is cyclic to mean that if the last operation of the schedule is processed, then a cycle will be created in the graph. It means, that $mvs(\tau)$ (icluding the last operation) is no longer DMV-serializable. Of course, the scheduler of the concurrency control algorithm Alg will abort the transaction that wants to execute the last operation, and therefore, it will maintain the acyclicity of $MVSSG(mvs(\tau))$.

Formally, a multiversion schedule state graph $MVSSG(mvs(\tau)) = (N, A)$ is a digraph. The set N of nodes consists of two types of nodes:

V1 for each transaction $T_{p_i} \in \tau$ whose operations appear in a history $mvs(\tau)$ there is a transaction node T_{p_i};

V2 for each data item version $x_{p_j}^j$ created by transaction T_{p_j}, committed in $mvs(\tau)$ there is a version node $x_{p_j}^j$.

A $MVSSG(mvs(\tau))$ is constructed as follows. When a first database operation of a transaction T_{p_i} appears in $mvs(\tau)$, add node T_{p_i} to the graph. Then add an arc or several arcs to the graph depending on the type of operation.

1. *Read operation:* $T_{p_i} : r(x)$
   If transaction T_{p_i} reads a version $x_{p_j}^j$ then:

   - add an arc $(x_{p_j}^j, T_{p_i})$ to the graph,
   - for each version $x_{p_k}^k$ committed in $mvs(\tau)$ such that $x_{p_k}^k$ is a successor of $x_{p_j}^j$ in $MVSSG(mvs(\tau))$, add an arc $(T_{p_i}, x_{p_k}^k)$ to the graph.

2. *Write operation:* $T_{p_i} : w(x)$
   Let $x_{p_i}^?$ denotes a new version of x created by $T_{p_i} : w(x)$. The following sets of arcs are added to the graph.

   - add an arc $(T_{p_i}, x_{p_i}^?)$ to the graph,
   - add a pair of arcs $(x_{p_j}^j, x_{p_i}^?)$ and $(x_{p_i}^?, T_{p_j})$ to the graph, where $x_{p_j}^j$ is the last version of x created by the operation $T_{p_j} : w(x)$ which imediately precedes the operation $T_{p_i} : w(x)$ in $mvs(\tau)$,
   - for each active transaction T_{p_k} that reads a version $(x_{p_j}^j$ that is a predecessor of $(x_{p_i}^?$ in the graph, add an arc (T_{p_k}, T_{p_i}) to the graph,
   - for each pair of versions $x_{p_i}^?, y_{p_i}^?$ created by the transaction T_{p_i}, add a pair of arcs $(x_{p_i}^?, y_{p_i}^?)$ and $(y_{p_i}^?, x_{p_i}^?)$.

3. *Commit operation:* $T_{p_i} : c$
   Let k denotes the index assigned to the version $x_{p_i}^?$ created by the committed transaction T_{p_i}. Modify $MVSSG(mvs(\tau))$ as follows:

   - if $x_{p_i}^?$ overwrites $y_{p_l}^l$ then:
     - add an arc $(y_{p_l}^l, x_{p_i}^?)$ to the graph,
     - if the graph contains a pair of arcs $(N_i, y_{p_l}^l)$, $(y_{p_l}^l, N_j)$, where $N_i, N_j \in N$, then add to the graph an arc (N_i, N_j),
     - delete all incoming and outgoing arcs of the version node $y_{p_l}^l$,
     - delete the version node $y_{p_l}^l$,
     - rename the version node $x_{p_i}^?$ to $x_{p_i}^k$,
     - enumerate all versions of data item y.

- if the graph contains a pair of arcs $(N_i, T_{p_i}), (T_{p_i}, N_j)$, where $N_i, N_j \in N$ and at least one of them is a transaction node, then add an arc (N_i, N_j) to the graph,
- delete all incoming and outgoing arcs of the transaction node T_{p_i},
- delete the transaction node T_{p_i}.

Now, consider the structure of $MVSSG(mvs(\tau))$ from the point of view of the relationship between an active transaction T_k (represented by the transaction node T_k) and a data item x represented by a sequence of versions nodes $x_{p_1}^1, x_{p_2}^2, \ldots, x_{p_g}^g$. From the point of view of T_k, versions of x can be divided into three classes: those which are predecessors of T_k in the graph, those which are successors of T_k in the graph and those which are unrelated to T_k.

If the current graph $MVSSG(mvs(\tau))$ is acyclic, there are only 7 possible structure describing the relationship between T_k and x. In case (1), all version nodes of x are unrelated to T_k. In case (2) version nodes of x are successors of T_k, whereas in case (3) version nodes of x are predecessors of T_k. In cases (4) and (5), part of version nodes of x is unrelated to T_k, the rest of them are either successors or predecessors of T_k in $MVSSG(mvs(\tau))$. In case (6) all version nodes are related to T_k. In case (7) part of version nodes is unrelated to T_k, others are either predecessors or successors of T_k in $MVSSG(mvs(\tau))$.

Consider a multiversion serializable schedule $mvs(\tau)$ represented by an acyclic graph $MVSSG(mvs(\tau))$. Assume that a transaction T_k is active and a continuation of $mvs(\tau)$ consists of only one operation — $T_k : r(x)$. Assume also the most general case of relationship between the transaction T_k and the data item x reprezented in Figure 2.

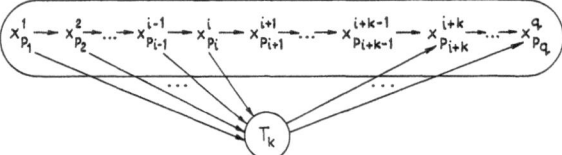

Fig. 2: Relationship between an active transaction T_k and a data item x

If transaction T_k reads any version $x_{p_1}^1, x_{p_2}^2, \ldots, x_{p_{i-1}}^{i-1}$, then, following the rules of $MVSSG(mvs(\tau))$ construction, it will be involved in a cycle in $MVSSG(mvs(\tau) + T_k : r(x))$. It means that the schedule $mvs(\tau) + T_k : r(x)$ is no longer DMV-serializable and transaction T_k must be aborted. On the other hand, if T_k reads any one version $x_{p_{i+k}}^{i+k}, x_{p_{i+k+1}}^{i+k+1}, \ldots, x_{p_g}^g$, then it will be also involved in a cycle in $MVSSG(mvs(\tau) + T_k : r(x))$ and it will have to be aborted. Therefore, to ensure DMV-serializability of the schedule $mvs(\tau) + T_k : r(x)$, transaction T_k has to read one of the versions: $x_{p_i}^i, x_{p_{i+1}}^{i+1}, \ldots, x_{p_{i+k-1}}^{i+k-1}$. This means that to ensure the safe continuation of T_k it is necessary to retain one of the above mentioned versions. We say that the set of versions $x_{p_{i+k}}^{i+k}, x_{p_{i+k+1}}^{i+k+1}, \ldots, x_{p_g}^g$ is a set of *useful versions* of a data item x of the active transaction T_k at time t. We denote it by $usv_x^t(T_k)$. A set $x \setminus usv_x^t(T_k)$ is a set of *unuseful versions* of a data item x of the active transaction T_k at time t. We denote it by $unv_x^t(T_k)$.

The sum $\bigcup_{x\in DB} unv_x^t(T_k)$ of sets of unuseful versions of all data items of the active transaction T_k, denoted $UNV^t(T_k)$, represents at a given moment t those versions which can be sefely discarded (overwritten) from DB from the point of view of the safe continuation of T_k. Thus, a sufficient condition for the safe version overwriting is given below.

Condition 1

Let $mvs(\tau)$ be a multiversion serializable schedule and T_k an active transaction in $mvs(\tau)$. If an overwrite protocol, at any time t of the continuation r, overwrites a version only from the set $UNV^t(T_k)$, then r is a safe continuation of T_k.

From the above condition follows that by the appropriate overwrite protocol we can always ensure that an active transaction T_k will never be rejected due to the unavailability of the suitable version to read.

Now, we would like to extend the result of the previous section to the case of multiple active transactions. Unfortunately, this is not possible. To illustrate the problem, consider the following example. Let $x = \{x_{p_1}^1, x_{p_2}^2, x_{p_3}^3\}$ and there are two active transactions T_i and T_j such that $usv_x^t(T_i) = \{x_{p_1}^1\}$ and $usv_x^t(T_j) = \{x_{p_2}^2\}$. Assume that one of the versions $x_{p_1}^1, x_{p_2}^2, x_{p_3}^3$ have to be overwritten in order to create a new version of a data item. The deletion of $x_{p_1}^1$ may cause the abortion of T_i, while the deletion of $x_{p_2}^2$ may cause the abortion of T_j. The version $x_{p_3}^3$ as the most current version of x is a useful version of any future transaction T_f which will appear later in the system. The deletion of this version will cause the abortion of any future transaction requiring access to the data item x. This means that we cannot ensure the safe continuation of transactions T_i, T_j and T_f after overwriting one of the versions.

A sufficient condition for the safe version overwriting for a set of active transactions may be defined as follows. Let M be a set of active transactions in $mvs(\tau)$ augmented by a fictitious transaction T_f representing future transactions in the system. For each data item $x \in DB$, at any point t at time, $usv_x^t(T_f)$ contains only one, last version of this data item. The definition of the condition is the following.

Condition 2

Let $mvs(\tau)$ be a multiversion serializable schedule and M an augmented set of active transactions in $mvs(\tau)$. If an overwrite protocol, at any time t of the continuation r, overwrites a version only from the set $\bigcap_{T_k \in M} UNV^t(T_k)$, then r is a safe continuation of transactions of M.

6 Dynamic overwrite protocol

A dynamic overwrite protocol follows directly from the formulation of Condition 2. However, to present this protocol we have to consider two particular cases:

1. The set $\bigcap_{T_k \in M} UNV^t(T_k)$ is non-empty;

2. The set $\bigcap_{T_k \in M} UNV^t(T_k)$ is empty.

In the first case, we dispose of a set of versions which can be safely overwritten by a new one. The choice of a version to overwrite has no importance from the point of view of DB performance.

In the second case, there is no version which can be safely overwritten. Despite this, we have to overwrite one of them. The choice of a version to overwrite is important from the point of view of DB performance. This choice depends on the DB performance evaluation criterion used in the analysis. For example, if we choose the minimalization of the number of transaction abortions, then we look for a version that is a useful version of the minimum number of active transactions.

Now, we can formally define the proposed dynamic overwrite protocol.

Dynamic overwrite policy (dop)

1. If the total number of valid versions of all data items is less than the system-imposed upper bound K, then a version created by a committed transaction is added to the database, otherwise,

2. it overwrites a version $x_{p_i}^i \in DB$ according to the following rules:

   - if the set $\bigcap_{T_k \in M} UNV^t(T_k)$ is non-empty, then $x_{p_i}^i$ is the oldest version contained in the set

   $$\bigcap_{T_k \in M} UNV^t(T_k)$$

   - if the set $\bigcap_{T_k \in M} UNV^t(T_k)$ is empty, then $x_{p_i}^i$ is chosen from one of sets $UNV^t(T_k)$, $k = 1, 2, \ldots, m$ in such a way that the criterion used to evaluate performance of $MVDBS$ is optimized.

The following example illustrates the construction of the $MVSSG(mvs(\tau))$ and the dynamic overwrite protocol.

Example 2

Consider the concurrent execution of transactions of the set τ from Example 1. We have shown before that if database operations of the set τ are processed in $MVDBS$ with the bound $K = 4$ and in accordance with $MVTO$ algorithm complemented by the nop, then transaction T_1 has to be aborted because of the lack of a suitable version of y to read.

Assume now that the sequence of database operations from Example 1 is processed according to $MVTO$ algorithm combined with the dop protocol. The consecutive steps of $MVSSG(mvs(\tau))$ construction are presented in Figure 3.

According to the step 1 of the dop, transaction T_0 creates new versions x_0^1 and y_0^1 of x and y. Similarly, transaction T_2 creates versions x_2^2 and y_2^2 of x and y. The state of $MVSSG(mvs(\tau))$ after T_2's commitment is represented in Figure 3.a. When transaction T_3 creates versions x_3^7 and y_3^7, the total number of valid versions is equal to K ($K = 4$) and two of them have to be overwritten in order to make space for x_3^7 and y_3^7. The state of $MVSSG(mvs(\tau))$ after commitment of T_3 is represented in Figure 3.b. There is only one active transaction in the system, namely T_1. It has already accessed data item x (it has read version x_0^1) and has not yet accessed data item y. From

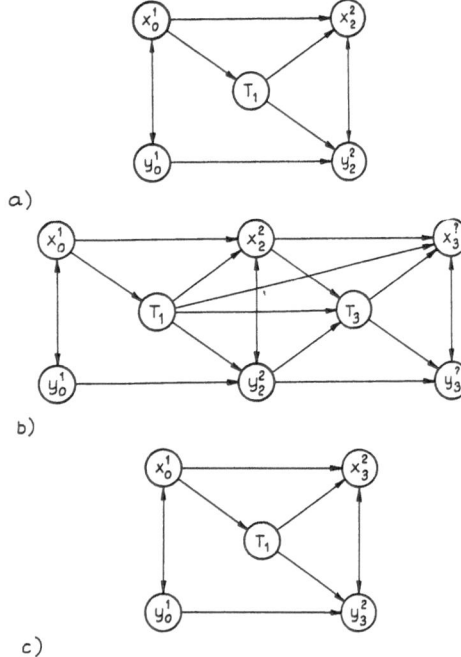

a)

b)

c)

Fig. 3: Construction of $MVSSG(mvs(\tau))$

$MVSSG(mvs(\tau))$ follows that: $usv_x^t(T_1) = \{x_0^1\}$ and $usv_y^t(T_1) = \{y_0^1\}$. Thus, $UNV^t(T_1) = \{x_2^2, x_3^?, y_2^2, y_3^?\}$. A set M consists of two transactions: T_1 and T_f. A set $UNV^t(T_f) = \{x_0^1, x_2^2, y_0^1, y_2^2\}$. Thus, $\bigcap_{T_k \in M} UNV^t(T_k) = \{x_2^2, y_2^2\}$. According to step 2 of the dop, versions $x_3^?$ and $y_3^?$ overwrite versions x_2^2 and y_2^2. New versions $x_3^?$ and $y_3^?$ obtain an index 2. The DB state is the following: $DB = \{(x_0^1, x_3^2), (y_0^1, y_3^2)\}$ (see Figure 3.c.). The last database operation of the input sequence, i.e. $T_1 : r(y)$, reads the version y_0^1.

The multiversion schedule produced by $MVTO$ algorithm complemented by the dop protocol is the following:

$T_0 : w(x,y) \quad T_0 : c \quad T_1 : r(x) \quad T_2 : r(x,y) \quad T_2 : w(x,y)$
$T_2 : c \quad T_3 : r(x,y) \quad T_3 : w(x,y) \quad T_3 : c \quad T_1 : r(y)$
$Rd_{mvs} = \{(T_0 : w(x), T_1 : r(x)), (T_0 : w(x), T_2 : r(x)),$
$(T_0 : w(y), T_2 : r(y)), (T_2 : w(x), T_3 : r(x)),$
$(T_2 : w(y), T_3 : r(y)), (T_0 : w(y), T_1 : r(y))\}$

7 Final conclusions

In this paper we have presented the novel dynamic overwrite protocol (dop) which compared to conventional natural overwrite protocol, used in practice, minimizes the number of transaction abortions caused by a bounded amount of space for holding data item versions. The main idea of this new overwrite protocol lies on the finding sets of data items versions which can be safely overwritten because no active transaction needs to access. We have shown in [8] how the presented overwrite policy can be efficiently combined with $MVTO$ concurrency control algorithms. The simulation analysis under development would have to check the usefulness of this approach.

References

[1] D. Agrawal, and S. Sengupta. *Modular Synchronization in Multiversion Databases: Version Control and Concurrency Control*, Proc. of the ACM-SIGMOD Conf. on Management of Data, pp. 74-83, (1989).

[2] P. A. Bernstein, and N. Goodman. *Multiversion concurrency control: theory and algorithms*, ACM Trans. on Database Systems 8,4, pp. 465-483, (1983).

[3] P. A. Bernstein, N. Goodman, and V. Hadzilacos. *Concurrency Control and Recovery in Database Systems*, Addison-Wesley Publ. Co. (1987).

[4] W. Cellary, E. Gelenbe, and T. Morzy. *Concurrency control in distributed database systems*, North-Holland Publ. Co., (1988).

[5] A. Chan, and R. Gray. *Implementing distributed read-only transactions*, IEEE Trans. on Software Engineering SE-11,2, pp. 205-212, (1985).

[6] T. Hadzilacos, and C. H. Papadimitriou. *Algorithmic aspects of multiversion concurrency control*, Journal of Computer and System Sciences 3,3, pp. 297-310, (1986).

[7] T. Harder, and E. Petry. *Evaluation of a multiple version scheme for concurrency control*, Information Systems 12, 1, pp. 83-98, (1987).

[8] Morzy, T., *On the use of the timestamp-ordering algorithm for concurrency control in K-version database systems*, Proc. Int. Congress on New Technologies for Software and Supercomputers Development, Caracas, (1989).

[9] S. Muro, T. Kameda, and T. Minoura. *Multi-version concurrency control scheme for a database system*, Journal of Computer and System Sciences 29, 2, pp. 207-224, (1984).

[10] Oracle Corporation, *Oracle Database Administrator's Giude*,(1983).

[11] C. H. Papadimitriou, and P. C. Kanellakis. *On concurrency control by multiple versions*, ACM Trans. on Database Systems 9, 1, pp. 89-99, (1984).

[12] C. H. Papadimitriou. *The theory of database concurrency control*, Computer Science Press, (1986).

[13] D. P. Reed. *Implementing atomic actions on decentralized data*, ACM Trans. on Computer Systems 1, 1, pp. 3-23, (1983).

[14] A. Silberschatz. *A multi-version concurrency scheme with no rollbacks*, Proc. ACM SIGACT-SIGOPS Symp. on Principles of Distributed Computing, Ottawa, pp. 216-223, (1982).

[15] Son, S.H., and Haghighi, N., *Performance evaluation of multiversion database systems*, Proc. 6th IEEE Data Engineering Conference, pp.129-136, (1990).

[16] R. Sun, and G. Thomas. *Performance results on multiversion timestamp concurrency control with predeclared write-sets*, Proc. 6th ACM SIGACT-SIGMOD-SIGART Symp. on Principles of Database Systems, San Diego, pp. 177-184,

A Temporal-Logic-Based Query Language for Querying Database Histories

Klaus Hülsmann[†]

TU Braunschweig, Informatik, Abt. Datenbanken
Postfach 3329, D–W3300 Braunschweig (Germany)
E-mail: huelsman@infbs.uucp

Abstract

In this paper, we present a language for querying temporal evolutions of databases. The underlying time model consists of sequences of database states. The general structure of the language is similar to traditional query calculi. Thus temporal queries can be specified in a descriptive logic–oriented way. The language allows arbitrary formulas of a first-order temporal logic as selection conditions. We define syntax and semantics of the language. Further, an algorithm is presented which evaluates temporal queries by scanning database state sequences in one pass from past to present.

key words: database history, database evolution, temporal database, temporal logic, query calculus, database behaviour

1 Introduction

Time is one major aspect of almost all areas of human life and activity. Humans act in, reason about and are influenced by time in a most fundamental way. Another fundamental issue in modern human life is information. Information is not just the basis for planning and decision making but more and more becoming an economic resource in itself. Of course, all kind of information is to a large extent time–related.

Large amounts of information are traditionally organized as databases. The major task of a database is to represent the relevant information about the application area in an appropriate way. It is the job of database design to organize the information in appropriate database structures. For doing this the underlying data model has to provide powerful modelling primitives.

Another important task of a database is to make stored information accessible to the users such that desired information can be extracted in an easy and natural way. This means, the data model must be accompanied by an expressive and powerful query language.

Within the database context, various aspects of time have been discussed. One direction is concerned with temporal databases. In a temporal database all temporal information is represented in one (the current) database state. The other direction is concerned with database behaviour. Here, time is represented by the temporal successorship of database states, i.e. the temporal information is not aggregated in one database state but in a sequence of database states including the current state at the last position.

The query language described in this paper is based on database state sequences. Its basic idea is to select "information units" which display a specific behaviour in time.

1.1 Temporal Databases

As already mentioned, temporal databases represent temporal information within one database state. Snodgrass & Ahn [25] distinguish between *transaction time valid time* and *user defined time*.

For example, we could think of inserting the information that John borrows a book which has to be returned at the first of March. In this case, valid time is the time John borrows the book. Transaction time is the time this information is inserted into the database. The date the book has to be returned is a user defined time.

Numerous attempts have been made to enhance data models and database technology with the capability to handle time. Many approaches extend the relational model [3, 7]. Research in this area faces the problem of preserving the orthogonality of the relational model.

Another example for temporal extensions is the Entity–Relationship model [5, 15]. Recently, also temporal deductive databases [1] have been subject to research.

1.2 Query Languages

Query Languages are usually closely related to the underlying data model. For the relational model two kinds of query formalisms can be distinguished. The first one consists of the class of algebra approaches, which allow to select information in an operational way by use of a couple of basic operations. Algebras are usually used for implementing query languages of the second kind of formalism. This formalism is called relational calculus. It comprises the two variants tuple calculus and domain calculus. The general form of expressions in tuple calculus is as follows:

$$\{x : s \mid \varphi(x)\}$$

Here, x is a variable of the tuple type s and $\varphi(x)$ is a first–order formula with x as its only free variable. The above expression selects the set of all tuples of type s which fulfill the formula $\varphi(x)$.

For temporal databases both kinds of formalism have been employed for defining query languages. For example Clifford & Tansel [3] and Lorentzos & Johnson [17] propose algebras for temporal databases. Gunadhi & Segev [9] discuss optimizations of a temporal algebra. Examples for calculus–based languages are TQUEL proposed by Snodgrass [24] or TSQL defined by Navathe & Ahmed [19].

1.3 Behaviour Specification

Database behaviour manifests itself in the evolution of the database contents in time. Evolutions can be described by database state sequences. According to the taxonomy of Snodgrass & Ahn, behaviour corresponds to transaction time.

Several logical formalisms for reasoning about evolutions have been developped. In [8] modal logic is used for specifying desired database behaviour. Similar lines are followed in [26] proposing deontic logic for specifying database behaviour in a less restrictive way. Another approach is temporal logic [18] which can be employed to reason about the actual behaviour of the database. The aim of the first two approaches is to impose a specific behaviour on the database. This semantics is not intended for temporal logic. A formula in temporal logic may be true or false for the actual behaviour of a database.

Temporal logic provides besides the usual logical connectives $\wedge, \vee, \neg$, etc. such operators as "always in the future holds", "sometime in the future holds", "in the next state holds", "sometime in the past holds", etc. It thus allows to express properties like *"Smith has never been a manager"* or *"All managers have sometime been in prison"*. But also the behaviour of temporal databases can be described in this framework.

Temporal logic has successfully been used to specify temporal integrity constraints on evolutions [22, 4]. In this context, temporal formulas are used to characterize the admissible database evolutions.

Another application for temporal logic is temporal deductive databases [1] where a database consists of temporal formulas.

[†]Supported by Deutsche Forschungsgemeinschaft under grant En184/1

1.4 Language for Behaviour Querying

In the presented framework queries are always formulated from the viewpoint of a current database state referring to *"present tense"* and inspect the history of the database. The idea how to do this is to combine tuple calculus and a subset of temporal logic only containing temporal operators which refer to the past (for short "temporal logic of the past"). So, again we have expressions of the form

$$\{x : s \mid \varphi(x)\}$$

Here, $\varphi(x)$ may be an arbitrary temporal formula characterizing the desired past behaviour of x.

The presented language contains tuple calculus as a sublanguage. Thus tuple calculus can be treated in the same semantical framework as queries on database histories. Tuple calculus queries are evaluated as usual in the current state, i.e. in the last state of the sequence.

We do not use original tuple calculus but a variant called EER calculus. This variant was developped by Hohenstein & Gogolla [10] for an extended Entity–Relationship model (for short *"EER model"*) and comprises rich possibilities for specifying queries and structuring their results. It contains tuple calculus as a subformalism.

1.5 Outline

The rest of this paper is organized as follows. In section 2, we give a brief discussion on database structures and state sequences. In sections 3 and 4, syntax and semantics of our temporal logic and query language are presented. Sections 5 and 6 give an outline of an evaluation method for the temporal logic and query language on database histories. In section 7 we give a brief discussion of possible applications of the presented language and describe enhancement possibilities of the presented algorithms. Finally, this paper ends with some conclusions.

2 Database Structures

The information a database has to provide is organized in specific structures described by a database schema. The database schema provides the language facilities, i.e. the functions and predicates to refer to the contents of a database.

2.1 Entity-Relationship Presentation

Well-known techniques to describe database schemas are Entity-Relationship approaches. In this subsection, we employ an extended Entity-Relationship model [10, 6] to describe an example schema.

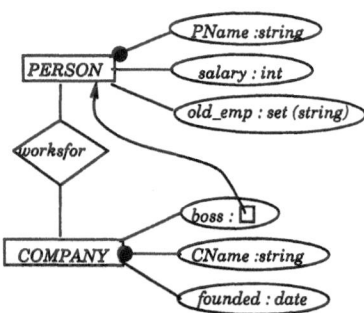

Besides the usual concepts of the Entity-Relationship model, this diagram contains a user defined datatype *date*, an object–valued attribute *boss* of the object type *COMPANY* and a multivalued attribute *old_emp*. Further concepts of this model are specialization and generalization, cardinality constraints and derived attributes.

2.2 Object Structures

In the example schema there can be distinguished between data sorts on the one hand and object and relationship sorts on the other. The language interfaces are defined by a couple of functions and predicates. In a logics framework such interfaces are called database signatures.

2.2.1 Data Sorts

The data sorts for the example schema are given in the following way:

$sorts : int, string, date, time, \ldots$
$functions :$
  $0 \; : \to int$
  $+ \; : \; int \times int \to int$
  $square \; : \; int \to int$
  $length \; : \; string \to int$
  $makedate \; : \; int \times int \times int \to date$
  $month \; : \; date \to string$
  etc.
$predicates :$
  $>, < \; : \; int \times int$
  $before \; : \; date \times date$

As usual functions without arguments represent constants, e.g. the function 0 represents the constant 0.

2.2.2 Object Sorts

The object sorts for the example schema are given in the following way:

$sorts : PERSON, COMPANY$
$functions :$
  $PName \; : \; PERSON \to string$
  $old\_emp \; : \; PERSON \to set(string)$
  $boss \; : \; COMPANY \to PERSON$
  $today \; : \to date$
  etc.
$predicates :$
  $worksfor \; : \; PERSON \times COMPANY$

There is a fundamental difference between data and object sorts, especially when dealing with behaviour aspects.

For data sorts the semantics is fixed once for the complete runtime of the database whereas the interpretation of the object sorts varies in time. For example the *square* of the number 5 is always 25 whereas the salary of the *PERSON* 'Smith' may change.

2.2.3 Sort Expressions

Besides the structures explicitly defined as data and object sorts, there are implicit structures which can be derived from them by use of the sort constructions $set(s)$, $bag(s)$, $list(s)$ and $prod(s_1, \ldots, s_n)$ which stand for finite sets, multisets, lists and the cartesian product.

The sort constructions induce functions and predicates on the resultant sorts. For example, *cnt* counts the number of elements in a set, bag or list, *sel* selects the i-th element of a list and $proj_i$ projects on the i-th place of a tuple. The functions *max* and *avg* compute the maximum and average of the elements of a set, bag or list. The function *max* needs a comparison predicate $\leq$ whereas *avg* requires operations for addition and division.

2.3 Database Behaviour

In the "time model" employed in this paper, the behaviour of a database is represented by a finite sequence of states.

$$\underline{\sigma} = < \sigma_1, \ldots, \sigma_n >$$

The current state is denoted by σ_n. The expression $\underline{\sigma}_i$ stands for the subsequence $< \sigma_1, \ldots, \sigma_i >$. A database state σ_i determines the semantics of a database signature. It is defined as a function mapping

- names of data sorts to sets
- names of object sorts to sets
- function symbols to functions and

- each predicate symbol $p : s_1 \times \ldots \times s_n$ to a set $\sigma_i(p) \subseteq \sigma(s_1) \times \ldots \times \sigma(s_n)$.

The predicates and functions for data sorts have a fixed semantics for all database states. The sets $\sigma_i(s)$ are not disjoint for different states. This allows state–independent object identification, which is an important prerequisite for dealing with object behaviour [23, 2].

For object sorts we have the restriction that objects once deleted are never inserted again, i.e. inserted objects are considered as new.

Terms are either function terms $f(t_1, \ldots, t_n)$ or query terms. They may contain free variables. By $free(t) \subseteq X$ the set of the variables occurring free in t is denoted. The set $X = \bigcup_s X_s$ is the union of the sets X_s containing the variables of sort s.

A substitution is a function ϑ mapping each variable $x \in X_s$ to a value or object of the corresponding sort, i.e. $\vartheta(x) \in \sigma_1(s) \cup \ldots \cup \sigma_n(s)$.

The semantics of a term t for a substitution ϑ in state sequence $\underline{\sigma}$ is then given by $\mu(\underline{\sigma}, \vartheta)(t)$. where $\mu(\underline{\sigma}, \vartheta)$ can be understood as an evaluation function for terms.

Note that terms are evaluated on state sequences. This is because the evaluation function has to be capable to handle temporal queries, too. However, function symbols are evaluated in the current state only, i.e. if the argument term is of the form $f(t_1, \ldots, t_l)$ where f is the name of a data or object function then $\mu(\underline{\sigma}, \vartheta)$ is defined as follows:

$$\mu(\underline{\sigma}, \vartheta)(f(t_1, \ldots, t_l)) = \sigma_n(f)(\mu(\underline{\sigma}, \vartheta)(t_1), \ldots, \mu(\underline{\sigma}, \vartheta)(t_l))$$

2.4 Query Terms

The following list may give an impression what kinds of queries on database behaviour are desirable.

1. *Select the set of 'Smith's former employers.*
2. *Select the maximum salary ever earned by some person.*
3. *Select the set of persons once having earned the maximum salary ever earned by some person.*
4. *Select the set of persons who have always been working for the same company.*
5. *Select the set of persons who have only been working for at most one company.*
6. *Select the date 'Smith' had the last change in salary.*
7. *Select for each company the set of its former employees.*
8. *Select each company and the $PNames$ of its former employees.*

It was already mentioned that queries are made from the viewpoint of the current state. The objects in the result sets must therefore be available in the current state, because only for current objects the corresponding functions and predicates are defined. Information about deleted objects can only be represented by data values because they are available for the whole database lifetime. Thus query no. 7 selects only current objects whereas query no. 8 also selects names of persons which are not present in the current state.

3 Temporal Logic

3.1 Syntax

If p is an n-ary predicate symbol and $t_1, \ldots, t_n$ are terms of appropriate types then $p(t_1, \ldots, t_n)$ is a basic formula.

If $\varphi, \varphi_1, \varphi_2$ are formulas then the following are formulas, too:

1. every basic formula

2. $\neg\varphi$, $(\varphi_1 \wedge \varphi_2)$, $(\varphi_1 \vee \varphi_2)$

3. $(\exists x \in t)\, \varphi$, $(\forall x \in t)\, \varphi$
   where t is either a term of sort $set(s)$, $bag(s)$ or $list(s)$ or the sort name s itself and x is a variable of sort s which has no free occurrence in t.

4. $(\mathbf{always}\,\varphi)$, $(\mathbf{sometime}\,\varphi)$, $(\mathbf{last}\,\varphi)$, $(\mathbf{weaklast}\,\varphi)$

Nothing else is a formula.

In the subsequent, brackets will be omitted if no ambiguity is possible. Sometimes we will use the notion *temporal formula* for explicitly referring to formulas which contain connectives of the last kind and *non–temporal formula* to refer to those ones which do not, respectively. By $free(\varphi)$ we will denote the variables occurring free in a formula.

The following example formula states that 'Smith' sometime earned a salary of 5000.

$$(\exists p \in PERSON)\, PName(p) = \text{``Smith''} \wedge \mathbf{sometime}\, salary(p) = 5000$$

3.2 Semantics

The fact that a temporal formula φ is valid for a given substitution ϑ is expressed as follows:

$$[\underline{\sigma}, \vartheta] \models \varphi$$

We assume ϑ to be defined in the current state for all variables occurring free in φ, i.e. for all $x \in free(\varphi)$ with sort s holds: $\vartheta(x) \in \sigma_n(s)$

The semantics of temporal formulas is defined as follows:

1. $[\underline{\sigma}, \vartheta] \models p(t_1, \ldots, t_l)$
   iff $(\mu(\underline{\sigma}, \vartheta)(t_1), \ldots, \mu(\underline{\sigma}, \vartheta)(t_l)) \in \sigma_n(p)$

2. $[\underline{\sigma}, \vartheta] \models \neg\varphi$
   iff not $[\underline{\sigma}, \vartheta] \models \varphi$

3. $[\underline{\sigma}, \vartheta] \models \varphi_1 \wedge \varphi_2$
   iff $[\underline{\sigma}, \vartheta] \models \varphi_1$ and $[\underline{\sigma}, \vartheta] \models \varphi_2$

4. $[\underline{\sigma}, \vartheta] \models \mathbf{always}\, \varphi$
   iff for all $i \in \{l, \ldots, n\}$ holds $[\underline{\sigma}_i, \vartheta] \models \varphi$ where σ_l is the earliest state in which $\vartheta(x)$ is defined for all variables in $free(\varphi)$

5. $[\underline{\sigma}, \vartheta] \models \mathbf{sometime}\, \varphi$
   iff exists $i \in \{l, \ldots, n\}$ such that $[\underline{\sigma}_i, \vartheta] \models \varphi$ where σ_l is the earliest state in which $\vartheta(x)$ is defined for all variables in $free(\varphi)$

6. $[\underline{\sigma}, \vartheta] \models \mathbf{last}\, \varphi$
   iff exists a previous state σ_{n-1} in which $\vartheta(x)$ is defined for all $x \in free(\varphi)$ and $[\underline{\sigma}_{n-1}, \vartheta] \models \varphi$

7. $[\underline{\sigma}, \vartheta] \models \mathbf{weaklast}\, \varphi$
   iff either a previous state σ_{n-1} in which $\vartheta(x)$ is defined for all $x \in free(\varphi)$ does not exist or otherwise $[\underline{\sigma}_{n-1}, \vartheta] \models \varphi$

8. $[\underline{\sigma}, \vartheta] \models (\exists x \in t)\, \varphi$
   iff exists a substitution ϑ' differing from ϑ only in the variable x such that $\vartheta'(x) \in \sigma_n(t)$ and $[\underline{\sigma}, \vartheta'] \models \varphi$

9. $[\underline{\sigma}, \vartheta] \models (\forall x \in t)\, \varphi$
   iff for all substitutions ϑ' differing from ϑ only in the variable x such that $\vartheta'(x) \in \sigma_n(t)$ holds: $[\underline{\sigma}, \vartheta'] \models \varphi$

3.3 Normal Form

The following so-called *recursion rules* allow temporal formulas to be split into a present part which must be valid in the current state and a historical part which has to be fulfilled by the database history.

$$\mathbf{always}\,\varphi \quad \Leftrightarrow \quad \varphi \wedge \mathbf{weaklast\ always}\,\varphi$$
$$\mathbf{sometime}\,\varphi \quad \Leftrightarrow \quad \varphi \vee \mathbf{last\ sometime}\,\varphi$$

By use of these rules, every temporal formula φ can be transformed to an equivalent formula $dtnf(\varphi)$ in so-called *temporal disjunctive normal form* (for short: DTNF). The algorithm to do this works as follows:

1. Until no changes occur, replace every temporal formula '$\mathbf{always}\,\varphi$' or '$\mathbf{sometime}\,\varphi$' not in the scope of another temporal operator by the right hand side of the corresponding recursion rule.

2. Eliminate all parentheses '(' and ')' not in the scope of a temporal operator. The result is a disjunction of conjunctions.

3. Replace subformulas '¬**weaklast** φ' and '¬**last** ψ' by '**last** ¬φ' and '**weaklast** ¬ψ', respectively.

4. For each conjunction, collect all subformulas bound by '**last**' or '**weaklast**', respectively, to two conjunctions bound by '**last**' or '**weaklast**'.

The resultant disjunctive temporal normal form looks as follows:

$$\bigvee_k \alpha_k \wedge \textbf{weaklast} \gamma_k [\wedge \textbf{last} \delta_k]$$

The parts bound by **last** are optional. A possibly missing part '**weaklast** γ_k' may be replaced by '**weaklast true**' which is valid for every state sequence.

Note, that the presented algorithm treats basic formulas and subformulas beginning with a quantifier as propositional variables, i.e. the internal structures of these constituents are not inspected.

Remark: The definitions of syntax, semantics and normal form for past temporal logic were carried over from [16] where these notions are defined for temporal logic of the future.

4 Temporal Queries

4.1 Syntax

We did already say that the language to be presented follows the line of traditional query calculi. The structure of queries is as follows:

$$\{t_1, \ldots, t_n \mid x_1 \in r_1, \ldots, x_k \in r_k : \varphi\}$$

Queries are terms of the sort $prod(s_1, \ldots, s_n)$. The constituents are:

- an *output list* consisting of terms $t_1, \ldots, t_n$ of sorts $s_1, \ldots, s_n$,

- a *declaration list* $x_1 \in r_1, \ldots, x_k \in r_k$ declaring the variables $x_1, \ldots, x_n$ of sorts $s_{x_1}, \ldots, s_{x_k}$ where r_i declares the *range* of x_i and is either a term of sort $set(s_{x_i})$, $bag(s_{x_i})$, $list(s_{x_i})$, or the sort name s_{x_i} itself, and

- a *qualification part* consisting of a temporal formula φ.

In the subsequent, we will occasionally use the terminology *temporal term* to refer to terms containing a temporal formula and *non-temporal term* to refer to those ones which do not.

For the declaration list we have the syntactical restriction that a variable x_i may not occur in the range definitions $r_1, \ldots, r_i$.

As ranges, arbitrary data or object sorts are allowed. The consequence is that the syntax does not prohibit unsafe queries, i.e. queries which have an infinite result. This is one of the differences between our language and the approach of [10] which was taken as a basis for developping it. In [10] safeness is achieved by prohibiting names of data sorts as ranges in the declaration list. If a variable of a data sort is needed, its range has to be specified by a term. Thus in the language of [10], terms have always a finite result.

Unfortunately, this solution would be too restrictive for temporal queries. Moreover, it is useless when evaluating queries by scanning the database sequence from past to present in one pass, since in the past it is not known which values or objects will be in the range at evaluation time. Thus all values of the sort must be considered anyway.

4.2 Semantics

The evaluation function for terms is extended for queries as follows:

$$\mu(\underline{\varrho}, \vartheta)(\{t_1, \ldots, t_n \mid x_1 \in r_1, \ldots, x_k \in r_k \; \varphi\}) =$$
$$\{\{\mu(\underline{\varrho}, \vartheta')(t_1), \ldots, \mu(\underline{\varrho}, \vartheta')(t_n) \mid$$
$$\vartheta' \text{ is a substitution with } \vartheta'(x) = \vartheta(x) \text{ for } x \notin \{x_1, \ldots, x_n\} \text{ such}$$
$$\text{that } \vartheta'(x_i) \in \mu(\underline{\varrho}, \vartheta')(r_i) \text{ for } i = 1 \ldots k \text{ and } [\underline{\varrho}, \vartheta'] \models \varphi\}\}$$

Double braces '{{' and '}}' indicate that the result is a bag.

Remark: The way to define syntax and semantics of a query language was carried over from [10] to the temporal case.

4.3 Examples

In this subsection, we demonstrate the query language by giving the formulation of the queries presented in subsection 2.4.

1. $\{emp \mid emp \in COMPANY, p \in PERSON:$
   $PName(p) = \text{"Smith"} \wedge$
   $\textbf{sometime } worksfor(p, emp)\}$

2. $max(\{sal \mid sal \in integer, p \in PERSON:$
   $\textbf{sometime } salary(p) = sal\})$

3. $\{p \mid m \in integer, p \in PERSON:$
   $m = max(\{s \mid s \in integer, p \in PERSON:$
   $\textbf{sometime } salary(p) = s\}) \wedge$
   $\textbf{sometime } salary(p) = m\}$

4. $\{p \mid emp \in \{c \mid c \in COMPANY : worksfor(p, c)\}$
   $p \in PERSON: \textbf{always } worksfor(p, emp)\}$

5. $\{p \mid p \in PERSON:$
   $cnt(\{s \mid s \in string:$
   $\textbf{sometime } (\exists c \in COMPANY$
   $worksfor(p, c) \wedge$
   $s = CName(c)\}) \leq 1\}$

6. $max(\{d \mid d \in date, s \in integer, p \in PERSON:$
   $PName(p) = \text{"Smith"} \wedge salary(p) = s \wedge$
   $\textbf{sometime } (d = today \wedge salary(p) \neq s)\})$

7. $\{c, \{p \mid p \in PERSON: \neg worksfor(p, c)$
   $\wedge \textbf{sometime } worksfor(p, c)\} \mid c \in COMPANY\}$

8. $\{c, \{n \mid n \in string:$
   $\neg(\exists p \in PERSON worksfor(p, c) \wedge n = PName(p)) \wedge$
   $\textbf{sometime} (\exists p \in PERSON$
   $worksfor(p, c) \wedge n = PName(p))\}$
   $\mid c \in COMPANY\}$

5 Temporal Logic Evaluation

The key to evaluating temporal formulas on state sequences are the corresponding disjunctive normal forms. Successive normal form construction allows to compute a kind of finite state machine, called *transition graphs*, for temporal formulas. A temporal formula is valid for a state sequence if a path to a corresponding node exists in the graph.

5.1 General Idea

A temporal formula is valid for a state sequence if at least one of the conjunctions of its disjunctive normal form is valid. For the moment let us assume the formula does not contain quantifiers. In this case, α_k is a conjunction of basic formulas whereas γ_k and δ_k are conjunctions of temporal formulas. The whole conjunction is valid if α_k is valid in the current state and additionally γ_k and δ_k are valid in the state sequence ending in the previous one. If this sequence is empty, i.e. if there is no previous state, γ_k is valid and δ_k, if existent, is not. If, otherwise, the sequence is not empty γ_k and δ_k have to be evaluated for the state sequence ending with the previous state. This can be done by computing $dtnf(\gamma_k \wedge \delta_k)$ and repeating the whole procedure for the shorter sequence.

5.2 Transition Graphs

The evaluation scheme sketched in the previous subsection successively computes new temporal formulas which remain to be evaluted in the sequence reduced by the last state.

There are only a finite number of different formulas which can be computed from an initial formula in this way. The transitions between these formulas can be represented in a graphical way by transition graphs.

A transition graph consists of the following parts:

1. A *directed graph* $G = (N, E)$ with nodes N and edges $E \subseteq N \times N$

2. A *node labelling* ν mapping every node to a temporal formula

3. An *edge labelling* η mapping every edge to a non–temporal formula

4. A set of *initial nodes* $I \subseteq N$

A transition graph is *consistently labelled* if for every node $k \in N$ the following property holds:

$$\nu(k) = \left(\bigvee_{l \in I, (l,n) \in E} \eta((l,k)) \wedge \text{weaklast } \nu(l) \right)$$
$$\vee \left(\bigvee_{l \in (N-I), (l,n) \in E} \eta((l,k)) \wedge \text{last } \nu(l) \right)$$

Finite, consistently labelled transition graphs can be computed from temporal formulas in the following way:

```
create a node n with label φ
for each node n ∈ N do
    compute dtnf(ν(n))
    for each conjunction αₖ ∧ weaklastγₖ do
        if no node l ∈ I with ν(l) = γ exists
            then create node l ∈ I with ν(l) = γₖ;
            create an edge e = (l, n) with η(e) = αₖ
    endfor;
    for each conjunction αₖ ∧ weaklastγₖ ∧ lastδ do
        if no node l ∈ N with ν(l) = γₖ ∧ δₖ exists
            then create node l ∈ N with ν(l) = γ ∧ δₖ;
            create an edge e = (l, n) with η(e) = αₖ
    endfor;
endfor;
```

Two simple, consistently labelled transition graphs are listed below.

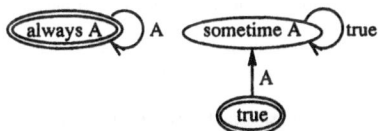

The double borderings indicate initial nodes.

5.3 Propositional Case

Assume we are given a temporal formula φ without any quantifiers. For evaluating this formula for a state sequence $\underline{\sigma}$ and substitution ϑ, we can use a consistently labelled transition graph.

The marking function

$$m_T(\underline{\sigma}, \vartheta, i)$$

yields for a substitution ϑ, state σ_i and sequence $\underline{\sigma}$ set of nodes whose labels are valid.

The marking at some state σ_i can be determined from the marking at state σ_{i-1} as follows:

$$m_t(\underline{\sigma}, \vartheta, i) = trans(m_t(\underline{\sigma}, \vartheta, i-1), \underline{\sigma}_i, \vartheta)$$

The *transition rule 'trans'* is defined as follows:

$$trans(L, \underline{\sigma}_i, \vartheta) = \{n \mid \exists l \in L : (l, n) \in E \wedge [\underline{\sigma}_i, \vartheta] \models \eta((l,n))\}$$

If σ_l is the first state in the sequence in which ϑ is defined for all variables in $free(\varphi)$ then

$$m_T(\underline{\sigma}, \vartheta, l) = trans(I, \underline{\sigma}_l, \vartheta).$$

I is the set of initial nodes of the transition graph.

A temporal formula can be evaluated by scanning the database sequence from 'past' to 'present' and computing the marking accordingly.

It follows from the definition of consistently labelled transition graphs that exactly those nodes are marked whose labels are valid for the sequence up to the corresponding database state. Thus holds:

$$[\underline{\sigma}_i, \vartheta] \models \nu(n) \text{ iff } n \in m_t(\underline{\sigma}, \vartheta, i)$$

Maintaining the marking for each substitution defined for the free variables allows to find all substitutions for which the formula is valid.

Remark: The definitions of transition graphs, consistently labelled transition graphs, the graph construction algorithm, the marking function and the transition rule were carried over from [21] where according notions are defined for temporal logic of the future.

5.4 First Order Case

We begin with the case that quantifications only occur outside the scope of temporal connectives. In this case, the formula can easily be transformed into prenex normal form, i.e. a formula of the following shape:

$$Q_1 x_1 \in t_1, \ldots, Q_n x_n \in t_n \varphi$$

Q_i is a quantifier $\exists$ or $\forall$ and x_i is a variable of sort s_i. The formula φ itself does not contain any quantifiers. Determining whether $Q_1 x_1 \in t_1, \ldots, Q_n x_n \in t_n \varphi$ is valid or not can be done as follows.

1. Compute the set of substitutions ϑ' with $\vartheta'(x) = \vartheta(x)$ for $x \notin \{x_1, \ldots, x_k\}$ and $[\underline{\sigma}, \vartheta'] \models \varphi$.

2. Evaluate the quantification part.

Since the algorithm for transition graph construction treats quantified subformulas in the same way as basic formulas, these subformulas occur inside the labels of the edges of the graph.

Their evaluation takes place by use of an own transition graph for each of them. Thus evaluating an edge label containing a quantified temporal formula can be done by inspecting its transition graph.

6 Query Evaluation

Evaluation of temporal queries basically relies on temporal logic evaluation. The algorithm presented in this section evaluates queries by scanning the database evolution in one pass from past to present.

The task of a query evaluation algorithm is to compute the result of a query which has to match the semantics given by:

$$\mu(\underline{\sigma}, \vartheta)(\{t_1, \ldots, t_n \mid x_1 \in r_1, \ldots, x_k \in r_k : \varphi\})$$

The general way to evaluate a temporal query is as follows:

1. Evaluate the declaration part: Determine all substitutions ϑ' differing from ϑ at most in the variables $x_1, \ldots, x_k$ such that $\vartheta'(x_i) \in \mu(\underline{\sigma}, \vartheta')(r_i)$.

2. Evaluate the qualification part: Select form the substitutions resulting from step 1 those ones with $[\underline{\sigma}, \vartheta] \models \varphi$

3. Evaluate the output list: For each of the substitutions remaining after step 2, add to the query result a tuple $(\mu(\underline{\sigma}, \vartheta')(t_1), \ldots, \mu(\underline{\sigma}, \vartheta')(t_n))$.

Each of the three components, i.e. output list, declaration and qualification may have to be evaluated on the whole database evolution.

A naive algorithm for their evaluation could be to evaluate each of them by scanning the database sequence in an own pass from past to present. This solution requires the whole database sequence to be available for the whole database lifetime, which is not the case for every application area of the language.

Therefore, the approach of this paper is to evaluate temporal queries in one pass. This is done by keeping the information which substitutions fulfill which temporal formula in which database states. This is done for every temporal formula occurring as qualification part of some subquery or of the query itself. With this information at hand, terms are evaluated as sketched above.

Of course, a formula may in turn contain temporal queries. The result of these queries is assumed to be at hand, too, i.e. they are assumed to be evaluated in a preceding step.

Step 2 of the evaluation algorithm is quite easy to realize. The only thing to be done is to inspect the marking of ϑ' for the transition graph of the the formula φ.

Step 3 can be realized by recursively applying the evaluation algorithm to the terms of the output list.

Step 1 needs more detailed explanation. The substitutions ϑ' are computed by successively evaluating the ranges r_i:

1. Initialize $\Theta_0 = \{\vartheta\}$

2. for i = 1 to k do
   compute the set
   $$\Theta_i = \bigcup_{\vartheta \in \Theta_{i-1}} \{\vartheta' | \vartheta'(x_i) \in \mu(\underline{\varrho}, \vartheta)(r_i) \wedge \vartheta'(x) = \vartheta(x) \text{ for } x \neq x_i\}$$
   endfor

3. The result is Θ_k.

Since each range definition r_i only depends on the variables $x_1, \ldots, x_{i-1}$ this algorithm computes the desired result, i.e. Θ_k contains all substitutions ϑ' differing from ϑ in at most the variables $x_1, \ldots, x_k$ such that $\vartheta'(x_i) \in \mu(\underline{\varrho}, \vartheta')(r_i)$.

7 Applications and Enhancements

In this section we discuss some possible extensions of the language and its application to temporal databases and database design.

7.1 Temporal Databases

There are two ways the query language can be applied to temporal databases.

One of them is to use it for querying the databases. In principle, the sketched evaluation method could be adopted for temporal databases, too, since their contents can be transformed into a sequence of snapshots. But in practice this method seems only useful for so-called *rollback databases* [25], which explicitly store database state sequences. For the other kinds of temporal databases it seems at least possible to translate the query language to the underlying query algebra.

Another application area is based on the fact that temporal databases not only store temporal data but themselves evolve in time. This means the behaviour of a temporal database can be described in the framework presented in this paper. Especially the relation of current temporal data to the history of the database can be expressed in terms of the query language. The language thus provides the means to define the formal semantics of a temporal database.

7.2 Database Design

A database may contain information referring to the past which must be modelled in the database schema. The attribute *old_emp* in the Entity-Relationship diagram in subsection 2.1 is an example for historical information. It refers to the former employers of a person.

The query language presented in this paper allows to express temporal information directly in terms of temporal queries. For our example *old_emp* is specified as follows:

$$old\_emp(p) = \{CName(e) \mid e \in COMPANY : \\ \mathbf{sometime}\, works for(p, e)\}$$

The presented evaluation method provides a one-pass evaluation from past to present and thus always only needs the current database state and some additional historical information for query evaluation. Furthermore, evaluation can be done automatically and thus assures temporal integrity constraints to be not violated.

Summarizing we can say, the query language is useful to define at database definition time the temporal information to be contained in the database. The evaluation schemes for queries are generated automatically at definition time, too.

7.3 Maintaining Temporal Information

Several authors discuss the problem of infinite data arising in the context of temporal query processing [1, 14]. This problem also occurs in the context of the query language of this paper.

For example, query number 2 in subsection 4.3 needs the marking for all substitutions of the variables *sal* and *p*, i.e. for each element of the set $\sigma_i(integer) \times \sigma_i(PERSON)$.

The same problem occurs with monitoring temporal integrity constraints which is based on transition graphs, too. The solution developped for this area also applies for temporal query evaluation [12, 13]. Its basic idea is to introduce so-called *descriptions* representing possibly infinite sets of substitutions by leaving the values for some variables open, e.g. $[*, *], [*, Smith], [3000, Smith]$.

Although infinite substitution sets can be represented by finitely many descriptions, infinitely many descriptions may generated by the evaluation algorithm. Whether this may occur or not depends on the structure of the underlying transition graphs and can be detected at query definition time. In [13] sufficient (but not necessary) criteria are presented for doing this. These criteria give rise to a syntactical definition of *temporally safe queries*.

The algorithm for description–based evaluation of transition graphs presented in [13] can be easily adopted for temporal query evaluation.

7.4 Optimization

Evaluation of temporal formulas consists of successively computing new markings. This is done by evaluating the transtion rule which in turn evaluates the edge lables of a transition graph. Evaluating the transition rule can be understood as evaluating a classical non-temporal query which determines the substitutions fulfilling the considered edge label. Thus classical query optimization methods apply to transition rule optimization, too.

Another source of optimization possibilities arises from the fact that in general, only small portions of the database change from one state to another.

This means for transition rule evaluation that only those substitutions have to be considered which depend on objects affected by the preceding update.

A similar problem is addressed in research on efficient checking of integrity constraints specified in first order logic [11, 20]. The algorithms developped for this task exploit the property that before the database update the formula to be checked was valid. The methods for checking space reduction and formula minimization developed for efficient integrity checking seem to apply for temporal query optimization, too.

8 Conclusions

This paper presents a temporal–logic–based query calculus for querying database histories. It provides a brief presentation of syntax and semantics of the language nd discusses a method for its evaluation. According to this method, query evaluation takes place by scanning database evolutions in one pass from past to present. The basic idea is to maintain for each database state the historical information needed for the queries to be evaluated. The structure of this information can be derived from the queries.

Several applications of the language are possible ranging from temporal database querying up to designing temporal information in merely traditional database contexts.

The presented evaluation method makes the language particularly useful for design purposes. It allows temporal information to be specified in terms of temporal queries. A centralized temporal query evaluation provides the temporal information in the current database state to be consistent with the actual history. This could otherwise only be ensured by designing the database update transactions such that historically consistent updates are guaranteed. Also for this task the presented evaluation scheme is applicable be it for being incorporated in the transaction specifications or for their verification.

References

[1] J. Chomicki and T. Imielinski. Temporal Deductive Databases and Infinite Objects. In *Proc. 7th ACM SIGACT-SIGMOD-SIGART Symp. on Princ. of Database Systems*, pages 61–73, New York (NY), 1988.

[2] J. Clifford. *Formal Semantics and Pragmatics for Natural Language Querying*. Cambridge University Press, Cambridge (UK), 1990.

[3] J. Clifford and A.U. Tansel. On an Algebra For Historical Relational Databases: Two Views. In S. Navathe, editor, *Proc. 1985 ACM-SIGMOD Int. Conf. on Management of Data*, pages 247–265, New York, 1985. ACM.

[4] H.-D. Ehrich, U. W. Lipeck, and M. Gogolla. Specification, Semantics, and Enforcement of Dynamic Database Constraints. In *Proc. Int. Conf. on Very Large Databases VLDB'84*, pages 301–308, Singapore, 1984.

[5] R. Elmasri, I. El-Assal, and V. Kouramajian. Semantics of Temporal Data in an Extended ER Model. In *Proc. 9th Int. Conf. on Entity-Relationship Approach*, Lausanne (CH), 1990.

[6] G. Engels, M. Gogolla, U. Hohenstein, K. Hülsmann, P. Löhr-Richter, G. Saake, and H.-D. Ehrich. Conceptual Modelling of Database Applications Using an Extended Entity-Relationship Model. Informatik-Bericht 90-05, Techn. Univ. Braunschweig, 1990. *submitted for publication*.

[7] S.K. Gadia. Weak Temporal Relations. In *Proc. 5th ACM SIGACT-SIGMOD-SIGART Symp. on Princ. of Database Systems*, pages 70–77, New York (NY), 1986.

[8] F. Golshani, T.S.E. Maibaum, and M.R. Sadler. A Modal System for Database Specification and Query Language Support. In *Proc. 9th Int. Conf. on Very Large Databases VLDB'83*, pages 331–339, Florence, (I), 1983.

[9] H. Gunadhi and A. Segev. Temporal Query Optimization in Scientific Databases. *Data Engineering*, 13:27–34, 1990.

[10] U. Hohenstein and M. Gogolla. A Calculus for an Extended Entity-Relationship Model Incorporating Arbitrary Data Operations and Aggregate Functions. In *Proc. 7th Int. Conf. on the Entity-Relationship Approach*, Rome, 1988. North-Holland, Amsterdam, 1988.

[11] A. Hsu and T. Imielinsky. Integrity Checking for Multiple Updates. In S. Navathe, editor, *Proc. 1985 ACM-SIGMOD Int. Conf. on Management of Data*, pages 152–168, New York, 1985. ACM.

[12] K. Hülsmann and G. Saake. Representation of the Historical Information Necessary for Temporal Integrity Monitoring. In F. Bancilhon, C. Thanos, and D. Tsichritzis, editors, *Proc. Int. Conf. on Extending Database Technology EDBT'90*, pages 378–392, Venice (I), 1990. LNCS 416, Springer-Verlag, Berlin, 1990.

[13] K. Hülsmann and G. Saake. Theoretical Foundations of Handling Large Substitution Sets in Temporal Integrity Monitoring. *Acta Informatica*, 28(4):365–407, 1991.

[14] F. Kabanza, J-M Stevenne, and P. Wolper. Handling infinite temporal data. In *9th Annual ACM SIGACT-SIGMOD-SIGART Symposium on Principles of Database Systems*, Nashville, TN, apr 1990.

[15] M.R. Klopprogge. TERM: An Approach to Include the Time Dimension in the Entity-Relationship Model. In *Proc. 2nd Int. Conf. on Entity-Relationship Approach*, October 1981.

[16] U. W. Lipeck and G. Saake. Monitoring Dynamic Integrity Constraints Based on Temporal Logic. *Information Systems*, 12:255–269, 1987.

[17] N.A. Lorentzos and R.G. Johnson. Extending Relational Algebra to Manipulate Temporal Data. *Information Systems*, 13:289–296, 1988.

[18] Z. Manna and A. Pnueli. Verification of Concurrent Programs: The Temporal Framework. In H.A. Maurer, editor, *6th Colloquium on Automata Languages and Programming, LNCS 71*, pages 385–409. Springer-Verlag, Berlin 1979, 1979.

[19] S.B. Navathe and R. Ahmed. TSQL: A Language Interface for History Databases. In *Proc. IFIP WG 8.1 Conf. on Temporal Aspect of Information Systems*, pages 109–122, Sophia Antipolis (F), 1987.

[20] J.-M. Nicolas. Logic for Improving Integrity Checking in Relational Databases. *Acta Informatica*, 18, 1982.

[21] G. Saake and U.W. Lipeck. Using Finite-Linear Temporal Logic for Specifying Database Dynamics. In E. Börger, H. Kleine Büning, and M.M. Richter, editors, *Proc. CSL'88 2nd Workshop Computer Science Logic*, pages 288–300, Berlin, 1989. Springer-Verlag.

[22] A. Sernadas. Temporal Aspects of Logical Procedure Definition. *Information Systems*, (5):167–187, 1980.

[23] A. Sernadas, C. Sernadas, and H.-D. Ehrich. Object-Oriented Specification of Databases: An Algebraic Approach. In P. Hammerslay, editor, *Proc. 13th Int. Conf. on Very Large Databases VLDB'87*, pages 107–116, Brighton (GB), 1987. Morgan-Kaufmann, Palo Alto, 1987.

[24] R. Snodgrass. The Temporal Query Language TQuel. In *Proc. 9th ACM SIGACT-SIGMOD-SIGART Symp. on Princ. of Database Systems*, pages 204–213, Waterloo (Ontario), 1984.

[25] R. Snodgrass and I. Ahn. A Taxonomy of Time in Databases. In S. Navathe, editor, *Proc. 1985 ACM-SIGMOD Int. Conf. on Management of Data*, pages 236–246, New York, 1985. ACM.

[26] R. Wieringa, J.-J.Meyer, and H. Weigand. Specifying Dynamic and Deontic Integrity Constraints. *Data & Knowledge Engineering*, 4(2):157–191, 1989.

Querying Incomplete Knowledge Bases with Abduction

Fiora Pirri
Dipartimento di Informatica e Sistemistica
Università di Roma "La Sapienza"
via Salaria 113, 00198 Roma, Italia
e-mail: pirri@vaxrma.infn.it

Clara Pizzuti
CRAI
Località S.Stefano
87036 Rende (CS), Italia
e-mail: clara@icsvmhpo.bitnet clara@crai.it

Abstract

A proposal for dealing with querying incomplete knowledge bases, as an abductive task, is presented. Abduction enhances reasoning capabilities allowing for an answer in all those situations in which the system does not have enough information and normally would fail. A method for the computation of abductive explanations which exploits logic programming is given. An application example pointing out the benefits of such an approach is shown.

Key words: abduction, explanations, logic programs, classical negation.

1 Introduction

In the last few years several research efforts have concentrated on describing databases as first order logical languages. The expectations of this research is to enhance the capabilities of database management systems with the espressive power of First Order Logic (FOL) to provide powerful systems that can be used in AI applications. In fact, while database management systems are able to manage efficiently large amounts of data, logic affords both an appropriate representation scheme of the application domain of knowledge and a computational model for *intelligent databases* or *knowledge bases (KB)*.

In this paper we shall examine incomplete KB [10], that is KB not having all the information necessary to answer a query. For example, the KB could know that Mary is either a teacher or a student, but also that she is neither a teacher nor a student. The reasons for the KB being incomplete may be manifold. The most important is that the KB undergoes a continuous evolution and an interactive system cannot wait for it to stabilize in a final and complete form since this may never happen. When a knowledge-based system depends on an incomplete KB, its reasoning capabilities are seriously compromised and, in order to overcome this, it must appeal to some kind of heuristics.

The approach suggested in this work is to provide the knowledge-based system with *abductive reasoning capabilities* so that, in the presence of incomplete information, it is able to abduce a consistent set of hypotheses, called abducibles, which permit to give an answer to the query, i.e. the answer is true under these hypotheses.

Abduction [11,5,8] is a form of hypothetical reasoning deriving a consistent set of hypotheses which, together with the knowledge on the world, account for observed events. This set of assumptions is considered an *explanation* of such events. In other words, given a theory Σ, describing the knowledge on the world, if it does not derive a formula C, to abduce C means to find those S such that $\Sigma \cup S \models C$. S is an hypothesis which, if known, sanctions the conclusion C.

Moving to databases, the theory is a description of the KB and the observation is a query which cannot be answered only on the basis of the information contained in the KB. The task is thus to find a set of abductive explanations which allows one to answer the query. For example, suppose that KB is

$$\{fly(tweety) \vee \neg bird(tweety), fly(tweety) \vee \neg haswings(tweety)\}$$

and we want to know if *tweety* flies. We cannot derive that *tweety* can fly, but there are two meaningful hypotheses which, if known, explain why tweety flies: one is that it is a bird, and the other that it has wings.

We found that, given a query, a suitable manipulation of the minimal models of the theory describing the KB allows us to derive the abducibles explaining the query. In order to obtain these models we exploit logic programming. In fact, these models are easily shown to correspond to the minimal three-valued stable models of a particular logic program associated with the theory. Three-valued stable models are an extension to two-valued stable models of [6,7] which allow one to deal with *unknown* values. Three-valued logics is particularly apt for dealing with databases where something is unknown to be either true or false and the distiction between *no* and *unknown* answers is important.

The paper is organized as follows: in Section 2 preliminary definitions and notations are given, in Section 3 the abductive framework is defined, in Section 4 the computation of abductive explanations with the proposed method is addressed and, finally, in Section 5 a brief description of the algorithm is presented.

2 Preliminaries

Let us start by defining our basic concepts and notation. We assume a first order language $\mathcal{L}$, without function symbols. Constant and variables (terms), predicate symbols, connectives and quantifiers are defined as usual. An *atomic formula* or *atom* is either a propositional letter, $A, \ldots, P, Q$ or a predicate symbol applied to terms of $\mathcal{L}$. A *literal* is either an atomic formula (positive literal) or the negation of an atomic formula (negative literal). A term, predicate or literal is *ground* if it is variable-free. A *clause* is a finite disjunction $\forall y_1 \cdots \forall y_r(L_1 \vee \cdots \vee L_n)$ of literals with no free variables occurring in $L_1, \ldots, L_n$. A *unit* clause is a clause with a single literal. A *Horn* clause is a clause with

---
*This work has been partially supported by "Progetto Finalizzato Sistemi informatici e Calcolo Parallelo" of C.N.R..

at most one positive literal. A *sentence*, denoted by lowercase greek letters ϕ, ψ,.., is a formula of $\mathcal{L}$ with no occurrence of free variables. In the following we assume that a theory Σ is a set of sentences of $\mathcal{L}$. $CNF(\phi)$ is a conjunction of disjunctions. Let $(\forall x)L_1, \ldots, L_n \supset L$ be a sentence ψ of $\mathcal{L}$ where $L, L_1, \ldots, L_n$ are literals. We call a *rule*, r, the notational variant of ψ written as $r : (\forall x)L \leftarrow L_1, \ldots, L_n$, where L is called the *head* of the rule, $L_1, \ldots, L_n$ the body of the rule and $\leftarrow$ is a sort of implication. Thus any sentence can be written as a rule. One of the central ideas of logic programming is to rely on a form of negation departing from classical logic, that is, negation as failure. Gelfond and Lifschitz, in [7] introduced explicitly negation as failure in the syntax of a rule, beside classical negation. In the sequel we use their notation. A *general logic program* is a set of rules of the form:

$$A \leftarrow A_1, \ldots, A_m, not\ A_{m+1} \ldots not\ A_n$$

where, for $1 \leq i \leq n$, A_i is an atomic formula.

An *extended logic program* is a set of rules of the form

$$L_0 \leftarrow L_1, \ldots, L_m, not\ L_{m+1} \ldots not\ L_n$$

where, for $0 \leq i \leq n$, L_i is a literal. Notice that while the symbol *not* is intended to be negation as failure, the symbol $\neg$, is intended as classical negation, implicitly expressed when a literal is negative, either in the body or in the head of a rule. A logic program is a finite (we do not consider the case of countably infinite) set of rules.

The declarative semantics of a logic program Π is given by the model-theoretic semantics based on Herbrand interpretations. The universe of a Herbrand interpretation is the set of variable-free terms of the language $\mathcal{L}_\Pi$ of a logic program Π, the Herbrand universe of a logic program Π is denoted by U_Π. The ground instantiation of a logic program, $ground(\Pi)$, is formed by substituting elements of the Herbrand universe for variables of the logic program in all possible ways. The Herbrand base, denoted by B_Π, is the set of all possible ground atoms of the language $\mathcal{L}_\Pi$, whose arguments are elements of U_Π. An *interpretation* I for Π is a set of ground atoms from $ground(\Pi)$; if, for every ground literal L of $ground(\Pi)$, either L or $\neg L$ is in I then the interpretation is called total, partial otherwise. In [3], Blamey shows that a partial interpretation can easily be translated into a three-valued total interpretation, partially ordered w.r.t. $* < T$, $* < F$, where $*$ stands for undefined: the truth-table is based upon the Kleene three-valued semantics; for a discussion see [9]. An Herbrand model $\mathcal{M}$ is an interpretation that makes every rule of $ground(\Pi)$ true, on the basis of two-valued truth-tables. A total model is a total interpretation. A partial interpretation of a program Π is a *partial model* $\mathcal{A}$ of Π iff $\mathcal{A}$ makes each rule of Π true on the basis of the Kleene truth-table.

A logic program Π is satisfiable iff it has a model $\mathcal{A}$, $\mathcal{A} \models \Pi$. The above declarative semantics holds for any set of sentences of $\mathcal{L}$ as well. A formula ϕ is a logical consequence of a set of formulae Σ ($\Sigma \models \phi$) iff, for each interpretation I, I is a model for Σ implies I is a model for ϕ.

The operator T_Π is a mapping $T_\Pi : 2_\Pi^B \to 2_\Pi^B$ on the complete lattice formed by the Herbrand interpretations of Π; a mapping $T_\Pi(I)$, where I is a subset of B_Π, is defined as follows: for any rule $A \leftarrow A_1, \ldots, A_m, not\ A_{m+1} \ldots not\ A_n$, there exists some substitution θ of ground terms for variables such that $A_1\theta, \ldots, A_m\theta$, $not\ A_{m+1}\theta, \ldots, not\ A_n\theta$ are true in I, then $A\theta$ is in $T_\Pi(I)$.

We recall the definition of stable model [6] and answer set [7]. Given a general logic program Π and an Herbrand interpretation

M, a *stable model* M of Π is $M = T_{\Pi_M}^\infty(M)$, where Π_M is defined to be:

$$\Pi_M = \{A \leftarrow A_1, \ldots, A_m \mid A \leftarrow A_1 \ldots A_m, not\ A_{m+1} \ldots not\ A_n$$

is a rule in $ground(\Pi)$ and $A_i \notin M$, for $m + 1 \leq i \leq n\}$

Let Π be a set of rules of the form:

$$L_0 \leftarrow L_1, \ldots, L_m$$

an *answer set* of Π is the smallest set I of literals from Π, satisfying the following two conditions:

(1) if $L_0 \leftarrow L_1, \ldots, L_m$ is in Π and $L_1, \ldots, L_m \in I$ then $L_0 \in I$.

(2) if for some atom P, P and $\neg P$ are both in I, then $I = \mathcal{L}_\Pi$.

Let M be a set of literals from Π and Π an extended logic program, then

$$\Pi^M = \{L_0 \leftarrow L_1 \ldots L_m \mid L_0 \leftarrow L_1 \ldots L_m, not\ L_{m+1} \ldots not\ L_n$$

is a rule in $ground(\Pi)$, $L_i \notin M$ for $m + 1 \leq i \leq n\}$

Π^M lacks the symbol *not*, so the answer set is well defined. Let M' be the answer set for Π^M. M is an answer set for Π precisely when $M' = M$.

Definition 1 *Given two total models $\mathcal{A}$ and $\mathcal{B}$ we say $\mathcal{A} \subseteq \mathcal{B}$ if the set of ground atoms of $\mathcal{A}$ is a subset of the set of ground atoms of $\mathcal{B}$.*

Definition 2 *Given two partial models $\mathcal{A}$ and $\mathcal{B}$ we say $\mathcal{A} \subseteq \mathcal{B}$ if the set of ground literals of $\mathcal{A}$ is a subset of the set of ground literals of $\mathcal{B}$.*

Definition 3 *A model $\mathcal{A}$ of Π is minimal if it is minimal in the $\subseteq$ ordering.*

3 Abduction

In this section a general specification for abduction is introduced together with a brief survey of the existing approaches.

Definition 4 *An abductive framework F_A is a couple $F_A = < \Sigma, \Delta >$ where Σ is a set of sentences of $\mathcal{L}$ and Δ is a set of literals of $\mathcal{L}_\Sigma$ called abducibles.*

Definition 5 *Given an abductive framework $F_A = < \Sigma, \Delta >$ and a sentence C (the observation), an explanation for C is a sentence ϕ, whose literals belong to Δ, iff*

1. $\Sigma \cup \{\phi\} \models C$;

2. $\Sigma \cup \{\phi\}$ is consistent;

3. ϕ is minimal, i.e. for every explanation ϕ' of C, if $\phi' \supset \phi$ then $\phi' = \phi$.

We say that an explanation is *trivial* when it is equivalent to the observation, i.e. when the observation is explained by itself.

Example 1 Let Σ be:
$\{(\forall x)(father(x) \vee \neg married(x) \vee \neg has\_family(x)),$
$(\forall x)(head\_of\_family(x) \vee \neg father(x) \vee \neg has\_salary(x))\}$ and we are given the query $\leftarrow head\_of\_family(john)$.

The minimal explanations for $head\_of\_family(john)$
$father(john) \wedge has\_salary(john)$,
$has\_salary(john) \wedge married(john) \wedge has\_family(john)$ and $head\_of\_family(john)$,
where $head\_of\_family(john)$ is the trivial explanation.

The difficulty of generating abductive explanations is well known. The problem, in fact, has been shown to be *NP-hard* [4,17]. The approaches to compute abductive explanations can be divided into two main classes: *logic programming* based and *clause* based. In the first one, explanations are computed using either *SLD-resolution* [5,16] or stable model semantics [8].

In particular, Shanahan [16] uses an extension to *SLD-resolution* so that whenever a subgoal Q cannot be resolved with any clause, it is added to a set of unit clauses Δ, called *residue*. It is this set of accumulated hypotheses that constitutes the requested explanation. The mechanism can be augmented to cope with *negation as failure*.

Eshghi and Kowalski [5] extend logic programming to include abduction with integrity constraints to simulate negation as failure by making negative conditions abducible and by imposing appropriate integrity constraints. These integrity constraints force the abducible $\neg Q$, renamed as Q^*, to be added to Δ if Q cannot be proved from $\Sigma \cup \Delta$.

Kakas and Mancarella [8] define a model-theoretic semantics, the *generalized stable model*, by adding the abducibles to the theory and searching for generalized stable models of this augmented theory. An observation has an abductive explanation if it is true in at least one of these models. Integrity constraints discard the non-allowed abducibles.

Bry [2] formalizes abduction as deduction in a meta-theory by applying a Prolog meta-interpreter to a set of meta-logical implications which define disjunctions processing and hypotheses generation. The meta-interpreter computes the minimal sets of atomic formulae logically consistent with the implications. The implications are specialized for the realization of intensional updates but they can be used for diagnosis as well. The construction of consistent hypotheses is quite similar to that of the Shannan's residue but, in this case, no extension to *SLD-resolution* is needed for achieving abductive reasoning.

In the clause-based approach the clauses are opportunely manipulated in order to obtain an explanation. In [15] Reiter and de Kleer introduce the *Clause Management System* as an extension of a traditional assumption-based truth-maintenance system. A *minimal support* for a clause C is found using the concept of *prime implicant* in a dual way with respect to the classical one.

A common drawback of all these approaches is that, assuming an abducible, because with present knowledge its negation cannot be proved, it does not prevent its later provability. Thus every time a new abducible is assumed, a consistency test is needed.

In the next section we propose a new approach to abduction which tries to overcome part of the outlined problems. Like Bry, we exploit Logic Programming and we don't need to extend it for dealing with abduction: while other logic-based approaches rely on resolution, our approach is model-based.

4 Computing Abducibles

In this section a new proposal for computing abductive explanations is introduced. The main idea is that explanations for a given observation can be built by examining the certain – even if incomplete – knowledge a database holds about the world. We suppose that, when the user asks a query (the observation), he does not keep in mind any particular hypothesis about it and he expects the KB system will provide him with all the possible explanations. By manipulating its knowledge, the KB system returns to the user a set of explanations among which the user can choose the most plausible one. Given a theory Σ, repre-

senting the KB, and a query $\leftarrow C$, where C is any clause, an explanation for C can be obtained by suitably manipulating the minimal models of such a theory augmented with the query $\leftarrow C$ and then discarding those explanations inconsistent with the theory. However we do not want to impose any restriction on the structure of Σ, thus it may happen that Σ is a general or extended logic program Π. Normally, stable model semantics fail to provide effective proof procedures for performing deduction and delivering an answer; we show that in order to perform abduction this semantics is adequate.

We showed [13] that minimal models of a theory coincide with partial stable models of a particular logic program associated with it. Thus, given an initial theory Σ – a set of sentences or a logic program – a particular class of logic programs is opportunely defined for the abductive reasoning. This class is called *satisfiability transformation class (STC)* because of the equivalence between the models of a set of sentences (in CNF) and the models of the corresponding set of rules; it is provided with a model-theoretic semantics, in particular with an extension to three-valued logic of the stable model semantics of [6,7].

The importance of this correspondence relies in that we can reduce the problem of finding a stable model for the class STC to the satisfiability problem; notice, in fact, that in [12] it has been shown that the problem "is $\mathcal{M}$ a stable model for P?" is Π_2^0-hard.

We devised an algorithm to find all the partial stable models which is proved sound and complete. The algorithm builds a tree with $\leftarrow C$ as root and nodes the literals appearing in Σ. A stable model is found if there is a path from the root to a leaf satisfying some properties.

Definition 6 *Let Σ be a set of clauses, a program, denoted by Π_Σ, of the Satisfiability Transformation Class STC is defined as follows: for every clause C of Σ we build as many rules as the number of literals of C where, in turn, every literal appears in the head of a rule, while the remaining literals constitute the body of the rule.*

Note that Σ and Π_Σ are equivalent. We show the transformation by means of an example.

Example 2 *Let Σ contain the only clause $\{teach(john, pascal) \lor teach(john, prolog)\}$, clearly Σ is equivalent to the program Π : $\{teach(john, prolog) \leftarrow \neg teach(john, pascal)\}$, where only classical negation is used. Then Π_Σ will be:*

$$\begin{cases} teach(john, prolog) \leftarrow \neg teach(john, pascal) \\ teach(john, pascal) \leftarrow \neg teach(john, prolog) \end{cases}$$

To transform a logic program into an STC program we cannot just complete every rule of the original program, we need first to rewrite it in clausal form.

Definition 7 *Let Π be a logic program, the program $\Pi' \equiv \Pi$ belongs to the STC class, iff Π' is built by the set of clauses Σ associated with Π.*

Example 3 *Let Π contain the only rule: $P \leftarrow \neg P$, then its corresponding STC program is Π' containing the only fact P.*

Notice that, while any extended program may be rewritten as a set of sentences in CNF in precisely one form, given a set of sentences $CNF(\Sigma)$, the most direct way to transform it into an

STC program Π_Σ is not to introduce negation as failure (thus leaving only classical negation). Moreover, if a negative atom $\neg P$ of $CNF(\Sigma)$ is represented in an STC program by $not\ P$, the resulting program is obviously different from the STC program obtained from $CNF(\Sigma)$ by representing $\neg P$ via classical negation. We treat this problem extensively in [14]. However we have shown that the correspondence between $CNF(\Sigma)$ and Π_Σ holds both for general and extended programs.

Definition 8 *The class STC is defined as the set of STC programs.*

We now introduce the semantic characterization of this subclass STC of logic programs by means of the partial stable model semantics. From the definition of stability transformation, we have that, given an STC logic program Π for any set M of ground literals:

$\Pi_M = \{A \leftarrow A_1, \ldots, A_m | A \leftarrow A_1, \ldots, A_m, not\ A_{m+1}, \ldots not\ A_n$
is a rule in $ground(\Pi)$ and $A_i \notin M$, for $m+1 \leq i \leq n\}$

and, if Π_M is a Horn program then it has a unique minimal Herbrand model; if this model coincides with M, then M is *a total stable set of* Π. In [6] M is called a stable model only if it is the unique stable set of Π; we do not use this restriction. A notion of partial stability is now given for the subclass STC.

Definition 9 *Given an STC logic program Π for any set M of ground literals*

$\Pi'_M = \{A \leftarrow A_1, \ldots, A_k | A \leftarrow A_1, \ldots, A_k, A_{k+1} \ldots A_m$ *is a rule in* Π_M *and* $A_i \notin M$, *for* $k+1 \leq i \leq m\}$

If M is the minimal Herbrand model of Π'_M then M is called a partial stable set of Π.

If Π is an extended program then Π'_M may still contain negation, i.e. classical negation, in such a case M cannot be a minimal Herbrand model and the definition of answer set is used. Notice that the transformation has eliminated negation as failure (not) and the undefined literals; thus if Π'_M is a set of ground rules containing classical negation ($\neg$) then M is said to be an answer set of Π, if M is the minimal set satisfying:

$$M = \{L_0 | L_0 \leftarrow L_1, \ldots L_n \in \Pi_M, L_1, \ldots L_n \in M\}$$

The given definition applies correctly to the STC class of programs whose rules can have classical negation in their heads. We showed in [13] that, if $\Pi \in STC$, then Π'_M, does actually have a unique minimal partial model. Moreover we showed that a partial stable model always exists for a program P belonging to the STC class:

Theorem 1 *Every logic program $\Pi_\Sigma \in STC$ has at least a non empty partial stable model.*

The proof, given in [13] is based on the following:

(a) we show that in a partial interpretation an empty model cannot exist, e.g. if Π is $P \leftarrow P$ we have a partial stable model $\{P\}$, corresponding to the supported model [1], while the two-valued (total) stable model does not exist. (b) Consider the set of sentences $CNF(\Sigma)$ associated with Π_Σ, since it is consistent then it has a model; take the minimal model $\mathcal{M}$ of Σ, since $\mathcal{M}$ is a partial model, for every clause C of Σ a ground literal from C must be in $\mathcal{M}$, we show that $\mathcal{M}$ is a partial stable set exploiting the symmetric construction of an STC program.

The importance of the above result relies on the fact that we manipulate models to perform abduction. Thus, if a non

empty partial model always exists, as we shall see in the sequel (Proposition 4), an explanation always exists.

Example 4 Let Σ be:

$\{\forall x(teach(x, pascal) \vee teach(x, prolog) \vee teach(x, italian)),$
$teach(john, prolog) \vee \neg teach(john, italian)\}$ by Definition 2 Σ holds two minimal two-valued models:

$M_a = \{teach(john, prolog)\}$ and $M_b = \{teach(john, pascal)\}$. These two models are also the minimal models of the program Π:

$teach(x, prolog) \leftarrow \neg teach(x, pascal), \neg teach(x, italian)$
$\neg teach(john, italian) \leftarrow \neg teach(john, prolog)$

notice that only M_a is an answer set of Π, interpreting negation as classical negation. In order to establish a semantic correspondence between Σ and Π we need to complete Π, by transforming it in an STC program. Let Π_Σ be:

$$\begin{cases} teach(x, prolog) \leftarrow \neg teach(x, pascal), \neg teach(x, italian) \\ teach(x, pascal) \leftarrow \neg teach(x, prolog), \neg teach(x, italian) \\ teach(x, italian) \leftarrow \neg teach(x, pascal), \neg teach(x, prolog) \end{cases}$$

$$\begin{cases} \neg teach(john, italian) \leftarrow \neg teach(john, prolog) \\ teach(john, prolog) \leftarrow teach(john, italian) \end{cases}$$

and consider the minimal three-valued models of Σ, they are: $M_1 = \{teach(john, prolog)\}$ and $M_2 = \{teach(john, pascal), \neg teach(john, italian)\}$, we show that they are also answer sets of Π_Σ. Notice that, since negation as failure does not appear in Π, we just need to apply the partial transformation to $ground(\Pi_\Sigma)$, with respect to M_1 and M_2 obtaining the two programs Π_{M_1} and Π_{M_2}, where the undefined literals have been eliminated.

Π_{M_1}:

$$\begin{cases} teach(john, prolog) \leftarrow \\ teach(john, pascal) \leftarrow \neg teach(john, prolog) \\ teach(john, italian) \leftarrow \neg teach(john, prolog) \\ \neg teach(john, italian) \leftarrow \neg teach(john, prolog) \end{cases}$$

and Π_{M_2}:

$$\begin{cases} teach(john, prolog) \leftarrow \neg teach(john, pascal), \neg teach(john, italian) \\ teach(john, pascal) \leftarrow \neg teach(john, italian) \\ teach(john, italian) \leftarrow \neg teach(john, pascal) \\ \neg teach(john, italian) \leftarrow \\ teach(john, prolog) \leftarrow teach(john, italian) \end{cases}$$

We can see that M_1 w.r.t. Π_{M_1} and M_2 w.r.t. Π_{M_2}, both satisfy the above conditions for an answer set. Moreover, the two answer sets of Π_Σ, defined in a three-valued interpretation, are exactly M_1 and M_2, in this way corresponding to the three-valued minimal models of Σ. Thus the semantic correspondence has been established.

In [7] it has been shown that every extended program can be reduced to a general program by a mapping that rewrites negative literals in positive form, thus every extended program can be seen as a general program. In the following we refer to general programs and hence to stable models, partial or total.

Proposition 1 *If $\mathcal{M}$ is a partial stable model of $\Pi_\Sigma \in STC$ then it is a minimal model of Π_Σ.*

The complete proof is given in [13]. The proof is based on the following:

(a) Since, by definition of partial stable model, $\mathcal{M}$ is a minimal model of the rules of Π_Σ not deleted from the partial stability transformation, we show that those deleted are satisfied in $\mathcal{M}$. (b) for every model $\mathcal{M}'$, s.t. $\mathcal{M}' \leq \mathcal{M}$ then $\mathcal{M}' = \mathcal{M}$.

Proposition 2 $\mathcal{M}$ is a partial stable model of $\Pi_\Sigma \in STC$ iff it is a minimal model of Σ.

The proof is given in [13] and is based on the equivalence between Π_Σ and Σ.

Proposition 3 Let Π be a logic program, and Π' its completion in an STC program. $\mathcal{M}$ is a partial stable model of $\Pi' \in STC$ iff it is a minimal model of Π.

The complete proof is given in [13], here we only sketch it; $\Rightarrow$ by Theorem 1 a partial stable model of Π' always exists (given a consistent program), the if-part, then, follows from Propositions 1 and 2 and adequate transformations. $\Leftarrow$ Let M be a minimal partial model of Π, we show that, by reducing Π to a set of clauses Σ it is a minimal model of Σ - where negation as failure and classical negation are treated homogeneously - by Proposition 2 it is a partial stable model of Π'.

Let $\leftarrow C$ be a query, with C a clause. If C is not derivable from Π, then it is known that $\Pi \cup \{\neg C\}$ is satisfiable. Thus if $M_1, \ldots, M_r$ are the partial stable models of $\Pi \cup \{\neg C\}$, it is possible to find the explanations for $\leftarrow C$ from such models.

If M_i is one of such models, let $Th(M_i)$ be the conjunction of all ground literals satisfied in M_i. We can now state the following:

Proposition 4 Let $M_1, \ldots, M_r$ be the stable models of $\Pi \cup \{\neg C\}$. Let S^* be :

$$S^* = CNF(Th(M_1) \vee \ldots \vee Th(M_r))$$

We call S^* a support set for explanations. Then the set S of explanations for C is

$$S = \{\neg\phi \ s.t. \ \phi \in S^* \wedge \neg\phi \ is \ consistent \ with \ \Sigma\}$$

The proof is given in [13].

We now give a method to find the set of consistent explanations. Let $S = \bigcup_{i=1}^{k} M_i$ be the union of these models. A bipartite graph G over Π is defined to be $G = < V_1 \cup V_2, E >$ where V_1 and V_2 are the nodes of the graph, $V_1 = \{P | P \in S\}$, $V_2 = \{M_i | M_i$ is a minimal model of $\Pi\}$ and $E = \{< P, M_i > | P \in M_i\}$, where if P and $\neg P$ are both present they are considered different nodes.

An *irredundant set* V_1^+ of the graph G is a subset of V_1 such that

i) $\forall M_i \in V_2 \ \exists$ an arc $< P, M_i >$ s.t. $P \in V_1^+$,

ii) V_1^+ is a set cover of V_2,

iii) if V_1' is a set cover then $V_1' = V_1^+$.

Consider the previous example:

Example 5 Let a query be $\leftarrow teach(john, italian)$. Adding the query to Π_Σ, it yields the two following answer sets (partial stable models):

$M_1 = \{\neg teach(john, italian), teach(john, prolog)\}$, and
$M_2 = \{\neg teach(john, italian), teach(john, pascal)\}$

where S^* is:

$\{\neg teach(john, italian), (teach(john, prolog) \vee teach(john, pascal))\}$
Taking the negation of each $\phi \in S^*$, we have the following supports:

(1) $teach(john, italian)$

(2) $\neg teach(john, prolog) \wedge \neg teach(john, pascal)$

We now compute which of the above supports are consistent explanations. Since the irredundant sets of the bipartite graph are $D_1 = \{teach(john, prolog), teach(john, pascal)\}$ and $D_2 = \{teach(john, prolog), \neg teach(john, italian)\}$, only the first support is a consistent explanation for $teach(john, italian)$, i.e. the trivial one.

Let now the query be $\leftarrow teach(john, pascal)$. By adding the query to Π_Σ, it yields only an answer set (partial stable model):

$M_1 = \{\neg teach(john, pascal), teach(john, prolog)\}$

thus S^* is:

$\{\neg teach(john, pascal), (teach(john, prolog)\} \ (teach(john, pascal) \vee teach(john, prolog))\}$.

Taking the negation of each $\phi \in S^*$ we have the following supports:

(1) $teach(john, pascal)$

(2) $teach(john, prolog)$

both of them are consistent explanations, the first one being trivial. We showed [13] that

• if $D_i = \{P_1, \ldots, P_s\}$ is an irredundant set of the graph G the formula $\psi = \neg P_1 \wedge \ldots \wedge \neg P_s$ is *bad*, i.e. it is inconsistent with Π

• Let ϕ be a clause that may explain C, $\Pi \cup \{\phi\}$ is inconsistent iff either ϕ is refutable or a *bad* formula ψ occurs in ϕ, i.e. all the literals of ψ occur in ϕ.

Notice that the problem of finding an irredundant set for bipartite graph is cubic in the dimension of V_i. We can therefore conclude this section by saying that the above method allows us to reduce the abduction problem to a) the satisfiability and b) the irredundant set problems, that are well studied from a tractability point of view.

5 Implementations

As said above, we defined a sound and complete algorithm to find the partial stable models of the logic programs of the STC class. Given a program Π_Σ, and a query $\leftarrow C$, the algorithm builds a tree with the root labeled $\neg C$ and nodes the literals appearing in Σ. The tree has as many levels as the number of clauses of Σ plus one, where the nodes of every level are the literals of the $i-th$ clause. A partial stable model is found if there exists a path $A = \{A_1^i, \ldots, A_m^j\}$ from the root to a leaf satisfying the following conditions:

(1) $\forall A_k^s \in A$, there does not exist a brother of A_k^s, already belonging to A, chosen at a previous level in the tree;

(2) $\forall A_k^s \in A$, $\neg A_k^l \notin A$, for every l.

(3) $\forall A_k^s \in A$, if $\neg A_k$ is in the body of a rule, having a literal A_m belonging to A as head, then there exists at least another rule $A_m \leftarrow L_1, \ldots, L_h$ such that for all i, $1 \leq i \leq h$, $L_i \neq A_k$ and $\neg L_i \notin A$.

It is worth noting that our heuristics consists in using the established equivalence between a given set of sentences $CNF(\Sigma)$ and the logic program $\Pi_\Sigma \in STC$. The algorithm has been implemented in C on a Macintosh and tested on small incomplete KBs. If the KB has few unknown values, i.e. almost all the information is available, the algorithm has good performances. In fact, to reduce the tree branching, during the tree construction a node is added only if conditions (1) and (2) are satisfied, thus, if there are enough known predicates, there will be a lot of cut branches. Therefore, visiting the tree can be done fast enough and, furthermore, the number of partial stable models is small. In this cases the answer time is very low. We are investigating the problem of reducing the set necessary to construct explanations by a method allowing to choose those stable models which contribute to the best approximate explanation.

6 Conclusions

The ubiquity of abductive inference in various aspects of intelligent behavior is widly recognized. In this paper a proposal for dealing with querying incomplete KBs, as an abductive task, is presented. Abduction enhances reasoning capabilities allowing for an answer when the system does not have enough information and normally would fail. A method for the computation of abductive explanations which exploits logic programming was given. The method has been tested on some sample applications.

7 Acknowledgements

We wish to thank Gigina Aiello, Carlo Batini and Luigi Palopoli for many useful discussions.

References

[1] K.R.Apt, H.A.Blair, A.Walker,"Towards a theory of declarative knowledge", in J.Minker ed. *Foundations of Deductive Database and Logic Programming*, pp.89-148, 1988, Morgan-Kaufmann.

[2] F. Bry, "Intensional Updates: Abduction via Deduction" D. Warren and P.Szeredi, eds, *Logic Programming: Proc. 7th Intl. Conf. on Logic Programming*, pp.561-575, Cambridge, MA, 1990, MIT Press.

[3] S. Blamey, "Partial Logic", *Handbook of Philosophical Logic* (D. Gabbay and F Guenthner Eds), Vol III, pp.1-71, Dordrecht, Hol., 1986.

[4] T. Bylander, D. Allemang, M.C. Tanner and J.R. Josephson, "Some Results Concerning the Computational Complexity of Abduction", *Proc. First Int. Conf. on Principles of Knowledge Representation and Reasoning*, Toronto, pp.44-54,1989, Morgan-Kaufmann.

[5] K. Eshghi and R.A. Kowalski, "Abduction Compared with Negation by Failure", *Proc. 6th Intl. Conf. on Logic Programming*, pp. 234-254, 1989, MIT Press.

[6] M. Gelfond and V. Lifschitz, "The Stable Model Semantics for Logic Programming", R.A. Kowalski and K.Bowen, eds, *Logic Programming: Proc. 5th Intl. Conf. on Logic Programming*, Cambridge, MA, pp.1070-1080, 1990, MIT Press.

[7] M. Gelfond and V. Lifschitz, "Logic Programs with Classical Negation", D. Warren and P.Szeredi, EDS, *Logic Programming: Proc. 7th Intl. Conf. on Logic Programming*, Cambridge, MA, pp.579-597, 1990, MIT Press.

[8] A.C. Kakas and P. Mancarella, "Generalized Stable Models: a Semantics for Abduction", L.C.Aiello ed. *Proc. ECAI 90*, pp. 385-391, London, 1990, Pitman.

[9] K. Kunen, "Signed Data Dependencies in Logic Programs" *The Journal of Logic Programming*, Vol. 7, 3, pp.32-86, 1989, Amst, North-Holland.

[10] H.J. Levesque, "The Logic of Incomplete Knowledge Bases", Brodie-Mylopoulos eds *On Conceptual Modeling*, pp.165-189, 1986, Springer-Verlag.

[11] H.J. Levesque, "A knowledge-level account of abduction" *Proc. IJCAI '89*, pp.1061-1067, Detroit, MI, 1989, Morgan-Kaufmann.

[12] W.Marek, V.S. Subrahmanian, "The relationship between logic program semantics and non-monotonic reasoning" *Logic Programming: Proc. 6th Intl. Conf. on Logic Programming*, pp.600-617, Cambridge, MA, 1989, MIT Press.

[13] F.Pirri and C.Pizzuti, '*Abductive Explanations through Partial Stable Models*, DIS, Technical Report,13, Oct., 1990, Università di Roma "'La Sapienza".

[14] F.Pirri and C.Pizzuti, "Abduction, Deduction and Negation as failure", submitted.

[15] R. Reiter, and J. de Kleer, "Foundations of Assumption-Based Truth Maintenance Systems: Preliminary Report", *Proc. of the National Conference on Artificial Intelligence*, pp.183-188, 1987, Seattle, WA.

[16] M. Shanahan, "Prediction is Deduction but Explanation is Abduction", *Proc. of the 8th National Conference on Artificial Intelligence*, 1990, pp. 1055-1060, Boston, Ma.

[17] B. Selman and H.J. Levesque, "Abductive and Default Reasoning: A Computational Core", *Proc. of the 8th National Conference on Artificial Intelligence*, pp. 343-348, 1990, Boston, Ma.

On Estimating COUNT, SUM, and AVERAGE
Relational Algebra Queries*

G. Ozsoyoglu[†], K. Du[†], A. Tjahjana[†], W-C Hou[‡], D. Y. Rowland[§]

ABSTRACT

CASE-DB is a relational database management system that allows users to specify time constraints in queries. For an aggregate query AGG(E) where AGG is one of COUNT, SUM and AVERAGE, and E is a relational algebra expression, CASE-DB uses statistical estimators to approximate the query. This paper extends our earlier work on statistical estimators of CASE-DB with the following features: (a) New statistical estimators for COUNT queries with projection, (b) Extending the methodology for SUM and AVERAGE aggregate queries, (c) New sampling plans based on systematic sampling and stratified sampling. We also present performance evaluation experiments of the estimators with the above extensions using artificial database instances.

1. Introduction

In real-time or time-constrained databases, queries have to be completed within a given time period. When an aggregate query in such an environment can not be evaluated within the given time period, one approach is to evaluate a statistical estimator, and produce a statistical estimate to the answer of the query. Such an approach has been proposed for COUNT relational algebra queries by Lipton and Naughton [LiNa 89], Lipton, Naughton and Schneider [LNS 90] and by us [HoOT 88, HoOT 89, HoO 91]. We have implemented our approach in a disk-based prototype DBMS, called CASE-DB and its main memory version, called CASE-MDB.

This paper extends our work on statistical estimators for aggregate relational algebra queries in CASE-DB with the following features.

1. **New statistical estimators for COUNT(E) queries with projection.** We introduce two new estimators, namely, the Jackknife estimator [BuOv 79], and the Chao's estimator [Chao 84].

2. **Extending the methodology for SUM and AVERage aggregate queries.** The previous works introduced estimators for COUNT queries. To obtain estimators for SUM(E) and AVG(E) queries where E has a projection operator, we use the double sampling technique with the acceptance/rejection method.

---
*This research is supported by the National Science Foundation under Grants IRI-8811057, IRI-9009897, and IRI-9008632.

[†]Department of Computer Engineering and Science, Case Western Reserve University, Cleveland, OH 44106.

[‡]Department of Computer Science, Southern Illinois University at Carbondale, Carbondale, IL 62901.

[§]D. Y. Rowland Associates, Cleveland Heights, OH.

3. **New sampling plans based on systematic sampling and stratified sampling.** Our earlier work used simple random sampling [HoOT 88], simple random sampling with an adaptive stopping criteria [LNS 90], and cluster sampling [HoO 91]. We now add systematic sampling and stratified sampling into the list of possible sampling techniques for aggregate query evaluation.

Section 2 introduces the new estimators for COUNT($\pi(r)$) queries. Generalization into estimators for COUNT(E) is given later in section 5. Section 3 introduces the double sampling approach to estimate SUM$_A$($\pi_X(r)$). In section 4, we briefly summarize systematic sampling and stratified sampling. Finally, in section 5, we present the algorithms for evaluating estimators for AGG(E) where AGG $\in$ {COUNT, SUM, AVE} and E is an arbitrary RA expression. Section 6 is the experimental results.

2. New Estimators for COUNT($\pi_X(r)$)

Consider the query COUNT($\pi_X(r)$). The projection operation on r may produce (and later eliminate) duplicate tuples. In the case that the sizes of distinct classes produced by projection are different, the duplication makes the probabilities of inclusion in the sample unequal; hence, introducing bias to the estimate for COUNT($\pi_X(r)$).

In our earlier work [HoOT 89] we used the Goodman's estimator [Good 49] to estimate COUNT($\pi_X(r)$). However, when the sampling fraction is low, Goodman's estimator is unstable for a population with heavy duplicates.

Below we present two different nonparametric estimators to estimate COUNT($\pi_X(r)$), namely, the Jackknife estimator and the Chao's estimator. K. P. Burnham and W. S. Overton [BuOv 79] use the Jackknife method to estimate the population size (e.g., in our case, $\pi_X(r)$ is the population, and COUNT($\pi_X(r)$) is the population size) when sample inclusion probabilities vary among population elements. Chao [Chao 84] proposes another nonparametric method to estimate the number of classes in a population. In what follows, we adapt the Jackknife and Chao's estimators to estimate COUNT($\pi_X(r)$).

2.1. Jackknife Estimators

The Jackknife estimator, denoted by $\hat{J}$, is developed by Burnham and Overton [BuOv 79] to be used for estimating the number of N distinct animals in live-trapping studies. The studies are done by trapping animals on c occasions. Capture frequencies, denoted by x_i for $i = 1, \cdots, c$, are then computed. Each x_i represents the number of animals captured exactly i times, while x_0 is the number of animals never trapped. Accordingly, $d = \sum_{i=1}^{c} x_i$ is the number of individuals seen during the study. Thus, $N = d + x_0$ is equal to the size of the animal population.

The animal population size estimation problem is mapped to our problem as follows: N is $COUNT(\pi_X(E))$; x_i is the number of tuples which appear exactly i times in the sample; x_0 is the number of distinct tuples which are not seen in the sample. As an analogy for c in our problem, we could theoretically have taken c as the size of the original sample (yielding many zero values for the x_i's). Equivalently, for convenience, we took c as the highest appearing frequency of sample elements. Therefore, in our problem: $d = \sum_{i=1}^{c} x_i$ equals the number of distinct tuples seen in the sample, and $N = d + x_0$ represents the number of distinct tuples in the population (i.e., $COUNT(\pi_X(E))$).

The kth order Jackknife estimator $\hat{J}_k$ of J_k is defined as

$$\hat{J}_k = d + \sum_{i=1}^{k} a_{ik} x_i \qquad (1)$$

where $a_{ik} = 0$ for $i > k$. The first three orders of the Jackknife estimators are [BuOv 79]

$$\hat{J}_1 = d + \frac{(c-1)}{c} x_1 \qquad (2)$$

$$\hat{J}_2 = d + \frac{(2c-3)}{c} x_1 - \frac{(c-2)^2}{c(c-1)} x_2 \qquad (3)$$

$$\hat{J}_3 = d + \frac{(3c-6)}{c} x_1 - \frac{(3c^2-15c+19)}{c(c-1)} x_2 + \frac{(c-3)^3}{c(c-1)(c-2)} x_3 \qquad (4)$$

From Burnham and Overton [BuOv 79], for any fixed value of c, the higher order Jackknife estimators (i.e., increasing k values) lead to greater bias reduction, but at the cost of increased sampling variance. Conversely, for any fixed value of k, as c increases, $\hat{J}_k$ is a consistent estimator of J asymptotically, and its sampling variance will decrease as c increases.

Clearly, one should choose [BuOv 79] a higher order Jackknife and a greater c if one wants to obtain a good bias reduction with small variance. But, Burnham and Overton suggest [BuOv 79] that there will generally be a minimum mean square error (MSE) at a small value of k; that is, there is a "best" $\hat{J}_k$ at a small order of Jackknife estimators. Experimental results show that the minimum MSE is usually achieved at k = 1,2 or 3.

A selection procedure was also presented by Burnham and Overton [BuOv 79] to select the "best" $\hat{J}_k$ among k = 1, 2, or 3. First, the null hypothesis is tested to investigate if there are any differences between the expected values of $\hat{J}_1$ and $\hat{J}_2$, i.e., test H_{o1}: $E(\hat{J}_2 - \hat{J}_1) = 0$ versus the alternative H_{a1}: $E(\hat{J}_2 - \hat{J}_1) \neq 0$. If H_{o1} is accepted, the interpretation is that the reduction in the absolute bias achieved by using $\hat{J}_2$ rather than $\hat{J}_1$ is small relative to the variance of $\hat{J}_2$. Since $\hat{J}_1$ has a smaller variance than $\hat{J}_2$, $\hat{J}_1$ is more preferable than $\hat{J}_2$, and it should be taken as the estimator.

The rejection of H_{o1} implies a significant decrease in absolute bias relative to the increased variance of $\hat{J}_2$. Therefore, $\hat{J}_2$ should be chosen instead of $\hat{J}_1$. However, the absolute bias may be reduced even further. Before choosing $\hat{J}_2$, $\hat{J}_2$ needs to be tested against $\hat{J}_3$. If this test results in rejection, the selection procedure continues. The selected $\hat{J}_i$ for i=1, 2, or 3, is called the Jackknife estimator. The general selection procedure for choosing $\hat{J}$ is given in [BuOv 79]. Algorithm JACKKNIFE-ESTIMATOR presented in Figure 2.1 shows the computation of the Jackknife estimator.

Algorithm JACKKNIFE-ESTIMATOR (x)

Input : An array x where each element x_i represents the number
   of distinct tuples appearing exactly i times in the sample.
Output : Jackknife estimator $\hat{J}$ of the number of distinct tuples.
begin

   Compute c which is the highest appearing frequency in the sample;
      {i.e., $x_i = 0$ for $i > c$}.
   $d := \sum_{i=1}^{c} x_i$;
   $\hat{J}_1 := d + \frac{(c-1)}{c} x_1$;
   $\hat{J}_2 := d + \frac{(2c-3)}{c} x_1 - \frac{(c-2)^2}{c(c-1)} x_2$;
   $\hat{J}_3 := d + \frac{(3c-6)}{c} x_1 - \frac{(3c^2-15c+19)}{c(c-1)} x_2 + \frac{(c-3)^3}{c(c-1)(c-2)} x_3$;

```
for k := 1 to 2 do
begin
      if TEST-NULL-HYPOTHESIS = "Accept"
         {E(Ĵ_{k+1} - Ĵ_k) = 0}
         then Ĵ(E) := Ĵ_k and exit;
end
   Ĵ(E) := Ĵ_3;
end
```

Figure 2.1. Algorithm for Computing the Jackknife Estimator $\hat{J}$

2.2. Chao's Estimator

Chao proposes a nonparametric method to estimate the number of classes in a population [Chao 84]. The method was intentionally devised for those cases where most of the information is concentrated on the first two occupancy numbers, i.e., x_1 and x_2. Chao's estimator, denoted by $\hat{C}$, is formulated as

$$\hat{C} = d + \frac{x_1^2}{2x_2} \qquad (5)$$

where d, x_1, and x_2 are as defined in Section 2.1. Clearly, Chao's estimator is easier to compute compared with Jackknife estimators. Comparison studies have shown that Chao's estimator has a better performance than the Jackknife estimator when (d, x_1, x_2) carry most of the information [Chao 84]. However, the estimator as formulated can easily give an infinite value when x_2 is equal to 0. The algorithm CHAO-ESTIMATOR for computing the Chao's estimator is presented in Figure 2.2.

Algorithm CHAO-ESTIMATOR(x)

Input : An array x where each its element x_i, $1 \leq i \leq c$, represents
   the number of tuples appearing exactly i times in the sample.
Output : Chao's estimator $\hat{C}$ of the number of distinct tuples.
begin

   Compute c which is the highest appearing frequency in the sample;
   $d := \sum_{i=1}^{c} x_i$;
   if $x_2 \neq 0$ then $\hat{C} := d + \frac{x_1^2}{2x_2}$;
   else Print ("error");
end

Figure 2.2. Algorithm for Computing the Chao's Estimator $\hat{C}$

3. Estimating $SUM_A(\pi_X(r))$ Using Double Sampling

Consider the query $SUM_A(\pi_X(r))$, where $A \subseteq X$. We would like to obtain a sample of tuples from r, where the inclusion probability of each distinct attribute A value in the sample is proportional to its frequency of occurrence in $\pi_X(r)$. For this purpose, we use the *acceptance/rejection* sampling method, which is a double sampling technique. This sampling technique was used by Olken and Rotem [OlkR 86] to estimate the cost of disk accesses in auditing and statistical analysis of large databases. The main steps of acceptance/rejection sampling are as follows.

1. Draw a reasonably large (e.g., 10%) simple random sample from r. Each tuple t_i in $\pi_X(r)$ has the inclusion probability of $\frac{N_{t_i}}{N}$, where N_{t_i} is the number of tuples in r with attribute X value of x_i, and N is the number of tuples in r.

2. Estimate the frequency distribution of each of the distinct tuples in $\pi_X(r)$ (i.e., obtain an estimate $\hat{N}_{t_i}$ for N_{t_i} for each t_i in $\pi_X(r)$).

3. Sample again from r with the acceptance probability $p_i = \frac{1}{\hat{N}_{t_i}}$ for a tuple of r whose X attribute values are x_i.

Hence, the inclusion probability for each distinct t_i in $\pi_X(r)$ is $p = (\frac{N_{t_i}}{N}) \times (\frac{1}{\hat{N}_{t_i}}) = \frac{1}{N}$. Moreover, the inclusion probability for each distinct value a of attribute A is $\sum_{i=1}^{N_a} \frac{1}{N} = \frac{N_a}{N}$ where N_a is the number of distinct tuples in $\pi_X(r)$ with attribute A value of a.

Let s denote the tuples that are sampled (and accepted) from r in step 3 of the acceptance/rejection sampling. Let N_s denote the number of tuples of s. Then the estimator for $SUM_A(\pi_X(r))$ we use is

$$S\hat{U}M_A(\pi_X(r)) = \frac{SUM_A(\pi_X(s)) \times C\hat{O}UNT_A(\pi_X(r))}{N_s} \qquad (6)$$

where $C\hat{O}UNT_A(\pi_X(r))$ is a nonparametric estimator from section 2 (such as the Jackknife estimator) for the total number of distinct tuples of $\pi_X(r)$. Also note that, $SUM_A(\pi_X(s))/N_s$ in the above equation is an unbiased estimator for $AVG_A(\pi_X(r))$, which has good performance even at very low sampling fractions. For example, at a sampling fraction of 5%, the relative error of $A\hat{V}G_A(\pi_X(r))$ is less than 2%.

4. New Sampling Plans

4.1. Sampling Plan Based on Systematic Sampling

Suppose we would like to draw a systematic sample from a population of size N. Assume that we have an ordering among the population elements. The systematic sampling procedure takes a unit at random from the first k elements and every k^{th} unit from there on. The performance of systematic sampling depends on the properties of the population [Coch 77], which may greatly improve the estimate for some populations, and it may deteriorate the estimate for others. Two main types of populations are **Random Order Populations** and **Ordered Populations**.

We obtain a systematic sample of size m from a relation r with N tuples ($N >> $ m) as follows. We take a tuple out at random from the first cluster of size c and every k^{th} thereafter. The period k of relation r is $\lfloor N/m \rfloor$. The first tuple in the sample is determined by drawing at random from the first c tuples of relation r, where c is

$$c = \begin{cases} k & \text{if k} = \frac{N}{m} \\ k + (N \bmod m) & \text{if k} \neq \frac{N}{m} \end{cases} \qquad (7)$$

4.2. Sampling Plan Based on Stratified Random Sampling

In stratified sampling, the population of N units is broken down into L non-overlapping subpopulations of $N_1, N_2, \cdots, N_L$ units, respectively. These subpopulations, called strata, are disjoint, i.e.,

$$N_1 + N_2 + \cdots + N_L = N \qquad (8)$$

It is known [Coch 77] that the variability or heterogeneity among the units of the population has an effect on the precision of an estimator. In addition to increasing the sample size, one possible way to obtain greater precision is to divide the population into several strata each of which is more homogeneous than the whole population and draw a sample from each of the stratum.

Stratified Relation : A stratified relation R is defined as a relation consisting of j, $j > 1$, non-overlapping subrelations (or strata) $s^1, s^2, \cdots, s^j$ with the following properties: (1) R $= s^1 \cup s^2 \cup \cdots \cup s^j$; (2) $s^m \cap s^n = \Phi$, $m \neq n$, $1 \leq m \leq j$, $1 \leq n \leq j$

Clearly, $N = N^1 + N^2 + \cdots + N^j$, where N is the number of tuples of the stratified relation R and N^j is the number of tuples of the subrelation s^j.

Our design utilizes the *proportional allocation* method: a sample from each stratum is allocated proportionally according to the size of the strata.

5. Generic Estimators for AGG Queries

In this section, we present the general methodology for estimating aggregate queries $AGG(E)$, where AGG $\in$ {SUM, COUNT, AVG}. The expression E in the query is an arbitrary relational algebra expression containing union ($\cup$), difference ($-$), intersection ($\cap$), selection (σ), projection (π), and natural join ($\bowtie$) operators. The attribute A is an output attribute of expression E.

5.1. Estimator for Select-Join-Intersection-Expressions

We first discuss the estimator for $AGG(E)$, where E is an expression with arbitrarily many select, join, and intersection operators. which, for simplicity, we will call an SJI-expression from now on.

Suppose that E has $n - 1$ join operators with relations denoted by $r_1, r_2, \cdots, r_n$. Let $|r_i|$ denote the number of tuples in r_i. An SJI-expression with n operand relations is modeled as an n-dimensional "point space" $r_1 r_2 \cdots r_n$. Given a tuple $t_i \epsilon r_i$, $1 \leq i \leq n$, if $E(\{t_1\}, \{t_2\}, \cdots, \{t_n\})$ produces an output tuple t, a "point" $p(t_1, t_2, \cdots, t_n)$ in the space is assigned a value of 1 (else 0) in the case of $AGG = COUNT$, or the attribute A value of the tuple t (else 0) in the case of $AGG = SUM_A$. $N = |r_1| \times |r_2| \times \cdots \times |r_n|$ is the total number of points in the point space $r_1 r_2 \cdots r_n$. Assume that the points in the point space of E are represented by $p_1, p_2, \cdots, p_N$. Let v_i denote the value of point p_i, $V(E) = v_1 + v_2 + \cdots + v_N$. One can see that $COUNT(r_1, r_2, \cdots, r_n)$ or $SUM(r_1, r_2, \cdots, r_n)$ is exactly $V(E)$. An estimator $\hat{V}(E)$ for $V(E)$ based on a simple random sample of m points from the space $r_1 r_2 \cdots r_n$ is then

$$\hat{V}(E) = N \frac{\sum_{i=1}^{m} v_i}{m} \qquad (9)$$

Intersection ($\cap$) is incorporated into the above approach by considering it as a special case of the join operation. Furthermore, by taking into account the qualification specified in the selection formula of the selection operator (σ) during the v_i value assignment process, the operator (σ) can also be incorporated into the methodology. Figure 5.1 gives the algorithm ESTIMATE-SJI-RANDOM(E) where E is an arbitrary SJI-expression.

Algorithm ESTIMATE-SJI-RANDOM(E, AGG, ATTR)
Input : An SJI-expression E, the aggregate function type AGG, and the aggregation attribute ATTR (if any).
Output : An estimate $A\hat{G}G(E)$ of $AGG(E)$.
begin
  Obtain a simple random sample of m points p_i, $1 \leq i \leq m$,
      from the point space $r_1 r_2 \cdots r_n$;
  {Note that each p_i uniquely identifies the ordered n-tuple $(t_1, t_2, \cdots, t_n)$
      such that $t_j \epsilon r_j, 1 \leq j \leq n$}
  case AGG of
      SUM: for each point p_i in the sample do
    if $E(\{t_1\}, \{t_2\}, \cdots, \{t_n\})$ produces an output tuple t then
          $v_i := t[ATRR]$ else $v_i := 0$;
      COUNT: for each point p_i in the sample do
    if $E(\{t_1\}, \{t_2\}, \cdots, \{t_n\})$ produces an output tuple
          then $v_i := 1$ else $v_i := 0$;
  endcase;
  return ($(N/m) \sum_{i=1}^{m} v_i$);
    {N is the total number of points in $r_1 r_2 \cdots r_n$}
end.

Figure 5.1. A Simple Random Sampling-Based Estimator Evaluation Algorithm for $AGG(E)$, where E is an SJI-expression

5.2. Estimator for Project-Select-Join-Intersection-Expressions

Let E be an expression with arbitrarily many project, select, join and intersection operators, which we call a PSJI-expression. The one-to-one relationship between the points in the point space and the output tuples of E is violated due to the duplication in the projected domain. Each group of duplicates eventually produces a single tuple in the projected result. For COUNT, we use the previously discussed nonparametric estimators, i.e., the Goodman's, the Jackknife and the Chao's estimators for estimating the number of distinct groups in the point space. For SUM, we generalize the double sampling technique. The algorithm ESTIMATE-PSJI-RANDOM of Figure 5.2 implements the estimation methodology for PSJI-expressions.

Algorithm ESTIMATE-PSJI-RANDOM (E, AGG, ATTR)
Input: A PSJI-expression E, the aggregate function type AGG, and the aggregation attribute ATTR (if any).
Output: An estimate $\hat{AGG}(E)$ of $AGG(E)$.
Global var: projector-estimator
begin
  case AGG of
    COUNT: begin
      Obtain a simple random sample of m points $p_\iota, 1 \leq \iota \leq m$,
        from the point space $r_1 r_2 \cdots r_n$;
        {Note that each p_ι uniquely identifies the ordered
        n-tuple $(t_1, t_2, \cdots, t_n)$ such that $t_j \epsilon r_j, 1 \leq j \leq n$}
      Initialize the multi-set MULTI-SET as empty;
      for each p_ι do
        if $E(\{t_1\}, \{t_2\}, \cdots, \{t_n\})$ produces an output tuple t_0
          then add t_0 into MULTI-SET;
      Scan MULTI-SET and compute $x_\iota, 1 \leq \iota \leq m$, which is
        the number of groups containing ι elements in MULTI-SET;
      case project-estimator of
        Jackknife: **return** (JACKKNIFE-ESTIMATOR(x));
        Chao: **return** (CHAO-ESTIMATOR(x));
        Goodman: **return** (GOODMAN-ESTIMATOR(x));
      endcase;
    endCOUNT;
    SUM: begin
      Obtain a simple random sample of M points $p_\iota, 1 \leq \iota \leq m$,
      from the point space $r_1 r_2 \cdots r_n$;   {M is pre-chosen}
      Initialize an array A as empty;
      for each p_ι do
        if $E(\{t_1\}, \{t_2\}, \cdots, \{t_n\})$ produces an output tuple t_0
          then add t_0 into A; {A is unsorted}
      Scan A and compute the frequency $f_{v_\iota}, 1 \leq \iota \leq M$;
      ACCEPTED-SUM := ACCEPTED-COUNT := 0;
      while ACCEPTED-COUNT < M do
        begin
          Sample randomly again from A with the
            acceptance probability $\frac{1}{f_{v_\iota}}$ for a tuple t;
          if t is accepted then
            begin
              ACCEPTED-SUM := ACCEPTED-SUM + t[ATTR];
              ACCEPTED-COUNT := ACCEPTED-COUNT + 1;
            end;
        end;
      $C\hat{OU}NT$:= ESTIMATE-PSJI-RANDOM (E, COUNT, ATTR);
      return ($C\hat{OU}NT \times$ ACCEPTED-SUM/ACCEPTED-COUNT);
    endSUM;
  endcase;
end.

Figure 5.2. A Simple-Random-Sampling-Based Estimator Construction Algorithm for $AGG(E)$, where E is a PSJI-expression

5.3. General algorithm for Estimating AGG(E)

We now incorporate difference $(-)$ and union $(\cup)$ operators into an SJI-expression E, and call such an expression a DUSJI-expression. We apply the **Principle of Inclusion and Exclusion** and the following equalities

$$AGG(r_1 \cup r_2) = AGG(r_1) + AGG(r_2) - AGG(r_1 \cap r_2)$$
$$AGG(r_1 - r_2) = AGG(r_1) - AGG(r_1 \cap r_2)$$

where AGG $\in$ {SUM, COUNT}. Clearly, we can compute $AGG(E_1 \cup E_2)$ and $AGG(E_1 - E_2)$ indirectly by making use of $AGG(E_1)$, $AGG(E_2)$, and $AGG(E_1 \cap E_2)$. Thus, to obtain an estimator for $AGG(E)$, where E is a DUSJI-expression, we decompose $AGG(E)$ into a set of subexpressions $AGG(E_i)$ combined by $+$'s and $-$'s, where E_i does not contain $\cup$'s and $-$'s. We call this transformation TRANSFORM(AGG(E)). When the projection operator is added into E, the transformation still works if projections do not precede differences in E^1. Thus, for each $AGG(E_i)$, the expression E_i is either an SJI or a PSJI-expression. The estimator for AGG(E) is then determined as

$$\hat{AGG}(E) = \sum_j (\pm) AGG(E_j).$$

Now we give the general algorithm for estimating AGG(E). Algorithm ESTIMATE-RANDOM of Figure 5.3 evaluates an estimator for $AGG(E)$ for any arbitrary RA expression E.

Algorithm ESTIMATE-RANDOM(E, AGG, ATTR)
Input: An arbitrary expression E; the aggregate function type AGG, and the aggregation attribute ATTR (if any).
Output: An estimate $\hat{AGG}(E)$ of $AGG(E)$, where AGG $\in$ {SUM, COUNT, AVG}.
begin
  case AGG of
    COUNT: begin
      TRANSFORM(COUNT(E));
      {Now, E is of the form $E_1 \theta E_2 ... \theta E_m$,
        where $\theta \in \{\cup, -\}$ and E_j is a SJI or PSJI exp. }
      for each E_j do
        case E_j of
          SJI-exp: $C\hat{OU}NT(E_j) :=$
              ESTIMATE-SJI-RANDOM($E_j, COUNT$, -);
          PSJI-exp: $C\hat{OU}NT(E_j) :=$
              ESTIMATE-PSJI-RANDOM($E_j, COUNT$, -);
        endcase;
      $C\hat{OU}NT(E) := \sum_j (\pm) C\hat{OU}NT(E_j)$;
    endCOUNT;
    SUM: begin
      TRANSFORM(SUM(E));
      for each E_j do
        case E_j of
          SJI-exp: $S\hat{U}M(E_j) :=$
              ESTIMATE-SJI-RANDOM($E_j, SUM, ATTR$);
          PSJI-exp: $S\hat{U}M(E_j) :=$
              ESTIMATE-PSJI-RANDOM($E_j, SUM, ATTR$);
        endcase;
      $S\hat{U}M(E) := \sum_j (\pm) S\hat{U}M(E_j)$;
    endSUM;
    AVG: begin
      S := ESTIMATE-RANDOM(E, SUM, ATTR);
      C := ESTIMATE-RANDOM(E, COUNT, -);
      $A\hat{V}G(E) := \frac{S}{C}$;
    endAVG;
  endcase
end.

Figure 5.3. A Simple-Random-Sampling-Based Estimator Construction and Evaluation Algorithm for $AGG(E)$, where E is an arbitrary RA-expression

6. Experimental Results

In this section, we report the experimental results with AGG queries. Due to space considerations, we only report (a subset of) the experimental results related to the new estimators and sampling techniques for COUNT and SUM queries. We discuss the experiments with a single RA operator and multiple RA op-

---

[1] We revise the expression and the estimator further when projections precede differences. See [HoOT 88] for details.

erators, separately. The two types of input relations used in the experiments have normal (correlated or uncorrelated) and uniform distributions over each column.

The precision of estimations here is measured in terms of the *relative error*. One way of measuring the relative error is to measure the *coefficient of variation*, denoted by e and, for our purposes, defined as

$$e = \frac{\sqrt{Var(A\hat{G}G(E))}}{AGG(E)} \quad (10)$$

where AGG $\in$ {SUM, COUNT, AVG}. $Var(A\hat{G}G(E))$ is the variance of the aggregate function $A\hat{G}G$.

6.1. COUNT on a Single Projection Operation ($\pi_{attr.}(r)$)

Here, we have used the Goodman's estimator, the Chao's estimator, and the Jackknife estimator to estimate $COUNT(\pi_{attributes}(r))$. Figures 6.1 and 6.2 contain the results of experiments using simple random sampling with normally distributed and uniformly distributed attribute values, respectively. The experimental results suggest that we use the Chao's estimator or Jackknife estimators in the case of low sampling fractions and selectivities. Otherwise, the Goodman's estimator is recommended.

6.2. SUM on a Single Projection Operation ($\pi_{attributes}(r)$)

In the experiments on $SUM(\pi_{attributes}(r))$, we have used an alternate estimator–the $\hat{D}$ estimator based on the double sampling and Chao's methods proposed in section 2. We have varied the distribution of attribute values, the variance of the input data in the case of normal distribution and selectivities.

Figures 6.3.a and 6.3.b show the results of the experiments using simple random sampling with normally distributed and uniformly distributed attribute values, respectively. The results show that the estimator performs better when the input data are uniformly distributed. At low selectivities, the estimator performs well. But, at high selectivities (sel ≥ 0.5), the relative errors are large in both normal and uniform cases.

6.3. COUNT and SUM on a Single Natural Join Operation ($r_1 \bowtie r_2$)

For the single natural join operation, we have concentrated on testing the performance difference between simple random sampling and systematic sampling. Since the experimental results for COUNT and SUM queries have quite similar characteristics, we only analyze the results for COUNT.

Figures 6.4.a and 6.4.b show the experimental results for COUNT with unordered input relations having simple random sampling and systematic sampling, respectively. Figures 6.5.a and 6.5.b show the experimental results for COUNT with ordered input relations using simple random sampling and systematic sampling, respectively.

From figures 6.4 and 6.5, we conclude that, when input relations are ordered, tuples selected by systematic sampling are more representative than those selected by simple random sampling.

6.4. Experimental Results for COUNT and SUM Estimators on Multiple RA operators

In addition to expressions having only a single RA operator, we have also performed experiments on COUNT and SUM queries with more than one RA operator. The expressions selected for our experiments are (1) $(r_1 \cap r_2) \bowtie r_3$, (2) $(r_1 - r_2) \bowtie r_3$ and (3) $(r_1 \cup r_2) \bowtie r_3$. Since the experimental results for COUNT and SUM have quite similar characteristics, we only show those

results for SUM. Experimental results for SUM using simple random sampling with normally and uniformly distributed data are shown in figures 6.6.a and 6..6.b, respectively.

6.5. Experiments with Stratified Random Sampling

It is often difficult to perform experiments with stratified random sampling since the experiments involve breaking down the input relations into smaller subrelations. Nevertheless, we now, for illustration purposes, provide the results of our experiments with stratified random sampling. We have chosen to use the selection (σ) operation for simplicity reasons. The experiments of this section are performed in order to give an insight as to how the stratified random sampling improves the precision of an estimate rather than to provide extensive evaluation of the stratified random sampling.

In figure 6.7, we show the results of the experiments. From figure 6.7, one can see that as the subrelations become more homogeneous (i.e., higher selectivity), the estimates with lower relative errors are obtained using the stratified random sampling as opposed to other sampling methods. In figure 6.7, we plot the relative errors corresponding toIn figure 6.7, we plot the relative errors corresponding to the stratified random sampling in thick lines in order to show the improvement in estimation by using the stratified random sampling.

7. References

[BuOv 79] Burnham, K.P., Overton, W.S , "Robust Estimation of Population Size When Capture Probabilities Vary Among Animals", Ecology, Vol. 60, 1979.

[Chao 84] Chao, A., "Nonparametric Estimation of the Number of Classes in a Population", Scand. J. Stat., Vol. 11, 1984.

[Coch 77] Cochran, W., "Sampling Techniques", Third Ed., John Wiley & Sons, Inc., 1977.

[Good 49] Goodman, L., "On the Estimation of the Number of Classes in a Population", Ann. Math. Stat., Vol. 20, 1949.

[HoOT 88] Hou, W-C., Ozsoyoglu, G., Taneja, B., "Statistical Estimators for Relational Algebra Expressions", ACM PODS Conference, March 1988.

[HoOT 89] Hou, W-C., Ozsoyoglu, G. Taneja, B., "Processing Aggregate Relational Queries with Hard Time Constraints", ACM SIGMOD Conference, May 1989.

[HoO 91] Hou, W-C., Ozsoyoglu, G., "Statistical Estimators for Aggregate Relational Algebra Expressions", To appear in ACM TODS Journal.

[Olke 86] Olken, F., "Physical Database Support for Scientific and Statistical Databases", Third Int. Scientific and Statistical Databases Workshop, 1986.

[OlkR 86] Olken, F., Rotem, D., "Simple Random Sampling from Relational Databases", Proc., VLDB Conf. 1986.

[LNS 90] R.Lipton, J.Naughton and D. Schneider, "Practical Selectivity Estimation through Adaptive Sampling", ACM SIGMOD, 1990.

[LiNa 89] R. Lipton and J. Naughton, "Query Size Estimation by Adaptive Sampling", ACM PODS, 1990.

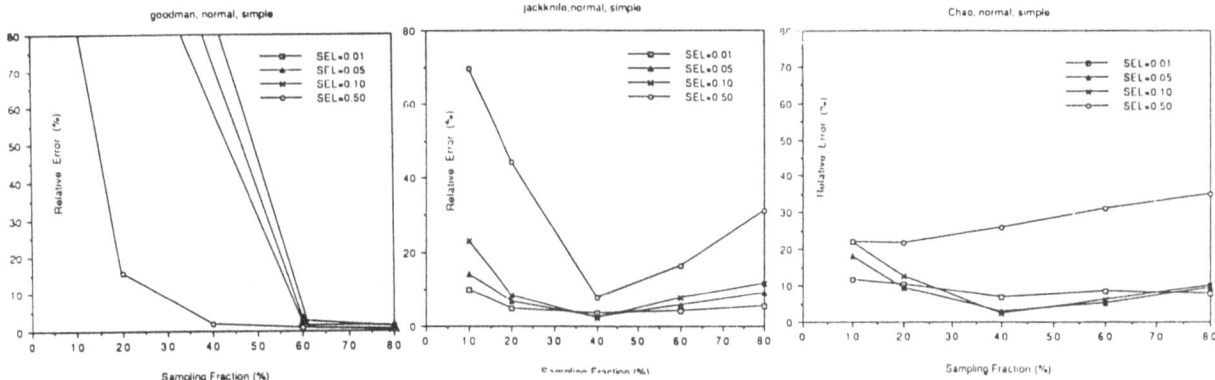

Figure 6.1. Behavior of the Relative Error e for COUNT on a Single
Projection Operation with Simple Random Sampling, and Normally
Distributed Input Relations

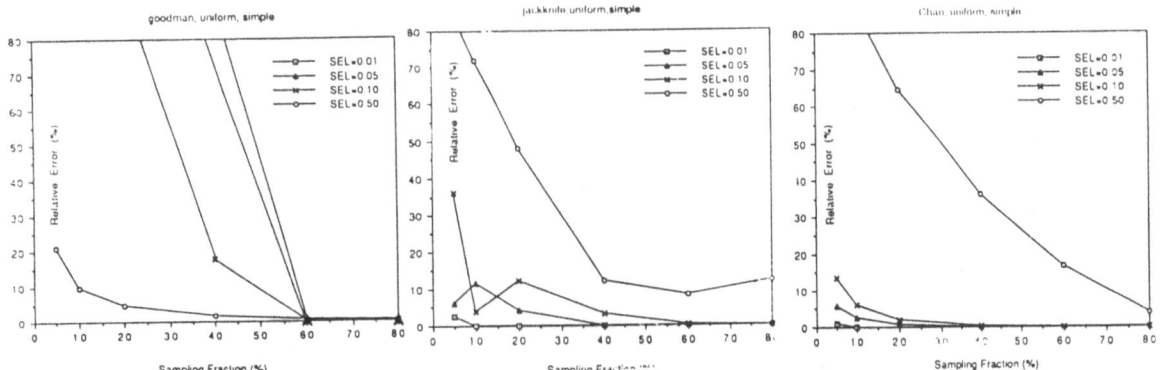

Figure 6.2. Behavior of the Relative Error e for COUNT on a Single
Projection Operation with Simple Random Sampling, and Uniformly
Distributed Input Relations

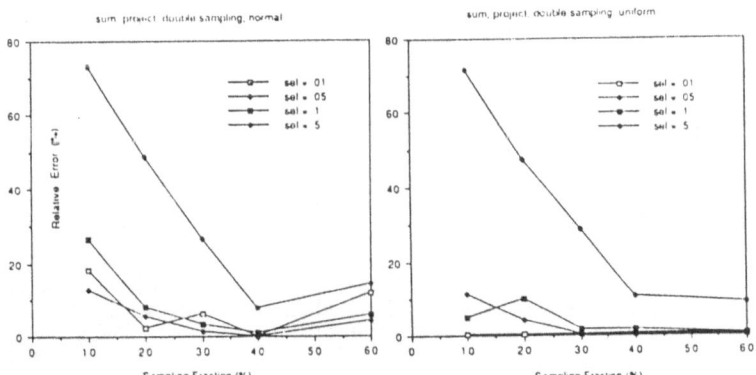

Figure 6.3. Behavior of the Relative Error e for SUM on a Single Projection
Operation with Simple Random Sampling

412

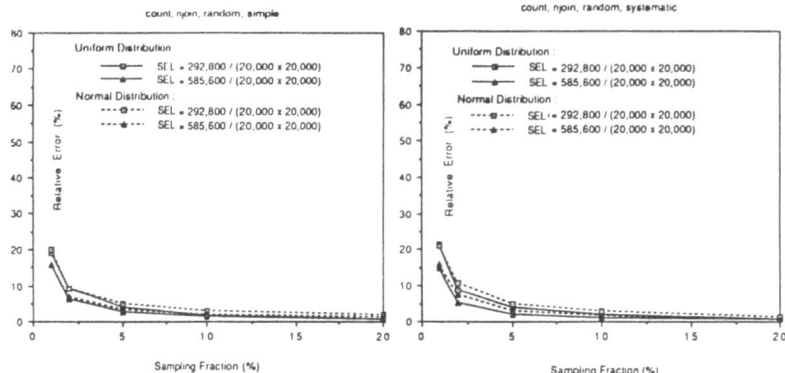

Figure 6.4. Behavior of the Relative Error *e* for COUNT on a Single
Projection Operation with Non-ordered Input Relations Using Simple
Random Sampling and Systematic Sampling

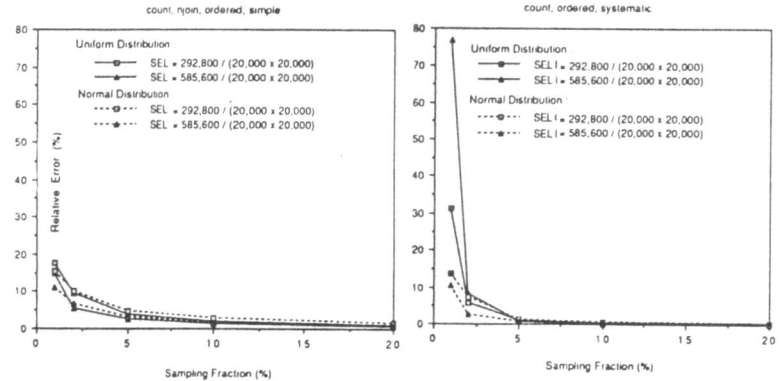

Figure 6.5. Behavior of the Relative Error *e* for COUNT on a Single
Projection Operation with ordered Input Relations Using Simple Random
Sampling and Systematic Sampling

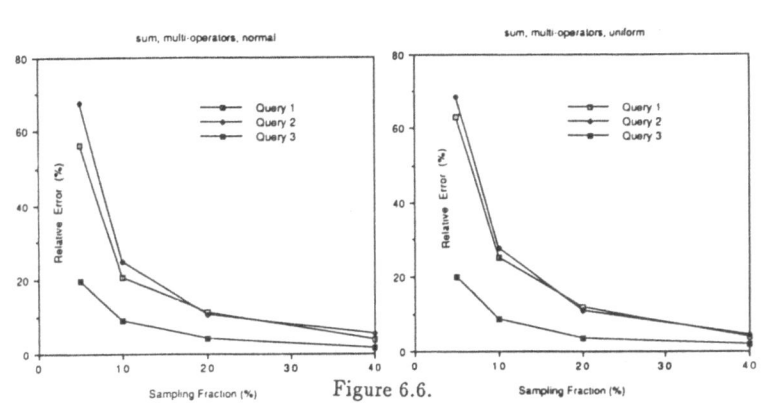

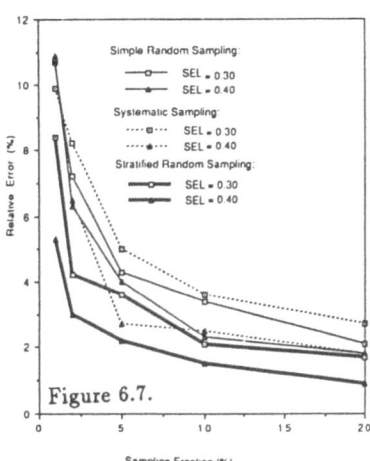

Figure 6.6. Behavior of the Relative Error *E* for SUM on Multiple RA
Operators with Normally and Uniformly distributed Data

Figure 6.7. Behavior of the Relative Error *E* for a Single Selection
Operation on Stratified Data with Various Sampling Methods

RECURSION WITH THE GRAPHICAL QUERY LANGUAGE CANDID

M. Schneider   C. Trépied

Laboratoire Informatique
Université de Clermont-Ferrand II
63177 Aubière Cedex (France)

ABSTRACT

CANDID is a graphical interface for data base manipulation designed for the final user. It is based on a generic semantic model using attributes and constructors. Each schema is represented by a graph where the nodes are associated to different object types and where the edges represent relationships between types. The graphical query language makes it possible to express a request by describing with a graph an object solution of the request. Specifying a request means the same as defining derived elements that can be incorporated definitively into the schema. This language is also characterized by the absence of boolean operators and quantifiers which are replaced by manipulations on Venn diagrams. This article shows how recursive requests can be expressed in CANDID through a tree-structure constructor.

1   Introduction

As information and communication functions grow, more elaborate human-computer interfaces need to be made available to final users. For some time now, progress has been made towards offering easy access interfaces to a data base for non-specialist users. Interfaces based on interactive graphical manipulations constitute an important class because of the obvious user-friendliness they can offer.

Several graphical interfaces have been proposed for the relational model: FORAL-LP, QBE [18], LAGRIF [12], PICASSO [9], ... Their power of expression is, in general terms, that of relational algebra. Simple extensions inspired from SQL (aggregate functions, grouping) have been proposed. Extensions allowing the formulation of recursive requests have also been studied and set up. The development of both semantic models ([8], [14]) and object-oriented DBMS have made it possible for a new generation of graphic interfaces to emerge (G.WHIZ [7], ISIS [6], SNAP [3], G+[4], QBD*[2], PASTA-3 [10], ...) in which CANDID takes place. Some of them (G.WHIZ, G+, QBD*) offer facilities to formulate recursive queries.

The graphical interface CANDID is based on a generic semantic model. A schema is represented graphically by means of a set of symbols which can be adapted. The graph of a schema is accompanied by a written description. The interface allows for the searching but also for the updating of information contained in the base. A request is expressed through a graph which uses the same symbolism as the schema graph. The principles of the graphical query language are as follows:

.replacement of the boolean operators and the quantifiers by manipulations on Venn diagrams;

.initiative coming preferably from the system;

.immediate graphical effect of any command;

.possibility of incremental composition for a request (by using previous requests).

We have shown [17] that CANDID makes it possible to express all algebraic operations for complex objects as defined in [1]. But CANDID offers more facilities, particularly for manipulating subtypes and for expressing recursive requests. Recursive requests are formulated on a tree structure derived with the hierarchisation constructor by using the underlying recursive relationship.

The article is organized as follows: Sections 2, 3, 4 give a rapid presentation of the model and the interface. Section 5 presents the graphical query primitives and section 7 deals with recursive requests.

2   Overview of the semantic model of CANDID

The semantic model of the CANDID system is a generic model for which a detailed description can be found in [17]. Here we shall simply illustrate its different concepts by means of the following example : the organization of a car rally (the "Paris-Dakar" rally for example). Different kinds of VEHICLEs can be used: motorbike, car, truck. The data base must allow to preserve the participants for each year of the rally (the RALLYMANs) and to follow the participants of the current rally (the COMPETITORs). A TEAM is made up of one or several competitors, the number of competitors depending on the type of vehicle (for example one for a motorbike, two for a car, three for a truck). A competitor must be recommended by a participant from one of the previous rallies. Finally any PERSON directly or indi-

414

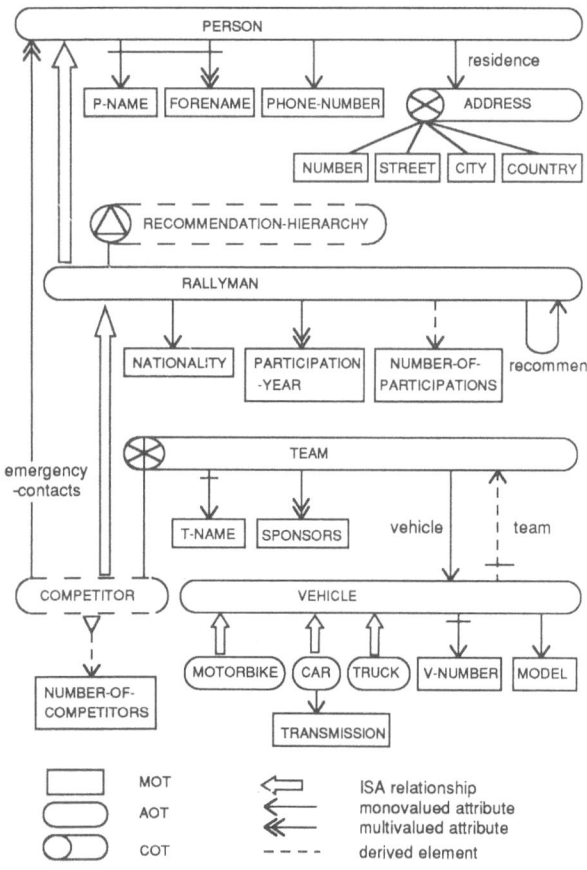

MOT   ISA relationship
AOT   monovalued attribute
           multivalued attribute
COT   - - - - derived element

Figure 1 . The conceptual schema of the database "RALLY"

rectly concerned by the rally (organizer, follower, person to contact in an emergency, ...) must be also to be memorized in the database. The conceptual schema of this data base is presented in figure 1.

The model distinguishes three kinds of types: the *mediatic object* type (MOT), the *abstract object* type (AOT) and the *constructed object* type (COT).

An MOT as its name shows, is used for input into and output from the database. It is the only type for which there is perfect equivalence between the object and its representation through a medium. Only an object of this type (an MO) can thus be entered or delivered directly through a medium. Several basic MOT are predefined : INTEGER, REAL, BOOLEAN, TEXT. Others MOT can be added (IMAGE, SOUND, ...). An MOT is represented by a rectangle (example: P-NAME).

An object of the type AOT cannot be printed or displayed on a screen but only described. In the real world which we want to model, an OA can exist in concrete form (material object) or in abstract form (idea, event). An AOT is described by its attributes. It is represented by a flattened ellipse. For example PERSON is an AOT.

An object of the type COT is constructed from other objects in the base. The semantics of this assembly is of course clear, being natural in the real world. Three construction relationships are defined: *aggregation*, *grouping*, *hierarching*. Grouping defines a CO as a set of objects (example: a TEAM is a set of COMPETITORS). Aggregation defines a CO as a n-tuple (example: an ADDRESS is a quadruplet (NUMBER, STREET, CITY, COUNTRY)). Hierarching defines a CO as a tree by using a succession relation (example: RECOMMENDATION-HIERAR-CHY defines several tree of rallymen by using the inverse relation of the "recommend-by" relation; the root of each tree is a participant to the first session of the rallye). A COT is represented by a flattened ellipse containing the symbol of the constructor type used.

An *attribute* is used to describe one aspect of an object type (the source type) by a semantic link with another object type (the target type). It is represented by an arrow from the source type to the target type. The target type may be identical to the source type. For example each rallyman is "recommended-by" another rallyman. An attribute can be viewed as an oriented relation between the source and the target. It is always possible to define the inverse attribute. An attribute can have an explicit name. Otherwise the attribute name is the same as that of the target type. Two kinds of attribute can be distinguished: *object attributes* and *class attributes*. An object attribute describes each object of the source type ("residence" of PERSON for example); a class attribute describes the class of the source type ("number-of-competitors" of COMPETITOR for example).

An attribute possesses several facets which describe it completely. Those appearing on the graph are the following: the *name*, the *target* type, the *cardinality*. A monovalued attribute sets up a relationship between a source type object and a single target type object. A multivalued attribute sets up a relationship between a source type object and several target type objects. Other facets can be defined on an attribute [17]. Several of them specify structural integrity constraints. Facets of the inverse are not independant of those of the direct attribute.

Any object possesses an identity and an aspect. Identity expresses the existence of the object. It is unique and invariable. It is controlled internally by the system. Aspect is expressed through the set of all attributes of the type. An object can have a double (another object with the same aspect). It is possible to forbid doubles. An object can have one or several *external identifiers*. An external identifier is formed on a subset of attributes. For example the name and the set of the associated forenames make it possible to identify a person from the RALLY database. An external identifier is represented graphically by a linear junction.

An ISA relationship between two object types indicates that any subtype object "is a" supertype object. For example RALLY-MAN is a subtype of PERSON. A subtype inherits all the object attributes of the supertype. With an ISA hierarchy (for example that of VEHICLE) the static constraints of covering (any supertype object is the occurrence of at least one of the subtypes) and of disjunction (a subtype object cannot be the occurrence of more than one subtype) can be specified. These constraints are defined graphically in CANDID using Venn diagrams.

An element is said to be derived if it is obtained from elements which already exist in the schema. A derivation rule is given to it. Our model allows for derived object types (subtype and COT) and derived attributes. The symbol for a derived element is drawn with dotted lines. For example COMPETITOR is a derived subtype defined by the rule: "RALLYMAN for which the set of PARTICIPATION-YEARs includes the current year".

For the purpose of the query facilities, CANDID defines automatically the inverse of each attribute. The name of the inverse is implicitly stated to *inv(direct-name)* if *direct-name* is the name of the direct attribute. Moreover a derived attribute *components* gives for each CO the lists of its components. The inverse attribute *inv(components)* gives thus the object in the composition of which a component participates. By using these different derived attributes, it is possible to access from a given type, any type connected with it. Types connected through ISA relationship are considered separately.

3 Screen composition

In the inquiry phase the terminal screen has four windows. At any time the user can change the size of a window or scroll its contents in any direction. Each window has a set of commands organized as scrolling menus. A general menu is present in each window allowing general manipulation without leaving the active window.

The *Schema Window* contains the graph of an external schema chosen by the user. This schema is constructed from a conceptual schema and can also contains the derived components created by the user while making inquiries on the base.

The user constructs progressively the graph of the request, through several stages, in the *Stage Window*.

The specification of a request is equivalent to the specification of derived elements of the schema (types or attributes), without the user being necessarily aware of this. To help the user, the interface offers a recapitulation in a summary form which is displayed in the *Recapitulation Window*.

The *Result Window* contains the result of the execution of the global request as specified in the Recapitulation Window. Results are displayed by using buckets like in EVER [13].

4 The inquiry model

The basic principle of inquiry in CANDID is that a request is expressed by describing an object solution of the request. The request must specify an *object for search* and among its components the objects for display and the operands of selection operations.

Example 1 : "Which rallymen have participated as often as the person recommending them? State the number of participations of the person recommending them". The request can be formulated in the following way:

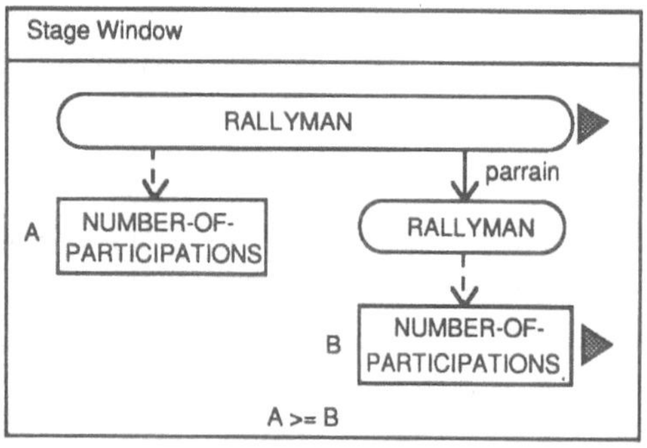

An object for search is a rallyman who has participated as often as the person recommending him. Its type is a subtype of the RALLYMAN type. The objects for display (identified by a small triangle) are its identifier (name and forenames) and the number of participations of the person recommending him.

The object for search is specified by constructing a request graph whose elements are similar as those of a schema graph. This graph comprises one or several components. A component is a tree where each node corresponds to an object type and each edge to a relationship (attribute relationship, construction relationship or ISA relationship). The root of the tree describes a unique object type. The tree is obtained from an initial object type (the root node) by applying successively the DEVELOP command. It is important to note that two "connected" types in the schema can always appear in the same component by derived attributes (inverse attributes, derived attributes in a construction).

The field of the request is the set of all the objects having the specified type.

When the graph has a unique component, the cardinality of the field is equal to the cardinality of the class of the root of the component.

When the graph has several components, the field of the request request is the cartesien product of the field of each component.

The field can be restricted by some conditions. The conditions are expressed through comparisons between elements of the same component or between elements of separate components.

An operand of a condition is designate by clicking a node on the request graph. This clicking has a specific semantics which is coherent with that of its component: It designates the object or the set of objects of the type selected, attached to a root type object through the semantic links of the path between the root and the node. This path comprises all the attributes encountered between the root type and the selected type. If at least one of these attributes is multivalued, the selection designates a set of objects (multivalued path). Otherwise the selection designates a unique object (monovalued path). Selecting the root of a component (zero path) designates an object of the root type.

All the elements specified during a stage can be re-used in the following stages. The Recapitulation Window contents is used as an extension of the external schema present in the Schema Window.

At the end of each stage, the user can view the result obtained with the request paraphrased in the Recapitulation Window (this result only exists if objects for display have been specified). He/she then can complete the request by extra stages.

5 The language primitives

We now make a few remarks concerning each primitive of the query language.

Enter: This allows one or several mediatic objects to be entered. Thus a constant is specified (object constant or set constant) which can be used with other primitives (eg. COMPARISON). The system displays a Venn diagram where the data is entered. Jokers can be used.

Display: This makes it possible to determine the "objects for display" in FT. These objects are indicated by a small triangle. Clearly only MOs can be displayed. By convention, if this command is used on an AOT or a COT, the external identifiers of these objects will be displayed.

Develop: This leads to a display of the graph of the type T selected by the user. The graph of a type comprises all of its attributes (specific, inherited, derived).

Stipulate: When a type T is selected by the user, this command leads to a display of:

.the ISA hierarchy for which T is the root,

.a combination of Venn Diagrams which represent the type T and its subtypes, respecting the constraints of covering and disjunction expressed in this hierarchy.

Comparison: This command makes it possible to express a binary comparison: t1 θ t2. Two steps are necessary: the first for stipulating the operands t1 and t2 (the user proceeds by selecting in the Stage Window); the second for choosing an expression t1 θ t2 in the list proposed by the system.

When a stage comprises several comparisons, the interface supposes that the corresponding boolean conditions are linked by logical ANDs. This interpretation corresponds to the usual comprehension in natural langage.

Combination: Here it possible to define a set through set operations on other already defined sets. This is simply carried out by clicking blocks on Venn diagrams (obtained, for example, with the command STIPULATE).

Function: This primitive makes it possible to evaluate a set of objects: type class or value of a multivalued attribute. The system proposes a list of evaluators appropriate to the type. The evaluator NUMBER (number of objects) is always proposed. The MOTs have specific evaluators (MAXIMUM, MINIMUM, AVERAGE, ... for numbers; THE LONGEST, THE SHORTEST, ...for strings). There are also functions for constructors.

Expression: With this function it is possible to specify an expression combining MOs of the same primary type (+, -, ... for numbers; CONCATENATION, ... for strings).

Grouping, Aggregation, Hierarchization: These concern explicit derivation primitives of new COTs.

6 Recursive requests

The specification and processing of recursive requests have been discussed in several graphical interfaces [2, 4, 7]. CANDID also allows certain possibilities in this area through the hierarchization constructor. Recursiveness is thus dealt with in CANDID through the manipulation of a constructed structure. This less functional view of recursiveness is coherent with the notion of a semantic model constructor. Moreover it leads to a certain "materialization" which is no doubt better suited to the final user. We shall now illustrate the possibilities of CANDID through a few examples.

6.1 Global manipulations of COs

The hierarchization constructor permits the definition of a constructed type CT on a basic type T by using a succession relation *succ* on the type T. Each CO is a tree such that:

.the root is a type T object which has no antecedent in *succ*;

.an internal node where a leaf is a type T object such that its father in the tree is its antecedent in *succ*.

This constructor presupposes that any object o, of type T, has no more than one antecedent in *succ*. An object o can thus only occur in a single CO. There are as many CO as there are type T objects which have no antecedent in *succ*. Clearly the objective of such a constructor is to be able to manipulate hierarchies induced by a succession relation.

For each component o of the basic type T, the system manages a monovalued derived attribute POSITION. POSITION is an aggregate object with two components: the root of the CO in which o occurs and the level of o in this CO.

This derived attribute allows for formulation according to

the simple recursive request concepts of CANDID as in the following example.

Example 2 : "Give the composition of the first five generations of each pioneer" (a pioneer is a competitor of the first generation of the rally; a pioneer does not have anyone recommending him).

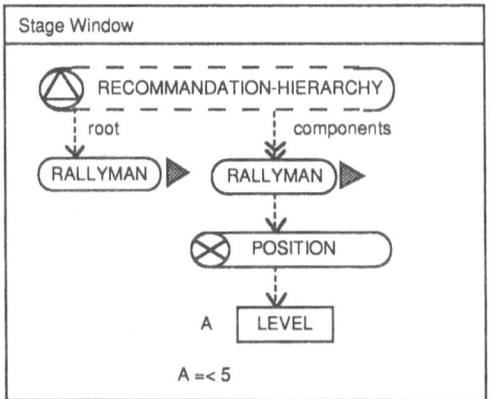

Extra restrictions on the root (for example: "1987 pioneers"; "pioneers whose number of participations is superior to five) and/or on the internal nodes (for example: "successors who participated in 1988") are specified without any further complexity. It is also possible to envisage an evaluation on all successorrs of a pioneer, through the primitive FUNCTION: total number of participations of successors, successor who has the greatest number of participations, … . Generally speaking, it is possible to draw up a list of all the components for each CO with various restrictions on the root and/or the other nodes, and to evaluate the resulting set.

6.2 Partial manipulations of COs

In a certain number of situations, it is useful to be able to manipulate just a subtree or a branch in one or several COs. For this purpose, CANDID offers a subtree derivation mechanism and a branch derivation mechanism.

Example 3: "List successors of rallymen whose name is DURAND".

The *root* attribute SUBTREE makes it possible to determine the root of each subtree. Several subtrees can be selected in one or several CO. The multivalued attribute *components* makes it possible to obtain all the component objects in each subtree. By convention the root is the root of each CO if *root* is not fixed.

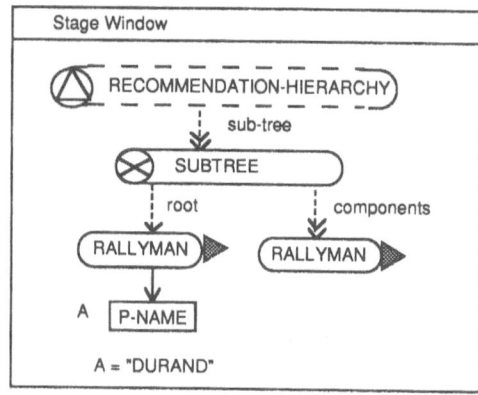

Example 4: "List the rallymen preceding DURAND".

The two attributes *beginning* and *end* of BRANCH can be used to fix the origin and the end of each branch. Several branches can be selected in one or several COs. The multivalued attribute *components* makes it possible to obtain all the component objects on each branch. By convention the origin is the root of each CO if *beginning* is not fixed, and the end is any descendant leaf of the origin if *end* is not fixed. The second case is thus equivalent to the processing of a subtree. The case where *beginning* and *end* are not fixed is equivalent to the complete processing of each tree.

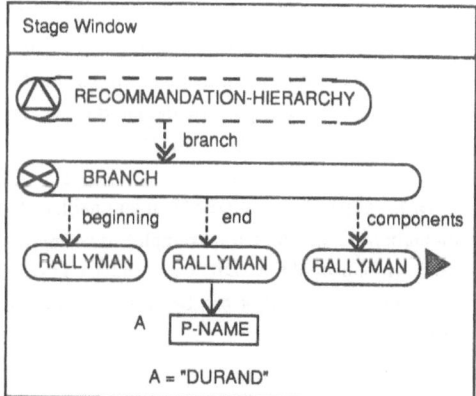

For the request in example 4, the graphical specification is no doubt more laborious than a functional specification. Graphical specification only becomes interesting for more complex requests.

7 Conclusion

Recursive requests are possible with CANDID with a structural approach through the hierarchization constructor. This approach consists in constructing the trees deduced from a relation of succession on objects of a basic type T, and in specifying a path on these trees. This formulation appears to be more cumbersome than a functional formulation for simple requests. However we do believe it is well-suited to the final user to the extent that it allows the problem to be approached in a more concrete way. But this point of view is debatable and needs to be confirmed (or refuted) experimentally.

This structural approach could be generalized within a much wider framework, where the relation s on objects of type T would no longer define a set of trees but a set of connected components in the graph (class(T), s). Primitives adapted to search for sets of remarkable nodes or particular paths could lead to the direct formulation of several graph problems.

We have not attempted to formally establish the power of expression of CANDID for recursive requests. As far as recursion is concerned, a formal approach is presented in [2] in order to compare the possibilities of the two graphical languages G+ and QDB*. This approach presupposes the definition of a textual language isomorphic to the graphical language. In order to apply a similar approach, we are defining a textual equivalent of CANDID.

Our objective through CANDID is not to elaborate a complete language. It is primarily intended for the final user and so it is vital to make the right compromise between power of expression and user-friendliness.

It is by no means easy to judge the ease of manipulation of such a language a priori. For the conception of CANDID we took inspiration from studies and previous experimentations [11, 5]. But it is only by experimenting that one will be able to come to a final conclusion. For this purpose the interface is currently being implemented on an APOLLO workstation.

We believe that this type of interface can be added to different types of DBMS: object-oriented DBMS, relational DBMS with object orientation (as in RM/T for example). It is important to note that the symbolism of CANDID can be adapted to different contexts as suggested in [15] or can be based on a compatible model [16].

References

[1] S. ABITEBOUL, S. GRUMBACH, "Bases de données et objets structurés", T.S.I., vol. 6, n° 5, pp 383-404, 1987.

[2] M. ANGELACCIO, T. CATARCI, G. SANTUCCI, "QBD*: A Graphical Query Language with Recursion", IEEE Transactions on Software Engineering, vol. 16, no. 10, October 1990.

[3] D.BRYCE, R.HULL, "SNAP: a Graphics-Based Schema Manager", 2nd International Conference on Data Engineering, IEEE, New-York, pp 151-164, Feb. 1986.

[4] I. F. CRUZ, A. O. MENDELZON, P. T. WOOD, "G+: Recursive queries without recursion", 2nd Int. Conf. Expert Database Syst., pp 355-368, Apr. 1988.

[5] Y. CORSON, "Ergonomie des langages de requête relationnels", T.S.I., vol. 2, n°5, pp 329-339, 1983.

[6] K.T. GOLDMAN, S.A. GOLDMAN, P.C. KANELLAKIS, S.B. ZDONIK, "ISIS: Interface for a Semantic Information System", Proceedings of the ACM SIGMOD International Conference on the Management of Data, New-York, 1985.

[7] S. HEILER, A. ROSENTHAL, "G. WHIZ, a Visual Interface for the Functional Model with Recursion", Proceedings of VLDB Conference, Stockholm, pp 209-218, 1985.

[8] R. HULL, R. KING, "Semantic Database Modeling: Survey, Applications, and Research Issues", ACM TODS, vol. 19, n° 3, pp 201-260, Sept. 1987.

[9] H. KIM, H.F. KORTH, A. SILBERSCHATZ, "PICASSO: a Graphical Query Language", Software-Practice and Experience, vol. 18(3), pp 169-203, March 1988.

[10] M. KUNT, "Description et évaluation de PASTA-3, une interface graphique de manipulation directe aux bases de données avancées", Sixièmes Journées Bases de Données Avancées, Montpellier, Septembre 1990.

[11] A. MICHARD, "A New Database Query Language for Non-Professional Users: Design Principles and Ergonomic Evaluation", Rapport de recherche n° 127, INRIA, Avril 1982.

[12] S. MIRANDA, J. NSONDE, "LAGRIF: a Pictorial Non-Programmer-Oriented Request Language for a Relational Data Base Management System", Improving Database Usability and Responsiveness, pp 173-204, 1982.

[13] P. PAUTHE, "EVER: un éditeur de V-relations", Thèse de 3ème cycle, n°3957, Université de Paris-Sud, Sept. 1985.

[14] W.D. POTTER, R.P. TRUEBLOOD, "Traditional, Semantic, and Hyper-Semantic Approaches to Data Modeling", Computer, pp 53-63, June 1988.

[15] W. F. RIEKERT, "The ZOO Metasystem: a Direct-Manipulation Interface to Object-Oriented Knowledges Bases", Institut für Informatik, Universität Stuttgart, 1986.

[16] M. SCHNEIDER, C.TREPIED, "A Graphical Query Language Based on an Extended E-R Model", 8th Int. Conf. on Entity Relationship Approach, pp 248-262, Toronto, 18-20 October 1989.

[17] C. TREPIED, "Un modèle de base de données sémantique et un langage graphique d'interrogation pour un environnement orienté utilisateur final", Thèse de Doctorat, Université de Clermont-Fd II, Janvier 1990.

[18] M.M. ZLOOF, "Query-By-Example: a Data Base Language", IBM Systems Journal, vol. 16, n°4, pp 324-343, 1977.

ADAMS: an Aggregate Data Management System with Multip Interaction Techniques

Fernando FERRI*, Patrizia GRIFONI^, Leonardo MEO-EVOLI^, Fabrizio L. RICCI^

^Consiglio Nazionale delle Ricerche, Istituo di Studi sulla Ricerca e
Documentazione Scientifica; Via Cesare de Lollis 12; 00185-Roma; Italy
*Università di Roma "La Sapienza", Dipartimento di Informatica e
Sistemistica; Via Salaria 113; 00198-Roma; Italy

ABSTRACT

The paper describes ADAMS (Aggregate Data Management System), a system for the definition and manipulation of Statistical Databases (SDB). ADAMS adopts different interface approaches according to the user profile. The System displays data by means of spreadsheet and simplify the user result analysis activity. The authors describe the models adopted for the representation of statistical information, manipulation and layout of statistical tables.

1 INTRODUCTION

The generic decision-making and evaluation process referring to trends in phenomena involves the exploitation or creation of data in the form of statistical tables (ST). Statistical Tables consist of data produced by a process of aggregating elementary data. To successfully manage, manipulate and query a Statistical Tables is a complex activity requiring a considerable knowledge of statistical problems.

The primary objective of the present paper is part of an applied research activity aimed at allowing computing resources to be exploited and the filing potential of personal computers to be used by professionals without any specific computer science training, but who are competent in the relevant application field.

The approach we have followed in the aggregate data management system project, once the user profile had been defined, was to provide the user with conceptual and visual tools for representing and manipulating data.

The steps followed in designing and implementing ADAMS involved:
- defining a logical (internal) model and an (external) user model of the aggregate data or statistical tables (§2)
- defining an algebra for manipulating such internal logical model
- defining the various user languages and techniques of interaction expressing such manipulations on the user external model (§3).
- defining the ADAMS system in terms of the functions provided, the type of user/system interaction and with reference to different user profiles.

ADAMS is a data management system whose main characteristic consists of the fact that it helps the user through the interaction and thus prevents any chance of error. The system has currently been implemented on a Macintosh platform although it is planned to implement it to other hardware platforms and operating systems in future.

This paper is organized as follows: section 2 consists of a presentation of the (internal) logical model and the user model. Section 3 contains a brief natural language description of the operators required for manipulation of the macro-data. This is followed by a presentation of the different ways in which the user interacts with the system. Section 4 illustrates windows and the system's manipulation environment and a description of a query session is described, showing the various functions ADAMS offers its users.

2 LOGICAL MODEL AND USER MODEL

ADAMS is a system which can be used to manage a statistical data base containing macro-data. The macro-data are obtained by the aggregation of data referring to individual events. The macro-data are described using other data, known as meta-data. Each Statistical Table (ST) is associated with a macro-datum and with the set of meta-data describing it. The meta-data identify respectively the ST variables characterizing the statistical phenomenon described in the table as well as the modalities associated with each variable, which identify the values of the variable itself. According to the MEFISTO logical model, a Statistical Table is defined as an ordered pair $<R,g>$, in which R is a relation having the variables of ST as attributes and g is the function which allows mapping from the meta-data (instances of R) to the summary values of the ST. Each ST is also univocally associated with a data type that expresses the aggregative function that has generated the table summary values.

Desease distribution		
Nº	year	
regions	1980	1981
Lazio	2148	1981
Piedmont	1523	1982
Lombardy	3263	4525
Campania	1695	2032
Basilicata	155	192
Sicily	2124	2557
Molise	221	258

Disease distribution		
Nº	years	
	1980	1981
	11129	14088

tab.2:distribution of disease by year

⬚ Data type ▦ Modality ⊠ Variables

tab1: example of a statistical table

An example of a Statistical Table is given in tab. 1: "Disease distribution" identifies the summary attribute associated with the statistical table in the case of viral hepatitis, "regions" and "years" are the variables, "1980" and "1981" represent the modalities of "year" and, lastly, "Lazio", "Piedmont", "Lombardy", "Campania", "Basilicata", "Sicily", "Molise" represent the modalities of the variable "regions". "N°" identifies the data type of the table and it is used to indicate that the values are absolute values obtained by count operations.

In order to represent the database the user makes use of a partially ordered, connected, direct and acyclic oriented graph model, the GRASS[7] graph. This graph is made up of the following node types:
- S nodes: identify the statistical phenomenon associated with the ST.
- T nodes: identify the ST of the databases and the relevant data type.
- A nodes: each ST can be structured using these nodes; they consist of the Cartesian product of all instances of the variables.
- C nodes: each of these nodes identifies a variable
- M nodes: each of these nodes identifies one of the values associated with a variable.

The GRASS nodes must respect the following connection rules:
- an S node can only have S nodes as ascendants and one or more S/T nodes as descendants
- a T node has no descendants and is connected with at least one S node and with a single A node.
- an A node can have A nodes as descendants and M nodes as ascendants
- each M node can have one or more C nodes as descendants and has no ascendants.

The nodes of a GRASS graph are the meta-data which allow the SDB to be described. Below is an example of an SDB represented by a GRASS graph (fig.1). The structure of an ST is described by the subgraph connected to the descending T node representing the table. The M nodes connected to a C node identify the modalities of the variable associated with the C node. At the interface level it was decided to represent the modalities referring to each variable in a dialogue box.

3 MANIPULATION

The user interacts with the System and manipulates the macro-data using the MEFISTO [8] algebra operators such as Summarization, Disaggregation, Reclassification, Restriction, Extension. A short description of these operators is given in the following.

Summarization. Summarization is one of the more frequently used operators. One table and one or more variables are involved in its application. The result produced will once again be a table obtained from the input table by eliminating the variables suppressed. Let us assume, for instance, that knowing distribution of viral hepatitis by region and by year (tab. 1), we wish to find out the number of patients by year and to discard the detail referring to the regions. In order to obtain the desired information we would have to, in this case, perform a summarization of tab. 1 with respect to the regions. The result is shown in tab. 2. As we can see the operator has not modified the data type in any way.

Disaggregation. Disaggregation allows us to recalculate the summary attribute of a table according to the law of distribution represented in the form of a suitable table. For example, if the number of viral hepatitis patients by year is known for 1980 and 1981 (Tab. 2) and the law of percentage distribution of the disease by age and year is known (tab. 3), it is possible to find out the number of patients by age and year using the disaggregation operator. The result is shown in tab. 4.
Reclassification. Reclassification allows the variable modalities to be grouped according to suitable relations of correspondence.

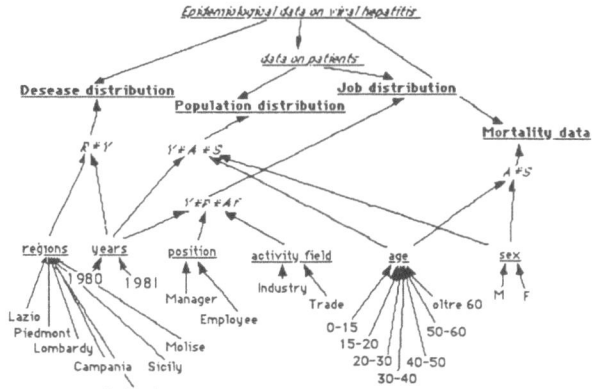

fig. 1: representation of the database using the GRASS graph

Disease distribution law		
%	years	
age	1980	1981
0-15	7.4	10.04
15-20	10.56	11.03
20-30	9.25	11.06
30-40	9.85	11.09
40-50	12.85	13.14
50-60	17.89	13.85
OVER 60	32.20	30.53

tab. 3: disease distribution by years and geographic area

Disease distribution law		
Number	years	
age	1980	1981
0-15	825	1415
15-20	1175	1555
20-30	1030	1558
30-40	1095	1562
40-50	1430	1888
50-60	1990	1952
OVER 60	3584	4158

tab.4: Disease distribution by years and age

relation	
person classes	age
children	0-15
adults	15-20
adults	20-30
adults	30-40
adults	40-50
adults	50-60
elderly	OVER 60

Disease distribution		
Number	years	
person classes	1980	1981
children	825	1415
adults	6720	8515
elderly	3584	4158

tab. 5: disease distribution by year and person classes

fig. 2: relation of correspondences between age classes and age

This operator allows a table to be completely reorganized by modifying its variables.

For example, if tab. 4 is known and you would like to know the distribution of viral hepatitis by year and person classes, it will be possible to reclassify the above table according to the relations between age and person classes fig. 2.

The resulting table is reported in tab. 5.

Extension. Extension uses two tables to produce a larger one. It involves tables defined using the same variables, but with different modalities. The result will again be a table in which the modalities referring to each variable are the result of modalities associated with those of the starting tables.

Let us assume, for instance, to have information referring to the distribution of viral hepatitis by geographic region and year in two different statistical tables, one for males and one for females (tabs. 6,7).

Number	years	
geograp hic area	1980	1981
centre	2148	147
north	4786	2574
south	2248	2800

tab.6: disease distribution in males by year and by geographic area

Number	years	
geograp hic area	1980	1981
centre	981	1066
north	2129	3933
south	1947	2239

tab.7: disease distribution in females by year and by geographic area

Male disease distribution sex=M

Female disease distribution sex=F

If it is desired to know disease distribution by geographic area, year and sex, an extension will be performed between the tables in tab. 6 and tab. 7 and the result will be as shown in tab. 8.

Disease distribution

No.		years	
sex	geogr area	1980	1981
F	centre	981	1066
	north	2129	3933
	south	1947	2239
M	centre	1167	1476
	north	2657	2574
	south	2248	2800

tab.8: disease distribution by year by geographic area and by sex

Disease distribution

Number	years	
person classes	1980	1981
elderly	3584	4158

tab.9: disease distribution by year in elderly

r1

person classes
elderly

<u>Restriction</u>. Restriction works on the cardinality of the variable domain and gives as result a table having the same variables as the starting table, but with a lower cardinality. Therefore, in the case in which a user has a statistical table and is interested in a subset of the information contained in it, the restriction operator will allow him to obtain a table in which only values referring to the modalities of interest are present. For example, on examining tab. 5, if we are interested to know the distribution of viral hepatitis for the elderly the restriction of tab. 5 on the relation r1 produces the result of tab. 9.

3.1 MANIPULATION USING MATHEMATICAL LINKS

Depending on the type of user profile [3] and thus on his level of experience, it is possible to interact in different ways with the System. In the case of an inexperienced user a graphical interaction is preferred. In ADAMS in particular each query can be edited by selecting the operands from among the icons of the GRASS graph. The query is represented by means of a model that uses an acyclic graph, VISTA [10]. Unlike the GRASS graph, in which the organization logical description of the database is represented, "VISTA" displays for the user to see the functional mathematical link between the result of each query and the tables present in the database which are involved in the above query. The query graph is defined as follows:
- each query is represented in tree form;
- the Mefisto operator referring to a query is associated with the root of the tree representing it;
- each descending node is a argument of the operator;
- each descending node may be the root of a query subtree;
- each leaf node is labelled with the meta-datum argument;
- any operator parameters are found to be associated with the node input arc;
- the VISTA graph represents one entire work session.

The inexperienced user interacts with the System following a graphical approach exclusively. He gradually learns the key words query language (described below) through, which is

used to achieve more rapid interaction with the System.

By way of example a query graph representing the query that produces the "population distribution" of viral hepatitis over the years is shown in fig. 3.

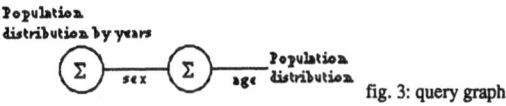

fig. 3: query graph

3.2 MANIPULATION OBTAINED USING A LANGUAGE INVOLVING THE USE OF KEY WORDS

An expert user can express his query using a language involving the use of key words: STAQUEL* [10]. This is a language which allows queries to be expressed using algebraic-functional type expressions like the following

$$r = F_1 P(O_{11}, ..., F_{1j1}(O_{1jm}, ...,) ..., O_{1n})$$

In the above expression r is the name used to identify the result of the query, F are the operators, p is the parameter of an operator and O is the operator argument. For example, using Staquel* syntax [10], the same query as in fig. 3 would have the following expression:

$$population\ distribution\ by\ year = \Sigma_{age}(\Sigma_{sex}(Disease\ Distribution)).$$

3.3 DIRECT MANIPULATION

Using direct manipulation it is possible to specify the query directly on the GRASS graph by modifying the graphic display of the SDB tables. Each modification will be the result of appropriate manipulation expressed using Mefisto algebra. Therefore, an appropriate set of rules have been laid down. The following are some significant examples:
- cutting an input edge in an A node means summarizing the tables on variables associated with ascending C nodes of A.
- replacing a C node means performing a reclassification.

Therefore it is possible to construct new ST without specifying the query with VISTA or STAQUEL. In fact a correspondence exists between the rules of direct manipulation and the MEFISTO operators. Let us assume once again, for example, that the aim is to express the query shown in fig. 3 where the user would like to know the viral hepatitis of population distribution by years. This may be achieved by eliminating the edges linking "age" and "sex" to the node A*E*S of the tree referring to the table "Population distribution", as you can see referring to the database of fig.1.

The result of the manipulation is represented according to GRASS by the "Population distribution by year" T node and its ancestor subgraph containing the C node "years" only (see fig. 6).

4   THE ADAMS SYSTEM

ADAMS is a system that enables the user to perform statistical table manipulations. It provides functions to express queries, to navigate through queries, to define a GRASS schema, and a sub-schema, to navigate through meta-data, to load tables, and finally to display tables and analyse data. In ADAMS the user interaction is supported by a multi-window graphical interface.

422

4.1 Windows and the manipulation environment

The ADAMS system provides an environment for specifying table manipulations both in the case of a direct manipulation approach or whenever the interaction is implemented using a key word and/or visual icon language. The interface windows used by the user for manipulation and querying are: the GRASS window, the VISTA window and the STAQUEL window, as well as the VISUAL DIRECT MANIPULATION window in the case of direct manipulation.

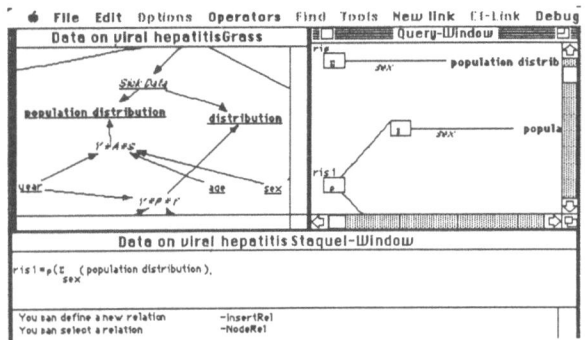

fig. 4: data base query interface

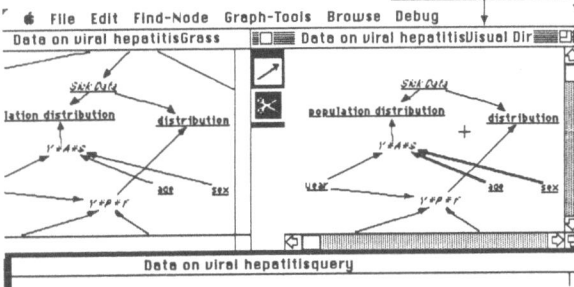

fig. 5: direct manipulation interface

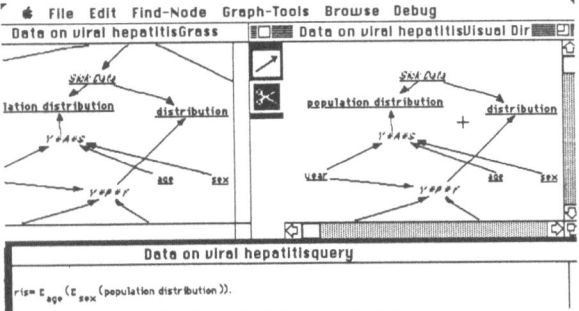

$r i s = \Sigma_{age} (\Sigma_{sex} (population distribution)).$

fig. 6: result of direct manipulation

In the GRASS window the logical schema of the SDB is displayed by means of the GRASS graph. Using the direct manipulation approach to query the statistical database, the user will have to display the SDB or a part in the VISUAL DIRECT MANIPULATION window and will thus be working on the nodes and edges used to represent it.

Should the approach followed involve expressing each manipulation with the query graph and/or STAQUEL, the interaction with the GRASS icons (representing the meta-data) will allow queries to be formulated, the SDB to be manipulated, as well as allowing the information associated with each icon to be ac-

cessed.

In the VISTA window a query is represented by means of a VISTA graph.

In the STAQUEL window each query is expressed using STAQUEL*[10] language expressions.

Furthermore, the interface is provided with a window referred to the GUIDE window on which the information helping the user through the interaction is displayed.

Whenever direct manipulation is not used, each query is expressed using a context-driven editor. The System makes it possible to select only the icons or menu options that respect the syntax and semantics of the current query and/or allows only expressions in which the names of identifiers congruent with the current query occur to be written. By moving into the VISTA window it is possible to navigate through the queries and display the way they are formulated, and also the structure of the results produced. Likewise, by shifting to the VISUAL DIRECT MANIPULATION window it is possible to navigate through the meta-data of the tables produced by the manipulation. The updating of any of the above windows produces feedback to update all the others.

4.2 DEFINING A QUERY

Let us now examine the database in which data are stored. Let us assume that the user is going to use the direct manipulation approach. If, he is interested to know the distribution of viral hepatitis by year (§ 3.3) he can cut the edge linking the nodes age and sex at the node Y*A*S and calculate the new table starting from the Population Distribution table (fig. 5). The result, displayed using GRASS, is shown in fig. 6. Let us now examine the case of a user that manipulates the SDB by editing the query graph and the corresponding STAQUEL expression. The display and interaction with the icons of the GRASS graph (representing the meta-data) are implemented in the window of the same name (fig. 4).

Let us assume that it is desired to know the number of viral hepatitis patients by year and person classes. The VISTA window will display the graph used to represent the query that involves Summarization and Reclassification the result of which identifies the information sought (fig. 4). It is worth mentioning that this is a complex query (i.e. one inside which a further query is expressed, namely summarization on sex). Associated with the node expressing the summarization is a labelled edge. The labelling of the edge allows us to identify the parameter referring to the summarization expressing the summarization variable. The query of fig.4 is still incompletely defined. In this state the context-driven editor allows only the relations which involve a variable of the current operand to be selected.

Σ_{sex}(Population Distribution).

The query as expressed using the graphical approach consists of the following steps:
1) assignment of a name to the result to be obtained;
2) specification of MEFISTO operator associated with the root node;
3) specification of the arguments. Note that each argument can have its own sub-query.

4.3   DEFINITION OF A GRASS SCHEMA

The System has an environment designed for the Table Administrator which allows the table schema of a data base to be defined. Each database table can be defined using the following steps:
- definition and positioning of T node;
- acquisition of information associated with T node (data type, name, description);
- definition of S nodes hierarchy;
- definition of hierarchic structure of A nodes;
.- definition of C nodes;
- definition of edges between C nodes and A nodes;
- acquisition of modalities associated with each C node.

As in query manipulation and expression, the system provides an editor also for the definition of the GRASS schema. Again the user is guided by screen messages indicating the operations allowed at any one time, as well as by icons representing the GRASS graph, which are selectable or not according to the manipulation in progress.

The interface implements three main windows: the GRASS window, the TOTAL SCHEMA window and the GUIDE window. The latter displays the messages used to guide the user through the interaction, while the TOTAL SCHEMA window is designed to display the SDB schema on a reduced scale and to highlight the current position of the GRASS window in the schema (fig. 7).

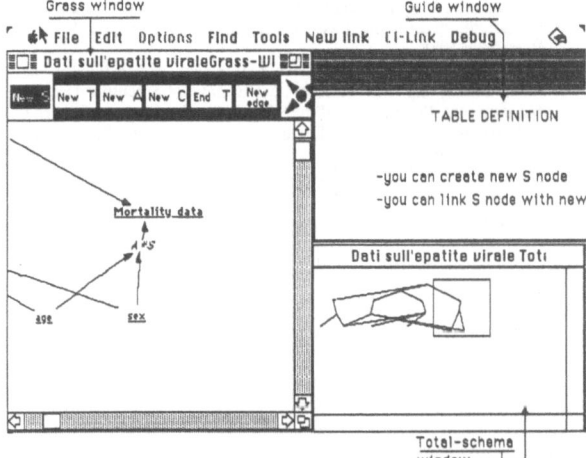

fig. 7: interface for database definition

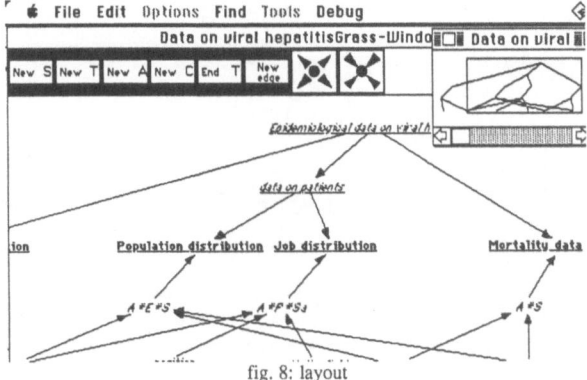

fig. 8: layout

4.4   FUNCTIONS AVAILABLE TO ALL USERS

The functions allowing navigation through meta-data (BROWSER), specifying a sub-set of the SDB (SUB-SCHEMA), displaying the GRASS graph (LAYOUT) and printing out one or more ST (PRINTING TABLE) are available to all users (from the end user to the database administrator).

4.4.1   Browser

The browser allows the user to navigate to the SDB schema using either the GRASS window and the classic approach involving scroll bars on the sides of the windows or the TOTAL SCHEMA window. Furthermore, starting from a given node, the user can move to another node by specifying the condition allowing the move to be made. Lastly, the System affords navigation through the set of relations representing links among modalities.

4.4.2   Sub-schema

Whenever the user needs to work on a sub-set of data and meta-data contained in the SDB, the System allows the tables of interest to be identified through the S nodes characterizing the phenomenon. In this case, ADAMS provides the user with a list of S nodes from which to select the root of the sub-schema of interest.

4.4.3   Layout

The position of the GRASS nodes and edges may be defined manually or automatically. In the first case the user, when the DBA itself or the end user, specifies the position of each GRASS node and edge. The System then ensures that the entire graph is sought and that the new positions are stored in memory (fig. 8). In the second case the System uses an automatic layout algorithm [4,5] which, by taking into consideration the relative positions of the nodes, minimizes the reciprocal distances between them and arranges the nodes in horizontal bands which are kept separate for each node type (fig. 8).

4.4.4   Setting up a printing table

The user may include the summary attributes of more than one table on the same printing format. In order to specify the printing format format of a table (printing table) an editor is used by means of which the reciprocal position of the summary attributes may be determined vis-à-vis variable positioning and vice versa. The position of each table is identified using a hierarchy of row and column variables [11].

Let us assume, for example, that a printing table is to be specified starting from the database set out in fig. 1. Once we have specified in the GRASS window the tables we wish to display on a single sheet, the user, using the interface in fig. 9, determines the position of the summary attributes, while the System positions the row and column attributes. On the other hand, the user is in a position to determine the position of the variables in such a way that the System will provide for the automatic positioning of the tables. Once the printing format has been decided the tables can be displayed in spreadsheet format (fig. 10) and the user can perform any necessary data analysis.

5 CONCLUSIONS

ADAMS allows a statistical database to be defined and the relative statistical tables to be manipulated by defining mathematical relations between meta-data. The system uses context-driven editors. The representation of the operations and meta-data is of the icon-graphical type to provide the less experienced users with editors using visual languages. Sometimes interaction may be specified using the direct manipulation approach. For more experienced users ADAMS provides a key word language which speeds up interaction and allows the same manipulations as those expressed in visual language to be expressed.

The strategy used was to select simple tools for representing the concepts needed by the user in the interaction. The explicitly mentioned concepts represented are: statistical tables, the statistical table manipulation, the relations between the modalities of the table variables, the structure of the results generated using the manipulations, the graphic set-up of the output printing format. A specific graphical display formalism is used for each of the above concepts. Work is now in progress on the possible extension of STAQUEL* using operators that modify the data type. However, this would require the existence of software modules associated with the MEFISTO operators that were capable of determining the correct resolution algorithm.

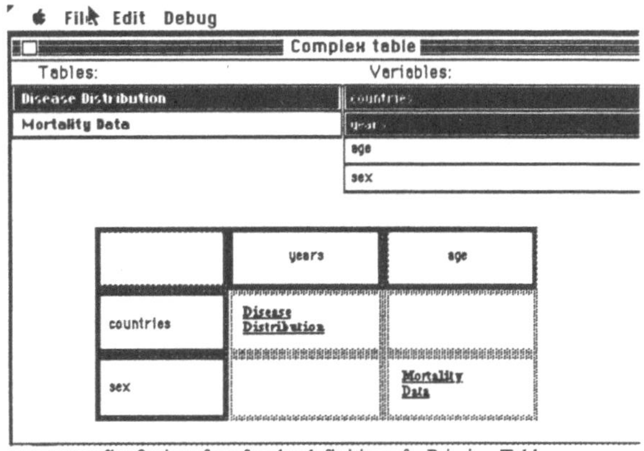

fig. 9.: interface for the definition of a Printing Table

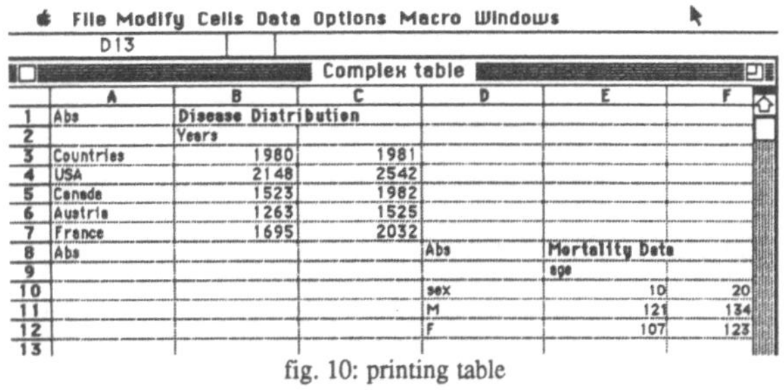

fig. 10: printing table

The system was implemented in an MPW environment using Pascal Object Oriented Language and the MacApp program library.

REFERENCES

[1] G. Bracaglia, Currò, A. D'Atri, P. Di Felice, F. L. Ricci, "Man-Machine interfaces to medical information system", Proc. VI IASTED International Symposium on Applied Informatics, 1988.

[2] A. D'Atri, L. Tarantino,"From Browsing to querying", Data Engeneering Bulletin, IEEE Computer society, vol.12, n°2, June 1989.

[3] W. W. Cotterman, K. Kumar, "User Cube: A Taxonomy of End Users", Comunication of the ACM, vol.32, Num.11, 1989.

[4] G. Di Battista, R. Tamassia, "Algorithms for Plane Representations of Aciclic Digraph", Theoretical Computer Science, 1988.

[5] G. Di Battista, "Automatic Drawing of Statistical Diagrams", Statistical and Scientific Database Management, Proceedings of the IV° Internat. Working Conference on SSDBM, Rome, June 1988, Lecture Notes in Computer Science, 339, Springer-Verlag, 1989.

[6] G.Falcitelli, L.Meo-Evoli, E.Nardelli, F.L.Ricci,"The Mefisto* model: an object-oriented representation for statistical data management",in "Data Analysis, Learning Symbolic and Numeric Knowledge", Nova Science Publishers, 1989.

[7] M. Rafanelli, F.L. Ricci: "Proposal of a logical Model for statistical database", Proceed of the I° Internat. Workshop on Statistical and Scientific Database Management, Los Altos (ca) 1983.

[8] E. Fortunato, M. Rafanelli, F. L. Ricci, A. Sebastio, "An Algebra for statistical data" Proceed . of the III Internat. Workshop on Statistical and Scientific Database Management, 1986.

[9] E. L. Hutchins, J. D. Hollan, D. A. Norman, "Direct Manipulation Interfaces", By "User centred system", LEA publishers, London, 1986.

[10] L.Meo-Evoli,"An aggregate database management system", Proc. VIII IASTED International Symposium on Applied Informatics, 1990.

[11] G. Ozsoyoglu, Z. M. Ozsoyoglu, F. Mata, "A language and a physical organization tecnique for summary tables", Proceed. of ACM SIGMOD Conference, 1985.

[12] M. Rafanelli, F. L. Ricci: "STAQUEL: A query language for statistical macro database management system", C.I.L. 85, Barcellona,1985.

[13] M.Rafanelli, F.L.Ricci,"A visual interface for browsing and manipulating statistical entities", Statistical and Scientific Database Management, Proceedings of the V° Internat. Working Conference on SSDBM, Rome, June 1988, Lecture Notes in Computer Science, 420, Springer-Verlag, 1990.

[14] M. Rafanelli, F. L. Ricci: "A functional model for statistical entiies". Database and Expert Systems Applications Proceedings of the DEXA 90, Springer-Verlag, 1990.

Juridical principles for juridical applications. The DERINFO methodology

Dr. Fernando Galindo

Seminario de Informática y Derecho

50009 Universidad de Zaragoza. España

ABSTRACT

Recent experiences with object-oriented programming, using the resources of artificial intelligence (knowledge representation, logic programming, expert systems, and natural language comprehension) show that it is possible to implement juridical applications, i.e. programs to assist juridical activities. There are applications which are about to be commercialised or used by governments. It is now the task of the legal philosophers to decide to what point these applications can or should be used, so as not to deviate from their original object, or from the nature of the law, or the support of justice. This means involving the programmers who design such programs in the juridical principles which the applications must enhance and respect. This is the object of the DERINFO methodology.

1   Introduction

Unlike traditional programming, which tends predominantly to satisfy technical requirements, and thus may be unsuitable for juridical applications, the aim of object-oriented programming is to construct programs which correspond as closely as possible to the nature of their functions, without introducing any modifications which might distort these functions. The difficulties with traditional programming are due to the fact that it is not easy to get a grip on the activities to be programmed in this field, given the impenetrability of the legal world, which operates with traditional categories, legal provisions, and the needs of a changing world [8]. In this field, as in others, systems analysis is not enough.

This is not surprising, considering that the juridical system involves individual citizens, who are the creators and the subjects of the law [14]. Furthermore, jurists, whose task is to express this world's characteristics, have only recently come to view juridical activities as worthy of consideration; there still exist juridical theories and practices which are more occupied with progressively purifying legal language and fitting it into traditional dogmatic categories than with elucidating the bases of these activities [9]. These are the difficulties facing a programmer who wishes to build a legal computer program.

For this reason, in order to ensure that applications are as operative as possible, and for the systems to be as complex and as close to their objective as possible,.it is necessary to take into account the proposals of professional legal philosophers whose brief is to study juridical practices and propose guidelines, so that the applications can be built in accordance with the juridical and political principles contained in the law.

This principle will be followed in this paper, which expresses the above-mentioned need while presenting the current status of the DERINFO (Derecho e Informática - Law and Computing) methodology, which was drawn up at the University of Zaragoza for the design of juridical applications.

2   The DERINFO methodology

The DERINFO methodology consists of a set of techniques used to build applications to be effective supports for juridical activities.

The DERINFO methodology consists of two types of techniques: juridical techniques and computational techniques. We will now describe the general principles underlying the juridical techniques.

These juridical techniques include the rules of the Philosophy of Law, specifically legal Methodology; the Dogmatic rules governing the construction of normative concepts and systems, and those governing forensic or processal practices or the "art of judgement" [3]. The computational techniques include: general rules for object-oriented programming, and the rules for artificial intelligence: knowledge representation, logic programming, expert systems and natural language comprehension (dialog modeling and interface construction). This paper is a presentation of the juridical techniques used by the DERINFO methodology.

With regard to the juridical techniques, an auxiliary instrument for all of them is the technique of social systems: a method which has practical uses in the juridical field [17], and is involved in building an application, enabling coherent proposals to be drawn up in line with the requirements imposed by the computational techniques.

To summarise the functions of the above-mentioned techniques, it is the task of the Philosophy of Law to establish each applications's particular nature: the type of activity which it must serve. This requires the application's designers and future users to study that activity, on the basis of theories in the Philosophy of Law and its Methodology, and to decide whether it involves retrieving legal texts, interpreting them, applying rules, or building dogmas or rules. Another function of the Philosophy of Law is to study the specific subject covered by the activities, and to elucidate its material or substantive qualities, both the nature of the situation governed by the law ("the nature of things") and the data about the contents of the laws governing that situation. Sociology can be of great importance here. Another task of the Philosophy of Law is to study the juridical and political consequences of these applications, and to find whether they modify the principles and values contained in the law, and whether they meet moral rules, insofar as this is applicable [5].

It is the task of Dogmatics (Legal Science) to establish a normative system in which both the substantive material and the juridical activity which are to be supported by the application can be expressed. Specifically, it must delimit the activity in terms of typical Dogmatic categories with regard to the type of social problem dealt with in the application. Thus it must help to conceptualize, providing structures of laws which will offer juridical solutions for the case, or problem for which the application is designed, in line with the different possible interpretations in a plural society [16]. Its proposals must be explicit, in a minimally controlled language, which is comprehensible to both jurists and computer programmers. It is not necessary to draw up a logical formulation of the type "a->b" [6].

The task of professional practice is to propose, in a minimally systematic way, the habits of work in relation to the most typical cases of the subject covered by the application. It's function is not to build philosophical or dogmatic theories, but simply to point to solutions for typical cases, and to lay down patterns for daily work on the basis of actual practice. In computational jargon, this is referred to as making heuristic knowledge explicit.

The DERINFO methodology, whose general principles with regard to juridical techniques are outlined above (a deeper treatment of which would require developing juridical proposals which go beyond the scope of this article), was drawn up by the Seminario de Informática y Derecho at the University of Zaragoza while developing a set of programs, research and reports aimed at assisting the jurist to access legal documentation, that is, to access the law. From a computational viewpoint, one of the substantive bases of this work is the prior existence of legal data banks. Before discussing what was done, it should be pointed out that the characteristics of typical democratic judicial practice (access, interpretation and application of law; construction of dogmas) and the requirements of the legal system of a democratic country, were respected at all times [5]

The activities of the Seminario can be summarised as follows:

a)   Research leading to the construction of programs - some prototypes, some working programs - to provide juridical users with access to juridical documentation on certain areas [SIREDOJ, ARPO I, ARPO II, DCA].

b)   Providing advice on the construction of computer systems for access to juridical data banks to be installed in Offices of the Public Administration [SIJA] or in Parliaments [SICA]. These programs would be used by jurists in the administration as part of their daily work. Their activities could involve interpretation or application of the law.

c)   Providing advice on the design of programs for assisting access to juridical data banks to be installed in private companies [SEDE]. These programs would be used by jurists employed by such companies, to devise the appropriate texts for particular contracts.

d)   Providing advice on the design of programs for assisting access to administrative data banks containing juridical and technical information (urban zoning regulations, technical regulations on building and environment) to be installed in Offices of the Public Administration [SIOTUA] These programs would be used by jurists in the Administration as part of their daily work.

e)   Providing advice on the design of programs for assisting access to private data banks containing tecnical, non-juridical data, to be installed in private companies [SEDE]. These programs would be used by jurists and technicians employed by such companies.

In describing the most important steps taken in developing these activities and programs, it should be pointed out that the basic problem, in any event, was agreeing on the nature of the object or function of the body requesting advice, and agreeing on the nature of the commission, in coherence with that function. Agreement must be reached in two contexts: the limits on the project's cost, and the guarantee that the final product will not adversely affect the body's juridical operation.

Continuing with the description of the steps involved in building programs and drawing up consultants reports, it should be stated that the first step was always a detailed juridical study of the activities the program was designed to assist, performed in conjunction with the jurists who would use the application. Particular attention had to be paid to the instructions given with the commission, to the organizational rulings and to the juridical practices in the institution. The second step involved studying the material or substantive law -the legal texts- governing the problem for which the program was to be designed or on which the consultants report was to be written.

An interview with the program's future users and of users of other applications currently in use was the basic initial information-gathering procedure. Other basic steps included observing the institution's operation, and considering the ends or interests which it is obliged to serve.

Once the object of the work, viewed as a social system participated by other social systems, had been delimited, it was necessary to study the juridical content of the material. This was carried out in conjunction with the jurists who would use the finished system. With the assistance of the dogmatics and the opinions of practical jurists other than the system's future users, subsystems were built consisting of rules which, in one or several of their elements, referred to the items or texts of the juridical documentation contained in the data banks. These systems respected the convictions, prejudices or valuations of the users (who are social systems).

The user's valuations were constantly used as the reference point for research, advice, prototypes and finished programs. The action or decision of a jurist is required at all times. In this sense, disputes or problems and open terms are never solved by the application or by the advisors, but are viewed as the sole responsibility of the jurist user or of the members of the institutions being advised [9].

Therefore, it is not surprising that the more precise and specific the terms of the commission, the more satisfactory was the result. Clear objectives reveal the easy and difficult cases, in juridical terms. Difficult questions are always solved by a jurist.

3   The SIREDOJ program

As an example of the current status of this research, we will describe the SIREDOJ program, for intelligent retrieval of juridical documents, which is currently at the prototype stage, and is being used as the test bench for the other systems under development.

From a juridical viewpoint, in its current state, a lawyer carries on a dialogue with the program, responding to its questions, to find whether, in a case regarding a dispute over the construction of a building, a suit can brought, and what type of suit, what procedure to follow, and the juridical documents (legal texts, jurisprudence and bibliographical references) which can be used as a basis for the suit.

We will now summarise what the program currently does, and what it is due to do in the near future.

As it stands, the progam invites the user to describe the case, and progressively builds up a formulation of the case in a form decided by the user by choosing between different options, so as to satisfy the premises on which the conclusion offered by SIREDOJ will be based. The conclusions consist of the limited set of extra-juridical and juridical solutions and law suits which can be implemented to solve the dispute between the parties as a result of constructing a building. The substantive description of the problem, and the link between premises and conclusions were performed by a professor of Civil Law, who is an expert in the general principles and doctrinal trends laid down by dogmatics with regard to obligations and contracts, and by a magistrate who is an expert in professional practice. This process has been described in other papers [4].

In the near future, this application will be able to do the following: Firstly, give replies which are more in coherence with the users' interests and convictions. In the application's current state, it assumes the user is a lawyer. In future, the user could also be a judge, technician (e.g. architect), a law lecturer or a law student. Depending on the type of user, the program will also provide texts containing claims, defenses, sentences, opinions, academic exercises (model solutions to cases) with a duly justified juridical content (jurisprudence and legislative texts).

The case, in the field of civil law, could involve disputes arising from contracts (any type of contract) and obligations in general. If the methodology is sufficiently well developed, it would not be difficult to solve problems such as personality and legal capacity, and later property, succession and family matters, or on any other type of dispute. The program's conclusions will depend on the data supplied and the object, action or conclusion which is desired. As is normally the case in practice, the main problem in taking advantage of the program is for the user to decide whether there are elements of proof for the premises proposed by the program.

With a view to finding the limits of research, future applications will deal with normative systems which conform to some of the different valuational domains from which juridical solutions can be supplied for disputes arising from building construction. These are domains -systems- of solutions (premises and conclusions) for typical cases [12], governed by efficacy [1] or other values: justice, rules of ideal communication [2], rules of "fairnes" [15] , or political ideologies [11] or moral convictions, which are congruent with the beliefs or principles of the program's users.

4   Juridical principles and applications for jurists

The example of SIREDOJ, and the DERINFO methodology which gave rise to it, lead to a reflection on their consequences for juridical practice. This is due to the fact that this type of methodology and application appear to affect several basic principles of law, in that the responsibility for juridical decisions appears to be transferred to computer programs. This objection is made from the standpoint that the law establishes that the final point of reference for the legitimation of juridical activities is the individual conscience, or the majority consensus (while respecting the view of minorities) on the criteria of justice which are recognised by the citizens of a given society.

To answer this objection, we should describe in detail what the DERINFO methodology and programs such as SIREDOJ actually do in this field.

If we consider the functions of SIREDOJ as described above, it is easy to see that its final aim is not to assist in activities which are the field of jurists, but to provide expert knowledge to jurists who are not experts in the field, for a problem which is not sufficiently covered by legislation.

The field covered by SIREDOJ, disputes arising from building construction, is not sufficiently covered by the Civil Code, and this fact is widely admitted. This is not surprising, since the Spanish Civil Code was promulgated in 1889. Construction techniques have changed radically since then. The result is a legal vacuum in building construction, an area of great economic and social importance. In the interim, jurisprudence has filled this legal vacuum, giving rise to numerous decisions which in fact constitute the current law on the subject.

As is easy to imagine, this law is difficult for the non-expert to approach. The SIREDOJ program therefore performs the function of providing knowledge to the non-expert, thereby improving juridical practice related to problems arising from building construction. Furthermore, this knowledge is within any jurist's reach: the program runs on a personal computer.

This means that the program has the virtue of instantaneously transmitting juridical experience and information to jurists who do not possess them. This improves professional practices, and thereby implements the principle that the laws which are obligatory for a society base their legitimacy on "the dialogue of all with all, without manipulation by power." [7].

But there are other conceivable uses of the SIREDOJ application, and the DERINFO methodology in general. The most obvious one is to meet routine requirements in juridical practice, and helping to make the practice of law more bureaucratic, by facilitating the automatic creation of documents and decisions. Another use would be to attack the principle of security: the point of reference for the activities served by these applications would not be the law or regulations, but the programs or creations made by anonymous individuals (jurists and programmers), who would be the "new legislators", legitimated not by the citizens' choice, but by the knowledge contained on an optical disk.

With regard to routine, this is not possible when the users are jurists. The work of a jurist is not routine. In contrast, the work of those who serve jurists (clerks of the Administration of Justice, for example) is routine. On the contrary, SIREDOJ increases the originality and complexity of the activities of jurists. We must consider that this program should be in the hands of all jurists, and not just of those with considerable resources, or of the Administration. This means that these systems would distribute knowledge and considerably increase the complexity and consistency of decisions, thereby increasing the rigour of the arguments which would be used in a dispute.

With regard to security, this innovation can bring the danger of violations of juridical security by the generation of possible legal provisions by people not entitled to do so, and which might not fit into real situations. This criticism is not consistent: if this were the case, a manual or book on "Responsibility in building construction" would attack the principle of security in the same way. The SIREDOJ program is no more than a good book, which can be brought up to date more easily than a paper-based book. With the existence of programs such as SIREDOJ, the DERINFO methodology is a computational technique to satisfy the values of the law for juridical offices, and not to adapt juridical activities to the requirements of a computer system.

SIREDOJ and DERINFO increase security and permit social consensus, by providing new arguments, which are present in the law, which are thus made explicit for all jurists. These applications increase the alternatives or ways of viewing social problems which were not apparent before, thereby bringing new peaceful solutions to disputes. Recall that all the decisions are made by the user.

These applications, on the other hand, enhance the exercise of freedom. As stated above, SIREDOJ cannot solve complex problems -it needs options to be defined by the user, and helps to clarify the problem if it is not sufficiently clear for the jurist. Therefore, the final reference point for the jurist user is still the individual conscience, considerably enhanced in this case.

Furthermore, while democratic principles are in force, these programs and methodology do not pose difficulties, but rather increase the clarity of terms, the generality, the use of empirical information, and the expansion of standard solutions to disputes. In other words, they increase justice. If trials are required by law to be by public hearing, in the form of a dialogue, implementing the principle of contradiction, the limit of these applications will always be in the publicity and in the nature of human dialogue, which they can never replace [13]. Things would be different if trials were initiated automatically by the Administration, without the knowledge of the parties to the dispute. Likewise, programs involving automation of numerical data, such as personal files or medical data, are a different situation entirely.

5   Conclusion

As the possibilities of technology advance, with the birth of new computer applications to assist intellectual activities, there is an increasing need to evaluate their consequences and to see if they fit in with the current situation and the accepted rules governing citizens' behaviour. In this sense, the methodology presented here, and proven in different governmental and juridical applications, guarantees that the programs created with its help will form part of the institution or function for which they are created, while not requiring the political and technical nature of the activities they serve to be adapted to the requirements of the computer system. This article has shown how the DERINFO methodology gives suitable guidelines for defining applications, for the concepts used in the programs and the techniques used to implement them, developed with the help of object-oriented programming and artificial intelligence. These guidelines consist essentially of developing the applications with the help of experts in the field, specifically of jurists with sufficient professional knowledge of the field in which the application is to be implemented.

REFERENCES

[1]   B. A. ACKERMAN, *Del realismo al constructivismo jurídico*, Barcelona, 1988, pp. 145-150

[2]   R.ALEXY, "Rechtssystem und praktische Vernunft", in *Rechtstheorie.*, 1987, pp. 407-417

[3]   R.DWORKIN, *Law's Empire*, Cambridge, 1986, p. 410

[4]   F.GALINDO, "PIDCA, a methodological prototype to build legal software", in *III International Conference on Logica, Informatica, Diritto*, vol. II, Florence,1989, pp. 419-438

[5]   F.GALINDO, "Jueces y Democracia. Criterios para una actividad judicial democrática", in *Anuario de Filosofía del Derecho*, VII, 1990, pp. 147-167

[6]   K.GÜNTHER, "Ein normativer Begriff der Kohärenz für einer Theorie der juristischen Argumentation", in *Rechtstheorie*, 20, 1989, p. 189

[7]   J.HABERMAS, *Nachmetaphysisches Denken*, Frankfurt, 1988, pp. 179-186

[8]   D.KENNEDY, "The Structure of Blackstone's Commentaries", in *Buffalo Law Review*, 28, 1979, pp. 211-213

[9]   L.LOMBARDI VALLAURI, "Informatics and 'political' or 'value' criteria of the legal decision", in *Artificial Intelligence and Legal Information Systems*, I, Amsterdam, 1982, pp. 61-72

[10]   L.LOMBARDI VALLAURI, "Jurisprudence", in *Archives de Philosophie du Droit*, 35, 1990, pp. 191-209

[11]   R.NOZICK, *Anarquía, Estado y Utopía*, México, 1988, p. 154ss

[12]   F.OST, M. van de KERCHOVE, *Entre la lettre et l'esprit*, Bruxelles, 1989, pp. 3-13

[13]   C.PERELMAN, *Ethique et droit*, Bruxelles, 1990, pp. 675-680

[14]   M.J.PERRY, *Morality Politics & Law*, Oxford, 1988, pp. 180-184

[15]   J.RAWLS, *Justicia como equidad. Materiales para una teoría de la justicia*, Madrid, 1986, p. 189

[16] T.SCHLAPP, *Theorienstrukturen und Rechtsdogmatik. Ansätze zu einer strukturistischen Theorienbildung*, Berlín, 1989, p. 215

[17] G.TEUBNER, *Recht als autopoietisches System*, Frankfurt, pp. 149s

A FORMAL MODEL FOR THE SUPPORT OF ANALOGICAL REASONING IN LEGAL EXPERT SYSTEMS

Matthias Baaz

Institut für Algebra
und Diskrete Mathematik
Technische Universität Wien
Wiedner Hauptstr. 8-10
A-1040 Wien
(Austria) 222/58801-5451

Gerald Quirchmayr

Forschungsinstitut für anwendungsorientierte
Wissensverarbeitung (FAW)
Johannes Kepler Universität
Altenbergstr. 69
A-4040 Linz
(Austria) 732-2468-882

ABSTRACT Formal models of decision making, and especially of legal reasoning, have with very few exceptions, so far largely ignored the importance of analogical reasoning. The goal of this paper is to describe how a model of analogical reasoning as it is used in legal decision making can be built around Gentzen's LK-calculus.

1. INTRODUCTION: EXPERT SYSTEMS AND ANALOGICAL REASONING

For the task of building expert systems in law, an analysis of the structure and the meaning of the concept of analogy is indispensible. The typical questions which have to be answered are such as "What is analogy?", "Which forms of analogy do exist?". Especially in the domain of law it is necessary to decide whether the formal model should only cover the similarity of facts or whether analogy should be dealt with at a higher level (cf. [6]). The approach described in this paper focusses on the analogy of decisions. The basic assumption is that decisions (mostly) have to be made from incomplete information. Therefore a decision is inferred from available knowledge and additionally made assumptions. If a decision is successful, it can be used as proof of the plausibility of the weakest assumptions that make the proof possible.

2. ABSTRACT FORMS OF DECISIONS

We base our formalization on a quantifier-free variant LK^* of LK, the famous calculus of Gentzen (cf. [5],[12]), that includes an extended form of resolution.

DEFINITION 1. The formal language of LK^* is constructed from the usual terms and predicate symbols together with the logical connectives $\neg, \wedge, \vee, \rightarrow$. Sequents $\Pi \Rightarrow \Gamma$ consist of (possibly empty) sequences of formulas Π, Γ. (The intended meaning is $\bigwedge_{A \in \Pi} A \rightarrow \bigvee_{A \in \Gamma} A$. Sequents consisting of predicates only correspond to clauses by

$$\Pi \Rightarrow \Gamma \simeq \bigvee_{A \in \Pi} \neg A \vee \bigvee_{A \in \Gamma} A.)$$

Logical axioms: $A \Rightarrow A$

Inference rules:

Logical rules:

L1 ($\neg$-left): $\dfrac{\Gamma \Rightarrow \Delta, D}{\neg D, \Gamma \Rightarrow \Delta}$;

($\neg$-right): $\dfrac{D, \Gamma \Rightarrow \Delta}{\Gamma \Rightarrow \Delta, \neg D}$;

L2 ($\wedge$-left): $\dfrac{C, D, \Gamma \Rightarrow \Delta}{C \wedge D, \Gamma \Rightarrow \Delta}$;

($\wedge$-right): $\dfrac{\Gamma \Rightarrow \Delta, C \quad \Gamma \Rightarrow \Delta, D}{\Gamma \Rightarrow \Delta, C \wedge D}$;

L3 ($\vee$-left): $\dfrac{C, \Gamma \Rightarrow \Delta \quad D, \Gamma \Rightarrow \Delta}{C \vee D, \Gamma \Rightarrow \Delta}$;

($\vee$-right): $\dfrac{\Gamma \Rightarrow \Delta, C, D}{\Gamma \Rightarrow \Delta, C \vee D}$;

L4 ($\rightarrow$-left): $\dfrac{\Gamma \Rightarrow \Delta, C \quad D, \Gamma \Rightarrow \Delta}{C \rightarrow D, \Gamma \Rightarrow \Delta}$;

($\rightarrow$-right): $\dfrac{C, \Gamma \Rightarrow \Delta, D}{\Gamma \Rightarrow \Delta, C \rightarrow D}$.

Structural rules:

S1 weakening

(w-left): $\dfrac{\Gamma \Rightarrow \Delta}{A, \Gamma \Rightarrow \Delta}$; (w-right): $\dfrac{\Gamma \Rightarrow \Delta}{\Gamma \Rightarrow \Delta, A}$;

S2 exchange

(exchange): $\dfrac{\Gamma \Rightarrow \Delta}{\Gamma' \Rightarrow \Delta'}$;

Γ' is rearrangement of Γ,
Δ' is rearrangement of Δ;

S3 factorization

(f-left): $\dfrac{A, A', \Gamma \Rightarrow \Delta}{A\sigma, \Gamma\sigma \Rightarrow \Delta\sigma}$;

(f-right): $\dfrac{\Gamma \Rightarrow \Delta, A, A'}{\Gamma\sigma \Rightarrow \Delta\sigma, A\sigma}$;

σ is most general unifier of A and A';

S4 resolution

(res): $\dfrac{\Gamma \Rightarrow \Delta, A \quad A', \Pi \Rightarrow \Lambda}{(\Gamma, \Pi)\sigma \Rightarrow (\Delta, \Lambda)\sigma}$;

σ is most general unifier of A and A'
(the numbers (i,j) of the formulas in Γ and Δ
are called the *index* of the inference).

DEFINITION 2. An LK*-*deduction* of H out of $H_1, \ldots, H_n$ is a tree of sequents such that

    a) the top nodes are axioms or variants of $H_1, \ldots, H_n$ by variable renaming;

    b) each other node is the direct consequence of its ancestor nodes;

    c) the bottom node is a sequent H' such that $H = H'\sigma$ for some σ.

Let $\sigma_1, \ldots, \sigma_n$ be all substitutions subsequently generated by the rule applications. The *total substitution* of the derivation is $\sigma\sigma_n \ldots \sigma_1$.

$H_1, \ldots, H_n \vdash H$ iff there is any derivation of H out of $H_1, \ldots, H_n$.

DEFINITION 3. Let $T(\Pi \to \Gamma) = \bigwedge_{A \in \Pi} A \to \bigvee_{A \in \Gamma} A$, $\bigwedge_{A \in \Pi} A$ is true for Π empty, $\bigvee_{A \in \Gamma} A$ is false for Γ empty. $T(\mathcal{K}) = \{T(H) \mid H \in \mathcal{K}\}$. $\mathcal{K}$ is a *valid consequence* of $\mathcal{L}$ ($\mathcal{L} \Vdash \mathcal{K}$) iff the universal closures of formulas in $T(\mathcal{L})$ imply all universal closures of formulas in $T(\mathcal{K})$.

THEOREM 1. $S_1, \ldots, S_n \vdash S \Leftrightarrow S_1, \ldots, S_n \Vdash S$.

Proof. Calculate the total substitution of the derivation and use the usual completeness theorem (cf. [12], Theorem 8.2) in connection with lifting lemma (cf. [2], Lemma 5.1) extended to LK*. □

DEFINITION 4. The *skeleton* of a deduction is

    a) a number (= an initial skeleton);

    b) of the form $\langle S, D \rangle$ where S is a skeleton and $D \in \{(\neg\text{-left}), (\neg\text{-right}), (\wedge\text{-left}), (\vee\text{-right}), (\to\text{-right}), (\text{w-left}), (\text{w-right}), (\text{f-left}), (\text{f-right})\}$;

    c) of the form $\langle S_1, S_2, D \rangle$ where S_1, S_2 are skeletons and $D = \{(\wedge\text{-right}), (\vee\text{-left}), (\to\text{-left})\}$;

    d) of the form $\langle S_1, S_2, (\text{res}), (i,j) \rangle$;

    e) of the form $\langle S, (\text{exchange}), i_1, \ldots, i_r, j_1, \ldots, j_s \rangle$, where $\{i_1, \ldots, i_r\} = \{1, \ldots, r\}$, $\{j_1, \ldots, j_s\} = \{1, \ldots, s\}$.

All initial skeletons within a given skeleton have to be different.

EXPLANATION. The skeleton of a deduction is an abstract description of the deduction without specifying assumptions and goal. For the general notion of skeleton cf. [11].

DEFINITION 5. A *decision path* is a quadruple $\langle A, B, C, D \rangle$ such that

    a) A is a skeleton of a deduction;

    b) B is a finite sequence of assignments $i : H_i$ of sequents to initial skeletons in A;

    c) C is a sequence of assignments $j : \Gamma_j$ of finite sets of constants Γ_j to initial skeletons which occur in A but not in B.

    d) D is a variable free non empty sequent.

We use the convention for b) and c) that in presence of several decision paths containing the initial skeleton k either always the same sequent H_k is assigned to k or always the same set of constants Γ_k is assigned to k.

EXPLANATION. The skeleton (A) represents the structure of a deduction together with the indices of the rule applications, but gives no information on initial and final clauses. The sequence of assignments (B) fixes some of the initial clauses of the skeleton. In interesting cases some of them remain unknown. (C) represents objects from which the "unknown" hypotheses are assumed to be independent. The final sequent (D) is fixed. Decision paths are formal objects and can therefore be treated in a formal manner.

The information given by facts and statements and the additional information given by the decision itself are used to derive the weakest preconditions of the decision. These weakest preconditions have to be accepted, because otherwise the decision itself would have to be rejected as false.

The initial sequents of the decision are usually at least known to be independent from certain elements, such as time, location, person, and other elements not occurring in the general form of the statements in the decision (in the decision path these elements are represented by C). Therefore the weakest preconditions are also considered as independent

3. WEAKEST PRECONDITIONS

For modelling analogy sets of decision paths and their interpretations have to be considered. Sets have to be used rather than isolated decisions, because the different decisions might influence each other.

DEFINITION 6. An *interpretation* $I(\mathscr{E})$ of a set of decision paths $\mathscr{E} = \{\ldots, \langle A_i, B_i, C_i, D_i \rangle, \ldots\}$ is a set of deductions in accordance with A_i and B_i with final sequents D_i. (Initial skeletons have to be realized by the same formulas throughout $I(\mathscr{E})$.) An *interpretation* of a decision path E is defined by $I(\{E\})$. (We write $I(E)$ instead of $I(\{E\})$.)

DEFINITION 7. The *propositional* (k, l)-*realization* of a skeleton S is constructed as follows (reducing S from outside to inside):

    1) Write $X_1, \ldots, X_k \Rightarrow Y_1, \ldots, Y_l$ as bottom node.

    2) Assume $U_1, \ldots, U_r \Rightarrow V_1, \ldots, V_s$ is constructed and that the subskeleton S' has to be reduced.

    a) S' is initial skeleton k:
$$U_1, \ldots, U_r \overset{k}{\Rightarrow} V_1, \ldots, V_s$$
is top node.

    b) $S' = \langle S'', D \rangle$, $D = (\neg\text{-left})$ (resp. $(\neg\text{-right})$, $(\wedge\text{-left})$, $(\vee\text{-right})$, $(\to\text{-right})$, (w-left), (w-right), (f-left), (f-right)): for the logical rules anywhere apply the following corresponding substitutions: $\{\neg U / U_1\}$ (resp. $\{\neg U / V_s\}$, $\{U \wedge V / U_1\}$, $\{U \vee V / V_s\}$, $\{U \to V / V_s\}$). Write

$$U_2, \ldots, U_r \Rightarrow V_1, \ldots, V_s, U$$
$$(\text{resp. } U, U_1, \ldots, U_r \Rightarrow V_1, \ldots, V_{s-1},$$
$$U, V, U_2, \ldots, U_r \Rightarrow V_1, \ldots, V_s,$$
$$U_1, \ldots, U_r \Rightarrow V_1, \ldots, V_{s-1}, U, V,$$
$$U, U_1, \ldots, U_r \Rightarrow V_1, \ldots, V_{s-1}, V,$$
$$U_2, \ldots, U_r \Rightarrow V_1, \ldots, V_s,$$
$$U_1, \ldots, U_r \Rightarrow V_1, \ldots, V_{s-1},$$
$$U, U_1, \ldots, U_r \Rightarrow V_1, \ldots, V_s,$$
$$U_1, \ldots, U_r \Rightarrow V_1, \ldots, V_s, V_s)$$

above the transformation of $U_1, \ldots, U_r \Rightarrow V_1, \ldots, V_s$, reduce the skeleton S' to S''.

c) $S' = \langle S'', S''', D \rangle$, $D = (\wedge\text{-right})$ (resp. $(\vee\text{-left})$, $(\rightarrow\text{-left})$): for the logical rules anywhere apply the following corresponding substitutions: $\{U \wedge V / V_s\}$ (resp. $\{U \vee V / U_1\}$, $\{U \rightarrow V / U_1\}$). Write
$$U_1, \ldots, U_r \Rightarrow V_1, \ldots, V_{s-1}, U \text{ and}$$
$$U_1, \ldots, U_r \Rightarrow V_1, \ldots, V_{s-1}, V$$
$$(\text{resp. } U, U_2, \ldots, U_r \Rightarrow V_1, \ldots, V_s \text{ and}$$
$$V, U_2, \ldots, U_r \Rightarrow V_1, \ldots, V_s,$$
$$U_2, \ldots, U_r \Rightarrow V_1, \ldots, V_s, U \text{ and}$$
$$V, U_2, \ldots, U_r \Rightarrow V_1, \ldots, V_s,$$

above the transformation of $U_1, \ldots, U_r \Rightarrow V_1, \ldots, V_s$, reduce the skeleton S' to S'' and S'''.

d) $S' = \langle S'', S''', (\text{res}), (i,j) \rangle$: write
$$U_1, \ldots, U_i \Rightarrow V_1, \ldots, V_j, U \text{ and}$$
$$U, U_{i+1}, \ldots, U_r \Rightarrow V_{j+1}, \ldots, V_s$$

above $U_1, \ldots, U_r \Rightarrow V_1, \ldots, V_s$.

e) $S' = \langle S'', (\text{exchange}), i_1, \ldots, i_r, j_1, \ldots, j_s \rangle$: write
$$U_{i_1}, \ldots, U_{i_r} \Rightarrow V_{j_1}, \ldots, V_{j_s}$$

above $U_1, \ldots, U_r \Rightarrow V_1, \ldots, V_s$ and reduce the skeleton S' to S''.

EXPLANATION. The propositional (k,l)-realization of a skeleton represents the propositional structure of any adequate derivation with this skeleton.

PROPOSITION 1: *If the construction of Definition 7 is impossible for some skeleton S and some (k,l), no set of decision paths containing $E = \langle S,B,C,D \rangle$ with $D = A_1, \ldots, A_k \Rightarrow B_1, \ldots, B_l$ has an interpretation.* □

Let any deduction that is an interpretation of the decision path $E = \langle S,B,C,D \rangle$ be given. The deduction is transformed into a propositional realization in a unique way if the total substitution (cf. Definition 2) is applied and atomic formulas are 1-1 replaced by propositional variables. This motivates the following definition.

DEFINITION 8. Let $E = \langle A,B,C,D \rangle$, $D = A_1, \ldots, A_k \Rightarrow B_1, \ldots, B_l$, be a decision path. E *determines* a propositional variable X in the (k,l)-realization of A iff X occurs in the top nodes fixed by B or in the bottom node.

DEFINITION 9. Let a set of decision paths
$$\mathscr{E} = \{\ldots, \langle A_i, B_i, C_i, D_i \rangle, \ldots\}$$
be given and let $i_1, \ldots, i_n$ be the sequence of numbers representing those sequents in $\mathscr{E}$ to which no sequents of B_i are assigned.

Variable-free sequents $H_{i_1}, \ldots, H_{i_n}$ are called *preconditions* of $\mathscr{E}$ iff

a) there exists an interpretation $I(\mathscr{E}')$ of
$$\mathscr{E}' = \{\ldots, \langle A_i, B_i', C_i, D_i \rangle, \ldots\}$$
where B_i' is the extension of B_i by $i_k : H_{i_k}$ for i_k occurring as initial skeleton in A_i and C_i is correspondingly restricted.

b) for each E in $\mathscr{E}$ the groups of propositional variables not determined by E are realized by a previously fixed list of zero-placed predicates.

EXPLANATION. The preconditions complete the incomplete information of $\mathscr{E}$. In case of not determined variables no information is given. So it is useful (cf. condition b)) to replace them by previously fixed zero-placed predicates.

DEFINITION 10. Let $\mathscr{L}^*$ be the extension of $\mathscr{L}$ by the set of new constants $\{c_i\}$ and let $\mathscr{E}$ be a set of decision paths. $W_1, \ldots, W_n$ are *weakest preconditions* for $\mathscr{E}$ and $\mathscr{L}$ iff

a) $W_1, \ldots, W_n$ are preconditions for E in the language $\mathscr{L}^*$;

b) For any sequence $H_1, \ldots, H_n$ of preconditions for $\mathscr{E}$, any H and any Γ in $\mathscr{L}$, the following holds:
$$W_1, \ldots, W_n, \Gamma \vdash H \Rightarrow H_1, \ldots, H_n, \Gamma \vdash H$$
using the same derivation with the exception that W_i is replaced by H_i.

EXPLANATION. If a decision path E is to be completed to a proof, the assumptions have to be made at least as strong as the weakest preconditions. The consequence is: if a decision path E is accepted as corresponding to a real conclusion, the weakest preconditions have to be accepted as true statements. (The definition of the weakest preconditions corresponds to the interrelation $\{(\exists x)A(x)\} \cup \Gamma \vdash B \Rightarrow \{A(t)\} \cup \Gamma \vdash B$ for any term t in usual first order predicate logic. If existential quantifiers have to be avoided (like in LK*), new constants have to be introduced.

THEOREM 2.

1. *It is decidable whether any interpretation for a set of decision paths $\mathscr{E}$ exists.*

2. *If an interpretation exists, the weakest preconditions in the extension $\mathscr{L}^*$ of $\mathscr{L}$ by $\{c_i\}$ can be constructed.*

Proof. Let $\mathscr{E} = \{\ldots, \langle A_i, B_i, C_i, D_i \rangle, \ldots\}$, let $i_1, \ldots, i_n$ be the sequence of numbers representing those initial sequents in A to which no sequents of B are assigned. Weakest preconditions are constructed as follows:

1) Construct the propositional realizations of A_i relative to D_i.

2) Identify the final sequents of the propositional realizations with D_i and identify the corresponding initial sequents with the sequents fixed by B_i using unification.

3) Replace remaining propositional variables by the previously fixed sequence of zero-placed predicates (these are the variables not determined by the skeleton, cf. Definition 8).

4) Let $W_{i_1}^*(\bar{x}), \ldots, W_{i_n}^*(\bar{x})$ be the resulting initial clauses not determined by B_i. Replace $\bar{x}$ by new constants $\bar{c}$.

The result is a sequence of weakest preconditions $W_{i_1}, \ldots, W_{i_n}$.

To prove 1 simply note that no interpretation is possible if this construction is not successful. Apply the usual lifting lemma to go back to the clauses fixed by B_i.

To prove 2 note that any sequence of preconditions $H_{i_1}, \ldots, H_{i_n}$ has the property

$$W_{i_1}^*(\bar{x})\sigma = H_{i_1}, \ldots, W_{i_n}^*(\bar{x})\sigma = H_{i_n}.$$

Assume $W_{i_1}, \ldots, W_{i_n}, \Gamma \vdash H$, where Γ and H do not contain the new constants. Assume that the new constants $\bar{c}$ have replaced $\bar{x}$ in the construction of weakest preconditions. Now replace $\bar{c}$ anywhere in the derivation by $\bar{x}\sigma$. Thus $H_{i_1}, \ldots, H_{i_n}, \Gamma \vdash H$ using the same derivation with the exception that W_i is replaced by H_i. □

COROLLARY. *The number of new constants needed to construct the weakest preconditions for the decision path E is bounded by the structure of E.*

4. ANALOGICAL REASONING

Using the notion of weakest precondition it is possible to reconstruct the "minimal" assumptions from a decision.

DEFINITION 11. *Simultaneous inversion of a set of conclusions:*
Let $\mathcal{E} = \{\ldots, \langle A_i, B_i, C_i, D_i \rangle, \ldots\}$ be a set of decision paths, let $W_1, \ldots, W_n$ be the weakest preconditions corresponding to initial skeletons $i_1, \ldots, i_n$ with assigned sets of constants $\Gamma_1, \ldots, \Gamma_n$ in $\ldots D_i \ldots$.
$\text{INV}(\mathcal{E}) = \{W_1', \ldots, W_n'\}$, where $W_1', \ldots, W_n'$ result from $W_1, \ldots, W_n$ by replacing all constants in $\Gamma_1, \ldots, \Gamma_n$ by new variables. (Note that $\text{INV}(\mathcal{E})$ may extend the formal language by new constants.)

We use the notion of inversion of sets of conclusions given by decision paths to define analogical reasoning.

DEFINITION 12. Let Γ be a set of accepted sequents; let $\mathcal{E}$ be a set of decision paths in $\mathcal{L}$ of accepted decisions.

A is derived from Γ and $\mathcal{E}$ by *analogical reasoning* iff
$$\Gamma \cup \text{INV}(\mathcal{E}) \vdash A$$
in the language extended by the adequate constants.

This concept of analogical reasoning depends on the following principle: *A successful conclusion based on non justified assumptions gives some kind of justification to these assumptions.*

5. ANALOGICAL REASONING IN LAW: RIGHTS OF FINDERS

A domain where analogies do even build the basis for any form of decision making is law. The common law system for example is based on the axiom that legal decisions can create new law. Therefore the weakest preconditions of a legal decision can also be given as specific weight which is unknown in other domains (cf. [3], [7]). This can easily be shown by a famous decision of Sir John Donaldson MR (cf. [10, p. 145], [4, p. 178]): The finder of a lost article does not commit a tort by taking it into his possession if he acts reasonable in an endeavour to find the true owner and does not intend to misappropriate it. If the article is found on the surface of the land, by a visitor entitled to be there, the finder usually has a better title in a public place, and the occupier a better title in a private place.

In Bridges v. Hawksworth (1851), the finder of a bundle of bank notes in a shop was held entitled as against the shopkeeper on the grounds that they were found in the *public* part of the shop.

We use the following constants and relations to formalize the decision:

F	...	finder
B	...	bundle of bank notes
PS	...	part of the shop
SK	...	shopkeeper
FOUND(x,y,u,v)	...	x was found by y in u belonging to v
PUBLIC(x)	...	x is a public place
ASSIGN(x,y)	...	the object x is assigned to the possession of y

The decision takes the form

$$\dfrac{\quad \dfrac{\overset{1}{\Rightarrow \textbf{FOUND(B,F,PS,SK)}} \quad \overset{2}{\text{assumption}}}{\textbf{PUBLIC(PS)} \Rightarrow \textbf{ASSIGN(B,F)}} \quad \overset{3}{\Rightarrow \textbf{PUBLIC(PS)}}}{\Rightarrow \textbf{ASSIGN(B,F)}}$$

2 is the assumption of the court, 1 and 3 are facts ("The bundle of bank notes was found in a part of the shop."; "This part of the shop was public."). The assumption is considered to be independent from the concrete parties and objects (B,F,PS,SK).

The decision path takes the form:

$$E = \langle \langle 3, \langle 1, 2, (\text{res}), (0,0)\rangle, (\text{res}), (0,0)\rangle,$$
$$1: \Rightarrow \textbf{FOUND(B,F,PS,SK)},$$
$$3: \Rightarrow \textbf{PUBLIC(PS)},$$
$$2: \{\textbf{B,F,PS,SK}\},$$
$$\Rightarrow \textbf{ASSIGN(B,F)}\rangle.$$

The propositional $(0,1)$-realization of the skeleton is

$$\dfrac{\quad \dfrac{\overset{1}{\Rightarrow X_1} \quad \overset{2}{X_1, X_2 \Rightarrow X_3}}{X_2 \Rightarrow X_3} \quad \overset{3}{\Rightarrow X_2}}{\Rightarrow X_3}$$

Unify 1 with $\Rightarrow \textbf{FOUND(B,F,PS,SK)}$, 3 with $\Rightarrow \textbf{PUBLIC(PS)}$.
$\text{INV}(E) = \{\textbf{FOUND}(x,y,u,v), \textbf{PUBLIC}(u) \Rightarrow \textbf{ASSIGN}(x,y)\}$
reconstructs the assumption of the court.

We use analogical reasoning to reconstruct the decision of Sir John Donaldson MR in Parker (**P**) v. British Airways Board (**BA**) (1982): A passenger in an executive lounge (**EL**) at Heathrow Airport found a gold bracelet (**BR**) on the floor. He was held to have a better title than the occupiers.

This decision can be formally represented as

$$
\cfrac{
\cfrac{\Rightarrow \text{FOUND}(\text{BR},\text{P},\text{EL},\text{BA}) \qquad \cfrac{\text{FOUND}(x,y,u,v),\ \text{PUBLIC}(u)}{\Rightarrow \text{ASSIGN}(x,y)}}{\Rightarrow \text{PUBLIC}(\text{EL}) \qquad \text{PUBLIC}(\text{EL}) \Rightarrow \text{ASSIGN}(\text{BR},\text{P})}
}{
\Rightarrow \text{ASSIGN}(\text{BR},\text{P})
}
$$

($\Rightarrow$ FOUND(BR,P,EL,BA) and $\Rightarrow$ PUBLIC(EL) are the facts of this case.)

(For an example of analogical reasoning modelling a construction of MARPOL international treaty on maritime pollution regulation concerning the dumping of waste from oil tankers in a logic programming framework cf. [1].)

6. IMPLEMENTATION

As the approach is based on sequents related to clauses, PROLOG can be recommended as a basis for implementation (cf. [9]). Analogical reasoning is most efficient when applied in an interactive system. That is why new forms of user interface design should be considered. In legal environments hypertext and hypermedia systems obviously are the future. Therefore a PROLOG version should be chosen which gives access to either GUIDE, MICROSOFT TOOLBOOK or Apple's HYPERCARD (cf. [8]).

7. CONCLUSION

In some fields of expert system design analogical reasoning has become a key aspect, because many decision makers, especially lawyers and business decision makers, do heavily rely on this concept. Therefore expert systems, which do include utilities for analogical reasoning, will certainly help to increase user acceptance.

Another aspect of analogical reasoning is the great flexibility, which can be added to traditional rule-based design. In the long run this concept will also be added to database systems, like rule-based design and object oriented design during the last years.

REFERENCES

[1] Baaz, M., Quirchmayr, G.: *A logic based model of legal decision making.* Proc. of the 10th Int. Workshop on Expert Systems and their Applications, Avignon, 1990.

[2] Chang, C.-L., Lee, R.C.-T.: *Symbolic Logic and Mechanical Theorem Proving.* Academic Press, New York and London, 1973.

[3] Cross, R.: *Precedent in English Law.* Clarendon Press, Oxford 1979.

[4] Dugdale, T., Furmston, M., Jones, F., Sherrin, C., Stanton, K.: *'A' level law.* London, Edinburgh, 1988.

[5] Gentzen, G.: *Untersuchungen über das logische Schließen.* Mathematische Zeitschrift, Vol. 39 (1934) 176-210 and 405-431.

[6] Hall, R.P.: *Computational approaches to analogical reasoning: a comparative analysis.* Artificial Intelligence 39 (1989) 39-120.

[7] Hart, H.L.: *The Concept of Law.* Oxford University Press, 1981.

[8] Kappes, C.A. and Quirchmayr. G.: *Artificial intelligence application in law and hypermedia.* In: Artificial Intelligence, Application and Neural Network, Zürich 1930, p. 231 ff.

[9] Kowalski, R.A.: *Directions for Logic Programming.* In: Brauer/Wahlster: *Wissensbasierte Systeme.* Springer IFB 155, München, 1987.

[10] Marsh, S.B. and Soulby, J.: *Outlines of English Law.* 4th edition, McGraw-Hill, London, 1987.

[11] Parikh, R.: *Some results on the length of proofs.* TAMS 177 (1973) 29-36.

[12] Takeuti, G.: *Proof Theory.* North-Holland, Amsterdam, 1975.

The effect of change on legal applications

Paul Bratley[1]   Daniel Poulin[2]   Jacques Savoy[1]

[1] Département d'informatique
[2] Centre de recherche en droit public
Université de Montréal, C.P. 6128, Succursale A
Montréal (Québec), Canada H3C 3J7

ABSTRACT

Change is a fact of life, in law as elsewhere. The law must be stable if it is to regulate effectively the affairs of those subject to it, yet it must be open to correction when its rules need revising. For designers of legal expert systems and legal hypertext systems, coping with change is a constant challenge.

A review of the recent literature suggests that this problem is just beginning to be taken seriously. We describe some of the difficulties which must be overcome, and review some suggested solutions. Our conclusion is that most of these provide little practical help, and that the problem is still entirely open.

1 Introduction

Change is a fact of life, in law as in any other field. The law must be stable if it is to regulate effectively the affairs of those subject to it, yet it must be open to correction when its rules need revising on account of errors, changing social reality or change of policies. In the rapidly-evolving modern world, such corrections are increasingly frequent, and a major item of social legislation may be amended several times a year, or even several times a month.

For designers of systems intended to give legal advice, or to help lawyers prepare cases and opinions, coping with change is a constant challenge. In a legal expert system, every change in the law can have repercussions on the knowledge base. In the worst case, it might require the entire knowledge base to be rebuilt. In a legal hypertext system changes in the law cause links to be deleted, added and changed. In both applications it must be possible to reconstruct the state of the system as it was at any previous time. The challenge is to make the necessary alterations at a minimum cost in effort, errors and inconvenience.

The long-term aim of our group in Montreal is to produce a system for lawyers which will integrate a legal expert system with a corresponding hypertext. For example, modules of the expert system may help in navigating through the hypertext and answer questions about the legal concepts involved; links in the hypertext will provide a way for the expert system to produce explanations of its conclusions and may help when the system has to be updated. Although we are still far from this goal, pilot projects are under way in the area of unemployment insurance. The need for a detailed study of the problems created by changes in the law was brought home to us last year, when the Canadian *Unemployment Insurance Act* was substantially amended. Overnight, many of the rules in our expert system needed revising, and a sizeable collection of cases which we had analysed in view of experiments in case-based reasoning became largely irrelevant.

Although most published work on legal expert systems pays lip service to the idea that they must be designed to cope with change, a review of the literature provided little practical guidance. The present paper is therefore an attempt to pose the problem more concretely. We first outline rapidly the kind of changes in the law that may be encountered, and indicate their effects on both the expert system and the hypertext components. Next we summarize the attitudes to change which we found in the literature. Finally, although we have no magic solutions to suggest, we indicate where future work should concentrate.

2 Legal change

The law is created and evolves through statutory changes, through bilateral or multilateral instruments, through the application of customs, and through precedents. For the purposes of this paper, we restrict ourselves mainly to the first form of creation of the law. The changes we encountered when the Unemployment Act was amended seem to fall into four rough categories.

Insignificant or minor changes

In one section of the Act, the order of the paragraphs has been inverted between the old and the new provisions. What is considered the main rule now precedes the exception. The terminology has been made "gender-neutral". In another, the words "who qualifies to receive benefit" have been added in a context where they were already implicit. In a third, the requirement that an applicant have twenty weeks of insurable employment before qualifying for a certain category of benefits is replaced by a table.

Reuse of existing concepts

In some cases tests or provisions already present in the Act are reused in a different context. For example, section 10(4) has been modified to include a provision already found elsewhere dealing with interruption of earnings.

Apparently innocuous changes with wider repercussions

The old Act provided that where the applicant refused work without good cause, lost his employment as a result of misconduct or left voluntarily, benefits would not be payable for a "penalty period [...] not exceeding six weeks." This provision now reads that the number of weeks of disqualification "shall be not less than seven and not more than twelve." On the surface, this looks like a minor change. For the expert, this is not the entire answer. Since the disqualification now lasts at least seven weeks, the expert expects that authorities deciding whether work was refused without good cause, whether the applicant misbehaved or whether he left voluntarily will interpret these clauses more restrictively to avoid imposing an unduly harsh penalty. Technical changes aimed at "tightening up" the Act thus lead to conceptual changes.

Modification or addition of concepts

Section 28(1) of the Act reads: "A claimant is disqualified from receiving benefits under this Part ... if he voluntarily left his employment without just cause." The voluntary character and the absence of just cause are concepts that are not directly observable but are left to be specified by decisions rendered in individual cases. They require "tests" in terms of directly observable facts.

Section 28 was further changed by the addition of a new paragraph, which reads:

> "(4) For the purpose of this section "just cause" [...] exists where, having regard to all the circumstances, [...] the claimant had no reasonable alternative to immediately leaving the employment."

This redefinition of the concept of "just cause" contains two new concepts, "no reasonable alternative" and "immediately," which must be included in our system.

Although these isolated examples cannot serve as a base for wide generalization, it does seem clear that the law generally tends to change incrementally, which means, in a majority of cases, without destroying the knowledge base on which it functions. Rather, the law builds on the existing base, accumulating and superposing rule upon rule. Moreover, it appears that statutory changes do not effectively change the law overnight. In many cases, the expert has no clear answer to the legal difficulties raised by a modifying provision. In such cases, he integrates the new rule into his knowledge base, but without necessarily drawing definite conclusions on its real impact, waiting for subsequent judicial or administrative determination.

Besides the numerous changes caused by major amendments to the relevant law, systems for legal applications must also deal with a constant flow of smaller ajustments. Since 1985, for instance, the Canadian Unemployment Act has been amended seven times, including the major overhaul discussed above. The associated Regulations have been changed on 35 occasions, or about once every two months. Evidence that this is not unusual is provided by [Bench-C. 91]. The authors of this paper, concerned with the field of work-related injuries, estimate that they will have to deal with about 20 new Statutory Instruments and 10 technical instructions each year, as well as several dozen relevant judgements, policy changes by the employer, and so on.

3 Effects of these changes

Insignificant changes in the law have –almost by definition– little effect on legal applications. In the expert system, at the most, some explanatory texts may have to be changed. The hypertext must also be brought up to date. Minor changes can be handled easily. As far as the expert system is concerned, they may require the addition of one or two local rules, but the knowledge base does not have to be restructured. Again, the hypertext component must reflect the changes.

Similarly it does not seem difficult to introduce new uses of existing concepts. This may simply require adding a reference to an existing set of rules in the expert system, or adding links to an existing module in the hypertext component. However it will often be necessary to review the existing rules and modules to ensure that they are sufficiently general to function in the new context. In every case re-using an existing concept requires that an expert jurist check to see that two apparently analogous concepts do not conceal an essential legal difference.

Other changes in the law are less easily handled; it is to these problematic instances that we wish to draw attention. Modifications whose effect is apparently minor, but which in fact change the law in unforeseen ways, may be encountered at any moment. Indeed the existence of such phenomena serves as a warning against adopting an unduly descriptive attitude to the law. Furthermore they underline the fact that the law may often be uncertain, and that this uncertainty must be reflected in the computer system.

Finally the introduction of new concepts, or major changes to existing ones, both require considerable effort. If this effort seems inevitable in the former event, since there is no way to avoid giving new rules to the expert system, and adding links to relevant jurisprudence in the hypertext component, in the case of a modification we may hope to do better. If expert lawyers bring their knowledge up to date by building on the base they already possess, it would seem wasteful to rebuild the expert system's knowledge base or the hypertext component's existing links by starting again from scratch. Yet it is not obvious how to do better than this. Even incorporating a restriction on an existing concept, as when "just cause" is defined more narrowly, seems to necessitate a complete restructuring of the rules and the links. To make matters worse, a truly useful legal expert system or legal hypertext system must be able to answer questions not only concerning the current state of the law, but also about the law which applied at some previous date. In any new structure of rules in the knowledge base, or of links in the hypertext component, it must therefore still be possible to reconstruct the previous states.

4 Some proposals for handling change

The design of a computerized system usually requires that the procedures to be computerized be relatively stable; alternatively, if the system lifetime is short, the profit to be realised makes the game worth the candle. Similarly, certain branches of the law, although subject to frequent modification, are nonetheless worth studying by researchers in artificial intelligence. This is particularly the case where the law affects large numbers of people, where the sums of money involved are enormous, and in areas which have resisted attack by more traditional techniques. Tax law and much social legislation are among those heavily used and frequently changed domains.

In such rapidly-evolving systems the methods used in artificial intelligence are often preferable to the procedural techniques of traditional computer programming; they are easier to adapt to less stable problem areas. In particular, artificial intelligence uses an explicit representation of the necessary knowledge, making it relatively easy to determine those areas of the knowledge base which correspond to a particular part of the problem domain. Thus when this domain is modified, it is easier to modify the corresponding structures in the knowledge base.

While it is certainly true that modifying a knowledge base is easier than modifying a program where the rules are represented implicitly, this does not mean that such modification is simple. The following paragraphs survey some proposals which have appeared in the recent literature.

Expert systems

[Smith 87] deals with an area which is particularly stable. The rules used in his "Nervous Shock Advisor" are constructed on the basis of a thorough analysis of all the relevant cases, of which there are only 74 this century. Such a system might almost be designed never to change. Any major modification of the law would require the whole analysis to be reworked.

The area chosen for Schlobohm and Waterman's EPS system [Schlo 87] is the rapidly changing law to do with estate planning. The knowledge is provided by an expert. However as tax law evolves rapidly, this approach led to problems. Schlobohm and McCarty subsequently described them in the following terms:

> [EPS] does not contain any knowledge about how the rules were obtained [...] As a result, human experts would have to modify the heuristic rules whenever the law changes, and the entire system containing the new rules would then have to be debugged. Finally, EPS [...] would be of little use to expert estate planners, since experts only need assistance when the law changes or when dealing with a novel client situation. [Schlo 89, p. 9]

More recently Schlobohm and McCarty proposed a new estate planning system: EPS II. In EPS II, the expert's heuristic knowledge is complemented by an explicit representation of the rules laid down by the *Internal Revenue Code*. Both these kinds of knowledge are expressed in the form of propositions in LLD, the *Language for Legal Discourse* [McCarty 89]. When the system is used, prototype solutions furnished by the human expert can be modified or "deformed" to satisfy the needs of the client and the constraints of the law. The authors show how certain kinds of change to the Code can be handled by EPS II. However not all changes can be taken care of in this way. Any modification of the Code which adds a new concept or radically changes an existing one is beyond the powers of EPS II.

In the area of statute law, one favourable approach to obtain an easily - modifiable system is to use a formalization which makes articles of the statute correspond to rules in the knowledge base. In a legal expert system based on such a formalization, every rule has an explicit link back to some clause of the legislation, of which it is a formal paraphrase. This is the line taken by Kowalski and Sergot and their team at Imperial College.

From the point of view of ease of maintenance, this is ideal. Modification of a paragraph in the text of the law simply implies that a corresponding modification has to be made in the associated rule in the knowledge base. However such a logical formalization cannot serve as the base of an expert system unless one adds a layer of heuristic knowledge, and other general knowledge of the kind used by jurists. Kowalski and Sergot admit that their model represents "a layman's reading of the provisions. This in itself renders our *British Nationality Act* program of limited practical value" [Kowalski 90, p. 207]. Such a program will need the help of a human expert, to correct, modify and augment the formalization; but once the formalization is augmented in this way, modifying the system following a change in the law implies modifying implicit or explicit rules which do not correspond directly to paragraphs in the law.

At the University of Liverpool, Bench-Capon's group also insist that the knowledge representation must be closely aligned to the sources of knowledge. In a recent paper [Bench-C. 91], they explicitly acknowledge the problem of coping with change, stating that "the greatest barrier to the routine use of knowledge based systems techniques for practical legal applications lies [...] in the problems associated with the maintenance of such systems." The group aim to provide tools to handle day-to-day changes due to minor modifications of the legal texts and the application of the law. It is still too early to judge the value of their techniques.

In the legal field, the case-based approach has been explored principally by Rissland's group at the University of Massachusetts. According to [Skalak 89], the weaknesses of legal expert systems that can be alleviated by case-based reasoning include their inertia, that is, the difficulty they have in assimilating new knowledge. The essential idea is that it is easier to add new cases to a collection than it is to add new rules to a rule-base. However, new "dimensions" of a legal concept may make their appearance, making it necessary to re-index all the cases using this new criterion.

Rissland and Skalak have also proposed using such a case-based reasoner with a more traditional rule-based system. In that context, they propose using ID5, a classification algorithm [Utgoff 89], to induce new rules corresponding to the modified case base. They have carried out a number of experiments with this in view [Skalak 90], so far with mixed results. We are forced to conclude with Rissland and Skalak that "there is no quick cure for this fundamental problem."

Hypertext systems

Legal applications offer an attractive field for the use of hypertext techniques. Shneiderman [Shneider 89] formulates the "golden rules of hypertext" for deciding when these techniques are applicable and when they are not. His rules may be summarized as follows: there exists a large body of information organized into numerous fragments; the fragments are related one to another; and the user needs only a small fraction of these fragments at any one time. A moment's thought is enough to show that legal texts satisfy these criteria. Statutes are divided into sections, paragraphs and articles, related to one another, and usually not all applicable at once; and a collection of cases can also be seen as a set of related opinions and commentaries on various aspects of the law.

It is therefore not surprising that the idea of using hypertext in a legal context is not new. [Yoder 89] provides an example in the area of patent law. Wahlgren [Wahl 89] has also studied different ways of decomposing the law to make a hypertext, and proposed a prototype to be combined with an expert system. A panel discussion at Hypertext '89 was devoted to systems combining expert systems with hypertext. However there seems to be little published work on dealing with change, and more particularly on how to take advantage of the complementary strengths of the two paradigms to deal more efficiently with changes in the domain concerned.

Nevertheless some light is thrown on the problem by [Delisle 87], who is concerned with a system for cooperative authoring of technical documentation. The proposed solution extends the notion of link and node by including a version tag for these components. On another level, some authors make a distinction between form and meaning to allow some links to be constructed heuristically. If such heuristic techniques can be implemented, they will help alleviate the problems caused by change. [Fung 90] establishes links between technical descriptions and the concepts involved; [Savoy 91] on the other hand links such descriptions to users' information needs.

Other references

Further references to the problem of dealing with change can be found in [Oskamp 90, Quast 89, Smits 89, Weusten 89] and in our own work [Poulin 88]. Oskamp devotes much of the penultimate chapter of her thesis to the problem of maintenance. Quast and de Wildt have built a rule base to deal with the concept of "commensurate work" in Dutch unemployment insurance law, based on an expert analysis of some 150 cases. They propose a structure which, they believe, will allow the rule base to be updated without a complete reorganization. Smits, Kracht and Weusten characterize the changes which may be necessary in a legal expert system, and propose some elementary measures to facilitate system maintenance.

In a more general context, the problem of change in a formal logical system has been studied by various authors. In classical logic, if new information contradicts previous assertions, then the system collapses completely. The aim of recent work has been to explore how contradictions can be avoided by withdrawing as few conflicting assertions as possible. Katsuno and Mendelzon [Katsuno 89] give an excellent introduction to this area which, while promising, is still far from having significant practical appliations.

5 Conclusion

The problem of adapting any computer system, expert system or hypertext to changes in the law is very real. Although some changes pose few problems, other essential aspects of the law, such as the existence of loosely-defined concepts, involve complex issues. The services of an expert jurist will be required throughout the life of the system, not simply when it is being created. And once the legal issues have been taken care of, many difficult technical problems remain.

For expert systems, structuring the rules of the system to correspond to the structure of legal texts, and taking advantage of the ability of case-based reasoning systems to integrate certain new cases without too much trouble, are approaches which, while useful, are for the moment limited. In the hypertext community, it is accepted that some systems will have to keep many versions of a text and "filter out" links and nodes which are not relevant in a given context. However there is no agreement on how to design the interface to such a multilayered system, nor how to structure it so that changes are easy. Finally, formal approaches to change in logical representations of knowledge also offer hope. However none of these lines of attack has yet proved its worth.

It remains to be seen if the whole is greater than the sum of the parts. Is it indeed true that combining a hypertext with an expert system can contribute to managing some of the links between the rules and the legal text? In the other direction, will the use of systems built round a knowledge base help edit the links in a hypertext following modifications in the law? These are some of the questions we intend –of necessity– to explore in the coming months.

6 Acknowledgements

The work described in this paper is supported by a grant from the Social Sciences and Humanities Research Council of Canada and by the Fonds FCAR of the Québec government under its program of *Actions structurantes*.

7 References

[Bench-C. 91] Bench-Capon, Trevor J.M; Coenen, Frans. Practical Application of KBS to Law: The Crucial Role of Maintenance. *Legal Knowledge Based Systems; Aims for Research and Development*; ed: C. van Noortwijk, A.H.J. Schmidt, R.G.F. Winkels, Lelystad, The Netherlands: Koninklijke Vermande Bv, 1991: 5-17.

[Delisle 87] Delisle, N.; Schwartz, M.; Contexts - A Partitioning Concept for Hypertext. *ACM Transactions on Office Information Systems*, 1987; 5(2): 168-186.

[Fung 90] Fung, R.M.; Crawford S.L.; Appelbaum L.A.; Tong, R.M. An Architecture for Probabilistic Concept-Based Information Retrieval, *Proceedings SIGIR'90*, September 1990, Brussels: 455-467.

[Katsuno 89] Katsuno, Hirofumi; Mendelzon, Alberto O. A Unified View of Propositional Knowledge Base Updates, *Proc. IJCAI 89*: 1413-1419.

[Kowalski 90] Kowalski, Robert; Sergot, Marek. The Use of Logical Models in Legal Problem Solving. *Ratio Juris*; 1990; 3(2): 201-218.

[McCarty 89] McCarty, L. Thorne. A Language for Legal Discourse - I. Basic Features. *Proceedings of the Second International Conference on Artificial Intelligence and Law*; 1989; University of British Columbia, Vancouver, BC: ACM Press: 180-188.

[Oskamp 90] Oskamp, Anja. *Het ontwikkelen van juridische expertsystemen* [Doctoral Thesis]. Deventer, The Netherlands: Kluwer, 1990.

[Poulin 88] Poulin, Daniel. *Étude des particularités du droit du point de vue de la conception d'un système expert et réalisation de Chomexpert* [Masters Thesis]. Montréal: Université de Montréal; May 1988.

441

[Quast 89]   Quast, Jeannette A.; de Wildt, Jaap H. Some Features of a Knowledge-Based System for the Dutch Unemployment Insurance Act. Forthcoming in: *Proceedings of the Third International Conference Logica Informatica Diritto – Expert Systems in Law*; November 1989; Florence, Italy.

[Savoy 91]   Savoy Jacques; Desbois Daniel. Bayesian Inference Networks in Hypertext, *Proceedings RIAO'91*, Barcelona (Spain), April 1991: 662-681.

[Shneider 89] Shneiderman, B.   Reflections on Authoring. Editing and Managing Hypertext; in E. Barrett (ed), *The Society of Text*, MIT Press, Cambridge MA, p. 115-131.

[Schlo 87]   Schlobohm, Dean A.; Waterman, Donald A. Explanation for an Expert System that Performs Estate Planning. Proceedings of the *First International Conference on Artificial Intelligence and Law*; 1987; Northeastern University, Boston: ACM Press: p. 18-27.

[Schlo 89]   Schlobohm, Dean A.; McCarty, L. Thorne. EPS II: Estate Planning With Prototypes. *Proceedings of the Second International Conference on Artificial Intelligence and Law*; 1989; University of British Columbia, Vancouver, BC: ACM Press: 1-10.

[Skalak 89]   Skalak, David B.; Rissland, Edwina L. Using Case-Based Reasoning to Extend the Expertise of Expert Systems. Forthcoming in: *Proceedings of the Third International Conference Logica Informatica Diritto – Expert Systems in Law*; November 1989; Florence, Italy.

[Skalak 90]   Skalak, David B.; Rissland, Edwina L. Inductive Learning in a Mixed Paradigm Setting. *Proc AAAI 90*: 840-847.

[Smith 87]   Smith, J.C.; Deedman, Cal. The Application of Expert Systems Technology to Case-Based Law. *Proceedings of the First International Conference on Artificial Intelligence and Law*; 1987; Northeastern University, Boston: ACM Press: p. 84-93.

[Smits 89]   Smits, Jan, M.; Kracht, Douwe. Experiences with a Methodology for Developing Advisory Systems for Legal Questions. Forthcoming in: *Proceedings of the Third International Conference Logica Informatica Diritto – Expert Systems in Law*; November 1989; Florence, Italy.

[Utgoff 89]   Utgoff, Paul E. Incremental Induction of Decision Trees. *Machine Learning*; 1989; 4: 161-186.

[Wahl 89]   Wahlgren, Peter. Hypertext and Legal Structures. Forthcoming in: *Proceedings of the Third International Conference Logica Informatica Diritto – Expert Systems in Law*; November 1989; Florence, Italy.

[Weusten 89]   Weusten, Marnix C. M. Maintenance of Knowledge in Advisory Systems on Legal Questions. Forthcoming in: *Proceedings of the Third International Conference Logica Informatica Diritto – Expert Systems in Law*; November 1989; Florence, Italy.

[Yoder 89]   Yoder, E.; Wettach, T.C. Using Hypertext in a Law Firm. *Proceedings Hypertext'89*, November 1989; Pittsburgh: 159-167.

An Expert Thesaurus for Ancient Law

Carla BASILI

Consiglio Nazionale delle Ricerche-ISRDS
Rome, Italy

Nicola PALAZZOLO

Università di Catania
Catania, Italy

Anna Maria TAMMARO

Univarsità di Firenze
Firenze, Italy

ABSTRACT

Problems related to Natural Language Processing can be treated only when knowledge can be limited to a specific domain. This is the case for the expert system IRIDA (Intelligent Information Retrieval for Ancient Law). The IRIDA knowledge base possesses all the requisites needed to facilitate intelligent information retrieval, together with the capability of analysing textual content. The terms of the domain have in fact already been identified and are contained in a hierarchical thesaurus. The term survey may be considered as practically definitive.

The present paper aims to illustrate the problems tackled, overall project architecture and the current state of implementation.

1   State of the art in the IRIDA project

1.1   The problems

In the course of recent international congresses it was pointed out that the problem of documentation, particularly of a bibliographic nature, in the field of ancient law, must be tackled with extreme urgency using state of the art technology. Increasing needs related to the quantity of the data, which are not always known outside the narrow circle of specialists in this particular field, as well as to the speed of retrieval, have basically shown up the comparative inadequacy and ineffectiveness of both traditional methods of bibliographic documentation and any "minimal" use of information scientific tools. It is now possible to make a quantum leap forward as a result of new developments in information technology (on-line computer networks, CD-ROMs, etc.), as well as of the refinement of techniques for storing and retrieving bibliographic information (thesauri, classifications, etc.).

Research on ancient law has developed around two quite different types of document collections: the bibliographic collection and ancient sources. The former (Bibliography) is a constantly expanding collection which is difficult to retrieve owing to the interdisciplinary nature of studies on the ancient world. Conversely, unlike other bibliographic collections, e.g. the physical or medical sciences, it possesses the characteristic of not "ageing"", even after many decades. The collection of the sources is, on the other hand, a "static" collection, in which, with very rare exceptions, it can be assumed that there will be no new additions in the coming decades. The starting hypothesis thus involved combining both the bibliographic collection and that of the sources into a single system so as to be able to get to the bibliography starting from a source cited in it, or else to display an ancient source cited in a bibliographic document. The rapid retrieval of the full literature referring to a given source of knowledge has, in fact, always been the primary need felt by ancient law researchers.

One further difficulty peculiar to the specific branch of ancient law is the fact that every concept is expressed in the first instance by means of a technical term in the original language (usually Latin), for which there is sometimes a modern technical term which is a full semantic equivalent of the original term and sometimes a modern term which only partly corresponds as it refers to concepts related to modern law rather than to ancient law. Likewise, in numerous cases, also in modern languages a term which in everyday language may seem to be the translation of another in technical language actually refers to a different concept because it denotes a completely different juridical situation. It may be said that between the "concept" and the "term" in many cases there is no absolute semantic correspondence.

1.2   Documentary collections and files.

The document base is comprised of three files integrated under the Superfind information retrieval program.

The bibliographic file currently comprises about 3000 monographs on Roman and ancient law drawn from the catalogue of the library of the Juridical Seminary of the University of Catania. It is already automated using the UNIBIBLIO and indexed using a specialized classification system. An optical reading system, running suitable font recognition software, so that the different fields can be identified right from the reading stage, allows a much larger collection to be added to the existing collection using the same information retrieval package. This collection consists of journal articles which have been systematically abstracted from the IURA bibliographic repertoire since 1950 and from the LABEO international repertoire since 1955 (about 20,000 titles). The IURA descriptions represent the semantically richer part of the collection owing to the presence of an abstract, while LABEO uses a limited number of controlled terms, corresponding to the headwords of the UNIBIBLIO classification, to indicate the contents. Many of the documents in the three collections also contain a reference to all the juridical sources cited in the text.

The sources file is composed of a large documentary collection (about 14 Mb) containing full-text Roman law sources stored electronically by a research group operating at the University of Linz (Austria) and transferred to the information retrieval package used. Other document collections referring to Latin literary sources available on commercial CD-ROMs are being acquired. Unlike other products it was in fact deemed necessary to store in memory all the sources referring to the history of the ancient world in the conviction that the juridical aspects cannot be separated from the other profiles used to analyse the societies of the past. However, this involves the difficult task of coding and normalizing quotations from the sources themselves as well, of course, as an enormous increase in the amount of data to be stored. Of course, the Greek sources, which nevertheless must be acquired, will involve even greater difficulty.

The thesaurus file consists of a structured set of terms (currently about 8000) representing a specific collection of disciplines referring to ancient law. The set is structured in the sense that all the terms are linked together by a tree classification structure (which reproduces the logical categories typical of the juridical disciplines) but also in the sense that the system makes provision for cross references between the common language terms used by the user to express his research needs and the controlled terms, which act as descriptions, or subjects, of the bibliographic documents. Creating the thesaurus involved

solving problems related to choosing the fundamental nodes of the scientific field considered. Whereas for single entries the choice has involved giving ancient criteria priority over modern ones, indicating the latter as associated concepts, wherever possible and useful, as far as the classification system is concerned, the choice was directed towards a system based on modern dogmatics, which is better suited to the explanatory schema normally employed by potential users. The integrated system thus allows the same classification scheme to be applied both to the sources and to the bibliography, without necessarily giving rise, as we shall see below, to the risk of an arbitrary indexing of the sources performed by the specialist. The risk of redundancy (which is inevitable in cases of any work dealing with several topics) is compensated by the absolute objectiveness of the references.

2   The IRIDA project development plan

The main activity is now to merge the three collections and to create a uniform indexing system. This sub-project is divided into the following implementation stages: inputting the UNIBIBLIO file, together with its own classification structure using the information retrieval software and the use of the same classification as a classification schema for the thesaurus; acquisition of the IURA and LABEO hard copy collections using optical readers and their indexing using the thesaurus created in the previous stages. The logical connection between the various collections is shown in fig. 1.

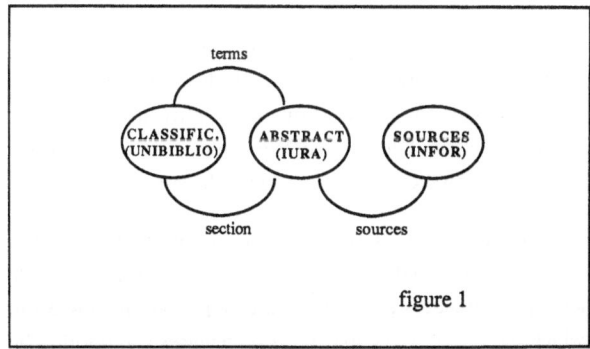

figure 1

The logical structure of the thesaurus has been inherited from the UNIBIBLIO classification. This classification consists of a hierarchy of terms, as in the following example:

section	6	Roman law
classes	6.6	private Roman law
subclasses	6.6.3	juridical facts
specifications	6.6.3.3	elements of juridical transactions
terms (related to the class)		causa lucrativa , causa in juridical transactions

The headword which identifies document content for LABEO corresponds to the headword of the thesaurus class notation, while the free language terms of the IURA abstract are mostly included among the related thesaurus terms. A preliminary comparison thus makes it possible to obtain proposed indexing in the case of matching terms. Comparison is useful also for the reverse flow, i.e. the enrichment of thesaurus terminology using both the significant words from the IURA abstracts and the full text of the sources.

This operation calls for considerable manual work both for checking and updating the indexing terms, which necessitates information retrieval software with powerful on-line updating capability, as well as thesaurus management software.

This led to the idea of using expert system technology in order to reduce the manual work required.

3   The expert system

The IRIDA expert system has a twofold purpose:
-   during data input the expert system is dedicated to automatic document indexing using text analysis and context analysis techniques;
-   at the operational stage the same knowledge base can be used for intelligent information retrieval, allowing a list of topics expressed in pre-coordinated controlled language (classification) to be matched with a list of potential, subsidiary topics contained within each class.

IRIDA also has the task of helping the user to refine his information needs interactively. By means of navigation through an expert thesaurus successive search topics are proposed for which the user is asked to express preferences and priority, in this way gradually refining and sharpening his information requirements.
Both the application aims of IRIDA lead to the need to assign an information content to the individual documents using a specialized knowledge base catering for the field of interest. Both automatic indexing based on context analysis and intelligent retrieval are non deterministic activities which thus cannot be performed using conventional programming languages.

In a scenario such as this the thesaurus comes to represent the backbone of the system's knowledge base.

3.1.   Thesaurus structuring for the purpose of the knowledge base

The careful development of a complex and structured thesaurus takes on an important role in the overall implementation of the system since, as we shall see, it represents the embryonic knowledge base of the IRIDA expert system.

The thesaurus currently being built is something more than a simple list of key-words or controlled vocabulary descriptors as is normally the case. It is a true hierarchical lexicon in that it is not restricted to recording the terms and compound expressions (syntagmas) of which its lexical units are composed but also expresses the semantic links between them. The act of looking up words associated through given semantic relations with a given technical terms circumscribes and delimits the semantic area of the concept to which the term refers. Therefore, within the thesaurus, the relations between a word and its associated terms makes it possible indirectly to determine the meaning of that word. The set of meaning relations the latter enters into with the other adjacent technical terms allows us to map out the knowledge field in which the topic of interest is situated.

The sole basis of the thesaurus is the relational and semantic aspect, avoiding as far as possible problems of definition and attempts at standardizing sectorial language. In fact, at this stage, terminological uniformity would involve linguistic problems (for instance, owing to the simultaneous presence of terms in Latin and in other modern languages), as well as theoretical problems, which are usually of little help in information retrieval and content analysis. The semantic networks it is intended to create are aimed at representing knowledge of a given sector of ancient law. The thesaurus is therefore a hierarchical lexicon composed of semantic networks (or microthesauri), each of which is composed of a set of nodes linked together by various relations. They are used to represent the meaning of the terms in the technical language.

In the first phase of the project the thesaurus relations were built up generically and comprehensively, and were essentially reduced to those of synonymy and quasi synonymy. Experience has shown that the smaller their number the greater their retrieval capacity, albeit at the cost of increased noise. Of course, there is a loss of concept intension and the precision of the conceptual grid is reduced. The present problem is that of deciding whether to go on working with a small number of comparatively generic relations that are sufficient to express the fundamental semantic nexi in the sector of ancient law, with a consequent loss of accuracy, and instead to use a much larger number, which will be of use in the automatic analysis of the documents. The possible risk is that of forcing the meaning of the terms used in that sectorial language with consequent silence at the reference level during the retrieval stage. For the time being it has been decided to sieve through the largest possible number of types of potentially usable semantic relations even though it may later be decided to exclude some or to group others together according to whether the ultimate aims will be directed mainly towards information retrieval or concept analysis.

The relations taken into account are those of synonymy in the broad sense, vertical hierarchical relations and relations of horizontal affinity.

Synonymy in the broad sense: this relation includes both synonymy in the narrow sense and near synonyms. Preferential synonymy has not been used, and a principal form has been selected which is usually expressed by the reciprocal relation Use (UF).

Hierarchical relations: hierarchical relations represent the backbone of a semantic network viewed vertically, and can be represented by a tree structure (e.g. a genealogical tree). Semantic trees are conventionally constructed starting from conceptual chains which proceed from broader or more general terms towards narrow or more specific terms. This relation is also known as hyponomy and is characterized by one salient feature: what is true from the point of view of the extension, insofar as it is included in that of a more general term, is true also from the point of view of intension, i.e. as a quality of the more specific term. The opposite is not true since the more specific term refers to a broader set of attributes.

The main drawback to the classical approach to hierarchical relations is probably that of having performed a single, comparatively undifferentiated semantic relation which was conceived of as a undistinguished container in which to include various different categories of the superordinate subordinate type which were essentially different, e.g. generic-specific, universal-particular, abstract-concrete, whole-part. The hierarchical network represents the framework of a semantic tree and as such should be refined more than the others if the aims are those of knowledge representation. A more accurate analytical distinction has thus been attempted at the level of the various hierarchical

type relations. Three have been identified, each made up of a pair of reciprocal relations:

1) BT/NT (Broader term-Narrower term): this is the classical relation of hyponomy defined in a narrower sense than in existing thesauri. The pair identifies only the genus-species relation between terms. For instance the relation:

Nomina transcripticia NT literal contracts

means that the first term is hierarchically subordinate and is a concept included in the superordinate term, or else is a type of literal contract, the hierarchically superordinate term. Thus interpreted, the relation is the same as the ISA relation, which is used in artificial intelligence for the structured representation of knowledge in the environment of semantic networks or frames. Conversely, the relation:

Literal Contracts BT Nomina transcripticia

will mean that Literal Contracts is the genus of the species Nomina transcripticia. The usefulness of having a pair of relations in the system instead of a single relation consists in the fact that, in this way, it is possible to "navigate" and perform inferences in both directions of the tree, top down and bottom up.

2) WH-PT (Whole-part): this is a semantic link of a hierarchical nature which however differs from the preceding one and is set up between two terms conceptually linked by a relationship of belonging expressed by the whole-part relation (total concept/partial concept). The pair is useful when it is a matter of terms, the meaning of which can be broken down into a series of components, each of which is expressed in turn by other terms. Thus the relation:

Pledge PT Real Contracts

means that the term 'Pledge' is hierarchically subordinate and identifies a part of the superordinate term Real Contracts. This relation is identical to the relation PARTOF used in the knowledge representation mechanisms. Conversely, the relation:

Real Contracts WH   Pledge, Deposito, Comodato, Mutuo,
                      Fiducia

means that Real Contracts is a whole with respect to Pledge, Comodato, Mutuo, Fiducia.

It should be noted that the definition of hierarchical relation expressed in terms of implication does not fit the case of PT very well. It is not always clear whether a term representing part of the meaning of another term can be said to semantically imply the latter and not vice versa.

3) ST/MB (Set-Member): one last type of hierarchical relation is exemplified by the relation linking together a term denoting the elements of a set and a term denoting a non defined member of the set itself. This pair must not be confused with the preceding one even if both may be expressed in terms of the concept of belonging:

Sacrilegium MB Individual Offences

means that the term Sacrilegium is lower down in the hierarchy and identifies a generic member of the set referred to by the hierarchically higher collective term 'Individual Offences'. Conversely, the relation:

Individual Offences ST Sacrilegium, Calumnia, Conspiratio,...

means that the term Individual Offences identifies the set, the elements of which are expressed by Sacrilegium, Calumnia, Conspiratio, etc. The pair is basically used to express the fact that the collective terms are hierarchically further up a hypothetical tree representation.

These three different pairs of hierarchical relations which reveal different aspects of the concept of superordinate-subordinate in a hierarchical conceptual structure share several fundamental logical properties: they are all irreflexive, asymmetrical and transitive relations. The property of transitiveness is particularly important because it sheds light on the capability of a node inside the semantic tree to "inherit" the relations and properties associated with another node should these two nodes be linked by a hierarchical chain of the type of those examined above.

Relation of association: within the construction of the tree structure of a semantic network another paradigmatic relation which may be used is the horizontal one. It is used to link those terms which may be considered as being on the same plane or level insofar as they are both subordinate with respect to the same higher level term.

The definition of this relation is defined as cohyponomy. Two terms are cohyponymous if they are in a NT or PT type relation with another term which is hyperonymous with them. On the other hand, there is no question of cohyponymy as far as the ST/MB pair relations are concerned since, in this case, the terms referring to one and the same collective noun would be mutually synonymous or quasi synonymous.

The relation is symmetrical but not transitive. It can be transitive only if we establish that each node in the network can have only one hierarchically superior level (single hierarchy tree or microthesauri).

Relations of this kind include:

1) TT (Top term): the general hierarchical structure of each of the semantic networks is completed by means of the information referring to the terms located at the root of the various conceptual trees. A thesaurus may be conceived of as being composed of the set of microthesauri (i.e. several semantic networks of hierarchical trees), each belonging to one of the terms presenting the highest degree of genericalness or TT.
2) Other horizontal semantic relations are those of opposition. They include: incompatibility, complementarity, antonymy, inversion.

Incompatibility occurs when the assertion of one of two elements implies the negation of the other. However, the negation of one does not imply the assertion of the other. Complementarity implies that the negation of the first term implies the assertion of the second and vice versa the assertion of the first implies the negation of the second. Antonymy implies a relation of semantic opposition between terms located along a graduable continuum. Inversion occurs when the terms are incompatible, non graduable or comparable and a rule of reciprocal substitutability is valid for them.

3) RT (Related term): the last semantic relation is the generic relation of association among terms. It indicates those terms which are connected with the descriptor given at the conceptual level or as a simple association of ideas without possessing hierarchical, synonymy or opposition relations. This type of relation is often used to link all those terms which, although not linkable in a more precise way by means of semantic relations examined above nevertheless display a kind of affinity of significance. It is no easy matter to establish this residual type of relation with any accuracy. It often remains vague and obscure. It is possible to use criteria of suitability with reference to the aims for which the thesaurus was constructed. By adopting a narrow criterion it is possible to avoid the noise generated by information dispersion, although the risk now becomes that useful information will be overlooked. However, the choice of a broad criterion increases the risk of a low capacity for conceptual precision.

4. The selected shell

4.1 LEONARDO overview

We are currently working towards the adoption of the LEONARDO shell produced by Creative Logic Ltd. LEONARDO actually uses the object-rule knowledge representation schema. The LEONARDO core consists of the "LEONARDO Development System" module which includes a knowledge editor, a natural procedural language which, among other things, provides access to external databases, to perform calculations and to obtain printouts. In particular, the system is equipped with an interface to three DBMS: Lotus, Btrieve and DataEase. The development module also contains the rule checking and validation functions, as well as the functions for maintaining the knowledge bases defined within the system. A second LEONARDO module provides ad hoc modules for the specific application. The latter include graphics, statistical and mathematical packages together with modules for interactive screen drawing for each of which specific help capabilities can be defined. The latter characteristic is of great assistance in developing a customized interface.

4.2 Structure of the LEONARDO knowledge base

A LEONARDO knowledge base is comprised of the MainRuleSet, objects and object frames. The MainRuleSet is the basic component of the knowledge base. Every application starts with the MainRuleSet which is a free format list of rule statements.

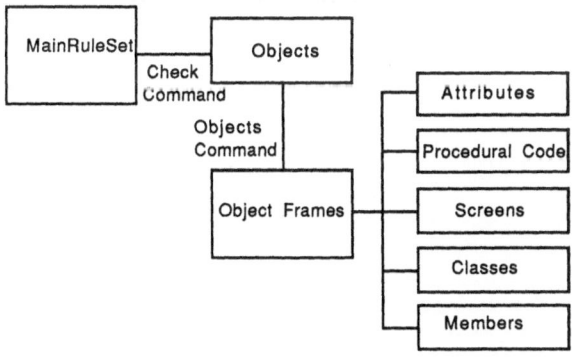

The basic LEONARDO *rules* are production rules of the usual form IF condition THEN result. The result could be a number of different things, for instance:

- assign a values to objects which can then used by other rules;
- invoke an input or output screen;
- execute a LEONARDO or external procedure;
- establish further tasks for LEONARDO to undertake.

The general syntax of a condition (antecedent clause) in a rule is:

<object>	<operator>	<objectı value>

while the result part (consequent clause) may have the following forms:

<object>	<operator>	<object ı constant ı expression>
ask	<object>	
say	<object>	
run	<procedure object>	([parameters])
use	<screen object>	

Wherever in the normal syntax of a rule can appear the name of an object, in so-called quantified rules can appear a slot referent. The use of slot referents gives rise to a more compact and flexible representation based on the dynamic slot value assignment mechanism.

Objects may be of various types and may have an associated object frame. The object frame contains all the information about an object. *Text, Real* and *List* objects are *value carrying objects*: their values are used and updated in rules, procedures and screens. A frame may contain an optional slot called *RuleSet* containing rules which derive the value of the object.

Procedural objects contain procedural code which may be executed from several points during knowledge base execution.

Screen objects are input and display screens generated using the LEONARDO Screen Designer.

Class and member objects contain information about objects and their relationships to each other. They contain slots defined by the system developer to describe the important attributes of the object.

4.3 The basic inference mechanism

The basic inference mechanism is depth-first backward chaining. However, when an object is instantiated, either through a rule or user query, forward chaining is triggered to maximise the use of the new data. After forward chaining is completed, backward chaining resumes. Backward chaining is also called goal-directed reasoning: an hypothetical solution (the goal) is assumed which the system will try to find evidence to prove. In this way a LEONARDO knowledge base needs a goal, that is a special rule which defines the objective of the knowledge base. This is the

448

seek directive. When LEONARDO executes a knowledge base it literally seeks for a value for the object named in the seek rule. In backward chaining it is assumed no data and only ask for the information needed to prove the evidence of a line of reasoning, therefore the system in turn receives an answer from the user and returns to evaluating a rule.

5   The IRIDA knowledge base under LEONARDO

The goal of the current IRIDA knowledge base implementation under LEONARDO is to define a search profile, i.e. a "search point of view" expressing the context of interest for the user. Such a point of view is comprised of one or more classification-code, followed by a list of terms which are consistent with the intersection or the union of different classification-codes.   The object "*search-context*" appears therefore in the seek directive and is defined with the following slots:

```
classification-codes:

terms:

notes:
```

In order to achieve such a goal, we have to distinguish two environments:

-    an *application control environment,* which includes a number of screen objects, value carrying objects and procedural objects; this environment constitutes the user interface and the query session supervisor;

-    a *knowledge environment,* including the semantic network of the terms and their classification structure; this environment is represented by means of class and member objects; particularly the member objects contain the following slots:

```
classes:
BT:
NT:
synonymous:
other_language_synonymous:
notes:
```

where each slot represents a semantic relationship between terms. Each slot points to a list object, containing the set of members in the slot relationship. Navigation through semantic objects is obtained by means of quantified rules and procedural objects.

At the current implementation stage the main effort was devoted to the declarative aspects of knowledge representation. In this approach a limited number of semantic relationship has been considered since the links between related terms are managed by means of a uniform structure.

REFERENCES

[1]   J.D.Ullman, Principles of Database and Knowledge-base Systems, Computer Science Press, 1989

[2]   C.Basili, N.Palazzolo, A.M. Tammaro, IRIDA: a project for Intelligent Information Retrieval, Convegno "Linguaggi Documentari e Basi di Dati, Roma, 3-4 dicembre 1990

[3]   C.Basili, A.M. Tammaro, ALTHES: un ipertesto per un thesaurus sui Diritti dell'Antichità Convegno "Linguaggi Documentari e Basi di Dati, Roma, 3-4 dicembre 1990

[4]   Menner J., La Attività della nostra sezione "Utilizzazione della elaborazione elettronica dei dati nel diritto romano". Retrospettiva e prospettive, in Proceedings of IV International Congress on the subject "Informatica e regolamentazioni giuridiche", II, 36.

[5]   Palazzolo N., - Tammaro A.M., Studio di un sistema integrato per il recupero dell'informazione bibliografica nel campo dei diritti dell'Antichità, in Proceedings of IV International Congress on the subject "Informatica e regolamentazioni giuridiche", II, 28.

[6]   T.C.Tan, M.Smith, M.Pegman, Conceptual retrieval using object-oriented approach, Proceedings of DEXA90, 1990

[7]   Petrucci P., The Thesaurus as a relational data model In Automated analysis of legal texts, ed. by Martino A., Socci F., Amsterdam North Holland, 1986.

[8]   L.Kerschberg (ed.), Proceedings from the Second International Conference on Expert Database Systems, Benjamin/Cummings Publishing Company, 1989

[9]   Gallizia A. (et al.), Per una classificazione automatica dei testi giuridici, Milano, Giuffrè, 1974, VII + 144 p.

[10]   Creative Logic Ltd, LEONARDO User's Guide, 1989

Designing a Hypermedia Information System

H.P. Frei, P. Schäuble

Swiss Federal Institute of Technology (ETH) Zurich
Department of Computer Science, 8092 Zurich, Switzerland

This paper addresses some problems arising when a Hypermedia Information System is designed. In contrast to authoring systems that primarily support document preparation, the system described here is intended mainly to support the administration of hypermedia information, i.e., storage and retrieval of as well as browsing in information. Since hypermedia information systems contain both structured and unstructured data, the integration of data base and information retrieval methods is an inevitable part of a multimedia retrieval function. In addition, adequate indexing methods and a novel similarity function are being developed. In order to study new methods, a hypermedia information system with real-world data is under development. This system will run on test data taken from an orthopedic clinic: medical histories mainly consisting of linked text portions but also graphics, slides, and video tapes.

1. Introduction

The purpose of a Hypermedia Information System is to provide access to stored hypermedia information. In particular, it has to allow the users of the system to *browse* through the information and to *search* for specified parts of the stored data. Hypermedia information is invariably partitioned into single information portions, so-called *nodes*. These nodes contain information of arbitrary types, i.e., text, graphics, images, or movies. The nodes themselves are connected by arcs, usually called *links*. These links allow the user to move through the hypermedia data collection at will and 'read' the content of the nodes he or she encounters.

At the present time, much effort goes into the development of hypermedia systems in order to support the *development* of hypermedia material. The aim is to assist producers of information when putting together diverse portions of information into complex but easy to perceive documents. Elaborate *editors* for various types of information (text, graphics, images, voice etc.) as well as their integration into a single system are the key to authoring tools such as Apple's HyperCard [6] and Xerox' NoteCard [8]. Through their use information collections are going to grow in the near future. The project described in this paper is not concerned with the preparation of hypermedia documents but with the *administration* of hypermedia collections.

Unfortunately, there are hardly any large collections of hypermedia documents available at the present time. For this reason we are employing test data taken from the orthopedic clinic Wilhelm Schulthess in Zurich. These test data consist of a great deal of medical data accumulated over the years. There are various sorts of forms, written reports including graphical information, x-rays, slides, and even video tapes of operations. Most of the information portions are connected in a natural way to other information portions resulting in a complex hypermedia web.

This paper is organized as follows. First, we point out our view of the characteristics of hypermedia information. Then we describe what the need of a user of a hypermedia information system is. As a consequence of these needs and as the main part of the paper, a retrieval mechanism is presented by means of an extension of a traditional data base query language. We conclude by presenting both the architecture of our system and the test data employed.

2. Hypermedia Information

In contrast to traditional documents whose structure is basically *linear*, i.e., a succession of linearly arranged information units, hypermedia information is *non-linear*. We call non-linear text documents *hypertext* documents. Various text portions are connected by so-called links that allow to quickly proceed from a current node to the logically or semantically connected nodes. [2].

If more than one information type is part of a document, we call it *multimedia*. This is often the case with traditional documents when they contain figures.

The combination of the properties of 'hyper' and 'multimedia' is called 'hypermedia'. This type of information is stored in hypermedia information systems. Let us first define more precisely the terms node, link, multimedia document, and hypermedia data collection:

• *Node:* A node is a portion of information. For instance linear texts, graphics, images, movies, audio recordings, spread sheets, or a mixture thereof may form nodes. A node may contain other nodes or parts of other nodes. Thus, words, phrases, rectangles of images, and parts ot audio or video recordings are also possible nodes.

- *Link:* A link consists of a source node, a target node, and possibly a description of the link. A link without a description is called a *referential link;* otherwise, it is called a *semantic link.*

- *Multimedia Document:* A multimedia document is a sequence of strictly linearly ordered nodes which are neither source nodes nor target nodes of links. These nodes may not contain subnodes. The essential property of a multimedia document is that it consists of *various types* of information.

- *Hypermedia Data Collection:* A hypermedia data collection consists of a set of nodes and a set of links. A link may neither originate in, nor point to, a node which is located outside of the collection.

Besides incorporating various information types like text, graphics, image, and sound, the most prominent property of a hypermedia document is its non-linearity. There may be links between any arbitrary two nodes and, therefore, between any arbitrary information portion independent of content or type. The links are the arcs of a *directed graph.* However, there is no more than one outgoing link per node. The links are either established automatically by a program or intellectually by an author or a reader.

Despite this clear definition and the simple mathematical interpretation as directed graphs, several kinds of links may exist depending on the nature of the connection to be expressed. In order to keep things simple, we restrict ourselves to two different kinds:

- *Referential Link:* The purpose of these links is mainly to allow comfortable reading of the information [12]; they are, for instance, established between the table of contents and the individual sections or between a citation and the corresponding bibliographic reference. In other words, a referential link may point to a node containing information related to the source node. In relational databases, referential links are usually represented as named correspondences.

- *Semantic Link:* The purpose of these links is to point to similar or more detailed information and to additional information on a specific topic. The description associated with these links may consist of a real-valued weight or a content-related topic. The weighting factor determines the strength of the relation between the two nodes. The content-related description determines the topic that justifies the link; it is usually expressed by means of features or descriptors.

Note that referential links are plain pointers which can be defined by means of the database schema. Conversely, the descriptions associated with the semantic links are established by special purpose indexing functions or even manually. The descriptions-- weighting factors and/or content-related topics--can be made available to the user or to retrieval algorithms. Semantic links represent a new type of automatic or manual indexing in so far as relationships between the nodes are assigned in addition to the plain descriptors which are used exclusively in traditional indexing.

A hypermedia node typically consists of *structured* and *unstructured* information. Structured information is stored in pre-defined data fields (mostly as records), unstructured information can be word sequences, graphics, images, or sound. They are stored in long fields. It goes without saying that structured information can be handled much easier than the unstructured information. Fortunately, there is more structured information contained in data collections than is usually assumed. Even a sound or image node often contains some structured information.

3. Users and Information Need

As with most computer applications we distinguish between *expert* and *casual* users. One of the aims of our system is to serve both. A query language with a high expressive power (vid. section 4) will allow an expert user flexibly to query the system. Likewise, a highly adaptable graphically oriented user interface will serve the casual user.

The services rendered by the system include browsing, data retrieval, information retrieval, and the combination of data and information retrieval. The non-linear structure of hypermedia information is particularly suited for *browsing* activities. Although browsing appears to be an unsystematic way of searching for information, our belief is that many user needs may be satisfied when a flexible browsing tool is available. This flexibility is most useful when the information need of the user is rather vague or when the user has a clear idea about where in the hypermedia web the desired information may be located.

A still open research issue is how to quantify the browsing effectiveness and how the browsing effectiveness is affected by the links. It is our intuition that users may benefit from links when browsing through a hypermedia data collection. However, little work has been done so far to measure the benefit of the links relative to the costs in establishing them.

Data retrieval means searching for *structured* information. This activity consists of data base searches which are naturally supported in a hypermedia environment because of the existence of so much structured information. A frequently occurring information need necessitates capabilities for the *statistical analysis* of stored data. How well this need can be satisfied depends on the expressive power of the query language.

Information retrieval means searching for *unstructured* information. There are well known techniques for searching through large texts and the rapid identification of keywords. However, most users are seeking a specific *concept* rather than the appearance of a single word. Texts are therefore usually indexed by means of content specific features. Typically, these features consist of so-called descriptors. Similarity measures are used to compare a query and a text. These similarity measures compare two--possibly weighted--sets of descriptors and deliver a sorted list of objects in descending order of similarity.

The combination of data retrieval and information retrieval requires the formulation of queries consisting of both precise and imprecise query components. We have designed our hypermedia information system to deal with such queries in an *integrated* manner. We decided to take a unified approach when extending a database query language so that it can also handle imprecise search criteria.

4. Retrieval of Hypermedia Information

As pointed out in the previous section, there are queries that simultaneously require arithmetic computations (e.g. sum, average), the selection of objects according to precise criteria (e.g. age of patient greater than 20 years), the selection of objects according to imprecise criteria (e.g. having pain in the back), and the ordering of the retrieved objects according to precise or imprecise search criteria (e.g. ordering by age or ordering by similar case histories). Arithmetic computations as well as selecting and sorting data items according to precise criteria can be expressed in a conventional database query language such as SQL. On the other hand, modern information retrieval systems accept imprecise search criteria. In particular, a query consists of weighted search criteria and the information retrieval system provides items which comply to these criteria to a varying degree.

Several attempts with the aim of incorporating imprecise search criteria into database query languages are known.

- The query languages proposed in [5] and [13] provide ranked output by means of the language constructs RANK_BY and RANK respectively. These extended query languages do not allow arithmetic computations on the data that has been retrieved by imprecise search criteria.

- The query language VAGUE [11] contains a SIMILAR-TO comparator which is determined by different metrics. The database administrator has to define for every domain D a metric M_D and a so-called radius r_D. Two attribute values v, $w \in D$ are considered as similar iff $M_D(v,w) \leq r_D$. A drawback of this approach is that finding appropriate similarity functions and radii is usually a difficult task. It is unlikely that the similarity functions and the radii provided by the database administrator will satisfy all users.

In our approach, a functional database query language is taken and its set of built-in functions is extended by a few *elementary similarity functions*. The following functions

$$sim_{txt}(q,d) \quad := \quad RSV(q,d)$$

$$sim_{num}(a,b,x,y) \quad := \quad \frac{exp(a-b(y-x)^2)}{1+exp(a-b(y-x)^2)}$$

$$sim_{date}(a,b,d,e) \quad := \quad sim_{num}(a, b, MJD(d), MJD(e))$$

are examples of such elementary similarity functions. The function sim_{txt} assigns the objects q and d of the class Text a real number $RSV(q,d)$ where $RSV(q,d)$ denotes the Retrieval Status Value of d with respect to q according to a specific information retrieval model [16]. Given two parameters a and b, the function

sim_{num} assigns the numbers x and y a real number $sim_{num}(a,b,x,y)$ which expresses how similar x and y are (Figure 1). The logistic function sim_{num} models a vague equality as pointed out in [5]. For $a \to \infty$, the similarity function sim_{num} converges to the Dirac δ function where $\delta(x,y) = 1$ if $x = y$ and $\delta(x,y) = 0$ if $x \neq y$.

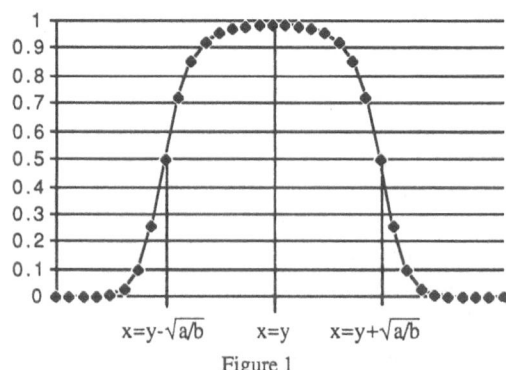

Figure 1

Analogously, the function sim_{date} determines the similarity of two dates where the function MJD determines for every date the Modified Julian Date, i.e. the number of mean solar days since 1/1/1950 00:00.

The elementary similarity functions compare simple (literal) objects. More sophisticated similarity functions which compare more complex objects can be defined by specifying derived functions or views as demonstrated in the example below. The realization of such similarity functions has two major advantages. First, no new language constructs are needed because existing concepts such as derived functions or views suffice. Since derived functions and views may have been defined by a user, every user can easily use his or her own set of similarity functions.

Example: We will use FQL* to define a non-elementary similarity function. FQL* is a Functional Query Language which is based on a data model supporting objects, classes (i.e. sets of objects), and bag functions that determine relationships between the objects [14]. FQL* is more expressive than the fixpoint query languages as shown in. As an example, let us create a hypothetical derived function op_sim which determines the similarity of two medical operations. Two operations are considered as similar if the operation reports are similar and if the ages of the patients are similar. We assume a database which has been generated by the following create statements.

create class Patient;
create class Operation;
create stored function ops: Patient $\to$ B(Operation);
create stored function birth_date: Patient $\to$ B(Date);
create stored function op_report: Operation $\to$ B(Text);

The function ops assigns every patient a bag (multiset) of operations. The function values have to be bags because the underlying model of FQL* is based on a complete lattice of bag functions [14]. The function birth_date assigns every patient a bag with a single date, i.e. the patient's date of birth. The function op_report assigns every patient a bag of text pieces which constitute the operation report. The following statement defines the derived function op_sim which determines the similarity of two operations. Given two operations x and y, the function op_sim returns a bag with a real number which is the estimated similarity of x and y.

> **create derived function**
> op_sim: Operation × Operation → B(real)
> **such that** op_sim(x,y) **contains**
> sim_txt(op_report(x),op_report(y)) *
> sim_date(365^2,1,birth_date(p),birth_date(q))
> **for each** (p,q) **in** Patient × Patient
> **where** (x **in** ops(p)) **and** (y **in** ops(q));

Given two operations x and y, the derived function op_sim selects from the class Patient those, possibly identical, patients p and q which have been operated in x and y respectively. Hereafter, the similarity of the operation reports of x and y and the similarity of the dates of birth of p and q are computed. The parameters a=365^2 and b=1 are such that $sim_{date}(365^2,1,bp,bq)$ >0.5 if the difference between the age of p and the age of q is less than one year. Finally, the product of these two similarities is put into the bag op_sim(x,y). In this way, the similarity op_sim(x,y) of two operations is high if both the similarity of the corresponding operation reports and the similarity of the ages of the corresponding patients are high.

Let x1 and x2 be two operations which have been retrieved earlier. The following query selects from the class Operation those operations which are more similar to x1 than x2 is similar to x1.

> **select** op_report(x) **into** R
> **for each** x **in** Operation
> **where** op_sim(x1,x) > op_sim(x1,x2)
> **order by** op_sim(x1,x) **desc**;

The answer to this query is a bag of operation reports that are stored in the bag variable R. The elements of the bag R are sorted in decreasing order of the similarity values op_sim(x1,x). The number of retrieved reports is obtained by the query

> **select** NumOfElems(R);

where the function NumOfElems counts the elements of a bag, e.g. NumOfElems({1,1,7}) = 3. *End of example*

We will use an information retrieval approach to define the similarity function sim_txt. An automatic indexing procedure assigns every object of the class Text a set of weighted features. The similarity between two text objects is obtained by determining the similarity of their features. We may think of the following types of features: Reduced words, phrases, descriptors, and numbers together with their units. Reduced words are obtained by removing the stop words first and then by reducing the remaining words by an appropriate word reduction algorithm (see references given in [19, pp.50] for English and German word reduction algorithms). There are several types of methods to identify phrases: Syntactic and non-syntactic methods [3], stochastic methods [1], and delimiter methods [9]. The identification of numbers and their units has been suggested by [10]. Finally, the similarity of two sets of weighted features can be modelled by an inner vector product as discussed in [16]. It is still an open research issue whether the features of the objects and their similarities depend on the links in the case of hypermedia documents (vid. Section 2). Preliminary results are presented in [4].

In this section, it was shown that information retrieval functionality can be added to a functional database query language by extending the set of built-in functions by a few elementary similarity functions. Further work is needed to model the similarity of images and spoken words. A possible approach to determine the similarities of audio recordings containing spoken words is discussed in [15]. Furthermore, the elementary similarity functions have to be evaluated on real data to see how well they perform.

5. The Architecture of the System

The Hypermedia Information System under development has two different types of user interfaces as shown in Figure 2. For various reasons we decided to adopt the well-known server-client architecture as the structure of our Hypermedia Information System. A high-level query language which includes the elementary similarity functions described in Section 4 is adopted.

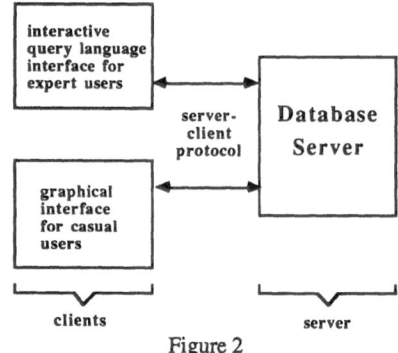

Figure 2

A still open research problem is the support of the evaluation of similarity based queries by the database server. A brute force approach would be the computation of all the similarity values by means of a highly parallel machine [18]. This approach causes an enormous overhead compared to inverted files. In contrast to the brute force approach, however, the inverted file approach is not feasable when the data are frequently updated. In what follows, we describe formally what we mean by an evaluation of a similarity based query. Let D be a domain and Φ be a set of features. For every object d ∈ D, there is a gauge function g_d: Φ → R, φ → $g_d(φ)$ which assigns every feature φ a weight $g_d(φ)$.

Furthermore, there is a similarity function

$$\text{sim}: D \times D \to R, (q,d) \to s(g_q, g_d)$$

where the function s determines the similarity sim(g,g') of two arbitrary gauge functions g: $\Phi \to R$ and g': $\Phi \to R$. The task to be supported by the database server is the following. Given an object $q \in D$ and a natural number k, find those k objects d_1, ..., $d_k \in D$ which have the highest similarity values sim(q,d_i) from among all objects in D.

In order to implement new access methods it is advantageous to rely on an extensible database kernel such as DASDBS [17] or StarBurst [7]. An extension of DASDBS is currently under development.

6 . A Specific Hypermedia Application

The test version of the hypermedia information system described above runs on a Sun workstation, employs X-Windows, and is mainly written in Modula-2 and C.

A test collection of medical data is being built up by scanning paper documents and digitizing slides. The actual information consists of formatted data, a great deal of unstructured texts, and associated images as can be seen in Figure 3. The conversion of paper into binary data is an expensive and time consuming process because parts of the scanned text data have to be completed and corrected manually. So far we included roughly 4 MByte of hypermedia information in our system which is only a small part of the 70,000 medical histories, 30,000 slides, 32,000 literature references, and 200 partially commented video tapes which form the medical data collection of the clinic with which we are cooperating.

Most of the referential links are created semiautomatically when the data are scanned into the system such as the links between associated paper forms and the pointers to x-rays and other images. However, some of the more useful semantic links have to be established by highly specialized personnel. Whether or not their efforts constitute enough added value to the information and can serve--at the same time--as increased indexing data is still being investigated.

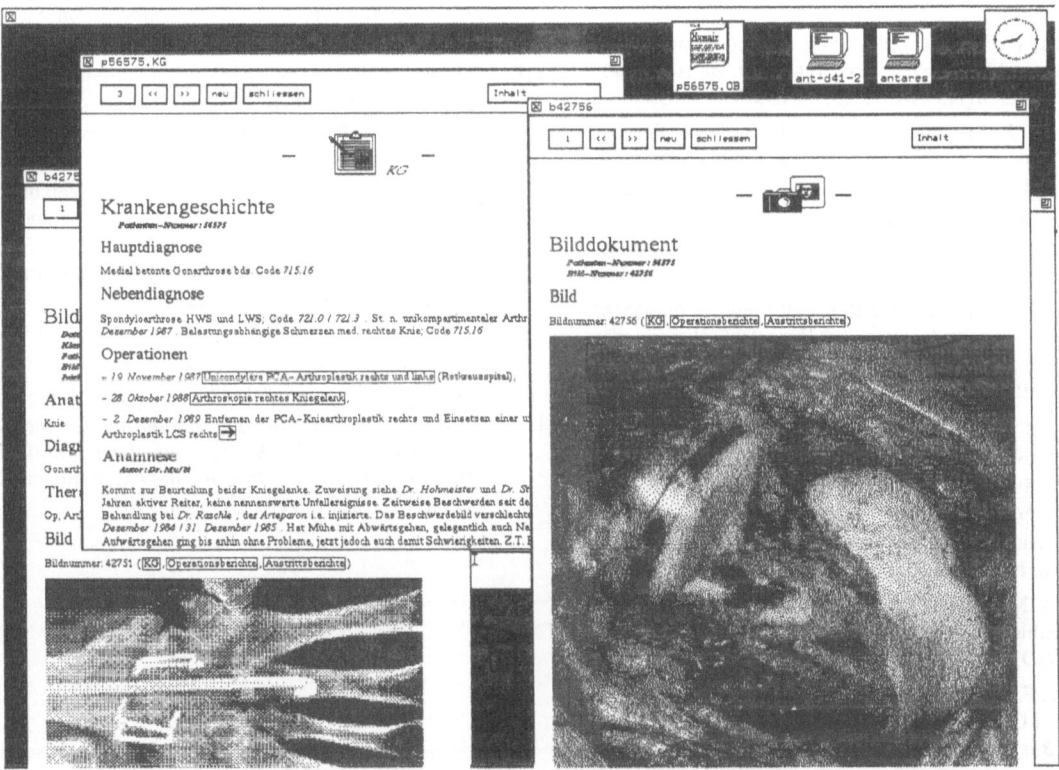

Figure 3

7. Conclusions

We described some design principles of a Hypermedia Information System that is intended primarily to support the storage of, retrieval of, and browsing in hypermedia data. Such data consist of a set of nodes and these nodes can be connected by so-called links.

One of the principle problems is to devise new methods for indexing a complex hypermedia web consisting of richly linked nodes. Related to this is the construction of retrieval algorithms that take into account both structured and unstructured information as well as the information conveyed by the links.

A user query typically consists of a mixture of precise and imprecise search criteria. Rather than treating these two parts separately, we chose a unified approach. A functional data base query language is extended by including a set of elementary similarity functions, thus adding information retrieval functionality. We showed how such a concept smoothly fits into a traditional query language. The concepts mentioned above are currently tested on real-world medical hypermedia data consisting of text, slides, x-rays, and videotapes.

References

[1]   Church, K.: A Stochastics Program and Noun Phrase Parser for Unrestricted Text. *Int. Conf. on Acoustics, Speech, and Signal Processing*, pp. 695-698, 1989.

[2]   Conklin, J.: Hypertext: An Introduction and Survey. *IEEE Computer 20*, No. 9, Sept. 1987, pp. 17-41.

[3]   Fagan, J.L.: *Experiments in automatic phrase indexing for document retrieval: A comparison of syntactic and non-syntactic methods*. PhD thesis, Department of Computer Science, Cornell University, TR 87-868, Sept. 1987.

[4]   Frei, H.P., Stieger, D.: The Retrieval View, a Component of the Document Architecture. *Hypertext/ Hypermedia '91*, Informatik-Fachberichte 276, Springer-Verlag, Berlin, 1991, pp. 99-108.

[5]   Fuhr, N.: A Probabilistic Framework for Vague Queries and Imprecise Information in Databases. *Proc. 16th Int. Conf. on VLDB*, Morgan Kaufmann Publishers, Palo Alto, CA, 1990, pp. 696-707.

[6]   Goodman, D.: *The Complete Hypercard Handbook*. Bantam, New York, 1987.

[7]   Haas, L.M, Freytag, J.C., Lohman, G.M., Pirahesh, H.: Extensible query processing in Starburst. *Proc. ACM SIGMOD*, Portland, OR, May 1989, pp. 377-388.

[8]   Halasz, F.G.: Reflections on NoteCards: Seven Issues for the next Generation of Hypermedia Systems. *Commun. ACM 31*, No. 7, July 1988, pp. 836-852.

[9]   Kienitz-Vollmer, B., Reichardt, J.: Bestimmung von Mehrwortgruppen mithilfe des Begrenzerverfahrens. Lustig, G. (ed.): *Automatische Indexierung zwischen Forschung und Anwendung*, Olm. Hildesheim, 1986, pp. 18-30.

[10] Mauldin, M.L.: *Information Retrieval by Text Skimming*. PhD thesis, Department of Computer Science, Carnegie Mellon University, 1989.

[11] Motro, A.: VAGUE: A User Interface to Relational Databases that Permits Vague Queries. *ACM TOIS 6*, No. 3, 1988, pp. 187-214.

[12] Raymond, D.R., Tompa, F.W.: Hypertext and the Oxford English Dictionary. *Commun. ACM 31*, No. 7, July 1988, pp. 871-879.

[13] Saxton, L.V., Raghavan, V.V.: Design of an Integrated Information Retrieval/Database Management System. *IEEE Transactions on Knowledge and Data Engineering 2*, No. 2, 1990, pp. 210-219.

[14] Schäuble, P., Wüthrich, B.: *On the Expressive Power of Query Languages*. Technical Report, ETH Zurich, Department of Computer Science, 1991.

[15] Schäuble, P., Glavitsch, U.: A Probabilistic Hypermedia Retrieval Model Based on Hidden Markov Models. *Proc. Workshop Intelligent Access to Information Systems*, Darmstadt, Nov. 1990.

[16] Schäuble, P.: *On the Compatibility of Retrieval Functions, Preference Relations, and Document Descriptions*. Technical Report No. 113, ETH Zurich, Department of Computer Science, 1989.

[17] Schek, H.-J., Paul, H.-B., Scholl, M.H., Weikum, G.: The DASDBS Project: Objectives, Experiences, and Future Prospects. *IEEE Transactions on Knowledge and Data Engineering 2*, No. 2, Special Issue on Prototype Systems, March 1990, pp. 25-43.

[18] Stanfill, C., Kahle, B.: Parallel Free-Text Search on the Connection Machine System. *Commun. ACM 29*, No. 12, Dec. 1986, pp. 1229-1239.

[19] Teufel, B.: *Informationsspuren zum numerischen und graphischen Vergleich von reduzierten natürlichsprachlichen Texten*. Informatik-Dissertationen ETH Zürich, No. 13, vdf Verlag, Zürich, 1989.

Querying in a Large Hyperbase

Michael Fuller   Alan Kent   Ron Sacks-Davis

James Thom   Ross Wilkinson   Justin Zobel

Department of Computer Science

Royal Melbourne Institute of Technology

GPO Box 2476V

Melbourne, VIC 3001

Australia

Abstract.

This paper proposes a query language and data organisation for large hyperbase systems. The language allows queries to involve the links as well as the text. The architecture allows the data to be efficiently indexed, as well as supporting multiple users.

Keywords: hypertext, information retrieval, query language.

1   Introduction

In hypertext, the order in which data is examined is determined by the user, rather than an author. The user controls the sequence of presentation of information by selectively following links to those parts of the body of information which are of interest.

This approach is rewarding when the database is small or has a very well understood structure such as that of an encyclopedia. However it is difficult to expect that in a larger, less-well structured database that an arbitrary node on a given topic can be found by browsing alone. For this reason, we investigate the use of querying in conjunction with browsing in a large hypertext database system, or *hyperbase* system.

In the next section we discuss the types of queries that might be desired. Following that, we introduce a formal node query language. In Section 4 we discuss how this language can be used and show how some sample queries may be formulated in this language. Next we discuss the architecture of the hyperbase in the light of the ramifications of this approach to querying. Finally, we describe a prototypical system that we have developed and offer some tentative conclusions.

2   Queries in Information Retrieval and Hypertext Systems

Querying has a long history in information retrieval and many forms of queries have been considered. The two most common types of queries are the Boolean query, such as "information AND retrieval", and weighted vectors, which indicate not only that a term is present in the query but also give its significance to that query. Boolean queries are used in most commercial information retrieval systems currently available. Weighted vectors are used in both the *vector space* method and the *probabilistic* method. See [6] for descriptions of these methods. Thus standard information retrieval systems allow the user to examine very large numbers of documents, and roughly determine their relevance to a given query.

In hypertext systems there is a wealth of further information available. The links present in a hypertext system reflect the conceptual and logical relationships which exist between separate nodes. Further, when a user makes a query which is dependent upon the current node, there is a great deal of internal context available which would normally be totally inaccessible in a standard query based system, and which could be used to dramatically improve the natural language understanding of the meaning of a query.

Hence, given the presence of links in a hypertext database, it would be useful to extend queries to take advantage of this rich source of contextual and conceptual information. Specifically, the domain and range of queries can be either constrained or extended by taking into consideration the presence and nature of links. An approach that incorporates hypertext links into a probabilistic model of information retrieval is provided in [1].

Another factor that distinguishes querying in a hypertext database from a standard text database is that most text databases consist of a large number of relatively small items. In some instances, the description of small items as "documents" may be appropriate, such as in the case of a large collection of essentially unrelated abstracts. Often this will be a purely arbitrary division of information, such as in the case where a text has been segmented into paragraphs or pages for convenience, or storage considerations. However sometimes a complex logical structure will exist. Hypertext systems can represent this structure very simply. Again, it would be clearly useful to allow the incorporation of this structural information in the construction of queries.

An alternative to information retrieval queries is to browse via hypertext links. This allows the structural information to be explicitly used, and takes into account contextual information. However, the problems of scale are considerable. Given a collection with 100,000 nodes, the ability to reach a given node from another via browsing is limited.

We want the best of both worlds: the ability both to browse and to query in context seamlessly. Thus we provide a sample set of queries which refer to both structure and context. We want to provide answers to these queries that use both the structure and context, as well as the text of the query.

- "I want all documents on robotic vision systems."

- "I want more information like this."

- "Show me a document about vision that is related to one that I have already looked at."

- "Show me a document about vision that is not related to one that I have already looked at."

- "Show me the node that I looked at before on robots."

Note that in a hyperbase system there also must be the usual ability to follow a link.

This set of queries assumes that the database is a set of documents, each of which is broken up into a set of nodes, with links of various types between these nodes. Note that two key terms have been used, namely "document" and "node". Also, the queries contain implicit references to links. Given this structure, queries requesting a document should either take the user to the start of the document or to a "header" node that might contain the title, an abstract and links to the text of the document.

Various techniques have been developed to address some of these issues. One technique developed for querying is described in [2]. All nodes are ranked against a given query. Weights are then modified by the weights of surrounding nodes. Another technique augments browsing using relational queries [4]. Using this technique, the structure of the hyperbase is stored in a relational database, which may be queried using SQL. It does not allow queries on the text in the nodes. Alternatively [7], it is suggested that user nodes and links be created temporarily for each query as part of a transient hypergraph.

3   A Node Query Language

Each of the above natural language queries, as well as "follow the link" queries, may be translated by a hyperbase system into queries in the following formal language. We first give definitions of nodes and links.

A **Node** is an object which has

- a (unique) Node Identifier,

- a Node Kind,

- Data,

- a list of Link References.

A **Link** is an object which has:

- a (unique) Link Identifier,

- a Node Reference A,

- a Node Reference B,

- a Link Kind for A→B

- a Link Kind for B→A

A 'Node Reference' is a Node Identifier.

A 'Link Reference' consists of:

- a Link Identifier,

- within-Node display information.

A 'Node' represents a conceptually-complete piece of data which is displayable in its entirety.

A 'Link' connects two nodes. It is traversable in either direction and each time a link is referred to, we are concerned with the kind associated with the chosen direction.

Now we introduce the types necessary for describing functions in our node query language:

- **node_list**
  (a list of nodes)

- **link_list**
  (a list of links)

Additionally, the following constants are used:

- **this_node**
  (The currently active node)

- **this_link**
  (Similarly, the particular link in which our user is interested)

- **specified_node_id**
  (A particular node, as specified at some higher level)

- **this_data**
  (The data associated with this_node)

- **history_list**
  (A list of previously visited nodes)

- **all_nodes**
  (All nodes in the database)

The functions are:

- **node_kind(node_list, kind) → node_list**
  (from node_list, extract nodes of a particular kind)

- **link_kind(link_list, kind) → link_list**
  (from link_list, extract links of a particular kind)

- **links_from(node_list) → link_list**
  (from node_list, extract links)

- **destination(link_list) → node_list**
  (determine destinations for these links)

- **rank(node_list, condition) → node_list**
  (rank a node_list against the specified condition)

- **match(node_list, condition) → node_list**
  (select nodes which 'match' the condition)

- **top(N, node_list) → node_list**
  (select the first N nodes on a list)

- **union(node_list, node_list) → node_list**
  (return the union of first list and second list)

- **intersect(node_list, node_list) → node_list**
  (return the intersection of first list and second list)

- **subtract(node_list, node_list) → node_list**
  (return the elements of first list that are not in the second)

4 Using the Query Language

Upon making a query in this language, the database is consulted and nodes satisfying this query are identified as answers. If there is a single answer node, this node is displayed. If there are many answer nodes, a new "query" node is created with links to each of the answer nodes. The query node stores the query and titles of the answer nodes. (This is similar to the approach described in [2].) This node is displayed. The node is associated with the user and may be discarded at the end of the session or maintained in a user database.

The functions described in the previous section have been selected to provide a basic class that we believe has the expressive power needed to both browse and query seamlessly. In practice a larger group of basic functions may be desirable. Due to the functional nature of the language, it is easy to define new functions. For instance if the nodes are arranged such that every sub-node of a document is linked to a document head node via a link of kind DOC_HEAD, we may define a function that obtains the document head nodes from a list of arbitrary nodes.

document(node_list) = destination(link_kind(links_from(node_list), DOC_HEAD))

Another simple example is to find related documents to the current node. We may define:

related_docs(node_list) = document(destination(link_kind(links_from(node_list), RELATED)))

We give no formal method of introducing recursion at this stage, however we recognise that such a facility would be useful.

Given the formal query language described in the previous section, we can now formulate the earlier queries as follows:

- "I want all documents on robotic vision systems."

  match(document(all_nodes), *robotic | vision | system*))

- "I want more information like this."

  top(10, subtract(rank(match(all_nodes, this_data), this_data), historylist))

- "Show me a document about vision that is related to one that I have already looked at."

  top(1, document(match(related_docs(historylist), *vision*)))

- "Show me a document about vision that is not related to one that I have already looked at."

  subtract(document(match(all_nodes, *vision*)), related_docs(historylist))

- "Show me the node that I looked at before on robots."

  top(1, match(historylist, *robot*))

As well, we can simply browse:

- Follow a link.

  destination(this_link)

The result of each of these queries would either be the creation of a query node in the event of there being many answer nodes, for example the first query, or would return and present the single answer node, for example the last query, and the browsing command.

5 The Database Architecture

Since the focus of this paper is to describe querying in a hyperbase, only an outline of the database architecture is provided here. A detailed description of a hyperbase system architecture can be found in [3].

In order to allow browsing and querying in a large scale hyperbase, we have developed an architecture to support these activities efficiently. Also, large systems are usually used by many people so multiple users must be supported as well. Each user must have the ability to annotate the material viewed, and as we have seen user queries result in user nodes and links being developed.

As a result, we have developed a database architecture that is composed of a main node database, a main link database, and user node databases and user link databases. The user databases contain any user defined nodes and links. The main databases are extensively indexed and are only updated in batch mode, whereas the user databases are interactively updated and only rudimentary indexing is maintained. The main node database must index on the text of each node, the kind of each node, and the node identifiers. The main link database must index on the identifiers, the link kinds and the node references.

We split the information into main and user databases for a variety of reasons. The extent of the indexing varies considerably. The main database is extensively indexed to optimize querying. This leads to batch updates. In contrast, the user databases are indexed less extensively with the aim of supporting rapid updates. This is done both to allow users to annotate, and also because each query may result in the addition of new information to the user databases. A reason for having separate databases for each user is that each user has a consistent view of the databases. As well, the integrity of the main database

458

is maintained whilst preserving the interactive nature of a hypertext system.

A key reason for separating the main databases and the user databases is the effect of querying. A query is matched against the main node database and the main link database and a set of nodes are identified. A user node is created and added to the user node database. A set of user links between the user node and the "answer" nodes is created and added to the user link table. Then, by default, the user node is displayed. When one of the answer nodes is requested, this will be done by selecting a link. This link is selected, and a node from the main node database is displayed.

6   A Sample System

To demonstrate the possibilities and flexibility inherent in the approach discussed, a simple hyperbase system has been developed which supports user driven browsing and user generated querying. This system provided both browsing and querying. Two hyperbases have been tested using this system: entries from the Unix manual, and the Bible. We shall discuss the latter as it is larger.

The text was broken up into books and chapters, reflecting the normal way of presenting and viewing the Bible. Each chapter in each book in the Bible was represented as a node in the hyperbase. These nodes fell hierarchically below nodes representing the various books which comprise the Bible. Links reflecting the logical structure of the Bible were made between the nodes representing chapters and the aggregate node representing the book of which that chapter was part. Similarly, links were placed between each book node and an aggregate node which served as a 'contents' page. To reflect the linear nature of the text of individual books, links were made between each chapter node and its (textually) preceding and subsequent chapter nodes, allowing the text to examined as a body. When the text was converted, 1,256 nodes and 40,946 links were created.

In accordance with the stated aims of supporting both efficient browsing and efficient querying, two types of indexes were used on the data. A linear hash index was employed to index the individual nodes and links, and a super-imposed coding signature file was created to index the text data within each node.

The main databases use superimposed coding to index the stopped and stemmed text of each node. Linear hashing is used for the identifiers of each node and link, and the source and destination node identifiers stored in each link. All node and link kinds are also indexed using superimposed coding. The databases are organised using a multi-level signature file organisation [5].

7   Conclusions

Very large hypertext systems need to augment browsing with querying strategies such as those developed in the information retrieval area. We have described a formal language for performing this task which

encapsulates the expressive power that we believe the language requires. A sample system has been described, verifying that this methodology is viable.

The approach described necessitates the introduction of user nodes and links. Since such entities are usually part of the "active" notion of a document database encouraged by hypertext, we feel this necessity is acceptable.

We have not dealt with many key issues involved with large hyperbase systems, such as the automatic generation of links and the provision of guides indicating the current location in the hyperbase. However, we have tried to ensure that our language and design allows flexibility in approaching these and other issues in the area of large hyperbases.

Acknowledgments. This research was supported by an AIRS grant from the Australian Commonwealth Department of Industry, Technology and Commerce, by a grant from the Australian Research Council, and by the Key Centre for Knowledge Based Systems.

References

[1] W. B. Croft, H. Turtle, *A Retrieval Model for Incorporating Hypertext Links.* Proceedings of Hypertext '89, 1989, pp. 213-224

[2] M. E. Frisse, *Searching for Information in a Hypertext Medical Book.* Proceedings of Hypertext '87, 1987, pp. 57-66

[3] J. Zobel, R. Wilkinson, J. Thom, R. Sacks-Davis, A. Kent, M. Fuller, *An Architecture for a Hyperbase System.* RMIT Computer Science Technical Report 42, 1991

[4] L. Gallagher, R. Furuta, P. D. Stotts, *Increasing the Power of Hypertext Search with Relational Queries.* Hypermedia, Vol. 2, No. 1, 1990, pp. 1-14

[5] A. J. Kent, R. Sacks-Davis, K. Ramamohanarao, *A Signature File Scheme Based on Multiple Organisations for Indexing Very Large Databases.* Journal of American Society for Information Science, Vol. 41, No. 7, 1990, pp. 508-534

[6] G. Salton, *Automatic Text Processing.* Addison-Wesley, Reading, Massachusetts, 1989

[7] M. A. Shepherd, C. R. Watters, Yao Cai, *Transient Hypergraphs for Citation Networks.* Information Processing and Management, Vol. 26, No. 3, 1990, pp. 395-412

InterSect: A General Purpose Hypertext System
Based on an Object Oriented Database

B. Wang   P.Hitchcock

Computer Science Department, University of York

Heslington, York, Y01 5DD, United Kingdom

wang@uk.ac.minster.york ph@uk.ac.minster.york

ABSTRACT

Most complicated documentation maintenance environments require sophisticated computer support systems for maintaining relationships between document types and document instances. Unfortunately, existing approaches are not sufficient to achieve this aim. Hypertext technology gives us the possibility to easily browse document contents but it lacks a mechanism for declaring the overall structure of the document and its relationships. Database management systems can model complex real world situations, but do not have *"the single coherent interface to the database which is the hallmark of hypertext"*[1]. In this paper, we propose a general hypertext-based documentation support system, *InterSect*, which uses an object oriented database as an information repository to support both the definition and manipulation of complex document structures. This prototype provides both hypertext and database views of documents, together with a versioning mechanism driven by a user defined schema for the overall document structure.

1   Introduction

Hypertext has become a popular approach for many computer applications. The main reason is that hypertext systems can help people to access related information more effectively. The fundamental basis of hypertext is not complicated: it organizes information into discrete *nodes* and each node can be joined by different types of *links*. However, current hypertext systems have several well-recognized problems[2], especially user *disorientation* in a hypertext network and the *cognitive overhead* for creating, managing and choosing links[1]. Much research has been devoted to solve these problems but only a small part of this has been concerned with using database technology. DBMSs have powerful abilities for managing structural data[3].

Object oriented database is currently an active research area. This is because object oriented concepts can more easily model the real world and capture its semantics than more traditional DBMSs. Besides this, the object oriented data model allows us to reuse components by producing enhancements based on the original. From the data processing point of view, object oriented databases can store many kinds of data, for example, text and graphics. Reference [4] gave a comprehensive review of using object oriented database to deal with multimedia applications.

Our approach uses object oriented ideas in order to build a general purpose hypertext system which can:

- Browse and search any kind of document type.

- Browse any instance of a document type and jump easily from one instance to another which may or may not have the same type.

- Provide a high level description of the document structure and complex relationships between its parts.

- Recover from any mistake made either by a user or by the system.

- Check consistency among document instances.

- Create any version of a document instance.

- Be application independent.

- Share data among a group of users

For this purpose we have built a 'prototype system, called *InterSect*, to meet the above requirements.

2   The Current Hypertext Data Model

In current hypertext systems, information is stored in discrete nodes and nodes are connected by links. The function of these links is to relate nodes into a meaningful whole. This kind of organization of discrete information is normally called the semantic network of a hyper document. However, in practice, most hypertext systems allow some nodes to play the role of high level nodes, such as the *browsers* and *fileboxes* in Node-Card. These high level nodes can be viewed as a image of the structure of the whole, or as some connected nodes, or simply as a container for a set of nodes. For example, in the NodeCard system, a *browser* is a node that contains a structural diagram of a network of corresponding information nodes. A filebox is also a special node which is used as a container in which to organize the collection of information nodes or other fileboxes. Most hypertext systems, such as HyperCard, HyperTIES and Intermedia, provide such abstraction mechanisms[5, 6, 7]. The following diagram shows the general hypertext data model of current hypertext systems:

460

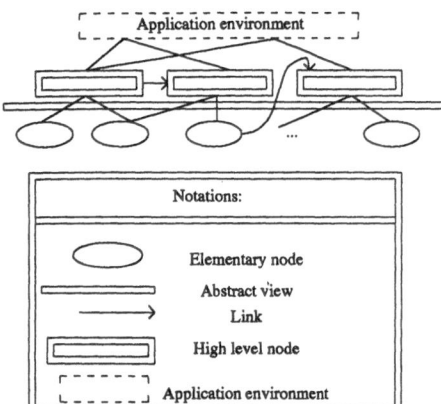

```
Notations:

⬭              Elementary node

▭              Abstract view

──────▶        Link

▱              High level node

┌ ─ ─ ─ ┐
└ ─ ─ ─ ┘      Application environment
```

Figure 1. The general hypertext data model

From this model, we can find several problems in current hypertext systems.

- *No semantics can be captured from this data model*

At the hypertext level we only know that there are one or more links between nodes. It is difficult to generalize this into a relationship which holds between all nodes of a similar type.

- *The high level node does not correctly model the hierarchical relation between nodes*

The high level nodes are only treated as containers for copies of the elementary nodes. Changes made to the high level node cannot be automatically reflected in the original elementary nodes in case these nodes are themselves linked elsewhere.

- *No schema definition for nodes and links*

Current hypertext systems have no schema definition mechanism like that of database systems. Modelling a hyper document is more or less a bottom-up approach. This implies that we should concentrate on how a document can be decomposed into different parts and then reorganize these individual parts by adding links between them. The key question here is that such analysis is **only** suitable and useful for that particular instance of a document, we cannot use the same structure for another document instance. In addition, when hypertext systems are used to model a large documentation environment such as the documentation of a software system, it is usually very hard to divide materials into separate nodes and to make links between them. If this is done, it will add an extra and unnecessary level of complexity[8].

- *No type definitions for node and link*

A node in the hypertext systems is a storage unit for storing a collection of data items. We cannot find out detailed information about its structure. Every node is treated as the same type. The same applies to links. The role of a link allows different kinds of nodes to be connected physically with each other. It cannot prevent meaningless links being made. For example, if an article is talking about how people teach animals and we make a link between people and animals, we don't know what this link means. If it represents the meaning that animals teach people, it is wrong.

Because of this lack of structure hypertext systems exhibit two well-known problems. These are *Cognitive Overhead* and *Disorientation*.

The cognitive overhead arises because links cannot reveal the semantic meanings between nodes. In authoring mode, mental effort is required to make such decisions as *how many elementary nodes are needed for maintaining a hyper document? How many links are required to connect created nodes?* and so on. In reading mode, mental effort is also needed for the decision of *how to travel the hyper space through the pre-defined link structure?*

As a result of the cognitive overhead, it is quite possible that users will be easily "lost in the hyperspace". This can arise from the confusion caused if the reader places a different interpretation on the hyper document structure than the author intended.

3 Extended Hypertext Data Model

We consider that the keys to solving these problems are that a powerful data model should be developed and that a suitable tool should be demonstrated to support such model.

The *InterSect_DM* is the data model of our prototype system *InterSect*. As we described above, the main reason for the problems of hypertext systems is that the data model of current hypertext systems is too simple. We have chosen an object oriented database as an information repository for our approach because of its superior capabilities for modelling semantics which are described by defining the appropriate database schema. For the *InterSect_DM*, we have the following aims in mind:

- The model will provide us with a high level description for any complex document-based application environment.

- The model will describe the hypertext style links between any instances as well as the relationship types between object types.

The model will have the following functions:

(1) Semantic representation can be supported.

(2) Node type and link type instead of individual nodes and links are used to represent the structure of a hyper document.

(3) A structured node type can be defined.

(4) Versions of nodes and links are supported.

(5) Arbitrary relationships can be represented between node types.

These functions are all based on object oriented concepts. *InterSect_DM* is an extension to the current hypertext data model which has added structured node type definition, version type definition, link type definition and other mechanisms which are necessary to meet the needs of the new generation hypertext system mentioned by[2].

3.1 Node type

A node type is an abstract data type which describes the structure of a component of a document. A document may have many different types of component. An individual instance of a node belongs to the corresponding node type. In *InterSect_DM*, nodes are the basic building blocks. Each node has a clear semantic meaning which the designer wants to express. The node type definition defined in *InterSect_DM* is different from the current hypertext approach in two ways: first, nodes can have attributes defined on them, these attributes can be viewed as *"filters"* for selecting all nodes with a particular property. Second, nodes may also have a special *"contents"* attribute whose value is of a multimedia data type. In *InterSect_DM* nodes act as hypertext nodes. If a node does not have a *"contents"* attribute, we regards this kind of node as a *"control"* node. The functions of a control node are: firstly to act as a semantic linkage between two node types. (the **impl** in *Module* example[9] plays a role of linking **module** and **bodies**) and secondly to provide existence constraints. This means that its existence may determine the existence of other nodes in order to maintain referential integrity. All node types are classified as either *primitive* node types or *structured* node types. Each type also has two variants: without contents (*controlled type*) and with contents. Each node belongs to exactly one node type. We use a software requirements document as a simple example of a structured node type. In a software documentation environment, a requirements document can be viewed as a composite document which consist of a functional requirement part (Fun_req), nonfunctional requirement part (NonFun_req) and so on. Using the definition of node type defined in *InterSect_DM*, the following diagram illustrates how this structure can be easily modeled.

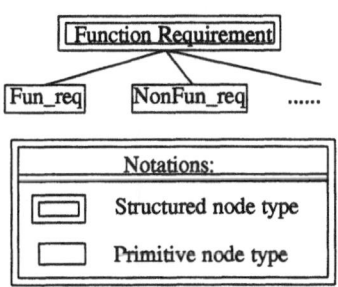

Figure 2. Example of a structured node type

In section 4, we illustrate in detail how *InterSect* deals with this kind of node type structure by using the example *Module* taken from[9].

3.2 Link type

In *InterSect_DM*, a link is defined as a structured object type in a object oriented way. At the moment, we only define two kinds of link types *annotation links* and *referential links* which are both subtypes of the super type *Links*. We can define more link types according to our needs in the future.

Annotation link

In *InterSect_DM*, the function of an annotation link is that it allows users to make annotations at any place within the contents of a node. We allow annotations to have versions. This mechanism means that users can make several annotations to the same piece of data within the contents of a node.

Referential link

A referential link allows any piece of data within the contents of a node to have a link with the contents of any other node, whether or not of the same type. Referential links have versions which imply that the same piece of data can link to several different node instances.

3.3 Attributes

Attributes can be viewed as *"filters"* for nodes. They can be attached to node types, link types and version types and can provide specific information about that particular node, link or version object.

3.4 Version type

A version is an object type. All node types can have corresponding versions, as do link types. Versions, or more precisely, version nodes or version links, must belong to their corresponding generic objects, the objects of which they are versions. However, as objects in their own right, a version can have its own attributes and contents if needed. In *InterSect*, version objects are treated in the same way as generic objects. There are also two kinds of version object types: *Version node without contents* and *Version node with contents*.

3.5 Relationship type

A relationship type defines the semantic relationships between node types. However, the *inclusion* relationship between the sub-node and its super-node is implicitly defined by the structured node type itself.

3.6 Application schema definition

The application schema definition is a logical framework of the application environment. It consists of all the definitions of node types, link types, version types and relation types.

4 Demonstration of *InterSect*

In this section we demonstrate a prototype tool called *InterSect*. *InterSect* is implemented in C++ on a Sun 3/50. We have successfully used it to produce a software documentation environment. In the rest of the paper, we will show how *InterSect* is used for inserting and browsing objects although we have also implemented a change operation. The particular example is taken from[9]. The document itself has a structure given by the schema. In addition to any hypertext link that may be created, there is a predefined relationship between the *specification* part of one document and the *implementation part* of another.

462

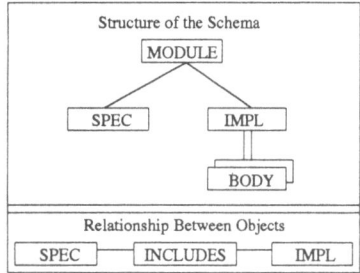

Figure 3. The module high level structure*

4.1 Editing the application schema

There are two ways to edit the application schema: *Edit Schema?* and *Input Schema?*. In *Edit Schema?* mode, an editor is called to edit the application schema. In *Input Schema?* mode, a file is named which contains the schema definition. Schema are defined in terms of the underlying database system. This is the object oriented DBMS called DAMOKLES.

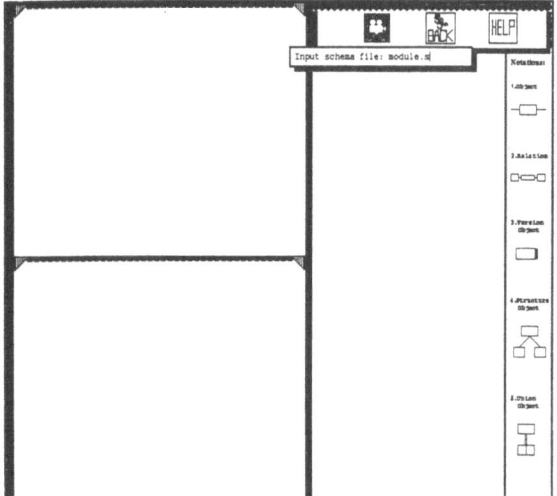

Figure 4. Input application schema

4.2 Displaying the structure of the defined schema

If the input schema is correct, *InterSect* displays its structure using the notations given down the right hand side of the screen.

4.3 Inserting the contents into the defined node type

There are two modes to insert an instance of a node type: *Insert General* and *Insert Version*. In the *Insert General* mode, there are two options: *Based or not based on the object*. If it is based on an object then this object is used as the basis for producing a new object by using the editor, otherwise the editor works on an empty object. *Insert Version* mode is similar, i.e *based or not based on the corresponding version*. If it is based on the version, *InterSect* will ask you to input the version number. If the

---

*A *MODULE* is a complex object type which has subtypes of *SPEC* (Specification) and *IMPL* (Implementation). The implementation is a union of *BODY* and *BODY.VERSION*. *BODY* is a version type definition. Subtypes are related by the *INCLUDE* relationship.

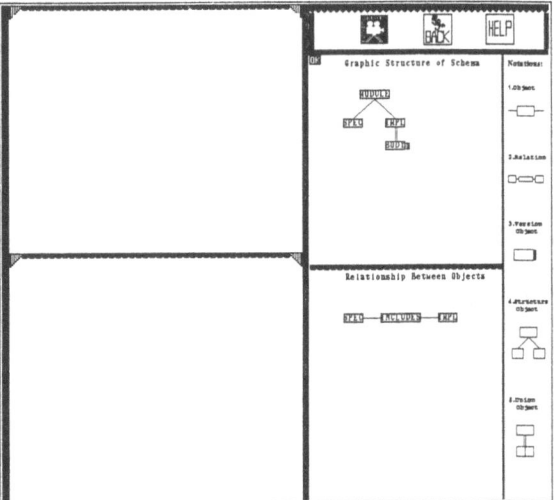

Figure 5. Structure of the defined node type**

defined node type is not a version type, *InterSect* will display a warning message. In any case, if the inserting, browsing or changing object does not match its type definition, or does not exist, *InterSect* will also give warnings. Figure 6 and figure 7 show the situation when a based object is inserted into *InterSect*.

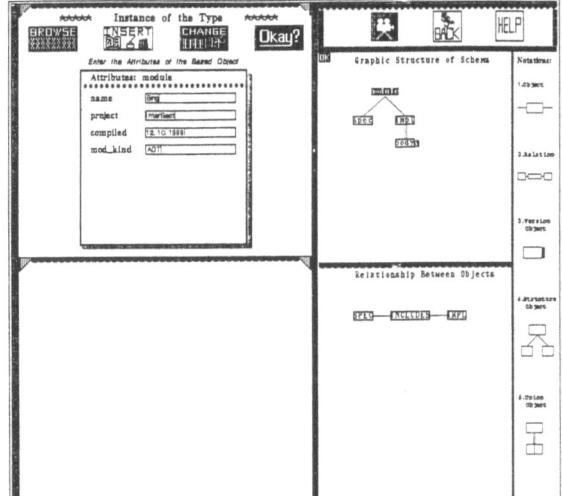

Figure 6. Entering the attributes of a based object

4.4 Constructing hypertext links in the contents of a node

Links can only be made during the process of inserting or changing an object. *InterSect* allows users to make two different kinds of links: *Annotation links* and *referential links*. In both cases, *InterSect* will ask you whether you want to make the version links or ordinary links.

**If the definition of the editing schema is not correct or the   file containing the schema does not exist, *InterSect* will give the following warning message:

Objects are not installed!

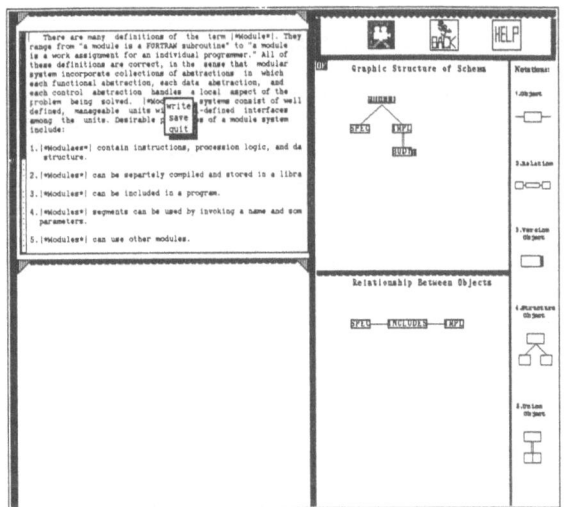

Figure 7. Entering the contents of a based object***

4.4.1 Annotation link

When making an annotation link, whether it is a version annotation link or a ordinary annotation link, *InterSect* will call an editor to edit the annotation. In figure 8, the screen of the annotation is chosen and highlighted in the top left quarter of the screen and the editor invoked in the bottom left to receive the annotation notes.

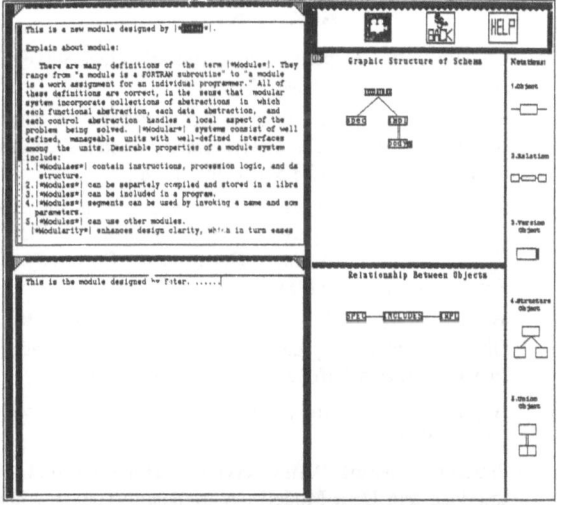

Figure 8. Entering an annotation link

***The *write* operation is used to store the final result but not to inherit the link structure defined on the based object. The *save* operation not only stores the contents but also inherits the link structure of the based object, i.e. the new object has the same link structure as its original based object but the contents are different.

4.4.2 Referential link

To make a referential link, the source of the link is highlighted in the top left of the screen. The user is prompted to select a versioned or non-versioned link and also for the type of the target instance. If this is correct then input moves to the bottom left of the screen where the attribute types of that node type are displayed. Values of these attributes are entered and used to identify the particular target of the referential link.

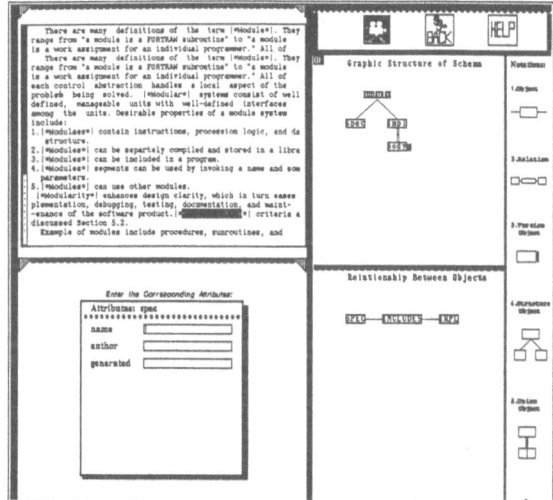

Figure 9 Editing a referential link

4.5 Browsing in *InterSect*

InterSect allows users to browse node types and instances.

4.5.1 Browsing types

InterSect provides four operations for browsing node types. These are, *What is this, What is type, Source* and *Execution*. They separately tell the browser what the defined node type means. The appropriate node type is selected from the schema display. Figure 10 show the *Source* of the node type *module*. Figure 11 shows *What is type* of *module*.

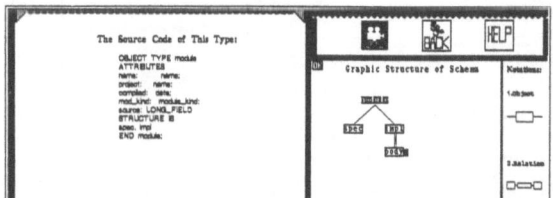

Figure 10. Source of the type *module*

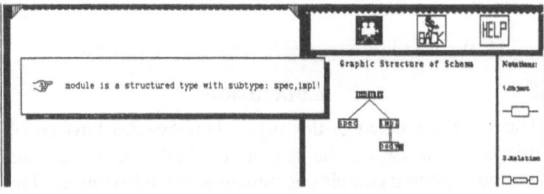

Figure 11. The type of the *module*

464

4.5.2 Browsing instance

Browsing instances is much like inserting instances as described above, there are four steps, first, identifying the kinds of object to be browsed, versioned or original; second, entering the corresponding attribute values into *InterSect*; third, the found object will be displayed on the screen; and finally, browsing the contents through the hypertext links, these are identified by surrounding the source text by a rectangle. If a hypertext link is selected, it is highlighted and the type required (*Annotation Link* or *Referential Link*) is displayed as a menu, as in figure 12.

Figure 12. The found object of type *module*

The appropriate target is produced in the bottom left of the screen as demonstrated by figure 13.

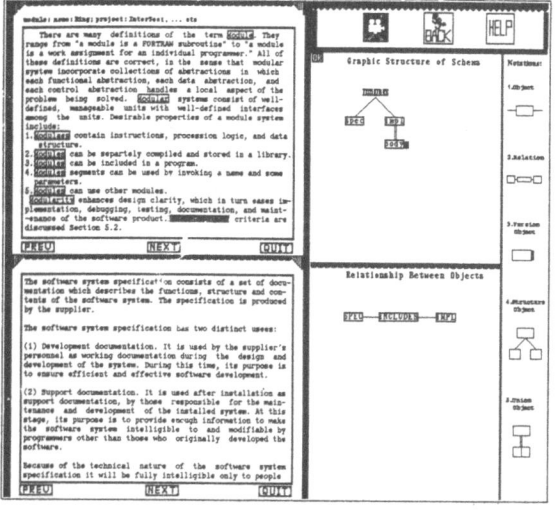

Figure 13. Referential link from the chosen part

5 Conclusion

The work presented in this paper demonstrates how an object oriented database can be used as the basis for an information base to support a complex documentation environment. Our first experiment with *InterSect* shows that the extended hypertext data model can support both the modelling of the application

and the hypertext structure of instances. We benefit from the mechanisms of the object oriented datanbase management system, especially the version mechanism and complex entity type definition mechanism. We are following this experimental approach because we would like to find out **practically** how object oriented database can support hypertext systems and how such a combination can be used as a solution to solve some of the problems of the next generation hypermedia systems proposed by Halasz[2].

InterSect is still a prototype system. Some mechanisms are not finished yet. For example, browsing a relationship type from the schema diagram. During the first stage of the implementation of *InterSect* , we have concentrated on *how object oriented database can support hypertext in a complicated documentation environment*. If it is successful, we will than consider how to build a graphic interface for the corresponding database function. However, the implementation will not be very difficult. When a relationship type is browsed, the corresponding database system calls will be invoked to check what objects are related with each other. Such information will be displayed on the screen for the user to browse. We would also like to define *InterSect_DM* using a formal notation.

Acknowledgments

This work has been carried out through the support of the **British Admiralty Research Establishment**. We are grateful for the useful suggestions from Dr. Martin Atkins in the first stage of the implementation of *InterSect*. Special thanks to Dr. Alan Brown for naming the prototype system.

References

1. Conklin, Jeff, "Hypertext: an Introduction and Survey", *IEEE Computer*, pp. 17-40 (Sept. 1987).

2. Halasz, F. G, "Reflections on Notecards: Seven Issues for the Next Generation of Hypermedia Systems", *Communications of the ACM* **31**(7) (July 1988).

3. Garg, Pankaj K, "Information Management in Software Engineering: A Hypertext Based Approach", *D.Phil thesis, Computer Science Department, University of Southern California* (1989).

4. Woelk, Darrell, Kim, Won and Luther, Willis, "An Object-Oriented Approach to Multimedia Database", *Proceedings of SIFMOD'86* (May 28-30, 1986).

5. Apple Computer, Inc., *Macintosh HyperCard User's Guide*, 1989.

6. Plaisant, Catherine, "An Overview of Hyperties, Its User Interface and Data Model", *Hypermedia/Hypertext and Object Oriented Database*, pp. 52-59 (Dec 1989).

7. Smith, K. E and Zdonik, S. B, "Intermedia: A Case Study of the Differences Between Relational and Object-Oriented Database Systems", *OOPSLA'87 Proceedings*, pp. 542-465 (Oct. 4-8, 1987).

8. Brown, P. J, "Hypertext: Dream and Reality", *Hypermedia/Hypertext and Object Oriented Database*, pp. 60-71 (Dec 1989).

9. *Damokles 2.0 - Reference Manual*, FZI, University of Karlsruhe (1988).

Knowledge Base Support for Hypermedia Co-Authoring

Stefan Eherer*

University of Passau
Innstr. 33, 8390 Passau, Germany
email: eherer@andorfer.fmi.uni-passau.de

Matthias Jarke

Informatik V, RWTH Aachen
Ahornstr. 55, 5100 Aachen, Germany
email: jarke@picasso.informatik.rwth-aachen.de

One of the many possible relationships between hypertext and knowledge representation is given by the utilization of process knowledge in the hypermedia authoring and document maintenance activity. The CoAUTHOR system has explored this relationship and demonstrates that process knowledge also provides additional access paths to a large hypermedia database, both from the viewpoint of content (idea processing) and from the viewpoint of static and dynamic document structure.

1 Introduction

Hypertext systems can be characterized by the interactions they provide. Systems like Document Examiner [26] and Hyperties [19] are intended to present hypertexts developed by a small group of experts, whereas the user shall only read them. On the other hand, systems like Augment [7], Guide [10], Intermedia [9], KMS [1], Neptune [4], NoteCards [12], and WE [20] provide facilities to edit hypertext documents, i.e. the users themselves are able to create nodes and links. KMS and NoteCards have been extended by components which support groups of users working with the system. However, none of them tries to control the usage of the system by integrating a knowledge base component.

Recently there has been increased interest in the interaction between formal knowledge representation and the informal semantics of hypermedia networks. Hypertext/Hypermedia can be understood as a semantic network where the nodes are arbitrary multimedia objects and edges may start/end within these objects. Firstly, it has proven useful to distinguish representational layers such as a base of chunks, the essential network structure, and various access paths or sequences to this structure [13]. Petrinet-like scripts appear as one attractive way to model these access paths. Second, hypermedia objects (individual nodes or subnets) often represent informally ideas whose essence can also be captured in some formal conceptual model. This relationship can be explored in two dimensions, either using hypermedia as an informal starting point for formal models, or by using a formal representation of ideas as a starting point for the development of hypermedia shows. Finally, experience in software engineering indicates that a lot can be gained by capturing at least certain aspects of the process of creating complex hypermedia bases, e.g. by relating ideas, structures, and the hypermedia base with each other as well as with information about the authors and their interaction.

The CoAUTHOR project, developed as part of the ESPRIT Technology Integration Project MULTIWORKS, has explored some of these relationships in the context of building an environment for hypermedia development. Besides the pure editing facilities, CoAUTHOR provides mechanisms to support the group processes which take place writing a document. Relating concrete nodes of the documents to the ideas they explore and their authors, the system documents the design history of each document. This is used for checking the consistency of the final document against its specification. To manage the accumulated knowledge adequately the system is based on a conceptual model of co-authoring, which is stored and maintained by a deductive object base. This object base also provides mechanisms to control the process of authoring.

In the following we motivate the development of such systems (section 2) and explain the conceptual model the system is based on (section 3). Section 4 deals with the implementation of the prototype system. An appendix contains a sample session.

2 Motivation

The intended application domain for CoAUTHOR is the production and maintenance of technical documentation. Recent years show a trend away from standard mass ware towards product customization. Products exist in a family of variants or versions which share a lot of common parts. Obviously, the documentation of such variants and versions can share a lot of common parts, too. The concept of hypermedia, i.e. linking small nodes containing text, graphics, images etc., seems to meet those needs.

On the other hand, personnel specialization requires large groups of experts to contribute to the documentation of products. Experts are often scattered geographically and work at different times. Therefore, authoring systems have to provide mechanisms to share results contributed at different times and locations, and to structure and coordinate distributed collaboration. However, there are situations which need direct communication between group members, e.g. solution of conflicts.

The CoAUTHOR system consists of the following subsystems to meet these requirements:
- a hypermedia system provides tools for editing, linking, storing, and retrieving concrete hypermedia chunks;
- to document and distribute results, a knowledge base management system has been connected to this hypermedia system;
- to support direct communication among group members, a simple real-time conference facility is provided.

This work was supported in part by the Commission of the European Community under ESPRIT contract 2105 (MULTIWORKS).
* Current Address: Informatik V, RWTH Aachen, Ahornstr. 55,
  5100 Aachen, Germany, email: eherer@picasso.informatik.rwth-aachen.de

3 Conceptual Model of Co-Authoring

CoAUTHOR's conceptual model [11] is a formal schema that defines how the co-authoring activity is organized and how its products - hypermedia documents - are structured and related to each other. It is not just a theoretical construct but is used directly by the knowledge base manager that administers the co-authoring process. There are two dimensions of conceptual models; first, a model of authoring including a document model, and second, a model of group work. Both of the models have been implemented in the knowledge representation language Telos [17] and are stored and maintained by the deductive object manager ConceptBase [14].

Our model of authoring is based on models developed for the generation of natural language text [15, 16] and on findings of Smith et al. [21] about the cognitive process of writing. It consists of the following three levels. At the top level of *idea processing* the issues are determined which should be covered by the resulting document. Hierarchical relations refine complex ideas into smaller ones, thus leading to a tree of ideas. Other relations of arbitrary, user-defined semantics expand this tree to a directed, possibly cyclic graph. At the middle level of *document design* a formal document structure has to be set up. Again, a tree of structure items is formed by hierarchical relations. Precedence relations indicating, that one structure item logically precedes another one, expand this tree to a directed, but now acyclic graph. Acyclic, because of no structure item should precede itself, not even through hierarchical relations. Each of these structure items has to be related to at least one idea of the idea processing level. Finally, at the bottom level of *document generation* structure items and their related ideas get implemented by appropriate hypermedia chunks or a net of chunks. Typed hypermedia links define relationships between chunks.

The hypermedia document model extends results of ESPRIT project MULTOS [22]. The MULTOS document model consists of conceptual, logical, and layout descriptions (the latter two according to the ODA [5] standard). The logical description deals with chapters, sections, paragraphs and so on, the layout description with page breaks, location of figures, footnotes etc., whereas the conceptual description models the content of the document (see [6] for a formal description of our hypermedia document model).

There is an overall class of objects, called CoAUTHOR_Object, with three subclasses according to the three levels of authoring: Idea, Structure, and HyperMediaObject.

Attributes of Idea objects are subIdea (representing a hierarchical relation between ideas), relatedTo (representing user defined relations between ideas), and refine (linking a HyperMediaObject to the Idea object containing a description of the intention of this idea).

Attributes of Structure objects are subStructure (representing a hierarchical relation between structures), precedeStructure (representing a precedence relation between structures), and relatedIdea (representing the link to the Idea object associated to this Structure object).

Finally, HyperMediaObjects have attributes relatedStructure (representing the link to the Structure object associated to this hypermedia chunk) and hypertextLinks (representing - at the conceptual side - the hypertext links between those chunks). See Figure 1 for a graphical illustration of the model of authoring.

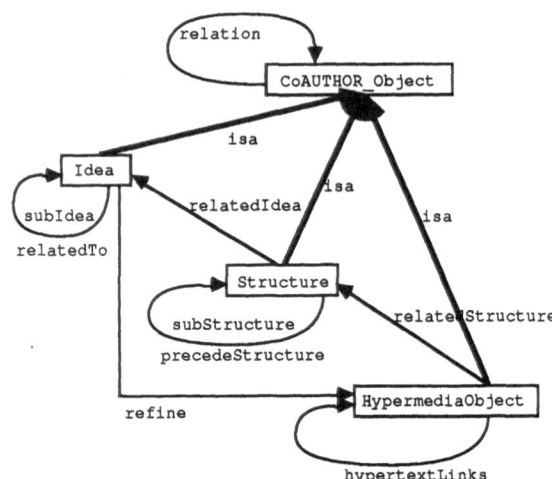

Figure 1: conceptual model of authoring

Only a few approaches have been suggested to support the group process of co-authoring documents. The Quilt system [8] models the social roles of group members and provides mechanisms for annotation, activity logging, and notification. The NoteCards system [23, 24] has been augmented by operations supporting collaboration, however, not collaboration of the authoring process itself but collaboration in using the system. InterNote [3] provides operators for commenting parts of documents and supports the revision of them. Our group work model is based on the above approaches along with ideas developed in [2, 25] regarding brainstorming and decision making scenarios.

Group work starts with the *generation* of individual contributions at each level of the authoring task, such as ideas, structures, and specific hypermedia chunks. This could be done at different times or within real-time conferences.

Each of the contributed objects and even the relations between them are open for *annotation* by other group members, again within conferences or asynchronously. Annotations may be the attachment of relevance assessments, critical comments, the augmentation by alternatives and so on.

Finally, the basic building blocks of a document have to be combined to form larger units on each of the three levels. This is essentially a *configuration* task. During this phase incomplete specifications, inconsistencies, and multiple solutions are likely to emerge. Negotiation-based alignment strategies support the resolution of those conflicts. As a result, ideas, structure objects, and concrete hypermedia chunks can be confirmed, modified or withdrawn.

Analogous to the model of authoring the model of group work has been implemented in Telos. A central aspect of this model is an overall Annotation class which is subclassed by a Pro, a Counter, and an Alternative class according to the *annotation* layer of the group work described above. Pro and Counter objects represent positive and negative comments attached to objects at every level of the authoring process. Alternative objects are designated to state common properties of two objects at any level. Each of these objects is related either to one of the specializations of CoAUTHOR_Object or any relation between those objects (figure 2).

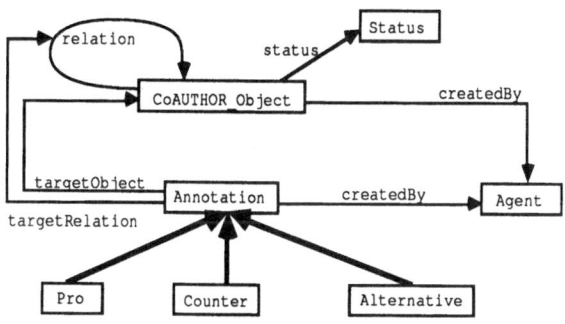

Figure 2: group model of authoring

4 Prototype Implementation

Figure 4 shows the architecture of the CoAUTHOR prototype. A graphic-based CoAUTHOR tool supports the instantiation of the conceptual model of co-authoring and real-time conferences and is connected to two servers:
- the deductive object base manager ConceptBase [14] managing the conceptual model and documenting the whole process of co-authoring, and
- the multi-media document server MULTOS [22] for storage and retrieval of concrete multi-media chunks.

The prototype was implemented in two major steps. First, the MULTOS system was extended by hypertext facilities and a connection to the ConceptBase system. Second, a specialized graphical tool was implemented which supports the instantiation of the integrated conceptual model of co-authoring and real-time conferences of the group.

To complement these tools, ConceptBase offers models and tools for the coordination of asynchronous group work, namely, for the sharing of tasks via a contract protocol, and for the sharing of results via a conflict-tolerating transaction protocol with automatic notification [18].

Another important part of the group model is the concept of agents, which are attached to each of the objects described above to assign authorship to objects, relations, and annotations. We have used a simple single level of agents with equal rights. It is not difficult to introduce a more sophisticated model of agents and actions, e.g social roles in the Quilt system [8].

For storing results of conflict resolution processes (like voting etc.) CoAUTHOR_Objects have an attribute status which can be either IN, OUT or PENDING. A status of IN (OUT) means, that there was a conflict and the group decided, that this object has (not) to be elaborated in the final document. A status of PENDING means, that further negotiations have to take place to solve the conflict. A missing status means, that the object is IN without any negotiation.

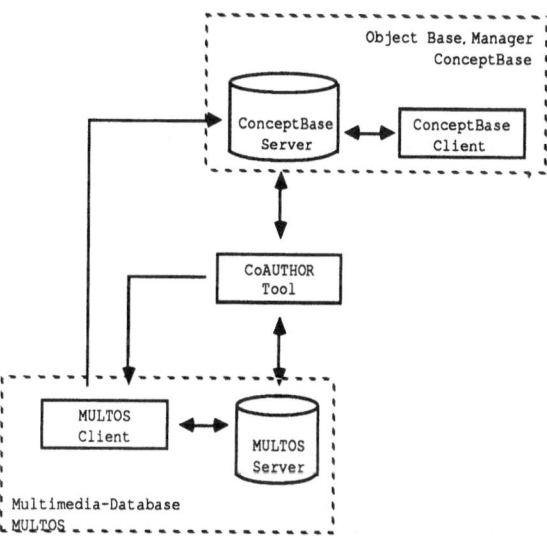

Figure 4: architecture of the first prototype

4.1 Extension of the MULTOS System

The MULTOS Document Editor has been extended by a hypertext link inset which stores some informations about the link style (text, button etc.), the displayed text portion, and the target of the link. The target information consists of the name of the document as stored within the knowledge base server. Thus, following such a link means asking the knowledge base for the unique MULTOS identifier of the target document, which is determined by the MULTOS server at document insertion time, retrieving the document from the MULTOS server, and, finally, displaying it in an editor window.

Each link is not only stored within the document but also represented within the knowledge base in order to allow access to links via the client tools of the knowledge base, e.g. querying, browsing, and the specialized graphical CoAUTHOR tool described in the next subsection.

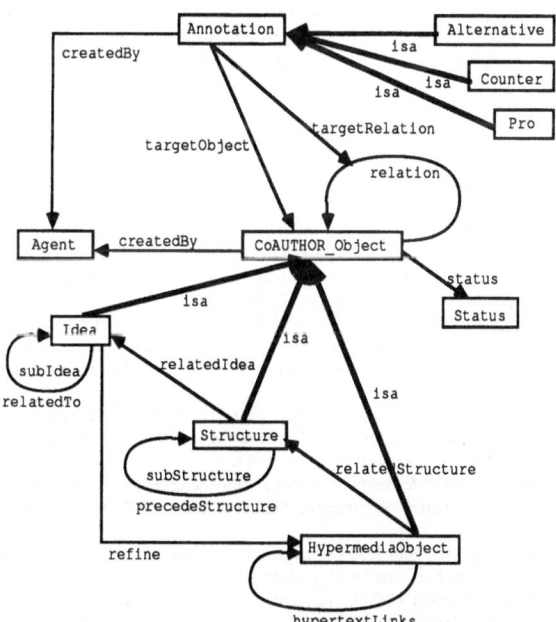

Figure 3: integrated model of co-authoring

Via these authorship links and the annotation links mentioned above the models of authoring and group work have been integrated. This integrated model serves as a formal backbone of the CoAUTHOR system (figure 3).

4.2 Implementation of the CoAUTHOR Tool

The CoAUTHOR tool manages the integrated model of co-authoring described in section 3. According to the three layers of the authoring model (idea processing, document design, document generation) the tool's window is divided into three major sections (see figure 5).

The IDEAS-section provides menu items for creating new ideas, relating them, and refining ideas by hypermedia chunks. Analogously, the STRUCTURES-section offers menu items for creating new structure objects and relating them. Additionally, structure objects can be related to ideas. The bottom HYPERMEDIA-section provides menu items for introducing documents created with the MULTOS document editor into the authoring model and for editing existing documents, editing in this context means retrieving the document from the MULTOS document server and displaying it on the screen.

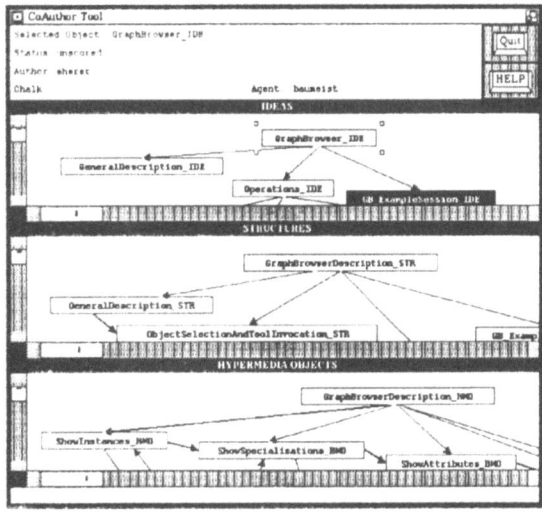

Figure 5: CoAUTHOR tool

To support the annotation phase of the group model, the tool provides menu items for attaching positive or negative comments to objects (ideas, structures etc.) or relations and for introducing alternatives to existing objects. Each comment consists of a brief description (the label of the comment object when it is displayed within the tool) and possibly some existing document which contains a more elaborated version of the comment.

To support the configuration phase of the group model, the CoAUTHOR tool provides a simple real-time conference facility. Several CoAUTHOR tools work on the same knowledge base and every change within one of the tools is passed onto the other tools. To handle parallel changes a simple chalkboard protocol has been implemented: only one of the group members can actually edit the knowledge base, the others can only see the changes made.

A conference is set up by the so-called master. The master has some additional facilities like grabbing the chalk or passing the chalk directly to a specific member.

To detect conflicts the tool provides a menu containing the following maintenance operators: the *Show Conflicts* operator returns all those objects and relations which have been assigned positive as well as negative comments; the *Show Alternatives* operator searches for those objects which are linked to an `Alternative` object; the *Show Open Issues* operator returns all those ideas, structure objects, and hypermedia objects whose status is PENDING.

5 Conclusion

We have shown, that the development of hypermedia documents is effectively supported by the integration of a knowledge base system and a hypermedia system. The knowledge base maintains a conceptual model which formally structures the informal ideas contained in the document. This formal structure is used to detect conflicts raised during the development process. It is also used to define new access paths to hypermedia documents. Access to nodes or subnets of a document is not only provided by the multimedia document server but also by the query facility of the knowledge base. Such queries may start from informal ideas which came up in the idea processing phase and may ask for all nodes or subnets which implement these ideas.

The conceptual model also contains knowledge about the steps performed by the group during the document development process. This process knowledge is used to support the collaboration of the group and, to a certain degree, control it. Policies with a stronger control may be defined in the knowledge representation language implemented by the knowledge base system. The observance of such policies may be enforced by the integrity checking component of the knowledge base and the user interface of the hypermedia system.

References

[1] R. M. Akscyn, D. L. McCracken, E. A. Yoder [1988]: KMS: A distributed Hypermedia System for Managing Knowledge in Organizations. In *Communications of the ACM*, Vol. 31, 7 (July 1988), pp. 820-835.

[2] M. P. Anderson [1970]: A Model of Group Decision. In R. S. Cathcart, L. A. Samovar (Eds): *Small Group Communication. A Reader*. Dubuque, Iowa: Brown, 1970, pp. 103-115.

[3] T. Catlin, P. Bush, N. Yankelovich [1989]: InterNote: Extending a Hypermedia Framework to Support Annotative Collaboration. In *Hypertext '89 Proceedings*, Nov. 5th-8th 1989, Pittsburgh, Pennsylvania, pp. 365-378.

[4] N. Delisle, M. Schwartz [1986]: Neptune: A Hypertext System for CAD Applications. In *ACM Transactions on Office Information Systems*, Vol. 6, 1 (January 1988), pp. 1-41.

[5] ECMA [1985]: *European Computer Manufacturers Association TC-29. Office Document Arcitecture*. Standard ECMA-101, Geneve, Sept. 1985.

[6] S. Eherer, K. Pohl [1991]: Introducing Abstraction into Hypermedia Documents. Submitted to Hypertext '91.

[7] D. C. Englebart [1984]: Authorship Provisions in Augment. *COMPCON 84: 28th IEEE Computer Society International Conference. Intellectual Leverage: The driving Technologies*. Feb. 27th-Mar. 1st 1984, San Francisco, CA, IEEE Computer Society Press, pp 465-472.

[8] R. S. Fish, R. E. Kraut, M. D. P. Leland, M. Cohen [1988]: Quilt - A Collaborative Tool for Cooperative Writing. In *Proceedings of the Conference on Office Information Systems*. Mar. 23rd-25th 1988, Palo Alto, California, pp. 30-37.

[9] L. N. Garret, K. E. Smith, N. Meyrowitz [1986]: Intermedia: Issues, strategies, and tactics in the design of a hypermedia system. In *Proceedings of the Conference on Computer Supported Cooperative Work*, Dec. 3rd-5th 1986, Austin, Texas, pp. 163-174.

[10] *Guide Users Manual*. Owl International, Bellevue, Wash., 1986.

[11] U. Hahn, M. Jarke, S. Eherer, K. Kreplin [1990]: CoAUTHOR - A Hypermedia Group Authoring Environment. In: J. Bowers, S. Benford (Eds.): *Studies in Computer Supported Cooperative Work: Theory, Practice and Design*. Amsterdam, North Holland, 1990.

[12] F. Halasz [1988]: Reflections on NoteCards: Seven Issues for the next Generation of Hypertext Systems. In *Communications of the ACM*, Vol. 31, 7 (Juli 1988), pp. 836-852.

[13] F. Halasz, M. Schwartz [1990]: The Dexter Hypertext Reference Model. In *Proceedings of the Hypertext Standardization Workshop*, Jan. 16th-18th 1990, National Institute of Standards and Technology, NIST Special Publication 500-178, Gaithersburg, MD.

[14] M. Jarke (Ed.) [1991]: *ConceptBase V3.0 User Manual*. University of Passau (Report MIP-9106).

[15] W. C. Mann, J. A. Moore [1981]: Computer Generation of Multiparagraph English Text. *American Journal of Computational Linguistics* Vol. 7 (1981), 1, pp. 17-29.

[16] K. R. McKeown [1985]: Discourse Strategies for Generating Natural-Language Text. *Artificial Intelligence* Vol. 27 (1985), 1, pp. 1-41.

[17] J. Mylopoulos, A. Borgida, M. Jarke, M. Koubarakis [1990]: Telos - a Language for Representing Knowledge about Information Systems. *ACM Transactions on Information Systems*, Vol. 8, 4 (October 1990).

[18] T. Rose, M. Jarke, M. Gocek, C. Maltzahn, H. W. Nissen [1991]: A Decision-Based Configuration Process Environment. *Software Engineering Journal*, Vol. 6, 1 (September 1991).

[19] B. Shneiderman [1987]: User interface design for the Hyperties electronic enceclopedia. In *Proceedings of the Hypertext '87 Workshop*, University of North Carolina, Chapel Hill.

[20] J. B. Smith, S. F. Weiss, G.J. Bolter, M. Lansman, D. V. Bea [1986]: *WE: A writing environment for professionals*. Tech. Rep. 86-025. Dept. of Computer Science. University of North Carolina, Chapel Hill, Aug. 1986.

[21] J. B. Smith, M. Lansmann [1988]: *A cognitive basis for a computer writing environment*. Tech. Rep. Dept. of Computer Science. University of North Carolina, Chapel Hill, 1988.

[22] C. Thanos (ed.) [1989]: *Multimedia Document Filing: The MULTOS Approach*. North-Holland, 1989.

[23] R. H. Trigg, L. Suchman, F. Halasz [1986]: Supporting Collaboration in NoteCards. In *Proceedings of the Conference on Computer Supported Cooperative Work*, Dec. 3rd-5th 1986, Austin, Texas, pp. 153-162.

[24] R. H. Trigg [1988]: Guided Tours and Tabletops - Tools for Communicating in a Hypertext Environment. In *ACM Transactions on Information Systems*, Vol. 6 (1988), 4, pp. 398-414.

[25] A. van de Ven, A. L. Delbecq [1971]: Nominal versus Interacting Group Processes for Committee Decision-Making Effectiveness. *Academy of Management Journal*, Vol. 14 (1971), 2, pp. 203-212.

[26] J. Walker [1987]: Document Examiner: Delivery interface to hypertext documents. In *Proceedings of Hypertext '87 Workshop*, University of North Carolina, Chapel Hill.

Appendix: CoAUTHOR Example Session

Assume, that a group of three authors has to write a documentation of the Editor of the ConceptBase user interface. First, in real-time conference, they elaborate the ideas which should be covered by the final document and create a document structure based on these ideas. Designing the concrete hypermedia chunks, based on the document structure, is done by the authors separately.

The group leader starts up a CoAUTHOR tool and introduces an initial idea object. The other group members also start up their own CoAUTHOR tools and the master sets up the

conference. The master chooses whose he wants to include into the conference and communicates his initial data to them (figure A1).

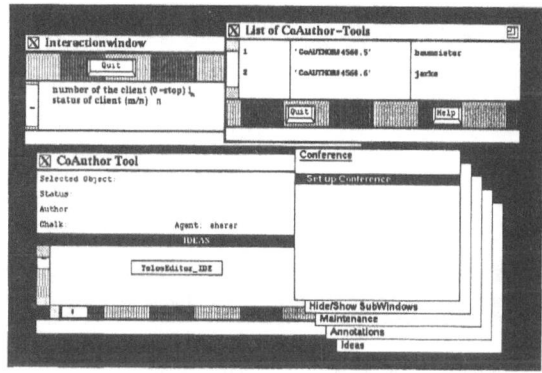

Figure A1: Setting up a conference

The master introduces a subidea of `TelosEditor_IDE` and specifys the name of the new idea, `EditingFacilities_IDE`. To elaborate its intention he attaches a previously created hypermedia object to his idea. The new objects are communicated to the ConceptBase server and to the other participants to guarantee, that each participant works on the same data.

Another participant looks at this refinement and makes a comment to the `EditingFacilities_IDE` object. He asks for the chalk and introduces his negative comment "Trivial". Giving "none" as attached document he indicates, that there is no further elaboration. Additionally, he introduces a subidea of `TelosEditor_IDE` called `EditorOperations_IDE`.

The third group member wants to endorse the `EditingFacilities_IDE` idea and attaches a positive comment "Needed" (figure A2). Now there are three idea objects, one of them refined and one of them with two comments attached.

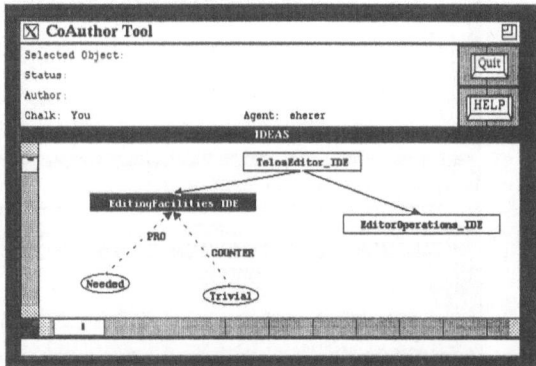

Figure A2: Situation after the idea processing phase

The master now asks the knowledge base for existing conflicts. Because of the negative and positive comments attched to the `EditingFacilities_IDE` object there actually is a conflict. The effected object is highlighted.

470

To solve this conflict the master selects the highlighted object and calls on the participants to vote. The new status of the object is communicated to the ConceptBase server as well as to every group member (figure A3).

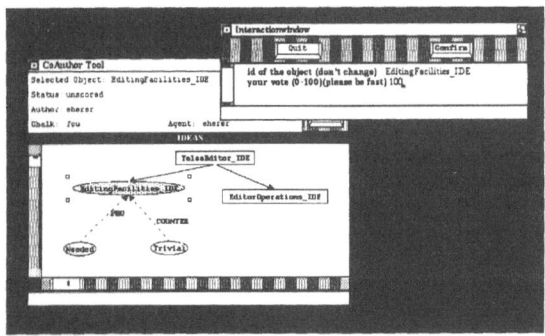

Figure A3: CoAUTHOR tool ready for voting

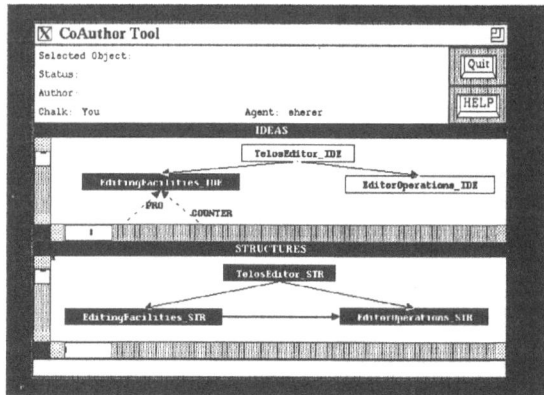

Figure A4: Situation after the document design phase

Now the group enters the process of document design. The master first grabs the chalk, creates a new structure object, `TelosEditor_STR`, and relates it to the existing `TelosEditor_IDE` idea object.

The group creates two additional structure objects, `EditingFacilities_STR` and `EditorOperations_STR`, as substructures of `TelosEditor_STR` and relates them to the idea objects `EditingFacilities_IDE` and `EditorOperations_IDE` respectively. The master asks for the chalk and creates a precedence relation from `EditingFacilities_STR` to `EditorOperations_STR`.

See figure A4 for the result of our sample document design process; there are three structure objects, all of them mapped to idea objects, and there is a precedence relation between two of them (displayed as a thick arrow).

The conference is closed now and the authors start up a new CoAUTHOR tool with `EditingFacility_IDE` and `EditingOperations_IDE` respectively as initial idea object.

One author invokes the MULTOS document editor and creates a new hypermedia chunk. He types in the text describing the editor operations, adds a screendump of the editor's window, and inserts the document into the MULTOS document server. He introduces the new chunk into the co-authoring process and relates it to 'his' structure object, `EditorOperations_STR`.

Simultaneously, the other author created a hypermedia chunk (called `EditorFacilities_HMO`) implementing the `EditorFacilities_STR` structure object and introduced it into the co-authoring process.

In order to configure the group document another conference is set up during which the group decides, that a hypermedia link should be created between `EditorFacilities_HMO` and `EditorOperations_HMO`. Figure A5 shows both new documents (`EditingFacilities_HMO` with the link in it) and the final status of the CoAUTHOR tools.

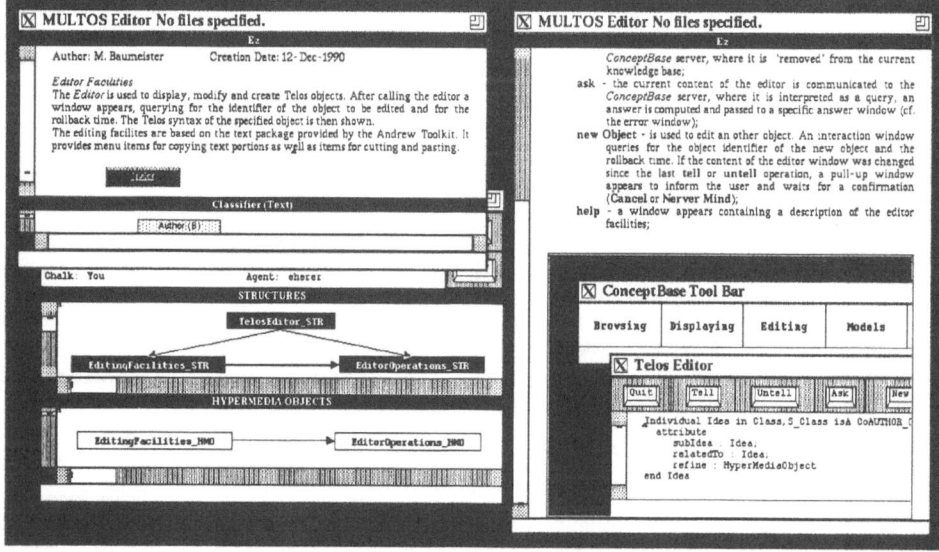

Figure A5: after creating a hypermedia object

Computer Supported Multimedia Environment
for Collaboration

Jože Rugelj

Jožef Stefan Institute
Jamova 39, 61111 Ljubljana
Slovenia

ABSTRACT

The impact of new technologies on the different aspects of collaboration and cooperation is concerned and some possible applications are proposed. An architectural model for CSCW systems is introduced. The management functions of a distributed conference environment are also proposed and a pilot conferencing system based on the above propositions is presented.

1   Introduction

It is hard to imagine a form of human activity that does not involve some kind of cooperation. The need for cooperation grows with the complexity of the work which is to be carried out. People working together have to agree on goals, make commitments to perform specific work, exchange reports on the progress of the work, coordinate the execution of sub-tasks, etc. All these activities are based on the exchange of information in different forms, i.e. they are based on communication. Voice and visual information, such as gestures, drawings and written notes, are still the most usual communication means.

Many aspects of the cooperation can be supported and enhanced by technologies. On the one hand, tools exist which help in creating, gathering, transforming, storing, and managing information, and on the other hand, there are means which allow geographically dispersed collaborators to exchange information in different forms.

Effective and cheap communication services are vital to economic performance and are therefore crucial to economic and social development. In West Europe, more than half the jobs are already related to information and services and involve the use of telecommunications in all its forms. Advanced infrastructure for information exchange and services will be as dominant in the next decades as canal, road and rail transport infrastructures were in the past centuries.

Development of digital electronic and optical technologies opens the way to greatly improved and economic voice, data and image communication. New developments include HDTV, digital recording and transmission of sound and pictures, optical fibres for very fast transmission of information, super fast computers and satellite broadcasting.

The usefulness of telecommunication services depends on wide-spread acceptance. Therefore, many activities have been undertaken in all parts of Europe to stimulate the dialogue between politicians, technologists, network operators and users to contribute to the emergence of a broad consensus on requirements and objectives.

2   Application of technology to collaboration

Until recently, computer based collaboration between geographically dispersed users has been limited primarily to electronic mail. This is due to the low throughput of the computer networks and the lack of standards for the interchange of computer processable multimedia information. In the last few years, new technologies appeared that greatly enhance data communication facilities and improve the human-machine interface. These improvements allow the introduction of real-time, synchronous communication techniques, using different communication media. Interactions can be supported that are "natural" to the user and make him "feel" like participating in a face-to-face meeting [1].

There are several areas of human activities where CSCW can have a particular impact on the efficiency and quality of work: medicine, education and training, all kinds of design, science and research, tourism and even marketing.

The use of computer systems in medical area has rapidly grown during the last few years. This is not restricted to image processing systems but also to other application fields. Nowadays, in the better equiped hospitals, most of the data concerning a patient can reside in a computer. Patient files consist of multimedia documents which comprise text, geometric graphic, raster graphic images, video recordings and audio information. Documents can be stored in a database, and can be retrieved for later or remote analyses by experts or special equipment.

In education, the use of CSCW systems render possible

472

engagement of the best lecturers and experts, and although they may live and work hundreds of miles away they need not travel. Interactive controlled multimedia courses can help students to study in an attractive and efficient way. In the design process as well as in the research, technical tools help involved people, even if they are geographically dispersed and each of them does not poses all expensive equipment and devices, to work on the same project simultaneously. They can share intermediate results and analyse them. Tourist agencies can use multimedia systems to present their programmes and the most attractive destinations. In this way a custumer can find only those details which are really interesting for him.

In order to offer requested high-quality services, CSCW systems ought to be based on the full understanding of the activities which are to be supported [2]. Therefore, human sciences such as psychology and sociology take an active part in the CSCW research. Architects and experts in the field of ergonomics are also expected to contribute to the design of the appropriate workspace [3].

3 Architectural Model for CSCW Systems

Our model for CSCW systems is significantly affected by considerations such as the distributed nature of CSCW, the concurrent access, the use of different media and the compatibility with the existing tools and applications [4].

The notion of shared workspace reflects the cooperation and the collaboration that take place in the CSCW environment. Concerning the lower layer communication facilities, the shared workspace makes use of the "ether" concept as defined in [5].

As regards the higher level tools, actors in the shared workspace see their interactions regulated by logical contexts with different degrees of shareability. When a software application package is shared by a multitude of participants both the information and information manipulation primitives are shared. In a more loosely coupled system, information sharing is accomplished through a common storage. The care of the overall coherence and consistency of shared information is taken by the transaction manager of the common data base. Finally, unrelated messages can be originated with replications and no attempt to maintain the consistency among such copies is necessary. This type of interactions may coexist and serve complementary purposes.

According to the above classification criteria, Garcia [6] proposes the following three classes of CSCW systems:

- application process sharing
- storage sharing
- electronic message sharing

Application process sharing implies the concurrent use of one or more processes by multiple clients. This can be implemented in different forms. A single instance of the shared application process can be accessed by different users or multiple instances of the same process can be maintained, each instance being accessed by a single user or a subset of users. In the latter case, the system must maintain the state consistency among all instances of the same process.

Storage sharing involves the use of centralized, partitioned, or replicated storage areas which can be supported by a centralized or distributed database system.

Electronic message sharing implies the distribution of a copy of the information to each collaborating party. This technique is exemplified by electronic mail and interactive file transfer. Nowadays, these two techniques represent the most popular form of information sharing.

Among the three forms of interaction involved in the shared workspace, new research challenges are stimulated by the application process sharing. In particular, our work focuses on multimedia desktop conferencing systems that are expected to support interactive, real-time communication. Conferencing systems suitable for small or medium-sized groups (2-10 persons) are supposed to be implemented on personal workstations equipped with some special devices for dealing with voice and video and interconnected across LANs, MANs and WANs. Application process sharing fits best into the conferencing environment since it allows other media such as voice or video to be included in the information sharing process. The application process the various kinds of information flow according to the rules of the conference scenario.

The users of a multimedia, distributed, computer-supported conference are expected to be given approximately the same opportunities for the exchange of control and information as they experience in a face-to-face meeting. The conferencing environment can be considered as the provider of a virtual meeting room [7] where tools in use during a real conference are emulated.

4 The Management of the Distributed Conference Environment

A general scheme for the distributed management of the shared workspace is proposed. Three main components can be identified: the management modules, the distributor modules and the communication networks.

4.1 The manager module

The management functions are incorporated in the conference manager which is implemented as a set of interconnected manager modules, one for each workstation.

There are three types of interfaces inside the manager

module. One interface is used for the communication with the user of the virtual meeting room. Commands and status reports concerning the conference are exchanged across this interface. This dialogue is supported by a dedicated management window on the screen of the workstation.

The second interface is used for the control of the distributor module, which in turn controls the input and the output data stream from the activated application programs and the multimedia device drivers which serve as the presentation tools of the virtual meeting room.

The third interface is devoted to the cooperation and the coordination of the management modules, which are distributed over the network. Network liaisons between such modules are established during the conference setup phase and remain active till its termination. A simple protocol is defined in support of this communication.

The distributed conference manager consists of identical management modules, but after the start of the meeting, one of them gets special rights and duties. It is usually the management module residing in the node where the meeting was first activated that acts as the chairman of the meeting. Its role is to resolve problems which appear during the meeting and can not be dealt with by automatic built-in mechanisms.

4.2 The distributor module

In general, the distributor module is responsible for the multicast of all types of data streams from the originator workstation to all other participants in the conference and for their selective reception by the receiving workstations.

Unlike other modules of general applicability, the distributor modules are very specific and strongly related to the user tools connected to them. The complexity of the distributor module depends on the available communication sublayer. If the multicast network facility is available, a multicast connection is established from the origin node to the other nodes. The byte stream is simply redirected to the multicast connection. If there is no multicast facility, a connection must be established to each participating node, and the data streams must be duplicated and sent across the individual connections.

On the receiving side, the distributor module is responsible for the selection and the adaptation of the incoming data stream to the specific requirements of its local environment. Moreover, it is responsible for the control of the backward traffic. The distributor module is connected to the manager module which controls all the activities of the distributor module.

When media such as voice or video are shared, the task to be executed by the distributor module is much more complex. However, a single network architecture can be used to distribute data, voice, and video signals. The sharing mechanism differs for the two media only in terms of performance

requirements and combination algorithms. Combination algorithms are used to compose common visual or aural information from different sources.

There are several strategies known how to select and how to add speech signals from different speakers which are to be transmitted over a common conference voice channel [8]. The video signals have to be handled differently because they cannot simply be added together. In [9] a new technique was presented which allows the composition of a digital video image from several different partial images. To reduce the network traffic, only some subset of the participants can be presented by full-motion images, while others can contribute their still images which are refreshed periodically. Some additional savings can be achieved by reducing the resolution of the video images.

4.3 Communication networks

There are generally two types of network connections in the conferencing environment, corresponding to two very different communication patterns.

The first type of connections is the so called control connection. Control connections are used to connect management modules for the exchange of control messages. The bandwidth needed is low, but a lot of acknowledgement and synchronization messages are exchanged. For such a traffic the ring topology is most suitable. It does not allow any parallelization in the message propagation, but it is very efficient as regards acknowledgement and synchronization. Although physical topologies may be of different nature, a virtual ring can be always defined on them.

The second type of network connections is used for bulk data traffic in the shared environment. High bandwidth is needed and because of real-time requirements and high-quality transmission media, no backward traffic is required. As indicated in the previous chapter, the tree topology is to be used for those purposes.

According to the relevant literature, [10], it is very important that users have, via the management modules of our scheme, direct control of the bandwidth allocation and the conference connections. The control is implemented in a distributed way, and each conferee is given the responsibility for the management of his own bandwidth needs and call control. These control issues could have significant implications for B-ISDN, since protocols for these control functions are still under definition.

5   A Pilot Conferencing System

A prototype of the proposed virtual meeting room has been implemented on Sun-3 workstations running the UNIX operating system [11]. It has been decided to adopt the X-window system [12] as a basic input-output environment. X is widely

474

used on various computer systems and appears to play the role of an industrial standard in the field. An important reason behind our decision is the fact that the X-window system is defined in terms of a network protocol. In particular, an asynchronous stream-based inter-process communication replaces the traditional procedure call or kernel call interface. An application can be bound to windows on any display in a network of workstations in a device-independent, network transparent fashion.

In order to support conference management functions the distributed conference manager, consisting of manager modules, was implemented as a well-known server process in each workstation. It is automatically loaded at computer startup time and is activated on user request or on the request from a remote manager module. The manager modules cooperate in the management of the virtual meeting room. The dialogue between the user and the manager module is supported by a dedicated management window on the screen which makes the communication convenient. All persons who have accepted the invitation to participate in the meeting are included in the environment of the virtual meeting room.

When the conference manager is created, various audio and video devices as well as application programs and multimedia drivers can be used in support of the cooperative work in a virtual meeting room. All these tools are controlled by the conference manager.

In the present state of our implementation, priority is given to the integration of existing application programs such as text editors, CAD packages, spreadsheets, and expert systems which are originally conceived for single-user operation.

We have implemented the distributor module for the class of the X-window applications. In order to clarify the details of our implementation, some components of the X-window system structure need to be recalled shortly.

The X-window system is based on the client-server model. There is a server in control of each physical display. The communication between a client application and a server takes place by means of a reliable duplex byte stream. Since such a facility can be offered by most networks, the X-protocol can be us d in very complex scenarios.

As mentioned above, those byte streams are intercepted and redirected by the distributor module. This is possible without changes in the application software, since the destination of the byte streams can be specified as an option at application startup. The complexity of the distributor module depends on the available communication sublayer and on the diversity of the physical displays used in the conference.

On the server side, the distributor module is responsible for the adaptation of the incoming byte stream to the specific requirements of its physical display. Moreover, it is responsible for the control of the backward traffic. The distributor module is connected to the manager module and allows events to be sent from the server to the client only when it is given the floor.

For each application, a new process is created within the distributor module and put under the control of the conference manager. Any participant can become the operator of a running application. The corresponding requests are queued and when the previous operator leaves the floor, the control is passed to the next applicant. The chairman has the right to reorder such queues and to set priorities. The interaction between the operator and his application are made visible to all participants.

During the meeting, provision is made for the exchange of short messages between selected participants.

5.1 Future Work

The next step of our implementation will deal with the integration of some multi-media devices such as voice compression cards, still image cameras and scanners. Although this is not expected to represent a technical difficulty, some real experience needs to be collected in order to properly devise the control mechanism and the human interface of the envisaged presentation tools. For this purpose, we plan to offer the system to volunteer users who will kindly experiment it. Their reaction is expected to help in the further evolution of the project. In particular, enhancements to be introduced at the network level in terms of multicast and synchronization services will be considered in the light of such an experience.

6 Slovene Experiences with Cooperative Technologies

In Slovenia, the research work in the area of CSCW is concentrated at the J. Stefan Institute of University of Ljubljana.

We gained early experience in this area in the European COST-11 project AMIGO (Advanced Messaging in Group Organizations), where different aspects of asynchronous group communications and conferencing systems were considered. We collaborate with the Joint Research Centre of CEC in Ispra, Italy, in the design of a multimedia conferencing system for long distance collaboration. We are also active participants in the COST-14 project, called Cooperative Technologies [13]. This allows us to keep track of current developments in the area, and to verify and mutually exchange the results of our work. We expect that the knowledge and skills gained in this way will help us to set up an adequate infrastructure and services for the CSCW support. Similarly, in the past, our participation in different European projects helped us to gain knowledge and to establish contacts with the experts in the area of computer networks. Thus, we were able to set up the E-mail system for academic community in Slovenia in spite of a very limited amount of money.

7   References

[1] K. A. Lantz: "An experiment in Integrated Multimedia Conferencing", *Proc. Conf. on CSCW '86*, December 1986, pp. 533-552

[2] L. Suchman: "Rediscovering Cooperative Work", *Proc. 1. European Conference on CSCW*, London, September 1989

[3] H. Krcmar: "Considerations for a Framework for CATeam Research", *Proc. 1. European Conference on CSCW*, London, September 1989, pp. 421-435

[4] J. Rugelj, A. Endrizzi: "The Functions and the Structure of Systems for CSCW", *EUR 13169, CEC-DG XIII*, Luxembourg-Brussels, 1990

[5] J. Rugelj, A. Endrizzi: "Multimedia Conference Across Wide-Area Networks", *Proc. 1. European Conference on CSCW*, London, September 1989, pp. 469-475

[6] J.J. Garcia-Luna-Aceves et al.: "An Open-Systems Model for Computer Supported Collaboration", *IEEE Proc. 2.Conf. on Computer Workstations*, 1988, pp.40-51

[7] J.R. Ensor et al.: "The RAPPORT Multimedia Conferencing System - a Software Overview", *IEEE Proc. 2. Conf. on Computer Workstations*, March 1988, pp. 52-58

[8] J. Nedergaard, H. Nielsen: "An All-Digital Audioconference System", *IEEE Proc. Intern. Zurich Seminar on Digital Comm.*, March 1990, pp.163-172

[9] S.M. Stevens: "Intelligent Interactive Video Simulation of Code Inspection", *Comm. ACM*, vol. 32, no. 7, July 1989, pp. 832-843

[10] S.R. Ahuja: "Network Support for Distributed Collaborations", *Gruopware Technology Workshop*, XEROX Parc, August 1989

[11] J. Rugelj, A. Endrizzi: "Conferencing via Workstations: Implementation Issues", *Eur. Workshop on CSCW in Research Labs*, Ispra, December 1989

[12] R.W. Scheifler, J. Gettys: "The X Window System", *ACM Trans. on Graphics*, vol. 5, no. 2, April 1986, pp. 79-109

[13] D.Barber, T.Kalin, A.Kündig, M. Purser, R. Speth: "Proposal for a new COST-Action in the area of Co-operation Technology (CO – TECH)", Zürich, March 1989

Expert Systems Development and Management, A Case Study

Per A. Zaring
Department of Computer Science
Chalmers University of Technology
S-412 96 Gothenburg
Sweden

Hans G. Vogt
Department of Production Engineering
Chalmers University of Technology
S-412 96 Gothenburg
Sweden

ABSTRACT

To describe the development of an expert system formally we cannot completely rely upon traditional software engineering conceptions. The question is that to what extent it is reasonable to borrow from already established disciplines to develop a new. To understand the problem situation we describe a computer supported method to choose tools and operational sequences for hole-machining, an activity which is representative when trying do define an understand the concept of *tacit knowledge*. The supporting system is presented as a frame of reference on which we apply one internal and one external view, i.e. we will adress some methodological problems concerning expert system development and a qualitative discussion of what properly managed expert systems could provide to the user.

1. INTRODUCTION

Making decisions is often a subtle process, requiring intelligence or worse still, common sense. No one has any idea yet how human beings think and make judgements in the way that they do, but at the very least one could say that we seem to have the abilities that lie beyond the scope of what we understand by computation. Still, numerous attempts have been, and are made, to reflect human intelligence by the use of *knowledge based systems*. One application area for such systems is *decision support*.

Here we shall not try to define this term but take a close look at a project where one such system were built, namely the rule based system IHOPE [13]. Our goal is to briefly describe the functioning of a computer supported system for choosing tools and operational sequences for machining of holes and to, in the last section, outline some future research issues that have shown important in order to make the system operationally usable. These issues include a critical discussion of the expert system concept based on our experiences from the development stages of this project.

The hole-machining process consists of a number of working steps and decisions that are to a great extent based on standardized default values referring to *normal conditions* [15] for tools, machines and workpiece materials. The evaluation of a finishing specification for a hole from drawing is a task which requires experience. The more experienced the engineer is the less there is a need for him to rely upon guidelines in the form of default values to make a decision and take an action, i.e. the greater his skill is in handling deviations from the norm. Thus the engineer often makes out his own standards and make decisions on a more *intuitive* basis to meet the situation at hand. He develops a type of *tacit knowledge* [3]. To succeed in formulating this knowledge explicitly and make it more generally available would mean qualitative as well as economic benefits in an operating environment.

2. THE PLANNING SUPPORT SYSTEM
2.1 Basic Components and Characteristics

As a starting point we have used a report that describes a systematic way to manually choose tools and combine them into sequences [14]. Initially this process is rather deterministic. All deterministic processes can suitably be represented using a procedural notation. In addition to automatize these basic steps our intent is to add knowledge to the computer based system that the engineer for the time being does not possess. The quality of the decision process will be enhanced.

This system should be regarded as a *decision support* system rather than a *decision making* system [9]. From the alternative solutions generated it can optionally make a choice or just rank them to facilitate a manual choice.

The ability to adjust the system behaviour and tune its performance to meet the situation at hand is one reason why we are mixing together various kinds of formalisms [6]. To the user the system is separated into three parts:

1. The update-system, that operates on the rawdata.

2. The sequence builder, that generates new solutions to unknown problems.

3. The reportgenerator with its report query management system(RQMS) and reportdatabase (RDS).

The purpose is that not only data stored in the databases should reflect specific needs within an organization but also that the interfaces should be customized in an easy manner to reflect different user requirements and to provide a *virtual memory* to the user.

Information is produced from data stored in the database containing raw data, i.e the standardized default values. The static facts are retrieved from the database while the declarative, heuristic knowledge components are expressed as rules. The rule based knowledge is classified as knowledge that is fragmentary, modular and often difficult, at a first sight, to place within a context. We could say that the system reflects reality by this mix of knowledge representations; a structured reality which corresponds to a specification of the problem and drawing, and an unstructured reality which corresponds to the operators mind and individual interpretation of the problem.

Buchanan [1] points out that *transparency* is the key idea for making the system understandable despite the complexity of the task. He argues that the system matures through incremental improvements, which require thorough understanding of previous versions and that the system improves through criticism from persons who are not familiar with the system specific details. One very important aspect for making a transparent system is that we must give the user the opportunity to examine *how* and *why* a certain rule is fired.

Thus the ability to trace the line of reasoning in this way makes it possible in the future to let the user of this system take greater part of the refinement of the knowledge base without having thorough understanding of all implementation details. The engineer himself might be capable of expanding the capacities of the system. During a session with IHOPE, approximately 3 minutes long, an operational sequence is created that fulfill a number of criteria. What criteria and to what extent they have influenced the solution is determined by the embedded rulebased system. The rules within the system are intended to emulate human reasoning or at least to support such. They reflect a number of situation-dependent parameters that might, in a specific situation, have influence on the operational sequence being created. This part of the system provides explanations of *why* and *how* certain actions are taken. This function, as well as many other functions described in this paper, is optional. To a well-trained eye the rulebased mechanism sometimes is redundant. Then as we shall see later, it is necessary to hide it from the user.

A complete and correct solution to a problem is given as a report. If a solution is accepted then the complete record is stored on file. We call this file *the report database* or **RDS**. The ability to *memorize* for future use is made possible through this file.

2.2 The Planning Process and The System Behaviour

The system provides aid to the process of incremental problem solving in a cyclic manner. By ranking and highlighting certain facts at certain decision points it enhances the perception of the user.

The rule base is with a few exceptions invoked during the creation of the operational sequence. Some rule sets are used early in the session to check correctness of starting parameters and to check the type of machine that the engineer has intended to use. The latter reduce the the span of decision alternatives considerably. This fact is of crucial importance since one of the great problems in many knowledge based applications is to avoid the *combinatorial explosion*, both within the machine and within the user's mind [8]. In our case this means a reduction of execution time by a factor of 10 compared to other systems based on for example pure Lisp-routines. In our implementation we avoid the resource consuming recursiveness of Lisp and similar languages. However, the most important benefit using an integrated development platform as ours is the ability to show and explain what is actually happening and to be sure that people can understand it and accept what they see.

It has shown that our way to represent data is suitable also for very moderate computer hardware. This is an important aspect when considering use and acceptance on a larger scale, beyond the laboratory.

In a situation where the IHOPE system runs operationally, it presents better solutions the more problems that have been solved and stored in the **RDS**. With enough cases stored, IHOPE might be capable of emulating expert knowledge [4] in the area of hole machining. Thus the system will seldom generate **completely** new sequences from beginning. Instead it will modify previously stored cases utilizing certainty factors referring to correctness, adequacy and grade of fitness. The meaning of these concepts are subject to future research and will not be discussed here. So, we can say that the system has the ability to learn from past experiences.

The solutions in the **RDS** are manipulated, ranked and weighted according to the wishes from a specific user in a specific moment through the **RQMS**. To this function we intend to add capabilities to provide the user with fast calculation power used in *whatif-analysis* where the value of one field in a stored record may be changed and the influence on other values are shown. The calculations are based on statistic inference from the stored historical data.

The IHOPE system constitutes a set of concepts that have never before been implemented as a decision support system. In the future the use of similar implementations is likely to be widespread which raises many questions to be answered. Below, we will adress some such issues that have occurred to us during our project. We shall discuss issues that originate from two perspectives; one internal view (systemic performance aspects) and one external view (aspects of this kind of system placed within a social context).

3. PROBLEMS OF SPECIAL INTEREST

In this section we will discuss some other than purely implementational aspects of expert system development. The topics are presented as brief notes and reflections on our work. Here we will give no solutions to the problems listed. Some of our standpoints might seem rather spectacular, as in the discussion of the impact of *Software Engineering* on expert system development. Other issues, such as the discussion on *knowledge elicitation*, are already regarded as **key concepts** within the area, and as such can be emphasized in our specific case of study. All of the subjects presented below should be regarded as future research issues within this project. No matter how well documented some of these topics are, there are obviously no thorough understanding available yet, that is possible to generalize to enough extent.

3.1 Effects of System Performance

Tacit knowledge is often referred to as concerning strategic issues within a system. It is applied in various managerial activities. This knowledge can be put in contrast to the knowledge required in e.g. engineering and accounting, where knowledge can be formalized and programmed [10]. As the benefits of pushing up productivity through mechanization have been exploited and the decrease in cost savings on this area have been realized in post industrial organizations, the major area for new benefits has become focused on increasing efficiency through quality improvements by the use of formalized knowledge -*information*.

The problem of formalization itself will not be discussed. Let us just assume that all knowledge cannot be formalized, but that knowledge based systems provide help to reach longer in this process and thus facilitates *communication* of more abstract phenomenas. What does this mean in practice? In the next three sections we will briefly present some empirical evidences of this.

3.1.1 Augmenting Professionalism by User Dialogue

In our area, manufacturing, we see a clear relationship between **quality of output** and and a certain type of **knowledge** that is possible to partly isolate by the use of expert system technology. The production engineer on the shop floor has proven to be a critical link in a chain where the overall requirements for a hole are made up, where the specification, the rough and the detailed design is carried out. His role is a critical one because in his work he can act in accordance with the specification or he can make own judgements of whether the specification in his hand is a meaningful specification or not, i.e. he may spoil all the previous work or correct all the previous work. In the area of hole machining the specification, in the form of a drawing, often have missing details for various reasons, these details can be considered as redundant information for some (highly skilled engineers) but for most this missing information is helpful and time saving. Furthermore, the calculations that he performs on the basis of the specification give results that are poorly optimized for a specific problem. As we said in the beginning of this paper these values are all standardized default values referring to **normal conditions**. A trained eye is able to fill in the blanks in the drawing and to differentiate (optimize) the results from the calculations which in practise often means the difference between low and high quality performance. This is an example of tacit knowledge that has not to be communicated vertically in the organization. Thus this knowledge does not have to be interpreted on different levels. This knowledge belongs to where it originates and is relevant in a very specific decision situation. Everybody's knowledge contains elements of *tacit* nature, self-evident experience, which can never be communicated to other people [16]. According to this argument we can see that our distinctly human gifts have been lifted out of the explicit, rational, and logical domain into the realm of intuitive, mystic knowledge, where no conscious mental activity goes on.

Queries vary from time to time from person to person. The system tells what the system knows, no matter the amount of stored knowledge. To make a query is to take an explicit action. Without an explicit action there will be no advises from the system. The latter means that the system operates as a coprocessor to the human, in a hidden manner only displaying some predefined results. This is the meaning of dialogue; only serve those who need to be served.

3.1.2 Scaling Up Operational Qualities

Where are the business benefits? Are there any savings from our system? There are numbers of ways in which cost savings can be realized; through reduced material costs, through aspects of competitive advantage or increased leveraged sales. The most important area for cost savings in our case can be found by realizing the ability to allow much lower skilled people to perform the same tasks as skilled ones and to make possible for skilled people to perform the same task much more quickly. Another very interesting area is the possibilities to use the IHOPE system as an educational platform for novices, i.e to let them act and observe under realistic circumstances.

3.1.3 The Persistence of Expertise

There have been and still are serious problems especially for knowledge-intensive areas within the industry to build up and keep the expertise within an organization. In the Swedish industry as well as in most of Europe there have been a long-term pressure to reduce the number of staff. Skill reductions and manpower reductions are obvious aspects of this. Systems like IHOPE offers possibilities to reduce the difficulties caused by this. The problem still remain and the effect of this rather new technology has not yet given what people were hoping for. This may due to lack of methods for managing expert system software in a proper manner, an issue to which we will return in a later section.

3.2 System Development

3.2.1 What models are available?

Many models for describing the software development process has been developed. Among certain general paradigms we find the *waterfall approach, Prototyping, System assembly from reusable components* and *Exploratory programming*. The waterfall model is well understood and wide spread. Here we will concentrate on the so called **Exploratory programming model** since it is obvious that this approach is the most common for the type of applications described in this paper. This model is based on the idea of development of an initial implementation and exposing this to user commitment and refining this according to the wishes from the user without using a formal plan for the activity. Exploratory programming is not specification-based. Since activities like verification and validation only are meaningful when a program is compared to its specification verification here is nonsense.

We must face the fact that there are AI-applications and knowledge based systems that are not intended as temporal systems running only for a limited period. People invest vast amounts of money to expand them and improve them. Does this approach hold also for large and long-lifetime systems?

We suggest that it does not because in exploratory programming, it is not cost-effective to produce a great deal of system documentation as the system is subject to such regular change. In order for this model to be used for large systems development, new management techniques will have to be established to control the development process. Exploratory programming tends to result in systems whose structure is not well-defined because the continual change corrupts the initial software structure.

3.2.2 System Development as a Learning Process

Our intention has been to codify the *tacit knowledge* described. This process has been carried out in an ad-hoc manner which means that no firm requirements for the system were specified at an early stage that could be used as a plan for the development. Dynamic requirements, increasing system size and human nature itself have forced the software process towards disorganization. As we build new systems we learn what we should have built. In fact, we often do not really understand what we really understand what we want or how to build it until we have finished. The evolutionary process is driven by requirements dynamics. Each new development uncovers new issues that lead to changes. In addition to being unplanned, changes are highly error-prone.

Because of the fuzzy nature of the tasks modelled whitin expert system development plans that relies upon a thorough requirement analysis cannot be developed. Without planning, the problems of scale are not understood or adequately anticipated. In large software systems, the most severe problems are not obvious until testing gets into trouble. Without a plan it has shown that we consider testing itself as the problem. Such irrational priorities produce increasingly chaotic behaviour.

3.3 Knowledge Acquisition

According to Hart [5] domain experts can have three different roles. These are: as a provider of information, as a problem-solver and as an explainer. In the first role and the last one problems of communication occur because in these roles more than one person is involved. The task is either to *provide someone* with information or to *explain* something to *somebody*. The process of *knowledge acquisition* is the most time consuming of our activities. Having collected enough information to make a computer implementation, a running version very often becomes an important communication channel between the knowledge engineer and the domain expert because it yields a visible and easily understandable interpretation of the problem. As the knowledge in the program accumulates and the problem becomes clearer we often find better ways to represent and process the knowledge. To express some chunk of knowledge as a rule in a rule set one must be sure that this knowledge is suited for that kind of representation. Problems of choosing representations, refining programs, determining what knowledge that in some sense can be regarded as fuzzy and communicating with domain experts all belongs to the knowledge acquisition process. The lack of methods and models in this area has, at the very minimum, been frustrating [2]. The rule formalism permits us to store and process single facts that we do not yet know how to handle within a context. This possibility facilitates the problem of visualizing abstract courses of events.

3.4 A Crisis within Expert System Development?

Through our work we have reached the conclusion that expert system development as well as *traditional* software system development requires professionals, skilled in software engineering†. In the previous we have mentioned the lack of

---

† The term *software engineering* should be interpreted in accordance with the definitions given in [11, 12] or similar.

methods to support different phases in the expert system development process. Below we shall continue that discussion from a software engineering point of view. What does a well engineered software system look like? A more general assessment of system quality requires the identification of common attributes which we would expect to find in all well engineered software. The last twenty years of work in the area of software enginnering has resulted in a rather well defined conception of what a good software look like. Ignoring functionality, there are four attributes which any well engineered software system should possess according to Sommerville [12].

1. The software should be maintainable. As long-lifetime software is subject to regular change it is important to write and document software in such a way that changes can be made without undue costs.

2. The software should be reliable.

3. The software should be efficient. Since attempting to maximize efficiency can make the software much more difficult to change, we primarily mean that a software system should not make wasteful use of system resources.

4. The software should offer an appropriate user interface. Much software is not used to its full potential simply because the interface offered makes it difficult to use.

How much attention is given to these attributes, especially the first three ones, by expert system developers? Here we will present some crisis-related issues that seem to be rather common but not well understood in our area. We find scarcely no evidence of commitment and action in the industry that successfully solve the problem of integrating knowledge based system applications in large scale with common software systems.

3.4.1 A New Software Crisis

The most fundamental reason for such a crisis is that programming methods and most existing software tools only adress the implementation part of the software development process. They provide no assistance to the software specifier and only limited assistance to the software designer [11].

In spite of the increasing number of high-level development platforms available on market and their user friendliness the problem remains the same; to end up with a smooth-running, well documented and understood, easy maintainable, portable, reliable and an **efficient** system. Good software engineering criterias are valid and should be followed also by expert system developers. Some might question this but that is because of lack of an holistic view; The systems are developed to serve a specific purpose and to be integrated within an already established organizational and technological culture.

3.4.2 The Problem of Standardization

What will happen when managers at different levels in an organization and specialists of various kinds within the same organization starts developing their own specialized applications on different hardware, using different methods and tools? Engineers probably choose a different type of development platform than the chief executive. The diversity of programming languages will reflect the variety of different computers in use. Some of them will be application-oriented higher level languages while others are implemented in assembler. Within a relatively short time there will be organizations that must be prepared to deal with a set of completely decoupled and autonomous systems running on the shop floor. On an operational level these organizations will show anarchistic tendencies.

While it is important to establish standards, it is also important to concentrate on those standards that can be implemented in a reasonable period and that will provide the most immediate benefit to the organization. Standards must be kept current. They should be modified based on the experiences in using and enforcing them, on the changes in available technology, and on the varying needs of the projects. Watts [7] suggests that in establishing new standards, it is rarely wise to adopt one from another organization because of the need for acceptance and enforcement from those who use the standards.

When bringing IHOPE into operation within different organizations we have often met a complicated situation where there exists standards that are old or developed by some no longer involved person. These organizations show an almost infinite number of representations and interpretations of partially overlapping tasks.

Until we understand and quantify the specification and design of expert system software and build tools to support this process, the software crisis can hardly be completely avoided.

3.5 The Need for a Framework

In our project we have succeeded in introducing the IHOPE-system to the real world. This is surely not to be generalized. As in any system only the strong will survive without the ability to adapt. As long as no standards are guiding expert system development, our main concern is and will be to try to adopt a frame of reference based on the well understood concepts of software enginnering, concepts that have been developed during the past twenty-five years. Our task will not be to justify the existence of the new tools and aids expert systems provide. We know they are powerful. Feigenbaum & McCorduck in their well known book, *The Fifth Generation* stated that knowledge is power and that machines that can amplify human knowledge will amplify every dimension of power. Donald Michie once formulated our intentions very clear:

It is not enough to know that a system contains expertise to believe in its solutions. The system itself must be based on stable conceptual foundations.

The study of the software engineering disciplines will provide guidance in this work.

As we can see the problem consists of two parts, firstly there are all the 'old' problems from the crisis in the 60's and secondly there are a series of new aspects that we have no knowledge about at all from this point of view.

These topics can be summarized as follows:

- The lack of methods to support exploratory programming [12].

- The impact of complexity when dealing with incremental system development. Do the rules of thumb from the area of software engineering still hold?

- The problem of integrating odd programming languages with an ordinary software environment.

- To investigate the efficiency aspects of non-efficient systems

4. CONCLUSIONS

We have briefly presented a computer supported method to choose tools and operational sequences for hole-machining. Initially we described the type of knowledge that we considered to be essential for this knowledge-processing system. This knowledge, i.e. domain specific knowledge, was characterized as *tacit knowledge* that gradually grows from experience. We argued that our ambition was to extract this knowledge and incorporate it in a computerized system. Subsequently we described the basic characteristics of the system. We concluded that the system was to be regarded as a decision support system rather than a decision making system according to the definitions given in [9].

480

Among a number of general system development paradigms we found the so called *Exploratory programming approach* to be the one best suited for describing the nature of expert system development. The resulting software structure from this model was said to be ill-structured. This means that maintenance of such systems is likely to be difficult and costly, particulary when, as is usual with large systems, the system maintainers are not the original developers. Most users of exploratory programming are highly qualified and skilled. The management of large systems involves a range of skill levels and it is not clear how feasible this approach will be for such an environment.

Subsequently we discussed some topics based on our own experiences from what we have seen from the usage of our system. Lower skilled people became able to produce high-quality output simply by providing them with an appropriate interface that encouraged their own creativity by dynamic interaction. Other aspects of the use of knowledge based systems and their impact on society were discussed.

Coming together with the expert system paradigm are are a number of new problems. From an historical point of view we should act with utmost care when introducing these new concepts to society. Nevertheless, today certain application domains are still to be found. It should however be mentioned the need for stable conceptual foundations to rely upon. A number of critical issues mainly concerning methodological aspects of expert system development were presented such as the lack of methods to deal with complexity within these systems, the management of large ill-structured systems and how to integrate different software development paradigms within one organization. No answers were given. Instead one should consider our discussion as an empirical survey where the results consists of certain highlighted questions.

REFERENCES

[1] Bruce G. Buchanan and Edward H. Shortliffe, *RULE-BASED EXPERT SYSTEMS, The MYCIN Experiments of The Stanford Heuristic Programming Project*, Addison Wesley (1984).

[2] Edward A. Feigenbaum and Pamela McCorduck, *The Fifth Generation*, Pan Books (1984).

[3] Bo Goranzon, *Datautvecklingens Filosofi*, Studentlitteratur (1983).

[4] Paul Harmon, Rex Maus, and William Morrissey, *EXPERT SYSTEMS, Tools&Applications*, Wiley (1988).

[5] Anna Hart, *Knowledge Acquisition for Expert Systems*, Kogan Page (1986).

[6] Clyde W. Holsapple and Andrew Winston, *Expert Systems using GURU*, Dow Jones-Irwin (1986).

[7] Watts S. Humphrey, *Managing the Software Process*, Addison-Wesley (1989).

[8] Peter Jackson, *Introduction to Expert Systems*, Addison Wesley (1986).

[9] Bengt G. Lundberg, "On the Evaluation of Heuristic Information Systems", *To be published in Decision Support Systems*, 1988.

[10] Herbert Simon, "The Structure of Ill-Structured Problems"", *Artficial Intelligence*, Vol. 4 no. NN (1973).

[11] Ian Sommerville and Ron Morrison, *Software Development with Ada*, Addison-Wesley (1987).

[12] Ian Sommerville, *Software Engineering 3 ed.*, Addison-Wesley (1989).

[13] Hans Vogt and Per Zaring, *A Computerized Interactive Hole Operation Planning Expert('IHOPE')*, Department of Production Technology and Department of Computer Science, Chalmers University of Technology (1990).

[14] Hans G. Vogt, "Choice of Tools and Operational Sequences for Machining of Holes", *IVF Result 77629*, Mekanforbundet, Stockholm, 1977.

[15] Hans G. Vogt, "Beeinflussung der Zerspanung bei der Innenbearbeitung insbesondere beim Gewindebohren", *Diss. CTH Department of Production Technology*, 1985.

[16] Yvonne Waern, *Cognitive Aspects of Computer Supported Tasks*, Wiley&Sons (1989).

Protein Function Database
as a Deductive and Object-Oriented Database

Hidetoshi Tanaka

Institute for New Generation Computer Technology (ICOT)
1-4-28, Mita, Minato-ku, Tokyo 108 Japan
htanaka@icot.or.jp

Abstract

This paper describes an experiment on a knowledge base approach to molecular biological databases, especially focusing on a protein function database.

Although there are many databanks of DNAs and proteins to support research in molecular biology, their integrated database is urgently requested, because redundancies and gaps among them prevent effectiveness of such data and knowledge.

For the integrated database, we take an approach to write various data and knowledge in a single knowledge representation language, $QUIXOTE$, which is designed at ICOT for deductive and object-oriented database (DOOD). As a protein function database is a typical one with complex data and inference rules, we start to describe it in $QUIXOTE$ as a part of the integrated database.

This paper describes motives for our experiments, status quo of biological database researches, features of $QUIXOTE$, the concept of a protein function database, examples of its representation in $QUIXOTE$, and evaluation.

1 Introduction

New concepts of database management systems (DBMS) are anxiously awaited in molecular biology. DBMS are used for storing and statistically analyzing data, both of which play important roles in molecular biological research. When we treat molecular biological data, we find that the traditional relational database model is not suitable for representing them. DNA sequences vary greatly in their length, and the feature descriptions of their regions overlap and are complicated. Amino acid sequences are generally shorter than DNA, but they have complex secondary and 3-D structures. The traditional model has many restrictions in itself to prevents natural representation of such data.

Besides, an integrated database of molecular biology is urgently required. There are various kinds of databanks* in molecular biology so that every time biologists have to use a new one, they are annoyed at understanding characteristics of each attribute: name, definition, syntax, and access methods.

In order to design an effective integrated database by means of a new concept, we have to do two works. Firstly, we should translate each existing databank into a database in new DBMS, so that syntactic mismatches would disappear. It is also important to discuss what kind of schema we should choose for them,

---

*In order to avoid semantical overloading of a term "database", I use a term "databank" for a collection of data and "database" for data related to a data model or DBMS

or how to parse valuable knowledge written in their comments. Secondly, we have to construct a knowledge base which has various knowledge items supplementary to them, so that semantic mismatches would be reduced. For example, if a certain attribute had its own rule to access data, or another table which explains meanings of its values, they act as knowledge to make its semantics clear.

At ICOT, we have several projects related to molecular biology, including the development of DBMS and the design of a knowledge representation language [12]. We have developed a DBMS, Kappa[17], based on a nested relational model, where GenBank and PIR are stored, and will develop some applications to help biologists. We are also developing a deductive and object-oriented database (DOOD)[16] language named $QUIXOTE$ [13].

Our research shows that it is not difficult to translate databanks whose schema are so concrete as ones mentioned above, into both Kappa and $QUIXOTE$.

Thus I proceed to the second issue, through providing formal function descriptions of DNAs or proteins as knowledge items. Function descriptions are what biologists really want to get and store, though it is not usefully acceptable in the existing databanks. These are so important to be written in a formal language, to be used in reasoning.

I choose a protein function database to build in a DOOD concept, as a first step to see following two points. First point is what kinds of knowledge are really useful for molecular biologists. I should provide an example knowledge base to get answers of this question. A protein function database seems useful in itself, in biochemistry or protein engineering. Second point is how efficiently we could adapt this new concept to molecular biological knowledge. One of the features of $QUIXOTE$ is natural representation and inference of complex objects. It seems a good example that representing chemical reactions which weave complicated networks.

This paper describes a tiny example of a protein function database in $QUIXOTE$, as an ingredient of an integrated knowledge base of molecular biology. Through this experiment I show the possibility of realization of integrated knowledge base as well as the usefulness of $QUIXOTE$.

I make a brief survey of molecular biological databases in Section 2, and explain how to represent the functions of proteins and show the configuration of the protein function database in Section 3. Introduction to the concepts and the features of $QUIXOTE$ is shown in Section 4, and an experimental description of protein functions, electron transfer through cytochromes for example, in Section 5. Section 6 is for the evaluation of the protein function database in $\mathcal{QUIXOTE}$ at the present and the future works, and Section 7 is for concluding remarks.

2   Molecular Biological Databases

I make a brief survey of researches in molecular biological databases. There are two points as I mentioned: new data models and integration of databases.

2.1   Data Models for Existing Databanks

Existing databanks [6] fall into roughly four categories: sequence, structure, map, and function.

The main problem in building the data model for sequence databases is how to represent feature descriptions of sequences. A relational model[2], CYC and interval calculus[9], and a nested relational model[17] have been tried.

How to represent "motifs" is another important issue. A motif is a sub-sequence of DNAs or amino acids representing a certain feature. It is usually represented in a syntax like regular expression at the present[11].

The data model for protein structure databank is also discussed: a deductive database[4] and an object-oriented database with a functional data model[3].

No adequate data model has been proposed for either map or function databases. Relational DBMS are usually used for them, enduring inconveniences.

Among data models mentioned above, object-oriented one is the most suitable to represent all databanks commonly. But provided that we require not only syntactic integration but also semantic one, the data model needs a certain mechanism to describe various relations between any attributes or any values easily.

I propose to use a deductive and object-oriented data model, which allows us to write any rules of attributes or values. It could be used efficiently in representing most data and rules in molecular biology.

2.2   Researches on Integrated Database

There are two kinds of trials to conquer impedance mismatches and realize an integrated database.

One is standardization. CODATA (Committee on Data for Science and Technology) in ICSU (International Council of Scientific Unions) proposed standardization of attributes so that it seems like one large database, which really consists of many databases[10]. NLM (National Library of Medicine) provides GenInfo Backbone Database[8]. They are built as a standardized primary databases, which are assumed to be a basis for secondary, value-added databases for each interest of biologists. In that sense, really convenient databases should be built by each biologist.

I choose another approach, to make an integrated knowledge base. It consists of two stages: to represent all facts in one language, and to supplement rules necessary to access facts, in the same language. The former corresponds to standardization, and realizes a syntactically integrated database. In the latter stage, supplementary knowledge items such as access methods for attributes or another table which explains its values as to relations, types, and other constraints or rules are provided.

A DOOD concept used in $\mathcal{QUIXOTE}$ has enough power to represent every data in existing databanks and most rules for them. Building a protein function database belongs to both stages. It is an ingredient of integrated database, as well as supplementary knowledge base for protein sequence or structure database.

3   Protein Function Database

A protein function database is the first step in the second stage toward an integrated knowledge base of molecular biology. I focus to represent chemical reactions, not only reactions among compounds but also relations among reactions. I show the reason why I choose chemical reactions, outline of an example, and how I design a total protein function database in $\mathcal{QUIXOTE}$.

3.1   Functions of Proteins

Proteins grouped by functions[5] and the corresponding properties to describe their functions are shown as follows:

Proteins:	Properties:
Enzymes	substrates, products, coenzymes, environments (ions, temperature, ...)
Transport	object, from, to, environments
Nutrient and Storage	place, environments
Contractile or Motile	place, environments
Structural	place, environments
Defense	object, place, environments
Regulatory	object, place, environments
Others	(?)

Function descriptions of proteins other than enzymes are expressed by names and environments, though the names vary in their meanings. I choose a methodology for representing enzyme function as a main issue. It is no more than chemical reaction expressions and the relations among them. They include the information of enzyme functions implicitly.

3.2   Reactions and Relations of Reactions

A scheme of a chemical reaction among compounds, concerning enzymes and co-enzymes is shown in the expression in Fig. 3.1. As all the attributes are multi-valued, even with an infinite structure, it is necessary to represent in complex objects. A proper frame-like language allows chemical reactions to be represented in the scheme in Fig. 3.1. It is enough to describe its static information.

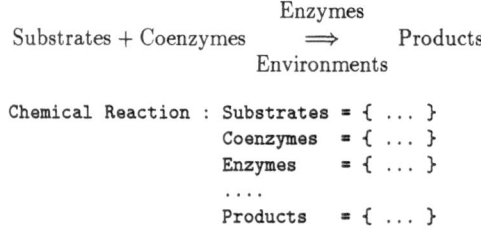

Fig. 3.1 Scheme of Chemical Reactions

The relations among reactions, such as electron transfer through cytochromes or the relation between catabolism and anabolism, is harder to describe than the reactions themselves. If we regard only compounds as entities, it would be a complicated description (see Fig. 3.2-(1)). It becomes easier however, once we regard each sort as an entity, such as cytochrome b or cytochrome c_1, and then regard each reaction as an entity, and so on (see Fig. 3.2-(2)). And it is sure that both representation are necessary, if we expect to get answer in both lower level (such as "oxidized cytochrome b") and higher level (such as "cytochrome b").

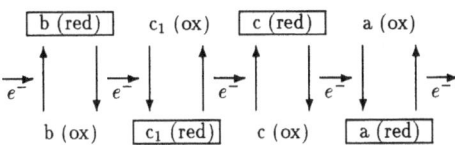

(1) All-in-one description

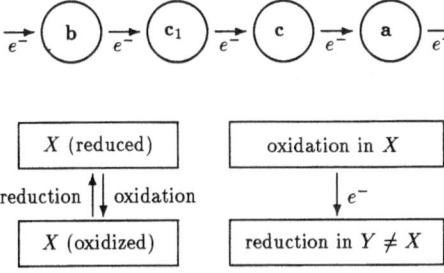

(2) Step-by-step description

Fig 3.2 Electron Transport through Cytochromes

Chemical reactions and the relations among them can be written in a frame-like language or scheme if we focus on the ability to answer questions on the function of the enzymes, namely static information as shown above. But once we have to get the relations among compounds or proteins, deductive features are mandatory, in tracing their connections or deducing from primitive knowledge such as a "step-by-step description" to appropriate knowledge such as an "all-in-one description" as shown in Fig. 3.2.

Hence we think DOOD is suitable, for it requires both object-oriented (or frame-like) and deductive features to represent molecular biological knowledge.

3.3 Design of a Protein Function Database

Fig. 3.3 shows the configuration for a protein function database which I plan to build in $\mathcal{QUIXOTE}$. $\mathcal{QUIXOTE}$ has a concept of modules (see Section 4), so each database module is designed to be independent.

In this system, GenBank and PIR are provided in the simplest schema, as near to the schema of original databanks as possible. The protein function database consists of several sub-modules: chemical reactions, relations among them, and the others that were enumerated before. The interface module shown in Fig. 3.3 inherits all other modules and is engaged in query processing. It has rules for getting questions, transforming them into proper queries, getting knowledge items in the implicit forms, and transforming those into proper answers.

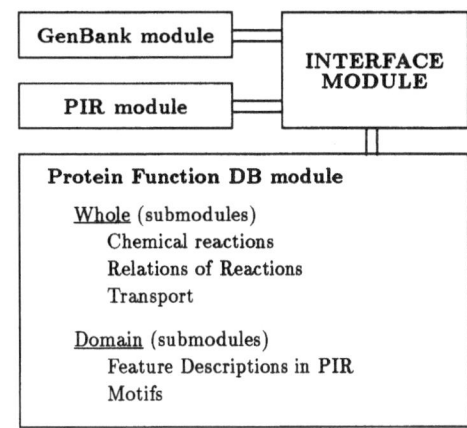

Fig 3.3 Protein Function Database in $\mathcal{QUIXOTE}$

4 $\mathcal{QUIXOTE}$: a DOOD Language

In [13] a new database language $\mathcal{QUIXOTE}$ has been proposed as a knowledge representation language, whose ancestors are languages for deductive and object-oriented databases [15] and natural language processing applications. It is shown more precisely in [14] and [7].

4.1 Object Terms and Properties

In $\mathcal{QUIXOTE}$, an object consists of the identifier named an object term and the attributes. Each attribute of them is a triple of a label, an operator and a value. An object term consists of the head and the attributes. For example:

$$head[lo1 = vo1, lo2 \leftarrow vo2, \ldots].$$

where $lo1$ and $lo2$ are labels, $vo1$ and $vo2$ are values, and $=, \leftarrow$ are operators. Values are also object terms so that complex objects can be represented. Object terms are partially ordered.

An object term can have attributes as follows:

$$o/[la1 = va1, la2 \rightarrow va2, \ldots].$$

where o is an object term, $la1$ and $la2$ are labels, $va1$ and $va2$ are values, and $=, \rightarrow$ are operators. Such a term is called an attribute term. The right hand side of / is a list of attributes. According to the order of object terms, attributes with $=$ or $\rightarrow$ are inherited from upper objects to the lower objects. As attributes in an object term cannot be updated, exception of inheritance is occurred at the object.

4.2 Rules

In $\mathcal{QUIXOTE}$, rules to create new objects can be written as follows:

$$new\_object \Leftarrow object, object, \ldots.$$

A new object is created if all the objects on the right hand side exist.

4.3 Constraints

In $\mathcal{QUIXOTE}$, an object term, an attribute term, and a rule can be written in a cannonical constraint form. For example, any rule can be written as follows:

$$o \mid \{c_0, \ldots\} \Leftarrow o_1, o_2, \ldots \parallel \{c_1, c_2, \ldots\}.$$

where $\{c_0, \ldots\}$ is a set of constraints of o, and $\{c_1, c_2, \ldots\}$ is a set of constraints of $o_1, o_2, \ldots$. Conditions in a chemical reaction can be written as a part of such constraints.

4.4 Modules

$\mathcal{QUIXOTE}$ has a concept of modules, each of which is a set of objects and rules. A submodule relation between modules makes rule inheritance possible. An object can have different states or properties in each module. Modules are written as follows:

$$\text{module\_id :: object.}$$
$$\text{module\_id :: rule.}$$

4.5 Features

A DOOD language $\mathcal{QUIXOTE}$ has various features as follows:

(1)	DDB	deductive features
(2)	Inheritance	inheritance mechanism in objects
(3)	Module	features of modules
(4)	Object-ID	representation of object identity
(5)	Constraints	representation of constraints
(6)	Infinite Terms	representation of circular structures
(7)	Exceptions	representation of exceptions

This list is explained in more detail in Section 6.

5 Representation in $\mathcal{QUIXOTE}$

I have tried several experimental descriptions of molecular biological knowledge, especially protein function, in $\mathcal{QUIXOTE}$. In this section, I show a small one which includes a lot of issues to discuss. I choose electron transfer through cytochromes for this purpose.

5.1 Electron Transfer

The respiratory chain of mitochondria contains a large number of electron carrying proteins, such as cytochromes. They act in sequence to transfer electrons from substrates to oxygen. The cytochromes are iron-containing electron transferring red or brown proteins that act in sequence to carry electrons from ubiquinone to molecular oxygen. They undergo oxidation and reduction as they carry electrons. There are three classes of cytochromes, a, b and c, distinguished by differences in their light-absorption spectra. Each cytochrome in its ferric [Fe(III)] form accepts one electron to become the ferrous form [Fe(II)]. [5]

I simply showed the sequence and the mechanism in Fig. 3.2.

5.2 Electron Transfer in $\mathcal{QUIXOTE}$

I described the electron transferring through cytochromes in $\mathcal{QUIXOTE}$ as simply as possible in Fig. 5.1.

```
-------------------------------------------------
m_1 :: {{
  e_transfer [l_donor= cyto_b, l_acceptor= cyto_c1].
  e_transfer [l_donor= cyto_c1,l_acceptor= cyto_c ].
  e_transfer [l_donor= cyto_c, l_acceptor= cyto_a ].
  cyto_b  =< cytochrome. %% cyto_b is a cytochrome.
  cyto_c1 =< cytochrome.
  cyto_c  =< cytochrome.
  cyto_a  =< cytochrome.
}}
m_2 >- m_1. %% m_1 is a submodule of m_2.
m_2 :: {{
  oxidation [l_object = X]
     <=e_transfer [l_donor = X, l_acceptor = Y].
  reduction [l_object = X]
     <=e_transfer [l_acceptor = X, l_donor = Y].
  oxidation =< reaction.
  reduction =< reaction.
  reaction.
  oxidation [l_object = X] /
     [l_source+ <- Y, l_product+ <- Z]||
     {Y =< X, Y!l_type = reduced, Z =< X,
     Z!l_type = oxidized}.
                   %% Y / [l_type = Y!l_type]
  reduction [l_object = X] /
     [l_source+ <- Y, l_product+ <- Z]||
     {Y =< X, Y!l_type = oxidized, Z =< X,
     Z!l_type = reduced}.
  cytochrome [l_type = reduced ].
  cytochrome [l_type = oxidized].
}}
-------------------------------------------------
```

Fig. 5.1 Electron Transfer through Cytochromes

The module m_1 describes only the flow of an electron, while m_2 shows its mechanism in detail.

In m_1, there are declarations on objects in this module: three objects under "electron_transfer" and four objects under "cytochrome". Attributes in a lower object (ex. cytochrome_b) inherit their values from the corresponding attributes in the upper object (ex. cytochrome).

In m_2, there are four groups of rules or facts. The first group contains rules that the oxidation occurs in the donor of electron transfer and the reduction in the acceptor. The second group contains declarations of oxidation, reduction and reaction. The third group shows simplified mechanisms of oxidation and reduction in cytochromes. The last group contains declarations of reduced type and oxidized type of cytochromes. The declaration that objects under cytochrome have both types is included.

If we ask module m_1 how the electron flows, it answers:

```
-------------------------------------------------
<Q>
? m_1 : e_transfer [l_donor = X, l_acceptor = Y].
<A>
e_transfer [l_donor = cyto_b,  l_acceptor = cyto_c1].
e_transfer [l_donor = cyto_c1, l_acceptor = cyto_c ].
e_transfer [l_donor = cyto_c,  l_acceptor = cyto_a ].
-------------------------------------------------
```

And if we ask m_2 its mechanism, it answers as follows: (Temporary rules can be put to queries)

```
--------------------------------------------------------
<Q>
? m_2 : e_transfer / [l_fromR = X, l_toR = Y].
  m_2 :: {{
    e_transfer [l_fromR = reduction [l_object = X],
                l_toR   = oxidation [l_object = Y] ]
         <= e_transfer [l_donor = X, l_acceptor = Y].
  }}
<A>
e_transfer [l_fromR = reduction[l_object = cyto_b],
            l_toR   = oxidation[l_object = cyto_c1] ].
e_transfer [l_fromR = reduction[l_object = cyto_c1],
            l_toR   = oxidation[l_object = cyto_c] ].
e_transfer [l_fromR = reduction[l_object = cyto_c],
            l_toR   = oxidation[l_object = cyto_a] ].
--------------------------------------------------------
```

6 Evaluation

I evaluate this work from two points of view: the needs, namely from a molecular biological point of view and the seeds, namely from a viewpoint of $\mathcal{QUIXOTE}$.

6.1 Influences on Molecular Biology

This paper describes only about chemical reactions in $\mathcal{QUIXOTE}$, which is so small part of our target, an integrated knowledge base, that I cannot discuss a lot from that point. Thus I evaluate only the result of Section 5.

For the molecular biology, the major benefit is that data which was difficult to store in databases can now be stored. It is also easy to retrieve whatever data we want when we use $\mathcal{QUIXOTE}$. It is powerful in knowledge description and enables us to retrieve complex data by means of the deductive mechanism.

The following are instances that can now be stored, other than chemical reactions.

(1) Formal descriptions of features in sequence databases

The feature descriptions in existing databanks are written mostly in English, not in formal languages. We can put an object term of $\mathcal{QUIXOTE}$ instead of English words, such as:

English: "essential myosin light chain, exon 1"

$\mathcal{QUIXOTE}$: "myosin[l_1 = essential, l_2 = light_chain, l_3 = exon, l_4 = 1]." or "essential_myosin[l_2 = light_chain, l_3 = exon, l_4 = 1]."

(2) Positions in features

Another issue is in describing positions of regions. Recent GenBank allows operators such as "join" or "one-of" to describe a region separated in several subregions. It is hard to represent naturally in both relational and nested relational models, while deductive representation is very easy in $\mathcal{QUIXOTE}$. Overton et al. also show the need for hierarchical representation in feature description and efficiency of an object-oriented database [9].

(3) Motifs

Each protein has domains which have certain functions. One of the main issues related to protein research is what kind of amino acid sequence represents a certain function. The sequences whose functions are known are called functional motifs. We also have structural motifs, which represent the local structure of proteins.

Many of both structural and functional motifs are known so far, but they are also written in some patterns, which are difficult for programs to use. [11].

Motifs have their own syntax which we have to remember to use them. So we could easily use motifs if we have the methods to access them or how to read them in a class and store motif data as its subclasses.

6.2 Features of $\mathcal{QUIXOTE}$

This table shows the features of $\mathcal{QUIXOTE}$ (see Section 4) and their usages and aims in this experiment.

Features	Usages	Aims
(1) DDB	relations among reactions reaction paths	primitive →appropriate trace paths
(2) Inheritance	sorts	reduce amount
(3) Module	knowledge modules	check inconsistency
(4) Object-ID	objects & modules	share objects
(5) Constraints	body of rules queries	represent a domain
(6) Infinite Terms	—	—
(7) Exceptions	—	—

Generally speaking, deductive mechanism enables to deduce appropriate knowledge from primitive knowledge, constraint representation is used in writing conditions efficiently, object identity is useful in sharing objects, and inheritance and the module reduce the amount of knowledge description, while the representation of exceptions and complex structure are not used well at the present.

(1) Deductive feature

We can deduce appropriate knowledge from primitive knowledge, so that we can store knowledge in primitive style. As I mentioned in Section 3, it reduce complicated knowledge such as electron transfer into several simple facts. ·

It is also useful when we search various paths, especially together with infinite term to represent a path including circles. But I defer this issue.

(2) Inheritance mechanism in object terms

The inheritance mechanism is used to reduce the amount of description of each object. For example, "cytochrome c" inherits all the properties of "cytochrome" so we can omit those properties in all objects under "cytochrome".

(3) Modules

It is important to make small modules of knowledge, so that we can easily check them and keep inconsistency within the module. As I mentioned in Section 3, we can store GenBank and PIR as modules, provide an interface module for them, add our own protein function database as another module and so on, without any trouble.

(4) Object identity

The object identifier in $\mathcal{QUIXOTE}$ has its name and property with which users can find a specific object from a pool of objects. It enables sharing a persistent object among programs. It makes compound objects to be represented efficiently.

486

(5) Constraints

Constraints are useful for writing complex attribute values such as specification of the range of a value, and condition to be satisfied in the body of a rule.

(6) Infinite Terms

It would be useful when we represent various paths including circles, for we can use infinite terms. But I defer this issue.

(7) Exception

I have not found any proper examples in molecular biology, though the well known example of birds and penguins are in a very near subject.

6.3 Future Works

There are three directions to proceed our researches.

(1) An useful tool for biologists

It is important for biologist's use to process quantity information. The chemical reaction has various quantity information, or stoichiometrical issues such as coefficient of each compounds or differences of free energy. Brutlag et al. employ the KEE system for this purpose[1].

Besides, We should estimate the performance of $\mathcal{QUIXOTE}$, and increase it.

(2) A more useful protein function database

Motifs are indispensable to describe functions of domains. We should look for the best way to represent them, to search the corresponding sequences efficiently.

Representation of complex structures, especially circular structures, should be tried and evaluated to see whether they are useful or not, for representing the result of searching various paths.

(3) An integrated knowledge base

It is important to increase its ingredients. For example, a genome map should be the next target to make an experimental representation.

And it is also important to increase its supplementary knowledge. We should research the way to extract such knowledge or rules, from biologists or from facts in databanks.

7 Concluding Remarks

I show the effectiveness and the possibility of an integrated knowledge base of molecular biology, through an example of a protein function database in $\mathcal{QUIXOTE}$.

I also introduced a DOOD language $\mathcal{QUIXOTE}$, designed at ICOT. Its great expressive power allows facts to be described in so many ways, that we are discussing a standard format for description. $\mathcal{QUIXOTE}$ is suitable for describing data and knowledge which could not be described before, and enables us to use them through programs.

Acknowledgements

The author wishes to thank Kazumasa Yokota, Hideki Yasukawa,and other people in the $\mathcal{QUIXOTE}$ project for their valuable comments on earlier versions of the paper, and people on the computer-biology mailing list for their many suggestions from the viewpoint of biology.

References

[1] Brutlag, D.L., Galper, A.R. and Millis, D.H.: "Knowledge-based Simulation of DNA Metabolism: Prediction of Enzyme Action", *CABIOS* No.7, Vol.9 (1991).

[2] Cinkosky, M.J. et al.: "GenBank/HGIR Technical Manual", *LA-UR* 88-3038 (LANL) (1988).

[3] Gray, P.M.D. et al.: "An Object-Oriented Database for Protein Structure Analysis", *Protein Engineering*, vol.3 no.4, pp.235-243 (1990).

[4] Kuhara, S., Satou, K., Furuichi, E. and Takagi, T.: "A Deductive Database System PACADE for Three Dimensional Structure of Protein", *Draft* (1990).

[5] Lehninger, A.L.: *Principles of Biochemistry*, Worth Publishers Inc. (1982).

[6] Lesk, A.M. (editor) : *Computational Molecular Biology, Sources and Methods for Sequence Analysis*, Oxford Univ. Press (1988).

[7] Morita, Y., Haniuda, H. and Yokota, K.: "Object Identity in $\mathcal{QUIXOTE}$", *IPSJ SIGDBS*, No.80 (Nov 1990).

[8] NCBI: "GenInfo Backbone Database", Version 1.59, *Draft* (Apr 1990).

[9] Overton, G.C., Koile, K. and Pastor, J.A.: "GeneSys: A Knowledge Management System for Molecular Biology", *Computers and DNA, SFI Studies in the Science of Complexity*, vol.VII, Addison-Wesley, pp.213-239 (1990).

[10] PIR-International (JIPID): *PIR Newsletter*, No.3 (June 1990).

[11] Trifonov, E.N. and Brendel, V.: *Gnomic - A Dictionary of Genetic Codes*, Balaban Publishers.

[12] Uchida, S. and Yoshida, K.: "The Fifth Generation Computer Technology and Biological Sequencing", *Proc. of Workshop on Advanced Computer Technologies and Biological Sequencing* (Nov 1988).

[13] Yasukawa, H. and Yokota, K.: "The Overview of a Knowledge Representation Language $\mathcal{QUIXOTE}$" *Draft*, (1990).

[14] Yasukawa, H. and Yokota, K.: "Labeled Graphs as Semantics of Objects", *IPSJ SIGDBS*, No.80 (Nov 1990).

[15] Yokota, K.: "The Outline of a Deductive and Object-Oriented Language: Juan", *IPSJ SIGDBS*, No.78 (Jul 1990).

[16] Yokota, K. and Nishio, S.: "Toward Integration of Deductive Databases and Object-Oriented Databases: A Limited Survey", *Proc. of Advanced Database System Symposium*, Kyoto (Dec 1989).

[17] Yokota, K. and Tanaka, H.: "GenBank in Nested Relation", *Joint Japanese-American Workshop on Future Trends in Logic Programming* (Oct 1989).

System Architecture and Specification of a Fast BOM Object Processor Using a Standard Relational Database Management System and a Main Memory Cache

Frank Steyer

TFH Berlin, Fachbereich 13 (Informatik)
Luxemburger Str. 10, D-1000 Berlin 65 (F.R.G.)

ABSTRACT

Based on standard relational tables, a more complex data structure (the directed ordered acyclic graph) together with its operational interface, is investigated. Linked lists are used for
representation and kept in cache memory, which
allows a much more efficient data retrieval.
These data structures have a wide range of applications, e.g. bill-of-material applications (BOM).

1   Introduction

Standard relational database systems have as
data structure flat tables which are very common
for many administrative tasks [3] . But data modelling in new fields of database applications,
e.g. engineering, CAD/CAM, requires the representation of more complex objects than in conventional applications.
A very useful data structure of a more complex
type is a directed ordered acyclic graph (DOAG)
which is very appropriate for bill of material
processing.

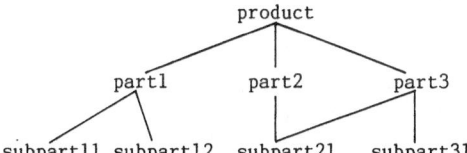

Fig.1: Bill of material (BOM) graph

In Fig.1 a product consists of three parts which
on their turn consist of subparts. In general it
must be accepted that the data structures of engineering applications should allow sub-assemblies
to be defined recursively, and other sub-assemblies to be shared or overlapping between assem-
blies [1] .
This data structure can be implemented and processed with flat tables. But the processing with
standard relational operators may produce run
time performance problems:
- A query, explosion of a product for example,
  would result in many sub-queries during the
traversal of the whole graph. Each sub-query has
to pass the process of syntactic and semantic
checking again.
- Each sub-query also means communication effort.
  Orders have to be sent from application to the
  RDBMS, intermediate and final results have to be
  sent back.
There are several suggestions to extend SQL by
transitive closure functions which support nested
objects [5] . This article presents another approach:
- The implementation of the DOAG structure as relational tables is kept.
- The relations are transformed to appropriate
  dynamic data structures.
- Operations on it are defined as a programming
  interface.
- A main memory cache is used to exploit more and
  more available hardware resources.
The concept of a main memory cache in this situation follows a suggestion e.g. by [2] .
The different aspects for the BOM processor in
terms of database design, system architecture,
operational interface, and storage administration
are discussed in the following chapters. A list
of open problems with possible solutions concludes
the paper.

2   Relational Design of Bill of Material Data

A tree and its common representation [4] is done
with two tables COMPONENT and ARTICLE. ARTICLE
contains the attributes of the articles, they represent the nodes in the graph. The connections
are contained in the COMPONENT table.

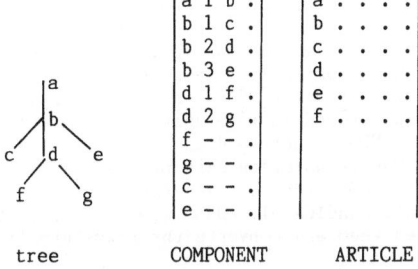

Fig.2: Tree and its relational representation

Note that by this technique (edge = node pair = table row) also a join of edges can be formulated.

table COMPONENT   table ARTICLE

Column name	Type	Column name	Type
artmajor	char(16)	artcode	char(16)
position	integer	artdesc	char(30)
artminor	char(16)	leadt	integer
qty	integer	price	money(16)

Fig.3: Table definitions [3]

3   System Architecture

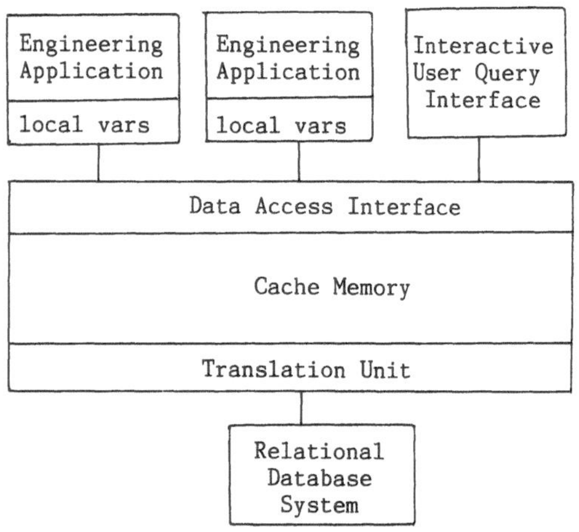

Fig.4: BOM Cache system architecture

The general system architecture for the BOM processor is shown in the above diagram. The processor is positioned between the application programs which access the structure data (COMPONENT table), and the RDBMS. The modules of the processor can be broadly classified under three areas: data access interface, cache memory, and translation unit.
The **data access interface** provides a programming interface for application programs. This programming interface consists of function calls of a standard programming language, for example C.
The **cache memory** holds the necessary information of the BOM structure data in main memory. The information stored in this unit is a conversion of the real BOM structure data lying on the RDBMS disks. The **translation unit** provides a buffer between the BOM processor and the underlying RDBMS. This unit handles all RDBMS specific requests, executes them and converts the rows into linked lists.

4   Data Access Interface

4.1 BOM System operations
There are functions necessary to start up, maintain, and shut down the BOM system as a whole.

- bom_start
The BOM cache system is initialized. Programming language definitions, database definitions, storage allocations are done, possibly with interaction.

- bom_stop
The BOM system is stopped.

- bom_clear
The cache with all structure data is cleared .

- bom_fill
The cache is filled with all structure information out of the COMPONENT table.

4.2 Accessing Single Nodes
To get the starting point for the tree operations, a function to find any article node, is provided:
bp_sel_node

4.3 Tree Operations
To search in structure data, the following functions are defined:

- bp_sel_top_down_one_level (use-what)
For one entry node all subordinate nodes of the next lower level are found.

- bp_sel_top_down_one_level_with_amount
For one entry node all subordinate nodes of the next lower level are found together with the necessary amount of subordinate parts (gross-demand).

- bp_sel_top_down_all_levels (use-what)
For one entry node all subordinate nodes down to the bottom level are found.

- bp_sel_top_down_all_levels_with_amount
For one entry node the set of all subordinate nodes down to the bottom level is found together with the necessary amount of subordinate parts.

- bp_sel_top_bottom_level_with_amount
For one entry node the set of all nodes on the bottom level is found together with the necessary amount of bottom parts (purchase list).

In the same way a set of functions for the upward direction can be defined, for example:

- bp_sel_bottom_up_one_level (where-use)
For one entry node all superordinate nodes of the next higher level is found.

- bp_fetch
After a call of a select function the output consists of a cursor. By repeated call of bp_fetch all parts are produced step-wise.

It is useful to control the order of returning the dependant parts by the parameters 'breadth' or 'depth' in the select function.

5   Cache Memory

5.1 Data Structure Mapping
From the description of the retrieval operations on BOM structure it is obvious that there is a need

for data to be logically arranged in 'use-what' as well as in 'where-use' manner to enable fast access. Both are implemented by linked lists.

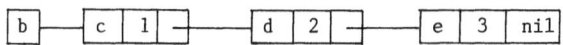

Fig.5: 'use-what' relation for article b

The 'where-use' relation of article c is similarly represented.

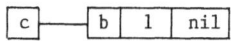

Fig.6: 'where-use' relation for article b

Furthermore an indexing mechanism id needed for quick access to the requested article node. This index uses the article code for its only key. The binary search tree index will be used because of its simplicity, fast access, and maintenance ease. To keep the search paths to a minimum, balancing is employed [7].

5.2 Article Node

The article node and the index information can be combined into one single node with the following shape:

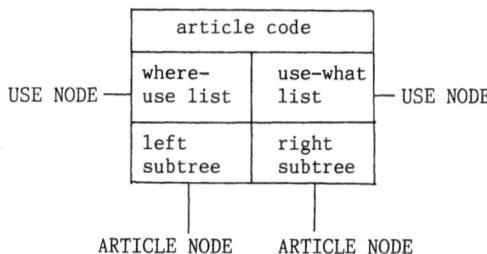

Fig.7: ARTICLE NODE

The size of the article node is 16 Bytes for the article code plus 4 times 4 Bytes for the pointers: 32 Bytes.

5.3 Use Node

The data for 'use-what' and 'where-use' operations are organized as linked lists with the following format:

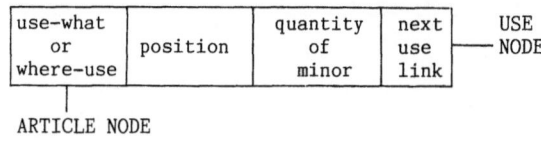

Fig.8: USE NODE

The size of the use node is 8 Bytes for the numeric values plus 2 times 4 Bytes for the pointers: 16 Bytes.
Based on the values given above, the space requirements depend on the number of articles only.
Per article one article node and two use nodes are necessary (32 Bytes + 2*16 Bytes = 64 Bytes). We get the function:

No. articles	10000	20000	30000	40000
Size in Bytes	640000	1280000	1920000	2560000

Fig.9: Storage requirements for a BOM cache

These are not too big requirements for main memory size. It should be noted that this number covers only the index and the minimal information for the structure records. Memory used for other supporting data and texts are not considered.

6 Translation Unit

To build up the BOM graph, the COMPONENT table has to be checked in three passes:
Pass 1 generates the article nodes, allocates storage, and constructs the binary tree. This makes up the basic skeleton (fig.10). **Pass 2** allocates storage for the where-use nodes, generates and connects them bottom-up-wise with the article nodes from pass 1. **Pass 3** does the same for the use-what nodes in the top-down direction.

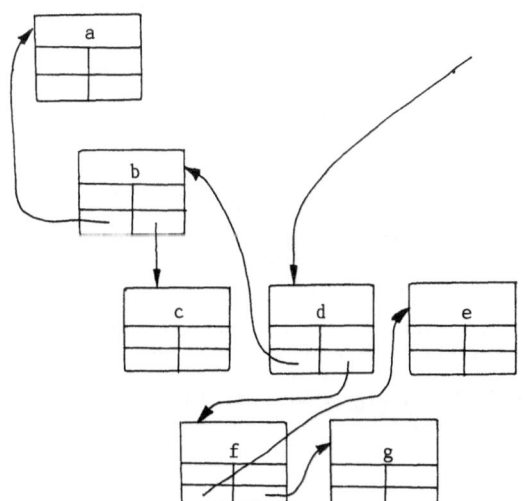

Fig.10: Binary tree for article nodes of fig.2

7 Present and Future Work

Presently, the BOM system is implemented with the following restrictions:
The generation of the dynamic data structure in

490

the cache is done once at the start up time of the
system as a whole, and it is there available for
several users in shared memory. It is assumed that
it fits completely there. If we deal with a restricted amount of main memory, some swapping strategy
has to be implemented.
We further assume that a BOM structure table is updated very seldom. So we presently do not consider
parallel updates. Another task of the future is the
implementation of a lock and refresh mechanism,
e.g. by a separate process.
Presently, we have two main interests:
Is the use of linked lists an appropriate implementation technique for the representation of complex data objects, for what types of objects, for
mixed types ?
Second, is the use of a main memory cache an appropriate architecture for significantly improving the
processing speed of complex objects ? Our test
cases cases contain trees with different levels and
fan-outs. In parallel we will implement a BOM system using the standard direct way with a large
database buffer only, and without a linked list
cache.

Acknowledgement: This paper is based on work done
together with Wilson Lee, Nixdorf Singapore, at
Nixdorf Computer Company [6] . The author wishes to
thank both. Errors are due only to the author.

References

[1] D. Batory and A. Buchmann, Molecular Objects,
    Abstract Data Types and Data Models: A Frame-
    work, Proc. VLDB, Singapore, 1984

[2] M. Hardwick, Why ROSE is Fast: Five Optimiza-
    tions in the Design of an Experimental Data-
    base System for CAD/CAM Applications, Proc.
    ACM SIGMOD Conference, San Francisco, 1987

[3] INFORMIX (SINIX) V2.0, SIEMENS AG, 1984

[4] G. Schlageter, W. Stucky, Datenbanksysteme:
    Konzepte und Modelle, Teubner, 1983

[5] D. Spooner, M. Hardwick, G. Samaras, Some Con-
    ceptual Ideas for Extending SQL for Object-
    oriented Engineering Database Systems, IEEE
    Conf. on Data and Knowledge Systems for Manu-
    facturing and Engineering, 1987

[6] F. Steyer, W. Lee, BOM Processor Cache Imple-
    mentation, Nixdorf Computer, 1990

[7] N. Wirth, Algorithmen und Datenstrukturen,
    Teubner, 1983

DATA MODELLING FOR INTERNATIONAL ORGANIZATIONS

August-Wilhelm Scheer   Stefan Spang

Institut für Wirtschaftsinformatik
Universität des Saarlandes
Im Stadtwald, Bau 14.1
D-6600 Saarbrücken (F.R.G.)

Abstract

There is a growing need in international organizations for sound solutions to the problems encountered when trying to design organization-wide information models. In the presented paper, the focus will be on the data side of the modelling effort as the key prerequisite for any integration approach.

In the paper, first a short outline of the data modelling technique and approach will be given. Next, the specific requirements on international organizations will be analyzed, and the effects on the data modelling effort will be examined. In this context, a methodological approach for modelling international organizations will be presented, along with tentative solutions for specific problems encountered when modelling particular aspects of the organization.

1 INTRODUCTION

In nowadays competitive business environments, there is increasing importance on managing complex international relationships. Internationally distributed production for international markets involving international distribution puts new requirements on the management of the manufacturing process. The efficiency of an enterprise operating in such an environment is increasingly depending on the availability of appropriate tools to manage this complexity. The stated goal, also for international organizations, is an overall integration of the company's activities. One aspect of integration certainly relates to the technical connection of previously isolated systems. In recent years, a vast variety of computerized systems has been developed to support specific activities within functionally oriented departments. But this tayloristic optimization has come to a point where no further improvements can be achieved [1]. The other side of integration deals with the underlying concepts that are the basis for the development of specific information systems. One cannot develop such systems without knowing where they will fit into the business process and what particular contribution they will make. Conceptual integration makes sure that information systems are designed within the context of a business process. In this way, systems do not support individual activities within isolated operating units, but stages within the process. As such, they are closely connected to the preceding and succeeding stages and, hence, assure the desired efficiency for this process. Data are not handed on from function to function, but regarded as an individual resource and organized independently from the requirements of specific functions [2]. This transition from an isolated department point of view to an overall perspective on the company's business is what conceptual integration is about.

Such a perspective is comprised of functional, data and organizational aspects [3],[4]. Figure 1 shows one alternative for such an architecture. As a foundation for conceptual integration, one has to design a model of the company that comprehensively reflects those aspects [5]. On the basis of this enterprise model, decisions can be taken to support the efficiency of the company's business. Of course, especially in an international organization, such an overall perspective still involves a lot of complexity. To reduce this complexity, the individual aspects of the whole may be described in separate models. Thus, a sound foundation for conceptual integration consists of a set of models describing the data, function, organization and resource view. These models are closely intertwined. It is just a matter of abstraction from the overall context that leads to individual models for each aspect. Those models help in abstracting what is important from a business perspective. They are intended to give a concise picture of the relevant aspects of reality, the emphasis of each model being on some particular perspective. In this way, data models, for example, aim at representing the business world exclusively from a data point of view, without considering functional and process issues.

From these considerations, several research issues arise:

- Are there differences in the modelling effort for international companies?
- Are those differences just due to the increased complexity, or are there more fundamental aspects involved, i.e. are the problems in modelling an international organization just a matter of degree or a matter of kind?

It turns out that internationally operating companies actually face specific problems that affect as well the data and the functional aspects of the business. There is a growing need in international organizations for sound solutions to the problems encountered when trying to design organization-wide information models. In the following, the focus will be on the data side of the modelling effort as the key prerequisite for any integration approach. There are two fundamental advantages a data model of the organization provides:

- On the one side, it can be used as a basis for the development of specific information systems that operate on the data described in the model.
- On the other side, even more important, it lays the foundation for general information management. It helps to control data redundancy and, as a basis for communication between different members of the company, the data model describes the universe of discourse when talking about the company.

492

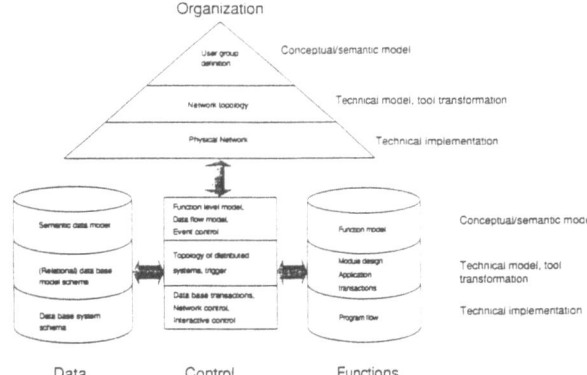

Fig. 1: Architecture of integrated information systems

This already shows the critical importance of a data model, especially within an international organization, where no single person can have expertise in every field of activity. In the following, a short outline of the data modelling technique and approach will be given. Next, the specific requirements on international organizations will be analyzed, and the effects on the data modelling effort will be examined. In this context, a methodological approach for modelling international organizations will be presented, along with tentative solutions for specific problems encountered when modelling particular aspects of the organization.

2   DATA MODELLING
The goal of a data model is to systematically describe all data that are relevant to the company's business, the internal structures as well as the linkages to the outside world. This description is not structured according to a data processing perspective, but strictly according to the application perspective. This approach is also termed "function-independent" because data are not organized with respect to the requirements of particular functions but rather from a general application point of view that combines the requirements of all individual functions that may occur within the enterprise.

2.1   A Data Modelling Technique
The technique most commonly used to represent the data aspect of an enterprise is the Entity-Relationship-Model (ERM), which was first presented by Chen in 1976 [6]. With all the extensions added since, it provides a very flexible and powerful means for representing logical data structures [7],[8],[9],[10],[11]. The elements of the ERM are entity types and relationship types. Entity types are used to refer to objects in real world (e.g., the entity type 'CUSTOMER' stands for all the individual customers of a company). Relationship types are used to express logical connections between the entity types (e.g., the two entity types 'CUSTOMER' and 'ORDER' might be connected by the relationship type 'places', so to express the fact that customers place orders). Entity types as well as relationship types can be further described by attributes (e.g., an attribute of the entity type 'customer' might be the customer's name, address etc.). In extended versions of the entity-relationship approach, relationship types can be reinterpreted as entity types, i.e. they can have relationships with other entities as well [12]. Another additional feature is the possibility of defining generalized

entity types to refer to more abstract concepts. By introducing a generalization operator, several types of entities with certain common attributes can be generalized into a higher-level entity type [13]. The concept of generalization is of particular importance in the context of designing enterprise-wide data models.
There are other techniques available, especially more implementation-oriented approaches like Bachmann. Experience has shown, however, that those approaches which originate from the technical world of hierarchical databases are not powerful enough to sufficiently represent the information relevant in the stage of conceptual modelling [14]. In the following, the focus will be on the extended Chen entity-relationship approach as described above.

2.2   A Data Modelling Process
The effort of designing a data model requires a sound procedure to assure consistency of the model. Experience has shown that it is best to first model the enterprise on an information object level, without assigning descriptive attributes to those objects in the first step. To efficiently guide the design process, area data models are developed for the individual functional areas of the enterprise (e.g., an area model for the sales and order processing, for production control, for warehousing etc.). Each area data model has to be consolidated in the overall enterprise-wide model to assure consistency. At this stage, precise definitions and descriptions of the information objects are of critical importance. Thus, relationships of information objects within one area model to objects of some other area model are revealed right away, and redundancy between the area models can at least be controlled, if not eliminated. Once the enterprise model is designed on an object level, the descriptive attributes are assigned to the established information objects.

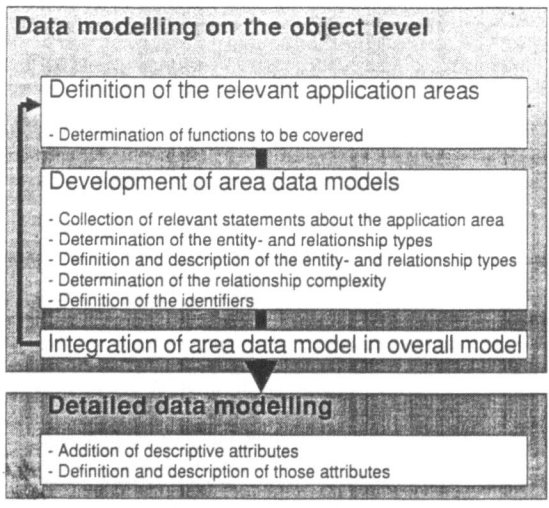

Fig. 2: Phases for the development of a data model

Figure 2 gives an overview on the modelling process. This process holds for the case of modelling an individual company and has been carried through in practice many times. The issue now is what modifications to this approach are necessary when modelling an international company.

3 INFLUENCING FACTORS FOR INTERNATIONAL ORGANIZATIONS

In order to examine the effects of internationality on the data modelling effort, it is necessary to give a working definition of just what makes an organization international. In the following, the main points that characterize such an organization will be discussed briefly.

3.1 Distributed Operating Units

The most prevalent property of an international organization is the international distribution of its operating units. Hence, an international company does not only sell to international markets, but runs operating units in the areas of sales, production, research and development on an international level. The geographic dispersion of the operating units itself already presents a cause for many problems. For it requires an internal communication infrastructure which is appropriate to timely convey any information relevant to the company's business to the respective addressee. The communication network is the central means of coordination for the company's activities and has to overcome aspects like time lag and multilinguality.

3.2 Markets

From the internationally distributed operating units, it is apparent that such an organization faces heterogeneous markets, too. In this context, all the problems of international marketing become important. The central task is to define a marketing mix which is appealing to customers from most heterogeneous cultural backgrounds. The composition of a successful mix requires expertise from those backgrounds, too, so that the responsibility for this task has to be allocated with the respective operating unit. But apart from finding the best marketing message, there is the additional problem if such a heterogeneous set of customers and customer groups can be described using the same criteria in the first place. This at least means that the properties used to describe the customer base have to be chosen very carefully, respecting all facets of the different customer backgrounds. It can also mean that there is actually just a very small set of common properties that can meaningful be assigned to all of the customers, and that a more differentiated description is required for each group individually.

In the context of heterogeneous markets, it is worth noting that a very complex distribution network has to be served by the organization, too. The complexity of the distribution network clearly depends on the overall strategy of the company: The problem is far less significant if the international organization views itself merely as some kind of holding, whereas the regional operating units serve their local market. In the opposite case, where an international network of operating units produces a common set of goods and services, which are distributed to an international market, the coordination of the distribution activities plays a central role in managing the company's business.

3.3 Stockholders

In an international organization, there probably is an international set of stockholders, too. Every one of them brings in specific interests which may well reflect political and social issues in the respective region. Hence, the process of finding the appropriate goals for the whole of the international organization is already a problem of its own. This especially holds for profit-oriented organizations, because the distribution of profits comes as a consequence of the distribution of tasks between the local operating units. Looking at the planning process in international organizations, it appears best to establish a basic set of common goals and then determine specific objectives for each operating unit individually. This again means more differentiation in the underlying information structure.

The case is different for non-for-profit organizations. They can keep up their general objectives for all of their operating units, which gives a much more homogeneous picture of the whole organization.

3.4 Personnel Profile

Another problem is presented by the heterogeneous personnel profile in an international organization. There is little chance of applying standard management techniques developed in one region all over the organization. Management has to take into account the diverse cultural background of the work force, which may well affect salary determination, working hours, and quality awareness. Like for the market and stockholder aspect, it is appropriate to just set general rules of management and then detail the specific management techniques and working conditions according to the respective context.

3.5 Legal and Regulative Environment

An international organization with widely distributed operating units has to respect a whole range of legal restrictions which hold for the respective region. Production techniques common in one area may be legally prohibited in another, so there is a completely different framework for each of the operating units. Assuming that the different units of the international organization still adhere to a set of common goals and tasks, it is very difficult to determine the specific functional profile of a particular unit. There are considerably less degrees of freedom for the allocation of tasks to operating units than there are in nationally restricted companies. This reduced flexibility makes the international organization vulnerable to external influences affecting one particular location.

4 EFFECTS OF INTERNATIONALITY ON DATA MODELLING

The explanations given above already indicated that internationality has effects on the organization's information structure and, hence, on data modelling. It also became apparent that those differences are not only due to the generally increased amount of data, but also to the necessity of accounting for more differentiated information structures. In the following, the specific effects on data modelling will be examined. The thesis is that internationality affects the data modelling process as well as the structure of the particular data models.

4.1 Modelling Approach

As a prerequisite for the further discussion, the overall objective of the modelling effort has to be determined. The hypothesis is that in the case of a truly international organization, it is best to allow for the cultural differentiations which express themselves in different languages and use and meaning of concepts. The task is not to create an overall artificial conceptual structure, with no exact correspondence to any of the source structures involved. Much rather, the goal is to first show the interrelationships between the diverse conceptual structures and, thus, provide some means for managing them. In some cases, it will turn out that there are actually common concepts involved, whereas in many others, representations from one conceptual structure only roughly approximate the seemingly analogous representations from some other structure. Considering the degree of natural language and common sense reasoning involved in communicating within an international organization, the task of creating some conceptual supersystem first is hardly feasible, and, second, does not promise very successful in the application either. Hence, the objectives when designing the data model for an international organization are

☐ Identify the similarities and analogies between the concepts commonly used, and

☐ Handle those similarities and analogies in the context of a model.

In the following, the consequences of those objectives on the modelling effort will be examined closer.

4.1.1 Generalization and Specialization
The first objective leads to the use of the modelling constructs. The examination of the modelling approach yields that the same technique of Extended Entity Relationship modelling can still be applied. The EERM is a general modelling language able to describe whatever data structure, so there is no reason for modifications. However, from the task requirements, the emphasis on the use of particular constructs changes. The task being the representation of similarities and analogies between already established concepts, and, hence, the creation of new linkage concepts, extensive use of the generalization and specialization operator is required. The concepts which are common in the context of the individual operating units are generalized to some more abstract concept, which represents the set of common properties applying for each underlying concept. Here, the idea of generalization is one of a generic entity type derived from a set of entity types with certain common attributes [15]. The idea is that the generalized concepts really serve as a link between the underlying concepts. It is not intended to replace the more concrete, locally specific concepts by the generalized concepts. This may only be done in cases where the general concept actually possesses the same properties as the underlying concepts.

4.1.2 Model Consolidation
The issue of identifying conceptual analogies also extends to the modelling process. Of course, one might argue that the task of consolidating different area models into one enterprise-wide data model for a locally restricted organization is analogous to the task of conceptually consolidating the models of individual organizational units into the model of an international organization. But from the definition of an international organization as given above, the issue is that, as opposed to the areas of an individual enterprise, the same areas are described from several different perspectives. Thus, production, marketing, order processing, warehousing etc. are all described from the point of view of every operating unit involved, creating a considerable diversity in the

respective area descriptions. Hence, the task in consolidating the models of the individual operating units is much wider, because virtually all concepts used will have a correspondent in some other operating unit. Figure 3 shows a modified approach to modelling an international organization.

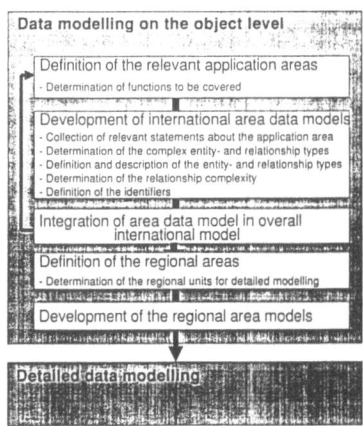

Fig. 3: Modified phases for the development of an international data model

From this, a two-stage approach is proposed: First establish a very rough organization-wide data model, containing the basic concepts the organization has to turn attention to. Those basic concepts and their relationships correspond to what is also called "business rules" of the overall organization [16]. With this framework, models for the individual operating units can be established, and this task is analogous to the design of an enterprise-wide data model for an individual company. But with the framework of the high-level organization model, the focal points of the modelling effort are known beforehand, and consolidation activities can start very early in the process of conceptual modelling.

4.1.3 Scope of the Model
The second issue of handling the interrelationships between the concepts in the context of a model immediately leads to the scope of "the model". From the fact that there are analogons across the different operating units for virtually every concept involved, it is obvious that "the model" of the international organization cannot be comprised of all the individual models plus the respective generalized concepts. In this case, it appears best to introduce a layer structure already in the stage of conceptual modelling. "The model" of the international organization on the top layer actually contains only generalized concepts and their relationships. The generalization/specialization operators on the middle layer only serve as a connection from the general model to the models of the individual operating units. The models of the individual operating units on the bottom layer, again, are designed like regular enterprise-wide data models. The relationship between the different layers is shown in figure 4. The difference to just combining existing enterprise-wide data models is that certain commonalities across the operating units were taken into account before starting the individual modelling effort, and that the generalized concepts do not appear in the same model as

the specialized concepts. This means that in some places - where it appears crucial to the whole of the organization - common concepts may be used, whereas in other areas, the individual concepts remain.

International Model

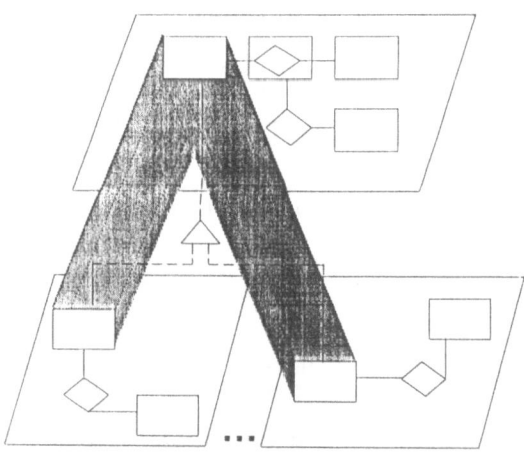

Regional Model 1   Regional Model n

Fig. 4: Relationship between model layers

4.2 Model Design

As pointed out above, the data modelling effort for an international organization requires a modified approach. Apart from this proceeding, specific problems are encountered within the particular stages of the model design, too.

4.2.1 Conceptual Differentiation

The heterogeneous information described with the model requires a powerful and flexible model structure. Thus, the degree of differentiation will generally be higher than in a regular enterprise-wide data model. Because of the structural diversity of the information to be captured in the structure, information carriers will move in status from attribute to entity type. In this way, for instance, it is possible to still keep the concept of "customer" or "business partner", although assigning different sets of descriptive attributes depending on the context of the organizational unit. For the descriptive attributes will become an entity type of its own, "customer properties", with a relationship to "customer". The entries in the relationship then depend on the particular operating unit. Figure 5 shows the alternative ways of representation.

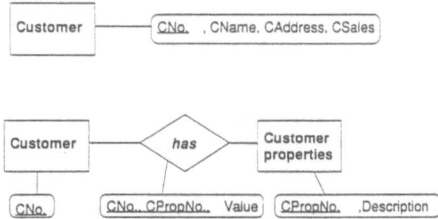

Fig. 5: Alternative ways of representing attributes

In addition, the generalized data model of the international organization will necessarily contain the concept of "operating unit". This concept has to be linked to all the other entity types which make up for the description of any individual operating unit. Thus, the generalized data structure is able to capture structurally different unit data structures within just one model. Depending on the particular organizational unit, the linkage to certain other concepts may not be filled. In this way, a mere sales unit would not have any entries in the structure's relationship between the concept of "operating unit" and the generalized concept "machine", whereas a production unit would heavily use this relationship.

4.2.2 Multilinguality

Apart from all the basic conceptual problems modelling, it is also necessary to decide on a language used within the modelling effort. For the generalized data model of the organization, it is obvious that it has to be described in the "official" common language of the organization. For the lower-level models, the decision clearly depends on organizational standards. Depending on the organization, it is perfectly conceivable that the detailed models will be designed in the same official language, too. But following the previous line of argumentation, the models for the individual operating units should be designed in the respective language, too. However, this would account for additional problems in the modelling effort, because the problem of translation across several languages would add to the problem of conceptual consolidation. As stated above, this decision also reflects the organization's own understanding of its degree of internationality. A company considering itself just as widely distributed branches of one particular national organization would certainly choose the first way, whereas an organization considering itself "truly" international would probably vote for the representation of the diverse cultural background as expressed in the use of different languages. One can assume, however, that in the course of time, more and more common concepts will arise, as cultural differentiation is reduced.

5 CONCLUSION

The above examination has tried to examine the issue of data modelling for international organizations. From a working definition of an international organization, the effects on the data modelling effort were derived. It turned out that there are not only problems of size and complexity, but also distinct structural and conceptual problems involved when modelling an international organization. A specific approach for modelling such an organization was presented. The approach draws on the same set of standard modelling constructs; differences can be found in the following areas:

❏ The emphasis on the use of specific constructs, especially the generalization operator, differs,
❏ the model structure is differentiated into layers of abstraction, from the generalized model of the international organization to the specialized model of the individual operating unit,
❏ the modelling process has to be extended by another stage of consolidation to connect the models of the operating units to the model of the organization.

It should be stated, that, in addition, the data modelling approach outlined above requires a sophisticated functionality to ensure consistency of the data base in the stage of model implementation. The task is in translating the contents of the individual data bases according to the rules described by the organization-wide model and its links to the individual models. Those rules are described by the generalization operators used as links between the individual models and the overall organizational model; they go beyond the integrity rules usually stated for a data base [17]. The description of this functionality and its translation mechanism is a necessary prerequisite for the implementation of the set of data models for an international organization as a basis for integrated information processing.

6 REFERENCES

[1]   Jorysz, H.R., Vernadat, F.B.: CIM-OSA Part 1: total enterprise modelling and function view. International Journal of Computer Integrated Manufacturing 3(1990)3-4, p. 144-156.

[2]   Scheer, A.-W.: Computer - A challenge for business administration. Berlin et al. 1985, p. 9.

[3]   Esprit Consortium AMICE: An Open Systems Architecture for CIM. New York et al. 1989, p. 52f.

[4]   Scheer, A.-W.: ARIS - Architektur integrierter Informationssysteme, Berlin et al. 1991.

[5]   Zachman, J.A.: A Framework for information systems architecture. IBM Systems Journal 26(1987)3, p. 276-292.

[6]   Chen, P.P.: The Entity-Relationship model: Toward a unified view of data. ACM Transactions on Database Systems 1(1976)1, p. 9-36.

[7]   Schlageter, G., Stucky, W.: Datenbanksysteme: Konzepte und Modelle. 2nd edition, Stuttgart 1983, p. 50.

[8]   Webre, N.W.: An Extended Entity Relationship Model and its Use on a Defense Project, in: Chen, P.P. (Ed.): Entity Relationship Approach to Information Modelling and Analysis. Proceedings of the 2nd International Conference on Entity-Relationship Approach (1981), Amsterdam et al. 1983, p. 193.

[9]   Sinz, E.J.: Das Strukturierte Entity-Relationship-Modell (SERM), Angewandte Informatik 30(1988), p. 191-202.

[10]   Elmasri, R., Weeldreyer, J., Hevner, A.: The Category Concept: An Extension to the Entity-Relationship Approach, Data & Knowledge Engineering 1(1985), p. 75-116.

[11]   Su, S.Y.W., Lo, D.H.: A semantic association model for conceptual database design, in: Chen, P.P (Hrsg.): Entity-Relationship Approach to Software Engineering (Proceedings of the International Conference on Entity-Relationship Approach to System Analysis and Design, Los Angeles 1979), Amsterdam et al. 1980, p. 169-192.

[12]   Scheer, A.-W.: Enterprise-wide data modelling - Information systems in industry. New York et al. 1989, p. 24.

[13]   Teorey, T.J., Wei, G., Bolton, D.L., Koenig, J.A.: ER Model Clustering as an Aid for User Communication and Documentation in Database Design. Communications of the ACM, 32(1989)8, p. 975-987.

[14]   Martin, J., McClure, C.: Structured techniques: the basis for CASE. Englewood Cliffs 1988, p. 324.

[15]   Teorey, T.J., Wei, G., Bolton, D.L., Koenig, J.A.: ER Model Clustering as an Aid for User Communication and Documentation in Database Design. Communications of the ACM, 32(1989)8, p. 978.

[16]   Appleton, D.S.: Business rules: The missing link. Datamation 30(1984)16, p. 145-150.

[17]   Jorysz, H.R., Vernadat, F.B.: CIM-OSA Part 2: information view. International Journal of Computer Integrated Manufacturing 3(1990)3-4, 157-167.

ISACS
An Integrated Surveillance and Control System

Jon Kvalem, Rolf-Einar Grini, Kjell Haugset

Institutt for energiteknikk
OECD Halden Reactor Project
N-1751 Halden, Norway

ABSTRACT

In this paper we report about application requirements and design principles used in the development of an integrated surveillance and control system, intended to be used by the operator of a Nuclear Power Plant. The system, for its own nature, is an example of a class of applications normally referred to as critical applications, and involve the use of both expert system and database technologies in a real-time process control environment.

1   Introduction

Information analysis and presentation are increasingly important activities in modern control rooms of industrial processes and power plants. The introduction of different Computerised Operator Support Systems (COSSs) in the control room, calls for a new approach in handling and presenting information to the operator. To deal with these problems, the project on the Integrated Surveillance and Control System (ISACS) was initiated at the Halden Reactor Project [1,2]. The ISACS concept is of general nature in industrial process and power plants, but our laboratory implementation is specialised towards nuclear power plants. In ISACS, information from several COSSs is collected, grouped, and presented in a uniform way. All visual information is presented to the operators on colour graphic CRTs.

ISACS consists of a number of modules, and of these the expert system called Intelligent Coordinator (IC) and the Common Database play central roles [3,4]. The IC receives input from the different COSSs, from the process, and from the operator. Sitting with the extract of available information, it can offer a concentrated overview of the status of the plant. In addition, it has access to detailed information which can be brought up on request.

The database management system of ISACS was required to be flexible in its handling of data. Due to the heterogeneous types of data which is included in the database, e.g. process related data, data from operator support systems, man-machine interface data etc., and to ease the integration of the different parts of ISACS, the use of a commercial system, with the necessary flexibility, seemed to be the solution with the most favourable cost-benefit ratio.

A demonstration version of ISACS, including the Intelligent Coordinator and the Common Database, is developed, preliminary tested in the Halden Man-Machine Laboratory and found satisfactory for a, on beforehand, specified scenario. The nucleus of the Halden Man-Machine Laboratory is a full-scale nuclear power plant simulator, which acts as the process in the laboratory implementation of ISACS.

2   System Structure

The multi-computer system which forms the basis for the implementation of the ISACS system, is a multi-vendor network-based system integrating conventional and knowledge processing capabilities.

It was required that ISACS was developed in such a way that optimal flexibility and modularity were maintained. It should be possible to:

- remove parts of ISACS for integration into other environments than the Halden Man-Machine Laboratory.

- remove one or several COSSs from an ISACS environment and integrate with other systems.

- easily include new COSSs into ISACS.

- easily expand ISACS with new functions.

To meet the requirements specified above, it is essential that:

- all communication between tasks in ISACS is message based.

- the interfaces between the different subsystems within ISACS are strictly defined.

- data are available in accessible databases.

The overall structure of the ISACS system, including data flow, is shown in figure 1. The real or simulated process data are continuously being updated in the Process Database, and hence made available to COSSs and the MMI. Some COSSs are running on a continuous basis, e.g. alarm filtering and fault detection systems, while some are triggered at events, e.g. diagnosis and prognosis systems. All COSSs access the Process Database for information and their produced information is delivered to the Common Database, where it can be accessed by the Intelligent Coordinator and the MMI. All information produced by the Intelligent Coordinator for presentation in displays is directed to the MMI via the Common Database.

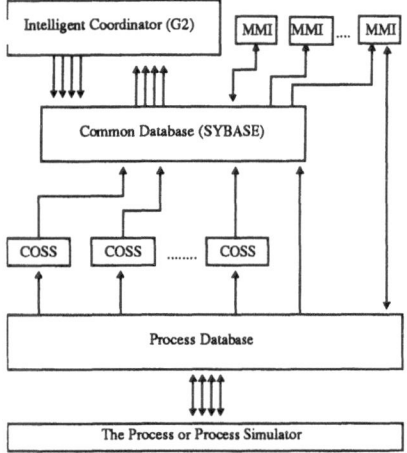

Figure 1. Overall structure of ISACS.

3   ISACS Databases

The use of commercial database systems in process control environments, as in ISACS, is not very often seen. Usually, commercial relational database systems are used in administrative application areas, while in the technical application area one, to a large extent, relies upon home-made solutions.

The wish for a system which has a uniform interface to the applications and a system which is, as far as possible, data

independent, motivated an examination of relational database systems. Three items were given special focus when choosing the relational database system for use in ISACS. Those items were: performance, distributed processing capabilities and the existence of a well-defined interface to applications written in conventional programming languages, such as C or FORTRAN. A careful study of relational database management systems resulted in the use of SYBASE for implementing the ISACS Common Database [5].

The nature of a relational database management system implies that handling cyclic updates of large amounts of measured data, as is the case in process control applications, is hard. Due to these limitations, ISACS requires a process database which is capable of handling cyclic updates of process signals and is capable of providing applications with updated values of process signals. In this way the process database will contain all process related signals, while the relational system will contain event-based information and all non time-critical information.

3.1   The Common Database

The Common Database in ISACS is the main repository of data to be shared by the different tasks. To avoid a tight coupling between tasks, a solution was chosen to let tasks deliver data to one central data pool, the Common Database, while other tasks are allowed to read the required data from this data pool. The data will typically be:

- a small selection of process data

- alarms from the different alarm systems

- diagnosis and prognosis data

- man-machine interface data

- operator actions

The different COSSs transfer all relevant data to the Common Database, from which the Intelligent Coordinator can access the data which it finds interesting at all times. In addition, the COSSs' data which are relevant for presentation in displays, can be accessed from the Common Database by the display systems.

Access to the Common Database by applications, e.g. COSSs, the Intelligent Coordinator and the MMI systems, is performed using the SYBASE functional library Open Client. As opposed to the embedded philosophy, the Open Client functions are called by applications and requires no pre-compilation. SQL-statements are given as parameters to these functions [6].

To avoid the interpretation of SQL procedures for each database access, the use of Stored Procedures, i.e. pre-compiled SQL procedures stored in the data dictionary, is extensively used in ISACS. By simply passing parameters to procedures ready for execution, performance is substantially enhanced. Specific SYBASE facilities for making high speed copying of bulks of data into the database is also being used to enhance performance further.

3.2 The Process Database

The Process Database in ISACS is an in-house made memory-resident database based on the FORTRAN COMMON block principle. The process simulator delivers updated signals at a 1.5 seconds fixed interval. The number of signals which are being updated every simulator cycle varies between a small number and several thousands, depending upon the changes in process state, since only changed signals are being updated.

The access to the Process Database takes place using a specially designed access library. This library provides applications with functions for both fetching and placing data from/ into the Process Database. All process signals are identified by a tag name, and a specially developed hashing algorithm is used for converting the tag names to unique database indexes. In this way process signals are accessed by direct reference.

A small selection of key process signals are, at pre-defined intervals, transferred from the Process Database into the Common Database. In this way they are made available to the Intelligent Coordinator and can be used for coordination and plant status identification purposes.

4 The Intelligent Coordinator

The Intelligent Coordinator (IC) continuously supervises messages coming in from COSSs. The contents of the messages are used to analyse current plant status which is represented by several specific parameters defined for ISACS. The IC activates passive COSSs when necessary, to get further information such as diagnosis, prognosis, or procedure recommendation. Another important aspect of the IC's role, is to interpret operator actions. When requested by the operator,

the IC must produce the requested information, coordinate the additional assessments and report the results.

When a COSS reports a planned or unexpected plant transient, the IC defines it as an event represented by an object in the knowledge base. All new information from the same or any other COSS, related to the same transient, will be tied to the already existing event. There may be several events present at the time, each representing a transient in the plant. The IC prioritises between the events to point out to the operator which are the most serious and should be concentrated on. A plant state will be defined, and recommendations for the operator about what to do to mitigate a failure will be given. Information created inside the IC will, in addition to data from the COSSs, be grouped and sent to the MMI.

G2 has been chosen as the implementation and development tool for the IC [7]. This is an expert system shell, specially constructed for real-time applications. It provides facilities for including the time aspect in the reasoning. This was very important when choosing G2, because of the dynamic character of the application. The implementation is object-oriented. Rules are written in a special G2 language, which also includes the use of procedures. An extensive use of WHEN-EVER <> DO <> type rules, results in an event based reasoning where rules are triggered only under certain circumstances. This is saving computer time compared to interval based triggering. The implementation of the IC is effectuated inside one knowledge base. The rules are organised in workspaces, where each workspace is related to one task or contains a collection of related items. The workspaces are organised in a hierarchy with one top-level workspace and subworkspaces, see figure 2. There are up to four levels in the hierarchy and a total number of approximately 60 workspaces. The hierarchy gives a well organised knowledge base in which it is easy to navigate through the workspaces. The maintenance of the hierarchy is made easier through the division into subworkspaces, as each subworkspace contains the knowledge associated with a specific function in the IC.

The interface towards the Common Database, is defined through sensor objects in G2. A sensor represents a variable to be transferred or received. Attributes in the sensor object defines a location in the Common Database. The values of the attributes may be static, which leads to one-to-one correspondence between a sensor and a location in the Common Database. However, the attribute may vary, which enables use of the same sensor to send values to different locations. The integration of the G2 Standard Interface and the SYBASE Open Client provides for an efficient way of communicating between the Intelligent Coordinator and the Common Database.

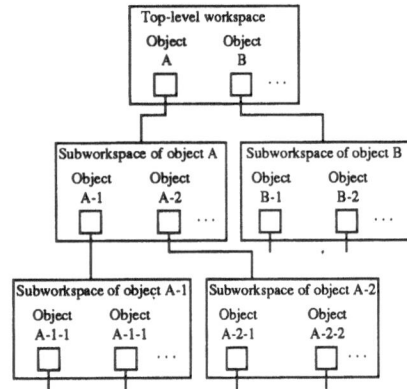

Figure 2. Workspace hierarchy of the Intelligent Coordinator.

5   The Man-Machine Interface

ISACS is intended to act as a single, integrated interface for the operator for all operational situations. As such, all information from the process, and all commands to the process will be passed through ISACS. Therefore, the design of the ISACS MMI is critical, as the operator's ability to interpret and control the process is entirely dependent on the MMI and its underlaying software.

The ISACS-1 MMI consists of a total of thirteen colour graphic screens. Five of them are showing ISACS driven overview information, while the rest are available to the operator for interaction with the process and the individual COSSs. Operator interaction with ISACS are taking place by using a context sensitive dynamic keyboard.

6   Conclusions and Status

A prototype, ISACS-1, has been made of the Integrated Surveillance and Control System, in which two major parts are the expert system named the Intelligent Coordinator, implemented in G2, and the Common Database, implemented in SYBASE. The choice of G2 has proved to be successful, with its capabilities for reasoning with time as a parameter. Communication between G2 and SYBASE has been realised and works satisfactorily through the use of the G2 Standard Interface package. One shortcoming, though, is that GSI does not permit external systems to set values in G2. This forces us to make G2 do time consuming polling in SYBASE looking for changes in the data.

ISACS belongs to a class of computer based systems with very little proven experience from the point of view of how to use traditional database technology. This is mainly due to the fact that in process control environments where the demand for real-time response is essential, home-made database solutions have been used in almost all situations. The reason for introducing a relational database in an environment like ISACS, was the need for a flexible and modern tool for handling the heterogeneous types of data which are present in the system. The preliminary experience, although thorough system testing has just been initiated, is rather good [8].

7   References

[1] Haugset K. et al., 1990. ISACS-1 Motivation, General Description. OECD Halden Reactor Project Technical Report HWR-265.

[2] Haugset K. et al., 1990. ISACS-1, The Prototype of an Advanced Control Room. IAEA International Symposium on Balancing Automation and Human Action in Nuclear Power Plants. Munich, 9-13 July 1990.

[3] Yamane N., Grini R.E., 1991. The Intelligent Coordinator Module of the Integrated Surveillance and Control System (ISACS-1). OECD Halden Reactor Project Technical Report, HWR-289.

[4] Kristiansen L.I., Kvalem I., Kvalem J., Swanberg B., 1991. ISACS-1 System Description. OECD Halden Reactor Project Technical Report HWR-290.

[5] SYBASE User's Manuals, 1989. SYBASE Inc., USA.

[6] SQL - American National Standard, ANSI X3.135, 1986.

[7] G2 User's Manuals, 1989. Gensym Corporation, USA.

[8] Fält C.O., Jensen L.S., Kvalem I., Kvalem J., 1991. Database Technology in Industrial Process Environments. OECD Halden Reactor Project Technical Report, HWR-291.

Constraint-Guided Scheduling
for Satellite Data Processing and Archiving

Jürgen Scholz[*], Paul Levi[**]

[*]German Aerospace Research Establishment, c/o Dr.R. Göbel, D–8031 Oberpfaffenhofen
[**]Technical University of Munich, Dep. of Computer Science, Orleansstr. 34, D–8000 München 80

Abstract

Production scheduling and controlling systems have become a useful tool to increase throughput, efficiency, and flexibility within complex production environments. One of the tasks of the "Facility Management System"(FMS) is to generate schedules for systems processing satellite data. Based on the requirements to the FMS a constraint-guided scheduler has been developed. A language that will be defined, allows the description of the scheduling problem with constraints, which can be logically combined within satisfiability specifications. Scheduling on this network of constraints falls into four levels: fixing islands of certainty, an analysis phase, computation of the scheduling sequence, and the scheduling main phase. Problems arising during constraint propagation are maintained by a rule-based repair component.

Keywords: CIM, scheduling, planning, constraints, constraint propagation

1 Introduction

In this paper we present a system for generating production schedules for the *German Processing and Archiving Facility* for ERS–1 satellite data(D–PAF). The scheduling procedure bases on constraint–guided scheduling, where one represents the scheduling problem by a network of restrictions. This representation allows the application of constraint satisfaction and constraint propagation techniques for supporting the scheduler.

We will start in this paper with a short introduction to the notion *scheduling* and *constraint satisfaction problems*. Following up is a brief description of the "Facility Management System"(FMS).

An additional requirement was to embed the network into a common CIM factory reference model. A large number of relations have been identified within this model, which are regarded as constraints. Upon these constraints, a language for the description of scheduling problems is defined. Several techniques of analysis and scheduling on the network are explained.

1.1 Scheduling

The *scheduling problem* is described by a set of tasks that have to be assigned to a set of resources with some constraints to be obeyed. The problem is therewith different from *configuration problems*, building up configurations from a set of components with respect to various requirements, and from *production systems*(in the classical sense of AI), which use operators to transform a start situation into a goal situation(e.g., STRIPS).

Scheduling algorithms are usually integrated into production planning and controlling system, as shown in fig.1. They work on a world model consisting of the description of the production environment(e.g., machines, resources, etc.) and production steps to be performed. The world model also represents the actual status of the production environment. The "output" of the scheduler is a production plan(schedule), i.e., a 1–to–n relation of resources and production steps with execution times assigned.

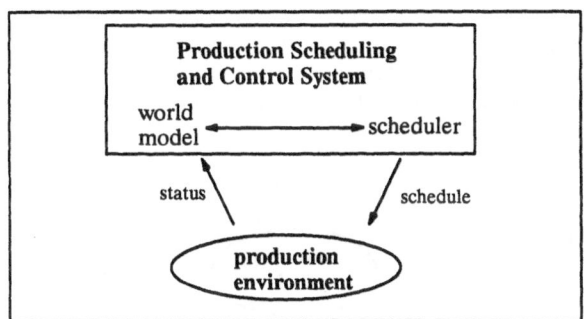

Figure 1: Architecture

1.2 Constraint Satisfaction Problems

Before introducing constraints and constraint networks in detail, we will give some brief notes on the notion used in this paper:

A constraint network consists of a set of variables and relations on these variables. Each of the relations is a *constraint*(or restriction) on its variables. Some simple constraints are, e.g.,

- $a + b = c; b < 7$

- production step A **before** production step B.

Constraints spread up networks by sharing variables. Then, a *constraint satisfaction problem(CSP)* is to find a consistent variable setting for all relations included in the network.

1.3 The Facility Management System

The German Processing and Archiving Facility(D-PAF) performs ground segment operations for ESA's first remote sensing satellite, ERS-1. This includes production and long-term archiving and retrieval of digital and image products derived from ERS-1's Synthetic Aperture Radar(SAR) and Radar Altimeter and Tracking(RAT) data, and product delivery to the customers.

The "Facility Management System"(FMS) is a knowledge-based production planning and controlling tool currently being integrated into the D-PAF. It has three main tasks:

- Scheduling of production resources and activities for about 70 workstations and several hundred peripherals.

- Monitoring of the hardware and order status.

- Production control and reactive schedule revision.

The constraint-guided scheduler described in this paper and the prototype that has been implemented are mainly based on the requirements to the FMS with respect to hardware and production step description representation(i.e., world modelling).

2 The Factory Reference Model

We used a very common "world model" to describe the scheduling environment. This factory reference model may also be part of a CIM shell, which is used to describe an entire manufacturing process from development to automatic construction.

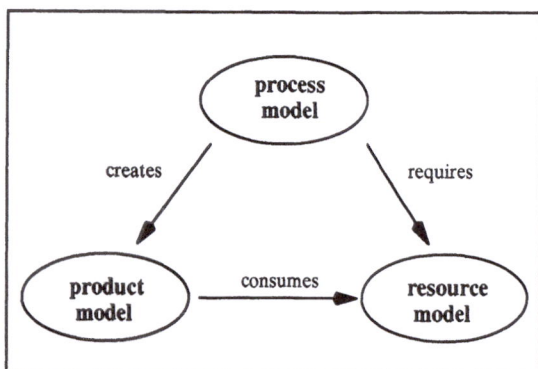

Figure 2: The Factory Reference Model

As shown in fig. 2, the reference model is divided up into three almost independent areas of information representing the information, material, and decision flow
In the remainder of this section, we will explain in brief the representation, elements, and attributes of the process, product, and resource model. Elements out of these models will be identified with nodes of a constraint network later.

2.1 The Process Model

The process model contains classes of static production step descriptions(type sequences) and classes of orders and

(dynamic) instances of production steps.
The necessity of static *production sequence descriptions* is obvious for the factory model. An instance contains at least the name of the production step, its minimum and maximum duration, several distinct sets of resources(i.e., raw materials, operators, machines, etc.) that are necessary to perform the step, resource dependencies, classes of input and output items(e.g., products), and information about set-up and transportation durations between successive steps.

An *order* is described by a list of instances of production steps(i.e., the production step sequences that have to be enforced in order to create the product), by an earliest start time(the placement date of the order), a latest finish times(the due date), and the priority of the order. Each *production step* out of a sequence refers to its static description, to instances of input and output items, and holds a list of assigned resources, and several specifications of its execution interval(i.e., earliest and latest start and finish time, planned start and finish time).

2.2 The Product Model

Products are the output of production steps. Several *types* and *product classes* will be distinguished which are represented by hierarchical models. The product type model subdivides the set of "real products" into type classes, independent of their current state. The latter is represented by the product class model, which falls into, e.g., stock, shipping, and temporary items. Instances of the product class model refer to a product type and contain, at least, a creation time, and the current and planned usages.

2.3 The Resource Model

The resource model describes the *hardware*, e.g., machines, workstations, and other resources(tools, materials, operators), etc., and the *organizational layout*.

Assuming that the descriptions of the production steps contain all necessary knowledge about the resources, only the *'usages'* of resources have to be considered. A usage contains, at least, its start and finish time, a type specification, the percentage of machine capability used, and the reference to the instance of the production step description.

3 A Language for the Description of Scheduling Problems

This section gives an overview on the model's constraints composing the network. For the description of scheduling problems we introduce satisfiability specifications and some kind of fuzzy logic.

3.1 Constraint Networks

A constraint network consists of variables, each associated with a domain, and of relations on the domains, which are applied on the variables. As long as binary relations are used, the problem may be seen as a graph. A solution of the network is a variable setting satisfying all relations. This process is known as a *constraint satisfaction problem*(CSP), for which standard algorithms can be applied. It emerged soon that binary relations are insufficient within the scheduling domain. Therefore, we consider n–ary relations in general.

3.2 Constraints within the Models

Before extending the notion of constraint networks, an overview on the constraints that we have identified within the scheduling domain is given. Each of the three models mentioned above has associated with it several *constraint classes*, further subdividing the internal and external relations of the the model under consideration. The following classifications have been chosen:

- Organizational goals
  These goals reflect concerns and objectives of a facility's management with respect to the performance of the factory. They also represent general criteria against which prospective schedules can be compared. Stating a goal, e.g., *minimize costs*, then may be seen as a constraint.

- Physical constraints:
  The relations of this class define functional limitations, e.g., of resources.

- Causal restrictions:
  This class describes conditions that have to be satisfied in order to generate a consistent schedule.

- Availability:
  Some relations have to be defined that declare the availability or unavailability of resource, e.g., due to maintenance requirements.

- Preferences:
  Usually, preferences express heuristic knowledge present in a given environment.

In the remainder of this paragraph, the constraints of the factory reference model are listed, of which some are explained in detail. Please note, that the list given does not claim to be complete. Further relations may have to be added with respect to other scheduling demands.

3.2.1 The Process Model Constraints

As a first example, we examine the **due date** constraint, which, as an organizational goal, represents the management's will to deliver a product right in time. It constraints the order and production step nodes(i.e., the objects of the knowledge base representing the order and the production step) by controlling the latest finish time slot(which is one of the variables of the production step). The relation is satisfied if the planned finish time of the last production step is less or equal the order's due date:

due_date(order[due date], step[planned finish time]) ⇔

step[planned finish time] $\leq$ order[due date].

Some of the constraints make it possible to compute new variable settings, e.g., the **processing time** constraint, which checks whether the reserved time interval is long enough to run the production step on the resource:

processing_time(step[start time, finish time, assigned resources]) ⇔

step[finish time] – step[start time]

$\leq f_{\text{execution duration}}$(step[assigned resources]).

Besides the relation, some kind of "code" is assigned to the constraint to compute lacking variable settings:

step[finish time] := step[start time] +

$f_{\text{execution duration}}$(step[assigned resources]).

step[start time] := step[finish time] –

$f_{\text{execution duration}}$(step[assigned resources]).

As most of the constraints, **due_date** and the **processing_time** are numeric constraints.

In contrast, some of the relations between nodes of the scheduling network are of symbolic kind. Consider a resource dependency between two production steps, "*if* step1 uses M1 or M2 *then* step2 has to use M3 or M4":

resource_dependency(step1[assigned resources],

step2[assigned resources]) ⇔

step1[assigned resources] $\in \{$M1, M2$\}$) and

step2[assigned resources] $\in \{$M3, M4$\}$.

The "code" of symbolic constraints is expressed using "look-up tables", containing on the left side the possible resource of step1 or step2 and on the other side the set of resources that has to be chosen.

The remaining organizational goals of the process model state goals that should be achieved within the production environment, e.g., not to excess a cost limit.

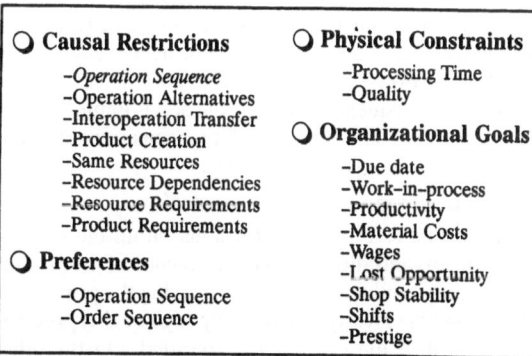

Figure 3: Process Model Constraints

The causal restrictions define the basic structure of the scheduling problem by describing the sequence and correct course of operations. Allen's temporal relations, i.e., before, after, during, etc., have been implemented to model the operation sequence. Causal restrictions usually dominate other classes of constraints.

The preference constraints of the resource model contain

504

heuristic knowledge on advantageous operation and order sequence.

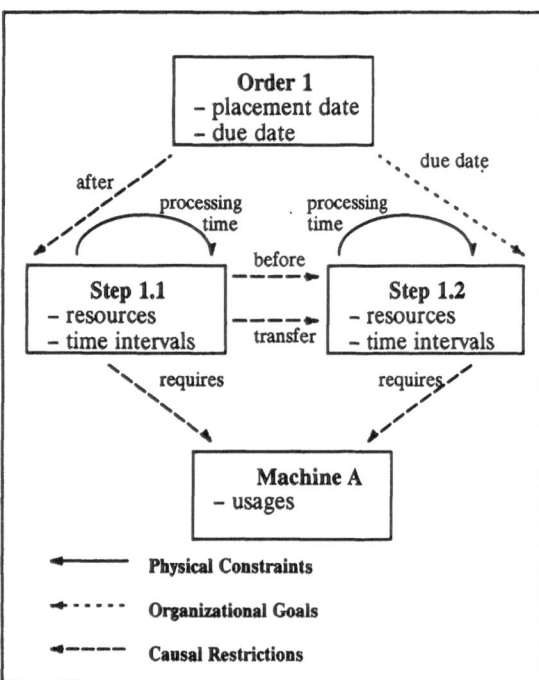

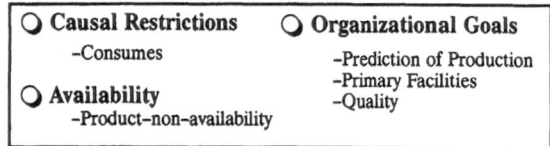

Figure 4: An Example

Fig. 4 shows a typical subnetwork of an order which limits the execution times of its production steps by specifying a **due date** and an **after** constraint. Both steps need some time to be performed(**processing_time**) and require machine A for execution. The sequence of the production is defined by the **before** constraint. The **transfer** relation constrains the start times of succeeding production steps.

3.2.2 The Product Model Constraints

Fig.5 shows a selection of constraints within the product model. The organizational goals directly control the production by setting production goals and defining the primary facilities within the factory. Additionally, high quality products are preferred, if the constraint is specified. On the other hand, a prediction of production is possible. The **consumes** constraint links the product to the resource model, by describing which resources, e.g., raw materials, are necessary to create a product.

○ **Causal Restrictions**	○ **Organizational Goals**
–Consumes	–Prediction of Production
○ **Availability**	–Primary Facilities
–Product-non-availability	–Quality

Figure 5: Product Model Constraints

3.2.3 The Resource Model Constraints

The management goals within this model optimize the usage of resources. From the parameters derived it is not only possible to achieve an estimation on resources needed, but also to reduce costs, e.g., if the resource inventory is limited. The physical constraints describe properties of machines. The unavailability of resources is expressed using availability constraints, e.g., for regularly machine maintenance.

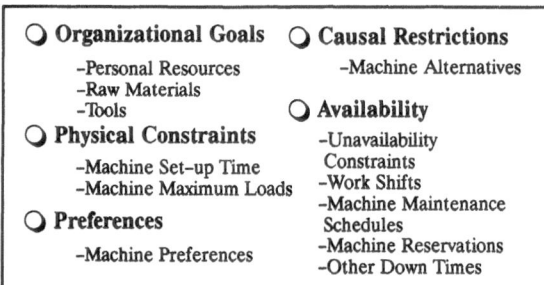

Figure 6: Resource Model Constraints

3.3 Satisfiability Specifications

The preceding approach does not satisfy the requirements to a constraint network for scheduling. Constraints should be combined in some way within the nodes they are associated to. Therefore, *satisfiability specifications* have been introduced, which allow the combination of relations with the operators AND, OR, and XOR.

An example from our scheduling domain clarifies this: Geocoding requires for its execution either the GPWS1, GPWS2, or GPWS3 workstation, and some of their peripherals, as shown in fig.7. In this way, we may also combine other constraints, e.g., to express that either the due date should be held or the costs should be minimized.

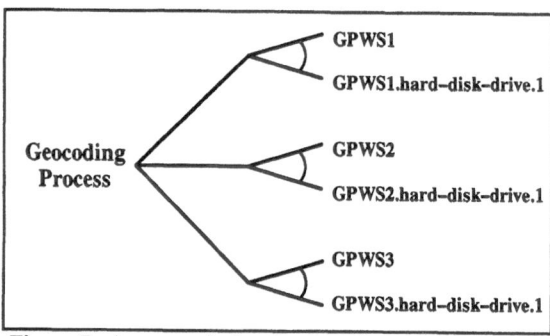

Figure 7: An example for the necessity of AND/OR expressions for scheduling

The example of fig. 7 will now be described as:

(OR (AND **requires**(geocoding[start time, finish time], GPWS1[planned usages])
  requires(geocoding[start time, finish time], GPWS1.hard–disk–drive.1[planned usages]))
 (AND **requires**(geocoding[start time, finish time], GPWS2[planned usages])
  requires(geocoding[start time, finish time], GPWS2.hard–disk–drive.1[planned usages]))
 (AND **requires**(geocoding[start time, finish time], GPWS3[planned usages])

requires(geocoding[start time, finish time],
  GPWS3.hard–disk–drive.1[planned usages])))

3.4 Fuzzy Relations

When working with relations within the scheduling domain, it emerges that, from time to time, not all relations can be satisfied, though the "plan" seems to be done. One might think about some of the *organizational goals* within a factory model, e.g., the goal to meet a due date:

If the product does not meet its due date, being finished, for example, one day too late, then this might be accepted, as long as other restrictions are not violated, e.g., some cost functions.

For this purpose we will allows fuzzy relations instead of common relations. A fuzzy relation maps a tuple of n elements into a real positive number from the interval [0, 1], instead of returning "true" or "false". This value specifies the degree of satisfaction of a fuzzy relation, i.e., 0 means: fuzzy relation not satisfied, 1 indicates full support.

Some constraints have *always* to be satisfied, especially the temporal relations between production steps.

The implementation of the FUZZY-AND, FUZZY-OR, and FUZZY-XOR operators, which are chosen instead of AND, OR, and XOR, depend on the type of scheduling problem. We may define that a FUZZY-AND expression is fulfilled as long as all constraints yield a *rating* greater than 0.5.

Therefore, every constraint has a *rating function* associated, which computes the rating of the current variable setting. For the **due_date** constraint a function could be:

if step[planned finish time] ≤ order[due date]
then 1
else   delay := step[planned finish time] –
              order[due date]
    if delay ≤ "one day"
    then 0.9
    else 1/delay
    endif
endif

In contrast, the rating function of a causal restriction(or of another constraint that must be satisfied), e.g., **before**, returns 0 if the relation is not fulfilled, and 1 else.

Additionally, *importances* may be assigned to constraints or constraint classes. On the one hand, very important constraints should be satisfied first. On the other hand, "bad" ratings of unimportant constraints may be *relaxed*.

4 The Scheduling Process

In this section, it is described how to schedule with networks of constraints. The process falls into four distinct levels, that are subsequently applied.

4.1 Initial State

The network has an initial state, from which scheduling starts, i.e., besides building up the network and specifying strategies and goals, some of the variables are bound, e.g.,:

▶ Every order has, at least, a placement date that corresponds to its earliest start time, and should have a due date, i.e., a latest finish time assigned.

▶ Working hours, machine operation times, and regular maintenance down times are fixed, if initially known; it may also be a goal of scheduling to derive these times.

▶ Management goals, e.g., limits for costs and productivity, have to be specified.

▶ Other events fixed within the schedule should be inserted, e.g., production steps that always run at the same time.

Putting these variable settings into the network does not mean that they cannot be relaxed or changed, but they represent a useful limitation of the search space.

4.2 Fixing Islands of Certainty
4.2.1 Process

The first measure to bound the search space of the network is to fix the so–called "islands of certainty", i.e., to propagate those variable settings defining the initial state of the scheduling problem.

We want to explain in brief the idea behind the propagation algorithm. Consider the job shop in fig. 8: The placement date of order 1 **meets** the earliest start time of step 1.1.The propagator now searches which other constraints are affected by this variable and finds the **processing_time** constraint of step 1.1.

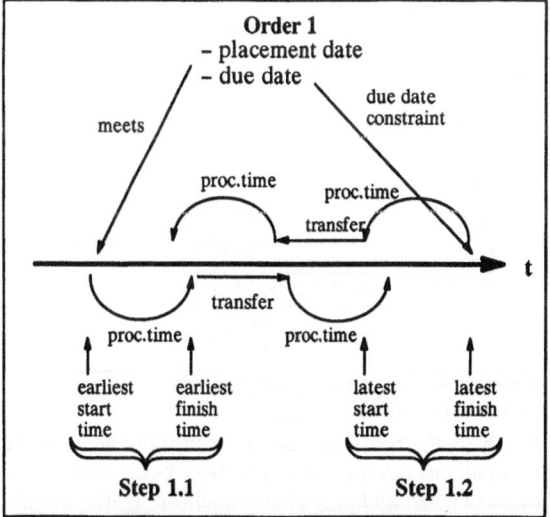

Figure 8: Propagation of placement date and due date

Now, the earliest finish time of this step can be computed. This invokes the application of the **transfer** constraint, fixing the earliest start time of step 1.2. In the same way, we propagate the due date backward(in time), computing the latest start and finish times of the production steps.

4.2.2 Results

At least, fixing islands of certainty leads to

☞ the propagation of placement date and due date of every order, fixing the earliest start and latest finish time of every production step by regarding predictions of minimal and maximal durations,

☞ he assignment of the most favorable resources to every production step, and to

☞ the propagation of the remaining variable settings, e.g., fixed production steps, maintenance intervals, etc.

4.3 Analysis Phases

The task of the analysis phase is to determine orders, which might violate their due date, and resource contention. From the results of this pre-analysis the scheduling sequence is derived.

4.3.1 Due Date Violations

The current method to determine orders, which might violate their due date, is to check what happens if the last production step finishes right at the due date. Therefore, a back-propagation of the due date is performed to find out, whether one of the affected constraints gets violated.

Thereby, the network is *interpreted*, i.e., propagation of values takes place in order to test whether certain variable settings are accepted by the network or not.

4.3.2 Resource Bottlenecks

A resource contention analysis is performed to determine possible bottlenecks. The analysis algorithm loops through all production step nodes and collects the required resources(via the **requires** constraint) and the associated time intervals as shown in fig. 9.

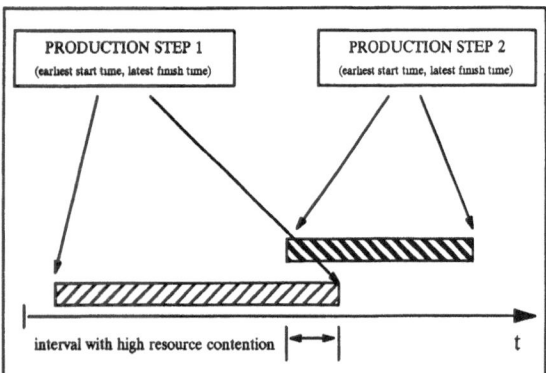

Figure 9: Resource contention analysis

4.3.3 Scheduling Sequence

Satisfying the relations within the constraint network may start at almost any point, but to achieve better results, a sequence of nodes and/or relations should be created, in which the results of the pre-analysis are applied. **Scheduling strategies** also have to be specified, e.g., a machine–oriented strategy, or an order–oriented strategy.

Scheduling strategies express a (user's) wish to emphasize one domain, i.e., to try to achieve good schedules for it. It should be clear that the constraints of the domain satisfied

at the beginning yield better ratings than those satisfied later. The strategies, therefore, lead to an order of objects to handle, respecting the results of the pre-analysis:

▪ The machine–oriented strategy sorts the list of all machines required by production steps, preferring those with high contention.

▪ An order–oriented strategy results in a sequence of all orders to manufacture, e.g., sorted by priority or closeness of due date first.

4.4 Scheduler Main Phase

The scheduling process, now, works on the sequence just created element–by–element. After an object from the sequence is chosen, the following steps have to be done:

- Find and rate all possible alternatives that would satisfy the constraints of the object, and
- propagate the best new variable settings.

4.4.1 Satisfying Constraints

As shown above, some of the constraints have "code" assigned, which enables the computation of lacking values. If a relation is not yet satisfied, the scheduler controller will first try to apply this code on the known variable settings. Note that, in most cases, this is possible if and only if $(n-1)$ of n variables are given. Conflicts arising on this level may either lead to the retraction of some variable settings or to an invocation of the rule–based repair component. If additional variable settings are computed, they have to be propagated through the network.

4.4.2 The Guide Operators

After islands of certainty have been fixed, there are no more variable settings to be propagated, i.e. that no additional constraints can be satisfied with an evaluation of the associated "code". Therefore, additional functions are introduced, called the *guides*. So, if not enough variables are bound, a *guide* function may return predictions on useful values. Two *guides*, one for each strategy, have been identified as being sufficient:

- A guide that is associated with the **contains** constraint, which says that a production step must run during its interval [earliest start time, planned finish time]. A valid planned start time must be within this interval.

- The guide of the **requires** constraint, expressing that a production step requires a resource during some time interval, is explained with fig. 10.

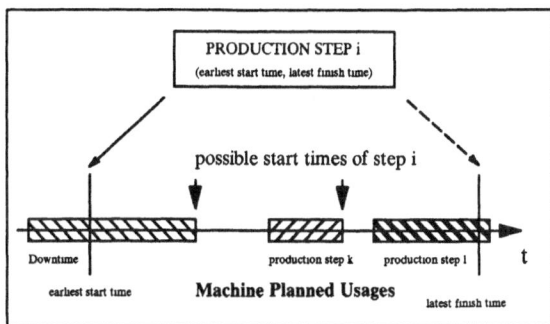

Figure 10: A guide for "requires"

4.4.3 Rule–Based Repair

If scheduling comes to a point where neither actions on constraint nor on satisfiability specification level yield feasible solutions, the rule–based repair is invoked. This maintenance level receives as input a list of constraints and variable settings that failed. Two main classes of problems have been identified:

▶ production steps that do not find a time interval to run on one of its possible machines and

▶ orders not meeting their due date.

Assume, that a production step does not find an interval to run on its most favorable machine:

> *if* "other machine possible"
> *then* "retract current assigned machine";
>   "use other machine"
> *else* "shift due date of order";
>   "use most favorable machine"
> *endif*

The rule says, that repair begins with the retraction of the current set of assigned resources, choosing the next set possible. If all sets of resources have been tested, search is re–invoked with the most preferred set of all resources, postponing the due date of the production step by a (user–specified) interval.

Other rules may retract the due date at once or shift one of the production steps that is blocking the current step.

4.5 Resulting Schedule

The scheduling process terminates after all decisions are made, i.e., all constraints and satisfiability specifications are satisfied: the constraint network is in a balanced state. The information needed to print out the schedule are stored within the nodes of the network:

☐ Orders and production steps hold the time they are performed and the resource(s) they use.

☐ The resource nodes have associated with them a list of usages, containing production steps, maintenance, down times, and other machine reservations. Gantt charts may be created with that information.

4.6 Implementation

A prototype version, CONSNET("**Cons**traint **net**works for scheduling"), of the scheduler described has been implemented on a SYMBOLICS 3620, using the Knowledge–Engineering Environment(KEE) and CommonLisp.

The computational results presented here refer to a job shop with ten orders, where every job has two or three production steps, and a choice among several sets of resource combinations, with a high contention for one machine and one peripheral. Half of the orders have a very close due date. The job shop needs about 250 relations to be described.

Using interpreted code without displaying the propagation, takes about 4 minutes for fixing islands of certainty, 20 seconds for pre–analysis, 1 second for the determination of the scheduling sequence, and between 20 and 30 minutes for scheduling the rest of the job shop, depending on the strategy and rules chosen. The tests lead to the following conclusions:

☞ The rule that uses other sets of resources instead of shifting or canceling the due date, yields better schedules, as long as enough possibilities for other resources are given.

☞ The machine–oriented strategies results in better schedules with reference to machine usages.

☞ High priority orders or orders with a close due date should be scheduled with the order–oriented strategy.

☞ Canceling the due date is only useful if all resources are highly contended. Low priority orders tend to violate their due date significantly, if they have no latest finish time.

Performance of CONSNET does not seem to be very good due to the long run time of the main scheduling algorithm, caused by the satisfaction routines and the propagation algorithm.

Literature

[1] M.S. Fox, S. F. Smith: *ISIS – a knowledge–Based System for Factory Scheduling*, Expert Systems **1** 1 July 1984, pp. 25 – 49

[2] H.W. Guesgen: *CONSAT: A System for Constraint Satisfaction*, Morgan Kaufman Publishers, 1989.

[3] P. Meseguer: *Constraint Satisfaction Problems – An Overview*, AICOM **2** 1, March 1989, pp. 3 – 16

[4] P.Levi: *Knowledge–Based Modelling for Computer–Integrated Manufacturing* in Robot Technologies and Application, ed. by U. Rembold, Ch.3 pp. 153 – 206, Marcel Dekker Inc., 1990.

[5] J.Scholz, *Constraint–Guided Scheduling for Satellite Data Processing and Archiving*, Master's Thesis, Technical University of Munich, November 1990.

[6] W.Rattei et al., *The German PAF for ERS–1: Architectural Design Document of the Facility Management System*, DLR 1990.

Acknowledgements

The work on this paper took place during the first author's time at D–PAF, which was made possible by Mr. J.Gredel and Mr. W.Rattei(DLR, WT–DA/IF). We would also like to thank Dr. Richard Göbel of DLR's AI group for discussion and comments on the work.

Building Adaptive Applications using Active Mediators

Tore Risch*
Hewlett-Packard Laboratories
1501 Page Mill Rd.,
Palo Alto, CA 94303

Gio Wiederhold
Department of Computer Science
Stanford University
Stanford, CA 94305

Abstract

We extend current DBMS technology to support applications in dynamic and heterogenous environments. Our approach raises the level of software support available from DBMSs to include an intermediate layer of software to *mediate* between databases and their use by applications and users. In particular we are demonstrating *active mediators*, where the application instructs a mediator to actively monitor databases for change in information that the application depends on. We identify how mediators can support applications that are sensitive to change.

A prototype platform for these classes of mediators has been developed. As a uniform interface language throughout the system we use OSQL, a declarative object-oriented query language. OSQL statements are optimized using concepts extracted from Datalog and relational database research.

1 Introduction

Future computing environments will have large numbers of workstations connected via communication networks. Workstations will have powerful computation capabilities; server stations store, maintain, and do inferences over local data- and knowledge-bases, or *information bases*. Each information base is maintained locally by human experts and is likely to be autonomous from other information bases. Data resources, servers, and applications are heterogeneous. The environment needs to support frequent changes and additions to these data and computation resources. Information and control often has to be exchanged among different information bases. We will have a large distributed *information network*, through which it is possible to access data stored in a variety of local forms, integrate the data, and obtain information without the use of human intermediaries, as is common today.

Wiederhold [26] has proposed to introduce an intermediate *mediator* layer of software between databases and their applications and users. The mediator layer insulates individual users and servers from the necessity to maintain detailed

---
*The work was done while visitiing the Hewlett-Packard Stanford Science Center.

models of the different and changing *data sources* within the information system.

We use the mediator concept to extend current DBMS technology to support such distributed, heterogeneous, and dynamic environments. Mediators make it easy to 'plug in' new data resources once there is a public interface protocol. In this work we focus on *active* mediators, where the application instructs a mediator to actively monitor databases for changes to information that the application depends on, and provide primitives for applications to adapt to these changes. We discuss what classes of mediator modules are needed to support active databases.

In Section 2 we motivate our work by describing a relevant real-life problem scenario. In Section 3 we describe the components of a mediator architecture serving as a platform to solve these real-life problems with references to related work. In Sections 4 and 5 we give an overview of the design of our mediator platform. Finally, Section 6 summarizes the work and indicates directions for future work.

2 A Scenario

To illustrate what new services are needed beyond what is provided by present DBMSs, it is fruitful to think of some possible problem scenarios. In this section we discuss one such scenarios, namely the problem of manufacturing production planning in a distributed environment with many independent production sites. The scenario mainly has grown out of discussions with people in HP Labs.

In our problem scenario we have a large corporation with production facilities distributed over many separate sites around the world. The computer environment is heterogeneous, different sites use different DBMSs. The hardware and software environments differ as well.

The corporation continuously receives orders that are composed of items that are produced at different sites. Often one has the choice to produce the same item at many sites, and one then makes choices depending on production costs, transportation costs, production capacity, etc. There are often dependencies between the production of order items, so that one site must wait for some other site to produce some subpart before the item can be made. The customers are promised delivery at some specific date, and it is important to neither deliver too early (because of cost of inventory) or too late.

When an order arrives, the possible production sites are polled to determine their capacities, costs, schedules, etc. Given this data and the customer's expectations, distributed production schedules for the order are produced for the various sites. We have implemented database support for executing such plans; we have not attacked the scheduling problem itself. The schedules are based on the polled data which occasionally change while the schedules are executed. Thus we have to be able to cope with world changes that may modify the plan while it is being executed. In the worst case some critical site may stop entirely and the plan will have to be completely redone. Because of the complexity of the planning problem, it is likely that the planning is broken down into many local interconnected planners, and normally not all of them have to be replanned at once.

Similar scenarios can be constructed for other related areas, e.g., computer network service planning systems, and project planning and tracking systems.

3 Mediator Classes

We will now continue by discussing a possible architecture covering the production planning scenario. architecture.

We have identified the following three classes of mediators (Figure 1):

Task Models

We break out domain knowledge now hidden in application programs and store them in a special kind of mediator which implements sharable and inspectable domain knowledge bases. We call such a domain knowledge base a *Task Model*. The task models allow us to maintain knowledge more easily by storing it in these limited-sized and specialized knowledge bases.

In our scenario, the actual task planners are application programs that generate plans for carrying out the distributed tasks as specified by users. The output of a task planner is a set of task models to be executed by the sites together. This interaction need not be completely automated; the plans could be done in cooperation with users, where the expert manually develops task models to carry out the plan.

While planners provide some of the most advanced and demanding applications for the mediator architecture, the architecture also supports ordinary application programs that retrieve distributed data through mediators, e.g. to produce weekly production summary reports.

We use extensions to OSQL, WS-OSQL, as the language to build task models. We have developed a platform for efficient representation of task models based on a main memory WS-OSQL compiler [15] integrated with Iris. An overview of this platform is given in Section 5. Related work includes work on extracting complex objects from databases [2, 22], structuring knowledge bases [25], and storing business rules in knowledge base modules [8]. Unlike these system we use the same extended OSQL query language as a uniform representation of both persistent data and task models. Task model OSQL queries are optimized using techniques from optimizing relational databases and Datalog [7, 20]. Our research aims at developing small, modular, inspectable, easily maintainable, and well integrated knowledge modules rather than large scale complex knowledge bases [12, 16].

Monitors

We need some mechanism to handle the problem of dynamically changing contents and locations of data. For example, when an initial scheduling plan is made, the assumption is that the data, critical for the execution of the plan, is not changing. In practice these data are frequently invalidated. Therefore the planner is notified when data is updated that was assumed to be constant when the plan was made. Now the plan must be adapted as well.

Mediators continuously monitor these invariant data and notify the planner when the invariants change to a significant extent. Let's call these mediators *monitors*. Traditional DBMSs are passive since they passively respond to requests from application programs. With monitors the database becomes an *active database*, because procedures of application programs are invoked from the DBMS, when triggered by state changes in data sources. This technique provides a way to pass control between cooperating application programs through a database.

We have extended OSQL to include primitives for monitoring state changes in Iris databases and implemented the extension for the Iris prototype [12, 13]. Related research includes work on coordinating long running activities [5, 23], blackboard architectures [11], forward chaining rule based systems[4], and constraint propagation languages[18]. We use the same extended OSQL language both for passive and active queries and both within task models and for persistent databases. We describe our database monitors in Section 4.

Integrators

The knowledge sources can be represented in different ways. For example, different sites may use different DBMSs and data models, similar data may be represented with different data formats, etc. We therefore need mediators that retrieve and combine results from different knowledge sources, check their consistency, and present a higher level view to applications [10]. We call these mediators *integrators*. Integrators decouple the application from the necessity to maintain

510

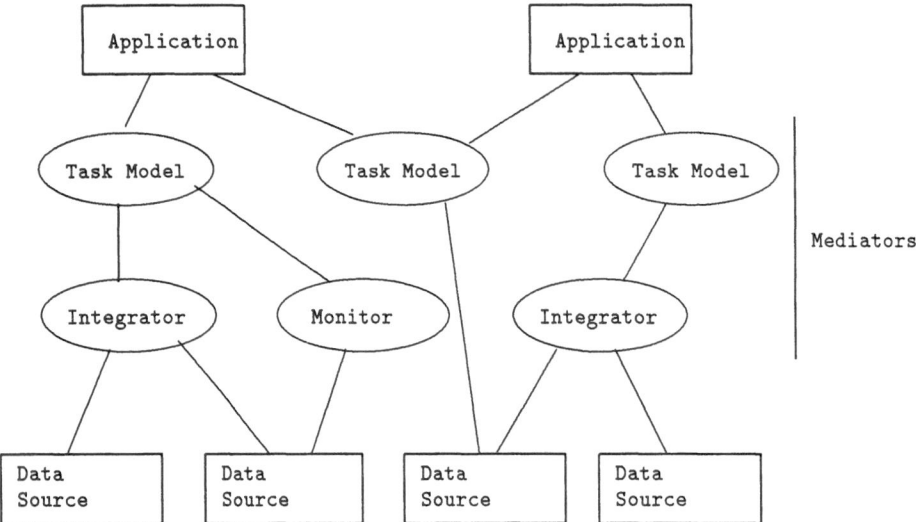

Figure 1: Examples of Mediators

multiple data models for all knowledge sources. The Pegasus project at HP Labs [1] aims at using OSQL to support such integrator models. We include its concepts here to make the overall picture complete.

Interface Language

Finally we need to define formal languages between the various mediator levels. The application programs need a standard interface language. Lower level software also needs well defined interfaces. For example, we need some standard way to interface new knowledge sources so that mediators 'understand' them. We are using an extended version of the OSQL language [3, 6, 9] as such a uniform interface language.

4 Monitors

Database change monitors are computer programs that observe changes in the contents of database access queries, e.g., the current price of some commodity, the highest paid employee in a department, or the expenses of a department relative to its sales. We have implemented database change monitors [13] within the object-oriented DBMS Iris [6].

We use non-procedural extensions to OSQL as the language to express what type of changes are of interest for a given application. This is achieved by the programmer specifying a query (view) whose result is monitored for change. The programmer thus registers interest in a class of database state changes and delegates to the DBMS to generate a plan to infer when these value states change because of database updates. The algorithms to track such value changes are complicated and depend on information outside of the scope of the programs interest. Hence the programmer should be

freed from having to specify their details. The system provides *monitor tuning parameters* that instruct the system to filter out insignificant state changes thereby decreasing the notification frequency.

The programmer must specify what happens when the value of a monitored view changes. A convenient way to do this is to specify a *tracking procedure* or *tracker*, which is a procedure of the application that is invoked by the DBMS when monitored data change. The DBMS thus keeps track of which tracking procedures monitor which object attributes and contains a mechanism to call the tracking procedures upon data changes. Monitoring processes are autonomous relative to updating processes, so that committing transactions need not wait for tracking procedures to finish, a distinction vis-a-vis POSTGRES triggering [19].

Possible tasks for tracking procedures include

- Notifying the end user that data have changed.

- Refreshing data browsers

- Modifying values in mediators.

- Changing processing heuristics in mediators.

- Changing stored abstractions in mediators.

- Informing applications that data views which the application depends on have changed.

We allow the programmer to specify the monitor tuning parameters *time intervals* and *tracking periodicity* Δt. If tuning parameters are specified the monitors are not triggered immediately when the database value state change happens, but will be delayed as specified. For example, in business situations, some monitors are best checked once a day or some time before the end of the week [23]. Some applications require the monitor to be notified every time there is a data change. Sometimes this checking must be done before committing the updating transactions, which can be very expensive. The programmer is given a primitive to make this choice.

A range interval, the *change significance* Δv, can be declared so that tracking procedures are not invoked unless the monitored value has changed more than the interval. The change significance is specified as absolute range limits, or as the variance relative to the magnitude of the value.

It is advantageous if the active DBMS can do this kind of *dynamic filtering* before notifying the application, in order to decrease the frequency of notification for intensively updated data. The application can dynamically change the difference interval to decrease the reactivity if it is performing some change-intensive task. Dynamic filtering is required, for example, by real-time monitoring AI systems where the tracker initiates time consuming reasoning activities [21].

5 Active Task Models

The DBMS architectures developed for conventional databases are not always feasible for supporting active databases. In particular, disk based databases are often too slow for applications requiring fast responses. Our architecture is a combination of traditional persistent data representation for conventional applications and main memory techniques for time critical mediators.

Task models represent domain knowledge bases. We represent our task models using the Iris data model whose lingua franca is the OSQL query language. Task models are presumed to contain moderate data volumes but complex structures. To obtain reasonable performance we need to represent task models in main memory. Therefore we have developed a main memory OSQL database implementation: WS-IRIS (Workstation IRIS) [15]. WS-IRIS is a fully operational DBMS for a workstation. WS-IRIS manages main-memory databases and, for better efficiency, it uses main memory data structures instead of the disk oriented data structures of classical DBMSs. It also provides transactions, limited concurrency control, logging, and recovery.

WS-IRIS contains an extensible cost-based query optimizer that translates queries in an extended OSQL dialect, WS-OSQL, into Datalog [20] programs for subsequent interpretation. It incorporates techniques for conventional query optimization, where effective for our main memory storage management. We also use optimization techniques tailored for the object-oriented nature of WS-OSQL.

The task model platform is interfaced with Iris so that data can be extracted from Iris databases into task models. With the Pegasus [1] extension to Iris we will be able to access heterogeneous data sources.

In order to support our scenario we also need to represent task models that are sensitive to changes both in underlying data sources and in local data. We therefore have implemented database change monitors both within WS-IRIS and in the IRIS prototype. Primitives have been added to OSQL to monitor changes of views of both local and global data. For example, a task model may have a set of rules for selecting a preferred part based on some local thresholds, e.g., maximum delivery time and failure rate. Using monitors the task model can instruct the system to execute some rule whenever some other part becomes the preferred one. The tuning parameters Δt and Δv add some stiffness to the system by filtering out temporary and insignificant data changes.

6 Discussion

We have described an architecture which has been implemented to support database applications that are sensitive to changes in an underlying heterogeneous data sources. Using such a system one writes applications that adapt to change rather than prohibit change as is customary in traditional database transaction systems. We used the mediator concept [26] to identify three kinds of mediators which we found important in such an architecture:

1. *Active Task Models* are domain knowledge bases which contain both conventional rules and rules sensitive to change in both local and external data.

   A planned generalization is to include the notion of time in the system in a coherent way in order to support rules that access timing information about data and knowledge [17, 24].

2. *Database Change Monitors* are mediators which detect changes in underlying data source by tracking changes in derived views. The monitors will notify the active task models when significant data changes are detected. The programmer specifies declaratively what constitutes significant change so that the monitors can filter insignificant notifications.

3. *Integrators* are mediators which, using schema integration and data conversion facilities [10], integrate heterogeneous data representations to be presented uniformly to other mediators.

512

As a common interface language to the different mediator modules we use extensions to OSQL [6], WS-OSQL [12]. The approach has been demonstrated by a prototype implementation, WS-IRIS (Workstation Iris) [12].

An important application area for active mediators is in the support of systems where persistent data is checked out into main memory *work areas*, which are here represented as active task models. During long sessions the user would work directly with specific and hence efficient active task models and only occasionally check data back into the central database. This complements the view object paradigm proposed by Wiederhold [22] and implemented in the PENGUIN project [2]. Here we provide the same uniform query language, OSQL, both for the shared database, the extraction of data into work areas, and for representing the work areas themselves.

Active task models also have applications in CAD/CAM and CASE systems, where a design is stored persistently in a database. A group of designers intend to work cooperatively on a specific design. They therefore check out the design into an active task model. The designers would work concurrently on the design in the active task model using some supporting software tools. The tools would use monitors to notify designers when some other designer modifies some data that is of interest. Winslett et al [27] describe an architecture for consistency maintenance in a design database, which could be supported by active task models.

An advantage with having data communicated between applications stored in a database is that the data then also is accessed using a query language instead of being hidden inside data structures within the applications. Having a query language permits a level of integration that is hard to obtain with direct use of communication protocols.

ACKNOWLEDGEMENTS:

The KSYS group at Stanford (supported partially by DARPA contract N39-84-C211) provided insights into the mediator concept. Peter Lyngbaek and the DTD group at HP Labs helped us understand Iris. Gio Wiederhold acknowledges support from HP Stanford Science Center and from NSF contract DMC 86-19595-A1.

References

[1] R.Ahmed, P.Desmedt, W.Kent, A.Rafii, W.Litwin, M.Shan: The Pegasus project: Information Management in a Heterogeneous Database Environment, *IEEE COMPCON*, March 1991.

[2] T.Barsalou, G.Wiederhold: Complex objects for relational databases, *Computer-Aided Design*, 22(8), Oct. 1990, pp. 457-468.

[3] D.Beech: A Foundation for Evolution from Relational to Object Databases, *Advances in Database Technology - EDBT '88*, Lecture Notes in Comp. Sc., Springer-Verlag, 1988, pp. 251-270.

[4] L.Brownston, R.Farell, E.Kant, N.Martin: *Programming Expert Systems in OPS5*, Addison-Wesley, Reading, Mass., 1985.

[5] U.Dayal, M.Hsu, R.Ladin: Organizing Long-Running Activities with Trigger and Transactions, *Proc. SIGMOD*, May 23-25, Atlantic City, 1990, pp. 204-214.

[6] D.Fishman et al: Overview of the Iris DBMS, in W.Kim, F.H.Lochovsky (ed.): *Object-Oriented Concepts, Databases, and Applications*, ACM press, Addison-Wesley Publ. Comp., 1989.

[7] R.Krishnamurthy, S.Zaniolo: Optimization in a Logic Based Language for Knowledge and Data Intensive Applications, *Advances in Database Technology - EDBT '88*, Lecture Notes in Comp. Sc., Springer-Verlag, 1988, pp. 16-33.

[8] P.Lucas, T.Risch: Representation of Factual Information by Equations and their Evaluation, *Proc. Intl. Conf. on Software Eng.*, Tokyo, Japan, Sept. 13-16, IEEE, New York, 1982, pp. 153-167

[9] P.Lyngbaek and the OODB Team at CSY: *OSQL: A Language for Object Databases*, Technical report, HP Labs, HPL-DTD-91-4, 1991.

[10] L.deMichiel: Performing Operations over Mismatched Domains, *Proc. of IEEE Data Eng. 5*, Los Angeles, Feb. 1989.

[11] P.Nii: The Blackboard Model for Problem Solving, *AI Magazine*, Vol. 7, No. 2, Spring 1986, pp. 38-53.

[12] T.Risch, R.Reboh, P.Hart, R.Duda: A Functional Approach to Integrating Database and Expert Systems, *Communications of the ACM* 31, 12 (Dec. 1988), pp. 1424-1437.

[13] T.Risch: Monitoring Database Objects, *Proc. VLDB*, Amsterdam, the Netherlands, 1989.

513

[14] T.Risch: *Tuning the Reactivity of Database Monitors*, Technical Report, HP Labs, HPL-90-17, 1990 (also part of [26]).

[15] T.Risch: *The Translation of Object-Oriented Queries to Optimized Datalog Programs*, Technical Report, HP Labs, HPL-DTD-91-9, 1991.

[16] E.H.Shortcliffe: *Computer-based medical consultations: MYCIN*, American Elsevier, New York, 1976.

[17] R.Snodgrass, I.Ahn: Temporal Databases, *IEEE Computer*, Vol. 19, No. 9, Sept. 1986, pp. 35–42.

[18] G.L.Steele Jr., G.J.Sussman: CONSTRAINTS, in *APL79 Conf. Proc.*, (Rochester, USA), pp. 208-225.

[19] M.Stonebraker: The design of POSTGRES, *Proc. SIGMOD*, 1986, pp. 340-355.

[20] J.D.Ullman: *Principles of Database and Knowledge-Base Systems*, Volume I and II, Comp. Sc. Press, 1988.

[21] R.Washington, B.Hayes-Roth: Input Data Management in Real-Time AI Systems, *11th Intl. Joint Conf. on Artificial Intelligence*, 1989, pp. 250-255.

[22] G.Wiederhold: Views, objects, and databases, *IEEE Computer*, 19(12), 1986, pp. 37-44.

[23] G.Wiederhold, X.Qian: Modeling Asynchrony in Distributed Databases, *3rd Intl. Conf. on Data Eng.*, Los Angeles, CA, Feb. 3-5, 1987, pp. 246-250.

[24] G.Wiederhold, S.Jajodia, W.Litwin: Dealing with Granularity of Time in Temporal Databases, *Nordic Conf. on Adv. Inf. Syst. Eng.*, Springer, 1991.

[25] G.Wiederhold, P.Rathmann, T.Barsalou, B.S.Lee, D.Quass: Partitioning and Composing Knowledge, *Inf. Systems*, Vol.15, No.1, 1990, pp. 61-72.

[26] G.Wiederhold, T.Risch, P.Rathmann, L.DeMichiel, S.Chaudhury, B.S.Lee, K.H.Law, T.Barsalou, D.Quass: *A Mediator Architecture for Abstract Data Access*, Stanford Comp. Sc. Dept., STAN-CS-90-1301, 1990.

[27] M.Winslett, K.Hall, D.Knapp, G.Wiederhold: Use of Change Coordination in an Information-rich Design Environment, *IEEE Design Automation Conf.*, Las Vegas, June 1989.

Hypertext for Hypertext: a Figured Thesaurus

Oreste Signore and Roberto Aulisi

CNUCE, Institute of CNR
via S. Maria, 36 - 56126 Pisa (Italy)

Valeria Ceccanti

Consorzio Pisa Ricerche
via Risorgimento, 9 - Pisa (Italy)

ABSTRACT

On the basis of a heraldic encyclopedia, a hypertext has been built. The existence of an exact heraldic grammar allows a classification of the coats-of-arms, but it is not easy to be used from not skillful users, and it makes particularly critic the user interface. The constitution of a figured thesaurus, hypertext structured, allowed the realization of a concept browsing interface, which accomplish the functions of didactic and support instrument for the formulations of queries.

INTRODUCTION

The starting point of this research* was a problem with which the scholars, particularly of history and art, have frequently to deal: that is the identification of a person, or at least of the family to which he belongs, on the basis of his coat-of-arms, and when only the coat-of-arms and anything else is known. A coat-of-arms can adorn a portrait, a painting, an altar, of which other documentary data are lacking (or they are unknown); therefore the coat-of-arms may represent the first access key for the right classification and study of that object, provided that it can be possible to know to whom it belongs.

---

* This work has been supported by a fellowship offered by the Consorzio Pisa Ricerche.
R. Aulisi worked mainly to the figured thesaurus and to the query interface. V. Ceccanti has gathered and organised the heraldic material and took care of developing the pertinent software. O.Signore designed the architecture and functionalities of the system.
We are also grateful to prof. Salvatore Settis (Scuola Normale Superiore), who proposed the topic and he incited us by his critical and constructive support. We wish at last to thank Mr. Umberto Parrini (Scuola Normale Superiore), for his cooperation in the scanning of images.

Heraldic encyclopedias are arranged in alphabetical order, therefore they are unsuitable to go back to the lineage starting from the graphic characteristics of the coat-of-arms. A traditional Information Retrieval approach appears unsatisfactory for several reasons:
- the description of a coat of arms, generally, should not leave out of consideration its image, as well as its links with news relative to the family or to other families which became related with it, or to the events which caused alterations to the coat of arms.
- It is not easy, in some cases, unless the user is a real scholar of the topic, to specify the kind of figure (natural or artificial) present in the coat of arms.
- The heraldic grammar, that is the language utilised to describe the arms, is not commonly known.

It results in that a file concerning the heraldic arms has clearly hypertextual and hypermedial characteristics, as it exhibits the interrelationship of many unstructured informations (historical documents, maps, descriptive texts, etc.).
Furthermore, considering the kind of potential users, it appears essential the availability of a fairly user friendly interface, which give also a supporting function for the learning of the heraldic grammar.

DATA AND THEIR CONCEPTUAL STRUCTURE

This work started from the study and deepening of the heraldic material through a careful bibliographic research: the classic texts of the italian heraldy ([3], [4], [5], [13]), as well as the more recent works ([1], [2], [9]) were examined and a look to the rich foreign literature in this field was taken ([6], [7], [8], [10], [11]). The informations which form the hypertextual data base were essentially deduced from the italian historical-noble Encyclopedia by Vittorio Spreti ([12]), whose work was taken as base, enriched by archive researches, mostly for what concerns the links among the various families and the events which caused alterations in the arms. This choice was essentially due to the fact that the Encyclopedia shows the arms drawing in black and white, clearly readable, ready to be directly inserted, by an inexpensive scanner, in HERMES.

A sample of about 380 arms, formed by all the arms belonging to the families included under the A letter of Spreti, was used.

From the study carried out it has been realized that all the possible data connected with a family can be articulated to form a single document, containing the arm's image and some essential informations (family name, escutcheon description, residence, noble titles, motto, crest and supports), in addition the historical informations about the family. The eventual references to other documents can be also considered as data; such references are evident on the escutcheon when it is composed by elements which are present on the escutcheon of other families (see fig. 1), as there are genealogical, vassallage, heredity connections with them; or such references are clearly related, together with some quotations, in the historical informations.

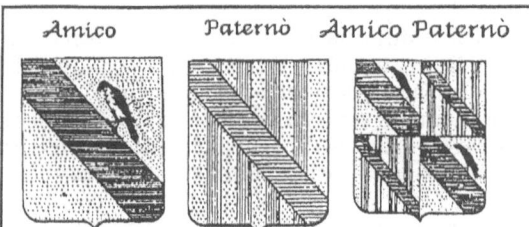

Fig. 1 - Example of clear connection on the arms

THE CHOISE OF THE APPROACH

The alternatives

To find the informations, in the hypertextual systems, two distinct stages are applied: at a first step a "satisfactory" entry point is obtained as reply to the user query; at a second step, starting from the entry point, we move in the hypertext. Therefore the main problem is to be able to obtain a satisfactory entry point. Such entry point should be given by a graphic identification.

Several alternatives were considered.

The implementation of an instrument based on the identification of the images, fit to isolate the essential elements of the graphic of the escutcheon and to codify them in a "loose" way, by associating the correct term of the heraldic grammar, or by calculating a codification function for the recognized element, has been discarded, because a standard for the graphics of the arms is lacking, and the implementation of the instrument should be of remarkable complexity.

A graphic editor, that is an instrument which should have been allowed the user "to build" graphically the arms, getting at the same time the description according to the heraldic grammar, would require a long serie of screens, also for simple arms. Apparently similar applications (e.g identikit), have less constitutive elements, with a lower number of dispositions and combinations (consider, as an example, the escutcheon in figure 2).

Fig. 2 - Example of an escutcheon graphic

However, it must be considered that to find the graphic of an escutcheon is equivalent to find the text of its description. The text of one description (called "blazon") is written according to the heraldic grammar and we may say that it creates, in a certain way, a controlled language, therefore suitable for the formulation of a query which gives good values of precision and recall.

All this series of considerations led to the decision of using the Information Retrieval techniques for the finding out of texts.

The role of the thesauri as user interface

The hypertextual instruments don't have powerful mechanisms of indexing and retrieval, as those usually present in the Information Retrieval systems. For the case under examination, the problem is complicated by the fact that we must be able to consider the inaccuracies which the user could make in any case, and with great facility. Such mistakes can be ascribed to two main classes:
- lack of precision of the utilized terms;
- incorrect identification of the element to be found.

In the Information Retrieval approach ([20], [21], [22], [25]), if the user cannot suitably express what he/she is looking for, the system cannot give adequate results. Therefore, the fundamental problem is to identify the contents of what he/she is looking for, to formulate the query and to begin a research per subject. In order to facilitate the user's research, it's useful to explicitly build in knowledge of synonyms, preference and hierarchical relationships among the terms, that is to create a thesaurus ([16]). A system of this type requires the user to move in the hierarchy of the concepts, usually top-down ([23]). Furthermore the thesauri are considered as integrating part of hypertextual systems, as they form the structure through which the users can move to select the fundamental parts of the documents under investigation ([24]).

The importance of a suitable user interface was emphasized since many years and from various authors, as also sophisticate systems, based on artificial intelligence techniques, give services which depend on the efficiency with which the system communicate with the user and therefore it is able to identify the descriptors which allow to compare the user's query with the content of documents.
In [17] is supported the thesis according to which a consistency in the knowledge representation between indexers and users can be obtained, provided that a semantic system of concepts is accessible to indexers and users. Considering the above, the authors think it is possible to implement intelligent interfaces which allow the user to be able of making significant researches using suitable descriptors, by creating a communication mechanism to fit the key concepts. One of the possible approaches are the graphic browsing oriented interfaces, where the browsing represents an informal or euristic research that, through a collection of well connected documents, allows to find the important information which is needed. Fundamental condition to implement a browsing interface is the availability of a high quality thesaurus. In the hypertexts and in the IRS the browsing has been used both for the assistance to query's formulation and the direct research of the information in the documents.
Some prototypes systems developed for the query formulation problem are CANSEARCH ([19]), CALIBAN ([15]), and COALSORT ([17]). Our system is for certain ways similar to CALIBAN and COALSORT for what concerns the manual construction of the query, and to CANSEARCH as regards to the query's composition on behalf of the system (query by browsing).

Therefore, in conclusion, the HERMES system is constituted by two components: the data 's hypertext and the graphic thesaurus (this realized at hypertext too). In following paragraphs the two components and the working of the integrated system will be separately illustrated.

THE HYPERTEXT OF HERMES

The structure

With reference to the abstract structure of the documents, it turned out natural to organize the hypertext on three types of cards:
• one *Coat of arms* card, which contains the arms image and some essential informations (family's name, arms's description, residence, supports, crests, mottoes and titles) made according to the heraldic grammar;
• one *Historical News* card, which contains the historical news pertinent to the family ;
• one *Additions* card, which may act as a repository of users' annotations.
The three types of cards were drawn to seem evidently different for structure and content, but "familiar" as regards to the interaction's type (mainly the disposition and meaning of the buttons).
The *Additions* card was conceived to allow the user to have a particularly active attitude towards the system, in order to catch his/her competences.

The navigation

The three different kind of cards are linked together in both directions, therefore it is possible to proceed immediately from one to another and consequently to look through the *Historical News* or *Coats of Arms* or *Additions* cards. The connection among the cards was clearly realized, by means of buttons, placed on the lower edge of the card, whose meaning appears evident from their icons (Fig. 3).
The various connections, relative to other families or further news, insert on this linear structure. For such connections a more transparent and immediate mechanism was chosen, by using "anchor points" embedded in the text or corresponding to some details of the images:
• in the fields containing text, all the words or expressions preceded and followed by the symbol @ act as anchor points.
• Some links which connect the single components of the arms to other cards were also defined on the

esctucheon image. To point out these links, it is suffcient to push the button *Links* and the escutcheon portions for which it was possible to define a connection with other cards will be highlighted. On the contrary, in case no link was found, the user receives a message. This solution was chosen to avoid the disappointment of repeated clicks on the image, without any reply from the system.

In order to avoid the problem known as being "*lost in the hyperspace*", the user is allowed to define bookmarkers (through the button *Remember*) every time the card under examination is interesting for him/her. Successively, the button *Return* allows to go backwards stopping only on the cards for which a bookmarker was formulated.

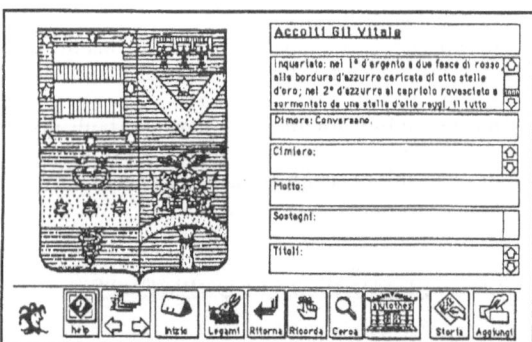

Fig. 3: Example of the card *Coat of Arms*

THE GRAPHIC THESAURUS

After an examination of the characteristics of escutcheon's descriptions and considering what stated in [14]), it was possible to conclude that as describing terms or key terms, present in the escutcheon's descriptions and (eventually) of crest and supports, have to be considered those words or series of words which exactly identify the fundamental elements of the graphic composition of the coat of arms (or the escutcheon's graphic, as minimum). Such elements are: the peculiar division of the escutcheon and pertinent fields of the parts, the peculiar heraldic figures present, the eventual honourables mentions.

In a description like: "*to the half black eagle, red tongued crowned of the field, coming out the partition*", it is easily seen that the most important term of the sentence is "*eagle*" as it identifies a definite heraldic symbol, all the others show some characteristics which refine the term *eagle*. The refinement can be of two types: for the colour and the peculiarity of the figure (generally of the element); therefore there are some relationships of narrower term between the more general term and more specific ones. If we indicate with **NTC** the relationship of narrower term for colour and with **NTP** the relationship of narrower term for peculiarity, we may see as we pass from *eagle* to *half eagle* by a **NTP** relationship, from *half eagle* to *black half eagle* with **NTC** relationship and so on.

The thesaurus structure is visualized to the user under a tree shape (Fig. 4), where the *classification's facets* are represented by the ellipses, and the *classes of descriptor terms* by the rectangles.

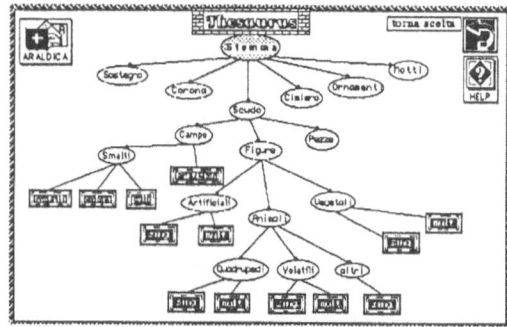

Fig. 4 - Visualization of the thesaurus

For each descriptor term, there is a leaf card, where the content of the broader term, NTC and NTP fields can or cannot be visualized, according to user's discretion. The passage from one term to the other happens simply by selecting the term which characterizes the leaf on which we want to position (Fig. 5).

Fig. 5 - A thesaurus leaf card, seen in *Query by browsing* mode.

THE INTEGRATED SYSTEM

The integrated system is composed by a main environment (**HERALDRY**) and a subordinate environment (**GRAPHIC THESAURUS**), both hypertext structured[1]. Only from the main environment it is possible to get the subordinate and this is possible immediately, on beginning of the system, and during the HERALDRY hypertext navigation.

The usage of the browsing interface

The thesaurus can be utilized either in *Didactic browsing* or in *Help for query* mode.

In case the **didactic browsing** was chosen, we navigate in the graphic Thesaurus, and starting from the visualization's card of the thesaurus we visit the cards of the descriptors terms, from which we may learn the heraldic term for a peculiar element, as well as peculiar rules of the nobility and an explanation of an eventual allegoric meaning.

In case we choose the **Help for query**, we may move in three different ways:
- *Query by browsing.*
  The system will take the job of composing the query according to the indications given from the user navigating in the thesaurus. On the cards of describing terms some new buttons are available, which allow to select the term considered more suitable (with or without its eventual synonyms) and put it in boolean AND/OR with the previous ones (see Fig. 5). The query expressed in this way can be later changed through a further navigating in the thesaurus.
- *Query by expert*
  The system has a card with which is possible to formulate a query through a description of "unknown" arms. The formulated query is *filtered* by the system in order to verify the exactness of the terms utilized (that is their existence in the thesaurus). If uncorrect terms are detected, a further dialogue takes place. All the terms which, even if aren't shown in the thesaurus, are anyway present in the escutcheon's descriptions, are placed in a suitable field, to allow an intervention of the

thesaurus's manager (inclusion of the term and its connections with other terms).
- *Query by novice*
  It differs from the previous case only because it allows to perform the query only in the Description field.

The **result** card is common to all the three ways, and shows the identifiers of the retrieved documents pertinent to the query.

Visit to the retrieved documents

To indicate that the cards are being visited coming from the subordinate environment, it was decided to change the number and type of buttons of the cards which form the physical document.
It is worthwhile to note:
- the appearance of a marker indicating that the card under examination is an element of the retrieved documents set;
- the possibility for the user to move both in the retrieved documents set and in the hypertext;
- the possibility to go back to the result card, to select a different entry point.

FUTURE DEVELOPMENTS

For the future, it's to be expected an increasing of data consistency, as the detail and structuration level of the informations seems to be sufficient to face the immediate requirements of the scholars. The task which, for the moment, seems to be more urgent is the development of the thesaurus, for which an expert's support is necessary.
The ways of navigating will be enriched, also basing on the more recent tendencies and experiences ([18]), in order to make some links more evident (think for instance to the possibility of visualizing a genealogical tree).
As regards to the support's functionality for the user, it has been thought to improve the help's functions, to realize a real didactic instrument and to allow the consultation of the hypertext with two different modalities:
- in *help* mode the user will receive informations about the meaning of the peculiar symbol represented or enamel;
- in *browse* mode the user will receive informations about the origin of the peculiar symbol and the reasons for which it has been represented on the escutcheon (marriage, honour, peculiar task etc.)

---

[1] The application has been developed using HyperCard™. The query and indexing facilities are provided by HyperKRS™.
All the terms are in Italian language.

It's also under study the implementation of indexing mechanisms more sophisticated than the simple extraction of words from the text, in order to allow the research basing on incomplete or "noisy" clauses, and the return of the documents according to the relevance to the query.

CONCLUSIONS

The hypertextual approach revealed itself fit to the management of a data base on heraldic arms, and allowed the gathering and the integration of different and connected data. The implemented system is available on low cost and high diffusion machines, while the new technology of optical disks has almost no limits for the development possibilities of the stored information.

The establishment of a thesaurus accompanied by figures, acting with browsing interface functions, resulted to be an efficient solution, and therefore represents the means through which it's possible to place at disposal of the data base manager as well as the user the same base of knowledge, increasing precision and recall.

The thesaurus represents also a didactic support instrument for the learning of the heraldic grammar.

REFERENCES

Heraldic literature

[1]   Bascapè G. C., Insegne e Simboli: araldica pubblica e privata medievale e moderna, Ministero per i Beni culturali e ambientali, Roma 1983.

[2]   Bascapè G. C., Sigillografia. Il sigillo nella diplomatica, nel diritto, nella storia, nell'arte, Antonio Giuffrè, Milano 1969.

[3]   Crollalanza G.B., Enciclopedia araldico-cavalleresca. Prontuario nobiliare, Pisa 1878.

[4]   Crollalanza G. B., Dizionario storico-blasonico delle famiglie nobili e notabili italiane, vol. I-III, Pisa 1886.

[5]   Manno A., Regolamento tecnico araldico della Consulta Araldica, Stab. Tip. Giuseppe Civelli, Roma 1906.

[6]   Menestrier V., Abrégé methodique des principes héraldiques, ou du veritable art du Blason, Amanlry t., Lyon 1681.

[7]   Pastoureau M., Les Armoiries, Editions Brepols, Turnhout 1976.

[8]   Pastoureau M., Traité d'Héraldique, Picard, Paris 1979.

[9]   Plessi G., Blasone e schedatura araldica, Quaderni della scuola di Paleografia ed Archivistica, Archivio di Stato di Bologna, Bologna 1963.

[10]   de Renesse T., Dictionnaire des figures héraldiques, vol 1-7, Société Belge de Librairie, Bruxelles 1894-1903.

[11]   Rietstap J. B., Armorial Général, vol. 1-2, G. B. van Goorzonen, Gouda 1884.

[12]   Spreti V. (a cura di): Enciclopedia storico-nobiliare italiana, Milano 1928-36

[13]   Spreti V.- Degli Azzi Vitelleschi G., Saggio di Bibliografia araldica italiana, supplemento alla Enciclopedia storico-nobiliare italiana, Arnaldo Forni Editore, Milano 1936.

[14]   Tribolati F., Grammatica araldica, Ulrico Hoepli, Milano 1892.

Scientific literature

[15]   Frei H.P., Jauslin J.F., Graphical presentation of of information and services: a user-oriented interface, Information Technology: Research and Development, N. 2, pp.23-42

[16]   International Standard ISO 2788, Documentation Guidelines for the establishement and development of monolingual thesauri, International Organization for Standardization, Svizzera (1986)

[17]   Monarch I, Carbonell J., CoalSORT: A Knowledge-Based Interface, IEEE Expert (Spring 1987), pp.39-53

[18]   Nielsen J.: The Art of navigating through Hypertext, Communications of the ACM, Vol. 33, N. 3 (March 1990)

[19]   Pollitt A.S., End user touch searching for cancer therapy literature-a rule based approach, in Proceedings of the Sixth Annual International ACM SIGIR Conference on Research and Development in Information Retrieval, Vol.17, N.4, (June 1983), pp.136-145

[20]   Salton G., McGill M.J., Introduction to modern Information Retrieval, McGraw-Hill, New York (1983)

[21]   Salton G.: Automatic text processing, Addison-Wesley (1989), ISBN 0-201-12227-8

[22]   Smith P.J., Shute S.J., Galdes D., Chignell M.H., Knowledge-Based Search Tactics for an Intelligent Intermediary System, ACM TOIS, Vol. 7, N. 3 (July 1989)

[23]   Thompson D., Interface design for an interactive information retrieval system: A literature survey and a research system description, J. Am. Soc. Inf. Sci. (1971), pp. 361-373

[24]   Trigg R.H., Weiser M.: TEXTNET: A network-based approach to text handling, ACM TOIS, Vol. 4, N. 1 (January 1986), pp. 1-23

[25]   Van Rijsbergen C.J.: Information retrieval, Second edition, Butterwoths, London(1979)

GNEIS: a Portable Natural Language Explanation Component for Expert Systems

Manfred Gehrke

Corporate Research-ZFE IS INF 23

Siemens AG, München

Abstract

GNEIS is the adaption of the Linguistic Kernel Processor (LKP), a general purpose natural langage processing system, to the expert system toolbox Domino Expert as an explanation module. The explanation of the decision made by the expert system is achieved by mapping the expert system predicates via several steps into a semantic form, the input to the generation component of the LKP. Adaption tools to construct the conversion rules and to build up the lexicon provide for the portability of this system.

1   GNEIS

Generating natural language explanations of expert system (ES) traces helps the user of an ES to understand the decisions of the system and shows him in the case of wrong deductions where to improve the rulebase[1]. A short glance at the translation into German of a rule of the ES ASTRA, an application to decide whether a company pollutes the air in its production process, shows this in fig. 1

(1)

    ES rule:

    if [anlage_ist_genehmigungsbedürftig(Anlage),
        trifft_stoe_fa_zu(Anlage,Entscheidung) ,
        check_if('==',Entscheidung,nein)]
    conclude stoe_fa_trifft_nicht_zu(Anlage)

    wenn die anlage genehmigungsbedürftig ist,
        über die anwendung der störfallverordnung
        entschieden wurde,
        die entscheidung negativ ist,
    dann gilt, dass die störfallverordnung nicht auf die
        anlage zutrifft,

if the production unit does need official approval,
and there was a decision made on the application
of emergency regulations,
and the decision was negative,
then the emergency regulations are not applicable
to the unit.

GNEIS (Generierung natürlichsprachlicher Erklärungen in Expertensystemen; *Generation of Natural Language Explanations in Expert Systems*), is an adaption of the application independent Linguistic Kernel Processor (LKP), developed at Siemens, to the ES tool box DOMINO-EXPERT [4], developed at Siemens Nixdorf Information Systems, of which ASTRA is an application.

Despite having a powerful component transforming the semantic form into a natural language surface string for the task of explanation it is equally important to map the ES rules into a semantic form. The conversion of an ES rule into a sentence is performed in several steps, resulting in well-defined intermediate representations. In a first step - the conceptual level - the ES rule is transformed by a set of application specific rules into a language related conceptualisation, where implicit arguments of an ES predicate are made explicit and the status of the arguments of the predicate are determined. This conceptualisation is then mapped into a semantic form, the quasi-logic form (QLF), where logical parameters, such as definiteness, focus, and tense are determined in a rule based manner. Onto the QLF the generator applies the grammar to produce the surface string of the translation into German. As this last step will be fully described in [2], only the main characteristics of the LKP are

---

[1]A more detailed discussion on the nature of explanation in expert systems can be found in [8], while [5] expands on natural language interaction with expert systems.

described here to allow for a more detailed description of the transformations into QLF.

The LKP is a system, implemented in PROLOG, to analyse and generate non-metaphorical language. The core of the LKP consists of a unification-based, declarative grammar description formalism (TUG; 'trace and unification grammar'). By now quite extensive grammar fragments for German and Chinese have been described in this formalism. Two compilers convert the grammar as well as the lexicon into formats suitable for the parser and the generator. The parser is based on the Tomita parser [8], whereas for the generator the starting point was [6]. The output of the parser as well as the input of the generator is a semantic form, that is identical to the QLF being developed at SRI Cambridge for the Core Language Engine [1].

During the development of the explanation component the parser turned out to be quite helpful to debug the system because parsing the expected explanation gives the adequate semantic structure as an intermediate fix-point.

2 Mapping an ES predicate into a language related conceptualisation

In this step an ES predicate as shown in fig. 1 is transformed into a language related conceptualisation, i.e. a structure from which a clause can be generated by adding the appropriate logical parameters. Thus at this level it is necessary to select the head of the clause to be constructed which is a verb. Also the status of the arguments of the ES predicate with respect to the head have to be determined, whether they fill an argument position in the clause, a modifier to an argument or whether they act as an adverbial.

The determination of argument positions is complicated by the fact that an ES predicate contains only those facts that are necessary to do its deductions, whereas for a proper explanation additional or other facts would be necessary. Thus these arguments implicite to the predicate have to be stated explicitly. Therefore for each predicate type a transformation rule[2] exists that associates a clause description with the predicate. A predicate type contains all predicates being associated with the same verb and possessing the same argument structure. The clause description provides for the verb, a feature determining whether the verb is to be modified by a modal verb, and a feature for possible sentence

modifiers. With the verb there is also given its argument structure, a reference, which argument position is filled by what argument of the ES predicate, and the implicitly stated arguments.

The transformation rule also contains rules to transform the arguments of the predicate which are used. Since the ES tool box includes a frame-based representation device where the static knowledge of the application is described, the types used there serve as restrictors in selecting the appropriate wording. The transformed argument is then unified with the clause description. In additional to the word and the concept class the description of an argument can contain the distinction whether an adjective is gradable or not, as well as number and determinacy, when this information is not deducible by general rules. Adverbials and prepositional modifiers also contain the appropriate preposition. Furthermore the arguments of the ES predicate are typed according to the role they play in the predicate. Possible types are class designator, role designator and value designator. These argument types are used later on to determine determinacy, number, topic and focus in a global manner.

3 Mapping into the semantic form

In this step the language-related conceptualisation of an ES predicate is mapped into a semantic representation, the QLF. Such a conceptualisation of an ES predicate can be seen as a partial description of a clause with the verb, its arguments and sentential modifiers being determined. But additional parameters, such as determinacy, number, topic, focus, tense, are still lacking.

The construction of the QLF out of the conceptualisation is accomplished in the following steps:

1. construction of a quantified term for each argument,

2. construction of the adverbial,

3. determination of tense and modality,

4. inclusion of adverbials and sentential modifiers.

The chunk of information that constitutes an argument and which is therefore to be transformed into a quantified term has with the exceptions discussed below the structure

---

[2]The construction of such transformation rules, which are highly application dependent and with which the system is provided with the necessary domain knowledge, is described in section 'Adaption Tools'.

[*head* , *modifier*$_1$,..., *modifier*$_n$],

where each modifier can also be modified by an adjective, genitive np, close apposition - the modifier being a name - or a pp. This structure is recursively converted into the appropriate terms with the correct embedding. Constructing these terms requires for nouns the determination of determinacy, number, topic and focus.

The markers for topic and focus are responsible for positioning an argument out of the default word order (external object > indirect object > direct object> inherent object), either into the 'vorfeld' (topic = yes), or by scrambling of the 'mittelfeld' (focus = yes)[3]. Thus nouns in a modifier position always have these markers set to 'no'. Since the default word order turns out to be sufficient in this application also the heads of an argument have these markers set to 'no'.

Number, if it is not supplied by the conceptualisation, is determined with respect to the type the argument has had in the ES predicate and the conceptual class. Thus class designators, role designators and implicite arguments as well as value designators being names are marked as singular. The determination of determinacy, that the distinction between a definite or an indefinite article is accomplished in the same way. Here the following heuristic rules are applied:

- role designators have always the marker 'def(betont)',

- names and class designators denoting some material have 'indef(_)',

- all other nouns denoting numbers or material have 'indef(mass)',

- otherwise nouns have 'def(unbetont)' as definiteness marker.

The argument of the definiteness marker comes into effect in prepositional phrases where some prepositions allow an incorporation of the article, if there is no stress on the article. The argument with 'indef' omits an indefinite article in the case of 'mass' at all. If the ES rule requires the negation of some argument, the following heuristic is used:

if there is a singular and definite value designator,
    then negate this argument using 'kein' ("no"),
    otherwise negate the clause using 'nicht' ("not").

Using these heuristics the following NPs will be generated:

1. *die Anlage*, if it is definite and singular

2. *zu der Anlage*, as 1. plus a preposition

3. *zur Anlage*, as 1. plus the preposition not stressed

4. *nicht die Anlage*, as 1. plus negation

5. *keine Anlage*, indefinite, singular, negated

6. *kohle*, massnoun

7. *nach dem Paragraphen*, as 2.

The last item in the table shows the necessity to supply a determinacy or number specification, because in legal texts references to sections usually have no article.

Thus the following conceptual form for an argument position

[[conc,implicite,anwendung,anwendung,_,_,_],
  [[conc,implicite,stoerfallverordnung,verordnung,_,_,_],
   [[conc,implicite,paragraph,paragraph,nach,_,indef],
    [conc,value,3,nummer,_,_,_]]],
  [[conc,role,anlage,anlage,aufdir,_,_],
   [conc,implicite,genehmigungsbeduerftig,
    genehmigungsbeduerftig,_,nongrad,_]]]

we get the QLF

qterm(qcat(no,no,def(unbetont),sg),X,
  and(and(and([anwendung,X],
      a_form(poss,M1,[M1,X,
        qterm(qcat(no,no,def(unbetont),sg),N1,
          [stoerfallverordnung,N1])])),
    a_form(nach,M2,[M2,X,
      qterm(qcat(no,no,indef(_),sg),N2,
        eapp([paragraph,N2],'3'))])),
  a_form(aufdir,M3,[M3,X,
    qterm(qcat(no,no,def(unbetont),sg),N3,
      and([genehmigungsbeduerftig,nil],
        [anlage,N3]))]))))

from which the complex np 2 is generated.

---

[3]'vorfeld' is the landing position for topicalisations, whereas 'mittelfeld' encloses the area between finite and infinite verb forms.

(2) die anwendung der störfallverordnung nach paragraph 3 auf die genehmigungsbedürftige anlage.
the application of the emergency regulations according to section 3 to the installation requiring official approval.

One exception from the treatment of arguments concerns the notoriously idiosyncratic verb 'sein' (to be) with adjectives. Here we adopt the view that 'sein' takes the adjective as an inherent object and that the adjective governs the objects. This treatment allows also for an elegant handling of cases like

(3) Die Adresse des Betriebes ist bekannt.
the address of the company is known vs.

(4) Die Adresse des Betriebes ist mir bekannt.
the address of the company is known to me.

Here at first the partial QLF for the adjective is constructed and then its arguments are transformed in the way described above, yielding in the following QLF for example 3

```
pres(sein(qterm(qcat(no,no,ex,sg),X,[event,X]),
    [bekannt,
        qterm(qcat(no,no,def(unbetont),sg),N1,
        and([adresse,N1],
            a_form(poss,M1,[M1,N1,
            qterm(qcat(no,no,def(unbetont),sg),
                N2,[anlage,N2])])))),nil,V])).
```

The other exception handles sentential arguments, i.e. subordinate clauses filling an argument position. A subordinate clause is always generated, whenever a clause description is recognized within another one. The transformation rules from the ES predicate into a conceptualisation have to construct the clause description for the subordinate clause and have to provide appropriate conjunction.

To construct the QLF for an adverbial one has to distinguish between a prepositional adverbial and an adjectival one. Since the necessary information to decide on is supplied by the conceptual form, the conversion is quite straightforward. The determination of tense and modality at least in the current application does not cause severe problems because the necessary information for both are given with the conceptual form. With all these partial structures given the QLF can be constructed.

4 Adaption Tools

At a first glance the construction of the transformation rules from ES predicates to conceptualisations in step I seems to be quite clumsy and error-prone. To circumvent this obstacle a tool has been developed to adapt the explanation system to a new application with which the transformation rules and the lexicon are built up semi-automatically. This adaption tool requires no detailed knowledge in linguistics.

For each ES predicate the user is at first asked for the appropriate verb and an example of the usage of the verb. From the example additional kinds of usage are derived and the user is asked whether they are acceptable. Having determined the argument structure of the verb the user is asked for language material to be associated with the argument positions. This can be an explicitly given argument of the ES predicate with a concept class and its type in the predicate being asked for, or an implicit argument for which the wording and the concept class is required. For the ES arguments left this procedure is repeated to determine whether they are used as modifiers for verb arguments or as adverbials. Here the user can also add additional material. Finally the user is asked for sentential modifiers, modal verbs and tense.

Since the basic lexicon contains only the closed word classes and some highly idiosyncratic verbs and adjectives, a lexicon entry is constructed for each word introduced during this procedure which is described in [3]. Only in cases where the required information can not be deduced, the possible forms are presented to the user to select the acceptable one. The user will be asked for the following facts to build up a complete lexical entry:

- verb: possibility of passive voice and types of sentential arguments, optional arguments, separable prefix,
- noun: type (count, abstract, mass, etc.), inflection, if not inferrable,
- adjective: governed (sentential) arguments in predicative use, gradability,
- adverb: position as sentential modifier.

With these tools the adaption to ASTRA consisting of about 250 rules and about 2000 different arguments for these predicates, required about 2 person-months including debugging.

524

5 Conclusion

From a bird's eye view GNEIS though lacking some modules, is already quite a practical explanation component. Extensions to the component go in two directions. On the hand one has to incorporate a text generation module to construct clause descriptions spanning more than one ES predicate. Text generation is not only a very interesting area of research in its own right, but also from a practical point of view, because explaining every ES predicate in great detail decreases the acceptance of the user as well. At the QLF level the text generation will be supported by a unified approach to represent arguments including nps, subordinate clauses and infinitive clauses. The inclusion of the discourse representation module which was developed in the WISBER Project, will allow the generation of pronouns when appropriate. Using such techniques a not so verbose paraphrase of 1 could be

(5) Die Anlage ist zwar genehmigungsbedürftig, aber
     da auf Nicht-Anwendung der Störfallverordnung
     entschieden wurde, trifft die störfallverordnung
     nicht auf diese anlage zu.,
     The production unit in fact does need official ap-
     proval, but because it has been decided not to apply
     the emergency regulations, therefore the emergency
     regulations do not hold for that unit.

On the other hand the reversibility of the whole process at least between the conceptual level and the surface string is an important goal for two reasons. Primarily it is very helpful in debugging the whole system. Secondly the level of language-related conceptualisations can be built up by describing the ES rules in natural language. The first step, the reversible mapping from QLF to German, is already provided by the LKP. The mapping between QLF and the language-related conceptualisations, which was to a small extent explored in an internal study, seems also to be feasible, because in this step only feature values are set in a rule-based manner. The remaining mapping onto an ES rule still has to be done by using well-known software engineering methods, but the gap between the expert and the expert system may be narrowed.

6 References

[1] Alshawi, H., Resolving Quasi Logical Forms, in: *Computational Linguistics*, 16:3, (1990), 133-144

[2] Block, H.U., Overview of the Linguistic Kernel Processor, (to appear)

[3] Block, H.U, Gehrke, M., Hunze, R., The Interactive Construction of the Lexicon for the LKP, (to appear)

[4] Elver, E., Bibel, W., Schneeberger, J., Domino Expert - Eine Toolbox zur Entwcklung von Expertensystemen, in: Nebendahl, D., (ed.), *Expertensysteme II*, Siemens, (1989), 227-270, (in german)

[5] Gehrke, M., Haugeneder, H., Böck, H., Elver, E., *Natürlichsprachliche Interaktion mit Expertensystemen*, Report INF2-NL-1-90, Siemens, 1990, (in german)

[6] Shieber, S.M., van Noord, G., Pereira, F.C.N., Moore, R.C., Semantic-Head-Driven Generation, in: *Computational Linguistics*, 16:1, (1990), 30-42

[7] Swartout, W.R., Knowledge Needed for Expert System Explanation, in: *Future Computing Systems*, 1:2, (1986)

[8] Tomita, M., An Efficient Augmented-Context-Free Parsing Algorithm, in: *Computational Linguistics*, 13:1-2, (1987), 31-46

SPREADVIEWS

Alessandro Campioli, Luciano Lucchesi

Systems & Management
Vicolo S.Pierino 4, 56100 Pisa, Italy

Franco Turini

Dipartimento di Informatica
Corso Italia 40, 56100 Pisa, Italy

Abstract

The data type spreadview is introduced. Spreadviews gather together features from the spreadsheet based technology and the relational data base field. Operations on spreadviews allow both the manipulation of data representation and the transformation of data via relational operations which are issued via a spreadsheet oriented interface.

0.   Introduction

In the Relational Data Bases context [6, 11, 12], the view concept has been developed to show data to the user. In fact, view definitions allow to show derived data, to hide undesirable data and so on, by means of classical operations of the relational algebra.

This work stems from a simple observation, that is that the partition of the view attributes in two orderly subsets, one depending from the other, allows one:

• to make use of a spreadsheet-like representation for the view, in which the independent attributes play the role of indexes, and the dependent attributes values play the role of cell contents;

• to define a set of view operations that make them a flexible and useful tool to represent and manipulate relational structures in a user friendly manner.

In our opinion, the data type defined in this way, which from now on will be called *spreadview*, combines the advantages and the features of the relational and of the spreadsheet representation/programming models.

The *spreadviews* semantics are derived from the relational model [5, 8, 2] in terms of information content, basic definitions and operations. The user-interface and the interaction style are derived from the spreadsheet model in terms of structure, incrementality, visualization and programming features.

In this paper the *spreadviews* and their operations are formally defined and their usefulness is shown via a number of examples of their use. We present also a sketch on how to provide formal semantics to spreadviews in terms of the standard notions of relational algebra. Indeed, spreadview operations can be considered, at least partly, a user oriented way of performing transformations on the relations in a data base.

In other words, the operations on spreadviews allow one to reorganize and manipulate data, which are presented in a spreadsheet like fashion and which are internally organized as relations in a relational data base. The operations on spreadviews may or may not affect the underlying relations. In fact, sometimes they only lead to a more suitable data presentation, whereas, in other cases, they actually trigger relational algebra operations on the underlying relations. Hence, spreadviews are not merely a spreadsheet like interface for relational data bases in that they allows data manipulation also at the presentation level. If, furthermore, spreadviews are also programmed in the spreadsheet style, as it will be discussed in section 4, the system presents the characteristics which are summarized below.

• The external presentation of data is in the spreadsheet like style.

• Data presentation and organization can be manipulated through specific operations.

• Automatic computation of new data is performed according to the spreadsheet model.

• Data are internally represented as relations and typical algebraic relational operations can be triggered by interacting at the presentation level.

The structure of the paper is as follows: section 1 defines in formal way the spreadview data type, section 2 introduces the operations defined on the spreadviews, in section 3 we give the semantics in relational terms of the spreadviews, while some interesting extension to the basic data type are exposed in section 4.

1.   Spreadview Definition

A *Spreadview* is a set of couples, called *τ-tuples*, in which the first component, *τ-tuple head*, plays the role of dependent side and the second, *τ-tuple index*, of the independent side.

$$spreadview = \{ \ \tau\text{-}tuples \ \} \quad \tau\text{-}tuple = head < index >$$

Two τ-tuples are different if their indexes are different, without considering their heads. Every index value is connected with a set of values of the head. Hence the head is joined to, or better depends on, from the values of the index itself. Sometimes, instead of this technical terminology, we shall use the terms cell contents instead of head and cell indexes instead of τ-tuple index. The following figure represents a spreadview containing the information concerning the timetable of the lessons held by the teachers during school.

Every non empty cell corresponds to a spreadview τ-tuple: the head of the τ-tuple is the cell content, and the index of the τ-tuple are the cell coordinates.

	Lang	Atkins	Tucker
III C	Mon., h 9	Tue., h11	Wed., h10 Thu., h10
IV C		Thu., h11 Thu., h12	
V C			Fri., h 9

In the example, the central cell of the spreadview coincides with the following τ-tuple:

$$\{(\text{Thu.},\text{h11}),(\text{Thu.},\text{h12})\} \ <\text{atkins},\text{IV C}>$$

This targeting idea sets in natural way a dependence between the two components of a spreadview element. In this case the head concerns the *days* and the *hours* values, while the index the *teachers* and the *classes*:

$$\{(\text{days},\text{hours})\} \ \leftarrow \ (\text{teachers},\text{classes})$$

Let D and I be respectively the spreadview dependent and independent side. They are composed by two orderly lists of *axes*:

$$D = T_1, T_2, ..., T_k \qquad k>0$$
$$I = X_1, X_2, ..., X_n \qquad n>0$$

the first ones are *dependent* axes, the second ones are *independent*. Each axis is defined as $ax(Type)$, where "Type" is an identifier, called *attribute*, which is defined on an elementary domain. This domain is therefore unstructured and enumerable. Each attribute is represented on a spreadview axis: its domain values will be the values represented on that axis.

Let $Dom(X)$ be the definition domain of the Att_X attribute of the X axis, let x_i denote the generic element of $Dom(X_i)$ and let τ be a set of elements belonging to the cartesian product of the domains concerning the dependent axes attributes, i.e.:

$$\tau = \{e_1, e_2, ..., e_r\}$$

where: $e_i = (t_1^{\ i}, t_2^{\ i}, ..., t_k^{\ i})$ and $t_j^{\ i} \in Dom(T_j)$

Def. (**Spreadview**)

A *spreadview* is a finite set, possibly empty, of elements, called *τ-tuples*, with the following form:

$$\tau < x_1, x_2, ..., x_n >$$

such that $\tau \neq \emptyset$.

The *spreadview type*, and therefore its τ-tuples type, will be denoted by the two lists of dependent and independent axes:

$$(T_1, T_2, ..., T_k < X_1, X_2, ..., X_n >)$$

or more simply with $(D < I >)$. The *degree*, or the *dimension*, of a spreadview is a pair of natural numbers, denoting the dependent and independent number of the axes respectively. A spreadview of (k,n) degree has therefore k dependent and n independent axes. The spreadview *cardinality* is the number of its τ-tuples.

The spreadview definition emphasizes the existence of two groups of data: the first group somehow depending from the second, the independent one, by which it is univocally indexed. This dependence link between the two groups is realized by the spreadview element, that is the τ-tuple. Here is an example of a spreadview definition concerning a school-timetable:

TimeTable (ax(Day), ax(Hour) <ax(Teacher),
        ax(Class), ax(Specialization), ax(Classroom)>)

TimeTable = {
  {(Mon.,h9)}   <Lang,III C,informatics,BM> ;
  {(Tue.,h11)}   <Atkins,III C,informatics,BM> ;
  (Wed.,h10),(Thu.,h10)}
                     <Tucker,III C,informatics,BM> ;
                   ⋮
  {(Fri.,h10)}   <Tucker,V C,electronics,CM> }

The spreadview representation consists of stacks of sheets. Each stack refers to one of n-2 independent axes which are not explicitly visualizable on a sheet.

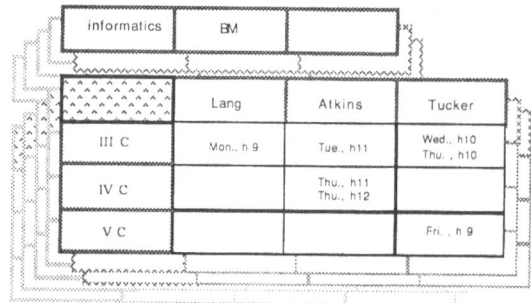

For simpleness we will always show just one bidimensional sheet for every examined spreadview.

2. Spreadview Operations

For the spreadview data type operations we will use the following notation:

- $Sv(T_1, ..., T_k < X_1, ..., X_n >)$ denotes the spreadviews set with dependent axes $T_1, .., T_k$ and with independent axes $X_1, ..., X_n$. The two lists identify the spreadview type. If it is not necessary to specify the single axes we will use $Sv(D < I >)$;
- Sv denotes the whole set of any type spreadviews;
- Ax denotes the generic axis set;
- $Attrs$ denotes the attribute set.

For notation convenience we will use $A(T_1,...,T_k < X_1,..., X_n >)$ instead of $A \in Sv(T_1,...,T_k < X_1, ..., X_n >)$.

2.1 Definition Operations

This class is composed only by the *create* and *delete* spreadview operations.

- $create : Ax^k \times Ax^n \times Name \ \rightarrow Sv \ (Ax^k < Ax^n >)$

- $delete : Sv \ \rightarrow$

The spreadview creation operation has k axes as parameters, that will be the dependent ones, and other n axes, that will be the independent ones, and, at last, an identifier which names the newly created spreadview. It will be a empty spreadview, with no τ-tuples.

The delete operation destroys the spreadview.

2.2 Modification Operations

The operations of this class modify the τ-tuple set of a spreadview.

- $insert : Sv \times \tau\text{-}tup \ \rightarrow \ Sv$

where *τ-tup* denotes a τ-tuple of the same type of the spreadview.

The insert operation has to put the specified τ-tuple values in the spreadview set. An insert operation does not necessarily result into the actual insertion of a new element in the spreadview. In fact such an insertion could only involve a spreadview τ-tuple head. This happens when an element with the same index is already in the spreadview. In this case, the insert operation merges the two heads . Now let us consider the TimeTable spreadview. The operation

TimeTable **insert** {(Mon.,h10)} <Lang,III C,informatics,BM >

does not insert a new τ-tuple, but it merges the τ-tuple with the one already existing in the spreadview, concerning the (Mon., h9) information.

∧∧∧∧∧	informatics	BM	

∧∧∧∧∧	Lang	Atkins	Tucker
III C	Mon. , h 9 Mon. , h10	Tue , h11	Wed. , h10 Thu , h10
IV C		Thu , h11 Thu , h12	
V C			Fri. , h 9

For all the TimeTable spreadview examples the reference sheet will be the above.

• *erase : Sv × τ-tup → Sv*

where *τ-tup* denotes a τ-tuple of the same type of the spreadview.

Analogously to the insert operation, erase does not necessarily modify the cardinality of the spreadview and its execution may modify only the τ-tuple head.

2.3 Basic Operations

This set of spreadview operations produces new spreadviews. This class concerns the basic operations of the spreadviews algebra.

• *change : Sv × Ax × Dest × Pos → Sv*

where: Dest = { dep, ind}.
 Pos ∈ N

- *Dest* indicates the dependent or independent side of destination in the axis shift.
- *Pos* denotes, inside the specified side, the axis position.

Given a spreadview, the change operation modifies its type by changing the axis position. Note that this change can involve either only the side of the specified axis or it can involve the two sides, by moving an axis from one side to another. The first case implies only a formal modification of the spreadview type, and a simple shift of values inside the τ-tuples. Spreadview dimension and cardinality remain the same. The second case, which is more interesting, transforms a dependent axis into an independent one, or viceversa. This process radically modifies the spreadview structure, and in particular the τ-tuples. The example below points out what happens in the second case (see the following picture):

TimeTable **change** ax(Day) **in** indep **of** 2 =
 TT(ax(Hour) <ax(Teacher), ax(Day), ax(Class),
  ax(Specialization), ax(Classroom)>)

The ax(Day) dependent axis becomes the second independent axis. The spreadview dimension is changed and it becomes (2-1,4+1). Normally, in this case, we have

III C	informatics	BM	

∧∧∧∧∧		Lang	Atkins	Tucker
Mon.		h 9 h10		
Tue.			h11	
Wed.				h10
Thu.				h10

an increase of the possible combinations of values on the independent side (and the creation of a new sheet stack for the changed axis). On the other hand we can easily observe an impoverishment of the information concerning the dependent side, now regarding only the lesson hours.

• *rename : Sv × Attrs × Attrs → Sv*

Rename operation gives a new name to an axis attribute, keeping its domain unchanged, but changing the spreadview type.

TimeTable **rename** Teacher **in** *School-master* =
 OS(ax(Day), ax(Hour) <ax(*School-master*),
  ax(Class), ax(Specialization), ax(Classroom)>)

• *plus : Sv(D<I) × Sv(D <I>) → Sv(D <I>)*

"A plus B" joins in *intelligent* way the A τ-tuples with B τ-tuples. In fact, if two τ-tuples with the same index exist, then their heads are merged obtaining a single τ-tuple. Note that, this is equivalent, from a visual point of view, to superpose the involved spreadviews representations.

• *minus : Sv(D <I>) × Sv(D <I>) → Sv(D <I>)*

Analogously to the previous union operation, the minus one gives the spreadview obtained by the intelligent difference between the τ-tuples of the two operands. In this way, for those τ-tuples having the same index, the difference is performed on the head sets.

• *project : Sv (D < I >) × Ax^S → Sv (D' < I' >)*

where Ax^S are s dependent and/or independent axes belonging to the spreadview.

This operation results in the spreadview projected only on the s specified axes. For example, let us suppose to execute:

project TimeTable **on** ax(Day), ax(Class), ax(Classroom)

Its result is the spreadview projected on the dependent axis with Day attribute, and on the independent axes with Class and Classroom attributes.

Such spreadview shows the *daily* distribution of the *classrooms* occupation by the *classes*.

∧∧∧∧∧	III C	IV C	V C
AM		Fri.	Thu. Fri.
BM	Mon. Wed. Tue. Thu.	Thu.	Fri.
CM	Wed.		

• *restrict : Sv(D < I>) × Pred(Att$_D$, Att$_I$) → Sv(D <I>)*

where Pred(Att$_D$, Att$_I$) denotes the predicate set defined on the attributes used on the axes.

Taken a spreadview and a predicate defined on the attributes represented on its axes, the restriction operation results in a spreadview containing all and only the τ-tuples whose values (i.e. the values in the τ-tuple of the predicate attributes) satisfy the predicate.

- $times : Sv(D' <I'>) \times Sv(D'' <I''>) \rightarrow Sv(D' \cdot D'' < I' \cdot I''>)$

where $\bullet$ denotes the juxtaposition operator, and the two spreadview operands must have all different axes.

The times operator results in the τ-tuple product of the two spreadviews. Product of τ-tuples means, first the indexes concatenation, and then the concatenation of the heads elements. The resulting spreadview dimension is given by the sum of the two operands dimensions (k1+k2, n1+n2); the cardinality is equal to the product of their cardinalities.

Let us consider the two following τ-tuples belonging to two spreadviews with axes whose attributes are all different:

{ (Wed., h10) , (Thu., h10) } < Tucker , informatics >
{ (III C) , (IV C) }   < BM , 30 seats >

A times operation on them gives the following τ-tuple:

{ (Wed., h10 , III C) , (Wed., h10 , IV C)
(Thu., h10 , III C) , (Thu., h10 , IV C) }
< Tucker , informatics , BM , 30 seats >

This operator is mainly used to derive others operators rather than for its direct use.

2.4 Derived Operations

The operations of this class are used to manipulate the spreadviews. Except for the update operation, they are derived by the basic ones, defined in the previous paragraph.

- $rot : Sv \times Ax \times Ax \rightarrow Sv$

The rotation exchanges the position of the two specified axes. This operation is the composition of two change operations, first on one axis, and then on the other one. So the considerations for the change operation are valid also for the rotation. In particular, also in this operation, the most interesting case is the rotation between axes belonging to different sides of the spreadview. This implies an exchange between two axes, from dependent into independent, or viceversa. The following operation:

TimeTable **rot** ax(Day) with ax(Class)

on the TimeTable spreadview, produces the spreadview showed below:

informatics	BM	

	Lang	Atkins	Tucker
Mon.	III C. h 9 III C. h10		
Tue.		III C. h11	
Wed.			III C. h10
Thu.		IV C. h11 IV C. h12	III C. h10
Fri.			V C. h 9

- $intersect : Sv(D<I>) \times Sv(D<I>) \rightarrow Sv(D<I>)$

A **intersect** B $\Leftrightarrow$ A **minus** (A **minus** B)

The intersect operator results in the intersection of the informations contained in the two spreadviews.

- $naturaljoin : Sv \times Sv \rightarrow Sv$

This operation allows to correlate τ-tuples of different spreadviews. The resulting spreadview axes are obtained by the union of the initial spreadviews axes; therefore the common axes appear only once. The τ-tuples are concatenated only for equal values concerning the equal axes, the other ones are discarded. It is worth to note that, different than relational algebra, the natural join is not a commutative operation, because the position of the common axes in the resulting spreadview makes reference to the position of the first operand. Obviously, the non commutativities property does not concern the contents of the resulting spreadview. The natural join operation is commutative apart from axes change. Also in the context of the spreadviews, the considerations valid for natural join in the relational algebra hold:

- if the two spreadviews do not have common axes, then the natural join becomes simply the times operation;
- by exploiting the equality of one or more axes, it is possible to execute a τ-tuple search which associates information belonging to spreadviews of different type.

Let us suppose to have two spreadviews. The first one, called LocalDistr, concerns the teacher distribution according to their home town and on the teaching subject.

	informatics	mathematics	electronics
livorno	Tucker Atkins		
pisa	Morgan	Turner Roper	Roberts
viareggio		O'Neil	Lang
tirrenia			Vane

LocalDistr(ax(Teacher) < ax(Subject), ax(Town) >)

While the second one, called NonResident, concerns the school-timetable of the non-resident teachers, that is the teachers who don't live in the town of the school.

The execution of this operation:

LocalDistribution **naturaljoin** NonResident = J_1

results in the J_1 spreadview, containing all the information about daily non-resident teachers shifts according to their lessons timetable.

	Mon.	Tue.	Wed.	Thu.	Fri.
Lang	h 9 h10	h11 h12		h 9	
Atkins		h11		h11 h12	h 9
Tucker	h 9 h12		h10 h11	h10	h 9 h10
O'Neil	h 9	h 9	h10	h10 h11	h12
Vane	h 9 h10	h11 h12		h10 h11	

NonResident (ax(Hour) <ax(Day), ax(Teacher)>)

A possible use of J_1 is the timetable optimization, i.e. avoiding that a non-resident teacher moves only for one lesson, or that he does not have useless free hours between two lessons. Below the resulting spreadviews for Monday is shown:

~~		
Mon.		

^^^^^^	informatics	mathematics	electronics
livorno	Tucker, h 9 Tucker, h12		
viareggio		O'Neil, h 9	Lang, h 9 Lang, h10
tirrenia			Vane, h 9 Vane, h10

3. Semantics of the Spreadviews in relational terms

Giving semantics to the spreadviews in relational terms means to represent the spreadview algebraic structure within, and through, the relational algebraic structure. Such structural representation has somehow to reproduce the form of the represented initial structure.

The *morphism* concept is just the formalization of this structural operation. Let *Rel* be the relational algebra and let $Sv°$ be the spreadviews subalgebra concerning only the basic operations excluding the "change" operation. *Rel* and $Sv°$ algebras have the same signature. Let us now define the following morphism:

$$svr : Sv° \rightarrow Rel$$

able to preserve the spreadviews informative contents. Such function is defined in a procedural way. Let us consider a generic spreadview $A(T_1, ..., T_k <X_1, ..., X_n>)$, and let us take its τ-tuple $a = \tau < x_1, ..., x_n>$, such that:

$$\tau = \{e_1, e_2, ..., e_m\} \quad \text{where} \quad e_i = (t_1^i, t_2^i, ..., t_k^i)$$

The following tuples set is then associated to the a τ-tuple:

t_1^1	...	t_k^1	x_1	...	x_n
t_1^2	...	t_k^2	x_1	...	x_n
:		:			
t_1^m	...	t_k^m	x_1	...	x_n

This tuples set is a real relation, indeed it is the relation equivalent to the a τ-tuple from the informations contents of view. It will be denoted with $svr.one(a)$. For each A τ-tuple we obtain one relation. The union of these is the relation associated to the whole A spreadview.

$$svr(A) = \bigcup_{a \in A} svr.one(a)$$

Intuitively, given the A spreadview, svr(A) is the correspondent relation having the same informations contents of A, but it is expressed in tuples form.

Theorem

The function $svr : Sv° \rightarrow Rel$ is a morphism.

Generally, the use of a morphism gives origin to different phenomena. The most interesting of them is the generation of a *congruence*, that is distinct points of the initial structure, in this case the spreadviews of the reduced algebra, are identified into the same point in its representation, that is in the same relation in the relational algebra. From an algebraic point of view, a function transforming an algebra in a other one, conserving its structure, must preserve all the correspondent operations of the two algebras. This means, informally, that working directly on the spreadviews is equivalent, as data integrity is concerned, to work on the correspondent relations containing the same information. This means that the difference between a spreadview and its associated relation is the

ability of the spreadviews of providing a more structured presentation of the data contained in the relation.

4. Beyond the Spreadview data type

In this section we describe some extensions to the spreadview concept.

Spreadview as ordered list.

The spreadview can be turned, from τ-tuples set, into an *ordered list* of τ-tuples. This is useful above all in its representation. In fact, the values on the axes are showed according to an order specified in their definition, which can be dynamically modified with a special operation. A ordered visualization of the data is often convenient and more immediately legible.

The Border.

The spreadview provides an interesting method to compute derived information. The method follows a logic scheme based on functions associated to the axes, and on the data organization inside a spreadview. The new values so computed, of any type, form the *Border set* and become the edge of the spreadview itself. Such set is paired off with the spreadview so to be its completion. In the following figure the Border is determined by:

^^^^^^	Mon.	Tue.	Wed.	Thu.	Fri.	card
Lang	h 9　h11 h10　h12		h15 h16	h10　h16 h11　h17	h10 h15	12
Atkins	h 9　h15 h10　h16	h11 h12		h11 h12	h10 h11	10
Tucker	h15 h16	h 9　h11 h10　h12	h10 h11	h10	h 9	10
O'Neil	h11.　h16 h17	h15 h16	h 9 h10	h11 h12	h 9　h15 h10　h16	13
Roper	h10 h11	h 9 h10	h 9　h11 h10　h12	h 9		9

free.m	Tucker	Lang O'Neil	Lang Atkins		Roper

- *card* which results in the number of weekly lesson hours held by every teacher;
- *free.m(orning)* which, for every day, results in the names of the teachers who haven't any lesson during the morning.

Tree-like domains.

Instead of the flat domains, used so far, we can use *tree-like domains* for the spreadviews axes. The tree-like approach is useful to model in an easier way real situations of elements belonging to a given taxonomy.

Spreadviews.programming

Analogously to the spreadsheet model, in which the cell contents can functionally depend on other cells contents the spreadview programming consists of defining functional relationships among the τ-tuples. These are called *derivation triples*.

$$derivation\ triples = (\ function\ ,\ indexes.list\ ,\ index\ )$$

A derivation triples imposes that a τ-tuple head (identified by *index*) functionally depends (through *function*) on other τ-tuple heads (identified by *indexes.list*). Let us suppose to have a spreadview concerning a school-timetable, with the subjects partitioned in theoretical and laboratory lessons.

SchoolSchedule (ax(Subject), ax(SubjectType)
                 <ax(Hour), ax(Day), ax(Class) >)

where SubjectType is an attribute defined on the domain {the , lab} denoting *theoretical* and *laboratory*.

The information concerning the technical subjects are printed in italic style.

U C

^^^^^	Mon.	Tue.	Wed.	Thu.	Fri.
h 9	stat., the	ital., the		syst., the	
h10		electr., the			
h11	mat., the		engl., the	inf., the	syst., the
h12	mat., the		engl., the		

Let us specify, on this spreadview, some derivation triples so to express the following fact: every theoretical lesson of a technical subject must be followed by a laboratory lesson of the same subject. Such a data derivation is achieved by means of this function:

lab.lesson : {(tech.subject , *the*)} → {(tech.subject , *lab*)}

allowing to specify the following derivation triples:

program(SchoolSchedule) = {
    (lab.lesson,   [(Mon.,h9)],   (Mon.,h10)) ;
    (lab.lesson,   [(Tue.,h9)],   (Tue.,h11)) ;
    (lab.lesson,   [(Thu.,h9)],   (Thu.,h10)) ;
    (lab.lesson,   [(Thu.,h11)],   (Thu.,h12)) ;
    (lab.lesson,   [(Fri.,h11)],   (Fri.,h12)) }

whose set constitutes the very *spreadview programming*. Given a spreadview, the operation:

$$apply : Sv \rightarrow Sv$$

applies its program yielding the spreadview *updated* in its τ-tuple contents, according to the functions specified in the triples. Among the derivation triples of a program, there is the possibility that the index lists intersect the indexes concerning the final τ-tuples. This can determine the modification of a τ-tuple identified by an index list of a derivation triples already evaluated. This will have to be evaluated once again. Then the triples are recursively applied until a *least fix point*, if it exists, is found.

The apply operation executed on the SchoolSchedule spreadview generates the below represented spreadview, where the underlined elements are those which are computed by the apply.

U C	

^^^^^	Mon.	Tue.	Wed.	Thu.	Fri.
h 9	stat., the	ital., the		syst., the	
h10	stat., lab.	electr., the		syst., lab.	
h11	mat., the	electr., lab.	engl., the	inf., the	syst., the
h12	mat., the		engl., the	inf., lab.	syst., lab.

Then, analogously to the spreadsheet model, we have seen that it is possible to program the spreadviews. In this sense it is easy to note that a spreadsheet is just a particular spreadview. The usual spreadsheet model is composed by a matrix of cells indexed by a triple (*letter* , *number* , *sheet*) → *cell*. A spreadsheet cell can contain alphanumeric values. Then the following spreadview:

Spreadsheet (ax(StringValueNil)
    < ax(Letters) , ax(Numbers) , ax(Sheets) >)

exactly defines the conventional spreadsheet in its common representation.

5. Conclusions

The spreadview idea is currently being used in the design and implementation of an updated version of the Logiform system [3]. Logiform is a powerful spreadsheet based system in which the programming of the computation is performed in a rule base fashion rooted in the logic programming approach.

The spreadview operations provide a complementary feature which allows the user to perform sophisticated rearrangements of the data in between the deductive computation steps performed by the system when applying the associated rules.

In the process of designing and implementing applications in the field of resource allocation (school timetables, software project management [1], crew formation for bus driving [4]) we have discovered that the ability of performing relational operations on the data is by no means less important than performing computations on the data in a rule based style.

The literature offers a few papers which present innovative spreadsheets and share some of the motivations of our work, although all of them stress the programming techniques of the spreadsheets rather than the manipulation of the spreadsheet itself. The Logicalc system [10] is implemented in Prolog and offers deductive features derived from it. In [7] a spreadsheet-like interface for Prolog is shown, while [9] describe research on logical spreadsheets performed at ECRC.

References

[1] Bertazzoni, C.and Giannotti, F. *RASP: a Resource Allocator for Software Projects*, Technical Report ESPRIT project 951 (PACT), System&Management (1988).

[2] Bjorner D.*Formalization of Database Models*, in Bjorner D. (a cura di) "Abstract Software Specifications", "Lecture Notes in Computer Science", Springer, Berlino 1980.

[3] Bonsignori A., Giannotti F., Lucchesi L., and Turini F., *The Logiform System*, Computers and Mathematics with Applications, Vol. 20, n° 9-10,1990

[4] P. Carraresi, G. Gallo, N. Ciaramella, P. Lullia, L. Lucchesi, *BDS: A system for the bus driver' scheduling problem integrating combinatorial optimization and logic programming*, Proceeding of 4th International Workshop on Computer Aided Scheduling of Pubblic Transport, Amburgo, 1987

[5] Codd E. F., *Extending the DatabaseRelational Model to Capture More Meaning*, ACM TODS 4, 397-434 (1979).

[6] Date C., *An Intoduction to Data Base Systems* voll. 1, 2; Addison-Wesley, Reading, Mass. 1983.

[7] van Emdem M.H., Ohki, M., and Takeuchi, A. *Spreadsheets with Incremental Queries as a User Interface for Logic Programming* New Generation Computing, 4, pp 287-304. 1986.

[8] Furtado A. L., *Formal Aspects of the Relational Model* Information Systems 3, 2, 131-40 (1978).

[9] Gallaire H., *Boosting Logic Programming*, in Proc. of the 4th International Conference on Logic Programming (J.L.Lassez, ed.), pp. 962-988. MIT Press. 1986.

[10] Kriwaczek F., *LogiCalc - A PROLOG Spreadsheet* M.I. News, no 9, The Turing Institute, Glasgow. 1985. Machine Intelligence 11, eds. J.E. Hayes, D. Michie and J. Richards, Oxford University Press, Oxford.

[11] Tsichritzis D. C., Lochovsky F. H., *Data Base Management Systems*, Academic Press, New York 1977.

[12] Ullman J. D., *Principles of Database Systems*, Computer Science Press, Potomac, Md 1983.

End-user Interface to Improve Microcomputer DBMS Efficiency

Juliana Peneva   Jordanka Angelova

Dept.of Software Engineering
Institute of Mathematics
Acad.G.Bontchev str.,bl.8
1113 Sofia, Bulgaria

ABSTRACT

Recently many microcomputer DBMSs were introduced. Due to a simplified design most of them lack tools for efficient query processing. The findings of good query evaluation strategies are up to end-users. So, to improve the query execution, there is a need of additional interfaces. Similar shells could be built on top of the microcomputer DBMS. In this paper the design of such a tool called Users Query Processor is presented. A concrete implementation of this shell for Oracle DBMS is described. Analytic estimates giving rise to the possibility of choosing the effective method for query evaluation and a brief overview of the incorporated algorithms are also given. Finally benchmark results for Oracle DBMS show that considerable performance advantages may be obtained.

I.INTRODUCTION

Recently research on end-user interfaces to databases received more support as important area for investigation [3,4]. It has to be pointed out that in the last decade major advances have been made in non-database related interfaces [1,4] such as spread sheets, WYSIWYG, Hypercad, etc. The need for better and easy-to-use database end-user interfaces of different types has been stressed [2,3]. The capability to handle graphics allows the creation of user-friendly interfaces making extensive use of windows, pull-down menus and icons [12]. At the same time alternative paradigms differing from the standard records- or files- oriented approaches to access the database are investigated [4]. Casual and occasional users also need languages which are easy to use and fit well with their problem domains [1].

On the other hand many DBMSs oriented toward microcomputers were introduced [7]. Usually they are based on the relational model [13] and have simplified structure.

Sophisticated storage management methods and different types of indexes are not incorporated in the systems due to the hard requirement for minimal code space usage. The retrieval of information from the database requires the user's knowledge of query language and underlying data. Moreover, most existing microcomputer databases lack means for appropriate data manipulation. Efficient query processing lies entirely on the end-user skill. Few of the microcomputer DBMS (Oracle, Ingress for PC [14]) posses specialized modules called Optimizers responsible to find suitable query execution strategies. In addition, query transformations preserving the original semantics to obtain better processing form could also be considered. Summarizing, the design of additional interfaces which are applied implicitly from the users and improve the query execution is necessary. Similar shells could be built on top of the microcomputer DBMS realizing an efficient query processing. In this way if an Optimizer in the microcomputer DBMS exists its possibilities are enlarged thus increasing the overall system productivity.

In this paper a tool called Users Query Processor is proposed. In Section II we present the design of the shell and its distinct components. In Section III a concrete implementation for Oracle DBMS is described. Analytic estimates giving rise to the possibility of choosing the effective method for query evaluation and a brief overview of the incorporated algorithms are also given. Benchmark results for Oracle relational DBMS are discussed in Section IV.

II.DESIGN OF THE USERS QUERY PROCESSOR FOR MICROCOMPUTER DBMS

Besides an Optimizer an overall systems productivity increase could be achieved by combining the following alternatives:

- well-grounded heuristic rules for which better query execution parameters are proven;

532

- equivalent query transformation;
- new methods to implement the basic relational operations.

The realization of these additional possibilities on top of the microcomputer DBMS is the aim of the designed users query interface (Fig.1):

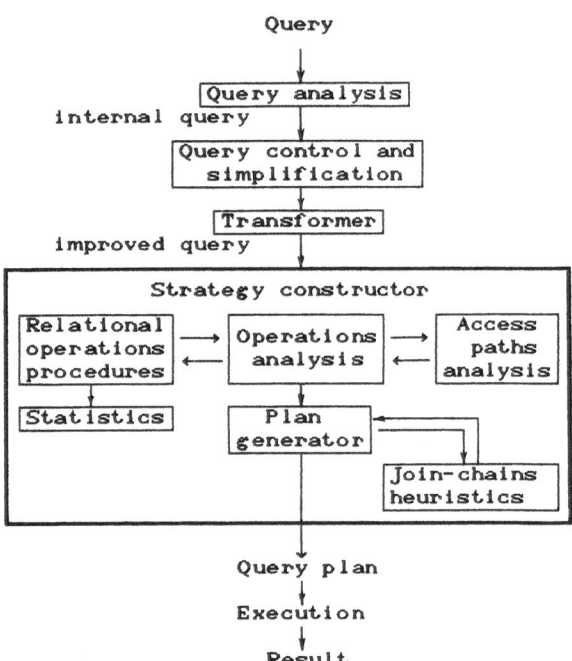

Figure 1. Users Query Interface

Brief description of the distinct components

1.Module for query analysis - it facilitates the users query assign by generating the relationships among the different relations automatically. Formal check of the request is performed. The internal query representation depends on the concrete DBMS and the query language.

2.Module for query control and simplification - this module examines the query correctness and simplifies it, if possible.

3.Transformer - its main task is to transform the users request by applying a well-grounded set of heuristic rules which preserve the query correctness but lead to a better execution form. These rules fit into two groups:

    a)rules transforming the query itself;

    b)rules transforming given query into an equivalent set of simpler for execution queries; this is especially important for the evaluation of views, aggregates and nested queries.

4.Strategy constructor - this module is not required when the DBMS has an Optimizer to find the efficient query execution strategy. Its main tasks are the following:

    a)arrangement of the database operations;

    b)analysis of the access paths and choice of the appropriate method for each relational operation;

    c)generation of query execution plan.

These tasks are performed by two modules:

    a)operations analyzer - it examines the improved internal query representation and maps the mentioned relations with their physical equivalents. In most microcomputer DBMS there is a set of basic operations which are implemented using rigid algorithms. New operations or alternative methods to realize them can be added. Furthermore the approach permits an enlargement of the query language and gives rise to the possibility for a choice of the best algorithm to perform given relational operation. To achieve this goal the operations analyzer communicates with other modules (access path analyzer, etc).

    b)query plan generator - the task of this module is to generate a query processing tree which models an effective sequence of the operations to the database. Although the resource usage is considerable and the optimization cost is high, exhaustive search of all possible query execution strategies to determine the best one is not performed. The join chains are defined by suitable heuristic rules. In this way a single query tree which is not the optimal one but it is enough effective is generated. The main features of the users query processor can be summarized as follows:

- universality - this shell can be applied to any relational microcomputer DBMS because it does not fix the internal query representation and the heuristic transformation rules;
- flexibility - design of different configurations is feasible;
- modularity;
- convenience to use the existing microcomputer DBMS Optimizer.

III.IMPLEMENTATION.

An experimental realization of the designed Users Query Processor has been made on top of Oracle DBMS for IBM PC/AT. The C language and Lattice C compiler to assure the connection with Oracle libraries have been used. The functions calls have been performed via the system interface Pro_C. As far as Oracle's DBMS Optimizer for finding efficient strategies can be used, only the following modules have been developed:

1.Query Analyzer - it communicates with the user in an on-line mode accepting the operation type and its parameters. An analysis of the operations is performed. A formal control of the query parameters, i.e. a check whether the relations and their attributes exist, data type correspondence is also done. The following commands are implemented:

- Help;
- Commit - declares the beginning of a transaction (one or several commands to the database);
- Rollback - cancels the database changes;
- Describe <table name> - describes a relation;
- Exec SQL - announces that one or several SQL commands are to be executed; the set of the permitted SQL commands is: Insert, Update, Delete, Select, Alter, Create, Drop;
- Autocommit - declares the end of a transaction.

In this way part of the SQL commands remains transparent to the casual end user. This allows easy data manipulation via the restricted command set. At the same time adding new commands to enlarge the shell possibilities is easy.

2.Transformer - it transforms fixed classes of queries into a better for execution form.

The experiments with Oracle DBMS and the analysis of the tracing files have pointed out that no preliminary transformation of the query to improve its execution is performed. Moreover there are some groups of requests such as nested queries with aggregates and views for which the Optimizer does not offer an optimal processing strategy. Aggregate functions are calculated repeatedly and the nested iteration method is the only method used in evaluating nested predicates. In addition existing access structures have to be used explicitly by the user to achieve better response time. So, in the Transformer algorithms as heuristic rules have been incorporated. They concern the following transformations of the Select operations:

- transformation of some types nested queries into equivalent ones expressing the semantics of nesting by joins;
- transformation of some classes of predicates including the operators Exist, Any, All into nested scalar or inclusion predicates;
- reordering of the predicates after the Where clause to achieve better usage of existing indices.

Further we would like to present part of the algorithms included in the Users Query Processor which concern nested queries. The basic structure of an SQL query is the SELECT-FROM-WHERE block [5,6]. Usually the WHERE clause specifies predicates of the form:

$$1. R_i.C_k \text{ op } X$$

where R_i is a relation in the database, C_k is the k-th column of R_i, X is a constant or a list of constants, and op is a scalar comparison operator. These predicates can be connected by Boolean functions.

$$2. R_i.C_k \text{ op } R_j.C_h$$

where R_i and R_j are relations, C_k and C_h are their attributes respectively, and op is a scalar comparison operator.

Nested predicates are obtained by substituting X with a new SELECT-FROM-WHERE block, i.e. $R_i.C_k$ op Q1. The first query block in a nested query is known as the outer query block and the next query block is known as the inner query block. As an example consider the following sample relations and query:

EMP (emp#,ename,dept#,salary,age,exp)
DEPT(dept#,dname,budget)

Q1: SELECT ename,salary, FROM EMP
    WHERE dept# IS IN

        SELECT * FROM DEPT
        WHERE budget>10000)

This is an example of a query with a single level of nesting. The terminology for nested SQL-queries is developed in [9]. We will be concerned with what is there termed type-J and type-JA nested queries.

A nested query Q is of type-J if the WHERE clause of the inner block contains a join predicate that references the relation of the outer block, and the relation is not mentioned in the inner FROM clause:

Q: SELECT <attr.list> FROM R_i
    WHERE P1 AND $R_i.C_h$ op Q1

Q1:SELECT $R_j.C_m$ FROM R_j
    WHERE P2 AND $R_j.C_k = R_i.C_p$

A nested query Q is of type-JA if the WHERE clause of the inner block contains a join predicate that references the relation of the outer block, and the inner SELECT clause consists of an aggregate function over the inner relation:

Q: SELECT <attr.list> FROM R_i
    WHERE P1 AND $R_i.C_h$ op Q1

Q1:SELECT agrf<$R_j.C_m$> FROM R_j
    WHERE P2 AND $R_j.C_k = R_i.C_p$

The standard method for processing such queries is by nested-iteration, i.e. by evaluating the inner block Q1 once for

534

each tuple of the outer block relation R_i, satisfying the predicate after the WHERE-clause. Although it proved a convenient way of viewing the semantics of a nested query, this method has poor performance. Obviously, an efficient way to obtain the answer of similar queries has to include techniques for calculating the aggregate function apart and to execute the inner query block as few times as possible.

Our algorithms are based on the idea to substitute the nested SQL query with a set of queries yielding the same result. According to the transformations proposed in [8,9,10] they also capture the semantics of the nested predicates by explicitly using joins but differ strongly in the way of intermediate query processing. The basis for the designed algorithms and the derived analytical estimates are the proved lemmas for equivalence [11] of the original and the transformed nested query. The presentation of the lemmas and estimates validity is beyond the scope of this paper.

The proved equivalence between a nested query of type-J or type-JA to proper sets of queries represents the basis for the designed algorithms:

ALGORITHM ALT_NEST_J

*Input:*Q - a type-J nested query
Algorithm:

Step 1. Create the temporary relation $Temp(C_m, C_k)$ with attributes C_m and C_k which contains all the tuples of R_j satisfying the predicate.

Step 2. Transform the nested query Q as follows:
a) add the relation TEMP after the relation R_i in the FROM clause;
b) substitute the predicate $R_i.C_h$ op Q1
with: $R_i.C_h op_1 Temp.C_m$ AND $R_i.C_p = Temp.C_k$.
where $p_1 = \begin{bmatrix} op & if & op \in \{<,>,=,\neq,\leq,\geq\} \\ = & if & op = \{CONTAINS, IS IN\} \end{bmatrix}$

Output: a set of queries {Q2,Q3} which are equivalent to Q, i.e. they yield the same result.

ALGORITHM ALT_NEST_JA

*Input:*Q - a type-JA nested query
Algorithm:

Step 1. Create the relation
$Temp(C_k \ aggr.f(R_j.C_m))$
with attributes C_m and C_k which contains all the tuples of R_j satisfying the predicate.

In this relation aggr.f($R_j.C_m$) is the aggregate function value computed for all the groups having equal value of the attribute $R_j.C_k$.

Step 2. Transform the nested query Q as follows:
a) add the relation TEMP after the relation R_i in the FROM clause;
b) substitute the predicate $R_i.C_k$ op Q1
with $R_i.C_h$ Temp.agr AND $R_i.C_p = Temp.C_k$.

*Output:*a set of queries {Q2,Q3} which are equivalent to Q, i.e. they yield the same result.

Further we would like to estimate the response time for a type-J or type-JA nested query performed by the nested iteration method and by the proposed algorithms. The goal is to obtain analytic estimations of the standard and the designed algorithms which can be incorporated into the Transformer. This will permit to choose the suitable processing strategy for the nested query. As an approximate measure for the response time the number of the fetched tuples has been used. If we suppose that card(R_i)=m and card(R_j)=n, the following statements were proved:

Statement I: For each integer m ≥ 9 and each integer n such that:
$$log(m)+6 \leq n \leq e^{m-3} - m.log(m)-1$$
the designed algorithm *ALT_NEST_J* gives better response time for type-J nested query than the nested iteration method.

Statement II For every integer m ≥ 10 and every n such that:
$$log(m)+7 \leq n \leq e^{m-4} - m.log(m)-1$$
the designed algorithm *ALT_NEST_JA* gives better response time for type-JA nested query than the nested iteration method. For a detailed description of the statements proof interested reader is referred to [11].

The transformation of some classes of predicates which include the operators Exist, Any, All into nested scalar predicates or into nested inclusion predicates is performed according to the algorithms developed in [10]. The transformed queries are evaluated using the standard or the proposed algorithms applying the analytic estimations.

IV.BENCHMARK RESULTS

Different series of experiments were carried out with type-J and JA nested queries in Oracle DBMS. Each query was evaluated using the proposed algorithms and the nested iteration method respectively.

Response time (sec)
for type-J nested query

The queries are:

Q1:SELECT * FROM T WHERE T.&1 IN

(SELECT S.&1 FROM S WHERE T.&2 = S.&2)

Q2:CREATE TABLE Temp AS

(SELECT DISTINCT &1,&2 FROM S)

Q3:SELECT T.* FROM T,Temp

WHERE T.&2=Temp.&2 AND T.&1=Temp.&1

In each experiment card(T) = m and card(S) = n are fixed; &1 and &2 are substituted by different attributes having integer values with an arbitrary distribution.

I series of experiments:
    m = 1000,n = 1000
Taking into account *Statement I* we obtain:
    ln(1000)+6 ≃ 13 ≪ n

Hence according to the analytic estimates algorithm *ALT_NEST_J* has to give better response times comparing to the standard one.

Table 1

Q1	Q2	Q3	Q2 + Q3
1.1	2.3	51.2	53.5
5.4	2.1	52.4	54.5
9.3	2.2	51.1	53.3
3.9	2.4	52.3	54.7
2.4	2.6	50.9	53.5
6.7	2.1	51.8	53.9

Improvement coefficient:

$$PP = \frac{\sum Cost_1(Q_i) - \sum Cost_2(Q_i)}{\max(\sum Cost_1(Q_i), \sum Cost_2(Q_i))} \cdot 100 \ \%$$

PP ≃ 54 %.

II series of experiments
    m = 100,n = 1000
Taking into account *Statement I* we obtain:
    ln(100) + 6 ≃ 11 ≪ n

Table 2

Q1	Q2	Q3	Q2 + Q3
15.4	2.1	6.1	8.2
17.9	2.2	6.2	8.4
15.0	2.1	6.4	8.5
17.3	2.0	6.2	8.2
17.3	2.2	6.1	8.3
18.3	2.4	6.2	8.6

Improvement coefficient:

PP ≃ 50 %.

III series of experiments:
    m = 10,n = 1200
Taking into account *Statement I* we obtain:
    ln(10) + 6 ≃ 8 ≪ n

but $e^7 - 10.ln(10) - 1 \simeq 1100 < n$.

Hence according to the analytic estimates algorithm *ALT_NEST_J* has to give worse response times comparing to the standard one.

Table 3

Q1	Q2	Q3	Q2 + Q3
1.9	2.3	1.6	3.9
2.0	2.2	1.7	3.9
1.8	2.0	1.6	3.6
1.9	2.0	1.8	3.8
2.1	2.2	1.9	4.1
1.7	2.0	1.5	3.5

Improvement coefficient:
PP ≃ -50 %.

Response time (sec)
for type-JA nested query

The queries are:

Q1:SELECT * FROM T WHERE T.&1 IN

(SELECT MIN(S.&1) FROM S WHERE T.&2=S.&2)

Q2:CREATE TABLE Temp AS

(SELECT &2,MIN(&1)agga FROM S GROUP BY &2)

Q3:SELECT T.* FROM T,Temp

WHERE T.&2=Temp.&2 AND T.&1=Temp.agga

IV series of experiments:
    m = 1000,n = 1000
Using *Statement II* we obtain:
    ln(1000)+7 ≃ 14 ≪ n.

Hence according to the analytic estimates algorithm *ALT_NEST_JA* has to give better response times comparing to the standard one.

Table 4

Q1	Q2	Q3	Q2 + Q3
40.1	2.3	3.5	6.2
201.1	3.2	8.2	11.4
6.6	2.1	2.1	4.3
201.9	3.2	8.2	11.4
6.6	2.1	2.1	4.2
37.4	2.3	3.1	5.4

Improvement coefficient:
PP ≃ 90 %.

V series of experiments:
    m = 10,n = 1000
Using *Statement II* we obtain:
    ln(10)+7 ≃ 9 ≪ n

but $e^6 - 10.\ln(10) - 1 \simeq 381 < n$.

Hence according to the analytic estimates algorithm *ALT_NEST_J* has to give worse response times comparing to the standard one.

Table 5

Q1	Q2	Q3	Q2 + Q3
2.9	2.3	0.5	2.8
3.0	3.2	1.1	4.3
2.3	2.1	0.4	2.5
3.1	3.2	1.1	4.3
2.3	2.1	0.4	2.5
3.0	2.3	0.5	2.8

Improvement coefficient:
PP $\simeq$ -14 % .

<u>V.CONCLUSION</u>

Most of the microcomputer DBMS do not offer tools to obtain an efficient query processing strategy. The finding of a comparatively good query evaluation plan has to be performed by the end-user and the solution heavily depends on its skill.

In the present paper we put forward a shell to improve the microcomputer DBMS productivity which can be built on top of the system, provides a good strategy for query processing and is user friendly. Its concrete realization for Oracle DBMS and the algorithms incorporated in it are reported. The benchmarks demonstrate that considerable performance improvement can be achieved.

<u>REFERENCES</u>

[1] Elmasri R., Navathe S. "Fundamentals of Database Systems", The Benjamin/ Cummings Publishing Company, 1989.

[2] Ullmann J. "Principles of Database and Knowledge-Base Systems", Vol.1, Computer Science Press, 1990.

[3] Zdonik S., Maier D. "Readings in Object - Oriented Database Systems" Morgan Kaufmann Publishers, 1990.

[4] The Laguna Beach Report, "Future Directions in DBMS Research", SIGMOD Record, Vol 18, 1, March, 1989.

[5] Astrahan M., Chamberlin D. "Implementation of a Structured English Query Language", Comm. ACM 18,10 1975, pp.580-588.

[6] Astrahan M. et al. "System R: A Relational Approach to Data Base Management", ACM Transactions on Database Systems Vol.1,2, 1976, pp.97-137.

[7]. Seymour J. "Programmable Databases: dBASE and its Challengers", PC Magazine, May 1988.

[8]. Bultzingloeven A. "Translating and Optimizing SQL Queries Having Aggregates", Proceedings of the 13-th International Conference on VLDB, Brighton, UK, 1987, pp.235-243.

[9]. Kim W. "On Optimizing an SQL-like Nested Query", ACM Transactions on Database Systems, Vol 7,3, 1982, pp.443-469.

[10] Ganski R., Wong H. "Optimization of Nested SQL Queries Revisited", ACM-SIGMOD International Conference on Management of Data, 1987, pp.23-33.

[11] Peneva J., Angelova J. "Efficient Evaluation of Nested SQL Queries", Proc. of the 13-th International Seminar on DBMS, Mamaia, Romania,1990.

[12] Agraval R. et al. "Ode-View: The Graphical Interface to Ode", Proc. of the 1990 ACM SIGMOD Conference on Management of Data, SIGMOD RECORD, Vol.19, 2, pp.34-44.

[13] Codd E. "The Relational Model, Version 2", Addison- Wesley, 1990.

[14] Harringhton J. "Relational Database Management for Microcomputers: Design and Implementation", Holt, Rinehart and Winston, 1988.

INTEGRATION OF DATABASE AND HYPERTEXTUAL TECHNOLOGIES IN DESIGNING A CLINICAL INFORMATION SYSTEM

A. CASANOVA *   N. DESSI'**

*Clinica Medica, Universita' di Cagliari, Via San Giorgio 8, 09124 CAGLIARI (ITALY)

** Centro di Calcolo Elettronico, Universita' di Cagliari, Via Universita' 40 ,09124 CAGLIARI (ITALY)

ABSTRACT

This paper presents a Clinical Information System (CIS) architecture which has the ability to integrate different functions performed by autonomous clinical structures. The basic idea is the use of hypertextual technologies, in order to model an effective management of complex objects (medical information) which interact in the context of hierarchical structures (clinical departments). The relational databases are shown to provide a reasonable platform to implement the presented architecture as well as to support medical information retrieval. Finally, the paper describes an application which is currently in use in a large academic clinic.

INTRODUCTION

The sanitary computerization presents two different and clear aspects. First, the clinical aspect that involves the planning of the activities which are required to meet medical care needs. Second, the organizational aspect of medical services. This aspect incorporates the definition of interrelations among divisions,departments and laboratories within an hospital as well as their individual roles and how they are coordinated to offer medical services (1). These aspects emphasize the need to introduce computer technology in medical practice, whose organizational framework has evolved from the original physician office to health care organizations of considerable size and complexity (2).

Despite this need,the traditional document-based medical record continues to be prevalent as method of information storage and retrieval. The clinical and the organizational aspects are not well integrated, although each one has its own characteristics.

Problems arise when interim reports are required and information holding in various forms is difficult to share between departments, divisions and laboratories. This is most likely a consequence of the nature of clinical decision making environment whose context is modified or advanced at different rates. The critical aspect of this environment seems to be the lack of a well-defined interface between various processes or clinical functions.

For example, a medical record may contain a large number of laboratory results, a set of patology reports and summaries of hospital admissions. In addition, the treatment of illness may require the ability to monitor patient progress throught the hospital on a division-by-division and on an examination-by-examination. The quality of the medical information stored about a patient must be maintained throughout the course of his illness. Some records (patient bills....) have no impact on the information processing related to patient care. However they should have a potential use in planning of the activity in terms of what,why and when a specific clinical function is required. In addition, current medical structures, like hospital themselves, seem to be in constant state of flux, because changes in patterns of medical care are associated with changes in the administrative structures of medical practice.

Also, the pattern of functions in which a sanitary structure is involved and the dissimilar characteristics of different types of structures would make a single database prohibitively large and difficult to manipulate (3).

For this reason, many database systems available to clinics are fragmented, that is, they are capable of supporting isolated clinical functions without mutual interconnection.

Although there has been important progress in the development of clinical information systems, there has been little change in the way that information system is designed.

538

Among the many factors responsible for this situation is the lack of modeling techniques as well as database management systems (4) needed for this kind of applications .

This paper presents a model for the specification of a Clinical Information System (CIS) that is rich enough to provide for all the usual database activities, such as querying and updating. Also, it has the ability to integrate functions performed by different autonomous clinical structures.

In order to offer an effective management of complex objects (medical information) which interact in the context of hierarchical structures (clinical departments), we suggest an hospital to be modeled as a system of functional relationships among the organizational structures supporting the effective implementation of clinical activities.

The basic idea is to represent the medical report processing as a hypergraph. Each node represents an text component of medical report and a hyperedge represents a functional relation among the clinical structures making up the medical report. This approach refers to the distinct cooperation of two technologies, one for system design and one for data management. In a simplified way , the hypertextual technology has an architectural role in designing the data model, the database technology supports the effective implementation of this model. The presented architecture structures information along two dimensions: vertically with the partitioning of the set of clinical components as hierarchically organized horizzontally with the introduction of a blackboard structure for distribuited information processing. Accordingly, the clinical information system takes the form of a distribuited database system, whose purpose is to automate clinical tasks and to support administrative and financial functions.

The presented architecture has been applied in developing the Clinical Information System currently in use in the Medical Clinic of our University.

THE CLINICAL INFORMATION SYSTEM ARCHITECTURE

If we consider a sanitary structure (administration, hospitals health centers,etc.), as a specialization of the concept of enterprise, we must look for the integration of information among each area that has to be computerized.This means that a database architecture for implementing clinical functions should support data and information exchange among clinical divisions as well as the functional description of the single clinical work structure. This integration is a key feature of both the practice of medicine and the administration of health care.

These considerations emphasize the distinction between the CIS logical structure (i.e. how should the CIS components cooperate with each other) and the physical representation associated with the implementation technology (i.e. how should a CIS be implemented).

Accordingly, the CIS model can be conceived as describing the channel of communication for the pattern of functions in which the clinical structure is involved. For this approach to work,we have considered a limited set of clinical functions, best divided into the following categories :

- Patient registration
- Medical history file -
- Diagnostic reporting
- Planning and control of patient flow
- Clinical administration

The related integration occurs at different levels: at the symbolic level of clinical work structures and at the operational level, when a unified medical report is the repository for all patient related information.

The pattern of functions in which a clinical system is involved suggests the clinical system can be divided into a number of smaller subsystems. Each subsystem corresponds to a physical clinical substructure (a department, a laboratory etc..) whose purpose is to automate a well-structured CIS function.

Our strategy for integrating CIS functions is that of a sparse multidimensional blackboard that is global to all the users, i. e. a blackboard structure in which several clinical substructures can take a turn in information processing or in inquirying about clinical activities. The blackboard is a functional structure, created in response to information needs of each clinical department. This unified frame in which different work structures can cooperate is the key feature of the proposed architecture whose schematic representation is given in Fig.1.

In order to protect confidentiality of medical records and to provide data integrity, communications among blackboards are done via blackboard interfaces,managed by the CIS administrator, whose blackboard is not accessible by clinical departments.

According to function required and under control of blackboard administrator, a blackboard can become central and can control activities of other blackboards. This organization assures that different needs of different clinical departments are met with regard to medical report.

The production of management reports (such a reports on the cost associated with each service provided by the clinic, on the type of resources being used by what patient etc.) is delegated to an administrative blackboard. It is capable of supporting functions of planning and controlling clinical resources.

The method of providing access to a specific blackboard is through standardized reports as well as prespecified scheduling functions. Each report is designed to suit the documentation patterns of each clinical substructure.

THE MEDICAL REPORT

While the blackboard as whole provides a structure for decentralizing the processing of a common set of relevant clinical data, its primary objective is to ensure that each clinical department can identify which particular report must be processed. This is achieved by associating each patient with a code called nosological number, which acts as a key to collect all patient related information. This means that there is a unique name and code associated with each patient item on each blackboard.

Both administrative and medical data for each patient are recorded on the encounter report with a definite structure and format. An encounter report is completed not only for each patient in the clinical department, but also for emergency department visits. The encounter report compiled by physician contains requests about tasks to be performed by various clinical departments as laboratory tests, physical examination etc.. Requests are automatically scheduled on the pertinent blackboard according to the clinical function required. Each request acts as trigger conditions that must be sactisfied by the pertinent clinical department. There are very large variations in the average lenght of time a trigger is sactisfied, because there are no two medical requests which have identical needs. One patient may be a transient who came only for a single laboratory test and another patient may require analysis lasting a number of days.

For the above reasons, at various stages of its development, the medical report is pending until all trigger are sactisfied. When all triggers of the specific patient are sactisfied, the medical report is stored in the medical history file and the blackboard areas are released and returned to free pool. This way, a trigger is intended to be a temporal link.

This dynamic allocation of medical report in the blackboard is an extremely important strategy. It guarantees that information is really current and available for review and data can be added from multiple sites.

The choice of the blackboard architecture is based on the observation that a medical report consists of a set of text components produced by different clinical substructures. Consequently, it is modular in nature and hierarchical in organization. This typical structure as well a success in hypergraph based models for database information structuring (5,6) allows us to describe the medical report processing both in terms of objects managed and functions performed. Like a hypertext, the medical report, expressed completely in a single document, is distribuited across many components. Each component has less information content than the medical report and needs to be linked with other components through organizational information.

Due to this active structure, a medical report is viewed as an hypertextual document whose nodes are text components and links represent the functional clinical structure.

This model of medical report is dependent on the modularity assumption as well on the link definition which is critical to the automatic organization and information retrieval and may impact greatly on report production.

As a pragmatic departure point in designing the Clinical Information System, we have chosen this hypertextual approach to model and to facilitate the visualization of report production.

Fig. 2 depicts the functional schema adopted and the clinical structures involved in medical report processing.

DEVELOPING THE RELATIONAL DATABASE STRUCTURE

The blackboard paradigm is a functional architecture which permits clinical structures to work cooperatively in a uniform structure. It allows a modular implementation as well as a system taylored according to the requirements of the organization. Note, however, that the implementation scheme of the blackboard can be identified at designing stage so that each clinical specialized subsystem can be implemented and integrated with due regard to the total structure.

The problem with this implementation is that each blackboard must handle all patient events and must be recoded whenever either changes.

While operative in a standardized and multi-user operating system environment (i.e., UNIX), relational databases offer a realistic platform for blackboard development and implementation. The relational data model allows a classification of clinical entities and functions involved and standard relational query language provides a uniform interface for data definition and data manipulation. In particular, we identify department and laboratory as organizational entities describing the clinical work structure. Patient related information constitutes medical-based entities and are intended to describe medical history, diagnostic information,laboratory test results ,e.t.c.). Each entity has an identifier that is completely unique (nosological number) as this will provide the link between blackboards holding nodes of the same medical report. Single facts about entities are connected to form a t-uple, similar t-uples are gathered to form relations with descriptive relation schemas and several relations will partecipate in a view.

The blackboard implementation is parallel to the one used by the relational database models to manage the facts and refers to the concept of context (7). As in the database a view is introduced to describe subsets of the content of the database, a context is introduced to partition the data instances and to cut across all the relationships in data model. It is the unified frame in which users of the same organizational entity can work cooperatively but independently.

If we adopt a relational model for the storage of facts about a patient, we can implement a blackboard as a set of database views that can be independently manipulated. Each user can derive a private view from the specified context, locking a view before updating its data. Each view is accessed directly and locked for the shortest possible amount of time. In practice, tables that contain data shared among concurrent users are immediatly updated, while updates on non-concurrent tables are buffered for later writing at the end of a session. The hierarchical structure among blackboards is implemented by the database administrator which defines the context availables by each clinical structure and resolves inter-context conflicts.

AN APPLICATION

The presented architecture has been applied in developing the Clinical Information System currently in use in the Medical Clinic of our University. Especially to model the real-world environment of the clinic, the architecture served as a suitable method for system development at various stages. The system development is done in UNIX environment and is based on the effective utilization of a relational database management system and specialized programs written in C.

Four clinic subsystems have already been developed and are in active operation within the clinic. These subsystems were designed with the presented set of clinic function in mind and serve departments as well as laboratories. The system differs information requirements due to distinct functions of various departement and laboratories and leads to different contexts each defined as a set of application dependent views. User views can be defined upon these by user themselves.

Access to all views is granted by the database administrator. Users can access the data from a terminal network. Updating and and data management is achieved by the use of cooperating transactions and applications which generate SQL statements dynamically.

Interactive documentation is performed by on-line transactions. It starts with the compilation of the encounter report identifying the patient. If the documentation unit with this identifiers already exists ,the transaction schedules other functions of the system. The identifiers allow a certain patient to be retrievable by each department of the clinic but departments are allowed to see only results about medical data or medical tests they asked for.

The system provides the capability to generate standardized management reports for day-to-day operations.

CONCLUSION

The presented paper enphasizes the integration of clinical functions by implementing a blackboard architecture. It constitutes a realistic proposal since the effective implementation has be done, based on the effective utilization of a relational database system. The decentralized architecture of the system permits the database to be reconfigured in response to user needs that are not adequately met by the actual system. Also,it is adaptable to changes or advances in computer technology.In particular, the standardized operating system environment and the modular system structure allows the integration with existing clinical subsystem or the integration with new subsystems considering advances in computer technology (i.e. workstations, multi-media information reporting, picture archiving.,e.t.c.).

REFERENCES

(1) RENNELS G.D. and SHORTLIFFE E.H. "Advanced Computing for Medicine", Scientific American, October :154-161,(1987).

(2) TOLCHIN, S.G. "An overview of an architectural approach to the development of the Johns Hopkins Hospital distributed clinical information system",J.Med.Syst. 10 (1986) 321-338.

(3) SAUTER K. "Integration by Distribution - a Contradiction or an Evolutionary Methodology to Develop Multi-Functional Health Information Systems?", Lecture Notes in Medical Informatics 25, Springer-Verlag (1985) 11-15.

(4) SMITH J.M. "Expert Database Systems : A Database Perspective" Proceeding from the First International Workshop on Expert Database Systems (1984).

(5) GARG P.and SCACCHI W. On Designing Intelligent hypertext System for Information management in Software Engineering", Proceedings of Hypertext '87 (Univ. North Carolina) (1987)

(6) TOMPA F.W. A Datamodel for Flexible Hypertext Database Systems, ACM Trans. Inf. Syst.,7,1 (Jan.1989),85-100

(7) DESLILE N.M. and M.D. SCHWARTZ, "Context - A Partitioning Concept for Hypertext", ACM Trans. Office Inf. Syst.,5,.2 (1987) 168-186.

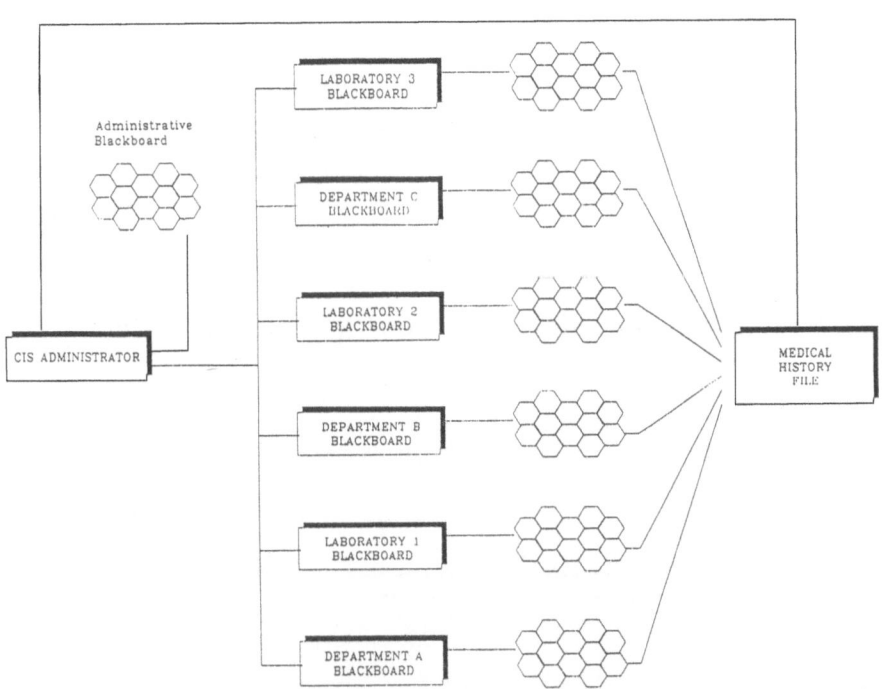

Fig.1 The CIS Blackboard Architecture

Subsystem Specific Blackboards

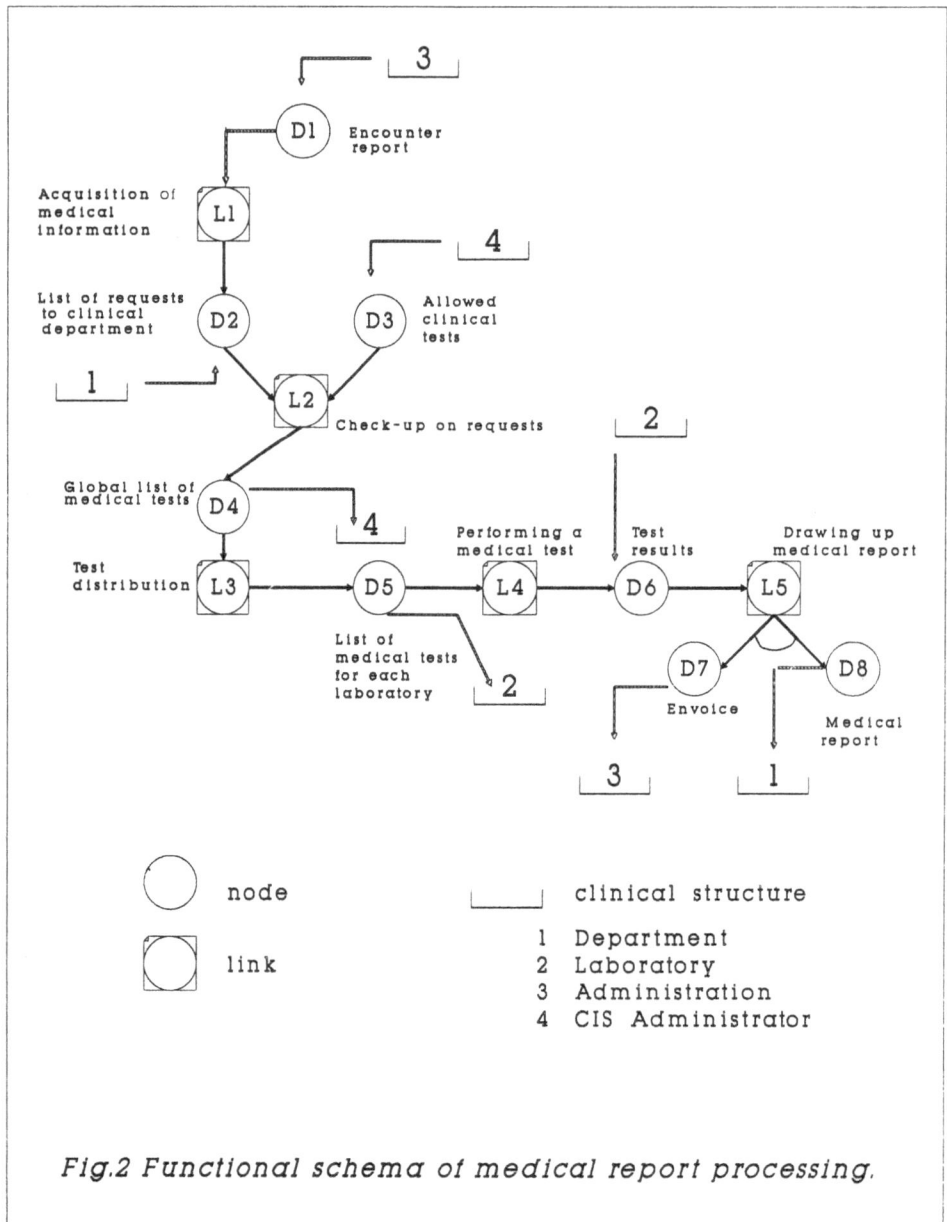

Fig.2 Functional schema of medical report processing.

RADES - Medical Assistance System for the Management of Irradiated Persons

Kindler H.*,**   Densow D.*   Fliedner T. M.*

* Institute of Occupational and Social Medicine of the University of Ulm
** Institute of Applied Knowledge Processing at the University of Ulm
Postfach 2060, D-7900 Ulm, kindler@dulfaw1a.bitnet

Abstract

A knowledge-based assistance system in medicine has for legal and ethical reasons special charges, i. e., transparency, explicability, and overrideability. An architecture to achieve these goals is proposed and discussed. A demonstrator for a knowledge-based assistance system for the medical management of accidentally irradiated persons (RADES) is presented.

Keywords

acute radiation syndrome, cognitive problem-solving model, knowledge-based assistance system, patient card metaphor user interface, sequential diagnosis

1. Introduction

Many medical expert systems have already been developed. In contrast to expert systems in industrial applications they have rarely been used in routine. Legal, ergonomic, and ethical charges imply special requirements which have for the most part not been fulfilled, yet. First, these requirements for knowledge-based assistance systems in medicine are listed. Next, the acute radiation syndrome as an exemplary medical domain for the demonstration of a knowledge-based assistance system in medicine is shortly described. Last, RADES a first demonstrator of an architecture of a medical knowledge-based assistence system meeting the medical demands is presented.

2. Requirements for a Knowledge-Based Assistence System in Medicine

As far as the results are concerned, expert systems that were previously constructed almost match the abilities of human experts. They were thought to be of use in domains in which physicians have a lack of expertise. The expert systems were designed to provide these physicians with the same level of knowledge as an expert. This lack of expertise is especially true concerning the management of radiation accidents.

But, for ethical, legal, and ergonomic reasons medical expert systems have rarely been used in practice, yet. Physicians are personally responsible for a patient's treatment even when applying complex technical aids. Thus, using a knowledge-based system the physician has to take the full responsibility for its application. In general physicians are not experienced computer users and have a lack of time. Therefore, technical aids have to be transparent, fully understandable, explicable, easily and quickly accessible for them. We use the term knowledge-based assistance system instead of expert system due to the role of a system which respects the above mentioned constraints being a cooperative assistant, who has a staff function, providing advice like a consultant, and having the same understanding of the problem. A relatively autonomous cognitive agent like former expert systems is difficult to apply in medicine for these reasons. Nevertheless, there is a need for cooperative intelligent agents, that assist the physician but leave the final decision to him.

In accordance to the hereinbefore named conditions the following design goals for knowledge-based assistance systems can be defined:

- authenticity meaning that the result of the reasoning process is correct and that the reasoning process is a good imitation of the human problem-solving process;

- transparency implying that all data which are important for one case have to be presented in a highly structured manner and the decision process has to be comprehensiable to the user;

- explicability consisting of the possibility to give "why"-explanations, strategic "how"-explanations, and other "how"-explanations;

- the possibility for the user to override the conclusions of the system;

- efficiency as short response time of the inference mechanism and as high information transfer capacity of the user interface; and

- ergonomics meaning that the user can rapidly gain a simple mental model of the functioning of the system and a user interface with a familiar metaphor.

The evaluation of former expert systems, e. g., MYCIN, has proved that their results of the problem-solving have been comparable to human experts' results [29]. This ability has been achieved by the application of formalized human knowledge in the form of rules. Nevertheless, their way of problem-solving has not been the way of humans' problem-solving because the knowledge was applied in a very mechanistic way by the inference mechanism. Thus, MYCIN has been restructured for tutorial purposes which require a high degree of transparency of the problem-solving process [4]. The successor of MYCIN, NEOMYCIN has used the fact that humans solve problems by the hierarchical decomposition in subtasks until means are found to solve the subtasks [1]. Imitating this strategy a higher authenticity of the problem-solving process itself and not only of the result is obtained, which is necessary for knowledge-based assistance systems. The decomposition and ordering of the tasks in NEOMYCIN is performed by strategic rules. Control tasks serve to structure the hierarchy and are composed of other tasks. For terminal tasks means are known to solve them. Those means are represented as knowledge sources. By the distribution of the knowledge base in several knowledge sources the efficiency of the reasoning process is increased, the response time is shortened, and the maintenance of the knowledge base is alleviated.

XPLAIN [28] has modeled the human problem-solving process as a hierarchical decomposition of complex tasks in simpler tasks, too. Both in NEOMYCIN and in XPLAIN "why"-explanations do not have to be prepared as canned text to explain the sense of incidentally asked questions. The task hierarchy serves to construct reasonable "why"-explanations.

The approaches of NEOMYCIN and XPLAIN restrict the modeling to problem-solving processes without iterative structures. In many medical disciplines problem-solving processes are iterative, e. g., electromyography and acute radiation syndrome. In electromyography diagnosis consists of a sequence of hypothesis and test cycles [13]. The problem-solving in the acute radiation syndrome is a sequence of diagnostic, prognostic and therapeutic tasks [9]. The underlying diagnostic strategies are subsummized as sequential diagnosis. An algorithm to perform sequential diagnosis in electric circuits has already been developed [16]. In principle, the algorithm describes the problem-solving strategy but the task concept is not explicitly represented. A cognitive problem-solving model allows the explicit representation as a task concept of the sequential diagnosis strategy rendering iterative steps possible [14]. In contrast to NEOMYCIN task types,

e. g., creation of a hypothesis, can be defined. These task types can be instantiated several times, e. g., creation of the third hypothesis, in order to represent similar task sequences. A cognitive problem-solving model is composed of

- a set of instantiable task types to deal with iteration in the diagnostic process,
- a set of strategic rules in first-order predicate calculus to decompose and arrange the tasks hierarchically, and
- a set of knowledge-sources to solve the terminal tasks.

A knowledge-based assistance system requires a cognitive problem-solving model in all domains in which sequential diagnosis is used to represent the problem-solving process explicitly.

A "How"-explanation, e. g., in MYCIN, is the tree of deductions leading to a certain value of a patient's property. A truth maintenance system will be necessary to give "How"-explanations if the inferences are performed with rules in first-order predicate calculus [6]. The first-order predicate calculus is an essential prerequisite in complex medical domains, e. g., electromyography and acute radiation syndrome. Using task types in a cognitive problem-solving model requires strategic knowledge in first-order predicate calculus, also. "How"-explanations on a strategic level are obtained by explicitly represented strategic knowledge. Due to the truth maintenance system the repetition of all inferences will be avoided if deductions of the knowledge-based assistance system have to be overridden.

In former expert systems, e. g., MYCIN [26], the user dialogue has been performed by written sentences in natural language. This approach has been disadvantageous because of the limited information exchange capacity. Thus, it has been difficult for the user to survey the state of the fact base and of the problem-solving process. An object-oriented graphical user interface for a knowledge-based assistance system is utilized to overcome this opacity by taking advantage of the enormous capacity of man's visual sense. "Why"-explanations are permanently given by the visualisation of the task hierarchy of the cognitive problem-solving model. In order to achieve a better understanding and handling of the user interface the patient card metaphor similar to the desktop metaphor [25] is introduced. On a set of register cards all the patient's data can be displayed in a highly structured form. The functions of the system are accessible by the object-oriented user interface, e. g., the "How"-explanations.

3. The Domain of Application - the Acute Radiation Syndrome

Radiation accidents have caused a sequence of clinical signs and symptoms in irradiated persons for which the term acute radiation syndrome has been introduced [19]. It can be characterised by a set of signs and symptoms, which forms the basis for a specific treatment. There are very important early signs and symptoms originating from blood cell changes, from responses of the skin, mucous membranes, and from the central nervous system that allow the physician to assess the severity of the acute radiation syndrome and its probable course of events. It is therefore important to control sequentially, on the basis of a time schedule depending on the severeness of the injury, the signs and symptoms.

Depending on the radiation dose and dose rate the tissues are damaged. The symptoms and signs of the damage occur with a specific delay. The development of an acute radiation syndrome is a dynamic process. Thus, signs and symptoms gain their specific relevance for diagnosis and therapy from their time of occurence.

The diagnostic strategy to solve the problem of the management of accidentally irradiated persons is sequential diagnosis [9]. After the acquisition of the first signs and symptoms an iteration of diagnostic and therapeutic tasks follows until the problem is solved. Thus, diagnosis and therapy run in parallel because the symptomatic treatment has to start before the definite diagnosis is obtained.

4. A Demonstrator of an Architecture of a Knowledge-Based Assistance System

4.1 Blackboard Control Architecture

An architecture and its implementation for a knowledge-based assistance system for the medical management of the acute radiation syndrome (RADES) are presented in accordance to the requirement analysis of chapter two. The knowledge engineering tool KEE™ has been choosen for the implementation. KEE™ offers a first-order predicate calculus inference mechanism, a truth maintenance system, an object-oriented representation of the fact-base, and an object-oriented user interface tool-kit. Providing these tools required for the construction of a knowledge-based assistance system increases the development efficiency.   -

A blackboard architecture provides the opportunity to represent complex problem-solving processes [8]. Especially, a blackboard control architecture similar to BB1 [10], that has already been used to implement sequential problem-solving strategies, is an appropriate mean to operationalize a cognitive problem-solving model. This architecture explains its problem-solving actions by showing how they fit into its underlying problem-solving strategy and by recursively explaining the problem-solving plan itself. A blackboard control architecture consists of a control and a domain blackboard. On the former the problem-solving plan, e. g., a task hierarchy of a cognitive problem-solving model composed of control and terminal

tasks, is explicitly represented. The domain blackboard serves to describe the patient's clinical status. The deductive knowledge is structured in knowledge sources. The strategic deductive knowledge, which is explicitly represented in first-order predicate calculus, is accumulated in a control knowledge source. The deductive domain knowledge in first-order predicate calculus is aggregated in domain knowledge sources. Each of them is a mean to solve a certain terminal task type. The control knowledge source primarily works on the control blackboard to develop the problem-solving plan and to trigger single domain knowledge sources depending on the activation state of the task hierarchy on the control blackboard. A natural representation of blackboard concepts can be easily obtained by object-oriented programming techniques [11]. Thus, KEE™ has formed a good basis to implement a blackboard control architecture in order to operationalize a cognitive problem-solving model explicitly representing the strategy of sequential diagnosis.

fig. 1, blackboard control architecture

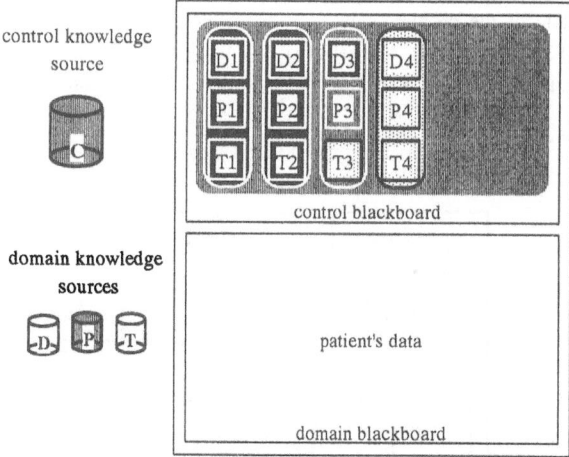

control knowledge source

domain knowledge sources

In fig. 1 the blackboard control architecture with an already developed task hierarchy of the cognitive problem-solving model on the control blackboard is shown. The big medium grey rectangle in the background represents the task "management of an irradiated person", which is decomposed in a sequence of four subtasks, the erect rectangles. Each of them is subdivided in three further subtasks, a sequence of diagnosis (D), prognosis (P), and therapy (T). The state of the execution of the tasks is indicated by different shades of grey. Tasks that have already been executed are depicted, dark grey, those which are actually under execution are indicated with medium grey, and those which are planned are represented light grey. Control tasks have rounded edges and terminal tasks have sharp edges. The terminal task actually under execution is the third prognosis "P3". The domain knowledge source "P", which serves to execute the task type prognosis, is activated. The domain knowledge sources diagnosis "D" and therapy "T" are inactive. The activation of the domain knowledge sources is controlled by the active control knowledge source "C" depending on the state of the task activation on the control blackboard. An example of a strategic rule of the control knowledge source "C" is shown in fig. 2.

fig. 2, strategic rule

If

a patient has an acute radiation syndrome of degree III on one of the days between the 3rd and 49th day after irradiation
then
plan a task of the type "diagnosis, prognosis, and therapy" and its subtasks for the following day.

It has been deduced, for instance, on the third day when executing the terminal task "P3" that the patient's acute radiation syndrome is of degree III. This is according to the state of the problem-solving of fig. 1 with the terminal task "P3" active. Thus, one set of conditions for the rule in fig. 2 leads to its firing. The consequences are the instantiation of a

control task and its terminal tasks "D4", "P4", and "T4" on the fourth day. It can be seen in fig. 1 that the instantiated tasks are planned, which is indicated by their light grey colour.

4.2 The User Interface

The patient card metaphor is applied for the user interface. A register card system is implemented with an object-oriented window system, e. g. in fig. 3 the register card of the patient's hematological data and in fig. 4 the register card with the management plan. Every card has a tab by which it can be rapidly accessed with a pointing device.

All the patient's properties important for the acute radiation syndrome are displayed on the register cards. Apart from those already mentioned cards there are others for the patient's primary data and his clinical symptoms and signs. Different displays [27] for different data types are provided, e. g., compare the time-value-plots for the hematological data in fig. 3 and the task hierarchies for the patient's management plan in fig. 4 displaying the state of the cognitive problem-solving model. The graphical display improves the physician's survey of the plan of management and over the patient's data by browsing through the register cards. The input of the data is performed with forms on the screen [17].

fig. 3, register card of the hematological data

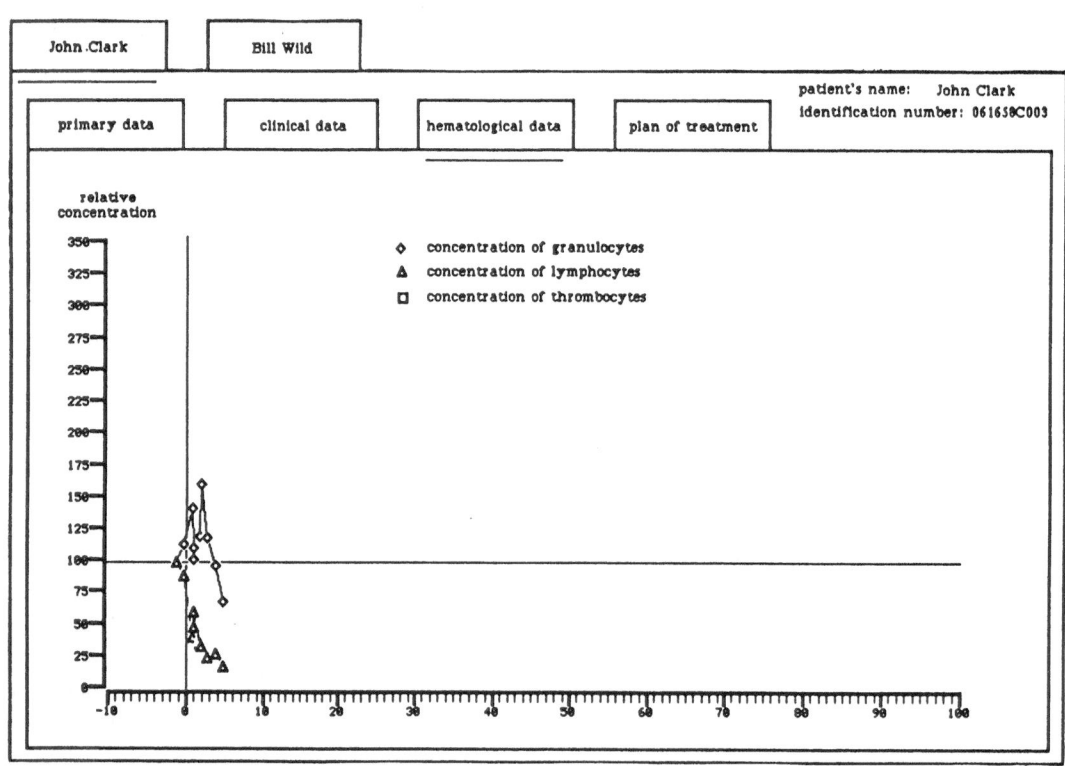

fig.4, plan of management

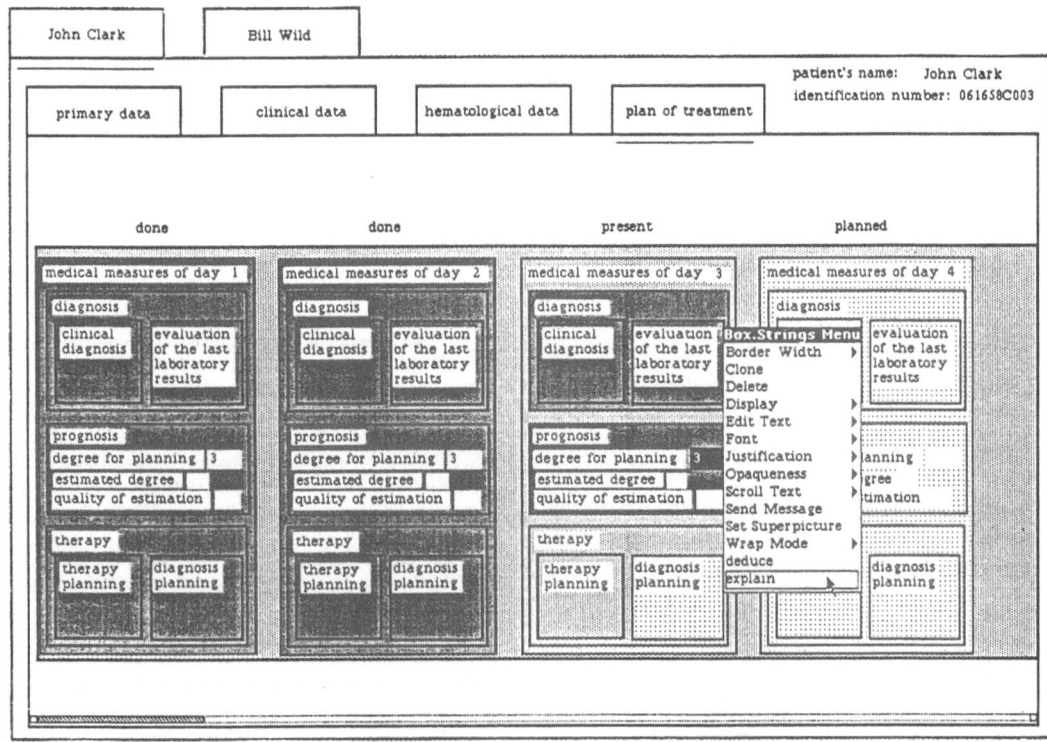

In fig. 4 the already developed management plan is displayed as a hierarchy of tasks, which is represented in the same manner on the control blackboard, according to the example in fig. 1. The explanation to the question "Why is a diagnostical question asked on day four?" is given by the task hierarchy and the strategic deductions which produced it, e. g., the rule in fig. 2 has fired because of degree III on the third day. A sound medical justification for the rule in fig. 2 can be given. The

fig. 5, "How"-explanation

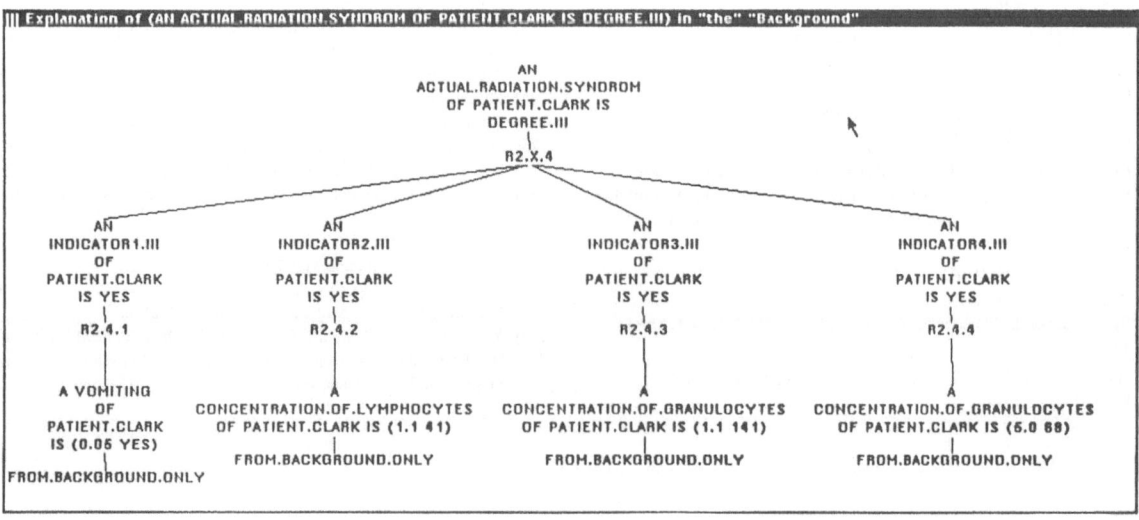

548

access to another functionality, e. g. a "How"-question, via the graphical user interface is shown in fig. 4. The user asks by utilizing a menu "How has the degree III of the patient's acute radiation syndrome on day three been deduced?" The answer is a visualized part of the reference graph of the truth maintencance system, see fig. 5. The rules deducing degree III are part of the domain knowledge source "P", see fig. 1. The degree III was deduced because all of the four indicators for a degree III of the acute radiation syndrome have been apparent. The rules which have served to deduce the evidence of the indicators can be justified pathophysiologically [15].

Due to the user interface management system methodology [23] the object-oriented knowledge-based module and the object-oriented graphical user interface are independant and communicate by message passing because of their object-oriented design. Thus, one knowledge-based module could have several graphical user interfaces dedicated to different groups of users. In KEE™ an object-oriented knowledge engineering tool and an object-oriented development kit for user interfaces are offered in one toolbox.

5. Conclusion

A first demonstrator of RADES with the above listed features has been implemented. The first results have shown to be rewarding. Due to the fact that the strategic and domain knowledge have only partially been implemented the system is still at the research stage. Objective evaluations of the problem-solving capacity with real cases and of the user interface with potential users have not been performed, yet.

6. Literature

[1]   Anderson J. R.: "Cognitive Psychology and its Implications", W. H. Freeman and Company, New York, 1985

[2]   Carroll J. M., McKendree J.: "Interface Design Issues for Advice-Giving Expert Systems", Communications of the ACM, vol. 30, no. 1, 1987

[3]   Chandrasekaran B., Tanner M. C., Josephson J. R: "Explaining Control Strategies in Problem-Solving", in "IEEE-EXPERT", vol. 1, no. 1, 1990, IEEE Computer Society Press

[4]   Clancey W. J., Letsinger R.: "NEOMYCIN: Reconfiguring a Rulebased Expert System for Application to Teaching", in: Clancey W. J., Shortliffe E. H. (Hrsg.): "Readings in Medical Artificial Intelligence: The First Decade", Addison-Wesley, Reading, 1984

[5]   Densow D., Kindler H., Fliedner T. M.: "RADES - Radiation Accident Decision Support System", Proceedings of the 10th International Symposium of the Electricity Section of the ISSA 1990, Vienna, to appear 1991

[6]   Doyle : "A Truth Maintenance System", Artificial Intelligence, vol. 12, North Holland, 1979

[7]   Elstein A. S., Shulman L. S., Spratka S. A.: "Medical Problem-Solving: An Analysis of Clinical Reasoning", Harvard University Press, Cambridge, 1978

[8]   Engelmore R. S., Morgan A. J., Nii H. P.: "Introduction", in Engelmore R. S., Morgan A. J. (eds.): "Blackboard Systems", Addison-Wesley, Wokingham, 1988

[9]   Fliedner T. M.: "Strategien zur strahlenschutzmedizinischen, ambulanten Versorgung von "Betroffenen" bei kerntechnischen Unfällen", in Messerschmidt O., Betz B., Fliedner T. M. (eds.): "Medizinische Erstmaßnahmen bei kerntechnischen Unfällen", Thieme, Stuttgart, 1981

[10] Hayes-Roth B.: "A Blackboard Architecture for Control", Artifical Intelligence, vol. 26, North Holland, 1985

[11] Hayes-Roth B., Hewett M.: "BB1: An Implementation of the Blackboard Control Architecture", in Engelmore R. S., Morgan A. J. (eds.): "Blackboard Systems", Addison-Wesley, Wokingham, 1988

[12] Kernavou E. T., Washbrook J.: "Deep and Shallow Models in Medical Expert Systems", in Sadegh-Zadeh K. (ed): "Artificial Intelligence in Medicine", vol. 1, no. 1, Burgverlag, Tecklenburg, 1989

[13] Kindler H.: "Controlling Qualitative Reasoning by a Cognitive Problem-Solving Model for Decision Support in Electromyography", Proceedings of the Workshop of Qualitative Reasoning and Decision Support Systems 1991, Toulouse, North Holland, Amsterdam, to appear 1991

[14] Kindler H.: "Wissensmodellierung als Grundlage eines intelligenten Tutors in der Elektromyographie", in Reuter A.: "20. GI-Jahrestagung", vol. 2, Springer, 1990

[15] Kindler H., Densow D., Fliedner T. M.: "Better Justifiability and Less Rules by Using Deep Knowledge", Proceedings of the 10th MIE 91, Vienna, Springer, to appear 1991

[16] Kleer, J. de, Williams B. C.: "Diagnosing Multiple Faults", Artificial Intelligence, vol. 32, North Holland, 1987

[17] Lane. C. D., Walton J. D., Shortliffe E. H.: "Graphical Access to Medical Expert Systems: II. Design of an Interface for Physicians", in Wagner G., Lindberg D. A. B. (eds.): "Methods of Information in Medicine", vol. 25, Schattauer Verlag, 1986

[18] Laurent J. P.: "La Structure de Contrôle dans les Systèmes Experts", in "Technique et Science Informatiques", vol. 3, no. 3, Afcet-Bordas, Paris, 1984

[19] Mettler jr. F. A., Kelsey C. A., Ricks R. C.: "Medical Management of Radiation Accidents", CRC Press, Fort Lauterdale, 1990

[20] Musen M. A.: "Automated Generation of Model-Based Knowledge-Acquisition Tools", Pitman, London, 1989

[21] Newble D., Clarke R.: "The Approaches to Learning of Students in a Traditional and an Innovative Problem-Based Medical School", Medical Education, vol 20, 1986

[22] Norman D. A., Draper S. W.: "User Centered System Design", Lawrence Earlbaum, Hillsdale, 1986

[23] Perlman G.: "Software Tools for User Interface Development", in Helander M. (ed.): "Handbook of Human-Computer Interaction", North-Holland, Amsterdam, 1988

[24] Ramsden P., Whelan G., Cooper D.: "Some Phenomena of Medical Students' Diagnostic Problem-Solving", Medical Education, vol. 23, 1989

[25] Shneiderman B.: "Designing the User Interface: Strategies for Effective Human-Computer Interaction", Addison-Wesley, Reading, 1987

[26] Shortliffe E. H.: "Computer-Based Medical Consultations: MYCIN", North Holland, New York, 1976

[27] Streveler D. J., Harrison P. B.: "Judging Visual Displays of Medical Information", Computing, vol. 2, no. 2, 1985

[28] Swartout W. R.: "XPLAIN: A System for Creating and Explaining Expert Consulting Systems", Artificial Intelligence, vol. 21, no. 3, 1983

[29] Yu. V., Buchanan B., Shortliffe E., Wraith E., Davis S., Scott R., Dohen A.: "Evaluating the Performance of a Computer-Based Consultant", Computer Programs in Biomedicine, vol. 9, 1979

A Temporal Model for Clinical and Resource Management in Vascular Surgery

Paul Soper*, Charles Ranaboldo†, Geetha Abeysinghe*

*Department of Electronics and Computer Science, Univeristy of Southampton, UK
†Department of Vascular Surgery, Royal South Hampshire Hospital, Southampton, UK

Abstract

A general formalism for temporal reasoning, the event calculus, is being applied to the development of medical knowledge bases and decision support tools in the domain of vascular surgery. After reviewing our initial feasibility study, the extensions we are undertaking are outlined: to model the patient record system in the event calculus; to devlop the event calculus for modes of temporal reasoning which occur; and to implement a prototype with improved retrieval for treatment planning. The resulting system, because it will provide an interface of sufficient flexibility, has the potential for widespread uptake in hospital practice and as a result may facilitate the collection of high quality clinical data. It is argued that such data is paramount for effective resource management and that therefore installation of the system will be attractive to hospital management as well as clinicians.

1 Introduction

The development of formalism to allow clinical decision making to be represented within a knowledge base for vascular surgery has led us to explore a general formalism for temporal reasoning. The results, presented in a previous paper[1], we believe provide a suitable platform for the development of a clinically useful system. During this initial work the relationship to other hospital activities, such as resource management, was also considered.

Artificial intelligence techniques have yet to be fully accepted as tools to facilitate medical practice. Many factors may be responsible for the slow uptake in comparison to that of industry or commerce, but one of the principle problems is that there is little perceived benefit to either hospital or clinicians. The application of artificial intelligence to routine clinical practice, for example our decision support system, may however facilitate other developments that are now beginning to get underway within the British health service.

Both the new programme of resource management and that of clinical audit require high quality detailed clinical data. Only doctors and others directly concerned with patient care can capture the information that is required with sufficient accuracy. Within the context of improved management of resources for health care the need for accurate information is becoming paramount.

The facilitation of clinical decision making, using artificial intelligence techniques, is based on the collection of patient data. Therefore the introduction of such a system can provide the mechanism and motivation for that data collection which in turn

can be used again for other activities such as clinical audit or resource management.

It is the attractions inherent to an artificial intelligence system itself which will probably dictate the success or failure of introducing such a system into routine clinical practice. It is not only the appearance of the user interface but also its flexibility which will influence its acceptance by those who use it. The system outlined below we believe has the necessary properties, primarily because of its support for temporal reasoning. Section 2 reviews our initial motivation and results on developing such as system, but it does not include a detailed description of the event calculus or of the formalisation of our initial system as a logic program which can be found in a previous paper [1] together with examples. Section 3 outlines our current research on the design of an extended system and Section 4 discusses the implications of the system for resource management.

2 Motivation and review of the initial system

Arterial disease is a modern epidemic of unparalleled proportions. In response the subspeciality of vascular surgery has rapidly expanded in an attempt to limit some of the worst effects of the disease. In the area of medical expert systems few have been created for use within surgical practice[2] and most of those that have have not been prospectively evaluated[3]. The aim of the present research is to develop a support environment which can improve the clinical management of patients as they are treated by a vascular surgery department.

We are developing a knowledge based system which has essentially two new aspects. Firstly we provide a general formalism for temporal reasoning and secondly we address the domain of vascular surgery, for which we know of no comparable system. The importance of relating the timing of events to a patient's clinical management has as yet received scant attention. From our early results we believe that our approach may provide considerable advantages in terms of both construction methodology and performance of the system[1].

The development of our knowledge based system is based upon experience with logic databases[4]. The general motivation behind this approach is that extended Horn clause logic should be investigated as a promising formalism for the development of knowledge based systems, since logic provides expressive knowledge representation, a rigorous framework and the implemented tools of logic programming. Furthermore it is argued that such systems should include a general framework for representing time, since reasoning about the change of a knowledge base over time is thought to be important for many applications[5].

The primary temporal formalism we have considered is the event calculus of Kowalski and Sergot[6] which, because it is expressed in classical logic, is better suited to logic programming than temporal logic[7]. Other related formalisms in particular Allen's logic[8] were shown by Sadri[9] to be cómparable to the event calculus. In the event calculus new knowledge is added to the knowledge base in the form of events and a meta-theory is used to describe the temporal relationship between classes of events, thus abstracting the specifically temporal reasoning from other aspects of the model. Typically events may be related causally, logically or by some protocol. There has been considerable recent work upon extending the event calculus, for example with transaction times[10] and hypothetical reasoning[11] and on applying it to new domains, for example air traffic control[12] and our work upon clinical patient management[1].

Our initial work has applied the above ideas of logic databases and event calculus to modelling the clinical pathway. We have shown how the event calculus can represent a simplified model in which specialists review patients at variable intervals depending upon previous investigation results and the clinical problem. The resulting formalisation is executable as a logic program. We also show how a useful support function, the recommendation of appropriate options at any time, can be built up on this basis. The motivation for starting this work was to provide a basis for extension of the system to support various medical tasks. These might include support for diagnosis, planning investigation and treatment, audit and research (see[13] for a recent discussion of medical descision making). In our current research we focus on providing flexible assimilation and retrieval of information normally recorded in the patients' notes and on developing improved modes of retrieval which are relevant for planning investigation and treatment.

3 Design of the extended system

We referred above to the argument that support for temporal reasoning in a knowledge base should be built into a general framework, in particular the event calculus, rather than added on ad hoc. Having decided on this framework our current research effort divides broadly into three strands: to model the patient record system in the event calculus; to develop the event calculus for modes of temporal reasoning which occur; and to implement a prototype with improved retrieval for treatment planning.

3.1 Modelling the domain

As a first step we attempt to represent the information collected in the paper-based clinical record. Rather than use a conventional database approach our task is to represent this information in the event calculus framework. The basic representation that we are developing is an inheritance hierarchy of case frames, each describing a class of event. For example a by-pass operation inherits cases such as time, clinician, patient as well as contributing specific cases such as material of graft, operation outcome[1]. Within this structure we still have the complex knowledge representation problem of choosing approriate cases. Studies are continuing that explore the effect upon this approach of improving the structure of the existing paper-based clinical record.

Although there is a great deal of information available about any individual patient, at any given moment, the clinical options for that patient within the context of vascular surgery are fairly limited. Our next step is to model the relations which are significant for selecting these options, and hence significant for patient management. The way these relations change with time is modelled in the event calculus by specifying the situations which initiate and terminate them. We are not able to give a complete prescription for choosing significant relations, but current diagnoses, current complaints and outcomes of treatments are included at the present stage.

3.2 Event calculus development

One of the characteristics of the event calculus is its extendability and, as noted above, some of the extensions are active areas of research. Our approach is to extend the basic formalism only as warranted by the problem. We can identify three kinds of change in our model:

- new event descriptions (input by the user) can initiate or terminate base relations

- ramification relations, which depend upon base relations, may change indirectly

- relations may change autonomously (without new events being input).

The first two types of change are the bread and butter of the event calculus and can be used to model complex inter-relations in a very clear way. The last type is an extension to the basic formalism which seems to be important for our problem. Typically knowledge about a patient's condition can only be relied upon for a certain length of time, after which it should be reassessed. We are modelling this form of behaviour as a simple form of autonomous change, associating reliability periods with different relations and contexts. We are likely to have to draw upon further extensions to the event calculus as we proceed.

3.3 Prototype for experimentation

The main clinical purpose of this system is to help optimise the treatment of patients with peripheral vascular disease. Our aim is to improve on the support offered in a conventional data base system by providing flexible assimilation and retrieval facilities to help clinicians involved in the decision making process. We are investigating various strategies for applying the knowledge in the system, including temporal knowledge, for guiding retrieval in a helpful way. For example a clinician might consult the system before seeing a patient and be presented with information relating to current diagnoses and recommended treatment options. He or she might then ask for an explanation of a recommendation. Such a request can be responded to by applying techniques developed for generating explanations from logic databases[14], but because of our event calculus formalism we are able to produce, in addition to rule traces, the sequence of related events which led to a conclusion. As well as being informative in itself this sequence of events provides access to the detailed information stored in the associated case frames. In addition to this idea we are prototyping a number of forms of flexible retrieval which exploit the event calculus, as well as providing output in a standardised format. The inclusion of reminders of due or overdue tasks is a straightforward extension.

4 Implications for resource management

In recent years there has been an increasing realisation that the funding for hospitals is finite and that the efficient utilisation of available resources is essential to the optimisation of patient care. The British hospitals resource management initiative aims to achieve this objective by gathering information about both clinical events for each patient and resources used in that patient's care. The resultant information is made available to both hospital managers and clinicians to help them make decisions about the future allocation of resources, or the impact of changing a treatment regime.

To make some of these decisions however information about the outcomes of treatment is also required, while other choices require comparisons to be made between treatments. A check upon the quality of results is also needed. At present clinical audit and clinical outcome procedures are being devised on an ad hoc basis to try to provided the necessary information.

Underpining these developments is the need for accurate information about a patient's problems and care. Although some computerised systems do exist in hospitals today, the overwhelming mass of information about any patient's care is contained within paper-based records. To make the changes that are necessary to implement procedures for resource management, clinical audit and clinical outcomes a considerable change in hospital practices will have to occur.

It is the accurate collection of patient data that will underpin these procedures. Only clinicans and others directly concerned with the moment to moment care of patients can be responsible for the data collection that is necessary. These professionals will not be prepared to alter their working practices to enable effective data collection unless there is a tangible reward to either themselves or to their patients. Their enthusiastic co-operation will be needed, however, to ensure that the computerised records are maintained to the necessary standard.

Existing database techniques are too inflexible to provide a realistic solution and also in themselves they do not have any spin off effects to attract clinicans to use them. The idea behind our approach is to provide a versatile system which might provide the catalyst for change that is needed, rather than attempt to force clinicians to adopt the conventional database approach.

The formalism outlined above we believe will provide the basis for an interface of sufficient flexibility to make the use of the underlying clinical knowledge base attractive to clinicians. This in itself will stimulate the use of the associated decision support system, which because of its inherent benefits will encourage further use of the system. As a spin off, through the use of the system, accurately collected information will become available for other activities such as clinical audit and resource management.

5 Conclusions

In its present form the system that we are developing shows, for the clinical management domain, how the event calculus affords an elegant method for modelling the interdependencies of properties which change with time and also for accessing historical information. In particular our model shows how the representation can be used to input, as event descriptions, some of the information currently kept in patient notes, access information in a flexible way, and model some aspects of the timing of clinical tests and treatments.

The results of prototyping the extended system will be potentially of direct benefit for development of knowledge based decision support tools for hospital surgical departments, with vascular surgery as the first instance. The Royal South Hampshire hospital aims to exploit the results to improve the quality of managment of patients with vascular disease, while at the same time contributing to more efficient utilisation of hospital resources. The potential of the system to provide accurate information as a spin off for other activities has not yet been explored but may act as an additional motivation for system uptake and utilisation.

There are many other directions in which the research might be further developed, including clinical research, information retrieval from a medical text base for educational purposes, and linking to medical systems in other domains such as the Oxford System of Medicine[15] for primary care.

References

[1] P. Soper and G. Abeysinghe and C. Ranaboldo, *Temporal aspects of a knowledge based system for the management of hospital patients*, DEXA 90, Springer-Verlag, 1990, 354-359

[2] P.Clifford and M.Chan and D. Hewett, *The acute abdomen: management with microcomputer aid*, Ann. R. Coll. Surg., 68, 1986, 182-184

[3] H. Lundsgaarrde, *Evaluating medical expert systems*, Soc. Sci. Med., 24, 10, 1987, 805-819

[4] H. Gallaire and J. Minker and J.M. Nicolas, *Logic and databases: A deductive approach*, Computing Surveys, June, 1984, 153-185

[5] R. Snodgrass and I.A. Ahn, *A taxonomy of time in databases*, Proceedings of ACM SIGMOD International Conference on Data, ACM, Austin, Texas, May, 1985, 236-246

[6] R.A. Kowalski and M.J. Sergot, *A logic-based calculus of events*, New Generation Computing, 4, 1, 1986, 67-95

[7] D. Gabbay, *The declarative past and imperative future: executable temporal logic for interactive systems*, Temporal Logic Specifications, LNCS 398, Springer-Verlag, 1989, 409-448

[8] J.F. Allen, *Maintaining knowledge about temporal intervals*, CACM, 26, 11, 1983, 832-834

[9] F. Sadri, *Three recent approaches to temporal reasoning*, Department of Computing, Imperial College, DoC 86/23, 1986

[10] S. M. Sripada, *A logical framework for temporal deductive databases*, Proceedings of VLDB, Morgan Kaufmann, 1988, 171-182

[11] K. Eshghi and R.A. Kowalski, *Abduction compared with negation by failure*, Fifth International Conference on Logic Programming, MIT Press, 1989

552

[12] J. M. Bedford and R.A. Kowalski and B.L. Rosser, *Representing change in air traffic flow management using the event calculus*, Colloquium on Temporal Reasoning, IEE, London, Digest No. 1990/024, 2/1-3, 1990

[13] M. O'Neil and A. Glowinski and J.A. Fox, *A symbolic theory of decision-making applied to several medical tasks*, Lecture Notes in Medical Informatics, Proceedings of AIME, Springer-Verlag, 1989, 62-71

[14] P. Hammond and M. Sergot, *APES: augmented prolog for expert systems*, Logic Based Systems Ltd, London, 1984

[15] A. Glowinski and M. O'Neil and J. Fox, *Design of a generic information system and its application to primary care*, Lecture Notes in Informatics, AI in Medicine 89, Springer-Verlag, 1989, 221-233

Preparing Medical Knowledge for
Diagnostic Expert Systems

Christian Stary

Florida International University
School of Computer Science
University Park
Miami, FL 33199
e-mail: stary@fiu.scs.edu

Karl Fasching

Technical University of Vienna
Department for Information Systems
Paniglgasse 16-187/1
1040 Vienna, Austria
e-mail: vexpert!fasching@relay.EU.net

ABSTRACT

The task of supporting medical diagnosis by computer applications is twofold: first, we have to accumulate and integrate medical knowledge into some kind of information system; secondly, we can apply these findings to actual patient data by generating and evaluating patient-specific hypotheses for diagnostics. This paper is focused on the initial task for computer-supported medical diagnosis. We present an approach to *organize* and later on, to *represent* medical knowledge in an information system, regardless to the original diagnostic problem domain.

Due to the knowledge we already have about medical decision making, the organization of medical knowledge can be predefined to a certain extent: Diagnostics requires several entrypoints to previously accumulated, and thus, case-independent medical knowledge: diseases, symptoms, factors like etiology, morphology, etc. Moreover, medical decision making requires not only the static coverage of the problem domain but also the representation of diagnostic procedures to support its dynamic aspects.

In order to meet these extraordinary requirements for the representation of medical knowledge we applied a comprehensive modelling technique, namely object-oriented design. It allows us not only to cover static properties as well as basic processes of medical diagnostics appropriately, but also to implement such a complex application accurately. For the representation of additional diagnostic heuristics and the design of working hypotheses by the diagnostician we have extended the representation schema by rules. Thus, for implementation a hybrid system, namely Prolog-DB (a data base coupled with a logical programming language) had to be used.

INTRODUCTION

Requirements. Medical diagnosis relies on the diagnostician's comprehensive knowledge, according to his/her practical experience and to his/her theoretical education. The latter mainly stems from text books and courses without contacting patients, whereas experience can only be accumulated by dealing with patients. Textbooks like Harrison's Textbook of Internal Medicine provide case-, i.e. patient-independent information, which can be considered the most general applicable form of medical knowledge. For individual cases, this knowledge has to be refined and evaluated by diagnostic procedures and strategies. However, both types of knowledge are used to generate and evaluate hypotheses concerning specific patients [2].

Although several medical information systems have been developed with the intention to provide accurate and comfortable access to medical knowledge for diagnostic support, medical practicioners mostly refused to use such diagnostic support tools steadily because of:

- inadequate access facilities and interface features, and

- orientation towards a particular medical problem domain [20].

Whenever a variety of diagnoses has to be evaluated[1] the diagnostician has to identify evaluation criteria to proceed. In a further step, all hypotheses have to be matched against these criteria. Since this step is not restricted to the initial diagnostic problem domain, a knowledge base is required which is not restricted to a certain problem domain. Rather, it has to offer structures to represent the entire medical knowledge [9]. In addition, the knowledge has to be accessible by certain entry-point like factors (e.g. etiology), findings, diseases, and diagnostic strategies (e.g. for the identification of differential diagnoses) [1].

Goals. According to the scenario above, and the fact that there is still a lack of frameworks for comprehensive representation of medical knowledge supporting diagnosis (see below), we developed a medical knowledge base which

- provides structures to represent the entire medical knowledge, regardless of the original diagnostic problem domain,

- supports not only the static description of diseases, symptoms, etc., but also

- the process of medical diagnosis (i.e. access by symptoms, diseases, signs, etc.), and

- takes into account several entry points for a variety of medical tasks, which have to be presented to the user by an appropriate user interface.

In order to cover all of these aspects, we could not simply apply a data model, data base language, representation schema, or knowledge engineering tool. For a serious approach we had to identify and to model carefully the interface between reliable medical knowledge and heuristics to support the process of finding a final diagnosis.

Procedure. We start with an evaluation of existing approaches (section 2). All of them pursue particular goals, like proving the adequacy of a representation technique. Since they do not provide concepts which are generally applicable for medical decision support, we had to develop knowledge structures which allow to represent general, i.e. case-independent medical knowledge (as it can be found in a medical text book) for diagnostic support. These structures can be applied to any particular medical problem domain. We will exemplify them by internal medicine (section 3).

---

[1] ,which is the usual way before making a final diagnostic decision,

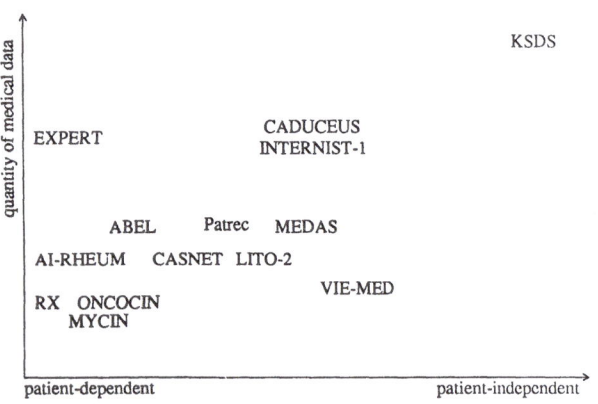

Figure 1: Categorization of Existing Approaches

In addition, we provide several access facilities (browser for diseases and symptoms, factor analyses, etc.) to support all procedural knowledge concerning medical decision making. It turns out that our initial chosen representation schema, namely object-oriented design has to be extended with rules (section 3.1). For implementation, the knowledge has been mapped to relations and horn clauses of PROLOG-DB, a relational data base management system providing an interface to Prolog. Thus, diagnostic strategies (represented by clauses) can immediately be applied to facts from the knowledge base (section 3.2).

Terminology. In order to avoid misunderstandings and ambiguities we have to clarify some medical terms. We give definitions according to [19]:

- A *disease* denotes all factors of an illness, including its course, etio-, morphology, etc., which are interpreted as an entity with more or less typical signs (symptoms).

- A *diagnosis* denotes a disease according to its nosology. A diagnosis concerns always a certain status (in contrast to a disease).

- *Diagnostics* covers all steps of identifying a final diagnosis on which treatment can be based.

- *Factors* are medical terms which describe and categorize diagnoses, examination or treatments, e.g. topography, morphology or etiology.

- An *examination* is every procedure, which can help to recognize a disease or a finding.

- A *symptom* is a sign of illness and can be identified by physical examination. All other signs, e.g. results of invasive examinations, are not considered to be symptoms.

EVALUATING PREVIOUS APPROACHES

In this section we review representation mechanisms which have been used for the development of medical knowledge bases. Due to the limited amount of space we can only sketch the main results of our review. For a detailed review of previous approaches the interested reader is referred to [7].

Most of our investigated approaches (Figure 1) pursued the goal to assist physicians and/or medical specialists in finding a diagnosis within a *limited medical problem domain*. Basically,

- different methods for knowledge representation have been used: rules (e.g. MYCIN [3]), objects (e.g. MEDAS [2]) or a combination of methods (e.g. RX [15]).

- several problem domains have been addressed: glaucoma diagnostics (CASNET [17]), rheumatology (RX [15], AI/REUM from EXPERT [12]), cancer (ONCOCIN [16]), and electrolytic systems ABEL [17].

Most of the investigated approaches introduced a concept for for hierarchical structuring of diagnoses (e.g. INTERNIST-1). Some of them concluded to structure also findings hierarchically, according to their degree of abstraction, e.g. MEDAS. Nearly all of them supported medical decision making by defining relationships between diseases and symptoms. A minor part of the mentioned approaches have been focused on general principles of knowledge-based diagnosis, e.g. Patrec, MDX [4, 22], LITO-2 [6]. Few approaches have taken into account the representation of therapeutic and diagnostic procedures, e.g, KSDS. As illustrated in Figure 1 systems like CADUCEUS and KSDS can be considered to provide the most comprehensive features for case-independent knowledge representation.

INTERNIST-1 [14] has been one of the first systems being used for diagnostics (in the field of internal medicine). It handles findings and diseases which are structured hierarchically according to their nosology (i.e. pathology). Diseases and findings are related by two different types of relationship: an *evoking strength* determines how "strong" the appearance of the disease can be assumed if the finding appears. Furthermore, the *frequency* of findings is specified. It is the inverse to the evoking strength. Finally, for each disease a profile comprising all possible findings is created. CADUCEUS [18, 17] succeeded INTERNIST-1 by enlarging the hierarchical structure for diagnoses. Diseases are ordered according to several factors (etiology, biological systems, etc). Causal links have been added to represent pathophysiological relationships. Despite this static representation of relationships, the system did not provide more flexible means to handle diagnostic procedures, working hypotheses, or strategies.

In KSDS [10] medical knowledge is organized by several concepts: diseases, groups of diseases, manifestations, diagnostic and therapeutic procedures, and attributes. These concepts correspond to nodes of a semantic network. Thus, a variety of relationships between diseases and manifestations as well as diseases and therapeutic procedures can easily be specified. A node description consists of four parts: a definition part for type description (e.g. diagnosis), a concept part containing the description of the concept (mainly attributes), a relationship part referring to all related nodes, and an explanation part for additional information. Although KSDS provides a rich set of descriptive items, the diagnostician cannot be supported with flexible mechanisms concerning the application of diagnostic strategies.

Thus, we had to develop a schema which combines traditional concepts used for information system design (i.e. providing specific data structures) with an adequate work space for diagnostic procedures (e.g. rules for heuristics).

DESIGN AND IMPLEMENTATION OF *UnPatient*

Since not all relevant diagnostic procedures can be structured by conventional data modelling techniques[2], we tried to identify computable structures, which do not render diagnosis difficult, but structure medical reality accurately.

Knowledge Representation

The evaluation of previous work (section 2) has shown the two key features of all diagnostic support systems: hierarchical structuring of diseases, and defining relationships between diseases and symptoms. By continuing this well established tradition and in order to enhance the flexibility of the knowledge base, we tried to define several hierarchies (e.g. for diagnoses, symptoms, examinations) which elements can be interpreted according to the needs of the diagnosticians.

555

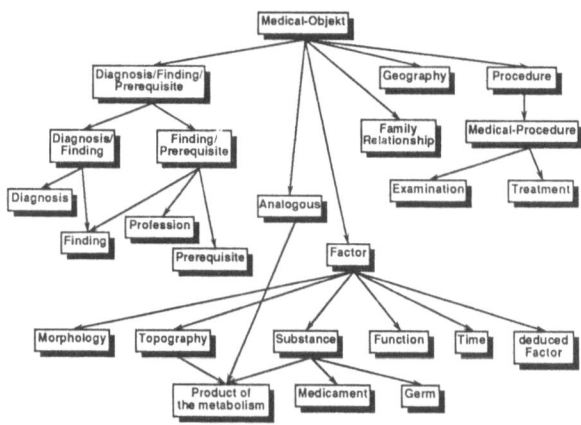

Figure 2: Knowledge Categorization in UnPatient

We decided to base our knowledge representation on objects and classes known from Object-Oriented Programming[3]. Although the object-oriented approach provides the required encapsulation for medical knowledge (e.g. certain parts of the organism can only be inspected by certain methods), we will have to extend this approach by a directly accessible control mechanism for the objects.

Figure 2 shows the most important part of our developed class hierarchy. It has been designed for the multiple interpretation of medical terms by diagnosticians. For instance, icterus, an ambiguous term in medical diagnostics, can appear as some kind of disease or as a finding. Such cases can be handled by multiple inheritance. The diagnostician is supported in his/her interpretation of medical terms according to the current diagnostic context, e.g. for the evaluation of differential diagnoses 'icterus' will be interpreted as a disease.

The most general class is denoted 'medical object'. The diagnostician is mainly concerned with the following subclasses: 'diagnosis/finding/prerequisite', 'factor', and 'procedure'. Whenever a symptom has to be evaluated, its status has to be clarified by analyzing medical facts represented by objects of the classes 'diagnosis', 'finding', and 'prerequisite'. If additional procedures for examination have to be performed, attributes of the class 'examination' are concerned. If procedures for treatment are concerned, objects of 'treatment' will be activated.

Figure 3 exemplifies a part of the representation of 'Hepatitis B'. Attributes and their values are illustrated by ellipses, whereas classes and objects are represented by rectangles. Arcs running into one direction denote the relationships between classes (as in Figure 2) and their instances, e.g. 'jaundice' is-a 'finding'. They are also used to demonstrate relationships between objects or classes and their attributes, e.g 'type of treatment'. Bidirectional arcs denote non-hierarchical relationships between classes , e.g. 'diagnosis/finding' and 'treatment of diagnosis/finding'.

Diagnostic Support by Means of Attributes. In order to support the diagnostician, diagnoses are not only described by conventional attributes like SNOMED-Codes (for factor classification) but also by the following attributes which turned out to be extremely helpful in daily diagnostic routines [9]:

[3]Object-oriented modeling allows to map medical objects like diseases or symptoms to computable structures: Properties (a number of attributes) and methods are associated with each object. Classes are sets of similar objects. In a class hierarchy, objects of superior classes inherit properties and methods to objects of classes below. Dynamic behaviour is supported by message exchange between objects to activate methods (e.g. diagnostic procedures).

- **Phase.** The course of a disease can be described by certain phases. According to its phase different symptoms may occur which have to be evaluated to exclude differential diagnoses.

- **Early Diagnosis Indicator.** In some cases, e.g. cancer, particular treatments may help to prevent spreading or extended damages of the organism. This indicator provides

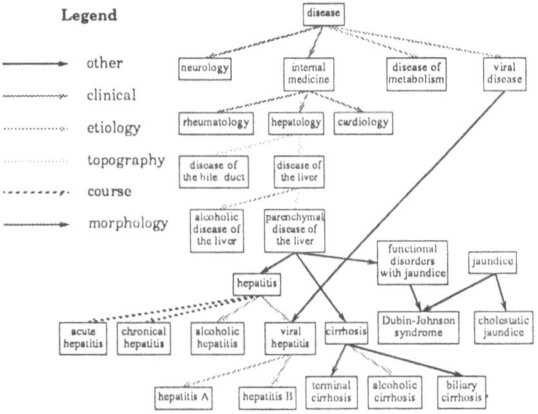

Figure 4: Relating Diagnoses and Findings

methods for prevention of worst cases, if such information is available.

- **Final Diagnosis Indicator.** This indicator tells the user of the knowledge base, whether the current diagnosis is a final one which cannot be refined for further diagnostic purposes (e.g. Hepatitis B). If the current diagnosis is not a final on, the diagnostician has to proceed with subclasses of the diagnoses' hierarchy (e.g. in the case of liver disease).

Factors like topography are primarily attached to findings. Usually, findings are results from examinations. Factors support the diagnosticians in providing several points of view to a finding. By following etiological or morphological differences of diagnoses the exclusion or the proof of hypotheses can be facilitated.

Diagnostic Support by Means of Relationships. In order to correlate symptoms to diseases we developed a particular structure, the 'disease-finding-graph'. Its nodes correspond to diagnoses and findings – as indicated in Figure 3 – by an instantiation of the class 'diagnosis-finding-relation', namely 'jaundice is a finding of hepatitis B'.

Figure 4 exemplifies the main relationships which have been defined between classes to support the diagnostic process: clinical, etiological, topographical, course and morphological relationships. For instance, 'Hepatitis B' is a parenchymal disease of the liver according to its *clinical* relation. It can be 'acute' or 'chronical' according to its *course.* 'Hepatitis B' is a viral disease according to its *etiology,* a.s.f. Such a comprehensive analysis can be performed for each finding and/or diagnosis whenever results of factor analyses are available.

Moreover, to exclude or prove certain diagnoses, the diagnostician can rely on the following relationships, which correlate findings and diseases:

- **Exclusion.** If an excluding finding has been found in the course of examinations concerning a particular disease, the current diagnosis can be excluded.

Class Level

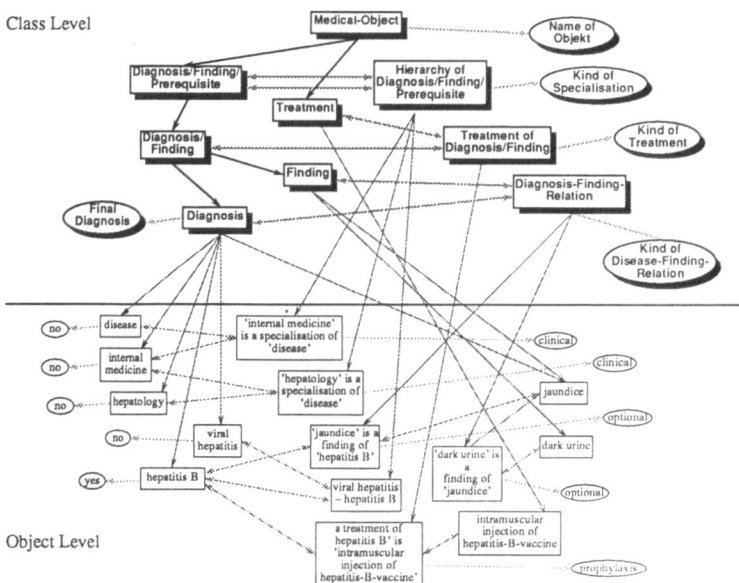

Object Level

Figure 3: Exemplified Instances

- *Obligation*. If a finding is marked to be mandatory for a disease, it has to become evident in the course of the investigated diagnosis.

- *Proof*. If a proven finding can be found in the evaluation of a diagnosis, the current diagnosis can be considered to be the ultimative result of the diagnostic procedure.

There are a lot more relationships and attributes like indicator-contra indicator, exclusive finding, probability, succeeding examination, and treatment, which could not be addressed here, and are innovations for diagnostic support. For a detailed discussion the interested reader is referred to [9] and [7].

Diagnostic Support by Means of Rules. Although object-oriented design supports data and control encapsulation, we can identify cases of medical decision making which cannot be handled by objects exclusively:

- Most of the diagnoses include constellations of findings, which cannot be described comprehensively by attributes and correlated methods:

    - To evaluate a diagnosis, e.g. breast cancer, specific relationships which are no built-in relationships, e.g. 'female ancestors', have to be prepared.

    - Particular constellations of symptoms can require to represent changes of values of attributes in the course of the disease. These values have not been covered by the initial acquisition process.

    - If constellations of new attributes, e.g., 'geographical location' and 'size of malignant melanoma' are considered to be relevant, they have to be formulated by additional means before a new relationship-class can be introduced.

    - If objects contain some composed items which follow particular rules for computation, we need a mechanism to formulate and update conditions and actions.

    - If temporal constraints appear which cannot be specified by message passing, additional control mechanisms are required, e.g. 'SGOP/SGPT can only be computed after all blood examinations have been completed'.

In order to meet the requirements listed above and in order to minimize efforts of updates concerning generic knowledge like classes, we introduced rules. Due to their structure and variety of applicability, rules are able to cover all properties, prerequisites, and relationships which are only valid under certain circumstances.

- In the development of diagnostic strategies, the diagnostician has to be supported to express newly acquired (meta-)knowledge. Rules provide this kind of support. The diagnostician is able to combine attributes from predefined objects to new structures and integrate them into new algorithms for computation. Moreover, temporal constraints concerning methods can be re-ordered and tested to develop alternative diagnostic strategies.

To generate complex rules, elements of the condition and the action part (i.e. findings, prerequisites, diagnoses, etc.) can be combined by the operators "and", "or" and "extra", where "extra" is used for identifying a valuation. For example, "Transaminases raised" is a combination of "SGOT raised" and "SGPT raised" - thus "Transaminases raised strongly" subsumes the increased SGOT and SGPT.

System Behaviour and Implementation

UnPatient provides a direct manipulation interface which supports the retrieval, acquisition, and updates of the entire medical knowledge. The diagnostician is able to browse the class hierarchy as well as its instances. In particular, the disease-finding-graph supports the explanation of correlations which have to be explicit for the evaluation of hypotheses.

In addition, the diagnostician can execute rules which process attributes of values retrieved from the stored objects. To accumulate and test diagnostic strategies he/she may formulate heuristics. Thus, he/she can contribute to a steady improvement of the quality of the knowledge.

UnPatient has been implemented in Prolog-DB, which allows to combine all pro's of logic programming and processing of knowledge stored in data base management systems [8]. Prolog-DB is based on a relational data base management system (db++) and Prolog. The entire object hierarchy has been mapped to db++-relations. The knowledge which has not been covered by the class definition has been represented by Prolog-clauses. Prolog-DB processes meta-rules with data from relations and results from database queries.

Relations. For example, the relation 'diagnosis-finding-graph (Diagnosis/finding, Subordered-diagnosis/finding, Type-of-sub-ordering)' represents the diagnosis-finding-graph. It contains the name of the medical term, one or more reference to sub-terms, and the type of relationship to the referred medical term, e.g., its succeeding element in the object hierarchy (if available) according to clinical criteria.

Relations which do not have to represent inherent features of object-oriented design (like the one above), comprise a more or less long list of attributes which may be handled by rules. For instance, the risk of performing a procedure is defined by the relation 'risk (Procedure, Topography, Substance, Valuation-Interval, Time, Result-Type, Frequency)'.

Rules are defined within the Prolog part of Prolog-DB. Thus, it is possible to embed static knowledge represented by relations into clauses which can also contain heuristics for diagnostics. If new information can be deduced from existing knowledge or new knowledge has been accumulated it can be represented by rules, too.

By introducing meta-levels, the diagnostician can map strategic knowledge concerning additional constraints and restrictions to control the execution of the derived knowledge.

CONCLUSION AND FUTURE RESEARCH

Since medical diagnostic support has to be based on more comprehensive knowledge bases than usually provided by applications designed for restricted problem domains, we introduced a concept for diagnostic problem domain- and case-independent information structuring. Moreover, it provides active support for the diagnostician to accumulate individual knowledge and to test diagnostic hypothesis.

Since encapsulation supports hierarchical structuring and explicit control of relationships, we decided to base the information system on object-oriented design techniques. To cover particular constraints concerning attributes and relationships, we had to extend it by rules. As an implication we had to use a hybrid knowledge representation language for implementation. Thus, the knowledge is mapped to relations and clauses of PROLOG-DB, a relational data base management system providing an interface to Prolog. Diagnostic strategies (represented by clauses) can immediately be applied to facts from the knowledge base.

Upcoming architectural questions concern the redesign of the user interface. The information system can not only support diagnosticians, but also provides the capability to support teachers and students in medicine, general practitioners, specialists and scientists. Moreover, the management of synonyma has been provided conceptually but has not been implemented up to now. Finally, we have to test the application's capability in complex diagnostic domains like malignant melanoma diagnosis [1, 21], where several diagnostic strategies have to be executed concurrently.

References

[1] Adolf, W.; Kokoschka, E.M.; Stary, Ch.: The Prospective Index Revisited (in German), in: Akt. Dermatologie, Vol. 14, No.6, pp. 151-153, June 1988.

[2] Ben-Bassat, M.: The Role of Expert Systems in Clinical Diagnosis: A Conceptual Model; in The 4th Jerusalem Conference in Information Technology; Tel Aviv University, University of California, IEEE, pp. 632-644; 1984.

[3] Buchanan B.G., Shortliffe E.H. (eds.); The MYCIN Experiments of the Stanford Heuristic Programming Project; Addison-Wesley Publishing Company, Inc.; 1985.

[4] B. Chandrasekaran, Jon Sticklen; Patrec: A Knowledge-Directed Database for a Diagnostic Expert System; in Computer, Vol. 17, No. 8, 1984.

[5] E. Charniak, D. McDermott; Introduction to Artificial Intelligence; Addison-Wesley Publishing Company, Inc.; 1985.

[6] C. Cravetto, L. Lesmo, R. Massa Rolandino, G. Molino, P. (LITO 2); in Proceedings of the 9th International Joint Conference on Artificial Intelligence, Vancouver, British Columbia, pp. 330-334, 1985.

[7] K. Fasching, Knowledge Acquisition and Representation for a Medical Knowledge Base; Master Thesis, Department of Applied Computer Science, Technical University of Vienna, 1990 (in German).

[8] G. Fleischanderl; PROLOG-DB - Pre-Compiler, User Manual, Version 1.0; Technical University of Vienna, Department for Applied Computer Science; 1987.

[9] W. Horak, E. Neuhold, Ch. Stary; Implementing A Medical Knowledge Base, A Feasible Study; Technical Report TR 25. 148, IBM-Laboratory Vienna, Austria, 1988.

[10] W. Horn, W. Buchstaller, R. Trappl; Knowledge Structure Definition for an Expert System in Primary Medical Care; in Proceedings of the 7th International Joint Conference on Artificial Intelligence, Vancouver, Canada, pp. 850-852; 1981.

[11] W. Kim, F. H. Lochovsky (Editors); Object-Oriented Concepts, Databases and Applications; Computer Systems Research Institute, Department of Computer Science, University of Toronto; 1989.

[12] L. C. Kingsland III; The Evaluation of Medical Expert Systems: Experience with the AI/RHEUM Knowledge-based Consultant System in Rheumatology; in Proceedings of the 9th International Joint Conference on Artificial Intelligence, Vancouver, British Columbia, pp. 292-295; 1985.

[13] R. A. Miller, H. E. Pople, Jr., Jack D. Myers; INTERNIST-1, an Experimental Computer-Based Diagnostic Consultant for General Internal Medicine; in The new England Journal of Medicine, pp. 468-476; 1982.

[14] Miller, R.A.: INTERNIST/CADUCEUS: Problem Facing Expert Consultant Programs, in: Meth. Inform. Med., Vol. 23, No. 1, 1984.

[15] P. L. Miller, P. R. Fisher; Causal Models in Medical Artificial Intelligence; in Proceedings of the 11th Annual Symposium on Computer Applications in Medical Care, IEEE, Washington D. C., pp. 17-22; 1987.

558

[16] M. Musen, D. M. Combs, J.D. Walton, E.H. Shortliffe, L.M. Fagan; OPAL: Toward the Computer-Aided Design of Oncology Advice System; in Proceedings of the 10th Annual Symposium on Computer Applications in Medical Care, IEEE, pp. 43-52, 1986.

[17] R.S. Patil, O. Senyk; Efficient Structuring of Composite Causal Hypotheses in Medical Diagnosis; in Proceedings of the 11th Annual Symposium on Computer Applications in Medical Care, IEEE, Washington D. C., pp. 23- 29; 1987.

[18] Harry E. Pople, Jr.; Heuristic Methods for Imposing Structure on Ill-Structured Problems: The Structuring of Medical Diagnostics; in Szolovitz P., ed. Artificial Intelligence in Medicine, Westview Press, pp. 119-190; 1982.

[19] ROCHE-Dictionary of Medicine; ed.: Hoffmann-La Roche-AG; Urban & Schwarzenberg, Munich; 1987 (in German).

[20] Singer, J.; Sacks, H.S.; Lucente, F.; Chalmers, T.C.: Physician Attitudes towards Applications of Computer Data Base Systems, in: JAMA, Vol. 259, pp. 1610-1614, 1983.

[21] Stary, Ch.; Adolf, W.: Computer - Supported Therapy Decision Making for the Malignant Melanoma of the Skin (in German), in: GI Informatik-Fachberichte, Vol. 127, eds.: Hommel, G.; Schindler, S., pp. 482-496, Springer, Berlin, October 1986.

[22] Gio Wiederhold, Robert L. Blum, Michael Walker; An Integration of Knowledge and Data Representation; in On Knowledge Base Management Systems: Integration Artificial Intelligence and Database Technologies, Brodie, Mylopolous and Schmidt (Eds.), Springer; 1986.

Symbolic computation in **RL/1**

S. van Denneheuvel   K. L. Kwast   P. van Emde Boas
Department of Mathematics and Computer Science
University of Amsterdam

F. de Geus   E. Rotterdam
Department of Medical Information Science
University of Groningen

Abstract

This article discusses the use of **RL/1** to build quantitative models and the application of these models to assist in decision making. A set of constraints constitutes a model. Constraint models can be extended and modified easily and the representation of model knowledge is separated from its use. The model knowledge is used by means of a constraint solver. This allows the application of the same knowledge for different purposes. In addition the knowledge representation allows the user to analyze relationships between variables and to infer new relationships that hold in special circumstances.

1 The rule language family RL

Recently, systems have emerged that allow declarative constraint processing (see for example Mathematica [9], Bertrand [5] and **CLP** [3]). Declarative constraint processing is also pursued in the rule language family **RL** (see [6], [7] and [8]), where knowledge can be represented in three different types of rules: *tabular rules*, *clauses* and *constraints*. Corresponding to these types of rules there are three areas of technology that support that style of knowledge processing in isolation: database systems, logic programming systems, and spreadsheets. The main goal of **RL** is to integrate these three technologies in one knowledge base system. In the current prototype **RL/1** we focus on the integration of a constraint solving subsystem with a relational database system; the associated language **RL/1** was presented previously at this conference [2]. All examples presented in this paper were processed successfully by this **RL/1** prototype.

In **RL/1** a distinction is made between *extensional* objects and *intensional* objects. Extensional objects correspond to base tables in the underlying relational database. Intensional objects are objects whose relations can be materialized by evaluation of their definition. An intensional object is defined by one or more *rules*, alternatively called clauses. A rule typically consists of a *rule head* and a *rule expression* separated by the keyword WHEN. The rule expression contains system defined primitives or invocations of intensional and extensional objects, separated by the conjunctive AND operator. Defining an intensional object with several rules expresses *disjunction* between the rules.

Queries in **RL/1** result in an answer relation which consists of attributes and a (possibly empty) set of tuples. Optionally the result of a query can be stored in an extensional table object (cf. [2]):

```
INFER ( attribute-list ) WHEN
    rule-exp [ TO table ]
```

The INFER query yields an answer relation with attributes equal to the attribute list between the INFER and WHEN keywords. The processing of queries requires one or more invocations of the constraint solver. The solver output is used to compile the query into a database request. Symbolic queries work by presenting this intermediate solver output to the user directly. They have the following format:

```
SYMINFER ( attribute-list ) WHEN
    rule-exp [ TO file ]
```

With the 'TO file' option the computed symbolic answer can be stored in a text file. Symbolic query commands produce the following answer:

```
con= Condition set
sol= Solution set
```

The solution set contains elements of the form $x = t$ with x a *wanted variable* and t a term. Wanted variables are variables that are to be eliminated from the constraint set. The condition part states under what additional restrictions the obtained solution is valid. The main goal of the constraint solver is to express the wanted variables in terms of *known variables*. Known variables are determined

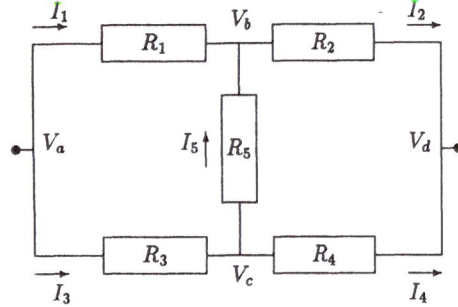

Figure 1: The bridge of Wheatstone

```
module wheatstone(number:v:i:r:va:vb:vc:
    vd:ve:i1:i2:i3:i4:i5:r1:r2:r3:r4:r5).
clause ohmlaw(v,i,r) when v=i*r.
clause circuit(va,vb,vc,vd,i1,i2,i3,i4,i5,
    r1,r2,r3,r4,r5) when
  ohmlaw(va-vb,i1,r1)
  and ohmlaw(va-vc,i3,r3)
  and ohmlaw(vc-vd,i4,r4)
  and ohmlaw(vb-vd,i2,r2)
  and ohmlaw(vc-vb,i5,r5)
  and i1+i5=i2
  and i4+i5=i3.
```

Figure 2: Representation in **RL/1**

by the rule expression of the query and wanted variables by the attribute list of the query. The capability to produce symbolic output is an important feature of the **RL/1** knowledge base system. It allows the user to analyze relationships between variables and to infer new relationships that hold in special circumstances.

2 Symbolic computation

Intensional objects are declarative representations of knowledge; therefore it is not known beforehand how the attributes of an object are invoked. As an application in the domain of electronics consider the circuit given in Figure 1 and its **RL/1** representation in Figure 2. In ancient history the bridge of Wheatstone was used to measure ohm resistance. In the setup, r_1 (or r_2) is a variable resistor and r_4 (or r_3) the unknown resistor. The component in the center is an ampere meter with resistance r_5. For the determination of the unknown resistor the variable resistor is adjusted so that no current flows through r_5. In this balanced state it can be shown that the Wheatstone relationship holds:

$$r_1/r_2 = r_3/r_4$$

To see if theory matches reality we apply 10 volt at the clamps of the circuit. When the values of all resistors are 200 ohm, the circuit should be in balanced state and as a consequence no current i_5 should flow through r_5 which indeed turns out to be the case:

```
infer(vb,vc,i1,i2,i5) when circuit(10,vb,vc,0,
    i1,i2,i3,i4,i5,200,200,200,200,200)
```

vb	vc	i1	i2	i5
5.000	5.000	0.025	0.025	0

If one of the resistors, say r_1, is taken unequal to the others, a small positive current flows through the center resistor:

```
infer(vb,vc,i1,i2,i5) when circuit(10,vb,vc,0,
    i1,i2,i3,i4,i5,400,200,200,200,200)
```

vb	vc	i1	i2	i5
3.846	4.615	0.015	0.019	0.003

Setting r_2 instead of r_1 to 400 ohm results in a negative current through the center resistor, as expected:

```
infer(vb,vc,i1,i2,i5) when circuit(10,vb,vc,0,
    i1,i2,i3,i4,i5,200,400,200,200,200)
```

vb	vc	i1	i2	i5
6.153	5.384	0.019	0.015	-0.003

As mentioned before, the constraint solver tries to eliminate wanted variables from the constraint set and all wanted variables are returned in the solution set. The solver also produces a condition set with expressions that only contain known variables. A *reduced model* of the circuit can be inferred by giving particular values for all resistors of the circuit. To obtain the reduced model the variables r_1, r_2, r_3, r_4 and r_5 are made wanted and all other variables known. The values of the resistors are presented to the solver in equations. The wanted variables are returned directly in the solution set and the condition set contains the reduced model for the circuit with the substituted resistor values (the '(*)' notation expands to all attributes of the involved object):

```
syminfer(r1,r2,r3,r4,r5) when circuit(*)
    and known9(va,vb,vc,vd,i1,i2,i3,i4,i5)
    and r1=200 and r2=200 and r3=200
    and r4=200 and r5=200
con=  -i3 + i4 + i5 = 0,
      i1 - i2 + i5 = 0,
      -200 * i5 - vb + vc = 0,
      200 * i2 - vb + vd = 0,
      200 * i4 - vc + vd = 0,
      200 * i3 - va + vc = 0,
      200 * i1 - va + vb = 0
sol=  r1=200,r2=200,r3=200,r4=200,r5=200
```

Since the clamps v_a and v_d are inputs of the circuit it should be possible, in the above reduced model where values are given for all resistors, to express all variables of the circuit in terms of v_a and v_d. The solver is actively directed towards this goal by making only v_a and v_d known:

```
syminfer(vb,vc,i1,i2,i3,i4,i5) when
   circuit(va,vb,vc,vd,i1,i2,i3,i4,i5,
      200,200,200,200,200)
   and known2(va,vd).
sol=  vb = 0.50000 * va + 0.50000 * vd,
      vc = 0.50000 * va + 0.50000 * vd,
      i1 = 0.00250 * va - 0.00250 * vd,
      i2 = 0.00250 * va - 0.00250 * vd,
      i3 = 0.00250 * va - 0.00250 * vd,
      i4 = 0.00250 * va - 0.00250 * vd,
      i5 = 0
```

Note that since the variables r_1, r_2, r_3, r_4 and r_5 do not appear in the query, their solution is not present in the symbolic output as in the previous query. Instead the values for the resistors were specified directly in the invocation of the object *circuit*. If one of the resistors is taken unequal, the reduced model is no longer symmetric:

```
syminfer(vb,vc,i1,i2,i3,i4,i5) when
   circuit(va,vb,vc,vd,i1,i2,i3,i4,i5,
      400,200,200,200,200)
   and known2(va,vd).
sol=  vb = 0.38461 * va + 0.61538 * vd,
      vc = 0.46153 * va + 0.53846 * vd,
      i1 = 0.00153 * va - 0.00153 * vd,
      i2 = 0.00192 * va - 0.00192 * vd,
      i3 = 0.00269 * va - 0.00269 * vd,
      i4 = 0.00230 * va - 0.00230 * vd,
      i5 = 0.00038 * va - 0.00038 * vd
```

It might be quite interesting to see if the Wheatstone relationship for r_4 can be inferred symbolically from the represented knowledge under the assumption that the circuit is in balanced state. This assumption yields a reduced model. We want to express r_4 in terms of r_1, r_2 and r_3 so these latter variables are specified as knowns and r_4 is specified as the only wanted variable. As an extra constraint we know that since the circuit is in balanced state no current flows through r_5:

```
syminfer(r4) when circuit(*) and i5=0
   and known3(r1,r2,r3).
sol=  r4=r2*r3/r1
```

To obtain this answer, the solver had to process the following constraint set:

$$v_a - v_b = i_1 * r_1, \ v_a - v_c = i_3 * r_3, \ v_c - v_d = i_4 * r_4,$$
$$v_b - v_d = i_2 * r_2, \ v_c - v_b = i_5 * r_5,$$
$$i_1 + i_5 = i_2, \ i_4 + i_5 = i_3, \ i_5 = 0$$

These equations are nonlinear by the occurrences of the terms $i_1 * r_1$, $i_2 * r_2$, $i_3 * r_3$, $i_4 * r_4$ and $i_5 * r_5$ (note that the known variables r_1, r_2 and r_3 are in fact not given as

a value and therefore contribute to the nonlinearity of the constraint system). Quick observation of the constraint set shows a total count of 14 variables of which 3 variables are known and the remaining 11 are unknown. There are 8 equations to express unknown variables in terms of known variables. A simple calculation predicts that we might eliminate 8 unknown variables by using the 8 equations and as a consequence we are left with $3 \ (= 11-8)$ unknown variables that can *not* be expressed in terms of known variables. Our hope is that r_4 is among the variables that can be expressed in terms of the known variables. In fact as we know from elementary physics, r_4 is the only variable that can be expressed in r_1, r_2 and r_3 [1].

3 A medical application

This section describes a physiological model of the human blood circulation and gas exchange. It is a simple model and therefore a poor reflection of reality, but it serves well to demonstrate how a model represented in constraints can be used for decision support in medicine. Variable names used in the model are abbreviated according to medical convention. A summary of the properties of the variables used is shown in Figure 4. The model consists of eleven equations; 6 describe the systemic and pulmonary circulation and the remaining 5 the gas exchange. Each model equation is presented together with some explanatory text. Figure 3 shows a graph representation of the model.

1. $VV = KV \times \ln(CVP)$
   A higher or lower venous volume (VV) results in a higher or lower central venous pressure (CVP). When VV gets larger, the veins are stretched and resist further filling. The above formula is derived from the assumption that the change in CVP due to a change in VV, is proportional to CVP: $\delta CVP / \delta VV \simeq CVP$.

2. $SV = KR \times \ln(CVP)$
   For the right side of the heart a similar formula can be assumed for the relationship between the stroke volume (SV) and the CVP. This formula has been chosen to keep the model simple. In reality the stroke volume increases initially, but it decreases again above a certain level of the central venous pressure. This relationship is known as the Starling curve.

3. $SV = KL \times \ln(PLA)$
   This relationship is the equivalent for the left side of the heart.

4. $PArtM - CVP = CO \times SVR$
   Ohm's law for the systemic circulation. The pressure difference between the mean arterial pressure

---

[1] As a comparison we ran this problem on a Mathematica system. After 91 seconds the system responded with a formula consisting of 15 subcases, none of which contained the desired relationship $r_4 = r_2 * r_3 / r_1$. The **RL/1** system computed the result in 7 seconds.

562

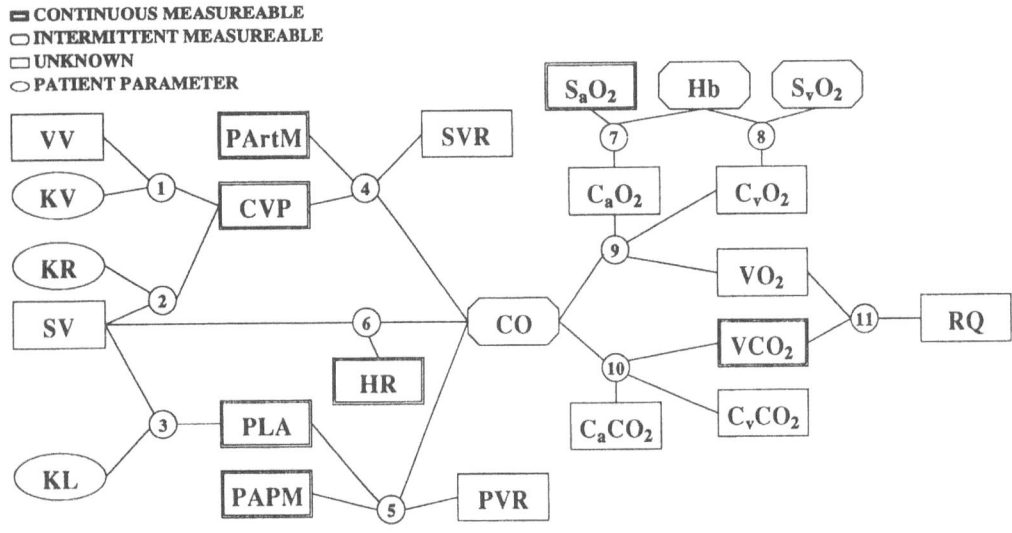

Figure 3: Graph representation of the model

(PArtM) and the CVP is equal to the cardiac output (CO) multiplied by the systemic vascular resistance (SVR).

5. $PAPM - PLA = CO \times PVR$

The equivalent relationship for the pulmonary circulation.

6. $CO = SV \times HR$

The CO is the volume of one heart stroke multiplied by the heart rate (HR).

7. $CaO_2 = 0.000134 \times Hb \times SaO_2$

The arterial oxygen concentration (CaO_2) is proportional to the haemoglobin concentration (Hb) multiplied by the fractional arterial oxygen saturation (SaO_2). The constant 0.000134 is in dl/g.

8. $CvO_2 = 0.000134 \times Hb \times SvO_2$

The equivalent relationship for the venous system.

9. $\dot{V}O_2 = (CaO_2 - CvO_2) \times CO$

The oxygen intake per minute ($\dot{V}O_2$) is equal to the difference in oxygen concentration between the arterial and the mixed venous blood multiplied by the CO.

10. $\dot{V}CO_2 = (CvCO_2 - CaCO_2) \times CO$

The expired carbon dioxide production per minute ($\dot{V}CO_2$) is supposed to be the difference in carbon dioxide concentration between the venous and arterial blood multiplied by the CO.

11. $RQ = \dfrac{\dot{V}CO_2}{\dot{V}O_2}$

The respiratory quotient (RQ) is defined as $\dot{V}CO_2$ divided by $\dot{V}O_2$. When no changes take place in the total body content of carbon dioxide, it has a constant value of 0.8, since the metabolic rate of oxygen used is proportional to the quantity of carbon dioxide produced.

4 Representation of the model

The physiological model is represented in **RL/1** by a single rule defining the intensional object s as shown in Figure 5. The '*' notation in the head of a rule indicates that all variables occurring in the associated rule expression are declared as attributes.

This section discusses two ways in which a physiological constraint model can be used to assist anaesthetists in decision making: (1) the interpretation of measurements, and (2) the prediction of effects of treatment.

The anaesthetist tries to gain insight in the development of the physiological condition of a patient by monitoring the trend of physiological variables. Unfortunately not all variables can be measured. A physiological model, like the one in Figure 5, can be used to derive values for non measurable variables from the ones measured.

The number of physiological variables which can be measured has increased over the past few decades. This development has raised a demand for computer systems that present all measured information in a coherent way (see e.g. [1] and [4]). The rapid development of new mea-

Abbreviation	units^a value	Name
CO	ml/min	Cardiac Output
CVP	mmHg	Central Venous Pressure
CaCO$_2$	ml/ml	Arterial CO$_2$ Concentration
CaO$_2$	ml/ml	Arterial O$_2$ Concentration
CvCO$_2$	ml/ml	Venous CO$_2$ Concentration
CvO$_2$	ml/ml	Venous O$_2$ Concentration
HR	B/min	Heart Rate
Hb	gr/dl	Haemoglobin concentration
KL	mmHg/ml	Left Heart parameter
KR	mmHg/ml	Right Heart parameter
KV	mmHg/ml	Venous system parameter
PAPM	mmHg	Mean Pulmonary Arterial Pressure
PArtM	mmHg	Mean Arterial Pressure
PLA	mmHg	Left Atrium Pressure
PVR	$\frac{mmHg}{(ml/min)}$	Pulmonary Vascular Resistance
RQ	—	Respiratory Quotient
SaO$_2$	%	Arterial O$_2$ saturation
SvO$_2$	%	Venous O$_2$ saturation
SV	ml	Stroke Volume
SVR	$\frac{mmHg}{(ml/min)}$	Systemic Vascular Resistance
$\dot{V}CO_2$	ml/min	Expiratory CO$_2$ Rate
$\dot{V}O_2$	ml/min	Inspiratory O$_2$ Rate
VV	ml	Venous Volume

Figure 4: Properties of model variables

---

^{a}mmHg = millimeter mercury, B = beats

surement equipment also requires that a computer system is adaptable to new measurement possibilities. Clearly this requirement is met by a declaratively represented model.

In our model physiological variables can be divided into four classes.

1. Continuously measurable variables: in the University Hospital of Groningen a computer system on the theatre stores average values for these variables at 1 minute intervals [4]. These sets of values can be used as input for interpretation.

2. Intermittently measurable variables: values of these variables can not be automatically measured, and the measurement methods available demand extra attention of the anaesthetist. They are therefore performed only when necessary. To determine bloodgasses for example, a sample of blood has to be taken. The time to analyze a blood sample in the laboratory averages to 18 minutes. Another example is cardiac output CO, which is measured by injecting cold fluid into the blood stream. This introduces extra volume and can therefore only be done a few times during an operation.

3. Patient parameters: variables whose values are characteristic for a particular patient and change so slowly

```
module phsystem(number:CaO2:CaCO2:CvCO2:
    CvO2:CO:CVP:HR:KL:KR:KV:PAPM:PArtM:PLA:
    PVR:RQ:Hb:SaO2:SvO2:SV:SVR:VCO2:VO2:VV).
table continuous(PArtM,CVP,PLA,PAPM,HR,
    SaO2,VCO2).
table intermittent(CO,Hb,SvO2).
table patient(KV,KR,KL).
table unknown(VV,SV,SVR,PVR,CaO2,CaCO2,
    CvO2,VO2,CvCO2,RQ).
clause s(*) when
/* 1*/    VV=KV*ln(CVP)
/* 2*/    and SV=KR*ln(CVP)
/* 3*/    and SV=KL*ln(PLA)
/* 4*/    and PArtM-CVP=CO*SVR
/* 5*/    and APM-PLA=CO*PVR
/* 6*/    and CO=SV*HR
/* 7*/    and CaO2=0.0001134*Hb*SaO2
/* 8*/    and CvO2=0.0001134*Hb*SvO2
/* 9*/    and VO2=(CaO2-CvO2)*CO
/*10*/    and VCO2=(CvCO2-CaCO2)*CO
/*11*/    and RQ=VCO2/CO2.
close.
```

Figure 5: The physiological model in **RL/1**

that they can be assumed constant with respect to other variables during an operation.

4. Unknown variables: variables that can be neither measured nor assumed to be constant.

In Figure 5 tables are defined to group continuously measurable variables, intermittently measurable variables, patient parameters and unknown variables respectively.

4.1 Interpretation

Anaesthetists are interested in the trend of the cardiac output (CO). An incidental measurement of CO, combined with values for the continuously measurable variables HR, CVP and PLA, determines the patient parameters KR and KL:

```
syminfer(KR,KL) when
  s(*) and CO=5000 and PArtM=72 and CVP=5
  and PLA=17 and PAPM=27
  and HR=72 and SaO2=0.99 and VCO2=200.
sol=  KR = 43.148259 , KL = 24.510842
```

By symbolic computation KR and KL can be expressed directly in terms of continuously measurable variables and CO:

```
syminfer(KR,KL) when s(*) and continuous(*)
  and known1(CO)
sol=  KR = CO * 1 / ln(CVP) * 1 / HR,
      KL = CO * 1 / ln(PLA) * 1 / HR
```

KR and KL are assumed to remain equal to the values computed for them since they are patient parameters. The values for KL and KR are used to construct a *reduced model* from the original one (cf. Section 2). Subsequent measurements for CVP, PLA and HR can be used to compute the CO. As shown below an estimate for the actual CO results.

```
syminfer(CO) when
   s(*) and PArtM=72 and CVP=5 and PLA=17
   and PAPM=27 and HR=72
   and SaO2=0.99 and VCO2=200
   and KR=43 and KL=24.5 and KV=2750
con=  FALSE
sol=  CO = 4997.788344
```

The condition contains FALSE, which indicates that an inconsistency is detected. The cause of this inconsistency can be ascertained by making both the continuously measurable variables and patient parameters known instead of supplying their values as in the previous query:

```
syminfer(CO) when s(*) and continuous(*)
   and patient(*)
con=  KR * ln(CVP) = KL * ln(PLA)
sol=  CO = HR * KL * ln(PLA)
```

The condition between KL, KR, CVP and PLA is not satisfied by the measured values.

4.2 Prediction

As an example of prediction of the effect of a treatment, consider a drug that increases the rigidity of the heart muscle. This results in a decrease of KL and KR. So our question is what the consequences are when KL and KR decrease by say 10%. To describe the qualitative consequences, an increase in variable x is denoted as $x\uparrow$ and a decrease as $x\downarrow$. The qualitative consequences of decreases in KR and KL are known to be $SV\downarrow$, $CO\downarrow$, $HR\uparrow$, $PARTM\downarrow$, $PAPM\downarrow$, $SVR\downarrow$, $PVR\downarrow$, $CVP\downarrow$, $PLA\downarrow$, $CvCO_2\uparrow$, $CvO_2\downarrow$, $SvO_2\downarrow$. As CVP and PLA decrease, the relative decrease in SV will be bigger than in KL and KR.

The quantitative model given is not refined enough to quantify all the changes listed above. Therefore some assumptions have to be made. When it is assumed that the continuously measurable variables keep their actual value, the effects of a 10% decrease in KL and KR are predicted by the following **RL/1** query:

```
syminfer(CO,SV) when
   s(*) and PArtM=72 and PLA=17 and PAPM=27
   and HR=72 and SaO2=0.99 and VCO2=200
   and KR=43*0.9 and KL=24.5*0.9 and KV=2750
sol=  CO = 4498.009505,
      SV = 62.472354
```

5 Conclusion

The language **RL/1** provides a framework in which algebraic constraints can be combined with relational databases. The prototype implementation **RL/1** contains a constraint satisfaction module that generates symbolic solutions, which were used to infer reduced models and analyze relationships between variables.

We used symbolic computation in a medical application to interpret patient measurements, to predict treatment effects and to trace inconsistencies between measurements. Substitution of measured variable values results in a reduced model. When it is assumed that variables of a particular class have kept the values that were last found for them, values of other variables can be inferred using the reduced model.

References

[1] Annejet P. Meyler, *Automation in Anesthesia, a Relief?; evaluation of a data acquisition and display system*, thesis of the university of Eindhoven, The Netherlands, ISBN 90-9001441-1, (1986).

[2] van Denneheuvel, S. & van Emde Boas, P., *The rule language RL/1*, A. M. Tjoa & R. Wagner (eds.), Database and Expert Systems Applications, Proc. of the International Conference, Vienna, Austria, Aug 1990, Springer Verlag Wien, 381-387, (1990).

[3] Jaffar, J. & Michaylov, S., *Methodology and Implementation of a CLP System*, Logic Programming, Proc. of the Fourth Int. Conf., Ed. Jean-Louis Lassez, 196-218, (1987).

[4] Karliczek, G. F., Geus, F. A., Wiersma, G., Oosterhaven, S. & Jenkins, I., *Carola, a computer system for automatic documentation in anesthesia*, Int. J. Clin. Monitoring and Computing 4, 211-221, (1987).

[5] Leler, Wm., *Constraint Programming Languages: Their Specification and Generation*, Addison-Wesly Series in Computer Science, Addison-Wesly, (1988).

[6] Van Emde Boas, P., *RL, a Language for Enhanced Rule Bases Database Processing*, Working Document, Rep IBM Research, RJ 4869 (51299), (1986).

[7] Van Emde Boas, P., *A semantical model for the integration and modularization of rules*, Proceedings MFCS **12**, Bratislava, Springer Lecture Notes in Computer Science **233**, 78-92, (1986).

[8] Van Emde Boas, H. & van Emde Boas, P., *Storing and Evaluating Horn-Clause Rules in a Relational Database*, IBM J. Res. Develop. **30** (1), 80-92, (1986).

[9] Wolfram, S., *Mathematica, A System for Doing Mathematics by Computer*, Addison-Wesly, (1988).

INEKS - an Information System for Medical Application

Roland Zimmerling

University of Oldenburg
Computer Science Department
P.O Box 2503
D-2900 Oldenburg

Abstract

This Paper describes the development of the information system INEKS for the Städtische Kliniken Oldenburg. After building the database with the relational database management system ORACLE and programming of the data input-component by the ORACLE-tool SQL*Forms the main topic of the development is the computer-aided, scientific evaluation of those data sets for research into the area cancer epidemiology (INEKS). Both classical, conventional applications (office automation, statistics) and tools will be developed for relating data pemanent saved in databases to temporal values, so as the researcher involved in medicine are able to verify their hypothesises. All results will be presented graphically by SQL*Graphics.

1 Preface

The increasing use of innovative medical techniques and new diagnostic technologies results in a fast growth in the amount of, above all, formated information and thereby to the necessity of using computer-aided information technology as data basc management systems.

Commercially available and efficient database systems are suitable for a consistent and persistent administration of the incurred information especially in the so-called standard applications (e.g. administration of basic patient data, examination results, sickness developments, and mainly statistical analyses).

Together with a medical partner, the Computer Science Department of Oldenburg University (Section: Information Systems, Prof. Dr. H.-J. Appelrath and Dr. R. Zimmerling) is developing the information system

INEKS *) - Informationssystem für epidemiologische Krebsregister
(information system for epidemiologic cancer register)

for medical applications. The relational database system ORACLE with a number of supplementary software tools is generally applied.

In developing the information system, tools are striven for which ought to make possible

1 user-friendly acquisition and maintenance of data,
2 persistent, consistent, multi-user administration of the well-structured data, equipped with data backup and data protection mechanisms,
3 rationalization of administrative work, as well as
4 an analysis of investigation results to support medical research and the elaboration of diagnosis and therapy.

Efforts for standardization of the medical information system on the one hand, and of the tools on the other hand, shall already receive attention in the developmental stage of the project in order to be able to use the developed concepts, methods and individual software components (possibly after application-specific adaptions) in other medical application spheres as well.

In addition, it is possible for the tools to contribute to medical training since the standardized and ergonomically matured user interfaces are also available for students and can serve the practice of interactive construction, of consistent altering and of intelligent analysis of medical data bases.

*) The Project INEKS are supported financially by the country Niedersachsen

2 Principles for the Development of the Information System

For the project INEKS the database system ORACLE, with the following supplementary software tools, was selected and purchased:
- SQL*Forms
- SQL*ReportWriter
- SQL*Menue
- Pro*C
- SQL*Graphics
- CASE.

In the logical design, the informational requirements of the considered part of the world (here: the medical world) are investigated in a systems analysis, irrespective of the applied data administration technology and described by means of a suitable data model (e.g. entity relationship model).

For the design of the information system the analysis results were described in a report /Appelrath/.

The physical design was carried out with pencil and paper, since at that time the design tool ORACLE*CASE was not yet available. The internal schema of INEKS was verified with the design tool GAMBIT.

GAMBIT is an interactive, graphical tool for the definition of schemas of relational databases (/Zehnder/). It monitors the consistency of the schema and allows the definition of additional transactions. Further, it provides a graphical representation of the defined entity block diagram.

The construction of the database was carried out with the DDL of the ORACLE component SQL*Plus.

The user interface for manual input of data, update and evaluation was implemented for present statistical purposes by means of SQL*Forms. Prefabricated masks in a familiar and comprehensible style are put at the user's dispoal, in which only the relevant data must be filled into the fields of the forms.

The lay-out of the monitor masks is oriented around aspects of contents:
- Related values are combined into components which consist of one or more forms, represent enclosed units as regards content and can be activated from a main menu.

- The order of the input fields for each component depends on the order of creation or the viewing order.

The lay-out of the masks takes into account both industrial standards (VDI norms 5005,1989 and DIN 55234, part 8) and results of ergonomic publications (/Smith/, /Spinas/) about questions of ergonomy. A mask type standardized for the medical database projects was developed (illustration 1).

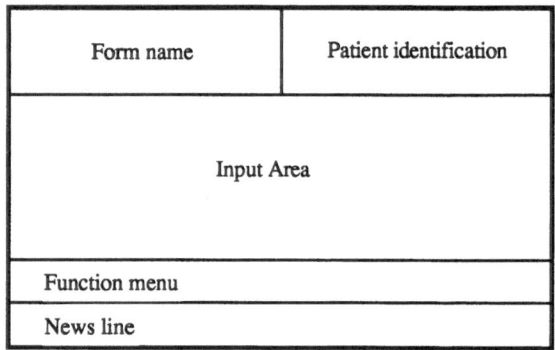

Figure 1: Generally used mask construction

Next to a chiefly alpha-numerical evaluation, graphical illustrations of the results are generated using SQL*Graphics. The necessary procedures are structured project-independently and uniformly to the greatest possible extent to guarantee a wide applicability as well as homogeneity in the lay-out.

3 The Medical Problem

Cancer epidemiology opens new horizons in fighting cancer at a time when - in view of the vital threatenings of the disease and despite some considerable progress - therapeutic efforts have, statistically, hardly any or no effect at all. Sensitive gauges for effects of preventive, diagnostic and therapeutic measurements in fighting cancer diseases are created by uniformly ascertained and therefore comparable registration of data.

In the Federal Republic of Germany, data are available only about cancer mortality. With regard to the incidence of cancer diseases, however, they are only of limited use since next to etiologic factors of the cancer disease, also regionally very different possibilities of medical diagnosis and therapy can influence mortality.

Other diseases, too, show a regionally quite different mortality frequency (e.g. lung cancer, cancer diseases of the gall-bladder, of the larynx, melanoms, cancer diseases of the mammary gland and the female sexual organs as well as of the male sexual organs and urinary tract, and above all malignant system diseases of the lymphatic tissue and leukaemias).

Research into the causes of all kinds of cancer disease is at present of a largely speculative nature and, applying conventional documentation techniques, gives no reason to expect any greater success. It is therefore essential to store in computer-assisted cancer registers extensive data about the real disease frequency in the single areas and to use modern information technology (database systems, expert systems) for analysis. Also, often discussed environmental factors (different forms of nutrition, consumption of alcohol, abuse of nicotine, radiation influences, especially by nuclear power stations) can only be recognized if more exact data about the disease incidents in a region are recorded and can be analyzed together with the supposed pathogenetical factors. Only thus can correlations to clinical data (primary stage of disease, therapeutical measurements, long-term progress) be established in order to intensify or improve preventative medical and therapeutical possibilities.

4 Information Requirements

The information system H.I.T.[1], which is used in the after-care centre of the Städtische Kliniken Oldenburg and other clinics in Niedersachsen, does not meet modern information-technical standards in decisive features (operating system, data model, data manipulation language). Despite the existence of an ANSI standard, the underlying programming language MUMPS[2] ensures no portability with regard to various target computers and limits the flexibility with regard to desirable possibilities of analysis, e.g. for epidemiologic cancer research.

The information system INEKS is being developed to complete and, if desired, at least partly replace H.I.T.
The data from the H.I.T. system shall be transferred into the INEKS database. A transfer program has to be developed which

---

[1] H.I.T. = Hannoversches Informationssystem für Tumordaten
Hannover information system for tumor data
[2] MUMPS = Massachusetts General Hospital Utility Multi Programming System /Wolters/

converts and transfers the H.I.T. data of the after-care centre into the INEKS database.
This base of data can be completed and extended through an input component programmed with SQL*Forms.

Furthermore, a programme for the Städtische Kliniken Oldenburg shall be developed to provide transference of data to the parent documentation 'Cancer' of the National Health Department.

For the support of epidemiologic cancer research, selected epidemiologic retrieval classes must be worked out which are realizable with the linguistic means of a database system or possible extensions. For the manipulation of the data in INEKS, from the aspect of epidemiological analysis, possible extensions of the data material must be carried out, especially with regard to regional quantities of influence. For all analysis results, graphical illustration should be made possible in order to increase their transparency.

5 System Description

So far, the following projects have been carried out, which are documented in the reports /Appelrath/, /Bergmann/, /Volbers/ and /Zimmerling/:
  - Data analysis in the after-care centre
  - Schema definition
  - Lay-out of the user interface
  - Transmission of H.I.T. data
  - Transmission of data to the National Health Department.

Data analysis and Definition of the schema

An evaluation of the H.I.T. data structures has shown that fundamental relations between entity sets cannot be constructed from the H.I.T. data since a structure of the data is carried out there in purely chronological order or according to sheets and to patients. The H.I.T. schema was therefore revised and incorporated in the INEKS schema taking into consideration
- the requirements for modification (especially expansion) of the existing data material
- the desired flexibility for analysis
- the modelling criteria of the applicable database systems and
- the accepted rules of relational modelling (normal-form theory).

568

The data recorded in the after-care centre were analyzed and assigned to the following entity sets (in brackets the DB-internal relation names of each; cf. figure 2):

Patient identification (patid):

This entity set contains the patient's personal data such as name and address.

Tumor/Diagnosis (tdiagnose):

Under this entity set information regarding a primary tumor and its diagnosis is combined, e.g. date of diagnosis and histology of the tumor.

Secondary manifestation (sekmf):

This entity set contains data about possible further tumors which are diagnosed, e.g. date and type of secondary manifestation.

Treatment (behandlung):

Information about the treatment (operation, radiation or systemic therapy) is recorded in this entity set, e.g. type of therapy, aim of therapy.

After-care (nachsorge):

Under this entity set information concerning the after-care dates and examinations of the patient are combined, e.g. start of after-care and after-care results.

Final (abschluß):

This entity set provides information as to when and why the registration of a patient was concluded.

Further data (w_daten):

This entity set contains additional information about the patient and the tumor diagnosis such as number of live-births and reason for registration.

Figure 2 shows the elaborated schema of the INEKS database in the form of an ER model, in which to the seven above-mentioned relations another seven (support) relations, implied by the design process are added.

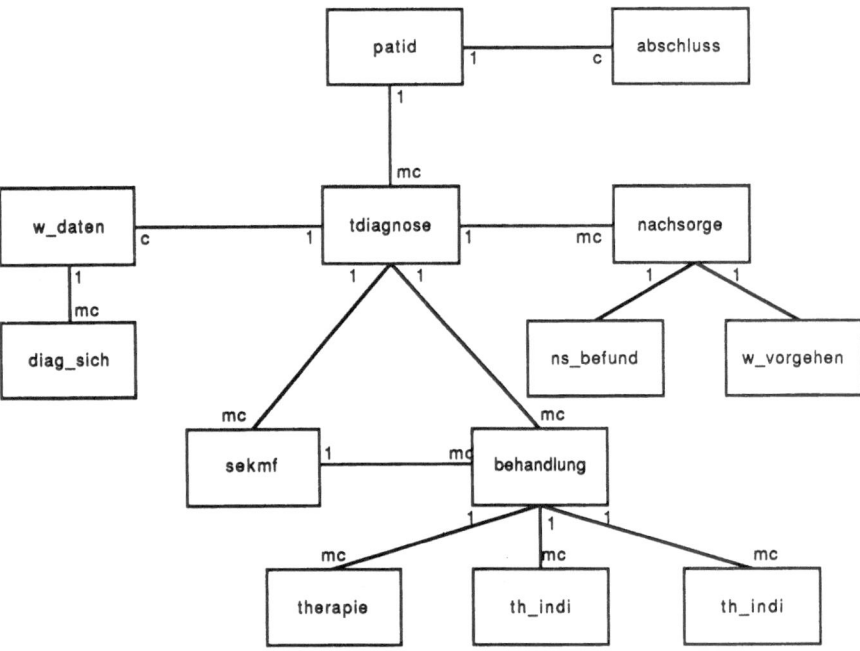

Figure 2: INEKS schema

The DB schema of INEKS thus comprises 14 relations with a total of 84 attributes.

In the meantime, data from about 8,000 patients has been transferred.

Transmission of H.I.T. data

The data stored in the information system H.I.T. should be transferred into the INEKS database. Therefore it was necessary to develop a program because the internal data representation of MUMPS was unknown. The H.I.T. data are given out and stored in a file named transfer file created by an MUMPS program. The transfer file consists of all attributes of a patient which needed by INEKS. The transfer file is structured like the relation structure of the INEKS database system. The attributes of each relation are linked to a join. The joins are chained to a linked list per patient. If a relation contains multiple tupels per patient the tupels are linked to an own list (cf. figure 3).

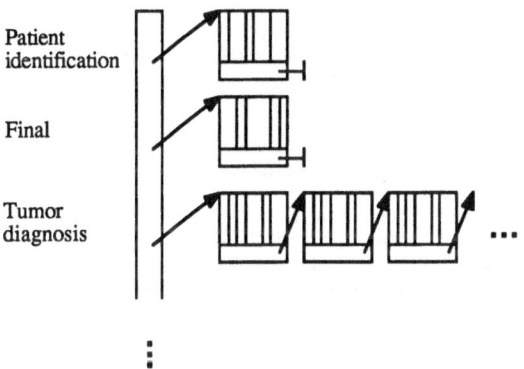

Figure 3: Structure of the transfer file

Next to generating the structure of the transfer file it is necessary to convert data types of some attributes, e.g. date of birth.

After generating the transfer file by MUMPS the data are read by a program written in PRO*C and inserted into the INEKS database.

6 Use of the INEKS Database for Epidemiological Cancer Research

There are analyses which do, for the most part, obtain their data from an underlying database, but would like to use in addition DB-external data, for example from files or main memory resident data structures such as records, arrays, or which shall be entered by keyboard for test purposes. This DB-external data is often not integrated in the DB because it is, for instance, only of temporary interest (and would not justify a laborious re-organisation of the DB schema), or because it would expand only a part of the DB by additional attributes and raise consistency problems (zero values!) for the remaining DB section.

Computer assistance in epidemiological cancer research attains a new quality only at the point when the data permanently stored in the INEKS database can be temporarily set in relation to hypothetical values. Assumptions of the doctors can thus be verified on the basis of the extensive stored data material and possibly gain relevance to a degree that justifies an extension of the database.

For this scenario of an integration of relational databases and DB-external data structures, three language levels can be identified:

- the relational data definition and manipulation (i.e. in general SQL-DDL and SQL-DML)
- the arrangement of suitable data structures and operations for the administration of the DB-extenal data
- the integrated entire layer for the retrieval and alteration of data which comes from the DB and/or are DB-external, i.e. this language shell encapsulates information about location and access mechanisms for all data.

The permeability between the DB system and DB-external administration component should be fulfilled in that views from the DB could be transformed into the DB-external data structures (update?, consistency?), and vice versa, stabilized, permanently interesting DB-external data could be adopted into the DB by adjustment of the schema.

For this, concepts, methods and languages (e.g. extended SQL) have to be developed which realize this described scenario under an application-dependent surface and which can be used in other applications with similar task profiles.

7   Concluding Remarks

By applying the information system INEKS in the Städtische Kliniken Oldenburg

1 computer-assisted data administration in the Clinics is extended,

2 a great amount of additional data is integrated which could not be considered with the previous documentation techniques because of their working restrictions,

3 any statistical analyses can be supported,

4 the visualization of the retrieval results is made possible, and

5 tools are provided which allow scientific analyses for the first time.

Providing application-dependent, ergonomically matured user interfaces, a high acceptance is expected which is not restricted to this particular application in the Städtische Kliniken Oldenburg, since from both the medical and informational aspects attention was paid to multi-function usability and portability.

References

/Appelrath/   Appelrath, H.-J., Volbers, H.
Systemanalyse INEKS Interner Bericht,
FB Informatik, Uni Oldenburg, 1990

/Bergmann/   Bergmann, B., Janßen, P.
Datentransfer H.I.T - INEKS
Praktikumsbericht,
FB Informatik, Uni Oldenburg, 1990

/Smith/   Smith, L.S., Mosier, J.N.
Guidelines for Designing User Interface Software
Bedford, Mass.: The MITRE Coorp., 1986

/Spinas/   Spinas, P., Troy, N., Ulich, P.E.
Leitfaden zur Einführung und Gestaltung von
Arbeit mit Bildschirmsystemen
München, CW-Publ., Zürich, Verlag Ind. Org.,
1983

/Volbers/   Volbers, H.
HIT-INEKS-Evaluation
Interner Bericht,
FB Informatik, Uni Oldenburg, 1989

/Wolters/   Wolters, E.
Programmieren in MUMPS - Mit zahlreichen
Übungsbeispielen
Hanser Studienbücher, Carl Hanser Verlag,
München 1988

/Zehnder/   Zehnder, C. A.
Informationssysteme und Datenbanken
Teubner, 4. Auflage, 1987

/Zimmerling/   Zimmerling, R.
Zwischenbericht INEKS
Interner Bericht,
FB Informatik, Uni Oldenburg, 1990

 # New by Springer-Verlag

Surveys on Mathematics for Industry

A new Journal

The main goal of this journal is to bridge the gap between university and industry by
- the presentation of mathematical methods relevant for industry
- the exposition of industrial problems which are of interest to mathematicians.

To achieve this goal, the journal publishes (exclusively in English):
● Surveys on new mathematical techniques
● Surveys on established mathematical techniques with a new range of applications
● Surveys on industrial problems for which appropriate mathematical models or methods are not yet available
● Articles comparing mathematical models or methods for particular industrial problems
● Articles describing mathematical modelling techniques
● Broad historical surveys
● Articles of general interest about the use of mathematics in industry
● Occasional book reviews and reports about conferences in the field of Industrial Mathematics.

ISSN 0938-1953   Title No. 724

Subscription Information:

1991. Vol. 1 (4 issues):
for institutional subscribers: DM 240,-, öS 1680,-, plus carriage charges
for individual subscribers: DM 144,-, öS 1008,-, plus carriage charges

Special rates for individual members of DMV, ECMI, GAMM, JSIAM, ÖMG, and SIMAI: DM 80,-, öS 560,-, plus carriage carges

Springer-Verlag Wien New York

Sachsenplatz 4–6, P.O. Box 89, A-1201 Wien · Heidelberger Platz 3, D-1000 Berlin 33
175 Fifth Avenue, New York, NY 10010, USA · 37-3, Hongo 3-chome, Bunkyo-ku, Tokyo 113, Japan

Computing

Archives for Informatics and Numerical Computation
Archiv für Informatik und Numerik

Presenting the latest research results from computer science and numerical computation, **Computing** is an international journal intended for professionals and students in all fields of scientific computing, for computer center staff, and software and hardware manufacturers. Each issue features original papers and short communications from a wide range of areas: discrete algorithms, symbolic computation, performance and complexity evaluation, operating systems, scheduling, software engineering, picture processing, parallel computation, classical numerical analysis, numerical software, numerical statistics, optimization, computer arithmetic, interval analysis, plotting.

ISSN 0010-485X   Title No. 607

Subscription Information:

1991. Vols. 46–47 (4 issues each):
DM 700,–, öS 4900,–
plus carriage charges

Springer-Verlag Wien New York